Per T. Cleve

Synopsis of the naviculoid diatoms.

Presented to the R. Swedish Academy of Sciences May 10, 1893

Per T. Cleve

Synopsis of the naviculoid diatoms.
Presented to the R. Swedish Academy of Sciences May 10, 1893

ISBN/EAN: 9783337724160

Printed in Europe, USA, Canada, Australia, Japan

Cover: Foto ©ninafisch / pixelio.de

More available books at **www.hansebooks.com**

SYNOPSIS

OF

THE NAVICULOID DIATOMS

BY

P. T. CLEVE.

PART I.

WITH 5 PLATES.

PRESENTED TO THE R. SWEDISH ACADEMY OF SCIENCES MAY 10, 1893.

STOCKHOLM 1894.
KUNGL. BOKTRYCKERIET. P. A. NORSTEDT & SÖNER

In carrying out this work I have been kindly assisted by several diatomists, who sent me for examination slides from their collections. Among them I name with recognition Prof. J. Brun, Mr Kinker, Mr. Le-Tourneur, Mr. J. D. Möller, Mr. P. Petit, Dr. Rae, Mr. Thum, Mr. E. Weissflog, Prof. Van Heurck and Mr. Ward. I am indebted to Mr. Julien Deby, who sent from his gigantic collection everything of interest to me, and to Mr. E. Grove, who not only sent me a large number of slides, but also took the trouble of revising the manuscript and the proofs. Materials from different parts of the world have been sent by Dr. Aurivillius (from Java), Mr. Beddome (from Tasmania), Mr. Dusén (from Cameroon), Captain G. C. Eckman (marine mud from the Atlantic and Mediterranean), Prof. Lagerheim (from Ecuador) and Dr. Norstedt (from Australia, New Zealand etc.). To Mr. Comber I am indebted for many fine photographs of several forms of interesting structure. To all these gentlemen I give my best thanks.

On the value of the characteristics.

It may be stated as an axiom that those characteristics are of the greatest importance which occur in the greatest number of forms, and on the other hand that the characteristics which occur in some, but not in all, of a number of forms otherwise nearly related are of less importance. The older authors as a rule attached but little importance to the more constant characteristics, but on the contrary gave much attention to trifling differences, because the latter are frequently more conspicuous than the former. They founded not only species but genera and divisions on characteristics, which were actually subject to variation in species otherwise identical. I will in the following pages treat of all characteristics which have been used for the description of species and genera.

Habit of life and growth. Most diatoms live in a free state, floating in the water, but many are attached to solid bodies in the water, some are stipitate on gelatinous stalks, and others enclosed in gelatinous tubes or masses of different shape and consistence. A careful examination shews that many of the attached or enclosed forms also occur in a free state; and that there are frequently very slight differences between species, which live attached or enclosed, and others which never occur in such a state. On the other hand forms, which are stipitate, or enclosed in tubes, belong to the most different types. For these reasons I regard as a characteristic of very little importance the mode of occurrence in free or attached state. At least, genera and species should not be founded on such characteristics alone. Genera, such as *Schizonema*, *Endostauron*, *Endosigma*, *Encyonema*, *Corconema*, are in my opinion not acceptable.[1]

Size. The limits of the dimensions of the forms of each species are in most cases pretty definite, the larger forms of each species being as a rule twice as large as the smallest. Still, in some cases the variability is more extensive and the followings may be cited as species in which the dimensions of the forms are subject to very considerable variation: Amphora ovalis, Achnanthes brevipes, Pinnularia viridis.

Form of the frustule. Most frustules of the Raphidieæ are straight, and nearly symmetrical, with the longitudinal and transverse axes, but a great number of forms are in some or other respects asymmetrical. A flexure of the frustule along the longitudinal, or the transverse axis, occur in the old genera *Cocconeis* and *Achnanthes* which have been distinguished hitherto principally by this characteristic. As to *Cocconeis* it seems probable that the flexure may be derived from the

[1] The gelatinous substance of the stipes of *Achnantes longipes* is intensely stained by hæmatoxyline, and no continuation of the substance of the stipes is visible in the interior of the frustule. On the other hand the stipes is not stained by Congo-red, methyle-green, eosine, and methylène-blue. The gelatinous tubes of Navicula (Schizonema) mollis are stained by hæmatoxyline, fuchsine, methyle-green and saffranine, but not by eosine. The tubes of Amphipleura (Berkelya) Dillwynii are stained by hæmatoxyline and methyle-green, but not by Congo-red. The gelatinous envelopes of Mastologia are stained by methyle-green, fuchsine and saffranine, but not by eosine and Congo-red.

form of the objects, to which these forms are attached by the lower valve, and in *Achnanthes* there are several forms, which owing to other important characteristics must be placed in this genus, although they are not at all genuflexed. Moreover genuflexed species occur in groups of allied forms the greater number of which are straight, for instance in the *Naviculæ lineolatæ*, *Nav. microstigmaticæ*, *Gyrosigma*, *Pleurosigma*, and in some species the degree of flexure seems to be subject to variation (for instance in *Gyrosigma arcticum*). The geniculated flexure is thus no generic characteristic, though in most cases of specific value.

Zone. The zone in the Raphidieæ is in most cases simple, that is without longitudinal divisions, but in many *Amphoræ*, in *Amphiprora* and in the group *Libellus* of the *Naviculæ microstigmaticæ* it is complex. This characteristic appears to be subject to very little variation and to be of importance in the limitation of genera. There are however in some cases small variations. The zone of *Amphora commutata* seems in some varieties to have, and in others not to have, faint divisions. *Amphora robusta* has usually no divisions, but in a variety from California there are longitudinal rows of alveoli on the zone. In the *Naviculæ microstigmaticæ* also, some allied forms have divisions and others are without them. Still we may consider the complexity of the zone as an important characteristic.

Outline of the valves. The outline of the valves of the naviculoid diatoms is very variable, presenting every intermediate passage from narrow linear to almost orbicular. The valves are non-constricted, constricted, or biconstricted, and, occasionally, some forms have 3 or 4 constrictions. Sometimes the valve is sigmoid.

The following schematic figures will illustrate the meaning of the terms used in my descriptions.

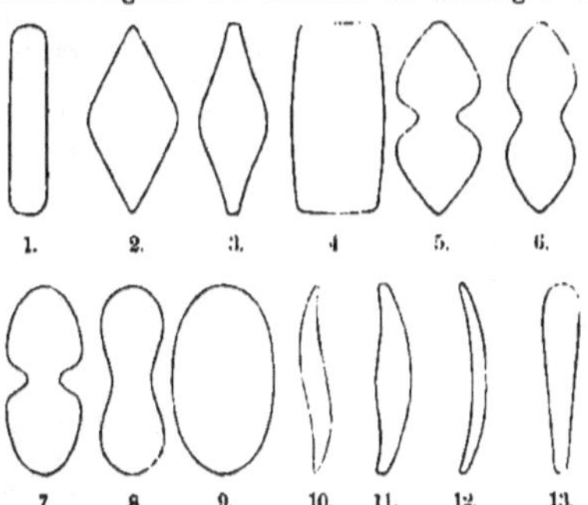

Outline of the valves. Fig. 1 Linear, 2 Rhomboidal, 3 Lanceolate, 4 Rectangular, 5 - 8 Panduriform with deltoid, subelliptical, tongue-shaped and broadly rounded segments, 9 Elliptical, 10 Sigmoid, 11 Cymbiform, 12 Lunate, 13 Clavate.

The *ends* of the valves also have a great variety of shapes, as

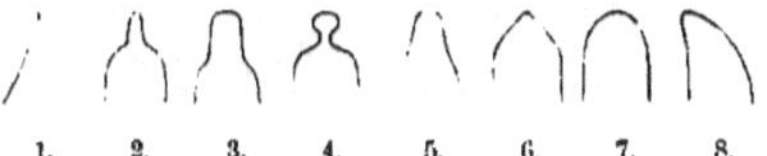

Ends of the valves. 1 Acuminate, 2 Apiculate, 3 Rostrate, 4 Capitate, 5 Truncate (subrostrate), 6 Cuneate, 7 Rounded obtuse, 8 Obliquely or unilaterally rounded.

The constancy of the outline is very different in different cases. Some species seem to be very constant in shape, as *Diploneis elliptica*, many species of *Pinnularia*, *Cocconeis* and *Amphora*.

But in other cases the form is subject to much change as, for instance, in *Navicula mutica.* The shape of the ends is frequently not constant, as in the genus *Neidium*, *Navicula viridula*, and others. In the same natural group of diatoms both the outline and the ends are frequently subject to much variation. I therefore conclude that though the shape of the valve may be of service to some extent as a specific distinction, it is of no real importance in limiting or defining genera.

On the *sigmoid flexure* of the valves have been founded the genera *Pleurosigma* and *Scoliopleura*. This characteristic is subject to great variation in *Pleurosigma*, some forms of which are almost straight. On the other hand widely different forms of other genera are sigmoid, as *Navicula Bacana*, *Navicula Sigma*, *Caloneis staurophora*. I have occasionally seen a sigmoid valve of *Frustulia Lewisiana* and one of *Navicula cincta var. Heufleri*. The sigmoid flexure of the valve can only be regarded as a specific characteristic.

The *symmetry* or *asymmetry* of the valve has been considered by HEIBERG, PFITZER and others as of great importance in the formation of families. But this can hardly be maintained, since we meet with forms both symmetrical and asymmetrical in the same species, as for instance *Trachyneis aspera*, *Frustulia vulgaris* and others; and there are asymmetrical species closely allied to symmetrical in the section *Naviculæ lineolatæ*, *Pinnularia*, *Caloneis* and others. The degree of asymmetry is also variable. This tends to shew that asymmetrical forms are derived from symmetrical and vice versa, and that in a natural system they cannot be placed in different families. As a generic distinction it may, when combined with other characteristics, be of value in certain cases.

A median *constriction* of the valve has been usually considered as an important characteristic, but it is not so, panduriform species being closely connected with others which are not at all constricted. *Dictyoneis marginata*, for instance, is usually deeply constricted, but varieties exist connecting this species with the non-constricted *D. Thumii*, which may therefore be considered as its variety. In the genus *Diploneis* very closely connected, constricted, and non-constricted forms exist. *Diploneis didyma* is usually panduriform, but in slightly brackish water the constriction becomes less distinct and, finally, not perceptible. We conclude thus that the outline of the valve in this respect is too variable to furnish generic distinctions, though in many cases, when constant, it may be a valuable specific characteristic.

Central nodule. The central nodule constitutes a more or less conical, interior silicious mass in the centre of the valve. In many cases it expands laterally into a *stauros*, and on this characteristic has been founded the genus *Stauroneis*. It is to be remarked that a stauroid nodule occurs in widely different forms, and that some really allied forms scarcely differ otherwise than in the presence or absence of a stauros. In such cases the stauros cannot be used as a generic distinction. As a specific characteristic it is in most cases very valuable, as it is very constant in the same species.

The central nodule extends not only transversely, but is in many cases prolonged into *horns*, as in *Diploneis*, in which they closely follow the median line. In other cases, as is *Dictyoneis*, larger forms of *Stauroneis*, *Frustulia*, the median line is enclosed between silicious ribs, in the middle frequently fused together with the central nodule, which thus seems to be elongated. The prolongation of the central nodule in such a manner reaches its maximum in *Amphipleura*, where the *forks* represent the horns of *Diploneis*. In the section *Naviculæ lyratæ* the horns are distant from the median line and developed into the lyriform markings, or large lateral, lunate areas, characterizing this section. The characteristics of the central nodule are subject to only slight variation and are therefore of importance.

Median line. The median line is in all probability a fissure of more or less complicated structure, and seems to afford valuable characteristics. In most of the *Mastogloiæ* it is undulating, also in *Navicula plicatula*. In *Pleurosigma*, *Gyrosigma*, and others, it is more or less sigmoid, but this characteristic, though valuable specifically, is not of sufficient constancy to afford generic distinction, sigmoid median lines occurring in forms nearly akin to others with straight median lines, as for instance *Navicula Raeana* and *Nav. Yarrensis*, *Nav. tumida* and *Nav. plicata*, *Navicula Sigma* and *Nav. superimposita*, *Cocconeis heteropleura* and *C. pellucida*.

The direction of the *terminal fissures* in most Naviculæ is the same in both extremities, but there are forms in which they are disposed in contrary directions. The latter characteristic on which GRUNOW was inclined to found a separate genus, *Pseudopleurosigma*, occurs in widely different groups, and it would not be in accordance with a natural system to class in one genus all forms with the terminal fissures in contrary directions. Such forms are frequently allied to others with the fissures in the same direction. On the other hand as a specific characteristic it seems to be of very great value.

Areas, or structureless parts of the valve, occur usually along the median line and around the central nodule. I call these areas *axial* and *central areas*. There are also, sometimes, *lateral* areas, or blank spaces on both sides of the median line, separated from the latter by a striated portion. The form, the presence, or absence, of such areas is in most cases a valuable specific characteristic, and, frequently, a useful distinction in groups of allied forms.

Longitudinal lines. In a great number of forms there occur lines, parallel to the median line, in some cases dilated into longitudinal bands or lateral areas, limiting an interior elevated or depressed portion. Although such longitudinal lines or lateral areas occur in certain groups of forms most of which are devoid of them, as in the *Naviculæ lineolatæ*, and in the whole group of the *Naviculæ lyratæ*, they are nevertheless in my opinion of great systematic importance. In the *Naviculæ lyratæ* the longitudinal lines or lateral areas are expansions of the central nodule, corresponding with the horns of *Diploneis*. In other cases they are merely non-striate portions of the valve, but in *Amphiprora*, *Diploneis*, *Caloneis* they are of a different nature. In *Amphiprora* they mark the limit between the elevated interior and the flatter exterior parts, which frequently have a different structure. They appear to be of the same nature in *Caloneis*. In *Diploneis* they limit a depressed portion, and the same is the case in several groups of *Amphora*, in which they are frequently so placed as to be distinctly seen only in favourable positions of the valve. In several cases the longitudinal lines are double. In *Diploneis* I call the space between the median line and the interior longitudinal line the *furrow*, and the space between two longitudinal lines the *lunula*. The presence or absence of longitudinal lines appears to me to be of very great importance in the construction of genera.

Structure of the valve. The valves of the naviculoid diatoms vary greatly in structure. In most cases the valves are decorated with small or large puncta, disposed in different manners. At present it seems to be generally admitted that these puncta are small cavities in the silicious mass of the valve. They are rarely scattered irregularly, but are usually arranged in transverse rows, more or less radiate or parallel, called *striæ*. The puncta are also so arranged as to form straight, or undulating, longitudinal rows, parallel to the median line, or decussating straight, or curved, rows as in *Pleurosigma* and others. When the puncta are large they are called *alveoli* and have the appearance of more or less quadrate spaces, as in several forms of *Diploneis* and *Amphora*. The silicious mass enclosing the alveoli in such cases has a reticulated appearance. I call these siliceous walls of the alveoli, if forming continuous silicious ribs, *costæ*. The strong, transverse silicious ribs of *Diploneis Crabro* are such costæ. The alveoli or puncta are frequently united, as in *Pinnularia*, *Caloneis* etc. In such cases the striæ appear to be channels, communicating with the interior, in the larger *Pinnulariæ*, by a larger *foramen* or *ocellus*. The outside part of the valve consists in several cases of a thin, minutely punctate stratum, usually seen only with difficulty. In a variety of *Diploneis splendida*, called *Dip. diplosticta*, there is such a finely punctate stratum outside the layer of alveoli. In the genus *Dictyoneis* it is also visible, the minute puncta forming transverse, and at the same time obliquely decussating striæ. This is also the case with the genus *Trachyneis*, where the fine puncta form longitudinal or somewhat oblique lines. In the group *Naviculæ lineolatæ* the transverse striæ are crossed by fine lines, which appear to be formed by closely crowded alveoli, as transitions exist from striæ of this nature to striæ composed of distinct puncta. In many forms there is an interior stratum, which may be isolated from the alveolar network. It is frequently found in preparations of *Trachyneis Debyi* and allied forms, and has been figured in A. SCHMIDT'S Atlas Pl. XLVIII f. 23. Also in *Navicula distans* this interior stratum occurs frequently in an isolated form.

In the most complicated cases, as in *Trachyneis*, we may distinguish three different strata, thus

1. The porous or ocelliferous interior stratum.
2. The alveolar stratum of reticulating costæ.
3. The exterior, minutely punctate stratum.

The structure of the valves presents characteristics which are of great importance for distinction both of species and genera. The coarseness of the structure may vary in the same species, though in most cases such variation is less than is usually believed. The direction of the striæ, the arrangement of their puncta, are characteristics subject to only very slight variation in the same species and in groups of allied forms.

Cell-contents. As is well known, the chromatophores of the diatoms present a great variation in different tribes, consisting in some of numerous granules, in others of one or two plates. To the latter type belong almost all the naviculoid diatoms, which have either one or two chromatophore-plates. The position and the form of these plates appear to be constant for groups of allied species, as is proved by the excellent researches of PFITZER. But the cell-contents are known only in a very limited number of forms, and the characteristics dependent on the cell-contents are, for the greatest number of forms, yet to be studied. The same is also the case with the reproduction by means of *auxospores*, and the characteristics, derived from the living cell, cannot for the present be used in the systematic arrangement of species, as they are too little known.

The characteristics derived from the structure of the valve are of the greatest importance in the definition of genera and families, and next to those, in my opinion, are the presence or absence of longitudinal lines, and the nature of the non-striate parts of the valve, or the areas.

An ideal system should take in consideration the evolution of the different forms, but in the present fragmentary state of our knowledge, such consideration cannot be more than an approximation wich may become closer to the truth as our knowledge of the forms becomes more extensive and perfect. The question which of the groups of forms are the highest and lowest may be answered by considering as the lowest those in which the characteristics are the least developed, and as the highest those in which the characteristics have attained their greatest evolution. But a greater development in one direction usually involves the slighter development, or obliteration, of other characteristics, so that one group may be the highest in some respects, and another in others. The changes of the organisms do not always indicate progress, but are frequently retrograde, especially where the mode of life has become parasitical. A natural system must consequently take account not only of the upward evolution, but also of the downward.

As the known diatoms probably represent merely a fraction of those, which exist and have existed, it will be necessary in constructing a natural system to fill the gaps with conjectures.

There can be no doubt that the naviculoid diatoms are most nearly connected with the *Nitzschiæ* among the diatoms without median line. The genera *Tropidoneis* and *Amphiprora* are very closely allied to several forms of *Nitzschia*. We meet in that genus with the carinated asymmetrical valves and the wing of *Tropidoneis*, also the complex zone and the carinal puncta of *Amphiprora*. In constructing a natural system then we may arrange the genera and groups in order of their relationship to the two genera above mentioned, and the following scheme shews how I suppose the different groups of the naviculoid forms to be related.

1. Nitzchieæ	Amphiprora (2) Auricula.
	Tropidoneis (4).
2. Amphiprora	.... Dictyoneis .... Mastoneis.
	.... Scoliotropis .... Gomphoneis.
	.... Pleurosigma (3). Toxonidea.
3. Pleurosigma	.... Naviculæ Decussatæ ... Anomoeoneis.
4. Tropidoneis	Naviculæ fusiformes (5).
	Naviculæ microstigmaticæ (7).
5 Naviculæ fusiformes	Naviculæ othostichæ.
	Gyrosigma.
	Frustulia (6).
	Cistula.
	Stenoneis.
6. Frustulia	Amphipleura.
	Brebissonia.
7. Naviculæ microstigmaticæ	Nav. minusculæ .... Microneis.
	Nav. decipientes (8).
	Nev. punctatæ (9).
	Anorthoneis.
	Eucocconeis.
	Halamphora.
	Oxyamphora.
	Amblyamphora.
	Psammamphora.
8. Naviculæ decipientes	Nav. bacillares.
	Nav. entoleiæ.
	Nav. mesoleiæ.
	.... Heteroneis.
9 Naviculæ punctatæ	Nav. lineolatæ (10).
	Nav. lyratæ (12).
	Nav. heterostichæ .. Actinoneis.
	.... Achnanthidium.
	.... Disconeis.
10. Naviculæ lineolatæ	Cymbella
	Gomphonema, Rhoicosphenia.
	Trachyneis.
	Nav. lævistriatæ (11).
11. Naviculæ lævistriatæ	Pinnularia.
	Cymbamphora.
	Archæamphora.
12. Naviculæ lyratæ	Diploneis (13).
	Pseudo-amphiprora (14).
13 Diploneis	Amphora .... Diplamphora.
	Cymatoneis.
	Scoliopleura.
	Nav. nicobaricæ.
	Nav. luxuriosæ.
14. Pseudo-amphiprora	Caloneis .... Neidium.
	.... Calamphora.
15.	.... Achnanthes .... Pleuroneis.
	.... Mastogloia.
16. Mastogloia	Cocconeis.
	Campyloneis.

Tropidoneis comprises both symmetrical not-winged and asymmetrical winged forms. The former appear to be related to the *Naviculæ microstigmaticæ* and *Nav. fusiformes*. As asymmetrical forms of the *Nav. microstigmaticæ* are to be considered the following sections of the old genus *Amphora: Oxyamphora, Amblyamphora, Psammamphora* probably also *Halamphora*. *Anorthoneis* is probably an asymmetrical form of *Nav. microstigmaticæ*. The *Nav. minusculæ*, of which *Microneis* and *Eucocconeis* appear to comprise degenerating forms, are probably also allies of *Nav. microstigmaticæ*. To the last named large section the *Nav. decipientes*, *Nav. entoleiæ* and *Nav. mesoleiæ* are certainly akin. *Heteroneis* may comprise degenerating forms allied to the same group.

From the *Nav. microstigmaticæ* the passage is gradual to the *Nav. punctatæ* and *Nav. heterostichæ* and the former section is very closely connected with the *Nav. lyratæ*. As degenerating forms are perhaps to be regarded *Disconeis* and *Achnanthidium*. Also some asymmetrical forms exist in the section *Nav. punctatæ*. Some *Cymbellæ* represent very likely asymmetrical forms of *Nav. punctatæ*.

The *Naviculæ Lyratæ* are by intermediate forms connected with *Diploneis*. Akin to the *Nav. lyratæ* I also consider *Pseudo-amphiprora*. The new groups *Amphora* and *Diplamphora*, broken out from the old genus *Amphora*, may be regarded as asymmetrical forms of *Diploneis*.

Pseudo-amphiprora is connected by intermediate forms with *Caloneis*, to which also *Neidium* seems to be allied.

The *Nav. lineolatæ* pass over to the group *Punctatæ* by transitional forms, and the former are also akin to *Trachyneis* (with the asymmetrical form *Amphora Clevei*). A part of the *Cymbellæ*, *Gomphonema*, *Rhoicosphenia* and *Amphora labuensis* may be considered as asymmetrical forms of the *Nav. lineolatæ*. Degenerated forms of the *Nav. lineolatæ* are probably to be found in *Actinoneis*.

On the other hand the *Nav. lineolatæ* are closely connected with the *Nav. lævistriatæ*, and those with *Pinnularia*, and I consider, with much hesitation, *Cymbamphora* as asymmetrical forms of the *Nav. lævistriatæ*.

I have no decided opinion as to the distantly related genera *Pleuroneis* and *Achnanthes* (sensu stricto). They seem in some way to be akin to the peculiar *Alloioneis Castracanei* Pantoc., which I know only from the figures. The structure resembles that of *Mastogloia Grevillei*. It may be possible that *Alloioneis Castracanei* connects *Achnanthes* and *Mastogloia*. The latter genus comprises forms with very different structure, which in some cases resembles that of the *Nav. orthostichæ* in others that of the *Nav. decussatæ* and *Pleurosigma*. Some forms of *Mastogloia* have the central nodule dilated into horns or connected with lateral areas as in the *Nav. lyratæ*. It might therefore be said that the *Mastogloiæ* belong to different types, but to prove this is not possible.

It is not easy to find in a natural system the place a form occupies, as the most important characteristics are usually the least striking. For practical purposes it is necessary to have an artificial classification in order to identify rapidly an unknown form, but it is by no means an easy task to construct an artificial key of such numerous and variable forms as the naviculoid diatoms. Still I have tried to compile an artificial key, which, however little rigorous it may be, will still be useful.

Artificial key of the groups and genera of naviculoid diatoms.

1.	Both valves similar	2.
	— — dissimilar	*Achnantheæ*.
2.	Frustules with a loculiferous rim	*Mastogloia*.
	— without — —	3.
3.	Valves symmetrical or almost so	4.
	— asymmetrical —	38.
4.	Valves with longitudinal lines	5.
	— without — —	13.
5.	Median line sigmoid	6.
	— — straight	8.
6.	Axial part of the valve elevated into a keel	*Amphiprora*.
	— — not — —	7.
7.	Structure double	*Scoliotropis*.
	— simple	*Scoliopleura*.[1]
8.	Central nodule with horns, enclosing the median line	*Diploneis*.
	— — without — — —	9.
9.	Central nodule stauroid	10.
	— not —	11.
10.	Striæ distinctly punctate	*Pseudo-amphiprora*.
	— not —	*Caloneis* (partim).
11.	Striæ distinctly punctate	12.
	— not — —	*Caloneis* (partim).[2]
12.	Valve with elevated ridges	*Cymatoneis*.
	without	*Neidium*.
13.	Structure double	14.
	— simple	16.
14.	Interior stratum with transverse costæ	*Mastoneis*.
	— — reticulate —	15.
15.	Reticulum of rounded meshes	*Dictyoneis*.
	— rhomboid or rectangular —	*Trachyneis*.
16.	Striæ apparently smooth	17.
	distinctly punctate or lineate	18.
17.	Valve more or less linear	*Pinnularia*.
	— — lanceolate	*Nav. lævistriatæ*.
18.	Median line sigmoid	19.
	— not —	20.
19.	Striæ decussating	*Pleurosigma*.
	transverse and longitudinal	*Gyrosigma*.

[1] *Caloneis staurophora*. — [2] *Nav. luxuriantes*, *Nav. nicobaricæ*.

20. { Valve with lateral areas uniting with the central area *Nav. lyratæ* (*Anomoeoneis* partim).
{ -- without — — — . . . . 21.

21. { Puncta arranged in decussating rows . . . . *Nav. decussatæ* (*Anomoeoneis* partim).
{ — transverse striæ . . . . 22.

22. { Striæ minutely and transversely lineate . . . . 23.
{ — punctatæ — — . . . . 24.

23. { Central nodule elongated . . . . *Brebissonia*.
{ — not — . . . . *Nav. lineolatæ*.

24. { Puncta arranged in longitudinal, almost straight rows . . . . 25.
{ — — — — undulating rows . . . . 28.

25. { Median line between siliceous ribs . . . . 26.
{ — not — — — . . . . *Nav. orthostichæ* (*Nav. fusiformes* partim).

26. { Punctation coarse . . . . *Cistula*.
{ — fine . . . . 27.

27. { Central nodule uniting with the ribs in a very elongated axial costa . . . . *Amphipleura*.
{ Central nodule not uniting with the ribs or uniting for a short way only . . . . *Frustulia* (*Nav. orthostichæ* partim).

28. { Striæ distinctly punctate . . . . 29.
{ — indistinctly or very finely punctate . . . . 32.

29. { Puncta coarse . . . . *Nav. punctatæ*.
{ — small . . . . 30.

30. { Median striæ of unequal length . . . . *Nav. heterostichæ*.
{ — — equal — . . . . 31.

31. { Valve very convex, and carinated . . . . *Tropidoneis*.
{ Valve slightly convex not carinated . . . . *Nav. microstigmaticæ* (*Nav. mesoleiæ* and *Nav. entoleiæ* partim).

32. { Terminal nodules incrassate or transversely dilated . . . . *Nav. bacillares*.
{ — not — — — . . . . 33.

33. { Median striæ more distant than the others *Nav. decipientes* (*Nav. microstigmaticæ* partim).
{ — not — — — . . . . 34.

34. { Axial area more or less lanceolate . . . . *Nav. entoleiæ*.[1]
{ — indistinct . . . . 35.

35. { Central area large . . . . 36.
{ — indistinct . . . . 37.

36. { Central area a transverse fascia . . . . *Stenoneis*.
{ — quadrate or rounded . . . . *Nav. mesoleiæ* (*Anomoeoneis* partim).

37. { Broad membranaceous forms . . . . *Nav. minusculæ*.
{ Narrow — — . . . . *Nav. fusiformes* (*Nav. microstigmaticæ* partim).

38. { Valve clavate . . . . 39.
{ -- not — . . . . 40.

39. { Structure: transverse striæ or rows of puncta . . . . *Gomphonema*.
{ — — costæ, alternating with double rows of puncta . *Gomphoneis*.

40. { Structure: decussating rows of minute puncta . . . . *Toxonidea*.
{ — transverse striæ or rows of puncta . . . . 41.

41. { Valve not strongly asymmetrical . . . . *Cymbella* (*Tropidoneis*, *Trachyneis*, *Nav. punctatæ* partim).
{ -- strongly asymmetrical . . . . 42.

42. { Median line on an elevated keel . . . . *Auricula*.[2]
{ — not — — . . . . *Amphora*.

Habitat and geographical distribution of diatoms.

A knowledge of the habitat and the geographical distribution of the diatomaceæ is of great importance, especially for geological researches. Fossil diatoms occur doubtless more frequently in geological strata than is usually believed, and may furnish the geologist with valuable evidence about the qualities of the water in which the sediments were deposited, whether fresh, brackish or

[1] *Navicula americana*. — [2] *Tropidoneis* partim and *Amphora Schmidtii*

strongly saline, and, in the latter case, whether the sea was tropical, temperate or arctic. There are also reasons to believe that the accurate investigation of the geographical distribution of the freshwater-forms will enable the geologist to ascertain the climate of the periods, when the fresh-water deposits were formed.

Considerations of that nature have induced me to pay much attention to the geographical distribution of the Diatomaceae. In the abundant literature upon the subject we find many lists of diatoms ocurring in certain seas, countries, and deposits, but I have intentionally made very little use of them, not being satisfied as to the accuracy of the determinations or limitations of species by the various authors. I have besides had sad experience how easily one may be deceived by slides of materials the loaclities of which are incorrectly named and which durnig the preparation have not been kept rigorously isolated from other materials. For such reasons I have relied mainly on my own observations only, though I still feel there may be among them some errors as to the localities, arising from the latter cause, as I had no opportunity of controlling the mode in which every slide, examined by me, had been prepared.

Many diatoms are cosmopolitan, occurring in all parts of the world, but there are on the other hand many species, genera and groups which occur only in certain seas and climates. The arctic sea has its characteristic form of *Triceratium arcticum* (or *Biddulphia Balæna*), *Campylodiscus Helianthus* and others. There are numerous common atlantic species which have never been found in the Arctic Sea. The tropical seas have their own peculiar species, not found in the Atlantic or in the arctic sea. The same is the case with several freshwater-forms. *Navicula* (*Diadesmis*) *confervacea*, *Achnanthes inflata*, *Ceratanlus lævis* occur in tropical or subtropical countries throughout the whole globe. Of *Tabellaria flocculosa*, one of the most frequent diatoms of Europe, not a trace has been found either in South America from Ecuador to Argentina or in Australia or New Zealand. *Gomphonema geminatum*, of frequent occurence in Scandinavia, Gt. Britain, and the Alps, does not live in the main-land of Europe. The same is the case with *Tetracyclus*, *Diatomella Balfouriana* and others. *Stauroneis Fulmen* and *St. Frauenfeldiana* are peculiar to the Australian region. I could easily multiply these examples, but they are enough to show that the study of the geographical distribution of the diatoms offers many points of interest.

I have examined a large number of samples of silurian clays and limestones, rhætic and cretaceous rocks of Sweden, but I never found in them a trace of a diatom. I have also searched for diatoms in the eocene and oligocene strata of Paris, but hitherto in vain, though I think it probable that they may yet be found there, as diatoms are found in the London clay of Sheppey. On the other hand fossil diatoms are very frequent in strata of the tertiary period in Barbados, Trinidad, New Zealand, Hungary, Japan, Denmark, etc. as is well known to every diatomist. If it be true, as PANTOCSEK believes, that the deposit of Kusnetzk belongs to the Trias, this is the oldest known diatomiferous rock, as the statement by CASTRACANE that diatoms occur in the carboniferous system has never been verified.

Some of the postglacial strata of Sweden are very rich in diatoms, and I have examined a considerable number of them. Among them the glacial clay and glacial marl have constantly been found by me free from diatoms, probably because the water, in which these deposits were formed, was too turbid for their growth. The strata, formed later than these, usually contain diatoms of both brackish and fresh-water habitat. The brackish-water-diatoms of the ancient baltic deposits comprise forms occuring in the present time in the southern part of the Baltic, as *Rhabdonema arcuatum* and *Coscinodiscus asteromphalus*, both characteristic fossils of the Litorina-epoch. The freshwater-species found in the Swedish post-glacial deposits are still living, but there are among them several peculiar species, not hitherto found in the southern or median part of the country, as *Pinnularia cardinalis*, *Navicula amphibola*, *Nav. Semen*, *Anomoeoneis serians* and others. Of interest is the occurrence of *Terpsinoe americana*, now extinct in Europe (or at least in northern Europe), in brackish or slightly brackish deposits of the Litorina-epoch. I have noticed this species in deposits from Warnemünde in Germany and from the eastern Smaland in Sweden.

The microscopical examination of the præ- and inter-glacial deposits of northern Germany and Denmark have furnished evidence that these strata were formed in inlets from the North Sea and not from the Arctic Sea.

All these facts prove of what importance the study of fossil diatomaceæ is becoming to Geologists.

Amphiprora Ehr. (1843).

Valve lanceolate, acute, convex. Axial part of the valve elevated into a sigmoid keel, usually separated from the lower part by a line of junction. Axial area indistinct. Central area small or none. Structure of the lower part of the valve: transverse striæ, rarely scattered puncta; structure of the keel: puncta in transverse or decussating rows. - Frustule strongly constricted in the middle. Junction between the keel and the lower part of the valve usually visible as a more or less sinuose line. Connecting zone complex, with more or less numerous, transversely striate divisions. — Cell-contents (of A. alata) a single chromotophore-plate along the zone. The division of the chromotophore begins from its ends (Pfitzer, Bau u. Entw. p. 94).

The name Amphiprora was given by Ehrenberg 1843 (Am. p. 122) to two naviculoid diatoms. *A. constricta*, the figure of which represents some species of Navicula in the frustular view, is slightly constricted in the middle. It seems impossible now to make out what form this name may denote. The other Amphiprora is, as the figures in the »Microgeology» shews, *Nav. Semen*. In the »Bacillarien» Kützing adds a third species, *A. alata*, which is distinguished by its sigmoid median line, and the lines on both sides of the median line, as well as by a complex connecting zone. Later on several other forms were described ass Amphiprora by Bailey, W. Smith, and others. W. Smith describes as *Amphiprora vitrea* a form with straight median line and not complex connecting zone. Forms of very heterogenous nature were thus thrown together in the genus Amphiprora. Rabenhorst tried 1864, (Fl. Eur. Alg. p. 257) to separate the forms with a sigmoid median line as a new genus. *Amphicampa*, which name Pfitzer 1871 (Bau und Entw. p. 94) changed to *Amphitropis*. — I consider that the name Amphiprora may be retained for the forms with sigmoid keel and complex zone, as *A. alata* is the first recognizable form described. For the other forms I have 1891 (Diatomiste 1, p. 51) proposed the name *Tropidoneis*.

The genus Amphiprora seems to be akin to the Nitzschieæ, and is on the other hand connected with *Auricula*. The complex zone, the single chromatophore, the puncta or lines on the keel remind one of the Nitzschieæ. In most species of Amphiprora the keel forms a well marked part of the valve, bordered by a junction-line, which is frequently denticulated or sinuose, and very suggestive of the alæ of Surirellæ. Whether this line projects into a true wing, I have not been able to discover. In all cases it occupies the same position as the wing of Surirellæ.

The structure of the valve is somewhat different in different sections. Three types may be distinguished: the type of *A. alata*, of *A. gigantea*, and of *A. Temperei*. In the first named the keel as well as the valve have transverse striæ. In larger forms of that type the striæ seem to be finely transversely lineate, with rather coarser puncta on the keel, which puncta appear to belong to an interior stratum. In the forms, of which *A. gigantea* is the type, the keel and the lower part of the valve have entirely different structure. The keel has puncta, disposed in obliquely decussating rows as in Pleurosigma, and the lower part of the valve has transverse striæ. In *A. Temperei* the keel has two rows of large stigmas and in addition very fine transverse striæ, while the lower part of the valve shews only fine scattered puncta.

Some few forms of Amphiprora live in fresh water, the greater part in brackish water, and some are purely marine. They occur in all parts of the world.

Artificial key.

1.	Keel with decussating rows of puncta	*A. gigantea* Grun.
	— without — — —	2.
2.	Keel with double rows of large marginal puncta	*A. Temperei* Cl.
	— without — — — —	3.
3.	Keel not separate from the lower part of the valve	4.
	— separate	5.
4.	Valve siliceous	*A. conspicua* Grev.
	— membranaceous	*A. Duseni* Cl.
5.	Keel and valve separated by a row of puncta	*A. margine punctata* Cl.
	— — — — — junction-line	6.
6.	Valve membranaceous	7.
	— solid	8.
7.	Junction-line with several denticulations	*A. ornata* Bail.
	— — one or no —	*A. paludosa* W. Sm.
8.	Margin of the valve crenulated	*A. crenulata* Temp.
	— — not —	9.
9.	Striæ of the keel obsolete	*A. Brebissoniana* Grev.
	— — distinct	10.
10.	Striæ on the keel wider than on the valve	*A. Kjellmanii* Cl.
	— — closer —	*A. kryophila* Cl.
	— and the valve æquidistant	11.
11.	Keel strongly sigmoid	*A. alata* Kütz.
	— slightly —	12.
12.	Striæ 6 in 0,01 mm.	*A. Meneghiniana* Grev.
	— 11 to 12 —	*A. lata* Grev.

1. **A. Paludosa** W. Sm. (1853). — Frustule membranaceous, in the zone-view deeply constricted, with rounded to truncate ends. B. 0,03 to 0,05 mm. Junction-line sinuose (or not). V. linear-lanceolate, with acute (or apiculate) ends. L. 0,055 to 0,13 mm. Median line strongly sigmoid. Striæ 19 to 20 in 0,01 mm., some of them frequently coarser than the others. — W. Sm. B. D. I. p. 44, Pl. XXXI f. 269. V. H. Syn. p. 121, Pl. XXII f. 10.

Brackish water: North Sea (Sweden! England! Belgium!) Cape May! Barbados!

Var. *bahusiensis* Cl. — Frustule strongly constricted. L. 0,08; B. 0,04 mm. Junction-line not sinuose and not punctate. Striæ 22 in 0,01 mm., those on the zone and the basal part of the valve more marked. Striæ of the keel faint, ending at the median line in very small puncta.

Marine: Sweden, Fiskebäckskil!

Var. *africana* Grun. (1879). — Frustule strongly constricted. L. 0,05 to 0,06; B. 0,03 mm. Junction-line not sinuose and not punctate. Striæ 20 in 0,01 mm., those on the keel with coarse puncta. — *A. pal. v. afr.* Grun. in Cl. M. D. N:o 196.

Brackish water: South Africa!

Var. *subsalina* Cl. — Frustule very thin, strongly constricted in the middle. L. 0,04; B. 0,03 mm. Junction-line with a large sinus. Striæ 23 in 0,01 mm. — Pl. I f. 1.

Brackish water: Artern, Saxony!

Var. *hyperborea* Grun. (1880). — Frustule slightly constricted in the middle. L. 0,065 to 0,07; B. 0,035 to 0,036 mm. Junction-line slightly sinuose. Striæ 27 to 28 in 0,01 mm. — *A. pal. var.? hyp.* Grun. A. D. p. 62. Pl. V f. 86.

Brackish water: Sea of Kara (Grun.).

Forma minuta Grun. (1884). — L. 0,035 mm. — *A. hyp. f. min.* Grun. Franz Josephs L. D. p. 54 (106), Pl. I f. 51.

Marine: Franz Josephs Land (Grun.).

Var. *Pokornyana* GRUN. (1860). — Frustule slightly constricted. L. 0,065 to 0,087; B. 0,02 to 0,027 mm. Junction-line slightly sinuose. Valve narrow, linear, with rostrate ends, and almost straight median line. GRUN. Verh. 1860 p. 569 Pl. VI f. 9.

Brackish water: Neusiedlersee (Hungary); Sea of Kara (GRUN.).

The above description is from the work of GRUNOW. In Cl. M. D. N:o 256 (Lymington, England) occurs a form, determined by GRUNOW as A. Pokorn. L. 0,09; B. 0,04 mm. Striæ 16 in 0,01 mm., coarsely punctate on the keel. Junction-line slightly sinuose. Keel strongly sigmoid.

Var. *punctulata* GRUN. (1880). — Frustule slightly constricted. L. 0,037 to 0,095 mm. B. 0,02 to 0,023 mm. Junction-line not sinuose, with a row of small puncta. Striæ about 27, on the keel 24 in 0,01 mm. — *A. pal. v. punct.* GRUN. A. D. p. 62, Pl. IV f. 84. Franz Josephs L. D. p. 53 (105), Pl. I f. 54, 55.

Brackish water: Sea of Kara! Franz Josephs Land (GRUN.), Cape Wankarema!

Var. *Nereis* LEWIS (1861). — Frustule strongly constricted in the middle. L. 0,05 to 0,114 mm Junction-line not sinuose, but with distant puncta. Striæ 22 in 0,01 mm. V. narrow, lanceolate, with sigmoid median line. — *A. Nereis* LEWIS. Proc. Acad. N. Sc. Philadelphia 1861 p. 64. — *A. plicata var. japonica* CASTR. Challenger Exp. D. p. 40, Pl. XXX, f. 8.

Marine: Atlantic coasts of N. America (LEWIS).

Var. *dilatata* PANT. (1891). — Frustule strongly constricted. L. 0,139. Height of the valve 0,025; at the constriction 0,0105 mm. Junction-line crenulated. Striæ 25 in 0,01 mm. — *A. dilatata* PANT. II. p. 55, Pl. X f. 179.

Brackish water: Hungary, fossil (PANT.).

This form only differs from var. Nereis by its somewhat larger size.

Var. *borealis* GRUN. (1880). — Frustule slightly constricted. L. 0,079 to 0,085; B. 0,028 to 0,03 mm. Junction-line slightly arcuate, not sinuose. Striæ on the keel 23, on the valve and the connecting zone 26 in 0,01 mm. — *A. pal. var.? borealis* GRUN. A. D. p. 62, Pl. IV f. 85.

Brackish water: Sea of Kara (GRUN.), Cape Wankarema!

Var. *duplex* DONK. (1858). — Frustule in L. 0,02 to 0,066; B. 0,01 to 0,04 mm. Junction-line arcuate, not sinuose. Striæ very fine. V. narrow, lanceolate, with strongly sigmoid median line. — *A. dupl.* DONK. T. M. S. VI p. 29, Pl. III f. 13. — *A. pal. v. dupl.* V. H. Syn. p. 121, Pl. XXII f. 15, 16.

Brackish water: Greenland! North Sea (Sweden! England, DONK., Belgium V. H.) Hungary, fossil (PANT.).

Var. *hyalina* EULENST. (1880). — As Var. duplex but smaller. L. 0,017; B. 0,035 mm. — *A. hyalina* EUL. in V. H. Syn. Pl. XXII f. 17.

Brackish water: Cette (GRUN.).

A. paludosa is a very variable species, closely connected with *A. alata*. Nearly akin to *A. paludosa*, perhaps a variety, is *A. Kützingiana* GREV. (1863 Edinb. N. Ph. J. XVIII p. 184 f. 6) from Queensland. The frustule is deeply constricted. L. 0,128 mm. The junction-line is not sinuose.

2. **A. Duseni** CL. N. SP. — Frustule membranaceous, strongly constricted in the middle, the segments being almost orbicular. L. 0,13; B. 0,11 at the constr. 0,07 mm. Zone with sigmoid longitudinal divisions, 2 in 0,01 mm., finely striate; striæ 17 in 0,01 mm. V. strongly compressed and elevated, without any junction-line. Striæ (at the keel) 12 in 0,01 mm., curved, towards the keel with distant puncta, 8 in 0,01 mm.

Brackish water (mouths of rivers): Cameroon (DUSÉN)!

3. **A. alata** KÜTZ (1844). — Frustule strongly silicious, constricted in the middle. B. 0,04. Junction-line not sinuose, but frequently with a row of large puncta. V. linear, with acuminate ends. L. 0,10 to 0,11; B. 0,02 mm. Median line strongly sigmoid. Basis of the keel linear, sigmoid.

Striæ 16 to 17 in 0.01 mm. finely lineate and, on the keel, with coarse puncta. — KÜTZ. Bac. p. 107 Pl. III f. 63. W. SM. B. D. I p. 44 Pl. XV f. 124. V. H. Syn. p. 121 Pl. XXII f. 11, 12.

Brackish water: North Sea (Bohuslän! England! France! Belgium V. H.). Mediterranean Sea (Peragallo). California!

Var. *intermedia* CL. V. in L. 0,11 to 0,15; B. 0,03; Height 0,025 to 0,03 mm. Striæ 11 in 0,01 mm.

Brackish water: New York! San Domingo (Witt Coll)!

Var. *pulchra* BAIL. (1850). Frustule strongly constricted. L. 0,27; B. 0,1 mm. Striæ 7 in 0,01 mm., on the keel with large puncta, 5 to 6 in 0,01 mm. — *A. pulchra* BAIL. Smiths. Contr. II p. 38 Pl. II f. 16, 18 (bad). V. H. Syn. Pl. XXII bis f. 1, 2, 4.

Brackish water: Atlantic coasts of N. America! San Domingo (Witt Coll.)!

Var. *japonica* CL. — V. in the zonal view strongly constricted. L. 0,085; B. 0,02 mm. Junction-line bisinuose on each side of the central nodule. Striæ 12 in 0,01 mm., coarsely punctate on the keel. — Pl. I f. 2.

Marine: Japan!

The smaller forms of *A. alata* appear to graduate into *A. paludosa*, so that there seems to be an uninterrupted series of forms from the gigantic Var. maxima to the very minute A. pal. var. hyalina. The Var. japonica may be regarded as a connecting link between *A. alata* and *A. ornata*. To the forms of *A. alata* belongs perhaps also *A. biharensis* PANT. III Pl. XLII f. 577.

4. **A. conspicua** GREV. (1861). V. linear-lanceolate, strongly convex. L. 0,06 to 0,13; B. 0,02 to 0,024 mm. Median line strongly sigmoid. Junction-line indistinct. Striæ 7 in 0,01 mm., some of them near the median line coarser, finely lineate; lineolæ about 25 in 0,01 mm. GREV. T. M. S. IX p. 86 Pl. X f. 16 (?). V. H. Syn. Pl. XXII bis f. 3.

Brackish water: Atlantic coasts of N. America! Brazil! Sierra Leone (GRUN), Cameroon!

5. **A. ornata** BAIL. (1852). — Frustule membranaceous, strongly constricted. L. 0,067; B. 0,05 mm. Junction-line deeply denticulate. Striæ 20 to 22 in 0,01 mm., finely punctate. BAIL. Smiths. Contr. II p. 38 Pl. II f. 15 to 23. V. H. Syn. p. 121 Pl. XXII bis f. 5. *A. fimbriata* CASTR. Voy. Challenger p. 40 Pl. XVII f. 15 (Surirella?).

Fresh water: Finland! Belgium (V. H.). North America (Michigan! Florida, BAIL).

6. **A. crenulata** TEMP. (1891). — Frustule deeply constricted. L. 0,037; B. 0,03 mm. Junction-line sinuose. Connecting zone with several longitudinal divisions, finely striate. Striæ 28 in 0,01 mm. V. lanceolate, with crenulated margins (denticulations 2 in 0,01 mm.), apiculate. L. 0,04; B. 0,014 mm. Median line strongly sigmoid. Basis of the keel biconstricted. Axial and central areas indistinct. Keel with transverse, punctate striæ, 16 in 0,01 mm. Lower part of the valve with numerous, strong, transverse lines. TEMP. Diatomiste I, p. 50 Pl. IX f. 9, 10.

Brackish water: New Guinea!

7. **A. Kjellmanii** CL. (1880). Frustule silicious, slightly constricted. L. 0,13; B. 0,04 mm. Junction-line undulated or not. Striæ coarser on the keel than on the valve, 12 or 13 (keel) to 17 (valve) in 0,01 mm. — CL. A. D. p. 14 Pl. IV f. 83.

Marine: Sea of Kara! Cape Wankarema!

Var. *glacialis* CL. (1883). — Frustule not constricted. L. 0,07; B. 0,015 mm. Striæ 14 (keel) to 19 (valve) in 0,01 mm. — CL. Vega p. 477 Pl. XXXV f. 12.

Marine: Cape Wankarema!

Var. *kariana* GRUN. (1880). Frustule slightly constricted. L. 0,061 to 0,07; B. 0,036, at the constriction 0,027 mm. Junction-line slightly sinuose. Striæ 10 or 11 (keel) to 17 or 18 (valve) in 0,01 mm. *A. kariana* GRUN. A. D. p. 61 Pl. IV f. 82. Franz Josephs L. D. p. 53 (105).

Marine: Franz Josephs Land (GRUN.).

Var. *subtilis* GRUN. (1884). — Frustule scarcely constricted. L. 0,04; B. 0,014 mm. Junction-line slightly undulated. Striæ 13 (keel) to 26 (valve) in 0,01 mm. V. in B. 0,08 mm. — *A. koriana v. subtilis* GRUN. Franz Josephs L. D. p. 105 (53) Pl. I f. 52, 53.

Marine: Franz Josephs Land (GRUN.).

Var. *striolata* GRUN. (1880). — Frustule rectangular, slightly constricted. L. 0,07; B. 0,023, at the constriction 0,015 mm. Junction-line not sinuose. Striæ 12 (keel) to 15 (valve) in 0,01 mm. those on the keel ending in small dots. — GRUN. A. D. p. 62 Pl. IV f. 81.

Brackish water: Sea of Kara (GRUN.).

8. **A. kryophila** CL. (1883). — Frustule slightly constricted. L. 0,13 to 0,16; B. 0,043 to 0,045; at the constriction 0,028 to 0,03 mm. Junction-line sinuose. Striæ on the keel 13 to 17 in 0,01 mm., ending in small puncta; striæ on the valve 10 to 14 in 0,01 mm. wider than on the keel. V. lanceolate, with strongly sigmoid median line. CL. Vega p. 477 Pl. XXXV f. 11.

Marine: Cape Wankarema!

A. kryophila is perhaps not specifically distinct from *A. Kjellmanii*, the only difference being that the striæ on the keel are closer than those on the valve; otherwise the two forms are perfectly similar. Both differ from *A. paludosa* in large size, more strongly silicious valves, and coarser striæ.

9. **A. lata** GREV. (1863). Frustule quadrate, strongly constricted. L. 0,075; B. 0,04, at the constriction 0,025 mm. Keel broad. Junction-line uniformly arcuate, not sinuose. Striæ on the keel 11 to 12 in 0,01 mm. ending in small puncta. Striæ on the valve of equal number, not distinctly punctate. Connecting zone with numerous, longitudinal divisions. GREV. Edinb. N. Phil. J. XVIII p. 38 f. 14. — Pl. I f. 5.

Marine: Balearic Islands! Queensland (GREV.).

The above description is from specimens from the Balearic Islands. GREVILLE does not give the number of striæ.

10. **A. Meneghiniana** GREV. (1863). Frustule broad, quadrate. L. 0,115 mm. Connecting zone with numerous longitudinal divisions. Junction-line uniformly arcuate. not sinuose. Striæ coarse 6 in 0,01 mm. — GREV. Edinb. N. Ph. J. XVIII p. 184 f. 7.

Marine: Queensland (GREV.).

11. **A. Brebissoniana** GREV. (1863). — Frustule strongly siliceous, deeply constricted, with broad truncate ends. L. 0,089 to 0,13; B. 0,066 mm. Junction-line not sinuose. Keel very elevated, bordered with a conspicuose hyaline margin, obsoletely striate, the striæ being visible only at the median line and at the junction-line. Striæ of the valve 7,5 in 0,01 mm., obscurely but coarsely punctate. — GREV. Edinb. N. Ph. J. XVIII p. 185 f. 8. — Pl. I f. 4.

Marine: South Pacific Ocean (GREV.), Sendaï, Japan, fossil (TEMPERE)!

12. **A. margine-punctata** CL. N. SP. — V. in L. 0,13; B. 0,04, at the constriction 0,015 mm. Keel very elevated, with a row of small marginal puncta, 8 in 0,01 mm., connected with similar rows of puncta at the basis of the keel. Lower part of the valve very narrow. Striæ on the keel 19 in 0,01 mm., curved and finely punctate. — Pl. I f. 3.

Marine: Java!

13. **A. Temperei** CL. (1890). — Frustule strongly constricted. L. 0,15; B. 0,055, at the constriction 0,027 mm. Junction-line obsolete, visible only near the central nodule. Keel with two rows of large puncta (4 in 0,01 mm.), striate; striæ 21 in 0,01 mm. V. with fine, scattered puncta. Connecting zone with numerous longitudinal divisions, transversely striate; striæ 20 in 0,01 mm. — CL. Diatomiste I p. 2 Pl. II f. 3.

Marine: Madagascar!

This is a very characteristic species, not closely connected with any other. The median line is strongly sigmoid.

14. **A. gigantea** Grun. (1860). — Frustule strongly constricted. L. 0,12 to 0,16 mm. Keel with a hyaline margin, broader towards the ends. Junction-line uniformly arcuate, not sinuose. Keel with puncta forming obliquely decussating rows, 13 to 15 in 0.01 mm. Striæ of the valve curved, divergent from the central nodule, about 14 in 0,01 mm., not decussating. Median line strongly sigmoid. Connecting zone with numerous longitudinal divisions. — Grun. Verh. 1860 p. 568 Pl. VI f. 12 (bad!). A. D. p. 63. — Pl. I f. 6. *A. gig. var. kerguelensis* Grun. A. D. p. 63 (1880).

Marine: Mediterranean Sea! Adriatic! Macassar Straits! Kerguelens Land!

This is a very large diatom, with somewhat thin silicious membrane. When dry the keel under a low power is yellow, and the valve hyaline.

Var. *tahitensis* Grun. (1880). — Frustule membranaceous. L. 0,06 (to 0,095); B. 0,04 mm. Keel strongly sigmoid. Striæ 18 to 22 in 0,01 mm. — A. D. p. 63.

Marine: China! Japan! Tahiti (Grun.).

Var. *æquatorialis* Cl. (1873). — L. 0,10 to 0,15 mm. Striæ 9 to 11 in 0.01 mm. — *Amphicampa æquatorialis* Cl. D. Sea of Java p. 12 Pl. III f. 17. *Amphipr. balearica* Grun. A. D. p. 63 (1880).

Marine: Balearic Islands! Adriatic! Java!

Var. *sulcata* O'Meara (1871). — L. 0,09 to 0,14 mm. Striæ 12 to 13 in 0,01 mm., on the connecting zone 20 in 0.01 mm. — *A. sulcata* O'M. M. J. (N. S.) Vol. XI p. 22 Pl. III f. 3. *A. pelagica* Brun. D. Esp. n. p. 8 Pl. XXII f. 3, 4 (1891).

Marine: Le Croisic! Balearic Islands! Seychelles! Cape Good Hope! Sumatra! Jamaica (Grove Coll.)!

Var. *decussata* Grun. (1880). — L. 0,063 to 0,065 mm. Keel slightly sigmoid. Striæ 21 to 24 in 0,01 mm. — *A. decussata* Grun. A. D. p. 63. V. H. Syn. Pl. XXII f. 13.

Marine: Coursélles (Grun.). Hungary, fossil (Pant.).

Var. *septentrionalis* Grun. (1880). — L. 0,076 to 0,18 mm. Striæ 20 to 23 in 0,01 mm. — *A. sept.* Grun. A. D. p. 63.

Marine: Finmark! Cape Wankarema!

Auricula Castr. (1873).

Valve more or less reniform or cymbiform, elevated into an asymmetrical, arcuate, but not sigmoid, keel. Median line not sigmoid, more or less biarcuate, with approximate central pores. Structure: transverse striæ, or more or less curved, irregular lines. Frustule usually globose, with complex connecting zone. Keels of both valves turned in the same direction.

The first known species was the diatom, described 1857 by Gregory as *Amphiprora complexa*. The genus Auricula was founded 1873 by Castracane (Atti del accad. pont. dei Lincei XXVI p. 406) for *A. Amphitritis*, which is evidently nearly akin to *A. complexa*. In Van Heurcks Synopsis (Pl. XXII bis f. 9, 10) Grunow has proposed the name *Amphoropsis* for two forms, of which one, *A. decipiens*, is related to Auricula, and the other, *A. recta*, is by me considered as belonging to Tropidoneis. As A. decipiens in my opinion cannot be separated from Auricula, I propose to reserve the name Amphoropsis for a section of Tropidoneis.

The valve of Auricula is keeled as in Amphiprora, but the keel is not sigmoid. In some species, which approach to Amphiprora, the keel is separated from the lower part of the valve by a line of junction. In other forms there is a gradual slope from the median line to the margin.

I have examined some living frustules of A. complexa. It has along the ventral side a single chromatophore-plate enclosed in a plasmatic mass, from which fine plasma-threads radiate towards the walls.

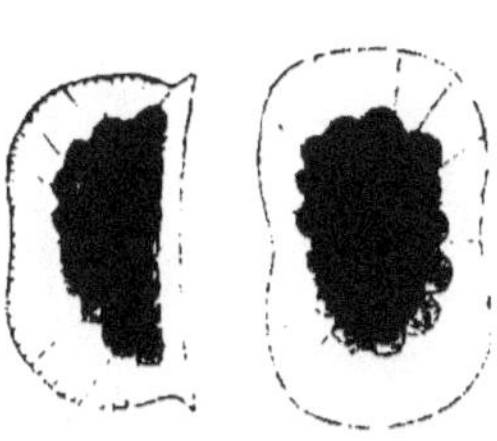

A. complexa, 500 times magnified

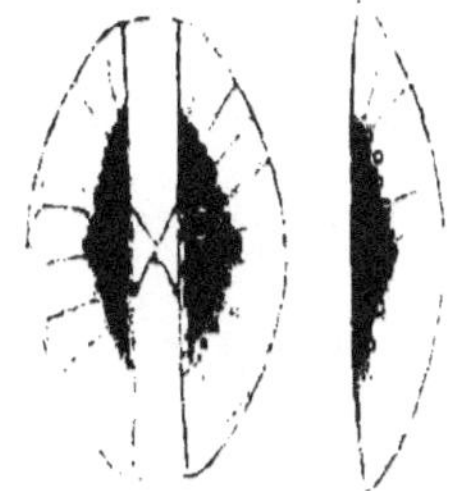

A. incerta, 500 times magnified

Of *A. incerta* I have had an opportunity of examining numerous living specimens. This species has also a single chromatophore-plate along the ventral side of the zone, enclosed in a plasma-mass which sends fine plasma-threads to the walls of the frustule. If the living frustules be suddenly killed by a boiling concentrated solution of mercuric chloride in alcohol, and then by washing freed from mercuric salt, they may be stained with different dyes. Carmine colours the nucleus, which is placed above the plate and on its centre. Stained with chrysoidine numerous granules in the plasma-mass take an intensely yellow colour, and are probably elaeoplasts, as fatty matters are intensely coloured by the dye.

Auricula minuta has also a single chromotophore-plate along the ventral side, and at the primordial stratum of the plasma a number of small granules, possibly geline-secreting organs.

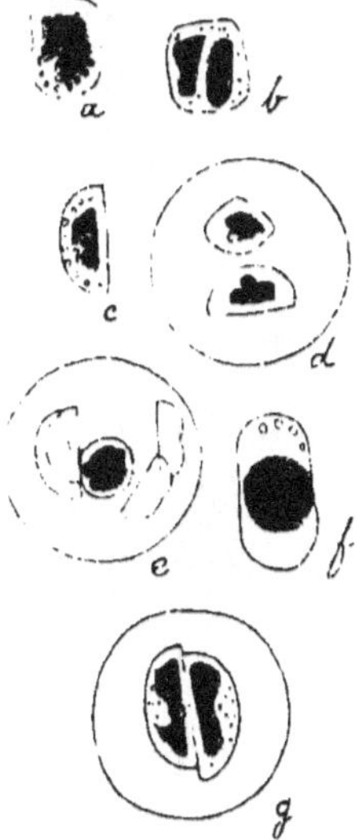

A minuta, 500 times magnified

Auxospores. In *A. minuta* a single globular auxospore is formed out of two frustules. In the annexed sketches *a* and *c* represent a frustule in living state, *b* a frustule in the state of division. Fig. *d* shews two frustules enclosed in a mucous mass, the first stage of the conjugation. In *e* the auxospore is formed and enclosed between the empty valves; *f* seems to represent an mature auxospore, and *g* two frustules, to judge from the size, probably formed out of the auxospore.

Some extreme forms of Auricula have a very peculiar appearance, but by intermediate steps they are connected on one hand with Amphiprora, on the other with Amphora, so nearly indeed that no line of demarcation may be traced between Amphora and Auricula.

All species of Auricula are marine and pelagic. Some forms are thin and membranaceous. Others have strong valves, but thin connecting zones, so that entire frustules are rarely to be found in gatherings which have been cleaned by means of acids.

Artificial key.

1.	Valve more or less boat-shaped	2.
	— — — reniform	4.
2.	Striæ 10 to 11 in 0,01 mm.	*A. coarctata* Br.
	— 20 to 22 —	3.
3.	Zone with a few larger stigmas	*A. pulchra* Grev.
	— without stigmas	*A. decipiens* Grun.
4.	Keel strongly inflected in the middle	5.
	— not, or slightly, inflected	6.
5.	Striæ 15 to 16 in 0,01 mm.	*A. intermedia* Lewis.
	Striæ very fine	*A. insecta* Grun.
6.	Striæ transverse	8.
	— curved, divergent towards the median line	7.
7.	Striæ coarse (8 in 0,01 mm.)	*A. Amphitritis* Castr.
	— finer (20 in 0,01 mm.)	*A. complexa* Greg.
8.	Valve large (L. 0,17 mm.)	*A. javanica* Cl.
	small (L. 0,02 to 0,03 mm.)	*A. minuta* Cl.

1. **A. (?) coarctata** Brun (1889). — V. lanceolate, acute. L. 0,115 to 0,135; B. 0,02; Height 0,025, at the constriction 0,013 mm. Median line highly elevated between the central nodule and the ends. Central area small, unilateral. Junction-line between the keel and the lower part of the valve very distinct, with a sinus on each side of the central nodule. Striæ 10 to 11 in 0,01 mm., convergent on both sides of the central nodule, punctate, puncta 12 to 13 in 0,01 mm. — *Amphiprora coarct.* Brun. D. foss. du Japon p. 14 Pl. III f. 12.

Marine: Japan, fossil and living (Brun)!

As the entire frustule is not known, it is impossible to decide whether this species, which has a great resemblance to a true Amphiprora, belongs to Auricula or to the sections Plagiotropis or Amphitropis of Tropidoneis. The incompletely described *Amphiprora nitida* Grev. (Edinb. N. Ph. J. XVIII p. 40 f. 18, 1856) has some resemblance to A. coarctata, but has not a complex zone.

2. **A. decipiens** Grun. (1882). — Frustule quadrate to rectangular, slightly constricted in the middle. L. 0,06 to 0,11; B. 0,05 mm. Junction-line distinct, sinuose. Central area indistinct. Striæ 20 in 0,01 mm., a little closer on the valve. Connecting zone, on the dorsal side, with broad divisions, about 3 in 0,001 mm., transversely striate; striæ 22 in 0,01 mm. Divisions narrow on the ventral side. *Amphoropsis decipiens* Grun. in Cl. M. D. N:o 309. V. H. Syn. Pl. XXII bis f. 11. *Amphiprora plicata* Greg. D. of Clyde p. 505 Pl. XII f. 57 (1857)?

Marine, æstuaries: Scotland!

3. **A. pulchra** Grev. (1863). — Frustule membranaceous, quadrate, slightly constricted. L. 0,075; B. 0,015 mm. Connecting zone with numerous divisions, about 5 in 0,01 mm., transversely striate; striæ about 22 in 0,01 mm. On the zone, close to the valve, are 3 or 4 large isolated stigmas. Valve with transversely dilated central nodule and elevated keel, bordered with a row of puncta, 6 in 0,01 mm. Striæ 22 in 0,01 mm. *Amphora pulchra* Grev. Edinb. N. Ph. J. XVIII p. 184 f. 2. — *Auricula pulc.* Pl. II f. 23.

Marine: Queensland (Grev.)! China! Macassar Straits (Grove coll.)! South Pacific Ocean (Van Heurcks coll.)!

The following incompletely described forms seem allied to this species: *Amphiprora lineata* Grev. (Edinb. N. Ph. J. XVIII p. 40 f. 19; 1863) and *Amph. Jolisiana* Grev. (l. c. p. 186 f. 11).

4. **A. insecta** Grun. (1876). — Frustule membranaceous, globose. L. 0,06 to 0,11; B. 0,04 to 0,05 mm. Median line strongly inflected towards the centre of the frustule. Central nodule

mucronate on inner side. Connecting zone complex, with 4 to 5 divisions in 0,01 mm. Along the keel is a row of puncta, 7 to 10 in 0,01 mm. Striæ 35 to 40 in 0,01 mm., extremely difficult to resolve. — *Amphora? insecta* A. S. Atl. XL f. 2, 3. *Amphora mucronata* H. L. Sm. Types N:o 38. Am. Qu. M. J. 1878 p. 17 Pl. III f. 9.

Marine and pelagic: Sweden, Gullmarsfjord on Zostera! Honduras (Grun.), Atlantic City (H. L. Sm.).

A probably allied, and very large, form is *Amphora? incerta* A. S. Atl. XL f. 1 from Baltschick. The specimen figured is too imperfect to admit of a description. It is probably the same species as *Amphiprora punctata* PANT. III Pl. XXXIX f. 547.

5. **A. complexa** GREG. (1857). — Frustule quadrate with rounded angles, constricted in the middle. L. 0,089 to 0,102; B. 0,07 mm. Connecting zone with 7 to 8 divisions (about 2 in 0,01 mm.) transversely striate. V. with reniform outline, and very excentric elevated keel, along which is a row of puncta, about 8 in 0,01 mm. Striæ of the valve curved and divergent from the central nodule, about 20 in 0,01 mm. — *Amphiprora complexa* GREG. D. of Clyde p. 508 Pl. XII f. 62. *Auricula Ostrea* TEMP. a. BRUN. D. foss. du Japon p. 25 Pl. IV f. 7 (1889)?

Marine, pelagic: Scotland! Balearic Islands! Rembang Bay (Debys Coll.)! Japan, fossil (Br. a. Temp.)? Barbados!

This species, remarkable for its excentric keel, is rarely found in entire frustules, the thin connecting zone being usually detatched in the course of preparation from the more silicious valves. A. Ostræa is in all respects similar to A. complexa, except as to the number of striæ, which according to BRUN and TEMPÈRE are only 7 to 9 in 0,01 mm.

6. **Auricula minuta** CL. N. SP. — Frustule quadrate with rounded angles. L. and B. 0,02 to 0,03 mm. Zone thin with about 7 divisions in 0,01 mm. V. reniform, very slightly indented in the middle. Margin with a row of puncta (7 in 0,01 mm.) along the median line. Striæ about 25 in 0,01 mm. delicate, almost parallel in the middle, curved at the ends. — Pl. I f. 7, 8.

Marine: Sweden, Gullmarsfjord on Zostera and among Amphipleura (Berkeleya) Dillwynii, frequent!

7. **A. intermedia** LEWIS (1865). — Frustule elongated, rectangular with rounded angles, very slightly constricted. L. 0,07; B. 0,03 mm. Median line strongly inflected towards the centre of the frustule. Along it is a row of puncta, 5 in 0,01 mm. V. in outline narrow, reniform. L. 0,07 to 0,11; B. 0,025 mm. Median line excentric, diverging from the central nodule towards the dorsal side of the valve. Striæ 15 to 16 in 0,01 mm. curved and divergent towards the median line. *Amphora intermedia* LEWIS. Proc. Philad. Ac. Nat. Sc. Pl. I f. 7 (1865). *Auricula japonica* BR. and TEMPÈRE, D. foss. du Japon p. 25 Pl. IV f. 8 (1889).

Marine: Adriatic! China! Japan, foss. (Br., Temp.), South Pacific Ocean (Van Heurcks Coll.)! Port Jackson! New Jersey (Lewis), Honduras (Grun.).

8. **A. javanica** CL. N. SP. Valve linear-lunate, very slightly constricted in the middle. L. 0,17; B. 0,026 mm. Median line very excentric not inflected, close to the margin of the valve and not bordered by a row of puncta. Striæ 8, 5 in 0,01 mm., almost transverse, finely punctate. Pl. II f. 22.

Marine: Sumbava (Kinker Coll.)!

9. **A. Amphitritis** CASTRAC. (1873). — V. reniform. L. 0,055; B. 0,025 mm. Keel very excentric, closer to the outer margin, to which its exterior wall is vertical. The interior wall seems to be elevated in the middle, and to slope gently towards the somewhat sinuose interior margin. Striæ about 8 in 0,01 mm., undulating, not distinctly punctate, on the interior wall of the keel alternately longer and shorter towards the keel, to which they diverge. — Castr. Atti del

accad dei n. Lincei 1873 p. 106 Pl. VII f. 2. Peragallo Villefranche D. p. 42 Pl. II f. 48. *A. Szontaghii* PANT. III Pl. VII f. 101 (1893).

Marine: Marocco! Balearic Islands! Adriatic!

To the genus *Auricula* may belong *Aur. Grunowii* Pant. III Pl. XXXI f. 453. *Amphiprora striata* Pant. III Pl. XXXIX f. 543 and *Amphiprora Pethöi* Pant. III Pl. XLI f. 565 all unknown to me.

Tropidoneis CL. (1891).

Valve elongated, lanceolate, more or less convex and acute, frequently with a wing, or longitudinal band, on one or both sides. Median line straight, on a central, or excentric, keel; its central pores approximate. Axial area indistinct. Central area small, rounded, or transversely dilated. Structure, fine puncta, forming transverse, not radiate, striæ, and longitudinal, more or less straight, much finer, striæ. Connecting zone not complex.

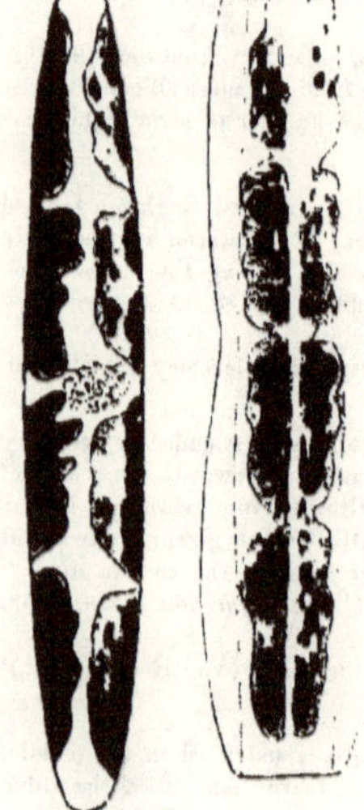

Tropidoneis elegans. 500 times magnified

Cell-contents. The cell of T. vitrea contains two chromatophore-plates along the connecting zone, they follow the interior of the larger side of the valve; and send some divisions into the keel (PFITZER: Bau und Entw., p. 93).

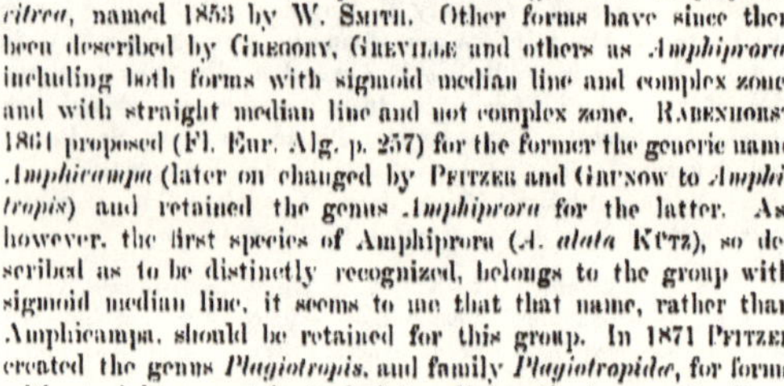

The plates of T. elegans are similar, but they have three deep constrictions nearly dividing them into almost equal patches, the margins of which are deeply indented. T. Lepidoptera has also two strongly indented or serrated plates along the connecting zone. At the ends of the frustule are numerous small granules in lively motion. T. conserta has an entirely different arrangement of the cellcontents, so that it seems questionable whether this species should not be placed in Auricula, the divisions of the zone being perhaps too delicate to be visible. T. conserta has along the neutral side of the zone a flat plasma-mass including two chromatophore-plates separated by a narrow, oblique fissure. The plasma-mass has a broad sinus at each end.

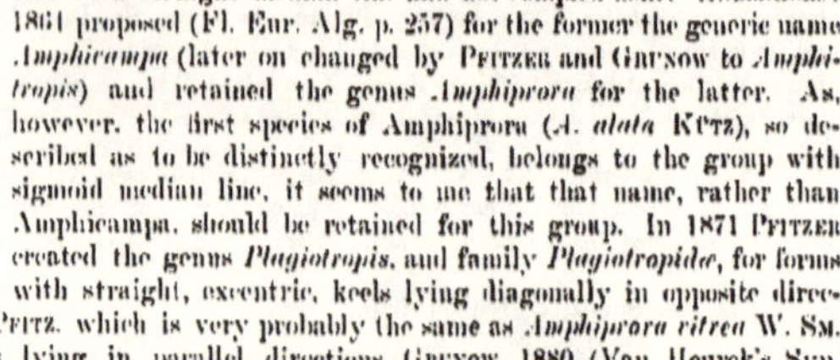

The first known species of this genus is *Amphiprora vitrea*, named 1853 by W. SMITH. Other forms have since then been described by GREGORY, GREVILLE and others as *Amphiprora*, including both forms with sigmoid median line and complex zone, and with straight median line and not complex zone. RABENHORST 1864 proposed (Fl. Eur. Alg. p. 257) for the former the generic name *Amphicampa* (later on changed by PFITZER and GRUNOW to *Amphitropis*) and retained the genus *Amphiprora* for the latter. As, however, the first species of Amphiprora (*A. alata* KÜTZ), so described as to be distinctly recognized, belongs to the group with sigmoid median line, it seems to me that that name, rather than Amphicampa, should be retained for this group. In 1871 PFITZER created the genus *Plagiotropis*, and family *Plagiotropidæ*, for forms with straight, excentric, keels lying diagonally in opposite directions, represented by *P. baltica* PFITZ. which is very probably the same as *Amphiprora vitrea* W. SM. For forms with excentric keels lying in parallel directions GRUNOW 1880 (Van Heurck's Syn. Pl. XXII bis.) created the genus (or more correctly subgenus of Amphora) *Amphoropsis*, in which he includes both forms with complex, and not complex, zones. In the year 1891 I (Diatomiste I p. 51) proposed to unite in one genus, *Tropidoneis*, the forms of Amphiprora with straight median line, those of Plagiotropis, and of Amphoropsis with non-complex zone.

The forms of Tropidoneis have boat-like valves, more or less strongly keeled. The keels are straight (not sigmoid) and either central (*Orthotropis*), or excentric. In the latter case they are either turned in opposite directions (*Plagiotropis*), or in the same direction (*Amphoropsis*). To treat these groups as different genera seems to me not to be natural; as the excentricity of the keel is subject to variation. On one or both sides of the keel there is frequently an expansion, or *wing*, which in the valvular view has the appearance of a longitudinal line. On the broader side of the

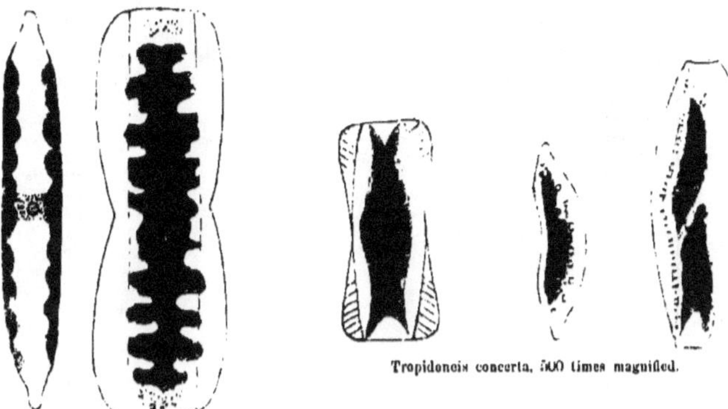

Tropidoneis concerta, 500 times magnified.

Tropidoneis Lepidoptera, 500 times magnified.

valves of Plagiotropis there is frequently a longitudinal band, the nature of which is not quite clear to me. It may be a wing, or a crest, as in many Nitzschieæ, or perhaps a furrow.

Tropidoneis has evidently a close affinity with the Nitzschiæ of the Grunowian divisions Bilobatæ and Pseudo-amphiprora. Among the Raphidieæ it may be akin to the carinated forms of Gyrosigma, or the so called Donkiniæ. It is also closely related to the Naviculæ of the section *fusiformes* which, although their valves are not keeled, agree with Tropidoneis in the nature of the sculpture of their values, in then non-complex zones, and in the approximate central pores of their median lines.

The species of Tropidoneis do not inhabit fresh water. Forms of the section Plagiotropis are very frequent in brackish water. The large, wingless forms of Orthotropis are pelagic in their habits, and the winged, marine. They occur in all parts of the world from the arctic seas to the tropical.

The forms of Tropidoneis are in many cases very imperfectly known, so that several species are to be regarded as doubtful. The study of them is difficult, especially as regards the nature of the wings, which require a favourable position of the valves for their examination.

Artificial key.

I. Orthotropis, median line central or nearly central.

1.	Valve without wings	2.
	with —	5.
2.	Valve moderately high	*T. adriatica* Cl.
	— very high	3.

3.	Valve thin	4.
	— solid	*T. solidula* Cl.
4.	Frustule in zonal view elliptical	*T. antarctica* Cl.
	— — rectangular	*T. membranacea* Cl.
5.	Valve nearly flat	*T. longa* Cl.
	— elevated	6.
6.	Wing close to the keel	*T. approximata* Cl.
	— not —	7.
7.	Central area indistinct or small	*T. Lepidoptera* Greg.
	— distinct —	*T. maxima* Greg.

II. **Plagiatropis** Pfitzer, median line excentric; keels of the valves in contrary directions.

1.	Striæ coarse and distant	*T. Zebra* Cl.
	— close	2.
2.	Striæ crossed by blank, longitudinal bands	*T. seriata* Cl.
	— not — — —	3.
3.	Valve not striate along the margin	4.
	— striate to the margin	5.
4.	Transverse striæ about 15 in 0,01 mm.	*T. japonica* Cl.
	— — — 19 —	*T. semistriata* Grun.
5.	Frustule constricted in the middle	6.
	— not or slightly	9.
6.	Wing or longitudinal band instinct	*T. samoensis* Grun.
	— — — distinct	7.
7.	Valve broad	*T. sumbavensis* Cl.
	— narrow	8.
8.	L. about 0,08 mm.	*T. gibberula* Grun.
	— 0,14 mm.	*T. chinensis* Cl.
9.	Valve narrow, almost linear	10.
	— broader, lanceolate	11.
10.	L. 0,2 to 0,27 mm.	*T. elegans* Greg.
	L. about 0,06 mm.	*T. pusilla* Greg.
11.	L. 0,06 mm.	*T. Van Heurckii* Grun.
	L. 0,09 to 0,2 mm.	12.
12.	Longitudinal band, if present, not interrupted	13.
	— — interrupted in the middle	*T. lata* Cl.
13.	Longitudinal striæ slightly finer than the transverse	*T. Kinkeriana* Cl.
	— much — —	*T. vitrea* W. Sm.

III. **Amphoropsis** Grun., median line excentric; keels of the valves turned in the same directions.

1.	Keels without coarse ribs	*T. recta* Greg.
	— with —	*T. concerta* Lewis.

1. **T. antarctica** Grun. (1878). — Frustule membranaceous, elliptical in outline. L. 0,19 to 0,24; B. 0,06 to 0,08 mm. Central area small, stauriform (the central nodule probably being a little transversely dilated). Transverse and longitudinal striæ 21 (16 to 18 Brun) in 0,01 mm., the median transverse striæ more distant than the others. — *Amphipr.? antarctica* Grun. in Cl. M. D. No. 125. *Navicula Challengeri* Grun. A. D. p. 64 (1880). *Stauroneis glacialis* Castrac. Voy. Challeng. D., p. 25. Pl. XXVII f. 11, 1886? *Amphipr. fragilis* Temp. n. Brun. D. fossiles du Japon, p. 14. Pl. IX f. 14 (1889).

Marine, pelagic: Antarctic Ocean! Japan, fossil (Brun.).

2. **T. membranacea** Cl. (1873). Frustule membranaceous, rectangular, very slightly constricted, with rounded angles. L. 0,25 to 0,35; B. 0,07 to 0,125 mm. Central area indistinct. Transverse striæ 20 to 24, longitudinal 30 to 32 in 0,01 mm. — *Amphiprora membranacea* Cl. D. of the Sea of Java p. 12, Pl. II, f. 18.

Marine, pelagic: Java! Sumbava (Kinker Coll.)! Colon (Deby Coll.)!

3. **T. solidula** Cl. N. Sp. — V. strongly silicious, in the zonal view linear, with straight dorsal margin, curved at the ends. L. 0,19; B. 0,02 mm. Central area indistinct. Transverse striæ 14 to 15 in 0.01 mm., composed of distinct puncta forming undulating longitudinal striæ, about 14 in 0,01 mm. — Pl. II f. 19, 20, 21.

Marine: Rembang Bay (Debys Coll.)!

4. **T. longa** Cl. (1873) — Frustule narrow, rectangular, with parallel margins, not constricted in the middle. L. 0,19 to 0,3; B. 0,025 to 0,036 mm. V. slightly convex, narrow, linear-lanceolate, acute. Wings distinct, on both sides of the median line. Central area large, transverse. Transverse striæ 16 in 0,01 mm. Longitudinal striæ about 28 in 0,01 mm. – *Amphiprora longa* Cl. D. of Arct. S. p. 20 Pl. III f. 15. — Icon. n. Pl. III f. 8.

Marine: Spitsbergen! Finmark! Greenland!

Var.? *gracilis* Grun. (1880). — V. in L. 0,2 to 0,28; B. 0,016 to 0,018 mm. Wings obsolete. Central area small, transversely dilated. Transverse striæ 16 to 17 in 0,01 mm., longitudinal finer. Frustule linear, somewhat constricted, B. 0,028 (ends) to 0,021 (middle) — *Amphipr. elegans v. gracilis* Grun. A. D. p. 64.

Marine: Adriatic (Grun.).

5. **T. Lepidoptera** Greg. (1857). — Frustule elongated, rectangular, strongly constricted in the middle. L. 0,12 to 0.20; B. 0,03 to 0,04, at the constriction 0.013 to 0,018 mm. Wings distinct, usually projecting above the central nodule. V. linear-lanceolate, with acute and frequently apiculate ends. L. 0,12 to 0,20; B. 0,018 to 0,022 mm. Central area indistinct, or small, and transversely lanceolate. Wing usually unilateral. Transverse striæ 20 to 21 in 0,01 mm., finely punctate. — *Amphiprora Lepidoptera* Greg. T. M. S. Vol. V. p. 76. Pl. I f. 39. D. of Clyde p. 505 Pl. XII f. 59 (not. *c*). Rabh. a. Jan. Honduras D. p. 3. Pl. III f. 5. V. H. Syn. p. 120 Pl. XXII f. 2, 3. *Amphipr. quarnerensis* Grun. Verh. 1860 p. 569 Pl. VII f. 1. *Amphipr. mediterranea* Grun. l. c. Pl. VII f. 3 (not V. H. Syn.)?

Marine: Finmark! North Sea (Sweden! England! France!) Adriatic! Macassar Straits! King George's Sound! Sumatra! Port Jackson! Galapagos Islands! Colon! Barbados!

Var. *samoensis* Grun. (1880). — Frustule elongated, strongly constricted in the middle. L. 0,2; B. 0,05 mm. Wings distinct, not projecting beyond the central nodule. V. lanceolate, acute. L. 0,2 to 0,26; B. 0,03 to 0,037 mm. Central area indistinct. Transverse striæ 15 to 16 in 0,01 mm. inside the wing, 14 in 0,01 mm. outside the wing. Wings on both sides of the median line. — *Amphipr. Lepidopt. var. samoensis* Grun. A. D. p. 65.

Marine: Samoa! Tahiti (Grun.), Honolulu (Grun.).

Var. *proboscidea* Cl. — V. linear-elliptical, apiculate. L. 0,075; B. 0,018 mm. Median line slightly excentric. Wing unilateral, at some distance from the median line. Central area small, orbicular. Striæ transverse, 16 in 0,01 mm., faint inside the wing.

Brackish water: Africa, Cameroon!

Var. *minor* Cl. — V. in L. 0,08; B. 0,013, at the constriction 0,01 mm. Wing unilateral. Striæ 20 in 0,01 mm.

Marine: St. Lunaire (Temp. Perag. Types N:o 292 as *T. Van-Heurckii*).

Var. *delicatula* Grev. (1863). — V. in L. 0,064 to 0,075; B. 0,015 mm. Striæ 26 in 0,01 mm. — *Amphipr. delic.* Grev. Edinb. N. Ph. J. XVIII p. 36 f. 15, 16.

Marine: Cette! Woodlark Island (Grev.), Labuan!

Amphiprora indica Grun. (Verh. 1860 p. 570, Pl. VI f. 13, Pl. VII f. 2) resembles Trop. Lepidoptera but is described as having a row of puncta along the median line. I have seen no specimen of this form, which Grunow does not mention in his synopsis of the Amphiproræ in A. D. — *Amphiprora didyma* W. Sm. (B. D. I p. 44, Pl. XV f. 125) has also puncta along the median line. This diatom may perhaps be a Nitzschia.

6. **T. approximata** Cl. N. Sp. — V. narrow, lanceolate, with acute ends, very convex. L. 0,2 to 0,3; B. 0,034 mm. Central area indistinct. Wing unilateral, close to the median line. Transverse striæ 19, longitudinal about 30 in 0,01 mm. — Pl. III f. 20, 21.

Marine: Rembang Bay (Deby Coll.)! Macassar Straits (Grove Coll.)! Colon (Deby Coll.)!

7. **T. adriatica** Cl. N. Sp. — Frustule narrow, linear, slightly constricted in the middle. L. 0,18; B. 0,025 mm. Wings indistinct. V. narrow lanceolate. L. 0,2; B. 0,018 mm. Central area small, transverse, narrowed towards the margin. Transverse striæ 15 to 16, longitudinal 27 in 0,01 mm. — Pl. III f. 22, 33.

Marine: Adriatic!

8. **T. maxima** Greg. (1857). Frustule strongly constricted in the middle. L. 0,13 to 0,17; B. 0,04 to 0,07, at the constriction 0,022 mm. Wings very distinct, projecting beyond the central nodule. V. lanceolate, acute. L. 0,22 to 0,24; B. 0,032 to 0,033 mm. Wing unilateral. Central area distinct, narrow, transversely lanceolate. Transverse striæ 15, longitudinal 21 in 0,01 mm., a little more distant outside the wing. — *Amphiprora maxima* Greg. D. of Clyde p. 507, Pl. XII f. 61. V. H. Syn. p. 120 Pl. XXII f. 4, 5. Grun. A. D. p. 65.

Marine: North Sea! Mediterranean Sea! Adriatic! Java! Macassar Straits (Grove Coll.)!

Var. *subalata* Cl. — L. 0,15 mm. Wing not projecting beyond the central nodule. Transverse striæ 19 in 0,01 mm., more distinct in the middle, punctate; puncta forming undulating, longitudinal rows, about 16 in 0,01 mm.

Marine: Macassar Straits (Grove Coll.)!

Var.? *decussata* Cl. — V. in L. 0,16; B. 0,024 mm. Transverse striæ 15 in 0,01 mm., punctate; puncta forming fine decussating lines, about 19 in 0,01 mm. — Pl. III f. 24, 25.

Marine: Seyshelles (Van Heurck Coll.)!

Var. *dubia* Cl. a. Grun. (1880). L. 0,072 to 0,09; B. 0,012 to 0,013 mm. Central area rounded. Transverse striæ 17 to 18 in 0,01 mm. — *Amphipr. maxima* var. *dubia* A. D. p. 65. Pl. V f. 89.

Marine: Finmark!

It seems to be generally considered that there are wings on both sides of the median line, but so far as I have seen, on examining a number of specimens, there is a wing only on one of the sides. The wings of one frustule are diagonal. The following insufficiently described and figured species seem to be akin to T. maxima: *Amphiprora oblonga* Grev. (T. M. S. XI p. 20, Pl. I f. 15, 1863). *Amphipr. eximia* Grev. (Edinb. N. Ph. J. XVIII p. 36 f. 13, 1863), *Amphipr. Wendtii* Witt (J. Mus. Godeffr. H. I p. 69 Pl. VIII f. 3, 1873).

9. **T. sumbavensis** Cl. N. Sp. — V. lanceolate, gibbous in the middle. L. 0,15; B. 0,03 mm. Central area unilateral, quadrate. Wing unilateral, very distinct. Transverse striæ 19 in 0,01 mm. Longitudinal striæ very fine.

Marine: Sumbava (Kinker Coll.)!

This form is evidently nearly akin to T. maxima.

10. **T. gibberula** Grun. (1882). Frustule rectangular, with rounded angles, constricted in the middle. L. 0,07 to 0,09; B. 0,017 mm. Wing slightly projecting outside the central nodule. V. narrow, lanceolate, with subcapitate ends, inæquilateral, the broadest side having a gibbosity in the middle. B. 0,02 mm. Striæ 16 in 0,01 mm. finely punctate. — *Plagiotropis gibberula* Grun. in Cl. M. D. N:o 309. V. H. Syn. Pl. XXII bis f. 12, 13.

Marine: Firth of Tay! China (Deby Coll.)!

11. **T. pusilla** Greg. (1857). — Frustule rectangular, with rounded angles, scarcely constricted in the middle. L. 0,055; B. 0,012 mm. V. narrow, lanceolate, unilaterally gibbous. Central area indistinct. Striæ 15 in 0,01 mm. *Amphipr. pusilla* Greg. D. of Clyde p. 504 Pl. XII f. 56.

Marine: North Sea (Coasts of Scotland! Belgium!)

12. **T. chinensis** Cl. N. Sp. — Frustule elongated, with rounded ends, constricted in the middle. L. 0,14; B. 0,03 mm., at the constriction 0,018 mm. V. narrow, lanceolate, acute, unilaterally gibbous. L. 0,14; B. 0,02 mm. Central area transversely lanceolate. Transverse striæ 18 in 0,01 mm., finely punctate. — Pl. III f. 5, 6, 7.

Marine: China (Deby Coll.)!

This form, which is somewhat doubtful as a species, resembles T. Lepidoptera.

13. **T. semistriata** Grun. (1879). — V. somewhat membranaceous, elongated, rectangular, slightly constricted. L. 0,075; B. 0,026 mm. V. lanceolate, acute. L. 0,09; B. 0,015 mm. Keel somewhat excentric. Transverse striæ 19 in 0,01 mm., not reaching the margin of the valve where is a broad blank band. — *Amphipr. semistriata* Grun. A. M. D. N:o 196. Icon. n. P. III f. 9, 10, 11.

Brackish water: South Africa!

14. **T. japonica** Cl. N. Sp. — V. strongly constricted in the middle. L. 0,11; B. 0,02 mm. Wing projecting beyond the central nodule. Transverse striæ 14 (wing) to 16 (keel) in 0,01 mm., not reaching the margin, where is a blank band. Longitudinal striæ fine, about 30 in 0,01 mm.

Marine: Sendaï, Japan, fossil (Brun Coll.)!

15. **T. elegans** W. Sm. (1856). — Frustule linear, rectangular, not constricted in the middle. L. 0,18; B. 0,04 mm. V. narrow, linear, very convex and inequilateral. L. 0,2 to 0,27; B. 0,013 mm. Wing on the broader part. Central area small, rounded. Transverse striæ 13 to 14 in 0,01 mm.; longitudinal striæ 23 in 0,01 mm. — *Amphipr. elegans* W. Sm. B. D. II p. 90. Greg. D. of Clyde. p. 505 Pl. XII f. 58, 58 b. V. H. Syn. p. 122 Pl. XXII f. 1, 6.

Marine: North Sea (Coast of Sweden! England! Belgium!) Mediterranean Sea! Adriatic!

Var. *Adriatica* Grun. (1880). — Frustule not constricted, narrowed towards the ends. L. 0,17 to 0,30; B. 0,035 to 0,05 mm. V. in B. 0,018 to 0,02 mm. Wing distinct. Central area small. Transverse striæ 13,5 in 0,01 mm. Longitudinal striæ finer but sharp. — *Amphipr. eleg. c. Adriatica* Grun. A. D. p. 64.

Marine: Adriatic (Grun.).

Var.? *Poscwitzii* Pant. (1889). L. 0,108; Height 0,0225, in the middle 0,0175 mm. Striæ 22,5 to 25 in 0,01 mm. punctate. — *Amphipr. (elegans var.?) Poscw.* Pant. II, p. 56 Pl. X. f. 181.

Marine: Hungary, fossil (Pantocsek).

It does not appear very probable that this form belongs to A elegans. The figure in Pantocseks work, although not clear, seems to represent some form of. T. vitrea.

16. **T. Van Heurckii** Grun. (1880). — Frustule nearly rectangular, not constricted. L. 0,06; B. 0,02 mm. On the broader side is a longitudinal band (wing?) forming a line, abruptly bent at about one third of the length of the value. Striæ 22 in 0,01 mm. — *Plagiotropis Van Heurckii* Grun. V. H. Syn. Pl. XXII bis f. 6 to 8.

Brackish water: Belgium!

17. **T. vitrea** W. Sm. (1853). — Frustule elliptical, truncate, very slightly constricted in the middle. L. 0,085 to 0,145; B. 0,03 to 0,04 mm. V. lanceolate, very asymmetrical. B. 0,012 to 0,018 mm. Central area indistinct. The broader side of the valve with or without a longitudinal band. Transverse striæ 18 in 0,01 mm. *Amphipr. vitrea* W. Sm. B. D. I, Pl. XXXI f. 270. *Plagiotropis vitrea* Grun. A. D. p. 67. V. H. Syn., Pl. XXII f. 7 to 9. *Plagiotr. baltica* Pfitzer: Bau und Entw. p. 94, 1871? *Plagiotr. vitrea* var. *Lindigii* Grun. A. D. p. 67.

Brackish water: North Sea (coasts of Sweden! Belgium! England!) Atlantic coast of North America! West Indies! California!

Var. *mediterranea* Grun. (1880). — Frustule nearly rectangular, slightly constricted in the middle. L. 0,075 to 0,15; B. 0,015 to 0,02 mm. The broader side of the valve with a longitudinal, broad, indistinctly punctate band. Transverse striæ 20, longitudinal 24 in 0,01 mm. — *Plagiotro-*

pis (baltica var.?) mediterranea GRUN. A. D. p. 66. *Amphiprora (Plagiotr.) medit.* GRUN. in V. H. Syn. Pl. XXII f. 14.

Marine: Mediterranean Sea (GRUN.), Adriatic (GRUN.), Samoa (GRUN.), Connecticut, Morris Creek!

Var. *scaligera* GRUN. (1880). — Frustule scarcely constricted. L. 0,1 to 0,13; B. 0,025 to 0,045 mm. The longitudinal band with coarse, transverse ribs. Striæ 17 to 18 in 0,01 mm. — *Plagiotr. (baltica var.?) scaligera* GRUN. A. D. p. 66, Pl. V f. 90.

Marine: Finmark!

The longitudinal band in this species appears to be subject to great variation. In the type it is always scarcely perceptible; in the varieties, it forms a broad band. — *Amphiprora? superba* GREV. (Edinb. N. Ph. J. XVIII p. 39 f. 17, 1863) represents probably a large form akin to T. vitrea.

18. **T. seriata** CL. (1892). — V. in the zonal-view linear, with straight dorsal margin, curved only at the ends, not constricted in the middle, very elevated and distinctly asymmetrical. L. 0,4; Height 0,04 mm. Transverse striæ 12 in 0,01 mm. crossed by several, blank, longitudinal bands. — CL. Diatomiste I p. 75 Pl. XII f. 2 to 4.

Marine: Connecticut! Colon! Jamaica!

This species, evidently akin to T. elegans, is remarkable for its large size and the peculiar striation; the striæ forming several longitudinal rows.

19. **T. Zebra** CL. (1892). — V. strongly asymmetrical, lanceolate. L. 0,18; B. 0,03 mm. Central area indistinct. There is a broad, marginal band on the broader side of the value. Striæ 5 to 6 in 0,01 mm. inequidistant, finely punctate, puncta 21 in 0,01 mm. — CL. Diatomiste I p. 75 Pl. XII f. 1.

Brackish water: Newark, N. Jers. fossil from the Champlain epoch ! Brazil, St Vincent!

20. **T. samoensis** GREV. (1880). — Frustule strongly constricted in the middle. V. in length 0,095 to 0,12; B. 0,023 to 0,027 mm. Longitudinal band very obscure. Striæ 16 to 19 in 0,01 mm. somewhat more distant in the middle, punctate. — *Plagiot. samoensis* GRUN. A. D. p. 67.

Marine: Samoa (GRUN.). West Indies (GRUN.).

21. **T. Kinkeriana** CL. N. Sp. — V. strongly asymmetrical, not constricted in the middle. L. 0,2; Height 0,032 mm. The broader side of the valve with a very broad band. Central area small, but distinct. Transverse striæ 14, longitudinal 17 in 0,01 mm. Pl. III f. 1, 2.

Marine: Sumbava (Kinker Coll.)!

22. **T. lata** CL. N. Sp. — V. not constricted. L. 0,135; Height 0,035 mm. On the broader side of the valve there is a band interupted in the middle. Transverse striæ 18 in 0,01 mm. punctate; puncta, about 23 in 0,01 mm., forming undulating, longitudinal rows. — Pl. III f. 3, 4.

Marine: Java, Rembang Bay (Deby Coll.)!

23. **T. recta** GREG. (1857). — Frustule rectangular, with rounded angles, slightly constricted in the middle. L. 0,08 to 0,09; B. 0,02 to 0,028 mm. V. strongly inequilateral, without distinct wing. Transverse striæ 21 to 24 in 0,01 mm. — *Amphipr. recta* GREG. T. M. S. Vol. V. p. 76 Pl. I f. 40. *Plagiotr. recta* GRUN. CL. M. D. N:o 310. *Amphoropsis recta* GRUN. V. H. Syn. Pl. XXII bis f. 9, 10.

Marine: Firth of Tay!

Var.? *subplicata* GRUN. (1880). — L. 0,051; B. 0,018 mm. Wing obscure. Transverse striæ 17 in 0,01 mm. — *Amphipr. plicata v. subplicata* GRUN. A. D. p. 65 Pl. V f. 88.

Brackish water: Sea of Kara (GRUN.).

24. **T. conserta** LEWIS. (1861). — Frustule membranaceous, rectangular, with rounded angles, slightly constricted in the middle. L. 0,08 to 0,16; B. 0,034 to 0,04 mm. V. lanceolate Keel with a number of coarse, radiate ribs. — *Amphipr. conserta* LEWIS. Proceed. Ac. Nat. Sc. of Philad. 1861, Pl. I f. 5.

Marine: Gullmarsfjord, Sweden! Atlantic coast of N. America (LEWIS.).

This species, which I have found at Fiskebäckskil (West-coast of Sweden) mong Zostera, is scarcely silicious, the frustules disappearing almost completely, if burnt on a glasscover.

This very interesting species, according to LEWIS lives in colonies, and forms curved filaments of 12 or more frustules. He figures such a colony in top-view, which shows that the frustules keep in contact by means of the wings.

Other species, which perhaps belong to Amphoropsis are *Amphipr.? paradoxa* GREV. (Edinb. N. Ph. J. XVIII p. 41 f. 21, 1863) remarkable for its coarsely moniliform striæ, and *Amph. Thwaitesiana* GREV. (l. c. p. 183 f. 9) notably distinguished by its strongly marked wings, which are striate, other parts of the valve not showing any striation.

Dictyoneis CL. (1890).

Valve elongated, panduriform or lanceolate. Median line straight with the terminal fissures usually in contrary directions. Valve with double structure; the upper stratum finely punctate, with puncta disposed in decussating rows; the interior stratum irregularly reticulate with rounded cellules. Marginal cellules frequently larger than the others, forming a row of false loculi. Connecting zone not complex.

The first known species of this genus is *Navicula marginata* LEWIS. The larger marginal cellules of several species give to the valves some appearance of *Mastogloia*, in which genus several forms of Dictyoneis have by various authors been placed. In the year 1877 GRUNOW expresses the opinion that the marginal cellules seem not to belong to a separate plate as in Mastogloia, but to the valve itself and proposes a new genus for *Mast.? reticulata* and the allied species. In the year 1890 I proposed (Diatomiste I p. 14) for this genus the name *Dictyoneis*, founded on the peculiar structure of the valve. Unfortunately I have in that paper committed an error, as I then supposed the stratum with coarse reticulations to be the upper instead of the lower.

The median line of most species of Dictyoneis is straight and ends in terminal fissures, turned in contrary directions. The central pores are moderately distant, except in D. naviculoides, where they are very approximate. On both sides of the median line are narrow structureless zones, which are more silicious than the other parts of the valve and are united to the central nodule.

The genus Dictyoneis is well distinguished from all the other naviculoid genera. Its systematical place is doubtful, as there are no intermediate forms connecting it with other diatoms. The structure of the outer stratum of the valve as well as the terminal fissures point perhaps to some relation to Pleurosigma.

The species are all marine and belong to warmer seas. Fossil forms occur at Oamaru and in Hungary.

This genus comprises forms, which are so closely connected, that the distinction of well defined species is very difficult, as is frequently the case with truly natural groups. Such characteristics as the outline of the valve, the coarseness of the reticulation etc. are very variable.

Artificial key.

1.	Marginal cellules larger than the others	3.
	— not — —	2.
2.	Valves panduriform	*D. jamaicensis* GREV.
	— lanceolate	*D. naviculacea* CL.
3.	Valve not constricted	*D. Thumii* CL.
	— slightly constricted	4.
	— strongly	6.

4. { Marginal cellules of unequal size . . . . *D. panduriformis*
  { — — equal — . . . . 5.

5. { Cellules of the valve 9 in 0,01 mm. . . . . *D. subconstricta* Cl.
  { — — — 17 — . . . . *D. Pantocseki* Cl.

6. { Segments narrow, linear . . . . *D. rugosa* Temp. a. Br.
  { — broad — . . . . 7.

7. { Marginal cellules about 5 in 0,01 mm . . . . *D. marginata* Lewis.
  { — — — 10 — . . . . *D. mastogloides* Pant.

1. **D. naviculacea** Cl. (1890). — V. elliptic-lanceolate. L. 0,09; B. 0,23 mm. Central nodule very small, surrounded by a moderately large, orbicular area. Terminal fissures indistinct, turned in the same direction. Cellules of the valve of about equal size, 10 in 0,01 mm. Transverse striae not seen. — Cl. Diatomiste I p. 15. Icon. n. Pl. V f. 34.

Marine: Pensacola, Florida!

This species, of which I have seen one specimen only, seems to be extremely rare.

2. **D. jamaicensis** Grev. (1868). V. strongly constricted in the middle with cuneate or elliptic-lanceolate segments and obtuse ends. L. 0,08 to 0,12; B. 0,024 to 0,032, at the constriction 0,013 to 0,02 mm. Terminal fissures in opposite directions. Cellules of the valve about 11 in 0,01 mm., obscure around the central nodule. Transverse striae 24 to 27 in 0,01 mm. — *Nav. jamaicensis* Grev. T. M. S. XIV p. 126 Pl. XII f. 23. *Nav. tortuosa* Leud.-Fortm. D. de Ceylan p. 34 Pl. II f. 26 1879 *Mastogloia? reticulata* Peragallo D. de Villefr. Pl. II f. 10, 1888. — Pl. V f. 32.

Marine: Mediterranean Sea! Adriatic! Red Sea (Van Heurck Coll.)! Ceylon! Sumatra (Deby Coll.)! Cebu (Grove Coll.)! New Guinea (Grove Coll.)! West Indies (Grev.).

Var. *gigantea* Cl. — L. 0,21; B. 0,045 at the constriction 0,022 mm. Cellules about 16 in 0,01 mm. Striae 25 in 0,01 mm.

Marine: Oamaru, New Zealand, fossil (Grove Coll.)! — Pl. V f. 35, 36.

3. **D. marginata** Lewis (1861). V. strongly constricted in the middle. L. 0,85 to 0,18; B. 0,024 to 0,044, at the constriction 0,008 to 0,022 mm. Segments cuneate to elliptical, with obtuse extremities. Terminal fissures in opposite directions. Marginal cellules of equal size, 4 to 5 in 0,01 mm. Cellules of the valve 8 to 12 in 0,01 mm.

The following forms may be distinguished.

1. { Marginal cellules forming a broad band . . . . Var. *spectatissima*.
  { — — — narrow — . . . . 2.

2. { Valve about 3 times longer than broad . . . . 3.
  { — — 4 — — — . . . . Var. *intermedia*.
  { — — 5 to 6 — — — . . . . 4.

3. { Segments cuneate . . . . Var. *typica*.
  { — elliptic-lanceolate . . . . Var. *Janischii*.
  { — elliptical with rounded ends . . . . Var. *Clevi*.

4. { L. 0,11 to 0,12 mm. . . . . Var. *commutata*.
  { L. 0,18 mm. . . . . Var. *gigantea*.

Var. *typica* Cl. — V. about 3 times longer than broad, deeply constricted, with cuneate, obtuse segments. L. 0,085 to 0,15; B. 0,024 to 0,037, at the constriction 0,008 to 0.015 mm. Marginal cellules 4 to 5 in 0,01 mm., forming a narrow band; cellules of the valve 8 to 12 in 0,01 mm., forming irregular, transverse rows. Transverse striae 26 to 27 in 0,01 mm. — *Navicula marginata* Lewis Proceed. Acad. Nat. Sc. Philad. 1861 p. 64 Pl. II f. 1. *Nav. strangulata* Grev. T. M. S. XIV p. 126 Pl. XII f. 24; 1866. - *Nav. reticulata* Grun. Hedwigia VI p. 26. *Mastogloia? reticulata* Grun. M. M. J. 1877 p. 175 Pl. CXCV f. 4. *Navic. Kossuthii* Pant. I p. 26 Pl. XVI f. 120; 1886. *Dictyoneis marginata* Cl. Diatomiste I p. 16 1890. A. S. Atl. Pl. CLX f. 20, 23, 28, 29. CLXXXVIII f. 47.

Marine: Mediterranean Sea, Alexandria (Deby Coll.)! Levant (Grove Coll.)! Delaware (LEWIS) Florida! West Indies! Colon! Gulf of Mexico! Java (ATL.) Fossil Szákal, S:t Peter, Hungary, (Pantocsek).

Var. *Janischii* CASTR. (1886). — Segments elliptic-lanceolate, obtuse. L. 0,1; B. 0,025 to 0,03, at the constriction 0,015 mm. Marginal cellules 4 to 4, 5 in 0,01 mm. Cellules of the valve 10 to 11 in 0,01 mm. Transverse striæ 26 to 27 in 0,01 mm. — *Navic. Jan.* CASTR. D. Voyage Challenger p. 29 Pl. XXX f. 5. *Mastogloia reticulata var. japonica* BRUN. D. fossiles du Japon p. 72; 1889. *Dictyoneis marginata* A. S. Atl. CLX f. 17, 18, 19, 21. *D. marg. v. Jan.* A. S. Atl. CLXXXVIII f. 50.

Marine: Madagascar (Brun Coll.)! Cebu! Java (Atl.), Japan (Atl.), Samoa (Atl.). Galapagos Islands! Bermudas (Castr.) Florida! Campeachy Bay! Colon (Deby Coll.)! Oamaru fossil, (Atl.)

Var. *Clevei* BRUN. (1889). — Segments broad, elliptical, with rounded ends. L. 0,11 to 0,125; B. 0,042, at the constriction 0,013 mm. Marginal cellules 3 to 4 in 0,01 mm. — *Mastogloia Clevei* BRUN a. TEMP. D. foss du Japon p. 39 Pl. IX f. 18. *D. margin. v. Clevei* A. S. Atl. CLXXXVIII. 46.

Marine: Java! Japan fossil and living, (BRUN).

Var. *intermedia* CL. — Segments narrow, elliptical. L. 0,12; B. 0,03, at the constriction 0,014 mm. Marginal cellules 4 in 0,01 mm. Cellules of the valve 10 in 0,01 mm. Transverse striæ 24 in 0,01 mm. — *Mastogloia Clevei* BRUN. A. S. Atl. Pl. CLX f. 34, 35.

Marine: Nossi Bé (Brun Coll.)! Japan (Atl.).

Var. *commutata* CL. — V. about 6 times longer than broad, gently constricted in the middle. Segments narrow, elliptical to elliptic-lanceolate. Ends obtuse. L. 0,11 to 0,12; B. 0,021 to 0,025, at the constriction 0,01 to 0,12 mm. Marginal cellules 5 to 6 in 0,01 mm. Cellules of the valve 12 in 0,01 mm. Transverse striæ 25 in 0,01 mm. — *Dictyoneis marginata f. elongata* A. S. Atl. CLX f. 30.

Marine: Manila (Deby Coll.)! Macassar Straits (Grove Coll.)! Sumbava (Kinker Coll.)! Campeachy Bay! Rio Janeiro (Deby Coll.)!

Var. *gigantea* CL. — V. as in the Var. commutata. L. 0,18; B. 0,044, at the constriction 0,022 mm. Marginal cellules 4 in 0,01 mm. Cellules of the valve 9 in 0,01 mm.

Marine: Oamaru, New Zealand, fossil (Grove Coll.)!

Var. *spectatissima* GREV. (1866). — V. strongly constricted, with cuneate, obtuse segments. L. 0,09 to 0,13; B. 0,03, at the constriction 0,013 mm. Marginal cellules broad, 4 in 0,01 mm. Cellules of the valve coarse, 8 in 0,01 mm. Transverse striæ 23 in 0,01 mm. — *Navic. spectatissima* GREV. T. M. S. Vol. XIV p. 84 Pl. IX f. 29. *Dictyoneis spect.* A. S. Atl. CLX f. 24 to 26, 32.

Marine: Zanzibar (Grev.) Seychelles (Van Heurcks Coll.)! Campeachy Bay (Atl.). Campeachy Bank (Atl.).

4. **D. Thumii** CL. (1890). — V. linear-lanceolate, with obtuse ends. L. 0,11 to 0,15; B. 0,022 to 0,032 mm. Terminal fissures in contrary directions. Marginal cellules 4 to 5 in 0,01 mm., of equal size. Cellules of the valve about 11 in 0,01 mm. Transverse striæ 24 to 25 in 0,01 mm. — Cl. Diatomiste I p. 15. Icon. n. Pl. V f. 33. A. S. Atl. CLXXXVIII f. 44, 45.

Marine: Red Sea (Atl.) Seychelles (Van Heurck Coll.)! Java! Cebu! China! Brazil. (Atl.).

D. Thumii is nearly akin to *D. marginata var. commutata*. The fig. 31 Pl. CLX and fig. 49 Pl. CLXXXVIII in A. S. Atl. seem to represent intermediate forms, as also *Pseudodictyoneis hungarica* Pant. III Pl. I f. 8.

5. **D. subconstricta** CL. N. Sp. — V. slightly constricted, with broad, elliptic-lanceolate segments. L. 0,055 to 0,083; B. 0,024 to 0,03, at the constriction 0,018 mm. Marginal cellules 4 in 0,01 mm. Cellules of the valve 9 in 0,01 mm. Transverse striæ 23 in 0,01 mm. — Pl. V f. 31.

Marine: Madagascar! Cebu! Campeachy Bay!

This form is nearly akin to *D. marginata var. Janischii* and is perhaps more correctly to be appreciated as a less constricted form of this variety.

6. **D. mastogloidea** PANT. (1886). — V. strongly constricted, with cuneate, obtuse ends. L. 0,078; B. 0,024; at the constirction 0,013 mm. Marginal cellules about 10 in 0,01 mm. Cellules of the valve 14 in 0,01 mm. — *Nav. mast.* PANT. I. p. 27 Pl. XXI f. 192.

Marine: Hungary, fossil (Pant.).

This species appears, to judge from the fig. in Pantocsek's work, to connect *D. marginata* and *D. jamaicensis*

7. **D. rugosa** TEMP. a. BRUN. (1889). — V. narrow, about 7 times longer than broad, gently constricted, and with linear, subtruncate segments. L. 0,2 to 0,225; B. 0,026 to 0,03, at the constriction 0,013 mm. Terminal fissures in contrary directions. Marginal cellules small, 5 in 0,01 mm. Cellules of the valve obscure. — *Mastogloia rugosa* TEMP. a. BRUN. D. foss. du Japon p. 39 Pl. IX f. 20. *Dictyoneis rugosa* CL. Diatomiste I. p. 17. A. S. Atl. CLX f. 33.

Marine: Japan, fossil (Temp. Br.).

8. **D. Pantocsekii** CL. (1890). — V. gently constricted, with tongue-shaped segments and obtuse extremities. L. 0,11; B. 0,034, at the constriction 0,027 mm. Median line with the terminal fissures in contrary directions and approximate central pores. Marginal cellules 5 in 0,01 mm., of equal size, forming an uninterrupted marginal band. Cellules of the valve about 17 in 0,01 mm., arranged in irregularly undulating transverse and longitudinal rows. Transverse striæ 25 in 0,01 mm. — *Navic. mastogloidea* PANT. II Pl. XXVI f. 387. *Dict. Pant.* CL. Diatomiste I p. 16.

Marine: Hungary, fossil!

9. **D. panduriformis** CL. (1881). V. slightly constricted, with tongue-shaped segments and obtuse ends. L. 0,097; B. 0,027, at the constriction 0,019 mm. Terminal fissures in contrary directions. Marginal cellules about 4 in 0,01 mm., af unequal size, absent in the middle and at the ends. Transverse striæ 20 to 21 in 0,01 mm. — *Mastogloia panduriformis* CL. N. R. D. p. 1 Pl. I f. 1. *Dict. pand.* CL. Diatomiste I p. 16; 1890.

Marine: Galapagos Islands!

Pleurosigma W. SM. (1852).

Valve linear to lanceolate, more or less sigmoid, symmetrical. Median line sigmoid with small central nodule and the ends turned in contrary directions. Axial area indistinct. Central area indistinct or small. Structure: small puncta disposed in transverse and oblique rows. No longitudinal lines. Frustule with narrow, simple zone, arcuate or not. — Cell-contents (of P. angulatum) two chromatophores, indented at their margins. The median part of each chromatophore branches into a large elongated lobe along the interior of one of the valves, and into two similar lobes on the other valve. Division begins by a fissure across the median lobe. After the division of the cell the parts of the chromatophore migrate to the inner side of the old valves (O. MÜLLER, Ber. d. Deutsch. Bot. Ges. 1883 p. 478).

The sigmoid Naviculæ were named *Navicula Sigma* by EHRENBERG. HASSALL (A. History of Brit. Freshw. Algæ 1845 p. 435) proposed for them the name *Gyrosigma*, which was adopted by RABENHORST (Die Süssw. Diat. 1853) but not by other diatomists, who preferred the newer name *Pleurosigma* formed 1852 by W. SMITH, who published the first monograph of the species (Ann. Mag. Nat. Hist. 2 ser. IX p. 1). The genus Pleurosigma, as accepted by all diatomists, includes forms with a structure of small puncta or alveoli, disposed in transverse rows, which are crossed by other rows, either longitudinal, or obliquely decussating. There are no intermediate forms between these two types, and I think they may justly be regarded as different genera. For the forms with the puncta in transverse and longitudinal rows, I adopt the name Gyrosigma, although, as GRUNOW remarks, this name involves a tautology. For the forms with the puncta disposed in transverse and oblique rows, I reserve the name Pleurosigma. In Pleurosigma I also include such of the forms of the Grunowian genus *Rhoicosigma*, as have the same disposition of the striæ as the true Pleurosigma. I have also included in Pleurosigma the Donkiniæ with decussating striæ. The generic name *Staurosigma* may be abolished as it was founded in 1860 by GRUNOW for Ehrenbergs *Stauroneis Sigma*, which is nothing but a frustule of *P. Normanii var. fossilis* (Perag. Monogr. de Pleuros. p. 26). For the few asymmetrical forms of Pleurosigma DONKIN proposed in 1858 (Trans. Micr. Soc. Vol. VI) the generic name *Toxonidea*. I felt at first inclined to include these forms in the genus Pleurosigma, but as such a change would be of little importance and the name Toxonidea is so generally in use, I have decided to retain the latter genus.

Pleurosigma, as here defined, comprises a large number of closely connected forms and is not nearly related to any known genus, with the exception of Toxonidea. Among the Naviculæ some few forms (N. Placenta EHB., N. Quincunx CL.) have the same disposition of the alveoli, but in other respects they are different. The same disposition of the alveoli is found also on the keel of *Amphiprora gigantea*, and in a few Mastogloiæ.

All true Pleurosigma-forms are marine. A few are pelagic in their habits. They occur in all parts of the world.

The distinction of species is a matter of difficulty. GRUNOW has in his monograph (Arct. Diat. 1880) used as characteristics for the groups the angle at which the oblique rows of puncta cross each other. PERAGALLO (Monographie du genre Pleurosigma, Diatomiste 1890—91) has adopted the same method, which I think cannot well be maintained as a natural arrangement.

Artificial key.

1. { Valve very slightly or scarcely sigmoid . . . . . 2.
   — sigmoid — . . . . . 11.
2. { Median line straight, central . . . . . 3.
   — — sigmoid — . . . . . 10.
3. { Ends rostrate . . . . . *P. cuspidatum* CL.
   — not . . . . . 4.
4. { Median oblique striæ more distant than the others . . . . . *P. nicobaricum* GRUN.
   — — — not — — — . . . . . 5.
5. { Transverse and oblique striæ equidistant . . . . . 6.
   — striæ closer than the oblique . . . . . 7.
6. { Valve rhomboid-lanceolate . . . . . *P. directum* GRUN.
   — narrow linear-lanceolate . . . . . *P. nubecula* W. SM.
7. { Ends with a lunate mark . . . . . *P. Endon* PANT.
   — without . . . . . 8.
8. { Valve lanceolate . . . . . *P. galapagense* CL.
   — narrow, linear-lanceolate . . . . . 9.
9. { Transverse striæ 19 in 0,01 mm . . . . . *P. Peragalli* BRUN.
   — — 23 — . . . . . *P. ibericum* PER.
10. { Median oblique striæ more distant than the others . . . . . 11.
   — not — — — . . . . . 12.
11. { Valve narrow-lanceolate . . . . . *P. naviculaceum* BRÉB.
   — broadly . . . . . *P. hungaricum* BR. a. CL.
12. { Ends rostrate . . . . . *P. lanceolatum* DONK.
   — not . . . . . 13.
13. { Ends acute . . . . . *P. pelagicum* PER.
   — obtuse . . . . . *P. marinum* DONK.
14. { Median line central . . . . . 15.
   — — excentric . . . . . 30.
15. { Valve 14 to 20 times longer than broad . . . . . *P. Clevei* GRUN. (*P. longum* var.)
   — 10 or less . . . . . 16.

16.	Median oblique striæ more distant than the others	17.
	— — — not	18.
17.	Valve linear-lanceolate	*P. australe* GRUN.
	— lanceolate	*P. Normanii* RALF.
18.	Transverse and oblique striæ equidistant	19.
	— striæ closer than the oblique	21.
	— more distant —	24.
19.	Valve narrow	*P. delicatulum* W. SM.
	— broad	20.
20.	Striæ 28 in 0,01 mm.	*P. javanicum* GRUN
	— 18 to 22 —	*P. angulatum* QUEK.
21.	Oblique striæ at an angle of 90°	22.
	— — — about 60°	*P. elongatum* W. SM.
22.	Ends with a lunate mark	*P. kerguelense* GRUN.
	— without —	23.
23.	Median line central at the ends	*P. longum* CL.
	— — excentric	*P. subrigidum* GRUN.
24.	Ends obtuse	25.
	— acute	28.
25.	Valve large, about 0,3 mm. in length	26.
	— small — 0,1 — or less	27.
26.	Valve straight	*P. rigidum* W. SM.
	— sigmoid	*P. prælongum* CL.
27.	Transverse striæ 24 in 0,01 mm.	*P. salinarum* GRUN.
	— — 27 —	*P. minutum* GRUN.
28.	Valve linear, strongly sigmoid at the ends	*P. Brunii* CL.
	— lanceolate — —	29.
29.	Transverse striæ 17 in 0,01 mm.	*P. Gründleri* GRUN.
	— — 21 to 24 —	*P. Stuxbergii* CL. & GR.
30.	Median line flexuose	*P. incertum* PER. (*P. falcatum* DONK).
	— — not	31.
31.	Median line enclosed between longitudinal lines	*P. Exul* CL.
	— — not — — —	32.
32.	Central area large	*P. umbilicatum* CL.
	— small or indistinct	33.
33.	Oblique striæ at an angle of 90°	34.
	— — — — less than 90°	37.
34.	Valve broad, lanceolate	35.
	— narrow, linear-lanceolate	36.
35.	Median oblique striæ more obtuse than the others	*P. majus* GRUN.
	— — — not —	*P. Heros* CL.
36.	Frustule arcuate	*P. Weissflogii* GRUN. (*P. formosum var. Arcus*).
	— not	*P. formosum* W. SM.
37.	Valve linear	38.
	— lanceolate	40.
38.	Valve carinated	*P. carinatum* DONK.
	— not	39.
39.	Median line strongly excentric	*P. obscurum* W. SM.
	— — excentric in the ends	*P. speciosum* W. SM.
40.	Ends subrostrate	*P. Æstuarii* BRÉB.
	— not	41.
41.	Valve rhomboidal	42.
	— narrow lanceolate	43.
42.	Transverse striæ about 17 in 0,01 mm.	*P. rhombeum* GRUN.
	— — — 24 —	*P. latum* CL.
43.	Striæ about 22 in 0,01 mm.	*P. acutum* NORM.
	— 20 —	*P. maroccanum* CL.

1. **P. Nubecula** W. SM. (1853). — V. narrow lanceolate, not, or slightly, sigmoid, with subacute ends. L. 0,095 to 0,16; B. 0,016 to 0,02 mm. Median line straight, central. Transverse and

oblique striæ equidistant, 20 to 24 in 0.01 mm.; angle about 60°. — *P. Nubecula* W. Sm. B. D. I p. 64 Pl. XXI f. 201. Grun. A. D. p. 52. Per. V f. 26. *P. Nub. var. parvula* Grun. A. D. p. 52. *P. Thumii* Castr. in Per. p. 14 Pl. V f. 25 (1891).

Marine: Finmark! North Sea! Adriatic (Grun.), Sumatra (var. in L. 0,14; B. 0,014 mm. Striæ 26 in 0,01 mm.)! California!

Var. *intermedia* W. Sm. (1853). — L. 0,14 to 0,44; B. 0,02 to 0,022 mm. Striæ 20 to 22 in 0,01 mm. — *P. interm.* W. Sm. B. D. I p. 64 Pl. XXI f. 200. V. H. Syn. p. 116 Pl. XVIII f. 6. Per. p. 13 Pl. V f. 27, 28.

Marine: North Sea! Port Jackson!

Var. *amphipleuroides* Grun. (1867). — L. 0,13 to 0,3 mm. Striæ 24 to 27 in 0,01 mm. — *P. interm. v. amphipl.* Grun. Hedwigia 1867 p. 29.

Marine: Honduras (Grun.).

Var. *subrecta* Cl. (1880). — L. 0,28; B. 0,022 mm. Transv. and obl. striæ $^{16}/_{17}$, $^{17}/_{18}$, $^{18}/_{19}$ in 0,01 mm. — *P. subrect.* Cl. A. D. p. 14 Pl. III f. 72. Per. V, 30. *P. elongatum var. balearica* Per p. 7 Pl. II f. 22.

Marine: Greenland! Finmark! Sea of Kara! Balearic Islands!

Var. *mauritiana* Grun. (Ms). — L. 0,13 to 0,16; B. 0,012 to 0,013 mm. Transv. and obl. striæ 22,5 in 0,01 mm.

Marine: Mauritius (Grun.).

There is no difference between *P. Nubecula* and *P. intermedium* except in the size. By its varieties *P. Nubecula* is closely connected with *P. elongatum*.

2. **P. Peragalli** Brun. (1891). — V. narrow lanceolate, gradually tapering from the middle to the obtuse ends. L. 0,3; B. 0,04 mm. Central nodule small, rounded. Median line straight, central. Transverse striæ closer than the oblique. Transv. and obl. striæ $^{19}/_{15}$ (Per). $^{21}/_{19}$ (Brun's fig.) in 0,01 mm. — *P. Perag.* Brun. in Per. p. 9 Pl. III f. 20. D. esp. n. Pl. XX f. 6.

Marine: Japan, fossil (Brun.).

Var. *perangusta* Cl. — L. 0,3; B. 0,018 to 0,024 mm. Transv. and obl. striæ $^{18}/_{15}$, $^{19}/_{16}$ in 0,01 mm.

Marine: China (Deby Coll.)! Balearic Islands!

Var. *gracilior* Cl. — L. 0,18; B. 0,012 mm. Transv. and obl. striæ $^{23}/_{19}$ in 0,01 mm.

Marine: China (Deby Coll.)!

This species seems to be nearest akin to *P. subrigidum* and *P. longum*. It has exactly the shape of *P. intermedium*, but the striation is different.

3. **P. ibericum** Per. (1891). — V. narrow lanceolate, with slightly rostrate, obtuse ends. L. 0,09 to 0,12; B. 0,015 to 0,02 mm. Median line central, slightly flexuose, curved at the ends. Transv. and obl. striæ $^{22}/_{20}$, $^{24}/_{22}$ (Per.), $^{25}/_{23}$ in 0,01 mm. Median striæ less acute. — Per. p. 8 Pl. III f. 12.

Marine: Balearic Islands!

4. **P. cuspidatum** Cl. (1881). — V. broad, lanceolate, scarcely sigmoid, with produced and rostrate ends. L. 0,077 to 0,1; B. 0,022 to 0,025 mm. Median line straight, central. Transv. and obl. striæ $^{19}/_{19}$, $^{20}/_{21}$, $^{19}/_{20}$, $^{21}/_{22}$, $^{24}/_{24}$ in 0,01 mm. — *P. lanceolatum var. cusp.* Cl. N. R. D. p. 5 Pl. I f. 7. Per. V. f. 16.

Marine: Firth of Tay! Port Jackson!

5. **P. directum** Grun. (1880). — V. rhombic-lanceolate, subacute. L. 0,243; B. 0,04 mm. Median line straight, central. Transv. and obl. striæ 18,5 in 0,01 mm. Angle 60°. Grun. A. D. p. 53. Cl. M. D. N:o 125. Per. V. f. 29.

Marine: Antarctic Ocean (Grun.).

6. **P. galapagense** Cl. N. Sp. — V. scarcely sigmoid, lanceolate, tapering from the middle to the subacute ends. L. 0,17; B. 0,046 mm. Median line straight, central. Transv. and obl. striæ $^{17}/_{14}$ in 0,01 mm. Angle about 90°. — Pl. IV f. 16.

Marine: Galapagos Islands!

This form is nearly akin to *P. nicobaricum*, but differs by the median striæ, which are not more distant than the terminal.

7. **P. Eudon** Pant. (1886). — V. scarcely sigmoid, lanceolate, tapering from the middle to the subacute ends. L. 0,28; B. 0,05 mm. Median line straight, central. Transv. and obl. striæ $^{13}/_{12}$ (on the fig. in Pant.). Ends of the valve with a lunate marking. — Pant. I p. 30 Pl. XXI f. 190. Per. III f. 21.

Marine: Hungary, fossil (Pant.).

8. **P. nicobaricum** Grun. (1867). — V. scarcely sigmoid, lanceolate, gradually tapering from the middle to the subacute ends. L. 0,14; B. 0,035 to 0,04 mm. Median line central, straight. Oblique striæ more distant in the middle. Transverse striæ coarser than the oblique (15 to 16 in 0,01 mm. according to Grun.). Transv. and obl. striæ $^{24}/_{20}$ in 0,01 mm. (Perag.). Median oblique striæ 20, terminal 24 in 0,51 mm. (Perag.). — *P. validum var.? nicob.* Grun. Novara p. 101 Pl. I. A. f. 20. *P. nicobar.* Grun. A. D. p. 51. Per. p. 10 Pl. IV f. 9. *P. affine var. nicob.* Grun. in V. H. Syn. Suppl. Pl. C. f. 34.

Marine: Nankoori, fossil (Grun.), Belgium (V. H.).

Var. *Sagitta* Brun. and Temp. (1889). — V. rhombic-lanceolate. L. 0,15 to 0,175; B. 0,03 to 0,036 mm. Median oblique striæ 12 to 14, terminal 17 to 20 in 0,01 mm. (Brun.). — *P. Sagitta* Brun. and Temp. D. foss. du Japon p. 49 Pl. IX f. 19. Per. IV f. 13.

Marine: Japan, foss. (Brun.).

Var. *hamulifera* Brun. (1889). — V. rhomboidal. L. 0,09 to 0,12; B. 0,025 to 0,03 mm. Median line central, straight, curved at the ends. Median oblique striæ more distant than the terminal striæ which are at an acuter angle. Transv. and obl. striæ $^{21}/_{21}$ (21 to 24 Brun) in 0,01 mm. — *P. hamuliferum* Brun. D. foss. du Japon p. 48 Pl. IX f. 5. Per. p. 13 Pl. V f. 31. *P. nicob. var. indica* Per. IV f. 12.

Marine: Japan (Brun.), China (Deby Coll.)! Sumatra (Per).

The original P. nicobaricum greatly resembles my *P. galapagense*, but according to Grunow (A. D.) it is nearly akin to *P. affine* and the fig. in V. H. Syn. evidently represents a form akin to *P. Normanii*. This is also the case with *P. Sagitta* Brun. As to *P. hamuliferum* I have not seen Brun's original specimens, and his description of the striation is incomplete. In Deby's collection I have seen a specimen closely resembling *P. hamuliferum* and evidently nearly akin to *P. Normanii*. It closely resembles *P. nicob. var. indica* Per. It seems probable that the original *P. nicobaricum* may be identical with *P. galapagense*, and that *P. nicob.* Grun. in V. H. Syn., Per, graduates into *P. Normanii*.

9. **P. naviculaceum** Bréb. (1854). — V. not, or slightly sigmoid, lanceolate, acute. L. 0,08 0,1; B. 0,015 to 0,02 mm. Median line strongly sigmoid. Median oblique striæ more distant than the terminal, which are at an acuter angle. Transv. and obl. striæ $^{18}/_{16}$, $^{19}/_{17}$, $^{20}/_{18}$. — *P. navic.* Bréb. Mém. de la Soc. du Cherb. 1854 f. 7. Grun. A. D. p. 51. V. H. Syn. Suppl. Pl. C. f. 35. *P. transversale* W. Sm. B. D. II p. 96 (1856). *P. japonicum* Castr. D. Challenger Ex. XXIX f. 14.

Marine: North Sea! Mediterranean! Ceylon! Java! Labuan!

Forma minuta. L. — 0,05; B. 0,015 mm. Transv. and obl. striæ $^{22}/_{20}$.

Marine: Sumatra! Bab el Mandeb.!

10. **P. hungaricum** Brun. and Cl. (1889). — V. broadly rhomboidal, slightly sigmoid, acute. L. 0,1 to 0,13; B. 0,045 to 0,06 mm. Median line strongly sigmoid. Central nodule orbicular. Median oblique striæ forming a larger angle than the terminal, which are more acute. Transv.

and obl. striæ $^{18}/_{15}$ ($^{20}/_{18}$ PERAG.) in 0,01 mm. — BRUN. and TEMP. D. foss. du Japon p. 48 Pl. IX f. 9. PER. p. 11 Pl. IV f. 14.

Marine: Hungary, Kekkö! Japan (BRUN.).

11. **P. pelagicum** PER. (1891). — V. scarcely sigmoid, lanceolate, acute. L. $0{,}16$ to $0{,}17$; B. $0{,}023$ to $0{,}025$ mm. Median line strongly sigmoid. Median oblique striæ not more distant than the others. Transv. and obl. striæ $^{21}/_{19}$, $^{22}/_{20}$. Angle about 65°. — *P. acutum var. australica* and *P. pelagicum* PER. p. 7 Pl. III f. 3.

Marine (pelagic.): Bay of Bengal! Java (Deby Coll.)!

This species was mistaken by me for *P. acutum* var. *austral.*, which is more like the fig. 2 Pl. III in PER. Monograph. It seems nevertheless akin to *P. acutum*, and to be related to that species as *P. naviculaceum* is to *P. Normanii.*

12. **P. lanceolatum** DONK. (1858). — V. scarcely sigmoid lanceolate, with slightly protracted acute ends. L. $0{,}08$ to $0{,}1$; B. $0{,}023$ to $0{,}025$ mm. Median line flexuose. Transv. and obl. striæ equidistant 20 to 22 in $0{,}01$ mm. Angle about 60°. — DONK. T. M. S. 1858 p. 22 Pl. III f. 4. GRUN. A. D. p. 53. PER. p. 12 Pl. V f. 14. *P. transversale β* ROPER M. J VI p. 25 Pl. III f. 11. *P. æstuarii* PER. V. f. 13?

Marine: Coasts of Scotland and England!

Var. *tahitensis* GRUN. (1880). — L. $0{,}118$; B. $0{,}016$ mm. Striæ 22 in $0{,}01$ mm. — *P. lanc. var. tahit.* GRUN. A. D. p. 53.

Marine: Tahiti (GRUN.).

The median striæ of *P. lanceolatum* are a little more distant than the terminal, which points to an affinity with *P. naviculaceum.* On the other hand it is nearly related to *P. æstuarii*, into which species it seems to graduate.

13. **P. marinum** DONK. (1858). — V. very slightly sigmoid, lanceolate, with obtuse ends. L. $0{,}11$ to $0{,}18$; B. $0{,}02$ to $0{,}03$ mm. Median line undulating, excentric towards the ends. Central nodule rounded. Transv. and obl. striæ $^{21}/_{18}$, $^{23}/_{20}$, $^{24}/_{23}$, $^{25}/_{21}$ (Barbados). — DONK. T. M. S. VI p. 22 Pl. III f. 3. PER. III f. 11. *P. mar. var. Antillarum* PER. p. 8 Pl. III f. 19. *P. mar. var. barbadensis* GRUN. A. D. p. 50.

Marine: Coasts of England and Scotland! Port Jackson! Labuan! Barbados!

Var. *italica* PER. (1891). — L. $0{,}3$ to $0{,}32$; B. $0{,}068$ mm. Central nodule quadrate. Transv. and obl. striæ $^{16}/_{14}$ (PER.), $^{18}/_{15}$ (PER.), $^{19}/_{17}$, $^{18.5}/_{16}$. — *Pl. ital.* PER. p. 8 Pl. III f. 10.

Marine: Gulf of Naples! Adriatic!

14. **P. Clevei** GRUN. (1880). — V. slightly sigmoid, very narrow, with attenuate ends. L. $0{,}14$ to $0{,}21$; B. $0{,}0095$ to $0{,}01$ mm. Median line central. Transv. and obl. striæ $^{24}/_{24}$ in $0{,}01$ mm. — GRUN. A. D. p. 52 Pl. III f. 70. PER. V. fig. 17, 18.

Marine: Sea of Kara (GRUN.).

Var. *sibirica* GRUN. Ms. — V. gradually tapering from the middle to the subacute ends. L. $0{,}2$; B. $0{,}011$ mm. Transv. and obl. striæ 28 in $0{,}01$ mm.

Marine: Cape Wankarema (GRUN.).

Var. *cornuta* GRUN. Ms. — V. narrow lanceolate, attenuate into long narrow beaks. L. $0{,}12$; B. $0{,}0075$ mm. Transv. and obl. striæ 25 in $0{,}01$ mm.

Marine: Coast of Northumberland (GRUN.).

Var. *fossilis* BRUN. (1891). Similar to var. cornuta. L. $0{,}2$; B. $0{,}015$ mm. Transv. and obl. striæ $^{23}/_{22}$ in $0{,}01$ mm. — PER. p. 13 Pl. V f. 19.

Marine: Japan, fossil (BRUN.).

15. **P. delicatulum** W. SM. (1852) — V. narrow lanceolate, slightly sigmoid, gradually tapering from the middle to the acute ends. L. $0{,}15$, to $0{,}28$; B. $0{,}02$ to $0{,}03$ mm. Median line

slightly excentric towards the ends. Transv. and obl. striæ 25 in 0,01 mm. — *P. delic.* W. Sm. Ann. Mag. Nat. H. [2] IX p. 6 Pl. I f. 5. B. D. I p. 64 Pl. XXI f. 202. Per. p. 13 Pl. V f. 20 to 22.

Brackish water: North Sea! Caspian Sea (Grun.), Red Sea (Grun.)! Massachusetts! Honduras (Grun.).

Var. *obtusiuscula* Grun. Ms. More obtuse. L. 0,165; B. 0,0195 mm. Striæ 22,5 in 0,01 mm.

Marine: Granton Quarry (Grun.).

Var. *africana* Grun. (1879). — L. 0,18 to 0,19; B. 0,014 to 0,018 mm. Transv. and obl. striæ $^{23}/_{24}$ in 0,01 mm. — Grun. in Cl. M. D. N:o 197.

Brackish water: South Africa!

Var. *americana* Cl. — L. 0,28; B. 0,02 mm. Transv. and obl. striæ 19 in 0,01 mm.

Brackish water: Quincy, Mass.!

16. **P. elongatum** W. Sm. (1852). — V. slightly sigmoid, elongated, gradually attenuate to the acute ends. L. 0,13 to 0,38; B. 0,024 to 0,03 mm. Median line central, slightly sigmoid. Transv. and obl. striæ $^{18}/_{16}$, $^{19}/_{18}$, $^{20}/_{17}$, $^{20}/_{18}$, $^{20}/_{19}$ in 0,01 mm. — W. Sm. Ann. M. Nat. H. [2] IX p. 6 Pl. I f. 4. B. D. I. Pl. XX f. 199. Per. III f. 5 to 8. *P. angulatum var. elongat.* V. H. Syn. p. 115 Pl. XVIII f. 7. *P. elongatum var. gracilis* Grun. Casp. Sea Alg. p. 115 Pl. III f. 7. Per. II f. 20, 21.

Brackish water: Spitsbergen! North Sea! Atlantic coast of North America! Mediterranean Sea! Adriatic! Java! Sumatra! China! Tahiti! Halle in Saxony! Baltic! Caspian Sea (Grun.) Médoc (Per.).

Var. *gracilescens* Grun. (1880). — V. very narrow, gently sigmoid, with acute ends. L. 0,204; B. 0,016 mm. Median line central. Transv. and obl. striæ $^{18,5}/_{16,5}$ in 0,01 mm. — *P. gracilescens* Grun. A. D. p. 50. Per. p. 7 Pl. III f. 9.

Marine: Seychelles (Grun.).

P. elongatum is very nearly akin to *P. delicatulum*, but the transverse striæ are a little closer than the oblique and it has a perfectly central median line. Still these characteristics seem not to be constant, as I have forms of the shape of *P. delicatulum* with the striation of *P. elongatum* (specimens from Java and Sumatra have the form of P. delicatulum and transv. obl. striæ $^{20}/_{17}$, $^{19}/_{17}$).

Var. *fallax* Grun. (1880). — V. gently sigmoid, narrow linear or lanceolate. L. 0,1 to 0,17; B. 0,022 to 0,024 mm. Median line sigmoid, central. Transv. and obl. striæ $^{23}/_{20}$, $^{24}/_{22}$, $^{23}/_{21}$ in 0,01 mm. — Grun. A. D. p. 50 Pl. III f. 66. Per. II f. 23.

Marine: Finmark, Sea of Kara (Grun.), Sumatra (Deby coll.)!

Specimens from Sumatra are much more narrow than the fig. in A. D. and resemble greatly *P. delicatulum*, but have the median line perfectly central.

Var. *kariana* Grun. (1880). — L. 0,2 to 0,21; B. 0,02 to 0,022 mm. Median line perfectly central. Transv. and obl. striæ $^{23}/_{19}$, $^{23}/_{20}$ in 0,01 mm. — *P. delic. var.? kariana* Grun. A. D. p. 50 Pl. III f. 69. *P. karianum* Per. p. 6.

Marine: Sea of Kara (Grun.).

This form connects *P. elongatum* with *P. longum*.

17. **P. longum** Cl. (1873). — V. narrow, linear-lanceolate, slightly sigmoid, with acute ends. L. 0,18 to 0,3; B. 0,018 to 0,021 mm. Median line central. Transv. and obl. striæ $^{19}/_{15}$, $^{20}/_{16}$, $^{21}/_{17}$ in 0,01 mm. — Cl. D. of Arct. Sea p. 19 Pl. III f. 14. Grun. A. D. p. 49 Pl. III f. 71. Per. II f. 2.

Marine: Greenland! Spitzbergen!

Var. *americana* Per. (1891). — V. narrow lanceolate, with acute ends. L. 0,35 to 0,4; B. 0,02 to 0,025 mm. Median line very slightly excentric at the ends. Transv. and obl. striæ $^{18}/_{14}$ (Per.) $^{17}/_{15}$ in 0,01 mm. — *P. decorum var. americ.* Per. p. 5 Pl. I f. 9.

Marine: Connecticut!

Var. *inflata* PER. (1891). — V. lanceolate, sigmoid, acute. L. 0,32: B. 0.04 mm. Transv. and. obl. striæ $^{14}/_{18}$ in 0,01 mm. — *P. decorum var. infl.* PER. p. 5 Pl. I f. 10.

Marine: Corsica (PER.).

18. **P. kerguelense** GRUN. (1880). — V. linear, elongated, slightly sigmoid, with obtuse ends. L. 0,27 to 0,38; B. 0,023 to 0,026 mm. Median line central, slightly sigmoid. Ends of the valve with a lunate marking. Transv. and obl. striæ $^{18}/_{13}$ in 0,01 mm. — GRUN. A. D. p. 49. PER. II f. 1.

Margine: Kerguelens Land!

19. **P. subrigidum** GRUN. (1880). — V. linear, gently sigmoid, with obtuse ends. L. 0,29 to 0,32; B. 0,028 to 0,03 mm. Median line central, slightly sigmoid at the ends. Transv. and obl. striæ $^{16.5}/_{13}$ (GRUN.) $^{10}/_{11}$, $^{18}/_{15}$. — GRUN. A. D. p. 49. PER. II f. 3.

Marine: North Sea! Mediterranean Sea! Sumatra (Deby coll.)!

All the above species from *P. Clevei* to *P. subrigidum* form a closely connected series. *P. subrigidum* is, by its striation and the excentricity of the median line towards the ends, connected with *P. speciosum*.

---

20. **P. salinarum** GRUN. (1878). — V. linear to narrow lanceolate, slightly sigmoid, obtuse. L. 0,104 to 0,13; B. 0,015 to 0,017 mm. Median line central, slightly sigmoid. Central nodule elongated. Transv. and obl. striæ $^{22}/_{25}$, $^{23}/_{26}$, $^{24}/_{27}$, $^{25}/_{28}$. — *P. delicatulum var. salin.* GRUN. Casp. Sea Alg. p. 116. *P. sal.* GRUN. A. D. p. 54. PER. VI f. 16.

Brackish water: Sweden, Lysekil! Kissingen (GRUN.). Caspian Sea (GRUN.), Bengal! Sumatra!

Var. *pusilla* GRUN. (1880). — L. 0,074 to 0,094; B. 0,012 to 0,018 mm. Transv. and obl. striæ $^{23}/_{25}$, $^{23}/_{26}$. — *P. pusillum* GRUN. A. D. p. 54. PER. VI, f. 15.

Fresh water: Bengal (GRUN.).

Var. *paradoxa* PER. (1891). — L. 0,044; B. 0,017 mm. Transv. and. obl. striæ $^{18}/_{20}$, $^{19}/_{21}$ in 0,01 mm. — *P. parad.* PER. p. 16 Pl. VI f. 13.

Marine: Connecticut, Morris Creek (PER.).

21. **P. prælongum** CL. N. Sp. — V. linear, slender, slightly sigmoid, with obtuse ends. L. 0,3 to 0,4; B. 0,03 to 0,035 mm. Median line central, slightly sigmoid. Transv. and obl. striæ $^{20}/_{23}$, $^{21}/_{24}$ in 0,01 mm. — Part II Pl. I f. 2.

Marine: Greenland! Spitsbergen! Finmark! Sea of Kara! Elephanta, Bombay (Grove coll.)!

This large form, widely distributed in the Arctic Seas, may be *P. Longine* W. SM. (Brightwell; M. J. VII p. 180 Pl. IX f. 7, 1859. PER. VIII f. 3) from the arctic regions. At least the outline and the median line are exactly similar. I know of no arctic form agreeing with the description of BRIGHTWELL. PERAGALLO believes that *P. Longine* may be a form of *P. robustum*, but the latter species occurs only in warmer seas and has an excentric median line.

22. **P. rigidum** W. SM. (1853). — V. linear lanceolate, almost straight, with truncate ends. L. 0,3 to 0,36; B. 0,04 to 0,054 mm. Median line central. Transv. and obl. striæ $^{18}/_{21}$, $^{19}/_{21}$, $^{20}/_{21}$, in 0,01 mm. — W. SM. B. D. I p. 64 Pl. XX f. 198. V. H. Syn. Pl. XIX f. 3. PER. VI f. 4 to 6.

Marine: North Sea! Mediterranean Sea! Adriatic! Red Sea! Samoa! West Indies! Colon! Magellhaëns Straits!

Var. *gigantea* GRUN. (1860). — More lanceolate, with obtuse ends. L. 0,44; B. 0,068 mm. Median line very slightly undulating, central, frequently bordered by a row of small dots. Transv. and obl. striæ $^{17}/_{18}$, $^{17}/_{20}$, $^{18}/_{20}$ in 0,01 mm. — *P. giganteum* GRUN. Verh. 1860 p. 558 Pl. VI f. 1 A. D. p. 53. PER. VI f. 2. *P. validum* Shadb. T. M. S. II p. 16 Pl. I f. 8 (1854)?

Marine: Java! Philippines! Samoa!

Var. *incurva* BRUN. (1891). — V. strongly sigmoid. — PER. p. 15 Pl. VI f. 7.

Marine: Japan, fossil (BRUN).

23. **P. Gründleri** Grun. (1880). — V. lanceolate, gently sigmoid, gradually tapering to the subacute ends. L. 0,36 to 0,46; B. 0,062 to 0,072 mm. Median line slightly sigmoid, central. Transv. and obl. striæ $^{17}/_{18}$ in 0,01 mm. Grun. A. D. p. 54. Per. p. 15 Pl. VI f. 1.

Marine: Campeachy Bay (Grun.).

This species is according to Peragallo nothing but a variety of *P. rigidum*. It seems me to be more nearly related to *P. strigosum*.

24. **P. australe** Grun. (1867). — V. linear, lanceolate, sigmoid, with obtuse ends. L. 0,08 to 0,11; B. 0,017 mm. Median line central, sigmoid. Central nodule large, rounded. Median striæ more distant than the terminal. Transv. striæ 21 to 23 in 0,01 mm.; obl. striæ 18 to 20 in the middle and 20 to 23 in 0,01 mm. at the ends. — Grun. Novara p. 21 Pl. I f. 18. A. D. p. 51. Per. IV f. 24 to 27. *P. æstuarii* var. Cl. D. of Java II f. 19. *P. æquatoriale* Cl. M. D. N:o 145, 146. 1878. *P. inflatum* Shadb. T. M. S. II p. 16 Pl. I f. 9 (1854)?

Marine (pelagic): Balearic Islands! Sumatra! Java! New Zealand (Grun.).

P. australe is very nearly connected with *P. naviculaceum* and with *P. Normanii*.

25. **P. Normanii** Ralfs (1861). — V. gently sigmoid, lanceolate, with subacute ends. L. 0,13 to 0,22; B. 0,027 to 0,036 mm. Median line sigmoid, central. Transv. striæ 19 to 21 in 0,01 mm. Obl. striæ 17 to 18 in the middle and 20 to 21 in 0,01 mm. at the ends. — Ralfs in Pritch. Inf. p. 919. *P. affine* Grun. A. D. p. 51 (1880). V. H. Syn. Pl. XVIII f. 9. Per. IV f. 5, 8. *P. affine var. Norm.* Per. IV f. 6, 7.

Marine: Spitsbergen! Davis Strait! North Sea! Mediterranean Sea! Red Sea! Java! Sumatra! Samoa! Atlantic coast of North America! Colon!

Var. *fossilis* Grun. (1880). — L. 0,15 to 0,22; B. 0,03 to 0,035 mm. Transv. striæ 17 in 0,01 mm. Obl. striæ 13 in the middle and 16 to 17 in 0,01 mm. at the ends. — *P. affine var. fossilis* Grun. A. D. p. 51. Per IV f. 16 to 18. *P. virginiacum* H. L. Smith (accord. to Perag.). *P. æstuarii var. intermedia* Grun. Novara p. 102. *P. neogradense* Pant. III Pl. XXI f. 315 (1893)?

Marine (fossil): Virginia! Nankoori (Grun.).

Var. *marylandica* Grun. (1880). — Rhomboidal-lanceolate, acute. L. 0,24 to 0,28; B. 0,03 to 0,044 mm. Transv. striæ 14 to 18 in 0,01 mm. Obl. striæ 13 to 17 in 0,01 mm. in the middle and closer at the ends. — *P. affine var. maryl.* Grun. A. D. p. 51. Per. p. 10 Pl. IV f. 15.

Marine (fossil): Nottingham, Maryland!

P. Normanii is one of the most common species, and connected with *P. australe* and *P. strigosum*, which latter has the same shape, and from which it may be distinguished by its median oblique striæ, which cross each other at the angle of 90 and become acuter towards the ends. It would be advisable to unite into one species *P. naviculaceum*, *P. australe* and *P. Normanii*. Peragallo mentions a form called *P. affine var interrupta* (Pl. IV f. 1, 2) which has an excentric median line. This form, as well as the specimen fig. 4, seems to me to be more akin to *P. decorum var. dalmaticum*.

26. **P. angulatum** Quekett (1848). V. rhomboidal-lanceolate, angular in the middle, with acute ends. L. 0,17 to 0,36; B. 0,036 to 0,05 mm. Median line central, slightly sigmoid. Central nodule small, rhombic. Transv. and obl. striæ equidistant 18 to 22 in 0,01 mm. Angle 60°. — *Navic. angulata* Quek. on the microscope p. 438 Pl. VIII f. 4 to 7 (according to W. Sm.). *P. angulatum* W. Sm. B. D. I p. 65 Pl. XXI f. 205. V. H. Syn. p. 115 Pl. XVIII f. 2 to 4. Per. V f. 3 to 5. *Nav. Thuringiaca* Kütz. (according to Grunow).

Marine: North Sea! Barbados!

Forma *undulata* Grun. (1880). V. with slightly undulate margins. Grun. A. D. p. 51. Per. Pl. V f. 6.

Marine: Bohuslän, Sweden! Belfast (Per.).

Var. *quadrata* W. Sm. (1853). — V. rhomboidal, broad, slightly sigmoid. L. $0{,}19$; B. $0{,}048$ mm. Median line central. Central nodule small, elongated. Transv. and obl. striæ $^{19}/_{18}$ in $0{,}01$ mm. — *P. angulatum* W. Sm. Ann. M. Nat. H. [2] IX p. 7 Pl. I f. 7 (1852). *P. quadr.* W. Sm. B. D. I p. 65 Pl. XX f. 204. Per. V f. 7, 8. *P. ang. var. quadr.* V. H. Syn. p. 115 Pl. XVIII f. 1.

Marine: North Sea!

Var. *strigosa* W. Sm. (1852). — Lanceolate, slightly sigmoid, gradually tapering to the subacute ends. L. $0{,}15$ to $0{,}28$; B. $0{,}03$ mm. Transv. and obl. striæ equidistant, 18 to 22 in $0{,}01$ mm. Angle about 60°. *P. strigosum* W. Sm. Ann. M. Nat. H. [2] IX p. 7 Pl. I f. 6. B. D. I p. 64 Pl. XXI f. 203; XXIII f. 203. Per. V f. 1, 2. *P. ang. var. strig.* V. H. Syn. p. 115 Pl. XIX f. 2.

Marine: North Sea! Mediterranean Sea! Adriatic! Red Sea! Ceylon! Java! South Africa! Brazil! Florida!

Var. *finmarchica* Cl. (1884). — Gently sigmoid, more obtuse. Median line excentric towards the ends. L. $0{,}17$ to $0{,}2$; B. $0{,}03$ mm. Transv. and obl. striæ $^{16}/_{15}$, $^{18}/_{17}$ in $0{,}01$ mm. — *P. Normanii* Cl. A. D. p. 14. Grun. A. D. p. 52 Pl. III f. 67. *P. Finm.* Grun. Franz Josephs Land D. p. 105 (53).

Marine: Finmark!

Var.? *convexum* Grun. (1880). — V. very convex. L. $0{,}225$; B. $0{,}02$ mm. Median line somewhat excentric at the ends. Transv. and obl. striæ $^{20}/_{18}$ in $0{,}01$ mm. — *P. strig. var.? convexa* Grun. A. D. p. 50.

Marine: Puerto Caballo (Grun.).

27. **P. minutum** Grun. (1878). V. lanceolate, gently sigmoid. L. $0{,}05$ to $0{,}065$; B. $0{,}011$ to $0{,}014$ mm. Median line nearly central. Transv. and obl. striæ $^{26}/_{28}$, $^{27}/_{28}$, $^{27}/_{29}$ in $0{,}01$ mm. — Grun. in Cl. M. D. 136. Icon. n. Pl. IV f. 19. *P. æstuarii var. minuta* Grun. A. D. p. 52. Per. V f. 15.

Brackish and marine: Sweden (Malmö! Lysekil, Grun.). Caspian Sea (Grun.), Balearic Islands (Per.).

This little form was placed by Grunow in the vicinity of *P. æstuarii*, with which it seems to me not to have any close relation, as it differs by its non-rostrate ends, the nearly central median line, and the finer striation. It may perhaps be a dwarf-form of *P. angulatum* (*strigosum*).

28. **P. (Rhoicosigma) Stuxbergii** Cl. and Grun. (1880). — V. narrow, lanceolate, gently sigmoid, acute. L. $0{,}19$ to $0{,}38$; B. $0{,}028$ to $0{,}032$ mm. Median line central. Central nodule small, rhomboid. Transv. and obl. striæ $^{23}/_{27}$, $^{24}/_{27}$, $^{25}/_{31}$ in $0{,}01$ mm. — A. D. p. 54 Pl. IV f. 74. Grun. Franz Josephs Land D. p. 105 (53) Pl. I f. 56. Per. VI f. 9, 10.

Marine: Franz Josephs Land (Grun.), Sea of Kara! Cape Wankarema!

Var. *minor* Grun. (1884). — L. $0{,}08$ to $0{,}11$; B. $0{,}016$ to $0{,}017$ mm. Transv. and obl. striæ $^{24}/_{32}$ in $0{,}01$ mm. — Grun. Franz Josephs Land D. p. 105 Pl. I f. 57. Per. VI f. 11.

Var. *rhomboides* Cl. (1880). — V. rhomboid-lanceolate, acute. L. $0{,}085$ to $0{,}135$; B. $0{,}02$ to $0{,}03$ mm. Median line central, almost straight. Transv. and obl. striæ $^{21}/_{23}$, $^{22}/_{24}$, $^{24}/_{25}$ in $0{,}01$ mm. — *P. rhomb.* Cl. A. D. p. 14, 54, Pl. IV f. 73. Per. VI f. 14.

Marine: Sea of Kara! Cape Wankarema!

Var. *latiuscula* Per. (1891). — V. lanceolate, slightly sigmoid, with somewhat obtuse ends. L. $0{,}16$; B. $0{,}026$ mm. Transv. and obl. striæ $^{23}/_{20}$ in $0{,}01$ mm. — *P. latiusculum* Per. p. 15 Pl. VI f. 12.

Marine: North Sea (Per.).

P. Stuxbergii, remarkable for its very fine oblique striæ, is not related to *P. delicatulum*, but to *P. acutum*. The var. rhomboides seems to connect it with *P. angulatum* v. *strigosa*.

29. **P. Brunii** CL. (1891). — V. linear, strongly sigmoid, suddenly attenuated to the acute ends. L. 0,42 to 0,45; B. 0,31 to 0,033 mm. Median line central. Central nodule small. Trans. and oblique striæ $^{27}{}_{32}$ in 0,01 mm. — PER. p. 16 Pl. VI f. 8.

Marine (pelagic): Bay of Bengal! Java!

30. **P. javanicum** GRUN. (1878). — V. narrow, lanceolate, gently sigmoid, acute. L. 0,125 to 0,144; B. 0,019 to 0,022 mm. Median line nearly central in the middle, excentric towards the ends. Transv. and obl. striæ equidistant, about 28 in 0,01 mm. *P. angulatum var. jav.* GRUN. in Cl. M. D. 145. *P. javanicum* GRUN. A. D. p. 52 (1880). Per. V f. 10.

Marine (pelagic): Java! China!

This species has the outline of *P. strigosum*, but is thinner (dry, yellowish) and more acute. It is most nearly akin to *P. acutum*. As *P. hyalinum*, GRUNOW describes in A. D. (p. 52) a similar, pelagic form from Triest (L. 0,085; B. 0,0105 mm.), the striation of which is too delicate for measuring.

31. **P. acutum** NORM. (1861). — V. lanceolate, gently sigmoid, acute. L. 0,24 to 0,3; B. 0,02 to 0,028 mm. Median line sigmoid, very excentric towards the ends. Transv. and obl. striæ $^{22}{}_{21}$, $^{22}{}_{19}$, $^{23}{}_{20}$ in 0,01 mm. — NORM. Pritch. Inf. p. 920. Per. III f. 1, 4. *P. acutum var. australasicum* GRUN. in Cl. M. D. 286 (1882).

Marine (pelagic): Europe (Norm.), Croisic (Per.). Java (Deby Coll.)! St Vincent, Australia! Yeddo Bay (Brun Coll.)!

This species is nearly akin to *P. javanicum* and *P. Stuxbergii*, from which latter it differs by its less acute oblique striæ and the excentricity of its median line towards the ends. The fig. 2 in PERAGALLO's monograph has the outline and median line of *P. Stuxbergii*, but the striation of *P. acutum*. The fig. 3 in the same monograph is another, allied form, described here as *P. pelagicum* PER. and formerly mistaken by me for *P. acutum var. australasicum* GRUN., which latter now seems to me to be identical with *P. acutum*.

32. **P. (Rhoicosigma?) maroccanum** CL. (1891). — V. narrow, lanceolate, gently sigmoid, gradually attenuated to the acute ends. L. 0,2 to 0,3; B. 0,02 to 0,037 mm. Median line somewhat excentric, sigmoid. Transv. and obl. striæ $^{19}{}_{18}$, $^{20}{}_{19}$ in 0,01 mm. Angle about 70 . *Rhoicosigma marocc.* Per. p. 32 Pl. IX f. 22.

Marine: Marocco! Gulf of Naples!

This form is doubtful as a species and requires further examination.

33. **P. æstuarii** BRÉB. (1849). — V. lanceolate, gently sigmoid, with slightly rostrate ends. L. 0,07 to 0,08; B. 0,017 mm. Median line more sigmoid than the valve, excentric. Transv. and obl. striæ equidistant, 19 to 21 in 0,01 mm. — *Navic. æst.* KÜTZ. Sp. Alg. p. 890. *P. æst.* W. SM. B. D. I p. 65 Pl. XXXI f. 275. Grun. A. D. p. 52. Per. p. 12 Pl. V f. 11 to 13. *P. candidum* SCHUM. Preuss. D. II Nachtr. Pl. II f. 57 (1867). *P. angulatum var. æst.* V. H. Syn. p. 115 Pl. XVIII f. 8.

Marine: North Sea! Adriatic (Grun.), Caspian Sea (Grun.). California!

This species has the striation of *P. angulatum* but, by the flexure of the median line, seems to be nearer akin to *P. lanceolatum*.

34. **P. latum** CL. (1880). — V. rhomboid-lanceolate, slightly sigmoid, gradually tapering to the subobtuse ends. L. 0,074 to 0,085; B. 0,02 mm. Median line slightly sigmoid, excentric towards the ends. Transv. and obl. striæ $^{21}{}_{22}$ in 0,01 mm. CL. A. D. p. 14, 51 Pl. III f. 68.

Marine: Finmark! California!

This form requires a closer examination.

35. **P. rhombeum** GRUN. (1880). — V. rhomboidal, sigmoid, often angular in the middle, and with obtuse ends. L. 0,12 to 0,26; B. 0,03 to 0,07 mm. Median line strongly sigmoid towards

the ends. Central area rather large, irregularly rhomboid. Transv. and obl. striæ $^{17}/_{15}$, $^{18}/_{16}$, $^{17}/_{17}$, $^{18}/_{18}$, $^{19}/_{19}$ in 0,01 mm. — *P. quadratum var.? rhombeum* GRUN. A. D. p. 50. *P. rhomb.* PER. III f. 13, 14.

Marine: Java! Labuan! Port Jackson! Aukland (Grun.), Samoa! China! Oakland, California!

P. rhombeum greatly resembles *P. quadratum* and *angulatum*, but differs by the more excentric median line and the coarser striation.

36. **P. obscurum** W. SM. (1852). — V. narrow linear, with unilaterally narrowed and rounded ends. L. 0,09 to 0,15; B. 0,01 mm. Median line strongly asymmetrical, near the ends close to the curved margin. Transv. and obl. striæ equidistant, 25 (Per.) to 29 (W. Sm.) in 0,01 mm. — W. Sm. Ann. M. Nat. H. [2] IX p. 8 Pl. I f. 11. B. D. I p. 65 Pl. XX f. 206. Per. I f. 14, 15. *P. macilentum* PER. p. 13, Pl. V f. 24 (1891).

Marine: England (W. Sm.). Balearic Islands (Per.).

Var. *barbadensis* CL. L. 0,14 to 0,18; B. 0,015 mm. Transv. and obl. striæ $^{19}/_{20}$, $^{20}/_{21}$ in 0,01 mm.

Marine: Barbados!

37. **P. (Rhoicosigma) falcatum** DONK. (1861). — V. linear, with unilaterally narrowed and rounded ends. L. 0,15 to 0,18; B. 0,015 mm. Median line flexuose in the middle, strongly excentric, following the curved margins of the ends. Striæ fine, oblique. — DONK. M. J. I p. 7 Pl. I f. 1. *Rhoic. falcat.* GRUN. Hedw. VI p. 20 (1867). Per. IX f. 25, 27.

Marine: Northumberland (Donk.).

Doubtful; specimens in GROVE's collection are *Gyrosigma arcticum* CL.

38. **P. (Rhoicosigma?) incertum** PER. (1891). — V. slender, sigmoid, acute. L. 0,33; B. 0,019 mm. Median line slightly sinuose, very excentric towards the ends. Transv. and obl. striæ $^{19}/_{17}$ in 0,01 mm. — Per. p. 32 Pl. IX f. 21.

Marine: Atlantic coast of North America!

39. **P. (Rhoicosigma) Weissflogii** GRUN. (1880). — V. linear, with unilaterally narrowed and rounded ends. L. 0,118 to 0,134; B. 0,018 to 0,019 mm. Median line excentric, and strongly sigmoid, closely following the curved margins for a considerable distance. Median oblique striæ cross each other in an angle of 90°; the terminal more acute. Transv. and obl. striæ $^{21}/_{15}$ in 0,01 mm. — *Rhoic. Weissfl.* GRUN. A. D. p. 54. Per. IX f. 23, 24.

Marine: Seychelles (V. H. coll.)!

40. **P. umbilicatum** CL. N. SP. V. linear, with unilaterally rounded and very slightly rostrate ends. L. 0,065 to 0,10; B. 0,015 mm. Median line strongly sigmoid, for a long distance closely following the convex margin of the valve. Central area unusually large, transverse and rounded. Transv. and obl. striæ equidistant, 22 in 0,01 mm. — Pl. IV f. 22.

Marine: Labuan!

This species is in form nearest to *P. Weissflogii*, but differs by the large area, and the close striation.

41. **P. Exsul** CL. N. SP. V. linear-lanceolate, gently sigmoid, with subacute ends. L. 0,18; B. 0,018 mm. Median line strongly sigmoid and excentric, enclosed between two longitudinal lines. Central nodule small, rounded. Transv. and obl. striæ $^{22}/_{23}$ in 0,01 mm. — Pl. IV f. 17.

Marine: Gulf of Naples (Deby Coll.)!

This species, of which I have seen only one specimen, has the outline of *P. formosum*, but has much closer striation, and longitudinal lines close to the median line.

42. **P. (Donkinia) carinatum** Donk. (1858). — V. very convex, unilaterally tapering from the middle to the acute ends. L. 0,1 to 0,13; B. 0,01 to 0,013 mm. Median line almost diagonal in the middle and then closely following the convex margins. Transv. and obl. striæ $^{19}_{18}$, $^{21}_{20}$ in 0,01 mm. — Donk. T. M. S. VI p. 23 Pl. III f. 5. *Donkinia car.* Ralf in Pritch. Inf. p. 921 (1861). Per. IX f. 6.

Marine: Sea of Kara! Davis Strait! North Sea! Balearic Islands! Japan, fossil (Brun coll.)!

43. **P. speciosum** W. Sm (1852). — V. linear, with unilaterally rounded ends. L. 0,18 to 0,27; B. 0,023 to 0,025 mm. Median line strongly excentric towards the ends. Transv. and obl. striæ $^{18}_{16}$, $^{19}_{17}$, $^{20}_{17}$, $^{20}_{18}$, $^{20}_{19}$ in 0,01 mm. — W. Sm. Ann. Mag. N. H. [2] IX p. 6 Pl. I f. 3. B. D. I p. 63 Pl. XX f. 197. Per. II f. 13 to 16.

Marine: North Sea! Mediterranean Sea! Red Sea! Java! Sumatra! Labuan! China! Port Jackson! Barbados!

Var. *gracilis* Per. (1891). — More narrow. L. 0,25; B. 0,015 mm. Transv. and obl. striæ $^{20}_{19}$ in 0,01 mm. Per p. 6 Pl. II f. 19.

Marine: Sumatra (Per.).

Var.? *Javanica* Per. (1891). — L. 0,07; B. 0,02 to 0,23 mm. Transv. and obl. striæ $^{20}_{19}$ in 0,01 mm. — Per. p. 6 Pl. II f. 17, 18.

Marine: Java, Sumatra (Per.).

Var.? *abrupta* Per. (1891). — Same as var. javanica, but with obliquely truncate ends. Per. p. 6. Pl. II f. 11.

Marine: Java, Sumatra (Per.).

Var. *mediterranea* Grun. (1880). — Linear, with unilaterally rounded ends. L. 0,21 to 0,32; B. 0,018 to 0,026 mm. Median line strongly excentric, coincident for a considerable distance with the convex margin. Transv. and obl. striæ $^{16.5}_{13.5}$, $^{18}_{11}$, $^{16}_{14}$ in 0,01 mm. — *P. obscurum var. medit.* Grun. A. D. p. 49. Per. II f. 5.

Marine: Mediterranean Sea! Seychelles (Grun.), Java!

Var. *pulchra* Grun. (1860). — V. and median line as in var. medit. L. 0,3 to 0,6; B. 0,023 to 0,04 mm. Transv. and obl. striæ $^{15}_{10}$, $^{11}_{11}$, $^{15}_{11}$, $^{16}_{22}$ in 0,01 mm. — *P. pulchr.* Grun. Verh. 1860 p. 556 Pl. VI f. 2. Per. I f. 8.

Marine: North Sea! Red Sea (Grun.), Java! Sumatra!

Var.? *tortuosa* Cl. (1881). — V. lanceolate, slightly sigmoid, with unilaterally rounded ends. L. 0,076; B. 0,012 to 0,013 mm. Median line strongly sigmoid and very excentric. Transv. and obl. striæ $^{22}_{20}$ in 0,01 mm. — *P. tort.* Cl. N. R. D. p. 5 Pl. I f. 6. Per. II f. 12.

Marine: Balearic Islands!

44. **P. majus** Grun. (1880). — V. lanceolate, gradually tapering from the middle to the obtuse ends, slightly sigmoid. L. 0,2 to 0,4; B. 0,024 to 0,052 mm. Median line nearly straight in the middle, excentric towards the ends. Oblique striæ form in the middle of the valve an obtuser angle than on other parts of the valve. Transv. and obl. striæ $^{15.5}_{13.5}$ (Grun.) $^{17}_{13}$, $^{17}_{14}$, $^{18}_{15}$, $^{20}_{18}$ in 0,01 mm. — *P. speciosum var.? major* Grun. A. D p. 49. *P. affine var. interruptum* Per. Pl. IV f. 1 to 3. *Pl. majus* Icon. n. Pl. IV f. 15.

Marine: Mediterranean Sea! Sumatra!

45. **P. Heros** Cl. N. Sp. — V. lanceolate, slightly sigmoid, gradually tapering from the middle to the obtuse ends. L. 0,4; B. 0,085 mm. Median line straight, somewhat excentric towards the ends. Transv. and obl. striæ $^{11}_{10}$ in 0,01 mm. — Pl. IV f. 20.

Marine: Macassar Straits (Grove's Coll.)!

This form is closely allied to *P. majus*, being somewhat broader. The striæ are coarser and in the same direction in the middle as elsewhere. It is also nearly akin to *P. formosum v. longissima*, which is more sigmoid and has a more excentric median line.

46. **P. formosum** W. Sm. (1852). — V. narrow, linear-lanceolate, gently sigmoid, gradually and unilaterally narrowed towards the ends. L. 0,14 to 0,53; B. 0,02 to 0,05 mm. Median line sigmoid, excentric, generally for a considerable distance coincident with the convex margin. Oblique striæ crossing each other at an angle of 90°. Transv. and obl. striæ $^{11}/_{10}$, $^{18}/_{14}$, $^{20}/_{16}$ in 0,01 mm. W. Sm. Ann. M. Nat. H. [2] IX p. 5 Pl. I f. 1. B. D. p. 63 Pl. XX f. 195. Grun. A. D. p. 48. V. H. Syn. p. 116 Pl. XIX f. 4. Per. I f. 3 to 5. *P. australicum* O. Witt. Mus. Godeff. p. 70 Pl. VIII f. 7 (1873). *P. decorum* W. Sm. I p. 63 Pl. XXI f. 196. Grun. A. D p. 49. V. H. Syn. p. 116 Pl. XIX f. 1. Per. I f. 11 to 13. *P. tahitense* O. Witt. Mus. Godeffr. p. 67 Pl. VIII f. 13 (1873).

Marine: North Sea! Mediterranean Sea! Red Sea! Java! China! Behrings Island! Sandwichs Islands! Galapagos Islands! West Indies!

Var. *dalmatica* Grun. (1880). — V. narrow, slender, acute, slightly sigmoid. L. 0,25 to 0,32; B. 0,03 mm. Median line slightly excentric. Transv. and obl. striæ $^{15}/_{12}$, $^{19}/_{14}$ in 0,01 mm. *P. decor. var. dalm.* Grun. A. D. p. 49. Per. II f. 6 to 9?. Icon. n. Pl. IV f. 21.

Marine: Balearic Islands! Adriatic (Grun.)!

Var. (*Rhoicosigma*) *Arcus* Cl. — V. arcuate. L. 0,2; B. 0,02 mm. Transv. and obl. striæ $^{18}/_{13}$ in 0,01 mm. — Pl. IV f. 18.

Marine: Macassar Straits (Grove Coll.)!

Var. *balearica* Per. (1891). V. linear, with unilaterally rounded ends. L. 0,35 to 0,51; B. 0,034 to 0,06 mm. Transv. and obl. striæ $^{13}/_{8}$, $^{14}/_{9}$, $^{15}/_{9}$ in 0,01 mm. - Per. p. 4 Pl. I f. 6, 7.

Marine: Mediterranean Sea (Per.), Singapore (Grove Coll.)!

Var. *longissima* Grun. (1880). — V. lanceolate, sigmoid. L. 0,4 to 0,78; B. 0,085 to 0,073 mm. Median line sigmoid, excentric at the ends. Transv. and obl. striæ $^{11}/_{10}$, $^{13}/_{11}$, $^{15}/_{12}$, $^{16}/_{14}$, $^{17}/_{13}$ in 0,01 mm. — Grun. A. D. p. 48. Per. p. 4 Pl. I f. 1, 2.

Marine: Puerto Caballo (Per.), Colon! Campeachy Bay! Samoa! China! Java! Galapagos Islands!

All the forms from *P. speciosum* are very nearly connected and might be united into one single species, characterized by the oblique striæ crossing each other at an angle of about 90°. Between *P. formosum* and *P. decorum* there is absolutely no specific difference, and by numerous varieties *P. formosum* graduates into *P. pulchrum* and *P. speciosum*. By the var. *dalmatica P. formosum* is connected with *P. subrigidum*, *P. longum* and *P. Peragalli*, which latter is intermediate in the passage to *P. Nubecula*. — *Donkinia reticulata* Norm. (Grev. in T. Bot. Soc. Ed. vol. VIII p. 237 Pl. III f. 13, 14. Pritch. Inf. 1861 p. 921) is probably akin to the last described species. It is a large form (L. 0,16 mm.) with very excentric median line and highly carinated valves. Oblique striæ about 8 in 0,01 mm. This form, found in Western Australia, is entirely unknown to me. A somewhat similar form occurs in Oamaru deposit but I have seen only some incomplete specimens. L. 0,2. Striæ 10 in 0,01 mm.

Toxonidea Donkin (1858).

Valve asymmetrical, thin. Median line arcuate, excentric. Axial area indistinct. Central area indistinct. Structure the same as in Pleurosigma. Zone not complex.

This genus comprises asymmetrical forms of Pleurosigma. The cell-contents are not known, but will probably offer some interesting peculiarities.

1. **T. insignis** Donk. (1858). — V. strongly asymmetrical, with almost straight dorsal and very convex ventral margin. Ends subrostrate. L. 0,12 to 0,13; B. 0,025 to 0,03 mm. Median line strongly excentric, coincident at the ends for some distance with the dorsal margin. Transv.

and obl. striæ $^{24}{}_{22}$, $^{22}{}_{21}$ in 0,01 mm. DONK. T. M. S. p. 21 Pl. III f. 2. V. H. Syn. p. 114 Pl. XVII f. 10. Per. IX f. 18, 19.

Marine: Coasts of Scotland and England! Belgium (V. H.)! Balearic Islands! Sumatra (Deby Coll.)!

Var. *madagascarensis* GRUN. (1891). — Dorsal margin concave. L. 0,017; B. 0,03 mm. Median line close to the dorsal margin. Transv. and obl. striæ $^{20}{}_{19}$ in 0,01 mm. — *T. madag.* Per. p. 28 Pl. IX f. 13.

Marine: Madagascar (Per).

Var.? *undulata* NORM. (1861). — Dorsal margin gibbous in the middle, ventral triundulate. L. 0,15; B. 0,032 mm. Transv. and obl. striæ $^{20}{}_{19}$ in 0,01 mm. — *T. undulata* PRIT. Inf. p. 920 Pl. VIII f. 46 (1861). Per. IX f. 12.

Marine: North Sea (NORM.).

T. insignis seems to graduate into *T. Gregoriana.*

2. **T. Gregoriana** DONK. (1858). — V. linear to semilanceolate, with unilaterally rounded ends, curved in the same direction. Dorsal margin straight, ventral slightly convex. L. 0,13 to 0,25; B. 0,022 to 0,03 mm. Median line arcuate, at the ends coincident with the margins. Transv. and obl. striæ $^{20}{}_{19}$, $^{21}{}_{21}$ in 0,01 mm. Donk. T. M. S. VI p. 19 Pl. III f. 1. Per. IX f. 16.

Marine: Coasts of Scotland and England!

Var. *balearica* CL. (1878). — Dorsal margin slightly concave. L. 0,17 to 0,22; B. 0,02 to 0,025 mm. Transv. and obl. striæ $^{17}{}_{18}$, $^{17}{}_{19}$ in 0,01 mm. — *T. balearica* CL. M. D. 154. Per. IX f. 14, 15.

Marine: Mediterranean Sea!

3. **T. Challengerensis** (CASTR. (1886). V. linear, narrow, inflated in the middle and at the ends. L. 0,3; B. 0,004 mm. CASTR. D. Exp. Chall. p. 39 Pl. XXVI f. 11, 15. Per. IX f. 17.

Marine: Tahiti (Castr.).

Caloneis CL. N. G.

Valve usually convex, of various shape, linear, lanceolate, panduriform, rarely sigmoid and asymmetrical. Striæ usually parallel, and divergent in the ends (rarely convergent), not distinctly (rarely finely) punctate, crossed by one or several longitudinal lines, which in some species increase to broad, lateral areas. Connecting zone not complex.

This genus comprises the groups *abbréviées*, *formosées*, *limosées* and *linéariées* of Navicula in the synopsis of VAN HEURCK, as well as the *quadriseriatæ* of GRUNOW. All these groups are intimately connected, however dissimilar the outline of the different species may be. Smaller forms of Caloneis with indistinct longitudinal lines closely resemble small Pinnulariæ, and certain of the panduriform species seem to be very closely connected with some marine, panduriform Pinnulariæ.

PFITZER, who has examined the cell-contents of *C. Silicula* places this specis in his genus *Neidium*, but it has no near affinity with that genus. According to PFITZER (Bau und Entw. p. 39) there are as in Neidium two chromatophores, lying closely along the inside of the connecting zone, which do not migrate to the valves, but are divided in situ by fissures parallel to the longitudinal axis of the cell. It thus appears that there are interior characteristics also, which distinguish Caloneis from Navicula. The cell-contents (of *C. blanda*, *C. Liber* and *C. formosa*) have also two chromatophore-plates along the connecting zone. Their margins are entire.

The form of the valve is as a rule linear, or lanceolate, and straight. A sigmoid species, *C. staurophora*, has hitherto been regarded as a *Pleurosigma*. This species has the ordinary form of a Pleurosigma, but the following important characteristics induce me to place it in Caloneis:

first, the presence of longitudinal lines and secondly, the striæ, which are not distinctly punctate, the striæ of all the species of Pleurosigma being punctate.

An asymmetrical tendency is slightly apparent in several forms of *C. Liber*, and is very decided in *C.* (*Alloioneis*) *curvinervis*. Among the Amphoræ are many forms with longitudinal lines, but no known species of that genus is closely connected with Caloneis. There are various transitions among the forms of Caloneis. Some species are slightly constricted in the middle or biconstricted, and thus connect the non-constricted forms with the panduriform or strongly biconstricted.

Closely connected with Caloneis is the genus *Pseudoamphiprora*, among the species of which *P. impleta* comes nearest. The principal distinction between these two genera consists in the nature of the striæ, which are punctate in *Pseudoamphiprora*. The transverse expansion of the central nodule of Pseudo-amphiprora is met with in some species of Caloneis, as for instance *C. Wardii*. — The terminal fissures in most forms of the type *C. Liber* are not very divergent from the direction of the median line, and being situated on the concave end of the valve, they have the appearance of short flexuose lines (see A. Schmidt's Atl. Pl. L.). In *C. abnormis* they are turned in contrary directions. In the forms of the type *C. Powellii* and in the panduriform species they are small and indistinct.

The striæ are as a rule transverse, in some forms slightly radiate, and are usually divergent at the ends, not convergent as in Pinnulariæ. They are generally smooth or not distinctly punctate, excepting in the doubtful *C. dispersa*, which has distinctly punctate striæ. — In addition to the nature of the striæ, the longitudinal lines are a very characteristic feature of Caloneis. In many species the valves are divided by these lines into an inner plane, or even concave, portion; and an outer portion which is convex and sloping. In other species the inner portion appears to be more elevated. Without transverse sections of the valves it is extremely difficult to ascertain which is the case; but as a rule the plane, or inclination, of the part of the valve which is within the longitudinal lines is different from that of the outside parts. Transitions of all kind occur, from the narrow true lines of *C. Liber* and others to the broad bands of *C. Castracanei*, *C. mirabilis* etc., shewing that, whether narrow or broad, these lines are of the same nature. — In *C. Madagascarensis* there are, in addition, other fainter, longitudinal lines, formed by knots on the striæ; and this fact seems to point to an affinity between *Caloneis* and *Tropidoneis* (T. lepidoptera, T. longa).

Artificial key.

1.	Central nodule stauroid	*C. Wardii* Cl.
	— not	2.
2.	Central area a transverse fascia	3.[1]
	— not —	19.
3.	Valve sigmoid	*C. staurophora* Grun.
	— straight	4.
4.	Linear or almost linear	5.
	Lanceolate, constricted or biconstricted	11.
5.	Striæ radiate	*C. Clevei* Lagst.
	parallel	6.
6.	Axial area rather broad	7.
	— — narrow or indistinct	8.
7.	Marine species	*C. latefasciata* Grun. (*C. formosa var. interrupta*).
	Freshwater species	*C. patagonica* Cl.
8.	Margins parallel	9.
	— slightly undulate	*C. Silicula* var.
9.	Striæ 15 in 0,01 mm.	*C. consimilis* A. S.
	— finer	10.

[1] To this division belongs *C. nubicola* Grun., which for want of figure and complete description cannot be enrolled in the key.

10.	Striæ about 21 in 0,01 mm.	*C. æmula* A. S.
	— 25 — —	*C. fasciata* Lagst.
11.	Valve lanceolate	12.
	— constricted	14.
	— biconstricted	16.
12.	Ends capitate	*C. Beccariana* Grun.
	— not —	13.
13.	Valve trochiform	*C. bolosensis* Pant.
	— elliptical-lanceolate	*C. bottaica* Cl.
14.	Axial area indistinct	*C. galapagensis* Cl.
	— — distinct or rather broad	15.
15.	Striæ 6 in 0,01 mm.	*C. scintillans* Br. a. Temp.
	9 —	*C. Hardmaniana* Cl.
	— 15 —	*C. galapagensis var. japonica.*
16.	Striæ 6 to 11 in 0,01 mm.	17.
	— about 20 in 0,01 mm.	18.
17.	Median segment large	*C. ophiocephala* Cl.
	— — small	*C. formicina* Grun.
18.	Longitudinal lines median	*C. claviger* Cl.
	— indistinct	*C. columbiensis* Cl. (*C. Schumaniana var. Heribaudi* Pérag.).
19.	Valve constricted	20.
	not —	30.
20.	Valve constricted in the middle	21.
	— biconstricted	25.
21.	Striæ 7 to 12 in 0,01 mm.	22.
	— about 22 —	*N. Liber var. Janischiana.*
22.	Area indistinct	*C. Liber var. Bleischiana.*
	— distinct	23.
23.	Central and axial area united in a narrow lanceolate space	24.
	Central area quadrate	*C. Powellii var. Bartholomei.*
24.	Longitudinal lines broad	*C. Musca* Greg.
	— narrow	*C. Kinkeriana* Truan
25.	Small forms (L. 0,03 to 0,04 mm.)	26.
	Larger —	27.
26.	Ends broad	*C. lobata* Schwartz.
	— acuminate	*C. egena* A. S.
27.	Axial area broad	*C. biclavata* Cl. a. Grove.
	— — narrow	28.
28.	Striæ about 8 in 0,01 mm.	*C. biconstricta* Grove a. Sturt.
	— 13 —	29.
	— — 19 —	*C. Schumanniana var. trinodis.*
29.	Longitudinal lines double	*C. eximia* Grun.
	— — single, inframarginal	*C. adenensis* Cl.
30.	Valve lanceolate, margins convex	31.
	— linear — parallel	49.
31.	Central area with lunate marks	32.
	— without —	33.
32.	Freshwater species	*C. Schumanniana* Grun.
	Marine	*C. samoensis* Grun.
33.	Valve asymmetrical	*C. carrinecria* Grun.
	symmetrical	34.
34.	Only the portion around the median line striate	*C. dispersa* Grove a. Sturt.
	Marginal portion of the valve striate	35.
35.	Longitudial lines broad	36.
	— — fine	38.
36.	Longitudinal lines dilated to broad, lunate areas	*C. kryophila* Cl.
	— — linear bands	37.
37.	Longitudinal bands and central areas united	*C. Castracanei* Grun.
	— — — — not	*C. biseriata* Pet.

Number	Character	Reference
38.	Axial and central areas indistinct	39.
	— area narrow, central area distinct	40.
	— and central areas united to a lanceolate space	44.
39.	Striæ 12 to 13 in 0,01 mm.	*C. tahitensis* Grun.
	— 20 to 21 —	*C. virginea* Cl.
40.	Central area large	41.
	— — small	42.
41.	Elliptical, obtuse	*C. brevis* Greg.
	Lanceolate, acute	*C. Duseni* Cl.
42.	Terminal fissures in contrary directions	*C. abnormis* Grun.
	— — the same —	43.
43.	L. 0,025 mm.	*C. ladogensis* Cl.
	L. 0,05 mm.	*C. Holstii* Cl.
44.	Longitudinal lines marginal or inframarginal	45.
	— — median	46.
45.	Breadth 0,009 mm.	*C. Lagerheimii* Cl.
	— 0,02 to 0,03 mm.	*C. latiuscula* Kütz.
46.	Longitudinal lines single	*C. amphisbæna* Bory.
	— — double or triple	47.
47.	Striæ 9 to 10 in 0,01 mm.	48.
	— 12 —	*C. bivittata* Pant.
48.	Longitudinal double-lines approximate	*C. permagna* Bail.
	— distant	*C. madagascarensis* Cl.
49.	Striæ very fine, 28 in 0,01 mm.	*C. lepidula* Grun.
	— distinct	50.
50.	Central area with longitudinal marks or rows of puncta	51.
	— — without — — —	55.
51.	Axial area narrow, central area rounded	*C. Liber* var.
	— and central areas united to a linear or lanceolate space	52.
52.	Valve with broad ends	53.
	— narrowed towards the ends	54.
53.	L. 0,05 to 0,06 mm.	*C. obtusa* W. Sm.
	L. 0,108 mm.	*C. Kainitzii* Pant.
54.	Striæ 7 or 8 in 0,01 mm.	*C. sectilis* A. S.
	— 10 to 12 —	*C. samoensis* Grun.
	— 20 — —	*C. alpestris* Grun.
55.	Longitudinal lines fine	56.
	— — broad	65.
56.	Axial area indistinct	57.
	Axial and central areas united in a linear or lanceolate space	64.
57.	Central area small or indistinct	58.
	— — orbicular	*C. Anderssoni* Cl.
58.	Striæ 8 to 10 in 0,01 mm.	59.
	— 11 to 20 —	61.
59.	Longitudinal lines double	*C. probabilis* A. S.
	— — single	60.
60.	Striæ parallel	*C. robusta* Grun.
	slightly radiate	*C. Eugeniæ* Cl.
61.	Valve gibbous in the middle and at the ends	*C. Silicula* Ehr.
	— with parallel margins	62.
62.	Freshwater species	*C. bacillaris* Greg.
	Marine —	63. [1]
63.	Longitudinal lines median	*C. Liber* W. Sm.
	— — marginal	*C. Spathula* Brun.
64.	Longitudinal lines median	*C. formosa* Greg.
	— — inframarginal	*C. Frater* Cl.

[1] In this division *C.? elongatula* Pant. may probably also be included.

65.	Axial area broad	*C. supergradata* Brun
	— — narrow or indistinct	66.
66.	Central area orbicular	67.
	— quadrate	68.
	— indistinct	70.
67.	Valve narrow	*C. blanda* A. S.
	broad, almost hexagonal	*C. quadriseriata* Cl. a. Grun.
68.	Longitudinal lines marginal	*C. Campbellii* Pet.
	— median	69.
69.	Longitudinal lines rather narrow	*C. Powellii* Lewis.
	— — — broad	*C. amica* Cl. a. Grun.
70.	Striæ about 21 in 0,01 mm.	*C. venusta* Pant.
	— 5 to 10 —	71.
71.	Striæ 5 in 0,01 mm.	*C. Zanardiniana* Grun.
	— 8 —	*C. Wittii* Grun.
	— 12 —	*C. sejuncta* A. S.

1. **C. lepidula** Grun. (1880). — V. narrow, linear, with broad, rounded ends. L. 0,02; B. 0,005 mm. Axial area indistinct; central small, orbicular. Striæ parallel, 27 to 30 in 0,01 mm. Longitudinal lines marginal. — *Nav. lep.* Grun. in V. H. Syn. p. 108 Pl. XIV f. 42.

Fresh water: Belgium (V. H.).

2. **C. bacillaris** Greg. (1856). V. linear, with rounded ends. L. 0,023 to 0,05; B. 0,005 to 0,006 mm. Axial area very narrow; central area small, sometimes unilaterally dilated to a fascia. Striæ 20 to 22 in 0,01 mm. almost parallel. — *Nav. bacillaris* Greg. M. J. IV Pl. I f. 24. V. H. Syn. Pl. XII f. 27.

Fresh water: Scotland (Greg.). Illinois (Grove Coll.)!

3. **C. fasciata** Lagstr. (1873). — V. linear to linear-lanceolate, with broad rounded ends. L. 0,023 to 0,037; B. 0,005 to 0,008 mm. Axial area indistinct or narrow. Central area a broad fascia. Longitudinal lines indistinct, striæ parallel 24 to 26 in 0,01 mm. — *Nav. fasciata* Lagst. Spitsb. D. p. 34 Pl. II f. 11. V. H. Syn. Pl. XII f. 34. *Nav. fonticola* Grun. V. H. Syn. Pl. XII f. 32 (1880). *Nav. fontinalis* Grun. V. H. Syn. p. 103 Pl. XII f. 33. *Nav. Bacillum var. inconstantissima* Grun. in V. H. Syn. Pl. XII f. 28. *Nav. Lacunarum* Grun. V. H. Syn. Pl. XII f. 31. *Stauroneis Bacillum* Grun. Verh. 1863 p. 155 Pl. IV f. 16. *Nav. (molaris var.?) abyssinica* Grun. in Martelli Florula Bogosensis p. 152 Pl. I f. 4 (1886).

Fresh or slightly brackish water: Spitsb.! Iceland! Scotland! Sweden! Finland! Belgium! Abyssinia (Grun.). N. Zealand! N. America, Hoboken. N. Jers! Dakota! Brazil! Ecuador! Argentina!

This little form has some resemblance to some small Pinnulariæ of the section Parallelistriatæ, so that Grunow (V. H. Syn. Pl. XII f. 34 text) considers the form from Spitsbergen to be a Pinnularia. I think it is more akin to *Nav. Bacillum.* The longitudinal lines are not distinct in most specimens, but I have seen such lines faintly on specimens from slightly brackish water at Pitea (Gulf of Bothnia), which I am unable to distinguish from the larger form, named by Grunow *Nav. Lacunarum.* As I can see no difference between *Nav. fasciata* and Grunows *Nav. fonticola*, *Nav. fontinalis* and *Nav. Lacunarum* I have united them.

A probably allied form is *Nav. Creguti* Hérib. a. Perag. (D. d'Auvergne p. 119 Pl. IV f. 17 and var. *lanceolata* f. 18) fossil in the Auvergne Deposits. The valve is more lanceolate, in L. 0,028 to 0,035 mm. The striæ are stated to be 12 to 15 in 0,01 mm. *Stauroneis acutiuscula* of the same author (p. 78 Pl. III f. 20) with 20 striæ in 0,01 mm. also fossil from Auvergne may be a form of *Caloneis fasciata*, or possibly of *Stauroneis (Pleurostauron) parvula* Grun., which I am unable to decide without original specimens.

4. **C. Beccariana** Grun. (1886). V. gibbous in the middle, with broad capitate ends. L. 0,026 to 0,074; B. 0,007 mm. Axial area narrow, central area a broad, transverse fascia. Striæ

21 in 0,01 mm. parallel. Longitudinal lines faint, median. — *Nav. Beccariana* GRUN. in Martelli Florula Bogosensis p. 153 Pl. I f. 5. Cal. B. Icon. n. Part. II Pl. I f. 7.

Brackish water: Calcutta! Abyssinia (GRUN.).

5. **C. Clevei** LAGST. (1873). V. convex, linear, with broad, subrostrate ends. L. 0,052 to 0,065; B. 0,011 to 0,014 mm. Axial area indistinct; central area a transverse fascia. Striæ 21 in 0,01 mm. (17,5 to 20 according to LAGERST.) slightly convergent in the middle and at the ends. Longitudinal lines distinct, submarginal. — *Nav. Cl.* LAGST. Spitsb. D. p. 34 Pl. I f. 10.

Fresh water: Spitsbergen!

6. **C. columbiensis** CL. N. Sp. — V. elongated, biconstricted, with cuneate ends. L. 0,044; B. 0,007 mm. Axial area narrow, somewhat broader in the middle, between the central nodule and the ends. Central area a broad, transverse fascia. Striæ almost parallel, 19 in 0.01 mm. Longitudinal lines indistinct. — Pl. III f. 34.

Fresh water: Columbia River, Oregon (Weissflog Coll.!)

I am unable to identify this form with any other, and it seems doubtful whether it belongs to this group of Navicula or to Pinnularia.

7. **C. lobata** SCHWARTZ (1877). V. small, short and stout, biconstricted, with broad, rounded-truncate ends. L. 0,03; B. 0,015 mm. Axial area narrow linear. Striæ fine, crossed by a median, longitudinal line. — *Nav. lobata* SCHW. in RAB. A. E. N:o 2481 (with fig.).

Marine? Vera Cruz.

I have not found this species in N:o 2481 of Rab. Dec. for which reason I am unable to decide if it be the same as *Nav. lobata* in CL. West. Ind. D. p. 7 Pl. I f. 8. They agree in size and outline but on the West Indian form no longitudinal lines have been observed.

8. **C. Silicula** EHR. (1843). V. elongated, gibbous in the middle with more or less clavate, obtuse ends. L. 0,033 to 0,08; B. 0,006 to 0,015 mm. Axial area indistinct or narrow; central area small and rounded, or a broad transverse fascia. Striæ 16 to 18 in 0,01 mm. almost parallel or slightly divergent in the middle and at the ends. Longitudinal lines marginal.

A. *Forms with small central area.*

Var. *alpina* CL. V. small, gibbous in the middle. L. 0,033 to 0,042; B. 0,0055 to 0,0075 mm. Axial area indistinct; central area very small. Striæ 19 to 22 in 0.01 mm. — *Nav. limosa* LAGERST. Spitsb. D. Pl. I f. 6. *Nav. Silicula* GRUN. in V. H. Syn. Pl. XII f. 21.

Fresh water: Spitsbergen! Norway, Dovre! Russian Lapland! Sweden, Arbra, Helsingland! Greenland!

Var. *gibberula* KÜTZ. — V. gibbous in the middle, with subcuneate ends L. 0,05 to 0,08; B. 0,01 to 0,015 mm. — *Nav. gibberula* KÜTZ. Bac. Pl. III f. 50 (1844). W. SM. B. D. I Pl. XVII f. 160. *Nav. limosa* KÜTZ Bac. p. 101 Pl. III f. 50 (1844). DONK. B. D. Pl. XII f. 6 b. *Nav. limosa genuina* GRUN. Verh. 1860 Pl. V f. 8 b. *Nav. limosa v. gibberula* V. H. Syn. Pl. XII f. 19.

Var. *genuina* CL. V. slightly gibbous in the middle, with subclavate, rounded ends. L. 0,05 to 0,08; B. 0,015 mm. Axial area narrow. — *Nav. Silicula* EHR. Am. p. 131. M. G. VI. 1 f. 16 etc. *Nav. limosa* DONK B. D. Pl. XII f. 6 a. V. H. Syn. Pl. XII f. 18.

The var. gibberula and genuina are very slightly different and graduate into each other completely. They occur in fresh, sometimes slightly brackish water: Sweden! Finland! England! Germany! Belgium (V. H.) Switzerland! Greenland! N. America! New Zealand!

Var. *undulata* GRUN. (1880). — V. elliptical, with very slightly undulated margin L. 0,05; B. 0,013 mm. — *Nav. limosa v. undulata* GRUN. V. H. Syn. Pl. XII f. 22.

Var. *inflata* GRUN. (1860). — V. elliptical-linear, very slightly gibbous in the middle. L. 0,05; B. 0,011 mm. — *N. lim. var. inflata* GRUN. Verh. 1860 Pl. V f. 8 c. *N. limosa var. subinfl.* GRUN. V. H. Syn. Pl. XII f. 20.

Var. *curta* GRUN. (1880). — V. linear-elliptical, with cuneate ends. L. 0,03; B. 0,012 mm. *Nav. lim. v. curta* GRUN. in V. H. Syn. Pl. XII f. 23.

Var. *capitata* LAGST. (1873). — V. strongly inflated in the middle and with broad, subtruncate ends. L. 0,06; B. 0,0075 mm. — LAGST. p. 31. Pl. I fig. 7 a.

Fresh water: Spitsbergen (LAGST.).

In Verh. 1860 GRUNOW describes two more varieties, named *truncata* and *bicuneata*, which however seem to be forms of Neidium.

B. *Forms with transverse fascia.*

Var. *minuta* GRUN. (1880). V. strongly gibbous in the middle, with clavate or cuneate ends. L. 0,022 to 0,033; B. 0,006 mm. Axial area indistinct. Striæ 21 to 22 in 0,01 mm. *Nav. ventricosa var. minuta?* GRUN. in V. H. Syn. Pl. XII f. 26.

Fresh water: Spitsbergen! Finland, Kuopio! Belgium (V. H.).

Var. *ventricosa* [EHB. 1830?] DONK. (1873). - Linear gibbous in the middle and at the rounded ends. L. 0,04 to 0,06; B. 0,009 to 0,011 mm. Axial area narrow. Striæ 18 to 20 in 0,01 mm. parallel or slightly radiate. — *Nav. ventricosa* EHB. Abh. 1830 p. 67? DONK. B. D. p. 74 Pl. XII f. 7. V. H. Syn. p. 103 Pl. XII f. 24. *Nav. Horvathii* GRUN. Verh. 1860 Pl. VI f. 18. Var. *Haslinszkyi* PANT. II p. 47 Pl. XI f. 193 (1889). *Nav. ventricosa var. subundulata* GRUN. A. D. p. 29 Pl. I f. 16. *Nav. neogena* PANT. III Pl. XVII f. 252; Pl. XXV f. 372 (1893)?

Fresh or brackish water: Sweden! Finland! Sea of Kara (GRUN.), England (DONK.) Japan!

Var. *truncatula* GRUN. (1880). V. elliptical, with rounded ends, not gibbous. L. 0,04; B. 0,01 mm. Axial area narrow. — *Nav. ventric. v. truncat.* GRUN. V. H. Syn. Pl. XII f. 25.

Var. *Kjellmaniana* GRUN. (1880). — V. gibbous in the middle with more narrow and rounded ends. L. 0,063; B. 0,0115 mm. Axial area narrow. Striæ 16 to 17 in 0,01 mm., slightly radiate. *Nav. vent. v. Kjellm.* GRUN. A. D. p. 29 Pl. I f. 17.

Marine: Finmark!

V. *Jenisseyensis* GRUN. (1880). — V. slightly gibbous in the middle. Ends rounded. L. 0,0445; B. 0,01 mm. Striæ 19 in 0,01 mm., parallel, slightly divergent at the ends. *Nav. ventric. v. Jeniss.* GRUN. A. D. p. 29 Pl. I f. 18.

Fresh water: Jenissey (GRUN.).

Var.? *subventricosa* GRUN. (1880). V. gibbous in the middle, with broad, rounded ends. L. 0,066; B. 0,0095 mm. Central nodule slightly dilated transversely. Axial area very narrow. Striæ 22 to 23 in 0,01 mm., convergent at the ends. *Nav. subventricosa* GRUN. A. D. p. 29 Pl. I f. 19.

Brackish water: Sea of Kara (GRUN.).

9. **C. tahitensis** GRUN. (1863). — V. lanceolate, inflated in the middle, with obtuse ends. L. 0,051 to 0,065; B. 0,002 mm. Axial and central areas indistinct. Striæ 12 to 13 in 0,01 mm., slightly radiate, finely punctate. Longitudinal lines median. *Nav. Tah.* GRUN. Verh. 1863 p. 152 Pl. V. f. 15. Nov. p. 19.

Fresh water: Tahiti (GRUN.).

This species is unknown to me, perhaps it is only a variety of N. Silicula.

10. **C. patagonica** CL. (1881). — V. convex, linear with cuneate ends. L. 0,057 to 0,09; B. 0,009 to 0,013 mm. Axial area narrow, but distinct. Central area a broad fascia, reaching to the margins. Striæ 13 to 14 in 0,01 mm., almost parallel, but radiate at the ends, crossed near the margin by a faint longitudinal line. - *Nav. viridis var. patag.* CL. Färskv. D. fran Grönl. och Arg. p. 12 Pl. XVI f. 3.

Fresh water, on moist rocks: Sierra Famatina, Rep. Arg.! Pichincha, Ecuador!

This remarkable freshwater-species may easily be mistaken for a *Pinnularia*, but the terminal striæ are radiate, not convergent as in the last named genus.

11. C.? **elongatula** Pant. (1889). V. linear, with rounded ends. L. 0,021; B. 0,008 mm. Axial area indistinct; central small, orbicular. Striæ 20 in 0,01 mm. parallel. Longitudinal lines? — *Nav. elongatula* Pant. II p. 45 Pl. III f. 40.

Brackish water: Hungary, foss. (Pant.).

The fig. of this species in Pantocseks work is not sufficient for determining the systematical place of this form, which seems to be related to *C. Silicula.* I have found in the deposit of Gyongyös Pata (Hungary) a form, which agrees with *N. elongatula* in outline and in the number of striæ, but is 0,04 mm. in length. In this form the striæ on both sides of the central nodule are interrupted by a short lunate, longitudinal line.

12. C. **Schumanniana** Grun. (1880). V. strongly inflated in the middle, with rounded obtuse ends. L. 0,037 to 0,05; B. 0,009 to 0,013 mm. Axial area indistinct or narrow. Central area lanceolate with a lunate marking on each side of the central nodule. Striæ 17 in 0,01 mm., radiate at the ends (very finely punctate?). Longitudinal lines indistinct. — *Nav. Trochus* Schum. P. D. I p. 189 f. 52. Greg. M. J. IV Pl. I f. 2 (1856). *Nav. Schumanniana* Grun. V. H. Syn. p. 99 Pl. XI f. 21.

Fresh water: Sweden, Ringsjön in Skane! Ladoga! Königsberg, fossil!

Var. *trinodis* Lewis (1861). — V. divided by two constrictions into three segments of equal size. Ends cuneate. L. 0,034 to 0,042; B. 0,011 mm. Striæ 18 to 20 in 0,01 mm. strongly radiate in the middle, almost parallel in the terminal segments. — *Nav. trinodis* Lewis Proc. Ac. n. sc. Philad. p. 66 Pl. II f. 6 (1861). *Nav. biconstricta* Grun. Casp. S. Alg. p. 15 Pl. III f. 6 (1878).

Fresh and brackish water: Caspian Sea (Grun.) N. America, Hudson River! Delaware! Dakota! Lake Pistaku, Illin.! Lost spring Ranch, Calif.!

13. C.? **bodosensis** Pant. (1893). — V. trochiform, obtuse. L. 0,077; B. 0,02 mm. Axial area lanceolate, dilated in the middle to a transverse fascia, and with an elongated marking on both sides of the central nodule. Striæ 17 in 0,01 mm. almost parallel. — *Nav. bodos.* Pant. III Pl. III f. 35.

Habitat?: Bodos (Pant.).

Var. *Heribaudi* Per. (1893). — V. in L. 0,07 to 0,09; B. 0,016 mm. biconstricted. Striæ 17 in 0,01 mm. *Nav. Her.* Perag. in Hérib. D. d'Auvergne p. 112 Pl. IV f. 8.

Fresh water: Puy de Dôme. Varennes (Brun Coll.)!

14. C. **alpestris** Grun. (1860). — V. linear, slightly gibbous in the middle, with rounded or subcuneate ends. L. 0,06 to 0,076; B. 0,008 to 0,009 mm. Axial and central area united in a narrow lanceolate space, having on each side of the central nodule a lunate marking. Striæ 20 in 0,01 mm. nearly parallel; slightly divergent at the ends. Longitudinal lines distinct, submarginal. *Nav. alpestris* Grun. Verh. 1860 p. 545 Pl. V f. 4. V. H. Syn. Pl. XII f. 30.

Fresh water, alpine regions: Swedens Lake Mälaren (in postglacial mud!), Austrian alps, (Grun.), Savoy!

Nav. alpestris var. tatrica Gutw. p. 20 Pl. I f. 17 — is no var. of *C. alpestris* and appears to be a Frustulia or Neidium, impossible to decide from the figures.

15. C. **nubicola** Grun. (1880). — V. slightly triundulated. Central area dilated transversely to a fascia, with lunate markings on both sides of the central nodule. — *Nav. nubicola* Grun. in V. H. Syn. Index to Pl. XII f. 30.

Fresh water: Turkestan (Grun.).

16. C. **Kainitzii** Pant. (1893). — V. elongated, gibbous in the middle, with broad, obtuse ends. L. 0,108; B. 0,02 mm. Axial area broad, linear-lanceolate, with an elongated marking on

each side of the median line. Striæ slightly radiate in the middle, elsewhere parallel, 19 in 0,01 mm. — *Nav. Kain.* PANT. III Pl. III f. 41.

Habitat?: Köpecz (PANT.).

17. **C. obtusa** W. SM. (1853). V. very convex, subrectangular, with broad, truncate ends. L. 0,05 to 0,06; B. 0,016 to 0,017 mm. Axial and central areas united in a moderately broad lanceolate space, in the middle of which is on each side of the central nodule a lunate marking. Striæ 17 in 0,01 mm. parallel or slightly divergent towards the ends. Longitudinal lines submarginal. *Nav. obtusa* W. SM. B. D. I p. 50 Pl. XVI f. 140 (1853). GRUN. Verh. 1860 p. 536 Pl. IV f. 39? *N. Hebes* RALFS Pritch. Inf. p. 896 (1861). DONK. B. D. p. 23 Pl. III f. 12.

Fresh water, especially in nothern regions. Greenland! Sweden, Lappland and Gotland! Russian Lappland! Norway, Dovre! Scotland!

This species is very characteristic and not closely akin to any known form. It seems to be an inhabitant of northern regions and is not mentioned by BRUN as occuring in Switzerland, nor by Belloc as occuring in the Pyrenées.

18. **C. Liber** W. SM. (1853). - V. linear, sometimes with slightly concave or convex margins, and rounded or subcuneate ends. L. 0,05 to 0,19; B. 0,008 to 0,032 mm. Axial area indistinct or very narrow. Central area indistinct or small. Striæ 13 to 20 in 0,01 mm. parallel, divergent at the ends. Longitudinal lines median, single or double.

A. Forms with linear, sometimes slightly constricted valves, and without lunate markings in the central area.

a) *Longitudinal lines single.*

Var. *linearis* GRUN. (1860). V. narrow, linear, with parallel margins and rounded ends. L. 0,054 to 0,12; B. 0,008 to 0,011 mm. Areas indistinct. Striæ 20 to 29 in 0,01 mm. Longitudinal lines median, frequently indistinct. *Nav. linearis* GRUN. Verh. 1860 p. 546 Pl. III f. 2. V. H. Syn. p. 105 Pl. XII f. 35. A. S. Atl. L. f. 38, 40.

Marine: Atlantic coasts of Europe, Africa and America (GRUN.), Ceylon! Singapore (BRUN Coll.!) Galapagos Islands! Peru (GRUN.), Honduras (GRUN.), Gulf of Mexico (ATL.).

Var. *genuina* CL. — V. linear, with parallel or slightly convex margins and more or less broad ends. L. 0,08 to 0,17; B. 0,013 to 0,024 mm. Axial area very narrow; central area small, orbicular, frequently somewhat asymmetrical. Striæ 13 to 20 in 0,01 mm. -- *Nav. Liber* W. SM. B. D. I p. 48 Pl. XVI f. 133. DONK. B. D. p. 62 Pl. IX f. 5. A. S. Atl. L. f. 16, 17, 18. A. S. N. S. D. II f. 45. V. H. Syn. p. 104 Pl. XII f. 36. *Nav. maxima* GREG. M. J. IV Pl. V f. 2 (1856). D. of Cl. p. 487 Pl. IX f. 18. A. S. Atl. L. f. 19 to 21, 37. N. S. D. II f. 44. *Nav. fortunata* Leud. Fortm. D. de Ceylan Pl. III f. 27 (1879).

Marine: Greenland! Spitsbergen! Finmark! Behrings' Island! North Sea! Mediterranean Sea! Red Sea! Seychelles! Cape of Good Hope! Ceylon! Singapore! Sidney! Port Jackson! Tasmania! Philippines! Japan! Campeachy Bay!

Forma tenuistriata CL. — L. 0,065 to 0,07; B. 0,015 mm. Striæ 25 to 26 in 0,01.

Marine: Labuan! Sandwichs Islands!

Forma convexa CL. — Convex. L. 0,11 to 0,13; B. 0,012 mm. Axial area somewhat broader. Striæ 16 to 20 in 0,01 mm. *Nav. Hauckii* CL. N. R. D. p. 9 Pl. II f. 27 (1881).

Marine: Gulf of Naples! Adriatic!

Var. *Holuboi* PANT. (1886). -- V. linear, with rostrate capitate ends. L. 0,159; B. 0,025 mm. Striæ 20 in 0,01 mm. - *Nav. (maxima var.?) Hol.* PANT. I p. 25 Pl. XVIII f. 165.

Marine: Hungary, fossil (Pant.).

Var. *relegata* CL. — V. slightly constricted in the middle, with cuneate ends. L. 0,15; B. 0,025 mm. Axial area linear-lanceolate. Striæ 12 to 13 in 0,01 mm., crossed by a median longitudinal line.

Marine: Redondo, Calif. fossil (Grove Coll.)!

b) *Longitudinal lines double.*

Var. *bicuneata* Grun. (1860). — V. broad, linear, with cuneate ends. L. 0,11 to 0,19; B. 0,018 to 0,032 mm. Striæ 15 to 17 in 0,01 mm. — *Nav. bicuneata* Grun. Verh. 1860 p. 546 Pl. III f. 4. A. S. N. S. D. Pl. II f. 44 (smaller form). *N. maxima* Donk. B. D. p. 60 Pl. IX f. 4. *N. Bleischii* A. S. Atl. L. f. 22, 23, 25.

Marine: North Sea! Baltjik, fossil (Atl.), Sumatra (Deby Coll.!) Samoa (Atl.), Seychelles! Colon (Deby Coll.)! Porto Seguro (Deby Coll.)!

Forma lanceolata. — V. shorter, with acuminate ends. L. 0,08 to 0,09; B. 0,032 mm. Striæ about 13 in 0,01 mm. — *Nav. excentrica* A. S. Atl. L. f. 6, 7.

Marine: Celebes (Atl.) Mazatlan (Atl.).

Var. *excentrica* Grun. (1860). — V. broadly linear to linear-elliptical, with rounded or cuneate ends. L. 0,09 to 0,14; B. 0,017 to 0,027 mm. Median line often slightly undulating. Central area frequently slightly dilated unilaterally. Striæ 20 to 22 in 0,01 mm. *Nav. excentrica* Grun. Verh. 1860 p. 545 Pl. III f. 1. *N. delata* A. S. N. S. D. p. 91 Pl. II f. 43 (1874). Atl. L. f. 30. *N. formosa v. fossilis* Pant. II p. 45 Pl. XX f. 310 (1889).

Marine: North Sea! Mediterranean Sea! Java (Kinker Coll.)! Japan (Atl.) Samoa! Colon (Deby Coll.)! Hungary, fossil (Pant.).

B. *Forms constricted in the middle. Central area without lunate markings.*

Var. *Janischiana* Rabh. (1862). — V. slightly constricted in the middle, with cuneate ends. L. 0,14; B. 0,035 mm. Median line slightly flexuose. Central area small, asymmetrical. Striæ 22 in 0,01 mm. Longitudinal lines faint, single. — *Nav. Jan.* Jan. Rab. Hond. p. 10 Pl. II f. 15.

Marine: Colon (Deby Coll.)!

Var. *Bleischiana* Jan. a. Rabh. (1862). — V. strongly constricted in the middle, with cuneate ends. L. 0,14 to 0,17; B. 0,025 (min.) to 0,042 (max.) in 0,01 mm. Areas indistinct. Striæ 12 in 0,01 mm. Longitudinal lines single, very distinct. — *Nav. Bl.* Jan. a. Rabh. Hond. p. 9 Pl. II f. 10. *Col. liber var. Bleisch.* Icon. n. Pl. IV f. 1.

Marine: Honduras (Jan. Rabh.) Nice (Deby, Brun. Van Heurck Coll.)! Redondo Calif. fossil (Grove Coll.)!

C. *Forms with lunate markings on the central area.*

Var. *elongata* Grun. (1874). — Linear, with parallel margins and broad rounded ends. L. 0,07 to 0,12; B. 0,018 to 0,009 mm. Axial area narrow; central area small with lunate markings on both sides of the central nodule. Striæ 15 to 18 in 0,01 mm. Longitudinal lines faint, median. — *Nav. elongata* Grun. in A. S., N. S. D. p. 91 Pl. II f. 42. A. S. Atl. L. f. 27.

Marine: North Sea! Mediterranean! Red Sea! Ceylon! Singapore! Japan! Galapagos Islands! Florida!

Var. *umbilicata* Grun. (1877). — V. linear, frequently slightly gibbous in the middle, with rounded ends. L. 0,13 to 0,16; B. 0,015 to 0,02 mm. Axial area narrow, but distinct, somewhat dilated in the middle, with linear markings on both sides of the central nodule. Striæ 12 to 15 in 0,01 mm. Longitudinal lines distinct. — *Nav. maxima var. umbilic.* A. S. Atl. L. f. 32, 33. *Nav. max. v. asiatica* Temp. Br. D. f. du Japon p. 72 (1889).

Marine: North Sea (Atl.) Bab el mandeb! Ceylon! Japan, fossil (Brun.) Colon (Deby Coll.!).

19. C. **robusta** Grun. (1877). — V. linear, narrowed towards the ends. L. 0,28 to 0,33; B. 0,04 to 0,035 mm. Axial area narrow, but distinct, slightly dilated around the central nodule. Striæ 9 to 11 in 0,01 mm. Longitudinal lines median, strong. — *Nav. robusta* Grun. in A. S. Atl. L. f. 1—2.

Marine: Zanzibar (Deby Coll.)! Java (Kinker Coll.)! Sumatra! Singapore! Samoa! Redondo, Calif. fossil (Grove Coll.)!

Var. *perlonga* PANT. (1889). — V. slightly gibbous in the middle. L. 0,4 to 0,5; B. 0,005 mm. Striæ 10 in 0,01 mm. — *Nav. perlonga* PANT. II p. 52; III Pl. XIV f. 209.

Marine: Hungary, fossil (Pant.).

Var. *subelliptica* CL. — V. linear-elliptical, frequently with subrostrate ends. L. 0,15 to 0,19; B. 0,037 to 0,04 mm. Areas broader. Striæ 11 to 12 in 0,01 mm. — A. S. Atl. L. 4, 5.

Marine: Raised Marsh (Atl.), Redondo and Santa Monica Calif., fossil (Deby Coll.)! Porto Seguro (Deby Coll.)!

This large and beautiful form is nearly connected with *C. Liber* and may be regarded as one of its many varieties.

20. **C. probabilis** A. S. (1877). — V. linear with subcuneate ends. L. 0,16 to 0,18; B. 0,028 to 0,03 mm. Axial area narrow. Central area small, subrhomboid. Median line slightly flexuose. Striæ 10 in 0,01 mm. Longitudinal lines double. — *Nav. prob.* A. S. Atl. L. f. 46.

Marine: Campeachy Bay (Atl.), Florida; Java (Grove Coll.)!

Also nearly akin to C. liber (var. bicuneata).

21. **C. Eugeniæ** CL. (1881). — V. linear, with rounded ends, very convex. L. 0,075 to 0,085; B. 0,017 mm. Axial area indistinct. Central area small, rhombic-orbicular. Median line slightly sinuose. Striæ 7 to 9 in 0,01 mm., slightly radiate in the middle, somewhat convergent at the ends, not distinctly punctate. Longitudinal lines distinct, submarginal. — *Nav. Eug.* CL. N. R. D. p. 7 Pl. II f. 16.

Marine: Galapagos Islands!

22. **C. virginea** CL. (1878). — V. lanceolate with acute or subrostrate and obtuse ends. L. 0,058 to 0,09; B. 0,027 to 0,025 mm. Axial area very narrow, slightly dilated unilaterally at the central nodule. Central pores approximate. Striæ 20 to 21 in 0,01 mm. parallel. Longitudinal lines faint, submarginal. — *Nav. virg.* CL. West Ind. D. p. 5 Pl. I f. 2. *Nav. parallela* CASTR. Voy. Challenger p. 31 Pl. XXVIII f. 12 (1886)?

Marine: West Indies, Virgin Islands! Bahamas (Grove Coll.)!

23. **C. eximia** GRUN. Ms. — V. divided by two deep constrictions into three segments of equal size. L. 0,11 to 0,12; B. 0,025 mm. Axial area narrow. Central area small, orbicular. Striæ 11 in 0,01 mm. radiate in the middle. Longitudinal lines double; the exterior stronger — Pl. IV f. 2.

Marine: Seychelles (Van Heurck Coll.)! Cebu (Grove Coll.)!

24. **C. clavigera** CL. N. Sp. — V. elongated, divided by two slight constrictions into one smaller median, and two larger terminal, segments. L. 0,115; B. 0015 (max.) mm. Axial area narrow. Central area a broad fascia. Striæ 20 in 0,01 mm., parallel, divergent at the ends. Longitudinal lines median. — Pl. IV f. 8.

Marine: Colon (Deby Coll.)!

This form may be regarded as a variety of *N. Liber*, with transverse fascia.

25. **C. (Pleurosigma) staurophora** GRUN. (1880). — V. sigmoid, lanceolate, gradually tapering from the middle to the acute ends. L. 0,1125; B. 0,014 mm. Median line central, sigmoid. Central area a broad, transverse fascia, reaching the margins. Striæ 14 in 0,01 mm. parallel, not punctate. Longitudinal lines closer to the median line than to the margin. Inside the longitudinal lines the striæ are fainter than outside. *Pleurosigma staurophorum* GRUN. A. D. p. 61. Perag. VIII f. 45.

Marine: Davis Strait (Grun.)

Var. *asiatica* TEMP. a. BRUN (1889) — L. 0,19 to 0,22; B. 0,025 to 0,028 mm. Striæ 16 to 18 in 0,01 mm. — *Pleur. asiaticum* D. f. du Japon p. 56 Pl. IX f. 1. Perag. VIII f. 44.

Marine: Japan, fossil.

26. **C. latefasciata** GRUN. (1880). — V. linear, with broad, rounded ends. L. 0,06 to 0,093; B. 0,012 to 0,017 mm. Axial area gradually enlarged from the ends to the middle. Central area a broad, transverse fascia. Striæ 16 to 20 in 0,01 mm. parallel. Longitudinal lines broad, submarginal. — *Nav. latef.* GRUN. A. D. p. 29 Pl. I f. 21.

Marine: Arctic America! Greenland! Sea of Kara! Cape Deschneff! Adriatic (Grun.).

27. **C. galapagensis** CL. (1881). — V. constricted in the middle, with tongue-shaped segments. L. 0,067 to 0,092; B. 0,025, at the constriction 0,009 to 0,011 mm. Axial area narrow. Central area a broad, transverse fascia. Median line with small and indistinct terminal fissures. Striæ 15 to 16 in 0,01 mm., not distinctly punctate, parallel. Longitudinal lines submarginal. — *Nav. Galapagens.* CL. N. R. D. p. 14 Pl. III f. 40.

Marine: Galapagos Islands!

Var. *contracta* GRUN. (1890). L. 0,062; B. 0,01 mm. Striæ 18 in 0,01 mm. — *Nav. contracta* A. S. Atl. CLX f. 13.

Marine: Campeachy Bay (Atl.).

Var. *japonica* CL. (1890). — L. 0,06 to 0,10; B. 0,019 to 0,023, at the constriction 0,01 to 0,014 mm. Axial area in each segment narrow lanceolate. Striæ 14 to 16 in 0,01 mm. Longitudinal lines marginal or inframarginal. *Nav. galap. v. jap.* A. S. Atl. CLX f. 16. *Nav. correpta* A. S. Atl. CLX f. 15.

Marine: China (Van Heurck Coll.)! Japan (Deby Coll., Brun Coll.)!

28. **C. consimilis** A. S. (1874). — V. linear, with parallel margins, narrowed towards the ends. L. 0,069 to 0,105; B. 0,013 mm. Axial area narrow; central area a transverse fascia. Striæ 13 to 16 in 0,01 mm. parallel. Longitudinal lines submarginal. — *Nav. consimilis* A. S N. S. D. p. 91 Pl. II f. 46.

Marine: North Sea! Balearic Islands!

29. **C. æmula** A. S. (1874). – V. linear, with parallel margins and rounded ends. L. 0,029 to 0,041; B. 0,07 mm. Axial area very narrow or indistinct. Central area a broad fascia. Striæ 19 to 23 in 0,01 mm. parallel. Longitudinal lines marginal or submarginal. — *Nav. æmula* A. S. N. S. D. p. 91 Pl. II f. 47. *Nav. subdirisa* GRUN. A. D. p. 29 Pl. I f. 20 (1880).

Marine: Sea of Kara (Grun.), Baltic (Grun.), Normandy (Grun.), Adriatic! Cape Deschneff! Arctic America! Greenland! Campeachy Bay (A. S.), Virgin Islands, West Indies!

Var. *major* CL. a. GROVE (1891). — L. 0,07; B. 0,085 mm. Striæ 18 in 0,01 mm. slightly radiate in the middle. — *Nav.* (*Caloneis*) *æmula var.? major* CL. a. GROVE Diatomiste I p. 67 Pl. X f. 8.

Marine: Macassar Straits!

30. **C. Wardii** CL. N. Sp. — V. linear, with cuneate ends. L. 0,04 to 0,09; B. 0,015 mm. Central nodule dilated transversely into a stauros, reaching the margin. Axial area narrow, linear. Longitudinal lines distinct, closer to the margin than to the median line. Striæ parallel, 19 in 0,01 mm. slightly divergent at the ends. — Pl. III f. 39, 40, 41.

Brackish water: Bristol, Conn. (Ward)! Hudson River (Ward)!

31. **C. formosa** GREG. (1856). — V. narrow lanceolate, with obtuse ends. L. 0,08 to 0,013; B. 0,015 to 0,026 mm. Axial and central area uniting into a narrow and irregularly lanceolate space, usually slightly dilated unilaterally in the middle. Striæ 14 in 0,01 mm., almost parallel, slightly radiate at the ends. Longitudinal lines median. *Nav. formosa* GREG. T. M. S. IV p. 42 Pl. V f. 6. A. S. Atl. L. fig. 9, 10. 12. 13. 14. 15. *Nav. oregonica* EHR. Ber. 1870 Pl. II: 1 f. 10. *Nav. liburnica* GRUN. V. H. Syn. p. 102 Pl. XI f. 3.

Brackish and marine: Greenland! North Sea! Baltic! Atlantic coasts of N. America! Cape Horn! Mediterranean Sea! Sierra Leone! Ceylon! Sidney! Sandwich Islands! California! Caspian

Sea (Grun.), Saxony! Great Salt Lake! Oregon, fossil! Guatemala, fossil! Mexico, fossil! Argentina, Rioja! Cameroon, Africa!

Var. *holmiensis* Cl. (1881). — L. 0,075 to 0,125; B. 0,02 to 0,03 mm. Area wider. Striæ 11 to 12 in 0,01 mm. Longitudinal lines faint or indistinct. *Nav. holm.* Cl. N. R. D. p. 8 Pl. II f. 18. *N. formosa* V. H. Syn. Pl. XI f. 2.

Brackish water: Baltic, (Vaxholm, Abo)!

Var. *interrupta* Cl. — L. 0,07; B. 0,013 mm. Axial area narrower. Central area a transverse fascia. Striæ 16 in 0,01 mm., parallel. Longitudinal lines median.

Brackish water: Yarra, S. Australia!

Var. *quadrilineata* Grun. (1879). — L. 0,044; B. 0,09 mm. Area narrow, lanceolate. Striæ about 17 in 0,01 mm. Longitudinal lines double. — *N. quadrilineata* Grun. Cl. M. D. N:o 204.

Brackish water: Oakland, Calif. (Grun.).

32. **C. (Alloioneis) curvinervia** Grun. (1878). — V. lanceolate, slightly asymmetrical, with obtuse ends. L. 0,068 to 0,115; B. 0,022 to 0,028 mm. Median line excentric, with arcuate components. Axial and central areas uniting in a narrow and asymmetrical lanceolate space. Striæ 8 to 9 in 0,01 mm. slightly radiate. Longitudinal lines distinct, median. — Grun. in Cl. W. Ind. D. p. 8 Pl. II f. 13.

Brackish water: Elephant Point, India (Grun.) Island of Rhea near Singapore!

33. **C. amphisbæna** Bory (1824). — V. elliptical, with capitate to rostrate ends. L. 0,06 to 0,08; B. 0,0225 to 0,03 mm. Axial and central area uniting in a large rhombic-lanceolate space. Striæ 16 to 17 in 0,01 mm. radiate to the ends. Longitudinal lines median. — *Navic. amphisb.* Bory Encycl. meth. T. 2 (according to Ehrenb.). *Frustulia depressa* Kütz. Dec. N:o 72 (1833) according to Lagerst. — *Nav. amphisbæna* W. Sm. B. D. I Pl. XVII f. 147 a. (1853). Grun. Verh. 1860 p. 534 Pl. IV f. 36. Donk. B. D. p. 36 Pl. V f. 13. V. H. Syn. p. 102 Pl. XI f. 7.

Fresh water: Sweden! England! Belgium (V. H.) Switzerland (Brun), Caspian Sea (Grun.).

Var. *fuscata* Schum. (1867). — V. rectangular, with rostrate ends. L. 0,04 to 0,045; B. 0,017 mm. Striæ 16 in 0,01 mm. *Nav. fuscata* Schum. Pr. D. II N. p. 57 Pl. II f. 43. Grun. A. D. p. 31 Pl. I f. 27.

Brackish water: Baltic (Schum.), Kara Sea (Grun.), Caspian Sea (Grun.).

Var. *subsalina* Donk. (1873). — V. elliptical with rostrate-apiculate ends. L. 0,07; B. 0,025 mm. Striæ 17 in 0,01 mm. *Nav. subsalina* Donk. B. D. p. 24 Pl. IV f. 2. *Nav. amphisbæna* W. Sm. B. D. I Pl. XVII f. 147 β. *Nav. amph. v. subs.* V. H. Syn. p. 102 Pl. XI f. 6. Dannf. Balt. D. Pl. II f. 14.

Brackish water: Greenland! Spitzbergen! Finmark! Bohuslän! north coasts of Britain (Donk). Baltic! Saxony, Mansfelderseen! Rostock, fossil!

Forma major. — V. lanceolate, with gradually attenuated ends. L. 0,1; B. 0,03 mm. — V. H. Syn. Pl. XI f. 4.

Brackish water: Belgium (V. H.).

Var. *Vukotinovicii* Pant. (1886). — V. lanceolate, subrostrate. L. 0,077 to 0,095; B. 0,029 to 0,032 mm. Area large, lanceolate. Striæ 12,5 to 15 in 0,01 mm., closer near the ends. — *Nav. Vuko.* Pant. I p. 29 Pl. I f. 7. II p. 54. Pl. XII p. 220.

Brackish water: Hungary, fossil!

Var. *liburnica* Grun. (1860). — V. broadly lanceolate. L. 0,05 to 0,11; B. 0,022 to 0,035 mm. Axial area narrow, slightly dilated in the middle. Striæ 16 to 17 in 0,01 mm. Longitudinal lines more approximate to the margin than to the median line. — *Nav. lib.* Grun Verh. 1860 p. 547 Pl. III f. 25.

Brackish: Adriatic (Grun.), Colon (Deby Coll.)! Calcutta (Deby Coll.)!

Var. *Fenzlii* Grun. (1863). Lanceolate, sometimes with subrostrate ends. L. 0,07 to 0,12; B. 0,028 to 0,042 mm. Area narrow, dilated around the nodule. Striæ 11 to 14 in 0,01 mm. Longitudinal lines median. — *Nav. elegans* Grun. Verh. 1860 p. 531 Pl. IV f. 37. *Nav. Fenzlii* Grun. Verh. 1863 p. 153. *Nav. amphisb. v. Fenzlii* Grun. in V. H. Syn. p. 102 Pl. XI f. 5. *N. Granowii* O'Meara B. D. p. 362 Pl. XXXI f. 17.

Brackish water: Neusiedler See. Hungary (Grun.), Rostock, fossil! Ceylon (Weissflog Coll.)! Calcutta (Deby Coll.)! Batavia! Jamaica! St Martin, W. Ind.! Guatemala, fossil! St. Monica, fossil (Dr. Rae Coll.)!

All these forms are closely connected, so that it seems to me impossible to regard them as distinct species. They are also nearly akin to the two following species, *C. bivittata* and *C. permagna*, of which the latter is, by intermediate forms, connected with *C. formosa*.

34. **C. bivittata** Pant. (1889). V. lanceolate. L. 0,08 to 0,15; B. 0,031 to 0,04 mm. Axial and central area uniting in a broad, lanceolate space. Striæ 10 (middle) to 12 or 13 (ends) in 0,01 mm., slightly radiate. Longitudinal lines double. — *N. (oregonica var.?) bivittata* Pant. II p. 43 Pl. V. f. 83.

Brackish and marine: Hungary, fossil! Atlantic City, N. Jers. foss. (Deby Coll.)!

35. **C. permagna** Bail. (1850). V. rhombic-lanceolate, sometimes with slightly triundulated margins. L. 0,15 to 0,22; B. 0,055 to 0,085 mm. Axial and central areas uniting in a more or less broad, irregularly lanceolate space. Striæ 9 to 10 in 0,01 mm. slightly radiate. Longitudinal lines broad or double, median. — *Pinnul. perm* Bail. Smiths. Cont. 1850 p. 40 Pl. II f. 28, 38. *Nav. permagna* Ralfs Pritch. Inf. p. 907. Lewis Proc. Ac. n. sc. Philad. 1861 p. 70 Pl. II f. 11. Greville T. M. S. XIV p. 127 Pl. XII f. 18 to 21, 1866. V. H. Syn. p. 102 Pl. XI f. 1.

Brackish water: Anvers (V. H.). N. America (New-York to Florida and Gulf of Mexico)!

This large and beautiful species passes over by intermediate forms to *N. formosa*, and seems also to be nearly akin to *C. bivittata*.

36. **C. Duseni** Cl. N. Sp. — V. rhombic-lanceolate, with subacute ends. L. 0,135; B. 0,038 mm. Axial area narrow. Central area moderately large, orbicular, without any markings. Striæ 13 in 0,01 mm., radiate, in the ends slightly convergent. Longitudinal lines approximate to the areas. Pl. IV f. 4.

Brackish water (mouths of rivers): Cameroon, Africa!

This species is named in honour of Mr Dusén, a swedish traveller in Western Africa, who procured me an interesting gathering from that country. This beautiful form greatly resembles *C. permagna*, but differs by the closener of its longitudinal lines to the areas.

37. **C. madagascarensis** Cl. (1890). V. broadly lanceolate. L. 0,095; B. 0,05 mm. Median line with distant central pores. Axial and central areas uniting in a narrow, lanceolate space. Median line bordered by thick silicious ribs. Striæ 9 in 0,01 mm. radiate troughout, indistinctly punctate. Longitudinal lines three, of which the median is the strongest (and differs from the others). — *N. madag.* Cl. Diatomiste I p. 23 Pl. IV f. 2.

Marine: Madagascar! Columbo, Ceylon (Letourneur Coll.)! Java!

This is a remarkable species, having some resemblance to *C. amphisbæna var. Fenzlii*, from which it is however quite distinct. Of the three longitudinal lines the median has the appearence of a narrow furrow, separating the flatter axial part of the valve from the sloping exterior part. The other lines are formed by small knots on the striæ.

38. **C. biclavata** Cl. a. Grove (1891). — V. convex, gibbous in the middle and with clavate ends. L. 0,12 to 0,16; B. 0,018 mm. Axial area broad, dilated around the central nodule to an irregularly rounded space. Striæ 10 in 0,01 mm., divergent in the ends, else almost parallel. Longitudinal lines distinct, median. — Cl. a. Grove Diatomiste I p. 66 Pl. X f. 7.

Marine: Macassar Straits (Grove Coll.)!

This is a remarkable form, not closely connected with any other known species. Perhaps *Stauroneis Bribissonii* CASTR. (Voy. Chall. Diat. p. 24 Pl. 15 fig. 4) may be the same, but the figure and description of that form are insufficient for identification.

39. **C. samoensis** GRUN. (1877). — V. linear to elliptic-linear, narrowed towards the ends. L. 0,085 to 0,115; B. 0,018 to 0,025 mm. Axial and central areas united in a narrow, irregularly lanceolate, space, having on each side of the central nodule a lunate or linear marking. Striæ 10 to 12 in 0,01 mm. slightly radiate at the ends. Longitudinal line median or submarginal. — *Nav. samoensis* A. S. ATL. L. f. 43, 44. *Nav. mammalis* CASTR. Chall. Voy. D. p. 30 Pl. XX f. 2 (1886)?

Marine: Ceylon! Amboina (Kinker Coll.), Java (Kinker Coll.)! Philippines! Labuan! Port Jackson! Samoa!

Var.? *bimaculata* PANT. (1889). V. elliptic-lanceolate. L. 0,064; B. 0,019 mm. Area lanceolate with markings on both sides of the central nodule. Striæ 14 to 15 in 0,01 mm. Longitudinal lines? - *Nav. bim.* PANT. II p. 42 Pl. XXIII f. 346.

Marine: Hungary, fossil (Pant.).

40. **C. sectilis** A. S. (1877). V. linear with rounded ends. L. 0,144; B. 0,023 mm. Axial and central areas uniting in a broad linear space, with a row of puncta along the median line. Striæ 7,5 in 0,01 mm., parallel. Longitudinal lines submarginal. *Nav. sectilis* A. S. ATL. L. f. 3.

Marine: Whatabevot, India (Atl.) Hungary, fossil (Pant.).

Var. *boryana* PANT. (1889). — L. 0,01 to 0,13; B. 0,02 to 0,024 mm. Area with a row of puncta on both sides of the central nodule. Striæ 8 to 9 in 0,01 mm. Longitudinal lines marginal or inframarginal. - *Nav. Boryana* PANT. II, XXVIII f. 407.

Marine: Gulf of Naples! Bory, Hungary, fossil! Galapagos Islands (Weissflog Coll.)!

Nav. parida PANT. III Pl. XXX f. 438 appears to be an allied but smaller form.

41. **C. Anderssonii** CL. (1881). — V. linear, with subcuneate ends. L. 0,075; B. 0,019 mm. Axial area narrow, dilated around the central nodule, to an orbicular space without markings. Striæ 6,5 to 7 in 0,01 mm., radiate at the ends, not punctate. Longitudinal lines inframarginal. *N. And.* CL. N. R. D. p. 11 Pl. III f. 28. *Cal. And.* Icon. n. Part. II Pl. I f. 8.

Marine: Galapagos Islands.

The fig. in Cl. N. R. D. is not quite exact, the axial area being too broad.

42. **C. Frater** CL. N. Sp. — V. convex, linear, with parallel margins and rounded cuneate ends. L. 0,1; B. 0,012 mm. Axial and central areas united in a narrow, lanceolate space, without markings. Striæ 8 in 0,01 mm., smooth, slightly radiate in the middle and at the ends. Longitudinal lines inframarginal. - Pl. III f. 26.

Marine: Galapagos Islands!

43. **C. Spathula** BRUN (1891). — V. linear, narrowed towards the ends. L. 0,15 to 0,16; B. 0,01 to 0,012 mm. Axial area linear, very narrow; central area indistinct. Striæ 12 in 0,01 mm. parallel, divergent at the ends finely punctate. Longitudinal line marginal or inframarginal — *Nav. spat.* BRUN. D. Esp. n. p. 40 Pl. XV f. 10.

Marine: Japan, fossil (Brun Coll.)!

44. **C. adenensis** CL. N. Sp. — V. elongated, slightly biconstricted, with cuneate ends. L. 0,07; B. 0,013 mm. Axial area narrow, irregularly dilated between the central nodule and the ends. Central area large, orbicular. Striæ 13 (middle) to 15 (ends) in 0,01 mm., radiate in the middle, transverse at the ends, not distinctly punctate. Longitudinal lines inframarginal. — Pl. III f. 33.

Marine: Between Aden and Bab el mandeb (Weissflog Coll.)!

45. **C. abnormis** Grun. (1878). — V. lanceolate, with broad, obtuse ends. L. 0,028 to 0,055; B. 0,007 to 0,009 mm. Axial area very narrow; central area small, orbicular. Median lines straight, with approximate central pores, and terminal fissures turned in contrary direction. Striæ 30 (Grunow) to 34 in 0,01 mm. transverse. Longitudinal lines faint, submarginal. — *Nav. abnormis* Grun. in Cl. M. D. N:o 142. A. D. p. 46. *Cal. abn.* Icon. n. Part. IV Pl. 1 f. 6, 7.

Marine: Bohuslän, Sweden!

46. **C. brevis** Grev. (1857). — V. elliptical, with rostrate, obtuse ends. L. 0,06 to 0,08; B. 0,022 to 0,03 mm. Median line with distant central pores. Axial area narrow, dilated in the middle to a large, orbicular space. Striæ 14 in 0,01 mm., almost parallel, not distinctly punctate. Longitudinal lines indistinct. — *Nav. brevis* Greg. D. of Clyde p. 478 Pl. IX f. 4. A. S. N. S. D. Pl II f. 15. Donk. B. D. p. 19 Pl. III f. 4. V. H. Syn. p. 97 Pl. XI f. 19. — *Nav. crassa* Greg. M. J. III p. 41 Pl. IV f. 18 (1855)?

Marine: Spitsbergen! Greenland! Finmark! North Sea! North Siberian Sea, Cape Deschniff! Löfänger, Angermanland, Sweden, (integlacial deposit)! Sydney (Thum.)!

Var. *vexans* Grun. (1880). — Elliptic-lanceolate, with broad, obtuse ends. — *Nav. brevis v. vexans* Grun. A. D. p. 30. A. S. N. S. D. Pl. II f. 14. *Nav. brev. v. elliptica* V. H. Syn. p. 97, Pl. XI f. 18.

Marine and brackish: Sea of Kara! Finmark! Japan (striæ 18 in 0,01 mm. Weissflog. Coll.)!

Var. *distoma* Grun. (1880). — V. elliptical, with broad ends. Central pores of the median line distant. Central nodule large, thick. Longitudinal lines distinct, single or double.

Forma latior: Broadly elliptical. L. 0,078; B. 0,026 mm. Striæ 13 to 14 in 0,01 mm. — *Nav. (brevis var.?) diatoma f. lat.* Grun. A. D. p. 31 Pl. 1 f. 25.

Brackish water: Sea of Kara (Grun.). Japan!

Forma angustior: Narrow elliptical. L. 0,068; B. 0,019 mm. Striæ 15 to 16 in 0,01 mm. *Nav. (brevis var.?) diatoma f. ang.* Grun. A. D. p. 31 Pl. 1 f. 26.

Brackish water: Jamal, Sea of Kara (Grun.).

Forma bicuneata Cl. — V. with parallel margins and cuneate ends. L. 0,085; B. 0,029 mm. Striæ 14 to 15 in 0,01 mm

Marine: Japan, fossil (Brun Coll.)! Sydney! China!

Nav. brevis and its varieties are nearly akin to N. *amphisbæna*.

47. **C. bottnica** Cl. N. Sp. — V. elliptic-lanceolate. L. 0,05; B. 0,018 mm. Central pores distant. Axial area broad, gradually dilated towards the middle, where it expands to a transverse fascia. Striæ 22 in 0,01 mm. slightly radiate towards the ends. Longitudinal line faint, marginal. — Pl. III f. 42.

Slightly brackish water: Gulf of Bothnia at Piteå!

48. **C. Lagerheimii** Cl. N. Sp. — V. elliptic-lanceolate convex, with obtuse ends. L. 0,042; B. 0,009 mm. Axial and central areas uniting in a lanceolate-linear space. Striæ 17 in 0,01 mm. very slightly radiate towards the ends. Longitudinal lines indistinct marginal, or inframarginal.

Fresh water: Ecuador. Quito (Lagerheim)!

49. **C. latiuscula** Kütz (1844). — V. elliptical to lanceolate. L. 0,075 to 0,09; B. 0,023 to 0,03 mm. Axial and central areas uniting in an irregularly lanceolate space. Striæ 18 to 21 in 0,01 mm. parallel, finely punctate. Longitudinal lines marginal or inframarginal. — *Nav. latiuscula* Kütz Bac. p. 93 Pl. V f. 40. Grun. Verh. 1860 p. 534 Pl. IV f. 38. Donk. B. D. p. 27 Pl. IV f. 7. *Nav. patula* W. Sm. B. D. I p. 49 Pl. XVI f. 139 (1853). V. H. Syn. Suppl. B f. 29.

Fresh water, larger lakes: Scotland; Sweden: Venern! Mälaren! Baltic, freshwater deposits of the Ancylus-epoch! Gotland! Switzerland (Lac des 4 cantons, Lac Leman)!

Var. *africana* CL. V. elliptic-linear, with broad and rounded ends. L. 0,13; B. 0,25 mm. Longitudinal lines crossing the striæ in their middle. Striæ 15 in 0,01 mm. Pl. IV f. 5.

Brackish water: Cameroon!

The var. africana merits perhaps to be considered as a distinct species.

50. **C. Holstii** CL. (1881). V. elliptical, with parallel margins and cuneate ends. L. 0,052 to 0,06; B. 0,016 to 0,02 mm. Axial area very narrow; central area small, rounded. Striæ 11 in 0,01 mm. almost parallel, not distinctly or finely punctate. Longitudinal lines marginal. — A. S. Atl. L. f. 48 (without name). *Nav. Holstii* CL. D. f. Grönl. and Argentina p. 11 Pl. XVI f. 1.

Fresh water: Greenland! Albany, Maine, fossil! Oregon (Atl.).

51. **C. Ladogensis** CL. (1891). V. broad, lanceolate, with subrostrate ends. L. 0,025; B. 0,011 mm. Axial area indistinct; central area small rounded, somewhat transverse. Striæ 17 in 0,01 mm. slightly radiate, finely punctate. Longitudinal lines marginal, faint. — *Nav. Ladog.* CL. D. of Finl p. 35 Pl. II f. 3.

Fresh water: Ladoga, on the surface of the lake!

52. **C.? dispersa** GR. and STURT (1887). — V. almost flat, elliptic-lanceolate, with subacute ends. L. 0,08; B. 0,027 mm. Median line straight, terminating close to the margin. Axial area narrow, dilated in the middle to a small rounded space. Striæ 27 in 0,01 mm., finely punctate, puncta forming undulating longitudinal lines. The striæ are confined to an irregular, lanceolate space around the axial area, the part outside of this space being irregularly and coarsely punctate. Longitudinal lines inframarginal. — *Nav. disp.* GR. and STURT. Queck. M. Cl. III (2) p. 132 Pl. X f. 10.

Marine: Oamaru, N. Zeeland, fossil!

This is remarkable species, which I have placed here only with hesitation. The longitudinal line is visible only in strongly oblique light. A somewhat similar form occurs at Monterey, which I know by a sketch sent by Grunow, who calls it *Mastogloia? decorata*. This form is smaller (L. 0,033; B. 0,013 mm.) and has a larger quadrate central area and probably coarser striæ.

53. **C.? sejuncta** A. S. (1874). — V. linear, with parallel margins and rounded cuneate ends. L. 0,04; B. 0,01 mm. Axial and central areas indistinct. Striæ 12 in 0,01 mm. transverse. Longitudinal lines broad, submarginal. *Nav. sejuncta* A. S. N. S. D. p. 87 Pl. I f. 18.

Marine: North Sea, Campeachy Bay (A. S.).

I have not seen this species, which A. SCHMIDT seems to consider akin to *Diploneis nitescens*. It seems to me more probable that it belongs to the group of *C. Powellii*. No indication of the nature of the striæ exists. If punctate this form may be a Diploneis; if smooth it belongs to the group of *C. Powellii*.

54. **C. blanda** A. S. (1874). — V. linear, with rounded ends. L. 0,05 to 0,13; B. 0,01 to 0,018 mm. Axial area narrow. Central area orbicular, large. Striæ 8 to 10 in 0,01 mm. parallel, radiate at the ends, not distinctly punctate. Longitudinal lines broad. *Nav. blanda* A. S. N. S. D. p. 90 Pl. II f. 27. *Pinn. crystadensis* GREG. T. M. S. 1856 p. 48 Pl. V f. 22?

Marine: North Sea! Black Sea! Ceylon! Seychelles! Amboina! Labuan! Tahiti!

55. **C. supergradata** BRUN. (1891). — V. convex, linear, with rounded ends. L. 0,115 to 0,135; B. 0,016 mm. Axial and central areas combined in a broad, linear space. Median line strongly flexuose. Striæ 6 in 0,01 mm., parallel smooth. Longitudinal lines broad, marginal. — *Nav. supergr.* BRUN. D. Esp. n. p. 40 Pl. XV f. 6.

Marine: Gulf of Naples! Port d'Alger (Brun). Bosphorus (Brun).

56. **C. Wittii** GRUN. (1881). — V. linear, slightly constricted in the middle, with subcuneate ends. L. 0,073; B. 0,014 mm. Axial and central areas indistinct. Striæ 8 in 0,01 mm., smooth, subparallel. Longitudinal lines broad, submarginal. — *Nav. Wittii* GRUN. in CL. N. R. D. p. 11 Pl. III f. 31.

Marine: Brazil (Grun.).

57. **C. Zanardiniana** GRUN. (1860). — V. linear, with slightly concave margins and subcuneate ends. L. 0,168; B. 0,019 mm. Axial area narrow, slightly dilated around the central nodule. Striæ 5 in 0,01 mm. Longitudinal lines broad, median. — *Nav. Zanard.* GRUN. Verh. 1860 p. 525 Pl. III f. 12.

Marine: Adriatic (Grun.).

58. **C. Campbellii** PETIT (1877). — V. with parallel or slightly concave margins and cuneate ends. L. 0,058 to 0,081; B. 0,019 to 0,022 mm. Axial area indistinct. Central area a subquadrate space with fragments of striæ. Striæ 8 in 0,01 mm. smooth, parallel. Longitudinal lines marginal. — *Nav. Campb.* PET. D. de Campb. p. 22 Pl. V f. 23.

Marine: Island of Campbell!

An examination of original specimens has convinced me that this species is nearly akin to *C. Powellii*.

59. **C. biseriata** PETIT (1877). — V. convex, lanceolate, gradually tapering from the middle to the ends. L. 0,055 to 0,074; B. 0,0176 mm. Axial area narrow. Central area a quadrate space. Median line with approximate central pores. Striæ 7 in 0,01 mm., smooth, slightly radiate throughout. Longitudinal lines broad, on one side of the median line uniting with the central area. — *Nav. biseriata* PETIT D. de Campb. p. 23 Pl. IV f. 15.

Marine: New Zealand!

60. **C. Powellii** LEWIS (1861). — V. linear, with parallel margins and cuneate ends. L. 0,05 to 0,13; B. 0,015 to 0,03 mm. Axial area indistinct or narrow. Central area quadrate. Striæ 7 to 11 in 0,01 mm., parallel, smooth. Longitudinal lines broad, uniting with the central area.

Var. *atlantica* CL. — L. 0,05 to 0,1 mm. Striæ 10 to 11 in 0,01 mm. — *Nav. Powellii* LEWIS Proced. Ac. nat. sc. Philad. p. 65 Pl. II f. 6. *Nav. sectilis var. Boryana* PANT. II p. 53 Pl. VIII f. 152 (1889).

Marine: Quincy, Mass! Long Island Sound! Hungary fossil (Pant).

Var. *galapagensis* CL. (1881). — L. 0,05 to 0,09; B. 0,013 to 0,02 mm. Striæ 8 to 9 in 0,01 mm. — *Nav. Pow. var. galapag.* CL. N. R. D. p. 11 Pl. III f. 30.

Marine: West Indies! Galapagos Islands!

Var. *Vidovichi* GRUN. (1863). — V. 0,1 to 0,15 mm. Striæ 6 to 7 in 0,01 mm. — *Nav. Vidovichi* GRUN. Verh. 1863 p. 150 Pl. XIII f. 4.

Marine: Adriatic (Grun.), Sumatra (Deby Coll.)! S. America (Deby Coll.)!

Var. *egyptiaca* GREV. (1866). — V. elongated, slightly constricted in the middle. L. 0,11 to 0,13; B. 0,02 mm. Axial area distinct. Central area irregularly quadrate. Striæ 6 in 0,01 mm. smooth, transverse. Longitudinal lines broad, united, or nearly so, with the central area. — *Nav. egyptiaca* GREV. T. M. S. XIV p. 127 Pl. XII f. 16—17. PERAG. D. de Villefr. p. 53 Pl. II f. 9.

Marine: Adriatic! Alexandria (Deby Coll.). Sumatra!

Var. *Bartholomei* CL. (1878). — V. panduriform. L. 0,055 to 0,07; B. 0,015 or 0,017 (max.) to 0,01 (min.) in 0,01 mm. Axial area distinct, but narrow. Central area quadrate. Striæ 7 to 8 in 0,01 mm. smooth, parallel. Longitudinal lines broad, marginal, united with the central area. — *Nav. Bartholomei* CL. W. Ind. D. p. 6 Pl. I f. 5. A. S. Atl. CLX f. 9.

Marine: West Indies! Porto Seguro (Deby Coll.)! Bahia (Deby Coll.)!

61. **C. Castracanei** Grun. (1881). — V. broadly linear to lanceolate, with obtuse ends. L. 0,07 to 0,135; B. 0,02 to 0,03 mm. Median line straight, with small, terminal nodules and large quadrate, central nodule. Axial and central areas uniting in a narrow, lanceolate space. Striæ 9 to 12 in 0,01 mm., slightly radiate throughout, smooth. Longitudinal lines broad, area-like, median, not united with the central area.

Var. *Philippinarum* Cl. — V. linear with gradually narrowed ends. L. 0,11; B. 0,02 mm. Striæ 12 in 0,01 mm.

Marine: Manilla (Deby Coll.).

Var. *Petitiana* Grun. (1881). — V. broadly linear, with cuneate ends and parallel margins. L. 0,07; B. 0,02 mm. Area crossed by faint striæ. Striæ 11 in 0,01 mm. *Nav. Pet.* Grun. in Cl. N. R. D. p. 12 Pl. III f. 34.

Marine: Cebu!

Var. *seychellensis* Grun. Ms. — Like var. Petitiana, but without faint striæ on the area. Striæ 10 in 0,01 mm.

Marine: Seychelles (Van-Heurck Coll.)!

Var. *caledonica* Cl. — V. narrow elliptical. L. 0,135; B. 0,03 mm. Striæ 10 in 0,01 mm.

Marine: New Caledonia (Kinker Coll.)!

Var. *genuina* Cl. — V. lanceolate. L. 0,1; B. 0,03 mm. Striæ 9 in 0,01 mm. — *Nav. Castracanei* Grun. in Cl. N. R. D. p. 12 Pl. III f. 33.

Marine: Australia (Grun.).

C. Castracanei is a large and beautiful form, and is connected by intermediate varieties with *C. Powellii*.

62. **C.? venusta** Pant. (1889). — V. linear, with rostrate ends. L. 0,037; B. 0,095 mm. Axial area narrow. Central area small, dilated on both sides of the median line to broad lateral areas. Striæ 21 to 22,5 in 0,01 mm., parallel, divergent towards the ends. Longitudinal lines marginal. — *Nav. venusta* Pant. II p. 54 Pl. V f. 81.

Marine: Hungary, fossil (Pant.).

I have not seen this species; the description being made from the figure in Pantocseks work, which shews some likeness to a small *C. Powellii*, with the striæ crossed by a narrow, marginal line.

63. **C. amica** Cl. a. Grun. (1881). — V. broad, slightly constricted in the middle, with cuneate ends. L. 0,075 to 0,095; B. 0,023 to 0,03 mm. Axial area very narrow. Central area large, quadrate, dilated to broad lateral areas on both sides of the median line. Striæ 7 to 8 in 0,01 mm. smooth, almost parallel. — *Nav. amica* Cl. a. Grun. in Cl. N. R. D. p. 12 Pl. III f. 37.

Marine: Tahiti!

C. amica is remarkable by the broad lateral areas, which are also very much developped in the following two species. These areas occupy the place of the longitudinal lines of the other species of this genus.

64. **C. quadriseriata** Cl. a. Grun. (1881). — V. broad, hexagonal, with parallel margins and large, cuneate ends. Median line with small terminal fissures and incrassate central nodule. L. 0,09 to 0,16; B. 0,035 to 0,047 mm. Axial area narrow. Central area large, orbicular. Striæ 7 to 8 in 0,01 mm., slightly radiate at the ends, elsewhere parallel, smooth. Longitudinal areas broad, linear, attenuated towards the ends. — *Nav. quadriseriata* Cl. N. R. D. p. 12 Pl. III f. 32. *Nav. duplex* Pant. III Pl. XLII f. 579 (1893).

Marine: Barcelona! Balearic Islands! Gulf of Naples! Levant (Grove Coll.)!

65. **C.? kryophila** Cl. (1883). — V. elliptic-lanceolate, with cuneate or obtuse ends. L. 0,05 to 0,08; B. 0,018 to 0,04 mm. Axial area narrow. Central area small, orbicular, dilated on both sides of the median line to large, lunate lateral areas, on which faint traces of the striæ

are visible. Striæ 8 to 9 in 0,01 mm. smooth, slightly radiate. — *Nav. kryoph.* Cl. Vega p. 473 Pl. XXXVII f. 43. Var.? *gelida* Cl. l. c. f. 42.

Marine: North Siberian Sea, Cape Wankarema! Ice from the east-coast of Greenland!

A very peculiar form, for which I can find no other natural place than this. The large lateral areas give this form some resemblance to *N. Hennedyi*, but nevertheless it cannot belong to the section Lyratæ of Navicula, as the structure of the striæ is entirely different. If this species really be a Caloneis, we have here the lateral lines in an extraordinary degree of development.

66. **C. Musca** Greg. (1857). — V. broad, panduriform, with cuneate or rounded ends. L. 0,04 to 0,07; B. 0,016 to 0,025 mm. Axial and central areas united in a broad lanceolate, space, sometimes constricted in the middle. Median line bordered by thick siliceous strings, with indistinct terminal fissures and approximate central pores. Striæ 7 to 8 in 0,01 mm., smooth, or more or less obscurely punctate. Longitudinal line broad, submarginal. — *Nav. Musca* Greg. D. of Clyde p. 479 Pl. IX f. 6. A. S. N. S. D. p. 86 Pl. I f. 15. Atl. CLX f. 1, 2, 10, 11, 12. *Nav. constricta* Grun. Verh. 1860 p. 535 Pl. III f. 18 (very bad). *Nav. intercedens* A. S. Atl. CLX f. 3, 4, 5. *Nav. musceformis* Pant. III Pl. XVII f. 256 (1893).

Marine: North Sea! Mediterranean Sea! Adriatic! Bab el mandeb! Ceylon! Seychelles! China! Japan! Galapagos Islands! Porto Seguro! West Indies!

Var. *intermedia* Cl. Strongly constricted, with elliptical segments. L. 0,06 to 0,09; B. 0,025 to 0,028 mm. Axial area narrow, lanceolate. Striæ 6 in 0,01 mm. Longitudinal lines broad, submarginal. — *Nav. Musca var. intermedia* A. S. Atl. CLX f. 7, 8.

Marine: Sumbava (Kinker Coll.)! Manila (Deby Coll.)! Samoa (Atl.).

Var. *mirabilis* Leud. Fortm. (1879). — V. panduriform with tongue-shaped segments. L. 0,077; B. 0,029 mm. Axial area narrow linear, slightly dilated around the central nodule. Striæ 7 (6 according to Leud.) in 0,01 mm. Longitudinal lines broad, submarginal. — *Nav. mirabilis* Leud. Fortm. D. de Ceylan p. 31 Pl. II f. 21. A. S. Atl. CLX f. 6.

Marine: Ceylon! Sumbava (Kinker Coll.)! Manila (Deby Coll.)! Sumatra!

Var. *eurynota* Cl. V. strongly constricted in the middle with elliptical segments. L. 0,08; B. 0,02 (max.) to 0,01 (min.) mm. Axial area very large. Striæ 6 in 0,01 mm. Longitudinal line narrow, median. Part II Pl. I f. 9.

Marine: Rio Janeiro (Deby Coll.)!

Var.? *margino-punctata* Grove a. Sturt (1887). V. slightly constricted in the middle, with cuneate or rounded ends. L. 0,055 to 0,11; B. 0,022 to 0,032 mm. Area broad and large. Striæ 10 in 0,01 mm., becoming faint towards the area. Longitudinal lines marginal. *Nav. margino-punctata* Gr. a. Sturt Journ.Quek. M. Club. III (2) p. 132 Pl. X f. 7. *Nav. margino-lineata* Gr. a. Sturt. l. c. f. 11. A. S. Atl. CLX f. 27.

Marine: Oamaru, New Zealand, fossil!

N. Musca is extremely variable and many of the varieties are very dissimilar in appearance, but there exist, so far as I can find, no characteristics of sufficient importance for their distinction as species. Nearly akin to *N. Musca* is also the following, which is described as a species, because it occurs in many different places with the same characteristics.

67. **C. Kinkeriana** Truan (1892). — V. panduriform, of the same outline as *Diploneis Kützingii*. L. 0,11 to 0,13; B. 0,04 (max.) to 0,018 (min.). Axial area broad, with rudimentary continuations of the striæ. Median line straight, enclosed between thick siliceous strings, with small terminal nodules and approximate central pores. Striæ 7 in 0,01 mm., smooth, or indistinctly granulate, radiate. Longitudinal bands narrow, nearer to the margin than to the median line. —

Cl. in Diatomiste I p. 76 Pl. XII f. 5. *Nav. Kink.* Pant. III Pl. XLII f. 571. *Nav. Venus* Pant. III Pl. XXIX f. 422 (1892)?

Marine: Guernsey (Grove Coll.)! Mediterranean Sea (Naples, Nice, Barcelona)! Moron. fossil (Truan).

This is certainly one of the most beautiful naviculoid diatoms. It was named by the late Mr. Truan *Nav. Kinkeriana*, a name given by Pantocsek to another Navicula (*N. Kinkerii* II, IX f. 169). For this reason I proposed to name it N. amoena, but having since separated the genus Caloneis from Navicula, I prefer the name given by Truan.

---

68. **C. biconstricta** Grove a. Sturt (1887). — V. biconstricted with orbicular median and elliptical terminal segments. L. 0,08; B. 0,016 mm. Axial area narrow; central area orbicular. Striæ 8 in 0,01 mm. Longitudinal line marginal. — *Nav. bic.* Grove a. Sturt. Quek. M. Club. III (2) p. 132 Pl. X f. 9.

Marine: Oamaru, New Zealand, fossil!

69. **C. formicina** Grun. (1878). — V. biconstricted, with small median and large terminal segments. L. 0,057 to 0,085; B. 0,012 (max.) to 0,004 (min.) mm. Axial area narrow, dilated in the middle to a transverse fascia. Striæ 6 in 0,01 mm., very delicately punctate. Longitudinal line inframarginal. Frustule rectangular. — *Nav. formicina* Grun. in Cl. West Ind. D. p. 6, f. 6. A. S. Atl. CLX f. 38 to 41.

Marine: Campeachy Bay (Grun.).

70. **C.? egena** A. S. (1890). — V. biconstricted, with the median segment smaller than the terminal, which are acuminate. L. 0,033; B. 0,005 mm. Axial and central areas united in a space of the same shape as the valve. Striæ marginal, 11 in 0,01 mm. Longitudinal line? — *Nav. egena* A. S. Atl. CLX f. 42, 43.

Marine: Campeachy Bay (A. S.).

71. **C. ophiocephala** Cl. a. Grove (1891). — V. very convex, divided by two constrictions into three segments, of which the median is almost orbicular, the terminal spathulate. L. 0,07 to 0,085; B. 0,013. Median line with indistinct terminal nodules, enclosed between strong siliceous strings. Axial areas in the terminal segments large, lanceolate. Central area very broad, having a lunate marking on each side of the central nodule. Striæ 11 in 0,01 mm. at the base of the segments, 13 at the ends, radiate, smooth. Longitudinal line narrow. — *Nav. ophiocephala* Cl. a. Grove Diatomiste I p. 57 Pl. IX f. 13.

Marine: Island of Rhea, Singapore! Java! Island of Muntok, Sumatra! Macassar Straits (Grove Coll.)!

---

72. **C.? scintillans** Temp. a. Brun. (1889). — V. strongly constricted in the middle. Segments rhomboidal with cuneate ends. L. 0,09 to 0,125; B. 0,025 to 0,035; at the constriction 0,012 mm. Median line enclosed between strong siliceous strings with small terminal fissures, turned in the same direction, and approximate central pores. Axial area narrow. Central area a broad, transverse fascia. Striæ 6 in 0,01 mm. smooth, slightly divergent in the middle of each segment. Longitudinal line(?) approximate to the axial area, indistinct. — *Nav. scint.* D. f. du Japon p. 45 Pl. V f. 5. A. S. Atl. CLX f. 36, 37.

Marine: Japan, fossil! Jedo (Atl.).

I am not quite sure whether this form belongs to Caloneis or to Pinnularia. On the fig. in D. f. du Japon a marginal longitudinal line is visible, but I have not seen this line on original specimens. It seems to me doubtful whether the line close to the axial area is the longitudinal line. If this form does not belong to Caloneis, it is a Pinnularia, and is then akin to *P. lobata* and *P. excellens*.

73. C.? **Hardmaniana** CL. V. Sc. — V. deeply constricted, with subelliptical segments, broadest at the base. L. 0,05; B. 0,016, at the constriction 0,005 mm. Median line with approximate median pores, and small terminal nodules. Axial area very broad, elliptical in each segment. Central area a broad, transverse fascia. Striæ 8 in 0,01 mm. at the base of the segments, 10 at the ends, smooth. Longitudinal lines indistinct. Part II Pl. I f. 10.

Marine: Campeachy Bay (Hardmans coll.)!

This species is akin to *C. scintillans* and may perhaps be a Pinnularia.

Additional.

74. C. **latevittata** PANT. (1893). V. with parallel margins and cuneate ends. L. 0,084; B. 0,0024 mm. Axial area narrow, slightly dilated around the central nodule. Striæ parallel throughout, 18 in 0,01 mm. not distinctly punctate. Longitudinal lines broad, nearer to the margin than to the median line. — *Nav. later.* PANT. III Pl. VIII f. 122.

Habitat? Hungary. Bodos (Pant.).

I have not seen this species, and am uncertain whether it is a Caloneis or a Neidium.

Neidium PFITZER (1871).

Valve elongated, linear to broadly lanceolate. Median line straight; its central pores turned in contrary directions; its ends with two lateral and one axial prolongations. On both sides of the median line are one or two longitudinal lines. Axial area narrow or indistinct. Central area orbicular or somewhat transversely dilated. Structure: distinct puncta, disposed in transverse, usually oblique, rows. Cell-contents: two chromatophores along the connecting zone, which do not migrate along the interior of the valve, and are divided by fissures parallel to the axis of the cell (PFITZER, Bau und Entw. p. 39). In conjugation two cells form two auxospores with transversely striate perizonium, which opens by an operculum (GRIFFITH, Ann. and Mag. n. hist. s. 2 Vol. XVI p. 92 Pl. II B 1855. DE BARY, Bot. Z. Beil. p. 62, 1858).

The genus Neidium was founded in 1871 by PFITZER (Bau u. Entw. p. 39) on the characteristics of the cell-contents, but the peculiarities of the valve are also sufficient for the distinction of Neidium as a genus. The median line has the central pores turned in contrary directions. The terminal nodules are also peculiar. The longitudinal lines point to some relation between Neidium and Caloneis, but the structure is different. The forms of Neidium have in the dry state usually a characteristic yellow colour. The striæ are coarsely, or at least distinctly, punctate and they usually cross the valve in an oblique direction. The puncta form also, on the other hand, more or less regular, longitudinal striæ.

Neidium is, as far I can see, not nearly akin to any other genus, although there are some relations to Caloneis, of which genus *C. Silicula* was by PFITZER included in Neidium. One species of Scoliopleura, viz. *S. Schneideri* GRUN., resembles Neidium in the oblique striation.

The numerous forms included in Neidium are so intimately connected, that all the species are more or less artificial and founded on variable characteristics, such as the form and outline of the valve. It seems from the observations of GRIFFITH that the mother-cells of the auxospore have rostrate, but the young cells, rounded ends. Strictly speaking, perhaps all the forms of Neidium ought to be treated as varieties of one species, but this course would make it difficult to discriminate between the numerous forms.

All the Neidia live in fresh water, some few also in brackish water. They occur in arctic as well as in tropical regions.

Artificial key.

1.	Valve elongated, 3 to 6 times longer than broad	2.
	— broad, 2 to 3	7.
2.	Margins parallel	. . 3.
	— convex	. . . . 4.
	— undulating	. . . . . . 5.
3.	Ends rounded	*N. bisulcatum* LAGST.
	cuneate . .	*N. amphigomphus* EHR.
	rostrate	*N. affine* EHR.
4.	Ends rounded . .	*N. Iridis* EHR.
	subrostrate .	. . . . *N. Iridis* var.
	— rostrate-capitate	*N. productum* W. SM.
5.	Ends broad, rounded	. *N. affine* var.
	— cuneate . .	. . . . 6.
6.	Striæ slightly oblique . .	. . . . *N. Hitchcockii* EHR.
	— strongly . .	*N. oblique-striatum* A. S.
7.	L. 0,03 to 0,04 mm.	. . . *N. dubium* EHR.
	L. 0,06 mm.	*N. dilatatum* EHR.
	L. 0,07 to 0,1 mm. . . .	. . *N. citreum* A. S.
	L. 0,16 mm.	. . *N. tumescens* GRUN.

1. **N. bisulcatum** LAGST. (1873). V. linear, with rounded ends. L. 0,04 to 0,07; B. 0,008 to 0,009 mm. Striæ 28 to 30 in 0,01 mm., distinctly punctate. — *Navic. bisulcata* LAGST. Spitsb. D. p. 31 Pl. I f. 8. A. S. Atl. XLIX f. 15, 17. *N. scita* W. SM. Ann. Mag. n. hist. XIX p. 10, Pl. II f. 4 (1857)?

Fresh water (alpine regions): Greenland! Spitsbergen! Beeren Eiland (Lagst.)! Dovre, Norway! Sweden (Areskutan, Westerbotten etc.)! Finland! Lac Gerardmer (Vosges)! Argentina!

2. **N. affine** EHR. (1843). V. linear, with rostrate ends.

Var. *longiceps* GREG. (1856). V. small, frequently with undulating margins. Ends broad, rostrate or rostrate-capitate. L. 0,03; B. 0,005 mm. Striæ very fine. — *Nav. longiceps* GREG. M. J. IV Pl. I f. 27.

Fresh water: Greenland! Scotland (Greg.)!

Var. *undulata* GRUN. (1860). V. slightly triundulate, with broad, rounded ends. L. 0,07; B. 0,013 mm. Striæ 24 in 0,01 mm. *Nav. aff. var. undulata* GRUN. Verh. 1860 p. 514. Pl. V f. 6. V. H. Syn. Pl. XIII f. 6.

Fresh water: Sweden (Cl. M. D. No 103), Belgium (V. H.).

Var. *amphirhynchus* EHR. (1843). — V. with protracted, rostrate-capitate ends.

Forma minor: L. 0,04 to 0,05; B. 0,008 to 0,013 mm. Striæ 25 to 27 in 0,01 mm.

Fresh water: Sweden (Upsala)! Astralia (Blue Mountains)!

Forma major: L. 0,09; B. 0,01 mm. Striæ about 16 in 0,01 mm. *Nav. affinis* EHR. Am. III: 1. f. 10 etc. *Nav. amphirhynchus* W. SM. B. D. XVI f. 142. DONK. B. D. p. 31 Pl. V f. 9. A. S. Atl. XLIX f. 27 to 30. *Nav. aff. var. amphirh.* GRUN. Verh. 1860 Pl. V f. 5, 11. *Nav. Iridis var. amphirh.* V. H. Syn. Pl. XIII f. 5.

Fresh water: Spitsbergen (Lagst.). Beeren Eiland (Lagst.). Scotland! England! Belgium (V. H.)! Sweden! Finland! New Zealand!

Var. *genuina* CL. V. with rostrate, less protracted ends.

Forma minor: L. 0,045 to 0,065; B. 0,008 to 0,013 mm. Striæ 22 to 29 in 0,01 mm. — *Nav. affinis* EHR. Am. II: 2. f. 7; 4 f. 4. KÜTZ. Bac. XXVIII f. 65. *Nav. affinis var.* A. S. Atl. XLIX fig. 20 to 23. *Nav. bisulcata var. turgidula* LAGST. Spitsb. D. p. 32 Pl. I f. 9.

Fresh water: Spitsbergen (Lagst.). Lappland! Finland (Tulomian Lappmark)! Italy (Atl.)! Australia (Blue Mountains and Tasmania)!

Forma media: L. 0,07 to 0,12; B. 0,017 to 0,02 mm. Striæ 18 to 19 in 0,01 mm., composed of puncta, 13 to 18 in 0,01 mm. — *Nav. affinis* GREG. M. J. 1851 II f. 8. GRUN. Verh. 1860 Pl. V f. 2. DONK. B. D. p. 33 Pl. V f. 8. *Nav. firma var. subampliata* GRUN. A. S. Atl. XLIX f. 19.

Fresh water: Greenland! Iceland! Spitsbergen (Lagst.)! England! Sweden! Finland! South Africa! Australia (Murray River)!

Forma maxima: L. 0,18 to 0,3; B. 0,04 mm. Striæ 12 to 17 in 0,01 mm. Puncta 11 to 15 in 0,01 mm. — A. S. Atl. XLIX f. 1.

Fresh water: Monticello, (fossil) New York!

3. **N. productum** W. SM. (1853). — V. subelliptical, with rostrate-capitate ends. L. 0,06 to 0,1; B. 0,02 to 0,025 mm. Striæ 17 in 0,01 mm. — *Nav. producta* W. SM. B. D. I p. 51 Pl. XVII f. 144. A. S. Atl. XLIX f. 37 to 39. GRUN. Verh. 1860 p. 543 Pl. IV f. 35. *Nav. Iridis var. producta* V. H. Syn. p. 104 Pl. XIII f. 3. *Nav. affinis* V. H. Syn. Pl. XIII f. 4.

Fresh water: England! Germany! Belgium (V. H.). Bengal!

This form graduates into *N. affinis var. amphirynchus.*

4. **N. oblique-striatum** A. S. (1877). — V. linear, slightly triundulate, with cuneate ends. L. 0,068 to 0,13; B. 0,015 to 0,022 mm. Striæ 14 to 20 in 0,01 mm. very oblique, coarsely punctate, puncta 17 to 18 in 0,01 mm. *Nav. obl. str.* A. S. Atl. XLIX f. 41, 42.

Fresh water: Demerara River!

5. **N. Iridis** EHB. (1843). — V. linear, subelliptical, with rounded ends. L. 0,09 to 0,17; B. 0,022 to 0,03 mm. Striæ slightly oblique, 16 to 19 in 0,01 mm., punctate; puncta 13 to 17 in 0,01 mm. — *Nav. Iridis* EHB. Am. p. 130 Pl. IV: 1, f. 2. KÜTZ. Bac. p. 92 Pl. XXVIII f. 42. DONK. B. D. p. 30 Pl. V f. 6. A. S. Atl. XLIX f. 2. V. H. Syn. XIII f. 1. *Nav. firma* KÜTZ. Bac. p. 92. Pl. XXI f. 10. W. SM. B. D. Pl. XVI f. 138. A. S. Atl. XLIX f. 3. *Nav. firma var. major* GRUN. Verh. 1860 p. 543 Pl. V f. 1. STRÖSE, Klieecken D. f. 5 a.

Fresh water: Franz Jos. Land (Grun.), Iceland! Sweden! Finland! England! Vosges! Switzerland (Brun). Belgium (V. H.). North America (French Pond. Monticello. Delaware)! Cape Horn (Petit). Australia (Blue Mountains)!

Var. *ampliata* EHB. (1842). — V. narrow, elliptical, with broad, subrostrate ends. L. 0,07 to 0,1; B. 0,023 to 0,026 mm. Striæ 16, puncta 17 in 0,01 mm. — *Nav. ampliata* EHB. Ber. 1842 p. 337 M. Geol. A. S. Atl. XLIX f. 4, 5. *Nav. affinis* W. SM. B. D. XVI f. 143. STRÖSE, Klieecken D. f. 12.

Fresh water: Sweden, Degernäs (Atl.); Holstein (Atl.). Houghton, Michigan N. A.!

6. **N. amphigomphus** EHB. (1843). — V. linear, with cuneate ends. L. 0,09 to 0,15; B. 0,022 to 0,04 mm. Striæ 16 in 0,01 mm. coarsely punctate, puncta 17 in 0,01 mm. — *Nav. amphigomphus* EHB. Am. II f. 27, III: 1 f. 8. KÜTZ. Bac. p. 93 Pl. XXVIII f. 40, 41. A. S. Atl. XLIX f. 32 to 34. *Nav. firma* DONK. B. D. p. 31 Pl. V f. 7. *Nav. affinis v. amphirhynchus* GRUN. Verh. 1860 p. 544 Pl. V f. 2. *Nav. dilatata* A. S. Atl. XLIX f. 9. *Nav. Iridis var. amphigomphus* V. H. Syn. p. 104 Pl. XIII f. 2.

Fresh water: Greenland! Spitsbergen (Lagst.)! Sweden! Finland! Belgium (V. H.)! Germany! Switzerland! North America (New Providence! Monmouth! Canada! Sierra Nevada!). South America!

7. **N. Hitchcockii** EHB. (1843). V. linear, biconstricted, with cuneate ends. L. 0,055 to 0,1; B. 0,015 mm. Striæ 20, puncta 20 in 0,01 mm. *Nav. Hitch.* EHB. Am. p. 130, M. G. V: 3 f. 11. DONK. B. D. p. 29 Pl. V f. 4. A. S. Atl. XLIX f. 35, 36.

Fresh water: Sweden! Scotland (Donk.)! Bengal! Australia (Murray River)! New Zealand! North America (Port Hope! Crane Pond! French Pond!).

N. Hitchcockii may be regarded as a undulate form of *N. amphigomphus.*

8. **N. dubium** EHR. (1843). V. elliptical, sometimes slightly biconstricted, with obtuse, subrostrate, or almost apiculate ends. L. 0,03 to 0,0375; B. 0,01 mm. Striæ 20 to 24 in 0,01 mm. *Nav. dubia* EHR. Am. p. 130 Pl. II f. 2. 8. KÜTZ. Bac. p. 96 Pl. XXVIII f. 61. GREG. M. J. 1856. IV Pl. I f. 3. SCHUM. P. D. 1 Nacht. p. 21 f. 25. A. S. Atl. XLIX f. 7, 8, 24 to 26. *Nav. Peisonis* GRUN. Verh. 1860 p. 544 Pl. III f. 28. *Nav. Iridis var. dubia* V. H. Syn. p. 104 Suppl. B. f. 32. *Nav. incurva var. minuta* GUTWINSKY Materyjaly p. 22 Pl. I f. 18.

Fresh, sometimes brackish water: Sweden (Westerbotten to Skane)! Gulf of Bothnia! Scotland (Greg.). Neusiedler See, Hungary (Grun.). Bengal! Australia (Blue Mountains)! New Zealand! North America (Port Hope. Ducks Pond, Lost Spring Ranch Cal.)! Surinam! Ecuador! Puerto Monte, Chile! Argentina!

9. **N. dilatatum** EHR. (1843). V. broadly elliptical, with subrostrate ends. L. 0,06 B. 0,025 mm. Striæ 16, puncta 17 in 0,01 mm. — *Nav. dilatata* EHR. Am. p. 130. A. S. Atl. XLIX f. 6.

Fresh water: Finland (Vasa! Pudasjärvi Atl.).

10. **N. citreum** A. S. (1877). V. broadly lanceolate. L. 0,07 to 0,10; B. 0,04 to 0,055 mm Striæ 16 to 17, puncta 17 to 19 in 0,01 mm. — *Nav. citrea* A. S. Atl. XLIX f. 12.

Fresh water: Demerara River!

11. **N. tumescens** GRUN. (1877). V. broadly lanceolate. L. 0,16; B. 0,06 mm. Striæ 16, puncta 17 in 0,01 mm. *Nav. firma var. tumescens* GRUN. A. S. Atl. XLIX f. 10.

Fresh water: North America (Bemis Lake! Cherryfield! Monmouth! Troy!).

Additional.

To Neidium perhaps belongs *Navicula includens* PANT. III (Pl. XIII f 201), unknown to the author.

Pseudoamphiprora CL. (1881).

Valve more or less lanceolate and convex. Median line straight. Central nodule transversely dilated into a stauros, not reaching the margin, but abutting on two longitudinal lines, one on each side of the median line. Axial area indistinct, central area a transverse fascia. Striæ nearly parallel, composed of fine puncta. Connecting zone not complex. — The cell-contents of *P. stauroptera* have two chromatophore-plates along the valves. They have entire margins and a deep, narrow sinus from the apices, below the median line. Their substance is thinner below the longitudinal lines.

In the year 1881 (New and rare D. p. 13) I proposed to include in a section Pseudo-amphiprora of Navicula a few forms, among which was *Amphora stauroptera* BAIL., synonymous with *Amphiprora lepidoptera* GREG. (D of Cl. Pl. XII f. 59 e) and *A. obtusa* GREG. (l. c. f. 60). This small group is very interesting and merits to be regarded as a separate genus, the systematic place of which is between *Naviculæ Lyratæ* and *Caloneis*.

All the species are marine and inhabit both arctic and tropical seas.

Artificial key of species.

1	Stauros narrow	*P. impleta* CL. a. GROV
	" broad .	. . . 2.
2.	V. with cuneate ends	*P. polygona* BRUN.
	V. lanceolate . . .	. . . 3

3. { V. very convex . . . . *P. crucifix* Br. a. Temp.
{ V. less convex . . . . 4.

4. { Striæ coarsely punctate . . . . *P. jugata* Cl.
{ — finely . . . . *P. stauroptera* Bail.

1. **P. impleta** Cl. a. Grove (1891). — V. elliptic-lanceolate. L. 0,13; B. 0,038 mm. Median line with very approximate central pores and indistinct terminal fissures. Stauros narrow dilated at the extremities. Striæ 12 in 0,01 mm., radiate throughout, finely lineate. Longitudinal lines 3 to 4 on each half of the valve, the most distinct connecting the ends of the stauros with the ends of the valve. — *Nav. impl.* Cl. a. Grove. Diatomiste I, p. 58 Pl. IX fig. 1.

Marine: Macassar Straits!

2. **P. polygona** Brun (1891). — V. broad with slightly convex margins and cuneate, obtuse, ends. L. 0,12 to 0,15; B. 0,035 to 0,05 mm. Median line with small terminal fissures, turned in the same direction, and not very approximate central pores. Stauros moderately broad. Striæ slightly radiate throughout, 16 in 0,01 mm., punctate, puncta 21 in 0,01 mm. Longitudinal lines not very distinct. — *Nav. pol.* Brun. D. Esp. n. p. 38 Pl. XV f. 9.

Marine: Japan, fossil!

The longitudinal lines are not so distinct as on the other species. In their place is a kind af low crest separating the interior part of the valve from the exterior steeply sloping part.

3. **P. stauroptera** Bail. (1854). — V. elliptic-lanceolate, with obtuse ends. L. 0,11 to 0,13; B. 0,03 to 0,035 mm. Stauros moderately broad. Striæ 14 to 18 in 0,01 mm., finely punctate, parallel. Longitudinal lines distinct, median. — *Amphora stauroptera* Bail. Smiths. Contr. VII p. 8 f. 14, 15 (1854). *Amphiprora lepidoptera* Greg. D. of Clyde p. 506 Pl. XII f. 59 c (1857). *Amphiprora obtusa* Greg. D. of Clyde l. c. fig. 60. A. S. N. S. D. III f. 1. *Nav. arctica* Cl. D. arct. S. p. 16 Pl. III f. 13 (1873). Lagerst. Boh. D. p. 46. Cl. N. R. D. p. 13.

Marine: Sea of Kara (Grun.). Finmark! North Sea! Nova Scotia (Bail). Sidney (Brun Coll.!).

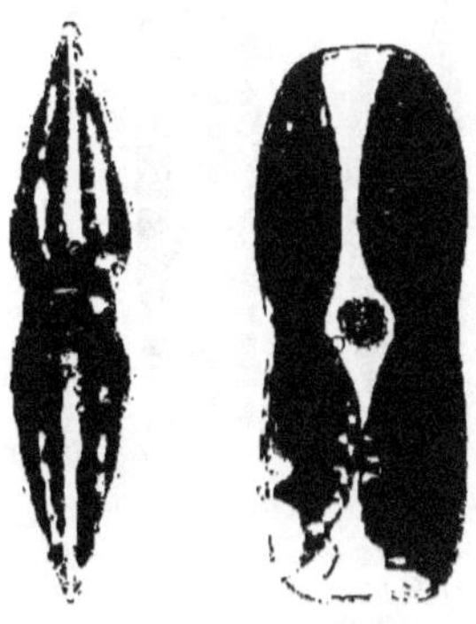

P. stauroptera 500 times magnified.

4. **P. jugata** Cl. (1881). — V. lanceolate, with obtuse ends. L. 0,068 to 0,093; B. 0,02 to 0,024 mm. Stauros of median breadth. Striæ 10 in 0,01 mm. parallel, more distinct outside the longitudinal lines, distinctly punctate; puncta about 12 in 0,01 mm. Longitudinal lines median. *Nav. jugata* Cl. N. R. D. p. 13 Pl. III f. 38.

Marine: Galapagos Islands!

Var. *Pensacolæ* Cl. (1881). — V. slightly triundulate, with subrostrate ends. L. 0,054; B. 0,015. Striæ 15 in 0,01 mm. — *Nav. Pensacolæ* Cl. N. R. D. p. 14 Pl. III f. 39.

Marine: Pensacola!

5. **P. crucifix** Temp. a. Brun. (1889). — V. very convex, narrow, lanceolate, with subacute ends. L. 0,12; B. 0,022 mm. Stauros moderately broad. Striæ 16 in 0,01 mm. parallel, punctate; puncta about 16 in 0,01 mm. Longitudinal lines marginal. — *Nav. cruc.* D. foss. du Japon p. 42 Pl. VII f. 10.

Marine: Japan, fossil!

To this genus probably belongs *Stauroneis decora* GREV. (T. Bot. Soc. of Edinb. Vol. VIII p. 236 Pl. III f. 11) from New Caledonia. It is very transparent, lanceolate, in length 0,14 mm. and has a short stauros not reaching the longitudinal ridges.

Scoliotropis CL. N. G.

Valve elongated symmetrical. Median line slightly sigmoid, especially towards the ends. On both sides of the median line is a longitudinal line. Structure double: coarser transverse costæ and finer puncta, disposed in obliquely decussating rows. Connecting zone with longitudinal rows of short striæ.

This genus has been formed for *Scoliopleura latestriata* GRUN. as this form is entirely different from the true Scoliopleura-forms in its structure, which is the same as in *Gomphoneis*, and in the complex nature of its connecting zone. Later on another, very interesting species, was discovered, unfortunately not yet found in entire specimens, *S. Gillesii*.

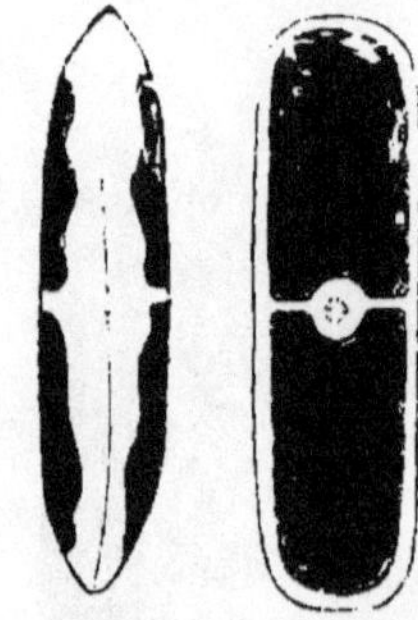

S. latestriata, 500 times magnified.

The frustules of *S. latestriata* have along the connecting zone on each side, two chromatophore-plates, the margins of which are gently undulating. In front-view the plates have a sinus around the central plasma-mass.

1. **S. latestriata** BRÉB. (1849). - V. linear, narrowed at the cuneate ends. L. 0,1 to 0,18; B. 0,025 mm. Median line strongly sigmoid. Structure: strong costæ, 7 in 0,01 mm., transverse, troughout, and minute puncta, 18 in 0,01 mm., forming obliquely decussating lines and alternating in double rows with the costæ. Connecting zone with several longitudinal rows of short striæ, about 25 in 0,01 mm. — *Amphipr. latestr.* BRÉB. in Kütz. Sp. Alg. p. 93. *Navic. convexa* W. SM. B. D. I p. 49 Pl. XVI f. 136 (1853). *Scoliopleura latestriata* V. H. Syn. p. 111 Pl. XVII f. 12.

Marine: North Sea (Sweden! England! Belgium!), Caspian Sea (Grun.). Atlantic coasts of North America! West Indies! California!

Var. *Amphora* CL. (1892). — V. asymmetrical, with a more convex dorsal side. Median line curved, with the terminations directed towards the same side. — *Scoliotr. latestr. var. Amphora* CL. Diatomiste I p. 78 Pl. XII f. 13.

Marine: Long Island Sound, New York!

I have only seen detached valves, of this variety, so I do not know whether both valves have the median lines on the same side of the frustule or not.

2. **S. Gilliesii** CL. a. COMBER N. SP. — V. convex, linear, tapering at the somewhat rounded ends. L. 0,2; B. 0,06 mm. Median line straight (sigmoid at the ends?). Central nodule small; its median pores turned in opposite directions. Axial and central areas indistinct. Costæ 7 in 0,01 mm. a little closer towards the ends, parallel, somewhat convergent at the ends, crossed by a longitudinal keel, enclosing a furrow broader than a half of the breadth of the valve. The costæ alternate with double rows of puncta, about 14 in 0,01 mm., forming longitudinal undulating rows. — Pl. I f. 16.

Marine: Jamaica (Comber Coll.)!

This species, named in honour of Captain GILLIES, who procured the material, is a very characteristic, large form, of which fragments only have been found. The median line seems to be curved, probably in contrary directions, at the ends. The median pores have the same characteristics as those of *Neidium*, and also the longitudinal keels or ridges, but the structure differs entirely from that of *Neidium* and agrees with that of *Diploneis*. In my opinion this remarkable form approaches nearer to *Scol. latestriata* than any other.

Gomphoneis Cl. N. Gen.

Valve elongated, clavate, or asymmetrical with the transverse axis. Median line straight, more or less oblique. Terminal fissures straight. Axial area narrow, linear. Central area small, rounded, with one or more stigmas. On both sides of the median line are longitudinal lines. Structure double: slightly radiate costæ, and fine puncta, forming obliquely decussating lines. — Zone broader in the upper than in the lower end, not complex. Cell-contents unknown.

I have formed this new genus for some species formerly considered as belonging to Gomphonema, but differing from it both in the structure and in the presence of the longitudinal lines. In these characteristics they agree nearly with Scoliotropis, but differ in the straight median line, and the asymmetrical form of the valve.

To Gomphoneis may perhaps also belong *Gomphonema eriense* Grun.

The few known species of Gomphoneis are all of fresh-water habitat and are found in North and Central America.

Artificial key.

1. { Central area on both sides of the central nodule with rows of stigmas . . *G. elegans* Grun.
   { — — — — — — — one or two stigmas . . . . . . 2.
2. { Costæ about 9 in 0,01 mm. . . . . *G. Mamilla* Ehb.
   { — 12 — — . . . . *G. herculeana* Ehb.

1. **G. elegans** Grun. (1880). V. sublanceolate, tapering from the gibbous middle to the broad rounded upper end, and to the narrower basis. L. 0,12 to 0,15; B. 0,028 to 0,03 mm. Median line broad (oblique). Axial area narrow; central area orbicular, with a circlet of stigmas. Costæ 10 in 0,01 mm., radiate in the ends. Puncta 22 in 0,01 mm. Longitudinal lines distinct, median. — *Gomphonema elegans* Grun. V. H. Syn. Pl. XXV f. 19.

Fresh water: Shasta Co. Cal. foss. (Cl. M. D. N:o 264). Pitt River, Oregon (Grove Coll.)!

2. **G. Mamilla** Ehb. (1854). V. lanceolate, gradually tapering to the obtuse, narrow ends. L. 0,09 to 0,15; B. 0,02 to 0,03 mm. Axial area narrow, linear. Central area small, rounded, with one or two stigmas. Costæ slightly radiate at the ends, 8 to 10 in 0,01 mm., alternating with double rows of fine puncta, forming obliquely decussating rows, 16 to 20 in 0,01 mm. Longitudinal lines marginal. *Gomphonema Mam.* Ehb. M. G. XXXVII: 2 f. 10. V. H. Syn. Pl. XXIII f. 1. *Gomphonema oregonicum var. maxima* Grun. V. H. Syn. Pl. XXIII f. 3.

Fresh water: Shasta Co. Calif., fossil! Pitt River, Oregon (Grove Coll.)!

3. **G. herculeanum** Ehb. (1845). V. clavate, with broad and rounded or subtruncate upper ends. L. 0,06 to 0,1; B. 0,02 to 0,022 mm. Axial area very narrow; central area small, rounded, with one stigma. Costæ slightly radiate at the ends, about 12 in 0,01 mm., alternating with double rows of puncta (about 22 in 0,01 mm.) forming obliquely decussating rows. Longitudinal lines faint, sometimes obsolete, median. — *Gomphonema hercul.* Ehb. Ber. 1845 (according to Chase). Grun. Casp. Sea Alg. p. 11. V. H. Syn. Pl. XXIII f. 2.

Fresh water: New York! Lake Erie (Cl. M. D. N:o 40)! Winnipeg River, Manitoba (Grove Coll.)!

Var. *robusta* Grun. (1878). — Broader, more clavate. — *G. herc. v. rob.* Grun. Casp. Sea Alg. p. 12 Pl. III f. 3.

Fresh water: Kamtschatka (Grun.).

Var. *clavata* Cl. — Broadest at the upper, rounded-truncate end. L. 0,11; B. 0,03 mm.

Fresh water: Pitt River, Col. (Grove Coll.)!

Naviculæ Luxuriosæ Cl.

Valve of elliptical outline, with depressed areas on both sides of the median line, separated by a more or less broad furrow from the marginal part. Axial and central area uniting in a narrow space around the median line. Structure: marginal, short striæ and on the depressed areas large distant puncta forming more or less regular longitudinal rows.

Only a few forms of this section are known, and it seems at present impossible to decide as to their affinities. They have some resemblance to *Diploneis nitescens*. The short marginal striæ are apparently smooth, but in a specimen of *N. luxuriosa* from China I have seen in the marginal furrow rows of distinct puncta in continuation of the marginal striæ.

1. **N. luxuriosa** Grev. (1862). V. elliptic-lanceolate, with obtuse, sometimes cuneate, ends. L. 0,06 to 0,09; B. 0,025 to 0,035 mm. Axial area narrow linear, slightly dilated in the middle. Striæ marginal, slightly radiate at the ends, 7 to 9 in 0,01 mm. Furrow with rudimentary, sometimes distinctly punctate, striæ. Depressed lateral areas large with 3 to 5 longitudinal rows of large puncta straight, or curved towards the median line. — *Nav. luxuriosa* Grev. T. M. S. XI p. 18 Pl. I f. 10, 11. *Nav. lux. var. cuneata* Brun. D. esp. n. p. 35 Pl. XVI f. 3.

Marine: N. S. Wales (Grev.). China! Japan (Brun Coll.)!

2. **N. decora** Grove and Sturt (1887). V. elliptical, with obtuse ends. L. 0,075 to 0,125; B. 0,03 to 0,045 mm. Median line straight; its terminal fissures turned in the same direction. Axial area distinct, linear, slightly dilated around the nodule. Marginal striæ 7 in 0,01 mm., apparently smooth, slightly radiate. Furrow crossed by faint striæ. Areas large, coarsely punctate; puncta forming 5 to 6 irregularly undulating longitudinal rows, or somewhat scattered. Grove and Sturt Quek. M. Cl. III (2) p. 133 Pl. X f. 13. A. S. Atl. CLXXIV f. 27.

Marine: Oamaru, New Zealand, fossil!

3. **N. trilineata** Grove and Sturt (1887). — V. elliptic-lanceolate. L. 0,1; B. 0,033 mm. Axial area narrow, slightly dilated towards the middle. Striæ 6 in 0,01 mm. crossed by two longitudinal blank bands, so that each half of the valve seems to bear three longitudinal rows of elongate, coarse puncta. Grove and Sturt Quek. M. Cl. III (2) p. 132 Pl. X f. 8.

Marine: Oamaru, New Zealand, fossil!

Naviculæ Nicobaricæ Cl.

Valve elliptical in outline. Median line with approximate central pores and large comma-like terminal fissures, bordered on both sides by a longitudinal row of large, sometimes confluent puncta. Axial and central areas united in a lanceolate space. Structure apparently smooth, distant striæ, radiate throughout.

This group comprises only two known species *N. Nicobarica* and *N. Ny*, of doubtful affinity to and other species. They have some resemblance to certain Diploneis forms, but the central and terminal nodules are very different. They seem to me provisionally to be nearest akin to *Diplon. bioculata* and *N. forcipata*, although the relation is a distant one.

1. **N. nicobarica** Grun. (1863). V. broadly elliptical. L. 0,0241 to 0,043; B. 0,015 to 0,03 mm. Median line with moderately approximate median pores and large comma-like terminal fissures, turned in the same direction. Axial and central areas uniting in a large lanceolate space, having on both sides of the median line a row of large, sometimes confluent puncta. Striæ 7 to 8 in 0,01 mm. smooth, radiate throughout. — Grun. Verh. 1863 p. 150 Pl. V f. 8. A. S. Atl VIII f. 57, LXX f. 35, 36. Cl. Vega p. 505 Pl. XXXV f. 16.

Marine: Ceylon! Nicobar Islands (Grun.), Celebes (Atl.), Cape of Good Hope (Atl.) Cape Horn (Petit).

2. **N. Ny** Cl. N. Sp. V. elliptical, with broad rounded ends. L. 0,04; B. 0,018 mm. Median line with large comma-like terminal fissures, turned in the same direction. Axial and central area united in a large lanceolate area having on both sides of the median line a row of small puncta, and around the central nodule a few larger stigmas. Striæ. 16 in 0,01 mm., apparently smooth. — Pl. I f. 24.

Marine: Java!

Cymatoneis Cl. N. G.

Valve more or less elliptical or lanceolate in outline, divided by one or several longitudinal ridges into two or more divisions. Median line with approximate central pores and elongated terminal fissures, at some distance from the ends of the valve. Axial area narrow, central small, usually rhomboidal. Structure: puncta disposed in transverse and straight longitudinal rows — Zone not complex.

This little group of very characteristic forms seems to be most nearly akin to Scoliopleura, although no species has any very close connection with that genus. The structure of the valve is the same as in *Scoliopleura Peisonis* and the ridges on both sides of the median line recall those of Scoliopleura. In several forms there is a tendency in the median line to be sigmoid.

1. **C. sulcata** Grev. (1863). — V. convex, with triundulated margins, and apiculate or subrostrate ends. L. 0,045 to 0,06; B. 0,025 to 0,033 mm. Axial area very narrow, dilated around the central nodule to a rhomboidal space. Median line slightly sigmoid; terminal fissures elongated, distant from the ends. Ridges two or three on each side of the median line. Striæ radiate at the ends, 8 to 11 in 0,01 mm.; puncta forming straight, longitudinal rows, 14 to 18 in 0,01 mm. — *Navic. sulcata* Grev. Trans. Bot. Soc. Edinb. Vol. VIII p. 235 Pl. III f. 10. Leud. Fortm. D. de Ceylan Pl. III f. 30. *Nav. triundulata* Grun. Hedwigia VI p. 27 (1867). M. M. J. 1877 Pl. CXCV f. 10. *Cymaton. sulc.* Pl. I f. 12. 13.

Marine: Mediterranean Sea! Seychelles (V. H. Coll.)! Madagascar (V. H. Coll.)! Ceylon! Labuan! Japan! Port Jackson! Java! China! Japan! New Caledonia (Grev.). Galapagos Islands! Honduras (Grun.), Campeachy Bay! West Indies! Florida!

Varies occasionally with a slight constriction in the middle and with quadri-undulated margins.

2. **C. quadrisulcata** Grun. (1867). V. elliptic-lanceolate, with slightly rostrate, obtuse ends. L. 0,05 to 0,09; B. 0,028 to 0,036 mm. Axial area indistinct; central area orbicular. Ridges two on each side of the median line. Striæ slightly radiate, 6 to 8 in 0,01 mm., punctate; puncta forming longitudinal rows. — *Nav. quadris.* Grun. Novara p. 101 Pl. I A f. 14.

Marine: S:t Pauls Island.

Grunow figures two specimens, which seem to belong to different species. The smaller resembles *C. sulcata* and may be a non-undulated variety of that species. The larger may be identical with the following, but I cannot identify them, as Grunow's figure shews two ridges of equal strength on both sides of the median line.

3. **C. circumvallata** Cl. N. Sp. V. linear-elliptical with broad, rounded, sometimes slightly rostrate ends. L. 0,055 to 0,075; B. 0,012 to 0,022 mm. Median line slightly sigmoid, with approximate central pores and prolonged terminal fissures. Axial area narrow; central rhomboidal. Ridges one or two on each side of the median line. Striæ 9 in 0,01 mm., parallel, radiate at the ends, punctate; puncta coarse, forming longitudinal rows, 14 in 0,01 mm. — Pl. I f. 10, 11.

Marine: Balearic Islands! Ceylon! Labuan! Japan (Brun Coll.)!

Diploneis Ehb. (1840).

Valve usually short, constricted in the middle, or not, generally with obtuse or rounded ends. Central nodule more or less quadrate, prolonged into *horns*, or processes, which enclose the median line. On both sides of the horns are depressions, or *furrows*, of more or less breadth. Structure: transverse finer striæ, or coarser costæ, which usually continue in a rudimentary state across the furrows, where they frequently give rise to a longitudinal row of large pearls. The transverse costæ are often crossed by one or more longitudinal costæ, giving the valve the appearance of being reticulated; or alternate with double rows of finer puncta, or *alveoli*. The cell-contents (of *D. fusca*, *D. Smithii*, *D. didyma*, *D. subcincta*, *D. chersonensis* and *D. constricta*) have two chromatophore-plates along the connecting zone. They are deeply indented and divided, sometimes in such a manner as to be split up into closely crowded and orbicular small discs.

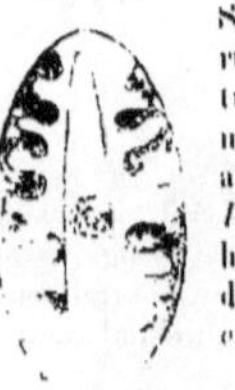

Diploneis Smithii. times magnified

The name *Diploneis* was given by Ehrenberg 1840, to some panduriform naviculoid diatoms. This characteristic is of no importance; but on the other hand, the central nodule, the furrows and the structure are so peculiar, that the genus Diploneis may be regarded as a well founded one.

The central nodule is, in the more typical forms, large and quadrate, with the angles prolonged into strong siliceous horns, enclosing the median line. In some few forms these horns are less distinct, as in *D. nitescens*. The horns correspond evidently to the lyre-shaped expansions or lateral areas in the section of Naviculæ Lyratæ, but in Diploneis the space between the horns and the median line is never punctate as in that group. There are a few forms which are intermediate between Diploneis and the Nav. lyratæ, viz. *Dipl. hyalina* Donk. and *D. Hudsonis* Grun. Outside the horns are depressed parts of the valve, *furrows*. These furrows have usually a longitudinal row of large pearls, formed by the continuation of the costæ of the valve. Sometimes there are double rows of pearls or alveoli. These furrows are to be found also in other genera, as in Scoliopleura, Cymatoneis, etc., and point to a relationship between Diploneis and those genera. Between the furrows and the exterior part of the valve is in several species a space, the *lunula*, of different structure from the outside part of the valve. Such lunulæ occur in *D. mirabilis*, *D. Crabro* and others.

The structure of Diploneis is very variable. In some forms, as in *D. hyalina*, the valve has fine striæ, which in *D. Hudsonis* are formed by obliquely decussating puncta. In other forms there are coarse costæ, not composed of puncta. The costæ frequently anastomose and seem then to be crossed by one or more, undulating, or straight, longitudinal ribs. When these longitudinal ribs are numerous, they form with the transverse costæ a network of quadrate alveoli. The costæ often alternate with double rows of puncta (alveoli), forming obliquely decussating rows. These alveoli seem to be formed by numerous small lateral branches from the costæ. A similar structure occurs in *Scoliotropis* and *Gomphoneis*. In the larger forms the transverse costæ alternate with large rounded pore-like markings, the *ocelli*, which evidently belong to an interior stratum of the valve. In *D. Crabro* and allied forms these ocelli form a marginal row, which in the middle approaches the central nodule. In other forms, as in *D. lesinensis*, they form several, more or less irregular, longitudinal rows. The ocelliferous stratum seems to correspond to the interior porous layer in *Trachyneis* and perhaps to the foramina of the larger *Pinnularia*.

Diploneis has, as already remarked, some affinity to the group of *Naviculæ lyratæ*, intermediate forms being *D. hyalina* and *D. Hudsonis*. It has also some relation to *Cymatoneis* and through that genus to *Scoliopleura*. Another genus, which has some relation to Diploneis, is Amphora, sensu strictiori. In the last named group we find the large central nodule, the lateral furrows, and, frequently, the reticulated structure of some Diploneis-forms; but there are no known intermediate forms between Diploneis and Amphora.

The systematic arrangement of the numerous forms of Diploneis is excedingly difficult. The species are very variable in size and in the coarseness of the structure. Moreover valves, which are uninjured often present a very dissimilar appearance to such as have been corroded by preparation. Several new species have been founded on corroded specimens of well-known species. Many, at first sight very distinct species, are connected by intermediate varieties. Although I have examined and figured a very large number of forms from all parts of the world, I must confess that my attempt to their classification still leaves much to desire.

Most species of Diploneis live in salt water. Brackish forms are *D. didyma*, *D. interrupta*, *D. Smithii* and frequently *D. elliptica*. The panduriform species are all marine or brackish, and *D. didyma* becomes almost elliptical in slightly brackish water. Fresh water species of Diploneis are few, but very frequent. The are all elliptical in outline.

Artificial key.

1.	Finely strate (striæ 17 to 24 in 0,01 mm.)	2.
	Coarsely — (costæ 3 to 17 in 0.01 mm.)	6.
2.	Striæ of distinct, coarse puncta	*D. ovalis* Hilse.
	not distinctly or finely punctate	3.
3.	Horns of the central nodule strong and distinct	4.
	— — — — not distinct	5.
4.	Transverse striæ crossed by oblique striæ	*D. Hudsonis* Grun.
	— — not — —	*D. hyalina* Donk.
5.	Furrows broad	*D. bioculata* Grun.
	— narrow	*D. oculata* Bréb.
6.	Transverse costæ not crossed by longitudinal, or not alternating with alveoli	7.
	— crossed by one or several longitudinal, or alternating with single or double rows of alveoli	25.
7.	Horns of the central nodule not distinct	*D. inscripta* Cl.
	— — — distinct	8.
8.	Furrows narrow	9.
	— broad	18.
9.	Valve constricted	14.
	— not or slightly	10.
10.	Valve elliptical	11.
	— linear-elliptical	12.
	— linear	13.
11.	Costæ 6 to 10 in 0,01 mm.	*D. suborbicularis* Greg. (*D. coffæformis* A. S.).
	12 to 18 —	*D. Puella* A. S.
12.	Fresh-water species	*D. Boldtiana* Cl.
	Marine	*D. advena* A. S.
13.	Horns parallel	*D. congrua* Jan.
	— divergent in the middle	*D. compar* Jan.
14.	Slightly constricted	*D. subunda* A. S.
	Strongly —	15.
15.	Ends rostrate	*D. laciniosa* A. S.
	not —	16.

16.	Costæ incrassate at the margin	*D. Adonis* Brun
	— not	17.
17.	Segments almost orbicular	*D. interrupta* Kütz.
	— elongate-elliptical	*D. Guinardiana* Brun.
18.	Valve not constricted	19.
	— panduriform	23.
19.	Valve very convex and thick	*D. circumnodosa* Brun.
	— not —	20
20.	Valve elliptical	*D. Cynthia* A. S.
	— linear	21.
21.	Furrows decreasing in breadth from the middle	*D. munda* Jan.
	— of equal breadth throughout	22.
22.	Central nodule small	*D. mediterranea* Grun.
	— large	*D. contigua* A. S.
23.	Furrow crossed by costæ	*D. Letourneurii* Cl.
	— without or with rudimentary costæ	24.
24.	Costæ 4 to 7 in 0,01 mm.	*D. musciformis* Grun.
	7 to 8	*D. constricta* Grun.
	— 11 to 12 —	*D. incurvata* Greg.
25.	Costæ crossed by a single longitudinal rib	26.
	— several — ribs	35.
	— alternating with double rows of alveoli	61.
26.	Valve not constricted	27.
	constricted	29.
27.	L. 0,02 to 0,05 mm.	28.
	L. 0,04 to 0,08 mm.	*D. lineata* Donk.
28.	Furrows broad	*D. discrepans* A. S.
	narrow	*D. Papula* A. S.
29.	Valve gently constricted	30.
	deeply —	34.
30.	Furrows decreasing in breadth from the middle	*D. Vetula* A. S.
	— of almost equal breadth	31.
31.	Furrows very broad	*D. binaria* A. S.
	— not —	32.
32.	Longitudinal rib in the middle of the striæ	33.
	— marginal	*D. subcincta* A. S.
33.	Rib narrow	*D. exemta* A. S.
	— broad	*D. demta* A. S.
34.	L. about 0,03 mm.	*D. bombiformis* Cl.
	L. 0,07 to 0,1 mm	*D. coarctata* A. S.
35.	Valve constricted	36.
	— not	50.
36.	Valve with ocelli	*D. areolata* Cl.
	— without	37.
37.	Valve strongly constricted	38.
	slightly	45.
38.	Segments orbicular	*D. Clepsydra* Cl.
	elliptical or deltoid	39.
39.	Costæ alternating with faint alveoli	*D. Præstes* A. S.
	— distinct —	40.
40.	Ribs forming undulating rows	*D. splendida* Greg.
	— — straight or curved	41.
41.	L. 0,01 or less	*D. Gründleri* A. S.
	L. larger	42.
42.	Furrows indistinct	*D. Weissflogii* A. S.
	distinct	43.
43.	Ribs two to five on each side of the median line	44.
	eight to ten	*D. Kützingii* Grun.
44.	Transverse costæ 5 to 8 in 0,01 mm	*D. Bombus* Ehr.
	8 to 13	*D. chersonensis* Grun.

45.	Longitudinal ribs 2 to 4 in 0,01 mm.	46.
	— — 5 to more —	47.
46.	Furrows broader in the middle	*D. Schmidtii* Cl.
	— not —	*D. Entomon* Ehr.
47.	Furrows broader in the middle	48.
	— not — —	49.
48.	Transverse costæ 6 to 9 in 0,01 mm.	*D. bomboides* A. S.
	— — 11 — —	*D. divergens* A. S.
49.	Transverse costæ 9 in 0,01 mm.	*D. didyma* Ehr.
	13 — —	*D. chinensis* Cl.
50.	Median line ending far from the margin	*D. microtatos* Pant.
	— — — near — —	51.
51.	Furrows abruptly dilated around the central nodule	52.
	— not — — — —	53.
52.	Transverse costæ about 7 in 0,01 mm.	*D. hyperborea* Grun.
	— — — 12 —	*D. vacillans* A. S.
53.	Furrows broad	54.
	— narrow	57.
54.	Freshwater species	*D. finnica* Ehr.
	Marine —	55.
55.	Longitudinal ribs few	*D. notabilis* Grev.
	— — numerous	56.
56.	Central nodule small	*D. Græffii* Grun.
	— — large	*D. fusca* Greg.
57.	Longitudinal ribs wider than the costæ	*D. domblittensis* Grun.
	equidistant with — or closer	58.
58.	Central nodule small	*D. litoralis* Donk.
	— large	59.
59.	Freshwater species	60.
	Marine —	*D. æstiva* Donk.
60.	Ribs as close as the costæ	*D. elliptica* Kütz.
	— closer than —	*D. Parma* Cl.
61.	Valve not or slightly constricted	62.
	— constricted	74.
62.	Valve elliptical	63.
	— elongated with parallel or slightly concave margins	73.
63.	Furrows narrow	64.
	— broad	67.
64.	Without ocelli	65.
	With ocelli	*D. biseriata* Cl. (*D. Crabro* var.)
65.	Furrows equally arcuate	*D. Smithii* Bréb.
	bent around the central nodule	66.
	— linear	*D. advena* var. *recta*.
66.	Central nodule large	*D. subovalis* Cl.
	— — rather small	*D. borealis* Grun.
67.	Furrows forming a large, orbicular space	68.
	— — an elliptical or lanceolate space	69.
68.	Furrows double	*D. mirabilis* Castr.
	— single	*D. Platessa* Cl. a. Grove.
69.	Horns distinct	70.
	— indistinct	72.
70.	Horns divergent	*D. Campylodiscus* Deby.
	— approximate	71.
71.	Furrows broader than 1/3 of the breadth of the valve	*D. Debyi* Pant.
	— narrower	*D. major* Cl.
72.	Freshwater species	*D. Mauleri* Brun.
	Marine —	*D. nitescens* Greg.
73.	L. 0,03 to 0,06 mm.	*D. Szontaghii* Pant.
	L. 0,08 to 0,21 mm.	*D. gemmata* Grev.

74. { Valve without ocelli . . . . 75.
{ — with — . . . . 76.

75. { Furrows narrow . . . . *D. dalmatica* Grun.[1]
{ — broad . . . . *D. Vespa* Cl.

76. { Ocelli in a marginal band . . . . *D. Crabro* Ehr.
{ — rows alternating with the costæ . . . . 77.

77. { Furrows broad . . . . *D. gemmatula* Grun.
{ narrow . . . . 78.

78. { Costæ 3 to 4 in 0,01 mm. . . . . *D. vagabunda* Grun.
{ 5 to 6 — . . . . *D. lesinensis* Grun.
{ 7 — . . . . *D. prisca* A. S.

D. Hudsonis Grun. (1892). — V. hyaline, elliptical, with more or less rounded ends. L. 0,036 to 0,05; B. 0,012 to 0,02 mm. Central nodule quadrate, its horns slightly divergent in the middle. Furrows forming a small, rhomboid, not striate, space around the central nodule. Parts outside the furrows striate. Striæ fine, 24 to 25 in 0,01 mm. slightly radiate at the ends, finely punctate; puncta forming obliquely decussating rows. *Navicula (Diploneis?) Hudsonis* (Grun.) Cl. in Diatomiste I p. 77 Pl. XII f. 8.

Brackish water: Hudson River!

This little form is very remarkable and not closely connected with any other known species. It seems to be most nearly related to *D. hyalina*, but there are considerable differences.

1. **D.? bioculata** Grun. (1881). — V. elliptical, with rounded ends. L. 0,02 to 0,036; B. 0,013 to 0,015 mm. Central nodule elongated; its horns close to the median line. Central pores distant, incrassate. Furrows broader than half of the breadth of the valve. Striæ 17 to 22 in 0,01 mm. not distinctly punctate, continued across the furrows to the median line, slightly radiate throughout. — *Nav. bioculata* Grun. A. S. Atl. LXX f. 9, 10, 11, VII f. 49?

Marine: Balearic Islands! Adriatic! Java! Port Jackson! Galapagos Islands!

Var. *vittata* Cl. L. 0,04; B. 0,015 mm. Central nodule very narrow; central pores distant. Furrow separated from the exterior part of the valve by a linear, broad band. Striæ 17 in 0,01 mm., on the furrows punctate. Pl. I f. 15.

Marine: Ceylon!

The exact place of this species is difficult to decide. The incrassated central pores recall those of *Nav. forcipata*, but nevertheless I believe it to be a Diploneis, akin to *D. hyalina*.

2. **D. inscripta** Cl. N. Sp. — V. lanceolate, subacute, convex. L. 0,065; B. 0,017 mm. Central nodule small; its horns close to the median line. Central pores approximate, incrassate. Furrows as broad as half of the valve. Striæ 10 in 0,01 mm. continued across the furrows, not distinctly punctate, parallel, very slightly radiate in the ends. — Pl. I f. 17.

Marine: Gulf of Naples! China!

This species seems to connect the genus *Cymatoneis*, to which it has some resemblance, with the forms of the group of *D. nitescens*.

3. **D. hyalina** Donk. (1861). — V. hyaline, thin, elliptical. L. 0,045 to 0,076; B. 0,014 to 0,026 mm. Central nodule somewhat elongated; its horns slightly divergent in the middle. Furrows much broader than half of the breadth of the valve. Striæ 22 in 0,01 mm., distinct outside, fainter in the furrows, fading away towards the horns of the median line. *Nav. hyalina* Donk. M. J. I p. 10 Pl. I f. 6. B. D. p. 5 Pl. I f. 1. A. S. Atl. LXX f. 1—5.

Marine: Finmark! North Sea!

[1] Var. of *D. Crabro*.

4. **D. coffæiformis** A. S. (1874). — V. broadly elliptical. L. 0,023 to 0,07; B. 0,01 to 0,033 mm. Central nodule quadrate to rectangular, with somewhat divergent horns. Furrows narrow. close to the horns. Striæ 8 to 10 in 0,01 mm., radiate at the ends, less distinct or imperceptible on the furrows, not alternating with puncta or alveoli. — *Nav. coffæiformis* A. S. N. S. D. p. 88 Pl. I f. 22 Pl. II f. 13. Atl. VIII f. 7.

Marine: North Sea! Gulf of Naples! Macassar Straits! Calif. Santa Monica, fossil (Deby Coll.).

Var. *densestriata* A. S. (1881). Striæ 10 in 0,01 mm. Lunulæ large. - *Nav. coff. v. dens.* A. S. Atl. LXX f. 54.

Marine: Jamaica (Atl.).

Var. *subcircularis* A. S. (1881). — V. orbicular. L. 0,04; B. 0,034 mm. Striæ 8 in 0,01 mm. — *D. coff. subc.* A. S. Atl. LXX f. 53.

Marine: ?

5. **D. suborbicularis** Greg. (1857). - V. elliptical with broad, rounded ends. L. 0,04 to 0,053; B. 0,024 to 0,032 mm. Central nodule large. quadrate; its horns divergent. Furrows linear, closely following the horns, with faint continuations of the costæ. or with a row of puncta. Costæ 6 to 9 in 0,01 mm. — *Nav. Smithii var. suborbicularis* Greg. D. of Clyde p. 487 Pl. IX f. 17. *Nav. suborbicularis* Donk. B. D. p. 9 Pl. I f. 9. A. S. N. S. D. Pl. I f. 21. Atl. VIII f. 2, 3. 5. not 4.

Marine: Davis Strait! North Sea! Corsica! Adriatic, Caspian Sea (Grun.). Ceylon! Madagascar! Singapore! Labuan! Galapagos Islands! Cape Horn (Petit). Brazil (Atl.). Gulf of Mexico (Atl.) North Carolina! Fossil: Hungary (Pant.), Sta Monica, Cal.!

Between *D. coffæiformis* and *D. suborbicularis* there is no sharp distinction, the furrows being broader, the horns of the central nodule more divergent and the costæ usually coarser in *D. suborbicularis* than in *D. coffæiformis.*

6. **D. compar** Jan. (1881). — V. linear, with broad, truncate ends. L. 0,05; B. 0,01 mm. Central nodule large, quadrate; its horns divergent at their basis. Furrows narrow, linear. Costæ about 13 in 0,01 mm. -- *Nav. compar* A. S. Atl. LXX f. 69.

Marine: ?

7. **D. advena** A. S. (1875). — V. linear-elliptical sometimes slightly constricted in the middle. L. 0,08 to 0,1; B. 0,026 to 0,035 mm. Central nodule small, quadrate, its horns parallel, approximate. Furrow narrow, linear. Costæ 9 in 0,01 mm., almost parallel, continuing across the furrow. — *Nav. advena* A. S. Atl. VIII f. 29; XII f. 41.

Marine: Cape Good Hope (Atl.), Madagascar! Java (Deby Coll.)! Japan (Deby Coll.)! Sandwich Islands (Atl.).

Var. *recta* Brun. a. Hérib. (1893). — L. 0,1 to 0,12; B. 0,02 to 0,023 mm. Costæ 7 in 0,01 mm. alternating with double rows of obscure puncta. about 14 in 0,01 mm. — *Nav. recta* Brun. a. Hérib. D. d'Auvergne p. 90 Pl. II f. 3.

Marine: Puy du Mur, Auvergne fossil (Br.). Morris Creek Conn. (Brun Coll.)!

Var. *sansegana* Grun. (1875). — V. linear-elliptical. L. 0,053; B. 0,018 mm. — *Nav. sansegana* Grun. A. S. Atl. VIII f. 27.

Marine: Adriatic (Grun.).

Var. *parca* A. S. (1875). — V. narrow, elliptical. L. 0,03 to 0,045; B. 0,016 mm. Furrows narrowed at the ends. Costæ 10 to 14 in 0,01 mm. *Nav. parca* A. S. Atl. VIII f. 20 to 22.

Marine: North Sea, Samoa, Campeachy Bank (Atl.).

8. **D. subnuda** A. S. (1875). — V. gently constricted, with elliptical segments. L. 0,076; B. 0,022; at the comtr. 0,015 mm. Central nodule small, its horns straight, approximate. Furrows linear, dilated in the middle. Costæ 10 in 0,01 mm. -- *Nav. subnuda* A. S. Atl. XII f. 44.

Marine: Mazatlan (Atl.).

Var. *densestriata* A. S. (1881). Smaller. Costæ 11 in 0,01 mm. *Nav. subnuda v. densestr.* A. S. Atl. LXIX f. 45.

Marine: California (Atl.).

9. **D. laciniosa** A. S. (1875). — V. strongly constricted in the middle, with rostrate ends. L. 0,033; B. 0,012; at the constr. 0,0076 mm. Central nodule very small; its horns parallel. Furrows narrow, not dilated in the middle. Costæ strongly divergent towards the margins, 12 in 0,01 mm. *Nav. lac.* A. S. Atl. XII f. 54.

Marine: Java (Atl.).

10. **D. congrua** Jan. (1881). — V. linear, with broad, capitate ends. L. 0,06; B. 0,0136 mm. Central nodule small; its horns parallel, approximate. Furrows very narrow, slightly dilated in the middle. Costæ 12 in 0,01 mm. — *Nav. congr.* Jan. A. S. Atl. LXX f. 66.

Marine: ?

This species is unknown to the author. The fig. in Atl. does not show the structure. Probably akin to *D. litoralis*.

11. **D. Cynthia** A. S. (1875). — V. narrow, elliptical, with rounded ends. L. 0,05 to 0,075; B. 0,018 to 0,025 mm. Central nodule small; its horns parallel, approximate. Furrows broad, linear, forming a narrow elliptical space, a third as broad as the valve. Costæ 7 in 0,01 mm., parallel, radiate at the ends, continued across the furrows. — *Nav. Cynthia* A. S. Atl. VIII f. 41.

Marine: Red Sea (Van Heurck Coll.)! Seychelles (Van Heurck Coll.)! Madagascar! Java! Tahiti! West Indies!

Var. *elongata* Cl. — L. 0,13; B. 0,038 mm. Costæ 13 in 0,01 mm.

Marine: Java!

Var. *sibirica* Cl. — L. 0,05; B. 0,017 mm. Costæ 11 in 0,01 mm.

Marine: Cape Wankarema!

Var. *minuta* Cl. L. 0,035; B. 0,01 mm. Costæ 15 in 0,01 mm. A. S. Atl. VIII f. 28.

Marine: Cape Good Hope (Atl.) Galapagos Islands!

12. **D. mediterranea** Grun. (1875). — V. linear with rounded or cuneate ends. L. 0,053; B. 0,021 mm. Central nodule small: its horns parallel. Furrows broad, with a row of puncta. Costæ 7 in 0,01 mm. *Nav. gemmata v. mediterranea* Grun. in A. S. Atl. VIII f. 42.

Marine: ?

13. **D. munda** Jan. (1881). — V. linear, with rounded ends. L. 0,047; B. 0,015 mm. Central nodule very small; its horns parallel, approximate. Furrows broadest in the middle, gradually tapering to the ends. Costæ 7 in 0,01 mm. marginal, not reaching the furrows. — *Nav. munda* A. S. Atl. LXX f. 70.

Marine: ?

The costæ are figured coarsely punctate, but nevertheless the general appearance of this species agrees most with *D. mediterranea*.

14. **D. contigua** A. S. (1875). — V. linear, with rounded or subcuneate ends. L. 0,066 to 0,14; B. 0,017 to 0,03 mm. Central nodule large, quadrate, with parallel, approximate horns. Furrows very broad, linear, crossed by rudimentary costæ or by a double row of large puncta. Costæ 6 to 7 in 0,01 mm. *Nav. cont.* A. S. Atl. VIII f. 43. *Nav. Thumii* Pant. I p. 29 Pl. X f. 85 (1886).

Marine: Japan (Deby Coll.)! Fossil: Oamaru N. Zeal.! S:t Peter, Hungary!

Var. *Zechenteri* Pant. (1886). — L. 0,072; B. 0,017 mm. Costæ 8 in 0,01 mm. *Nav. Zechenteri* Pant. I p. 30 Pl. XIV f. 118.

Marine: Hungary, fossil (Pant.).

Var. *Eudoxia* A. S. (1875). — V. linear, with rounded ends. L. 0,07 to 0,085; B. 0,017 to 0,022 mm. Costæ 6 to 7 in 0,01 mm. Furrows narrower, than on the type. — *Nav. mediterranea* A. S. N. S. D. Pl. II f. 10. *Nav. Eudoxia* A. S. Atl. VIII f. 40, LXX f. 71.

Marine: Morocco! Balearic Islands! Red Sea! Bab el mandeb! Madagascar! Ceylon! Galapagos Islands! Monterey (Atl.). Fossil: Szákal, Hungary!

Var. *Eugenia* A. S. (1875). — V. with subcuneate ends. L. 0,06; B. 0,017 mm. Costæ 7 to 8 in 0,01 mm. — *Nav. Eugenia* A. S. Atl. VIII f. 44.

Marine: Ceylon (Leuduger Fortm.) Macassar Straits! Campeachy Bay (Atl.).

There is, so far as I can see, no specific distinction between the above forms, which I regard as belonging to *D. contigua*. They are perhaps all only smaller, and corroded, forms of *D. gemmata*.

15. **D. circumnodosa** Brun. (1891). — V. very convex and thick, linear, with broad, rounded ends. L. 0,1; B. 0,023 mm. Central nodule short and broad; its horns divergent at the nodule. Furrows very broad. Costæ 7 in 0,01 mm., continued across the furrows as rows of three large puncta. — *Nav. circumn.* Brun. Esp. n. p. 33 Pl. XVI f. 2.

Marine: Japan, fossil (Brun Coll.)!

16. **D. Letourneuri** Cl. N. Sp. — V. elongated, very slightly constricted in the middle, with broad, rounded ends. L. 0,07; B. 0,023; at the constr. 0,02. Central nodule elongated quadrate; its horns nearly parallel. Furrows very broad. Costæ 9 in 0,01 mm. almost parallel, continued across the furrows, smooth. Pl. I f. 18.

Marine: Columbo, Ceylon (Letourneur Coll.)!

17. **D. muscæformis** Grun. (1875). — V. gently constricted in the middle, with cuneate ends. L. 0,07 to 0,095; B. 0,03 to 0,04 at the constr. 0,024 to 0,037 mm. Central nodule quadrate, with approximate, scarcely divergent horns. Furrows 1/2 to 1/3 as broad as the valve. Costæ 4 to 7 in 0,01 mm., with faint continuations across the furrows.

Var. *placida* A. S. L. 0,09 mm. Costæ 4 to 4,5 in 0,01 mm. — *Nav. placida* A. S. Atl. CLXXIV f. 2.

Marine: Galapagos Islands! San Pedro Calif. fossil (Kinker Coll.)! Oamaru New Zealand, fossil (Atl.).

Var. *genuina* Cl. Costæ 7 in 0,01 mm. — *Nav. muscæform.* A. S. Atl. XIII f. 42, 47.

Marine: Campeachy Bay! Java!

Var. *constricta* Grun. Ends rounded. L. 0,05 to 0,06; B. 0,018 to 0,019 at the constr. 0,013 to 0,015 mm. Costæ 6 to 7 in 0,01 mm. — *Nav. constricta* Grun.? A. S. Atl. XII f. 65; LXIX f. 12.

Marine: Balearic Islands! Sansego (Atl.). Seychelles (Van Heurck Coll.)! Madagascar! Sumbava (Kinker Coll.)! Japan (Deby Coll.)! Leton Bank (Atl.).

Var. *pusilla* Cl. V. slightly constricted. L. 0,02; B. 0,010 mm. Costæ 9 in 0,01 mm.

Marine: Galapagos Islands!

This form is doubtful as a species, having very much the appearance of strongly corroded valves of other species as *D. Beyrichiana* and allied forms. Grunow mentions a form from the Caspian Sea in length 0,038 mm. and with 12 costæ in 0,01 mm., which seems not to belong to *D. muscæformis*.

18. **D. constricta** Grun. (1860). — V. gently constricted in the middle, with subcuneate ends. L. 0,08 to 0,15; B. 0,023 to 0,03, at the constr. 0,02 to 0,025 mm. Central nodule quadrate, its horns parallel, approximate. Furrows very broad. Costæ 7 to 8 in 0,01 mm., very faint on the furrows, radiate at the ends. — *Nav. constricta* Grun. Verh. 1860 p. 535 Pl. III f. 18 (according to V. H. T 103). *Nav. Musca* Donk. B. D. p. 50 Pl. VII f. 6 (1873). *Nav. Donkinii* A. S. N. S. D. Pl. I f. 12 (1874); II f. 8. Atl. XII f. 63, 64.

Marine: Finmark! North Sea! Balearic Islands! Ceylon! Florida!

Forma minuta. L. 0,035; B. 0,014; at the constr. 0,013 mm. Costæ 13 in 0,01 mm.

Marine: Madagascar!

Var. *distans* Cl. — Horns of the central nodule divergent.

Marine: Norway! (L. 0,052; B. 0,02; constr. 0,018 mm. Costæ 9 in 0,01 mm.) Hungary, Szákal! (L. 0,04; B. 0,016 constr. 0,015 mm. Costæ 10 in 0,01 mm.) Galapagos Islands! (L. 0,032; B. 0,013; constr. 0,011 mm. Costæ 12 in 0,01 mm.).

19. **D. incurvata** Greg. (1856). — V. elongated, panduriform. L. 0,06 to 0,07; B. 0,013 to 0,017; constr. 0,01 to 0,012 mm. Central nodule small, quadrate; its horns parallel. Furrows broad, linear, not costate or punctate. Costæ 11 to 12 in 0,01 mm., parallel, slightly radiate at the ends. — *Nav. inc.* Greg. T. M. S. IV p. 11 Pl. V f. 13. Donk. B. D. p. 49 Pl. VII f. 4. A. S. N. S. D. Pl. I f. 10, 11; II f. 6.

Marine: Finmark! North Sea! Morocco! Florida! Galapagos Islands! Cape of Good Hope!

20. **D. interrupta** Kütz (1844). — V. deeply constricted, its segments broadly elliptical to orbicular, with rounded ends. L. 0,029 to 0,072; B. 0,012 to 0,024; at the constr. 0,007 to 0,013 mm. Central nodule elongated, quadrate, its horns parallel. Furrows linear, narrow. Costæ 8 to 12 in 0,01 mm., divergent, usually interrupted or not reaching the margin in the middle of the valve. — *Nav. interr.* Kütz Bac. p. 100 Pl. XXIX f. 93. Donk. B. D. p. 47 Pl. VII f. 2. Grun. Verh. 1860 p. 531 Pl. V f. 20. Lagst. Spitsb. D. p. 28 Pl. II f. 6. A. S. N. S. D. Pl. I f. 8. Atl. XII f. 3, 4, 5, 11; LXIX f. 24. V. H. Syn. p. 89 Pl. IX f. 7, 8. *Diploneis didyma* Ehb. Abh. Berl. 1870 Pl. II f. 13. W. Sm. B. D. XVII f. 151 *a'*. *Nav. Puella* A. S. Atl. LXIX f. 25. *Nav. interr. v. Novæ Zealandiæ* A. S. Atl. XII f. 12.

Brackish water: Spitzbergen! Beeren Eiland (Lagst.). Kara! Finmark! North Sea! Baltic (Tornea to Rügen)! Mediterranean Sea! Red Sea (Grun.), Java! Samoa! Australia! Auckland (Grun.), Cape Good Hope (Atl.), Atlantic coast of America! Greenland! Arctic America! Franzenbad! Halle! Great Salt Lake!

Var. *Tallyana* Grun. (1882). — Costæ interrupted in the middle, outside the furrow. — *Nav. interr. v. Tall.* Grun. F. D. Öst. Ung. p. 150 Pl. XXX f. 59.

Brackish water: Tallya, Hungary, fossil (Grun.).

Var. *zanzibarica* Grun. (1875). — V. deeply constricted. L. 0,05 to 0,07; B. 0,02 to 0,033; at the constr. 0,009 to 0,017 mm. Segments nearly orbicular. Horns of the central nodule divergent. Costæ 7 to 8 in 0,01 mm. (according to A. S. Atl. alternating with rows of puncta). — *Nav. interr. v. zanz.* A. S. Atl. XII f. 1, 2.

Brackish and marine: Zanzibar (Atl.), Carpentaria, Australia (Atl.).

Var.? *Weisneri* Pant. (1886). — V. less constricted. L. 0,021 to 0,032; B. 0,01 to 0,014; at the constr. 0,012 mm. Segments tongue-shaped. Horns somewhat divergent. Costæ 10 to 12,5 in 0,01 mm. — *Nav. Weisneri* Pant. I p. 29 Pl. XVIII f. 158. *Nav. interr. var. fossilis* Pant. II p. 48 Pl. VI f. 112; Pl. XII f. 208, 215 (1889).

Brackish water: Hungary fossil!

Var.? *Gorjanovicii* Pant. (1886). — V. gently constricted, with elliptical segments. L. 0,022 to 0,036; B. 0,012 to 0,014; at the constr. 0,007 to 0,009 mm. Horns slightly divergent. Costæ 8 to 12,5 in 0,01 mm. not interrupted in the middle. — *Nav. Gorjanovicii* Pant. I p. 25 Pl. IX f. 81. *Nav. Heerii* Pant. II p. 47 Pl. XI f. 195; Pl. XII f. 210 (1889). ?*Nav. Gorjanov. var. major* Pant. II p. 46 Pl. V f. 78.? *Nav. suspecta? var. Czekehazensis* Pant. II p. 44 Pl. IV f. 56.

Brackish water: Hungary, fossil (Pant.)!

Var. *clavcula* A. S. (1875). — V. deeply constricted, with almost orbicular segments. L. 0,036; B. 0,018, at the constr. 0,009. Costæ 8 to 9 in 0,01 mm. not interrupted in the middle. — *Nav. clavc.* A. S. Atl. XII f. 33, 34.

Marine: Australia (Atl.).

Diploneis interrupta is a very variable species, and appears to graduate into *D. incurva*. The specimens in the deposits of Hungary are corroded, so that it is not easy to decide whether they really belong to *D. interrupta* or not. So far as I can see from the descriptions and figures, there is no difference between *Nav. Wiesneri* and *Nav. interrupta var. fossilis* PANT. The same is also the case with the nearly related forms *Nav. Heerii* and *Nav. Gorjanovicii* PANT.

21. **D. Guinardiana** BRUN. (1889). — V. elongated, panduriform, with narrow elliptical segments. L. 0,08 to 0,095; B. 0,018 to 0,028; at the constr. 0,009 to 0,017 mm. Central nodule small, quadrate; its horns parallel, approximate. Furrows very narrow, linear. Costæ 8 in 0,01 mm. smooth, almost parallel. *Nav. Guin.* BRUN. a. TEMP. D. de Japon p. 45 Pl. V f. 9.

Marine: Madagascar! Sumbava! Macassar Straits! Japan, fossil (Brun).

22. **D. Adonis** BRUN. (1889). — V. stout and panduriform. L. 0,1 to 0,125; B. 0,035 to 0,045; at the constr. 0,024 to 0,028 mm. Segments elliptical. Central nodule large, quadrate; its horns divergent. Furrows narrow linear. Costæ 5 in 0,01 mm. smooth, curved; strongly incrassate at the margin of the valve (or in certain focus alternating with a punctum). — *Nav. Adonis* BRUN a. TEMP. D. f. du Japon p. 41 Pl. V f. 3.

Marine: Mexilones! Iquique! Yedo, fossil (Brun).

Var. *gibbosa* BRUN (1889). — Segments deltoid. — *Nav. Adonis v. gibb.* BRUN l. c. f. 2.

Marine: Mexillones, Peru!

Var. *Ganymedes* CL. — L. 0,07 to 0,1; B. 0,025 to 0,03; at the constr. 0,017 to 0,022. Costæ 7 to 8 in 0,01 mm.

Marine: Peru (Mexillones! Iquique!) Madagascar (Kinker Coll.)!

Var. *Oamarnensis* CL. — L. 0,045 to 0,05; B. 0,015 to 0,018; at the constr. 0,01 to 0,012 mm. Costæ 9 in 0,01 mm. — *Nav. Apis* GROVE a. STURT. A. S. Atl. CLXXIV f. 13.

Marine: Oamaru, New Zealand, fossil!

D. Adonis comprises a series of forms from the small var. *Oamarnensis* to the large typical *D. Adonis*, which are doubtful as species, as they have very much the appearance of being corroded.

23. **D. lineata** DONK. (1858). — V. elliptical to linear-elliptical. L. 0,04 to 0,08; B. 0,019 to 0,032 mm. Central nodule quadrate; its horns convergent at the ends. Furrows rather narrow, smooth, or with one to two rows of puncta. Costæ 9 to 10 in 0,01 mm., crossed by a longitudinal line, smooth. *Nav. lineata* DONK. T. M. S. VI p. 32 Pl. III f. 17. B. D. p. 8 Pl. 1 f. 8. A. S. N. S. D. Pl. I f. 16, 17. Atl. VII f. 44, LXIX f. 31; LXX f. 67. *Nav. adriatica* GRUN. Verh. 1860 p. 525 Pl. III f. 17.

Marine: North Sea (Coasts of Scandinavia and England)! Mediterranean Sea (Balearic Islands, Gulf of Naples)! Adriatic!

Forma pusilla CL. — L. 0,032; B. 0,014 mm. Costæ 11 in 0,01 mm.

Marine: Galapagos Islands!

24. **D. Vetula** A. S. (1875). — V. elliptical, very slightly constricted in the middle with broad rounded ends. L. 0,05; B. 0,024 mm. Central nodule broad, quadrate, its horns parallel. Furrows broadest in the middle, gradually tapering to the ends. Costæ 10 in 0,01 mm., crossed near the margin by a line. — *Nav. Vetula* A. S. Atl. XII f. 49.

Marine: Sansego (Atl.).

25. **D. Papula** A. S. (1875). — V. elliptical. L. 0,023; B. 0,01 to 0,011 mm. Central nodule small; its horns somewhat divergent. Furrows linear, narrow. Costæ about 13 in 0,01 mm. crossed by one longitudinal line. — *Nav. Papula* A. S. Atl. VII f. 45 to 47.

Marine: Samoa (Atl.) Campeachy Bay (Atl.).

26. **D. subcincta** A. S. (1874). — V. slightly constricted in the middle, with more or less distinctly cuneate ends. L. 0,06 to 0,092; B. 0,0235 to 0,025; at the constr. 0,02 to 0,022 mm. Central nodule large, quadrate; its horns parallel or convergent at the ends. Furrows moderately broad, narrowed at the ends with faint traces of costæ. Costæ 6 to 7 in 0,01 mm., crossed by a longitudinal line. — *Nav. subcincta* A. S. N. S. D. Pl. II f. 7. Atl. XIII f. 41; LXIX f. 32. GRUN. D. Franz Josephs Land p. 56 (1) Pl. 1 f. 38. 39. *Nav. didyma* LAGST. Boh. D. f. 4 *a*.

Marine: Franz Josephs Land (Grun.). Kara! Finmark! North Sea! Balearic Islands! Adriatic! Madagascar! Monterey, Cal.! Fossil: Aegina (Atl.), Japan (Brun a. Temp.), Maryland (Deby Coll.)! St. Monica (Deby Coll.)!

27. **D. discrepans** A. S. (1875). — V elliptical. L. 0,03; B. 0,011 mm. Central nodule broad, quadrate, its horns divergent at their basis, convergent at the ends. Furrows broad. Costæ 11 in 0,01 mm., crossed by a longitudinal costa(?). — *Nav. discr.* A. S. Atl. VIII f. 8.

Marine: Campeachy Bank (Atl.).

Unknown to the author. The description is from the fig. in atlas and I am not sure if the longitudinal line across the costæ really be a costa.

28. **D. binaria** A. S. (1875). — V. slightly constricted, with broad, rounded ends. L. 0,042; B. 0,022; at the constr. 0,02 mm. Central nodule large, quadrate, its horns parallel, approximate. Furrows very broad, not dilated in the middle, with double longitudinal rows of puncta. Costæ 6 in 0,01 mm. crossed by a longitudinal costa. — *Nav. binaria* A. S. Atl. XII f. 62.

Marine: Java (Atl.).

29. **D. demta** A. S. (1881). — V. sligthly constricted. L. 0,116; B. 0,037; at the constr. 0,03 mm. Central nodule large, quadrate: its horns parallel. Furrows broad, linear. Costæ 6 in 0,01 mm. crossed by a broad longitudinal costa(?). — *Nav. demta* A. S. Atl. LXIX f. 34.

Marine, fossil: St. Monica, Cal. (Atl.).

Unknown to the author. The fig. in Atl. does not distinctly show if the longitudinal band is, as here accepted, a costa or a row of ocelli. In the latter case this form may probably be placed near *D. Pandura*.

30. **D. exemta** A. S. (1875). — V. panduriform, with tongue-shaped segments. L. 0,085 to 0,136; B. 0,032 to 0,042; at the constr. 0,026 to 0,03 mm. Central nodule quadrate, rather large; its horns parallel. Furrows linear. Costæ 5 in 0,01 mm., crossed by a longitudinal line, on the furrows faint or reduced to puncta. — *Nav. exemta* A. S. Atl. XI f. 28, 29.

Marine: Tamatave (Brun Coll.)! Tahiti! Kerguelens Land (Rae Coll.)! Campeachy Bay! Fossil: Oamaru, New Zealand! S:ta Monica (Deby Coll.)!

Var.? *crabroniformis* GRUN. (1875). — L. 0,083; B. 0,025: at the constr. 0,016. Costæ 6 in 0,01 mm. — *Nav. crabronif.* Atl. XI f. 24.

Marine: Gulf of Mexico (Atl.).

Var. *digrediens* CL. — L. 0,048 to 0,065; B. 0,022; at the constr. 0,01 to 0,014 mm. Horns somewhat divergent. Costæ 8 in 0,01 mm.

Marine: China (Thum.)! Hungary, fossil (Deby Coll.)!

31. **D. coarctata** A. S. (1875). — V. deeply constricted in the middle. L. 0,07 to 0,1; B. 0,026 to 0,035; at the constr. 0,0136 to 0,018 mm. Central nodule quadrate, with parallel horns. Furrows narrow, linear, with a row of large puncta. Costæ 3—4 in 0,01 mm., crossed by a longitudinal line. — *Nav. coarct.* A. S. Atl. XI f. 30, 31, 32, LXIX f. 11.

Marine: Campeachy Bay (Atl.), Cape Horn (Petit). Hungary, fossil (Pant.).

This is a very suspicious form. The figure recently published by A. SCHMIDT in Atl. (CLXXIV f. 22) has very much the appearance of being a strongly corroded specimen of *D. Crabro var.* or of *D. Dirhombus*, if that form be anything but a small *D. Crabro*.

32. **D. bombiformis** Cl. N. Sp. — V. deeply constricted in the middle, with broad segments. L. 0,032; B. 0,014 mm. Central nodule small, its horns strongly divergent. Furrows narrow. Costæ 8 in 0,01 mm. crossed by a longitudinal line. — Pl. I f. 26.

Marine: Macassar Straits (Grove Coll.)!

This form may be a small variety of *D. Bombus*.

33. **D. Clepsydra** Cl. N. Sp. — V. strongly constricted, with almost orbicular segments. L. 0,07; B. 0,032; at the constr. 0,016 mm. Central nodule large, quadrate; its horns divergent in the middle. Furrows narrowed in the middle and at the ends, crossed by faint costæ. Costæ 7 in 0,01 mm. strongly radiate, alternating with single rows of alveoli. — Pl. I f. 29.

Marine: Madagascar!

34. **D. Præstes** A. S. (1875). — V. elongated, slightly constricted, with narrow elliptical segments. L. 0,07 to 0,12; B. 0,019 to 0,025; at the constriction 0,015 to 0,017 mm. Central nodule small, quadrate; its horns parallel. Furrows linear, moderately narrow. Costæ almost parallel, 6 to 7 in 0,01 mm., alternating with rows of indistinct puncta. — *Nav. Præstes* A. S. Atl. XII f. 57, 58.

Marine: Gulf of Naples (Thum.)! Alexandria (Deby Coll.)! Red Sea (Deby Coll.)! Mazatlan (Atl.). Campeachy Bay (Atl.).

D. Præstes is nearly allied to *D. Guinardiana*, from which it differs by somewhat coarser costæ and the rows of alveoli alternating with the costæ. It seems to be very probable that *D. Guinardiana* is only a corroded *D. Præstes*.

35. **D. Entomon** (Ehb. 1844) A. S. — V. elongated, slightly constricted in the middle, with tongue-shaped segments. L. 0,072 to 0,15; B. 0,028 to 0,042; at the constr. 0,026 to 0,35 mm. Central nodule large, quadrate, its horns parallel. Furrows moderately wide, linear, forming a space of about a third of the width of the valve, often dilated around the central nodule. Costæ 6 to 8 in 0,01 mm. parallel, at the ends divergent, anastomosing with a few (1 to 4) longitudinal, irregularly undulating, more or less distinct, costæ. — *Dipl. Entomon* Ehb. Berl. Ber. 1844 accord to Chase. *Nav. Entomon* A. S. N. S. D. Pl. I f. 13, 14; Atl. XIII f. 48, 49. *Nav. bomboides var. media* Grun. A. D. p. 41 Pl. III f. 51. *Nav. bomboides* A. S. Atl. XIII f. 38.

Marine: Arctic America! Spitsbergen! Kara! Finmark! North Sea! Mediterranean Sea! Adria! Samoa! Sidney! China! Japan! Behrings Island! Mexillones, Peru (Deby Coll.)! Fossil: Brünn, Tegel! Bory, Hungary!

D. Entomon is not a sharply defined species, graduating as it seems into *D. splendida*, with which many of its varieties are closely connected.

36. **D. splendida** Greg. (1856). — V. elongated, panduriform. L. 0,055 to 0,22; B. 0,02 to 0,05; at the constr. 0,015 to 0,03 mm. Central nodule large, quadrate; its horns parallel. Furrows narrow, linear, not dilated around the central nodule. Transverse costæ 5 to 8 in 0,01 mm.; crossed on each side of the median line by 4 to 6, slightly curved or undulating longitudinal costæ. — *Nav. splendida* Greg. T. M. S. IV p. 44 Pl. V f. 14. V. H. S. Pl. IX f. 4. A. S. N. S. D. Pl. I f. 3, 4, Pl. II f. 2. Atl. XIII f. 31, 32, 34. *Nav. Entomon* Donk. B. D. p. 49 Pl. VII f. 5. *Nav. didyma var.* Greg. T. M. S. IV p. 45 Pl. V f. 16. *Nav. gemmatula* Cl. Quek. M. Cl. II (2) p. 167 Pl. XII f. 1 (1885). *Nav. Taschenbergeri* A. S. Atl. CLXXIV f. 9; 1892 (a large and coarse form). *N. margaritifera* Pant. III Pl. XXXV f. 494 (1893)?

Marine: Greenland! Spitsbergen! Beeren Eiland! Finmark! North Sea! Ceylon! Madagascar! Java! Sumatra! Port Jackson! Japan! Sandwich Islands (Atl.). West Indies! Florida! Fossil: Moravian Tegel! S:a Monica, Calif.!

Var. *Puella* A. S. (1875). — L. 0,0636 to 0,106; B. 0,0166 to 0,026; at the constrict. 0,0075 to 0,015 mm. Transverse costæ 6 to 9 in 0,01 mm.; longitudinal 2 to 3 on each side of the median line, less distinct. *Nav. Puella* A. S. Atl. XII f. 13; LXIX f. 15. *Nav. excenta* A. S. N. S. D. p. 85. Pl. II f. 5 (1874). Atl. LXIX f. 13.

Marine: North Sea (A. S.); Sorrento (Atl.), Campeachy Bay (Atl.), California (Atl.).

Under the name *Nav. Puella* A. SCHMIDT seems to have confounded different forms. The figs. 14 and 15 Pl. XII probably do not represent the same form as the fig. 13. The fig. 13, which I regard as the most typical, is evidently a small variety of *D. splendida*. A. SCHMIDT seems also to have denoted two different species as *Nav. excenta*.

Var. *diplosticta* A. S. (1875). — With fine puncta above the reticulation of the costæ. — *Nav. diplosticta* A. S. Atl. XIII f. 25 to 30; LXIX f. 22, CLXXIV f. 10 (no punctation visible).

Marine: Campeachy Bay (Atl.), Gulf of Mexico (Atl.), Java, Samoa (Atl.), Cape Horn (Petit).

Var.? *Hugnaldii* PANT. (1889). — V. slightly constricted. L. 0,091 to 0,15; B. 0,028 to 0,04; at the constr. 0,027 to 0,028 mm. Central nodule quadrate, with parallel horns. Furrows narrow, linear, with a row of puncta. Transverse costæ radiate at the ends, 8 to 10 in 0,01 mm., crossed on each side of the median line by about 8 longitudinal, slightly undulating costæ. — *Nav. Haynaldi* PANT. II p. 47 Pl. XXIV f. 361.

Marine: Hungary, Bory, fossil!

The fig. in PANTOCSEK'S work is not very clear. The above description is from specimens from Bory, which agree in all eventials with *D. splendida*, being only a little less constricted and having finer structure than usual.

Var.? *prominula* A. S. (1875). — V. strongly constricted. L. 0,042; B. 0,019; at the constr. 0,013 mm. Transverse costæ 8 in 0,01 mm., crossed by some few longitudinal costæ. *Nav. prominula* A. S. Atl. XIII f. 15.

Marine: Kings Mill Island (Atl.).

This form requires a more accurate examination before its true place in the system can be determined.

Var.? *ilesdiana* PANT. (1886). — L. 0,07 to 0,1; B. 0,026 to 0,03; at the constr. 0,02 to 0,028 mm. Segments tongue-shaped. Transverse costæ 8 in 0,01 mm.; longitudinal numerous, about 8 on each side of the median line. — *Nav. ilesd.* PANT. I p. 42 Pl. XVII f. 152.

Marine: Hungary, fossil (Pant.). Baltjik, fossil! Russia, fossil (Deby).

Nav. Margarita A. S. (Atl. CLXXIV fig. 17) seems to be akin to var. *ilesdiana*. I have not seen any form exactly resembling this, but I think it very probable, that the figured specimen would in another focus have very much the same appearance as some of the numerous varieties of *D. splendida*.

37. **D. bomboides** A. S. (1874). — V. panduriform, with subelliptical to tongue-shaped segments. L. 0,09 to 0,13; B. 0,04 to 0,055; at the constr. 0,03 to 0,035 mm. Central nodule strong, quadrate; its horns parallel. Furrows linear, somewhat dilated around the central nodule. Transverse costæ 6 to 7 in 0,01 mm, crossed by numerous slightly undulating, longitudinal costæ, about 6 in 0,01 mm. — *Nav. bomboides* A. S. N. S. D. Pl. I f. 2. Atl. XIII f. 36. V. H. Syn. Suppl. B f. 19. *Nav. didyma* W. SM. B. D. XVII f. 154 a*. *Nav. Williamsonii* V. H. Syn. Pl. IX f. 3.

Marine: North Sea! Alexandria (Deby Coll.)! Zanzibar (Atl.). Madagascar! Ceylon! Philippines! Sydney! China! Japan! Galapagos Islands! Campeachy Bay!

Var. *madagascarensis* CL. — V. short, slightly constricted, with broad, tongue-shaped segments. L. 0,04 to 0,085; B. 0,022 to 0,043; at the constr. 0,02 to 0,035 mm. Transverse costæ 7 to 9 in 0,01 mm., slightly radiate. Longitudinal costæ almost straight, curved outwards in the middle of the valve. — A. S. Atl. LXIX f. 35 (small form). — Pl. I f. 22.

Marine: Madagascar (Kinker a. Brun Coll.)! Cape Good Hope (Atl.)! Manilla (Deby Coll.)!

Forma minor Cl. — L. 0,03 to 0,045; B. 0,015 to 0,025; at the constr. 0,013 to 0,02 mm Central nodule small. Transverse costæ 11 in 0,01 mm.; longitudinal 9 in 0,01 mm.

Marine: Tahiti! Madagascar!

The f. minor may be the same as *Nav. futilis* A. S. Atl. XIII f. 17 from Zanzibar, but the furrows are not drawn as dilated around the nodule.

Var. *moesta* A. S. 1881. — V. slightly constricted. L. 0,09; B. 0,034; at the constr. 0,029 mm. Transverse costæ 7 in 0,01 mm. — *Nav. moesta* A. S. Atl. LXIX f. 18, 19.

Marine, fossil: Baltjik (Atl.).

D. bomboides is very nearly akin to *D. splendida*, from which it differs only in the furrows which are slightly dilated around the nodule, a characteristic which seems to be variable. To judge from specimens from Bory Deposit in Hungary *Nav. andesitica* Pant. (1889, II p. 42 Pl. XXVII f. 390) seems to be somewhat corroded specimens of *D. bomboides* with rather closer costæ.

38. **D. divergens** A. S. (1875). — V. more or less constricted in the middle, with elliptical to tongue-shaped segments. L. 0,038 to 0,045; B. 0,018 to 0,02; at the constr. 0,012 to 0,013 mm. Central nodule small, quadrate; its horns divergent at the basis, convergent at the ends. Furrows linear, broader around the central nodule, forming a lanceolate space. Transverse costæ 11 in 0,01 mm., crossed on each side of the median line by about 5 longitudinal, slightly curved costæ. — *Nav. divergens* A. S. Atl. XII f. 50, 51.

Marine: Mediterranean Sea!

Var. *digrediens* A. S. (1881). — V. less constricted. L. 0,04; B. 0,019; at the constr. 0,017 mm. Transverse costæ 13 in 0,01 mm. Longitudinal costæ less distinct. — *Nav. digrediens* A. S. Atl. LXIX, f. 26, 27.

Marine: Tahiti! Baltjik, foss.!

39. **D. Schmidtii** Cl. N. Sp. — V. slightly constricted in the middle, with broad tongue-shaped segments. L. 0,027 to 0,075; B. 0,011 to 0,038; at the constr. 0,0105 to 0,027 mm. Central nodule small, quadrate; its horns divergent in the middle. Furrows broader in the middle, narrower at the ends, with faint traces of the costæ. Transverse costæ 8 to 9 in 0,01 mm. crossed on each side of the median line by 3 to 4 more or less undulating longitudinal costæ. — A. S. Atl. XII f. 48; LXIX f. 23 (small, but typical). XIII f. 18, 19. — Icon. n. Pl. I f. 20, 21.

Marine: Seychelles! Madagascar! Port Jackson! Tahiti! Galapagos Islands!

This form is nearly akin to *D. divergens*. The fig. 18, 19 Pl. XIII in A. S. Atl. greatly resembles larger specimens of *D. Schmidtii*, but has not divergent horns. *Nav. rana* A. S. Atl. LXIX f. 36 is probably also nearly related.

40. **D. chinensis** Cl. N. Sp. — V. slightly constricted, with broad, rounded ends. L. 0,055; B. 0,02; at the constr. 0,013 mm. Central nodule elongated, quadrate; its horns parallel. Furrows narrow, linear, not dilated in the middle. Costæ 13 in 0,01 mm., alternating with single rows of alveoli, about 16 in 0,01 mm. — Pl. I f. 25.

Marine: China (Thum).

41. **D. Grundleri** A. S. (1873). — V. deeply constricted, very convex. Segments semi-orbicular to broadly tongue-shaped, often of inequal size. L. 0,04; B. 0,02; at the constr. 0,01 mm. Central nodule quadrate, large, with divergent horns. Furrows narrow, broader in the middle. Transverse costæ 7 in 0,01 mm., crossed by 2 to 4 longitudinal costæ, usually interrupted in the middle of the valve. — *Nav. Grundl.* A. S. Zeitschr. f. ges. Naturw. 1873 p. 407 Pl. VI f. 5, 6. Atl. XII f. 35, 36.

Marine: Balearic Islands! Bab-el-Mandeb! Philippines! Atlantic coast of N. America! Para River (A. S.).

42. **D. didyma** Ehr. (1840). — V. slightly constricted in the middle, with tongue-shaped segments. L. 0,05 to 0,09; B. 0,017 to 0,036 mm. Central nodule moderately large, its horns not divergent. Furrows narrow, linear. Transverse costæ 8 to 10 in 0,01 mm., crossed by numerous, slightly undulating, longitudinal costæ. — *Pinnularia didyma* Ehr. Kreideth. p. 75. *Nav. didyma* W. Sm. B. D. XVII f. 154 a. A. S. Zeitschr. f. ges. Naturw. 1873 p. 405 Pl. VI f. 1. A. S. N. S. D. Pl. I f. 7. Atl. XIII f. 1. 2. 3. V. H. Syn. p. 90 Pl. IX f. 5. 6. Suppl. B. f. 20. *N. Bombus* Donk. Pl. VII f. 7 b, 8 b.

Brackish and marine: Greenland! Spitsbergen! Kara! Finmark! Baltic (from Westerbotten to Rügen). Caspian Sea (Grun.). Black Sea! Ceylon! Tahiti! Japan! Cape Horn (Petit). West Indies!

D. didyma is a variable species, related to the var. *elesdiana* of *D. splendida* and to certain forms of *D. Bombus*. The outline of the valve becomes less panduriform and almost elliptical as the water becomes less salt. The varieties in the northern part of the Bay of Bothnia where the water is almost fresh are almost elliptical and closely connected with *D. domblittensis*.

43. **D. Bombus** Ehr. (1844). — V. deeply constricted, with suborbicular or elliptical segments often of inequal size. L. 0,065 to 0,13; B. 0,022 to 0,045; at the constr. 0,012 to 0,025 mm. Central nodule large: its horns divergent in the middle, approximate at the ends. Furrows narrow, linear. Transverse costæ 5 to 8 in 0,01 mm. crossed by 2 to 5 curved, longitudinal costæ. Central alveoli distant from the margin. — *Dipl. Bombus* Ehr. Berl. 1844 p. 84 (accord. to Chase). M. G. Pl. XIX f. 31. *Nav. Bombus* Greg. D. of Clyde p. 484 Pl. IX f. 12. Donk. B. D. p. 50 Pl. VII f. 7 a. V. H. Syn. p. 90 Suppl. B f. 22, A. S. Atl. LXIX f. 28, 29. *Nav. gemina* A. S. Zeitschr. f. ges. Naturw. 1873 p. 405 Pl. VI f. 2. N. S. D. Pl. I f. 1, II f. 1. Atl. XIII f. 4, 5, 6, 7, 8, 9. *Nav. abnormis* Castr. Chall. Exp. XXVIII f. 19.

Marine: Finmark! North Sea! Marocco! Mediterranean Sea! Adriatic! Black Sea! Caspian Sea (Grun.)! Madagascar! Java! Japan! Samoa! Galapagos Islands! Cape Horn (Petit), Brazil (Atl.), Florida! Campeachy Bay! Fossil: Aegina (Ehb., Atl.).

Var. *egena* A. S. (1875). — L. 0,038 to 0,047; B. 0,015 to 0,02; at the constr. 0,006 to 0,012 mm. Transverse costæ 8 to 9 in 0,01 mm. crossed on each side of the median line by about 3 longitudinal costæ. — *Nav. gemina v. egena* A. S. Atl. XIII f. 10.

Marine: Balearic Islands! Madagascar! Manilla! China! Japan!

Var. *densestriata* A. S. (1875). — L. 0,045 to 0,056; B. 0,018 to 0,026; at the constr. 0,011 to 0,015 mm. Costæ 8 to 9 in 0,01 mm. — *Nav. gemina v. densestr.* A. S. Atl. XIII f. 11, 12. *Nav. didyma* A. S. Atl. LXIX f. 30.

Marine: Marocco! Seychelles (Van Heurck Coll.)! California (Atl.).

Var. *bullata* Cl. — L. 0,15; B. 0,047 in 0,01 mm. Horns with a row of large puncta. Costæ 5 to 7 in 0,01 mm.

Marine: Adriatic! Red Sea (Deby Coll.)! California!

44. **D. Kützingii** Grun. (1860). — V. strongly constricted, with deltoid-elliptical segments. L. 0,063 to 0,15; B. 0,03 to 0,055; at the constr. 0,014 to 0,035 mm. Horns of the central nodule parallel. Transverse costæ 6 to 8 in 0,01 mm., crossed by numerous (8 to 10) longitudinal, almost straight or slightly undulating costæ. — *Nav. Kützingii* Grun. Verh. 1860 p. 532 Pl. III f. 15. A. S. Atl. XIII f. 22, 23, 24. Pant. I Pl. XXIX f. 299.

Marine: Balearic Islands! Gulf of Naples! Black Sea! Red Sea (Deby Coll.)! Cape of Good Hope! Bermuda (Rae Coll.)! Valparaiso (Atl.), Galapagos Islands! Fossil: Hungary (Pant.), Aegina (Atl.).

Var. *bullata* Cl. — Horns with a row of large puncta.

Marine: Gulf of Naples! Red Sea (Deby Coll.)!

D. Kützingii is very nearly akin to *D. Bombus var. densestriata*, but it is larger and the horns of the central nodule are parallel.

45. **D. chersonensis** GRUN. (1875). — V. panduriform, usually slender, with subelliptical segments. L. 0,055 to 0,15; B. 0,02 to 0,06; at the constr. 0,012 to 0,03 mm. Central nodule with parallel, approximate horns. Furrows very narrow, linear. Transverse costæ 8 to 13 in 0,01 mm., crossed by 2 to 5, not undulating, almost straight longitudinal costæ. — *Nav. cherson.* GRUN. A. S. Atl. XII f. 40, LXIX f. 21. *Nav Apis.* A. S. N. D. Pl. I f. 9. Atl. XII f. 18 to 23, 25.

Marine: North Sea! Mediterranean Sea! Zanzibar (Atl.). Ceylon! Philippines! China! Tahiti! Galapagos Islands! West Indies! Florida! Cape Horn (Petit). Fossil: S:ta Monica Calif.

This very widely distributed species is usually regarded as *Nav. Apis* of EHRENBERG. I am unable to make out what this name, as is the case with so many others of the names given by EHRENBERG, may denote. *Nav. Apis* of DONKIN (B. D. p. 48 Pl. VII f. 3) and of SCHMIDT (Atl. XII f. 16; LXIX f. 41, 43, 44) are unknown to me. Specimens from England in the collection of GROVE are identical with *D. incurvata*. *D. chersonensis* is nearly akin to *D. splendida*, intermediate forms being frequent. Such a form is the fig. 24 Pl. XII in A. S. Atl. and *Nav splendida var. ovata* A. S. (Atl. XIII f. 13, 14, 16, 33, 35). To *D. chersonensis* belongs most likely *Nav Hantkenii* PANT. (II p. 46 Pl. VIII f. 150). On corroded specimens the longitudinal costæ are less distinct and the transverse more or less fragmentary. Such corroded specimens form Bruns *Nav. pedalis* (D. esp. nouvelles p. 36 Pl. XVI f. 10; 1891. A. S. Atl. CLXXIV f. 14, 15; 1892), original specimens of which I had an opportunity of examining.

46. **D. Weissflogii** A. S. (1873). — V. strongly constricted, with subelliptical segments. L. 0,033 to 0,11; B. 0,014 to 0,035; at the constr. 0,009 to 0,025 mm. Central nodule with approximate horns. Furrows not distinct from the other rows of alveoli. Transverse costæ 7 to 8 in 0,01 mm., crossed by numerous equidistant, straight, longitudinal costæ, curved outwards in the middle of the valve. On the middle of the valve the costæ are slightly divergent and not, or only close to the central nodule, crossed by longitudinal costæ. — *Nav. Weissflogii* A. S. Zeitschr. f. ges. Natur. 1873 p. 406 Pl. VI f. 3, 4. A. S. Atl. XII f. 26 to 32. V. H. Syn. p. 90 Suppl. B. f. 21. *Nav. diversa* GREV. Ed. N. Ph. J. XVIII p. 186 f. 14; 1863.?

Marine: Bab el mandeb! Madagascar! Ceylon! Singapore! Philippines! Samoa! Tahiti! Sandwich Islands (Atl.), Gulf of Mexico! Florida! North Carolina!

47. **D. areolata** CL. N. Sp. — V. moderately constricted, with subelliptical segments. L. 0,13; B. 0,045; at the constr. 0,028 mm. Central nodule large, its horns almost parallel. Furrows linear, with strongly marked transverse costæ. Transverse costæ 4 in 0,01 mm., crossed by a few, slightly curved longitudinal costæ, 3 in 0,01 mm., which are interrupted in the middle of the valve. The rectangular areolæ, formed by the two sets of costæ are large and have in their middle one or two ocelli. — Pl. I f. 28.

Marine: S:ta Monica, Calif., fossil (Deby Coll.)!

------

48. **D. domblittensis** GRUN. (1882). — V. elliptical. L. 0,02 to 0,045; B. 0,015 to 0,022 mm. Central nodule large, quadrate. Furrows narrow, of equal breadth the whole length. Transverse costæ 10 in 0,01 mm. anastomosing and thus producing more or less regular longitudinal rows of elongated alveoli, about 7 in 0,01 mm. No fine punctation visible. — *Nav. elliptica v. domb.* GRUN. Foss. D. Öster. Ung p. 156 Pl. XXX f. 60. *Nav. hilarula* PANT. III Pl. XV f. 230 (1893). *Dipl. domb.* Icon. n. Pl. II f. 2.

Fresh or slightly brackish water: Sweden. Lefrasjön in Skane! Mälaren! Domblitton, foss.! Gulf of Bothnia! Common in the Baltic deposits of the Ancylus-epoch!

This form seems to be closely connected with *D. didyma*, of which it may be a non-constricted freshwater form. GRUNOW considers it as connected with *D. notabilis*.

49. **D. elliptica** Kütz. (1844). — V. elliptical, with broad and rounded ends. L. 0,02 to 0,087; B. 0,011 to 0,02 mm. Central nodule of medium size quadrate. Furrows narrow, of the same breadth throughout. Transverse rows of puncta 10 to 13 in 0,01 mm. Alveoli 10 to 14 in 0,01 mm. forming irregular longitudinal rows. — *Nav. elliptica* Kütz. Bac. p. 98 Pl. XXX f. 55? V. H. Syn. Pl. X f. 10 (upper figure). A. S. Atl. VII f. 29, 32. *Nav. elliptica var. minor* Grun. Foss. D. Österr. Ung. p. 145. *Nav. ovalis* W. Sm. B. D. I p. 48 Pl. XVIII f. 153 *a'*? *Nav. elliptica* W. Sm. B. D. II p. 93.

Fresh water: Iceland! Sweden! Finland! Germany! England! New Zealand! North America (New York)! Ecuador!

Var. *grandis* Grun. (1882). — L. 0,065 to 0,13; B. 0,033 to 0,045 mm. Transverse and longitudinal rows of alveoli 10 in 0,01 mm. — *Nav. ellipt. var. grandis* Grun., Foss. D. Österr. Ung. p. 145. *Nav. præclara* Pant. III Pl. XI f. 182 (1893).

Brackish water: Hungary, fossil!

Var. *ladogensis* Cl. (1891). — L. 0,06; B. 0,025 mm. Transverse costæ 9 in 0,01 mm. irregularly anastomosing with a few longitudinal undulating costæ. — Cl. D. of Finland p. 43 Pl. II f. 9.

Fresh water: Ladoga!

Var. *Ostracodarum* Pant. (1893). — V. elliptical, tapering from the middle to the ends. L. 0,045; B. 0,027 mm. Transverse rows of alveoli 6 in 0,01 mm. — *Nav. ostrac.* Pant. III Pl. IX f. 145.

Habitat:? Köpecz, Hungary, fossil (Pant.).

50. **D. Puella** (Schum. 1867?) Cl. — V. elliptical. L. 0,013 to 0,025; B. 0,008 to 0,014 mm. Central nodule large, quadrate. Furrows narrow, of the same breadth throughout. Costæ 12 to 18 in 0,01 mm. Alveoli indistinct. — *Nav. Puella* Schum. Preuss. D. II Nachtr. f. 39? *Nav. elliptica var. minutissima* V. H. Syn. p. 92 Pl. X f. 11.

Fresh water: Spitzbergen! Sweden! Finland! Berlin! Hungary, fossil (Grun.).

This species, differing only in its small size and indistinct alveoli, is closely connected by intermediate forms with *D. elliptica*. *Navicula Puella* A. S. is quite another form (see page 88).

51. **D. Boldtiana** Cl. (1891). — V. elongate-elliptical. L. 0,03; B. 0,0012 mm. Central nodule small, quadrate. Furrows of equal breadth throughout. Costæ 14 in 0,01 mm. No distinct alveoli. — Cl. D. of Finl. p. 43 Pl. II f. 12.

Fresh water: Finland!

52. **D. oculata** Bréb. (1854). — V. elongate-elliptical. L. 0,015 to 0,02; B. 0,006 to 0,007 mm. Central nodule small. Furrows very narrow. Costæ 23 in 0,01 mm. Alveoli very small. — *Nav. oculata* Bréb. in Desm. Crypt. N:o 110. Journ. Quek. M. Cl. 1870 f. 5. V. H. Syn. Pl. IX f. 10.

Fresh water: France.

53. **D. ovalis** Hilse (1861). — V. broadly elliptical, not constricted in the middle. L. 0,035 to 0,048; B. 0,02 to 0,026 mm. Central nodule very large, rounded. Furrows very narrow, closely following the central nodule and its horns. Transverse rows of alveoli 13 to 19 in 0,01 mm. radiate at the ends. Puncta 13 to 20 in 0,01 mm. forming irregular longitudinal rows. — *Pinnularia ovalis* Hilse in Rab. A. E. 1025. *Nav. ovalis* A. S. Atl. VII f. 33, 34, 35, 36. W. Sm. B. D. XVII f. 153 *a*? Cl. D. of Finland p. 44 Pl. II f. 13. *Nav. elliptica* A. S. Atl. VII f. 30. V. H. Syn. Pl. X f. 10 (lower fig.). *Nav. Carpathorum* Pant. III Pl. XVII f. 246 (1893)?

Fresh water: Sweden (Lapland, Gotland, Billingen)! Finland (Russian Lapland)! Norway (Dovre)! Saxony! Alps of Switzerland! Australia, Daintree River!

Var. *pumila* Grun. (1882). L. 0,02 to 0,022; B. 0,008 to 0,088 mm. Rows of alveoli 16 to 18 in 0,01 mm. *Nav. ovalis var. pum.* Grun. Foss. D. Österr. Ung. p. 150 Pl. XXX f. 61. *Nav. Parmula* Bréb. (according to Grunow).

Fresh water: Hungary, foss. (Grun.). Baku (Grun.).

Var. *oblongella* NÆGELI (1849). — V. linear elliptical. L. 0,02 to 0,038; B. 0,0065 to 0,01 mm Rows of alveoli 13 to 19 in 0,51 mm. Puncta 20 to 25 in 0,01 mm. *Nav. oblongella* NÆG. KÜTZ Sp. Alg. p. 890. V. H. Syn. Pl. X f. 12. *Nav. ovalis var. fossilis* PANT. II p. 51 Pl. VI f. 115 (1889)?

Fresh water: Iceland! Finland! Paris! Königsberg, fossil!

54. **D. notabilis** GREV. (1863). — V. elliptical. L. 0,025 to 0,08; B. 0,02 to 0,035 mm. Central nodule large, quadrate. Furrows linear, arcuate, moderately broad. Transverse costæ 7 to 10 in 0.01 mm. alternating with large, elongated alveoli, forming 4 to 5 longitudinal, undulating rows, more close towards the margins.

Forma genuina — Rows of alveoli one to three along the margin and one along the furrow. *Nav. notab.* GREV. T. M. S. XI p. 18 f. 9. A. S. Atl. VIII f. 46, 47, 48.

Forma expleta A. S. (1874). — Rows of alveoli filling the whole space between the furrow and the margins. — *N. notabilis var. expleta* A. S. N. S. D. I f. 20, II f. 11. Atl. VIII f. 49 to 52.

Marine: North Sea! Mediterranean Sea! Black Sea! Red Sea! Ceylon! Madagascar! Cape of Good Hope! Java! Labuan! Sandwich Islands! West Indies! Brazil!

55. **D. Grælli** GRUN. (1875). — V. elongated elliptical. L. 0,065 to 0.12; B. 0.025 to 0,042 mm. Central nodule small, rounded quadrate. Furrows broad, gradually narrowed from the middle and crossed by faint prolongations of the costæ. Costæ 7 to 8 in 0,01 mm., alternating with single rows of quadrate alveoli, 8 to 11 in 0,01 mm. and forming 7 to 8 longitudinal rows on each side of the furrows. — *Nav. Græffii* A. S. Atl. VII f. 5, 6.

Marine: Bab el mandeb! Seychelles! Madagascar! Manilla! Java! Sumbava! Labuan! Japan (Atl.), Samoa (Atl.), Tahiti!

Forma minor. — L. 0,06; B. 0,018 mm. — A. S. Atl. VIII f. 33.

Marine: Campeachy Bank (Atl.).

This species seems to be intermediata between *D. notabilis* and *D. fusca*.

56. **D. fusca** GREG. (1857). — V. elliptical or subrectangular, not constricted. L. 0,07 to 0,14; B. 0,038 to 0,075 mm. Central nodule moderately large, quadrate. Furrows broad, gradually tapering from the middle and crossed by faint prolongations of the costæ, frequently alternating with double rows of obliquely disposed puncta. Costæ 6 to 10 in 0,01 mm. alternating with rows of more or less quadrate alveoli, forming more or less regular, longitudinal rows, equidistant with, to twice as close as, the costæ.

Var. *Pelagi* A. S. (1875). — V. rhombic-elliptical. L. 0,055 to 0.066; B. 0,035 to 0,04 mm. Central nodule large, rounded quadrate. Furrows broad, semilanceolate, crossed by rows of alveoli. Costæ 7 in 0,01 mm. Alveoli 9 in 0,01 mm. forming longitudinal rows, parallel with the margins. — *Nav. Pelagi* A. S. Atl. VII f. 25, 26.

Marine: Campeachy Bay! Colon (Deby Coll.)! Tahiti!

Var. *nigricans* PANT. (1893). — V. narrow elliptical. L. 0,25; B. 0,07. Transverse and longitudinal rows of alveoli 6 in 0,01 mm. — *Nav. nigricans* PANT. III Pl. XL f. 552.

Marine: Bory, Hungary, fossil (Pant.).

Var. *pseudofusca* PANT. (1886). — V. nearly orbicular. L. 0.052 to 0,087; B. 0,037 to 0,066 mm. Costæ in the middle 9 at the ends 13 in 0,01 mm. Furrows forming a large rhomboid space. Longitudinal rows of alveoli about 10 in 0,01 mm. — *Nav. pseudofusca* PANT. I p. 28 Pl. XIII f. 109.

Marine: Hungary, fossil (Pant.).

Var. *norvegica* CL. — L. 0.085 to 0,01; B. 0,045 to 0,055 mm. Costæ and longitudinal rows of alveoli 10 in 0,01 mm. — *N. fusca* A. S. Atl. VII f. 2, 3.

Marine: North Sea! Hungary, fossil (Deby Coll.)!

Var. *subrectangularis* CL. — V. more or less rectangular. L. 0.85 to 0.13; B. 0,037 to 0,056 mm. Costæ and longitudinal rows of alveoli 8 in 0.01 mm. — *Nav. fusca* A. S. Atl. VII f. 4. *N. Smithii* DONK. B. D. p. 6 Pl. I f. 4.

Marine: North Sea! Balearic Islands! Sumatra (Deby Coll.)!

Var. *Gregorii* Cl. — V. elliptical to subrectangular. L. 0,17; B. 0,08 mm. Costæ and longitudinal rows of alveoli 7 in 0,01 mm. — *Nav. Smithii var. fusca* Greg. D. of Clyde IX f. 15.

Marine: North Sea! Gulf of Naples (Deby Coll.)!

Var. *delicata* A. S. (1874). — Elliptical. L. 0,07 to 0,13; B. 0,038 to 0,08 mm. Costæ 7 to 10 in 0,01 mm. Longitudinal rows of alveoli 10 to 15 in 0,01 mm. — *Nav. fusca var. delicata* A. S. N. S. D. I f. 26. Atl. VII f. 1, 7, 8.

Marine: North Sea (A. S.), Adriatic! Sumatra! Hungary, fossil (Deby Coll.)!

Var. *tenuipunctata* Cl. — V. elliptical. L. 0,07 to 0,14; B. 0,032 to 0,07 mm. Costæ 6 to 9 in 0,01 mm. Longitudinal rows of alveoli 12 to 18 in 0,01 mm. — *Nav. fusca* V. H. Syn. Suppl. B. f. 24.

Marine: Gulf of Naples! Sumatra (Deby Coll.)! South Sea (Van Heurck Coll.)! Mexillones guano (Deby Coll.)!

Var. *Van Heurckii* Cl. — V. elongated, very slightly constricted. L. 0,08; B. 0,025 mm. Costæ 8 in 0,01 mm. Alveoli 20 in 0,01 mm. — Pl. I f. 19.

Marine: South Sea (Van Heurck Coll.)!

Var. *subfusca* Pant. (1893). — Narrow elliptical. L. 0,055; B. 0,017 mm. Transverse rows of alveoli 5, longitudinal 7 in 0,01 mm. — *Nav. subfusca* Pant., III Pl. XL f. 553.

Habitat:? Asopallaga-Serges (Pant.).

Var. *oamaruensis* Cl. — V. narrow elliptical. L. 0,11; B. 0,03 mm. Central nodule elongated rounded. Furrows very broad, about a fourth of the breadth of the valve. Costæ 8 and longitudinal rows of puncta 16 in 0,01 mm. — Pl. II f. 3.

Marine: New Zealand, Oamaru, fossil!

Var. *japonica* Cl. — L. 0,11; B. 0,055 mm. Costæ 6 and longitudinal rows of alveoli 13 in 0,01 mm. Furrows separated from the other parts of the valve by a row of foramina and crossed by transverse single rows of large puncta. — Pl. I f. 23.

Marine: Sendaï, Japan, fossil (Tempère).

Nav. præfluu Pant. (III Pl. XV f. 232) appears to be a form of *D. fusca*.

57. **D. æstiva** Donk. (1858). — V. elliptical. L. 0,037 to 0,065; B. 0,018 to 0,038 mm. Central nodule large, elongated. Furrows narrow of equal breadth throughout. Costæ 8 to 12 in 0,01 mm. Alveoli of equal or double number in 0,01 mm. — *Nav. æstiva* Donk. T. M. S. VI p. 32 Pl. III f. 18. B. D. p. 6 Pl. I f. 3. A. S. Atl. VII f. 8, 10, 11; VIII f. 26, 31.

Forma α. Costæ and alveoli of equal number.

Marine: Singapore (costæ and alveoli 9 in 0,01 mm.). Manilla (c. a. alv. 10 in 0,01 mm.). Colon (c. a. alv. 12 in 0,01 mm.) all in Deby Coll.!

Forma β. Alveoli twice as close as the costæ.

Marine: West coast of Sweden (L. 0,04 mm. Costæ 12 in 0,01 mm.). Sumatra (L. 0,06 mm. Costæ 8 in 0,01 mm. Deby Coll.)!

58. **D. litoralis** Donk. (1870). — V. elliptical. L. 0,027 to 0,07; B. 0,015 to 0,033 mm. Central nodule small, elongated, rounded rectangular. Furrows very narrow, parallel and close to the horns. Costæ 11 (typical) to 14 in 0,01 mm. Alveoli 22 (typical) to more in 0,01 mm., forming longitudinal rows. — *Nav. litoralis* Donk. B. D. p. 5 Pl. I f. 2. V. H. Syn. Suppl. B. f. 25. A. S. Atl. VIII f. 23 to 25. *Nav. litor. var. subtilis* A. S. N. S. D. Pl. I f. 24, 25. *Nav. Ovulum* Grun. Verh. 1860 p. 519 Pl. III f. 19?

Marine: Arctic America! Finmark! North Sea! Sea of Kara! Cape Deschneff! Adriatic! Java! Tahiti! Port Jackson! West Indies!

Var. *hospes* A. S. (1875). — V. subhexagonal. L. 0,05; B. 0,023 mm. Costæ 11, alveoli 13 in 0,01 mm. — *Nav. hospes* A. S. Atl. VIII f. 32.

Marine: Samoa (Atl.), Java!

59. **D. hyperborea** Grun. (1860). — V. elliptical. L. 0,1; B. 0,049 mm. Furrows abruptly bent around the large central nodule. Costæ 7 in 0,01 mm. — *Nav. hyperborea* Grun. Verh. 1860 p. 531 Pl. III f. 16. *Nav. propinqua* A. S. Atl. VII f. 13?

Marine: Bohuslän, Sweden (Grun.).

Var. *excisa* A. S. (1874). V. slightly constricted in the middle. L. 0,09; B. 0,03 mm. Costæ 9 in 0,01 mm. — *Nav. fusca var. excisa* A. S. N. S. D. II f. 9.

Marine: North Sea (Atl.).

60. **D. vacillans** A. S. (1875). — V. elongated elliptical, constricted, or not constricted. L. 0,04 to 0,06; B. 0,014 to 0,016 mm. Furrows dilated in the middle, forming in the middle of the valve a lanceolate space. Costæ 9 to 14, alveoli 15 to 21 in 0,01 mm. Alveoli forming longitudinal rows parallel with the margins of the areas.

Forma α. V. constricted in the middle. — *Nav. vacillans* A. S. Atl. VIII f. 61; XII f. 42, 43, 52, 53.

Marine: Ceylon (Leuduger Fortm.) Rodriguez! Cape Good Hope (Atl.), Japan (Atl.), Samoa (Atl.), Sandwich Island (Atl.). Cape Horn (Petit), Campeachy Bank (Atl.), California (Atl.).

Forma β. V. not constricted in the middle. — A. S. Atl. VIII f. 34, 35, 36. *Nav. parca var. producta* Pant. II p. 52 Pl. VIII f. 148 (1889).

Marine: North Sea (Atl.). Marocco! Balearic Islands! Macassar Straits! Colon (Deby Coll.)! Campeachy Bay (Atl.).

Var. *delicatula* Cl. — not constricted. Striæ 13 to 14 in 0,01 mm. A. S. Atl. VIII f. 37.

Marine: Cape Good Hope (Atl.).

Var. *renitens* A. S. (1875). — V. strongly constricted. L. 0,05; B. 0,018 mm. Costæ 10 in 0,01 mm. — *Nav. vacill. v. renitens* A. S. Atl. XII f. 55.

Marine: Celebes (Atl.).

Var. *corsicana* Grun. (1878). — V. slightly constricted. L. 0,065; B. 0,022 mm. Costæ 8, alveoli 18 in 0,01 mm. — Cl. M. D. N:o 153.

Marine: Corsica! Seychelles (Van Heurck Coll.)! Campeachy Bay!

Var.? *minuta* Grun. (1880). — V. slightly constricted. L. 0,014 to 0,02; B. 0,0045 mm. Costæ about 16 in 0,01 mm.. — *Nav. vacillans f. minuta* (*N. Pfitzeriana* O. W.) V. H. Syn. p. 90 Pl. IX f. 9.

Marine: Belgium (V. H.).

61. **D. Parma** Cl. (1891). V. broadly elliptical. L. 0,03; B. 0,02 mm. Central nodule moderately large, rounded quadrate. Furrows arcuate, equally bent, approximate to the horns. Costæ 14 in 0,01 mm. Alveoli 20 in 0,01 mm., forming longitudinal rows. — Cl. D. of Finland p. 43 Pl. II f. 10.

Fresh water: Sweden, Lake Rosslängen i Kalmar Län! Finland, Åbo, Viando!

Similar to *D. finnica* but only half the size and with costæ and alveoli twice as close.

62. **D. finnica** Ehb. (1838) Cl. — V. broadly elliptical. L. 0,05 to 0,055; B. 0,034 to 0,036 mm. Central nodule small, elongated. Furrows broad, with arcuate exterior margins enclosing a large, lanceolate space, about one third of the valve. Costæ 7 in 0,01 mm. Alveoli 12 in 0,01 mm. forming longitudinal or near the margin obliquely decussating rows. — *Cocon. finnica* Ehb. Inf. p. 194. M. G. XVII, 2 f. 19. *D. finnica* Cl. D. of Finland p. 43 Pl. II f. 11.

Fresh water: Sweden, Lake Roslängen! Degernäs in Westerbotten, fossil! Finland! U. States Albany, Maine, fossil! Crane Pond, fossil! Canada, fossil!

63. **D. microtatos** Pant. (1886). — V. orbicular. L. and B. 0,034 to 0,04 mm. Central nodule large, not sharply defined. Median line with distant central pores, and ending at a considerable distance from the margin. Furrows broad; their outer margins enclosing an elliptical

space, half as broad as the valve and crossed by somewhat radiate rows of alveoli. Rows of alveoli 8 in 0,01 mm. Alveoli 8 in 0,01 mm. *Nav. microtatos* PANT. I p. 27 Pl. IX f. 80.

Marine: Szákol, Hungary, foss.! South Naparima, Trinidad, foss. (Deby Coll.)!

Var. *Christianii* T. C. L. 0,045; B. 0,04 mm. Median rows of the alveoli at the margin alternately longer and shorter, 11 in 0,01 mm. - *Raphidodiscus Marylandica, Christianii and Febigerii* T. C. Microscope 1889, according to Wolle D. of N. Am. Pl. LXXXIV f. 1 to 4. Icon. n. Pl. II f. 1.

Marine: Cambridge, Maryland, fossil (Deby Coll.)!

64. **D. Smithii** BRÉB. (1856). V. elliptical. L. 0,027 to 0,05; B. 0,015 to 0,035 mm. Central nodule small. Terminal nodules close to the ends. Furrows narrow, close to the horns. Costæ 7 to 11 in 0,11 mm. alternating with double rows of alveoli disposed in obliquely decussating lines, twice or more as close as the costæ. – *Nav. elliptica* W. SM. B. D. I p. 48 Pl. XVII f. 152 *a*. *N. Smithii* BRÉB. in W. SM. B. D. II p. 92. *N. Smithii v. borealis f. minor* GRUN. Franz Josephs Land D. Pl. I f. 41. *N. Smithii* A. S. Atl. VII f. 16, 17. N. S. D. I f. 19.? *N. Scutellum* V. H. Syn. Pl. IX f. 11.? *Nav. Smithii var. lævis* Dannf. Baltic D. p. 30 Pl. II f. 15.

Marine and brackish: Franz Josephs Land (Grun.), Spitzbergen! Sea of Kara! Finmark! Baltic! Gulf of Bothnia! North Sea! Mediterranean Sea! Madagascar! Seychelles! Tasmania! Java! New Zealand! Colon! Campeachy Bay!

Nav. Dóczyi (PANT. II p. 45 Pl. XIV f. 247, 1889) from Bremia in Hungary, seems to be a finely costate variety of *D. Smithii*. Its length is 0,052 and its breadth 0,017 mm. The costæ are 14 to 16,5 in 0,01 mm. and are described as indistinctly punctate.

65. **D. subovalis** CL. N. Sp. V. elliptical. L. 0,38; B. 0,019 mm. Central nodule large, rounded. Furrows narrow, closely following the central nodule and its horns. Costæ 10 in 0,01 mm., alternating with double rows of alveoli, forming oblique lines, about 18 in 0,01 mm. — Pl. I f. 27.

Fresh water: New Zeeland, Paeroa.

This form resembles *D. ovalis* in its shape and large central nodule, but has the structure of *D. Smithii*.

66. **D. borealis** GRUN. (1884). — V. elongate-elliptical. L. 0,65 to 0,078; B. 0,025 to 0,0265 mm. Central nodule elongated. Furrows narrow, dilated around the central nodule and crossed by costæ, interrupted by a longitudinal band. Costæ 10 in 0,01 mm., alternating with rows of alveoli, forming oblique longitudinal lines, about 24 in 0,01 mm. — *Nav. Smithii var. borealis* GRUN. Franz Josephs Land D. p. 56 (4) Pl. I f. 40. *Nav. fusca* DONK. B. D. Pl. I f. 5.?

Marine: Franz Josephs Land (Grun.), Matotschin Sharr. Sea of Kara! Gullmarefjord! Java (var. L. 0,042; B. 0,017 mm. Costæ 8 puncta 17 in 0,01 mm.).

Var. *subconstricta* CL. — V. slightly constricted in the middle. L. 0,58; B. 0,02 mm. Costæ 10, alveoli 24 in 0,01 mm. Furrows narrow, the costæ not interrupted by a longitudinal band.

Marine: Campeachy Bay!

This form resembles *D. vacillans*, from which it differs by the alveoli forming oblique rows. The fig. 14 and 15 Pl. VII in A. S. Atl. seem to belong to *D. borealis*.

67. **D. major** CL. N. Sp. — V. elliptical. L. 0,07 to 0,17; B. 0,037 to 0,06 mm. Central nodule large, rounded quadrate. Terminal nodules distant from the ends. Furrows rather broad; their outer margins enclosing a space 1/4 to 1/3 as broad as the valve, crossed by costæ and double rows of alveoli. Costæ 5 to 7 in 0,01 mm. alternating with double rows of alveoli, 7 to 15 in 0,01 mm., forming oblique lines. — *Nav. Smithii* A. S. Atl. VII f. 19, (typical)! 22, 21, 18. V. H. Syn. Pl. IX f. 12. Suppl. Pl. B. f. 23.

Marine: North Sea! Marocco! Barcelona! Madagascar! Macassar Straits! Sumatra! China! Japan! Australia! Sta Monica, Calif. fossil! Colon!

Var. *permagna* PANT. (1889). — V, elliptical, very large. L. 0,014 to 0,2; B. 0,075 mm. Costæ 4.5 to 5 in 0,01 mm. alternating with double rows of alveoli, about 9 in 0.01 mm. — *Nav. fusca var. permagna* PANT. II p. 46.

Marine: Bory, Hungary, fossil!

D. major is usually considered as a larger form of *D. Smithii*, with which it is intimately connected. Still I find it desirable to separate them, as the structure of *D. major* is much coarser.

68. **D. Platessa** CL. and GROVE. N. Sp. — V. broadly elliptical-lanceolate. L. 0,06; B. 0,045 mm. Central nodule rounded-quadrate. Furrows very broad, their outer margins enclosing a lanceolate space 3/4 as broad as the valve and crossed by costæ. Costæ 7 to 8 in 0,01 mm., alternating with double rows of alveoli (16 in 0,01 mm.) forming obliquely decussating lines. — Pl. II f. 6.

Marine: Manilla (Deby Coll.)! Macassar Straits (Grove Coll.)!

69. **D. mirabilis** CASTR. (1886). — V. elliptical-orbicular. L. 0,065 to 0,08; B. 0,055 to 0,062 mm. Central nodule moderately large, quadrate. Furrows very broad, double, the outer margins of the exterior enclosing a broadly lanceolate space, about 3/4 as broad as the valve. The interior furrows are crossed by costæ, the exterior of costæ, alternating with double rows of alveoli. Costæ 7 in 0,01 mm. alternating with double rows of alveoli 14 in 0,01 mm. forming obliquely decussating lines. — *Nav. mirabilis* CASTR. Voyage Challenger D. p. 34 Pl. XXX f. 10.

Marine: Madagascar (Brun Coll.)! Zebu (Castr.).

70. **D. Vespa** CL. N. Sp. — V. panduriform, with subrhomboid segments. L. 0,05; B. 0,012 at the constr. 0,06 mm. Central nodule small, its horns approximate. Furrows broad, of the same shape as the valve, crossed by costæ. Costæ 11 in 0.01 mm. alternating with double rows of small puncta, arranged in obliquely decussating rows. — Pl. II f. 5.

Marine: Java!

71. **D. nitescens** GREG. (1857). — V. elliptical-lanceolate. L. 0,05 to 0,09; B. 0,022 to 0,036 mm. Central nodule small, its horns not very distinct. Furrows wide. Their outer margins enclosing a lanceolate space, 1/2 or more as broad as the valve, crossed by costæ, frequently alternating with double rows of alveoli Costæ 6 to 8 in 0,01 mm. alternating with single or near the margin double rows of alveoli, 14 to 16 in 0,01 mm. — *Nav. Smithii var. nitescens* GREG. D. of Clyde p. 487 Pl. IX f. 16. *Nav. nitescens* DONK. B. D. p. 8 Pl. I f. 7. A. S. Atl. VII f. 38 to 41, VIII f. 14 to 16. *Pinnularia arraniensis* O'M. M. J. VII p. 116 Pl. V. f. 6. *Nav. adriatica* GRUN. Verh. 1860 p. 525 Pl. III f. 17.

Marine: North Sea! Morocco! Adriatic! Sebastopol! Moravian Tegel (fossil)! Seychelles! Madagascar! Sumbava! Singapore! Australia! Sandwich Islands! S:ta Monica, fossil! Colon! Campeachy Bay!

Var. *fossilis* PANT. (1889). — L. 0,099; B. 0,041 mm. Costæ 7,5 to 8,5 in 0,01 mm. Alveoli not distinct. — *Nav. nitescens var. fossilis* PANT. II p. 51 Pl. IX f. 163.

Marine: Hungary, fossil (Pant.).

Var. *fuegiana* P. PETIT (1888). — L. 0,062; B. 0,0255 mm. Costæ 10 in 0,01 mm. — *Nav. nitescens var. fuegiana* PETIT Cape Horn D. p. 122 Pl. X f. 6.

Marine: Cape Horn.

Var. *serratula* GRUN. (1875). — V. lanceolate. L. 0,09; B. 0,021 mm. Central nodule small, rounded; its horns indistinct, very approximate to the median line. Furrows broad, forming a lanceolate space, crossed by faint costæ, alternating with double rows of indistinct alveoli. Costæ 6 in 0,01 mm. alternating with (single?) rows of alveoli, 11 in 0,01 mm. — *Nav. serrat.* A. S. Atl. VII f. 42, 43 VIII f. 11.

Marine: Campeachy Bay! Colon (Deby Coll.)!

D. nitescens is remarkable for the week development of the central nodule, the horns of which are scarcely distinct. In this respect it comes near to *D. inscripta* CL. On corroded specimens the alveoli are indistinct.

72. **D. dalmatica** GRUN. (1860). — V. slightly constricted, with cuneate segments. L. 0,058 to 0,062; B. 0,014 to 0,017; at the constr. 0,012 to 0,014 mm. Central nodule small, rounded elongated; its horns indistinct, close to the median line. Furrows narrow, not dilated in the middle, crossed by faint costæ. Costæ 8 in 0,01 mm., alternating with double rows of alveoli. — *Nav. dalm.* GRUN. Verh. 1860 p. 525 Pl. III f. 14. A. S. Atl. VIII f. 58, 59. *N. Hornigii* PANT. III Pl. XVI f. 241 (1893)?

Marine: Morocco! Balearic Islands! Adriatic (Grun.), Bab el Mandeb! Macassar Straits! Campeachy Bay!

Var. *Vulpecula* A. S. (1875). — V. deeply constricted, with semilanceolate segments. L. 0,062; B. 0,017; at the constr. 0,012 mm. Central nodule small, its horns indistinct. Furrows linear, moderately broad, near the horns with traces of the costæ. Transverse costæ parallel, 8 in 0,01 mm., alternating with indistinct (double?) rows of puncta. — *Nav. Vulp.* A. S. Atl. XII f. 56.

Marine: Celebes (Atl.), Java!

73. **D. Mauleri** BRUN. (1880). — V. elliptical. L. 0,037 to 0,05; B. 0,013 to 0,015 mm. Central nodule large, rounded; its horns indistinct, close to the median line. Furrows broad, forming a narrow elliptical space, half as wide as the valve, with two rows of large puncta. Costæ 7 in 0,01 mm. alternating with double rows of alveoli, 10 in 0,01 mm. — *Nav. Mauleri* BRUN. D. des Alpes p. 77 Pl. I f. 18. D. espèces n. p. 35 Pl. XV f. 7.

Lacustrine: Lac Leman! Sahara (Brun), Bottom-mud from Vettern! Of frequent occurrence in the Baltic deposits of the Ancylusepoch.

Var. *borussica* CL. (1882). — L. 0,025 to 0,037; B. 0,011 to 0,012 mm. Costæ 7 to 8 in 0,01 mm. alternating, with (single?) rows of indistinct alveoli. — *Nav. borussica* CL. Phys. Oek. Gesellsch. zu Königsberg XXII p. 139. A. S. Atl. VIII f. 17, 19. *Nav. Mauleri* PANT. III Pl. VII f. 105; Pl. IX f. 150.

Slightly brackish water: Gulf of Bothnia at Nedre Kalix! Domblitton, Prussia fossil! Rammer Moor (Atl.).

74. **D. Debyi** PANT. (1886). — V. lanceolate, with obtuse ends. L. 0,1; B. 0,03 mm. Central nodule rounded quadrate; its horns slightly divergent in the middle, approximate. Furrows very broad, with a row of strong puncta (reduced costæ). Costæ slightly radiate, 4 in 0,01 mm., alternating with rows of alveoli. — *Nav. Debyi* PANT. I p. 23 Pl. XV f. 136.

Marine: Szákal, Hungary, fossil (Pant.).

Var. *elliptica* CL. — V. narrow elliptical. L. 0,1; B. 0,035 mm. Furrows broad. Costæ 5 in 0,01 mm. continued across the furrows and alternating with double rows of small alveoli. — Pl. II f. 4.

Marine: Red Sea (Deby Coll.)!

75. **D. gemmata** GREV. (1859). — V. broad, linear, with rounded or cuneate ends and parallel or slightly concave margins. L. 0,085 to 0,24; B. 0,03 to 0,065 mm. Central nodule large, quadrate; its horns parallel, closely approximate to the median line. Furrows broad, linear, filling a third or less of the surface of the valve. Costæ 3 to 6 in 0,01 mm., alternating with double rows of twice as close alveoli. Along the horns of the central nodule is a row of short, but strong costæ.

Var. *fossilis* PANT. (1886). — V. slightly constricted in the middle. L. 0,16 to 0,24; B. 0,045 to 0,065 mm. Costæ 3 in 0,01 mm. — A. S. Atl. LXX f. 74. *Nav. gemmata var. fossilis* PANT. I p. 25 Pl. XX f. 181.

Marine, fossil: Hungary (Deby Coll.)! Moravian Tegel! Moron (Atl.).

Var. *typica* Cl. — V. not constricted. L. 0,085 to 0,19; B. 0,03 to 0,05 mm. Costæ 4 in 0,01 mm. — *Nav. gemmata* Grev. Ed. N. Ph. J. X July 1859 p. 30 Pl. IV f. 7. *Nav. gemmata var. biseriata* Grun. Novara 100 Pl. I A f. 16. *Nav. gemmata var. spectabilis* Grun. A. S. Atl. VIII f. 38? *Nav. Basilica* Brun. D. espèces n. p. 32 Pl. XV f. 14 (1891)? *Nav. pseudogemmata* Pant. III Pl. XXIX f. 420 (1893).

Marine: Gulf of Naples! Nossibé! South Sea (Van Heurck Coll.)! Galapagos Islands! Campeachy Bay! West Indies! Fossil: Hungary (Pant.), Moravian Tegel! Nankoori! Californian Guano (Grev.).

In the coll. of Prof. Brun I have seen a specimen from Sendaï, which agrees with his *Nav. Basilica* and is only a somewhat elliptical form of *D. gemmata*.

Var. *minor* Cl. — L. 0,09 to 0,16; B. 0,027 to 0,035 mm. Costæ 5 in 0,01 mm. — A. S. Atl. LXX f. 73.

Marine: Balearic Islands! Madagascar! Colon (Deby Coll.!). Jamaica (Atl.).

Var. *punctata* Cl. — L. 0,14; B. 0,045 mm. Costæ 5 in 0,01 mm. Furrows with transverse rows of large puncta. Costæ alternating at their interior ends with one or in the middle with two large ocelli.

Marine: San Pedro, Calif. (Kinker Coll.)!

Var. *spectabilis* Grun. (1860). — L. 0,062 to 0,17; B. 0,025 mm. Costæ 3 to 5 in 0,01 mm. continued across the furrows. — *Nav. spectabilis* Grun. Verh. 1860 p. 533 Pl. III f. 11. *Nav. Grunowii* Rabh. Fl. E. Alg. p. 203 (1864).

Marine: Adriatic (Grun.), Sumbava (Kinker Coll.)! Fossil: S:t Peter, Hungary.

Var. *oamaruensis* Cl. — V. slightly constricted. L. 0,16; B. 0,04 mm. Horns of the central nodule more distinct and distant. Furrows with faint markings of the costæ which become strong along the horns. Costæ 5 in 0,01 mm. alternating near the furrows with two large ocelli.

Marine: Oamaru, New Zeeland, fossil!

Var. *madagascarensis* Cl. — V. narrow, very slightly constricted. L. 0,13; B. 0,024 mm. Horns distinct and somewhat distant. Furrows with two longitudinal rows of puncta along the horns. Costæ 6 in 0,01 mm.

Marine: Tamatave (Kinker Coll.)!

Var. *pristiophora* Jan (1881). — V. distinctly constricted in the middle. L. 0,1 to 0,15; B. 0,025 to 0,036 mm. Costæ 5 to 6 in 0,01 mm. — *Nav. pristiophora* A. S. Atl. LXX f. 72.

Marine: Morocco! Porto Seguro (Deby Coll.)! Leton Bank (Atl.).

Forma minuta Cl. — L. 0,057; B. 0,015 mm. Costæ 7 in 0,01 mm.

Marine: Macassar Straits!

D. gemmata is very variable, and by the form madagascarensis nearly connected with *D. contigua*, which may perhaps be only corroded specimens of D. gemmata.

76. **D. Szontaghii**, Pant. (1886). — V. elliptic-linear, with broad, rounded ends. L. 0,03 to 0,06; B. 0,016 to 0,022 mm. Central nodule large, quadrate; its horns distinct and distant from the median line. Furrows narrow, linear, with a row of large puncta (spaces between the rudimentary costæ). Costæ 5 in 0,01 mm. alternating with double rows of twice as close alveoli (on corroded specimens alternating with single rows of larger puncta). — *Nav. Szont.* Pant. I p. 29 Pl. III f. 25. Pl. XXVIII f. 284. Icon. n. Pl. II f. 7.

Marine: Sumbava (Kinker Coll.)! Hungary, fossil!

77. **D. Campylodiscus** Grun. (1875). — V. suborbicular. L. 0,038 to 0,05; B. 0,026 to 0,03 mm. Central nodule large, quadrate, its horns strong, distant, and convergent in the middle. Furrows broad, with faint costæ. Costæ 4 in 0,01 mm. alternating with double rows of faint alveoli. — *Nav. suborbicularis var. Nankoorensis* Grun. Novara p. 100 Pl. I A. f. 15 (1867). *Nav. Campylod.* Grun. A. S. Atl. VIII f. 9, 10, 12, LXX f. 64, 65. *Cocconeis coelata* Walker Arn. M. J. II p. 234 Pl. X f. 5, 6 (1862)?

Marine; Bab el Mandeb! Seychelles! Madagascar! Philippines! Tahiti! Galapagos Islands! Mazatlan (Atl.). Cape Horn (Petit). Campeachy Bay (Atl.). Fossil: Nankoori (Grun.).

78. **D. Crabro** Ehr. (1844). — V. constricted or not. L. 0,04 to 0,2 mm.; B. 0,018 to 0,06 mm. Central nodule large, quadrate with parallel horns. Furrows narrow linear, with a row of large puncta. Lunulæ none or more or less large. Costæ 3 to 8 in 0,01 mm. alternating with double rows of alveoli outside of the lunulæ. Ocelli forming a marginal band, bent inwards toward the central nodule.

This species comprises a considerable number of forms, differing in size, number of costæ, breadth of lunulæ and in the amount, or absence, or constriction of the middle. The forms also present a very different appearance, according as they are uninjured or corroded. Having compared a very large number of different forms I am unable to make distinct species of them, all being more or less connected and differing only in characteristics, which are subject to great variation.

If only a few extreme forms be examined, it is easy to found on them apparently well defined species, but the greater the number of intermediate forms observed, the greater becomes the difficulty of finding any definite distinctions between them. There are all intermediate transitions from purely elliptical to strongly constricted forms, from forms with no lunulæ to others with broad lunulæ; as to the ocelli I am not yet convinced of their value as specific characteristic. In most forms they occur as a marginal band, but there are forms without them, either because they originally had none or because the ocelli have been destroyed in preparation.

I have distinguished the following forms, which diatomists, fond of speciesmaking, may consider as specifically distinct.

A. *Forms with no, or very narrow lunulæ.*

Var. *limitanea* A. S. (1875). — V. panduriform, with narrow elliptical segments. L. 0,08 to 0,11; B. 0,024 to 0,032, at the constriction 0,017 to 0,025 mm. Central nodule small, quadrate. Lunulæ very narrow. Costæ 6 to 7 in 0,01 mm. alternating with double rows of alveoli, about 14 in 0,01 mm. Ocelli forming a narrow band along the margin. — *Nav. lim.* A. S. Atl. XI f. 23. LXIX f. 14 (optime) (not f. 12).

Marine: Seychelles (Van Heurck Coll.)! Sumbava (Kinker Coll.)! Singapore! Java! China! Kerguelens Land! Fossil: Atlantic City N. Jers. (Deby Coll.)!

The fig. 23 in A. S. Atl. is not sufficiently characteristic, but the fig. 14 Pl. LXIX represents very well the form, which I understand to be *limitanea*. It differs from Var. *Pandura* by smaller size and closer costæ. Otherwise, there is, as far as I can see, no difference.

Var. *Pandura* Bréb. (1854). V. constricted, with elongated, tongue-shaped segments. L. 0,106 to 0,212; B. 0,038 to 0,053; at the constriction 0,023 to 0,044 mm. Central nodule of median size. Lunulæ none. Costæ 4 to 5 in 0,01 mm. alternating with double rows of fine puncta about 10 in 0,01 mm. — *Nav. Pandura* Bréb. D. de Cherb. f. 4. A. S. N. S. D. Pl. II f. 3 (optime!) Atl. XI f. 1, 2, 9 (4, 8 corroded). V. H. Syn. Pl. IX f. 1. Truan and Witt D. von Jeremie Pl. IV f. 14 (corroded). *Pinnul. Pandura var. elongata* Greg. D. of Clyde Pl. IX f. 22. *Nav. Crabro* Donk. B. D. p 46 Pl. VII f. 1. *Nav. nitida* Greg. T. M. S. IV p. 44 Pl. V f. 12*. *Nav. Mantichora* Pant. III Pl. XXXV f. 190; 1893 (corroded).

Marine: North Sea! Mediterranean Sea! Adriatic! Red Sea! Madagascar! Sumbava! Society Islands! Galapagos Islands! Magellhaëns Strait! Bolivia! Campeachy Bay! West Indies!

As *Nav. navigans* Brun a form has been figured in A. S. Atl. CLXXIV f. 1, which seems to belong to Var. Pandura. The figure is too indistinct for identification. Perhaps fig. 3, *Nav. sideralis* A. S., may be the some form in a very corroded state.

Var. *expleta* A. S. (1881). — V. slightly constricted, with broad, tongue-shaped segments. L. 0,07 to 0,12; B. 0,032 to 0,033; at the constr. 0,027 to 0,03 mm. Costæ 5 in 0,01 mm. alternating with double rows of somewhat coarse puncta (8 to 11 in 0,01 mm.). — *Nav. expleta* A. S. Atl. LXIX f. 7. 8.

Marine: Zanzibar! Celebes (Atl.), Society Islands!

This form differs from *var. Pandura* by its shorter, less constricted valves.

Var. *Didelta* Cl. — V. slightly constricted, with almost triangular segments. L. 0,085; B. 0,04; at the constriction 0,028 mm. Costæ 8 in 0,01 mm. — Pl. II f. 8.

Marine: Sumbava (Kinker Coll.)!

Var. *subelliptica* Cl. — V. elongated, not at all, or very slightly, constricted. L. 0,15; B. 0,052. Costæ 3 to 4 in 0,01 mm. alternating with double rows of coarse puncta, about 8 in 0,01 mm. — Pl. II f. 11.

Marine: South America, fossil! Macassar Straits (corroded form with 4 to 5 costæ in 0,01 mm. in Grove Coll.)! Galapagos Islands (perfectly elliptical form. L. 0,08; B. 0,04 mm. Costæ 5 in 0.01 mm. Ocelli not distinct).

Var.? *Pandurella* Cl. — V. strongly constricted with subelliptical segments. L. 0,038 to 0,075; B. 0.011 to 0,022; at the constriction 0,007 to 0.013 mm. Costæ 8 to 9 in 0,01 mm. alternating with double rows of puncta, about 20 in 0.01 mm. Rows of ocelli indistinct. — Pl. II f. 9.

Marine: Indian Ocean (Deby Coll.)! China! Galapagos Islands!

This form resembles in all respects the *var. Pandura*, but is much smaller and has closer costæ. As I have not seen any rows of ocelli I am doubtful whether this form is to be regarded as belonging to this group; nevertheless it is related to the *var. Pandura* as the *var. suspecta* to the *var. separabilis* and the *var. Dirhombus* to the *var. multicostata*.

B. *Forms with moderately vide lunulæ.*

Var. *separabilis* A. S. (1875). — V. gently constricted with elliptical segments. L. 0,08 to 0,16; B. 0.033 to 0,05; at the constriction 0,026 to 0,032 mm. Costæ 5 to 6 in 0,01 mm. Lunulæ narrow. — *Nav. Crabro* Grev. M. J. V. p. 7 Pl. III f. 11. *Nav. Grevillei* Donk. B. D. p. 47. *Nav. separabilis* A. S. Atl. XI f. 3, 5, 6, 7, 10, 17. — *N. Crabro var. Japonica* A. S. Atl. CLXXIV f. 4?

Marine: Pelew Island (Atl.). Singapore (Deby Coll.)! Puerto Caballo (Atl.), Campeachy Bay (Atl.), Trinidad (Grev.).

This form is intermediate between *var. Pandura* and *var. multicostata*.

Var. *hungarica* Cl. — V. elliptical, not constricted. L. 0,06; B. 0.03 mm. Row of ocelli marginal, not bent toward the central nodule. Costæ 5 in 0.01 mm. Lunulæ narrow. Pl. II f. 10.

Marine: Szákal (Hungary, fossil)! Galapagos Islands!

Var. *gloriosa* Brun (1891). - V. slightly constricted, vith tongue-shaped segments. L. 0,11 to 0,2; B. 0.04 to 0,074: at the constriction 0,025 to 0,06 mm. Central nodule large. Lunulæ narrow. Costæ 3 to 3.5 in 0.01 mm. alternating with double rows of large puncta, about 8 in 0,01 mm. Ocelli usually indistinct. — *Nav. gloriosa* Brun D. esp. n. p. 34 Pl. XV f. 8.

Marine: Mexillones Bolivia! Hakodadi, Japan (Deby Coll.)!

This is the stoutest and most beautiful of all the forms of *D. Crabro*. The outline varies. Some specimens are deeply and abruptly constricted, others scarcely constricted. The ocelli are usually not distinct, but in some specimens easily seen. The breadth of the lunulæ is also variable.

Var.? *suspecta* A. S. (1875). — V. strongly constricted, with elliptical segments. L. 0.046 to 0,092; B. 0,012 to 0,03; at the constriction 0,006 to 0.016 mm. Costæ 5 in 0,01 mm. Ocelli not distinct. — *Nav. suspecta* A. S. Atl. XI f. 12, 13. 26, 27. *Nav. gloriosa var. inflata* Brun D. esp. n. p. 34 Pl. XV f. 12.

Marine: Manilla (Deby Coll.)! Singapore (Van Heurck Coll.)! Java! Japan (Atl.), Galapagos Islands! Mexillones, Bolivia (Brun Coll.)! Campeachy Bay (Atl.).

I have placed this form among the varieties of *D. Crabro*, only with hesitation, as I never observed on it the marginal row of ocelli, by which the other forms are characterized.

To this group of forms belongs probably *D. ornata* (*Nav. ornata* A. S. Atl. LXIX f. 5. *N. ornata spirifera* A. S. Atl. CLXXXIV f. 25) from S:ta Monica and Monterey in California. It is a large and beautiful form, of which only corroded specimens seem to be known. At least I have hitherto not seen any uninjured specimen.

C. *Forms with broad lunulæ.*

Var. *multicostata* Grun. (1860). — V. strongly constricted, with elliptical to rhomboid segments. L. 0,09 to 0,21; B. 0,03 to 0,06; at the constriction 0,018 mm. Lunulæ very broad. Costæ 4 to 5 in 0,01 mm. — *Nav. multicostata* Grun. Verh. 1860 p. 524 Pl. III f. 13. A. S. Atl. XI f. 14, 15, 16, 18, 19, 20, CLXXIV f. 6, 7. *Nav. Crabro* A. S. Atl. LXIX f. 1, 2. V. H. Syn. p. 83 Pl. IX f. 2. A. S. N. S. D. Pl. I f. 5, 6 II f. 4 (corroded). *Nav. crabro var. oranensis* Atl. LXIX f. 3 (corroded). *Nav. polita* Brun D. esp. n. p. 37 Pl XV f. 1 (corroded).

Marine: North Sea (Norway)! Mediterranean Sea! Red Sea! Madagascar! Ceylon! Labuan! Java! Samoa! Sandwich Islands (Atl.)! Galapagos Islands! Cape Horn (Petit)! West Indies! Fossil Hungary! Moravian Tegel! Oran (Atl.). Ægina (Atl.), Nankoori! S:ta Monica Cal.

Var. *nankoorensis* Grun. (1881). - V. less constricted, with cuneate ends. L. 0,12; B. 0,053; at the constriction 0,042 mm. Costæ 4,5 in 0,01 mm. — *Nav. Crabro var. nankoor.* A. S. Atl. LXIX f. 4 (corroded).

Marine: Nankoori, fossil (Atl.).

Var. *O'Meari* Grun. Ms. -- V. elliptical, not constricted. L. 0,135; B. 0,058 mm. Lunulæ very broad. Costæ parallel, 4 in 0,01 mm. — Pl. II f. 12.

Marine: Macassar Straits (Grove Coll.)! Seychelles (Grun.), South Sea (Van Heurck Coll.)!

Grunow sent me several years ago a sketch of an elliptical Diploneis from Seychelles under the name of *Nav. O'Mearii*, which agrees in essential points with the form from Macassar Straits, having, as it has, very broad lunulæ, filling almost the whole valve. L. 0,09; B. 0,03 mm. Costæ 6 in 0,01 mm.

Var.? *Gibelii* A. S. (1874). — V. slightly constricted, with tongue-shaped segments. L. 0,09; B. 0,033; at the constriction 0,026 mm. Lunulæ broad, forming a biconstricted space. Costæ 4 in 0,01 mm. — *Nav. Gibelii* A. S. Probet. f. 13 Pl. XII f. 73.

Marine: Campeachy Bay (Atl.).

Var. *minuta* Cl. — L. 0,056; B. 0,024; at the constr. 0,016 mm. Costæ 6 in 0,01 mm. A. S. Atl. XII f. 71.

Marine: Samoa (Atl.).

Var. *perpusilla* Cl. — L. 0,04; B. 0,018; at the constriction 0,012 mm. Costæ 8 in 0,01 mm. — A. S. Atl. XII f. 72.

Marine: North Sea (Atl.).

Var.? *confecta* A. S. (1875). — V. small. L. 0,04; B. 0,009; at the constriction 0,0075 mm. Lunulæ very large. Costæ 9 in 0,01 mm. — *Nav. confecta* A. S. Atl. XII f. 46.

Marine: Campeachy Bay (Atl.).

Var.? *Dirhombus* A. S. (1875). — V. strongly constricted, with subrhomboid segments. L. 0,076 to 0,13; B. 0,024 to 0,038; at the constriction 0,012 to 0,015 mm. Lunulæ large, lunate. Costæ 4 to 6 in 0,01 mm Ocelli not distinct. *Nav. Dirh.* A. S. Atl. XI f. 21, 22; LXIX f. 9 (10 corroded).

Marine: Gulf of Mexico (Atl.), Pelew Island (Atl.).

The connection of this form with the others is not certain, as the figures in Atl. do not shew the marginal row of ocelli. It seems as if this form were to *var. multicostata* what *var. suspecta* is to *var. separabilis*. *Dipl. coarctata* may be a corroded *Dirhombus*, which however am unable to decide, not having had an opportunity of comparing specimens.

79. **D. biseriata** Cl. N. Sp. — V. elliptical or slightly constricted. L. 0,11 to 0,13; B. 0,047 to 0,06 mm. Central nodule large, quadrate, its horns almost parallel. Furrows linear,

narrow, with a row of large granules, formed by the continuation of the costæ. Costæ 3 to 4 in 0,01 mm. alternating with double rows of coarse puncta. Lunulæ none or narrow. Ocelli forming a marginal band, and, besides, a band along the furrows or lunulæ.

This species, which is intermediate between *D. Crabro* and *D. vagabunda*, differs from *D. Crabro* in nothing but the double rows of ocelli. The form of the valve is variable, usually elliptical, but in some specimens panduriform. The lunulæ are indistinct in some forms, narrow in others. It would be admissible to group the forms of this species together with the forms of *D. Crabro*. The *var. Kinkeriana* and *galapagensis* are analogous to the Pandura-series, the *var. lata* to the separabilis-series.

Var. *Galapagensis* CL. — V. not constricted, elliptical. L. 0,12; B. 0,05 mm. Costæ 4 in 0,01 mm. alternating with double rows of coarse puncta. Lunulæ very narrow. Ocelli forming a marginal and an interior row. — Pl. II f. 16.

Marine: Galapagos Islands!

Var. *lata* CL. — V. elliptical, not constricted. L. 0,11; B. 0,048 mm. Costæ 4 in 0,01 mm. Lunulæ moderately broad. — Pl. II f. 14.

Marine: Galapagos Islands!

The fig. 12 Pl. CLXXIV in A. S. Atl. represents doubtless a small, but strongly corroded form of *D. biseriata*.

80. **D. vagabunda** BRUN (1892). — V. panduriform with tongue-shaped segments. L. 0,13 to 0,17; B. 0,06; at the constriction 0,043 mm. Central nodule large, quadrate; its horns nearly parallel. Furrows narrow, linear, with a row of large granules. Lunulæ very narrow or not distinct. Costæ 3 to 4 in 0,01 mm., alternating with double rows of coarse puncta. Ocelli forming a marginal band and several oblique or curved rows besides. — *Nav. vagabunda* BRUN A. S. Atl. CLXXIV f. 5. *Dipl. vag.* Icon. n. Pl. II f. 13, 15.

Marine: Tamatave (Kinker Coll.)! Fossil: S:ta Monica, S:n Pedro (Kinker Coll.) Calif.!

D. vagabunda is a transitional form from *D. biseriata* to *D. gemmatula* (*var. Beyrichiana*).

81. **D. prisca** A. S. (1875). — V. slightly constricted, with tongue-shaped or cuneate, obtuse segments. L. 0,07 to 0,08; B. 0,029 to 0,03 mm., at the constriction 0,02 to 0,027 mm. Central nodule quadrate; its horns parallel and approximate. Furrows narrow, linear, with a row of large puncta. Transverse costæ 7 to 8 in 0,01 mm. alternating with double rows of puncta, about 16 in 0,01 mm. and ocelli, 4 to 5 in 0,01 mm. — *Nav. prisca* A. S. Atl. Pl. XII f. 66 to 68 (69?).

Marine: Nottingham (Maryland)! Atlantic City, N. Jers. (Grove Coll.), Richmond, Va! always fossil.

This species is very nearly akin to *D. gemmatula* from which it differs by the narrow furrows. The exterior stratum with small alternating puncta is usually preserved in *D. prisca*, but never found on *D. gemmatula*, which may be a consequence of the state of preservation and preparation.

82. **D. gemmatula** GRUN. (1875). — V. slightly constricted, with tongue-shaped to broadly cuneate segments. L. 0,07 to 0,15; B. 0,033 to 0,062; at the constr. 0,027 to 0,05 mm. Central nodule large; its horns almost parallel. Furrows usually broad, and somewhat dilated in the middle, with a row of large puncta. Costæ 5 to 7 in 0,01 mm. alternating with rows of more or less numerous, large ocelli.

Var. *hungarica* CL. — V. moderately constricted. L. 0,08; B. 0,025; at the constr. 0,018 mm. Ocelli forming one row along the margin and one along furrows.

Marine: Szákal, Hungary, fossil!

Akin to *Nav. expedita* A. S. (Atl. LXIX f. 6) from Moron.

Var. *Grunowii* CL. — V. very slightly constricted, with broad tongue-shaped segments. L. 0.07 to 0,09; B. 0,033 to 0,039; at the constr. 0,03 to 0,037 mm. Furrows very broad. Costæ 5,5 to 7 in 0,01 mm. alternating with ocelli, forming some few more or less undulating, longitudinal rows. — *Nav. gemmatula* GRUN. A. S. Atl. XIII f. 20, 21 (37, 40?). *Nav. lacrimans* A. S. Atl. XII f. 61.

Marine: Balearic Islands! Red Sea! Mauritius! Tamatave! Sumatra! Yokohama! Samoa! Campeachy Bay (Atl.). Fossil: Moravian Tegel! S:ta Monica, Calif. (Deby Coll.)!

Var. *lacrimans* A. S. (1875). — V. elongated, slightly constricted in the middle. L. 0,09 to 0,14; B. 0,031 to 0,045; at the constr. 0,025 to 0,04 mm. Furrows broad. Costæ 5 in 0,01 mm. Ocelli about 4 in 0,01 mm., forming longitudinal rows. — *Nav. lacrimans* A. S. Atl. XII f. 59, 60. *Nav. gemmatula* CL. D. of Mor. Tegel Pl. XII f. 1. *Nav. lacr. var. fossilis* PANT. II p. 49 Pl. II f. 18. *Nav. Taschenbergeri* A. S. Atl. CLXXXIV f. 8 (1892).

Marine: Tamatave (Deby Coll.)! Campeachy Bay! Colon! Fossil: Szákal, Hungary! Moravian Tegel!

Var. *Beyrichiana* A. S. (1861). — V. slightly constricted, with cuneate ends. L. 0,09 to 0,144; B. 0,35 to 0,062; at the constr. 0,027 to 0,053 mm. Furrows of median breadth, distinctly dilated around the central nodule. Costæ 6 in 0,01 mm. alternating with rows of large ocelli (about 5 in 0,01 mm.). — *Nav. Beyrichiana* A. S. Atl. LXIX f. 16, 17.

Marine: Gulf of Naples! Madagascar! Java! China! Indian Ocean (Deby Coll.)! Cape Horn (Petit). Fossil: Hungary! Ægina (Atl.).

Forma minor PANT. (1886). — V. nearly elliptical. L. 0,069; B. 0,034 mm. Costæ and ocelli about 5,5 in 0,01 mm. — *Nav. Beyr. var. minor* PANT. I p. 23 Pl. III f. 31.

Marine: Hungary, fossil (Petit).

Var. *Moravica* CL. — V. slightly constricted, with broad, cuneate ends. L. 0,16; B. 0,068; at the constr. 0,06 mm. Costæ 4 in 0,01 mm. Ocelli scattered, 2 to 3 in 0,01 mm.

Marine: Moravian Tegel (Deby Coll.)!

83. **D. lesinensis** GRUN. Ms. — V. elongated, usually very slightly constricted, with broad, tongue-shaped segments. L. 0,072 to 0,22; B. 0,03 to 0,057; at the constr. 0,028 to 0,051 mm. Central nodule small, its horns parallel, approximate. Furrows narrow, linear, scarcely dilated in the middle, with a row of large puncta or rudiments of the costæ. Costæ 5 to 6 in 0,01 mm. alternating with rows of large and close ocelli (5 to 7 in 0,01 mm.) and double rows of small, sometimes little distinct, alveoli (about 12 to 18 in 0,01 mm.). — Pl. II f. 17, 18.

Marine: Balearic Islands! Gulf of Naples! Adriatic! Red Sea! Sumatra (Deby Coll.)! Philippines (Rae Coll.).

D. lesinenses has the form and appearance of a large *D. Entomon*.

Additional.

Navicula Budayana PANT. III Pl. IV f. 57 (1893) seems to belong to the varieties of *D. elliptica*.

Navicula elliptica var. fossilis PANT. III Pl. II f. 32 perhaps a small form of *D. Smithii*, which I am unable to decide as the minute structure is not visible on the figure.

Navicula perrasta PANT. III Pl. XXXVI f. 510 a large form, very similar to *D. major var. permagna*, but the alveoli are drawn as forming single rows.

Scoliopleura Grun. (1860).

Valve elongated, convex. Median line sigmoid. Central nodule small. Median line enclosed between two approximate longitudinal lines or ridges. Structure, fine puncta disposed in transverse and longitudinal rows. Connecting zone simple or without longitudinal divisions.

The genus Scoliopleura was founded 1860 by Grunow (Verh. p. 554) for Naviculæ with sigmoid median line, such as *Nav. Jenneri* and *Nav. convexa* W. Sm. (B. D.), with the bent of the lines of both valves in contrary directions. The genus comprises very different forms, so that I have separated from it forms without longitudinal ridges along the median line. *Sc. convexa* (or *latestriata*) differs from the other species by its structure, for which reason I have formed for it the genus *Scoliotropis*. With regard to the affinities, *Scoliopleura*, as defined above, appears to be distantly allied to *Caloneis*, and to *Diploneis*.

1. **S. Schneideri** Grun. (1878). — V. elliptic-lanceolate, subacute. L. 0,14; B. 0,04 mm. Median line slightly sigmoid. Median pores in opposite directions. Terminal nodules small. Transverse striæ 18 (14 according to Grun.) in 0,01 mm. oblique, distinctly punctate, puncta forming longitudinal, undulating rows, 14 (13 according to Grun.) in 0,01 mm. — *Nav. Schn.* Grun. Casp. Sea Alg. p. 16 Pl. III f. 1.

Brackish water: Caspian Sea!

This is a very remarkable form. The median transverse striæ form oblique lines across the valve, as in some forms of Neidium; at the ends they are almost parallel.

2. **S. Peisonis** Grun. (1860). — V. narrow, elliptical, with rounded ends. L. 0,035 to 0,08; B. 0,01 to 0,018 mm. Median line strongly sigmoid. Striæ 14 to 16 in 0,01 mm., transverse, distinctly punctate; puncta forming regular, longitudinal striæ, 18 in 0,01 mm. — Grun. Verh. 1860 p. 554 Pl. V f. 25. — Icon. N. Pl. I f. 14.

Brackish water: Neusiedler See, Hungary (Grun.), Salt Lake, Utah!

3. **S. elegans** Cl. N. Sp. — V. slightly sigmoid, lanceolate, gradually tapering from the middle to the somewhat obtuse ends. L. 0,15; B. 0,03 mm. Median line sigmoid at the ends; its central pores approximate; its terminal fissures in contrary directions. Longitudinal lines closely approximate to the median line. Central area indistinct. Transverse striæ 17, longitudinal 25 in 0,01 mm. — Pl. I f. 9.

Marine: Java!

Naviculæ Fusiformes Cl.

Valve narrow, linear to lanceolate, usually thin or slightly silicious. Median line with closely approximate central pores. Axial and central areas indistinct. Striæ parallel, usually fine, not crossed by longitudinal lines, finely punctate; puncta usually arranged in longitudinal, straight rows.

This small group comprises both marine and brackish forms, akin to *N. inornata* of the Section *Naviculæ entoleiæ*, which also has approximate central pores. On the other hand this group is also allied to the Section *Naviculæ orthostichæ*.

Artificial key.

1. { Valve attenuated towards the ends, narrow lanceolate . . . . 2.
{ — linear, with broad ends . . . . 5.

2. { Ends subcapitate . . . . *N. nuda* PANT.
   { — acute . . . . 3.

3. { Striæ about 12 in 0,01 mm. . . . . *N. lucida* PANT.
   { — 17 — . . . . *N. Schmidtii* LAGST.
   { — — 24 — . . . . *N. Acus* CL.
   { — — 30 — . . . . 4.

4. { Longitudinal striæ closer than the transverse . . . . *N. fusiformis* GRUN.
   { — — more distant . . . . *N. Frauenfeldii* GRUN.

5. { Ends rostrate . . . . *N. crassirostris* GRUN.
   { — obtuse or truncate . . . . 6.

6. { Terminal fissures in contrary directions . . . . 7.
   { — — indistinct . . . . *N. Lineola* GRUN.

7. { Striæ all parallel . . . . *N. parallelistriata* PANT.
   { Median striæ radiate . . . . *N. heteroflexa* PANT.

1. **N. fusiformis** GRUN. (1877). — V. narrow, lanceolate, gradually tapering from the middle to the acute ends. L. 0,115 to 0,15; B. 0.01 mm. Central pores very approximate. Striæ transverse, 33 in 0,01 mm., longitudinal 36 in 0,01 mm. — *Berkeleya Fusidium* GRUN. Hedw. 1867 p. 17. *Amphipleura danica* KÜTZ Bac. p. 103 Pl. XXX f. 38 (1844)? *N. fus.* GRUN. M. J. 1877 p. 178 Pl. CXCV f. 11.

Marine: Honduras (Grun.).

Var. *ostrearia* GAILLON (1820). — L. 0,068 to 0,073; B. 0,006 to 0,007 mm. Striæ transverse 36 in 0,01 mm. — *Vibrio ostrearius* GAILLON (accord. to Grun.). — *Nav. ostrearia* Turp. Dict. d'hist. nat. 11 Pl. 1 f. 2 (accord. to Grun.). *N. fusif. v. ostrearia* GRUN. M. M. J. 1877 p. 178 Pl. CXCV f. 12. V. H. Syn. Pl. XIV f. 33.

Marine: North Sea (West coast of Sweden)! Loire infér. (Grun.), Marseille (Grun.), Triest (Grun.).

This species lives on oyster-beds and according to BORNET the oysters become greenish by feeding on this diatom. Living frustules have two chromatophore-plates along the connecting zone. The cell-sap has, especially towards the ends, a peculiar blue colour.

2. **N. Frauenfeldii** GRUN. (1863). — V. lanceolate. L. 0,1 to 0,16; B. 0,019 to 0,025 mm. Central pores very approximate. Transverse striæ 29 in 0,01 mm., longitudinal more distant. — *Amphipleura Frauenfeldii* GRUN. Verh. 1863 p. 144 Pl. V f. 8. *N. Frauenf.* GRUN. M. M. J. 1877 p. 179.

Marine: Indian Ocean (Grun.).

3. **N. nuda** PANT. (1889). — V. narrow, lanceolate, with subcapitate ends. L. 0,037; B. 0,007 mm. Striæ not observed. — PANT. II p. 51 Pl. VI f. 108.

Brackish water: Hungary, fossil (Pant.).

This species is unknown to me and the description and figure are not sufficient for diagnosis.

4. **N. Acus** CL. N. Sp. — V. narrow, lanceolate, acute. L. 0,09; B. 0,009 mm. Central pores approximate. Terminal fissures elongated. Axial and central areas indistinct. Striæ 24 to 25 in 0,01 mm., equidistant, in the middle slightly radiate, elsewhere transverse, or nearly so — Pl. III f. 29, 30.

Marine: Balearic Islands!

As *N. Acus* CL. 1880 (A. D.) is the same as *N. inornata* GRUN. the name Acus may be used for this form, which differs from *N. fusoides* GRUN. (1880) by the absence of longitudinal lines and by its indistinct area.

5. **N. Schmidtii** LAGST. (1876). — V. narrow, lanceolate, with somewhat obtuse ends. L. 0,06 to 0,075; B. 0,009 to 0,011 mm. Central pores approximate. Striæ about 17 in 0,01 mm., transverse. — N. (without name) A. S. N. S. D. Pl. III f. 7, 8 (1874). *N. Schm.* Ldt. Boh. D. p. 45.

Marine: Bohuslän (Ldt).

I do not know this species, which seems doubtful. The fig. in A. S. is not sufficient, and the description of LAGERSTEDT may belong to some form of *Nav.* (Schizonema) *ramosissima*. The fig. 7 in A. S. shews two longitudinal lines crossing the striæ on each side of the median line, which suggests some affinity to Caloneis, if this character is not due to an optical illusion.

6. **N. lucida** PANT. (1893). — V. narrow, lanceolate, subacute. L. 0,2; B. 0,022 mm. Axial area very narrow, not dilated in the middle. Transverse striæ 12 in 0,01 mm. almost parallel throughout. — PANT. III Pl. XVIII f. 264.

Habitat? »Bodas» fossil (Pant.).

Under the name *N. inculta* Pantocsek figures (III Pl. XIV f. 216) a similar, but smaller and more finely striate form, with subrostrate ends.

7. **N. parallelistriata** PANT. (1889). — V. linear, attenuated towards the broad, obtuse ends. L. 0,069; B. 0,017 mm. Central pores approximate, terminal in contrary directions. Axial area linear, narrow. Striæ 17,5 in 0,01 mm. parallel. — PANT. II p. 52 Pl. II f. 26.

Brackish water: Hungary, fossil (Pant.).

8. **N. heteroflexa** PANT. (1889). — V. linear-lanceolate, with broad, rounded ends. L. 0,074 to 0,11; B. 0,011 to 0,013 mm. Median pores approximate; terminal in contrary directions. Axial area very narrow, linear. Striæ 22 (28 accord. to Pant.) in 0,01 mm. (the median shorter than the others) radiate in the middle, parallel towards the ends. — PANT. II p. 47 Pl. II f. 34.

Brackish water: Hungary, fossil!

Var. *constricta* PANT. (1889). — V. slightly constricted in the middle, with cuneate ends. L. 0,05 to 0,06; B. 0,011 to 0,012 mm. Striæ 25 to 30 in 0,01 mm. — PANT. Pl. II f. 27, 33.

Brackish water: Hungary, fossil (Pant.).

Var. *minor* PANT. (1889). — V. linear-lanceolate. L. 0,048; B. 0,0095 mm. Striæ 22 to 25 in 0,01 mm. — PANT. II Pl. IX f. 162.

Brackish water: Hungary, fossil (Pant.).

This species is one of the most remarkable Naviculæ. Although in some respects divergent from the rest of this group, especially by its radiate median striæ, I have placed it here, as it seems to be more akin to N. parallelistriata than to any other species.

9. **N. crassirostris** GRUN. (1880). — V. linear, with prolonged, rostrate and obtuse ends. L. 0,046; B. 0,0073 mm. Median line with approximate central pores. Areas indistinct. Striæ transverse, 27 in 0,01 mm. — GRUN. A. D. p. 45 Pl. III f. 57.

Brackish water: Kara (Grun.).

Var. *Maasöensis* GRUN. (1880). — More elongated and with narrower ends. Striæ about 25 in 0,01 mm. — GRUN. A. D. p. 46.

Marine: Finmark (Grun.).

10. **N. Lincola** GRUN. — (1884). — V. linear with rounded ends. L. 0,016 to 0,051; B. 0,0025 to 0,003 mm. Central pores approximate. Striæ extremely fine(?) — GRUN. Franz Jos. Land D. p. 104 (52) Pl. I f. 45, 46.

Marine: Franz Josephs Land (Grun.).

Var. *perlepida* GRUN. (1884). — V. with somewhat constricted ends. L. 0,02 to 0,034; B. 0,002 to 0,0033 mm. — *N. perlepida* GRUN. Franz Jos. Land, D. p. 104 (52) Pl. I f. 44.

Marine: Franz Josephs Land (Grun.).

Naviculæ Orthostichæ CL.

Valve usually elongated, lanceolate to linear. Median line with small or elongated central nodule, sometimes transversely dilated into a stauros, and with small or indistinct terminal fissures.

Central pores of the median line approximate. Structure: small puncta arranged in parallel, transverse and longitudinal rows, crossing each other at a right angle. Axial and central areas small or indistinct. Connecting zone not complex.

This group is closely related to the Section Fusiformes, by the approximate central pores and the structure of the valve, but the longitudinal striæ of the valve are less distinct in Fusiformes. Some forms of Orthostichæ seem to be connected with *Gyrosigma*. The smaller forms of this section, *Nav. gregaria* to *N. microrhynchus*, have no distinct longitudinal striæ, but have been placed here, as they seem to be connected with *Nav. halophila*. On the other hand they appear to come near to *Nav. cryptocephala* of the section Lineolatæ. Some species have transversely dilated central nodules, and have been considered as belonging to the genus *Stauroneis*, but there is very little resemblance between there forms and the true *Stauroneis* (division of *Microstigmaticæ*), in the structure of the valve, which is the same as in other orthostichæ.

Artificial key.

1.	Central nodule dilated into a stauros	11.
	— not —	2.
2.	Longitudinal striæ indistinct	3.
	— — distinct	6.
3.	Striæ uninterrupted in the middle	4.
	— interrupted	5.
4.	Ends acute	*N. microrhynchus* GRUN.
	— rostrate to capitate	*N. gregaria* DONK.
5.	Striæ crossed by a longitudinal depression	*N. Wankaremæ* CL.
	— not — — —	*N. Kryokonites* CL.
6.	Terminal striæ convergent	*N. halophila* GRUN.
	— — not —	7.
7.	Valve broadly linear, with broad ends	*N. portomontana* CL.
	linear or lanceolate, narrowed towards the end	8.
8.	Transverse striæ more distant than the longitudinal	*N. cuspidata* KÜTZ.
	— closer — — —	*N. Perrottetii* GRUN.
	— equidistant with —	9.
9.	Ends acute	*N. vitrea* CL.
	— rounded	10.
10.	Striæ 15 in 0,01 mm.	*N. Kjellmanii* CL.
	— closer	*N. O'Mearii* GRUN.
11.	Stauros short	*N. balearica* CL.
	reaching half way to the margin	*N. quarnerensis* GRUN.
	pervious — — —	12.
12.	Valve rhombic-lanceolate	*N. Stodderi* GREENL.
	— linear or linear-lanceolate	13.
13.	Longitudinal striæ more distant than the transverse	*N. sulcata* CL.
	— — closer — — —	14.
14.	Transverse striæ 12 in 0,01 mm.	*N. crucigera* W. SM.
	— — about 26 in 0,01 mm.	*N. Spicula* HICKIE.

1. **N. gregaria** DONK. (1861). V. lanceolate, with rostrate-capitate ends. L. 0,015 to 0,035; B. 0,005 to 0,009 mm. Transverse striæ 16 to 22 in 0,01 mm. Longitudinal striæ indistinct. DONK. M. J. I p. 10 Pl. I f. 10. B. D. p. 43 Pl. VI f. 13. V. H. Syn. p. 85 Pl. VIII f. 12 15. *Nav. cryptocephala* W. SM. B. D. Pl. XVII f. 155. Pedicino Ischia II f. 9—11: *Nav. lanceolata* W. SM. B. D. p. 46 Pl. XXXI f. 272? *Nav. veneta* SCHUM. P. D. II N. Pl. II f. 30. *Nav. Granum Arenæ* SCHUM. P. D. N. II p. 56 Pl. II f. 36 (1867)?

Brackish water: Sweden (Bohuslän)! England! Saxony (Salines Dürrenberg)! Belgium (V. H.) France! South Africa! Argentina!

Var. *thurholmensis* DANNF. (1882). — V. lanceolate, with more distinctly capitate ends. L. 0,02; B. 0,005 mm. Striæ 26 in 0,01 mm. — *Nav. thurholmensis* DANNF. Balt. D. p. 27 Pl. 1 f. 11. *N. lævis* PANT. II p. 50 Pl. XXV f. 366?

Brackish water: Bay of Finland (Danuf.).

N. gregaria connects *N. cryptocephala* of the section Lineolatæ with *N. halophila*, so that it might perhaps have been placed as well there as here. Its parallel striæ seem however to indicate a closer relation to *N. halophila*.

2. **N. Wankaremæ** CL. (1883). — V. narrow, lanceolate, with obtuse, prolonged ends. L. 0,035; B. 0,007 mm. Median line with approximate median pores. Axial area indistinct. Central area a broad, transverse fascia. Striæ parallel, about 30 in 0,01 mm., obsolete between the margin and the median line. Longitudinal striæ not seen. — *N. Kryokonites? var. Wankaremæ* CL. Vega p. 473 Pl. XXXVII, f. 47.

Marine: Cape Wankarema, North Siberian Sea!

The accurate place in the system, which this form occupies, is difficult to decide. I have placed it here, at it seems to be nearest akin to *N. gregaria*.

3. **N. Kryokonites** CL. (1883). — V. lanceolate, obtuse. L. 0,084; B. 0,011 mm. Central area a transverse, broad fascia. Striæ 22 in 0,01 mm. — CL. Vega p. 473 Pl. XXXVII f. 44.

Marine: Cape Wankarema!

Var. *subprotracta* CL. (1883). — V. rhombic-lanceolate, with subcapitate ends. L. 0,033; B. 0,007 mm. Striæ 22 in 0,01 mm. — CL. Vega l. c. f. 46.

Marine: Cape Wankarema!

Var. *semiperfecta* CL. (1883). — V. rhombic-lanceolate. L. 0,028; B. 0,008 mm. Central area a unilateral fascia. — CL. Vega l. c. f. 45.

Marine: Cape Wankarema!

4. **N. microrhynchus** GRUN. (1882). — V. narrow lanceolate, with acute, prolonged ends. L. 0,024; B. 0,004 mm. Median pores approximate. Striæ 16 (middle) to 17 (ends) finely punctate. — GRUN. Foss. D. Öst. Ung. p. 149 Pl. XXX f. 46.

Slightly brackish water: Hungary, fossil (Grun.).

N. microrhynchus is according to Grunow related to *N. Baluheimii*, which I have placed among the Microstigmaticæ because of its wider central striæ and its, (somewhat indistinct) complex, connecting zone. *N. microrhynchus* PANT. (II p. 51 Pl. III f. 38; Pl. VIII f. 145, 1889) is, if the figures in Pantocsek's work be accurate, not the species of Grunow, which has no axial area.

5. **N. halophila** GRUN. (1881). — V. rhombic-lanceolate, subacute. L. 0.05; B. 0,01 to 0,012 mm. Striæ 19 to 20 (16 according to V. H. Syn.) in 0,01 mm. convergent at the ends, elsewhere parallel. Longitudinal striæ fine. — *N. cuspidata var. haloph.* GRUN. in V. H. Syn. p. 100 Suppl. Pl. B. f. 30. *N. protracta forma minor* PANT. III Pl. XX f. 301 (1893)?

Brackish water: Sweden, Sturkö in Blekinge! England, Hull! Belgium (V. H.) Saxony (Mansfelderseen)! France, Medoc!

6. **N. cuspidata** KÜTZ. (1834). — V. rhombic-lanceolate, with acute ends. L. 0,07 to 0,15; B. 0,017 to 0,03 mm. Transverse striæ 14 to 19, longitudinal 26 in 0,01 mm. *Bacillaria fulva* NITSZCH. p. p. 1817 (according to Kütz.). *N. fulva* DONK. B. D. Pl. VI f. 9? *Frustulia cuspidata* KÜTZ. Syn. Pl. II f. 26. *Nav. cuspidata* KÜTZ. Bac. p. 94 Pl. III f. 24, 37. W. SM. B. D. I p. 47 Pl. XVI f. 131. DONK. B. D. p. 39 Pl. VI f. 6. GRUN. Banka D. Pl. II f. 16. Fresenius Senckenb. Abh. IV Pl. IV f. 18. Ströse Klicken f. 22. V. H. Syn. p. 100 Pl. XII f. 4. *Nav. Reinickeana* RABH. Alg. Sachs. N:o 802 (1859). *Vanheurckia cuspidata* BRÉB. Ann. Soc. phyto. et microgr. de Belgique Vol. I p. 205 (1868).

Fresh water: Sweden! Finland! Germany! France! Switzerland! Bengal! Japan! New Zealand! Australia (Murray River)! Guatemala, fossil! Ecuador! Dakota! Illinois!

Var. *danaica* Grun. Ms. — Smaller, with somewhat obtuse ends. L. 0,07 to 0,09; B. 0,017 to 0,02 mm. Transverse striæ 16 to 17, longitudinal 21 to 27 in 0,01 mm.

Fresh water: Greenland! Danas pond, Massachusetts (Grun.).

Var. *ambigua* Ehb. (1843). — Lanceolate, rostrate. Striæ finer. — *Nav. amb.* Ehb. Am. II: 2, f. 9? Ktz. Bac. p. 95 Pl. XXVIII f. 66. W. Sm. B. D. I Pl. XVI f. 149. Donk. B. D. p. 39 Pl. VI f. 5. Pedicino Ischia D. Pl. II f. 4, 6. V. H. Syn. p. 100 Pl. XII f. 5. *N. sphærophora* Donk. B. D. Pl. V f. 10? *N. birostrata* Greg. M. J. III p. 40 Pl. IV f. 15 (1855). *N. quarnerensis* Grun. Verh. 1860 p. 530 Pl. III f. 8? *Vanheurckia amb.* Bréb. Ann. Soc. phyto. et micro. de Belgique I p. 206 (1868).

Fresh water: Sweden! Belgium (V. H.), Italy (Pedic.), Japan! New Zealand! Argentina!

Var. *Héribaudi* Perag. (1893). — Median striæ somewhat radiate and more distant than in the type. — Hérib. D. d'Auvergne p. 108 Pl. IV f. 16.

Fresh water: Auvergne, fossil.

As *Bacillaria fulva* Nitzsch is an older name than *N. cuspidata*, it would have been more correct to name this species *N. fulva*, but on the other hand it is so extremely difficult to make out what the names of the older authors denote, and the name *N. cuspidata* has been so commonly adopted, that to do so would make the synonymy still more intricate. I prefer therefore the generally accepted name. *N. cuspidata* is variable as to the outline, and it can hardly by doubted that *N. cuspidata* and *N. ambigua* should be united into one species. It frequently occurs in the forms of *N. cuspidata* that the interior of the valve is provided with strong transverse costæ. Such monstrosities have been named *Surirella craticula* Ehb., *Craticula Ehrenbergii* Grun., *Stictodesmis craticula* L. Sm. *Stictodesmis Febigerii* (Deby Coll. = craticular state of the var. danaica). Their true nature has been shewn by Pfitzer (Bau u. Entw. p. 104). See also Hériband D. de d'Auvergne p. 107 Pl. IV f. 15.

7. **N. Perrotettii** Grun. (1867). — V. rhombic-lanceolate, with slightly rostrate ends. L. 0,12 to 0,185; B. 0,03 to 0,04 mm. Transverse striæ 13 to 14, longitudinal striæ 11 to 12 in 0,01 mm. *Craticula Perrotettii* Grun. Nov. p. 20 Pl. I f. 21. *Nav. Perrotettii* Grun. M. J. 1877 p. 172. — Icon. n. Pl. III f. 12. *Nav. Pangeroni* Leud. Fortm. D. de la Malaisie p. 52 Pl. II f. 9.

Slightly brackish water: Italy (Grun.), Philippines (Dr. Rae Coll.)! Java (Leud. Fortm.). New Guinea (Tempère)! Senegal (Grun.)! Rio Purus, Brazil (Deby Coll.)! Lake Pistaku, Illinois (Grove Coll.)!

8. **N. Stodderi** Greenl. (1861). — V. lanceolate with acute ends. L. 0,09; B. 0,014 mm. Central nodule dilated to a stauros, reaching the margin; terminal nodules small; terminal fissures nearly straight. Transverse striæ 18 to 19 (22 according to Lewis) in 0.01 mm. longitudinal about 13 in 0,01 mm. — *Stauroneis Stodderi* Greenl. in Lewis Proc. Ac. Philad. 1861 Pl. II f. 6.

Fresh water: French pond, Maine! Waltham, Mass.!

Var. *insignis* Grun. Ms. — V. rhombic-lanceolate. L. 0,09; B. 0,021 mm. Transverse striæ 16 in 0,01 mm.; longitudinal 7 to 8 in 0,01 mm. — *Stauron. lineolata* Ehb. Am. II: 1 f. 19? *N. Stodd. v. ins.* Pl. III f. 13.

Slightly brackish water: Bengal!

9. **N. sulcata** Cl. (1881). — V. linear, with subacute ends. L. 0,088 to 0,109; B. 0,008 to 0,009 mm. Central nodule transversely dilated to a stauros reaching the margin. Transverse striæ 21, longitudinal 13 to 14 in 0,01 mm. — *Stauron. sulcata* Cl. N. R. D. p. 14 Pl. III f. 46.

Marine: Balearic Islands!

10. **N. Spicula** Hickie (1873). — V. narrow lanceolate, with subacute ends. L. 0,05 to 0,13; B. 0,004 to 0,013 mm. Central nodule dilated into a stauros, reaching the margin. Transverse striæ 25 to 29, longitudinal finer. Frustules free. — *Stauroneis Spicula* Hickie Month. M. Journ.

XII p. 290 (according to V. H. Syn.). V. H. Syn. p. 68 Pl. IV f. 9. *Staur. hyalina* DANNF. Balt. D. p. 32 Pl. III f. 20 (1882)?

Marine and brackish water: Arctic America! Cape Wankarema! Sea of Kara! England (V. H. T.).

11. **N. crucigera** W. SM. (1856). V. narrow lanceolate, with acute ends. L. 0,08 to 0,11; B. 0,01 mm. Central nodule dilated to stauros, reaching the margin. Transverse striæ 12, longitudinal 25 to 28 in 0,01 mm. Frustule free or enclosed in gelatinous tubes. — *Schizonema cruc.* W. SM. B. D. II p. 74 Pl. LVI f. 354; LVII f. 356. V. H. Syn. p. 110 Pl. XVI f. 1.

Marine and brackish water: Gulf of Bothnia! Firth of Tay! Bohuslän! Mouth of Loire (Grun.), Saxony (salines of Dürrenberg)!

N. crucigera, which occurs in gelatinous tubes and for that reason has been regarded as a *Schizonema*, is closely connected with *N. Spicula*, which (always?) occurs free. The striation is much coarser in *N. crucigera* than in *N. Spicula*.

12. **N. balearica** CL. (1881). — V. narrow lanceolate, with acute ends. L. 0,11; B. 0,013 mm. Central nodule dilated to a short stauros. Transverse striæ 26, longitudinal 23 in 0,01 mm. — *Stauroneis balear.* CL. N. R. D. p. 14 Pl. III f. 41.

Marine: Balearic Islands!

13. **N. quarnerensis** GRUN. Ms. — V. membranaceous, linear-lanceolate, gradually tapering from the middle to the subacute ends. L. 0,14; B. 0,02 mm. Central nodule small, transversely dilated to a very narrow stauros, reaching half way to the margins. Transverse striæ 24, longitudinal 18 to 20 in 0,01 mm. — Pl. III f. 14.

Marine: Adriatic (Grun.), Seychelles (V. H. Coll.)! Sumatra (Deby Coll.)!

GRUNOW has sent me a sketch of this diatom with the name *Stauroneis quarnerensis*. As it evidently belongs to this group I have changed the name to *Navicula quarn.* It is true that this name has been used by GRUNOW for an other form, but as that is probably identical with *N. cuspidata var. ambigua*, I think it admissible to use the name *N. quarnerensis* for this species.

14. **N. vitrea** CL. (1880). — V. narrow lanceolate acute. L. 0,15 to 0,2. B. 0,22 mm. Transverse striæ 19 to 20, longitudinal 21 in 0,01 mm. — *Pleurosigma vitrea* CL. A. D. p. 15 Pl. IV f. 78. GRUN. A. D. p. 60. PÉRAGALLO Pleur. VIII f. 9.

Marine: Sea of Kara! Cape Wankarema! Adriatic (Grun.).

15. **N. O'Mearii** GRUN. (1880). — V. narrow-lanceolate, with rounded ends. L. 0,059 to 0,068; B. 0,009 to 0,0115 mm. Transverse striæ 17; longitudinal 19 in 0,01 mm. — GRUN. A. D. p. 61. CL. Vega p. 496. *Pleur. O'M.* PÉRAG. Pleur. VIII f. 10.

Marine: Seychelles (Grun.), Australia (Grun.).

Var. *minor* CL. (1883). — L. 0,05; B. 0,011 mm. Transverse striæ slightly radiate, 16 in 0,01 mm. Longitudinal striæ 18 in 0.01 mm. — CL. Vega p. 496.

Marine: Port Jackson!

16. **N. Kjellmanii** CL. (1880). — V. linear lanceolate, with subacute ends. L. 0,168; B. 0,0264 mm. Transverse striæ 15 in 0,01 mm.; longitudinal of equal number, slightly inflexed towards the central nodule. — *Pleurosigma (Nav.?) Kjellm.* CL. A. D. p. 14 Pl. IV f. 80. *Pleur. Kjellm.* PÉRAG. Pleur. Pl. VIII f. 8. *Nav. Vegæ* CL. Vega p. 474.

Brackish water: Sea of Kara.

Var. *subconstricta* GRUN. (1883). — V. linear, slightly constricted in the middle, with subcuneate ends. L. 0,156; B. 0,015 mm. Transverse striæ 15,3; longitudinal 14,3 in 0,01 mm. — *Nav. Vegæ v. subc.* Vega p. 474.

Marine: North Siberian Sea, Cape Wankarema (Grun.).

N. Kjellmanii, O'Mearii and *vitrea* are closely connected and form a peculiar group intermediate between *Gyrosigma* and *Navicula*, having the structure of the former and the straight median line of the latter. I have proposed (1883 Vega p. 474) to include these forms in a Section *Vegæ*, but I now prefer to connect them with the other species of *N. orthostichæ*.

17. **N. porto-montana** Cl. N. Sp. — V. broad, linear, slightly gibbous in the middle, with broad rounded ends. L. 0,07; B. 0,017 mm. Median line with approximate median pores and bordered by a narrow silicious rib. Terminal nodules thick, terminal fissures indistinct. Transverse striæ 19 to 20, longitudinal 19 in 0,01 mm. The puncta close to the median line are larger than the others. Pl. III f. 36.

Fresh water: Puerto Monte, Chile, fossil (Kinker Coll.)!

Gyrosigma Hassall (1845).

Valve more or less elongated and sigmoid. Central nodule small. Ends of the median line in contrary directions. Central area small or indistinct. Axial area indistinct. Structure: puncta disposed in transverse and longitudinal rows. — *Cell-contents* (of the freshwater forms) with two chromatophores along the connecting zone, which long before the division of the cell are transversely cut off and migrate in pairs to the inside of the valve. The opening between the halves of the chromatophores becomes oblique, and each half increases to a chromatophore. The margins of the chromatophores entire (Pfitzer, Bau und Entw. p. 57). Marine species (G. balticum) have irregularly serrated chromatophores the indentations being directed towards the central nodule. The median part of the chromatophores is obliquely striate, their substance being alternately thicker and thinner. The striæ of the two chromatophores cross each other in an oblique angle (O. Müller Ber. d. Deutch. Bot. Ges. 1883 p. 481).

The sigmoid Naviculæ were named *Navicula Sigma* by Ehrenberg. Hassall proposed for them the name *Gyrosigma*, which was adopted by Rabenhorst (Die Süssw. Diat. 1853), but not by other diatomists, who prefered the newer name *Pleurosigma*, formed by W. Smith, 1852, who published the first monograph of the species (Ann. Nat. Hist. 2 ser. IX p. 1). The genus Pleurosigma, as accepted by all diatomists, includes forms with a structure of small puncta or alveoli, disposed in transverse rows, which are crossed by other rows, either longitudinal, or obliquely decussating. There are no intermediate forms between these two types, and I think they may justly be considered as different genera. For the forms with the puncta in transverse and longitudinal rows, I adopt the name *Gyrosigma*, although, as Grunow remarks, this name involves tautology. For the forms with the puncta disposed in transverse and oblique rows I reserve the name *Pleurosigma*. — Among the forms of Gyrosigma are several with carinated valves, for which Ralfs 1861 (Pritch. Inf. p. 920) proposed the generic name *Donkinia*. In my opinion this genus is not acceptable, as founded on a characteristic which is subject to too much variation. The same may be the case with *Rhoicosigma*, proposed 1867 by Grunow (Hedwigia VI p. 10) for forms with geniflexed or arcuate frustules. The genus Rhoicosigma seems at first sight to be better founded, as the valves of the same frustule of *R. compactum* are (as Peragallo has shewn) dissimilar. But on the other hand some forms (as *R. robustum*) have evidently similar valves. Besides, the flexure of the frustule differs in different species to all degrees. The manuscript-name *Endosigma* Bréb. for the forms living like Schizonema, in gelatinous tubes is not admissible, on the same grounds as Schizonema, Colletonema, Endostauron etc. — From Gyrosigma may be removed *Pleurosigma staurophorum* Grun., which has no close affinity to any of the other forms, but has the characteristics of Caloneis, being a sigmoid form of that genus. — The division of the sigmoid forms of Navicula into two groups, founded on the disposition of the puncta in transverse and longitudinal, and in transverse and oblique, rows, was first proposed by W. Smith, and has been accepted by all later diatomists. In the year 1880 Grunow published (in Arctische Diat.) an elaborate monograph, in which he introduced a classification, founded on the relative number of the transverse and the longitudinal or oblique striæ. This classification has been adopted by PERAGALLO, who published 1891 (in Diatomiste) a monograph of Pleurosigma and the allied genera Donkinia, Rhoicosigma and Toxonidea. — It seems to me that to separate the species in accordance with the relative number of the transverse and longitudinal striæ is much too artificial a method, although this characteristic may in many cases be useful. *Gyros. Fasciola* offers a striking illustration of how unnatural such a classification based on the relative number of the striæ may be. In the type the longitudinal striæ are closer than the transverse, but in the var. *sulcata* the transverse are closer than the longitudinal striæ. In some cases moreover the relation between the transverse and longitudinal striæ may be vitiated by inevitable errors in their counting. These reasons have induced me not to adopt the classification of GRUNOW and PERAGALLO. I prefer as bases of classification the outline of the valve and the flexure of the median line.

The variation of the forms in Gyrosigma is very great, and the species pass over into each other in so many cases that it is very difficult to define them.

Gyrosigma is related to Tropidoneis by the carinated forms (Donkinia). On the other hand it is related to the Naviculæ orthostichæ. The peculiar *G. spectabile* has a central nodule, which closely resembles that of the above named section (as of Nav. cuspidata).

The majority of forms, belonging to Gyrosigma live in brackish water, but a few are inhabitants of fresh, and salt. water.

Artificial key.

1.	Median line central	2.
	— — excentric	10.
2.	Ends protracted into beaks	3.
	— not — —	6.
3.	Beaks short and stout	*G. distortum* W. SM.
	— long — narrow	4.
4.	Valve abruptly attenuated into beaks	*G. macrum* W. SM.
	— gradually —	5.
5.	Valve narrow (B. 0,005 to 0,01 mm.)	*G. prolongatum* W. SM.
	— broader (B. 0,015 to 0,024 mm.)	*G. Fasciola* EHR.
6.	Valve linear	12.
	— lanceolate, tapering from the middle	7.
7.	Longitudinal striæ wider than the transverse	8.
	— equidistant with —	9.
	— — narrower than the —	10.
8.	Transverse striæ about 14 in 0,01 mm.	*G. attenuatum* KÜTZ.
	— — — 17 —	*G. litorale* W. SM.
9.	Transverse striæ about 14 in 0.01 mm.	*G. Terryanum* PER.
	— — 17 to 23 —	*G. acuminatum* KÜTZ.
	— — about 28 —	*G. glaciale* CL.
10.	Transverse striæ about 13 in 0,01 mm.	11.
	— — — 21 —	*G. Kützingii* GRUN.
	— — — 24 —	*G. Febigeri* GRUN.
	— — — 27 —	*G. diaphanum* CL.
11.	Central area small	*G. Strigilis* W. SM.
	— — large, oblique	*G. Baileyi* GRUN.
12.	Valve about 15 times longer than broad	*G. tenuissimum* W. SM.
	— — 10 — — —	13.
13.	Transverse and longitudinal striæ equidistant	14.
	— striæ wider than the longitudinal	15.
14.	Central area large, oblique	*G. plagiostomum* GRUN.
	— — small —	*G. balticum* EHR.

15. { Size small (L. 0,06 to 0,2 mm.) . . . . 16.
{ — large (L. 0,3 to 0,5 mm.) . . . . 18.
16. { Valve with gradually narrowed ends . . . . *G. Spencerii* W. Sm.
{ — — obliquely rounded . . . . 17.
17. { Length 0,06 mm. . . . . *G. scalproides* Rabh.
{ — 0,14 — . . . . *G. Temperei* Cl.
18. { Transverse striæ about 9 in 0,01 mm. . . . . *G. Grovei* Cl.
{ — — 18 — . . . . *G. spectabile* Grun.
19. { Median line sinuose . . . . *G. diminutum* Grun.
{ — not . . . . 20.
20. { Valve very narrow, 17 or more times longer than broad . . . *G. lineare* Grun.
{ — less narrow . . . . 21.
21. { Median line slightly excentric . . . . 22.
{ — — coincident with the margin . . . . 24.
22. { Striæ equidistant . . . . 23.
{ Transverse striæ wider than the longitudinal . . . . *G. arcticum* Cl.
23. { Striæ about 12 in 0,01 mm. . . . . *G. robustum* Grun.
{ — — 20 — . . . . *G. Wansbeckii* Donk.
24. { Frustule arcuate . . . . 25.
{ — not . . . . 26.
25. { Valve broad, unilaterally rounded . . . . *G. compactum* Grev.
{ — narrow, lanceolate . . . . *G. mediterraneum* Cl.
26. { Transverse and longitudinal striæ equidistant . . . . *G. rectum* Donk.
{ — striæ narrower than the longitudinal . . . . *G. angustum* Donk.

1. **G. acuminatum** Kütz. (1833). — V. sigmoid, lanceolate, gradually tapering to the obtuse ends. L. 0,1 to 0,18; B. 0,015 to 0,02 mm. Median line central, sigmoid. Transverse and longitudinal striæ equidistant, about 18 in 0,01 mm. *Frustulia acuminata* Kütz. Linnæa VIII p. 555 Dec. N:o 84 (accord. to Lagst.). *Pleuros. acuminatum* Grun. A. D. p. 56. V. H. Syn. 117 Pl. XXI f. 12. Per. VII f. 36. 37. *Pleur. lacustre* W. Sm. B. D. I Pl. XXI f. 217. *Pleur. transsylvanicum* Pant. III Pl. VI f. 94?

Fresh water: Sweden! England! Saxony!

Var. *curta* Grun. (1880). — L. 0,063 to 0,086; B. 0,0145 mm. Ends subrostrate, obtuse. Striæ 18 in 0,01 mm.

Fresh water: Holstein (Grun.).

Var. *gallica* Grun. — V. sigmoid, lanceolate, with attenuate, subacute ends. L. 0,011 to 0,155; B. 0,011 to 0,018 mm. Median line sigmoid, central. Longitudinal and transv. striæ equidistant 20 to 21 in 0,01 mm. — *P. scalprum var. gallica* Grun. V. H. T. N:o 172. *P. gallic.* Per. VII f. 2.

Fresh and brackish water: Sweden (Hernösand, fossil, Rimforsa i Vestergötland, Ringsjön)! France (V. H. T.), Argentina!

Var. *Brebissonii* Grun. (1880). — V. sigmoid, linear-lanceolate, with subacute ends. L. 0,086 to 0,104; B. 0,011 to 0,013 mm. Median line central, sigmoid. Transverse and longit. striæ equidisstant, 22 to 23 in 0,01 mm. — *Pleuros. balticum* γ W. Sm. B. D. XXII f. 207 γ. *P. Bréb.* Grun. A. D. p. 56. Per. VII f. 29, 30? *P. balt. var. Bréb.* V. H. Syn. p. 117 Pl. XXI f. 6. *P. scalprum* Rabh. A. Eur. N:o 2013 (accord. to Grun.).

Fresh or slightly brackish water: Spitzbergen! Sweden! Paris! Saxony! Argentina!

2. **G. Terryanum** Per. (1891). — V. slightly sigmoid, tapering from the middle to the obtuse ends. L. 0,4 to 0,45; B. 0,038 to 0,041 mm. Median line central, flexuose near the central nodule, which is obliquely elongated. Transverse and longit. striæ equidistant, 14 in 0,01 mm. — *Pleuros. Terr.* Per. p. 18 Pl. VII f. 21.

Marine: Connecticut!

3. **G. Baileyi** Grun. (1880). — V. broadly lanceolate, strongly sigmoid, with subacute ends. L. 0,08 to 0,13; B. 0,018 to 0,021 mm. Median line central, sigmoid. Central nodule large,

elongated and oblique. Transverse striæ radiate in the middle and 11 to 16 in 0,01 mm., but 18 in 0,01 mm. at the ends. Longitud. striæ 18 in 0,01 mm. — *Pleur. Bal.* Grun. A. D. p. 59 Per. VIII f. 11.

Brackish water: Bengal (Grunow).

4. **G. Strigilis** W. Sm. (1852). — V. narrow, lanceolate, sigmoid, gradually tapering to the subacute ends. L. 0,25 to 0,36; B. 0,03 to 0,034 mm. Median line central, slightly flexuose. Transverse striæ more distant than the longitudinal. T.S. : L.S. $^{12}/_{15}$, $^{13}/_{15}$, $^{14}/_{16}$ in 0,01 mm. *Pleur. Strig.* W. Sm. Ann. Mag. N. H. (2) IX p. 8 Pl. II f. 4. B. D. I p. 66 Pl. XXII f. 208. Per. VIII f. 4. 5.

Brackish water: Baltic! North Sea! English Channel (W. Sm.), Batavia!

Var. *Smithii* Grun. (1880). — L. 0,15 to 0,025; B. 0,012 to 0,018 mm. T.S. : L.S. $^{12}/_{18}$, $^{14}/_{18}$ in 0,01 mm. *Pleur. Smithii* Grun. A. D. p. 58.

Brackish water: Java! Bengal (Grun.). South America (Grun.).

Var.? *tropica* Grun. (1860). — Ends obtuse. L. 0,16 to 0,3; B. 0,023 to 0,033 mm. Transv. striæ about 21 in 0,01 mm. — *Pleur. tropicum* Grun. Verh. 1860 p. 559 Pl. III f. 34. Per. VIII f. 7.

Marine: Red Sea (Grun.). West Indies (Grun.).

Var.? *capensis* Petit (1891). — L. 0,3; B. 0,017 mm. T.S. : L. S $^{10}/_{13}$, in 0,01 mm. *Pleur. cap.* Per. p. 21 Pl. VIII f. 6.

Marine: Cape Good Hope (Petit).

5. **G. Kützingii** Grun. (1860). V. gently sigmoid, lanceolate, with acute ends. L. 0,08 to 0,12; B. 0,012 to 0,015 mm. Central nodule somewhat elongated. Median line central, sigmoid. Transv. striæ slightly radiate in the middle, more distant than the longitudinal. T.S. : L.S. $^{21}/_{25}$, $^{20}/_{24}$, $^{22}/_{26}$, $^{23}/_{26}$ in 0,01 mm. — *Pleur. Kützingii* Grun. Verh. 1860 p. 561 Pl. VI f. 3. *P. Spencerii var. Kütz.* Grun. A. D. p. 59. V. H. Syn. p. 118 Pl. XXI f. 14. Per. VIII f. 22. *P. gracilentum* Rabh. Alg. Europ. N:o 1066 (1861). *P. Wormleyi* Sulliv. - *P. Spencerii var. acutiuscula* Grun. in V. H. Types N:o 183.

Fresh water: Sweden (Lake Mälaren)! Finland! Belgium (V. H.), Saxony! East Indies (Grun.)! Japan! Tasmania! New Zealand (Grun.). Waltham in Massachusetts! Hudson River! Argentina!

6. **G. Febigerii** Grun. (1879). — V. lanceolate, gently sigmoid, subacute. L. 0,11 to 0,15; B. 0,0145 to 0,015 mm. Central nodule rounded. Median line sigmoid, central. T.S. : L.S. $^{24}/_{29}$ in 0,01 mm. — *Pleur. Febig.* Grun. Cl. M. D. N:o 223. A. D. p. 60. *P. Spencerii var.? Febig.* Per. VIII f. 28.

Marine: California (Grun.).

7. **G. diaphanum** Cl. N. Sp. — V. lanceolate, sigmoid, subobtuse. L. 0,085; B. 0,015 mm. Median line central, sigmoid. Centralnodulerounded. T.S. : L.S. $^{25}/_{30}$ in 0,01 mm. — Part II Pl. I f. 6.

Marine: Isle de Bréhat, France! Gullmarefjord, Sweden!

8. **G. (Rhoicosigma) glaciale** Cl. (1883). — V. thin, lanceolate, gently sigmoid, gradually tapering to the acute ends. L. 0,143; B. 0,019 mm. Median line very slightly sigmoid. Transv. and longit. striæ equidistant, 28 in 0,01 mm. *Pleur. glaciale* Cl. Vega p. 476 Pl. XXXV f. 13. Per. VII f. 15.

Marine: Cape Wankarema!

9. **G. attenuatum** Kütz. (1833). — V. gently sigmoid, lanceolate, gradually tapering from the middle to the obtuse ends. L. 0,18 to 0,24; B. 0,025 mm. Median line gently sigmoid, central. Longitudinal striæ stronger and more distant than the transverse. T.S. : L.S. $^{14}/_{10}$, $^{14}/_{12}$, $^{16}/_{11}$ in 0,01 mm. — *Frustulia attenuata* Kütz. Dec. N:o 83 (accord. to Lagst.). *Pleur. atten.* W. Sm. B. D. I p. 68 Pl. XXII f. 216. V. H. Syn. p. 117 Pl. XXI f. 11. Per. VII f. 9. *P. Hippocampus* W. Sm.

Ann. Mag. N. H. [2] X p. 10 Pl. II f. 9 (1852). B. D. I. c. f. 215. V. H. Syn. p. 117 Pl. XX f. 3. Per. VII f. 1 to 7. *P. att. var. caspia* Grun. Casp. Sea Alg. p. 18 Pl. III f. 8. Per VII f. 8.

Fresh and brackish water: Sweden! Finland! England! Saxony! Belgium (V. H.), France! Baltic! North Sea! Caspian Sea (Grun.).

Var. *Scalprum* Gaill. a. Turp. (1827). — L. 0,12 to 0,15; B. 0,019 mm. T.S. : L.S. 19/16, 17/14. *Nav. Scalprum* Gaill. a. Turp. Mém. du Muséum XV Pl. X. XI f. 3 (accord. to Kütz.). *P. acuminatum* W. Sm. B. D. I p. 66 Pl. XXI f. 209. Grun. A. D. p. 55. Per. p. 17 Pl. VII f. 3. *Pl. Kochii* Pant. III Pl. IX f. 153 (1893)??

Brackish and marine: North Sea!

10. **G. litorale** W. Sm. (1852). — V. sigmoid, lanceolate, with attenuate, slightly rostrate ends. L. 0,11 to 0,19; B. 0,022 to 0,045 mm. Median line sigmoid, central. Longit. striæ very strong and distant. T.S. : L.S. 17/10 in 0,01 mm. — *P. litorale* W. Sm. Ann. and Mag. N. Hist. [2] IX p. 10 Pl. II f. 8. B. D. I p. 67 Pl. XXII f. 214. Per. VII f. 1.

Marine: North Sea! English Channel (W. Sm.), Mediterranean Sea (Per.).

11. **G. distortum** W. Sm. (1852). V. lanceolate, slightly sigmoid. Ends more or less abruptly produced into short, obtuse beaks, turned in contrary directions. L. 0,07 to 0,12; B. 0,017 mm. Median line sigmoid, central. Transv. striæ more distant than the longit. T.S. : L.S. 23/27, 25/28. *Pleur. dist.* W. Sm. Ann. Mag. Nat. Hist. [2] IX p. 7 Pl. I f. 10; B. D. I p. 67 Pl. XX f. 210. Per. VIII f. 32.

Marine: Spitzbergen! North Sea! English Channel (W. Sm.), Ionian Archipelago (Grun.). Cameroon, Africa!

Var. *Parkeri* Harrison (1860). L. 0,08 to 0,15; B. 0,015 to 0,025 mm. T.S. : L.S. 19/22 (Grun.), 20/24, 21/27, 23/24 in 0,01 mm. *Pleur. Park.* Harr. M. J. 1860 p. 104. Grun. A. D. p. 57. V. H. Syn. p. 118 Pl. XXI f. 10. Per. VIII f. 33.

Fresh and brackish water: Baltic! England! Belgium!

Var. *stauroneoides* Grun. (1880). — Central nodule transversely dilated. T.S. : L.S. 24/21 0,01 mm. — *Pleur. Park. var. stauron.* Grun. A. D. p. 57.

Brackish water: Hudson River (Grun.).

12. **G. Fasciola** Ehr. (1839). — V. lanceolate, attenuated into long, linear beaks, curved in opposite directions. L. 0,09 to 0,15; B. 0,015 to 0,024 mm. Median line central, straight in the middle of the valve. T.S. : L.S. 21/24, 23/22 in 0,01 mm. — *Ceratoneis Fasciola* Ehr. Abh. 1839 (accord. to Chase). *Pleur. Fasciola* W. Sm. B. D. I p. 67 Pl. XXI f. 211. Grun. A. D. p. 58. V. H. Syn. p. 119 Pl. XXI f. 8. Hendry T. M. Soc. 1862 X p. 152. Per. VIII f. 36 to 38.

Marine: Spitsbergen! North Sea! California! Barbados!

Var. *sulcata* Grun. (1880). — Longitudinal striæ strong. T.S. : L.S. 19/15 (Grun.), 20/17, 23/16 in 0,01 mm. — *P. (Fasc. var.?) sulcatum* Grun. A. D. p. 55 Pl. IV f. 75. V. H. Syn. XXI f. 7. Per. VIII f. 43.

Marine: Sea of Kara (Grun.), Spitsbergen! Firth of Tay (Grove), Mouth of Seine!

Var *tenuirostris* Grun. (1880). — L. 0,14 to 1,16; B. 0,011 to 0,012 mm. T.S. : L.S. 22/19, 23/20 in 0,01 mm. — *P. (Fasc. var.?) tenuirostris* Grun. A. D. p. 55 Pl. IV f. 76. Per. VIII f. 42.

Marine: Sea of Kara (Grun.).

Var. *arcuata* Donk. (1858). V. lanceolate. Ends more suddenly produced into long, narrow beaks curved in contrary directions. L. 0,1 to 0,115; B. 0,012 mm. Median line central, straight. Transv. striæ 24 to 25 (Grun.) in 0,01 mm.; longitudinal finer. — *Pleur. arcuat.* Donk. T. M. S. VI p. 25 Pl. III f. 10. Per. VIII f. 34, 35.

Marine: Coast of Sweden (Grun.)! England (Donk.).

Gyros. Fasciola is intimately connected with *G. distortum var. Parkeri*, and by the Var. *tenuirostris*, with *G. macrum*.

13. **G. macrum** W. Sm. (1853). — V. narrow, lanceolate, abruptly attenuated into very long and narrow beaks, curved in contrary directions. L. 0,2 to 0,27; B. 0,01 mm. Median line central. Transv. striæ 27 to 28 in 0,01 mm., longitudinal more than 30 in 0,01 mm. *Pleur. macr.* W. Sm. B. D. I p. 67 Pl. XXXI f. 276. V. H. Syn. p. 119 Pl. XXI f. 9. Per. VIII f. 41.

Marine: Sea of Kara (Grun.), North Sea! Mediterranean Sea (Grun.).

14. **G. prolongatum** W. Sm. (1852). — V. narrow, lanceolate, gradually attenuated into long beaks, curved in contrary directions. L. 0,11 to 0,25; B. 0,005 to 0,015 mm. Transverse striæ 21 to 22 in 0,01 mm., longit. finer. — *Pleur. prol.* W. Sm. Ann. Mag. Nat. Hist. [2] IX p. 9 Pl. II f. 7. B. D. I p. 67 Pl. XXII f. 212. Per. VIII f. 39.

Marine: North Sea! Balearic Islands!

Var. *closteroides* Grun. (1884). — Beaks turned in the same directions. Transv. striæ 22 in 0,01 mm. — *Pleur. prol. var. closteroides* Grun. Franz Josephs Land D. p. 105 (53) Pl. I f. 58. Per. VIII f. 40.

Marine: Coasts of England (Grun.).

15. **G. tenuissimum** W. Sm. (1853). — V. very narrow, linear-lanceolate, slightly sigmoid, acute. L. 0,11 to 0,22; B. 0,005 to 0,015 mm. Median line central. Transv. striæ 18 to 22 in 0,01 mm. longitud. finer. — *Pleur. tenuiss.* W. Sm. B. D. I p. 67 Pl. XXII f. 213. Per. VIII f. 13.

Marine: Sea of Kara! East coasts of England (W. Sm.), Triest! California!

Var. *subtilissima* Grun. (1880). — L. 0,137; B. 0,0065 mm. Transv. striæ 27 in 0,01 mm. — *Pleur. ten. var. subt.* Grun. A. D. p. 58.

Marine: Sea of Kara (Grun.).

Var. *hyperborea* Grun. (1880). — V. linear, sigmoid. L. 0,084 to 0,094; B. 0,006 to 0,007 mm. T.S. : L.S. $^{21}/_{23}$, $^{22}/_{24}$ in 0,01 mm. — *Pleur. ten. var. hyperb.* Grun. A. D. p. 58 Pl. IV f. 77. Per. VIII f. 14.

Marine: Sea of Kara (Grun.).

Gyros. tenuissimum connects *G. prolongatum* with *G. Spencerii* by the Var. *hyperborea*.

16. **G. Spencerii** W. Sm. (1852). — V. linear-lanceolate, sigmoid, obtuse. L. 0,078 to 0,22; B. 0,012 to 0,025 mm. Median line central. Transv. striæ more distant than the longitudinal. T.S. : L.S. $^{11}/_{22}$, $^{21}/_{21}$, $^{22}/_{24}$ in 0,01 mm. — *Pleur. Spencerii* W. Sm. Ann. Mag. Nat. Hist. [2] IX p. 12 Pl. II f. 15. B. D. I p. 68 Pl. XXII f. 218. *P. Spenc. var. Smithii* Grun. A. D. p. 59. V. H. Syn. p. 118 Pl. XXI f. 15. Per. VIII f. 21, 23. *P. Spenc. var. Arnottii* Grun. A. D. p. 59, *P. Spenc. var. borealis* Grun. A. D. p. 60. Per. VIII f. 15. *P. Spenc. var. Antillarum* Grun. A. D. p. 60. *P. Spenc. var. curvula* Grun. A. D. p. 60. V. H. Syn. p. 118 Pl. XXI f. 3, 4, 5. Per. VIII f. 20, 24.

Brackish water: Spitsbergen! Sea of Kara! North Sea! Saxony! Canada! New York! West Indies! Bombay (Grove Coll.)!

Var. *exilis* Grun. (1880). — L. 0,05 to 0,055; B. 0,007 mm. Transv. striæ 28 to 29 in 0,01 mm. — *P. Spenc. var. exilis* Grun. A. D. p. 60. Per. VIII f. 25.

Brackish water: Normandy (Grun.). Tasmania!

Var. *minutula* Grun. (1880). — L. 0,06; B. 0,01 mm. T.S. : L.S. $^{23}/_{25}$, $^{24}/_{26}$ in 0,01 mm. — *P. Spenc. var. min.* Grun. A. D. p. 60.

Brackish water: Elbe (Grun.).

Var. *nodifera* Grun. (1880). — V. linear, slightly sigmoid, obtuse. L. 0,06 to 0,1; B. 0,011 mm. Median line central. Central nodule surrounded by an elongated, oblique area. Transv. striæ slightly radiate in the middle. T.S. : L.S. $^{17}/_{22}$, $^{20}/_{23}$ in 0,01 mm. — *P. nodif.* Grun. A. D. p. 59. *P. Spenc. var. nod.* V. H. Syn. p. 118. Pl. XXI f. 13. Per. VIII f. 26.

Fresh water: Mouth of Elbe (Grun.), Belgium (V. H.), Samoa (Grun.).

17. **G. Grovei** Cl. (1891). — V. linear, sigmoid at the attenuated, obliquely rounded, ends. L. 0,4 to 0,6; B. 0,03 to 0,06 mm. Central nodule obliquely elliptical. Median line central, scarcely flexuose. T.S. : L.S. $^{9}/_{13}$ in 0,01 mm. *Pleur. Grovei* Per. p. 22 Pl. VIII f. 1.

Brackish water: Java! Singapore!

18. **G. spectabile** Grun. (1891). — V. sigmoid, linear, obtuse. L. 0,3 to 0,34; B. 0,04 mm. Median line central, sigmoid, enclosed between two siliceous strings. Central nodule small, elongated. Terminal areas large. T.S. : L.S. $^{18}/_{23}$ in 0,01 mm. *Pleur. spect.* Per. p. 21 Pl. VII f. 14.

Brackish water: Brazil!

This isolated species is very interesting, as the central nodule and the median line recall those of Frustulia and Naviculæ Orthostichae.

19. **G. scalproides** Rabh. (1861). — V. slightly sigmoid, linear, with obliquely rounded ends. L. 0,058 to 0,068; B. 0,01 mm. Median line straight. Central nodule elongated. Median transv. striæ somewhat radiate. T.S. : L.S. $^{22}/_{20}$ in 0,01 mm. — *Pleur. scalproides* Rabh. Alg. Eur. N:o 1101. Grun. A. D. p. 60. V. H. Syn. p. 119 Pl. XXI f. 1. *P. Spencerii var. scalpr.* Per. VIII f. 31.

Fresh water: Germany! U. States, Kansas River! Cameroon, Africa!

Var. (*Endosigma*) *eximia* Thw. (1856). — V. linear, obliquely truncate. L. 0,06 to 0,08; B. 0,009 to 0,01 mm. Median line straight, somewhat excentric in the ends. T.S. : L.S. $^{23}/_{27}$, $^{25}/_{28}$ in 0,01 mm. Frustules enclosed in gelatinous tubes. — *Colletonema exim.* Thw. in W. Sm. B. D. II p. 69 Pl. LVI f. 350. *Pleur. exim.* V. H. Syn. p. 119 Pl. XXI f. 2. Per. VIII f. 47.

Fresh water: Sweden (Gulf of Bothnia, Upsala)! England (W. Sm.), Belgium (V. H.), Bengal!

Var. *obliqua* Grun. (1880). — V. linear, obliquely truncate. L. 0,089; B. 0,0145 mm. Central area elongated, oblique. Median line straight, curved at the ends, central. T.S. : L.S. $^{22}/_{24}$ in 0,01 mm. — *Pleur. obl.* Grun. A. D. p. 56. Per. VII f. 34.

Brackish water: Sierra Leone (Grun.). U. States! Savannah, Ga.!

20. **G. Temperei** Cl. (1893). — V. linear, with obliqely truncate and rounded ends. L. 0,14; B. 0,014 mm. Median line central, straight, curved only at the ends. Central nodule small, elongated. T.S. : L.S. $^{27}/_{30}$. — Diatomiste II p. 55 Pl. III f. 3.

Brackish water: Connecticut!

This form has nearly the same outline as *P. balticum*, but is smaller and has closer striation.

21. **G. plagiostomum** Grun. (1880). — V. linear, with obliquely rounded ends. L. 0,1; B. 0,013 mm. Median line central, slightly flexuose. Central nodule large, elongated and oblique. Transv. and longit. striæ equidistant, 18 to 19 in 0,01 mm. *Pleur. plag.* Grun. A. D. p. 56. Per. VII f. 33.

Marine: Seychelles (Grun.). Sierra Leone! Barbados!

Pleur. scioteuse Sulliv. (1854 Sillim. J. XXVII p. 251; Grun. A. D. p. 59), which seems to be the same as *Pl. Wansbeckii* Per. VII f. 25, 26, is probably only a variety of *G. plagiostomum*. Specimens from Hudson River (Icon. nost. Part II Pl. I f. 5) differ from that form in their somewhat larger size (L. 0,14 to 0,16; B. 0,016 to 0,018 mm. T.S. : L.S. $^{16}/_{18}$, $^{18}/_{19}$ in 0,01 mm.).

22. **G. balticum** Ehr. (1830). — V. linear, with obliquely truncate and obtuse ends. L. 0,2 to 0,4; B. 0,024 to 0,040 mm. Median line slightly excentric and somewhat flexuose. Central area small, oblique. Transv. and longit. striæ equidistant, 11 to 16 in 0,01 mm. — *Nav. baltica* Ehr. Abh. 1830 p. 114 (accord. to Chase). *Pleur. balticum* W. Sm. B. D. I 66 p. XXII f. 207. Jan. Rabh. Honduras D. Pl. III f. 3. V. H. Syn. p. 117 Pl. XX f. 1. Per. VII f. 19, 20. *P. Makron* Johnst. M. J. VIII p. 15.

Brackish and marine: Baltic! North Sea! Caspian Sea (Grun.). Mediterranean Sea! Adriatic! Red Sea! Java! Sumatra! Sandwich Islands! Samoa! Magellans Strait! Brazil! West Indies! Atlantic coasts of U. States!

Var. *similis* GRUN. (1880). — V. linear, with obtuse ends. L. 0,10 to 0,2; B. 0,02 to 0,024 mm. Median line central, slightly sigmoid, ending below the apices of the valve. Central area small. Striæ equidistant, 16 to 17 in 0,02 mm. — *Pleur. simile* GRUN. A. D. p. 56. PER. VII f. 27.

Fresh or brackish water: Lagos (Grun.), Java! Samoa (Grun.), Tasmania! China! Barbados!

Var. *sinensis* EHR. (1847). — V. gibbous in the middle and with incrassate ends. L. 0,1 to 0,2; B. 0,013 to 0,022 mm. Median line strongly flexuose. T.S. : L.S. $^{15}/_{17}$ in 0,01 mm. *Nav. sin.* EHR. Ber. 1847 p. 485 (accord. to Chase). M. G. XXXIV, 7. f. 11. PER. VII f. 11. *Pl. sin. var. calcuttensis* GRUN. A. D. p. 57. PER. VII f. 12.

Var. *californica* GRUN. (1879). — V. linear, slightly sigmoid, with gradually attenuated ends. L. 0,25 to 0,28; B. 0,028 mm. Transv. and longit. striæ equidistant, 14 to 15 in 0,01 mm. — *Pleur. balt. var. calif.* GRUN. in Cl. M. D. N:o 246. PER. VII f. 22.

Brackish water: California!

23. **G. diminutum** GRUN. (1880). — V. linear, with obliquely truncate and rounded ends. L. 0,1 to 0,11; B. 0,016 mm. Median line strongly flexuose, excentric towards the ends. T.S. : L.S. $^{18}/_{22}$, $^{19}/_{21}$, $^{23}/_{26}$ in 0,01 mm. — *Pleur. (balt. var.?) dim.* GRUN. A. D. p. 56. PER. VII f. 31, 32.

Marine: Balearic Islands! Adriatic (Grun.)!

Var. *constricta* GRUN. (1880). — V. gibbous in the middle and at the ends. L. 0,1; B. 0,013 mm. T.S. : L.S. $^{21}/_{23}$ in 0,01 mm. — *Pleur. (balt. var.?) constr.* GRUN. A. D. p. 57. PER. VII f. 13. *Pleur. reversum* GREG. D. of Clyde p. 530 Pl. XIV f. 105. PER. VII f. 10?

Marine: Adriatic (Grun.).

Pl. biharense PANT. III Pl. XLII f. 581 seems to be an akin form.

24. **G. Wansbeckii** DONK. (1858). — V. linear, tapering towards the slightly curved and obliquely rounded ends. L. 0,11 to 0,17; B. 0,015 mm. Median line excentric, sigmoid. T.S. : L.S. $^{18}/_{20}$, $^{20}/_{18}$ in 0,01 mm. *Pleur. balt.* β W. SM. B. D. Pl. XXII f. 207 β. *Pl. Wansb.* DONK. T. M. S. VI p. 24 Pl. III f. 7. PER. VII f. 23. 24.

Brackish and marine: Sea of Kara! North Sea!

Var. *Peisonis* GRUN. (1860). — L. 0,09; B. 0,01 mm. T.S. : L.S. $^{21}/_{25}$, $^{21.5}/_{26}$ in 0,01 mm. — *Pleur. Peis.* GRUN. Verh. 1860 p. 562 Pl. VI f. 8. *P. Spencerii var. Peis.* GRUN. A. D. p. 60. PER. VIII f. 27.

Brackish water: Sonderburg (Grun.), Neusiedler See, Hungary (Grun.)!

Var. *subsalina* PER. (1891). — L. 0,12 to 0,17; B. 0,012 mm. T.S. : L.S. $^{18}/_{22}$. — *Pleur. Spencerii var. subs.* PER. p. 24 Pl. VIII f. 16, 17.

Brackish water: Médoc, France (Per.).

25. **G. (Rhoicosigma) arcticum** CL. (1873). - V. slightly sigmoid, tapering from the middle to the subacute or obliquely rounded ends. L. 0,07 to 0,2; B. 0,014 to 0,02 mm. Median line more sigmoid than the valve, sometimes slightly sinuose. T.S. : L.S. $^{21}/_{28}$, $^{21}/_{30}$, $^{23}/_{30}$ in 0,01 mm. Frustule more or less arcuate to almost straight. — *Rhoicosigma arcticum* CL. D. Arc. Sea p. 18 Pl. III f. 16. PER. X f. 16, 17.

Marine: Greenland! Spitsbergen! Sea of Kara! Finmark! Grip in Norway! Firth of Tay! Barbados! Kerguelens Land!

This species varies in amount of flexure. Specimens from Kerguelens Land, named by GRUNOW *Donkinia subflexuosa* (Icon. n. Part II Pl. I f. 3, 4), are straight, so also are specimens from Barbados, but otherwise they differ in nothing of importance. The ends are subacute or obliquely rounded according to the position of the valve.

As a Var. *irregularis* PERAGALLO has (p. 33 Pl. X f. 18) figured an asymmetrical form from the North Sea, which requires a more accurate study.

26. **(Donkinia) rectum** DONK. (1858). — V. convex, linear, straight. with obliquely rounded ends. L. 0,11 to 0,23; B. 0,013 to 0,02 mm. Median line strongly excentric and sigmoid. Transverse

and oblique striæ almost equidistant, 19 to 20 in 0,01 mm. — *Pleur. rectum* DONK. T. M. S. VI p. 23 Pl. III f. 6. *Amphiprora Ralfsii* ARNOTT M. J. VI p. 91 (1858) ad spec. authentica. *Donkinia recta* V. H. Syn. p. 119 Pl. XVII f. 9. PER. IX f. 4. *P. Lorenzii* GRUN. Verh. 1860 p. 558 Pl. VI f. 4. PER. VII f. 17.

Marine: North Sea! Mediterranean Sea! Adriatic! Labuan! China! Port Jackson! Florida!

Var. *intermedia* PER. (1891). — V. more lanceolate, with less asymmetrical ends. — *Donkinia recta var. int.* PER. p. 30 Pl. IX f. 7, 8.

Marine: Cherbourg (Per.). Firth of Tay!

Var. *Thumii* CL. (1891). L. 0,1 to 0,13; B. 0,011 to 0,012 mm. T.S. : L.S. $^{25}{}_{21}$, $^{28}{}_{28}$, $^{28}{}_{27}$ in 0,01 mm. — *Donkinia Thumii* PER. p. 30 Pl. VII f. 28, IX f. 10.

Marine: Balearic Islands! Seychelles! Sumatra!

Var. *minuta* DONK. (1858). — Smaller. L. 0,06; B. 0,012 mm. Striæ 19 in 0,01 mm. *Pleur. minutum* DONK. T. M. S. VI p. 24, Pl. III f. 8. *Donkinia min.* RALFS in Pritch. Inf. p. 921 (1861). PER. IX f. 9.

Marine: Newcastle! Firth of Tay!

27. **G. lineare** GRUN. (1880). — V. narrow, linear, almost straight, unilaterally narrowed towards the ends. L. 0,17 to 0,26; B. 0,01 to 0,015 mm. Median line sigmoid, strongly excentric. T.S. : L.S. $^{20}{}_{24}$, $^{21}{}_{26}$ in 0,01 mm. — *Rhoic. lineare* GRUN. A. D. p. 59. PER. IX f. 11 (median line incorrectly represented as central).

Marine: Adriatic! Seychelles (Grun.), Port Jackson! Colon!

Var. *longissima* CL. (1881). — V. very narrow, with obliquely rounded ends. L. 0,16 to 0,17; B. 0,007 mm. T.S. : L.S. $^{18}{}_{21}$, $^{22}{}_{22}$ in 0,01 mm. — *Pleur.* (*Donk.?*) *long.* CL. N. R. D. p. 6 Pl. I. f. 8. PER. VII f. 16.

Marine: Mediterranean Sea (Gulf of Naples, Balearic Islands)!

28. **G. angustum** DONK. (1858). — V. very convex, thin, linear, with unilaterally attenuate, acute ends. L. 0,126 to 0,14; B. 0,015 mm. Median line diagonal in the middle and then marginal. T.S. : L.S. $^{28}{}_{22}$ in 0,01 mm. *Pleur. angustum* DONK. T. M. S. VI p. 24 Pl. III f. 9. *Donkinia angusta* RALFS in Pritch. Inf. p. 921 (1861). PER. IX f. 3.

Marine: England (Donk.), Balearic Islands!

Var. *sumatrana* CL. — Less convex. L. 0,14; B. 0,018 mm. T.S. : L.S. $^{29}{}_{21}$ in 0,01 mm. Median line less excentric.

Marine: Sumatra (Deby Coll.)!

29. **P. (Rhoicos.) compactum** GREV. (1857). — Frustule arcuate, with dissimilar valves. V. short, linear, unilaterally attenuated to the obliquely rounded ends. L. 0,089 to 0,4; B. 0,015 to 0,05 mm. Upper valve with straight diagonal, median line T.S. : L.S. $^{16}{}_{22}$, $^{14}{}_{23}$, $^{16}{}_{21}$, $^{17}{}_{20}$ in 0,01 mm. Lower valve with strongly excentric and sigmoid median line. T.S. : L.S. $^{16}{}_{22}$, $^{17}{}_{19}$, $^{17}{}_{22}$, $^{18}{}_{22}$, $^{19}{}_{21}$, $^{19}{}_{24}$ in 0,01 mm. — *Lower valve: Pleur. comp.* GREV. M. J. V. p. 12 Pl. III f. 9. *Donkinia comp.* RALFS in Pritch. Inf. p. 921 (1861). *Rhoic. comp.* GRUN. M. M. J 1877 p. 182. PER. p. 33 Pl. X f. 7, 8. *Rhoic. oceanicum* PER. l. c. f. 5, 12, 15. *Rhoic. corsicanum* PER. l. c. *Rhoic. Antillarum* CL. West. Ind. D. p. 9 Pl. II f. 14. *Pleur. Smithianum* CASTR. Voyage Challenger D. p. 38 Pl. XXVIII f. 6? *Donkinia antiqua* GROVE and STURT J. Queck. M. Cl. III [2] p. 133 (1887)? — *Upper valve: Rhoic. Reichardtianum* GRUN. Hedwigia VI p. 11 (1867). M. M. J. 1877 p. 181 Pl. CXCV f. 19. *Rhoic. compactum* PER. p. 33 Pl. X f. 6, 8, 10, 13.

Marine: La Rochelle (Petit Coll.)! Mediterranean Sea! Adriatic! Red Sea! Sumatra! Philippines! Port Jackson! Samoa! Tahiti! Galapagos Islands! Honduras (Grun.). West Indies!

Var. *constricta* GRUN. (1877). - V. slightly constricted in the middle, with subcuneate ends. L. 0,13; B. 0,02 mm. T.S. : L.S. $^{17}{}_{19}$, $^{18}{}_{20}$ in 0,01 mm. — *Rhoic.* (*Reichardtii var.?*) *constr.* GRUN. M. M. J. 1877 p. 181.

Marine: Honduras (Grun.)! Adriatic (Grun.)!

This species is very variable as to size and number of the striæ, so that I cannot admit the separation of *Rhoic. compactum* and *Rhoic. oceanicum* PER. According to PERAGALLO *Gyr. compactum* has 20 to 24 transverse and closer longitudinal striæ, but I have not seen such closely striate forms, which are said to be frequent. Most specimens I have seen agree with *Rhoic. oceanicum*. The fact that the valves of the same frustule are dissimilar, discovered by PERAGALLO, is of great interest. The striation of the valves is somewhat dissimilar. On specimens from La Rochelle I counted on the lower valve 19 transv. and 24 longit. striæ in 0,01 mm. and on the upper valve 16 transv. and 23 longit. striæ in 0,01 mm.

30. **G. (Rhoicosigma) mediterraneum** CL. (1877). — V. narrow, with acute ends. L. 0,18 to 0,24; B. 0,022 to 0,0025 mm. Median line diagonal in the middle and then marginal. T.S. : L.S. $^{18}/_{25}$, $^{19}/_{26}$, $^{19}/_{27}$ in 0,01 mm. — *Rhoic. medit.* CL. T. R. M. S. 1877 p. 182. N. R. D. p. 6 Pl. I f. 9. PER. IX f. 29 to 32.

Marine: Balearic Islands! Adriatic! Sumatra (Deby Coll.)! Java!

Var. *calcarea* BRUN (1891). V. smaller, with less acute ends and less asymmetrical median line. T.S. : L.S. $^{20-5}/_{27}$ in 0,01 mm. — PER. p. 32 Pl. IX f. 28.

Marine: Japan, fossil (Per.).

Var. *chinensis* CL. — L. 0,14; B. 0,018 mm. Median line as in the type. T.S. : L.S. $^{23}/_{30}$ in 0,01 mm.

Marine: China (Deby Coll.)!

31. **G. (Rhoicosigma) robustum** GRUN. (1880). — V. narrow lanceolate, sigmoid, gradually tapering from the middle to the acute ends. L. 0,27 to 0,6; B. 0,04 to 0,06 mm. Median line sigmoid, excentric. T.S. : L.S. $^{11}/_{12}$, $^{12}/_{13}$, $^{13}/_{13}$ in 0,01 mm. — *Pleur. (Rhoic.?) robustum* GRUN. A. D. p. 58. *Rhoic. robustum* PER. X f. 2, 3.

Marine: Mediterranean Sea! Java! Singapore! Samoa! Galapagos Islands! Campeachy Bay!

Var. *inflexa* PER. (1891). — Valve more narrow and sigmoid. — PER. p. 34 Pl. X f. 4.

Marine: Mediterranean Sea!

Frustulia AG. (1824).

Both valves similar. Central nodule small, indistinct or elongated. Median line enclosed between two siliceous ribs. Terminal nodules small, sometimes elongated; terminal fissures not distinct. No axial or central area. Structure: puncta arranged in transverse and longitudinal striæ. Connecting zone simple. Cellcontents: two endochrome-plates along the interior wall of the connecting zone, in the middle of the valve separated a from the wall by hemispherical plasma-masses. On division of the plates, they do not move in the cells; the fission begins at the ends of the plate (PFITZER Bau u. Entw. p. 58). On conjugating, two frustules form by their cell-contents a mass, which is transformed into two cylindrical bodies, with obtuse, rounded ends, coarsely transversely costate, parallel to the empty valves. The ends of these bodies form, later on, caps, which are thrown off. The bodies become conical, and gradually the valves are developed, one after the other. When full-grown they are twice as long as the mother-cells (PFITZER Bau u. Entw. p. 58).

From the description of the cell-contents and the process of conjugation it seems that Frustulia and Navicula differ considerably in these respects.

Some species of Frustulia (of the group of *F. rhomboides*) are, as far as regards the valve, nearly akin to the *Naviculæ orthostichæ* and, on the other hand to *Amphipleura*. The central nodule, usually small, becomes in same forms (*N. rhomboides var. amphipleuroides*) united to the strong siliceous strings, which enclose the median line, as in Amphipleura, but the central nodule is in the latter genus much larger. Several species of Frustulia (as *F. vulgaris*) live enclosed in gelatinous tubes and have been considered as belonging to a separate genus (*Colletonema* THW.); others live in gelatinous masses (*Frustulia* AG., EHB., KÜTZ.). No generic distinctions may be founded on such characteristics. BRÉBISSON founded 1868 (Ann. de la Soc. phytol. et microsc. de Belgique. Vol. I p. 201) the genus *Van Heurckia* on the peculiar structure of the central nodule and the median line. With PFITZER I am inclined to retain the old name *Frustulia*.

Artificial key.

1.	Valve rhomboid to lanceolate	2.
	— linear to elliptic-linear	4.
2.	Size small. L. 0,028 to 0,03 mm.	*F. styriaca* GRUN.
	— larger. L. 0,05 or more	3.
3.	Median striæ slightly radiate	*F. vulgaris* THW.
	— parallel	*F. rhomboides* EHB.
4.	Terminal nodules near the margin	*F. interposita* LEWIS.
	— — distant from —	*F. Lewisiana* GREV.

1. **F. styriaca** GRUN. (1880). — V. narrow rhombic-lanceolate. L. 0,028 to 0,03; B. 0,005 to 0,006 mm. Central nodule elongated. Striæ slightly radiate, also at the ends, about 24 (middle) to 27 (ends) in 0,01 mm. — *Nav. (Vanheurckia?) styriaca* GRUN. V. H. Syn. Pl. XVII f. 7, 8.

Fresh water?

I have not seen this species, which has the appearance of a small *F. rhomboides*.

2. **F. vulgaris** THW. (1847). V. narrow-lanceolate, with subrostrate, obtuse ends. L. 0,05–0,07; B. 0,011 mm. Central nodule elongated. Striæ 24 (middle) to 34 (ends) in 0,01 mm., slightly radiate in the middle, transverse at the ends. Frustules enclosed in unbranched gelatinous tubes. — *Colletonema vulgaris* THW. Ann. N. H. (2) I Pl. XII f. 4. W. SM. B. D. II p. 70 Pl. LVI f. 351. GRUN. Banka D. II f. 15. *Nav. dirhynchus* DONK. B. D. Pl. V f. 3 (1871) Ehb.? Kütz? *Vanheurckia vulgaris* V. H. Syn. p. 112 Pl. XVII f. 6.

Fresh water: Sweden! Norway! Finland! Saxony! Belgium (V. H.), Switzerland (Brun.), Siberia! Japan! Bengal! Australia (Orara River, Blue mountains etc.)! Tasmania! Ecuador!

Var. *asymmetrica* CL. V. elliptical, asymmetrical, with obtuse ends. Median line excentric, more approximate to the less convex margin. Terminal nodules at some distance from the ends of the valve. Striæ 22 to 30 in 0,01 mm., somewhat radiate in the middle and closer at the ends, punctate; puncta arranged in longitudinal undulating rows, 19 to 23 in 0,01 mm. — Pl. V f. 29.

Brackish water: Sierra Leone! Cameroon! Tasmania! Newark N. Jers. fossil (Champlain epoch)!

3. **F. rhomboides** EHB. (1843). — V. rhombic-lanceolate, with obtuse ends. L. 0,07 to 0,16; B. 0,015 to 0,03 mm. Central nodule small or elongated. Transverse striæ parallel, 23 to 24 in 0,01 mm.; longitudinal striæ 20 to 25 in 0,01 mm. — *Nav. rhomboides* EHB. Am. III: 1 f. 15? W. SM. B. D. I Pl. XVI f 129. GRUN. Banka D. Pl. II f. 14. *Vanheurckia rhomb.* BRÉB. Ann. Soc. phyto. et micr. de Belgique Vol. I p. 201 (1868). V. H. Syn. p. 112 Pl. XVII f. 1, 2.

Fresh water: Sweden! Finland (from Russian Lapland to Abo)! England! Belgium (V. H.), Bengal! Australia (Daintree River, Blue Mountains)! New Zealand! Greenland! Canada! Sierra Nevada! White Mountains! Demerara River! Brazil!

Var. *lineolata* EHB. (1843). V. with several coarse longitudinal furrows. — *N. lineolata* EHB. Am. Pl. I: a f. 4 a? M. G. Pl. XVI: 1 f. 3 etc.

Fresh water: Sweden (Degernäs, fossil)! Bengal! New Zealand, fossil!

Var. *oregonica* CL. — V. narrow. L. 0,1; B. 0,015 mm. Transverse striæ 30, longitudinal 25 in 0,01 mm.

Fresh water: Oregon, fossil!

Var. *amphipleuroides* Grun. (1880). — L. 0,13; B. 0,02 mm. Central nodule elongated; median line slightly excentric. Transverse striæ 23, longitudinal striæ 18 to 19 in 0,01 mm. *Vanheurckia rhomb. var. amphipl.* Grun. A. D. p. 47 Pl. III f. 59.

Fresh water: Finland (Russian Lapland, Ladoga)! Mouth of Jenissey! Vancouver Island (Grove Coll.)!

Var. *saxonica* Rabh. (1851). — V. lanceolate, with rostrate ends. L. 0,05 to 0,07; B. 0,013 to 0,02 mm. Striæ fine, 34 to 35 (V. H. Syn.). — *Frustulia saxonica* Rabh. (Bac. exc. N:o 42. Fl. E. Alg. p. 227). Grun. Banka D. Pl. I f. 13. *Nav. crassinervia* Bréb. in W. Sm. B. D. p. 47 Pl. XXXI f. 271 (1853). Grun. Verh. 1860 p. 518 Pl. V f. 12. Donk. B. D. p. 42 Pl. VI f. 12. *Vanheurckia crass.* Bréb. Ann. Soc. phyto. et microgr. de Belgique Vol. I p. 204 (1868).

Fresh water: Spitsbergen (Lagerst.), Beeren Eiland (Lagerst.), Sweden! Finland! Germany! Australia (Blue Mountains, Daintree River)! New Zealand! Bengal!

Var. *viridula* Bréb. (1849). — Frustules in gelatinous tubes. V. elongated, with broad, obtuse ends. L. 0,08 to 0,11; B. 0,015 mm. Striæ 28 to 30 in 0,01 mm. (V. H.). — *Colleton. viridulum* Bréb. in Kütz. Sp. A. p. 105. *Vanheurckia virid.* Bréb. Ann. Soc. phyt. et micr. de Belgique Vol. I p. 203 (1868). V. H. Syn. p. 112 Pl. XVII f. 3. *Frustulia torphacea* A. Br. in Rabh. Alg. Sachs. N:o 761 (1858).

Fresh water: Germany! France (Bréb.).

4. **F. interposita** Lewis (1865). — V. linear-elliptical, with broad, rounded ends. L. 0,12 to 0,13; B. 0,025 to 0,027 mm. Central nodule small, terminal nodules small, approximate to the ends. Transverse striæ 20, longitudinal 18 in 0,01 mm. — *Nav. interposita* Lewis Proc. Ac. Philad. 1865 Pl. II f. 19. *Nav. Martonfii* Pant. III Pl. XVII f. 247 (1893)?

Brackish water: Sierra Leone! Bombay (Grove Coll.)! Savannah Ga.! Oakland, Calif.! South America (Lewis), Hungary, Tallya fossil (Grun.).

Var. *labuensis* Cl. (1883). — Narrow elliptic-lanceolate with obtuse ends. L. 0,065 to 0,072; B. 0,015 mm. Transverse striæ 17; longitudinal 18 to 21 in 0,01 mm. *Nav. O'M. var. lab.* Cl. Vega p. 496.

Marine: Labuan!

Var. *incomperta* Lewis (1865). — Transverse striæ about 27, longitudinal 22 to 23 in 0,01 mm. — *Nav. incomperta* Lewis l. c. f. 20.

Brackish water: Atlantic coasts of U. States (Lewis).

Var. *Julieni* Brun a. Hérib. (1893). — L. 0,07; B. 0,012 to 0,017 mm. Transverse striæ about 28, longitudinal 20 in 0,01 mm. — *N. Jul.* Brun a. Hérib. D. d'Auvergne p. 199 Pl. VI f. 8, 9.

Brackish water: Auvergne, fossil!

5. **F. Lewisiana** Grev. (1863). — V. linear, with broad, rounded ends. L. 0,19 to 0,21; B. 0,035 to 0,038 mm. Central nodule small, terminal nodules elongated and linear, at some distance from the ends. Transverse striæ parallel in the middle, convergent at the ends, 24 in 0,01 mm. Longitudinal striæ 25 in 0,01 mm. irregularly undulating. — *Nav. n. sp.* Lewis Proced. Ac. Nat. Sc. Phil. Pl. II f. 3 (1861). *Nav. Lewis.* Grev. T. M. S. XI p. 15 Pl. I f. 7 (1863). *Vanheurckia Lewisiana* Bréb. Ann. Soc. phytol. et microgr. Belgique Vol. I p. 202 (1868).

Brackish water: Sierra Leone! Cameroon! India (Wallich), Batavia! Sendaï. Japan, fossil! Brazil (Brun Coll.)! Florida and Georgia (Lewis).

Stenoneis Cl. N. Gen.

Valve narrow, with rounded ends. Central and terminal nodules very small. Median line indistinct, bordered by two strong linear silicious ribs. Structure: fine, transverse, striæ. Axial area indistinct.

This genus includes one species only, which I cannot place in any other group. The thick lines on both sides of the median line seem to point to some relation to Frustulia.

1. **S. inconspicua** Greg. (1857). — V. linear, frequently gibbous in the middle, with broad, rounded ends. L. 0,05; B. 0,007 mm. Central nodule very small; terminal nodules small, somewhat distant from the ends. Median line bordered by two strong, siliceous ribs. Axial area indistinct. Central area a broad, transverse fascia. Striæ 26 in 0,01 mm., parallel throughout. — *N.? inconspicua* Greg. D. of Clyde p. 478 Pl. IX f. 3. *N. Fistula* A. S. N. S. D. Pl. II f. 29 (1874). *Stenon. inconsp.* Icon. n. Pl. V f. 28.

Marine: North Sea! Scotland (Greg.), Bohuslän! Balearic Islands!

Var. *Baculus* Cl. (1883). — L. 0,065; B. 0,007 mm. Striæ 19 in 0,01 mm., crossed in the middle by a narrow lateral area. — *N. Baculus* Cl. Vega p. 474 Pl. XXXVII f. 51.

Marine: North Siberian Sea, Cape Wankarema!

Cistula Cl. N. G.

Valve broad (of the only known species, rectangular). Central nodule very small. Median line between two siliceous ribs; its central pores very approximate. Structure: slightly radiate striæ, crossed by several longitudinal, blank bands.

This group contains but one species, which I am unable to place in any other. The peculiar form of the median line is nearly the same as in *Stenoneis* and *Frustulia*.

1. **C. Lorenziana** Grun. (1860). — V. rectangular, sometimes slightly gibbous in the middle and at the ends. Striæ slightly radiate throughout, 17 in 0,01 mm., composed of elongated puncta, arranged in regular longitudinal rows, 12 in 0,01 mm., angularly bent in the middle. — *Nav. Lorenziana* Grun. Verh. 1860 p. 547 Pl. III f. 3. *Nav.? Cistella* Grev. T. M. S. XI p. 19 Pl. I fig. 12 to 14 (1863). *Cistula Lor.* Icon. n. Pl. I f. 31.

Marine: South coast of England (Roper), Balearic Islands! Adriatic! Queensland (Grev.)! Port Jackson! Campeachy Bay!

Brebissonia Grun. (1860).

Valve symmetrical, lanceolate or subrhomboid. Central nodule elongated. Terminal fissures almost straight. No longitudinal lines. Structure: coarse, transverse, costate striæ and very fine puncta arranged in very fine longitudinal striæ. Connecting zone simple. Cell-contents: a single chromatophore-plate as in Cymbella.

The only species of this genus was in 1838 described by Ehrenberg as *Cocconema Boeckii*. It was in 1858 placed by W. Smith in the genus *Doryphora* together with *Rhaphoneis amphiceros*. Grunow in 1860 formed for this species the genus *Brebissonia* (Verh. 1860 p. 512), principally characterized by the occurrence of the symmetrical frustules on gelatinous stalks. Heiberg in 1863 placed it in *Navicula*, a genus to which it has scarcely any affinity, and from which, according to the researches of Pfitzer (Bau u. Entw. p. 76) it differs greatly in its cell-contents, which are similar to those of *Cymbella*. There is no doubt good reason for placing it in the separate genus *Brebissonia*. By its elongated central nodule it seems to approach to *Amphipleura*, but the structure of the valve is different, and is more like that of the group *Lineolatæ* in the *Naviculæ*. It is at any rate an isolated form of doubtful place in the system. The only known species occurs in brackish water attached by gelatinous stalks to water-plants.

1. **B. Boeckii** EHR. (1838). — Frustule stipitate. V. lanceolate. L. 0,12; B. 0,023 mm. Central nodule elongated. Terminal fissures straight, at a short distance from the ends. Striæ 10 (middle) to 13 (ends), radiate at the ends. Puncta of the exterior stratum forming fine lineolæ, about 30 in 0,01 mm. — *Cocconema Boeckii* EHR. Inf. Pl. XIX f. 5. *Doryphora Boeckii* W. SM. B. D. Pl. XXIV f. 223. *Brebissonia Boeckii* GRUN. Verh. 1860 p. 512.

Brackish water: Baltic (from Roslagen and Bay of Finland to Kiel)! Coasts of England! Connecticut to North Carolina!

Var. *minor* CL. — L. 0,058; B. 0,016 mm. Striæ in the middle 12, at the ends 15 in 0,01 mm.

Brackish water: Amsterdam (Kinker Coll.)!

Amphipleura KÜTZ (1844).

Valve elongated, fusiform or linear, without longitudinal lines or ridges. Central nodule elongated into a rib, extending throughout the whole valve, furcate towards the ends. Structure: very fine puncta arranged in parallel, transverse and straight longitudinal striæ. Cell-contents: two endochrome-plates along the inside of the connecting zone. Median plasma-mass distinct. On conjugating two cells give origin to two auxospores (»Berkeleya Dillwynii» Lüders Beob. p. 59).

The genus *Amphipleura* was founded in 1844 by KÜTZING (Bac. p. 103) for *Frustulia pellucida*, known already by him in 1833. *Nitzschia Sigma*, under the name of *Amphipleura rigida*, was also included in the new genus. According to KÜTZING and all later authors (compare the ideal section in VAN HEURCK synopsis Pl. XVII f. 14 A) the valve of Amphipleura has on both sides of the axis an elevated line or ridge, which I have always failed to discover. Certain small forms of *Amphipleura* live in gelatinous tubes, and for these the genera *Berkeleya* GREV. (1827), *Rhaphidogloea* (KÜTZ. 1844) were founded. They have also been included in *Schizonema*, *Micromega*, *Bangia*, *Monema*, *Conferva* etc., but there is no more reason for separating these forms from *Amphipleura* than for distinguishing *Encyonema*, *Endosigma*, *Endostauron*, *Schizonema* and *Colletonema* from *Cymbella*, *Gyrosigma*, *Navicula* and *Frustulia*. The frustules of the forms living in tubes are exactly similar to those of the true *Amphipleura*, only smaller. The shape of the gelatinous tubes is in my opinion of little importance. GRUNOW in 1880 (Bot. Centralblatt) wrote an elaborate monograph of these forms, to which I refer.

The diatoms most nearly akin to *Amphipleura* are to be found in the genus *Frustulia*. In this genus one meets with forms, having a small central nodule and obscure median line, enclosed between two, strong interior silicious ridges, forming at the ends of the valve a »porte-crayon»-shaped figure. In some forms the central nodule becomes fused together with the siliceous ridges. If the fusion extends farther, we get the forms of the central nodule, characterizing *Amphipleura*. The »forks» in *Amphipleura* correspond to the »port-crayons» in *Frustulia* and to the »horns» in *Diploneis*. Another genus, to a certain degree akin to *Amphipleura* is *Brebissonia*. Perhaps the curious and isolated *Hydrosilicon* BRUN, (*Amphiprora rimosa* O'MEARA) may be a distant relative. *Amphipleura Debyi* appears in some respects to be intermediate.

All species of Amphipleura, except *A. Debyi*, are nearly related, have the same important characteristics, and differ only in the size, some slight differences in the outline, the length of the forks, and number of striæ. They inhabit fresh as well as brackish or salt water. Fresh-water forms are larger, live free or enclosed in mucous, amorphous masses, the marine live enclosed in tubes. Of the freshwater-forms those living in warmer or tropical countries are the largest and in structure coarsest.

1. *Smaller, marine or brackish forms, enclosed in gelatinous tubes* **(Berkeleya, Raphidogloea).**[1]

1. **A. rutilans** TRENTEPOHL (1806). — V. short and narrow, obtuse, linear-elliptical or linear-lanceolate. L. 0,015 to 0,035; B. 0,004 to 0,006 mm. Forks about 1/3 as long as the length of the valve. Striæ 28 in 0,01 mm., slightly radiate at the ends. — *Conferva rutilans* TRENT. in Roth Cat. III p. 179. *Berkeleya Dillwynii* V. H. Syn. p. 113 Pl. XVI f. 15. *Schizonema Dillw.* W. SM. B. D. II p. 77 Pl. LVIII f. 366. *Berkel. obtusa* V. H. Syn. l. c. f. 16 and var. *adriatica* f. 17, 18.

Brackish and marine: Baltic (Gulf of Bothnia, at Tornea, Gotland, Bay of Finland)! Caspian Sea (Grun.)! North Sea, English Channel! Mediterranean Sea! Japan!

Var. *antarctica* (HARW.) GRUN. 1881. — Striæ 36 in 0,01 mm. — *Berkel. antarct.* GRUN. in V. H. Syn. Pl. XVI f. 20. *Berk. Harveyana* GRUN. l. c. 14. *Berk. parasitica* GRUN. l. c. f. 19. *Berk. finnica* DANNF. Baltic D. Pl. II f. 19 (1882)?

Marine: North Sea (Grun.), Falklands Islands (Grun.), Friendly Islands (Grun.).

2. **A. micans** LYNGB. (1819). V. linear, with broad and rounded ends, elongated. L. 0,065 to 0,125; B. 0,01 mm. Forks more than 1/3 of the length of the valve. Striæ about 27 in 0,01 mm. *Bangia micans* LYNGB. Tentamen hydrophytol. p. 84 Pl. XXV. *Berkeleya mic.* GRUN. in V. H. Syn. p. 113 Pl. XVI f. 11. *Berk. pumila* V. H. Syn. l. c. f. 13. *Berk. adriatica* GRUN. in T. R. M. S. 1877 p. 180 Pl. CXCV f. 15.

Marine: North Sea! Mediterranean Sea (Grun.). Adriatic (Grun.).

Var. *fragilis* (GREV.) GRUN. Striæ 32 to 36 in 0,01 mm. *Berkel. fragilis* GREV. Scot. Crypt. Fl. Pl. 294. V. H. Syn. Pl. XVI f. 12.

Marine: North Sea (Grun.), Mediterranean Sea (Grun.).

2. *Larger, brackish or freshwater forms, free or in mucous masses* **(Amphipleura).**

3. **A. pellucida** KÜTZ. (1833). — V. fusiform, acute. L. 0,08 to 0,14; 0,007 to 0,009 mm. Forks 0,02 mm. Transverse striæ 37 in 0,01 mm. *Frustulia pelluc.* KÜTZ. Linnea VIII Pl. 13 f. 11. Dec. N:o 83 (1834) accord. to Lagerst. *A. pellucida* KÜTZ. Bac. p. 103 (1844). W. SM. B. D. XV f. 127. GRUN. Verh. 1862 p. 154. GRUN. T. R. M. S. 1877 p. 179. V. H. Syn. p. 113 Pl. XVII f. 14, 15 A.

Fresh and slightly brackish water: Baltic (Gotland, Dannf. Torneå!), Sweden (Mälaren, Vestergötland)! Finland! Belgium (V. H.), England (W. Sm.), Austria (Grun.), Switzerland (Brun.), Japan!

Var. *brasiliensis* CL. — L. 0,009; B. 0,01 mm. Forks 0,015 to 0,03 mm. Transverse striæ 33, longitudinal 27 in 0,01 mm. — *A. Lindheimeri* GRUN. in Cl. M. D. N:o 298.

Fresh water: Brazil! Ecuador!

Var. *Lindheimeri* GRUN. (1862). L. 0,15 to 0,16; B. 0,024 mm. Forks 0,036 mm. Terminal nodules short, rounded. Transverse striæ 26 longitudinal 26 in 0,01 mm. — *A. Lindheim.* GRUN. Verh. 1862 p. 155 Pl. XIII f. 11. T. R. M. S. 1877 p. 179 Pl. CXCV f. 13.

Fresh water: Texas (Grun.). Costa Rica (Grove).

Var. *intermedia* GRUN. (1877). — L. 0,019 to 0,2; B. 0,013 to 0,015 mm. Forks 0,044 mm. Terminal nodules short rounded. Striæ somewhat finer than in var. Lindheimeri. — GRUN. T. R. M. S. 1877 p. 179.

Fresh water: Oregon, fossil (Grun.).

Var. *oregonica* GRUN. (1877). — 0,33; B. 0,027 mm. Forks 0,063 mm. Terminal nodules elongated, linear. Striæ as in var. Lindheimeri. — GRUN. l. c. p. 179.

Fresh water: Oregon, fossil (Grun.).

[1] See GRUNOWS Monograph in Bot. Centralblatt 1880 N:o 47/48.

Var. *maxima* H. L. SMITH (1886). — L. 0,37; B. 0,04 mm. Forks 0,01 mm. Striæ 32 in 0,01 mm. — *A. maxima* WALKER and Chase N. R. D. p. 2 Pl. II f. 5.

Fresh water: Oregon, fossil.

Var. *Truani* V. H. — V. fusiform, acute. L. 0,26; B. 0,023 mm. Forks 0,006 mm. Terminal nodules elongated. Transverse and longitudinal striæ 26 in 0,01 mm. — *A. Lindheimeri var. Truani* V. H. T. N:o 166. TRUAN D. Astur. Pl. II f. 34, 35 (according to De Toni). *A. pell. var. Tr.* Icon. n. Pl. VI f. 1.

Fresh water: Spain!

Var. *recta* KITTON (1884). — V. linear, with gently cuneate ends. L. 0,226; B. 0,019 mm. Forks 0,05 mm. Terminal nodules elongated. Striæ 26 in 0,01 mm. — KITTON J. Quekett M. C. (2) II p. 21 Pl. IV f. 4.

Marine: Japan (Kitton).

Var. *Schumannii* GRUN. (1877). — L. 0,18 to 0,02; B. 0,014 mm. Striæ 16 in 0,01 mm. *A. pellucida* SCHUM. Preuss. D. II N. p. 53 Pl. I f. 9. *A. Schum.* GRUN. T. R. M. S. 1877 p. 180.

Brackish water: Baltic (Schum.)

4. **A. Weissflogii** GRUN. (1877). — V. linear, with rounded ends. L. 0,19 to 0,25; B. 0,012 to 0,013; Forks 0,06 to 0,08 mm. Striæ 25 in 0,01 mm. — GRUN. T. R. M. S. 1877 p. 180 Pl. CXCV f. 14.

Fresh water: Oregon, fossil (Grun.).

5. **A. hungarica** PANT. (1889). V. narrow fusiform, obtuse. L. 0,08 to 0,1; B. 0,014 mm. Forks a third as long as the valve. Striæ 11 in 0,01 mm. *Berkeleya hung.* PANT. II p. 55 Pl. IX f. 165.

Marine: Hungary, fossil (Pant.).

A similar form, but with a longitudinal line (?) on each side of the median line is *Berkeleya neogradensis* PANT. III Pl. XXXVI f. 508 (1893).

6. **A. Debyi** LEUD. FORTM. (1892). — V. gibbous in the middle and with very long and narrow protracted ends, of unequal length. L. 0,22; B. 0,02 mm. Forks very elongated. Margin of the valve with coarse »pearls» (loculi?). Striæ not seen. — LEUD. FORTM. D. de la Malaisie p. 22 Pl. II f. 10.

Marine: Sumatra (Leud. Fortm.).

I have had no opportunity of examing this very curious diatom, which to judge from the figure seems to have a loculiferous marginal rim as in Mastogloia.

Naviculæ Mesoleiæ CL.

Valve symmetrical, linear to elliptical, with usually obtuse or rostrate ends. Axial area narrow or indistinct. Central area large, quadrate, or a transverse fascia. Striæ usually fine, punctate and radiate throughout. Connecting zone not complex.

This Section comprises a number of usually small forms, inhabiting fresh, rarely salt water. By *N. Papula* and *N. bacilliformis* this section is closely connected with *Naviculæ bacillares*. There is also some relation between some species of this group and of the section *Naviculæ punctatæ*.

Artificial key.

1.	Valve constricted in the middle	*N. binodis* EHR.
	— not — — —	2.
2.	Length about 0,12 mm.	*N. Szaboi* PANT.
	— — 0,01 mm. or less	3.
3.	Terminal nodules with lateral expansions	*N. Papula* KTZ.
	— — without —	4.

4.	Central area reaching nearly to the margin	5.
	— — not more than half the breadth of the valve	9.
5.	Valve trochiform	*N. Lagerheimii* CL.
	— elliptical	6.
6.	Central area with a single marginal stria	7.
	— — without — —	8.
7.	Isolated stria on one side only	*N. asymmetrica* PANT.
	— — — both sides	*N. alvacea* BERKEL.
8.	Striæ 20 in 0,01 mm.	*N. obliqua* GREG.
	— 27 — —	*N. Rotæana* RABH.
9.	Central area with a stigma	*N. mutica* KÜTZ.
	— without —	10.
10.	Ends capitate	*N. Heufleriana* GRUN.
	— not	11.
11.	Length about 0,04 mm. or more	*N. bacilliformis* GRUN.
	— 0,025 mm.	*N. Haradaæ* PANT.
	— 0,014 to 0,02 mm. or less	12.
12.	Ends rostrate	13.
	— rounded	15.
13.	Valve biconstricted	*N. nivalis* EHB.
	— elliptical to lanceolate	14.
14.	Striæ distinct	*N. Kotschyi* GRUN.
	— very delicate	*N. depressa* CL.
15.	Valve centrally gibbous	*N. Seminulum* GRUN.
	— not —	*N. minima* GRUN.

1. **N. minima** GRUN. (1880). — V. linear with broad rounded ends. L. 0,015; B. 0,0045 mm. Central area small, quadrate. Striæ 26 in 0,01 mm., more distant in the middle of the valve, radiate throughout. — *N. minutissima* GRUN. Verh. 1860 p. 552 Pl. IV f. 2. *N. minima* GRUN. in V. H. Syn. p. 107 Pl. XIV f. 15, 16. *N. Saugerri var.* GRUN. in V. H. S. f. 16 b. *Synedra pusilla* KÜTZ. (according to Grun.).

Fresh water: Belgium (V. H.).

Var. *atomoides* GRUN. (1880). — V. elliptical. L. 0,008; B. 0,004 mm. Striæ 27 to 30 in 0,01 mm. — *N. atomoides* GRUN. in V. H. Syn. Pl. XIV f. 12–14.

Fresh water: Belgium (V. H.).

2. **N. Seminulum** GRUN. (1860). — V. sublinear, gibbous in the middle, with broad, subtruncate ends. L. 0,015; B. 0,004 mm. Central area quadrate, not very large. Striæ 20 in 0,01 mm., radiate throughout. — *N. Seminulum* GRUN. Verh. 1860 p. 552 Pl. IV f. 3. LAGST. Spitsb. D. Pl. II f. 9. V. H. Syn. p. 107 Pl. XIV f. 8, 9. *N. Saugerri* DESMAZ in V. H. Syn. f. 8 a'.

Fresh or slightly brackish water: Spitsbergen (Lagst.), Sweden (Bollnäs in Helsingland, Koön in Bohuslän)! Belgium (V. H.), Japan! Greenland!

Var. *fragilarioides* GRUN. (1880). — Striæ somewhat coarser. — Grun. in V. H. Syn. f. 10.

3. **N. Rotæana** RABH. (1852). — V. elliptical with rounded ends. L. 0,013 to 0,024; B. 0,006 to 0,008 mm. Central area large and broad, reaching near to the margin. Terminal fissures of the median line in contrary direction. Striæ about 28 in 0,01 mm., radiate throughout. — *Stauroneis Rotæana* RABH. HEDW. I p. 103 Pl. XIII f. 7 (1852). GRUN. Verh. 1860 p. 565 Pl. VI f. 14. *Stauron. minutissima* LAGST. Spetsb. D. p. 39 Pl. I f. 13 (1873). *Stauron. ovalis* GREG. M. J. IV Pl. I f. 36 (1856). *Stauron. Cohnii* BRUN D. des Alpes p. 91 Pl. IX f. 10 (1880). *Navic. Rotæana* V. H. Syn. Pl. XIV f. 17–19.

Fresh water: Spitsbergen (Ldt), Sweden! Finland! Austrian alps (Grun.).

Var. *excentrica* GRUN. (1880). — Median line somewhat excentric. — GRUN. in V. H. Syn. XIV f. 20.

Var. *oblongella* GRUN. (1880). — Valve narrow elliptical. — GRUN. in V. H. S. XIV f. 21. *Nav. oblongella* GRUN. Verh. 1860 p. 551 Pl. IV f. 4?

4. **N. Haradaæ** PANT. (1893). — V. broadly elliptical, with broad, rounded ends. L. 0,025; B. 0,018 mm. Axial area indistinct. Central area large, somewhat transverse, half as broad as the valve. Striæ 20 in 0,01 mm. radiate throughout. — PANT. III Pl. VI f. 100.

Habitat? »Sentenaï» (Pant.).

5. **N. depressa** CL. (1891). — V. elliptical, with rostrate ends. L. 0,022; B. 0,009 mm. Surface of the valve depressed between the margin and the longitudinal and transverse area. Central area about $^1/_3$ of the breadth of the valve. Striæ 27 in 0,01 mm., more distant (about 24 in 0,01 mm.) in the middle, slightly radiate, especially near the ends. — CL. D. of Finl. p. 35 Pl. II f. 4.

Fresh water: Sweden, Åreskutan in Jämtland! Wernamo, fossil! Finland (Imandrian Lapland, Suomenniemi, fossil)!

6. **N. binodis** EHR. (1840). — V. strongly constricted in the middle, with rostrate-capitate ends. L. 0,025; B. 0,008 mm. Axial area indistinct. Central area small. Striæ about 30 in 0,01 mm., sligthly radiate. — EHR. Ber. 1840 p. 18. W. SM. B. D. I p. 53 Pl. XVII f. 159. GRUN. Verh. 1860 p. 551 Pl. II f. 42. DONK. B. D. p. 38 Pl. VI f. 3. V. H. Syn. p. 108, Suppl. Pl. B. f. 33.

Fresh water: England (Sm.), Belgium (V. H.), Switzerland! Japan!

7. **N. (Dickieia) ulvacea** BERKL. (1844). — V. linear-elliptical, with rounded ends. L. 0,025 to 0,035; B. 0,008 to 0,012 mm. Axial area indistinct. Central area a narrow, transverse fascia furcate at the margin. Striæ 16 in 0,01 mm., slightly radiate at the ends. Frustules in leaf-like, flat and stipitate gelatinous mass, in length about 1 to 5 cm. — *Dickieia ulv.* BERKL. in Kütz. Bac. p. 119. V. H. Syn. Pl. XVI f. 10.

Marine: Scotland (Dickie), Ireland (O'Meara), Balearic Islands!

8. **N. asymmetrica** PANT. (1893). — V. narrow elliptical, obtuse. L. 0,025; B. 0,01 mm. Central area a broad fascia, reaching the margins, where is, unilaterally, in the middle of the area a single stria. Striæ radiate, 19 in 0,01 mm. — PANT. III Pl. VII f. 110.

Habitat? »Sentenaï» (Pant.).

9. **N. mutica** KÜTZ (1844). — V. of variable shape, elliptic-lanceolate, frequently with undulated margins. L. 0,013 to 0,033; B. 0,007 to 0,014 mm. Axial area narrow. Central area large, transversely dilated, with an isolated punctum on one side of the central nodule. Striæ 18 to 20 in 0,01 mm. radiate at the ends, distinctly punctate. A few of the median striæ shorter than the rest. — KÜTZ Bac. p. 93 Pl. III f. 32 (according to Arnott). GRUN. A. D. p. 40.

Forma Cohnii HILSE (1860). — V. elliptic-lanceolate, with rounded ends. — *Stauron. Cohnii* HILSE Beitr. p. 83. *N. mutica v. Coh.* V. H. Syn. p. 95 Pl. X f. 17. *Stauron. polymorpha* LAGST. Spitsb. D. p. 39 Pl. I f. 12.

Brackish water: Spitsbergen! Belgium (V. H.), Bengal! Daintree River, Australia! Lost Spring Ranch, Calif.!

Forma Göppertiana BLEISCH (1861). — V. lanceolate. - *Stauroneis Semen* EHR. M. G. XXXVIII A 20 f. 1 (1854)? *Stauron. Göppertiana* BLEISCH Rabh. A. E. N:o 1183 (1861). *Nav. mutica* GRUN. Verh. 1860 p. 538 Pl. V f. 16. *Stauron. Cohnii* SCHUM. Tatra p. 78 Pl. IV f. 61. *N. mut. v. Göppertiana* V. H. Syn. p. 95 Pl. X f. 18, 19.

Fresh or brackish water: Belgium (V. H.), Nova Scotia! West Indies! Ecuador!

Forma producta GRUN. (1880). - V. lanceolate, with broad, truncate ends. — GRUN. A. D. p. 41.

Forma ventricosa KÜTZ (1844). — V. inflated, with capitate ends. L. 0,016 to 0,022; B. 0,06 to 0,08 mm. Striæ 17 in 0,01 mm. — *Stauron. ventric.* KÜTZ Bac. p. 105 Pl. XXX f. 27. GREG. M. J. IV Pl. I f. 10 (1856). *Nav. (St.) vent.* V. H. Syn. p. 96 Pl. IV f. 1 b.

Brackish water: Argentina!

Var. *Peguana* Grun. (1879). V. lanceolate, slightly triundulate with subacute ends. L. 0,04; B. 0,01 mm. Striæ in the middle 15 at the ends 20 in 0,01 mm. — Grun. Cl. M. D. N:o 188.

Brackish water: Bengal!

Var. *Legumen* Cl. — V. linear, triundulate, with cuneate, acute ends. L. 0,035; B. 0,009 mm. Striæ 21 in 0,01 mm.

Fresh water: Surinam!

Forma undulata Hilse (1860). — V. with three to four undulations on the margins. — *Stauroneis undulata* Hilse Beitr. p. 83. *Nav. mutica v. undulata* Grun. A. D. p. 41. V. H. Syn. p. 95 Pl. X f. 20 c.

Brackish water: South Africa! Ecuador!

N. mutica is a very variable species, having the appearance of a Stauroneis, under a low power. All varieties have the unilateral isolated punctum in the area.

10. **N. Kotschyii** Grun. (1860). — V. lanceolate, rostrate, with obtuse ends. L. 0,0136 to 0,022; B. 0,0054 to 0,0068 mm. Axial area narrow. Central area large transversely dilated, without an isolated punctum. Striæ 19 to 23 in 0,01 mm., closer near the ends, radiate, distinctly punctate. — Grun. Verh. 1860 p. 538 Pl. IV f. 12. A. D. p. 41. *Nav. Kotschyana* V. H. Syn. Pl. X f. 22.

Fresh water, hot springs: Buda-Pest!

11. **N. Heufleriana** Grun. — V. inflated, with large capitate and flattened ends. L. 0,0244 to 0,032; B. 0,008 to 0,009 mm. Axial area indistinct. Central area large, almost quadrate, without an isolated punctum. Striæ 16 in 0,01 mm. *Stauron. Heufleriana* Grun. Verh. 1863 p. 155 Pl. IV f. 10. *St. Heufleri.* V. H. Syn. Pl. IV f. 1 a.

Fresh water: Tyrol (Grun.).

This form is very nearly connected with *N. mutica var. ventricosa*, almost only difference being absence of an isolated punctum in the central area.

12. **N. nivalis** Ehb. (1854). V. with triundulate margins and rostrate-truncate ends. L. 0,0122 to 0,018; B. 0,0054 mm. Axial area indistinct, central area large, rounded-quadrate, without an isolated punctum. Striæ 18 to 19 in 0,01 mm. radiate to the ends and composed of distinct puncta, 18 to 24 in 0,01 mm. - Ehb. M. G. XXXIII B. a f. 5. *N. quinquenodis* Grun. Verh. 1860 p. 522 Pl. III f. 33. Verh. 1863 p. 149 Pl. IV f. 9. Cl. D. of Finland p. 33 Pl. II f. 5. *N. undosa* Donk. B. D. p. 37 Pl. VI f. 1 (1871).

Fresh water: Sweden (Upsala)! Finland! Belgium (V. H.). Brünn (Grun.). Blue Mountains, Australia!

13. **N. obliqua** Greg. (1856). — V. broad, elliptic-lanceolate. L. 0,04; B. 0,016 mm. Median line slightly sigmoid, with the ends in contrary directions. Axial area very narrow or indistinct; central area a broad transverse fascia, almost reaching to the margin, where it becomes somewhat wider. Striæ 21 in 0,01 mm., in the middle a little more distant, almost parallel, distinctly punctate: puncta about 21 in 0,01 mm., arranged in somewhat undulating longitudinal rows. — *Stauroneis obliqua* Greg. M. J. IV p. 11 Pl. I f. 35. *N. obl.* Icon. n. Pl. V f. 26.

Fresh water: Scotland (Loch Leven) Greg., Engl. Windermere, Grove Coll.! Sweden, bottom-mud from Vettern!

Gregory's figure shews no structure and a decided sigmoid bent of the median line. The above description is from a specimen in Groves collection, which perfectly agrees with the description of Gregory. On original specimens from Loch Leven in Deby's collection I could not distinctly see the sigmoid flexure of the median line. Neither could I find the median line sigmoid on specimens from Abo (Diat. of Finl. p. 34 Pl. III f. 1), Oregon and the mouth of the Jenissey. Having had no opportunity of reexamining these specimens I am unable to state whether I am guilty of a mistake on this point, or these forms represent a variety with straight median line. In all cases the above description refers to a specimen, doubtless identical with *Stauroneis obliqua* Greg.

14. **N. Szaboi** PANT. (1889). V. linear elliptical, with rounded ends. L. 0,123; B. 0,029 mm. Central area large, dilated outwards. Striæ 12 in 0,01 mm. parallel, convergent at the ends, punctate, puncta forming longitudinal rows. — PANT. II p. 54 Pl. VI f. 120.

Brackish water: Hungary fossil (Pant.).

This species is unknown to me and I have placed it with some hesitation in this section as it seems to be most nearly related to *N. obliqua.*

15. **N. Lagerheimii** CL. N. Sp. — V. rhomboid, very dilated in the middle, with truncate ends. L. 0,027 to 0,033; B. 0,013 to 0,014 mm. Axial area very narrow; central area a broad transverse fascia, reaching nearly to the margin, without an isolated punctum. Striæ 18 in 0,01 mm., radiate at the ends, coarsely punctate; puncta about 16 in 0,01 mm.

Fresh water (moist rocks): Ecuador, Pichincha!

This species has the outline of *Anomoeoneis Follis* and is remarkable for its large central area. The central nodule seems to be stauroid.

16. **N. bacilliformis** GRUN. (1880). — V. linear, with broad, rounded ends, frequently somewhat gibbous in the middle and at the ends. L. 0,032 to 0,045; B. 0,009 to 0,01 mm. Central area rectangular, half as broad as the valve. Striæ 12 to 15 in 0,01 mm. at the middle, 20 to 22 in 0,01 mm. at the ends, where they are radiate and curved. — GRUN. A. D. p. 44 Pl. II f. 51. V. H. S. Pl. XIII f. 11. PANT. III Pl. III f. 49.

Fresh water: Norway, Dovre (Grun.). Finland! Australian Alps (Riewa Lagoons)! Ecuador!

17. **N. Pupula** KÜTZ. (1844). — V. linear, frequently gibbous in the middle, with broad, rounded or subtruncate ends. L. 0,022 to 0,037; B. 0,007 to 0,009 mm. Terminal nodules with two lateral expansions. Central area about $^1/_2$ as broad as the valve, quadrate. Striæ 13 to 15 in 0,01 mm. at the middle, 22 to 23 in 0,01 mm. at the ends, radiate at the ends, very finely punctate. — KÜTZ. Bac. p. 93 Pl. XXX f. 40. *N. Pup. var. genuina* GRUN. A. D. p. 45 Pl. II f. 53. V. H. Syn. p. 106 Pl. XIII f. 15, 16. *Stauroneis Wittrockii* LDT. Spitsb. D. p. 38 Pl. II f. 15 (1873) (perhaps N. bacilliformis). *Stauroneis tatrica* GUTWINSKY Mat. fl. Galicyi 1890 p. 24 Pl. I f. 20 (perhaps N. bacilliformis)? *Schizostauron? tatric.* DE TONI Notarisia 1890 p. 196.

Fresh water: Spitzbergen! Sweden! Finland! Norway! Belgium! England! Bengal! Australian Alps! Japan! New Zealand! Sandwich Islands! South Africa! Greenland! Kansas! Argentina! Ecuador!

Var. *rectangularis* GREG. (1854). — V. linear with broad, subrostrate ends. — *Stauroneis rectangularis* GREG. M. J. II Pl. IV f. 17. *N. Pup. v. rect.* GRUN. A. D. p. 45.

Fresh water: Scotland (Greg.).

Var. *bacillaroides* GRUN. (1880). — V. linear with rounded ends. — GRUN. A. D. p. 45.

Naviculæ Entoleiæ CL.

Valve symmetrical, linear-lanceolate or fusiform to elliptical, rarely constricted. Median line with somewhat distant central pores. Axial and central areas combined in a more or less broad, lanceolate space. Striæ fine, finely punctate, radiate at the ends. Connecting zone not complex.

This section comprises forms in some respects intermediate between those of the sections *Nav. microstigmaticæ* and *Nav. lævistriatæ.* Some of them appear to be related to the *Nav. fusiformes,* but differ in the more distant central pores and in the axial area.

The species of this section partly inhabit fresh, and partly salt water. Some of the small fresh-water species usually grow in filaments, and are then called *Diadesmis.*

Artificial key.

1.	Small forms L. 0,02 mm. or less	2.
	Larger — L. 0,04 or more	7.
2.	Striæ 13 to 16 in 0,01 mm.	3.
	— much finer	4.
3.	Striæ nearly parallel	*N. Scutum* V. H.
	— radiate	*N. infirma* Grun.
4.	Striæ about 21 in 0,01 mm.	*N. confervacea* Kütz.
	— — 33 — —	5.
5.	Valve gibbous in the middle and at the ends	*N. contenta* Grun.
	— — — — but not at the ends	6.
6.	Valve sublinear	*N. Flotowii* Grun.
	— subelliptical	*N. perpusilla* Grun.
7.	Valve with undulated margins	*N. polygibba* Pant.
	— — non — —	8.
8.	Valve elliptical with rounded ends	9.
	— lanceolate or fusiform	11.
9.	Terminal fissures in contrary direction	*N. fallax* Cl.
	— — the same —	10.
10.	Puncta twice as close as the striæ	*N. Beta* Cl.
	— as close as the striæ	*N. Hochstetteri* Grun.
11.	Valve broadly lanceolate	12.
	— narrow — or fusiform	16.
12.	Puncta forming straight, longitudinal rows	*N. Iota* Cl.
	— undulating — —	13.
13.	Area broad	14.
	— narrow	15.
14.	Striæ 10 in 0,01 mm.	*N. semitecta* A. S.
	— 13 —	*N. occidentalis* Cl.
	— 19 —	*N. definita* Grove a. Sturt.
15.	Valve rostrate	*N. mocsarensis* Pant.
	obtuse	*N. Bäumleri* Pant.
	— acute	*N. Kappa* Cl.
16.	Valve fusiform	17.
	— narrow lanceolate	*N. Foliola* Brun a. Temp.
17.	Striæ radiate in the ends	*N. monmouthiana* Grun.
	— almost parallel	18.
18.	Striæ »crossed by two lines»	*N. fusoides* Grun.
	— not	*N. inornata* Grun.

1. **N. contenta** Grun. (1880). — V. linear, gibbous in the middle, with broad capitate ends. L. 0,007 to 0,01; B. 0,002 to 0,0025 mm. Axial area narrow, linear, slightly dilated in the middle. Striæ almost parallel 36 in 0,01 mm. *N. trinodis* V. H. Syn. Pl. XIV f. 31 a. *N. contenta* Grun. in V. H. Syn. p. 109.

Fresh water (on moist rocks and mosses): Sweden (Trollhättan)! Finland (Åbo)! Belgium (V. H.), Salzburg! Amsterdam Island!

Var. *biceps* Arnott Ms. — V. not gibbous in the middle. — *Diadesmis biceps* Arnott (according to Grun.). *Nav. trinodis var. biceps* V. H. Syn. XIV f. 31 b.

Fresh water: Belgium (V. H.), Ecuador!

2. **N. (Diadesmis) Flotowii** Grun. (1880). — V. narrow, lanceolate, with broad, obtuse ends. L. 0,015; B. 0,004 mm. Area narrow, lanceolate. Striæ radiate, 35 in 0,01 mm. — Grun. V. H. Syn. p. 109 Pl. XIV f. 41.

Fresh water: Belgium (V. H.), France (V. H. T.).

3. **N. perpusilla** GRUN. (1860). — V. subelliptical, gibbous in the middle and with broad, subtruncate ends. L. 0,012; B. 0,004 to 0,005 mm. Area lanceolate, narrow. Striæ about 30 in 0,01 mm., radiate throughout. — GRUN. Verh. 1860 p. 552 Pl. IV f. 7. V. H. Syn. Pl. XIV f. 22, 23.

Fresh water (on moist rocks, earth etc.): Scotland (Aberdeen)! Sweden (Taberg in Småland)! Finland (Lapland to Åbo)! Arctic America!

4. **N. (Diadesmis) confervacea** KÜTZ (1844). V. thick, lanceolate, obtuse. L. 0,02; B. 0,005 to 0,007 mm. Area lanceolate. Striæ 20 to 22 in 0,01 mm. radiate throughout, finely punctate. Frustules cohering in long bands. — KÜTZ Bac. p. 109 Pl. XXX f. 8. GRUN. Novara p. 21 Pl. I f. 19. *N. (Diad.) conf.* V. H. Syn. XIV f. 36.

Fresh water, tropics: Jamaica! Rio Janeiro! Marquesas Island! Sandwich Islands!

Var. *peregrina* W. SM. (1861). — V. elliptical. L. 0,012 to 0,015; B. 0,006 to 0,0065 mm. Striæ 22 in 0,01 mm. — *Diadesmis peregrina* PRITCH Inf. p. 923. GRUN. Novara Pl. I f. 20. *Nav. confervacea var. peregrina, et hungarica* GRUN. in V. H. Syn. Pl. XIV f. 37, 38.

Fresh water: Rangoon! Australian Alps (Riewa Lagoon)! Tahiti (Grun.), Jamaica! Ecuador!

5. N. **Scutum** (SCHUM.?) V. H. (1880). — V. narrow elliptical, with rounded ends. L. 0,03; B. 0,01 mm. Area narrow, lanceolate, dilated around the central nodule. Striæ 16 in 0,01 mm., very slightly radiate, finely punctate. — SCHUM. Pr. D. p. 188 f. 45 (1862)? V. H. Syn. p. 98 Pl. XI f. 14.

Fresh water: Belgium (V. H.).

N. Scutum V. H. and *N. infirma* GRUN. are, as far as I may judge from the descriptions and the figures, closely akin, the only difference being that the striæ of the former are less radiate. The *Nav. Scutum* SCHUM. from the Königsberg deposit has about the same size, and 14 striæ in 0,01 mm., but no area, so it seems doubtful whether it be the same species as Van Heurck's. The *Nav. Scutum* SCHUM. is perhaps a form of *Cocconeis Placentula*. Another small form of about the same outline and size and with 15 parallel striæ in 0,01 mm., but without area is *Nav. ignobilis* PANT. (II p. 48 Pl. XXV f. 367, 1889) from the brackish strata of Kavna, Hungary. A similar form is *N. debilis* PANT. III Pl. VI f. 98. Having had no opportunity of examining these forms I am unable to decide whether or not they are identical.

6. **N. infirma** GRUN. (1882) — V. linear elliptical, with rounded ends. L. 0,02; B. 0,007 mm. Area narrow, lanceolate. Striæ 13 (middle) to 17 (ends) in 0,01 mm. radiate throughout and finely punctate. — GRUN. Foss. D. Öster. Ung. p. 146 Pl. XXX f. 53.

Fresh water: Hungary fossil (Dubravica Grun.).

7. **N. inornata** GRUN. (1880). — V. fusiform, convex. L. 0,05 to 0,09; B. 0,008 mm. Median line with approximate central pores. Area narrow, lanceolate. Striæ 19 to 21 in 0,01 mm. at the middle, 23 to 24 in 0,01 mm. at the ends, almost parallel. — GRUN. A. D. p. 46 Pl. III f. 56. *N. Acus* CL. A. D. p. 14 Pl. III f. 55. *N. Hahnii* PETIT Cape Horn D. p. 124 Pl. X f. 11 (1888). *N. filiformis* PANT. III Pl. XXXIX f. 538 (1893)?

Marine: Finmark! Bohuslän! Mediterranean (Pithuisian Island)! Ile de Brehat, Manche! Cape Horn!

N. inornata seems to have a longitudinal line crossing the striæ, but this line is an optical illusion, arrising from the convexity of the valve. This species forms a passage from this group to the section N. fusiformes, which has no distinct area, parallel striæ, and very approximate central pores.

8. **N. fusoides** GRUN. (1880). — V. narrow, linear-lanceolate, with more or less obtuse ends. L. 0,05 to 0,12; B. 0,007 to 0,012 mm. Axial area narrow. Striæ 21 to 25 in 0,01 mm. slightly radiate, crossed by two longitudinal lines. — *N. subula* GRUN. Verh. 1860 p. 548 Pl. III f. 24. *N. fusoides* GRUN. A. D. p. 46.

Marine: Bohuslän (Grun.), Mediterranean Sea (Grun.).

I have not seen this species, which according to GRUNOW resembles *N. inornata*. The two distinct longitudinal lines seem to indicate that *N. fusoides* is a Caloneis.

9. **N. Follola** BRUN a. TEMP. (1889). — V. narrow-lanceolate, subacute. L. 0,08 to 0,1; B. 0,015 to 0,017 mm. Central pores of the median line distant., Striation fine, most visible near the margin. BRUN a. TEMP. D. f. du Japon p. 43 Pl. VII f. 15.

Marine: Japan, fossil (Brun a. Temp.).

I have not seen this species, which is not sufficiently figured and described to acertain its proper place.

10. **N. monmouthiana** GRUN. (1880). — V. fusiform. L. 0,082 to 0,09; B. 0,011 to 0,022 mm. Median line with somewhat distant central pores and small comma-like terminal fissures turned in the same direction. Area linear. Striæ 16 (middle) to 20 (ends) in 0,01 mm., almost parallel in the middle, radiate at the ends. GRUN. A. D. p. 16. Icon. n. Pl. V f. 20.

Fresh water: N. America fossil (Cherryfield. Monmouth)!

11. **N. Bäumleri** PANT. (1886). — V. elliptic-lanceolate, with obtuse ends. L. 0,096 to 0,11; B. 0,018 mm. Area narrow, linear-lanceolate. Striæ 9 in 0,01 mm. almost parallel in the middle, radiate at the ends, coarsely punctate; puncta 13 in 0,01 mm., forming longitudinal undulating rows. PANT. I p. 22 Pl. XII f. 108; II Pl. XXIII f. 317.

Marine: Hungary, fossil (Pant.).

Var. *interrupta* PANT. (1886). — Striæ 12 to 14 in 0,01 mm. crossed by a marginal line. — PANT. I l. c. f. 103.

Marine: Hungary, fossil (Pant.).

I have not seen this species, which I have provisionally placed in this section. It is perhaps akin to *Nav. rhombica*. The terminal fissures seem, according to the fig. 103 in Pantocseks work, to be turned in contrary directions.

12. **N. occidentalis** CL. N. Sp. — V. lanceolate, with slightly protracted ends. L. 0,04 to 0,045; B. 0,015 to 0,02 mm. Axial area moderately broad somewhat dilated in the middle. Striæ 13 in 0,01 mm. radiate throughout coarsely punctate; puncta about 16 in 0,01 mm.

Fresh water: Pitt River (Oregon), fossil (Grove Coll.)!

This species has some resemblance to *N. lacustris*, from which it differs by its much broader area.

13. **N. semitecta** A. S. (1874). — V. lanceolate. L. 0,042; B. 0,013 mm. Area lanceolate, broad. Striæ 10 in 0,01 mm., slightly radiate throughout, coarsely punctate. — A. S. Atl. Probetafel f. 11.

Marine: Campeachy Bay (Atl.).

I do not know this species, which may perhaps be a Mastogloia.

14. **Navicula Iota** CL. N. Sp. — V. elliptic-lanceolate, gradually tapering from the middle to the subacute ends. L. 0,1; B. 0,021 mm. Median line with somewhat distant central pores and small terminal fissures. Axial area broad, lanceolate. Striæ 13,5 (middle) to 16 (ends) in 0,01 mm., slightly radiate throughout, of equal length in the middle, distinctly punctate; puncta 16 in 0,01 mm. arranged in regular, longitudinal rows. Pl. V, f. 22.

Marine: Madagascar (Van Heurck Coll.)!

15. **N. Kappa** CL. N. Sp. — V. narrow lanceolate, with elevated, acute ends. L. 0,17; B. 0,028 mm. Median line with transversely dilated median pores and elongated terminal fissures, turned in the same direction. Area narrow near the ends of the valve, gradually widened towards the middle. Striæ 16 in 0,01 mm., not closer near the ends, of equal length and slightly radiate

in the middle, transverse at the ends, punctate, puncta, 14 in 0,01 mm. forming undulating longitudinal rows. — Pl. V f. 21.

Marine: Oamaru, New Zealand, fossil!

16. **N. definita** GROVE a. STURT (1887). — V. elliptic-lanceolate. Ends obtuse and with short diaphragms. L. 0,15; B. 0,04 mm. Median line with the terminal fissures in contrary directions. Area linear-lanceolate, broad. Striæ 18 in 0,01 mm., not closer near the ends, punctate; puncta, 17 in 0,01 mm., forming longitudinal undulating rows. GROVE a. STURT Q. M. Cl. III p. 73 Pl. VI f. 11.

Marine: Oamaru, New Zealand, fossil!

Var. *intermedia* CL. — V. subelliptical, with rounded ends. L. 0,09; B. 0,028 mm. Striæ 18 in 0,01 mm., crossed near the margin by a line. Pl. V f. 24, 25.

Marine: Oamaru, New Zealand fossil (Tempère)!

The *var. intermedia* is a form connecting *N. fallax* with *N. definita*.

17. **N. fallax** CL. N. Sp. — V. elliptic-lanceolate, with rounded ends. L. 0,085; B. 0,032 mm. Median line with the terminal fissures in contrary direction. Area very broad, lanceolate. Striæ 20 in 0,01 mm., radiate throughout, punctate; puncta about 23 in 0,01 mm. The striæ seem to be crossed near the margin by a fine line. Pl. V f. 27.

Marine: Oamaru, New Zealand, fossil (Grove Coll.)!

This interesting species seems at the first view to be *Nav. nebulosa*, having the outline and marginal striate band of the latter, but a closer inspection shews that it is entirely different, having no rows of striæ along the median line. In fact it is nearly akin to *N. definita*.

18. **N. Hochstetteri** GRUN. (1863). — V. elliptical with broad, rounded ends. L. 0,027 to 0,057; B. 0,019 to 0,032 mm. Area broad, subrhomboidal. Striæ 15 (middle) to 20 (end) in 0,01 mm. radiate throughout, in the middle alternately longer and shorter, distinctly punctate: puncta about 17 in 0,01 mm., and close to the area uniting into short lines. — GRUN. Verh. 1863 p. 153 Pl. V f. 2. Novara p. 19. A. S. Atl. VIII f. 53—55.

Marine: Nicobar Island (Grun.), Java! Carpentaria Bay (Atl.). California (Sn Pedro, fossil, Kinker Coll.)! Cape Horn (Petit). Brazil (Atl.).

Var. *placita* GROVE a. STURT (1887). — L. 0,045; B. 0,025 mm. Striæ 14 (middle) to 19 (ends) in 0,01 mm., a few only in the middle being shorter than the others, punctate; puncta 14 in 0,01 mm. — *N. placita* GROVE a. STURT Q. M. Cl. III p. 133 Pl. X f. 14.

Marine: Oamaru, New Zealand, fossil!

As GRUNOW has already remarked there is no specific distinction between *N. placita* and *N. Hochstetteri*. Nearly akin to *N. Hochstetteri* is *N. Beta*, which differs only by its less coarsely punctate striæ.

19. **N. Beta** CL. N. Sp. — V elliptical, with broad rounded ends. L. 0,043; B. 0,025 mm. Median line with the terminal fissures in the same direction. Area broad, lanceolate. Striæ 13 (middle) to 17 (ends) in 0,01 mm. radiate at the ends, in the middle alternately longer and shorter, finely punctate; puncta about 26 in 0,01 mm. — Pl. V f. 30.

Marine: Japan (Tempère)!

20. **N. polygibba** PANT. (1893). — V. lanceolate subapiculate, ends; margins with four undulations. L. 0,055; B. 0,025 mm. Axial area narrow, not dilated in the middle. Striæ radiate throughout, 16 in 0.01 mm. punctate; puncta 16 in 0,01 mm. — PANT. III Pl. V f. 85.

Habitat:? Kavna-Bremia, Hungary, fossil.

Unknown to the author. It has a considerable likeness to *N. mutica var. undulata*.

21. **N. mocsarensis** PANT. (1893). — V. broad, elliptic-lanceolate, rostrate. L. 0,053; B. 0,026 mm. Axial area narrow, dilated towards the middle, where it expands into a somewhat trans-

verse central area. Striæ 9 in 0,01 mm., radiate throughout, coarsely punctate; puncta 12 in 0,01 mm. — PANT. III Pl. XXIII f. 340.

Habitat:? Moesár. (Pant.).

This form resembles *N. amphibola* or *N. Placentula*. Unknown to the author.

Naviculæ Bacillares CL.

Valve linear to elliptical, usually with broad and rounded ends. Median line straight, enclosed by siliceous thickenings. Terminal nodules incrassate. Axial area usually narrow or indistinct; central area very small. Structure: fine transverse striæ, more distant in the middle than elsewhere, slightly radiate throughout and curved, very finely punctate. Connecting zone simple.

This section comprises forms, which are nearly akin to the *N. mesoleiæ*, and it would perhaps be more natural to include in this group *N. Pupula* and *N. bacilliformis*, which are closely connected with *N. Pseudobacillum*. On the other hand, the nature of the striæ, which are more distant in the middle, indicates a relationship to the section *N. decipientes*. In the section Bacillares I have included a form, which in some respects is aberrant from the rest, viz. *N. americana*, which has a broad, axial area and almost equidistant striæ. Nevertheless, this form is connected by *N. Lambda* with *N. Bacillum*, and I think it better to place it in this group rather than in the section *N. mesoleiæ*, with which it has still less affinity, or to form a separate group for this single species as VAN HEURCK has done in his synopsis.

Artificial key.

1.	Axial area broad	*N. americana* EHR.
	— narrow or indistinct	2.
2.	Central and terminal areas with stigmas	*N. trinotata* PANT.
	— without —	3.
3.	Terminal nodules laterally expanded	*N. Pseudobacillum* GRUN.
	— — not — —	4.
4.	Length 0,06 to 0,1 mm.	5.
	— 0,055 or less	6.
5.	Valve linear	*N. Lambda* CL.
	— elliptical	*N. Rioja* CL.
6.	Terminal fissures comma-like	*N. subhamulata* GRUN.
	— not prolonged	*N. Bacillum* GRUN.

1. **N. americana** EHR. (1843). — V. broad, linear, with rounded ends. L. 0,055 to 0,1; B. 0,014 to 0,017 mm. Central nodule strong, with one or two pore-like puncta. Axial and central areas uniting in a very broad space, somewhat dilated in the middle. Striæ 16 in 0.01 mm., of equal length, parallel in the middle, radiate in the ends. — EHR. Am. p. 129 M. G. II: 2, f. 16. V. H. Syn. p. 105 Pl. XII f. 37. *N. am. var. bacillaris* HÉRIB. a. PÉRAG. D. d'Auvergne p. 116 Pl. IV f. 13. *N. am. var. minor* HÉRIB. a. PERAG. l. c. f. 12 (1893).

Fresh water: Sweden (Lake Rosslängen in Calmar län)! Finland (Abo)! Belgium (V. H.), Australian Alps (Riewa Lagoons)! America (Crane Pond, Boxford, Mass. etc.)!

This species is very characteristic and not to be mistaken for any other. It is widely distributed, but seems to be rare everywhere.

2. **N. Lambda** CL. N. Sp. — V. linear slightly constricted in the middle, with broad, rounded ends. L. 0,05 to 0,1; B. 0,016 mm. Terminal fissures straight in the thick nodules. Axial area narrow but distinct, linear; central area small orbicular. Striæ 13 (middle) to 20 (ends) in 0,01 mm. divergent in the middle, parallel at the ends, distinctly but finely punctate. — Pl. V f. 19.

Fresh water: Demerara River!

3. **N. Riojæ** CL. (1881). — V. elliptical, with rounded ends. L. 0,06 to 0,07; B. 0,023 to 0,024 mm. Median line in a thick silicious rib, combining the large central nodule with the thick terminal nodules. Terminal fissures slightly curved. Axial and central area united in a linear space very slightly dilated in the middle. Striæ 17 (middle) to 19 (ends) in 0,01 mm., radiate throughout, indistinctly punctate, crossed by a shallow, longitudinal depression. - CL. D. fr. Grönl. and Argentina p. 12 Pl. XVI f. 2.

Fresh water: Argentina (Sierra Famatina)!

4. **N. Bacillum** EHB. (1843). — V. linear with rounded ends. L. 0,035 to 0,055; B. 0,01 to 0,015 mm. Median line in a thick siliceous rib. Axial area narrow slightly enlarged around the central nodule and expanded at the ends on each side to the full width of the valve. Striæ 14 (middle) to 20 (ends) very slightly radiate. — EHB. Am. Pl. IV: 5, f. 8. GRUN. A. D. p. 44 Pl. II f. 50. V. H. Syn. p. 105 Pl. XIII f. 8. Ströse Kliecken f. 8. *N. lævissima* DONK. B. D. p. 28 Pl. V f. 2 1871?

Fresh water: Sweden (Skåne)! Finland! Siberia, Mouth of Jenissey (Grun.). North Australia! New Zealand!

Var.? *mexicana* GRUN. (1880). — V. gibbous in the middle. L. 0,05; B. 0,01 mm. Terminal nodules larger; area abruptly dilated around the central nodule. Striæ 18 in 0,01 mm., closer at the ends, in the middle frequently alternately longer and shorter. - GRUN. A. D. p. 44.

Fresh water: Mexico, fossil (Grun.).

Var. *Gregoryana* GRUN. (1880). — V. slightly constricted in the middle. — *N. Bacillum* GREG. M. J. IV, Pl. I f. 4 (1856). *N. bac. var. Greg.* GRUN. A. D. p. 44.

Fresh water: Loch Leven, Scotland Greg.

Var. *minor* V. H. (1885). — V. half as large as the typical form. Striæ 16 (middle) to 20 (ends) in 0,01 mm. — V. H. Syn. p. 105 Pl. XIII f. 10.

Fresh water: Belgium (V. H.).

Var. *lepida* GREG. (1856). — V. elliptical with rounded ends. L. 0,02 to 0,025; B. 0,01 mm. Axial area indistinct, central small. Striæ 17 (middle) to 26 (ends) in 0,01 mm., slightly radiate throughout. *N. lepida* GREG. M. J. IV Pl. I f. 25. V. H. Syn. Pl. XIII f. 12. Icon. n. Pl. V f. 14.

Fresh water: Sweden (Hernösand foss.)! Finland (Abo)! Scotland (V. H. T.). Argentina (Sierra Famatina)!

5. **N. trinotata** PANT. (1893). — V. linear, with broad, rounded ends. L. 0,056; B. 0,014 mm. Axial area narrow, slightly dilated in the middle, where is an unilateral stigma. Near the ends of the median lines is also an elongated stigma, placed on contrary sides of the median line. Striæ 21, somewhat radiate in the middle, else parallel. — PANT. III Pl. IX f. 152.

Habitat? Köpecz (Pant.).

6. **N. Pseudo-bacillum** GRUN. (1880). — V. linear-elliptical, with rounded ends. L. 0,035 to 0,045; B. 0,01 to 0,015 mm. Terminal nodules with two lateral expansions. Axial area narrow, central area small, rounded. Striæ in the middle 13 (Grun. 21 V. H.) in 0,01 mm. at the ends 20 (Grun. 24 V. H.) in 0,01 mm.: radiate throughout, very finely punctate. — *N. lævissima* KÜTZ. Bac. p. 96 Pl. XXI f. 14 (1844)? V. H. Syn. Pl. XIII f. 13? *N. leptogongyla* EHB. p. p.? according to Grun. *N. Granum* SCHUM. P. D. II N. p. 58 Pl. II f. 46? according to Grun. *N. lævissima* and *N. Pseudo-bac.* GRUN. A. D. p. 45 Pl. II f. 52 1880. *N. Pseudo-bac.* V. H. Syn. p. 106 Pl. XIII f. 9. *N. Bacillum var. β* Ströse Kliecken f. 9?

Fresh water: Sweden (Borås)! Finland! Belgium (V. H.). Java, foss.! Japan! New Zealand! Australian Alps! Canada, foss.!

This species described and figured by GRUNOW in A. D. was at first believed by him to be *N. lævissima* KÜTZ. But as this name may denote some form of *N. Silicula* GRUNOW proposed the name *N. Pseudobacillum*. The same form has been since figured in V. H. Syn. f. 9, but on the same plate GRUNOW figures (f. 13) a smaller form as *N. laevissima* KÜTZ. In this, somewhat obscure figure, the lateral extensions of the terminal nodules are not visible, and it seems uncertain whether it may be a variety of *N. Pseudobacillum* or of *N. Bacillum* or perhaps *N. subhamulata*.

7. **N. subhamulata** GRUN. (1885). — V. linear, slightly gibbous in the middle, with broad, rounded ends. L. 0,02; B. 0,005 mm. Terminal nodules not laterally extended. Terminal fissures comma-like. Axial area indistinct, central very small. Striae about 26 in 0,01 mm. slightly radiate throughout. Frustule with triundulated margins. — GRUN. in V. H. Syn. p. 106 Pl XIII f. 14.

Fresh water: Belgium (V. H.).

Naviculæ Decipientes GRUN. (1880).

Valve lanceolate to linear, with subacute to truncate, frequently rostrate or capitate, ends. Axial and central areas small or indistinct. Terminal nodules not very thick. Central nodule frequently transversely dilated. Structure: finely punctate striae, slightly radiate or almost parallel, more distant in the middle, than at the ends. Connecting zone not complex.

This group is nearly akin to the *Nav. bacillares*, which differ in the incrassate terminal nodules, and also to *Nav. microstigmaticae*. Some few forms are slightly asymmetrical and have for this reason been considered as *Cymbellae*, but they are, no doubt, more closely allied to the symmetrical forms of this section. On the other hand some *Cymbellae* (as *C. aequalis*) appear to be related to species of this group.

Artificial key.

1.	Valve acute . . .	*N. ramphoides* PANT.
	— obtuse	. . . . . . 2.
2.	Median line broad, flexuose .	*N. Semen* EHR.
	— straight, filiform	3.
3.	Margins undulated	4.
	— not —	. . . . 5.
4.	Valve lanceolate	. . *N. integra* W. SM.
	— linear . .	. *N. Lagerstedtii* CL.
5.	Ends rostrate or capitate .	. . . . 6.
	— not —	. . . . 9.
6.	Median striae alternately longer and shorter . .	*N. inflata* DONK.
	not — — — —	. . . . 7.
7.	Striae 20 or less in 0,01 mm. . .	. . . . 8.
	— 30 or more —	*N. subtilissima* CL.
8.	Striae radiate throughout . .	*N. Lundströmii* CL.
	parallel at the ends . . .	*N. protracta* GRUN.
9.	Linear-elliptical with broad ends	. . . *N. seminoides* CL.
	Lanceolate — narrow —	. *N. brasiliana* CL.
10.	Valve lanceolate . . .	. *N. Cruciculа* W. SM.
	linear	. . . . 11.
11	Valve centrally gibbous	*N. gibbula* CL.
	not	. . . . 12.
12.	Median striae shortened	. *N. subinflata* DONK.
	— not —	. *N. Kälfrensis* GRUN.

1. **N. Semen** EHR. (1843). — V. elliptic-lanceolate, with broad, almost truncate, frequently slightly rostrate, ends. L. 0,05 to 0,09; B. 0,023 to 0,029 mm. Median line flexuose. Axial area narrow, linear; central area small, orbicular. Striae in the middle 8 in 0,01 mm., of equal length,

radiate; terminal striæ 13 in 0,01 mm., slightly convergent; all finely punctate. EHB. Am. I: 2. f. 17. M. G. XVI. I f. 11? W. SM. B. D. I p. 50 Pl. XVI f. 141. DONK. B. D. p. 21 Pl. III f. 8. A. S. Atl. LXXII f. 1. GRUN. Franz Josephs Land D. p. 99 (17) Pl. I f. 31. *Amphiprora navicularis* EHB. Micr. G. III: 1, f. 10, 11.

Fresh water: Franz Josephs Land (Grun.). Sweden (Lule Lappmark living, common in post-glacial, lacustrine deposits)! Finland, foss.! England (Hull) Donk., Germany, Harz (Atl.); Bohemia, Eger fossil! North America: common in diatomaceous earths (Nova Scotia, Canada West, Washington territory etc.)!

What Nav. Semen of EHRENBERG may denote is impossible to decide, as the figures published by EHRENBERG cannot be recognized. The figure in W. SMITH Brit. Diat. is not good, but leaves little doubt that the author meant the same species, which now is generally believed to be N. Semen. On the other hand there can be no doubt that *Amphiprora naviculoides* of EHRENBERG is the same species as our N. Semen. N. Semen seems to be a northern species, rarely found living, but frequently in postglacial deposits of Scandinavia and North America. It is not mentioned by BRUN as an inhabitant of the Alps, nor by BELLOC as occurring in the Pyrenées. Its occurrence in a living state in the Harz is an interesting fact and suggests that it may be a survival from the post-glacial epoch.

2. **N. (Diadesmis) seminoides** CL. & GROVE N. Sp. — V. elliptic-lanceolate, with truncate ends. L. 0,027 to 0,045; B. 0,01 to 0,012 mm. Axial area narrow linear, suddenly dilated to a small, orbicular central area. Striæ in the middle 16 in 0,01 mm., alternately longer and shorter, divergent; striæ at the ends about 23 in 0,01 mm. slightly convergent, all finely punctate.

Slightly brackish water: West Indies, Jamaica (Grove Coll.)! Ecuador!

This small form resembles in outline *N. Semen*. The frustules form in living state coherent filaments.

3. **N. brasiliana** CL. (1881). V. lanceolate, with subacute ends, often slightly asymmetrical. L. 0,035 to 0,065; B. 0,012 to 0,018 mm. Median line straight: its terminal fissures in the same direction. Axial area narrow, linear, somewhat dilated around the central nodule. Striæ in the middle 18 in 0,01 mm., divergent alternately longer and shorter; towards the ends 21 to 22 in 0,01 mm.; at the ends convergent; all distinctly punctate; puncta (on the median striæ about 18 in 0,01 mm.) forming undulating, longitudinal rows. *Cymbella brasil.* CL. N. R. D. p. 1 Pl. I f. 4.

Fresh water: Brazil! Calif. (St. Rosa in Grove Coll.)! Ecuador in mineral springs at Tesalia Prov. Pichincha!

4. **N. inflata** DONK. (1870). V. lanceolate with capitate ends. L. 0,022 to 0,026; B. 0,007 to 0,008 mm. Axial area indistinct, central area small, irregular. Striæ in the middle 19 in 0,01 mm., somewhat divergent and of unequal length; other striæ 22 to 23 in 0,01 mm., convergent at the ends, all indistinctly punctate. — DONK. B. D. p. 21 Pl. III f. 9 (nec Kütz. = *N. hungarica?*) Cl. D. of Finl. p. 37 Pl. II f. 2 (1891).

Fresh water: Ireland (Lough Mourne foss. Donk.), Sweden (Lake Rosslängen in Kalmar län, Rimforsa in Westergötland)! Finland, foss.! N. America (Houghton, Michigan, foss.)!

5. **N. ramphoides** PANT. (1889). — V. narrow, rhombic-lanceolate, with acute ends, very convex. L. 0,086 to 0,09; B. 0,013 mm. Median line with approximate central pores. Axial area indistinct. Central area (by the distant median striæ) a narrow transverse fascia. Striæ about 14 in 0,01 mm. (the median more distant) very slightly radiate, at the ends transverse, indistinctly punctate. — PANT. II p. 53 Pl. V f. 97, 98.

Brackish water: Hungary, fossil!

6. **N. Crucicula** W. SM. (1853). — V. lanceolate to elliptic-lanceolate, with somewhat obtuse ends. L. 0,045 to 0,07; B. 0,015 to 0,019 mm. Central nodule transversely dilated. Axial and

central areas indistinct. Striæ about 16 in 0,01 mm. the median stronger and more distant, very slightly radiate, at the ends parallel, all finely punctate. — *Stauroneis Cruicula* W. Sm. B. D. I p. 60 Pl. XIX f. 192. Ldt. Spitsb. D. p. 37 Pl. II f. 14. *N. cruc.* Donk. B. D. p. 44 Pl. VI f. 14. V. H. Syn. p. 96 Pl. X f. 15. *Stauroneis dilatata* W. Sm. B. D. l. c. f. 191?

Brackish water: Spitsbergen! Baltic! Coasts of the North Sea (Sweden! England! Belgium V. H.), Atlantic coasts of North America!

Var. *obtusata* Grun. (1880). — Smaller, broadly lanceolate, with rounded obtuse ends. L. 0,025 to 0,05; B. 0,01 to 0,016 mm. Striæ 17 in 0,01 mm. — *Nav. Crucic. var. obt.* Grun. A. D. p. 35 Pl. II f. 37.

Brackish water: Grun.

Var. *minuta* Grun. (1860). V. broadly lanceolate, with slightly rostrate ends. — L. 0,02; B. 0,01 mm. Striæ 19 in 0,01 mm. — *Staur. Crucicula var. minuta* Grun. Verh. 1860 p. 567 Pl. VI f. 15.

Marine: Adriatic (Grun.).

7. **N. gibbula** Cl. N. Sp. V. linear, slightly gibbous in the middle, with broad, truncate ends. L. 0,033 to 0,043; B. 0,0085 to 0,01 mm. Axial area indistinct. Central area very small, rounded. Striæ 16 (middle) to 21 (ends) radiate in the middle, where they are of equal length, slightly radiate in the ends, distinctly punctate, puncta (about 22 in 0,01 mm.) forming longitudinal rows. — *N. gibberula* Lagst. Spitsb. D. p. 30 Pl. I f. 7 (1873). — *N. gibbula* Icon. n. Pl. V f. 17.

Fresh water (moist earth etc.): Spitsbergen! Beeren Eiland (Ldt.).

Var. *oblonga* Lagst. (1873). — V. linear not gibbous in the middle. — *Nav. gibberula var. oblonga* Lagst. l. c. p. 31.

Fresh water: Spitsbergen (Lagst.).

Var. *capitata* Lagst. (1873). — V. strongly gibbous in the middle, with dilated, rounded truncate ends. *N. gibberula var. capitata* Lagst. l. c. p. 31 Pl. I f. 7 *a'*.

Fresh water: Spitsbergen (Lagst.), Beeren Eiland (Lagst.).

8. **N. Lundströmii** Cl. (1880). — V. linear-lanceolate, with subrostrate, broad ends. L. 0,034 to 0,051; B. 0,011 to 0,013 mm. Median line with the terminal fissures in the same direction. Axial area narrow, slightly dilated around the central nodule. Striæ 16 (middle) to 20 (ends) in 0,01 mm., radiate throughout, finely punctate, in the middle of equal length. — Cl. A. D. p. 13, 36, Pl. II f. 39.

Brackish water: Sea of Kara (Jamal)!

Var. *Frieseana* Grun. (1879). — V. with broad rostrate-capitate ends, slightly asymmetrical. L. 0,032 to 0,048; B. 0,012 to 0,015 mm. Striæ 16 to 18 in 0,01 mm. (middle) or 20 to 22 in 0,01 mm. at the ends, in the middle radiate and of equal length, at the ends radiate, distinctly punctate, puncta (about 20 in 0,01 mm.) forming undulating longitudinal rows. — *Cymbella Frieseana* Grun. in Cl. M. D. N:o 261. Icon. n. Pl. V f. 18.

Brackish water: Finmark (Tana Elf)!

9. **N. protracta** Grun. (1880). — V. linear, with rostrate and truncate ends. L. 0,022 to 0,035; B. 0,008 to 0,01 mm. Axial area very narrow; central very small. Striæ 12 (middle) to 20 (ends) in 0,01 mm., slightly radiate in the middle, transverse at the ends, coarsely punctate, puncta about 17 in 0,01 mm. *N. Cruc. var.? prot.* Grun. A. D. p. 35 Pl. II f. 38. V. H. Syn. p. 96 Suppl. Pl. B f. 27. Foss. D. Öster. Ung. p. 116 Pl. XXX f. 17. *N. Troglodytes* Pant. II p. 51 Pl. XI f. 184 (1889)?

Brackish water: Salines of the mainland of Europe (Grun.), Belgium (V. H.), Hungary, foss. (Pant.) Cameroon!

Var. *maxima* Cl. — L. 0,08; B. 0,016 mm. Striæ about 14 to 15 in 0,01 mm.

Fresh water: Rio Purus, Brazil (Deby Coll.)!

10. **N. integra** W. SM. (1856). — V. lanceolate-elliptical, margins with 3 to 5 undulations, and rostrate-apiculate ends. L. 0,027 to 0,03; B. 0,008 to 0,009 mm. Axial area indistinct, central very small. Striæ about 23 in 0,01 mm., more distant in the middle, slightly radiate at the ends. — *Pinnularia rostrata* GREG. M. J. IV Pl. I f. 14 (1856). *Pinn. integra* W. SM. D. II p. 96. *Nav. integra* RALFS. in Pritch. p 895 (1861). DONK. B. D. p. 40 Pl. VI f. 8. GRUN. A. D. p. 36. V. H. Syn. p. 96 Pl. XI f. 22. *Cymbella integra* A. S. Atl. Pl. LXXI f. 61—66. *Stauroneis Janischii* RABH. Alg. Eur. 848 (1859)?[1]

Brackish water: Holstein! England (W. Sm.). Belgium (V. H.).

11. **N. Lagerstedtii** CL. N. Sp. — V. linear with triundulated margins and broad, obtuse ends. L. 0,026; B. 0,006 mm. Areas indistinct. Striæ 11 (middle) to 15 (ends) in 0,01 mm. slightly radiate, parallel at the ends. — *Nav. sp.* LAGST. Spitsb. D. p. 35 Pl. II f. 12 (1873).

Fresh water: Spitsb. (Lagst.).

12. **N. subtilissima** CL. (1891). — V. linear, with capitate ends. L. 0,032; B. 0,005 mm. Axial area indistinct, central small. Striæ about 40 to 45 in 0,01 mm. in the middle stronger, more distant and more radiate; other striæ slightly radiate. — CL. D. of Finl. p. 37 Pl. II f. 15. *Stauroneis linearis* LAGST. Spitsb. D. p. 37 Pl. II f. 13?

Fresh water: Finland (Imandra Lappmark)! Sweden (Westerbotten, Degernäs)! Spitsbergen (Lagst.).

13. **N. Kälfvensis** GRUN. Ms. — V. linear with rounded ends. L. 0,02; B. 0,005 mm. Areas indistinct. Striæ 24 (middle) to 27 (ends) in 0,01 mm.

Fresh water: Kälfva, Ålands socken. Sweden, fossil (Grun.).

14. **N. subinflata** GRUN. (1883). — V. linear, more or less gibbous in the middle, with rounded ends. L. 0,025 to 0,04; B. 0,008 mm. Axial area indistinct, central small irregular. Striæ about 19 in 0,01 mm., almost parallel. The three or four median striæ are shorter and much more distant than the others. Frustule in the zonal view rectangular; the connecting zone with faint longitudinal lines. — GRUN. in Cl. Vega p. 470 Pl. XXXVII f. 50.

Marine: Cape Wankarema! Arctic America! Norway, Grip!

Var. *elliptica* CL. — V. elliptical with rounded ends. L. 0,035; B. 0,013 mm. Striæ 20 in 0,01 mm.

Marine: Adriatic (Cl. M. D. N:o 210).

Naviculæ Microstigmaticæ CL.

Valve elongated, usually lanceolate to linear, never panduriform. Axial area narrow or indistinct. Central area small and rounded, or a transverse stauros. Structure: small, but distinct, puncta arranged in parallel, or slightly radiate, transverse striæ, and undulating longitudinal rows, the median transverse striæ not alternately longer and shorter, connecting zone complex or simple.

This large section comprises a number of species, hitherto placed in *Navicula*, *Stauroneis*, *Pleurostauron*, *Schizostauron* and *Schizonema*. The may be classed in the following divisions:

1. *Stauroneis*. Central nodule transversely dilated into a simple stauros. No diaphragms at the ends of the valve. Connecting zone simple.

2. *Pleurostauron*. Like Stauroneis, but with diaphragms at the ends of the valve.

3. *Schizostauron*. Central nodule transversely dilated into a furcate or bifid stauros.

[1] To judge from the figure. I have not seen any specimens in the material.

4. *Libellus*. Zone complex or with longitudinal divisions. Central nodule dilated into a stauros, or not dilated.

5. *Microstigma*. Zone simple. Central nodule not transversely dilated.

This division of the whole group cannot be completely carried out at present, as the connecting zones of many species have not been observed. I consequently class all the forms now in two groups, viz. those with transversely dilated central nodules in Stauroneis, and those without such dilated central nodules in Microstigma; at the same time indicating as far as can yet be made out to which of the five groups named above each species belongs.

The genus *Stauroneis* (EHR. 1843) has always been regarded as distinguished from Navicula by the transversely dilated central nodule; but the difference between a dilatation of the nodule itself, or *stauros*, and a more transverse extension of the central area, or *fascia*, has not hitherto been strictly carried out, and several forms with transverse areas only have been placed in Stauroneis. These I now remove to Pinnularia or Navicula.

Still, if we include in Stauroneis all the naviculoid forms which have transversely dilated central nodules, we shall not have a natural genus, as it will comprise species of Trachyneis, Mastoneis, Pseudoamphiprora, and other groups. All these I also remove to their respective groups and confine Stauroneis to such forms as possess the structure described above as belonging to the Microstigmaticæ.

Stauroneis has affinities with Amphora, particulary with the group Psammamphora, in which the structure is identical, and in which occur species with and without a stauros, which may be regarded as asymmetrical forms of Stauroneis and Microstigma.

In all the true species of Stauroneis the striæ are radiate at the ends. This is the case also in the group *Pleurostauron*, which is nearly related to Stauroneis and passes over into it by gradual transitions.

Many species of both these groups are met with in fresh water in all countries, arctic or tropical, a few inhabit brackish waters, but there is scarcely any undoubted marine species.

The fresh water species of *Schizostauron* are closely allied to those of Pleurostauron, but I am not sufficiently acquainted with the marine species of the former to be able to speak as to their affinities.

The division *Libellus* comprises forms with and without stauros. They are all marine and some of them live enclosed in gelatinous tubes, for which reason they have been classed in the very unnatural genus Schizonema. As there are free forms, so closely connected with those living in gelatinous tubes, that they cannot be specifically distinguished, there is no reason to retain the genus Schizonema. As early as 1873 I proposed the generic name Libellus for Naviculæ with complex zone, but this view was not accepted until recently by De Toni, who placed in this genus *N. aponina*. Whether this be admissible or not I cannot say, as I have not examined this species sufficiently; but as it is figured in VAN HEURCKS Synopsis as having subsidiary longitudinal lines it may belong to Caloneis.

The species of Libellus are no doubt closely connected with those of the division Microstigma, in which are some forms the zone of which has longitudinal rows of short striæ (*N. auklandica* and *N. Garkeana*). Still closer allied are the forms of the section *Oxyamphora* among the asymmetrical naviculoid diatoms. The same structure exists in these Amphoræ as in Libellus; the zone is similar and there are in Oxyamphora species with, and without stauros, exactly as in Libellus. Most forms of Libellus have the terminations of the median line at some distance from the ends of the valve.

The division *Microstigma* comprises forms without stauros, and with a simple connecting zone, which however, as stated above, has in some species longitudinal rows of short striæ. I have enclosed in this division several forms, classed in different genera by authors, as *Scoliopleura tumida*, and *Rhoiconeis Garkeana*, the former having a sigmoid median line, the latter arcuate frustules. On the sigmoid median line alone no natural genus can be founded, forms with a sigmoid median line occuring in the groups *Lævistriatæ* (*N. Bacana*), *Caloneis* (*C. staurophora*), *Lineolatæ*, *Eucocconeis* etc. Moreover there are gradual transitions from forms with sigmoid median line to forms with straight median line and terminal fissures in contrary directions (*N. auklandica*) while many such forms are closely connected with others having the terminal fissures in the same direction. In *N. tumida* some specimens occur in which the median line is scarcely sigmoid.

As to *Rhoiconeis*, this genus is also inadmissible, as it contains widely different forms, and the degree of flexure in the frustule varies in the same species. Some forms of the section *Lineolatæ* are more or less arcuate, and in Gyrosigma and Pleurosigma we meet with species, which in some varieties are straight, in others arcuate.

Microstigma is doubtless akin to Libellus and has also a resemblance to the symmetrical forms of Tropidoneis, which differ principally by their highly elevated valves. Among the other groups of Navicula, Microstigma has affinities with the *Decipientes* and *Fusiformes*, the former having the median striæ wider (as in *N. tumida*), the latter having the puncta arranged in longitudinal rows; and with the *Entoleiæ*, which have a distinct axial area. In fact it is impossible to trace any absolute limit between these groups of forms.

Artificial key.

1.	Central nodule stauroid	2.
	— — not	29.
2.	Stauros bifid	24.
	— not	3.
3	Ends of the valves with diaphragms	17.
	— — — without	4.
4.	Ends protracted	5.
	— not —	7.
5.	Stauros broad	*S. dilatata* Ehr.
	— narrow	6.
6.	Striæ 15 in 0,01 mm.	*S. Phyllodes* Ehr. (*S. anceps var. nobilis*).
	— 20 to 30 in 0,01 mm.	*S. anceps* Ehr.
7.	Size small (L. 0,015 to 0,025 mm.)	8.
	— median (L. about 0,05 mm.)	10.
	— large (L. 0,07 to 0,2 mm.)	16.
8.	Linear-elliptical	*S. septentrionalis* Grun.
	Lanceolate	*S. perpusilla* Grun.
	Elliptical	9
9.	Striæ about 18 in 0,01 mm.	*S. kryophila* Grun.
	— 22 —	*S. perminuta* Grun.
10.	Ends broad, capitate or truncate	11.
	— obtuse or rounded	12.
	— cuneate	*S. Demeraræ* Cl.
	— subacute	15.
11.	Striæ 14 to 19 in 0,01 mm.	*S. desiderata* Cl.
	— 29 — —	*S. pachycephala* Cl.
12.	Stauros small and short	*S. pellucida* Cl.
	— pervious	13.
13.	Zone broad with numerous distinct divisions	*S. Biblos* Cl.
	— narrow with faint divisions	14.
14	Stauros broad	*S. Gregorii* Ralfs.
	— narrow	*S. constricta* W. Sm.
15.	Striæ 17 to 18 in 0,01 mm.	*S. salina* W. Sm.
	— 23 — —	*S. africana* Cl.
16.	Linear	*S. Schinzii* Brun.
	Rhomboid-lanceolate	*S. Phoenicenteron* Ehr.
17.	Apiculate	*S. Smithii* Grun.
	Non-apiculate	18.

18. { Valve biconstricted . . . 19.
{ — not — . . . 20.

19. { Small (L. 0,03 to 0,04 mm.) . . . *S. Legumen* Ehb.
{ Large (L. 0,2 mm.) . . . *S. Fulmen* Btw.

20. { Valve fusiform . . . *S. Frauenfeldtiana* Grun.
{ — rhombic-lanceolate . . . *S. acuta* W. Sm.
{ — lanceolate or linear-lanceolate . . . 21.

21. { Large (L. 0,12 to 0,2 mm.) . . . *S. javanica* Grun.
{ Small (L. less than 0,07 mm.) . . . 22.

22. { Striæ about 15 in 0,01 mm. . . . *S. oblonga* Grun.
{ — fine 23 . . . 23.

23. { Ends rostrate . . . *S. parvula* Grun.
{ non-rostrate . . . *S. obtusa* Lagst.

24. { Branches of the stauros parallel . . . *S. Sagitta* Cl.
{ - divergent . . . 25.

25. { Freshwater habitat . . . 26.
{ Marine . . . 27.

26. { Ends rostrate . . . *S. Crucicula* Grun.
{ — non-rostrate . . . *S. undicola* Cl.

27. { Valve lanceolate, subrostrate . . . *S. Reichardtiana* Grun.
{ broadly elliptical . . . 28.

28. { Stauros with very divergent branches . . . *S. Lindigiana* Grun.
{ — — less — — . . . *S. ovata* Grun.

29. { Median line sigmoid or with the terminal fissures in contrary directions . . . 30.
{ — not sigmoid . . . the same — or indistinct 31.

30. { Median line sigmoid . . . *N. tumida* Bréb.
{ - — straight . . . *N. aucklandica* Grun.

31. { Ends with diaphragms . . . *N. inelegans* Grove & Sturt.
{ — without - . . . 32.

32. { Median line flexuose . . . *N. plicatula* Grun.
{ — — straight . . . 33.

33. { Frustule arcuate . . . *N. Garkeana* Grun.
{ — not . . . 34.

34. { Striæ very fine (28 to 30 in 0,01 mm.) . . . 35.
{ — 15 to 20 in 0,01 mm. . . . 37.

35. { Zone broad . . . *N. Hyalosira* Cl.
{ — narrow . . . 36.

36. { Ends acute . . . *N. aponina* Kütz.
{ — rostrate-capitate . . . *N. Balnheimii* Grun.

37. { Valve linear, obtuse . . . *N. Scopulorum* Bréb.
{ — — lanceolate . . . 38.
{ — rhombic — . . . 39.
{ — elliptic — . . . *N. suavis* Cl. & Grove.
{ — rostrate . . . *N. Jimboi* Pant.

38. { Zone broad . . . *N. complanata* Grun.
{ · narrow . . . *N. plicata* Donk.

39. { Frustules in gelatinous tubes . . . *N. Grevillei* Ag.
{ — free . . . 40.

40. { Obtuse . . . *N. Weissflogii* Grun.
{ Acute or subacute . . . 41.

41. { Median line reaching to the ends . . . *N. Libellus* Greg.
{ — — not — — . . . 42.

42. { Terminal fissures indistinct . . . *N. rhombica* Greg.
{ — book-shaped . . . *N. hamulifera* Grun.

1. **S.? pellucida** Cl. (1883). — V. elliptical, with broad, rounded ends, thin and convex. L. 0,053 to 0,06; B. 0,016 to 0,023 mm. Median line with the terminal fissures indistinct because the convexity of the valve. Central nodule transversely dilated to a short stauros. Axial area indistinct; central small. Striæ 16 to 21 in 0,01 mm. obscure, punctate.

Forma arctica. Stauros narrow. Striæ 19 to 21 in 0,01 mm. — *S. pellucida* CL. Vega p. 475 Pl. XXXV f. 10.

Marine: Cape Wankarema (North Siberian Sea)!

Forma mediterranea. Stauros broad, irregularly subquadrate. Striæ 16 in 0,01 mm.

Marine: Barcelona! Balearic Islands!

This is a curious form, not closely connected with any other known species, so that its position in a natural system is uncertain. I have placed it here only provisionally. It always occurs very sparingly.

2. **S. (Libellus) constricta** (EHR. 1843?), W. SM. (1853). — V. membranaceous, linear, convex, sometimes constricted in the middle, with subacute, rounded or subcuneate ends. L. 0,05 to 0,14; B. 0,0075 mm. Stauros pervious, narrow linear. Axial area indistinct. Striæ 25 to 27 in 0,01 mm. transverse. Frustule with complex connecting zone. — *Stauron. constricta* EHR. Am. Pl. I: 2 f. 12 b.? *Amphiprora constricta* W. SM. B. D. I Pl. XV f. 126. *Stauron. amphoroides* GRUN. in A. S. Atl. XXVI f. 35 to 39. *Nav. simulans* DONK. B. D. p. 60 Pl. IX f. 3 (1873)?

Marine or brackish: Davis Strait! North Sea (coasts of Sweden, England, Normandy)! Adriatic (Grun.).

It is not very probable that *St. constricta* of EHRENBERG represents this species, whatever it may be.

3. **S. (Libellus) Biblos** CL. (1892). — V. thin and very convex, linear-elliptical with obtuse ends. L. 0,055; B. 0,015 mm. Central pores approximate. Central nodule transversely dilated into a narrow stauros. Terminal nodules distant from the ends of the valve. Striæ about 30 in 0,01 mm. composed of fine puncta somewhat less close, forming undulating, longitudinal rows. Frustule quadrate. Zone broad, with numerous longitudinal divisions. — CL. Diatomiste I p. 77 Pl. XII f. 9, 10.

Marine (pelagic.): Barbados!

This species is of interest as it has a very complex connecting zone and at the same time a well developed stauros. The former characteristic as well as the sculpture of the valve and the distant terminal nodules, prove that it is nearly akin to *N. rhombica*. The latter characteristic shews an affinity to *Stauroneis salina*.

4. **S. (Libellus) africana** CL. (1881). — V. lanceolate, with subacute ends, convex. L. 0,05 to 0,06; B. 0,01 to 0,013 mm. Stauros narrow, pervious. Striæ 23 in 0,01 mm. transverse. Connecting zone with faint longitudinal divisions. — CL. N. R. D. p. 15 Pl. III f. 42.

Brackish water: South Africa! Ceylon (Weissflog Coll.)!

Var. *acuminata* GRUN. — V. acuminate. Striæ 23 in 0,01 mm. GRUN. in V. H. T. N:o 137.

Marine: Norfolk.

This species is intermediate between *S. constricta* and *S. salina*, having the fine striæ of the former and the form of the latter. It is more silicious than *S. constricta*.

5. **S. salina** W. SM. (1853). — V. lanceolate, with subacute ends. L. 0,05 to 0,08; B. 0,012 to 0,014 mm. Axial area indistinct. Stauros narrow, slightly dilated towards the margins, pervious. Striæ 17 to 18 in 0,01 mm. transverse, finely punctate. — W. SM. B. D. I p. 60 Pl. XIX f. 188. V. H. Syn. p. 68 Pl. X f. 16. LAGST. Boh. D. p. 47 f. 5.

Marine: North Sea! Mediterranean Sea (Balearic Islands)! Black Sea (Sebastopol)!

Var.? *latior* DANNF. (1882). - V. broadly lanceolate, with rostrate ends. Striæ? - DANNF. Balt. D. p. 32 Pl. III f. 21.

Brackish water: Baltic, Bay of Finland (Dannf.).

6. **S. Gregorii** RALFS (1861). — V. lanceolate, gradually tapering from the middle to the obtuse ends. L. 0,05 to 0,1; B. 0,01 to 0,013 mm. Stauros broad, pervious. Striæ 16 to 20 in

0,01 mm. almost parallel. — RALFS Prich. Inf. p. 913. *St. Amphioxys* GREG. T. M. S. IV p. 48 Pl. V f. 23 (1856). *St. Gregorii* GRUN. A. D. p. 47 Pl. III f. 64 (1880). V. H. Syn. p. 68 Suppl. Pl. A. f. 4.

Brackish water: Sea of Kara! North Sea (coasts of Sweden! Scotland! and Belgium V. H.). Black Sea (Sebastopol)! Caspian Sea (? Grun.). Atlantic coast of N. N. America (Cape May)!

S. Gregorii differs from *S. salina* by its broad stauros. Probably a variety with more lanceolate outline is *S. pacifica* CASTR. (Chall. Voy. p. 23 Pl. XX f. 9), which is too insufficiently described for identification.

A small form of *S. Gregorii* from the mouth of the Somme has been named by GRUNOW (in Cl. M. D. 217, 255) var. *diminuta*.

7. **S. perminuta** GRUN. (1881). — V. elliptical, with rounded ends. L. 0,013 to 0,025; B. 0,005 to 0,007 mm. Stauros narrow, pervious. Striæ 22 to 23 in 0,01 mm. slightly radiate. — GRUN. in Cl. D. fr. Grönl. Arg. p. 12 Pl. XVI f. 9.

Brackish water: South Africa (Grun.). Patagonia (Arroyo de Olivera)!

8. **S. perpusilla** GRUN. (1884). — V. lanceolate. L. 0,018 to 0,02; B. 0,0038 mm. Stauros narrow, pervious. Striæ not seen. — GRUN. Franz Josephs Land D. p. 105 (53) Pl. I f. 50.

Marine: Franz Josephs Land (Grun.).

Var. *obtusinscula* GRUN. — V. shorter, with more obtuse ends. GRUN. l. c. f. 49.

Marine: Franz Josephs Land (Grun.).

9. **S. desiderata** CL. (1880). — V. linear to lanceolate with broad, capitate ends. L. 0,05; B. 0,016 mm. Terminal fissures of the median line hook-shaped and turned in contrary directions. Stauros narrow, linear, reaching nearly to the margins. Striæ 14 to 19 in 0,01 mm. slightly radiate, especially at the ends, very finely punctate. CL. in A. D. p. 14 Pl. III f. 58.

Brackish and marine: Sea of Kara! Behrings Island!

10. **S. septentrionalis** GRUN. (1884). — V. linear-lanceolate. L. 0,024; B. 0,0048 mm. Stauros narrow, not reaching the margin. Striæ 23 in 0,01 mm. transverse, in the middle subradiate. GRUN. Franz Joseps Land D. p. 105 (53) Pl. I f. 48.

Marine: Franz Josephs Land (Grun.).

11. **S. kryophila** GRUN. (1884). — V. elliptic-lanceolate, with obtuse ends. L. 0,019; B. 0,007 mm. Stauros narrower towards the margins. Striæ in the middle 16, at the ends 20 in 0,01 mm. slightly radiate, distinctly punctate. - GRUN. Franz Josephs Land D. p. 105 (53) Pl. I f. 47.

Marine: Franz Josephs Land (Grun.).

12. **S. pachycephala** CL. (1879). V. linear, gibbous in the middle, with broad, capitate ends. L. 0,04 to 0,055; B. 0,007 to 0,009 mm. Median line with contrary and hook-shaped terminal fissures. Stauros pervious. Striæ about 29 in 0,01 mm. radiate. - CL. M. D. N:o 197. N. R. D. p. 15 Pl. III f. 43.

Brackish water: South Africa! Tasmania!

13. **S. Schinzii** BRUN. (1891). — V. linear, somewhat gibbous in the middle and at the broad, rounded ends. L. 0,13 to 0,17; B. 0,011 to 0,12 mm. Stauros pervious. Terminal fissures turned in the same direction. Terminal nodules large. Axial area narrow, linear. Striæ 19 to 20 in 0,01 mm. slightly divergent in the middle and slightly convergent at the ends, distinctly punctate. Puncta 19 to 20 in 0,01 mm. arranged in irregular, longitudinal rows. BRUN. D. espèces n. p. 38 Pl. XVI f. 1.

Fresh water: South West Africa (Brun Coll.)!

This form is very distinct from all other known species. The narrow axial area is bordered by conspicuous thick silicious ribs.

14. **S. Demeraræ** Cl. N. Sp. — V. linear, gibbous in the middle, with broad cuneate ends. L. 0,045; B. 0,009 mm. Stauros linear, pervious. (Terminal fissures, not seen). Striæ very fine, transverse in the middle, slightly radiate at the ends. — Pl. III f. 15.

Fresh water: Demerara River!

Of this species, remarkable for its form. I have seen only a few specimens, in which I have not succeeded in making the terminal fissures visible, for which reason the description is somewhat incomplete.

15. **S. anceps** Ehr. (1843). — V. lanceolate to linear-lanceolate, with rostrate or rostrate-capitate ends. L. 0,024 to 0,13; B. 0,006 to 0,017 mm. Stauros linear, reaching the margin or not. Axial area indistinct. Striæ 20 to 30 in 0,01 mm. slightly radiate, finely punctate. *S. anceps* Ehb. Am. Pl. II: 1, f. 18.

S. anceps is extremely variable, and it does not appear to me possible to separate the forms into definite species. The numerous fresh-water species of Stauroneis, named by Ehrenberg, are founded on very slight differences in the outline, which is very variable, and they cannot be identified, as no indication of the number of striæ exists. Moreover the forms included here under the name of *S. anceps*, pass gradually, without any limit, into others, which can scarcely be distinguished from smaller forms of *S. Phoenicenteron*. The simplest method had perhaps been to unite S. anceps and S. Phoenicenteron, but the species would then have comprised, as extremes, very different forms. From a practical point of view it seems to be best to arrange the forms into a few varieties, however arbitrary the limits may be. The central nodule reaches usually to the margin of the valve and corresponds to a transverse area, which however, is frequently narrower than the central nodules. Under good lenses the marginal part of the stauros seems to be covered with shorter striæ.

A. *Lanceolate forms, with more or less protracted, not capitate ends.*

Var. *siberica* Grun. (1880). — V. lanceolate. L. 0,064; B. 0,015 mm. Stauros not reaching to the margin. Striæ very fine (more than 30 in 0,01 mm.). — Grun. A. D. p. 48 Pl. III f. 65.

Fresh water: Mouth of Jenisey (Grun.).

Var. *hyalina* Br. a. Perag. (1893). — V. lanceolate, with very protracted ends. L. 0,04 to 0,085; B. 0,009 to 0,012 mm. Stauros pervious. Striæ very fine. — Br. a. Perag. in Hérib. D. d'Auvergne p. 78 Pl. III f. 19.

Fresh water: Puy de Dôme, fossil (Hérib.), Australia (Blue Mountains, Rieva Lagoons, Austr. Alps)!

Var. *gracilis* (Ehb. 1843?). — V. lanceolate. L. 0,04 to 0,05; B. 0,008 mm. Stauros pervious. Striæ 27 in 0,01 mm. — *S. grac.* Ehb. Am. Pl. I: 2, f. 14 etc.

Fresh water: Dovre, Norway!

Var. *birostris* (Ehb. 1843?). — V. lanceolate. L. 0,065 to 0,13; B. 0,014 to 0,017 mm. Striæ 24 in 0,01 mm. distinctly punctate. — *S. birostris* Ehb. Am. Pl. II: 2 f. 1? *S. anceps var.* Cl. D. f. Grönland and Argentina p. 12 Pl. XVI f. 5. *St. gallica* Hérib. a. Perag. D. d'Auvergne p. 77 Pl. III f. 21 (1893).

Fresh water: Puy de Dôme, fossil (Hérib.), Waltham, Mass.! Argentina, Rioja!

Var. *derasa* Grun. Ms. — V. narrow lanceolate, with somewhat protracted ends. L. 0,05 to 0,07; B. 0,008 to 0,01 mm. Stauros broad pervious. Striæ about 26 in 0,01 mm. visible only along the median line.

Fresh water: Förarm in Asnen, Sweden, fossil!

Var. *linearis* Ehb. (1843). — V. with parallel margins, rostrate. L. 0,045 to 0,05; B. 0,008 to 0,012 mm. Striæ 20 to 25 in 0,01 mm. — *S. linearis* Ehb. Am. 1: 2, f. 11 etc.? *S. anceps var. lin.* V. H. Syn. p. 69 Pl. IV f. 7, 8.

Fresh water: Holstein! Belgium (V. H.), Australia, Blue Mountains!

Var. *obtusa* GRUN. Ms. — V. linear, with broad, rostrate ends. L. 0,024; B. 0,006 mm. Striæ 21 in 0,01 mm. closer towards the ends (24 in 0,01 mm.).

Fresh water: Sandwich Islands, Mauna Kea (Cl. M. D. N:o 141).

Var.? *nobilis* SCHUM. (1867?). — V. lanceolate, rostrate. L. 0,11; B. 0,023 mm. Stauros narrowed towards the margins. Striæ 16 in 0,01 mm., slightly radiate, composed of coarse, elongate puncta, 15 in 0,01 mm., arranged in oblique, somewhat undulating rows. — *S. nobilis* SCHUM. P. D. II Nachtr. p. 59 Pl. II f. 60?

Slightly brackish water: Kläckeberga, Kalmar län, Sweden, fossil (Ancylus-epoch)!

I am not convinced that this form is really the same as SCHUMANN's, the puncta of which are figured as arranged in obliquely decussating rows as in Pleurosigma Else the outline and the size agree pretty well with SCHUMANN's figure.

B. *Forms with capitate ends.*

Var. *elongata* CL. — V. narrow linear-lanceolate. L. 0,055; B. 0,009 mm. Striæ 26 in 0,01 mm. — *S. linearis var.* in Cl. M. D. N:o 56.

Fresh water: Germany!

Var. *amphicephala* KÜTZ. (1844). — V. lanceolate. L. 0,04 to 0,08; B. 0,009 to 0,015 mm. Striæ 21 to 22 in 0,01 mm. distinctly punctate. — *S. amph.* KÜTZ. Bac. p. 105 Pl. XXX f. 25. *S. anceps* W. SM. B. D. I Pl. XIX f. 190. V. H. Syn. p. 69 Pl. IV f. 4, 5. *S. linearis* GRUN. Verh. 1860 Pl. VI f. 11.

Fresh water: Spitsbergen! Sweden (Westerbotten to Småland)! Belgium (V. H.), England (W. Sm.), Switzerland (Brun), Japan! Bengal! Greenland! Maine! California! Brazil! Ecuador!

Var. *recta* CL. — V. linear. L. 0,045; B. 0,009 mm. Striæ 23 in 0,01 mm.

Fresh water: Kuopio, Finland!

Var. *fossilis* CL. (1891). — V. lanceolate, with flattened, capitate ends. L. 0,09; B. 0,016 mm. Striæ 23 in 0,01 mm. — CL. D. of Finland p. 40 Pl. II f. 18.

Fresh water: Sweden (Degernäs in Westerbotten, fossil; Lake Rosslängen)! Finland (Savitaipale, foss.)!

Var. *argentina* CL. (1881). — V. lanceolate. L. 0,065; B. 0,013 mm. Stauros not reaching to the margins. Striæ 16 in 0,01 mm. — *S. gracilis var. arg.* CL. D. från Grönl. och Argentina p. 12 Pl. XVI f. 4.

Fresh water: Sierra de Velasco, Argentina!

16. **S. Phyllodes** EHR. (1843). — V. lanceolate, with protracted, obtuse ends. L. 0,105; B. 0,025 mm. Stauros narrower towards the margins. Striæ 15 (middle) to 18 (ends) in 0,01 mm. radiate throughout, punctate; puncta about 15 in 0,01 mm., arranged into irregularly undulating rows. — EHR. Am. Pl. II: 1, f. 16 etc.? Icon. n. Pl. III f. 27. *S. Sieboldii* EHR. M. G. Pl. XXXIV: 8, f. 12?

Fresh water: Demerara River!

17. **S. dilatata** EHR. (1843). — V. with parallel margins and rostrate, truncate ends. L. 0,065 to 0,068; B. 0,018 to 0,02 mm. Stauros broad, linear, reaching near to the margin. Striæ 18 in 0,01 mm., radiate throughout, distinctly punctate, puncta 24 in 0,01 mm., forming undulating, longitudinal rows. — EHR. Am. I: 2 f. 12. CL. A. D. p. 48 Pl. III f. 62.

Fresh water (larger lakes): Sweden, Mälaren! Finland, Ladoga! Siberia. Mouth of Jenissey!

18. **S. Phoenicenteron** EHR. (1843). — V. lanceolate, usually with slightly protracted, obtuse ends. L. 0,07 to 0,2; B. 0,028 to 0,04 mm. Stauros linear. Striæ radiate throughout 13 to 21 in 0,01 mm. distinctly punctate, puncta forming undulating, longitudinal lines. — EHR. Am. Pl. II: 5 f. 1 etc.

Var. *amphilepta* Ehb. (1843). — L. 0,07 to 0,1; B. 0,015 to 0,02 mm. Striæ and puncta 18 to 21 in 0,01 mm. — *S. amph.* Ehb. Am. I: 2 f. 9? M. G. Pl. XIV f. 18? Hérib. D. d'Auvergne p. 77 Pl. III f. 18 (1893). *S. gracilis* W. Sm. B. D. XIX f. 186. *S. lanceolata* Grun. Verh. 1860 p. 563. *S. borgana* Pant. III Pl. V f. 78; 1893 (*S. javanica?*).

Fresh water: Sweden! Finland! Holstein! England (Sm.), Greenland! Australia, Murray River!

Var. *genuina* Cl. — L. 0,1 to 0,15; B. 0,03 to 0,04 mm. Striæ 14 to 17, puncta about 12 in 0,01 mm. — *S. phoenicenteron* W. Sm. B. D. Pl. XIX f. 185. Grun. Verh. 1860 p. 563. V. H. Syn. p. 67 Pl. IV f. 2. Pant. III Pl. VIII f. 134. *S. Brunii* Per. in Hérib. d'Auvergne p. 76 Pl. III f. 22 (1893).

Fresh water: Sweden! Finland! England! Belgium (V. H.), Switzerland! North America (Canada, Calif.)! Brazil! Argentina! New Zealand!

Var. *Baileyi* Ehb. (1843). — L. 0,15 to 0,2; B. 0,045 mm. Striæ and puncta 12 to 11 in 0,01 mm. — *S. Bail.* Ehb. Am. p. 143. *S. pteroidea* Bail. (accord. to Ehb.) M. G. Pl. XIV f. 5.

Fresh water: North America (Cherryfield etc. fossil)!

19. **S. (Pleurostauron) parvula** Grun. (1878). — V. linear-lanceolate, with obtuse or slightly rostrate ends. L. 0,02 to 0,025; B. 0,005 mm. Stauros broad, pervious. Striæ 23 in 0,01 mm. radiate. — Grun. in Cl. M. D. N:o 139.

Fresh water: Berlin!

Var. *prominula* Grun. Ms. — Linear, with rostrate ends. L. 0,02 to 0,04; B. 0,004 to 0,008 mm. Striæ 25 to 28 in 0,01 mm.

Fresh or slightly brackish water: Greenland! Finmark, Tana Elf (Grun.), Gulf of Bothnia!

Var. *producta* Grun. (1880). — V. linear lanceolate, with rostrate ends. L. 0,03 to 0,04; B. 0,008 mm. Striæ 18 to 20 in 0,01 mm. — *Stauron. producta* Grun. in V. H. Syn. Pl. IV f. 12.

Fresh water: Sweden Skåne! Holstein! (Grun.).

As *S. parvula* Janisch has described, but not figured, a form from Angamos Guano (Charac. d. Guano II p. 14), which cannot be identified, for which reason Grunow's name may be retained. — *S. parvula* Grun. differs from *S. producta* only by its smaller size and finer striæ, and they may be united. The var. producta is nearly akin to, and seems to graduate into *S. Legumen*.

20. **S. (Pleurostauron) oblonga** Grun. (1867). — V. linear, with broad, rounded ends. L. 0,038 to 0,05; B. 0,0122 mm. Stauros linear, reaching to the margin. Striæ transverse, 15 in 0,01 mm. — Grun. Nov. p. 20 Pl. I f. 15.

Fresh water: Java, foss. (Grun.).

I have not succeeded in finding this form in the edible earth from Java, and cannot say anything about its affinities.

21. **S. (Pleurostauron) obtusa** Lagst. (1873). — V. linear-lanceolate, with broad, obtuse, not rostrate ends. L. 0,06 to 0,07; B. 0,01 mm. Stauros broad, reaching to the margin, where it becomes somewhat broader. Striæ 19 to 21 in 0,01 mm. — Lagst. Spitsb. D. p. 36 Pl. I f. 11.

Fresh water: Spitsbergen (Lagst.).

A similar form from Australia (Blue Mountains) has slightly rostrate ends. Another similar form, but with narrow, subacute ends, is described by Lewis (Proc. N. Sc. Philad. 1865 Pl. II f. 14) as a variety of *S. Legumen*.

22. **S. (Pleurostauron) Legumen** Ehb. (1843). — V. elongated, biconstricted. Median inflation not larger than the others. Ends rostrate. L. 0,03 to 0,035; B. 0,008 mm. Stauros reaching nearly to the margin and not dilated outwards. Striæ 27 in 0,01 mm., slightly radiate. Frustules coherent in short bands. — *Stauroptera Legumen* Ehb. Am. p. 135 Pl. I: 2, f. 5 (fide Kütz.). *Stauroneis Leg.* Kütz. Bac. p. 107 Pl. XXIX f. 11. Greg. M. J. IV Pl. I f. 9. V. H. Syn. p. 69 Pl. IV f. 11.

Fresh or slightly brackish water: Sweden, Åreskutan! Gulf of Bothnia! Lake Älmten in Småland! Scotland (Greg.). Belgium (V. H.).

S. Legumen is nearly akin to *S. parvula* and may be regarded as a biconstricted variety of that species. If so Legumen should be the specific name.

23. **S. (Pleurostauron) Smithii** Grun. (1860). — V. rhomboid-lanceolate, with slightly triundulate margins; the median inflation being larger. Ends apiculate. L. 0,02 to 0,03; B. 0,007 mm. Stauros narrow, reaching to the margins. Striæ 28 to 30 in 0,01 mm., almost parallel. — *S. linearis* W. Sm. B. D. p. 60 Pl. XIX f. 193 (1853). *S. Smithii* Grun. Verh. 1860 p. 464 Pl. VI f. 16. V. H. Syn. p. 69 Pl. IV f. 10. *Pleurostauron linearis* Hilse Rab. A. E. N:o 1161 (1861).

Fresh or slightly brackish water: Sweden, Gulf of Bothnia! Upsala! Saxony! Belgium (V. H.), England! Illinois! Surinam!

This is a small, very characteristic form, which occurs isolated among other diatoms.

24. **S. (Pleurostauron) Frauenfeldiana** Grun. (1867). — V. fusiform, subacute. L. 0,07 to 0,11; B. 0,008 to 0,009 mm. Stauros strong and dilated at the margins. Striæ 21 in 0,01 mm. parallel, minutely punctate. — *Pleuros. Frauenf.* Grun. Nov. p. 21 Pl. I f. 13.

Fresh water: Java (fossil)! New Zealand!

25. **S. (Pleurostauron) javanica** Grun. (1867). — V. lanceolate with rounded obtuse ends. L. 0,12 to 0,21; B. 0,027 to 0,04 mm. Stauros linear, reaching the margin. Striæ 12 to 14 in 0,01 mm. slightly radiate, punctate; puncta about 13 in 0,01 mm. — *Pleurost. javanic.* Grun. Novara p. 21 Pl. I f. 14. *S. Szontaghii* Pant. III Pl. VIII f. 143 (1893).

Fresh water: Europe, Hungary, Bory (fossil)! Java! Australia (Blue Mountains)! Nova Scotia! Canada! Chicago, interglacial peat!

This form is scarcely specifically distinct from *S. acuta*, although its form is nearly the same as that of *S. phoenicenteron*.

26. **S. (Pleurostauron) acuta** W. Sm. (1853). — V. rhombic-lanceolate, gradually tapering from the middle to the narrow, obtuse ends. L. 0,08 to 0,15; B. 0,015 to 0,04 mm. Stauros broad, dilated outwards, reaching the margin. Striæ 12 to 16 in 0,01 mm. composed of distinct puncta, 12 to 16 in 0,01 mm. Frustules coherent in short bands. — W. Sm. B. D. I p. 59 Pl. XIX f. 187. V. H. Syn. p. 68 Pl. IV f. 3. *S. Kochii* Pant. III Pl. VI f. 92 (1893).

Fresh water: Franz Josephs Land (Grun.), Sweden! Finland! England! Belgium (V. H.), Germany! Greenland! Nova Scotia! Canada! Massachusetts! Argentina! Australia! New Zealand!

Var. *Terryana* Temp. — V. in L. 0,35; B. 0,055 mm. Striæ and puncta 13 in 0,01 mm.

Brackish water: Connecticut!

Var. *undulata* Cl. — V. with triundulate margins. L. 0,16; B. 0,03 mm. Diaphragms broad. Striæ 15 to 16, puncta 15 in 0,01 mm.

Fresh water: Murray River, Australia!

27. **S. (Pleurostauron) Fulmen** Btw (1859). — V. elongated, biconstricted. Median inflation of about the same size as the others. Ends capitate. L. 0,2 to 0,22; B. 0,0028 to 0,03 mm. Stauros reaching to the margins and somewhat dilated outwards. Striæ 15 in 0,01 mm., slightly radiate, punctate; puncta 13 in 0,01 mm. forming undulating, longitudinal rows. — Btw M. J. VII p. 180 Pl. IX f. 6.

Fresh water: Java (foss.)! N. Zealand! Australia (Carpentaria Bay, Murrey River)!

St. Fulmen is very nearly akin to *S. acuta* and might be regarded as a variety. There is the same relation between *S. Fulmen* and *S. acuta* as between *S. Legumen* and *S. parvula*.

Subdivision Schizostauron GRUN.

In the year 1867 GRUNOW founded (Hedwigia VI p. 28) this genus for some marine diatoms from Honduras. The diagnosis is »Frustulia naviculacea, valvis ovatis vel lanceolatis, nodulo centrali transversim dilatato, lineari, utroque fine bifido (vel laciniato fimbriato)».

The last characteristic »nodulo laciniato fimbriato» refers to *S. fimbriatum*, which has since been discovered to be the upper valve of *Achnanthes danica*. The other species named by GRUNOW *S. Lindigianum*, *S. ovatum* and *S. Reichardtianum* are entirely unknown to me. I have since found three species of fresh water habitat, which agree with Stauroneis, but have a cloven stauros.

28. **S. Sagitta** CL. (1881). — V. lanceolate, with slightly triundulate margins and apiculate ends having short diaphragms. L. 0,03 to 0,04; B 0,006 to 0.01 mm. Stauros bifid with parallel branches. Striæ slightly radiate, 21 in 0,01 mm. — CL. N. R. D. p. 15 Pl. III f. 45.

Slightly brackish water: Tana Elf in Finmark! Gulf of Bothnia!

This little form has a great resemblance to *S. Smithii*, but has coarser striæ and a bifid stauros.

29. **S. Crucicula** GRUN. (1881). — V. lanceolate, with rostrate, obtuse ends, having narrow diaphragms. L. 0,03; B. 0,009 mm. Stauros bifid with divergent branches. Striæ radiate, 25 in 0,01 mm. — *Schizost. Crucic.* GRUN. in Cl. N. R. D. p. 16 Pl. III f. 44.

Fresh water: Merrimac River! Rio Purus, Brazil!

30. **S. andicola** CL. (1881). — V. convex, linear with rounded ends. L. 0,032 to 0,036; B. 0,007 to 0,008 mm. Terminal fissures in contrary directions. Stauros bifid, its branches divergent. Striæ almost transverse, 22 in 0,01 mm. — *S. andic.* CL. Diat. fr. Groen. and Argentina Pl. XVI f. 8.

Fresh water: Sierra de Velasco, Argentina! Cameroon!

31. **S. Lindigiana** GRUN. (1867). — V. broadly elliptical or suborbicular. L. 0,029; B. 0,021 mm. Median line complex. Central nodule transversely dilated, at the ends bifurcate; its branches parallel to the margin. Striæ 36 in 0,01 mm. parallel. — *Schiz. Lindigianum* GRUN. Hedwigia VI p. 28. *S. Lindigii* GRUN. T. R. M. S. 1877 p. 181 Pl. CXCV f. 17.

Marine: Honduras (Grun.).

32. **S. ovata** GRUN. (1867). — Valve, size and median line as in *S. Lindigiana*. Stauros linear, with short, slightly divergent branches prolonged to the margins of the valve. Striæ 26 in 0,01 mm. parallel. — *Schiz. ovatum* GRUN. Hedwigia VI p. 28.

Marine: Honduras (Grun.).

33. **S. Reichardtiana** GRUN. (1867). — V. broadly lanceolate, with subrostrate ends. L. 0,026 to 0,036; B. 0,016 to 0,019 mm. Median line straight. Central nodule transversely dilated, bifurcate, with arcuate, divergent branches. Striæ 12 in 0,01 mm. punctate, subradiate. — *Schiz. Reichardtianum* GRUN. in Hedw. Vol. VI p. 28 (name only). *Schiz. Reichardii* GRUN. T. R. M. S. 1877 p. 181 Pl. CXCV f. 18.

Marine: Adriatic (Grun.).

Subdivisions Microstigma and Libellus.

34. **S. Scopulorum** BRÉB. (1849). — V. linear, slender, often gibbous in the middle and at the ends, with broad, rounded ends. L. 0,1 to 0,26; B. 0,009 to 0,016 mm. Median line with approximate central pores and distant terminal nodules. Terminal fissures indistinct. Axial area indistinct; central very small. Striæ 18 to 20 in 0,01 mm. radiate in the middle, convergent at the ends, distinctly punctate, puncta about 19 in 0.01 mm., forming undulating longitudinal rows. — BRÉB. in Kütz. Sp. Alg. p. 81. GRUN. Verh. 1860 p. 547 Pl. III f. 6. DONK. B. D. p. 73 Pl. XII

f. 5. *Pinnularia Johnsonii* W. SM. B. D. XIX f. 179 (1853). *Nav. Johns.* V. H. Syn. p. 99 Suppl. B. f. 28.

Brackish water: S. coasts England (W. Sm.), Mediterranean Sea! Adriatic! Sumatra! Labuan! Japan (Deby Coll.)! East Cape. North Siberia! Brazil (Deby Coll.)!

Var. *belgica* V. H. (1885). — V. linear slightly gibbous in the middle. L. 0,06 to 0,07; B. 0,0075 mm. Striæ 24 in 0,01 mm. — *N. John. v. belg.* V. H. Syn. Suppl. B. f. 29.

Marine: Belgium!

Var. *fasciculata* GRUN. (1879). — V. linear, not gibbous in the middle. L. 0,08 to 0,12 mm. Striæ in the middle 16 to 18, at the ends 21 in 0,01 mm. - GRUN. in Cl. M. D. N:o 178.

Brackish water: Bengal!

N. Scopulorum is a very characteristic form, which seems not to be very nearly allied to any other species but the following. It occurs frequently with numerous transverse siliceous bars, or in a craticular state, and has then been named *Climaconeis Frauenfeldii* GRUN. Verh. 1862 p. 421 Pl. IV f. 2. *Cl. Lorenzii* GRUN. l. c. Pl. V f. 7. *Cl. linearis* JAN. Rab. Hond. p. 6 Pl. II f. 2 (1862). *Stictodesmis australis* GREV. Ed. N. Phil. J. XVIII p. 34 Pl. I f. 1—4 (1863).

Var. *perlonga* BRUN (1891). — V. very narrow, linear. L. 0,33 to 0,4; B. 0,007 mm. Striæ in the middle 18, in 0,01 mm., almost parallel, at the ends 20 in 0,01 mm. convergent, punctate, puncta about 27 in 0,01 mm. — BRUN D. Esp. n. p. 39 Pl. XV f. 2. *N. famelica* CASTR. Osserv. Ciclopb. p. 9 (1889) accord. to De Toni.

Marine: Gulf of Naples (Brun Coll.)!

35. **N. Weissflogii** GRUN. (1878). — V. rhomboid, with obtuse ends. L. 0,08 to 0,085; B. 0,026 to 0,034 mm. Median line with distant median and terminal pores. Terminal fissures indistinct. Axial area indistinct.; central area small and elongated. Striæ 15 (middle) to 20 (ends) in 0,01 mm., radiate at the ends, punctate, puncta 11 in 0,01 mm. forming longitudinal undulating rows. — *Brebissonia? Weissflogii* GRUN. in Cl. West. Ind. D. p. 7 Pl. I f. 9.

Marine: Campeachy Bay! Colon (Deby Coll.)!

This species is scarcely a Brebissonia, but in my opinion nearer akin to *N. rhombica*, having as the last, the terminal nodules at some distance from the ends, and the striæ more distant in the middle.

36. **N. (Libellus) rhombica** GREG. (1855). — V. rhombic-lanceolate, with subacute ends. L. 0,055 to 0,125; B. 0,018 to 0,024 mm. Median line with the terminal nodules at some distance from the ends. Terminal fissures indistinct. Axial area indistinct. Central area small, orbicular. Striæ 14 (middle) to 17 (ends) in 0,01 mm. nearly parallel on the middle part of the valve, convergent in the ends, punctate, puncta 13 in 0,01 mm. forming undulating longitudinal rows. Frustules in zonal view quadrate, with complex connecting zone. GREG. M. J. III p. 40 Pl. IV f. 16. T. M. S. IV p. 38 Pl. V f. 1.

Marine: Coasts of Scotland (Greg.), Greenland! Sumatra! Japan (fossil, Tempère)!

Var. *japonica* BRUN 1891. — L. 0,13 to 0,2; B. 0,035 to 0,05 mm. Striæ 13 (middle) to 14 (ends) in 0,01 mm. — *Schizonema Japonicum* BRUN D. Esp. n. p. 43 Pl. XIV f. 6.

Marine: Sendaï, Japan, fossil!

The living frustules of *N. rhombica* have two deeply indented plates along the connecting zone.

N. rhombica wiht cell-contents 500 times magnified.

37. **N. (Schizonema Libellus) Grevillei** AG. (1830). — V. lanceolate-elliptical, with obtuse ends. L. 0,03 to 0,07; B. 0,015 mm. Median pores distant, terminal pores at some distance from the end. Axial area indistinct, central area small. Striæ 18 to 20 in 0,01 mm. (closer, 20 to 27

in 0,01 mm. at the ends), the 4 to 5 median striæ being stronger and more radiate than the others, which become transverse towards the ends. Connecting zone with numerous longitudinal divisions. Frustules enclosed in mucous tubes of various shape. — *Schizonema Grev.* AG. Consp. p. 18. W. SM. B. D. II p. 77 Pl. LVIII f. 364. GRUN. A. D. p. 42. V. H. Syn. p. 110 Pl. XVI f. 2. *Schizonema sectio comoidea* GRUN. Bot. Centr. 1880. *Schiz. comoides* V. H. Syn. XVI f. 3. *Schiz. apiculatum* and var. V. H. Syn. l. c. f. 4—8. *Navic. Delognei* V. H. Syn. p. 110 Pl. XI f. 13.

Marine: Spitsbergen! Finmark! North Sea! Coasts of England (Sm.), Arctic America! Greenland! Cape Deschneff (North Siberian Sea)! West Indies! Kerguelens Land! California!

N. Grevillei is closely connected with *N. rhombica*, and it is questionable whether they should not be united. A great number of species of Schizonema have been founded on the shape of the gelatinous tubes, in which the frustules are enclosed in the living state. As the frustules of these forms are in all essential respects similar, there seems to be no sufficient reason for adopting these species.

38. **N. Libellus** GREG. (1857). — V. rhombic-lanceolate, convex, with acute ends. L. 0,065 to 0,15; B. 0,016 to 0,035 mm. Terminal nodules near the ends; terminal fissures indistinct. Axial and central areas indistinct. Striæ 13 to 14 in 0,01 mm., on larger form, or about 18 in 0,01 mm. on smaller forms, very slightly radiate, almost parallel at the ends, distinctly punctate, puncta (13 to 16 in 0,01 mm.) forming undulating, longitudinal rows. Connecting zone with numerous, longitudinal divisions. — GREG. D. of Cl. p. 528 Pl. XIV f. 101. *N. rhombica* DONK. B. D. Pl. IX f. 1.

Marine: Scotland (Greg.), Macassar Straits! Oamaru, fossil! Sendaï, Japan, fossil!

N. Libellus is very similar to *N. rhombica*, but has the terminal nodules closer to the ends and the striæ almost parallel at the ends. The terminal fissures are difficult to observe as the ends of the valve are curved downwards.

39. **N. (Libellus) complanata** GRUN. (1867). — V. linear-lanceolate, acute. L. 0,035; B. 0,005 mm. Striæ 18 to 19 in 0,01 mm. Frustule rectangular. L. 0,054; B 0,033 mm. Connecting zone with numerous, longitudinal divisions. — *Amphora complanata* GRUN. Hedwigia VI p. 25. A. S. Atl. XXVI f. 45. *Navic.? compl.* GRUN. A. D. p. 42 (1880).

Marine: Davis Strait! Sea of Kara (Grun.), Finmark! Bohuslän! Adriatic (Grun.).

Var. *subinflata* GRUN. (1875). Frustule rectangular. L. 0,04; B. 0,012 to 0,018 mm. Slightly inflated in the middle. — *Amphora subinfl.* GRUN. A. S. Atl. XXVI f. 48, 49.

Marine: Adriatic (Grun.).

Var. *hyperborea* GRUN. (1884). — Frustule rectangular. L. 0,05; B. 0,0165 mm. Striæ 24 in 0,01 mm. — *Amphora hyperborea* GRUN. Franz Josephs Land D. p. 55 (3) Pl. I f. 10.

Marine: Franz Josephs Land (Grun.), Sweden, Fiskebäckskil!

Nav. complanata is nearly akin to *N. Libellus*, but is no Amphora, though the frustules have some resemblance to that genus. The valves are rarely met with and difficult to observe. *N. subinflata* and *hyperborea* are scarcely specifically distinct.

The living frustule has two chromatophore-plates, each extending along the connecting zone from the ends towards the central nodule.

N. complanata with cell-contents 500 times magnified.

40. **N. (Libellus) Hyalosira** CL. (1822). — V. convex, thin, lanceolate, rostrate or with rounded ends. L. 0,025 to 0,03; B. 0,0066 mm. Striæ 29 in 0,01 mm. punctate. Frustule slightly siliceous, quadrate. L. 0,025; B. 0,017 mm. Connecting zone broad, with numerous and distant longitudinal divisions. — CL. M. D. N:o 309. Diatomiste I p. 77 Pl. XII f. 11.

Marine: Firth of Tay! Cresswell (Deby Coll.)!

41. **N. (Libellus) aponina** Kütz. (1836). — V. narrow, lanceolate, acute. L. 0,025; B. 0,004 mm. Axial and central areas indistinct. Striæ about 30 in 0,01 mm. Connecting zone longitudinally striate. — *Brachysira aponina* Kütz. Dec. N:o 153 (according to Lagst.). *Nav. apon.* Kütz. Bac. p. 91 Pl. IV f. 1. V. H. Syn. Pl. XII f. 15. Lagst. Öfvers. af K. Sv. Vet.-Akad. Förh. 1884 Pl. X f. 8. *Libellus apon.* De Toni Atti del R. Inst. de Scienze (ser. VII) VII p. 967.

Hot springs: Abano (Italy).

The above description is from the figure in V. H. Syn. as I have had no opportunity of examining this species.

42. **N. (Libellus) Bulnheimii** Grun. (1880). — V. linear-lanceolate, with rostrate to capitate ends. L. 0,02; B. 0,003 mm. Areas indistinct. Striæ parallel, 30 in 0,01 mm., the two median stronger. — Grun. in V. H. Syn. p. 108 Pl. XIV f. 6 a.

Salines: Sulza (Rabh. Alg. 1301)!

Var. *belgica* Grun. — V. with somewhat obtuse ends. Connecting zone with fine, longitudinal striæ (V. H. Types N:o 143).

Marine: Ostend.

43. **N. (Libellus) hamulifera** Grun. (1880). — V. lanceolate, sometimes slightly asymmetrical, with subacute ends. L. 0,051 to 0,058; B. 0,012 to 0,014 mm. Median line with somewhat approximate central pores. Its terminal fissures distinct, hook-shaped, turned in the same direction and at some distance from the ends of the valve. Areas indistinct. Striæ in the middle 19 to 21 in 0,01 mm. slightly radiate, at the ends 25 in 0,01 mm., parallel, punctate; puncta, about 20 in 0,01 mm., forming undulating longitudinal rows. — Grun. A. D. p. 44. Icon. n. Pl. III f. 16, 17, 18.

Marine: Mediterranean Sea (Grun.), Adriatic (Grun.), Sebastopol! Ceylon (Weissflog Coll.)! Java! Barbados!

Var. *interrupta* Cl. — L. 0,1; B. 0,02 mm. V. as in *N. Libellus*. Striæ interrupted on each side of the median line by a narrow longitudinal area. Striæ 20 to 21 in 0,01 mm. Puncta 23 in 0,01 mm. — Pl. III f. 19.

Marine: Japan!

N. hamulifera closely resembles *N. Libellus* and is characterized by its hook-shaped, terminal fissures.

44. **N. (Libellus) plicata** Donk. (1873). — V. linear, convex, with obtuse ends. L. 0,06 to 0,08; B. 0,012 to 0,016 mm. Terminal nodules close to the ends. Areas indistinct. Striæ in the middle 17 to 19 in 0,01 mm., almost transverse, at the ends 20 to 21 in 0,01 mm., also transverse, finely punctate, puncta about 18 in 0,01 mm. forming longitudinal, undulating rows. Frustule in the zonal-view with fine, longitudinal striæ on the connecting zone. — Donk. B. D. p. 59 Pl. IX f. 2. Grun. A. D. p. 36.

Marine: Kara Sea (Grun.), England! Scotland! Baltic (Grun.), Balearic Islands! Triest (Grun.), Labuan! Brazil!

Var. *sumatrana* Cl. — V. very convex with more acute ends. L. 0,13 to 0,17; B. 0,017 to 0,02 mm. Axial area indistinct; central small, orbicular. Striæ 15 (middle) to 16 (ends) in 0,01 mm. transverse throughout, coarsely punctate, puncta about 17 in 0,01 mm., forming undulating longitudinal rows. — *N. arcia* Castr. D. Challenger Exp. p. 31 Pl. XX f. 8 (1886)?

Marine: Island of Muntok, Sumatra (Grove Coll.)! Java!

45. **N. Garkeana** Grun. (1863). — V. linear, with obtuse ends. L. 0,04 to 0,095; B. 0,011 to 0,015 mm. Axial area indistinct; central very small, elongated. Striæ 18 to 19 in 0,01 mm., almost parallel, distinctly punctate; puncta about 20 in 0,01 mm., forming longitudinal rows. Frustule in zonal-view arcuate, subrectangular, with broad connecting zone, on which are 2 to 4 rows of short striæ (13 in 0,01 mm.). — *Rhoiconeis Gar.* Grun. Verh. 1863 p. 148 Pl. IV f. 12.

Marine: Behrings Strait! Kamortha! California! North Pacific Ocean (Grun.).

This species is remarkable for its arcuate valves, but in its essential characteristics seems to be nearest allied to *N. plicata*.

46. **N. suavis** CL. and GROVE N. Sp. — V. elliptic-lanceolate, flat. L. 0,115; B. 0,04 mm. Axial area very narrow. Central area small, rounded. Median line ending close at the margin. Striæ 18 in 0,01 mm. equidistant throughout, finely punctate; puncta about 18 in 0,01 mm., somewhat coarser around the central nodule, forming undulating longitudinal rows. — Pl. III f. 31, 32.

Marine: Oamaru, New Zealand, fossil (Grove Coll.)!

47. **N. plicatula** GRUN. Ms. — V. elliptic-lanceolate, with subacute ends, convex, with a more or less distinct longitudinal depression on each side of the median line. L. 0,075 to 0,115; B. 0,02 to 0,025 mm. Median line with approximate central pores and small terminal nodules at the ends of the valve, flexuose. Areas indistinct. Striæ 15 to 19 in 0,01 mm. at the middle, slightly divergent, and 18 to 20 in 0,01 mm. at the ends, parallel, and finely, but distinctly punctate. — Pl. III f. 28.

Marine: Gulf of Naples! Balearic Islands! Madagascar! Seychelles! Japan (Brun Coll.)!

This is a very characteristic species, remarkable for its undulating median line.

48. **N. inelegans** GROVE and STURT (1887). — V. lanceolate, gradually tapering from the middle to the somewhat obtuse ends, where are short transverse diaphragms. L. 0,18; B. 0,03 mm. Median line with elongated central nodule and small terminal nodules at the ends of the valve. Terminal fissures indistinct. Areas indistinct. Striæ 13 in 0,01 mm. radiate at the ends, sometimes crossed on each side of the central nodule by a short and narrow lateral area, punctate; puncta, about 15 in 0,01 mm., forming undulating longitudinal rows. — GROVE and STURT Q. M. Cl. J. III p. 132 Pl. X f. 6. Icon. n. Pl. V t. 16.

Marine: Oamaru, New Zealand, fossil!

This species is a very characteristic form, remarkable for the diaphragms in the ends, as in Pleurostauron. It bears some resemblance to *N. Kappa* of the same habitat.

49. **N. (Scoliopleura) tumida** BRÉB. (1849). — V. lanceolate, gradually attenuated to the subacute ends. L. 0,1 to 0,16; B. 0,025 mm. Median line slightly sigmoid. Axial area very narrow; central area small, somewhat elongated. Striæ 13 to 14 in 0,01 mm., in the middle where a few frequently are shorter than the others, more distant, slightly radiate (at the ends transverse) finely punctate. Frustule in the zonal-view rectangular with rounded angles. Connecting zone slightly oblique, not complex. — BRÉB. in Kütz. Sp. Alg. p. 77. *N. Jennerii* W. SM. B. D. I p. 49 Pl. XVI f. 134 (1853). *Scoliopleura tumida* V. H. Syn. p. 112 Pl. XVII f. 11, 13. PANT. III Pl. XVII f. 245.

Marine and brackish: Franz Josephs Land (Grun.), North Sea! Sebastopol! Ceylon! Sydney!

Var. *adriatica* GRUN. (1860). — V. 0,027; B. 0,008 mm. Median line strongly sigmoid. Striæ 12 in 0,01 mm. — *Scoliopleura adriatica* GRUN. Verh. 1860 p. 554 Pl. V f. 21.

Marine: Adriatic (Grun.).

I have seen a few living specimens of *N. tumida*. They had along the zone two chromatophore-plates, with entire margins. Each plate contained a row of 6 large, orbicular pyrenoids. At the ends of the frustules a number of small granules in lively motion was visible.

N. tumida with cell-contents 500 times magnified.

50. **N. auklandica** Grun. (1863). — V. linear, with broad rounded ends, convex. L. 0,05 to 0,06; B. 0,018 mm. Median line straight, somewhat excentric; its terminal fissures turned in contrary directions and of somewhat unequal length. Axial area indistinct; central very small. Striæ 10 (middle) to 14 (ends) in 0,01 mm., slightly radiate throughout, punctate, puncta about 18 in 0,01 mm. Frustule rectangular with rounded corners, somewhat constricted in the middle. Connecting zone with several longitudinal rows of short striæ (Grun.). Grun. Verh. 1863 p. 151 Pl. V f. 14. Novara p. 17. Icon. n. Pl. V f. 15.

Marine: Auckland (Grun.), Port Jackson! Australia!

A very characteristic species, which seems to be related to *N. tumida*.

51. **N. Jimboi** Pant. (1893). V. lanceolate, rostrate, obtuse. L. 0,042; B. 0,019 mm. Axial area indistinct. Central area small, transverse, with a stigma, close to the central nodule. Striæ 13 in 0,01 mm. radiate, but parallel at the ends, punctate; puncta about 16 in 0,01 mm. — Pant. III Pl. V f. 81.

Habitat?: Sentenaï (Pant.).

This form resembles *N. mutica*, which also has a stigma on the central area, but the central area of *N. Jimboi* is very small. It is doubtful whether it should be placed in this group.

Cymbella Ag. (1830).

Valve elongated, boat-shaped or more or less asymmetrical to the longitudinal axis. Median line excentric. The terminal nodules near the ends of the valve, and the terminal fissures turned to the dorsal, or ventral, side, or straight. Structure transverse, usually radiate, rows of puncta, or finely lineate striæ on both sides of the median line. Connecting zone not complex. Cell-contents a single chromatophore, the longitudinal axis of which follows the dorsal part of the connecting zone. The chromatophore covers the inside of the frustule, with the exception of the ventral part of the connecting zone and the branches of the median line. The division of the chromatophore begins in the ends of the plate on the dorsal side. In conjugating, the mother-cells, usually produced by division of a parent cell, and enclosed in a gelatinous mass produce two auxospores, parallel to the mother-cells. Before conjugation the cell-contents of one of the mother-cells is divided into two masses, each of which unites with a similar mass of the other mother-cell.

As early as 1817 Nitszch described some Cymbellæ under name the of *Bacillaria fulva* and *B. phoenicenteron*, and in 1829 Ehrenberg founded the genus *Cocconema* for the stipitate forms. Agardh in 1830 founded the genus *Cymbella* (Consp. crit. 1) for diatoms with frustula elliptica, libera vel muco amorpha involuta, binatim conjuncta. Some of the species included by Agardh in this genus belong doubtless to what we now name *Cymbella*. Later on, in 1830, Kützing created the genus *Encyonema* for the cymbelloid forms included in gelatinous tubes. Most authors since then have adopted these three genera and have regarded as Cymbella, forms which live free; as Cocconema, forms attached to gelatinous stalks; and as Encyonema, forms included in tubes. The valves of all these forms are in all essential points similar, and frustules of stipitate or enclosed forms frequently occur free; for which reasons Heiberg (Consp. Crit. Diat. p. 107) 1863 united them in one genus, for which he considered the name Cymbella more adequately fitting, although a little more recent than Cocconema. There can be no doubt as to the advisability of uniting Cymbella and Cocconema, but some hesitation may be felt in uniting Encyonema which has somewhat differently shaped terminal fissures. On the other hand transitions exist between the downward turned terminal fissures of Encyonema and the reflexed fissures of Cymbella, as for instance in *C. helvetica;* and I think it most convenient to follow the proposition of Heiberg.

The most characteristic feature of Cymbella is the asymmetrical form of the valves, but this characteristic is subject to much variation. There are all transitions from boat-like to almost symmetrical naviculoid forms. On the other hand several species in other groups of naviculoid diatoms are more or less decidedly asymmetrical. For instance, all the larger forms of Pinnularia shew a tendency to asymmetry. The same is the case with numerous varieties of *Trachyneis aspera*. All the Amphoræ are asymmetrical, and usually in a more decided manner than the Cymbellæ. From some groups of the old genus Amphora the Cymbellæ differ only by their connecting zone not being complex. From other groups of the same genus the distinction is attended with more difficulty, especially in the new group *Cymbamphora*, the valves of which are still more asymmetrical, having the median line close to the ventral margin. But the Cymbamphoræ are marine or brackish, while the Cymbellæ usually are of fresh-water habitat.

The structure of the Cymbellæ consists of puncta disposed in rows or of transverse striæ, which are more or less transversely lineate. The striæ in the middle of the valve are radiate and somewhat more distant than in other parts of the valve. In the ends they are parallel or radiate. They either reach the median line, or end at some distance from it, leaving a narrow axial area, frequently dilated around the central nodule. In some species there is a shallow depression on the ventral side of the central nodule, the median ventral striæ appearing to be crossed, below the central nodule, by a semicircular furrow. In one division of Cymbella there is in the middle of the central nodule or on its ventral side a peculiar punctum or pore, for which I use the name *stigma*. If the stigma is below the nodule, a fine, fissure-like line proceeds from it into the nodule. The median line is in some species oblique and therefore broad, shewing a complex structure, as in some Pinnularias. The terminal nodules are usually close to the end of the valve, and the fissures, especially in the boat-like forms, reflexed to the dorsal side. In the naviculoid forms it is comma-like, and in *C. helvetica* straight, in the direction of the median line, thus forming a passage to Encyonema, which has the terminal fissures bent downwards.

The Cymbellæ are certainly nearly akin to the Naviculæ of the section *Lineolatæ*. *Navicula dicephala* is closely connected with *C. amphicephala*, and *C. naviculiformis*, and with these a number of forms are more or less related:

Navicula dicephala

Cymbella amphicephala — Cymbella naviculiformis

C. Ehrenbergii — C. tumida — C. heteropleura

C. aspera — C. Cistula — C. oregonica

C. lanceolata — C. Janischii.

Cymb. microcephala shews some signs of affinity to *Navicula Bulnheimii*, and we may thus trace passages to a number of forms

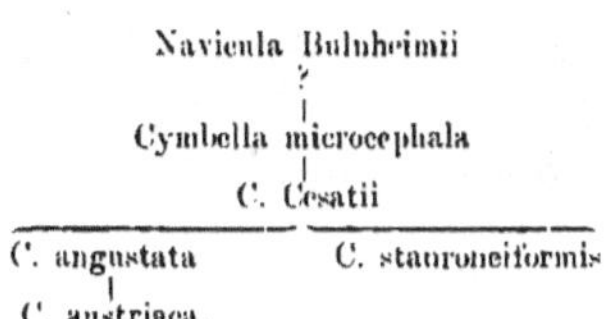

Cymbella alpina is an isolated form, without, so far I can see, any close relation to the *Lineolatæ*, although the structure of the striæ is the same as in the typical form of that group of Navicula. *Cymb. sinuata* is also an isolated form, which seems to have its nearest relatives in Gomphonema.

69. **M. Braunii** GRUN. (1863). — V. elliptic-lanceolate. L. 0,04 to 0,095; B. 0,014 to 0,027 mm. Central nodule large, quadrate, prolonged into narrow horns, as to form a lyriform figure. Loculi 4,5 to 6 in 0,01 mm. quadrate, equal, or the median larger, forming a band ending near the extremities. Striæ 18 to 22 in 0,01 mm. parallel, radiate towards the ends, finely punctate; puncta about 25 in 0,01 mm. — Verh. 1863 p. 156 Pl. IV f. 2. DANNF. Balt. D. Pl. I f. 4. V. H. Syn. p. 71 Pl. IV f. 21, 22. A. S. Atl. CLXXXV f. 39, 40, 45; CLXXXVIII f. 4 to 12. *M. Kinsmanni* LEWIS Proced. Ac. Nat. Hist. Philad. p. 13 Pl. II f. 15 (1865).

Brackish water: Spitsbergen! Baltic! Caspian Sea! Saxony! North Sea! Mediterranean, Adriatic and Black Seas! Red Sea (Grun.). Japan! Pensacola! Cape May (Lewis).

70. **M. Debyi** CL. (1892). — V. narrow, rhombic-lanceolate. L. 0,055; B. 0,014 mm. Median line strongly flexuose. Central area quadrate, expanded into narrow, linear lateral areas, parallel to the median line. Loculi 8 in 0,01 mm. quadrate, forming a narrow band reaching to the ends. Striæ 15 in 0,01 mm. slightly radiate, finely punctate. — Diatomiste I p. 161 Pl. XXIII f. 11. *Nav. perducta* PANT. III Pl. XVIII f. 262 (1893). *M. rhomboidalis* PANT. III Pl. XLI f. 563 (1893)?

Marine: Karand, Hungary, fossil (Deby Coll.)!

71. **M. baltjikiana** GRUN. (188 ?). — V. elliptical to elliptic-lanceolate, subacute. L. 0,042; B. 0,02 mm. Median line undulating. Central area broad, transverse, merging into two narrow, lunate lateral areas. Loculi 6 to 8 in 0,01 mm., equal, rectangular, forming bands, ending at some distance from the apices. Striæ 16 to 17 in 0,01 mm., slightly radiate, coarsely punctate; puncta about 16 in 0,01 mm. *M. Braunii var. baltjikiana* GRUN. in V. H. Types N:o 545. *M. baltj.* A. S. Atl. CLXXXVIII f. 2. Icon. n. Pl. II f. 11. *M. Pethöi* PANT. III Pl. XXXVII f. 519 (1893). *M. neogena* PANT. III Pl. XLI f. 559 (1893). *M. Kinkerii* PANT. III Pl. XLI f. 562 (1893). *Navicula Orphei* PANT. III Pl. XLII f. 580 (1893).

Marine: Baltjik, foss.!

Var. *bullata* CL. Areas with some few scattered, large puncta. L. 0,09; B. 0,024 mm. Striæ 17 in 0,01 mm. Puncta 16 in 0,01 mm.

Marine: Russia, fossil (Deby Coll.)!

72. **M. Macdonaldii** GREV. (1865). — V. lanceolate to rhomboid, subacute. L. 0,035 to 0,045; B. 0,013 to 0,017 mm. Median line slightly undulating. Central nodule transversely dilated into a broad stauros. Loculi 3 in 0,01 mm., decreasing in size towards the extremities and with slightly rounded interior edges. Striæ 22 in 0,01 mm. slightly radiate throughout, crossed by large, semi-lanceolate areas, punctate; puncta about 22 in 0,01 mm. forming somewhat undulating longitudinal rows. — T. Bot. Soc. Edinb. Vol. VIII p. 237 Pl. III f. 15. A. S. Atl. CLXXXVII f. 42, 43. Icon. n. Pl. II f. 21.

Marine: Corsica! Adriatic! Philippines! Australia (Grev.).

73. **M. euxina** CL. (1892). — V. lanceolate. L. 0,07; B. 0,026 mm. Median line undulating. Axial area narrow. Central nodule transversely dilated into a short stauros. Axial area narrow; central area prolonged into the narrow, lunate lateral areas. Loculi 5 in 0,01 mm. equal, quadrate, forming a band reaching nearly to the ends. Striæ 17 in 0,01 mm. coarsely punctate; puncta about 18 in 0,01 mm. forming undulating longitudinal rows. Axial striæ short. — Diatomiste I p. 160 Pl. XXIII f. 9.

Marine: Baltjik, fossil!

74. **M. entoleia** CL. (1892). — V. lanceolate. L. 0,07; B. 0,025 mm. Loculi 4 in 0,01 mm. of equal size, rectangular, forming bands ending at some distance from the extremities. Median line undulating. Axial area lanceolate, moderately broad. Striæ 17 in 0,01 mm. punctate; puncta, about 14 in 0,01 mm., forming longitudinal undulating rows. — Diatomiste I p. 160 Pl. XXIII f. 8. A. S. Atl. CLXXXVIII f. 15 to 17.

Marine: Baltjik, foss.!

A similar, not described, and insufficiently figured, form seems to be *M. obtusa var. fluviatilis* BRUN in A. S. Atl. CLXXXVIII f. 18.

75. **M. antiqua** CL. (1893). V. rhomboid. L. 0,08; B. 0,03 mm. Median line slightly undulating. Axial area a narrow, lanceolate space. Loculi 6 in 0,01 mm., equal, quadrate, forming a band inside the margin and ending at some distance from the extremities. Striæ 18 in 0,01 mm. parallel, very slightly radiate at the ends, punctate; puncta 18 in 0,01 mm., forming undulating longitudinal rows. - Diatomiste II p. 16 Pl. I f. 19.

Marine: Karand, Hungary, fossil (Deby Coll.)!

76. **M. cruciata** LEUD. FORTM. (1879). — V. rhomboid. L. 0,085 to 0,122; B. 0,053 to 0,057 mm. Central nodule transversely dilated into a stauros, not reaching to the margins. Median line slightly undulating. Loculi? Lateral areas large, semilanceolate, crossed by faint striæ. Striæ marginal and axial. Marginal striæ 8 to 9 in 0,01 mm. punctate; puncta 12 in 0,01 mm. Axial striæ short. *Nav. cruc.* LEUD. FORTM. D. Ceylan p. 25 Pl. II f. 19. *Mast. cruc.* CL. Diatomiste I p. 65 Pl. X f. 4 (1891). A. S. Atl. CLXXXVII f. 50.

Marine: Ceylon (Le Tourneur Coll.)! Manilla (Deby Coll.)! Philippines!

77. **M. Craveni** LEUD. FORTM. (1879). -- V. rhombic-lanceolate. L. 0,111; B. 0,056 to 0,06 mm. Median line almost straight. Central area irregularly rounded, moderately large. Loculi? Lateral areas large, with numerous and irregular longitudinal rows (about 7 in 0,01 mm.) of elongated puncta. Striæ marginal and axial. Marginal striæ 12 in 0,01 mm. punctate; puncta about 14 in 0,01 mm. — *Navicula Crav.* LEUD. FORTM. D. Ceylan p. 25 Pl. II f. 20. *Mastogl. Crav.* CL. Diatomiste I p. 66 Pl. X f. 5.

Marine: Colombo, Ceylon (Le Tourneur Coll.)!

78. **M. Leudugeri** CL. a. GROVE (1891). V. rhombic-lanceolate. L. 0,12; B. 0,06 mm. Median line undulating. Central area small, subquadrate. Axial area very narrow. Loculi 3 in 0,01 mm., quadrate, equal, forming a band, reaching to the extremities. Lateral areas broad, semilanceolate, with numerous longitudinal rows (about 7 in 0,01 mm.) of short striæ. Striæ marginal and axial, 14 in 0,01 mm. punctate; puncta 15 in 0.01 mm. forming undulating, longitudinal rows. — Diatomiste I p. 65 Pl. X f. 3. A. S. Atl. CLXXXVI f. 13.

Marine: Macassar Straits! Singapore! Java!

79. **M. lemniscata** LEUD. FORTM. (1879). — V. rhombic-lanceolate. L. 0,05 to 0,088; B. 0,025 to 0,043 mm. Median line slightly undulating. Loculi 5 to 6 in 0,01 mm. quadrate, forming a band reaching to the ends. Central area small, quadrate. Lateral areas large, semilanceolate, with a few (3 to 4) longitudinal rows of short striæ. Striæ 15 to 16 in 0,01 mm. punctate; puncta 15 to 20 in 0,01 mm. - - D. de Ceylon p. 35 Pl. III f. 29. A. S. Atl. CLXXXVI f. 14. Icon. n. Pl. II f. 26. *M. decora* LEUD. FORTM. l. c. f. 32.

Marine: Madagascar (Van Heurck and Kinker Coll.)! Ceylon! Sumbava (Kinker Coll.)! Manilla (Deby Coll.)! Macassar Straits (Grove Coll.)! Carpentaria Bay! Japan! Colon (Deby Coll.)!

80. **M. javanica** CL. (1893). V. rhomboid-lanceolate. L. 0,11; B. 0,032 mm. Median line slightly undulating. No axial or central areas. Loculi 3 in 0,01 mm. equal, rectangular, forming a narrow band, reaching to the ends. Striæ 16 in 0,01 mm. parallel, slightly radiate at the ends, composed of elongated puncta, forming longitudinal, parallel, straight rows, 12 in 0,01 mm. Surface of the valve with a shallow, narrow, longitudinal depression, close to the median line. The longitudinal rows of puncta are more distant on the depression. — A. S. Atl. CLXXXVIII f. 38. Icon. n. Pl. II f. 22, 23.

Marine: Java! Sumatra (Grove Coll.)!

49. Median striæ more distant than the others . . . . 50.
— — not — — — . . . . *C. incerta* Grun.

50. Central area dilated to the ventral margin . . . . *C. sinuata* Greg.
— — not — . . . *C. æqualis* W. Sm.

51. Valve almost symmetrical . . . . 52.
— decidely asymmetrical . . . . 53.

52. Central area large . . . . *C. Mölleriana* Grun.
— — small . . . . *C. lacustris* Ag.

53. Axial area narrow . . . . 54.
— — moderately broad . . . . 56.

54. Length about 0,03 to 0,04 mm. . . . . 55.
— — 0,06 to 0,07 mm. . . . . *C. borealis* Cl.

55. Striæ 5 in 0,01 mm. . . . . . *C. alpina* Grun.
— about 10 in 0,01 mm. . . . *C. æqualis* W. Sm.

56. Axial area dilated to a small central area . . . . 57.
— — not — — — . . . . 58.

57. Striæ coarsely punctate . . . . *C. Hauckii* V. H.
— finely . . *C. Reinhardtii* Grun.

58. Length about 0,03 mm. . . . . *C. leptoceros* Grun.
— — 0,06 mm. . . . . *C. austriaca* Grun.

59. Median ventral striæ ending in isolated puncta . *C. tumidula var. salinarum.*
— not . . . . 60.

60. Terminal nodules distant from the ends . . . . *C. Cesatii* Rabh.
— — approximate to — . . . . 61.

61. Median line straight, strongly excentric . . . . 62.
— — subarcuate, nearly central . . . . 63.

62. Valve broad. B. 0,02 mm. . . . . *C. Triangulum* Ehb.
— narrow. B. less than 0,01 mm. . . . . . *C. hebridica* Greg.

63. Central area not dilated in the middle . . . . *C. acutiuscula* Cl.
— — abruptly dilated into a central area . . . . 64.

64. Large. L. 0,05 to 0,1 mm. . . . . 65.
Small. L. 0,03 to 0,04 mm. . . . . 66.

65. Striæ about 10 in 0,01 mm. . . . . *C. acuta* A. S.
— — 17 — — . . . . *C. oregonica* Cl.

66. Central area rounded . . . . *C. lapponica* Grun.
— — dilated outwards . . . . *C. stauroneiformis* Lagst.

1. **C. microcephala** Grun. (1880). — V. almost symmetrical, linear, with rostrate-capitate ends. L. 0,015 to 0,023; B. 0,003 to 0,004 mm. Median line almost central, straight; its central pores approximate. Axial and central areas indistinct. Striæ 24 to 30 in 0,01 mm. almost parallel. — Grun. in V. H. Syn. p. 63 Pl. VIII f. 36 to 39. *C. minuscula* A. S. Atl. IX f. 58 to 61?

Fresh water: Greenland! Scotland! Sweden (Vernamo, fossil)! Belgium (V. H.), Ecuador, Banos!

2. **C. (Encyonema) Cesatii** Rabh. (1853). — V. nearly symmetrical, narrow lanceolate, gradually tapering from the middle to the acute ends. L. 0,045 to 0,05; B. 0,006 to 0,007 mm. Median line almost central, with approximate central pores and slightly curved terminal fissures at some distance from the ends. Axial area narrow; central area small. Striæ radiate throughout, about 19 in 0,01 mm., very finely punctate. — *Nav. appendiculata* Grun. Verh. 1860 p. 552 Pl. IV f. 29. *Nav. Cesatii* Rabh. Süssw. D. p. 39 Pl. VI f. 89. V. H. Syn. p. 88 Pl. VIII f. 35. *Cymbella Cesatii* Grun. A. S. Atl. LXXI f. 48, 49.

Fresh water: Greenland! Iceland! Swedish and Russian Lappland! Scotland! Sweden (Wenern)! Belgium (V. H.), Piedmont (Rabh.), Canada!

This form, easily recognized by the distance of its terminal nodules from the ends of the valve, is so slightly asymmetrical, that one might regard it as a Navicula. It seems to be an inhabitant principally of northern or alpine regions. In Verh. 1860 (p. 571 Pl. VII f. 16) Grunow mentions a *Colletonema dubium* as occurring together with *C. Cesatii* (his *Nav. appendiculata*) and with frustules of the same appearance. It seems then probable that the frustules of *C. Cesatii* occur enclosed in gelatinous tubes.

3. **C. angustata** W. SM. (1853). — V. almost symmetrical, with, usually, slightly triundulate margins and capitate ends. L. 0,03 to 0,05; B. 0,008 mm. Median line almost central, straight; its central pores approximate and its terminal fissures in the ends of the valve. Axial area very narrow or indistinct, not dilated in the middle. Striæ about 16 in 0,01 mm., slightly radiate throughout. — *N. angustata* W. SM. B. D. I Pl. XVII f. 156. *C. æqualis* A. S. Atl. IX f. 69. *C. æqu. var. hybrida* GRUN. A. S. Atl. LXXI f. 50. *Navic. inæquilatera* LAGST. Spitsb. D. p. 33 Pl. II f. 10.

Fresh water (alpine and arctic regions): Greenland! Spitsbergen! Scotland, England (W. Sm.), Norway (Dovre)! Sweden (Gellivara, Degernäs, Loka, Förarm in Åsnen, fossil)! Finland (Imandra to Karelen and Aland)!

4. **C. Schmidtii** GRUN. (1875). — V. almost symmetrical, broadly linear, with triundulate margins and cuneate ends. L. 0,026; B. 0,009 mm. Median line almost central, slightly flexuose. Axial and central areas indistinct. Striæ about 14 in 0,01 mm., slightly radiate. — GRUN. in A. S. Atl. IX f. 48.

Brackish water: Neusiedler See, Hungary (Atl.).

5. **C. obtusiuscula** (KÜTZ. 1844?) GRUN. 1875. V. slightly asymmetrical, broad, almost elliptical, with subrostrate ends. L. 0,027; B. 0,012 mm. Median line almost central, straight. Axial area very narrow; central area small and orbicular. Striæ 12 in 0,01 mm., slightly radiate. — KÜTZ. Bac. p. 79 Pl. III f. 68. A. S. Atl. IX f. 49.

Fresh water: Steinitz See (Atl.).

6. **C. alpina** GRUN. (1863). — V. slightly asymmetrical, lanceolate, with convex dorsal and ventral margins and slightly obtuse ends. L. 0,023 to 0,04; B. 0,008 to 0,01 mm. Median line straight, slightly excentric. Axial area very narrow, not dilated in the middle. Striæ 5 in 0,01 mm., very slightly radiate, finely transversely lineate. — GRUN. Verh. 1863 p. 148 Pl. IV f. 19. A. S. Atl. LXXI f. 44, 45. BRUN. Diat. des Alpes p. 62 Pl. III f. 7.

Fresh water (alpine regions): Tyrol (Grun.), Switzerland (Brun), Savoy!

This little species is very characteristic, not nearly akin to any other *Cymbella*, and distinguished by its unusually coarse and lineate striæ. It is an habitant of alpine regions only. The fine lineation of the striæ appears to indicate a relationship to the group *Naviculæ lineolatæ*, but there is no closely allied from in that group.

7. **C. borealis** CL. (1891). V. slightly asymmetrical, linear-lanceolate, gradually tapering from the middle to the obtuse or slightly capitate ends. L. 0,06 to 0,07; B. 0,007 to 0,09 mm. Median line almost central, straight. Axial area very narrow, slightly or indistinctly dilated in the middle. Striæ 10 (middle) to 13 or 14 (ends) in 0,01 mm., very slightly radiate throughout, very finely lineate. — CL. D. of Finl. p. 46 Pl. II f. 19.

Fresh water: Russian Lapland!

8. **C. delicatula** KÜTZ. (1849). — V. narrow, lanceolate, slightly asymmetrical, obtuse. L. 0,022 to 0,03; B. 0,005 to 0,006 mm. Striæ 18 or 20 (dorsal) to 21 (ventral) in 0,01 mm., delicate. — KÜTZ. Sp. Alg. p. 59. A. S. Atl. LXXI f. 54, 55. V. H. Syn. p. 62 Pl. III f. 6.

Fresh water (moist rocks etc.): Norway (Dovre, Brevig)! Sweden (Lapland to Skane)! France! Savoy! Genève!

This species is recognized by its narrow, almost linear, lanceolate valves and by its close and delicate striæ. It is nearly connected with *C. lævis*, which has broader valves and somewhat coarser striæ. Intermediate forms exist between both.

As *Cymbella elegans* CRAMER has issued in Rabh. Alg. Eur. N:o 1441 (1863) a sample containing several Cymbellæ, as *C. Cistula, C. helvetica, C. delicatula, C. lævis, C. affinis, C. leptoceras, C. amphicephala* and *C. aspera*. As no description or figure of *C. elegans* is given, it is impossible to determine what form the name denotes.

9. **C. lævis** NAEGELI (1849). — V. strongly asymmetrical, semilanceolate, gradually tapering from the middle to the ends. Dorsal margin arcuate; ventral margin straight or slightly convex in the middle. L. 0,025 to 0,035; B. 0,007 to 0,008 mm. Median line somewhat excentric and slightly arcuate. Axial area indistinct. Striæ of the dorsal side 13 (middle) to 15 (ends) in 0,01 mm., slightly radiate. Striæ of the ventral side 16 (middle) to 17 (ends) in 0,01 mm. almost parallel and finely punctate. — NAEG. in Kütz. Sp. Alg. p. 59. V. H. Syn. p. 62 Pl. III f. 7. A. S. Atl. IX f. 35.

Fresh water: Norway (Dovre)! Sweden (Gellivaara to Örtofta in Skåne)! Finland (Lapland to Karelen)! Scotland! Zürich (Grun.), Tours du Rhône!

10. **C. pusilla** GRUN. (1875). — V. asymmetrical, narrow, semilanceolate, with subacute ends and arcuate dorsal, straight or slightly convex ventral, margin. L. 0,23 to 0,04; B. 0,005 to 0,0075 mm. Median line straight, strongly excentric. Axial area very narrow, not, or slightly, dilated around the central nodule. Striæ 15 to 18 (middle) or 16 to 20 (ends) in 0,01 mm., radiate in the middle, transverse at the ends. — GRUN. in A. S. Atl. IX f. 36, 37. V. H. Syn. Pl. III f. 5.

Brackish water: Sweden (Baltic: Gothland, Malmö)! Halle! Neusiedler See (Grun.), Caspian Sea (Grun.), Normandy! Belgium (V. H.), Bayonne (Atl.). Sardinia (Grun.), Mouth of Jenissey! South Africa! Ecuador!

11. **C. yarrensis** A. S. (1881). — V. narrow, semilanceolate, acute. L. 0,075 to 0,11; B. 0,012 to 0,015 mm. Median line nearly central; its terminal fissures in the ends. Axial area narrow, linear, dilated in the middle to an elongated central area. Striæ 11 in 0,01 mm., somewhat more distant in the middle, where they are radiate, parallel in the ends. — *Encyon? yarrense* A. S. Atl. LXXI f. 16.

Slightly brackish water: Yarra-Yarra (Australia)! Tasmania!

12. **C. rupicola** GRUN. (1881). — V. slightly asymmetrical, lanceolate, gradually tapering from the middle to the subacute ends. L. 0,027 to 0,034; B. 0,0045 to 0,0055 mm. Median line almost central, straight. Axial area narrow, not dilated in the middle. Dorsal striæ 12 (middle) to 15 (ends) in 0,01 mm. slightly radiate. Ventral striæ 16 in 0,01 mm. slightly radiate — GRUN. in A. S. Atl. LXXI f. 70, 71.

Fresh water (moist rocks): Arctic America! Scotland (V. H. Types), Salzburg (Atl.).

This species is very nearly akin to *C. lævis* and differs scarcely in anything except the less asymmetrical valves.

13. **C. Reinhardtii** GRUN. (1875). — V. slightly asymmetrical, elliptic-lanceolate, with convex dorsal and ventral margins. Ends obtuse. L. 0,03 to 0,06; B. 0,008 to 0,014 mm. Median line nearly central, straight. Axial area narrow, gradually dilated to the middle, where it expands to a moderately large central area. Striæ 10 (middle) to 13 or 14 (ends) in 0,01 mm. The median striæ are more distant than the rest and slightly radiate. Towards the ends the striæ become almost parallel. — A. S. Atl. IX f. 27. CL. M. D. N:o 132.

Fresh water: Norway (Romsdalen)! Steinitz Sea (Atl.).

The above description is from specimens in Cl. M. D. 132, determined by GRUNOW as *C. Reinhardtii*.

14. **C. leptoceros** (EHR. 1843?) GRUN. — V. asymmetrical, lanceolate, with slightly gibbous ventral margin and obtuse, sometimes slightly attenuated ends. L. 0,02 to 0,04; B. 0,008 to 0,01 mm. Median line slightly arcuate. Axial area linear, not dilated around the central nodule.

Striæ 9 or 11 (middle) to 12 (ends) in 0,01 mm. slightly radiate, especially near the ends, punctate; puncta about 22 in 0,01 mm. — *Cocc. lept.* EHR. Am. Pl. I: 2 f. 30. *Cy. leptoc.* V. H. Syn. p. 62 Pl. II f. 18, III f. 21 (f. curta) Suppl. A. f. 2 (f. elongata). *Cy. hungarica* PANT. II p. 40 Pl. I f. 14 (1889)?

Fresh water: Rostock (foss.). Belgium! Hungary foss. (Pant.)? Mexico, foss.!

Var. *minor* GRUN. (1882). — L. 0,026; B. 0,007 mm. — GRUN. Foss. D. Österr. Ung. p. 142 Pl. XXIX f. 32.

Fresh water: Hungary, fossil (Grun.).

Var. *angusta* GRUN. (1882). — L. 0,021 to 0,04; B. 0,005 to 0,01 mm. Striæ 12 to 15 in 0,01 mm. — GRUN. Foss. D. Österr. Ung. p. 142 Pl. XXIX f. 33. 34.

Fresh water: Greenland! Hungary, fossil (Grun.). Geneva! Savoy!

Var. *excisa* PET. (1877). — Ventral margin indented in the middle. — *C. turgida var. excisa* PET. Bull. Soc. Bot. de France 1877 Pl. I f. 2. A. S. Atl. LXXI f. 35. GRUN. Foss. D. Österr. Ung. p. 142.

Fresh water: Marly, near Paris (according to Grunow).

The most marked characteristic of *C. leptoceros* is the distinct axial area, which seems to become much reduced in some of the varieties, named by GRUNOW, especially in the var. *excisa* which I have placed here on the authority of GRUNOW. Specimens of that var. from Marly (Cl. M. D. N:o 195) agree in my opinion with *C. tumidula* GRUN.

The following forms, found in a fossil state in Hungary and described by PANTOCSEK seem to be nearly akin to *C. leptoceros*.

C. karnensis PANT. (II p. 40 Pl. XI f. 186). — L. 0,025; B. 0,0075 mm. Striæ 15 in 0,01 mm.

C. Neupaueri PANT. (II p. 40 Pl. XI f. 187). — L. 0,027; B. 0,0095 mm. Striæ 15 in 0,01 mm.

Specimens from Gyöngiös-Pata, which I have examined, are scarcely distinguishable from *C. leptoceros* in Van Heurck's Types.

15. **C. austriaca** GRUN. (1875). — V. asymmetrical; with arcuate dorsal margin and slightly convex ventral margin. Ends obtuse and rounded. L. 0,045 to 0,088; B. 0,012 to 0,017 mm. Median line somewhat excentric, nearly straight, broad (oblique). Axial area distinct, linear, not widened in the middle. Striæ 11 or 13 (dorsal) to 13 or 14 (ventral) in 0,01 mm., radiate throughout, punctate; puncta about 21 in 0,01 mm. — GRUN. in A. S. Atl. IX f. 10, LXXI f. 67 to 69.

Fresh water: Tyrol (Atl.), Switzerland (St. Gingolf, Engadine)!

Var. *prisca* GRUN. (1882). — L. 0,05 to 0,078; B. 0,013 to 0,019 mm. Median line slightly arcuate. Area slightly dilated on the dorsal side of the central nodule. Striæ 9 (middle) to 11 (ends) in 0,01 mm., punctate. Puncta 23 in 0,01 mm. — GRUN. Foss. D. Österr. Ung. p. 143 Pl. XXIX f. 29.

Fresh water: Hungary, fossil (Grun.).

Var. *excisa* GRUN. (1882). — Smaller. Ventral margin indented. — GRUN. Foss. D. Österr. Ung. Pl. XXIX f. 27. PANT. III Pl. I f. 11.

Fresh water: Hungary, fossil (Grun.).

C. austriaca, which seems to inhabit the alps only, is characterized by its median line, being oblique and therefore broad in the middle between the central and terminal nodules, by its distinctly punctate striæ and non-rostrate ends. It is evidently akin to *C. leptoceros*. *Cymb. Erdöbenyana* PANT. (II p. 40 Pl. XI f. 198; 1889) agrees completely with *C. austriaca*, as I have convinced myself by examining specimens from Erdöbenye.

16. **C. Stodderi** CL. (1881). — V. slightly asymmetrical, narrow, lanceolate, with subrostrate ends. L. 0,075 to 0,09; B. 0,015 mm. Median line almost central, straight; its terminal fissures approximate to the ends. Axial area moderately broad, linear-lanceolate, not abruptly dilated around the central nodule. Striæ strongly radiate in the middle, 10 or 11 (middle) to 12 (ends) in 0,01 mm., not distinctly punctate. — CL. N. R. D. p. 5 Pl. I f. 5. CL. M. D. N:o 212, 274.

Fresh water: Monmouth (Maine), Bemis Lake (White Mountains)! Caldas (Brazil)!

This species is probably akin to *Nav. Monmouthiana* GREV., and its place here is somewhat doubtful.

17. **C. amphioxys** KÜTZ. (1844) GRUN. — V. almost symmetrical, narrow linear-lanceolate, with subrostrate ends. L. 0,07; B. 0,007 mm. Median line almost central, straight. Axial area narrow; central area indistinct. Striæ 17 in 0,01 mm. slightly radiate in the middle and slightly convergent in the ends, not distinctly punctate. — *Navic. amphioxys* KÜTZ. Bac. p. 91 Pl. XXVIII f. 37? *Cymb. navic. var. amphioxy* GRUN. in Cl. M. D. N:o 273 (1879).

Fresh water: Degernäs, Westerbotten, Sweden, fossil!

This form, frequent in Cl. M. D. N:o 273, seems not to be akin to *C. naviculacea*, but rather to the group of *Navicula radiosa*, having, like those, the terminal striæ convergent.

18. **C. acuta** A. S. (1881). — V. almost symmetrical, lanceolate, with acute ends. L. 0,05 to 0,085; B. 0,016 to 0,02 mm. Median line almost central, straight. Axial area narrow, linear, in the middle dilated to a rhomboid-orbicular central area. Striæ 9 to 11 in 0,01 mm., very finely punctate. — *C. americana var. acuta* A. S. Atl. LXXI f. 75 to 78.

Fresh water: Sweden (Lake Rosslängen in Calmar Län)! Mouth of Jenissey! Demerara River!

19. **C. acutiuscula** CL. N. Sp. — V. slightly asymmetrical, lanceolate, gradually tapering from the middle to the acute ends. L. 0,07 to 0,095; B. 0,02 to 0,022 mm. Axial area narrow, lanceolate, not (or on the ventral side slightly) dilated around the central nodule. Striæ 9 to 10 (middle) or 11 (ends) in 0,01 mm., slightly radiate in the middle, parallel at the ends, coarsely punctate; puncta 17 to 20 in 0,01 mm. — Pl. IV f. 26.

Fresh water: Crane Pond! Waltham, Mass.!

This species is nearly akin to *C. acuta*, but has broader area and more coarsely punctate striæ.

20. **C. Hauckii** V. H. (1888). — V. asymmetrical-lanceolate, with arcuate dorsal margin, slightly convex ventral margin and obtuse, not rostrate ends. L. 0,07 to 0,08; B. 0,018 to 0,02 mm. Median line slightly asymmetrical, almost straight. Axial area narrow, lanceolate, scarcely dilated on the dorsal, but distinctly on the ventral side of the central nodule. Striæ 10 (middle) to 18 (ends) in 0,01 mm., radiate throughout, coarsely punctate; puncta about 18 in 0,01 mm. — V. H. in Hauck and Richter Phycoth. univ. N:o 117. Notarisia 1888 p. 622. Icon. n. Pl. IV f. 21.

Fresh water: Triest!

The above description is from original specimens in Van Heurck's collection. *C. Hauckii* is similar to *C. acutiuscula*, but the striæ are radiate in the ends, where they are much closer than in the middle. *C. Lindsayana* GREV. (Trans. Bot. Soc. Edinb. Vol. VIII p. 234 Pl. III f. 5 to 8) has the same size and outline as *C. Hauckii*, but, according to GREVILLE, somewhat coarser striæ. The description and figures given by GREVILLE are not sufficient for identification.

21. **C. amphicephala** NAEGELI (1849). — V. slightly asymmetrical, with arcuate dorsal and almost straight ventral margin. Ends rostrate to rostrate-capitate. L. 0,025 to 0,04; B. 0,009 to 0,01 mm. Median line slightly excentric, almost straight. Axial and central areas indistinct. Striæ 12 or 14 (dorsal) to 16 (ventral) in 0,01 mm., more distant in the middle than elsewhere, slightly radiate. — NAEG. in Kütz. Sp. Alg. p. 890. A. S. Atl. IX f. 62, 64 to 66; LXXI f. 52. V. H. Syn. p. 61 Pl. II f. 6. *C. naviculiformis* HEIB. Consp. Crit. p. 108 Pl. I f. 2.

Fresh water: Spitsbergen! Iceland! Sweden (Areskutan, Upsala, Billingen, Gulf of Bothnia)! Denmark! Holstein! England! Saxony! Belgium (V. H.), Switzerland! Ispahan (Atl.), Tasmania! New Zealand! Brazil!

Var. *subundulata* CL. — V. linear, with slightly triundulate margins and capitate ends. L. 0,04; B. 0,007 mm. Striæ in the middle 16, at the ends 18 in 0,01 mm.

Fresh water: Norway, Dovre!

Var. *hercynica* A. S. (1875). — V. rostrate. L. 0,029; B. 0,01 mm. Striæ about 13 in 0,01 mm. — *C. herc.* A. S. Atl. IX f. 30, 31. *C. abyssinica* GRUN. in Martelli Florula bogosensis p. 151 Pl. I f. 3 (1886).

Fresh water: Juliushall, Harzburg (Atl.), Ringsjön (Sweden)! Abyssinia (Grun.).

22. **C. lata** GRUN. Ms. — V. slightly asymmetrical, broadly lanceolate, with subrostrate to rostrate ends. L. 0,042 to 0,056; B. 0,016 to 0,018 mm. Median line almost straight and central. Axial area narrow, linear, slightly dilated around the central nodule. Striæ 9 (middle) to 12 (ends) in 0,01 mm. slightly radiate in the middle, almost parallel at the ends, finely punctate. Pl. IV f. 27.

Fresh or slightly brackish water: Sweden (Gulf of Bothnia at Piteå; Öre sjö, near Borås)! Ladoga! Domblitten, Rostock and Lüneburg, fossil!

This species resembles in outline *C. Ehrenbergii*, but is much smaller and has less distinctly punctate striæ.

23. **C. Cucumis** A. S. (1875). V. broad, with convex dorsal and almost straight or slightly convex ventral margin. Ends rostrate-truncate. L. 0,07 to 0,09; B. 0,024 mm. Median line almost central, slightly arcuate. Axial area narrow, slightly dilated around the central nodule. Striæ 8 to 9 (dorsal) to 10 (ventral) in 0,01 mm. punctate; puncta 12 in 0,01 mm., more distant on the median ventral striæ. — A. S. Atl. IX f. 21, 22.

Fresh water: Bengal (Atl.), Cameroon!

24. **C. Ehrenbergii** KÜTZ. (1844). V. asymmetrical, elliptic-lanceolate, with slightly rostrate, obtuse ends. L. 0,09 to 0,14; B. 0,028 to 0,038 mm. Median line slightly excentric, straight. Axial area narrow, but distinct, slightly dilated around the central nodule. Striæ 7 to 9 in 0,01 mm. slightly radiate throughout, coarsely punctate; puncta 13 to 16 in 0,01 mm. *Navic. inæqualis* EHR. Inf. Pl. XIII f. 18 (1838). *Cymb. Ehrenb.* KÜTZ. Bac. p. 79 Pl. VI f. 11. W. SM. B. D. I Pl. II f. 21. A. S. Atl. IX f. 6 to 9; LXXI f. 71. V. H. Syn. p. 61 Pl. II f. 1.

Fresh water: Iceland! Sweden (from Lapland to Skåne)! Norway! Finland! England! Belgium (V. H.). Paris! Germany! Switzerland! North America (Crane Pond, Lost Spring Ranch, Washington territory, St. Rosa Cal.)!

Var. *delecta* A. S. (1875). V. asymmetrical-lanceolate, with slightly rostrate ends. L. 0,063 to 0,085; B. 0,019 to 0,024 mm. Axial area narrow, not, or slightly, dilated around the central nodule. Striæ 8 to 9 (middle) to 11 (ends) in 0,01 mm. — *Cymb. delecta* A. S. Atl. IX f. 17. *C. Ehrenbergii var.* Atl. LXXI f. 80. *C. Ehrenb. var. minor* V. H. Syn. II f. 2.

Fresh water: Greenland! Königsaue (Atl.), Puerto Monte, Chili (Atl.), Victoria, Splitters Creek (Austr.)!

25. **C. lapponica** GRUN. (1879). — V. almost symmetrical, sublanceolate, gradually tapering from the middle to the acute ends. L. 0,033 to 0,037; B. 0,008 to 0,0085 mm. Median line almost central, straight. Axial area narrow; central area rather large, rounded. Median striæ 16 in 0,01 mm., terminal striæ about 21 in 0,01 mm., finely punctate. — GRUN. in Cl. M. D. N:o 271. Pl. IV f. 28.

Fresh water: North Iceland! Repats in Gellivare, Luleå Lapmark, fossil, Sweden!

This species has never been described or figured, but I suppose that GRUNOW denotes this form, which occurs sparingly in Cl. M. D. N:o 271. This species seems to connect *C. Cesatii* with *C. stauroneiformis*.

26. **C. stauroneiformis** LAGST. (1873). V. lanceolate, almost symmetrical, with nearly obtuse, attenuated ends. L. 0,038 to 0,04; B. 0,009 to 0,011 mm. Median line almost central, straight. Axial area very narrow; central area large, quadrate, somewhat broader outwards, not reaching to the margins. Striæ 16 to 17 in 0,01 mm., slightly radiate, finely punctate. — LAGST. Spitsb. D. p. 45 Pl. I f. 15. A. S. Atl. LXXI f. 62, 63.

Fresh water: Beeren Eiland (Lagst.), Spitsbergen!

27. **C. naviculiformis** Auersw. (1861). — V. elliptic-lanceolate, slightly asymmetrical, with rostrate-capitate ends. L. 0,03 to 0,047; B. 0,01 to 0,018 mm. Median line almost central, nearly straight. Axial area narrow, linear, suddenly dilated in the middle to an orbicular space. Striæ in the dorsal side 14 (middle) to 18 (ends) in 0,01 mm., on the ventral side 14 in 0,01 mm. — Auersw. Rabh. Alg. E. N:o 1065. V. H. Syn. Pl. II f. 5. *C. cuspidata* W. Sm. B. D. I Pl. II f. 22 a'. *C. anglica* Lagst. Spitsb. D. p. 42 Pl. II f. 18 (1873). A. S. Atl. IX f. 63. V. H. Syn. Pl. II f. 5.

Fresh water: Greenland! Spitsbergen! Beeren Eiland (Lagst.). Norway (Romsdalen, Dovre)! Sweden! Finland! Holstein! Harz (Atl.). Jenissey! New-Zealand! Australia!

Heiberg (Consp. Crit. p. 108) remarks that *Cymb. cuspidata* W. Sm. is not the species of Kützing, but possibly *C. naviculiformis*, of which he gives several figures (Pl. I f. 3), which however are much more similar to *C. amphicephala* than to this species. Lagerstedt proposed the name *C. anglica*, believing it to be identical with the species of W. Smith, which is too indistinctly figured for identification. *C. naviculaeformis* closely resembles *C. amphicephala*, from which it is distinguished by the larger central area.

28. **C. hybrida** Grun. (1878). V. linear, almost symmetrical, with rostrate ends. L. 0,015; B. 0,009 mm. Median line almost central and straight. Axial area narrow; central area large, subquadrate. Striæ 11 in 0,01 mm. almost parallel, finely punctate. — Grun. in Cl. M. D. N:o 161. Icon. nostr. Pl. IV f. 23.

Fresh or very slightly brackish water: Sweden (Gothland, Lefrasjön in Skåne)!

29. **C. spuria** Cl. N. Sp. - V. asymmetrical, lanceolate, with subrostrate ends. L. 0,05 to 0,06; B. 0,013 mm. Median line very slightly arcuate, almost central. Axial area narrow, gradually dilated towards the middle. Striæ 12 (dorsal, median) to 13 (ventral and dorsal, terminal) in 0,01 mm., slightly radiate in the middle, almost parallel in the ends, finely but distinctly punctate.

Fresh water: Talbot (Victoria, Australia)! Pichinicha (alpine region of Ecuador)!

30. **C. cuspidata** Kütz. (1841). V. broadly linear-lanceolate, slightly asymmetrical, with rostrate-capitate ends. L. 0,04 to 0,095; B. 0,014 to 0,024 mm. Median line slightly excentric, straight. Axial area narrow, linear; central area rather large, orbicular. Striæ 9 or 10 (middle) to 12 or 14 (ends) in 0,01 mm. radiate, finely lineate. Kütz. Bac. Pl. III f. 40. Heib. Consp. p. 109 Pl. I f. 4. A. S. Atl. IX f. 50 (typical) 53 to 55. V. H. Syn. p. 61 Pl. II f. 3.

Fresh water: Sweden (Lappland to Upsala and Westergötland)! Norway (Finmark, Dovre)! Finland! Paris! Belgium (V. H.). England! Germany! Italy! Greenland! Canada! Massachusetts! Jenissey! Kamtschatka! Japan! New Zealand!

Var. *obtusiuscula* Grun. (in V. H. Types N:o 19). L. 0,06 to 0,08; B. 0,019 to 0,02 mm. Ends more rounded.

Fresh water: England (V. H. T.).

31. **C. heteropleura** Ehr. (1843). — V. slightly asymmetrical, lanceolate, with rostrate and truncate to subrostrate, obtuse ends. L. 0,12 to 0,15; B. 0,033 to 0,04 mm. Median line almost central, straight. Axial area distinct, linear. Central area large, slightly transversely dilated. Striæ 9 to 10 in 0,01 mm. slightly radiate throughout, punctate; puncta 9 to 13 in 0,01 mm. — *Pinnularia heteropleura* Ehr. Am. p. 133. M. G. V: 2 f. 11. *Cymb. het.* Kütz. Bac. p. 79. A. S. Atl. IX f. 4, 5.

Fresh water (arctic and northern regions): Greenland! Norway (Dovre)! Sweden (Lappland)! Russian Lappland!

Var. *subrostrata* Cl. — V. with scarcely rostrate, obtuse ends. L. 0,19 to 0,20; B. 0,045 mm. Striæ 9 in 0,01 mm. coarsely punctate; puncta 9 to 13 in 0,01 mm. — *Cymb. heteropleura* A. S. Atl. IX f. 3.

Fresh water: Canada! Danas Pond! Cherryfield!

Var. *minor* Cl. — V. with rostrate and truncate ends. L. 0,06 to 0,08; B. 0,015 to 0,022 mm. Striæ 9 in 0,01 mm., coarsely punctate; puncta 18 to 21 in 0,01 mm. — *Cymb. Ehrenb.* var. Lagst. Spitsb. D. p. 42 Pl. II f. 17. *Cymb.* A. S. Atl. IX f. 51, 52.

Fresh water: Spitsbergen! Beeren Eiland (Lagst.), Norway (Dovre)! Scotland (Lough Mourne, foss.)! Jenissey! St. Fiora, Italy (foss.)!

The typical *C. heteropleura* is a large and characteristic boreal form. The var. minor occurs at Hjerkin in Dovre and cannot be distinguished from specimens in St. Fiora deposit. The latter variety differs from *C. cuspidata* in nothing except the somewhat different shape of the ends and the more coarsely punctate striæ. *C. americana* A. S. (Atl. IX f. 15, 20) seems to be intermediate between *C. cuspidata* and *C. heteropleura var. minor.* A similar form occurs in New Zealand at Horawarra.

32. **C. oregonica** Cl. N. Sp. — V. slightly asymmetrical, lanceolate, gradually tapering from the middle to the acute ends. L. 0,1; B. 0,02 mm. Median line almost central. Axial area narrow, slowly dilated to the middle, where it suddenly expands to a large, subrectangular, central area. Striæ 17 (middle) to 20 (ends) in 0,01 mm. radiate throughout, punctate; puncta about 18 in 0,01 mm. forming longitudinal rows. Pl. IV f. 25.

Fresh water: Oregon, fossil!

33. **C. Mölleriana** Grun. (1875). — V. nearly symmetrical, somewhat irregularly lanceolate, obtuse. L. 0,05 to 0,06; B. 0,01 to 0,012 mm. Terminal nodules of the median line at some distance from the ends. Axial area narrow; central area large, orbicular. Striæ 12 to 13 in 0,01 mm., radiate throughout. — Grun. in A. S. Atl. IX f. 71 to 75.

Fresh water(?): Wedel in Holstein (Atl.).

It seems doubtful whether this form, which I know only from the figures in A. S. Atlas, really be a Cymbella. It has more of the appearance of some form belonging to the group of *Navicula viridula*, but the striæ are radiate at the ends.

34. **C. (Encyonema) lacustris** Ag. (1824). — V. lanceolate, scarcely asymmetrical, with obtuse or truncate ends. L. 0,03 to 0,06; B. 0,01 mm. Median line nearly central; its terminal nodules very distant from the ends. Axial area narrow; central area small, irregular. Striæ about 9 in 0,01 mm., divergent in the middle, convergent at the ends, in the middle alternately longer and shorter, transversely lineate; lineolæ about 28 in 0,01 mm. — *Schizonema lacustre* Ag. Syst. p. 10. A. S. Atl. LXXI f. 1 to 5. V. H. Syn. Pl. XV f. 40. *Colletonema subcoherens* Thwaites in W. Sm. B. D. II p. 70 Pl. LVI f. 353. *Encyonema Ungeri* Grun. in A. S. Atl. X f. 63. *Colletonema lacustre* V. H. Syn. p. 111.

Fresh or slightly brackish water: Hungary (Plattensee Cl. M. D. N:o 108), England (W. Sm.). Gulf of Bothnia!

The frustules of this species live enclosed in mucous tubes. The structure of the valve shews that it is nearly akin to the Naviculæ lineolatæ.

35. **C. (Encyonema) prostrata** Berk. (1832). — V. strongly asymmetrical, semielliptical, with obtuse ends, frequently inclined downwards. L. 0,04 to 0,1; B. 0,025 to 0,03 mm. Median line straight; its terminal nodules considerably distant from the ends. Axial area narrow; central area small, orbicular. Striæ about 7 in 0,01 mm., in the middle of inequal length, and radiate at the ends convergent, transversely lineate. — *Monema prostratum* Berk. Brit. Alg. Pl. IV f. 3. *Gloeonema Leibleinii* Ag. Consp. p. 31? *Encyonema paradoxum* Kütz. Bac. p. 82 Pl. XXII f. 1 (1844). *Encyon. prostratum* Ralfs Ann. N. Hist. (1) XVI Pl. XVIII f. 3 (1845). W. Sm. B. D. II

p. 68 Pl. LIV f. 345. A. S. Atl. X f. 64 to 69; LXXI f. 6 to 9. V. H. Syn. p. 65 Pl. III f. 9 to 11. *Cymbella Encyonema* Heib. Consp. p. 110 (1863). *Encyonema maximum* Wartm. Rabh. Alg. Eur. N:o 1248 (1862).

Fresh or slightly brackish water: Sweden (Gulf of Bothnia, from Westerbotten to Roslagen; Lake Mälaren)! Finland (Abo, Ladoga)! England! Belgium (V. H.), France! Switzerland (Brun). Germany! Hungary (Plattensee, Grun.). Italy (St. Fiora, foss.).

36. **C. (Encyonema?) inelegans** Cl. N. Sp. — V. boat-shaped, with arcuate dorsal margin, straight or slightly concave ventral margin, and broad, rounded, somewhat reflexed ends. L. 0,055 to 0,065; B. 0,02 mm. Median line parallel to the ventral margin, very excentric. Terminal fissures comma-like; terminal pores near the ends. Axial area linear, rather broad. Striæ on the dorsal side 10 (middle) to 12 (ends) slightly radiate; striæ on the ventral side 8 in 0,01 mm., radiate in the middle, parallel in the ends, coarsely punctate: puncta 17 to 18 in 0,01 mm. Pl. V f. 1.

Fresh water: Fall River, Oregon, foss. (Grove Coll.)!

37. **C. (Encyonema) Triangulum** Ehb. (1845). V. broad, asymmetrical, lanceolate with acute ends. L. 0,04 to 0,05; B. 0,02 mm. Median line straight, dividing the valve into a ventral part half as broad as the dorsal. Terminal fissures in the ends of the valve. Axial area very narrow; central area small or indistinct. Striæ 9 to 11 in 0,01 mm. almost parallel or slightly radiate in the ends, coarsely punctate; puncta about 10 in 0,01 mm. *Gloeonema Triangulum* Ehb. Abh. 1845 p. 77. M. G. XXXV A. 7 f. 10. *Encyon. Triang.* Kütz. Sp. Alg. p. 62. A. S. Atl. X f. 54; LXXI f. 10.

Fresh water: North America, New York and Pensacola (Atl.), Michigan, Dakota and Lost Spring Ranch Calif.! Tasmania, Campbell Town, fossil!

38. **C. (Encyonema) turgida** Greg. (1856). V. lunate, with strongly arcuate dorsal, centrally gibbous ventral margin, and acute ends. L. 0,05 to 0,10; B. 0,012 to 0,023 mm. Median line straight, dividing the valve into a ventral part of about half the width of the dorsal. Terminal fissures in the ends, comma-like, turned downwards. Axial area distinct, linear, scarcely dilated in the middle. Striæ 7 to 9 in 0,01 mm., radiate in the middle and, on the dorsal side, at the ends, parallel or convergent at the ends on the ventral side, punctate; puncta 13 to 18 in 0,01 mm. Greg. M. J. IV p. 5 Pl. I f. 18. *Encyon. turg.* A. S. Atl. X f. 49 to 53. V. H. Syn. p. 65 Pl. III f. 12.

Fresh water: Sweden! Finland! Mouth of Jenissey! Scotland (Greg.). East Indies! Java! Australia (Murray River)! Tasmania! New Zealand! North America (California, Mexico)! Guatemala! Ecuador! Argentina!

This species is very variable and graduates into the following. The largest and most typical specimens occur in California, Mexico and Ecuador. European specimens are smaller and can only with difficulty be distinguished from the following species.

39. **C. (Encyonema) ventricosa** Kütz. (1834). V. lunate, with straight or centrally gibbous ventral margin and subacute ends, usually turned downwards. L. 0,015 to 0,036; B. 0,007 to 0,011 mm. Median line approximate to the ventral margin. Terminal nodules and fissures at the ends of the valve. Axial area very narrow or indistinct. Striæ 10 to 16 in 0,01 mm. slightly radiate, finely punctate. Frustules enclosed in branched mucous tubes. — *Frustulia ventricosa* Kütz. Syn. p. 11 f. 7. *Cymb. ven.* Bac. p. 80 Pl. VI f. 16. *Encyon. ventric.* V. H. Syn. p. 66 Pl. III fig. 15 to 17, 19. *Encyon. prostratum* Kütz. Bac. p. 82 Pl. XXV f. 7 (1844). *Encyon. cæspitosum* Kütz. Sp. Alg. p. 61 (1849). W. Sm. B. D. II p. 68 Pl. LV f. 346. V. H. Syn. p. 65 Pl. III f. 14; Suppl. A f. 3. A. S. Atl. X f. 57, 58; LXXI f. 11, 12. *Encyon. Auerswaldii* Rabh. Süssw. D. p. 24 Pl. VII f. 2 (1853). *Cymbella maculata* W. Sm. B. D. I Pl. II f. 23. *Cymb. affinis var. semicircularis* Lagst. Spitsb. D. p. 43 Pl. II f. 20. *Cocconema Lunula* Ehb. Am. Pl. I: 1, f. 15 (1843). *Encyon.*

Lunula A. S. Atl. X f. 42, 43; LXXI f. 14, 15, 32 to 34. *Cymb. Lunula* RABH. Alg. Eur. N:o 1166 (1861). *Cymb. silesiaca* BLEISCH RABH. Alg. Eur. N:o 1802 (1865). A. S. Atl. X f. 59. *Cymb. minuta* HILSE RABH. Alg. Eur. N:o 1261 (1862). A. S. Atl. LXXI f. 30, 31. *Cymb. variabilis* WARTM. RABH. Alg. Eur. N:o 803 (1859).

Fresh water: Spitsbergen! Norway (Dovre, Christiania)! Sweden (Lapland to Skane)! Finland! Gulf of Bothnia (from Haparanda to Roslagen)! England! Belgium! France! Germany! Switzerland! East Indies! Japan! Australia! Tasmania! New Zealand! Greenland! Mexico! California! Ecuador!

Var. *ovata* GRUN. (1875). — V. with convex ventral margin. Median line almost in the middle of the valve. — *Encyon. caespit. var. ovata* A. S. Atl. X f. 45, 46. V. H. Syn. Pl. III f. 13.

Fresh water: Sweden (Gulf of Bothnia)! Germany, Atter See (Atl.), Belgium (V. H.).

Var. *obtusa* GRUN. (1875). — V. elongated, obtuse. — *E. caespit. var. obtusa* GRUN. in A. S. Atl. X f. 47, 48.

Fresh water: Rome (Atl.). Rammer Moor (Atl.).

Most authors regard the forms of *C. ventricosa* as belonging to two different species, *Encyonema ventricosum* and *E. caespitosum*, the former being smaller and with the median line closer to the straight ventral margin, the latter a little larger, with the median line somewhat more distant from the ventral margin, which is slightly gibbous in the middle. I am unable to find any definite limit between these species, and as their distinctive characteristics are very trifling and subject to great variation, I have united them.

40. **C. (Encyonema) Jordani** GRUN. Ms. — V. with very elevated dorsal margin, more or less gibbous ventral margin and truncate to capitate ends. L. 0,02 to 0,032; B. 0,008 to 0,009 mm. Areas indistinct. Median line straight; its terminal fissures turned downwards. Striæ about 16 in 0,01 mm., radiate in the middle, very finely punctate. — Pl. V f. 3, 4.

Fresh water: Otago, New Zealand (Weissflog Coll.)!

41. **C. (Encyonema) hebridica** GRUN. (1877). — V. elongated, lunate, with arcuate dorsal and slightly convex ventral margin and subacute ends. L. 0,03 to 0,04; B. 0,007 to 0,008 mm. Median line straight, dividing the valve so that the ventral part is half as broad as the dorsal. Terminal fissures in the ends. Axial area very narrow; central area small or indistinct. Striæ about 10 in 0,01 mm. distinctly punctate. — *Encyon. hebridicum* (GREG.) GRUN. Cl. M. D. N:o 37. CL. D. of Finl. p. 48 Pl. II f. 16, 17.

Fresh water: Sweden (Lulea Lapmark, foss.)! Finland (Russian Lapland; Nyland and Viborg foss.)!

This form, which appears to be pretty constant, occurs in northern regions. It connects *E. ventricosum* with *E. gracile*. In A. SCHMIDTS Atl. IX f. 11 is figured a large form from Ohlajärri (Orrjärvi, Finland?), which seems either to be a forma maxima of *C. hebridica* or a new species.

42. **C. (Encyonema) gracilis** RABH. (1853). — V. narrow, slender, with gently arcuate dorsal and straight ventral margin. Ends acute. L. 0,03 to 0,056; B. 0,007 to 0,01 mm. Median line more approximate to the ventral than to the dorsal margin; its terminal nodules distant from the ends. Areas indistinct. Striæ 10 to 13 in 0,01 mm. — *Encyon. gracile* RABH. Süssw. D. Pl. X f. 1. A. S. Atl. X f. 36, 37, 39, 40. V. H. Syn. Pl. III f. 20 to 21. *Cymbella scotica* W. SM. B. D. I p. 18 Pl. II f. 25 (1853). *Cymb. lunata* W. SM. Ann. Mag. Nat. Hist. [2] XV Pl. IX f. 15 (1855). V. H. Syn. Pl. III f. 23.

Fresh water, especially alpine regions: Norway (Finmark, Dovre)! Sweden (Lapland, Småland)! Finland! Scotland! Savoy! Tasmania! New Zealand! Greenland! White Mountains!

43. **C. (Encyonema) norvegica** GRUN. (1875). — V. asymmetrical, linear, with obtuse, broad ends. L. 0,04 to 0,05; B. 0,007 to 0,008 mm. Median line straight, nearly axial, with the

terminal nodules at some distance from the ends. Axial area narrow, central area small, orbicular. Striæ 11 to 15 in 0,01 mm. slightly radiate in the middle, where they are more distant, parallel at the ends. — GRUN. in A. S. Atl. X f. 41. CL. M. D. N:o 268.

Fresh water (alpine regions): Greenland! Iceland! Norway (Dovre, Romsdalen)! Sweden (Pauträsk, Wilhelmina socken)!

C. norvegica is nearly akin to *C. gracilis* and differs principally by its more linear form and broad, rounded ends.

14. **C. incerta** GRUN. (1878). V. linear, slightly asymmetrical, with broad, obtuse ends, slightly arcuate dorsal margin and almost straight ventral. L. 0,04 to 0,07; B. 0,009 mm. Median line almost central. Axial area narrow, not dilated in the middle. Striæ 11 to 16 in 0,01 mm., equidistant in the middle, where they are parallel, and slightly radiate at the ends. — *C. Pisciculus var. incerta* GRUN. Cl. M. D. N:o 96. CL. D. fr. Grönl. och Argent. p. 13 Pl. XVI f. 12. *C. subæqualis var. incerta* GRUN. in V. H. T. N:o 30.

Fresh water, northern or alpine regions: Norway (Dovre, Hammerfest)! Sweden (Lapland)! Finland (Russian Lapland)! Scotland (V. H. T.).

Var. *naviculacea* GRUN. (1879). With somewhat wider axial area and finer striæ, about 18 in 0,01 mm. — *C. (Pisciculus var.) naviculacea* GRUN. in Cl. M. D. N:o 272. CL. D. fr. Grönl. och Argentina p. 13 Pl. XVI f. 11.

Fresh water: Greenland! Norway (Dovre)! Sweden (Lapland to Jämtland)! Finland (Russian Lapland)!

15. **C. æqualis** W. SM. (1856). V. linear-lanceolate, with arcuate dorsal, straight or slightly convex ventral margin, and broad, obtuse, or almost truncate ends. L. 0,03 to 0,045; B. 0,006 to 0,011 mm. Median line straight, near to the ventral margin, broad (oblique). Axial area narrow, not, or slightly, dilated in the middle. Striæ 11 or 14 (middle) to 14 or 16 (ends) in 0,01 mm., slightly radiate, obscurely punctate; puncta about 16 in 0,01 mm. — W. SM. B. D. II p. 84. *Cymb. obtusa* GREG. M. J. IV Pl. I f. 19 (1856). V. H. Syn. p. 61 Pl. III f. 1 *a*. A. S. Atl. IX f. 41 to 45; LXXI f. 72? *Cymb. subæqualis* GRUN. V. H. Syn. Pl. III f. 2, 4 Suppl. A f. 1 (1880).

Fresh water: Greenland! Iceland! Scotland and England! Sweden (Lapland to Skåne, Gothland)! Norway (Dovre, Stavanger, foss.)! Belgium (V. H.). Saxony! Switzerland! Michigan!

Var. *florentina* GRUN. (1880). — V. less asymmetrical, almost lanceolate. Striæ finer, 15 in 0,01 mm. — *Cymb. subæqualis var. florentina* GRUN. in V. H. Syn. Pl. III f. 3.

Fresh water: S:ta Fiora, foss. (Grun.).

Var. *diminuta* GRUN. — L. 0,015; B. 0,004 mm. Striæ 12 to 15 in 0,01 mm. — *Cymb. obtusa var. diminuta* GRUN. in V. H. T. N:o 129.

Fresh water: England (V. H. T.).

C. æqualis W. SM. is usually believed to denote the same species as *C. angustata*, but as the ends are described as obtuse and the striæ are coarse, 12 in 0,01 mm., it is evident that this is a mistake, and that SMITH meant the form described above as *C. æqualis*. GREGORY's figure of *Cymb. obtusa* is small and not very characteristic, but agrees pretty well with this species. Between *Cymb. subæqualis* GRUN. and *Cymb. obtusa* GREG. as represented in VAN HEURCK's Synopsis I am unable to discover any specific distinction. As limited here *Cymb. æqualis* is a common form, distinguished by its linear form and almost truncate ends. The median striæ are more distant than the others and radiate.

16. **C. sinuata** GREG. (1856). — V. linear, slightly asymmetrical, frequently gibbous in the middle on the ventral side, with broad, obtuse ends. L. 0,012 to 0,026; B. 0,004 to 0,005 mm. Axial area narrow; central area large, on the ventral side reaching to the margin. Striæ 9 to 11 0,01 mm., almost parallel. — GREG. M. J. IV Pl. I f. 17. *C. abnormis* GRUN. in V. H. Syn. Pl. III f. 8 (1880). *Gomphonema asymmetricum* GUTW. p. 28 Pl. I f. 24?

Fresh water: Sweden (Mälaren, Westergötland, Småland)! Finland (Abo)! Scotland (Greg.). Ireland! New Zealand!

Var. *antiqua* GRUN. — V. with subcapitate ends. L. 0,032 to 0,033; B. 0,008 mm. Striæ 7 to 8 in 0,01 mm., finely punctate. — *C. abn. var. ant.* GRUN. Foss. D. Öster. Ung. p. 111 Pl. XXIX f. 31.

Fresh water: Hungary, fossil (Grun.).

Var.? *fossilis* PANT. (1893). — Linear with slightly rostrate ends. L. 0,05; B. 0,01 mm. Central area a transverse fascia. Striæ 8 to 9 in 0,01 mm. — *Cymb. abnormis var. fossilis* PANT. III Pl. XVII f. 255.

Fresh water: Hungary, fossil (Pant.).

This little form is of interest as it has some resemblance to a Gomphonema, in its unilaterally dilated central area. The fig. given by GREGORY is not as good as desirable, but there can hardly exist any doubt that GREGORY really meant this species.

47. **C. tumidula** GRUN. (1875). — V. asymmetrical, linear-lanceolate, with rostrate ends. L. 0,033 to 0,035; B. 0,007 to 0,009 mm. Dorsal margin arcuate, ventral straight, or somewhat gibbous in the middle. Median line somewhat excentric, straight, with approximate central pores. Axial areas indistinct; central area indistinct or on the dorsal side only. Striæ on the dorsal side 13 (middle) to 15 (ends) in 0,01 mm., on the ventral side 14 in 0,01 mm., slightly radiate throughout, finely punctate. On the ventral side of the central nodule are two puncta at the ends of the two median striæ. — GRUN. in A. S. Atl. IX f. 33. V. H. T. N:o 27.

Fresh water: Rostock, fossil! Oxford! Triest (Atl.), Paris, Marly (Cl. M. D. 195)!

Var. *salinarum* GRUN. (1875). — V. asymmetrical, lanceolate, with subacute, not rostrate ends. L. 0,027 to 0,04; B. 0,008 to 0,01 mm. Axial area narrow, slightly dilated on the dorsal side around the central nodule. Striæ 11 or 12 (middle and dorsal) to 15 (ventral) in 0,01 mm. — *C. salinarum* GRUN. A. S. Atl. IX f. 28. V. H. T. N:o 26.

Brackish water: Bay of Finland (Dannf.), Saule (Atl.), Italy!

C. tumidula seems to connect *C. amphicephala* with *C. turgidula*, *C. affinis* etc. As far I can see, there is no other difference between *C. tumidula* and *C. salinarum* than the somewhat different shape of the ends. The above descriptions are from original specimens in VAN HEURCK's Types.

48. **C. turgidula** GRUN. (1875). — V. asymmetrical with more or less rostrate, obtuse, or truncate ends. L. 0,032 to 0,05; B. 0,01 to 0,015mm. Axial area very narrow. Striæ in the middle on the dorsal side 9 to 10 in 0,01 mm, at the ends about 11 in 0,01 mm. finely punctate, puncta about 21 in 0,01 mm. At the ventral side of the central nodule are two small puncta, ending the median striæ. — GRUN. A. S. Atl. IX f. 23 to 26.

Fresh water: Bengal (Atl.), New Zealand! Niagara falls! Porto Rico! Ecuador. Chimborazo! Argentina!

C. turgidula is nearly related to *C. affinis*, but is larger and has 2 puncta below the central nodule.

49. **C. affinis** KÜTZ. (1844). — V. more or less broad, semielliptical to semilanceolate with almost straight ventral margin and slightly rostrate, obtuse or subtruncate ends. L. 0,025 to 0,04; B. 0,007 to 0,01 mm. Median line slightly arcuate, excentric. Axial area very narrow, not dilated around the central nodule. Striæ 10 or 11 (dorsal side) to 12 (ventral side) in 0,01 mm. a little closer at the ends, slightly radiate, finely punctate. On the ventral side of the central nodule is a small isolated punctum ending the median stria. — KÜTZ Bac. p. 80 Pl. VI f. 15? W. SM. B. D. I Pl. XXX f. 250? A. S. Atl. IX f. 29, 38*; LXXI f. 28, 29. V. H. Syn. p. 62 Pl. II f. 19. V. H. Types N:o 26. *Cymb. truncata* GREG. M. J. III p. 39 Pl. IV f. 3 (1855)? *Cocconema nanum* HANTZSCH Rab. A. E. N:o 1321 (1862). A. S. Atl. LXXI f. 27. *Coccon. gibbum* A. S. Atl. X f. 27. *Cymb. affinis var. tumida* LAGST. Spitsb. D. p. 43 Pl. II f. 19?

Fresh water: Sweden (Uppland to Skane, Gothland, Gulf of Bothnia)! Finland! Holstein! England! Belgium (V. H.). Germany! Switzerland! Italy! Mouth of Jenissey! Japan! Australia (Lake Muir)! New Zealand! New York! Argentina!

Cymb. affinis is a variable species, connecting *Cymb. turgidula* with *Cymb. parva*. The ventral margin is sometimes indented in the middle. Such a form has been figured by Grunow in Foss. Diat. Österr. Ung. Pl. XXIX f. 26 and is probably identical with *Cymb. exisa var. major* Gutwinsky Materialy p. 25 Pl. I f. 21.

50. **C. parva** W. Sm. (1852). V. semilanceolate, with slightly rostrate, obtuse to subtruncate ends. L. 0,03 to 0,05; B. 0,01 to 0,012 mm. Median line somewhat arcuate and broad (oblique). Axial area narrow, very slightly dilated in the middle. Striæ 9 or 10 (median, dorsal) to 13 (ventral and terminal) in 0,01 mm., very slightly radiate, obscurely punctate. There is no punctum on the ventral side of the central nodule. — *Cocco. parvum* W. Sm. B. D. I p. 77. Pl. XXIII f. 222. A. S. Atl. X f. 14, 15. Grun. Franz Josephs Land D. p. 97 (45) Pl. I f. 9. *Cymb. cymbyformis var. parva* V. H. Syn. p. 64 Pl. II f. 11. *Cocconema pachycephalum* Rabh. Alg. Eur. N:o 1107 (1861).

Fresh water: Greenland! Franz Josephs Land (Grun.). Sweden (Lapland to Skåne)! Norway (Finmark to Christiania)! Finland! England! Germany! Belgium! France! Switzerland! Savoy! Italy! Mouth of Jenissey! North America, Winnepeg!

Var. *hungarica* Grun. (1875). — L. 0,024 to 0,04; B. 0,009 to 0,01 mm. Area dilated on the dorsal side of the central nodule. Striæ 10 in 0,01 mm. — *Coccon. hungaric.* Grun. in A. S. Atl. IX f. 38. X f. 16, 17; LXXI f. 37, 38.

Fresh water: Norway (Brevig)! Platten See, Hungary (Grun.).

Cymb. parva is in the living state stipitate. It is closely akin to *Cymb. affinis* and *Cymb. cymbiformis*, differing from both by the want of a punctum at the end of the median central stria.

51. **C. Botellus** Lagst. (1873). V. arcuate, with parallel margins and rounded ends. L. 0,024 to 0,034; B. 0,006 to 0,007 mm. Median line slightly excentric, arcuate. Axial area narrow, not dilated around the central nodule. Striæ 10 to 11 in 0,01 mm., very slightly radiate, not distinctly punctate. — *Cymb. variabilis var. Botellus* Lagst. Spitsb. D. p. 14 Pl. II f. 22. *Cymb. bot.* A. S. Atl. LXXI f. 39.

Fresh water: Arctic America! Beeren Eiland (Lagst.). Spitzbergen!

52. **C. cymbiformis** (Ag. 1830?) Kütz. (1833). — V. boat-shaped, with straight, sometimes slightly gibbous, ventral margin and obtuse or truncate ends. L. 0,05 to 0,1; B. 0,01 to 0,012 mm. Median line slightly arcuate, broad (oblique); its terminal fissures reflexed. Axial area narrow; central area small. Striæ 8 to 9 in 0,01 mm. somewhat closer at the ends, finely lineate (lineolæ 20 in 0,01 mm.). On the ventral side of the central nodule is an isolated punctum at the end of the median stria. — Ag. Consp. p. 10 (1830)? *Frustulia coffeæformis* Kütz. Dec. N:o 11 (1833) according to Lagst. *Frust. cymb.*? Kütz. Linn. VIII p. 539 Pl. XIII f. 10. *Coccon. cymbiforme* W. Sm. B. D. I p. 76 Pl. XXIII f. 220? A. S. Atl. IX f. 76 to 79; X f. 13. *Cymb. cymbif.* V. H. Syn. p. 63 Pl. II f. 11 a, b, c.

Fresh water: Iceland! Norway (Finmark to Brevig)! Sweden! Finland! England! Belgium (V. H.). France! Germany! Switzerland! Hungary (Dubravica, foss. Grun.). Socotra (Kitton). Japan! Tasmania! Argentina!

C. cymbiformis is very similar to *C. helvetica*, but differs by the reflexed terminal fissures and from *C. helvetica*, as well as from *C. parva*, by the isolated punctum below the central nodule.

53. **C. Beccarii** Grun. (1886). — V. clavate, and at the same time boat-shaped, with one half longer than the other. L. 0,054 to 0,08; B. 0,014 mm. Median line arcuate, almost in the middle of the valve. Axial area narrow, not dilated around the central nodule. Striæ 11 to 16

in 0,01 mm., slightly radiate throughout, distinctly punctate. No isolated punctum below the central nodule. — GRUN. in Martelli Florula Bogosensis p. 152 Pl. I f. 1, 2.

Fresh water: Abyssinia (Grun.).

54. C. **Cistula** HEMPR. (1828). — V. boat-shaped, with concave, centrally slightly gibbous, ventral margin, and truncate or rounded, obtuse ends. L. 0,07 to 0,16; B. 0,018 to 0,025 mm. Median line arcuate, broad, bent downwards near the central nodule. The central pores distant, and the terminal fissures reflexed. Axial area narrow, linear, slightly dilated on the dorsal side of the central nodule. Striæ 7 to 9 in 0,01 mm. coarsely lineate; lineolæ 18 to 21 in 0,01 mm. On the ventral side, near the central nodule, the striæ are interrupted by a narrow depression, so that below the central nodule is a segmental row of 2 to 5 puncta. — *Bacillaria Cistula* HEMPR. a. EHR. Symb. Phys. phyto. Pl. II, IV f. 10. *Coccon. Cistula* W. SM. B. D. XXIII f. 221. A. S. Probet. f. 16 Pl. X f. 1—5, 24—26. *Cymb. Cistula* V. H. Syn. p. 64 Pl. II f. 12 13. *C. Cistula var. maculata* A. S. Atl. LXXI f. 21. GRUN. Franz Josephs Land D. p. 97 (45) Pl. I f. 8. *C. Cistula var. fusidium* HÉRIB. a. PERAG. D. d'Auvergne p. 71 Pl. III f. 12. *Coccon. arcticum* A. S. Atl. LXXI f. 25. *Coccon. cornutum* GREG. M. J. IV Pl. I f. 11 (1856)?

Fresh and slightly brackish water: Spitsbergen! Norway (Dovre, Stavanger, foss.)! Sweden (Lapland to Skåne), Bay of Bothnia (from Piteå to Uppland and Helsingfors)! Finland! England! Holstein! Belgium! France! Germany! Switzerland! Italy! Mouth of Jenissey! Kamtschatka! Japan! Yarkand! America (Winnepeg, Vancouver, Massachusets, Illinois, California, Mexico)!

Var. *maculata* KÜTZ. (1834). — V. broader and shorter than in the type. L. 0,045 to 0,082; B. 0,013 to 0,015 mm. Striæ 9 to 12 in 0,01 mm. Lineolæ 24 in 0,01 mm. No row of puncta below the central nodule. — *Frustulia maculata* KÜTZ. Dec. N:o 85 (1834) according to Lagst. *Cymb. maculata* A. S. Atl. X f. 6; LXXI f. 20, 22. *Cymb. Cistula var. mac.* V. H. Syn. p. 64 Pl. II f. 16, 17. *Cymb. Bouleana* BR. a. HÉRIB. D. d'Auvergne p. 220 Pl. VI f. 14 1893 (ad spec. auth.). *Cymb. Pauli* HÉRIB. a. PERAG. D. d'Auvergne p. 70 Pl. III f. 11 (1893).

Fresh water: Franz Josephs Land (Grun.), Spitsbergen! Sweden (Vestergötland, Smaland)! Finland! England! France! Germany! Greenland! Argentina!

Var. *sibirica* GRUN. (1880). — V. with rounded, not rostrate ends. L. 0,08; B. 0,024 mm. Median line strongly arcuate. Striæ 10 (middle) to 12 (ends) in 0,01 mm. lineate (lineolæ about 20 in 0,01 mm.) interrupted in the ventral side of the central nodule by a narrow depression. — *Coccon. Cistula var. sib.* GRUN. A. D. p. 25 Pl. I f. 11.

Fresh water: Mouth of Jenissey!

Var. *arctica* LAGST. (1873). — V. boat-shaped, with strongly arcuate dorsal, and slightly concave ventral, margin. Ends truncate. L. 0,032 to 0,07; B. 0,007 to 0,015 mm. Median line strongly arcuate, broad; its terminal fissures reflexed. Axial area narrow. Striæ 9 to 13 in 0,01 mm. finely lineate. No row of puncta on the ventral side of the central nodule. — *Cymb. variabilis var. arctica* LAGST. Spitsb. D. p. 14 Pl. II f. 21. *Cymb. arctica* A. S. Atl. X f. 12; LXXI f. 23, 24.

Fresh water: Beeren Eiland (Lagst.), Spitsbergen! Russian Lapland! Mouth of Jenissey!

Var.? *truncata* BRUN (1880). — V. with slightly arcuate dorsal margin, straight ventral margin and very broad, truncate ends. L. 0,045 to 0,075 mm. Striæ 8 to 10 in 0,01 mm. No row of puncta below the central nodule. — BRUN D. des Alpes p. 58 Pl. III f. 2.

Fresh water: Switzerland (Brun.).

C. Cistula is a very variable species, graduating, as it appears, to *C. cymbiformis*. Its most distinctive characteristic, the row of puncta below the central nodule, is not present in some of its varieties. The *var.? truncata* is remarkable for its outline and resembles very much the smaller *C. curta* A. SCHM. (Atl. IX f. 47. L. 0,02; B. 0,01 mm.) unknown to me.

55. C. **Stuxbergii** CL. (1880). — V. with strongly arcuate dorsal margin, almost straight ventral margin, and rostrate, truncate ends. L. 0,055 to 0,075; B. 0,02 mm. Median line strongly arcuate, with reflexed terminal fissures. Axial area indistinct, slightly dilated on the dorsal side

around the central nodule. Striæ 14 to 15 in 0,01 mm. radiate in the middle, almost parallel at ends, very finely punctate, crossed on the ventral side below the central nodule by a narrow depression. — *Coccon. Stuxb.* CL. A. D. p. 13 Pl. I f. 10. *Cymb. St.* Icon. n. Pl. V f. 2.

Fresh water: Mouth of Jenissey!

56. **C. Sturii** GRUN. (1882). V. boat-shaped, with truncate ends. Dorsal margin arcuate, ventral margin straight, somewhat gibbous in the middle. L. 0,19 to 0,25; B. 0,032 mm. Median line slightly arcuate, dilated towards the ends; its terminal fissures reflexed. Axial area narrow linear, gradually dilated towards the middle and the ends. Striæ 7 or 8 (middle) to 10 or 12 (ends) in 0,01 mm. punctate (puncta about 14 in 0,01 mm.), crossed near the central nodule on the ventral side, and sometimes on the dorsal side, by a narrow depression. GRUN. Foss. D. Österr. Ung. p 140 Pl. XXX f. 35. PANT. III Pl. XIX f. 287.

Fresh water: Hungary, fossil!

This species is very characteristic, distinguished from all others by its median line becoming wider towards the ends. It has the outline of *C. lanceolata*, and the row of puncta of *C. Cistula*.

57. **C. lanceolata** EHR. (1838). V. boat-shaped, with arcuate dorsal margin, slightly concave, centrally gibbous, ventral margin, and obtuse ends. L. 0,08 to 0,16; B. 0,024 to 0,03 mm. Median line slightly arcuate with reflexed terminal fissures. Axial area very narrow; central area small, elongated. Striæ 9 to 10 in 0,01 mm. slightly radiate, punctate, puncta 15 to 18 in 0,01 mm. — *Coccon. lanceolatum* EHR. Inf. p. 224 Pl. XIX f. 6. W. SM. B. D. I Pl. XXIII f. 219. A. S. Atl. X f. 8—10. *Cymb. lanc.* V. H. Syn. p. 63 Pl. II f. 7. *Coccon. Boeckii* GRUN. in A. S. Atl. X f. 11 (1875). *Coccon. variabile* CRAMER. Rab. A. E. 1216 (p. p. C. cymbifera).

Fresh water, especially larger lakes, often slightly brackish water: Sweden (Lapland to Skane)! Gulf of Bothnia! Norway (Finmark to Laurgård)! Finland (Ladoga, Onega)! Siberia! Holstein! Britain! France! Belgium (V. H.). Switzerland! Vienna! Socotra (Kitton).

Var *cornuta* EHR. (1843). L. 0,15 to 0,20; B. 0,027 to 0,029 mm. Striæ 7 or 8 (middle) to 10 or 11 (ends) in 0,01 mm. punctate; puncta 10 to 12 in 0,01 mm. — *Coccon. cornutum* EHR. Am. p. 124. M. G. XV. A f. 94. *Cymb. lanc. var. cornuta* GRUN. Foss. D. Österr. Ung. p. 141.

Fresh water: Ireland, Toome Bridge, Mourne Mountains (Grun.), Lüneburg (Grun.).

Var. *fossilis* PANT. (1889). L. 0,127; B. 0,021 mm. Striæ 11 (middle) to 8 (ends) in 0,01 mm. — PANT. II p. 40.

Brackish water: Hungary, fossil (Pant.).

58. **C. helvetica** KÜTZ. (1844). — V. boat-shaped, with gently arcuate dorsal margin and straight, frequently slightly gibbous ventral. Ends rounded obtuse. L. 0,036 to 0,085; B. 0,01 to 0,015 mm. Median line slightly asymmetrical and almost straight. Terminal fissures in nearly the same direction as the median line. Axial area narrow, very slightly dilated around the central nodule. Striæ 9 to 11 in 0,01 mm. closer towards the ends; puncta about 16 in 0,01 mm. There are no isolated puncta below the central nodule. KÜTZ. Bac. p. 79 Pl. VI f. 13. V. H. Syn. p. 64 Pl. II f. 15. A. S. Atl. X f. 20 to 21, 22 (*Cymb. scotica*) f. 23 (*Coccon. laeve*); LXXI f. 19.

Fresh water: Greenland! Norway (Finmark, Stavanger, foss.)! Sweden (Lapland to Skane)! Gulf of Bothnia (Haparanda, Pitea), Finland! Scotland! Belgium (V. H.), Germany! France! Switzerland!

Var. *curta* CL. — L. 0,045; B. 0,012 mm. Central area smaller than in the type, or indistinct. Striæ 12 in 0,01 mm. less distinctly punctate than in the type. *C. turgidula* GRUN. in Cl. M. D. N:o 95.

Fresh water: Holstein!

Var.? *Balatonis* GRUN. (1875). — Dorsal margin strongly arcuate, ventral slightly gibbous. L. 0,09; B. 0,026 mm. Striæ about 8 in 0,01 mm. *Cymb. Bal.* GRUN. A. S. Atl. X f. 19.

Fresh water: Platten See, Hungary (Grun.).

Cymbella helvetica is a very common species, easily recognized by its straight terminal fissures. Under the name *Encyonema Gerstenbergeri* GRUNOW has described (Banka D. p. 9 Pl. I f. 11; 1865) a form, remarkable for the terminations of the median line, which are unusually distant from the ends of the valve. I have seen from various localities several specimens closely agreeing with the figure published by GRUNOW, and I have convinced myself that these are abnormal forms of *C. helvetica*.

* **C. hevesensis** PANT. (1889). V. boat-shaped, with obtuse ends. L. 0,062; B. 0,013 mm. Median line bent; its central pores very distant. Axial area narrow, slightly dilated around the central nodule. Striæ 11,5 to 13,5 in 0,01 mm. slightly radiate, punctate. — PANT. II p. 40 Pl. III f. 53.

Brackish water: Hungary, fossil (Pant.).

This species is unknown to me. The fig. and description given by PANTOCSEK are insufficient for deciding as to its relations to other boat-shaped Cymbellæ.

* **C. Chyzerii** PANT. (1889). — V. boat-shaped, with the ventral margin slightly gibbous in the middle. Ends subrostrate, obtuse. L. 0,0825; B. 0,0145 mm. Median line arcuate, its central pores approximate. Axial area narrow, not dilated in the middle. Striæ 10 to 12,5 in 0,01 mm. Ventral striæ crossed by a black line (?) — PANT. II p. 40 Pl. XI f. 191.

Brackish water: Hungary, fossil (Pant.).

This species is unknown to me. The description and the figure given by PANTOCSEK are insufficient for ascertaining its relations to other boat-shaped Cymbellæ. It may come near to *C helvetica*, *C. lanceolata*, *C. cymbiformis*.

59. **C. aspera** EHB. (1840). V. boat-shaped, with strongly arcuate dorsal margin and straight, centrally gibbous ventral margin. Ends obtuse, rounded. L. 0,15 to 0,18; B. 0,033 mm. Median line arcuate. Axial area linear, slightly dilated in the middle. Striæ 7 to 9 in 0,01 mm. slightly radiate, punctate; puncta 12 to 15 in 0,01 mm. No row of isolated puncta on the ventral side. — *Coccon. asperum* EHB. Ber. 1840 M. G. V: 1 f. 1 etc. PETIT Journ. de Microgr. 1878 Mars et Avril f. 3. HÉRIB. D. d'Auvergne Pl. III f. 10. *Cy. lanceol. var. aspera* BRUN D. des Alpes p. 57 Pl. IX f. 16? *Cy. gastroides* KÜTZ. Bac. p. 79 Pl. VI f. 4 *b* (1844). A. S. Atl. IX f. 1, 2; X f. 7. V. H. Syn. p. 63 Pl. II f. 8. GRUN. Franz Josephs Land D. p. 97 (45) Pl. I f. 7. *C. gigantea* PANT. III Pl. XXI f. 321 (1893)?

Fresh water: Franz Josephs Land (Grun.), Iceland! Norway (Dovre, Laurgaard)! Sweden (Lapland to Skåne)! Finland! France! Britain! Belgium! Germany! Switzerland! Savoy! Italy! Japan! New Zealand!

Var. *minor* V. H. (1880). — Smaller, with strongly arcuate median line. L. 0,07 to 0,08 mm. — *Cy. gastr. forma minor* V. H. Syn. p. 63 Pl. II f. 9.

Var. *neogena* GRUN. (1882). — L. 0,175; B. 0,033 mm. Striæ about 8 in 0,01 mm., 12 in 0,01 mm. towards the ends, punctate; puncta about 14 in 0,01 mm. *Cy. gastroides var. neogena* GRUN. Foss. D. Öster. Ung. p. 141.

Fresh water: Hungary, fossil (Grun.).

Var. *dubravicensis* GRUN. (1882). — L. 0,168; B. 0,027 mm. Terminal nodules very strong, at some distance from the ends, surrounded by short striæ. Striæ 6 to 9 in 0,01 mm.; their puncta 14 to 17 in 0,01 mm. — *Cy. gastr. var. dubr.* GRUN. Foss. D. Öster. Ung. p. 141 Pl. XXIX f. 30. PANT. III Pl. XVII f. 251.

Fresh water: Hungary, fossil (Grun.).

Var.? *crassa* GRUN. (1882). — V. short and broad with rounded obtuse ends. L. 0,073; B. 0,024 mm. Median line strongly arcuate. Axial area narrow. Striæ 6 or 7 (middle) to 9 (ends) in 0,01 mm. punctate; puncta 16 to 17 in 0,01 mm. The striæ are on the ventral side crossed by a short depression. — GRUN. Foss. D. Öster. Ung. Pl. XXIX f. 28.

Fresh water: Hungary, fossil (Grun.).

Var. *bengalensis* GRUN. (1875). - V. less asymmetrical, almost boat-shaped, with straight or slightly centrally gibbous ventral margins. Ends obtuse. L. 0,08 to 0,11; B. 0,024 to 0,027 mm. Median line slightly arcuate. Axial area linear, scarcely dilated around the central nodule. Striæ 7,5 (middle) to 9 (ends) in 0,01 mm., coarsely punctate; puncta 12 to 13 in 0,01 mm. — *C. beng.* GRUN. in A. S. Atl. IX f. 12. 13; LXXI f. 79. KITTON Linn. Soc. Bot. XX Pl. XLVIII f. 6 (1884). CL. M. D. N:o 194.

Fresh water: Bengal! Socotra (Kitton).

C. aspera is a very common species, easily recognized by its boat-shaped outline, its coarsely punctate striæ and always distinct area. It appears to be more closely akin to *C. Ehrenbergii* than to the boat-shaped *C. lanceolata*, *C. Cistula* etc. It seems questionable whether the *var. crassa*, which I have not seen, really belongs to *C. aspera*. It may possibly be more akin to *C. Cistula*.

' **C. salina** PANT. (1889). — V. boat-shaped, with arcuate dorsal margin, straight ventral margin and obtuse ends. L. 0,0585; B. 0,013 mm. Median line arcuate. Axial area distinct linear, slightly dilated around the central nodule. Striæ 12,5 to 13 in 0.01 mm. punctate. PANT. II p. 40 Pl. I f. 9.

Brackish water: Hungary, fossil (Pant.).

This species is not known to me, but seems, to judge from the fig. in PANTOCSEK's work to be allied to *C. aspera*, from which it differs by smaller size and closer striæ.

60. **C. tumida** BRÉB. (1849). — V. boat-shaped with slightly centrally gibbous ventral margin. Ends rostrate-truncate. L. 0,05 to 0,1; B. 0,018 to 0,022 mm. Median line arcuate. Axial area narrow, linear, suddenly dilated around the central nodule to an orbicular or subquadrate central area. A stigma with a fine fissure below the central nodule. Striæ 8 or 9 (middle) to 10 or 12 (ends) in 0,01 mm., radiate, towards the ends almost parallel, distinctly punctate; puncta about 20 in 0,01 mm. — *Coccon. tumidum* BRÉB. in Kütz Sp. Alg. p. 60. *Cy. tum.* V. H. Syn. p. 64 Pl. II f. 10. *Cocc. gibbum* A. S. Probst. f. 17. *Cy. stomatophora* GRUN. in A. S. Atl. X f. 28 to 30. *Coccon. stomat.* GRUN. A. D. p. 26.

Fresh water: Sweden (Westergötland, Göteborg)! Holstein (V. H. T.). Belgium (V. H.), Germany! France! Mouth of Jenissey! Japan! Bengal! New Zealand! Australia, Victoria! America (Illinois, California)!

Var. *borealis* GRUN. (1880). — Ends obliquely truncate, not rostrate. Striæ 8 in 0,01 mm. — *Cocc. stomat. var. borealis* GRUN. A. D. p. 26.

Fresh water: Sweden (Grun.). Niagara Falls!

Var. *gibba* GRUN. (1880). — Dorsal margin with 3 to 4 undulations. Striæ 8 to 9 in 0,01 mm. *Coccon. stomat. var. gibba* GRUN. A. D. p. 26.

Var. *fossilis* GRUN. (1880). — V. with less rostrate and more rounded ends. Stigma with shorter fissure than in the type. *Coccon. stomat. var. fossilis* GRUN. A. D. p. 26.

Fresh water: Habichtswald, fossil (Grun.).

61. **C. australica** A. S. (1875). — V. boat-shaped with centrally gibbous ventral margin and truncate or rounded obtuse ends. L. 0,1 to 0,14; B. 0,026 to 0,03 mm. Median line arcuate. Axial area linear, suddenly dilated around the central nodule to an orbicular space. A stigma with a distinct fissure below the central nodule. Striæ 7 (middle) to 9 (ends) in 0,01 mm. slightly radiate in the middle, parallel at the ends, coarsely punctate; puncta about 13 in 0,01 mm. — *Cocc. austr.* A. S. Atl. X f. 34. 35. CL. M. D. N:o 295.

Fresh water: Australia! New Zealand!

62. **C. punctifera** CL. N. Sp. — V. boat-shaped, with truncate ends. L. 0,13; B. 0,02 mm Median line arcuate; terminal fissures reflexed. Axial area linear, suddenly dilated to an orbicular central area. Stigma in the middle of the central nodule, without distinct fissure. Striæ 8 in 0,01

mm. a little closer towards the ends, where they are strongly radiate, distinctly punctate; puncta 15 in 0,01 mm.

Fresh water: Oregon, fossil!

63. **C. mexicana** EHR. (1844). — V. lunate with rounded truncate ends. L. 0,09 to 0,14; B. 0,026 to 0,036 mm. Median line bent, with reflexed terminal fissures. Axial area narrow linear, central small, orbicular. Stigma in the middle of the central nodule, without distinct fissure. Striæ 7 (middle) to 9 (ends) in 0,01 mm. radiate in the middle and alternately longer and shorter, nearly parallel at the ends, coarsely punctate. Puncta 12 to 13 in 0,01 mm. — *Coccon. mexicanum* EHR. Ber. 1844 p. 342. A. S. Atl. X f. 32, 33; LXXI f. 82. *Cymb. kamtschatica* GRUN. in A. S. Atl. X f. 31.

Fresh water: Washington Territory! Vancouver Island! Mexico. California and Guatemala fossil! Kamtschatka!

There is, so far I can see, no other difference between *C. mexicana* and *C. kamtschatica* than that the latter is somewhat smaller and has rather closer striæ and puncta.

64. **C. Janischii** A. S. (1881). — V. lunate, with rounded ends. L. 0,2; B. 0,05 mm. Median line arcuate, with strong terminal nodules and reflexed terminal fissures. Axial area narrow, linear, slightly dilated around the central nodule. Stigma in the middle of the central nodule, without distinct fissure. Striæ 8 to 9 in 0,01 mm., in the middle radiate and of unequal length, towards the ends almost transverse, distinctly punctate; puncta 10 to 12 in 0,01 mm. *Cocc. Jan.* A. S. Atl. LXXI f. 81.

Fresh water: Pitt River, Oregon (Grove Coll.)! San Francisco (Atl.).

Additional.

C. conifera BRUN (1893). — V. slightly asymmetrical, with arcuate dorsal and gibbous ventral margin. Ends apiculate. L. 0,04 to 0,05; B. 0,012 to 0,018 mm. Median line slightly arcuate, somewhat excentric. Axial area narrow, linear, not dilated around the central nodule. Striæ 9 to 10 in 0,01 mm., slightly radiate throughout, coarsely punctate; puncta 20 in 0,01 mm. — HÉRIB. D. d'Auvergne p. 220 Pl. VI f. 7.

Fresh water: Cantal, fossil!

Species not described and too imperfectly figured to be admitted in the above monograph.

C. affinis PANT. III Pl. IV f. 52.
C. austriaca var. fossilis PANT. III Pl. VIII f. 133.
— — *var. latestriata* PANT. III Pl. I f. 9.
C. Badayiana PANT. III Pl. XV f. 233 (C. Ehrenbergii var.?).
— — *var. gracilior* PANT. III Pl. XXIV f. 363.
C. capitata PANT. III Pl. X f. 160.
C. Cistula var. hungarica PANT. III Pl. III f. 40 (C. helvetica?).
C. Clementis PANT. III Pl. XX f. 303 (C. Cistula var.?).
C. cymbiformis PANT. III Pl. X f. 174.
— — *var. producta* PANT. III Pl. XXIII f. 346.
C. Grunovii PANT. III Pl. XIX f. 283 (C. Cistula var.?).
C. helvetica var. fossilis PANT. III Pl. IX f. 158.
C. inflata PANT. III Pl. VI f. 95.
C. Jimboi PANT. III Pl. VIII f. 130 (C. Cistula?).
C. Kockii PANT. III Pl. I f. 2 (C. Cistula var. maculata?).

C. lanceolata var. fossilis PANT. III Pl. XXIII f. 344.
var. robusta PANT. III Pl. XXIII f. 350.
C. marina PANT. III Pl. XIX f. 274 (Amphora augusta var.?).
C. obtusa PANT. III Pl. V f. 79.
C. pachyptera PANT. Pl. XXI f. 304, 316.
C. Peragalli PANT. III Pl. XLII f. 584.
C. perfecta PANT. III Pl. XVII f. 249 (C. cymbiformis var.?).
C. platonica PANT. III Pl. XX f. 297 (C. aspera var.?).
C. praeclara PANT. III Pl. XXXVI f. 512 (resembles C. lanceolata but has closer striæ).
C. Rakoczyana PANT. III Pl. VIII f. 121 (C. Cistula var. maculata?).
C. simplex PANT. III Pl. XXI f. 308 (C. ventricosa?).
C. Staubii PANT. III Pl. VIII f. 131 (C. leptoceras var.?).
C. Szontaghii PANT. III Pl. X f. 161 (Amphora augusta var.?).
C. suavis PANT. III Pl. XV f. 229 (akin to C. leptoceras?).
C. turgida PANT. III Pl. VI f. 103 (C. parva?).
C. valida PANT. III Pl. IX f. 154 (C. aspera var.?).
C. vegeta PANT. III Pl. XXIV f. 359.

Gomphonema AGARDH (1824).

Valve more or less elongated, clavate, or asymmetrical to the transverse axis. Structure: transverse slightly radiate striæ or rows of puncta. Connecting zone not complex, broader in the upper than in the lower end. Cell-contents a single chromatophore, leaving only a narrow parietal plasmaband along one side of the zone, deeply sinuose below the median line. On conjugation two auxospores are formed by two mother-cells, parallel to them. The plane of division of the primordial cell is at right angles to the plane of division of the mothercells (PFITZER Bau u. Entw. p. 88).

The large *G. geminatum* was observed as early as 1773 by O. F. MÜLLER, who named it *Vorticella pyraria*. The genus Gomphonema was established 1824 by AGARDH for two species, and since then a large number of species have been formed by EHRENBERG, KÜTZING and others, unfortunately founded on trifling characteristics. For forms living, as Diadesmis, in bands of closely connected frustules, EHRENBERG created (1843) the genus *Sphenosira*. KÜTZING founded (1844) the genus *Sphenella* for free-living forms and RABENHORST (1853) the genus *Gomphonella* for forms, which live in gelatinous masses. HEIBERG (1863) maintained, with justice, that these genera are not admissible, as they are founded on characteristics, which occur in the same species. An attempt to arrange systematically the known species of Gomphonema was made (1878), by GRUNOW in his description of the algæ of the Caspian Sea, and since then he has given a number of most valuable figures in VAN HEURCK's Synopsis Plates XXIII, XXIV and XXV. As among them there are several species from America, which, while having the general outline of Gomphonema, differ in their structure, and in the presence of longitudinal lines, similar to those of Scoliotropis and Caloneis, I now exclude these forms, and place them in a separate genus *Gomphoneis*. Recently BRUN has described, as *G. cantalicum*, a species, which seems to be allied to Gomphoneis, as it shews across the striæ a longitudinal line, but the striation of this species is in all other respects quite different from that of Gomphoneis.

The valve of Gomphonema is asymmetrical to the transverse axis, and is usually broader in the upper portion, with a wedge-shaped lower end. The central nodule is nearer to the upper end, or *apex*, than the lower, or *basis*. Many species are asymmetrical also to the longitudinal axis, but in a less visible degree, as PFITZER first pointed out, with a parallel asymmetry, like that of the Cymbellæ. Some varieties are even slightly cymbelliform. In many species there is on one side of the central nodule an isolated punctum, or *stigma*, as in several Cymbellæ, and in others a unilateral row of stigmas. GRUNOW has formed for the species with stigmas the group *Asymmetrica*, and for those without stigmas the group *Symmetrica*, which names may in view of maintaining the analogy with the Cymbellæ be adventageously changed to *Stigmatica* and *Astigmatica*.

There is a great resemblance between the cell-contents of Gomphonema and Cymbella, the structure is the same in both genera, and they are no doubt nearly connected. We have in *Cym. Beccarii* GRUN. a form, which is asymmetrical to the transverse axis, and, there are several other Cymbelloid varieties of Gomphonema. *Gomph. Cymbella* BRUN may be considered as an intermediate link between the two genera.

The outline of the forms of Gomphonema is very variable, and older authors have paid too much attention to it in forming new species. There exist in the same species all possible transitions, from purely clavate, to strongly biconstricted forms, so that outline only cannot be regarded as a good specific distinction.

Most species of Gomphonema inhabit fresh water, some brackish water, and there are also purely marine forms, the latter being all astigmatical. They are usually attached by dichotomously branched gelatinous stalks to algæ, stones, leaves of water-plants etc. Some forms are inbedded in gelatinous masses, but frustules of attached species occur also occasionally free.

Artificial key.

I. Stigmatica.

1.	Median striæ alternately longer and shorter	2.
	— — not — — —	3.
2.	L. 0,1 to 0,12 mm.	*G. geminatum* LYNGB.
	L. 0,05 mm.	*G. constrictum* EHR.
3.	Axial area distinct or broad	4.
	— — indistinct or narrow	7.
4.	Area linear	5.
	— lanceolate	6.
5.	Ends subacute or apiculate	*G. validum* CL.
	— broadly truncate	*G. Berggrenii* CL.
6.	Striæ about 12 in 0,1 mm.	*G. ventricosum* GREG.
	— — 8 —	*G. oxycephalum* CL.
7.	Central area transverse	8.
	— — small and rounded or indistinct	12.
8.	Central area unilateral	9.
	— — bilateral	10.
9.	Ends apiculate	*G. Augur* EHR.
	rostrate to truncate	*G. angustatum* KÜTZ.
	— broad, rounded-truncate	*G. subtile* EHR.
10.	Central area narrow	*G. gracile* EHR.
	— broad	11.
11.	Striæ coarsely punctate	*G. semiapertum* GRUN.
	— obscurely —	*G. intricatum* KÜTZ.
12.	Valve biconstricted	*G. acuminatum* EHR. (*G. subclavatum var. Mustela*).
	— not —	13.
13.	Ends capitate	*G. sphærophorum* EHR.
	apiculate	*G. apicatum* EHR.
	— rounded	14.
14.	Striæ coarsely punctate	*G. lanceolatum* EHR.[1]
	— finely or obscurely	15.

[1] *G. cantalicum* BR. a. HÉRIB.

15.	Valve cymbiform	*G. Cymbella* Brun.
	— clavate	*G. subclavatum* Grun.
	lanceolate	16.
16.	Striæ radiate	*G. eriense* Grun.
	— almost transverse	*G. parvulum* Kütz.

Astigmatica.

1.	Axial area narrow or indistinct	2.
	— distinct	5.
2.	Central area distinct	3.
	— — indistinct	*G. exiguum* Kütz.
3.	Valve lanceolate	*G. transsylvanicum* Pant.
	— clavate	*G. olivaceum* Lyngb.
	— linear-clavate	*G. peruvianum* Grun.
	— linear, with broad apex and basis	4.
4.	Central area rounded	*G. Salinarum* Pant.
	— — a transverse fascia	*G. æstuarii* Cl.
5.	Axial area narrow, dilated in the middle	*G. kamtschaticum* Grun.
	— broad	6.
6.	Striæ 21 to 22 in 0,01 mm.	*G. abbreviatum* Kütz.
	— 16 to 18	*G. brasiliense* Grun.
	6 in —	*G. Puiggarianum* Grun.

1. **G. eriense** Grun. (1878). — V. lanceolate, slightly clavate with rounded, obtuse ends. L. 0,032 to 0,042; B. 0,013 to 0,014 mm. Axial area narrow, linear; central area small, rounded, with a distinct stigma. Striæ radiate, 14 to 16 in 0,01 mm. — Grun. Casp. Sea Alg. p. 12. V. H. Syn. XXIII f. 10.

Fresh water: Lake Erie, N. America (Grun.).

This species in unknown to me, but to judge from the figure, it is not closely allied to any other Gomphonema.

2. **G. parvulum** Kütz. (1844). V. lanceolate-clavate, with rounded or rostrate to capitate apex, gradually tapering from the middle to the narrow often subcapitate basis. L. 0,02 to 0,03; B. 0,006 to 0,007 mm. Axial area indistinct; central area indistinct or small and unilateral. Stigma frequently indistinct. Striæ 13 to 15 in 0,01 mm., almost transverse, indistinctly punctate. — *Sphenella parvulum* Kütz. Bac. p. 83 Pl. XXX f. 63. *Gomphon. parvulum* V. H. Syn p. 125 Pl. XXV f. 9. *G. parv. var. subcapitata* V. H. Syn. f. 11. *G. parv. var. lanceolata* V. H. Syn. f. 10. *G. Lagenula* V. H. Syn. Pl. XXV f. 7, 8.

Fresh water: Sweden! England! Belgium (V. T.), France! Athens! Italy! Sandwich Islands! Tahiti! New Zealand! New Jersey! Dakota! Jamaica! Brazil! Ecuador!

Var. *subelliptica* Cl. V. elliptic-lanceolate almost symmetrical, with scarcely rostrate apex. L. 0,015; B. 0,005 to 0,006 mm. Striæ 13 to 14 in 0,01 mm.

Fresh water: Greenland! Falmouth! Tasmania!

Var. *exilis* Grun. — V. subclavate, narrow, linear-lanceolate, with rounded, not rostrate apex. L. 0,02 to 0,005 mm. Striæ 18 to 19 in 0,01 mm. Grun. Casp. S. Alg. p. 10.

Fresh water: Rimforsa in Westergötland, Sweden (Grun. ad. icon. in litt).

Var. *exilissima* Grun. V. narrow, lanceolate, subclavate, with slightly rostrate ends. L. 0,02; B. 0,005 mm. — Grun. in V. H. Syn. Pl. XXV f. 12 (V. H. T. 17).

Fresh water: England! Ecuador!

Var. *micropus* Kütz (1844). — V. slightly clavate, lanceolate, with obtuse apex and subacute basis. L. 0,025 to 0,03; B. 0,007 to 0,008 mm. Striæ 8 to 13 in 0,01 mm. Central area unilateral, narrow. *G. micropus* Kütz Bac. p. 84. V. H. Syn. p. 125 Pl. XXIV f. 46, XXV f. 4, 5, 6.

G. angustatum var. intermedia GRUN. in V. H. Syn. Pl. XXIV f. 47, 48. *G. angustum* BRÉB. (fide Grun.).

Fresh water: Finland! Sweden. Upsala! Gothland. Visby in slightly brackish water (a var. with coarse striæ, 8 in 0,01 mm.), Kansas River! Ecuador!

Var.? *tergestina* GRUN. (1880). — V. lanceolate, with obtuse, truncate ends. L. 0,015; B. 0,004 mm. Central area unilateral, very broad, reaching to the margin. Striæ 14 in 0,01 mm. *G. semiapertum var. tergestina* GRUN. in V. H. Syn. Pl. XXV f. 40.

Triest (Grun.).

3. **G. angustatum** KÜTZ (1844). — V. slightly clavate, linear, with broad, rostrate to subcapitate apex and basis. L. 0,03 to 0,04; B. 0,007 mm. Axial area not distinct; central area unilateral, stigma indistinct. Striæ transverse 10 to 12 in 0,01 mm. indistinctly punctate. - *Sphenella angustata* KÜTZ Bac. p. 83 Pl. VIII f. 6. *G. commune* RABH. Fl. E. Alg. p. 283 (1864). *G. angusta* V. H. Syn. p. 126 Pl. XXIV f. 49, 50.

Fresh water: Sweden! England! Belgium (V. H.). France! Germany!

Var. *producta* GRUN. (1880). — V. L. 0,02 to 0,025. Ends rostrate to capitate. — *Gomph. commune* LAGST. Spitsb. D. p. 40 Pl. I f. 14. *G. ang. var. prod.* V. H. Syn. Pl. XXIV f. 52 to 55.

Fresh water: Spitzbergen! Sweden! Finland! Neuchâtel! Tasmania! Arctic America! Winnipeg River! Brazil!

Var. *obtusata* KÜTZ (1844). — V. distinctly clavate, with broad, subrostrate ends. L. 0,025 to 0,03 mm. Striæ 9 to 10 in 0,01 mm. — *Sphenella obtusata* KÜTZ Bac. p. 83 Pl. IX f. 1. *Gomph. ang. var. obtus.* V. H. Syn. Pl. XXIV f. 43 to 45. *Sph. obt.* and *S. vulgaris* SCHUM. I Nacht. Pl. II f. 14, 15. *Sphenella naviculoides* HANTZSCH in Rab. Dec. N:o 1322 (1862).

Fresh water: Thüringen!

Var. *æqualis* GREG. (1856). — V. with capitate-rostrate apex and basis. L. 0,03 to 0,035; B. 0,006 mm. Striæ 10 to 12 in 0,01 mm. — *G. æquale* GREG. M. J. IV Pl. I f. 41. *G. angust. var.? æqualis* GRUN. V. H. S. Pl. XXV f. 3.

Fresh water: Scotland (Greg.).

Var. *subæqualis* GRUN. (1880). V. as in var. producta. Striæ 14 in 0,01 mm. — GRUN. V. H. Syn. Pl. XXV f. 1.

Fresh water.

Var. *Sarcophagus* GREG. (1856). — V. linear with rostrate, broad apex and basis. L. 0,024 to 0,04; B. 0,006 to 0,007 mm. Striæ 8 in 0,01 mm. — *G. Sarcophagus* GREG. M. J. IV Pl. I f. 42. *G. ang. var. Sarcoph.* V. H. Syn. Pl. XXV f. 2. *G. Lagenula* SCHUM. III Nacht. Pl. II f. 8?

Fresh water: Sweden (Rimforsa in Westergötland, Alnarp)! Scotland (Greg.).

Var. *undulata* GRUN. Ms. V. triundulate. L. 0,02 to 0,028; B. 0,006 mm. Striæ 10 in 0,01 mm.

Fresh water: Laurgaard in Norway (Grun.).

Gomph. angustatum is a very variable species, passing over by its varieties to *Gomph parvulum var. micropus.* By the var. undulata it seems to be connected with *Cymbella abnormis.*

4. **G. intricatum** KÜTZ (1844). — V. sublinear, slender, slightly gibbous in the middle, with obtuse apex and basis. L. 0,03 to 0,07; B. 0,005 to 0,008 mm. Axial area distinct, but narrow; central area transverse, broad. Striæ 10 in 0,01 mm., subparallel, obscurely punctate. — KÜTZ Bac. p. 87 Pl. IX f. 4. V. H. Syn. p. 126 Pl. XXIV f. 28, 29. *G. gracile* SCHUM. II Nacht. Pl. I f. 18 *a*.

Fresh water: Sweden! Russian Lapland! Finland! Hungary. Dubravica, fossil (Grun.), Ecuador (reg. trop.)!

Var. *pumila* GRUN. (1880). — L. 0,03; B. 0,005 mm. Striæ 10 in 0,01 mm. — GRUN. in V. H. Syn. Pl. XXIV f. 35, 36. *G. gracillimum* SCHUM. II Nacht. Pl. I f. 18 *b*?

Fresh water: Belgium (V. H.), England, Cirencester! Hungary. Dubravica, foss. (Grun.).

Var. *dichotoma* KÜTZ (1833). — L. 0,04 to 0,06; B. 0,008 mm. Striæ 11 to 13 in 0,01 mm. — *G. dichot.* KÜTZ. Syn. D. p. 569 f. 48. Bacil. p. 85 Pl. VIII f. 14. W. SM. B. D. Pl. XXIX f. 241? *G. intr. var. dich.* V. H. Syn. p. 125 Pl. XXIV f. 30—31. *G. pulvinatum* AL. BR. in Rab. Süssw. D. p. 58 (1853). V. H. Syn. f. 32 to 34.

Fresh water: Finland! Zürich! Australia (Victoria, Lake Muir, Tasmania)!

Var. *fossilis* PANT. (1889). — L. 0,045; B. 0,0075 mm. Striæ 10 to 12.5 in 0,01 mm., the median more distant, 7.5 in 0,01 mm. — PANT. II p. 56 Pl. XI f. 201.

Brackish water: Hungary, foss. (Pant.).

Var. *Vibrio* EHB. (1843). — V. very slender and narrow, linear, slightly gibbous in the middle, with rounded-truncate often gibbous ends. L. 0,08 to 0,011; B. 0,01 to 0,012 mm. Striæ 10 in 0,01 mm. distinctly punctate. — *G. Vibrio* EHB. Verb. p. 128 Pl. II: 1 f. 40. Microg. W. SM. B. D. Pl. XXVIII f. 212. V. H. Syn. Pl. XXIV f. 26—27. *G. Cygnus* SCHUM. P. D. p. 187 Pl. IX f. 26?

Fresh water: Finland! Germany, Erlaf See (Grun.). Hungary, Dubravica, fossil (Grun.), Seychelles!

To this species probably belongs *G. hungaricum* PANT. III Pl. II f. 28 (1893).

5. **G. subtile** EHB. (1843). — V. narrow, elongated biconstricted, with broad, rounded-truncate apex. L. 0,045; B. 0,007 mm. Axial area indistinct; central area narrow, unilateral, transverse. Striæ 12 in 0.01 mm., almost transverse, distinctly punctate. — EHB. Am. p. 128. GREG. M. J. IV Pl. I f. 12. SCHUM. P. D. I Nacht. Pl. II f. 19. V. H. Syn. Pl. XXIII f. 13, 14.

Fresh water: Scotland! Finland! Holstein! Bengal!

Var. *Sagitta* SCHUM. (1863). — As the type, but with cuneate apex. — *G. Sagitta* SCHUM. P. D. p. 187 Pl. IX f. 29. V. H. Syn. Pl. XXIII f. 27.

Fresh water: Prussia (Schum.).

6. **G. semiapertum** GRUN. (1880). — V. elongated, clavate, with broad apex and basis. L. 0,06 to 0,07; B. 0,011 to 0,013 mm. Axial area distinct, linear; central area a large, transverse fascia, with a distinct stigma on one side and frequently marginal striæ on the other. Striæ 10 to 11 in 0,01 mm., slightly radiate, punctate; puncta about 21 in 0,01 mm. — GRUN. in V. H. Syn. Pl. XXIV f. 42. CL. M. D. N:o 264.

Fresh water: California, Shasta Co (Grun.). Oregon, Pitt River (Grove Coll.)!

7. **G. gracile** EHB. (1838). — V. elongated, linear to lanceolate, with acute to subacute apex and basis. L. 0,025 to 0,07; B. 0,04 to 0,0111 mm. Axial area very narrow; central area narrow, transverse. Striæ transverse, 9 to 15 in 0.01 mm.

Var. *cymbelloides* GRUN. Ms. — V. slightly asymmetrical to the longitudinal axis, with gently curved dorsal margin and nearly straight ventral margin. L. 0,05; B. 0,005 mm. Striæ about 16 in 0,01 mm.

Fresh water: Norway, Dovre! Sweden, Helsingland, Arbra!

Var. *aurita* AL. BR. (1853). — V. narrow, linear-lanceolate. L. 0,024 to 0,04; B. 0,005 to 0,006 mm. Striæ 15 to 16 in 0.01 mm. Living cells with two horn-like processes at the end. *G. aur.* AL. BR. in Rabh. Süssw. D. p. 59 Pl. VIII f. 3. V. H. Syn. XXIV f. 15 to 18. *G. angustum* SCHUM. I Nachtr. Pl. II f. 17?

Fresh water: Baden, Titisee (A. Br.). Finland! Norway, Dovre! Iceland! U. St. Benis Lake, White Mountains!

Var. *dichotomum* W. SM. (1853). — Linear-lanceolate, slightly clavate, with obtuse ends. L. 0,04 to 0,05; B. 0,007 mm. Striæ 12 to 14 in 0,01 mm. finely punctate. — *G. dichotomum* W. SM. Br. D. I p. 79 Pl. XXVIII f. 240. *G.* (*gracile var.?*) *dichotomum* V. H. Syn. Pl. XXXV f. 19 to 21. *G. tenellum* W. SM. B. D. Pl. XXIX f. 243? *G. Vibrio* SCHUM. Tatra Pl. III f. 38? *G. hebridense* HÉRIB. D. d'Auvergne p. 61 Pl. III f. 9?

Fresh water: Sweden! Finland! England! Dubravica, Hungary, foss. (Grun.). Celebes! Hawaji! New Zealand! Australia (Daintree River! Mitchell River! Australian Alps! Tasmania!) Nova Scotia! Illinois! Mexico! Jamaica! Ecuador!

Var. *major* GRUN. (1880). V. slender, lanceolate. L. 0,07 to 0,10; B. 0,011 mm. Striæ 9 to 10 in 0,01 mm. distinctly punctate. — GRUN. in V. H. Syn. Pl. XXIV f. 12. *G. hebridense* GREG. M. J. II Pl. IV f. 19?

Fresh water: New Zealand! Rhode Island! Demerara River!

Var.? *lanceolata* KÜTZ. (1844). V. lanceolate-clavate, with apiculate apex. L. 0,055; B. 0,01 mm. Axial area narrow; central area narrow, transverse. Striæ 16 in 0,01 mm. KÜTZ. Bac. p. 87 Pl. XXX f. 59. V. H. Syn. XXIV f. 11. *G. Turris var. apiculata* GRUN. D. of Banka p. 10 Pl. I f. 12.

Fresh water: Trinidad (Kütz, Grun.), Banka (Grun.).

Var. *naviculacea* W. SM. (1856). — V. almost symmetrical to the transverse axis, lanceolate. L. 0,035 to 0,047; B. 0,007 to 0,01 mm. Striæ 11 to 14 in 0,01 mm., indistinctly punctate. W. SM. B. D. II p. 98. V. H. Syn. XXIV f. 13, 14.

Fresh water: Edinburgh Bot. Garden (W. SM.)! New Zealand!

G. gracile comprises a large number of closely connected forms, some of which are nearly akin to *G. intricatum*, some to *G. lanceolatum* EHR.

8. **G. Cymbella** BRUN (1891). — V. linear, slightly clavate with obtuse apex and basis, slightly lunate. L. 0,05 to 0,065; B. 0,011 mm. Axial area narrow. Central area transverse not reaching the margin, with a conspicuous stigma. Striæ almost parallel 6 to 7 in 0,01 mm. — BRUN D. esp. n. p. 28 Pl. XIX f. 2.

Fresh water: South Africa, Rio de la Plata, Cape Horn (Brun).

9. **G. lanceolatum** EHR. (1843). — V. lanceolate, clavate, gradually tapering from the middle to the obtuse apex and basis. L. 0,027 to 0,07; B. 0,01 mm. Axial area narrow linear. Central area small, rounded, with one unilateral stigma. Striæ 12 to 13 in 0,01 mm., slightly radiate, coarsely punctate; puncta 22 to 24 in 0,01 mm.; the median stria opposite to the stigma shortened. — EHR. Am. Pl. II: 1 f. 37. *G. affine* KÜTZ. Bac. p. 86 Pl. XXX f. 54 (1844). V. H. Syn. Pl. XXIV f. 8 to 10. *G. Szaboi* PANT. III Pl. II f. 34 (1893)?

Fresh water: Mexico! Jamaica! Ecuador! Lake Tacarigua, Trinidad (V. H. Syn.). Marquesas Islands! New Zealand!.

Var. *insignis* GREG. (1856). — At the type, but with coarser striæ, 9 to 10 in 0,01 mm.; puncta 18 to 22 in 0,01 mm. — *G. insignis* GREG. M. J. IV Pl. I f. 39. V. H. S. Pl. XXIV f. 39 to 41.

Fresh water: Scotland (Greg.), Bengal! Victoria, Australia! Ecuador, San Nicolas!

Var. *bengalensis* GRUN. (1880). — More clavate. L. 0,03 to 0,057; B. 0,009 mm. Striæ 8 to 9 in 0,01 mm. indistinctly punctate. — *G. bengalense* GRUN. in V. H. Syn. Pl. XXIV f. 37, 38.

Fresh water: Bengal (V. H. Syn.).

G. lanceolatum is nearly akin to *G. gracile*, some of its forms being exceedingly difficult to distinguish from several varieties of that species. Some forms are, on the other hand, very similar to forms of *G. subclavatum*.

10. **G. subclavatum** GRUN. (1878). — V. clavate, with broad rounded apex and somewhat narrower basis, gibbous in the middle. L. 0,035 to 0,07; B. 0,008 to 0,01 mm. Axial area narrow; central area rounded, with distinct stigma. Striæ strong, 9 to 13 in 0,01 mm. obscurely punctate, almost transverse, the median ones often shortened. — *G. longiceps* EHR. *var. subclavata* GRUN. Casp. S. Algæ p. 10. *G. montanum v. subclav.* GRUN. in V. H. Syn. p. 125 Pl. XXIII f. 39—43., XXIV f. 1. *G. commutatum* GRUN. V. H. Syn. Pl. XXIV f. 2. Fr. Jos. Land D. p. 98 (46) Pl. I f. 12. *G. longiceps* EHR. M. G. Pl. VII: 3, B f. 9 (1854)? SCHUM. P. D. p. 187 Pl. IX f. 27? *G. Cygnus* Ströse Kliecken f. 17. *G. calcareum* CL. a. M. D. N:o 137. *G. dichoto-*

num β sessile Kütz. (fide Grun.). *G. Brébissonii* Kütz. (fide Grun.). *G. mexicanum* Grun. in V. H. Syn. Pl. XXIV f. 3. *G. Kinkerianum* Pant. III Pl. X f. 162, 165.

Fresh water: Sweden! Finland! Holstein! Belgium (V. H.). France! England! Neusidler See (Grun.), Iceland! Argentina! Chimborazo, Ecuador! Sandwich Islands! Tasmania! Auckland! California!

Var. *obliqua* Grun. (1881). — Cymbelloid bent, asymmetrical to the longitudinal axis. — Grun. Fr. Josephs L. D. p. (98) 46.

Var. *acuminata* Hérib. a. Perag. (1893). Lanceolate, tapering towards the narrow ends. — *G. subclav. var. acum.* Hérib. a. Perag. D. d'Auvergne p. 55 Pl. III f. 8.

Fresh water: Auvergne, fossil.

Var. *Mustela* Ehr. (1854). Biconstricted, with gibbous, obtuse apex. — *G. Must.* Ehr. M. G. Pl. VII: a, B. f. 9. Schum. P. D. p. 187 Pl. IX f. 30. V. H. Syn. Pl. XXIV f. 4 to 7. *G. Sagitta* Schum. P. D. III Nachtr. Pl. II f. 16?

Fresh water: Beeren Eiland (Lagst.). Finmark! Norway. Dovre! Finland! Gulf of Bothnia!

Forma curvata Br. a. Perag. (1893). Frustules in front-view curved. — Hérib. D. d'Auvergne p. 59 Pl. III f. 6, 7.

Fresh water: Auvergne, fossil.

Var. *montana* Schum. (1867). — Biconstricted, with protracted subtruncate or obtuse apex. Schum. Tatra p. 67 Pl. III f. 35. V. H. Syn. p. 124 Pl. XXIII f. 33 to 36. *G. acuminatum var. submontana* Gutwinsky Fl. Galiz. p. 28 Pl. I f. 23.

Fresh water: Galiz. (Schum.). Belgium (V. H.), Hungary, fossil (Grun.), Demerara River!

G. subclavatum by its variety *montana* makes complete transition to *G. acuminatum*, the latter comprising forms with acute, the former with obtuse ends.

11. **G. acuminatum** Ehr. (1838). V. clavate, more or less biconstricted, with apiculate apex, and narrow basis. L. 0,03 to 0,07; B. 0,009 to 0,01 mm. Axial area narrow or indistinct; central area short and narrow, unilateral. Striæ 10 to 11 in 0,01 mm., slightly radiate, the median stria opposite to the stigma being shortened. — Ehr. Inf. p. 217 Pl. XVIII f. 4. W. Sm. B. D. I Pl. XXVIII f. 238 *a, a'*.

Forma trigonocephala Ehr. (1854). — V. not distinctly biconstricted. Apex cuneate. — *G. trig.* Ehr. M. G. Pl. VI: I f. 36. V. H. Syn. Pl. XXIII f. 18.

Forma Brébissonii Kütz. (1859). — V. slightly biconstricted, with cuneate apex. — *G. Bréb.* Kütz. Sp. Alg. p. 66. V. H. Syn. XXIII f. 23 26. *G. ac. var. Clavus* V. H. Syn. Pl. XXIII f. 20. *G. acum.* W. Sm. B. D. Pl. XXVIII f. 238 *a''*.

Forma coronata Ehr. (1840). — V. strongly biconstricted, with broad, apiculate apex. — *G. coron.* Ehr. Abh. 1840 p. 211. *G. acum.* W. Sm. B. D. Pl. XXVIII f. 238 *β*. V. H. Syn. p. 124 Pl. XXIII f. 15. Petit Lac des Vosges f. 2. Ströse Klieken f. 16. *G. acum.* V. H. Syn. Pl. XXIII f. 16. *G. acum. var. laticeps* V. H. Syn. l. c. f. 17.

Forma pusilla Grun. (1880). — As the f. coron. but smaller. L. 0,03; B. 0,008 mm. — *G. acum. var. pus.* Grun. V. H. Syn. Pl. XXIII f. 19.

Fresh water: Spitzbergen (Lagst.). Sweden! Finland! Belgium (V. H.), England, (Sm.), Germany! Switzerland! France! Spain! Canada! Massachusetts! Illinois!

Var. *elongata* W. Sm. (1855). — V. slender, elongated, strongly gibbous in the middle and at the apex. L. 0,07 to 0,11; B. 0,012 to 0,017 mm. Striæ 12 in 0,01 mm. coarsely punctate; puncta about 20 in 0,01 mm. — G. *elongat.* W. Sm. Ann. N. Hist. 1855 p. 6 Pl. I f. 4. B. D. II p. 99. *G. acum. var. elong.* V. H. Syn. Pl. XXIII f. 22. *G. Brébissonii* Greg. M. J. II Pl. IV f. 13 (1854)? *G. acum. var. intermedia* Grun. in V. H. Syn. Pl. XXIII f. 21.

Fresh water: Scotland! Finland! Vosges!

Var. *Turris* Ehr. (1843). V. very slightly biconstricted with cuneate or apiculate apex. L. 0,04 to 0,06; B. 0,013 mm. Striæ 10 to 11 in 0,01 mm. *G. Turris* Ehr. Am. p. 128. M. G. Pl. XIV f. 70, 71. V. H. Syn. Pl. XXIII f. 31.

Fresh water: Finland (Padasjoki)! Bengal! Australia, North Australia! Murray River! Australian Alps! New Zealand! Houghton, Michig.! Illinois! California! Demerara! Rio Janeiro! Ecuador!

G. acuminatum comprises a number of forms, exceedingly variable in size and outline, passing over to *G. subclavatum var. montana* by the forma Brébissonii, and to *G. Augur* by smaller forms of the var. Turris.

12. **G. Augur** Ehb. (1840). V. clavate, with broad, truncate-apiculate apex and narrow basis. L. 0,03 to 0,05; B. 0,009 to 0,01 mm. Axial area narrow; central area narrow, unilateral Striæ 10 in 0,01 mm. slightly radiate. — Ehb. Ber. 1840 p. 211. M. G. XVII: 1, f. 35. V. H. Syn. p. 124 Pl. XXIII f. 29. *G. Augur var. Gautieri* V. H. Syn. p. 124 Pl. XXIII f. 28. *G. nasutum* Ehb. Am. p. 128. M. G. VI: 1 f. 37?

Fresh water: Belgium (V. H.), Ceyssat, Puy de Dôme foss.! Maine, Bridgetown! Waltham Mass.! Mexico! Seychelles!

G. Augur is closely connected with *G. acuminatum var. Turris*, of which it may be regarded as a form with non-constricted valves.

G. apicatum Ehb. (1841). — V. clavate, not biconstricted, with acuminate apex. L. 0,022 to 0,025; B. 0,006 to 0,007 mm. Axial and central areas indistinct. Striæ 14 in 0,01 mm. almost transverse, near the end slightly radiate, not distinctly punctate. — Ehb. Abh. 1841 p. 416 (accord. to Chase) M. G. IX: 1 f. 41? Cl. D. of Finl. p. 48 Pl. III f. 20, 21. *G. cristatum* W. Sm. B. D I Pl. XXVIII f. 239? Heib. Consp. D. D. V f. 17?

Fresh water: Finland!

G. apicatum is nearly connected with *G. acuminatum f. trigonocephala*, but has finer striæ.

13. **G. validum** Cl. N. Sp. — V. elongated, gently biconstricted, with rostrate-apiculate apex. L. 0,065; B. 0,01 mm. Axial area linear, moderately broad, not dilated in the middle. Stigma often indistinct. Striæ 6 to 7 in 0,01 mm., distinctly punctate, of equal length, transverse, but radiate at the apex. — Pl. V f. 9.

Fresh water: Japan, fossil in lignite (Brun Coll.)! Demerara River!

Var. *elongata*. — V. very slightly biconstricted, with subcuneate apex. L. 0,14; B. 0,0113 mm. Striæ 5,5 in 0,01 mm. Pl. V f. 8.

Fresh water: Demerara River!

G. validum has the outline of *G. subclavatum var. montana*, from which it differs by its coarser striæ and broader axial area.

14. **G. sphærophorum** Ehb. (1845). — V. clavate, with capitate apex and narrow basis. L. 0,035 to 0,047; B. 0,01 mm. Axial area indistinct. Central area small, rounded. Striæ 11 in 0,01 mm., nearly transverse, punctate. — Ehb. Ber. 1845 p. 78 (fide Chase), V. H. Syn. Pl. XXIII f. 30.

Fresh water: Finland (Aland)! New York (Niagara Falls! Genessee Falls)! Lake Pistaku (Illinois)!

G. sphærophorum is nearly akin to *G. Turris*, from which it differs scarcely by anything but the capitate apex.

15. **G. Berggrenii** Cl. N. Sp. — V. clavate, with broad subtruncate and usually constricted apex. Basis much narrower, obtuse. L. 0,047 to 0,05; B. 0,011 to 0,012 mm. Axial area narrow, linear, somewhat dilated around the central nodule. Stigma distinct. Striæ coarse, 10 to 11 in 0,01 mm. distinctly punctate, slightly radiate. — Pl. V f. 6, 7.

Fresh water: New Zealand (Waitangi! Lake Rotorua! etc.).

G. Berggrenii resembles in outline *G. constrictum* and *G. subclavatum*, but differs from the former by the median striæ not being alternately longer and shorter, and from the latter by its much broader ends and more distinct axial area.

16. **G. constrictum** EHR. (1830). — V. clavate, gibbous in the middle, with broad, rounded-truncate apex and narrower basis. L. 0,04 to 0,06; B. 0,01 mm. Axial area narrow linear; central area narrow, star-like. Stigma distinct, unilateral. Striæ 10 to 12 in 0,01 mm., slightly radiate, in the middle alternately longer and shorter, coarsely punctate. EHR. Abh. 1830 W. SM. B. D. Pl. XXVIII f. 236. V. H. Syn. p. 123 Pl. XXIII f. 6. *G. pohliæforme* KÜTZ. Dec. N:o 25 (1833). *G. subramosum* KÜTZ. Dec. N:o 152 (1836) fide Lagst. *G. constr. var. subcapitata* GRUN. V. H Syn. f. 5.

Fresh water: Sweden! England! Belgium (V. H.), Switzerland! Jenissey! Australian Alps! North Australia! Tasmania! Illinois!

Var. *capitata* EHR. (1838). — V. very slightly or not constricted, clavate with broad apex. — *G. capitatum* EHR. Inf. Pl. XVIII f. 2. W. SM. B. D. Pl. XXVIII f. 237. V. H. Syn. p. 123 Pl. XXIII f. 7. PETIT Lac des Vosges f. 3. *G. turgidum* EHR. M. G. Pl. II: 2 f. 40. V. H. Syn. Pl. XXIII f. 11. *G. italicum* KÜTZ. Bac. p. 85 Pl. XXX f. 75. V. H. Syn. Pl. XXIII f. 8. *G. clavatum* EHR. Inf. p. 218 Pl. XVIII f. 6. V. H. Syn. Pl. XXIII f. 9.

Fresh water: Sweden! Gulf of Bothnia! Finland! England! Belgium (V. H.), France! New Zealand! Canada, foss.! New York, foss.! Argentina! Ecuador!

G. constrictum is a very common species with very variable outline. Typical specimens are strongly biconstricted, but all possible intermediate forms exist to the quite unconstricted var. capitata. The characteristic present in all these forms is the stellate central area arising from the median striæ being alternately longer and shorter.

17. **G. geminatum** LYNGB. (1819). — V. strongly biconstricted, with broad, subtruncate apex and less broad, obtusely truncate basis. L. 0,1 to 0,12; B. 0,03 to 0,04 mm. Axial area narrow, linear; central area rounded, stellate at its margin, with one or, usually, several, stigmas, disposed in a longitudinal row on one side of the central nodule. Striæ 10 in 0,01 mm. radiate at the ends, in the middle alternately longer and shorter, coarsely punctate; puncta 12 in 0,01 mm. — *Vorticella pyraria* MÜLL. 1773 (fide Kütz.). *Echinella geminata* LYNGB. Tent. Hydroph. p. 210. *Gomph. gem.* AG. Syst. p. 12 (1824). W. SM. B. D. Pl. XXVII f. 235.

Fresh water on stones in rivulets and lakes: Spitsbergen, Beeren Eiland (Lagst.), Färöar (Lyngb.), Scotland! Ireland (Kütz.), Sweden! Finland! France, Cantal (Hérib.), Spain, Aragonia (Mouzón), Switzerland (Brun), Vancouver Island!

Var. *sibirica* GRUN. (1878). — V. slightly or indistinctly biconstricted, with broad end. L. 0,08 to 0,09; B. 0,035 mm. Stigma single. Striæ 9 to 10 in 0,01 mm. — GRUN. Casp. See Alg. p. 11. *G. gem. var. hybrida* GRUN. V. H. Syn. Pl. XXIII f. 4. Franz Josephs Land D. p. 97 (45) Pl. I f. 11.

Fresh water: Ochotsk (Grun.), Franz Josephs Land (Grun.), Jenissey!

Var. *curvirostra* TEMP. and BRUN (1889). — V. deeply biconstricted, arcuate. L. 0,012 to 0,145 mm. Central area with a single stigma. Striæ 6 to 8 in 0,01 mm. — *G. curvirostrum* TEMP. and BRUN D. f. du Japon p. 38 Pl. IX f. 4.

Fresh water: Yedo foss. (Temp. and Brun).

G. geminatum, the largest of all species of this genus, is a northern and alpine form, being very common in Scotland, Sweden and Finland, where it occurs attached to stones by strong stalks. Between the strongly biconstricted type and the broadly clavate var. sibirica all kinds of intermediate forms exist. The var. curvirostra is a cymbelloid form, such as occurs also among the forms of other species.

18. **G. ventricosum** GREG. (1856). — V. lanceolate-clavate, with broad, obtuse apex and narrower basis. L. 0,035 to 0,055; B. 0,01 mm. Axial area linear lanceolate. Central area rounded, with one distinct stigma. Striæ 11 to 13 in 0,01 mm., radiate, finely punctate; puncta about 24 in 0,01 mm. — GREG. M. J. IV Pl. I f. 40. V. H. Syn. Pl. XXV f. 13. CL. M. D. N:o 93.

Fresh water: Scotland (Greg.). Norway! Sweden! Finland! Jenissey! Kamtschatka! Waltham, Massachusetts!

Var. *maxima* CL. — V. more lanceolate. L. 0,08; B. 0,017 mm. Striæ 12 in 0,01 mm. coarsely punctate; puncta 15 in 0.01 mm. — Pl. V f. 13.

Fresh water: Pitt River, Oregon (Grove Coll.)!

Var. *tasmanica* CL. — V. nearly lanceolate. L. 0,07; B. 0,015 mm. Striæ about 9 in 0,01 mm., coarsely punctate; the median, on one side of the valve, alternatelty longer and shorter.

Fresh water: Campbell Town, Tasmania, fossil!

Var. *ornata* GRUN. (1880). — Lanceolate, gradually tapering from the middle to the obtuse apex and basis. L. 0,06 to 0,1 mm. B. 0,011 to 0,013 mm. Axial and central areas combined in a narrow, lanceolate space. On one side of the central nodule is a row of 3 to 5 stigmas, on the other none, or one to two, stigmas. Striæ 10 in 0,01 mm. coarsely punctate; puncta 18 in 0,01 mm. — GRUN. in V. H. Syn. Pl. XXV f. 15. *G. dubravicense* PANT. III Pl. XX f. 294, 296 (1893)?

Fresh water: Guatemala, foss.!

The typical forms of *G. ventricosum* belong to northern countries and for that reason it is doubtful whether the varieties should not be considered as distinct species, although the differences are only trifling.

19. **G. oxycephalum** CL. N. Sp. — V. large, gradually tapering from the middle to the acute apex. Basis obtuse to truncate. L. 0,09 to 0,13; B. 0,018 to 0,026 mm. Axial and central areas uniting in a lanceolate space, with one (or two) stigma on one side of the central nodule. Striæ 8 in 0,01 mm., slightly radiate at the ends, distinctly punctate; puncta 21 in 0,01 mm. — Pl. V f. 10.

Fresh water: Demerara River!

20. **G. Salinarum** PANT. (1889). — V. linear, more or less gibbous in the middle, with almost equally broad, rounded obtuse apex and basis. L. 0,038 to 0,051; B. 0,0075 to 0,008 mm. Terminal fissures of the median line distant from the ends. Axial area narrow linear, suddenly dilated around the central nodule to an orbicular space. Striæ 10 to 12 in 0.01 mm., obscurely punctate, slightly radiate in the middle and at the ends. — *G. olivaceum var. salinarum* PANT. II p. 56 Pl. IX f. 160; XI f. 199; XVIII f. 287. *G. olivaceum var. fossilis* PANT. II p. 56 Pl. XII f. 204. *G. salsa* PANT. II p. 56 Pl. XVII f. 285. *G. Salin.* Icon. n. Pl. V f. 11, 12.

Brackish water: Baltic at Rügen! Hungary fossil (Gyöngyös Pata! etc.).

Var. *staurophora* PANT. (1889). — Central area a transverse fascia. — *G. oliv. var. staur.* PANT. II p. 56 Pl. XII f. 206.

Brackish water: Hungary fossil (Pant.).

G. Salinarum seems me to be perfectly distinct from *G. olivaceum* by the distant terminal fissures, the broader axial area, the central orbicular area and the more distant striæ. The outline of the valve is, as in most species of Gomphonema, variable. Between *G. salsa* PANT. and *G. oliv. var. fossilis* PANT. I am unable to find any difference from the descriptions and the figures.

21. **G. transsylvanicum** PANT. (1893). — V. lanceolate, scarcely clavate, tapering from the middle towards the obtuse ends. L. 0,084; B. 0.0168 mm. Axial area narrow; central area large, irregular. Striæ about 10 in 0,01 mm., radiate in the middle, where they are of unequal length, parallel towards the ends, not distinctly punctate. — PANT. III Pl. XIV, 219, 220.

Fresh water?: Köpecz (Pant.).

Unknown to the author.

22. **G. olivaceum** LYNGB. (1819). — V. clavate, rarely sublanceolate, with broad, rounded, obtuse apex and narrower basis. L. 0,015 to 0,025; B. 0,005 to 0,007 mm. Axial area indistinct; central area rectangular. Striæ 13 to 14 in 0,01 mm., curved or radiate in the middle of the valve, elsewhere almost transverse, not distinctly punctate. — *Echinella oliv.* LYNGB. Tent. Hydr. D. p. 209 Pl. LXX f. c 1 to 3. *G. oliv.* KÜTZ. Alg. Dec. N:o 13 (fide Lagst.). W. SM. B. D.

P. XXIX f. 244. V. H. Syn. p. 126 Pl. XXV f. 20 to 27. *G. sphaerelloides* SCHUM. Pr. D. I Nachtr. p. 19 f. 16. *G. subramosum* KÜTZ. (fide Grun.). *Sphenella vulgaris* KÜTZ. (fide Grun.).

Fresh and brackish water: Sweden! Germany! Switzerland! England!

Var. *baltica* CL. (1868). — V. clavate. L. 0,04; B. 0,0075 mm. Central area small. Striæ 16 to 17 in 0,01 mm. — *G. balticum* CL. Sv. och Norsk D. p. 231 Pl. IV f. 10 to 16.

Brackish water: Baltic (from Westerbotten to Gothland)!

Var. *calcarea* CL. (1868). — V. clavate; L. 0,022 to 0,047; B. 0,005 to 0,008 mm. Central area small. Striæ 12 to 13 in 0,01 mm. *G. calcareum* CL. Sv. och Norsk D. p. 231 Pl. IV f. 7.

Fresh water (on moist limestone-rocks): Gothland!

Var. *stauroneiformis* GRUN. (1878). V. lanceolate. L. 0,033 to 0,07; B. 0,01 to 0,012 mm. Striæ 10 to 13 in 0,01 mm. GRUN. Casp. See Alg. p. 9 Pl. III f. 2.

Brackish water: Caspian Sea (Grun.).

Var. *tenellum* KÜTZ. (1844). — V. small, clavate. L. 0,012 to 0,025; B. 0,003 to 0,0035 mm. Striæ 14 in 0,01 mm. — *G. ten.* KÜTZ. Bac. p. 84 Pl. VIII f. 8. V. H. Syn. Pl. XXIV f. 22 to 25.

Fresh water: Finland, Abo! Australian Alps!

G. olivaceum lives usually in rivulets by slender stalks attached to stones and forming brownish masses about 1 centim. in diameter. The var. calcarea was found on limestone-rocks on Gothland, fixed by long stalks and forming thick gelatinous masses. The var. baltica is common in the Baltic and the Gulf of Bothnia, where it occurs attached by elongated gelatinous stalks to Zostera and Potamogeton. The *G. tenellum* is not quite clear to me. What I suppose to be KÜTZINGS species is doubtless a very small *G. olivaceum*, but in the Syn. of Van Heurck GRUNOW places *G. tenellum* among the asymmetrical Gomphonemas, so it is possible that *G. tenellum* KÜTZ. is a small *G. intricatum*.

23. **G. Aestuarii** CL. (1893). — V. linear, narrow, slightly clavate, with obtuse end and basis. L. 0,02 to 0,028; B. 0,002 to 0,0035 mm. Axial area indistinct; central area a broad transverse fascia. Striæ parallel (the median radiate) 20 in 0,01 mm. Ends of the valve with rudimentary diaphragms. CL. Diatomiste Vol. II p. 55 Pl. III f. 4.

Marine: Hastings (Comber Coll.)!

24. **G. exiguum** KÜTZ. (1844). — V. narrow, clavate with obtuse, sometimes slightly rostrate apex. L. 0,009 to 0,03; B. 0,002 to 0,003 mm. Axial area narrow, not dilated in the middle. Striæ 18 in 0,01 mm. transverse. KÜTZ. Bac. p. 84 Pl. XXX f. 58. V. H. Syn. p. 126 Pl. XXV f. 34. *G. hyalinum* Heib. Consp. D. D. p. 96 Pl. V f. 18 (1863). *G. exiguum var. digitatum* V. H. Syn. f. 35, 36; *var. telegraphicum* (KÜTZ.) V. H. l. c. f. 37; *var. minutissimum* (KÜTZ.) V. H. l. c. f. 38; *var. perpusilla* GRUN. V. H. l. f. 39.

Marine: Coasts of Denmark (Heib.), England! Belgium (V. H.).

This minute species is probably widely distributed, but from its smallness rarely met with in cleaned materials. Between the many varieties in V. H. Syn. I am unable to find any difference except in the number of the striæ, and the size.

Var. *pachyclada* BRÉB. (1838). V. linear-clavate. L. 0,015 to 0,034; B. 0,005 mm. Striæ 16 in 0,01 mm. — *G. pach.* BRÉB. Considér. p. 21 (fide Chase). V. H. Syn. XXV f. 31, 32.

Marine: Coasts of Normandy (Bréb., Grun.), Cape Wankarema! Behrings Island!

Var. *arctica* GRUN. (1880). — V. broad, clavate. L. 0,02 to 0,035; B. 0,006 to 0,008 mm. Striæ 16 to 20 in 0,01 mm. almost transverse. — *G. arct.* GRUN. V. H. Syn. Pl. XXV f. 30. Franz Josephs Land D. p. 102 (50) Pl. I f. 13.

Marine, arctic regions: Franz Josephs Land (Grun.), Nova Zembla! Cape Wankarema!

25. **G. kamtschaticum** GRUN. (1878). — V. elongated, clavate, with rounded apex and narrower basis. L. 0,03 to 0,07; B. 0,005 to 0,011 mm. Axial area distinct, linear, dilated around the central nodule. Striæ 12 to 16 in 0,01 mm. radiate in the middle, very finely punctate. —

GRUN. Casp. Sea Alg. p. 12. V. H. Syn. XXV f. 29. *G. antarcticum* O'MEARA L. Soc. XV p. 56 Pl. I f. 3 (1877)?

Marine: Arctic America, Bessels Bay! Esquimaux Harbour (Grun.), Iceland! East Cape! Behrings Island!

Var. *sibirica* GRUN. (1878). V. less clavate, striæ less radiate. — GRUN. in Cl. M. D. 315 to 318.

Marine: Cape Wankarema!

Var. *californica* GRUN. (1880). — Almost linear, with obtuse and rounded ends. L. 0,03; B. 0,006 mm. Striæ 15 in 0,01 mm. - GRUN. in V. H. Syn. Pl. XXV f. 28.

Marine: San Francisco (Grun.).

G. Kamtschaticum is by the *var. calif.* nearly connected with *G. exig. var. pachyclada*, the two latter varieties being distinguished only by the somewhat more visible axial and central area of the former. In the Cape Wankarema material occur forms of *G. kamtschaticum* with unilateral axial area.

26. **G. peruvianum** GRUN. (1880). — V. linear, clavate. L. 0,03; B. 0,005 mm. Axial area narrow; central subquadrate. Striæ 9 in 0,01 mm. — GRUN. in V. H. Syn. Pl. XXV f. 33.

Marine: Peru (Grun.).

27. **G. abbreviatum** (AG. 1831?) KÜTZ. (1844). — V. clavate, with broad, rounded end and narrow, obtuse basis. L. 0,016 to 0,028; B. 0,005 mm. Axial and central areas uniting in a broad, linear-lanceolate space. Striæ 21 to 22 in 0,01 mm. transverse, radiate in the end. — *Licmophora minuta* KÜTZ. Dec. N:o 23 (1833) fide Lagst. *G. abbreviatum* AG. Consp. p. 34? KÜTZ. Bac. p. 84. GRUN. Casp. Sea Alg. p. 13. V. H. Syn. Pl. XXV f. 16.

Fresh or slightly brackish water: Weissenfels (Kütz.), Dubravica, Hungary, fossil (Grun.). Gulf of Bothnia at Torneå!

28. **G. brasiliense** GRUN. (1878). — V. lanceolate, obtuse. L. 0,025 to 0,034; B. 0,005 to 0,0055 mm. Axial and central areas uniting in a broad, lanceolate space. Striæ 16 to 18 in 0,01 mm. short. GRUN. Casp. Sea Alg. p. 13. *G. abbr. var. bras.* V. H. Syn. Pl. XXV f. 17.

Fresh water: Brazil, Cuba, Bengal (Grun.).

Var. *Demeraræ* GRUN. Ms. — V. sublanceolate with subrostrate apex. L. 0,038 to 0,058; B. 0,008 to 0,012 mm.

Fresh water: Demerara River (Grun.).

29. **G. Puiggarianum** GRUN. (1880). — V. linear-lanceolate, with truncate apex and basis. L. 0,05; B. 0,008 mm. Axial area broad, lanceolate. Striæ 6 in 0,01 mm. marginal. GRUN. in V. H. Syn. Pl. XXV f. 18.

Fresh water: Brazil (Grun.).

Var. *æquatorialis* CL. — V. small. L. 0,025; B. 0,005 mm. Area less broad. Striæ 8 to 9 in 0,01 mm.

Fresh water: Ecuador, San Nicolas!

Additional.

G. cantalicum BRUN a. HÉRIB. (1893). — V. lanceolate, slightly clavate, gradually tapering from the middle to the rounded obtuse ends. L. 0,16 to 0,225; B. 0,025 to 0,032 mm. Axial area narrow, linear, not dilated in the middle where there is, unilaterally, a stigma. Striæ 12 in 0,01 mm. almost parallel, slightly radiate at the ends, coarsely punctate; puncta about 14 in 0,01 mm., arranged in slightly undulating longitudinal rows. Across the striæ and in the middle between the median line and the margin there is a shadowy longitudinal line. — BRUN a. HÉRIB. D. d'Auvergne p. 219 Pl. VI f. 11.

Fresh water: Cantal, fossil!

Var. *costalonga* BRUN a. HÉRIB. (1893). — Valve very slightly curved. Longitudinal lines more distinct. — l. c. f. 13.

Var. *major* BRUN a. HÉRIB. (1893). — L. 0.23 mm. — l. c. f. 12.

A very remarkable species. It does not belong to Gomphoneis as the striæ are composed of simple rows of puncta.

Trachyneis CL. N. GEN.

Valve naviculoid, more or less elongated, frequently asymmetrical on both sides of the longitudinal axis. Valve (often) with an interior coarsely dotted stratum, a median stratum of more or less transverse flexuose strong costæ, anastomosing, where they bend towards each other and thus forming a network of diamond-shaped or rectangular alveoli, and an exterior stratum with very fine puncta forming longitudinal, sometimes slightly oblique, fine striæ. — *Cell-contents:* T. aspera v. genuina has two chromatophore-plates along the connecting zone. The margins of the plates are strongly indented.

The type of this genus, *Nav. aspera* EHR. is very variable and widely distributed. The peculiar structure of this species makes it necessary to form for it and the allied species a separate genus. Under a low power the valve seems to be covered with elongated or rhomboid puncta, more or less distinctly disposed in quincunx, these puncta being the diamond-shaped alveoli formed by the anastomoses of the costæ. The fine puncta of the exterior stratum are visible only with difficulty, and, under certain illumination, give to the elongated puncta the appearance of being transversely lineate (See Van Heurck Suppl. Pl. B f. 26). The interior stratum of the valve may sometimes be separated, as is shewn by the fig. 23 Pl. XLVIII of A. S. Atl.

I suppose that the division Lineolatæ of Navicula may be regarded as having the nearest relations to Trachyneis, especially the forms of that group, which have divided striæ. A structure somewhat similar to that of Trachyneis is to be found in Mastoneis and Dictyoneis. All the species of this genus are marine. They occur in all seas, arctic as well as tropical.

Most forms of Trachyneis are so closely connected and subject to transitions as to make the distinction of well founded species very difficult. The variability of some species is considerable. In certain species there is a remarkable tendency to asymmetry, some varieties having a very excentric median line, or asymmetrical axial area; but such forms, for which the genus *Alloioneis* was created, are so closely connected with other, nearly, or perfectly, symmetrical forms, that no specific distinction can be founded on this character. The arrangement of the alveoli in oblique, or straight longitudinal rows, seems to afford some distinction; but this characteristic is also subject to great variation, and in some forms we find that the rows are oblique near the central area, and longitudinal elsewhere.

Artificial key.

1. { Central area small . . . . *T. velata* A. S.
   { — — large . . . . 2.
2. { Central area a transverse, outwards dilated fascia . . . . 3.
   { — rounded . . . . 4.
3. { Stauros not reaching to the margin . . . . *T. aspera* EHR.
   { — reaching — — . . . . *T. tumidula* GREV.
4. { Alveoli in decussating rows . . . . 5.
   { — — longitudinal — . . . . *T. Johnsoniana* GREV.
5. { All alveoli in decussating rows . . . . 6.
   { Alveoli at the margin in decussating, in the middle in straight rows . . . . *T. Brunii* CL.

6. { Axial area indistinct . . . . *T. Clepsydra* DONK.
{ — — linear, frequently unilateral . . . . 7.

7. { Alveoli in regularly decussating rows . . . . *T. Debyi* LEUD. FORTM.
{ — — irregularly — — . . . . *T. Antillarum* CL.

1. **T. aspera** EHB. (1843). — V. elliptic- to linear-lanceolate or elongated rhomboid. L. 0,06 to 0,3; B. 0,024 to 0,05 mm. Ends obtuse or rounded. Axial area very narrow or linear and unilateral. Central area a broad stauros, widened and truncate outwards. Alveoli forming transverse striæ, radiate throughout, 6 to 18 in 0,01 mm. in more or less oblique rows.

Symmetrical forms.

Var. *genuina* CL. — V. linear-lanceolate, obtuse. L. 0,15 to 0,2; B. 0,028 to 0,033 mm. Alveoli close. Rows of alveoli 7 to 10 in 0,01 mm. Longitudinal fine striæ distinct, 26 in 0,01 mm. — *Stauroptera aspera* EHB. Am. Pl. I f. 1, 2. *Nav. aspera* V. H. Syn. Pl. X f. 13. Suppl. B. f. 26. A. S. Atl. XLVIII f. 15, 21, 22. DONK. B. D. Pl. X f. 1. *Nav. pseudo-aspera* PANT. III Pl. XVIII f. 258 (1893).

Marine: North Sea! Singapore (Atl.). Amboina (Kinker Coll.)! Sydney! Japan, fossil (Brun Coll.)! Mexillones guano (Deby Coll.)!

Var. *vulgaris* CL. — V. elliptic- or linear-lanceolate. L. 0,11 to 0,2; B. 0,02 to 0,035 mm. Axial area indistinct or very narrow. Alveoli close. Rows of alveoli about 10 in 0,01 mm. Longitudinal fine striæ about 25 in 0,01 mm. — *Nav. aspera* A. S. XLVIII f. 2 to 6.

Marine: Arctic America! North Sea! Cape of Good Hope! New Zealand! Samoa! New Caledonia! Java! Galapagos Islands!

Var. *Neumeyeri* JANISCH (1876). — V. large, lanceolate. L. 0,3; B. 0,05 mm. Axial area narrow. Rows of alveoli about 9 in 0,01 mm. — *Nav. Neum.* A. S. Atl. XLVIII f. 1.

Marine: Cape Horn (Petit).

Var. *robusta* PETIT (1877). — V. narrow, elliptical, with acute or subcuneate ends. L. 0,09 to 0,14; B. 0,028 to 0,035 mm. convex, with a longitudinal depression on each side of the median line. Axial area indistinct. Alveoli forming three longitudinal bands and somewhat radiate striæ, 6 (middle) to 8 (ends) in 0,01 mm. — *Stauroneis robusta* PETIT D. de Campbell p. 27 Pl. V f. 16.

Marine: Campbell Island (Petit Coll.)!

Var. *angusta* CL. — V. narrow, linear-lanceolate. L. 0,12; B. 0,018 mm. Rows of alveoli 11 in 0,01 mm.

Marine: Sumbava (Kinker Coll.)! Colon (Deby Coll.)!

Var. *contermina* A. S. (1876). — V. narrow elliptical. L. 0,048; B. 0,011 to 0,012 mm. Axial area narrow. Striæ in slightly radiate, transverse, rows, about 10 in 0,01 mm., crossed by a few longitudinal blank bands. — *Nav. contermina* A. S. Atl. XLVIII f. 17, 18.

Marine: Japan (Atl.), Cape Horn (Petit).

Var. *pulchella* W. SM. (1853). — V. narrow, elliptical, gradually tapering towards the obtuse ends. L. 0,075 to 0,085; B. 0,015 to 0,02 mm. Axial area indistinct. Alveoli close, forming oblique, and slightly radiate, transverse rows, 13 to 16 in 0,01 mm. — *Stauroptera Achnanthes* EHB. Am. p. 135 Pl. III: 3 f. 7? M. Geol. XVII: 1 f. 10? *Stauroneis pulchella* W. SM. B. D. I p. 61 Pl. XIX f. 194. *Navicula aspera* DONK. B. D. X f. 1 *b*. *Stauroneis pygmæa* CASTR. Voyage Challenger p. 25 Pl. XXIX f. 7. A. S. Atl. XLVIII f. 12, 13 (no name).

Marine: North Sea! Philippines! Samoa! Sandwich Islands!

Var. *residua* A. S. (1876). — V. narrow, linear-lanceolate. L. 0,1; B. 0,012 mm. Axial area indistinct. Rows of alveoli 18 in 0,01 mm. — *Nav. residua* A. S. Atl. XLVIII f. 29.

Marine: Japan (Atl.), Cape Horn (Petit).

Asymmetrical forms.

Var. *californica* CL. — V. linear-lanceolate, obtuse. L. 0,17 to 0,22; B. 0,03 to 0,035 mm. Axial area linear, unilateral. Alveoli close, disposed in irregular, longitudinal rows, and slightly radiate, transverse rows, 6 to 7 in 0,01 mm.

Marine, fossil: Japan (Brun Coll.)! San Pedro (Kinker Coll.)! S:ta Monica Cal. (Deby Coll.)!

Var. *derasa* CL. — V. linear, obtuse. L. 0,22; B. 0,023 mm. Axial area broad and irregular, unilateral. Central area a broad fascia, reaching to the margin. Alveoli close, forming oblique rows and slightly radiate, at the ends parallel, rows, 7 in 0,01 mm.

Marine: Madagascar (Kinker Coll.)!

Var. *intermedia* GRUN. (1876). — V. narrow lanceolate to elliptic-linear. L. 0,1 to 0,19; B. 0,019 to 0,026 mm. Axial area narrow, unilateral. Alveoli forming longitudinal or oblique rows, and transverse, slightly radiate rows, 7 to 9 in 0.01 mm. — *Nav. aspera var. interm.* GRUN. A. S. Atl. XLVIII f. 14. Franz Josephs Land D. Pl. I f. 20. *Nav. aspera var. hungarica* PANT. II p. 42 Pl. X f. 180 (1889).

Marine: Greenland! Spitzbergen! Franz Josephs Land (Grun.), Finmark! Sea of Kara! Cape Deshneff! North Sea! Fossil: St. Peter, Hungary! Brünn! Sendaï, Japan!

Var. *oblonga* BAIL. (1854). — V. linear, with subcuneate ends, and frequently with a median gibbosity. L. 0,17 to 0,22; B. 0,04 to 0,05 mm. Axial area narrow, linear, unilateral. Alveoli close, in oblique and transverse rows, the latter slightly radiate, 7 to 10 in 0,01 mm. *Stauroptera oblonga* BAIL. Smiths. Contr. 1854 p. 10 f. 17. *St. oblonga?* A. S. Atl. Pl. XLVIII f. 16. *Stauroneis oblonga* CASTR. Voy. Challenger p. 24 Pl. XX f. 7 to 11.

Marine: Sydney! Kerguelens Land! South America, fossil!

Var. *rhombica* CL. — V. rhomboid. L. 0,12; B. 0,055 mm. Ends acute. Median line excentric. Axial area linear, unilateral. Central area large. Costæ near the margin transverse, 9 in 0,01 mm. Alveoli arranged in oblique rows, crossing each others in an angle of about 80°, 6 in 0,01 mm.

Marine: Galapagos Island!

Var. *perobliqua* CL. — V. linear, gradually tapering towards the obtuse ends. L. 0,158; B. 0,02 mm. Median line very excentric. Axial area indistinct. Alveoli arranged in obliqe and transverse rows, the latter 8 to 9 in 0,01 m. m. — Pl. III f. 37.

Marine: Macassar Straits (Grove Coll.)!

Var. *Amphora* BRUN (1891). — V. strongly asymmetrical. L. 0,09 to 0,14 mm. Axial area irregular, unilateral. Central area small. Alveoli arranged in oblique and transverse rows, the latter 6 in 0,01 mm. — *Nav. Amphora* BRUN De espèces n. p. 32 Pl. XV f. 3.

Marine: Port au Prince and King Georgs Sound (Brun).

Var. *Schmidtiana* GRUN. (1876). — Lanceolate, somewhat gibbous in the middle, obtuse. L. 0,08 to 0,11; B. about 0,017 mm. Axial area linear, unilateral. Alveoli distant, disposed in 2 to 3 longitudinal rows and in transverse rows, 9 to 12 in 0,01 mm. — *Nav. Schm.* A. S. Atl. XLVIII f. 19, 20.

Marine: Campeachy Bay! Galapagos Islands!

2. **T.(?) tumidula** GRUN. (1860). — V. gibbous in the middle and with broad, truncate ends. L. 0,025; B. 0,011 mm. Axial area indistinct; central area a broad fascia, reaching the margin, where it is dilated. Rows of alveoli radiate, 13 in 0,01 mm. *Stauroneis tumid.* GRUN. Verh. 1860 p. 566 Pl. VI f. 10.

Marine: Red Sea (Grun.).

I have not seen this form, which, to judge from GRUNOW's description, seems to belong to Trachyneis.

3. **T. Clepsydra** DONK. (1861). — Frustule rectangular, constricted in the middle. V. convex, linear lanceolate, with obtuse or subtruncate ends. L. 0,11 to 0,13; B. 0,02 mm. Median line

central; its terminal fissures laterally expanded. Axial area indistinct; central area rounded-quadrate. Alveoli disposed in oblique and transverse rows, the latter curved and slightly radiate, 10 in 0,01 mm. — *Nav. eleps.* DONK. M. J. I n. s. p. 8 Pl. I f. 3. B. D. p. 63 Pl. X f. 2. A. S. Atl. XLVIII f. 7—8 (no name).

Marine, aestuaries: Coasts of Scotland and England! Cape Horn (P. Petit).

Var. *scotica* A. S. (1876). — Smaller, more linear. L. 0,055 to 0,09; B. 0,015 mm. — *Nav. scotica* A. S. Atl. XLVIII f. 9—11. CL. M. D. N:o 303.

Marine: Scotland!

4. **T. Debyi** LEUD. FORTM. (1892). — V. linear-lanceolate, convex, gradually tapering towards the obtuse ends. L. 0,15 to 0,30; B. 0,025 to 0,04 mm. Axial area narrow linear, symmetrical; central area orbicular. Alveoli disposed in oblique and transverse rows, the latter parallel, 8—9 in 0,01 mm. Longitudinal fine striæ about 20 in 0,01 mm. — *Nav. clepsydra* A. S. Atl. XLVIII f. 39.

Marine and brackish: Red Sea! Sumatra (Grove Coll.)! Java (Kinker Coll.)! Singapore! China (Penang Harbour Dr. Rae Coll.)! Australia (St. Vincent, Atl.)!

Var. *osculifera* CL. — Axial area unilateral; central area with a linear marking on both sides of the central nodule. — *Alloioneis Debyi* LEUD. FORTM. D. de la Malaisie p. 18 Pl. II f. 5.

There can be no doubt that *T. Clepsydra* and *T. Debyi* are distinct species. The fig. 38 in A. S. Atl., (*Nav. cleps. var.?*) appears to be a variety of *T. aspera*, or perhaps a new species.

5. **T. Johnsoniana** GREV. (1863). — V. elliptic-lanceolate, with obtuse or subrostrate ends. L. 0,09 to 0,11; B. 0,033 to 0,037 mm. Axial area indistinct; central area, large, widened and rounded outwards. Alveoli disposed in longitudinal and transverse rows; the former about 6 in 0,01 mm.; the latter radiate throughout, 8—10 in 0,01 mm. Longitudinal fine striæ 25 in 0,01 mm. — *Nav. Johns.* GREV. T. M. S. XI p. 17 Pl. I f. 8. *Nav. Sieboldii* PANT. III Pl. XX f. 293 (1893)? *Trach. Johns.* Icon. n. Pl. III f. 38.

Marine: Java (Deby Coll.)! Queensland (Grev.). Port Jackson! New Zealand (Grev.). Japan, Sendaï Dept (Brun Coll.)!

The valve is sometimes slightly asymmetrical, the median line being excentric. The central area, rounded in typical specimens, is in some varieties dilated and truncate outwards, so that *T. Johnsoniana* is closely connected with *T. aspera*.

6. **T. Brunii** CL. (1891). — V. broadly elliptical. L. 0,068; B. 0,034 mm. Axial area indistinct; central area large, transverse, rounded outwards. Alveoli disposed in two to three longitudinal rows along the median line, in oblique rows towards the margin. Transverse rows of alveoli slightly radiate throughout, 9 (middle) to 12 (ends) in 0,01 mm. Longitudinal fine striæ about 26 in 0,01 mm. — *Nav. Brunii* CL. in Brun D. espèces n. p. 33 Pl. XVI f. 4.

Marine: Japan (Brun Coll.)! China!

This species has some resemblance to *Nav. Ovum Paschale* (A. S. Atl. Pl. VIII f. 56) also from Japan, but this form, unknown to me, has not the large central area of *T. Brunii*. It seems, nevertheless, probable that *Nav. Ovum Paschale* is a form of *Trachyneis*.

7. **T. Antillarum** CL. (1878). — V. linear-lanceolate to linear-elliptical, with obtuse ends. L. 0,12 to 0,17; B. 0,026 to 0,032 mm. Median line somewhat excentric. Axial area more or less broad, irregularly linear and unilateral. Central area rounded, unilateral, on the opposite side of the axial area. Alveoli disposed in longitudinal flexuose or irregularly oblique rows. Transverse rows slightly radiate throughout 9 to 10 in 0,01 mm. — *Alloioneis* (*Navicula?*) *Antillarum* CL. West. Ind. D. p. 8 Pl. II f. 11.

Marine and brackish: Campeachy Bay! West Indies! Florida! Red Sea! Bab el Mandeb! Madagascar! Singapore! Java! Sumatra! China!

Var. *Kurzii* GRUN. (1878). — V. rhombic-lanceolate, with rounded ends. L. 0,09 to 0,105; B. 0,036 mm. Median line strongly excentric. Axial area semilanceolate, unilateral. Alveoli disposed in oblique rows, crossing each other in an angle of about 80°, and about 7 in 0,01 mm. Transverse costæ marginal, 10—11 in 0,01 mm. — *Nav.* (*Alloioneis?*) *Kurzii* GRUN. in Cl. West Ind. D. p. 8 Pl. II f. 12.

Brackish water: Elephant Point, India (Grun.), Singapore! Sumatra (Grove Coll.)!

8. **T. velata** A. S. (1876). — V. lanceolate, gradually tapering to the obtuse ends. L. 0,07 to 0,13; B. 0,02 to 0,022 mm. Axial area very narrow or unilateral; central area small, rounded. Alveoli rectangular, disposed in irregular, oblique rows and in transverse rows; the latter almost parallel or slightly radiate at the ends, 15—16 in 0,01 mm. Fine longitudinal striæ 25 in 0,01 mm. — *Nav. velata* A. S. Atl. Pl. XLVIII f. 33—34; f. 35—37 (no name). *Nav. australis* PETIT Cape Horn p. 125 (1888).

Marine: Cape Good Hope (Atl.), Madagascar! Mauritius! Ceylon! King Georges Sound (Grove Coll.)! Sumatra! Java! China! Japan! Sandwich Islands! New Caledonia! Cape Horn (Petit).

Additional.

Under the name *Navicula Paludinarum* PANTOCSEK has recently figured an apparently very curious form, which ought perhaps to be included in a proper genus. The valve is lanceolate, obtuse. L. 0,115; B. 0,038 mm. Axial area moderately broad, slightly dilated in the middle. Striæ costate, 8 in 0,01 mm., radiate throughout and alternating with single rows of large ocelli(?) — PANT. III Pl. IX f. 144. Var. *gracilior* l. c. Pl. XI f. 186. Fresh water? Bodos (Pant.).

Having had no opportunity of examining this remarkable form I am unable to decide as to its place in the system.

Mastoneis Cl. N. Gen.

Valve with double structure. The exterior stratum with transverse striæ, composed of puncta; the interior with transverse costæ, directed from the margin, where they are thicker, towards the median line.

The only known species has been placed by GREVILLE and GRUNOW in the genus *Stauroneis*, but it has no close relation to any species of that genus, and the peculiar structure of the valve makes it advisable to form for it a new genus. I am unable to point out any close relation between this form and any other, although its general appearance has some resemblance to some Mastogloiæ.

1. **M. biformis** GRUN. (1863). — V. elliptical with rostrate extremities. L. 0,08 to 0,09; B. 0,032 to 0,035 mm. Median lines with approximate median pores and small terminal fissures, turned in the same direction. Central nodule transversely dilated into a very short stauros. No axial area. Striæ slightly radiate, 15 (middle) to 18 (ends) in 0,01 mm. punctate; puncta about 20 in 0,01 mm. Costæ 8—9 in 0,01 mm. — *Stauroneis biformis* GRUN. Verh. 1863 p. 154 Pl. IV f. 7. *Stauroneis australis* GREV. Ed. N. Ph. J. V. XVIII p. 187 f. 13 1863.

Marine: Queensland (Grev.), Red Sea (Kinker Coll.)! Port Jackson! Labuan!

Plate I.

PLATE I.

Fig. 1. Amphiprora paludosa var. subsalina CL. — Artern, $^{500}/_{1}$ . . .
2. A. alata var. japonica CL. — Japan, $^{500}/_{1}$ . . . .
3. A. marginepunctata CL. — Japan, $^{500}/_{1}$ . . . .
4. A. Brébissoniana GREV. — Sendaï, $^{500}/_{1}$ . . . .
5. A. lata GREV. — Balearic Islands, $^{500}/_{1}$ . . . .
6. A. gigantea GRUN. — Macassar Straits, $^{500}/_{1}$ . . . .
7, 8. Auricula minuta CL. — Bohuslän, $^{1000}/_{1}$ . . . .
9. Scoliopleura elegans CL. — Java, $^{500}/_{1}$ . . . .
10. Cymatoneis circumvallata CL. — Labuan, $^{1000}/_{1}$ . . . .
11. Japan, $^{1000}/_{1}$ . . . .
12. C. sulcata GREV. — Madagascar, $^{500}/_{1}$ . . . .
13. var. — Japan, $^{1000}/_{1}$ . . . .
14. Scoliopleura Peisonis GRUN. — Utah, $^{1000}/_{1}$ . . . .
15. Diploneis bioculata var. vittata CL. — Ceylon, $^{850}/_{1}$ . . . . .
16. Scoliotropis Gilliesii CL. (schematic) — Jamaica, $^{500}/_{1}$ . . . .
17. Diploneis inscripta CL. — China, $^{500}/_{1}$ . . . .
18. D. Letourneurii CL. — Ceylon, $^{500}/_{1}$ . . . .
19. D. fusca, var. Van Heurckii CL. — South Sea, $^{1000}/_{1}$ . . . . .
20. D. Schmidtii CL. — Galapagos Islands, $^{500}/_{1}$ . . . .
21. — Seychelles, $^{500}/_{1}$ . . . .
22. D. bomboides var. madagascarensis CL. — Madagascar, $^{500}/_{1}$ . .
23. D. fusca var. japonica CL. — Sendaï, $^{500}/_{1}$ . . . .
24. Navicula Ny CL. — Java, $^{1000}/_{1}$ . . . .
25. Diploneis chinensis CL. — China, $^{500}/_{1}$ . . . .
26. D. bombiformis CL. — Macassar Straits, $^{1000}/_{1}$ . . . .
27. D. subovalis CL. — New Zealand, $^{1000}/_{1}$ . . . .
28. D. areolata CL. — S:ta Monica, $^{500}/_{1}$ . . . .
29. D. Clepsydra CL. — Madagascar, $^{500}/_{1}$ . . . .
30. Navicula lauta GRUN. — South Yarra, $^{500}/_{1}$ . . . .
31. Cistula Lorenziana GRUN. — Campeachy Bay, $^{1000}/_{1}$ . . . . .
32, 33. Navicula mediterranea BRUN a. CL. — Naples, $^{500}/_{1}$ . . .

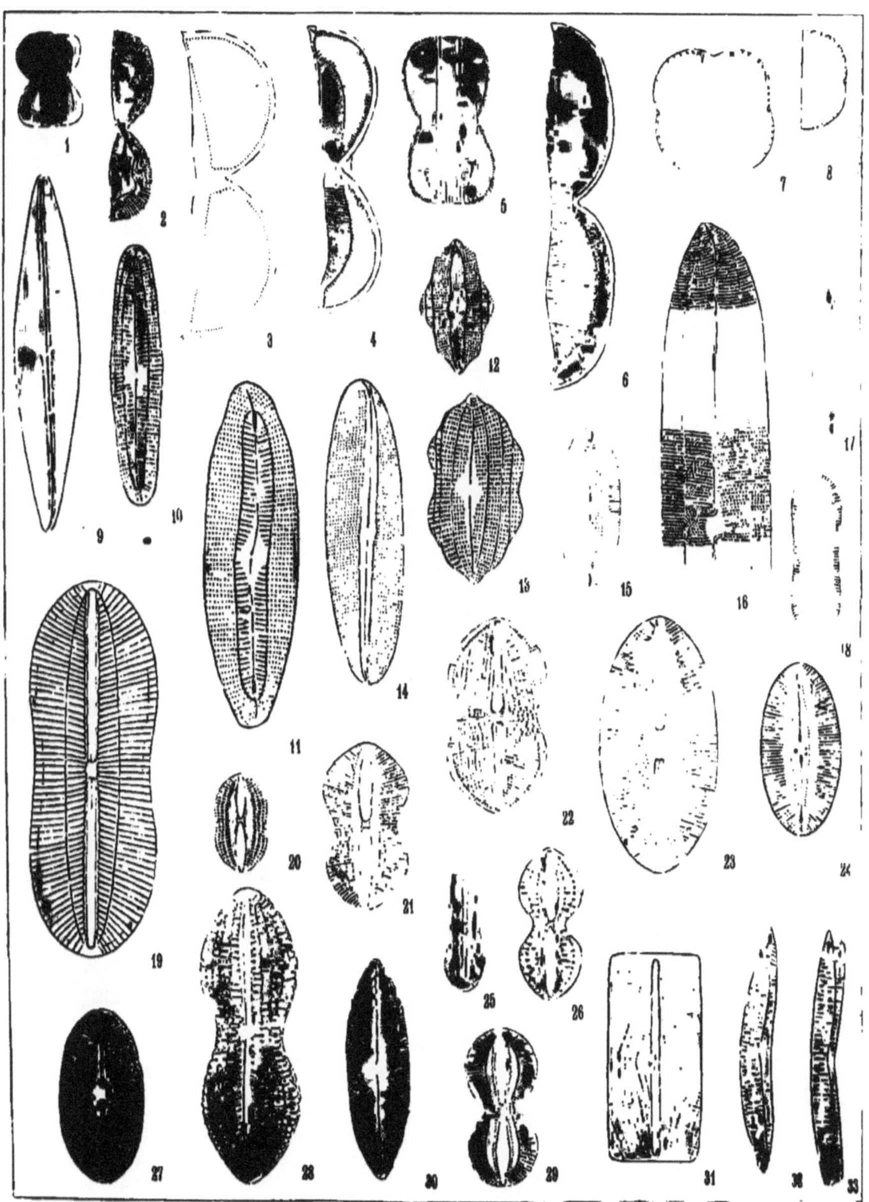

Del. P. T. Cleve

Ljustr. Gen. Stab. Lit. Anst. Sthlm.

Plate II.

PLATE II.

		Page.
Fig. 1.	Diploneis Microtatos var. Christiani T. C. — Maryland. $\frac{1000}{1}$	96.
2.	D. domblittensis GRUN. — Lefra sjö, Sweden, $\frac{1000}{1}$	91.
3.	D. fusca var. oamaruensis CL. — Oamaru, $\frac{500}{1}$	94.
4.	D. Debyi var. elliptica CL. — Red Sea, $\frac{500}{1}$	98.
5.	D. Vespa CL. — Java $\frac{1000}{1}$	97.
6.	D. Platessa CL. and GROVE — Macassar Straits, $\frac{500}{1}$	97.
7.	D. Szontaghii PANT. — Sumbava, $\frac{500}{1}$	99.
8.	D. Crabro var. Didelta CL. — Sumbava, $\frac{500}{1}$	101.
9.	D. Crabro var. Pandurella CL. — China, $\frac{500}{1}$	101.
10.	D. Crabro var. hungarica CL. — Szákal, $\frac{500}{1}$	101.
11.	D. Crabro var. subelliptica CL. — Galapagos Islands, $\frac{500}{1}$	101.
12.	D. Crabro var. O'Meari GRUN. — Macassar Straits, $\frac{500}{1}$	102.
13.	D. vagabunda BRUN. — S:n Pedro Calif., $\frac{500}{1}$	103.
14.	D. biseriata var. lata CL. — Galapagos Islands, $\frac{500}{1}$	103.
15.	D. vagabunda BRUN. — S:ta Monica, Calif., $\frac{500}{1}$	103.
16.	D. biseriata var. galapagensis CL. — Galapagos Islands $\frac{500}{1}$	103.
17, 18.	D. lesinensis GRUN. — Adriatic	104.
19.	Tropidoneis solidula CL. — Rembang Bay, $\frac{500}{1}$	25.
20, 21.	» » (parts of the valve) $\frac{1000}{1}$	
22.	Auricula javanica CL. — Sumbava, $\frac{500}{1}$	21.
23.	A. pulchra GREV. — Macassar Straits, $\frac{500}{1}$	20.

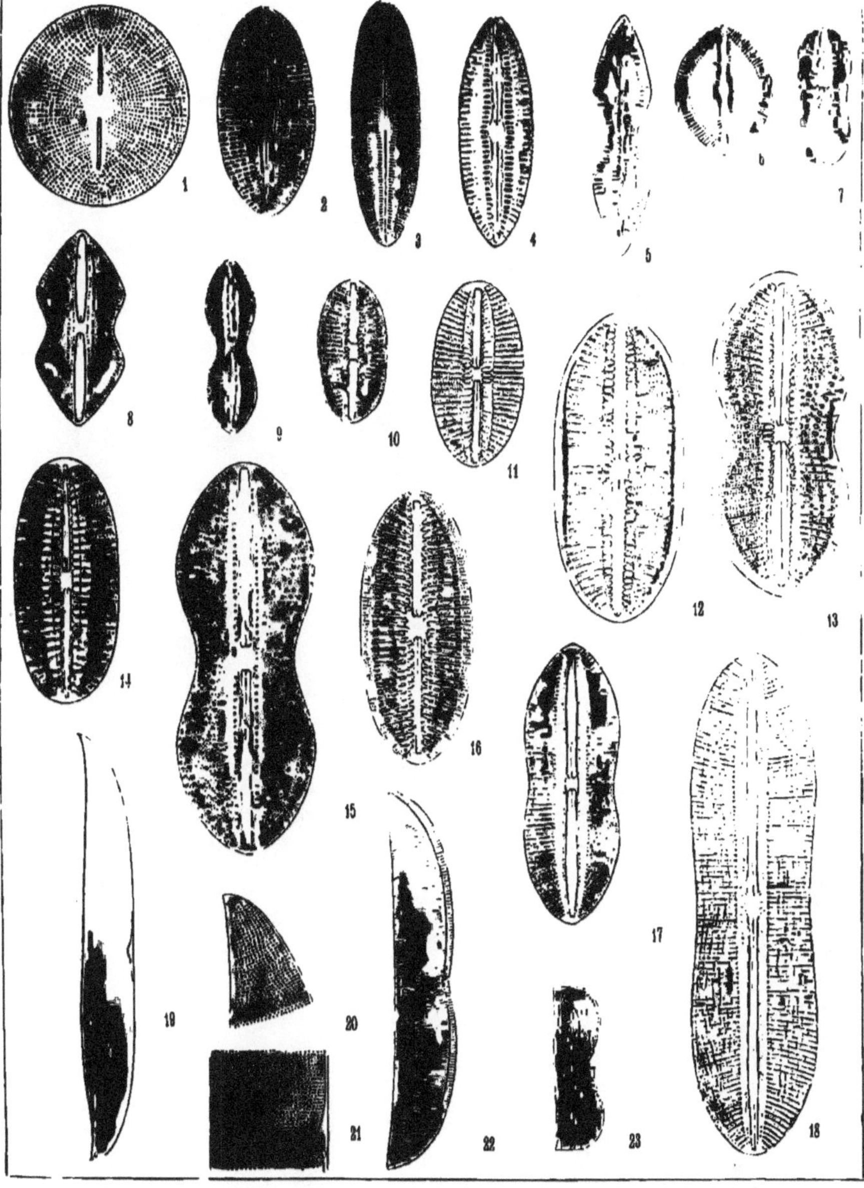

1
2
3
4
5
6
7
8
9
10
11
12
13
14
15
16
17
18
19
20
21
22
23

Plate III.

PLATE III.

Fig. 1. Tropidoneis Kinkeriana CL. — Sumbava, $^{500}/_{1}$

» 2. » » (structure) $^{1000}/_{1}$

» 3. T. lata CL. — Rembang Bay, $^{500}/_{1}$

4. (Part of the valve) $^{1000}/_{1}$

5, 6. T. chinensis CL. — China, $^{500}/_{1}$

7. » (part of the valve) $^{1000}/_{1}$

8. T. longa CL. — Finmark, $^{500}/_{1}$

9, 10, 11. T. semistriata GRUN. — South Africa, $^{500}/_{1}$

» 12. Navicula Perrotettii GRUN. — Brazil, $^{500}/_{1}$

13. » Stodderi v. insignis GRUN. — Bengal, $^{500}/_{1}$

» 14. » quarnerensis GRUN. — Sumatra, $^{500}/_{1}$

» 15. (Stauroneis) Demeraræ CL. — Demerara, $^{500}/_{1}$

» 16. hamulifera GRUN. — Balearic Islands $^{500}/_{1}$

17. Barbados, $^{500}/_{1}$

18. (part of the valve) $^{1000}/_{1}$

19. var. interrupta CL. — Japan, $^{500}/_{1}$

20. Tropidoneis approximata CL. — Rembang Bay, $^{250}/_{1}$

21. » » (part of the valve) $^{1000}/_{1}$

22, 23. adriatica CL. — Adriatic, $^{250}/_{1}$

» 24. maxima var. decussata CL. — Seychelles, $^{500}/_{1}$

25. » direction of the striæ

» 26. Caloneis Frater CL. — Galapagos Islands, $^{500}/_{1}$

27. N. (Stauroneis) Phyllodes EHB. — Demerara, $^{500}/_{1}$

» 28. N. plicatula GRUN. — Naples, $^{500}/_{1}$

29. N. Aeus CL. — Balearic Islands, $^{500}/_{1}$

30. (parts of the valve) $^{1000}/_{1}$

31. N. suavis CL. and GROVE. — Oamaru, $^{500}/_{1}$

32. (parts of the valve), $^{1000}/_{1}$

33. Caloneis adenensis CL. — Bab-el-mandeb, $^{500}/_{1}$

34. C. columbiensis CL. — Columbia River, $^{1000}/_{1}$

» 35. N. Rho CL. — Canton River, $^{500}/_{1}$

36. N. portomontana CL. — Puerto Monte. $^{1000}/_{1}$

37. Trachyneis aspera var. perobliqua CL. — Macassar Straits, $^{500}/_{1}$

38. T. Johnsoniana GREV. — Sendaï, $^{500}/_{1}$

» 39, 40. Caloneis Wardii CL. — Connecticut, $^{500}/_{1}$

41. (part of the valve) $^{1000}/_{1}$

» 42. C. bottnica CL. — Piteå, $^{1000}/_{1}$

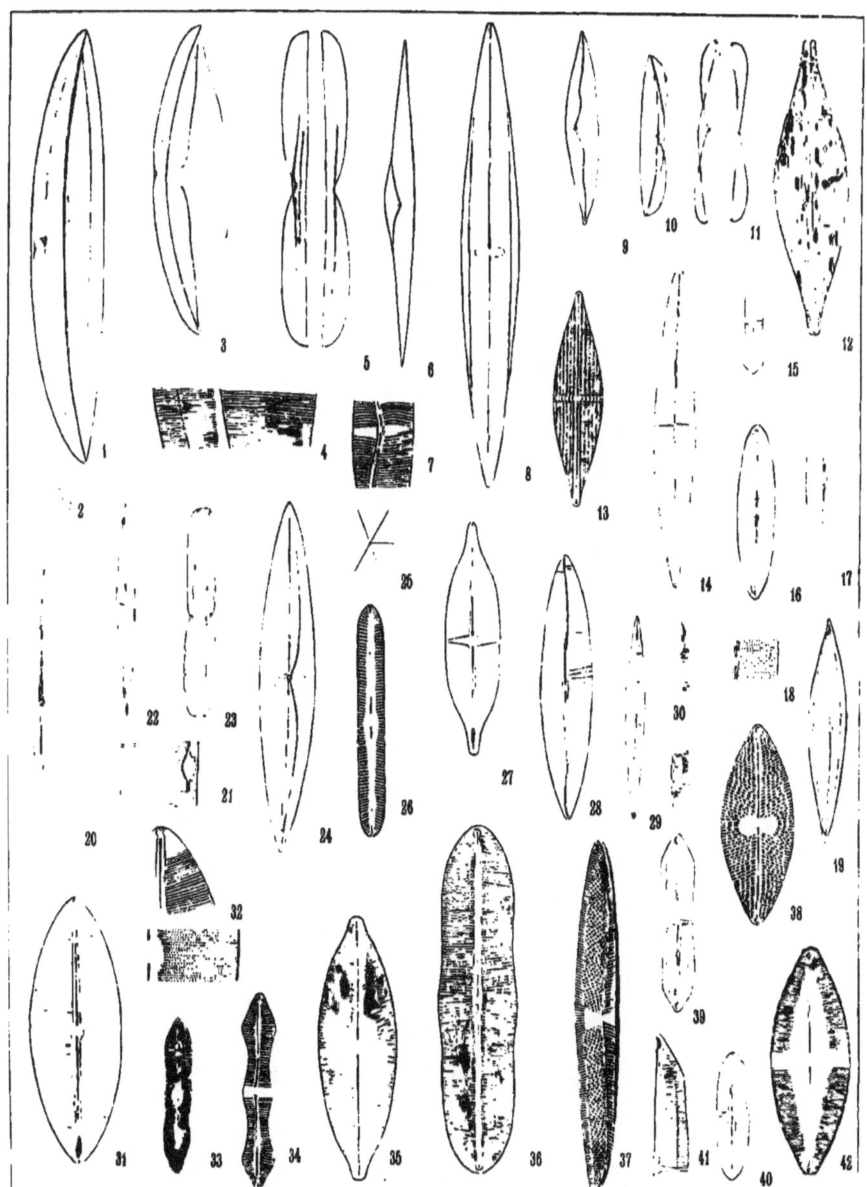
1
2
3
4
5
6
7
8
9
10
11
12
13
14
15
16
17
18
19
20
21
22
23
24
25
26
27
28
29
30
31
32
33
34
35
36
37
38
39
40
41
42

Plate IV.

PLATE IV.

Fig. 1. Caloneis Liber var. Bleischiana JAN. and RABH. — Nice. $^{500}/_{1}$
2. C. eximia GRUN. Cebu, $^{500}/_{1}$
3. C. clavigera CL. — Colon, $^{500}/_{1}$
4. C. Dusenii CL. — Cameroon, $^{500}/_{1}$
5. C. latiuscula var. africana CL. — Cameroon, $^{500}/_{1}$
6, 7. C. abnormis GRUN. — Lysekil, $^{1000}/_{1}$
8. Navicula H. album CL. — China, $^{500}/_{1}$
9. „ „ (part of the valve) $^{1000}/_{1}$
10. N. Ypsilon CL. — Bory, $^{500}/_{1}$
11. N. clavata var. rhombica CL. — Morocco, $^{500}/_{1}$
12. N. venustissima KITTON — Hongkong, $^{500}/_{1}$
13. N. irrorata var. elliptica CL. — Hungary, $^{500}/_{1}$
14. N. Hennedyii var. Centraster CL. — Mexillones, $^{500}/_{1}$
15. Pleurosigma majus GRUN. — Sumatra. $^{225}/_{1}$
16. P. galapagense CL. — Galapagos Islands, $^{500}/_{1}$
17. P. Exsul CL. — Naples, $^{500}/_{1}$
18. P. formosum var. Arcus CL. — Macassar Straits, $^{500}/_{1}$
19. P. minutum GRUN. — Malmö, $^{500}/_{1}$
20. P. Heros CL. — Macassar Straits, $^{225}/_{1}$
21. P. formosum var. dalmatica GRUN. — Balearic Islands, $^{225}/_{1}$
22. P. umbilicatum CL. — Labuan, $^{500}/_{1}$
23. Cymbella hybrida GRUN. — Fårön, $^{1000}/_{1}$
24. C. Hauckii VAN HEURCK — Triest, $^{1000}/_{1}$
25. C. oregonica CL. — Oregon $^{1000}/_{1}$
26. C. acutiuscula CL. — Waltham Mass. $^{1000}/_{1}$
27. C. lata GRUN. — Piteå, $^{1000}/_{1}$
28. C. lapponica GRUN. — Gellivaara, $^{1000}/_{1}$

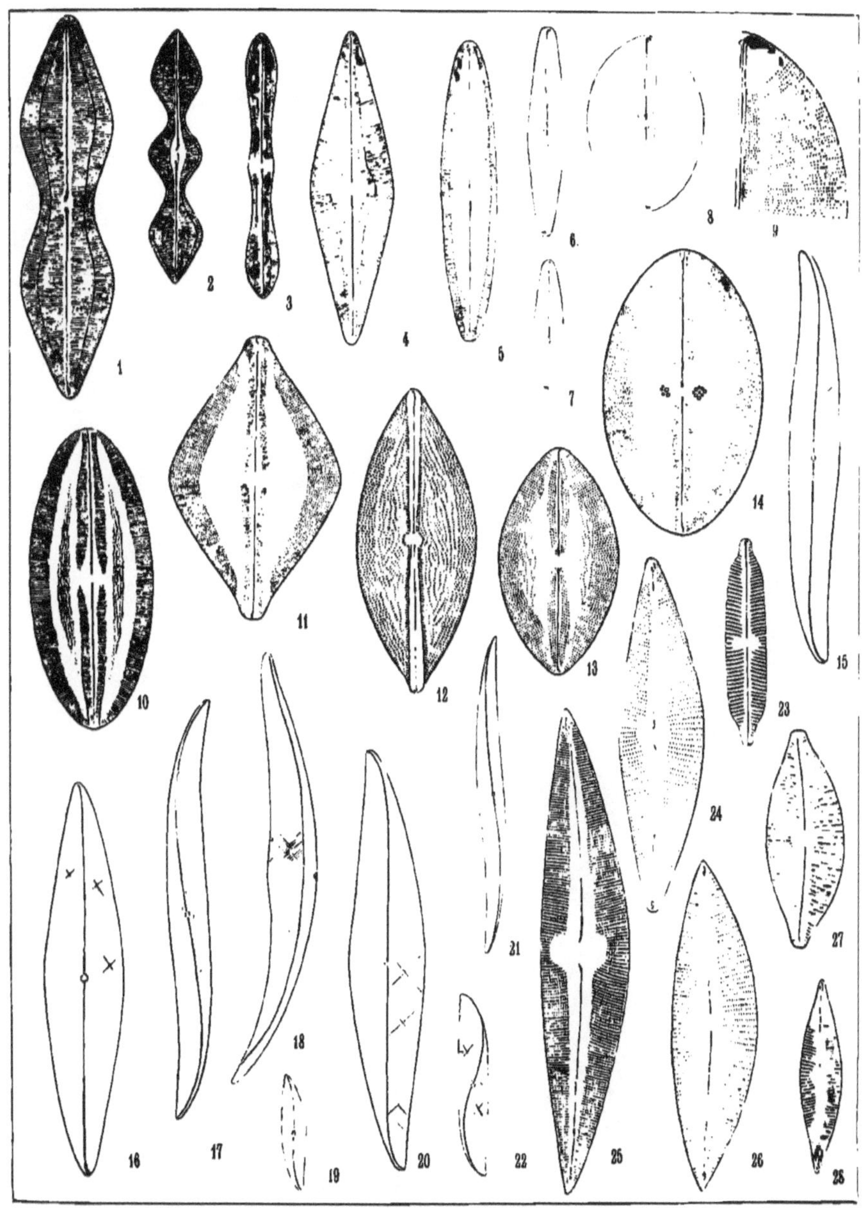
1
2
3
4
5
6.
7
8
9
10
11
12
13
14
15
16
17
18
19
20
21
22
23
24
25
26
27
28

Plate V.

PLATE V.

Fig.		Page
Fig. 1.	Cymbella inelegans CL. — Pitt River, $^{1000}/_1$	168.
2.	C. Stuxbergii CL. — Jenissey, $^{1000}/_1$	173.
3, 4.	C. Jordani GRUN. — Otago, New Zealand, $^{1000}/_1$	169.
5.	Navicula Lunula CL. — Java, $^{1000}/_1$	Part II.
6, 7.	Gomphonema Berggrenii CL. — New Zealand, $^{1000}/_1$	185.
8.	G. validum CL. var. elongata CL. — Demerara, $^{500}/_1$	185.
9.	G. validum CL. — Demerara, $^{500}/_1$	185.
10.	G. oxycephalum CL. — Demerara, $^{500}/_1$	187.
11, 12.	G. Salinarum PANT. — Rügen, $^{1000}/_1$	187.
13.	G. ventricosum var. maxima CL. — Pitt River, $^{1000}/_1$	187.
14.	Navicula Bacillum EHB. var. lepida GRUN. — Lojo Finland, $^{1000}/_1$	137.
15.	N. aucklandica GRUN. — Port Jackson, $^{1000}/_1$	156.
16.	N. inelegens GROVE & STURT var. Oamaru, $^{500}/_1$	155.
17.	N. gibbula CL. — Spitsbergen, $^{1000}/_1$	140.
18.	N. Lundströmii var. Friesana GRUN. — Finmark, $^{1000}/_1$	140.
19.	N. Lambda CL. — Demerara, $^{1000}/_1$	136.
20.	N. monmouthiana GRUN. — Monmouth, $^{1000}/_1$	134.
21.	N. Kappa CL. — Oamaru, $^{1000}/_1$	134.
22.	N. Iota CL. — Madagascar, $^{500}/_1$	134.
23.	» (structure) $^{1000}/_1$	»
24.	N. definita GROVE & STURT var. intermedia CL. — Oamaru, $^{500}/_1$	135.
25.	» » (structure) $^{1000}/_1$	
26.	N. obliqua GREG. — Windermere, $^{1000}/_1$	130.
27.	N. fallax CL. — Oamaru, $^{500}/_1$	135.
28.	Stenoneis inconspicua GREG. — Balearic Islands, $^{1000}/_1$	124.
29.	Frustulia vulgaris var. asymmetrica CL. — Newark, $^{500}/_1$	122.
30.	Navicula Beta CL. — Japan, $^{1000}/_1$	135.
31.	Dictyoneis subconstricta CL. — Madagascar, $^{500}/_1$	31.
32.	D. jamaicensis GREV. — Alexandria	30.
33.	D. Thumii CL. — China, $^{500}/_1$	31.
34.	D. naviculacea CL. — Pensacola, $^{500}/_1$	30.
35.	D. jamaicensis var. gigantea CL. — Oamaru, $^{500}/_1$	30.
36.	» » » (structure) $^{1000}/_1$	

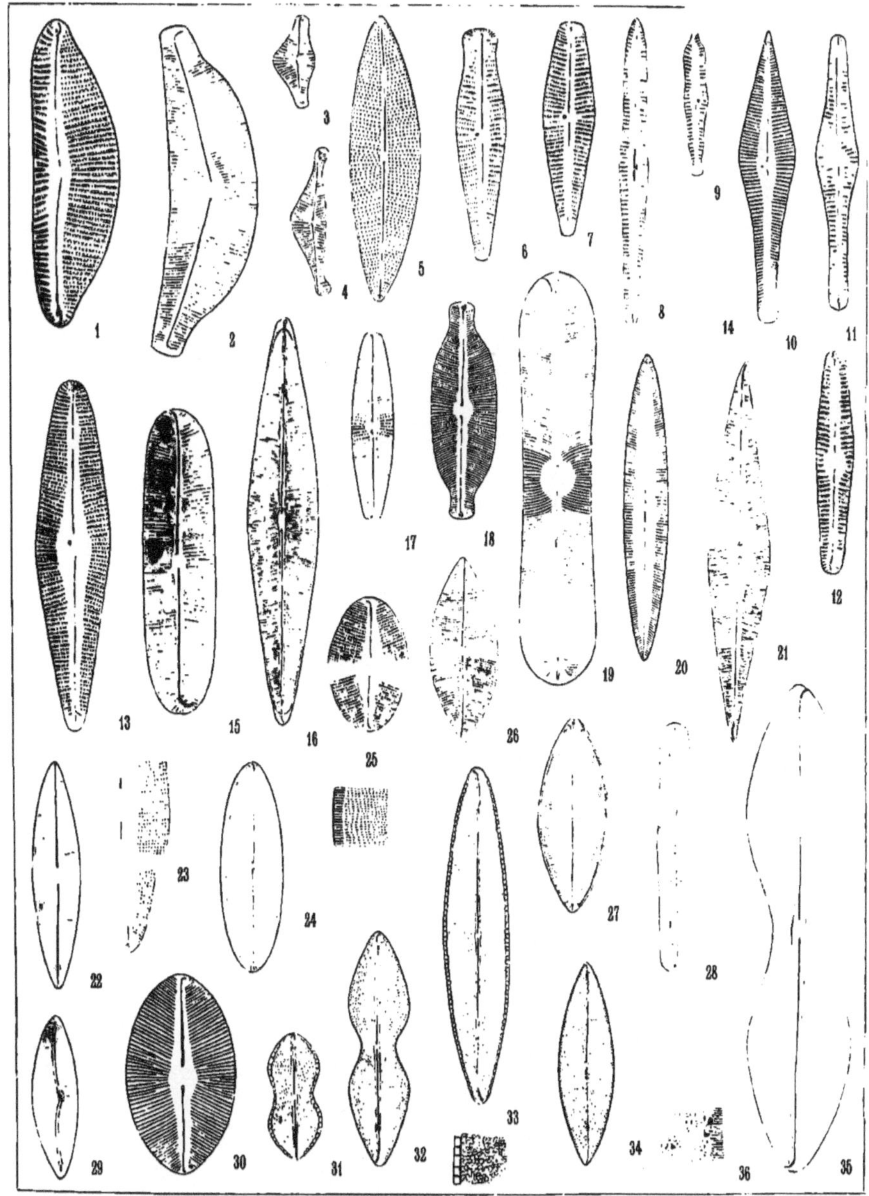
1
2
3
4
5
6
7
8
9
10
11
12
13
14
15
16
17
18
19
20
21
22
23
24
25
26
27
28
29
30
31
32
33
34
35
36

Corrigenda.

Page 19, line 4 and 5, instead of *A. incerta* read *A. insecta*

Page 23, line 7, instead of Tropidoneis concerta read Tropidoneis conserta

P. T., Synopsis of the Naviculoid diatoms.

SYNOPSIS

OF

THE NAVICULOID DIATOMS

BY

P. T. CLEVE.

PART II.

WITH 4 PLATES.

RESENTED TO THE R. SWEDISH ACADEMY OF SCIENCES MAY 10, 1893.

STOCKHOLM 1895.
KUNGL. BOKTRYCKERIET. P. A. NORSTEDT & SÖNER.

Naviculæ Minusculæ Cl.

Valve small, broadly lanceolate to elliptical, slightly silicious. Areas indistinct. Structure slightly radiate, very fine or indistinct striæ. Connecting zone not complex.

The species of this group are usually of extremely small size, and live in fresh or salt water.

Artificial key.

1.	Marine species	2.
	Fresh-water species	3.
2.	Valve elliptical	*N. debilissima* Grun.
	— lanceolate	*N. bahusiensis* Grun.
3.	Striæ coarse (17 in 0,01 mm)	*N. lucidula* Grun.
	— fine (30 and more in 0,01 mm.)	4.
4.	Valve elliptical	5.
	— lanceolate	8.
5.	Striæ indistinct	*N. pelliculosa* Bréb.
	— about 30 in 0,01 mm.	6.
6.	Striæ radiate	*N. atomus* Naegeli.
	— parallel	7.
7.	Valve broadly elliptical	*N. muralis* Grun.
	— narrow	*N. exilissima* Grun.
8.	Valve broadly lanceolate	*N. minuscula* Grun.
	- narrow	*N. microcephala* Grun.

1. **N. pelliculosa** (Bréb.) Hilse (1862). — V. very slightly silicious, elliptical, with broad and rounded ends. L. 0,009; B. 0,004 to 0,005 mm. Striæ extremely fine. — *Frustulia pellic.* Bréb. (according to Grunow). *Frustulia sp.* Grun. Verh. 1860 p. 573 Pl. VII f. 18. *Nav. pell.* Hilse Rabh. A. E. № 1265. V. H. Syn. Pl. XIV f. 32.

Fresh water: Germany (A. E.), France (Bréb.).

2. **N. debilissima** Grun. (1884). — V. elliptic-lanceolate L. 0,007; B. 0,005 mm. Striæ not seen. — Franz Jos. Land D. p. 104 (52) Pl. I f. 42.

Marine: Franz Josefs Land.

3. **N. muralis** Grun. (1880). — V. elliptical, with rounded ends. L. 0,006 to 0,012; B. 0,004 mm. Areas indistinct. Striæ very slightly radiate, about 30 in 0,01 mm. — V. H. Syn. Pl. XIV f. 26 to 28. *N. Atomus* Schum. P. D. I Nachtr. p. 21 f. 24?

Fresh water.

4. **N. exilissima** Grun. (1880). — V. linear-elliptical. L. 0,005 to 0,01; B. 0,003 mm. Areas indistinct. Striæ about 40 in 0,01 mm., almost parallel; the median more distant. — V. H. Syn. p. 108 Pl. XIV f. 30.

Fresh water: Belgium (V. H.).

5. **N. microcephala** Grun. (1880). V. lanceolate, obtuse. L. 0,014; B. 0,003 mm. Areas indistinct. Striæ nearly parallel, about 30 in 0,01 mm. — V. H. Syn. Pl. XIV f. 29. *Achnanthidium micror.* W. Sm. B. D. II p. 31 Suppl. Pl. LXI f. 380 (1856)?

Fresh water.

6. **N. Atomus** Naegeli (1849). — V. elliptical, with rounded ends, slightly silicious. L. 0,004 to 0,008; B. 0,0025 to 0,004 mm. Areas indistinct. Striæ about 30 in 0,01 mm. strongly radiate throughout. — *Synedra At.* Naegeli in Kütz Sp. Alg. p. 40 (according to Grunow). *N. At.* Grun. Verh. 1860 p. 552 Pl. IV f. 6. V. H. Syn. p. 107 Pl. XIV f. 24, 25.

Fresh water (Moist earth etc.): Belgium (V. H.).

7. **N. (Diadesmis) lucidula** Grun. (1880). — V. elliptical, with broad, rounded ends. L. 0,015 to 0,019; B. 0,0085 to 0,01 mm. Areas indistinct. Striæ 17 in 0,01 mm. slightly radiate throughout, distinctly punctate, puncta forming longitudinal rows, about 17 in 0,01 mm. — V. H. Syn. Pl. XIV f. 40.

Fresh water.

8. **N. minuscula** Grun. (1880). — V. elliptic-lanceolate, with obtuse ends. L. 0,012; B. 0,005 mm. Areas indistinct. Striæ about 30 in 0,01 mm. almost parallel. — V. H. Syn. Pl. XIV f. 3.

Fresh water.

9. **N. bahusiensis** Grun. (1880). — V. broadly lanceolate, with subrostrate ends. L. 0,013 to 0,02; B. 0,006 mm. Areas indistinct. Striæ 25 in 0,01 mm. almost parallel. — *N. minusc. v. bah.* V. H. Syn. Pl. XIV f. 2.

Marine: West coast of Sweden!

Var. *istriana* Grun. (1880). — V. more lanceolate. Striæ 22 in 0,01 mm. — V. H. Syn. Pl. XIV f. 4.

Marine: Adriatic (Grun.).

Var. *arctica* Grun. (1884). — V. broadly lanceolate. L. 0,02 to 0,021; B. 0,0095 mm. Striæ 21 in 0,01 mm. radiate throughout. — Fr. Jos. Land, D. p. 104 (52) Pl. I f. 43.

Marine: Franz Josefs Land (Grun.).

Naviculæ Decussatæ Grun. (1860 p. p.).

Valve elongated, elliptical, or lanceolate, symmetrical, not sigmoid. Structure: puncta arranged in obliquely decussating rows.

This small group comprises three isolated forms, which seem not to be allied to each other. *N. Placentula* is a fresh-water species, perhaps akin to the *Punctatæ*, although it has no nearly allied species in that group. *N. decussata* is too imperfectly described to decide what are its affinities. The termination of the median line at a distance from the ends suggests an affinity to the section *Microstigmaticæ* (division *Libellus*). *N. Quincunx* is an entirely isolated form, the structure of which recalls that of some Mastogloiæ, but from the straight median line it may be inferred that it really is a Navicula.

1. **N. Placenta** Ehb. (1854). — V. elliptical, with rostrate-capitate ends. L. 0,037 to 0,039; B. 0,015 to 0,017 mm. Axial area indistinct. Central area small, orbicular. Transverse striæ 22 (middle) to 27 (ends) in 0,01 mm. slightly radiate. Oblique striæ curved, crossing each other at an angle of about 80°. — M. G. XXXIII, 12 f. 23. Lewis Proc. acad. nat. sci. Philad. p. 7 Pl. II f. 7 (1865). Grun. A. D. p. 47 Pl. III f. 60. *N. apiculata* Greg. M. J. IV p. 4 Pl. I f. 13 (1856). *N. Rostellum* W. Sm. B. D. II p. 93 (1856). Grun. Verh. 1860 p. 550 Pl. IV f. 10. Donk. B. D. p. 40 Pl. VI f. 7.

Fresh water: Finmark! Scotland! Lule Lappmark! Finland, Kuopio! Hungary, Neusiedler-see (Grun.), New Zealand!

This species seems not to be allied to any other.

2. **N. decussata** (KÜTZ 1859?) PETIT (1877). — V. narrow elliptical. L. 0,03 to 0,039; B. 0,0077 mm. Median line ending at a considerable distance from the margin of the valve. Axial and central areas indistinct. Puncta disposed in obliquely decussating rows. — KÜTZ Sp. alg. p. 70? PETIT Ile Camph. D. p. 23 Pl. IV f. 11.

Marine: New Zealand (Pet.).

I am not acquainted with this species, which in the outline, and the distance between the ends of the median line and the margin, has some resemblance to *Navicula Grevillei*.

3. **N. Quincunx** CL. (1892). — V. lanceolate. L. 0,085; B. 0,024 mm. Axial area indistinct; central area very small, orbicular. Transverse striæ 17 in 0,01 mm. almost parallel. Puncta 12 in 0,01 mm., forming oblique rows (14 in 0.01 mm.) crossing each other at an angle of about 80°. — Diatomiste I p. 76 Pl. XII f. 6.

Marine: China (Van Heurck Coll., Deby Coll.)!

Anomoeoneis PFITZER (1871).

Valve usually lanceolate, not constricted. Central nodule small. Median line central. Structure: small puncta, arranged in transverse, frequently marginal, striæ, and longitudinal, undulating or oblique rows. Axial area narrow. Central area unilaterally dilated, or uniting with lateral areas in a lyriform space. Cell-contents (in *A. sphærophora*) with a single chromatophore-plate, along the inside of one of the walls of the zone and of the valves. The plate has a narrow and deep fissure along the zonal-wall and opposite to the side with the asymmetrical central area, broader sinuses along the ends of the median line and, a sinus below the central area (Pfitzer, Bau u. Entw. p. 78). — In conjugation *A. serians* is similar to *Frustulia* (CARTER).

This genus was founded by PFITZER especially for *Nav. sphærophora* and probably for *Nav. sculpta*, principally on the cell-contents. As to *Nav. serians* PFITZER hesitates to place it either in this genus or in *Neidium*. There is no resemblance between *Nav. serians* and the forms of *Neidium*, but its structure agrees more with that of *A. sphærophora*, so it may be placed in the neighbourhood of the latter, although it has not the unilaterally dilated central area of the latter. Some of the Naviculæ, recently described by PANTOKSEK, seem to be related to *A. sphærophora* and I have included them in Anomoeoneis.

As this genus is founded principally on the characteristics of the cell-contents, and those of most of the species have not yet been examined, the genus is not well established and requires further examination of living specimens.

Artificial key.

1.	Valve with rostrate or capitate ends	2.
	— — non- non- —	5.
2.	Larger forms. L. 0,04 to 0,08 mm.	3.
	Smaller L. 0,02 to 0,03 mm.	4.
3.	Central area rounded, asymmetrical	*A. sphærophora* KÜTZ.
	— — a transverse fascia	*A. menilitica* PANT.
	— — dilated to lunate lateral areas	*A. sculpta* EHR.
4.	Valve trachiform	*A. Follis* EHR.
	— lanceolate	*A. exilis* GRUN.
5.	Valve linear, slightly biconstricted	6.
	— lanceolate, not biconstricted	7.

6.	Central pores approximate	*A. bipunctata* Grun.
	— distant	*A. zellensis* Grun.
7.	Central area a transverse fascia	*A. Macraeana* Pant.
	— — not dilated	8.
8.	Ends acute	*A. serians* Bréb.
	— obtuse	9.
9.	Larger forms L. 0,1 mm.	*A. polygramma* Ehr.
	Smaller — L. 0,02 to 0,05 mm.	*A. brachysira* Grun.

1. **A. sphærophora** Kütz (1844). — V. elliptic-lanceolate with rostrate-capitate ends. L. 0,055 to 0,08; B. 0,017 to 0,02 mm. Axial area narrow, linear. Central area irregularly rounded, larger on one side of the valve than on the other. Striæ slightly radiate throughout, 16 in 0,01 mm. — *Navic. sphærophora* Kütz Bac. p. 95 Pl. IV f. 17. W. Sm. B. D. 1 Pl. XVII f. 148. V. H. Syn. p. 101 Pl. XII f. 2. A. S. Atl. XLIX f. 49—51.

Fresh or slightly brackish water: Sweden! England! Switzerland! East Indies! New Zealand! Illinois! Guatemala! West Indies (St. Martin! Jamaica!) Ecuador!

Var. *biceps* Ehr. (1843). — Smaller. L. 0.04; B. 0.013. Striæ finer. *Nav. biceps* Ehr. Am. p. p. Schum. 1 Nachtr. p. 21 f. 26. A. S. Atl. XLIX f. 52. *N. sphæroph. v. minor* V. H. Syn. Pl. XII f. 3. *N. sphæroph. subcap.* Grun. Foss. D. Öst. Ung. p. 157.

Slightly brackish water: Franzenbad (Atl.). Eger foss!

2. **A. sculpta** Ehr. (1840). — V. lanceolate, with protracted, rostrate, and obtuse ends L. 0,07 to 0,1; B. 0,025 to 0,036 mm. Axial area narrow, linear, bordered by a single row of puncta, 16 in 0,01 mm. Central area uniting with large, lunate lateral areas, of which one expands in the middle to the margin. Striæ 15 to 16 in 0,01 mm., slightly radiate, distinctly punctate; puncta crowded near the margin, distant towards the lateral areas, where they are arranged in oblique, somewhat undulating rows. *Nav. sculpta* Ehr. Ber. 1840 p. 18. M. G. X: 1, f. 5. Fresenius Senckenb. Abh. IV Pl. IV f. 14 to 16. A. S. Atl. XLIX f. 46 to 48. V. H. Syn. p. 100 Pl. XII f. 1. Pant. II, XI f. 191. *N. rostrata* Kütz. Bac. p. 94 Pl. III f. 45 (1844). Donk. B. D. p. 15 Pl. II f. 9. Grun. Verh. 1860 p. 540. *N. tumens* W. Sm. B. D. Pl. XVII f. 150 (1853).

Brackish water: Baltic! Franzenbad! Mansfelder Seen! Neusiedler See (Grun.), Belgium (V. H.), S:ta Fiora (Ehb.), England! Hungary fossil (Pant.), New Zealand! Ecuador!

Var. *major* Cl. — L. 0,12 to 0,15; B. 0,04 to 0,05 mm. Lateral areas almost similar. Striæ 13 in 0,01 mm.

Brackish water: S:ta Rosa, Calif. (Grove Coll.)! Guatemala, fossil!

A. sculpta is nearly akin to *A. sphærophora*, from which it is distinguished by larger size and the large, lunate lateral areas, which are in typical specimens somewhat dissimilar, one of them extending in the middle to the margin. *A. sculpta* is also related to *A. polygramma*, together with which form it usually occurs, and which differs by its not protracted ends. Both are to be considered as forms of the same species.

3. **A. polygramma** Ehr. (1843). — V. narrow-elliptical, with obtuse, not protracted ends. L. 0,08 to 0,13; B. 0,023 to 0,03 mm. Axial area narrow, linear, bordered with a single row of puncta. Central area transverse, uniting with narrow, somewhat asymmetrical lateral areas. Striæ about 14 in 0,01 mm. very slightly radiate throughout and composed of distant puncta, arranged in longitudinal, undulating rows. — *Stauroneis polygramma* Ehr. Am. II: 6, f. 30. *Nav. costata* Kütz. Bac. p. 93 Pl. III f. 56 (1844). *N. bohemica* Ehr. Mic. G. X: 1 f. 4 a (1854). Fresenius Senckenb. Abh. IV Pl. IV f. 10 to 13. A. S. Atl. XLIX f. 43 to 45. *N. fossilis* Ehr. Mic. G. X: 1. f. 6 (1854). *N. pannonica* Grun. Verh. 1860 p. 541 Pl. IV f. 40. *N. trigramma* Fresenius Senckenb. Abh. IV Pl. IV f. 1 to 9 (1862).

Brackish water: Sweden! Franzenbad! Eger! Neusiedler See (Grun.). Catania fossil (Grun.), Cuba (Ehb.). Utah!

4. **A. Macraeana** Pant. (1889). — V. rhomboid-lanceolate, gradually tapering to the not protracted ends. L. 0,119 to 0,17; B. 0,027 to 0,033 mm. Axial area narrow linear. Central area a transverse fascia, reaching on one side to the margin, on the other nearly to the margin. Striæ 18 in 0,01 mm., transverse in the middle and convergent at the ends, composed of elongated puncta forming undulating, longitudinal rows, about 14 in 0,01 mm. — *Nav. Macraeana* Pant. II Pl. VIII f. 155.

Brackish water: Hungary, Gyöngyös Pata!

5. **A. menilitica** Pant. (1889). — V. lanceolate with rostrate, obtuse ends. L. 0,038; B. 0,016 mm. Axial area linear. Central area a transverse fascia. Striæ 20 in 0,01 mm. composed of distant puncta. — *N. menil.* Pant. II p. 51 Pl. II f. 30.

Brackish water: Hungary, fossil (Pant.).

I have not seen this form, which seems to be nearly akin to *A. sphærophora var. biceps*. *Nav. irrorata var. fossilis* Pant. (Pl. VIII f. 147) seems to be also related to the above species.

6. **A.? serians** Bréb. (1844). V. rhomboid-lanceolate with acute ends. L. 0,06 to 0,08; B. 0,012 mm. Axial area linear-lanceolate. Striæ 24 in 0,01 mm. slightly radiate throughout, composed of elongated puncta, forming longitudinal rows. — *Navicula serians* Bréb. in Kütz Bac. p. 92 Pl. XXX f. 23. W. Sm. B. D. XVI f. 130. Donk. B. D. p. 41 Pl. VI f. 10. Grun. Verh. 1860 Pl. V f. 13. V. H. Syn. p. 101 Pl. XII f. 7. *N. lineolata* Ehb. 1843 fide Kütz. *N. punctulata* Ehb. M. G. XVI: 1, f. 1 1854.

Fresh water, northern or alpine regions: Greenland! Lapland! Scotland! England, Cornwall! Belgium (V. H.), Switzerland! Sierra Nevada! New Hampshire (foss.)! Blue Mountains, Australia! New Zealand (foss.)!

This well-known species occurs rarely living except in nothern or alpine regions. It is of frequent occurence in diatomaceous earths from Scandinavia and North America.

7. **A.? brachysira** (Bréb. 1853) Grun. — V. rhomboid, more or less obtuse. L. 0,022 to 0,028; B. 0,006 to 0,009 mm. Axial area narrow; central small. Striæ 26 to 27 in 0,01 mm. — *Navicula brachysira* Bréb. in Rabh. Süssw. D. p. 39 Pl. V f. 11 c, d, e. Grun. V. H. Types N:o 39. *C. serians v. minor* and *minima* Grun. in V. H. Syn. Pl. XII f. 8, 9. *Cymbella Beverleiana* A. S. Atl. LXXI f. 56 to 61 (1881).

Fresh water: Greenland! Lapland! Finland! Scotland!

A. brachysira in V. H. Syn. Suppl. B f. 31 seems, so far I can see, to be the same as *A. serians*. *A. brachysira* differs from *A. serians* only in its smaller size, its somewhat finer striæ and especially its obtuse ends. There is a tendency to asymmetry in the valves, which induced A. S. to regard such forms as belonging to *Cymbella*.

8. **A.? zellensis** Grun. (1860). — V. linear, slightly biconstricted, with rostrate, broad and obtuse ends. L. 0,032; B. 0,005 mm. Striæ 30 in 0,01 mm. Axial area indistinct; central small. — *Nav. zellensis* Grun. Verh. 1860 p. 521 Pl. III f. 34. V. H. Syn. Pl. XII f. 14. *N. tabida* Rylands (according to Grunow).

Fresh water: Germany, Erlaf See (Grun.), Scotland! Greenland! Michigan!

This form is nearly connected with *A. brachysira* and *A. serians*.

9. **A.? Follis** Ehb. (1838). — V. rhomboid, with strongly dilated middle, and obtuse, usually capitate ends. L. 0,04; B. 0,017 mm. Central area small, lanceolate. Striæ 24 in 0,01 mm., radiate in the middle, transverse in the ends. — *Navic. Follis* Ehb. Inf. p. 179 M. G. XVI: 1, f. 14 etc. Donk. B. D. p. 44 Pl. VI f. 15. *N. Trochus* Kütz Bac. p. 99 Pl. III f. 59.

Fresh water: Sweden (Lapland, Småland)! Finland! Scotland! Norfolk, England (Donk.) New Hampshire! Sierra Nevada!

A. Follis is intimately connected with *A. serians* and *A. exilis* and might, as the latter, be considered as a variety of *A. serians.* Perhaps *Nav. pyrenaica* W. SM. (Ann. Mag. Nat. Hist. XIX, 1857, p. 8 Pl. II f. 5) is an intermediate form between *A. Follis* and *A. serians*, which cannot be decided by the figure in SMITH's paper.

10. **A.? exilis** (KÜTZ 1844). GRUN. (1860). — V. narrow-lanceolate with protracted, capitate ends. L. 0,021 to 0,028; B. 0,005 mm. Axial and central areas indistinct. Striæ about 30 in 0,01 mm. — *Nav. exilis* KÜTZ Bac. p. 95 Pl. IV f. 6 p. p. GRUN. Verh. 1860 p. 553 Pl. IV f. 30. V. H. Syn. p. 101 Pl. XII f. 11, 12. *Colletonema exile* GRUN. Verh. 1860 p. 571 Pl. VII f. 15? *Achnant. microcephalum* W. SM. B. D. LXI f. 380?

Fresh, frequently slightly brackish water: Greenland! Norway, Dovre! Sweden, Lapland! Russian Lapland! Gulf of Bothnia! Nordhausen (KÜTZ).

Var. *thermalis* GRUN. (1880). — Lanceolate with less protracted, obtuse ends. L. 0,024; B. 0,006 mm. Striæ 27 in 0,01 mm. — *N. serians var. thermalis* GRUN. V. H. Syn. Pl. XII f. 10.

Habitat?

Var. *gomphonemacea* GRUN. (1880). — V. lanceolate with rostrate ends, slightly asymmetrical to the transverse axis. L. 0,022; B. 0,006 mm. Striæ 30 in 0,01 mm. radiate in the middle, closer towards the ends. — *Gomphonema? citreum* GRUN. Casp. See Alg. p. 13. *N. gomphonemacea* GRUN. V. H. Syn. Pl. XII f. 13.

Fresh water: Erlaf See near Mariazell (Grun.).

By the var. *thermalis A. exilis* is closely connected with *A. brachysira* and *A. serians.*

11. **A.? bipunctata** GRUN. (1881). — V. linear, slightly biconstricted, with cuneate, broadly truncate ends. L. 0,035; B. 0,006 mm. Median line with approximate central pores. Axial area narrow. Central area a broad, transverse fascia. Striæ about 30 in 0,01 mm. almost parallel, very slightly radiate in the ends, punctate. — *Nav. bip.* V. H. Syn. Pl. XIII f. 7.

Habitat?

This species is unknown to me, and the diagnosis has been constructed from the figure in V. H. Syn.

Naviculæ Heterostichæ CL.

Small, more or less elliptical, forms. Axial area narrow. Central area usually distinct. Structure: fine striæ, in the middle of the valve alternately longer and shorter, towards the ends finer and radiate, finely, but usually distinctly, punctate; puncta forming undulate longitudinal rows.

The species of this small group are closely connected with *Naviculæ punctatæ*, from which they differ by the very fine punctation of the striæ. Among the *Naviculæ lineolatæ* are several similar forms, for instance *N. bottnica*, but they differ by the direction af the terminal striæ.

The few species of this section live in fresh water or in the mouths of rivers.

Artificial key.

1. { Valve biconstricted . . . *N. Tau* CL.
   { — not — . . . 2.
2. { Ends rostrate . . . 6.
   { — not — . . . 3.
3. { Central area indistinct . . . *C. cocconeiformis* GREG.
   { — — orbicular . . . 4.
4. { Median striæ more coarsely punctate than the other . . . *N. limicola* CL.
   { — not . . . 5.

5. { Puncta forming longitudinal rows parallel to the margins of the valve . . *N. Theta* CL.
{ — not — — *N. scutiformis* GRUN.

6. { Striæ very fine, about 30 in 0,01 mm. . *N. Pusio* CL.
{ — coarser, about 17 in 0,01 mm. . *N. surinamensis* CL.

1. **N. Theta** CL. (1893). — V. elliptical. L. 0,055; B. 0,028 mm. Axial area narrow, linear; central area small, orbicular. Striæ radiate (in the ends nearly parallel) in the middle, where they are alternately longer and shorter, 20 in 0,01 mm. at the ends 25 in 0,01 mm., distinctly punctate; puncta 21 in 0,01 mm. forming longitudinal rows parallel with the margin. — Diatomiste II p. 56 Pl. III f. 5.

Fresh water: Oregon, fossil.

2. **N. limicola** CL. (1893). — V. elliptical, with rounded, obtuse ends. L. 0,046; B. 0,017 mm. Axial area narrow, linear. Central area moderately large, orbicular. Striæ about 25 in 0,01 mm., gently curved and radiate at the ends, finely but distinctly punctate. Median striæ more coarsely punctate than the others. — Diatomiste II p. 14 Pl. I f. 12.

Mouth of rivers: Cameroon, Africa (leg. Dusén).

3. **N. Pusio** CL. N. Sp. — V. elliptical, with broad rostrate ends. L. 0,018; B. 0,007 mm. Axial area very narrow. Central area small. Striæ very fine, about 30 in 0,01 mm. radiate at the ends, in the middle alternately longer and shorter, closer towards the ends. Pl. II f. 3.

Fresh water: Rotorua Lake, N. Zealand (leg. Berggren).

N. arcuata PANT. III Pl. VI f. 97 represents a similar, but larger form. L. 0,03; B. 0,016 mm. Striæ 27 in 0,01 mm.

4. **N. cocconeiformis** GREG. (1856). V. elliptical to rhomboidal, obtuse. L. 0,026 to 0,032; B. 0,009 to 0,013 mm. Central pores of the median line distant. Axial area indistinct; central area small, elongated. Striæ 25 to 29 in 0,01 mm., radiate at the ends, in the middle of unequal length, finely punctate. — M. J. IV, I. f. 22. GRUN. Verh. 1860 p. 550 Pl. IV f. 9. DONK. B. D. p. 22 Pl. III f. 11. LAGST. Spitsb. D. p. 32 Pl. II f. 8. V. H. Syn. Pl. XIV f. 1.

Fresh water, especially in arctic or alpine regions: Spitsbergen! Norway, Dovre! Finland (Russian Lappland to Abo). Sweden! Scotland! France (Vosges)! Oregon, foss.!

5. **N. scutiformis** GRUN. (1881). — V. elliptical, with broad, rounded ends. L. 0,04; B. 0,024 mm. Central pores of the median line distant. Axial area very narrow, linear; central area large, orbicular. Striæ 18 to 20 in 0,01 mm. (in the middle, closer towards the ends), strongly radiate; the median of unequal length, not more coarsely punctate than the others. — A. S. Atl. LXX f. 62.

Fresh water: Stavanger, Norway (A. S. Atl.). Lule Lappmark! Umeå, Sweden, fossil!

6. **N. Tau** CL. (1893). - V. elongated, slightly biconstricted, with cuneate ends. L. 0,037; B. 0,01 mm. Axial area very narrow; central area of medium size, rounded. Striæ 20 in 0,01 mm. radiate at the ends; in the middle of unequal length. -- Diatomiste II p. 14 Pl. I f. 11.

Fresh water: Demerara River!

7. **N. surinamensis** CL. N. Sp. — V. elliptic-lanceolate with rostrate, broad ends. L. 0,027; B. 0,013 mm. Median line with the terminal fissures in contrary direction. Axial area indistinct or very narrow. Central area small. Striæ 17 in 0,01 mm., in the middle alternately longer and shorter, radiate at the ends. — Pl. II f. 4.

Fresh water: Surinam!

Naviculæ Lineolatæ Cl.

Valve elongated, rarely constricted, sigmoid or asymmetrical. Axial area usually indistinct or narrow, rarely wide. Central area small or large. Structure: radiate or parallel striæ, finely and transversely lineate, the lineation always closer than the striæ. Connecting zone not complex. *Nav. distans* and *N. directa* have two chromatophore-plates along the connecting zone. Their margins are not indented. *N. (Schizonema) mollis* has the same arrangement of the cell-contents.

This section corresponds to the groups *Radiosæ*, *Retusæ* and *Directæ* of Grunow and comprises a very large number of forms, frequently nearly connected or passing into each other. Their most characteristic feature is the lineation of the striæ. The latter are usually radiate in the middle of the valve and divergent, parallel or convergent at the ends. In several forms the striæ are parallel throughout. In those forms in which the median striæ are radiate, they are also frequently alternately longer and shorter.

This group is connected by a few forms (*N. Placentula*) with the Naviculæ Punctatæ. As a rule the Lineolatæ incline to a lanceolate or linear outline, while the Punctatæ are elliptical. The principal distinction between both groups is that the striæ of the Punctatæ are composed of distinct puncta, usually as widely apart as the striæ, but in the Lineolatæ the puncta are much closer, the distance between the lineolæ being less than the distance between the striæ. In some cases (for instance *Nav. tuscula*) the striæ are crossed by longitudinal blank lines and have then very much the appearance of the striation in the section Punctatæ. Such forms may in most cases be distinguished from the Punctatæ by the terminal striæ being parallel or convergent.

Among the asymmetrical diatoms there is a close relation between the *Cymbellæ* and this section, both having in many cases an exactly similar striation. Several intermediate forms exist. For instance *Nav. dicephala* is nearly akin to *Cymbella anglica*, and the frustules of *Cymbella Ungeri* are frequently so nearly symmetrical, that this species might be classed among the Lineolatæ. Among the *Amphoræ* there is one species only, as far as I know, which seems to be closely akin to the Lineolatæ (*Amphora labuensis*). Passages between the perfectly symmetrical and decidedly asymmetrical are offered by *Nav. mediterranea* and *Nav. toxonidea*.

The forms of this group, which have the striæ crossed by several longitudinal blank lines, suggest a connection with the genus *Trachyneis*.

The species of the group Lævistriatæ are no doubt nearly connected with those of the Lineolatæ. They have the same general outline, and the striæ are in similar directions, but those of the former are apparently smooth.

Artificial key.

1	Median line sigmoid	*N. Sigma* Brun.
	— straight	2
2	Axial area distinct or broad	3
	— — very narrow or indistinct	16.
3.	Axial area bilateral	4.
	— unilateral	*N. scalarifer* Brun.[1]
4	Axial area asymmetrical	*N. irregularis* Pant.
	— symmetrical	5
5.	Valve constricted in the middle	*N. Chi* Cl.
	— not —	6.

[1] Besides: *N. irregularis* Pant., *N. superba* Cl., *N. transitans var. incudiformis*, *var. asymmetrica*, *N. spuria var asymmetrica*, *N. imperfecta* Cl., *N. monodon* Brun, *N. Anthracis* Br. and Cl., *N. valida* Cl.

6.	Valve with undulate margins	*N. Sancti Thomæ* Cl.
	— — non — —	7.[1]
7.	Fresh water habitat	*N. ludloviana* A. S.
	Marine	8.
8.	Striæ not reaching to the margin	*N. subalata* Grun.
	— reaching	9.
9.	Ends obtuse	10.
	— acute	14.
10.	Ends broad, rounded	11.
	— not very broad	12.
11.	Axial area gradually dilated to the middle	*N. jamalinensis* Cl.
	— — abruptly — — a central area	*N. opima* Grun.
12.	Size small. L. about 0,05 mm.	13.
	— large. L. about 0,1 mm.	*N. distans* W. Sm.
13.	Axial area lanceolate	*N. Nicæensis* Per.
	— — abruptly dilated into an orbicular central area	*N. salva* A. S.
14.	Striæ radiate throughout	*N. Platessa* Cl.
	— transverse in the ends	15.
15.	Striæ crossed by a blank band	*N. Bruchii* Grun.
	— not — — —	*N. Amicorum* Grun.
16.	Striæ radiate	17.
	— parallel	82.
17.	Terminal striæ parallel or convergent	18.
	— — radiate	51.
18.	Terminal striæ crossed by a lunate band	*N. annulata* Grun.
	— — not — —	19.
19.	Terminal striæ genuflexed	*N. oblonga* Kütz.
	— — not —	20.
20.	Striæ crossed by lateral areas or by narrow blank bands	30.
	— not — — — — — —	21.
21.	Median striæ of unequal length	22.
	— — equal —	36.
22.	Valve lanceolate, rostrate-capitate	28.
	— — not — —	23.
23.	Valve acute	24.
	— obtuse	25.
24.	Median striæ alternately longer and shorter	*N. Salinarum v. intermedia.*
	— — shorter than the others	*N. notabilis* Pant.
25.	Striæ fine, 20 in 0,01 mm.	*N. bottnica* Grun.
	— coarse, 8 to 9 mm.	26.
26.	Striæ coarsely lineate	27.
	— finely —	*N. digito-radiata* Greg.
27.	Striæ 6 in 0,01 mm.	*N. peregrina* Ehr.
	— 9 — —	*N. Reinhardtii* Grun.
28.	Terminal striæ strongly convergent	*N. Wilczekii* Grun.
	— — parallel	29.
29.	Length 0,028 to 0,037 mm.	*N. Salinarum* Grun.
	— 0,115 mm.	*N. Rho* Cl.
30.	Striæ crossed by a lateral area	31.
	— — two or more blank bands	34.
31.	Valve obtuse	32.
	— acute	33.
32.	Valve linear, with rounded ends	*N. obtusa* Cl.
	— lanceolate	*N. Haueri* Grun.
33.	Lateral area unilateral	*N. Anthracis* Br. a. Cl.
	— areas bilateral	*N. Bruchii* Grun.
34.	Longitudinal bands two on each side	35.
	— — several —	*N. Tuscula* Ehr.

[1] Conf. *N. basaltæ proxima* Br. and *N. aquitaniæ* Br. (additional).

35.	Central area small or indistinct	. . . . *N. multiseriata* Grun.
	— — orbicular —	*N. maculosa* Donk.
36.	Size small. L. 0,018 to 0,04 mm.	. 37.
	large. L. 0,05 mm. and more . .	43.
37.	Striæ 11 in 0,01 mm.	38.
	— 6 to 10 mm.	. . 40.
38.	Median striæ stronger . . .	*N. cincta* Ehb.
	— — not	. . . . . . 39.
39.	Ends obtuse .	. . . . . . *N. Beckii* Pant.
	— acute	*N. ammophila* Grun.
	— subcapitate .	*N. cryptocephala* Kütz.
40.	Striæ coarsely lineate .	. . . . 41.
	— apparently smooth	. . . . 42.
41.	Valve rhomboidal . .	. . . . *N. Raphoneis* Grun.
	— elliptic-lanceolate	*N. Formenteræ* Cl.
42.	Terminal striæ strongly marked	. *N. hungarica* Grun.
	— — not — —	*N. costulata* Grun.
43.	Ends protracted . . .	. . . . 52.
	— not —	. 44.
44.	Central area distinct	46.
	— — not —	. . . . . . 45.
45.	Marine habitat	. . . . *N. spuria* Cl.
	Fresh water —	. *N. radiosa* Kütz.
46.	Striæ coarsely lineate	. . . 47.
	— finely —	. . . . . 49.
47.	Marine habitat . .	. . . . 48.
	Fresh water	*N. vulpina* Kütz.
48.	Valve narrow lanceolate, not very convex	*N. pinnata* Pant.
	— broadly — convex	. . *N. fortis* Greg.
49.	Valve not very convex	. *N. arenacea* Bréb.
	— convex, with conical ends . . .	. . . . 50.
50.	Ends very elevated and compressed .	. *N. compressicauda* A. S.
	— not — — —	. . . . 51.
51.	Central area small .	. *N. cancellata* Donk.
	— — large	. *N. Centraster* Cl.
52.	Ends subrostrate, obtuse . .	. . . . . *N. viridula* Kütz.
	— non-rostrate	. . . . 53.
53.	Ends subcapitate .	*N. rhynchocephala* Kütz.
	— acute .	. . *N. gotlandica* Grun.
54.	Frustule arcuate .	. . . . . . 55.
	— non —	. . . . . . 56.
55.	Striæ about 18 in 0,01 mm.	*N. genuflexa* Kütz.
	— — 10 —	*N. Bolleana* Grun.
56.	Striæ crossed by lateral areas or blank bands .	. . . 57.
	— not — — — —	61.
57.	Striæ crossed by a single, narrow area	. . 58.
	— — — several longitudinal bands	. . . . . . 60.
58.	Apiculate	. *N. Galea* Brun.
	Non-apiculate	. . . . 59.
59.	Axial part of the valve elevated	. . *N. superimposita* A. S.
	— — — — not —	. . . *N. Phi* Cl.
60.	Blank lines straight .	. . . . *N. arata* Grun.
	— undulating	. . . . . 61.
61.	Axial area unilateral . . .	. . . . 62.
	— areas bilateral	. . . . 63.
62.	Valve slightly convex	. . . . . . *N. imperfecta* Cl.
	— very —	. . *N. monodon* Grun.
63.	Valve slightly convex	. *N. consors* A. S.
	— very —	. *N. guttata* Grun.

No.	Character	Result
64.	Valve rostrate	65.
	— non —	73.
65.	Median striæ alternately longer and shorter	66.
	— — not — — — —	69.
66.	Striæ coarsely lineate	67.
	— finely —	68.
67.	Central area with stigmas	*N. Clementis* Grun.
	— without —	*N. leptostigma* Ehr.
68.	Striæ about 9 in 0,01 mm.	*N. Gastrum* Ehr.
	— — 17 — —	*N. platystoma* Ehr.
69.	Valve linear	*N. falaisiensis* Grun.
	— lanceolate to elliptical	70.
70.	Valve very convex	*N. crucifera* Grun.
	— not —	71.
71.	Striæ coarsely lineolate	*N. Placentula* Ehr.
	— finely —	72.
72.	Central area small	*N. anglica* Ralfs.
	— — large	*N. dicephala* W. Sm.
73.	Median striæ alternately longer and shorter	76.
	— — not — — — —	74.
74.	Size small. L. 0,02 mm.	*N. arenariæformis* Pant.
	— larger. L. 0,06 to 0,1 mm.	75.
75.	2,5 to 4 times longer than broad	*N. valida* Cl. a Grun.
	5 to 6 — — — —	*N. Hasta* Pant.
76.	Central area small or indistinct	77.
	— — medium sized or large	80.
77.	Ends conical	*N. inflexa* Greg.
	— not —	78.
78.	Striæ slightly radiate	*N. arenicola* Grun.
	— strongly —	79.
79.	Fresh water habitat	*N. lanceolata* Kütz.
	Marine	*N. solaris* Greg.
80.	Striæ coarse 5 to 6 in 0,01 mm.	81.
	— finer 10 in 0,01 mm.	*N. oriformis* Cl.
81.	Striæ coarsely lineate	*N. pennata* A. S.
	— finely —	*N. consanguinea* Cl.
82.	Size small, L. less than 0,05 mm.	83.
	— larger. L. more —	86.
83.	Striæ 15 in 0,01 mm.	84.
	— 22 to 28 mm.	85.
84.	Lineolæ forming longitudinal striæ	*N. mollis* W. Sm.
	— not — — —	*N. incerta* Grun.
85.	Frustules in gelatinous tubes	*N. corymbosa* Ag.
	— — the interior of algæ	*N. nidulans* Cl.
86.	Frustule arcuate	*N. sibirica* Grun.
	— not —	87.
87.	Striæ crossed by lateral areas or blank bands	97.
	— not — — — — —	88.
88.	Striæ coarsely lineate	*N. Satura* A. S.
	— finely —	89.
89.	Lineolæ forming oblique or longitudinal fine striæ	103.
	— not	90.
90.	Valve very convex	91.
	— not —	93.
91.	Valve asymmetrical	*N. Scoliopleura* A. S.
	— symmetrical	92.
92.	Frustule arcuate	*N. Cubitus* Br. a. Temp.
	— not —	*N. Northumbrica* Donk.
93.	Valve linear	*N. jejuna* A. S.
	— lanceolate or rhomboidal	94.

94. { Habitat: fresh-water . . . . *N. gracilis* Ehr.
   — marine . . . . 95.

95. { 3 to 4 times longer than broad . . . . 96.
   4 to 6 — — . . . . *N. transitans* Cl.
   6 to 7 — — — — . . . . *N. Zosterei* Grun.
   10 — — — . . . . *N. directa* W. Sm.

96. { Valve rhomboidal . . . . *N. superba* Cl.
   — lanceolate . . . . *N. gelida* Grun.

97. { Striæ between the margin and the axis faint . . . . 98.
   — unilaterally crossed by an area . . . . 99.
   — crossed by undulating, blank bands . . . . 100.

98. { Central nodule a short stauros . . . . *N. finmarchica* Cl. a. Grun.
   — — not stauroid . . . . . *N. transitans* v. *derasa* (*N. kariana* v. *detersa*).

99. { Valve about 10 times longer than broad . . . . *N. directa* v. *lucus*.
   — — 5 to 6 — — — . . . . . . *N. transitans* v. *incudiformis*.[1]

100. { Valve very convex . . . . 101.
   — not — . . . . 102.

101. { Valve fusiform . . . . *N. citriscala* Brun.
   — linear . . . . *N. mediterranea* Bn. a. Cl.

102. { Valve linear with cuneate ends . . . . *N. trigonocephala* Cl.
   — lanceolate . . . . *N. transitans* v. *erosa*.

103. { Lineation oblique . . . . *N. Kepesii* Grun.
   — straight . . . . 104.

104. { Valve narrow lanceolate . . . . *N. ramosissima* Ag.
   — broadly — . . . . *N. Kariana* Grun.

1. **N. cryptocephala** Kütz. (1844). — V. lanceolate, with rostrate-capitate ends. L. 0,025 to 0,035; B. 0,005 to 0,007 mm. Axial area indistinct. Central area small, somewhat transverse. Striæ 16 to 18 in 0,01 mm., radiate in the middle, slightly convergent in the ends, finely lineate. — Bac. p. 95 Pl. III f. 26. Donk. B. D. p. 37 Pl. V f. 14. V. H. Syn. p. 84 Pl. VIII f. 1, 5. *Nav. mutica* Rabh. Alg. Sachs. N:o 965.

Fresh water: Sweden! England! Belgium (V. H.). Germany! France! Arctic America! Greenland! Argentina! Japan!

Var. *veneta* Kütz. (1844). — Smaller, with scarcely capitate ends. L. 0,025; B. 0,005 mm. Striæ 14 in 0,01 mm. *N. veneta* Kütz. Bac. p. 95 Pl. XXX f. 76. Pedicino Ischia Pl. II f. 9 to 12? Donk. B. D. p. 43 Pl. VI f. 13? *N. crypt. v. veneta* V. H. Syn. p. 85 Pl. VIII f. 3, 4, Pl. XIV f. 34.

Brackish water: Sweden. Malmö! Venice (Kütz).

Var. *pumila* Grun. (1880). — V. rhombic-lanceolate. L. 0,016 to 0,023; B. 0,006 to 0,007 mm. Striæ about 15 in 0,01 mm. — V. H. Syn. Pl. VIII f. 6, 7. XIV f. 35. *N. Rhombulus* Schum. P. D. II N. p. 56, Pl. II f. 35 (1867)? *N. Lancettula* Schum. P. D. II N. Pl. II f. 34. *N. cryptoc. v. Lancettula* V. H. Syn. Pl. VIII f. 11. *N. pumila v. fossilis* Pant. III Pl. V f. 75 (1893)?

Brackisch water: Triest!

Var. *perminuta* Grun. (1880). — V. lanceolate, not capitate. L. 0,008 to 0,011; B. 0,003 mm. Striæ about 20 in 0,01 mm. — V. H. Syn. Pl. XIV f. 7.

Var. *exilis* Kütz (1844 p. p. accord. to Grunow). V. lanceolate, with subrostrate, obtuse ends. L. 0,018 to 0,019; B. 0,005 mm. Striæ about 19 in 0,01 mm. — V. H. Syn. p. 85 Pl. VIII f. 2, 4.

Fresh water: Belgium (V. H.). Somme! Triest!

2. **N. gotlandica** Grun. (1878). — V. narrow, lanceolate, with protracted, subacute ends. L. 0,05 to 0,06; B. 0,008 mm. Axial area indistinct; central area small, orbicular. Striæ 11 (middle) to 18 (ends) in 0,01 mm. radiate in the middle, convergent in the ends. — Cl. M. D. N:o 161. V. H. Syn. Pl. VIII f. 8.

Slightly brackish water: Sweden, Gothland! Tasmania!

[1] *N. irregularis* Pant. *N. superba v. elliptica*.

3. **N. rhynchocephala** Kütz (1844). — V. lanceolate, with protracted, usually subcapitate ends. L. 0,04 to 0,06; B. 0,01 to 0,013 mm. Axial area indistinct. Central area orbicular. Striæ 10 to 12 in 0,01 mm., in the middle radiate and more distant, convergent at the ends, coarsely lineate. — Bac. Pl. XXX f. 35. W. Sm. B. D. Pl. XVI f. 132. Donk. B. D. p. 38 Pl. VI f. 4. Grun. A. D. p. 33 Pl. II f. 33. V. H. Syn. p 84 Pl. VII f. 31. *N. cryptoc. v. rhynchoc.* Strösse Kliecken Pl. I f. 3.

Fresh or slightly brackish water: Finmarken! Sea of Kara! Gulf of Bothnia! Sweden! Belgium (V. H.), Saxony! Cape Deschneff! Arctic America! Dakota! Illinois! South Africa! Australian Alps!

Var. *amphiceros* Kütz (1844). — V. broader lanceolate. Ends not distinctly capitate. Striæ 8 to 10 in 0,01 mm. — *N. amph.* Kütz. Bac. p. 95 Pl. III f. 39. A. S. Atl. XLVII f. 25, 26. V. H. Syn. p. 84 Pl. VII f. 30.

Brackish water: Gulf of Bothnia! England! Belgium (V. H.). Sandwich Islands!

N. rhynchocephala and *var. amphiceros* pass into each other; the latter graduates into *N. avenacea* and *N. viridula*, the former is closely connected with *N. cryptocephala*.

4. **N. avenacea** Bréb. (1878). — V. lanceolate, with acute ends. L. 0,04 to 0,05; B. 0,008 to 0,01 mm. Axial area indistinct; central area orbicular, large. Striæ 10 or 12 (middle) to 13 (ends) in 0,01 mm., finely lineate, radiate in the middle, slightly convergent in the ends. Grun. Caspian Sea Alg. IV f. 23. *N. viridula v. av.* V. H. Syn. p. 84 Pl. VII f. 27. *Pinnul. silesiaca* Bleisch (according to Grun.). *Schizonema Smithii* (Ag.) V. H. Syn. p. 110 Pl. XV f. 33.

Brackish water: Falaise (Bréb.), England! Belgium (V. H.), Black Sea! Caspian Sea (Grun.). East Cape! Tasmania!

N. avenacea connects *N. viridula* with *N. rhynchocephala*.

5. **N. viridula** Kütz (1844). V. broadly lanceolate, with subrostrate, obtuse ends. L. 0,05 to 0,07; B. 0,01 to 0,015 mm. Axial area indistinct. Central area large, orbicular. Striæ 10 in 0,01 mm., coarsely lineate, radiate and more distant in the middle, slightly convergent in the ends. — Bac. p. 91 Pl. XXX f. 47. Grun. A. D. p. 33 Pl. II f. 35. V. H. Syn. p. 84 Pl. VII f. 25. *Schizonema Thwaitesii* V. H. Syn. Pl. XV f. 38, 39.

Fresh and slightly brackish water: Sweden! England! Belgium (V. H.), Finland! Salzburg! Sandwich Islands! — Australian Alps! Murray River! — Arctic America!

Var. *slesvicensis* Grun. (1880). — V. linear-lanceolate, with broad, rostrate ends. L. 0,03 to 0,05; B. 0,009 to 0,011 mm. Striæ 8 to 9 in 0,01 mm. — *N. sles.* Grun. in V. H. Syn. p. 84 Pl. VII f. 28, 29. *N. virid. f. minor* A. S. Atl. XLVII f. 48. V. H. Syn. p. 84 Pl. VII f. 26. *Pinnul. silesiaca* Fresenius Senckenb. Abh. IV. Pl. IV f. 27.

Brackish water: Finland! Holstein! Belgium (V. H.), Greenland!

Var. *abbreviata* Grun. Ms. — V. linear, with rostrate and subcapitate ends. L. 0,016 to 0,03; B. 0,0055 to 0,007 mm. Central area small. Striæ 16 to 17 in 0,01 mm.

Brackish water: Gulf of Bothnia, Torneå! South Africa! Bengal!

Var. *rostellata* Kütz (1844). — V. lanceolate, with attenuated, subrostrate ends. L. 0,04 to 0,065; B. 0,01 mm. Striæ 10 to 11 in 0,01 mm. — *N. rost.* Kütz Bac. p. 95 Pl. III f. 65. A. S. Atl. XLVII f. 27 to 30. *N. rhynchoc. v. rost.* Grun. A. D. p. 33. V. H. Syn. p. 84 Pl. VII f. 23, 24.

Brackish water: England! Belgium (V. H.). Marseilles (Atl.), East Cape! Japan!

The variety *rostellata* is a transitional form between *N. viridula* and *N. amphirhynchus var. amphiceros.*

6. **N. vulpina** Kütz (1844). V. lanceolate, gradually tapering from the middle to the obtuse ends. L. 0,09; B. 0,014 to 0,016 mm. Axial area very narrow; central area large, orbicular. Striæ 10 to 11 in 0,01 mm., radiate in the middle, convergent in the ends, coarsely lineate; lineolæ

24 in 0,01 mm. forming longitudinal, fine rows. — Kütz Bac. p. 92 Pl. III f. 43. V. H. Syn. p. 83 Pl. VII f. 18. *N. viridula forma major* A. S. Atl. XLVII f. 53, 54.

Fresh water: Sweden! Finland! Ireland (Lough Mourne)! Domblitten, fossil! Arctic America! Greenland! Michigan! New Zealand!

Var. *oregonica* Cl. — Linear with broad, truncate ends. L. 0,095; B. 0,013 mm. Striæ 11 in 0,01 mm. — A. S. Atl. XLVII f. 55, 56 (without name).

Fresh water: Oregon, fossil!

7. **N. costulata** Grun. (1880). — V. rhombic-lanceolate, with acute ends. L. 0,015 to 0,02; B. 0,0015 to 0,005 mm. Axial area narrow; central area a transverse fascia. Striæ 8 to 10 in 0,01 mm., slightly divergent in the middle, distant. Terminal striæ not more strongly marked than the others. — A. D. p. 27. V. H. Syn. p. 85 Suppl. A. f. 15. Grun. Foss. D. Öst. Ung. p. 156 Pl. XXX f. 45.

Slightly brackish water: Sweden (Gulf of Bothnia)! Holstein (Grun.). Belgium (V. H.).

8. **N. hungarica** Grun. (1860). — V. linear lanceolate, with broad, obtuse ends. L. 0,015 to 0,02; Br. 0,005 to 0,006 mm. Axial area very narrow; central area small. Striæ 8 to 9 in 0,01 mm., distant, slightly divergent in the middle and convergent in the ends, where there are on both sides of the terminal nodule one or two more strongly marked striæ. — *Pinnul. pygmæa* Ehr. M. G. X: 1 f. 9 (1854). *Nav. hungarica* Grun. Verh. 1860 p. 539 Pl. III f. 30. Foss. D. Öster. Ung. p. 156 Pl. XXX f. 42. A. D. p. 27.

Slightly brackish water: Gulf of Bothnia (Torneå)! Holstein! Franzenbad (fossil)! Neusiedlersee (Grun.). Dakota! Illinois! Ecuador! Argentina!

Var. *capitata* Ehr. (1848). — V. gibbous in the middle and with subcapitate ends. — *Pinn. capit.* Ehr. Ber. 1848 (accord. to Chase) M. G. XXXVII: 2 f. 9; XXXV A. I f. 4. *Pinn. signata* Ehr. M. G. XXXIV 6 A. f. 7 (1854). *Pinn. garganica* Rabh. Süssw. D. VI f. 41 (1853). *Nav. inflata* W. Sm. B. D. I Pl. XVII f. 158 (1853). *Nav. globiceps* Lagst. Spitsb. D. p. 27 Pl. II f. 5 (1873). *Nav. humilis* Donk. B. D. p. 67 Pl. X f. 7 V. H. Syn. p. 85 Pl. XI f. 23.

Fresh water: Beeren Eiland (Lagst.). Sweden; England! Belgium (V. H.). Japan!

Var. *lüneburgensis* Grun. (1882). — V. lanceolate, with subacute ends. Foss. D. Öster. Ung. p. 156 Pl. XXX f. 43—44.

Brackish water: Finmark (Tana Elf)! Holstein (Grun.). Germany (Domblitten, Oberrohe, fossil)! Bombay (Grun.).

The *var. lüneburgensis* is very similar to *Nav. costulata*. Probably *Gomphonema naviculoides* Ströse Klieken D. Pl. I f. 18 is this form.

9. **N. cincta** Ehr. (1854). — V. linear-lanceolate, with obtuse ends. L. 0,02 to 0,04; B. 0,005 to 0,006 mm. Axial area indistinct; central area small, transverse. Striæ 12 to 17 in 0,01 mm. strongly radiate in the middle, slightly convergent at the ends. The median striæ are more distant and more strongly marked than the others. — *Pinnul. cincta* Ehr. M. G. X: 2 f. 6. *N. cincta* V. H. Syn. p. 82 Pl. VII f. 13, 14. *P. Heufleri* Pedicino Ischia Pl. II f. 17. *N. Kützingiana* H. L. Smith Am. Q. J. M. 1878 p. 13 f. 3. *Pinnul. nana* Greg. accord. to Grun. A. S. N. S. D. II f. 23, 24 (without name)?

Fresh and brackish water: Sweden! Finland! Holstein! England! Belgium (V. H.), Bavaria! Switzerland! East Cape! Japan! N. America, Kansas! Vancouver Island!

Var. *Heufleri* Grun. (1860). — L. 0,022 to 0,032; B. 0,004 mm. Central area small. Striæ 10 in 0,01 mm. — *Nav. Heufleri* Grun. Verh. 1860 p. 528 Pl. III f. 32. *N. cincta v. Heufl.* V. H. Syn. p. 82 Pl. VII f. 12, 15.

Fresh and brackish water: Sweden (Malmö)! Belgium (V. H.), Triest! Ecuador!

Var. *leptocephala* Bréb. (1880). — V. lanceolate, with slightly rostrate and obtuse ends. L. 0,025; B. 0,006 mm. Striæ 13 in 0,01 mm. — *N. leptoceph.* Bréb. in Kütz Herb. accord. to Grun. V. H. Syn. p. 82 Pl. VII f. 16.

Belgium (V. H.).

Var. *Cari* Ehb. (1838). — V. narrow lanceolate. L. 0,046; B. 0,007 mm. Central area distinct, transverse. Striæ 17 in 0,01 mm. — *N. Cari* Ehb. Inf. p. 174. M. G. XII f. 20. V. H. Syn. VII f. 11.

Fresh water: Habichtwalde, fossil (Ehb.). Australia, Daintree River!

Var. *angusta* Grun. (1860). — V. linear-lanceolate, obtuse. L. 0,05 to 0,065; B. 0,005 to 0,006 mm. Central area distinctly transverse. Striæ 12 to 13 in 0,01 mm. — *N. angusta* Grun. Verh. 1860 p. 528 Pl. V f. 19. *N. Cari v. ang.* V. H. Syn. Pl. VII f. 17.

Fresh water: Austrian Alps (Grun.), Vosges (Lac de Gerardmer)! Ecuador!

N. Cari connects *N. cincta* with *N. radiosa* and might as well be regarded as a variety of the latter, distinguished principally by its somewhat transverse central area.

10. **N. radiosa** Kütz (1844). — V. narrow, lanceolate, gradually tapering from the middle to the subacute ends. L. 0,045 to 0,09; B. 0,012 to 0,019 mm. Axial area indistinct. Central area very small, rhomboidal. Striæ 11 to 12 in 0,01 mm, strongly radiate in the middle and convergent at the ends, finely lineate. — Bac. p. 91 Pl. IV f. 23. *Pinn. radiosa* and *P. acuta* W. Sm. B. D. p. 56 Pl. XVIII f. 171, 173. *N. radiosa* Grun. Verh. 1860 p. 526. A. S. Atl. XLVII f. 50 to 52. V. H. Syn. p. 83 Pl VII f. 20. *Pinn. acuta* Ströse Klieken f. 2.

Fresh water: Spitsbergen (Lagerst.). Sweden! Norway! Finland! England! France! Switzerland! Saxony! Japan! South Africa! Illinois! Michigan! Brazil! Argentina! Ecuador!

Var. *dubraciensis* Grun. (1882). — V. broadly lanceolate. L. 0,072 to 0,085; B. 0,011 mm. Striæ 13 in 0,01 mm., more distant in the middle, distinctly lineate; lineolæ 25 in 0,01 mm. — F. D. Öst. Ung. p. 144 Pl. XXX f. 49. *N. Dubrav.* Pant. III Pl. XIX f. 281 (1893).

Fresh water: Hungary, fossil (Grun.).

Var. *subrostrata* Cl. — Linear with subrostrate, obtuse ends. L. 0,085; B. 0,011 mm. Striæ 10 in 0,01 mm. — *Pinnul. tenuis* Greg. M. J. II Pl. IV f. 9 (1854)?

Fresh water: Crane Pond (N. Am.)!

Var. *tenella* Bréb. (1849). — Lanceolate with acute ends. L. 0,03 to 0,065; B. 0,005 to 0,006 mm. Striæ 15 to 18 in 0,01 mm. — *N. tenella* Bréb. in Kütz Sp. Alg. p. 74. *N. radiosa v. ten.* V. H. Syn. p, 84 Pl. VII f. 21, 22.

Fresh water: Sweden! Finland! Belgium (V. H.). Japan! Australia (Daintree River)! Tasmania! Greenland! Argentina!

Pantocsek describes as *N. tenella var.? fossilis* (II p. 54 Pl. V f. 91) a form with broad axial area, which, if the figure be exact, cannot belong to *N. radiosa.*

Var. *minutissima* Grun. (1882). — 0,017 to 0,027; B. 0,0035 to 0,004 mm. Striæ 14 to 19 in 0,01 mm. — F. D. Öst. Ung. p. 144.

Fresh water: Hungary, fossil (Grun.), Rostock, fossil!

This var. seems rather to belong to *N. cryptocephala v. veneta.*

11. **N. gracilis** Ehb. (1830). — V. almost linear, obtuse. L. 0,035 to 0,05; B. 0,0065 to 0,01 mm. Axial area indistinct; central area distinct, transverse. Striæ 11 to 12 in 0,01 mm., in the middle slightly radiate, elsewhere almost parallel. — Ber. 1830 Inf. p. 176 Pl. XIII f. 2(?) Grun. Verh. 1860 p. 526 Pl. IV f. 27. V. H. Syn. p. 83 Pl. VII f. 7, 8.

Fresh water: Sweden! Finland! Denmark! Normandy! Arctic America! Argentina, Sierra Famatina!

Var. *schizonemoides* V. H. (1880). — Frustules enclosed in unbranched, gelatinous tubes. Central area somewhat smaller. — *Colletonema neglectum* Thwaites in W. Sm. B. D. II p. 70 Pl. LVI

f. 352 (1856). *Schizon. neglectum* V. H. Syn. Pl. XV f. 37. *N. gracilis v. schizon.* V. H. Syn. p. 83 Pl. VII f. 9, 10.

Fresh water: England! Belgium (V. H.).

N. gracilis is very similar to larger varieties of *N. cincta* and to some forms of *N. radiosa* from which it may be distinguished by its less radiate striæ, and larger, transverse central area.

12. **N. peregrina** Ehb. (1843). — V. lanceolate with obtuse ends. L. 0,08 to 0,15; B. 0,021 to 0,028 mm. Axial area distinct, narrow. Central area large, somewhat transverse, subrectangular. Striæ in the middle 5 to 6 in 0,01 mm. radiate, and frequently alternately longer and shorter, towards the ends transverse, and at the ends (8 in 0,01 mm.) convergent, distinctly lineate; lineolæ about 25 in 0,01 mm. — *Pinn. peregr.* Ehb. Am. I: 1 f. 5, 6. W. Sm. B. D. I Pl. XVIII f. 170. *N. peregr.* Kütz Bac. p. 97 Pl. 28 f. 52. A. S. Atl. XLVII f. 57—60.

Brackish water: Sea of Kara! Baltic! North Sea! Saxony! Adriatic (Grun.). Arctic America! Greenland! Atlantic coasts of United States! Argentina! Cape Wankarema! Japan! Batavia!

Var. *kefringensis* Ehb. (1840). — Smaller. L. 0,044 to 0,09 mm. Striæ 7 (middle) to 8,5 (ends). — *Pinn. kefr.* Ehb. Ber. 1840 p. 20 (accord. to Kütz). M. G. X: 2. f. 4, 5. *Nav. kefr.* Kütz Bac. p. 97 (1844). A. S. Atl. XLVII f. 61, 62.

Brackish water: Firth of Tay! Franzenbad, fossil!

Var. *polaris* Lagst. (1873). — V. subelliptical, with broad, obtuse ends. L. 0,051 to 0,072; B. 0,014 to 0,016 mm. Striæ 6 (middle) to 8 (ends) in 0,01 mm. — *N. polaris* Lagst. Spitsb. D. p. 24 Pl. II f. 3. Boh. p. 33.

Brackish water: Spitsbergen! Beeren Eiland (Lagst.), Bohuslän (Lagst.).

Var. *calcuttensis* Grun. Ms. — V. lanceolate. L. 0,05 to 0,06; B. 0,017 mm. Striæ 9, lineolæ 21 in 0,01 mm. Axial area unilateral, not dilated in the middle. Central area small, also unilateral. — Pl. II f. 2.

Brackish water: Calcutta!

Var. *Meniscus* Schum. (1867). — V. elliptic-lanceolate. L. 0,036 to 0,066; B. 0,01 to 0,019 mm. Striæ 7 to 8,5 in 0,01 mm. — *N. Meniscus* Schum. P. D. II N. p 55 Pl. II f. 32 (*N. Sambiensis* f. 37? *N. aperta* f. 49, *N. Cyprinus* f. 50?). Grun. A. D. p. 33. A. S. Atl. XLVII f. 47 (without name). *N. peregr. v. M.* V. H. Syn. p. 82 Pl. VIII f. 19.

Brackish water: Sea of Kara (Grun.), Baltic (Schum., Grun.), Königsberg, fossil! Cuxhaven (Atl.), Cape Wankarema!

Forms with asymmetrical axial area occur at Cape Wankarema.

Var. *Menisculus* Schum. (1867). — V. elliptic-lanceolate, frequently slightly rostrate. L. 0,018 to 0,04; B. 0,01 to 0,011 mm. Axial area indistinct; central area small. Striæ 9 to 12 in 0,01 mm., finely lineate. — *N. Menisc.* Schum. P. D. II N. p. 56 Pl. II f. 33. *N. peregr. v. Menisculus* V. H. Syn. p. 82 Pl. VIII f. 20, 21, 22. *N. Gastrum v. Upsaliensis* Grun. in Cl. M. D. No 242. *N. peregr. menisculus f. Upsaliensis* V. H. Syn. p. 82 Pl. VIII f. 23, 24. *N. pressa* Pant. III Pl. XXIV f. 362 (1893)?

Fresh and slightly brackish water: Sweden! Baltic! Königsberg and Domblitten, fossil! Belgium (V. H.). France (Paris, Normandy)! Saxony! Vienna (Grun.). Argentina (Sierra Velasco)!

By the var. *Menisculus N. peregrina* seems to pass into *N. cryptocephala var. veneta.*

13. **N. Haueri** Grun. (1882). — V. lanceolate, with obtuse ends. L. 0,08 to 0,12; B. 0,017 to 0,019 mm. Axial area narrow. Central area large, transverse. Striæ 8 in 0,01 mm. radiate and more distant in the middle, convergent in the ends, finely lineate, and crossed on both sides of the median line by a narrow, blank area. — F. D. Öst. Ung. p. 143 Pl. XXX f. 48. Pant. III Pl. VIII f. 135.

Brackish water: Hungary, fossil (Dubravica, Grun., Bory)!

This species, distinguished by the blank band across the striæ, is nearly akin to *N. peregrina.*

14. **N. Anthracis** BRUN a. CL. (1889). — V. lanceolate, acute. L. 0,05 to 0,06; B. 0,014 to 0,018 mm. Axial area unilateral. Central area also unilateral, but on opposite side to the axial area and connected with a narrow longitudinal area. Striæ 7 (middle) to 8 (ends) in 0,01 mm. radiate in the middle, transverse at the ends, coarsely lineate; lineolæ 20 in 0,01 mm. — D. f. du Japon p. 41 Pl. V f. 6. *N. Flattii* PANT. III Pl. XXII f. 330 (1893).

Fresh water (marine?): Japan, fossil!

15. **N. maculosa** DONK. (1871). — V. broadly linear, with apiculate ends. L. 0,045 to 0,068; B. 0,013 mm. Axial area narrow; central area orbicular. Striæ 10 in 0,01 mm. radiate in the middle, transverse at the ends, finely lineate, crossed by two undulating, narrow, lateral areas. — B. D. p. 25 Pl. V f. 1. *N. albinensis* GRUN. Franz Jos. Land D. p. 103 Pl. I f. 29 (1884).

Marine: Scotland!

Original specimens of Donkins *N. maculosa* in Deby's Collection agree perfectly with original specimens of Grunows *N. albinensis*.

16. **N. tuscula** EHB. (1840). — V. elliptical, with protracted, capitate ends. L. 0,05; B. 0,015 mm. Axial area narrow; central area large, transverse, subrectangular. Striæ 12 to 14 in 0,01 mm. radiate in the middle, transverse at the ends, very finely lineate and crossed by several irregularly undulating longitudinal bands. — *Pinnularia tuscula* EHB. Ber. 1840. *Stauroptera tuscula* EHB. M. G. VI: I f. 13 *a*. *Stauroneis punctata* KÜTZ. Bac. p. 106 Pl. XXI f. 9 (1844). W. SM. B. D. I Pl. XIX f. 189. DONK. B. D. p. 36 Pl. V f. 12. *Navicula tuscula* V. H. Syn. p. 95 Pl. X f. 14. *Stauroneis meniscus* SCHUM. Preuss. D. p. 189 Pl. IX f. 54 (1862)? *Navic. tumida var. subsasla* Ströse Klieken Pl. I f. 10?

Fresh or slightly brackish water (larger lakes): Spitsbergen (Lagst.), Beeren Eiland (Lagst.), Iceland! Sweden (Mälaren, Wenern, Ringsjön)! Finland! Gulf of Bothnia (Tornea, Pitea)! England! Belgium (V. H.). Switzerland (Brun), Illinois! Fossil at Königsberg! Klieken! Rostock! S:ta Fiora!

According to Grunow (F. D. Öst. Ung. p. 145) the cell-contents of Nav. tuscula are very different from those of other species of Naviculæ.

17. **N. Salinarum** GRUN. (1880). — V. elliptic-lanceolate, with protracted, capitate ends. L. 0,023 to 0,037; B. 0,01 to 0,012 mm. Axial area indistinct; central area distinct, orbicular. Striæ 14 to 16 in 0,01 mm., distinctly lineate, in the middle strongly radiate and alternately longer and shorter, in the ends transverse. — A. D. p. 33 Pl. II f. 34. V. H. Syn. p. 82 Pl. VIII f. 9. *N. Carassius* GRUN. Verh. 1860 p. 537 Pl. III f. 31; Pl. IV f. 11.

Brackish water: Spitsbergen! Sea of Kara! Finmarken! Sweden (Malmö)! Holstein! Belgium (V. H.), England! Saxony! Neusiedlersee, Hungary (Grun.).

Var. *intermedia* GRUN. (1880). — V. lanceolate, with subcapitate ends. L. 0,035 to 0,04; B. 0,007 mm. Striæ 14 (middle) to 18 (ends), in the middle alternately longer and shorter, strongly radiate, in the ends convergent. — *N. cryptocephala v. int.* GRUN. in V. H. Syn. Pl. VIII f. 10.

Fresh water: Sweden, Ringsjön in Skåne! New Zealand!

By the var. *intermedia* is *N. Salinarum* connected with forms of *N. cryptocephala* as well as with *N. notabilis* PANT.

18. **N. Rho** CL. N. Sp. — V. lanceolate, rostrate, obtuse. L. 0,115; B. 0,026 mm. Axial area very narrow, in the middle dilated into a large orbicular central area. Striæ 11 in 0,01 mm., distinctly lineate (lineolæ 25 in 0,01 mm.), in the middle strongly radiate and alternately longer and shorter, in the ends transverse. — Part. I Pl. III f. 35.

Mouth of rivers: China, Canton River!

This species resembles *N. elegans*, but differs by the distinctly lineate striæ.

19. **N. notabilis** PANT. (1889). — V. lanceolate, acute. L. 0,04 to 0,056; B. 0,009 to 0,012 mm. Axial area indistinct; central area small, somewhat transverse. Striæ 10 to 11 (12,5 Pant.)

in 0,01 mm. more distant in the middle, where they are radiate and alternately longer and shorter. Terminal striæ transverse. — PANT. II. p. 51 Pl. V f. 95.

Brackish water: Hungary, fossil!

20. **N. Wilczekii** GRUN. (1884). — V. elliptic-lanceolate, with protracted, rostrate ends. L. 0,07; B. 0,026 mm. Axial area narrow. Central area subrectangular. Striæ 10 in 0.01 mm. finely punctate, in the middle more distant (8 in 0,01 mm.) alternately longer and shorter, radiate; strongly convergent at the ends, where they are closer (16 to 17 in 0,01 mm). — Franz Jos. Land D. p. 98 Pl. I f. 36.

Fresh water: Franz Josefs Land (Grun.).

21. **N. bottnica** GRUN. (1880). — V. lanceolate, obtuse. L. 0,04 to 0,065; B. 0,01 to 0,013 mm. Axial area indistinct. Central area orbicular. Striæ 20 in 0,01 mm. very finely punctate, in the middle strongly radiate and alternately longer and shorter, at the ends convergent. — A. D. p. 32 Pl. II f. 32. V. H. Syn. Pl. VII f. 33.

Brackish and marine: Finmark! Coast of England! Baltic (from Piteå to Gothland)! Greenland! Canada! Maine!

22. **N. digito-radiata** GREG. (1856). — V. lanceolate, obtuse. L. 0,06 to 0,07; B. 0,012 to 0,018 mm. Axial area narrow. Central area small, irregular. Striæ 9 in 0,01 mm., very finely lineate, in the middle radiate and alternately longer and shorter, at the ends transverse. — *Pinn. dig.* M. J. IV Pl. I f. 32. *N. dig.* A. S. N. S. D. p. 92 Pl. III f. 4. V. H. Syn. p. 86 Pl. VII f. 4. *Pinnul. viridula* EHR. Abh. Berl. Ak. 1870 II f. 12. *N. dig. v. angustior* GRUN. A. D. Pl. II f. 31.

Marine and brackish: Spitsbergen! Finmarken! Sea of Kara! North Sea! Saxony! Caspian Sea (Grun.). Arctic America! New York! Fossil, Hungary (Grun.).

Var. *Cyprinus* (EHR. 1843?) W. SM. (1853). — V. slightly gibbous in the middle. L. 0,06 to 0,08; B. 0,0125 to 0,0275 mm. — *Pinn. Cypr.* EHR. Am. I: 2 f. 7? W. SM. B. D. I Pl. XVIII f. 176. *N. digito-r. var. Cypr.* V. H. Syn. p. 86 Pl. VII f. 3.

Marine: North Sea! England (W. Sm.), Belgium (V. H.).

Var. *Seychellensis* CL. — As the type. L. 0,04; B. 0,01 mm. Striæ 12 to 13 in 0,01 mm.

Marine: Seychelles (V. H. Coll.)!

Under the name *N. Gurovii* PANTOCSEK (III Pl. IV f. 58) has figured a form, which seems to be a new species, akin to *N. digito-radiata* or *N. peregrina*. It is broadly, almost rhomboid, lanceolate. L. 0,065; B. 0,02 mm. Striæ 6 in 0,01 mm. the median of unequal length.

23. **N. Reinhardtii** GRUN. (1860). — V. elliptical to lanceolate, with broad, obtuse ends. L. 0,04 to 0,07; B. 0,014 to 0,017 mm. Axial area very narrow. Central area irregular, transversely dilated. Striæ 9 in 0,01 mm., coarsely lineate, in the middle alternately longer and shorter, strongly radiate, in the ends transverse. — *Stauroneis Reinhardtii* GRUN. Verh. 1860 p. 566 Pl. VI f. 19. *Nav. vernalis* DONK. M. J. 1869 p. 293 Pl. XVIII f. 5. *Nav. Reinh.* V. H. Syn. p. 86 Pl. VII f. 5, 6. *Stauroptera truncata* RABH. Süssw. D. Pl. IX f. 12 (1853) Alg. Sachs. N:o 848.

Fresh water: Sweden! England! Belgium (V. H.). Germany! Switzerland!

Var. *gracilior* GRUN. (1880). — V. lanceolate, narrowed towards the ends. L. 0,06 to 0,07; B. 0,013 mm. Striæ 8 to 9 in 0,01 mm. *N. digito-radiata var. striolata* GRUN. A. D. p. 32. *N. Reinh. var. gracilior* V. H. Syn. p. 87.

Fresh water, occurring with the type.

Var. *jenisseyensis* GRUN. (1880). As var. gracilior, but with only few shorter median striæ. L. 0,132; B. 0,016 mm. A. D. p. 32.

Fresh water: Mouth of Jenissey (Grun.).

N. Reinhardtii is very similar to *N. digito-radiata*, from which it differs by its fresh water habitat, and its more coarsely lineate striæ, and to *N. Gastrum*, which has striæ radiate throughout.

24. **N. oblonga** Kütz (1833). — V. linear-lanceolate, with truncate ends. L. 0,07 to 0,2; B. 0,014 to 0,024 mm. Axial area very narrow. Central area suborbicular. Striæ 7 to 8 in 0,01 mm., very finely lineate, the median more distant and strongly radiate, the terminal convergent and angularly bent. — *Frustulia oblonga* Kütz Dec. N:o 71 (accord. to Lagst.). *N. oblonga* Kütz Bac. p. 97 Pl. IV f. 21. Grun. Verh. 1860 p. 523. A. S. Atl. XLVII f. 63 to 68. V. H. Syn. p. 81 Pl. VII f. 1. Pant. III Pl. VIII f. 142. *Pinnul. oblonga* W. Sm. B. D. XVIII f. 165.

Fresh or very slightly brackish water: Sweden! Finland! Saxony! Belgium (V. H.). England! Switzerland (Brun.), Illinois! Fossil: Dubravica, Hungary (Grun.), Mexico and Guatemala!

Var. *lanceolata* Grun. (1860). — Shorter and broader lanceolate. — Verh. 1860 p. 523 Pl. IV f. 25.

Var. *acuminata* Grun. (1860). — Almost linear, with cuneate, obtuse ends. — l. c.

Fresh water: Austria (Grun.).

Var. *nodulosa* Grun. (1860). — As the var. acuminata, but with triundulate margins. — l. c.

Fresh water: Frankfurt am Main.

25. **N. falaisiensis** Grun. (1880). — V. narrow, lanceolate, with subrostrate, obtuse ends. L. 0,025; B. 0,005 mm. Axial area indistinct. Central area small, rounded. Striæ about 20 in 0,01 mm., slightly radiate throughout. — V. H. Syn. Pl. XIV f. 5.

Fresh water: Greenland! England (V. H. T.), Belgium (V. H.).

Var.? *Lanceola* Grun. (1880). — V. linear with more distinctly rostrate ends. L. 0,03; B. 0,004 mm. Striæ 23 in 0,01 mm. more radiate — V. H. S. Pl. XIV f. 6 *B*.

N. falaisiensis is according to Grunow nearly related to *N. Bahuheimii*.

26. **N. arenicola** Grun. (1882). — V. linear, frequently slightly gibbous in the middle, with broad, rounded ends. L. 0,02; B. 0,005 mm. Axial and central areas indistinct. Striæ 13 or 14 (middle) to 21 (ends) in 0,01 mm. very finely lineate, slightly radiate throughout. — *Amphiprora arenaria* Bréb. in Rab. A. E. N:o 2150. *N. arenicola* Grun. F. D. Öst. Ung. p. 149 Pl. XXX f. 76, 77.

Marine (aestuaries): Coasts of France and England (Grun.). Firth of Tay!

27. **N. dicephala** (Ehb. 1836?) W. Sm. (1853). — V. linear to linear-lanceolate with capitate-rostrate ends. L. 0,025 to 0,04; B. 0,01 to 0,0125 mm. Axial area indistinct. Central area large, transverse and rectangular. Striæ 9 to 11 in 0,01 mm. radiate throughout. — *Pin. diceph.* Ehb. Inf. p. 185. Am. II: i f. 29? *N. dicephala* W. Sm. B. D. I p. 87 Pl. XVII f. 157. Grun. A. D. p. 34. V. H. Syn. p. 87. Pl. VIII f. 33, 34. Ströse Klicken D. f. 4.

Fresh water: Sweden! England! Saxony! Switzerland (Brun.), Hungary, Dubravica, fossil (Grun.), Kamtchatka! Japan! Illinois! Ecuador!

Var. *elginensis* Greg. (1856). — L. 0,024 to 0,03; B. 0,01 to 0,0105 mm. Striæ 12 to 14 in 0,01 mm. transverse at the ends. — *Pinn. elginensis* Greg. M. J. IV Pl. I f. 33. Grun. A. D. p. 35.

Fresh water: Scotland, Ben Lawers fossil (Grunow), Finland, Pudasjärvi, fossil!

Var. *subcapitata* Grun. (1882). — V. with broadly truncate ends. — F. D. Öst. Ung. p. 156 Pl. XXX f. 54.

Fresh water: Hungary, fossil (Grun.).

N. dicephala is very nearly connected with the Cymbellæ, which, besides its great resemblance to *Cym. anglica*, is proved by its cell-contents (see A. S. Atl. Pl. LXXII f. 29–33; Grun. F. D. Öst. Ung. XXX f. 55). There is only one chromatophore-plate, in the middle separated by a plasmatic mass from the zone, and on the dorsal side deeply cloven by a linear fissure.

28. **N. lanceolata** (Ag. 1827?) Kütz (1833). — V. lanceolate. L. 0,03 to 0,05; B. 0,008 to 0,01 mm. Axial area indistinct. Central area distinct, orbicular. Striæ 12 (middle) to 15 or 16 (ends) in 0,01 mm., strongly radiate throughout. — *Frustulia lanceolata* Agardh Flora X p. 626?

KÜTZ. Dec. N:o 72 according to Lagst. *Pinnularia viridula* W. SM. B. D. XVIII f. 175. *N. lanceol.* A. S. Atl. XLVII f. 49. GRUN. A. D. p. 35. V. H. Syn. p. 88 Pl. VIII f. 16 (17 forma curta). LAGST. Öfvers. K. Sv. Vet.-Akad. Förh. 1884 X f. 5 *a*. *N. cryptoc. v. rhynchoc.* Ströse Klieken D. f. 3 *b*.

Fresh water: Sweden! Finland! Germany! England! Belgium (V. H.). Japan! Australia, Mitchell River!

Var. *tenella* A. S. (1876). — V. narrow lanceolate. L. 0,035; B. 0,006 mm. — *N. tenella* A. S. Atl. XLVII f. 45, 46.

Fresh water: Sweden, Loka (Atl.).

Var. *phyllepta* KÜTZ. (1844). — L. 0,03 to 0,033; B. 0,008 to 0,009 mm. Striæ 18 in 0,01 mm. *N. phyllepta* KÜTZ. Bac. p. 94 Pl. XXX f. 56. V. H. Syn. p. 88 Pl. VIII f. 40.

Brackish water: Belgium (V. H.). Saxony (Saline Dürrenberg)!

Var. *arenaria* DONK. (1861). — L. 0,05 to 0,06; B. 0,01 mm. Striæ 9 to 10 in 0,01 mm. — *N. arenaria* DONK. M. J. I p. 10 Pl. I f. 9. B. D. p. 56 Pl. VIII f. 5. A. S. Atl. XLVII f. 38, 39, 40. *N. lanc. v. aren.* V. H. Syn. p. 88 Pl. VIII f. 18.

Marine: Baltic (Gothland)! North Sea!

Var. *Cymbula* DONK. (1869). — V. lanceolate. L. 0,055; B. 0,011 mm. Axial area indistinct. Central area small, orbicular. Striæ 8 (middle) to 10 (ends) radiate throughout, coarsely lineate. — *N. Cymbula* DONK. M. J. 1869 p. 294 Pl. XVIII f. 6. V. H. Syn. Pl. VII f. 32.

Fresh water: England (Donk.). Finland! Japan!

Var.? *latior* DANNF. (1882). — V. broadly lanceolate, with capitate ends. L. 0,026; B. 0,01 mm. Striæ 22 in 0,01 mm. — *N. cryptocephala v. latior* DANNF. Baltic D. p. 26 Pl. II f. 12.

Brackish water: Baltic (Helsingfors, Gothland) Dannf.

As Dannfeldts fig. shews the striæ radiate at the ends, this form has been classed here under *N. lanceolata*.

Var. *hordeiformis* PANT. (1889). — L. 0,026; B. 0,008 mm. Striæ 10 to 12,5 in 0,01 mm. — *N. hordeiformis* PANT. II p. 48 Pl. XI f. 197.

Brackish water: Hungary, fossil (Pant.).

29. **N. anglica** RALFS (1861). — V. elliptical, with capitate ends. L. 0,04; B. 0,014 mm. Axial area very narrow. Central area small. Striæ 9 to 12 in 0,01 mm. radiate throughout, finely lineate, in the middle of equal length. — *N. tumida* W. SM. B. D. I p. 53 Pl. XVII f. 146 (1853). *N. tumida genuina* GRUN. Verh. 1860 p. 537 Pl. IV f. 43 *a*. *N. anglica* RALFS in Pritch. Inf. p. 900. DONK. B. D. p. 35 Pl. V f. 11 *a*. V. H. Syn. p. 87 Pl. VIII f. 29, 30. *N. gastrum v. anglica* GRUN. A. D. p. 34.

Fresh water: Sweden! Finland! England! Illinois! Ecuador!

Var. *minuta* CL. — L. 0,025; B. 0,008 mm. Striæ 15 to 17 in 0,01 mm.

Fresh water: Finland, Lake Lojo near Abo! Jamaica!

Var. *subcruciata* GRUN. — L. 0,014 to 0,024; B. 0,007 mm. Area more transverse. — GRUN. in V. H. Types N:o 99.

Slightly brackish water: England (V. H. T.).

Var. *subsalsa* GRUN. 1860. — V. lanceolate with rostrate, not capitate ends. L. 0,03; B. 0,011 mm. Striæ 9 to 11 in 0,01 mm. — *N. tumida v. subsalsa* GRUN. Verh. 1860 p. 537 Pl. IV f. 43 *b*, *c*. A. D. p. 34. *N. anglica* DONK. B. D. Pl. V f. 11 *b*. *N. anglica v. subsalina* GRUN. in V. H. Syn. p. 87 Pl. VIII f. 31.

Slightly brackish water: Neusiedler See (Grun.), Shienitzer See, Prussia (Grun.).

The var. *subsalsa* is nearly akin to *N. dicephala* and connects this species with *N. Gastrum*.

30. **N. Gastrum** EHR. (1843). — V. lanceolate to elliptical, with slightly rostrate, obtuse ends. L. 0,024 to 0,045; B. 0,012 to 0,018 mm. Axial area very narrow. Central area large irregular, somewhat transverse. Striæ 8 to 10 in 0,01 mm., finely punctate, in the middle usually

alternately longer and shorter. — *Pinn. Gastrum* EHR. Am. III: 7 f. 23. M. G. V: 1 f. 12. Ströse Klieken D. f. 1 *b*. *N. Gastrum* DONK. B. D. p. 22 Pl. III f. 10. GRUN. A. D. p. 31. V. H. Syn. p. 87 Pl. VIII f. 25, 27. PANT. III Pl. III f. 48. *Nav. exigua* PANT. III Pl. III f. 45 (1893). *N. varians* GREG. T. M. S. III p. 10 Pl. II f. 27, 28 (1855). *N. Hoffmannii* PANT. II p. 47 Pl. XIV f. 245 (1889)?

Fresh water: Sweden! Finland! England! Ireland! Belgium (V. H.). Sea of Kara! Cape Deschneff! New Zealand! Illinois!

Var. *Jenisseyensis* GRUN. (1880). — Lanceolate. L. 0,038 to 0,065; B. 0,011 to 0,017 mm. Striæ about 9 in 0,01 mm. more distant in the middle, where there are only a few shorter ones among the longer, very finely lineate. — A. D. p. 31 Pl. I f. 28. *N. Basilica* Pant. III Pl. VIII f. 129 (1893)?

Fresh or brackish water: Jenissey (Grun.). Cape Deschneff! New Zealand! New Caledonia (Kinker Coll.)!

Var. *latiuscula* GRUN. (1880). — V. lanceolate. L. 0,024 to 0,06; B. 0,012 to 0,017 mm. Striæ 10 to 11 in 0,01 mm. The median striæ not alternately longer and shorter. — A. D. p. 31. Ströse Klieken D. f. 1 *a*.

Fresh and slightly brackish water: Sea of Kara! Sweden (Upsala, Ronneby, Kalmar, fossil)! Finland! East Cape, East Siberia! Cuxhaven (Grun.). Oberrohe and Klieken, fossil!

Var. *exigua* GREG. (1854). — V. lanceolate with subrostrate or subcapitate ends. L. 0,017 to 0,03; B. 0,009 to 0,012 mm. Striæ 12 to 14 in 0,01 mm *Pinnul. exigua* GREG. M. J. p. 99 Pl. IV f. 14. *N. Gastr. v. exigua* GRUN. A. D. p. 31. V. H. Syn. Pl. VIII f. 32.

Fresh or brackish water: Gulf of Bothnia (Torneå! Piteå!) Finland, Lake Lojo, Åbo! Hungary, fossil (Grun.). New Zealand!

Var. *borgana* PANT. (1889). — V. capitate. L. 0,046 to 0,06; B. 0,017 to 0,02 mm. Striæ 7,5 to 8,5 in 0,01 mm. radiate, coarsely punctate, puncta 17 to 18 in 0,01 mm. Median striæ alternately longer and shorter. — PANT. II p. 46.

Marine: Hungary, fossil (Pant.).

30. **N. Placentula** EHR. (1843). — V. elliptic-lanceolate, with rostrate, obtuse ends. L. 0,05 to 0,06; B. 0,016 to 0,028 mm. Axial area narrow, but distinct. Central area irregular, transverse. Striæ 6 to 9 in 0,01 mm., radiate throughout, coarsely lineate or punctate, shortened in the middle, but not alternately longer and shorter. — *Pinnul. Plac.* EHR. Am. III: 7 f. 22. M. G. XII f. 19. GRUN. A. D. p. 31 Pl. II f. 36. *N. pusilla* DONK. B. D. p. 20 Pl. III f. 6 *b*? *N. Gastrum v. Plac.* V. H. Syn. p. 87 Pl. VIII f. 26, 28. *N. Gastrum f. minor.* GRUN. F. D. Öst. Ung. XXX f. 51.

Fresh water: Cassel Polierschiefer (Ehb.). Ireland Antrim Co.! Jenissey! New Zealand! California! Oregon! Puerto Monte! Ecuador!

Var, *lanceolata* GRUN. (1860). — V. broadly lanceolate. Ends not rostrate. L. 0,04; B. 0,016 mm. Striæ 7 to 8 in 0,01 mm. — *N. tumida var. lanceolata* GRUN. Verh. 1860 p. 537 Pl. IV f. 44. A. D. p. 31.

Brackish water: Sea of Kara! Skienitz See near Berlin (Grun.), Neusiedlersee (Grun.).

Nav. Placentula is very nearly akin to *Nav. Gastrum*, and it is questionable whether they should not be united in one species. The median striæ are in *Nav. Gastrum*, but not in *Nav. Placentula*, alternately longer and shorter, but this characteristic is subject to great variation, the var. *Jenisseyensis* having only a few, and the var. *latiuscula* no, shorter median striæ. Of more importance is it that *Nav. Placentula* has coarsely lineate, or almost punctate striæ. *Nav. anglica* is nearly akin to *Nav. Gastrum* and might be considered as a variety of it. There exists in fact no limit between these three species; *Nav. Placentula* appears to be akin to *Nav. leptostigma*, which has finer, distinctly punctate, striæ and that to *Nav. platystoma*, the striæ of which are very finely punctate. On the other hand *N. Placentula* is by its coarsely punctate striæ allied to the section *Punctatæ*, among which *Nav. amphibola* is nearly akin to *Nav. Placentula*. Smaller forms of *Nav. Gastrum* closely resemble smaller forms of *Nav. peregrina var. Menisculus*, from which they differ by the terminal striæ being radiate throughout, but this characteristic is sometimes exceedingly delicate.

32. **N. leptostigma** Ehb. (1854). — V. elliptical, with more or less broad, rostrate ends. L. 0,038 to 0,048; B. 0,015 to 0,02 mm. Axial area indistinct. Central area large, orbicular. Striæ 14 in 0,01 mm., radiate throughout, distinctly punctate (puncta about 22 in 0,01 mm.) in the middle alternately larger and shorter. — *Pinnul. leptost.* Ehb. M. G. XXXIII: 12 f. 25. *Nav. lept.* Icon. n. Pl. I f. 37.

Fresh water: Oregon, fossil!

33. **N. platystoma** Ehb. (1838). V. elliptic-lanceolate, with broad, rostrate ends. L. 0,037 to 0,05; B. 0,017 mm. Axial area narrow. Central area large, transversely dilated, subrhomboidal. Striæ 17 in 0,01 mm., very finely lineate, radiate throughout. Among the median striæ a few shorter frequently occur. — Ehb. Inf. 178 Pl. XIII f. 8. M. G. XIII f. 6 *b*. Cl. A. D. p. 14 Pl. III f. 61. *N. macromphala* Schum. Preuss. D. II N. p. 55 Pl. II f. 29 (1867)?

Fresh and slightly brackish water: Sweden (Lake Mälaren, Gulf of Bothnia, Gotland in the Baltic)! Mouth of Jenissey! Michigan!

Var. *bengalensis* Grun. Ms. V. subrhomboidal, with broad, rounded ends. L. 0,03; B. 0,012 mm. Striæ distinctly punctate.

Fresh water: Bengal (Grun.).

34. **N. oviformis** Cl. N. Sp. — V. elliptic-lanceolate. L. 0,045; B. 0,018 mm. Axial area narrow, linear; central area large, orbicular. Striæ 10 in 0,01 mm., radiate throughout, finely lineate, not alternating in length in the middle. — Pl. II f. 4.

Marine: Madagascar (Van Heurck Coll.)!

35. **N. arata** Grun. (1882). - V. lanceolate, gradually tapering from the middle to the obtuse ends. L. 0,06 to 0,067; B. 0,018 to 0,02 mm. Axial area narrow; central area orbicular. Striæ 8 to 9 in 0,01 mm. closer towards the ends, all radiate and distinctly punctate. Across the striæ on each side of the median line are 3 to 4 narrow longitudinal clear areas. — *N. Tuscula v. arata* Grun. F. D. Öst. Ung. p. 145 Pl. XXX f. 58. Pant. III Pl. XXIII f. 342.

Brackish or fresh water: Hungary, Dubravica fossil (Grun.), Hudson River (Grun.).

This species can scarcely be a variety of *N. tuscula*, the terminal striæ being radiate. It seems rather to belong to the group of *N. Gastrum*.

36. **N. Clementis** Grun. (1882). — V. slightly asymmetrical, broadly lanceolate, with rostrate, obtuse ends. L. 0,04 to 0,045; B. 0,012 to 0,015 mm. Axial area narrow. Central area small, orbicular, with 2 isolated puncta on one side of the central nodule. Striæ 8 to 10 in 0,01 mm. in the middle, where they are alternately longer and shorter, 16 in 0,01 mm. towards the ends. All striæ are strongly radiate and finely punctate. -- F. D. Öst. Ung. p. 144 Pl. XXX f. 52.

Fresh water: Dubravica, Hungary, fossil! Cheshire, England (V. H. T.).

This species is akin to *N. Placentula* and at the same time to *N. Demeraræ* of the section Punctatæ, the latter having also isolated puncta on the central area.

37. **N. arenariæformis** Pant. (1889). — V. lanceolate, obtuse. L. 0,02; B. 0,011 mm. Axial area distinct; central area small. Striæ 12,5 in 0,01 mm., strongly radiate to the ends, the median striæ alternately longer and shorter. — Pant. II p. 42 Pl. VIII f. 140.

Brackish water: Hungary, fossil (Pant.).

38. **N. ludloviana** A. S. (1876). — V. lanceolate, with obtuse, subtruncate ends. L. 0,09; B. 0,03 mm. Axial area distinct, dilated around the central nodule. Striæ 8 (middle) to 9 (ends)

in 0,01 mm., radiate throughout, finely lineate, the median alternately longer and shorter. Atl. XLVI f. 15.

Fresh water: Fort Ludlow (Atl.), Shasta Co. Calif., fossil! Oregon! Minnesota (interglacial deposit)!

39. **N. valida** CL. a. GRUN. (1880). V. slightly asymmetrical, elliptic-lanceolate. L. 0,057 to 0,11; B. 0,022 to 0,026 mm. Axial area narrow, asymmetrical. Central area irregular, somewhat asymmetrical. Striæ 7,5 to 8 in 0,01 mm., distinctly lineate, radiate throughout, the median alternately longer and shorter. — A. D. p. 32 Pl. II f. 29. CL. Vega p. 466.

Marine: Sea of Kara! Cape Wankarema!

Var. *minuta* CL. (1883). L. 0,025; B. 0,013 mm. Striæ 8 in 0,01 mm., not alternately longer and shorter. — Vega p. 466.

Marine: Cape Wankarema!

Var.? *capensis* CL. — L. 0,056; B. 0,019 mm. Striæ 8 in 0,01 mm. not distinctly lineate, radiate throughout. Axial area symmetrical. Central area larger.

Marine: Cape of Good Hope!

The type is most nearly akin to *N. Gastrum var. Jenisseyensis* but has more distinctly lineate striæ. The var. *capensis* is very doubtful as a form of *N. valida*.

40. **N. Hasta** PANT. (1893). — V. lanceolate, gradually tapering from the middle to the subacute ends. L. 0,07 to 0,09; B. 0,015 mm. Axial area narrow, slightly dilated in the middle. Striæ 9 in 0,01 mm. strongly radiate throughout and coarsely lineate. Among the median striæ some few shorter ones are intercalated. — PANT. III Pl. V f. 74; Pl. XIV f. 213.

Habitat?: Köpecz, Hungary, fossil (Pant.).

41. **N. imperfecta** CL. (1883). — V. elliptical to elleptic-lanceolate, frequently with subrostrate ends. L. 0,065; B. 0,03 mm. Axial area unilateral, narrow. Central area small. Striæ 8 in 0,01 mm. radiate throughout, finely lineate and crossed by several longitudinal and undulating narrow blank bands. — Vega p. 466 Pl. XXXVI f. 34.

Marine: Sea of Kara! Cape Wankarema!

This form is very nearly akin to *N. valida*, from which it differs by its striæ being divided into 2 to 4 lengths, as the striæ of *N. maculosa* DONK.

42. **N. consors** A. S. (1876). — V. narrow elliptic-lanceolate, obtuse. L. 0,06 to 0,1; B. 0,015 to 0,02 mm. Axial area narrow; central area transverse, rectangular. Striæ 8 in 0,01 mm., radiate throughout, finely lineate and crossed by 3 to 4 irregularly undulating, longitudinal bands. Atl. XLVIII f. 24, 25, 26, 27. *N. Lendugeri* CL. Vega p. 505 Pl. XXXVI f. 22 (1883).

Marine: Ceylon! Samoa (Atl.), Sandwich Island (Atl.), Singapore (Atl.), Java!

43. **N. (Rhoiconeis) genuflexa** KÜTZ (1844). V. convex, elliptic-linear, with obtuse ends. L. 0,02 to 0,043; B. 0,004 to 0,005 mm. Axial area indistinct. Central area small, orbicular. Striæ 18 in 0,01 mm., a little closer at the ends, radiate throughout. Frustule arcuate. L. 0,02 to 0,03; Height 0,01 mm. — Bac. p. 101 Pl. XXI f. 6. *Rhoiconeis genuflexa* GRUN. Verh. 1863 p. 147.

Marine: Peru (Grun.), New Zealand (Grun.), Port Jackson! Samoa! Labuan! Ceylon!

44. **N. (Rhoiconeis) Bolleana** GRUN (1863). — V. linear-lanceolate, with obtuse ends. L. 0,045 to 0,095; B. 0,01 to 0,011 mm. Axial area very narrow; central area large quadrate. Striæ 8 (middle) to 11 (ends) in 0,01 mm. not distinctly lineate, radiate throughout. Frustule with broad connecting zone, arcuate. — *Rhoiconeis Bolleana* GRUN. Verh. 1863 p. 147 Pl. IV f. 11. A. S. Atl. XLVII f. 18 (striæ strongly punctate)? *N. Index* TEMP. a. BRUN D. foss. du Japon p. 44 Pl. V f. 5 (1889).

Marine: Greenland! Spitsbergen! Finmark! Sea of Kara! Cape Deschneff! Behrings Island! Japan, fossil! Pacific Ocean (Grun.).

N. Bolleana has somewhat dissimilar valves, the concave having more strongly radiate striæ than the convex. Original specimens of *Nav. Index* TEMP. a. BRUN are perfectly similar to specimens of *N. Bolleana*, determined by GRUNOW.

45. **N. incerta** GRUN. (1880). — V. linear, with slightly convex margins and obtuse ends. L. 0,015; B. 0,006 mm. Axial and central areas indistinct. Striæ 15 in 0,01 mm., scarcely radiate. — V. H. Syn. p. 107 Pl. XIV f. 43.

Marine: Belgium (V. H.).

A small form, remarkable for its coarse striæ, unknown to the author. Its place in the system is doubtful.

46. **N. (Schizonema) corymbosa** C. AG. (1824). V. narrow, lanceolate, obtuse. L. 0,01; B. 0,002 mm. Axial and central areas indistinct. Striæ 23 in 0,01 mm. very slightly radiate. — *Schizonema corymbosum* AG. Syst. Alg. p. 11. V. H. Syn. Pl. XVI f. 21.

Marine: Japan (Grun.).

The frustules live in hair-fine branched tubes.

47. **N. (Schizonema) mollis** W. SM. (1856). — V. lanceolate, obtuse. L. 0,027 to 0,032; B. 0,006 to 0,007 mm. Axial and central areas indistinct. Striæ 14 to 16 in 0,01 mm. radiate in the middle, elsewhere parallel, finely lineate; lineolæ forming longitudinal striæ. — *Schizon. molle* W. SM. B. D. II p. 77 Pl. LVIII f. 365. V. H. Syn. Pl. XV f. 22, 23. *S. albicans* V. H. Syn. l. c. f. 20. *S. torquatum* V. H. Syn. l. c. f. 21.

Marine: Arctic Amercia, Cape Sabine! Bohuslän! North Sea! Adriatic!

The frustules are crowded in very branched, soft tubes, forming branches 15 to 30 cmt. long.

A form intermediate between *N. mollis* and *N. ramosissima* is *S. setaceum* V. H. Syn. XV f. 13. The frustules of this form live crowded in stiff, olive-green coloured, arborescent and very branched tubes.

48. **N. (Schizonema) nidulans** CL. (1892). — V. narrow linear-lanceolate. L. 0,026; B. 0,005 mm. Axial and central areas indistinct. Striæ 22 in 0,01 mm., parallel. Frustules inhabit the interior of marine algæ. — CL. Diatomiste I p. 78 Pl. XII f. 12.

Marine: South coast of Australia, in the thallus of a Chylocladia, sent by Prof. J. AGARDH!

49. **N. (Schizonema) ramosissima** AG. (1824). — V. linear-lanceolate, with obtuse ends. L. 0,051 to 0,072; B. 0,01 to 0,008 mm. Axial and central areas indistinct. Striæ 12 to 13 in 0,01 mm. parallel, finely lineate, lineolæ forming longitudinal striæ, about 30 in 0,01 mm.

Forma caspia GRUN. (1878). — L. 0,038 to 0,052; B. 0,007 to 0,008 mm. Striæ 12 in 0,01 mm. — Casp. Sea Alg. p. 19 Pl. IV f. 21.

Brackish water: Caspian Sea (Grun.).

Forma genuina CL. — L. about 0,05 mm. — *Schiz. ram.* C. A. Syst. Alg. p. 11. V. H. Syn. p. 110 Pl. XV f. 4. 5.

Marine: North Sea!

Forma amplia GRUN. (1880). — L. 0,08 to 0,072; B. 0,007 to 0,008 mm. Striæ 10 to 12 in 0,01 mm. *Schizon. amplius* V. H. Syn. Pl. XV f. 3. — A. S. N. S. D. III f. 5.

Marine: North Sea! Canada! Mauritius!

N. ramosissima lives enclosed in gelatinous tubes on the various forms of which a great number of species and varieties has been founded (see GRUNOW's paper in Botan. Centralbl. 1880). As mentioned above, this species is nearly akin to *N. mollis*, and on the other hand to smaller forms of *N. directa var. subtilis*, from which *N. ramosissima* can scarcely be distinguished.

50. **N. directa** W. Sm (1853). — V. narrow, gradually tapering from the middle to the acute ends, about 10 times longer than broad. Central pores of the median line approximate. Axial area indistinct; central area small. Striæ 4 to 11 in 0,01 mm., distinctly transversely lineate.

Var. *subtilis* Greg. (1857). — L. 0,09 to 0,012; B. 0,008 mm. Striæ 10 to 11 in 0,01 mm., finely lineate. — *Pinn. subtilis* Greg. D. of Clyde p. 488 Pl. IX f. 19. *N. directa var. subt.* Cl. Vega p. 467. *Pinnul. acutiuscula* Greg. T. M. S. IV p. 48 Pl. V f. 21 (1856)?

Marine: Iceland! Scotland (Greg.). Sea of Kara! Cape Wankarema!

Var. *genuina* Cl. — L. 0,07 to 0,125; B. 0,008 to 0,012 mm. Striæ about 8 in 0,01 mm., finely lineate. — *N. directa* W. Sm. B. D. I p. 56 Pl. XVIII f. 172. A. S. Atl. XLVII f. 4. 5. *N. dir. v. augusta* Grun. A. D. p. 39.

Marine: Spitsbergen! Finmark! Sea of Kara! Cape Deschneff! North Sea! Yokohama! Arctic America! Greenland!

Var. *remota* Grun. (1880). L. 0,16 to 0,2; B. 0,015 mm. Striæ 4 to 5 in 0,01 mm., coarsely lineate; lineolæ 17 to 21 in 0,01 mm. A. S. N. S. D. III f. 2. Atl. XLVII f. 1. 2, 8, 9. *Pinn. longa* Greg. T. M. S. IV p. 47 Pl. V f. 18 (1856)?

Marine: Spitsbergen! Finmark! Sea of Kara! Mediterranean Sea! Red Sea! Gulf of Mexico (Atl.), Colon! Campeachy Bay (Atl.).

Var. *lucus* A. S. (1876). — L. 0,13 to 0,15; B. 0,018 mm. Central area on one side of the central nodule dilated to a short longitudinal space. Striæ 4 to 4,5 in 0,01 mm. Lineolæ about 24 in 0,01 mm. *N. lucus* A. S. Atl. XLVII f. 7.

Marine: Mediterranean Sea (Atl.), Sumbava (Kinker Coll.)! Colon!

Var. *javanica* Cl. — L. 0,15; B. 0,01 mm. Striæ 5 in 0,01 mm. finely lineate.

Marine: Sumbava (Kinker Coll.)!

N. directa is a very variable species, of which I have seen strictly typical specimens only from the Arctic Sea and the North Sea. Specimens from other localities are suspicious. As to *N. longa* Greg. I have not seen any form accurately agreeing with the fig. of Gregory, which has radiate striæ. *Pinnul. eriophila* Castrac. (Challenger Voyage D. p. 26 Pl. XV f. 2) is probably a form of N. *directa*.

51. **N. Kepesli** Grun. (1884). — V. linear, narrow. L. 0,085 to 0,095; B. 0,008 mm. Areas indistinct. Striæ 12 to 13 in 0,01 mm. transverse, finely lineate, forming oblique striæ. — Franz Jos. Land D. p. 103 Pl. I f. 37.

Marine: Franz Josefs-Land (Grun.).

52. **N. jejuna** A. S. (1876). — V. narrow, linear, with rounded or somewhat cuneate ends. L. 0,1 to 0,12; B. 0,01 mm. Axial area indistinct. Central area small, elongated. Striæ 5 in 0,01 mm., parallel, or slightly radiate throughout, distinctly lineate. Atl. XLVI f. 76. Castr. Challenger Voy. p. 33 Pl. XX f. 12, XXVIII f. 11.

Marine: Java (Atl.), Sumatra (Grove Coll.)! Singapore! Macassar Straits! Japan!

53. **N. trigonocephala** Cl. (1883). — V. linear, with cuneate ends. L. 0,05 to 0,065; B. 0,01 to 0,012 mm. Axial area indistinct. Central area small. Striæ 10 to 12 in 0,01 mm., almost parallel, transversely lineate, crossed by several undulating, narrow longitudinal bands. — Vega p. 468 Pl. XXXVI f. 29.

Marine: Cape Wankarema!

54. **N. transitans** Cl. (1883). — V. lanceolate, 4 to 6 times longer than broad. L. 0,065 to 0,09; B. 0,016 to 0,02 mm. Axial area indistinct. Central area small, orbicular. Striæ 7 to 9 in 0,01 mm. parallel, distinctly lineate. — Vega p. 467 Pl. XXXVI f. 31.

Marine: Cape Wankarema!

Var. *derasa* Grun. (1880). — Striæ crossed on each side by a more or less narrow lateral area. L. 0,055 to 0,067; B. 0,0145 to 0,015 mm. Striæ 8,5 or 12 (middle) to 10 or 14 (ends) in 0,01 mm. — *N. derasa* Grun. A. D. p. 39 Pl. II f. 46. *N. trans. v. derasa* Cl. Vega p. 467 Pl. XXXVI f. 32.

Marine: Sea of Kara! Cape Wankarema! Cape Deschneff!

Forma minuta. — L. 0,035; B. 0,012 mm. Striæ 12 in 0,01 mm. — Cl. Vega p. 467 Pl. XXXVI f. 37.

Marine: Cape Deschneff!

Forma gracilenta Grun. (1880). — V. narrower, with prolonged ends. L. 0,065 to 0,075; B. 0,009 to 0,011 mm. Striæ 10,5 to 11 in 0,01 mm. — *N. derasa var.? gracilenta* Grun. A. D. p. 40.

Marine: Sea of Kara (Grun.).

Var. *incudiformis* Grun. (1883). — Axial area unilateral, irregular, linear. Striæ on the side, opposite to the axial area, crossed by a more or less broad lateral area, usually uniting with the central area. — *N. incus v. abbreviata* Grun. A. D. p. 39 Pl. II f. 43. *N. incudiformis* Grun. in Cl. Vega p. 467 Pl. XXXVI f. 26, 30.

Marine: Cape Wankarema!

Var. *erosa* Cl. 1883. — Striæ 7,5 to 10 in 0,01 mm., crossed by several narrow, undulating, longitudinal bands. — *N. erosa* Cl. Vega p. 468 Pl. XXXVI f. 28.

Marine: Cape Wankarema!

Var. *asymmetrica* Cl. (1883). — Axial area unilateral, irregularly linear. Striæ 9,5 in 0,01 mm. as in var. erosa. *N. asymmetrica* Cl. Vega p. 468 Pl. XXXVI f. 27.

Marine: Cape Wankarema!

55. **N. finmarchica** Cl. a. Grun. (1880). — V. lanceolate, with obtuse ends. L. 0,03 to 0,042; B. 0,0115 to 0,013 mm. Central nodule transversely dilated to a short stauros. Striæ 12 to 14 in 0,01 mm., slightly radiate, apparently smooth, crossed by a narrow, arcuate lateral area. *Stauroneis finm.* Cl. a. Grun. A. D. p. 47 Pl. III f. 63.

Marine: Finmark! Bohuslän!

It is difficult to find the proper place in the system for this little form. There is no allied species in Stauroneis, nor any other naviculoid form, to which it seems to be related, with the exception of *N. transitans var. derasa f. minuta*, from which it differs by its stauros and apparently smooth striæ. This form is neither a Mastogloia nor an Achnanthes, both valves being similar.

56. **N. kariana** Grun. (1880). V. broadly lanceolate, slightly rostrate. L. 0,085 to 0,09; B. 0,024 to 0,026 mm. Median line with approximate central pores. Axial area indistinct; central area small, orbicular. Striæ 12,5 to 14 in 0,01 mm., parallel, finely lineate; lineolæ forming longitudinal striæ, about 27 in 0,01 mm. — A. D. p. 39 Pl. II f. 44.

Marine: Frans Josefs Land! Sea of Kara! Cape Wankarema!

Var. *detersa* Grun. (1883). – Striæ crossed by a more or less large lateral area. — Cl. Vega p. 469 Pl. XXXVI f. 36. Franz Jos. Land D. p. 103 Pl. I f. 23, 24.

Marine: Franz Josefs-Land (Grun.). Cape Wankarema!

Var. *frigida* Grun. (1880). L. 0,044 to 0,07; B. 0,012 to 0,013 mm. Striæ 15 or 16 (middle) to 17 or 18 (ends) in 0,01 mm. very slightly radiate throughout, finely lineate; lineolæ forming longitudinal striæ, about 26 in 0,01 mm. — A. D. p. 39. Franz Jos. Land D. p. 103 Pl. I f. 25.

Marine: Sea of Kara! Franz Josefs-Land!

57. **N. gelida** Grun. (1884). V. lanceolate, with slightly rostrate ends. L. 0,03 to 0,065; B. 0,009 to 0,015 mm. Axial area indistinct. Central area very small, orbicular. Striæ 9 to 12 in 0,01 mm., finely lineate; lineolæ not forming longitudinal striæ. — Franz Jos. Land D. p. 103 Pl. I f. 27, 28. *N. kariana v. curta* Cl. Vega p. 470 Pl. XXXVII f. 40 (1883).

Marine: Davis Strait! Franz Josefs-Land (Grun.). Cape Wankarema! Cape Deschneff!

Var.? *subimpressa* GRUN. (1880). — V. lanceolate. L. 0,065; B. 0,016 mm. Striæ 11 to 12 in 0,01 mm., crossed by a longitudinal line. — *N. subimpr.* GRUN. A. D. p. 39 Pl. II f. 45.

Marine: Sea of Kara (Grun.).

Var.? *tenuis* CL. (1883). — V. elliptic-lanceolate, with a longitudinal impression on both sides of the median line. L. 0,038; B. 0.015 mm. Striæ 18 in 0,01 mm., unilaterally interrupted by a narrow transverse fascia. — *N. subimpressa var. tenuior* CL. Vega D. p. 470 Pl XXXVII f. 49.

Marine: Cape Deschneff!

58. **N. irregularis** PANT. (1889). — V. narrow, lanceolate, with subacute ends. L. 0,126; B. 0,021 mm. Axial area broad on one side of the median line, narrow on the other. Striæ 7 to 10 in 0,01 mm. almost parallel, alternately longer and shorter, on one side of the median line crossed by a linear lateral area. — PANT. II p. 49 Pl. XXX f. 424.

Marine: Hungary, fossil (Pant.).

I have not seen this species, but to judge from the figure it seems to be akin to *N. transitans var. asymmetrica*. Somewhat similar is *N. primordialis* PANT. (III Pl. XXV f. 382).

59. **N. (Rhoiconeis) sibirica** GRUN. (1882). — V. lanceolate, subacute. L. 0,04 to 0,06; B. 0,01 mm. Axial area indistinct; central area large, subquadrate. Striæ 10 (at the ends 10 to 11) in 0,01 mm. almost parallel throughout, distinctly lineate. Frustules arcuate, with narrow connecting zone. — *Rhoiconeis Bolleana var.? sibirica* GRUN. in CL. M. D. N:o 302. CL. Vega p. 469 Pl. XXXVII f. 38.

Marine: Cape Wankarema!

Var. *asymmetrica* CL. 1883. — Axial area unilateral, narrow. Striæ 11 in 0,01 mm. — *N. Bolleana v. asym.* CL. Vega p. 469 Pl. XXXVII f. 39.

Var. *mediterranea* CL. — V. narrow, rhombic-lanceolate acute. L. 0,1; B. 0,013 mm. Central area rounded. Striæ 7 in 0,01 mm., distinctly lineate; lineolæ about 27 in 0,01 mm.

Marine: Gulf of Naples!

N. sibirica resembles *N. Bolleana*, but differs by its more parallel striæ and by the narrow connecting zone. The *N. Zostereti* A. S. N. S. D. III f. 3 seems to belong to *N. sibirica*.

60. **N. (Rhoiconeis) superba** CL. (1883). — V. rhomboidal with subacute ends. L. 0,06; B. 0,02 mm. Axial area unilateral, more or less narrow. Central area small, somewhat transverse. Striæ 8 to 10 in 0,01 mm., parallel, finely lineate, frequently crossed, on one side of the median line by an irregular, narrow lateral area. — Vega p. 468 Pl. XXXVI f. 23.

Marine: Cape Wankarema!

Var. *elliptica* CL. (1883). — V. elliptical. L. 0,065; B. 0,02 mm. Striæ 10 in 0,01 mm.

Marine: Cape Wankarema!

The valves of this species seem to be somewhat dissimilar, the concave having more distant striæ, frequently crossed unilaterally by a narrow area.

61. **N. (Rhoiconeis) obtusa** CL. (1882). — V. linear with broad, rounded ends. L. 0,055 to 0,075; B. 0,014 to 0,018 mm. Axial area narrow, unilateral, irregular. Central area small. Striæ 11 in 0,01 mm., slightly radiate in the middle, and convergent at the ends, frequently crossed by irregular longitudinal, narrow bands. — CL. a. M. D. N:o 315 to 318. CL. Vega p. 469 Pl. XXXVI f. 25.

Marine: Cape Wankarema!

62. **N. ammophila** GRUN. (1882). — V. linear-lanceolate, subacute. L. 0,017 to 0,03; B. 0,005 mm. Axial and central areas indistinct. Striæ 10 to 11 in 0,01 mm., finely lineate, in the middle subradiate, at the ends transverse (12 to 13 in 0.01 mm.). — F. D. Öst. Ung. p. 149 Pl. XXX f. 66 to 69.

Marine and brackish: Coasts of England and Sweden (Grun.), Hungary, Tallya, fossil (Grun.).

Var. *intermedia* Grun. (1882). Striæ in the middle 12 to 13, at the ends 15 in 0,01 mm. *N. cancellata f. minuta* Grun. A. D. p. 37 Pl. II f. 41 (1880). *N. amm. f. minuta* Grun. F. D. Öst. Ung. p. 149 Pl. XXX f. 71 to 73. Pant. II p. 41 Pl. XI f. 190.

Marine: Finmark (Grun.). North Sea (Grun.). Cape Deschneff! Hungary, fossil (Pant.).

Var. *degenerans* Grun. (1882). — L. 0,014 to 0,02; B. 0,004 to 0,005 mm. Striæ very finely lineate, slightly radiate, 14 or 15 (middle) to 18 or 19 (ends) in 0,01 mm. Foss. D. Öst. Ung. p. 149 Pl. XXX f. 74, 75.

Marine: Coasts of England (Grun.). Sweden! Hungary, fossil (Grun., Pant.).

Var. *flanatica* Grun. (1860). V. lanceolate with attenuate, acute ends. L. 0,054; B. 0,008 mm. Striæ 9 to 11 in 0,01 mm. *N. flanatica* Grun. Verh. 1860 p. 527 Pl. III f. 9. *N. cancellata v. scaldensis* V. H. Syn. p. 86 Suppl. Pl. A f. 17.

Marine: Belgium (V. H.). Adriatic (Grun.).

63. **N. Beckii** Pant. (1889). — V. narrow, lanceolate with obtuse ends. L. 0,035; B. 0,008 mm. Axial area distinct; central area small. Striæ 12,5 to 15 in 0,01 mm. radiate in the middle, transverse at the ends. — Pant. II p. 42 Pl. XI f. 188.

Brackish water: Hungary, fossil (Pant.).

According to Pantocsek this form seems to be akin to *N. ammophila*.

64. **N. cancellata** Donk. (1873). — V. narrow, linear-lanceolate, convex, with subacute or subcuneate ends. L. 0,06 to 0,09; B. 0,012 mm. Axial area indistinct; central area small. Striæ 5,5 to 6,5, finely, but distinctly, lineate (lineolæ about 18 in 0,01 mm.) slightly radiate in the middle, transverse at the ends. — *N. truncata* Donk. M. J. I p. 9 Pl. I f. 4 (1861). *N. cancellata* Donk. B. D. p. 55 Pl. VIII f. 4 *a, b*. — A. S. N. S. D. II f. 36, 37. Atl. XLVI f. 29, 30. V. H. Syn. p. 86 Suppl. Pl. A f. 16. *N. canc. v. genuina* a. *impressa* Grun. A. D. p. 36. *N. fortis?* A. S. Atl. XLVI f. 36. *N. impressa* Lagst. Boh. D. p. 33 f. 3. A. S. Atl. XLVI f. 31, 34.

Marine: Finmark! Sea of Kara! Greenland! North Sea! Mediterranean Sea! Bab el Mandeb! Madagascar! Labuan! China! Galapagos Islands!

Var. *maroccana* Cl. — L. 0,095; B. 0,016 mm. Striæ 5 in 0,01 mm. coarsely lineate; lineolæ about 23 in 0,01 mm., crossed at the ends (below the margin) by a broad and short blank space.

Marine: Morocco!

The blank space at the ends of the valve is visible only in the zonal view.

Var. *Gregorii* Ralfs (1861). — V. lanceolate, subacute. L. 0,03 to 0,05; B. 0,007 to 0,0075. Striæ 6,5 to 8 in 0,01 mm. — *Pinnul. apiculata* Greg. M. J. III p. 41 Pl. IV f. 21 (1855)? *N. Gregorii* Ralfs Pritch Inf. p. 901. *N. canc. v. Greg.* Grun. A. D. p. 37. A. S. Atl. XLVI f. 41, 42, 71, 72.

Marine: Spitsbergen! Sea of Kara! North Sea (Atl.). Baltic (Atl.). Cape Deschneff! Sandwich Islands! New Caledonia! Tahiti! Kerguelen's Land! Galapagos Islands!

Var. *retusa* Bréb. (1854). — V. narrow, linear, with rounded or subcuneate ends. L. 0,05 to 0,075; B. 0,0075 to 0,011 mm. Striæ 6 to 7 in 0,01 mm. *N. retusa* Bréb. D. de Cherb. f. 6. Donk. M. J. I (N. S.) p. 14 Pl. I f. 17 (1861) B. D. p. 64 Pl. X f. 3. A. S. N. S. D. Pl. II f. 30. Atl. XLVI f. 45, 46, 74, 75. *N. cancellata v. Schmidtii* Grun. A. D. p. 36. *N. retusa v. subretusa* V. H. Syn. p. 77 Suppl. A f. 10 (V. H. T. N:o 74).

Marine: Spitsbergen! North Sea! Baltic (Atl.). Cape Deschneff!

N. retusa Grun. in A. D. p. 38 is another species, *Pinnularia? ambigua* Cl. *N. retusa* V. H. Syn. seems to be another form, as the striæ are described as smooth. The figures of Brébisson and Donkin are insufficient, so that it is doubtful, what the original *N. retusa* may be.

Var. *subapiculata* Grun. (1880). V. linear, with apiculate ends. L. 0,03 to 0,04; B. 0,006 to 0,008 mm. Striæ 8 to 9 in 0,01 mm. *N. Gregorii* A. S. N. S. D. II f. 22. A. S. Atl. XLVI f. 66 to 68. *N. cancell. v. subapic.* Grun. A. D. p. 37.

Marine: Sea of Kara! Baltic (Atl.), Firth of Tay (Atl.).

65. **N. inflexa** Greg. (1856). — V. narrow, elliptic-lanceolate, with obtuse, conical ends. L. 0,033 to 0,045; B. 0,0075 to 0,0085 mm. Axial area indistinct, central area small, rounded. Striæ 11 in 0,01 mm. strongly radiate throughout, distinctly lineate; lineolæ 23 in 0,01 mm. — *Pinn. inflexa* Greg. T. M. S. IV p. 48 Pl. V f. 20. *N. inflexa* Donk. B. D. p. 54 Pl. VIII f. 2. A. S. Atl. XLVI f. 69, 70.

Marine: Sea of Kara! North Sea!

N. inflexa v. Biharensis Pant. II p. 48 Pl. III f. 36 from Bremia seems to be another species, as it has scarcely any resemblance to *N. inflexa*.

66. **N. northumbrica** Donk. (1861). — V. very convex, narrow lanceolate, with acute ends. L. 0,046 to 0,076; B. 0,008 to 0,01 mm. Axial area indistinct; central area small, rounded. Striæ 10 to 11 in 0,01 mm. (the median stronger and more distant) very slightly radiate in the middle, transverse at the ends, lineate; lineolæ 25 in 0,01 mm. Frustule quadrate. — Donk. M. J. I p. 9 Pl. I f. 5. B. D. p. 54 Pl. VIII f. 1. A. S. XLVII f. 19, 20.

Marine: North Sea!

This species is remarkable for the extreme convexity of its valves, from which cause it is very difficult to find a specimen in the valvular view.

67. **N. (Rhoiconeis) Cubitus** Temp. a. Brun (1889). — V. very convex, linear-lanceolate with acute, excavate ends. L. 0,09 to 0,095; B. 0,013 mm. Axial area indistinct. Central area a narrow, transverse fascia, arising from the two distant median striæ. Terminal areas large, triangular spaces (visible only in the zonal view). Striæ 6 in 0,01 mm., parallel, coarsely lineate; lineolæ 21 in 0,01 mm. Frustule arcuate. D. foss. du Japon p. 42 Pl. V f. 8.

Marine: Japan, fossil!

68. **N. Zostereti** Grun. (1860). — V. slightly convex, narrow lanceolate, subacute. L. 0,065 to 0,14; B. 0,011 to 0,022 mm. Axial area indistinct; central area very small, orbicular. Striæ 7 in 0,01 mm. (a little more close towards the ends) transverse, and slightly curved, lineate; lineolæ 23 in 0,01 mm. — Verh. 1860 p. 528 Pl. IV f. 23. A. S. Atl. XLVII f. 42, 43, 44.

Marine: Adriatic (Grun.), Bab el Mandeb! Ceylon! Labuan! Java! China! Japan (Atl.), Sandwich Islands (Atl.), Brazil (Atl.), Atlantic City, fossil!

Var. *seychellensis* Cl. — L. 0,065; B. 0,011 mm. Striæ 12 in 0,01 mm.

Marine: Seychelles (Van Heurck Coll.)!

N. Zostereti is very similar to *N. directa*, but has more convex valves and slightly radiate, striæ curved towards the ends, finely lineate.

69. **N. spuria** Cl. N. Sp. — V. rarrow, lanceolate, acute. L. 0,09 to 0,15; B. 0,013 to 0,021 mm. Axial area indistinct. Central area small, irregularly rounded. Striæ 7 in 0,01 mm., slightly radiate in the middle, transverse at the ends, coarsely lineate; lineolæ 21 to 24 in 0,01 mm.

Marine: Mediterranean Sea (Gulf of Naples)! Adriatic! New Caledonia (Kinker Coll.)! Galapagos Islands (Weissflog Coll.)!

Var. *asymmetrica* Cl. — Axial area narrow, unilateral. Striæ on the side opposite to the axial area, crossed by an irregular, narrow lateral area. L. 0,15; B. 0,022 mm. Striæ 6 in 0,01 mm., lineolæ 27 in 0,01 mm.

Marine: Hungary, fossil (Karnaud Deposit in Deby Coll.)!

N. spuria resembles *N. directa*, from which it differs by its slightly radiate striæ, and *N. pennata*, from which it differs by its small central area. From *N. Zostereti* it may be distinguished by its coarsely lineate striæ and from *N. distans* by its indistinct axial area.

70. **N. fortis** Greg. (1856). — V. very convex, elliptic- to rhombic-lanceolate, obtuse. L. 0,05 to 0,089; B. 0,01 to 0,017 mm. Axial area indistinct; central area small, orbicular. Striæ 8 to 9 in 0,01 mm. slightly radiate in the middle, transverse at the ends, coarsely lineate; lineolæ 24 in

0,01 mm. — *Pinn. fortis* GREG. T. M. S. IV p. 47 Pl. V f. 19. *N. fortis* DONK. B. D. p. 57 Pl. VIII f. 8. A. S. Atl. XLVI f. 37 to 39. *Pinn. constricta* O'MEARA M. J. VII p. 17 Pl. V f. 8 (1867).

Marine: Spitsbergen! Finmark! North Sea! Greenland!

71. **N. Formenteræ** CL. (1881). — V. elliptic-lanceolate obtuse. L. 0,03 to 0,037; B. 0,013 to 0,015 mm. Axial area indistinct. Central area large quadrate. Striæ 6 in 0,01 mm., radiate throughout, coarsely lineate; lineolæ about 21 in 0,01 mm. *N. Fromenteræ* CL. N. R. D. p. 10 Pl. II f. 24. Icon. n. Pl. I f. 33. A. S. Atl. XLVI f. 7 (without name).

Marine: Balearic Islands! Campeachy Bay (Atl.).

72. **N. satura** A. S. (1876). — V. narrow elliptical, with rounded ends. L. 0,075; B. 0,021 mm. Axial area indistinct; central area large. Terminal nodules very distant from the ends. Striæ 5,5 in 0,01 mm. parallel, coarsely punctate. — Atl. XLVI f. 27.

Marine: Cape of Good Hope (Atl.), Cape Horn (Petit).

73. **N. crucifera** GRUN. (1876). — V. broadly linear, with apiculate ends. L. 0,05 to 0,07; B. 0,017 to 0,019 mm. Axial area very narrow; central area large, quadrate. Striæ 5 to 6 in 0,01 mm., slightly radiate throughout, coarsely lineate; lineolæ 22 in 0,01 mm. In the zonal view the frustule is quadrate and has irregularly triangular terminal areas or blank spaces. *N. rostellata* A. S. N. S. D. Pl. II f. 31 (1874). *N. crucifera* GRUN. A. S. Atl. XLVI f. 50—53 (1876). *N. apiculata var. maculifera* GRUN. A. D. p. 37 (1880). *N. bicuspidata* CL. a. GRUN. N. R. D. p. 10 Pl. II f. 25 (1881).

Marine: North Sea! Baltic (Atl.). Naples! Sumatra (Deby Coll.)!

This species is considered to be the same as *N. apiculata* BRÉB. Diat. de Cherbourg 1859 f. 5 and *Pinn. rostellata* GREG. D. of Clyde Pl. IX f. 20 (1857), but these figures shew no central area.

74. **N. Scoliopleura** A. S. (1876). — V. linear, with apiculate ends. L. 0,083; B. 0,0167 mm. Median line slightly flexuose, with distant terminal nodules. Axial area narrow, linear; central area large, somewhat transverse. Striæ 7 in 0,01 mm., parallel throughout (finely lineate?) Atl. XLVI f. 63.

Marine: Campeachy Bay (Atl.).

75. **N. solaris** GREG. (1856). — V. lanceolate, obtuse. L. 0,088 to 0,114 mm. Axial area narrow; central area small, orbicular. Striæ 14 in 0,01 mm., strongly radiate throughout. — T. M. S. IV p. 43 Pl. V f. 10.

Marine: Scotland (Greg.).

This form is entirely unknown to me. To judge from the figure it has some resemblance to *N. baltica*, but if it be *N. baltica*, the fig. is very far from accurate. In A. S. Atl. XLVI f. 16 is a form from New Providence named *N. solaris?* but the striation is much too coarse for the *N. solaris* of GREG.

76. **N. centraster** CL. N. Sp. — V. convex, linear lanceolate, obtuse. L. 0,07 to 0,11; B. 0,012 to 0,015 mm. Axial area indistinct, or narrow and unilateral. Central area large, orbicular. Striæ 7 to 8 in 0,01 mm. strongly radiate in the middle, where they are more distant, transverse at the ends, finely lineate; lineolæ about 30 in 0,01 mm. — Pl. I f. 35.

Marine: Japan! Madagascar! Auckland!

This species resembles *N. inflexa* GREG. but has more distant, and very finely lineate, striæ.

77. **N. pennata** A. S. (1876). — V. linear-lanceolate, subacute. L. 0,068 to 0,095; B. 0,011 to 0,014 mm. Terminal fissures small, close to the ends of the valve. Axial area narrow or indistinct; central area large, quadrate. Striæ 5 to 6 in 0,01 mm., radiate throughout, coarsely lineate; lineolæ 20 in 0,01 mm. — Atl. XLVIII f. 41, 42, 43.

Marine: Morocco! Mediterranean Sea! Adriatic (Atl.). Hungary, fossil! Gulf of Mexico (Atl.). West Indies! Pensacola, Florida!

Var. *maxima* CL. — V. narrow, rhombic-lanceolate. L. 0,12 to 0,17; B. 0,021 to 0,024 mm. Axial area narrow, unilateral. Striæ 4,5 to 5 in 0,01 mm., coarsely lineate; lineolæ 17 to 18 in 0,01 mm. — Pl. I f. 36.

Marine: Adriatic! Gulf of Naples! Sumatra (Deby Coll.)! Indian Ocean (Deby Coll.)!

Var. *Kinkeri* PANT. (1889). — V. slightly sigmoid. L. 0,1 to 0,109; B. 0,016 to 0,018 mm. Striæ 5 in 0,01 mm., coarsely lineate. — *N. Kinkeri* PANT. II p. 49 Pl. IX f. 169. *Scoliopleura Szakalensis* PANT. II p. 55 Pl. VIII f. 154.

Marine: Petersburg, Va. foss.! Szákal, Hungary, fossil!

78. **N. pinnata** PANT. (1889). — V. narrow, lanceolate. L. 0,062; B. 0,0125 mm. Axial area distinct; central small. Striæ 7,5 in 0,01 mm. slightly radiate in the middle, transverse at the ends, coarsely lineate. — PANT. II p. 52 Pl. XX f. 308.

Marine: Hungary, fossil (Pant.).

I have not seen this species, which appears to differ from *N. pennata* principally by its less radiate striæ and the more distinct axial area.

79. **N. consanguinea** CL. C. Sp. — V. convex, linear lanceolate, obtuse. L. 0,10 to 0,12; B. 0,016 mm. Axial area very narrow. Central area large, quadrate. Terminal fissures bayonet-shaped, distant from the ends of the valve. Striæ 6 in 0,01 mm., slightly radiate throughout, not distinctly lineate. — A. S. N. S. D. Pl. II f. 32 (without name).

Marine: North Sea (A. S.), Morocco!

80. **N. compressicauda** A. S. (1874). — V. very convex, lanceolate, obtuse, with elevated conical ends. L. 0,11 to 0,19; B. 0,024 mm. Median line with distant terminal nodules, which are strongly marked. Axial area very narrow; central area orbicular. Striæ 6 in 0,01 mm., radiate in the middle, transverse at the ends, indistinctly lineate. — N. S. D. p. 91 Pl. II f. 35. Atl. XLVI f. 62.

Marine: North Sea! Morocco! Balearic Islands! Sendai, Japan, fossil (Brun.).

81. **N. annulata** GRUN. (1880). — V. rhomboidal, obtuse, flat. L. 0,05 to 0,076; B. 0,025 to 0,03 mm. Median line with somewhat distant central pores and terminal pores approximate to the ends. Axial area very narrow; central area large, transverse. Striæ 7 in 0,01 mm. slightly radiate, apparently smooth, crossed at the ends of the valve by a semicircular blank narrow space. — A. D. p. 37. Icon. n. Pl. I f. 38.

Fresh water: Demerara River!

This species is an isolated form, the systematic place of which is doubtful. It is no Achnanthes, both valves being similar.

82. **N. (Alloioneis) mediterranea** BR. a. CL. (1891). — V. very convex, linear, obtuse, asymmetrical. L. 0,09 to 0,13; B. 0,0012 to 0,0018 mm. Median line excentric. Axial area indistinct or narrow. Central area small, unilateral. Striæ 5 to 6 in 0,01 mm., very finely lineate, crossed at least on one side of the valve by one to three narrow, undulating blank bands. — — BRUN D. espèces nouv. p. 35 Pl. XV f. 11. Icon. n. Part. I Pl. I f. 32, 33.

Marine: Balearic Islands! Gulf of Naples! Indian Ocean (Deby Coll.)! Sydney (Brun.).

Nav. mediterranea KÜTZ is a small form, not determinable by the fig. in Bac. Pl. III f. 17. *N. medit.*, GRUN. 1874 belong to the genus *Diploneis*. The figure in BRUN's D. esp. is not quite characteristic, the asymmetry being not sufficiently marked.

83. **N. (Alloioneis) scalarifer** BRUN (1891). — V. narrow, fusiform, acute, very convex and somewhat asymmetrical. L. 0,085 to 0,1; B. 0,01 to 0,012 mm. Median line with distant terminal nodules. Axial area linear, unilateral. Striæ 4 to 5 in 0,01 mm., parallel throughout, finely

lineate and crossed by an infra-marginal lateral area. V. in the zonal view slightly constricted in the middle with broad, obliquely truncate ends. Striæ crossed by a broad lateral area. — D. espèces N. p. 38 Pl. XV f. 4.

Marine: Japan, fossil (Brun.).

84. **N. (Alloioneis) vitriscala** BRUN (1891). — V. narrow, fusiform, acute, very convex. L. 0,2 to 0,22; B. 0,015 to 0,022 mm. Median line slightly undulating; terminal nodules distant. Axial and central areas uniting in a narrow, lanceolate space. Striæ fragmentary, finely lineate. V. in zonal view broad, not constricted in the middle, with obliquely truncate ends, where are large terminal areas, having in their centre a stigma. Along the interior margin is a band of parallel not interrupted striæ (14 in 0,01 mm.) outside which the striæ are fragmentary. — D. esp. n. p. 41 Pl. XV f. 5.

Marine: Japan, fossil!

85. **N. superimposita** A. S. (1874). — V. lanceolate (occasionally with slightly undulated margins) with obtuse ends. L. 0,058 to 0,125; B. 0,012 to 0,018 mm. Terminal nodules distant. Axial area narrow; central area large, quadrate. Striæ 5,5 to 7 in 0,01 mm., finely lineate, slightly radiate and crossed by a longitudinal area. N. S. D. p. 90 Pl. II f. 34. Atl. XLVI f. 61. PERAG. D. de Villefr. p. 53 Pl. III f. 29?

Marine: Baltic (A. S.), Norway! Morocco! China!

86. **N. Sigma** BRUN (1891). — V. very convex, lanceolate, sigmoid, with obtuse ends. L. 0,12 to 0,17; B. 0,03 to 0,035 mm. Axial area narrow, linear; central area large, quadrate. Median line with approximate central pores and distant terminal nodules. Striæ 6 in 0,01 mm., slightly radiate, coarsely lineate (lineolæ 17 in 0,01 mm.), crossed by a lateral area. V. in zonal view broad, with obliquely truncate ends, slightly constricted middle, and with a very broad lateral area. — D. espèces n. p. 39 Pl. XVI f. 5.

Marine: Gulf of Naples! Messina (Brun), Athens (Brun).

87. **N. Phi** CL. N. Sp. — V. convex, narrow, lanceolate, obtuse. L. 0,08; B. 0,015 mm. Axial area narrow, unilateral; central area large, uniting with the lateral areas. Median line with somewhat distant central pores and comma-like terminal fissures. Striæ 10 in 0,01 mm., radiate throughout, coarsely lineate; lineolæ 24 in 0,01 mm. The striæ are crossed on each side of the median line by a moderately broad, linear lateral area and probably also by another infra-marginal area. — Pl. I f. 34.

Marine: Seychelles (V. H. Coll.)!

This species is very similar to *Caloneis biseriata* PETIT, which has smooth striæ.

88. **N. Galea** BRUN (1891). V. broadly elliptical, with rostrate ends, convex. L. 0,06 to to 0,075; B. 0,03 to 0,035 mm. Median line with approximate central pores and somewhat distant terminal nodules. Axial area narrow; central area large, quadrate, uniting with the lateral areas. Striæ 7 in 0,01 mm. slightly radiate throughout, coarsely lineate and crossed by broad, linear, lateral areas. D. espèces n. p. 34 Pl. XVI f. 7.

Marine: Gulf of Naples! Palermo, Tangier, Arzila (Brun).

89. **N. guttata** GRUN. (1878). — V. very convex with conical ends, elliptic-lanceolate, obtuse. L. 0,057 to 0,06; B. 0,011 to 0,014 mm. Median pores approximate. Axial area indistinct; central area large, somewhat transverse and quadrate. Striæ 7 to 8 in 0,01 mm. slightly radiate, crossed by 3 to 4, irregularly undulating, narrow lateral areas, so that they have the appearance of being composed of 3 to 4 elongated large puncta. Lineation of the striæ fine. — CL. M. D. N:o 151 to 155. A. S. Atl. XLVI f. 10 (without name).

Marine: Balearic Islands! Sansego (Atl.).

Var. *maxima* CL. — V. less convex, lanceolate, acute. L. 0,13; B. 0,03 mm. Striæ 6,5 in 0,01 mm. almost parallel, composed of about 7 elongated puncta, lineate, lineolæ about 27 in 0,01 mm.

Marine: Gulf of Naples (Brun's Coll.)!

Var.? *Peragalli* BRUN (1891). — V. rhomboidal, acute; the axial part forming a distinct keel especially towards the ends. L. 0,08 to 0,11; B. 0,025 to 0,030 mm. Striæ 7 in 0,01 mm. slightly radiate, composed of about 7 elongated puncta, crossed by fine lineolæ, about 27 in 0,01 mm. — *N. Peragalli* BRUN D. espèces n. p. 37 Pl. XVI f. 12.

Marine: Gulf of Naples! Athens (Brun).

90. **N. (Alloioneis) Monodon** BRUN (1891). — V. very convex, narrow, rhombic-lanceolate, subacute. L. 0,06 to 0,09; B. 0,011 mm. Central nodule strong, elevated with a pore in the middle. Terminal nodules distant. Axial area asymmetrical narrow, slightly dilated around the central nodule. Striæ 6 to 8 in 0,01 mm. crossed by undulating, narrow, longitudinal areas. V. in zonal view broad, slightly constricted in the middle, with obliquely truncate ends. Central nodule forming a conical projection, perforated by a tube. Striæ composed of elongated puncta. — Diat. espèces n. p. 36 Pl. XVI f. 8.

Marine: Japan (Brun)!

This is one of the most remarkable naviculoid diatoms, diverging from all other known forms by its central nodule, forming a conical, perforated projection on the outside of the valve.

91. **N. distans** W. SM. (1853). — V. lanceolate, gradually tapering from the middle to the obtuse ends. L. 0,09 to 0,13; B. 0,017 to 0,02 mm. Axial area gradually dilated towards the middle, where it expands to a large, rounded quadrate space. Striæ 5 to 6 in 0,01 mm., radiate throughout, strongly lineate; lineolæ 21 in 0,01 mm. — *Pinn. distans* W. SM. B. D. I p. 56 Pl. XVIII f. 169. *N. distans* A. S. Atl. XLVI f. 11 to 14. N. S. D. II f. 38 (without name). V. H. Syn. p. 87 Suppl., Pl. A f. 18. *N. dist. v. borealis* GRUN. A. D. p. 38 Pl. II f. 42.

Marine: Frans Josefs Land (Grun.), Spitsbergen! Finmark! Greenland! North Sea!

N. distans seems to belong to the Arctic Sea and Northern Atlantic. I have not seen typical specimens from other seas.

92. **N. subalata** GRUN. (1880). — V. lanceolate, obtuse. L. 0,08; B. 0,02 mm. Median line with approximate central pores and distant terminal nodules. Axial area linear distinct. Central area large, somewhat transverse. Striæ 6 in 0,01 mm. radiate throughout, transversely lineate; lineolæ 22 in 0,01 mm. The striæ in the middle do not reach the margin, so that the valve seems there to be bordered by a hyaline rim. A. D. p. 38. Icon. n. Pl. I f. 32.

Marine: Seychelles (Van Heurck Coll.)!

An original sketch by GRUNOW agrees perfectly with the specimen in Van Heurck Collection, which has distinctly lineate striæ. According to GRUNOW they are smooth.

93. **N. salva** A. S. (1876). V. elliptic-lanceolate, sometimes with slightly triundulated margins and subrostrate ends. L. 0,038 to 0,06; B. 0,02 to 0,022 mm. Median pores approximate; terminal nodules distant. Axial area narrow, linear. Central area large, quadrate. Striæ 8 in 0,01 mm. radiate throughout. — Atl. XLVI f. 23.

Marine: Balearic Islands! Campeachy Bay (Atl.). Florida!

94. **N. opima** GRUN. (1867). — V. elliptic-lanceolate, with rounded, obtuse ends. L. 0,06 to 0,11; B. 0,017 to 0,025 mm. Central pores approximate; terminal fissures almost straight, large, at some distance from the ends of the valve. Axial area broad, linear. Central area large, orbicular. Striæ 6 to 8 in 0,01 mm., more distant in the middle; strongly radiate throughout, lineate; lineolæ 24 in 0,01 mm. — *N. fortis var.? opima* GRUN. Novara p. 100 Pl. I *A* f. 13. *N. opima* A. S. Atl. XLVI f. 24, 25, 26. *N. fortis* A. S. Atl. XLVI f. 19, 20, 21, 22.

Marine: Greenland! Davis Straits! Grip in Norway! Baltic (Atl.), Barcelona!

95. **N. Rhaphoneis** (EHR. 1854?) GRUN. (1866). — V. rhombic-lanceolate. L. 0,027; B. 0,011 mm. Axial area indistinct; central area small. Striæ 8 in 0,01 mm., radiate in the middle, transverse at the ends, coarsely lineate; lineolæ about 20 in 0,01 mm. — *Pinnularia Rhaph.* EHR. M. G. XXXV: 9, f. 7? *N. Rhaph.* GRUN. Novara p. 19. Icon. n. Pl. I f. 30. *N. Pacifica* GRUN. Nov. Pl. I f. 17.

Marine: Samoa! Tahiti (Grun.), Jamaica!

96. **N. Bruchii** GRUN. (1881). — V. lanceolate, acute. L. 0,044 to 0,06; B. 0,012 to 0,018 mm. Axial and central areas uniting in a narrow, lanceolate space. Striæ 7 in 0,01 mm. abbreviate, and radiate in the middle, transverse at the ends, lineate; lineolæ 18 in 0,01 mm. The striæ are crossed by a narrow longitudinal band. — CL. N. R. D. p. 13 Pl. III f. 35.

Marine: Labuan! Manila (Deby Coll.)! China (Thum.)? Tahiti (Grun.).

97. **N. multiseriata** GRUN. (1881). — V. lanceolate, with protracted ends. L. 0,04; B. 0,012 mm. Axial and central areas indistinct. Striæ 9 in 0,01 mm., slightly radiate, crossed by two narrow longitudinal bands. — CL. N. R. D. p. 13 Pl. III f. 36.

Marine: Tongatabu (Grun.).

98. **N. Amicorum** GRUN. Ms. — V. elliptic-lanceolate, acute. L. 0,0155 to 0,038; B. 0,008 to 0,015 mm. Central pores approximate. Axial and central areas uniting in a lanceolate space. Striæ 8 to 9 in 0,01 mm. radiate throughout, coarsely lineate. Lineolæ 20 in 0,01 mm. — Pl. I f. 31.

Marine: Tahiti! Galapagos Islands!

Var. *madagascarensis* CL. — V. lanceolate. L. 0,065; B. 0,013 mm. Striæ 8 in 0,01 mm., radiate in the middle, elsewhere parallel.

Marine: Madagascar (V. H. Coll.)!

99. **N. nicæensis** PERAG. (1888). — V. rhombic-lanceolate, obtuse. L. 0,055; B. 0,015 mm. Axial and central areas uniting in a lanceolate space. Striæ 10 in 0,01 mm., radiate throughout, granulate. — D. de Villefr. p. 46 Pl. II f. 8.

Marine: Mediterranean Sea (Peragallo).

100. **N. Platessa** CL. (1881). — V. broadly lanceolate, with acuminate ends. L. 0,028 to 0,03; B. 0,015 to 0,018 mm. Median pores approximate. Terminal nodules distant. Axial and central areas uniting a large, lanceolate space. Striæ 8 in 0,01 mm. lineate, lineolæ 20 in 0,01 mm. — N. R. D. p. 9 Pl. I f. 12.

Marine: Galapagos Islands!

101. **N. Sti Thomæ** CL. (1878). — V. lanceolate with triundulated margins and rostrate ends. L. 0,055 to 0,061; B. 0,02 to 0,025 mm. Central pores approximate, terminal nodules near the margin. Axial and central areas uniting in a large, lanceolate space, considerably dilated in the middle. Striæ 6 in 0,01 mm., radiate throughout, distinctly lineate. — West Ind. D. p. 6 Pl. I f. 4.

Marine: West Indies!

102. **N. Jamalinensis** CL. (1880). — V. elliptical, with broad, rounded ends. L. 0,03 to 0,065; B. 0,016 to 0,027 mm. Median pores approximate; terminal nodules very distant from the ends. Axial and central area uniting in a very large, lanceolate space. Striæ 7 in 0,01 mm. radiate throughout, coarsely lineate; lineolæ about 20 in 0,01 mm. — A. D. p. 13 Pl. II f. 40.

Marine: Sea of Kara! Cape Deschneff! China! Indian ocean (Grove Coll.)!

Var. *simiæcultus* BRUN (1891). — L. 0,05 to 0,06; B. 0,024 to 0,03 mm. Striæ 5 in 0,01 mm. Median line somewhat asymmetrical. Area with a large dot on each side of the median line. — *N. simiæ cultus* BRUN D. espèces n. p. 39 Pl. XVI f. 13.

Marine: Japan, fossil (Brun)!

Var. *schizostauron* Cl. — L. 0,038; B. 0,02 mm. Striæ 7 in 0,01 mm. Lineolæ 20 in 0,01 mm. Central nodule lyriformly dilated.

Marine: China (Thum.)!

103. **N. Chi** Cl. N. Sp. — V. broad, constricted in the middle, with apiculate ends. L. 0,05; B. 0,027, at the constriction 0,021 mm. Central pores approximate, terminal nodules near the ends. Axial and central areas uniting in a large space, crossed by faint continuations of the striæ. Striæ 9 (middle) to 12 (ends) in 0,01 mm. radiate in the middle, transverse at the ends, very finely lineate. — Pl. I f. 29.

Marine: Balearic Islands! Gulf of Naples!

This form may easily be mistaken for *N. Excl*, but it has no axial band of striæ. Besides, the striæ are very finely lineate.

Additional.

104. **N. Aquitaniæ** Brun a. Hérib. (1893). — V. narrow elliptic-lanceolate, with obtuse ends. L. 0,17 to 0,24; B. 0,034 to 0,045 mm. Axial area in width about a third of the breadth of the valve, lanceolate, slightly dilated in the middle. Striæ 10 in 0,01 mm. slightly radiate in the middle, where some few are shorter than the others, convergent and genuflexed in the ends, punctate; puncta about 16 in 0,01 mm. — D. d'Auvergne p. 81 Pl. II f. 4.

Brackish water: Auvergne, fossil!

A very remarkable species, the terminal striæ of which are genuflexed as in *N. oblonga*. Varies with undulating margins (var. *undulata* Brun). At the inner ends of the striæ there is a narrow blank band or depression.

105. **N. basaltæ proxima** Brun a. Hérib. (1893). — V. linear, with cuneate ends and parallel or slightly concave margins. L. 0,075 to 0,09; B. 0,014 to 0,018 mm. Axial area narrow, dilated to a large central area. Striæ 10 in 0,01 mm., radiate in the middle, convergent in the ends, finely punctate. — D. d'Auvergne p. 89 Pl. II f. 5.

Brackish water: Auvergne, fossil!

Naviculæ Punctatæ.

Valve usually symmetrical, elliptical to lanceolate, with broad and rounded or, frequently, rostrate ends, rarely constricted in the middle, or with undulate margins. Median line usually central; central nodule not stauroid or dilated in lyriform processes; terminal fissures turned in the same or, sometimes, in contrary, directions. Axial area narrow or indistinct. Central area usually small, rarely transverse, and never dilated to a transverse fascia. Structure: distinct puncta arranged in transverse rows (striæ) radiate at the ends and in the middle of equal or unequal length, and, besides in longitudinal, undulating, rarely straight, rows. No longitudinal lines or lateral areas (except in *N. carinifera* and *N. interlineata*). Connecting zone not complex, usually narrow. Cell-contents unknown.

This section, characterized by the distinct puncta composing the striæ, comprises two, not sharply distinct, divisions — forms with the median striæ of equal length, and forms with the median striæ alternately longer and shorter. The former division is very nearly akin to the Lyratæ, which differ in the lateral areas. In many forms of the Punctatæ there is a tendency to form lateral depressions or areas, where the puncta are less crowded, which suggests a passage to such forms of Lyratæ as *N. irrorata*, *N. fluitans* and others. Some forms are distinctly intermediate between the two sections, as *N. carinifera*.

The division, comprising forms with the median striæ of equal length, is not to be considered as a series of forms starting from the same point as the Lyratæ, but rather as a parallel row of allied forms. For instance the following forms may be regarded as nearly connected:

Lyratæ.	Intermediate.	Punctatæ.
N. Lyra.	*N. carinifera.*	*N. scandinavica.*
N. connectens.	*N. conciliaus.*	*N. diffusa.*
N. Schaarschmidtii.		*N. transfuga.*
N. fluitans.		*N. transfuga var. Neupaueri.*
N. abrupta.		*N. granulata.*

There seems also to be some connection between the Punctatæ and the Lineolatæ. Thus *N. amphibola* is no doubt akin to *N. Gastrum*. Several species of Cymbella, which have distant puncta (*C. aspera*, *C. mexicana* etc.) seems also to be related to Punctatæ, but they have broader axial areas. The same is also the case with the Entoleiæ, among which are some coarsely punctate forms.

With the Microstictæ the connection is less evident, the forms of that section generally having the puncta closer than the striæ. In the Mesoleiæ there are also some small forms, which might be placed in this section, for instance *N. nivalis* and others.

The Heterostichæ are apparently akin to the forms of the division, which have the median striæ alternately longer and shorter, but they have a finer punctation and the striæ are closer towards the ends.

Most forms of the section Punctatæ are marine, a few only living in fresh water. Some are decidedly inhabitants of brackish water. They occur in all zones and seas.

Artificial key.

1.	Valve symmetrical	3.
	— asymmetrical	2.
2	Ends broad	*N. Grundleri*, Cl. a. Grun.
	Ends acute	*N. Lunula* Cl.
3	Striæ of equal length	18.
	— unequal — (at least in the middle)	4.
4	Ends cuneate	*N. Eta* Cl. (*N. humerosa* var.).
	— rostrate	5
	— not cuneate or rostrate	9.
5.	Striæ 8 to 9 in 0,01 mm.	6.
	— 12 — —	7.
	— 16 — —	8.
6.	Terminal fissures in the same directions	*N. humerosa* Bréb.
	— — — contrary —	*N. Alpha* Cl.
7.	L. 0,03 mm.	*N. Delta* Cl.
	L. 0,07 mm.	*N Xi* Cl.
8.	L. about 0,04 mm.	*N. pusilla* W. Sm.
	L. about 0,08 mm.	*N. Delawarensis* Grun.
9.	Valve elliptical	10.
	lanceolate	14.
10.	Puncta elongated	*N. Macandrina* Cl.
	— round	11.
11.	Length about 0,05 mm	12.
	— 0,07 mm.	13.
12.	Median striæ more coarsely punctate than the others	*N. scintillans* A. S.
	— not — —	*N. scutelloides* W. Sm.
13.	Without central area	*N. neogradensis* Pant.
	With — —	*N algida* Grun.

14. Length about 0,1 mm. . . . . 15.
— — 0,06 mm. . . . . 16.

15. Striæ 8 in 0,01 mm. . . . . *N. latissima* GREG.
— 17 — — . . . . *N. My* CL.

16. Central area bordered with a circlet of elongated puncta . . . . . *N. Zeta* CL.
— — not — — — . . . . 17.

17. Central area large . . . . *N. Febigerii* CL.
— — small . . . . *N. Neumayeri* PANT.

18. Valve biconstricted . . . . *N. Novæ Guineensis* TEMP.
— constricted in the middle . . . . 19.
— not constricted . . . . 21.

19. Puncta large, irregular . . . . *N. bilobata* LEUD. FORTM.
— arranged in transverse rows . . . . 20.

20. Transverse rows of puncta 6 in 0,01 mm. . . . . . *N. ceylanensis* LEUD. FORTM.
— — — 12 — — . . . . *N. sublyrata* GRUN.

21. Valve rostrate . . . . 22.
— not — . . . . 31.

22. Central area large . . . . 23.
— — small or indistinct . . . . 25.

23. Puncta closer than the striæ . . . . . *N. amphibola* CL. (*N. Galikii* PANT.).
— and striæ equidistant . . . . 24.

24. Puncta forming straight longitudinal rows . . . . . . *N. Gamma* CL. var.
— — curved — — . . . . . *N. baccata* BRUN. a. TEMP.
— — undulating — — . . . . . . *N. maculata* BAIL.

25. L. 0,03 mm. . . . . 26.
L. 0,04 to 0,1 mm. or more . . . . 27.

26. Striæ 10 in 0,01 mm. . . . . *N. Omicron* CL.
— 17 — — . . . . *N. Omega* CL.

27. Ends apiculate . . . . *N. diffusa* A. S. (*N. conspersa* PANT.)
— not — . . . . 28.

28. Terminal fissures large, hook-shaped . . . . *N. arabica* GRUN.
— — small . . . . 29.

29. Terminal fissures in contrary directions . . . . *N. Epsilon* CL.
— — — the same — . . . . 30.

30. Puncta equidistant . . . . *N. monilifera* CL.
— more crowded at the margin and the median line . . . . *N. transfuga* GRUN.

31. Valve elliptical . . . . 32.
— lanceolate . . . . 39.

32. Puncta irregular . . . . *N. margaritifera* TRUAN. a. WITT.
— in transverse rows . . . . 33.

33. Puncta closer than the striæ . . . . *N. Jentzschii* GRUN.
— equidistant with the striæ, or wider . . . . 34.

34. Length 0,02 to 0,04 mm. . . . . 35.
— 0,06 to 0,1 mm. . . . . 36.

35. Puncta near the median line in longitudinal straight rows . . . . *N. fraudulenta* A. S.
— not forming straight rows . . . . *N. torneensis* CL.

36. Puncta wider than the striæ . . . . . . *N. sparsipunctata* GROVE a. STURT.
— not — — . . . . 37.

37. Puncta in slightly curved longitudinal rows . . . . *N. Schulzii* KAIN.
— undulating — — . . . . 38.

38. Central area transverse . . . . *N. oscitans* A. S.
— — rounded . . . . *N. glacialis* CL.

39. Freshwater habitat . . . . 40.
Marine — . . . . 42.

40. Central area small . . . . 41.
— — large . . . . *N. Gamma* CL.

41. Puncta in straight longitudinal rows . . . . *N. Tuscula* PANT.
— — undulating — . . . . *N. lacustris* GREG.

42. Axial area narrowed towards the middle and the ends . . . . . *N. granulata* BAIL.
— — not — — — — — . . . . . . 43.

43. { Central area large . . . . . . N. Grovei Cl.
{ — — small . . . . . . 44.
44. { Striæ crossed by a blank band . . . . . . N. interlineata Grove a. Sturt.
{ — not — — — . . . . . . 45.
45. { Valve with shallow depressions on each side of the median line . . . . N. impressa Grun.
{ — without . . . . . . 46.
46. { Median portion of the valve elevated at the ends . . . . . . N. carinifera Grun.
{ — — not — — . . . . . . 47.
47. { Striæ radiate . . . . . . 48.
{ — almost parallel . . . . . . 49.
48. { Puncta equidistant . . . . . . N. punctulata W. Sm.
{ — closer at the margin and axis . . . . . . N. brasiliensis Grun.
49. { Striæ 9 in 0,01 mm. . . . . . . 50.
{ — 11 to 14 — . . . . . . 51.
50. { Central area orbicular . . . . . . N. doljensis Pant.
{ — transverse . . . . . . N. Brunii Pant.
51. { Valve rhombic-lanceolate . . . . . . N. Pi Cl.
{ — elliptic-lanceolate . . . . . . N. scandinavica Lagst.

1. **N. scutelloides** W. Sm. (1856). — V. orbicular. L. 0,015 to 0,027; B. 0,013 to 0,02 mm. Axial area indistinct; central area indistinct or irregular. Striæ 10 in 0.01 mm. radiate throughout, the median striæ of unequal length. Puncta of the striæ coarse, 10 in 0,01 mm. — M. J. IV Pl. I f. 15. — Schum. Pr. D. I N. p. 20 f. 22. A. S. Atl. VI f. 34. Ströse Klicken Pl. I f. 11.

Fresh and slightly brackish water: Sweden (Gulf of Bothnia! Lake Mälaren! Ronneby, fossil! etc.), Finland, fossil! Germany, Domblitten, foss. (Atl.), England!

Var. *mocarensis* Grun. (1882). — Striæ very distant, alternating with short, marginal striæ. — Foss. D. Öst. Ung. Pl. XXX f. 65.

Fresh water: Hungary, fossil (Grun.).

Var. *minutissima* Cl. (1881). — Diam. 0,008 mm. Striæ obsolete. — D. f. Grönl. Argentina p. 12 Pl. XVI f. 10.

Fresh water: Greenland! Finland.

2. **N. scintillans** A. S. (1881). — V. elliptical, with broad, rounded ends. L. 0,038; B. 0,026 mm. Axial area indistinct; central area small, somewhat transverse. Striæ 10 (middle) to 12 (ends) in 0,01 mm. in the middle of unequal length, coarsely punctate, the puncta in the middle of the valve larger. — Atl. LXX f. 61.

Marine: Campeachy Bay.

3. **N. neogradensis** Pant. (1886). — V. elliptic-lanceolate. L. 0,057; B. 0,034 mm. Axial area narrow; central area indistinct. Striæ 7 in 0,01 mm., radiate throughout, alternating with short marginal striolæ. Puncta of the striæ 7 in 0,01 mm. — *Cocconeis neogr.* Pant. I p. 31 Pl. XIII f. 111.

Marine: Hungary, fossil (Pant.).

There is no reason for placing this species in Cocconeis. It seems nearly akin to *Nav. punctulata*, and to the following.

4. **N. algida** Grun. (1884). — V. broadly elliptical, with rounded ends. L. 0,07 to 0,085; B. 0,035 to 0,04 mm. Axial area very narrow. Central area not well defined, the median part of the valve being an irregular space with scattered puncta. Striæ 9 to 10 in 0,01 mm., radiate throughout, coarsely punctate, alternating with short marginal striolæ. — Fr. Jos. Land D. p. 56 Pl. I f. 31. *Nav. glacialis* Cl. M. D. N:o 302. Vega p. 471.

Marine: North Siberian Sea!

5. **N. glacialis** Cl. (1873). — V. elliptical. L. 0,06 to 0,11; B. 0,03 to 0,066 mm. Axial area linear, narrow. Central area orbicular. Striæ 12 in 0,01 mm., radiate throughout, punctate;

puncta forming undulating longitudinal rows, about 8 in 0,01 mm. — *Coccon. gl.* Cl. D. Arct. Sea p. 14 Pl. III f. 12. *N. sp.* A. S. Atl. VI f. 39. *N. gl.* Grun. Fr. Jos. Land D. p. 55. Petit Cape Horn D. p. 123 Pl. X f. 16, 17 (1888). Icon. n. Pl. I f. 28. *N. kerguelensis* Castr. Challenger Voy. D. Pl. XXVIII f. 16 (according to Petit).

Marine: Greenland! Spitsbergen! Matotschin Scharr! Cape Horn (Petit), Kerguelens Land (Castr.).

Var. *septentrionalis* Cl. — V. smaller. L. 0,04 to 0,05; B. 0,035 mm. Puncta in the median part of the valve scattered or forming short, undulating rows. — A. S. Atl. VI f. 37.

Marine: Arctic America! Greenland! Spitsbergen! Sea of Kara! Cape Horn (Petit).

The original figure in D. of the Arct. Sea shews a marginal rim, which I have since found to be occasioned by the zone. There is no rim on detached valves. The var. *septentrionalis* connects the type with *N. algida.*

6. **N. Xi** Cl. N. Sp. — V. elliptic-lanceolate, with rostrate ends. L. 0,055 to 0,075; B. 0,022 to 0,032 mm. Axial area narrow; central large, orbicular. Striæ 12 to 13 in 0,01 mm. radiate throughout. Puncta 12 in 0,01 mm. Among the median striæ are some few shorter ones.

Marine (Mouth of rivers): Sierra Leone (Deby Coll.)! Cameroon!

7. **N. Delta** Cl. (1893). — V. elliptical, with rostrate ends. L. 0,032; B. 0,016 mm. Axial area narrow; central orbicular. Striæ 12 in 0,01 mm., radiate throughout, coarsely punctate; puncta 12 in 0.01 mm., equidistant. Among the median striæ there are some few shorter ones. — Diatomiste II p. 14 Pl. I f. 10.

Marine: Ceylon (Weissflog Coll.)!

8. **N. pusilla** W. Sm. (1853). — V. elliptical to lanceolate, with more or less distinctly rostrate ends. L. 0,03 to 0,047; B. 0,015 to 0,025 mm. Axial area narrow; central area small, orbicular. Terminal fissures in the same direction. Striæ 13 to 18 in 0,01 mm. radiate throughout, in the middle of unequal length; puncta distinct, 16 to 20 in 0.01 mm. — B. D. I p. 52 Pl. XVII f. 145. V. H. Syn. p. 99 Pl. XI f. 17. *N. tumida var. genuina* Grun. Verh. 1860 p. 537 Pl. IV f. 43 *a*; *v. subsalsa* Grun. f. *b. c.* — *N. pus. var. spitsbergensis* Grun. A. D. p. 40 (Cl. M. D. N:o 158).

Fresh or slightly brackish water: Spitsbergen (Grun), England! Arctic America! Mouth of Jenissey! Bahamas! Surinam! Tasmania! Cameroon!

Var. *lanceolata* Grun. (1860). Lanceolate, with slightly or scarcely rostrate ends. L. 0,04; B. 0,015 mm. Striæ 11 in 0,01 mm. — A. D. p. 40 Pl. II f. 47. *N. gastroides* Greg. M. J. III p. 40 Pl. IV f. 17 (1854). *N. pulchra* Greg. T. M. S. IV p. 42 Pl. V f. 7 (1856). *N. tumida v. lanceolata* Grun. Verh. 1860 p. 537 Pl. IV f. 44. *N. tum. v. subsalsa* Ströse Klieken f. 10.

Brackish water: Germany, Berlin (Grun.), Klieken, foss. (Ströse), Sweden, Lysekil! Hungary, Neusiedlersee (Grun.), Mouth of Jenissey!

Var. *jamalinensis* Grun. (1880). V. lanceolate with broad rostrate ends. L. 0,04; B. 0,016 mm. Central nodule incrassate around the median pores. Striæ 13 in 0,01 mm. — A. D. p. 40 Pl. II f. 48.

Brackish water: Sea of Kara (Grun).

9. **N. Demeraræ** Grun. (1893). — V. broadly lanceolate, with acute or obtuse ends. L. 0,046 to 0,065; B. 0,017 to 0,03 mm. Axial area narrow or indistinct. Central area large, irregular, with one, or a few, larger puncta near the central nodule. Terminal fissures in contrary direction. Striæ 15 to 17 in 0,01 mm. somewhat closer near the ends, radiate, punctate; puncta 19 in 0,01 mm. Median striæ of unequal length, terminal striæ parallel. — Diatomiste II p. 14 Pl. I f. 9.

Fresh water: Demerara River! Surinam (Kinker Coll.)!

10. **N. delawarensis** Grun. (1893). — V. elliptic-lanceolate, with subrostrate ends. L. 0,085 to 0,1; B. 0,044 mm. Median line with distant central pores. Axial area narrow. Central area

large, rounded. Striæ 14 to 15 in 0,01 mm., closer (about 18 in 0,01 mm.) near the ends, radiate at the ends, coarsely punctate; puncta about 11 in 0,01 mm. forming undulating, longitudinal rows. Median striæ alternately longer and shorter. — Diatomiste Vol. II p. 13 Pl. I f. 7, 8.

Brackish water: Mouth of Delaware (Grun.) Connecticut!

11. **N. Febigerii** Cl. (1881). — V. lanceolate, with obtuse ends. L. 0,054 to 0,06; B. 0,02 mm. Axial area indistinct; central area large and irregular. Striæ 14 to 16 in 0,01 mm., not closer near the ends, *strongly* radiate, parallel at the ends, composed of large puncta, about 14 in 0,01 mm. Median striæ of unequal length. — N. R. D. p. 9 Pl. II f. 21.

Marine: California! Japan!

N. Febigeri resembles the lower valve of *Achnanthes danica*, but it is a true Navicula, both valves being similar.

12. **N. Neumayeri** Pant. (1893). — V. lanceolate, subobtuse. L. 0,056; B. 0,022 mm. Axial area very narrow; central area small, rounded. Striæ 10 in 0,01 mm. radiate throughout, punctate; puncta 10 in 0,01 mm. Among the median striæ a few shorter are intercalated. — Pant. III Pl. IV f. 64.

Marine: Bory, Hungary, fossil (Pant.).

13. **N. Zeta** Cl. N. Sp. — V. lanceolate, with obtuse ends. L. 0,065; B. 0,022 mm. Median line with short terminal fissures, turned in the same direction. Axial area narrow. Central area orbicular, bordered by somewhat elongated puncta. Striæ 17 (middle) to 21 (ends) in 0,01 mm., radiate, parallel at the ends, coarsely punctate, puncta about 17 in 0,01 mm., forming undulating longitudinal rows. A few of the median striæ shorter than the others.

Brackish water: Barbados (Weissflog Coll.)!

Var. *mexicana* Cl. — V. with broader ends. L. 0,06; B. 0,019 mm. Striæ 15 (middle) to 20 (ends) in 0,01 mm. The median striæ not alternating with shorter striæ. Central area with blank spaces on both sides of the rows of elongated puncta.

Brackish water: Mexico (Weissflog Coll.)!

14. **N. My** Cl. N. Sp. — V. lanceolate, gradually tapering from the middle to the rounded and obtuse ends. L. 0,11; B. 0,024 mm. Axial area narrow; central area small, elongated. Striæ 14 (middle) to 20 (ends) in 0,01 mm. radiate at the ends and gently curved, punctate, puncta about 16 in 0,01 mm. Median striæ of unequal length. Pl. I f. 17.

Marine: China (Deby and Van Heurck Coll.)!

In outline and striation this species has some resemblance to *N. bottnica*, but it is much larger, has more distant puncta and the terminal striæ are radiate.

15. **N. mæandrina** Cl. (1893). — V. elliptical, with rounded ends. L. 0,045 to 0,065; B. 0,021 to 0,031 mm. Axial area narrow. Central area orbicular, moderately large. Striæ 19 to 21 in 0,01 mm., radiate throughout, composed of elongated puncta, forming undulating, longitudinal rows, about 9 to 10 in 0,01 mm. Median striæ alternately longer and shorter. — Diatomiste II p. 13 Pl. I f. 6.

Fresh water: Oregon, fossil!

The place of this form among the *Punctatæ* is somewhat uncertain. The elongated puncta suggest that it may be akin to *Nav. Tuscula*, which may be decided by examination of specimens in highly refractive media. The puncta will then perhaps be found to be finely, transversely lineate, in which case its place is near to *N. Tuscula*.

16. **N. Eta** Cl. (1893). — V. subhexagonal or broadly linear, with cuneate ends. L. 0,044; B. 0,019 mm. Axial area distinct, linear, slightly dilated in the middle. Striæ 16 (middle) to 20 (ends) radiate throughout, punctate; puncta about 21 in 0,01 mm. — Diatomiste II p. 13 Pl. I f. 5.

Marine: Red Sea! Japan!

This species has the appearance of a small *N. humerosa*, from which it differs by finer striæ and closer punctation.

17. **N. conspersa** PANT. (1893). V. broad, with almost parallel margins and slightly apiculate ends. L. 0,063; B. 0,033 mm. Axial area narrow, very slightly dilated in the middle. Striæ 11 in 0,01 mm., radiate at the ends, in the middle of equal length, punctate; puncta 13 in 0,01 mm. — PANT. III Pl. XI f. 184.

Habitat?: »Köpecz» (Pant.).

Resembles *N. humerosa*, but the median striæ are of equal length.

18. **N. humerosa** BRÉB. (1856). V. broad, with parallel margins and rostrate to cuneate, obtuse ends. L. 0,05 to 0,1; B. 0,03 to 0,042 mm. Axial area narrow, linear. Central area orbicular or somewhat transversely dilated. Median line frequently with incrassate central pores and hookshaped terminal fissures turned in the same direction. Striæ 9 to 10 in 0,01 mm. radiate or parallel in the ends, punctate; puncta 10 to 16 in 0,01 mm., forming undulating, longitudinal rows. Median striæ of unequal length. — SM. B. D. II p. 93. DONK. B. D. p. 18 Pl. III f. 3. A. S. Atl. VI f. 3, 4, 5. V. H. Syn. p. 98 Pl. XI f. 20. *N. quadrata* GREG. T. M. S. IV p. 11 f. 5 (1856). *Stauroneis erythræa* GRUN. Verh. 1860 p. 567 Pl. VI f. 17. *N. bengalensis* GRUN. in A. S. Atl. VI f. 1, 2 (1875). *N. Kamorthensis* GRUN. Verh. 1863 p. 152 Pl. V f. 16. A. S. Atl. VI f. 8, 8*?

Marine and brackish: Spitsbergen! Sea of Kara! Finmark! Baltic! North Sea! Mediterranean Sea! Black Sea! Caspian Sea (Grun.), Red Sea! Seychelles! Nicobar Islands! Sumatra! Java! Labuan! Sydney! Cameroon!

Var. *constricta*. — V. slightly constricted in the middle. — Sumbava (Kinker Coll.)! Gulf of Naples (Brun Coll.)!

Var *Fuchsii* PANT. (1889). — Puncta nearest to the areas elongated. — *N.* (*latissima var.?*) *Fuchsii* PANT. II p. 45 Pl. X f. 170.

Marine: Hungary, fossil (Pant.).

N. humerosa is somewhat variable in the outline and the punctation of the striæ. *N. Kamorthensis* in A. S. Atl. has somewhat convex margins. Similar specimens from Samoa (Van Heurck Coll.) differ in nothing else from *N. humerosa*. *N. humerosa* is allied with *N. punctulata*, which has, occasionally, longer and shorter striæ intermixed in the middle. On the other hand it is closely connected with *N. latissima*.

19. **N. monilifera** CL. — V. broad, with almost parallel margins and rostrate ends. L. 0,077 to 0,1; B. 0,03 to 0,05 mm. Axial area narrow; central area orbicular, moderately large. Striæ 8 in 0,01 mm. radiate throughout. Puncta 7 to 8 in 0,01 mm. — *N. granulata* BRÉB. in DONK. T. M. S. VI p. 17 Pl. III f. 19 (1858). B. D. p. 17 Pl. III f. 1. V. H. Syn. p. 98 Pl. XI f. 15. *N. granul. c. javanica* LEUD. FORTM. D. de Malaisie p. 17 Pl. II f. 2 (1892)?

Marine: North Sea! Ceylon! Madagascar!

Var. *heterosticha* CL. — Striæ 8 in 0,01 mm., in the middle alternately longer and shorter. Puncta 10 to 11 in 0,01 mm. — *N. granulata* A. S. Atl. VI f. 15, 16.

Marine: Hungary, fossil (Deby Coll.)!

N. monilifera is closely akin to *N. humerosa*, from which it differs principally by its coarser punctation. The median striæ are in most specimens of equal length, but this is subject to great variation and some shorter rows of puncta are occasionally intermixed in the middle of the valve. As the name *N. granulata* was used by BAILEY 1854 for another species, I have been obliged to change the name.

20. **N. latissima** GREG. (1856). — V. elliptic-lanceolate. L. 0,05 to 0,13; B. 0,04 to 0,05 mm. Axial area narrow, distinct. Central area orbicular. Striæ 7 or 8 (middle) to 9 or 10 (ends) in 0,01 mm., radiate, at the ends parallel, punctate; puncta about 11 in 0,01 mm. The

median striæ of unequal length. — T. M. S. IV p. 40 Pl. V f. 4, 4*. RALFS in Pritch Inf. VII f. 70. A. S. N. S. D. I f. 30. Atl. VI f. 7. DONK. B. D. p. 17 Pl. III f. 2. PANT. III Pl. XLI f. 568. *Pinnul. divaricata* O'MEARA M. J. VII p. 116 Pl. V f. 7 (1867).

Marine: Finmark! North Sea! Naples! Sebastopol! Ceylon! China! Japan! Hungary, foss.!

Var. *capitata* PANT. (1889). — V. with capitate ends. L. 0,109; B. 0,048 mm. Striæ 10,5 in 0,01 mm. — PANT. II p. 49; III Pl. XXXII f. 461.

Marine: Hungary, fossil (Pant.).

Var. *minor* PANT. (1889). — V. elliptic-elongated, with capitate ends. L. 0,075; B. 0,03 mm. Striæ 10,5 in 0,01 mm. — PANT. II p. 49.

Marine: Hungary, fossil (Pant.).

Var. *elongata* PANT. (1889). — V. elliptic-lanceolate. L. 0,14; B. 0,06 mm. Striæ 10 to 11 mm. Puncta 10 to 11 in 0,01 mm. — *N. humerosa v. elongata* PANT. II p. 48 Pl. X f. 175.

Marine: Hungary, fossil:

21. **N. Alpha** CL. (1893). — V. broadly lanceolate, with obtuse, subrostrate ends. L. 0,062; B. 0,03 mm. Median line with incrassate central pores, and the terminal fissures turned in contrary directions. Striæ 7 in 0,01 mm., a little closer at the ends (9 in 0,01 mm.), radiate, coarsely punctate; puncta 8 in 0,01 mm. Median striæ of unequal length. — Diatomiste II p. 13 Pl. I f. 4.

Marine: Japan!

22. **N. Jentzschii** GRUN. (1882). — V. elliptical, with rounded ends. L. 0,017 to 0,02; B. 0,009 to 0,0115 mm. Axial and central areas indistinct. Striæ 8 or 10 (middle) to 12 or 16 (ends) in 0,01 mm., frequently closer on one side of the valve, radiate throughout, punctate; puncta 22 in 0,01 mm. — Foss. D. Österr. Ung. p. 156 Pl. XXX f. 64.

Fresh or slightly brackish water: Domblitten, fossil (Grun.), Finland, Åbo! Sweden, Mälaren! Gulf of Bothnia!

This species seems to connect the *Punctatæ* with *N. lucidula* and *N. Atomus* among the *Minusculæ*.

23. **N. torneensis** CL. (1891). — V. lanceolate, with obtuse ends. L. 0,017 to 0,024; B. 0,008 to 0,01 mm. Axial area indistinct, central area small. Striæ 14 in 0,01 mm., radiate at the ends, coarsely punctate; puncta about 14 in 0,01 mm. — D. of Finl. p. 33 Pl. II f. 6.

Slightly brackish water: Gulf of Bothnia (Tornea, Piteå)!

Var. *åboensis* CL. (1881). — V. elliptical. L. 0,012; B. 0,008 mm. — l. c. f. 7.

Fresh water: Finland, Lake Lojo near Åbo!

24. **N. lacustris** GREG. (1856). — V. lanceolate, with subacute or subrostrate ends. L. 0,035 to 0,055; B. 0,016 to 0,018 mm. Axial area narrow; central area small, but distinct, orbicular. Terminal fissures seem to be turned in contrary directions. Striæ 14 to 16, radiate at the ends, distinctly punctate; puncta about 18 in 0,01 mm., larger near the areas. — M. J. IV Pl. I f. 23. CL. D. of Finl. p. 34 Pl. II f. 14.

Fresh water: Scotland, Loch Leven! Lule Lapmark! Finland! Germany, Oberrohe! Canada, Port Hope!

25. **N. Toulae** PANT. (1893). — V. lanceolate. L. 0,056; B. 0,021 mm. Axial area indistinct. Central area small, rounded. Striæ 10 in 0,01 mm. radiate throughout, composed of somewhat elongated puncta (9 in 0,01 mm.) arranged in almost straight longitudinal rows. Median striæ shortened. PANT. III Pl. XII f. 196.

Fresh water?: Hungary, Köpecz (Pant.).

26. **N. Gamma** CL. (1893). — V. lanceolate, with subrostrate ends. B. 0,036; B. 0,014 mm. Terminal fissures in contrary direction. Axial area indistinct; central area large, orbicular or

somewhat transverse. Striæ 12 (middle) to 13 (ends) in 0,01 mm. radiate throughout, coarsely punctate; puncta 14 in 0,01 mm. — Diatomiste II p. 12 Pl. I f. 2.

Slightly brackish water: Amatitlan, Guatemala, fossil!

Var. *rectilineata* Cl. (1893). — L. 0,032; B. 0,014 mm. Striæ 16 in 0,01 mm. composed of puncta, 17 in 0,01 mm., arranged in straight, longitudinal rows. — Diatomiste Vol. II p. 12 Pl. I f. 1.

Brackish water: Cameroon, Africa!

27. **N. amphibola** Cl. (1891). — V. elliptic-lanceolate, with rostrate, truncate ends. L. 0,037 to 0,07; B. 0,02 mm. Axial area narrow, but distinct. Central area rectangular, transversely dilated, broader outwards. Striæ 9 to 10 in 0,01 mm. radiate throughout, punctate; puncta 12 to 15 in 0,01 mm. *N. punctata v. asymmetrica* Lagst. Spitsb. D. p. 29 Pl. II f. 7 (1873). *N. Gastrum v. styriaca* Grun. Foss. D. Öst. Ung. p. 144 Pl. XXX f. 50 (1882). Franz Jos. Land D. p. 98 Pl. I f. 35. *N. amphibola* Cl. D. of Finl. p. 33 (1891). *N. styriaca* Pant. III Pl. VI f. 102; Pl. XII f. 194; Pl. XX f. 298 (1893).

Fresh water: Franz Josefs-Land (Grun.) Spitsbergen! Beeren Eiland (Lagerst.), Sweden. Alnarp, Skåne! Finland! Hungary, fossil (Grun.), S:ta Rosa, Calif.! Chicago foss.!

28. **N. Gálikii** Pant. (1889). — V. elliptic-lanceolate, rostrate. L. 0,034; B. 0,015 mm. Axial area narrow. Central area transversely dilated. Striæ 7,5 to 8 in 0,01 mm., radiate throughout. Puncta 10 in 0,01 mm. *N.* (*Gastrum var.?*) *Gálikii* Pant. II p. 46 Pl. XI f. 192.

Brackish water: Hungary, fossil (Pant.).

Probably the same as *N. amphibola*.

29. **N. Grovei** Cl. (1893). — V. broadly lanceolate, with obtuse ends. L. 0,06; B. 0,03 mm. Axial area narrow. Central area large, transversely dilated, and widened outwards. Terminal fissures in the same direction. Striæ 16 in 0,01 mm., radiate throughout. Puncta equidistant, 15 in 0,01 mm. Among the median striæ a few shorter are intermixed. — Diatomiste II p. 15 Pl. I f. 14.

Marine: Oamaru, N. Zealand, fossil!

This species seems to be akin to *N. transfuga var. Neupaueri*.

30. **N. baccata** Temp. a. Brun (1889). — V. broad, with parallel or slightly convex margins and cuneate or rostrate, obtuse or truncate ends. L. 0,05 to 0,055; B. 0,025 to 0,027 mm. Terminal fissures in the same direction. Axial area linear. Central area large, orbicular. Striæ 5,5 in 0,01 mm., radiate throughout. Puncta 6 in 0,01 mm. forming somewhat curved, longitudinal rows. — D. foss. du Japon p. 42 Pl. V f. 10.

Marine: Japan, fossil! Colon (Deby Coll.)!

31. **N. Schulzii** Kain (1889). — V. elliptical with rounded, obtuse ends. L. 0,12; B. 0,04 mm. Axial area distinct, narrowed towards the central and terminal nodules. Central area large, somewhat transverse. Terminal fissures turned in the same direction. Striæ 7 in 0,01 mm., radiate throughout. Puncta 6 in 0,01 mm., forming somewhat curved, longitudinal rows. — Bull. Tor. Bot. Cl. March 1889 p. 75 Pl. 89 f. 2 (according to Wolle Am. D. Pl. XXIV f. 5). *N. confoederata* Pant. III Pl. XXXIV f. 481 (1893).

Marine: Atlantic City, N. Jersey, fossil (Deby Coll.)!

Var. *californica* Cl. — V. elliptical, with subacute ends. L. 0,096; B. 0,042 mm. Striæ 5, puncta 5 in 0,01 mm. — Pl. I f. 26.

Marine: San Pedro, Calif. fossil (Kinker Coll.)!

Var. *marylandica* Cl. V. broadly elliptic-lanceolate, with obtuse ends. L. 0,09; B. 0,05 mm. Striæ 6 in 0,01 mm. Puncta 6 to 7 in 0,01 mm., largest at the margins and gradually decreasing in size towards the areas, forming irregular longitudinal rows.

Marine: Nottingham, Maryland, fossil (Dr. Rae Coll.)!

32. **N. maculata** Bail (1850). V. lanceolate, with subrostrate ends. L. 0,09 to 0,12; B. 0,035 to 0,015 mm. Axial area linear, narrow. Central area large, somewhat transverse. Striæ 6,5 in 0,01 mm. radiate throughout. Puncta 6 to 7 in 0,01 mm. forming undulating, longitudinal rows. — *Stauroneis maculata* Bail. Smiths Contr. 1850 p. 40 Pl. II f. 32. *N. Fischeri* A. S. Atl. VI f. 38 (1875).

Marine: Marble Head, Mass.! Pensacola, Florida!

Var. *caribæa* Cl. (1875). — L. 0,056 to 0,1; B. 0,025 to 0,04 mm. Striæ and puncta 7 in 0,01 mm. Central area small. *N. carib.* Cl. West Ind. D. p. 5. A. S. Atl. VI f. 10 12.

Marine: West Indies! Florida! Zanzibar (Atl.). Labuan! Port Jackson!

33. **N. Omicron** Cl. N. Sp. — V. elliptical, with apiculate ends. L. 0,028; B. 0,011 mm. Axial and central areas indistinct. Striæ 10 in 0,01 mm. slightly radiate throughout. Puncta 10 to 11 in 0,01 mm. — Pl. I f. 11.

Marine: Galapagos Islands!

34. **N. Omega** Cl. (1893). — V. broadly elliptical-lanceolate, with rostrate ends. L. 0,026; B. 0,015 mm. Axial area indistinct. Central area very small, rounded. Terminal fissures at distance from the ends. Transverse striæ 17 in 0,01 mm., slightly radiate throughout, coarsely punctate. Puncta 17 in 0,01 mm., forming nearly straight, longitudinal rows. — Diatomiste II p. 56 Pl. III f. 6.

Marine: Etretat (Temp. Perag. Types N:o 406).

35. **N. diffusa** A. S. (1874). — V. with parallel margins and apiculate ends. L. 0,072; B. 0,03 mm. On each side of the median line is a longitudinal depression. Axial area narrow; central area distinct. Striæ 9 in 0,01 mm., radiate throughout. — Atl. II f. 28. Perag. Villefr. p. 49 Pl. III f. 30.

Marine: Gulf of Mexico (Atl.), Mediterranean Sea (Perag.).

Var.? *balcarica* Cl. — V. in L. 0,052; B. 0,022 mm. Axial area indistinct; central small. Striæ 11 in 0,01 mm. Puncta 12 in 0,01 mm. forming undulating longitudinal rows. Valve without longitudinal depressions.

Marine: Balearic Islands!

Var. *minor* Cl. — L. 0,037; B. 0,015 mm. Striæ 13; puncta 16 in 0,01 mm.

Marine: Java!

36. **N. sublyrata** Grun. (1883). — V. elongated, constricted in the middle. L. 0,046; B. 0,01, at the constriction 0,007 mm. Axial area indistinct. Central area very small. Striæ 12 in 0,01, parallel, distinctly punctate. — Cl. Vega p. 496 Pl. XXXV f. 17.

Marine and brackish: North America (Grun.), Labuan!

37. **N. ceylanensis** Leud. Fortm. (1879). V. elongated, constricted in the middle; segments lanceolate. L. 0,16; B. 0,04, at the constriction 0,024 mm. Areas indistinct. Striæ 6 in 0,01 mm. transverse, coarsely punctate; puncta forming longitudinal rows. — D. de Ceylon p. 26 Pl. II f. 25.

Marine: Ceylon (Leud. Fortm.).

38. **N. bilobata** Leud. Fortm. (1879). — V. strongly constricted in the middle, with broadly elliptic-lanceolate segments. L. 0,07; B. 0,0255, at the constriction 0,0115 mm. Areas indistinct. Valve with large irregular puncta. — D. de Ceylon p. 24 Pl. II f. 24.

Marine: Ceylon (Leud. Fortm.).

N. bilobata and *N. ceylanensis* are unknown to the author and may possibly represent some forms of Dictyoneis.

39. **N. punctulata** W. SM. (1853). — V. elliptic-lanceolate, with subrostrate ends. L. 0,04 to 0,06; B. 0,025 to 0,03 mm. Axial area narrow or indistinct. Central area small, orbicular. Striæ 10 to 13 in 0,01 mm., radiate throughout. Puncta 10 in 0,01 mm. equidistant. Among the median striæ there are a few shorter frequently intermixed. — B. D. I p. 52 Pl. XVI f. 151. *N. marina* RALFS Pritch. Inf. p. 903 (1861). DONK. B. D. p. 19 Pl. III f. 5. A. S. Atl. VI f. 9. V. H. Syn. p. 98 Pl. XI f. 16.

Marine and brackish: Greenland! Finmark! Sea of Kara! North Sea! Caspian Sea (Grun.). Massachusetts! Florida! Barbados! South Africa! Mediterranean Sea! Ceylon! Port Jackson! California!

Var. *cluthensis* GREG. (1857). — V. elliptical, with rounded ends. L. 0,045 to 0,05; B. 0,025 mm. Axial area indistinct or narrow. Central area indistinct or small, orbicular. Striæ 10 to 14 in 0,01 mm., radiate throughout, punctate; puncta 12 to 13 in 0,01 mm. — *N. cluthensis* GREG. D. of Clyde p. 478 Pl. IX f. 2. *N. Cl. v. maculifera* CL. N. R. D. p. 9 Pl. II f. 23. *N. erythræa* GRUN. Verh. 1860 p. 539 Pl. V f. 17.

Marine and brackish: Finmark! North Sea! Baltic! Cape Horn (Petit), Madagascar! Ceylon! Nicobar Island! Tahiti!

Var. *finmarchica* GRUN. (1880). — L. 0,036 to 0,047; B. 0,022 to 0,024 mm. Striæ 11 to 12 in 0,01 mm. Central area indistinct. — *N. cluth. v. finm.* GRUN. A. D. p. 40 Pl. II f. 49.

Marine: Finmark (Grun.).

Var. *striolata* GRUN. (1884). — Striæ 14 in 0,01 mm. Puncta 8 in 0,01 mm. forming longitudinal rows. — *N. cluth. v. striol.* GRUN. Franz Jos. Land D. 1884 p. 104. CL. M. D. N:o 156.

Brackish water: Fiskebäckskil, Sweden.

Var. *Novæ Zealandiæ* GRUN. (1884). — L. 0,029; B. 0,015 mm. Striæ 11 (middle) to 14 (ends) in 0,01 mm. Central area indistinct. Valve with a marginal furrow. — *N. cluth. v. Novæ Zeal.* GRUN. Franz Jos. Land D. p. 104.

Marine: N. Zealand (Grun.).

Var. *pagophila* GRUN. (1884). — L. 0,031; B. 0,014 mm. Areas indistinct. Striæ 14 in 0,01 mm., distinctly punctate. — *N. cluth. v. pagophila* GRUN. Franz Jos. Land D. p. 104 Pl. I f. 30.

Marine: Franz Jos. Land.

The name *N. punctulata* was given 1842 by EHRENBERG to a form, which, to judge from the figure in the Micro-geologie is doubtless *Anomoeoneis sculpta*. As this species is not included in Navicula, I think it advisable to retain the name, given by W. SMITH. Between *N. punctulata* and *N. Cluthensis* there are no distinctions other than the form of the ends, which are subrostrate in the former and broadly rounded in the latter. This characteristic is so trifling that I have united them. Among the median striæ a few shorter are usually intermixed, which with other characteristics shews that *N. punctulata* is nearly akin to *N. humerosa*. By the var. *cluthensis* it is also related to *N. glacialis* CL. As *N. cluth. var. minuta* I, in 1881 (N. R. D. p. 10 Pl. II f. 22), described a small form with more distinct axial area. It does not belong to the section *Punctatæ*, and, as it is not sufficiently characterized, may be dropped.

40. **N. brasiliensis** GRUN. (1863). — V. lanceolate or elliptic-lanceolate, sometimes with subrostrate ends. L. 0,054 to 0,16; B. 0,027 to 0,055 mm. Terminal fissures in the same direction. Axial area indistinct. Central area small, rounded, frequently slightly transversely dilated. Striæ 8 to 12 in 0,01 mm. slightly radiate throughout. Puncta close towards the margins, more distant in the median part of the valve, where they form longitudinal, undulating rows. — Verh. 1863 p. 152 Pl. V f. 10. Novara p. 19. A. S. Atl. Pl. VI f. 19 to 25, 31 to 33.

Marine: Atlantic coast of N. America (Connecticut, North Carolina)! West Indies! Campeachy Bay! Brazil! Bab el Mandeb! Zanzibar (Atl.), Madagascar! Ceylon! Singapore! Labuan! China! Japan! New Caledonia! Samoa! Sandwich Islands (Atl.).

Var.? *bicuneata* Cl. — V. with parallel margins and cuneate ends. L. 0,10 to 0,12; B. 0,04 mm. Axial area linear. Central area transversely dilated, small. Striæ 8 in 0,01 mm., the median more approximate and more closely punctate. Pl. I f. 19.

Marine: Pensacola! Connecticut!

This variety, determined by Grun. as *N. arabica*, has nearly the same outline as f. 28 Pl. VI in A. S. Atl.

Var. *fossilis* Pant. (1889). — V. with cuneate ends. L. 0,027; B. 0,014 mm. Axial area distinct, not dilated around the central nodule. Striæ 12,5 in 0,01 mm. — Pant. II p. 43 Pl. V f. 82.

Marine: Hungary, fossil (Pant.).

41. **N. scandinavica** Lagst. (1876). — V. elliptic-lanceolate, with rostrate ends. L. 0,063 to 0,105; B. 0,028 to 0,034 mm. Axial area indistinct. Central area small, transverse. Striæ 12 to 14 in 0,01 mm. almost parallel, distinctly punctate; puncta about 13 in 0,01 mm. — *N. lacustris* A. S. N. S. D. p. 88 Pl. I f. 29 (1874) Atl. VI f. 30. *Stauroneis scandin.* Lagst. Boh. D. p. 47. *Staur. dilatata* Ströse Klicken f. 28? *Staur. Eichhornii* Schum. Pr. D. p. 189 Pl. IX f. 55 (1862)?

Marine: North Sea (Bohuslän, Norway)!

This species is probably allied to *N. carinifera*. There is on each side of the median line a narrow, longitudinal depression, which extends to the margin.

42. **N. carinifera** Grun. (1874). — V. lanceolate, with the axial part elevated towards the ends. L. 0,09 to 0,11; B. 0,03 to 0,04 mm. Axial area indistinct; central area small, transverse. Striæ 9 to 10 in 0,01 mm., slightly radiate, distinctly punctate; puncta 15 in 0,01 mm. — A. S. Atl. II f. 1.

Marine: Balearic Islands! Campeachy Bay! West Indies! Florida!

Forma minor. — L. 0,072; B. 0,024 mm. Striæ 11 in 0,01 mm. less distinctly punctate. — A. S. Atl. II f. 2.

Marine: Campeachy Bay (Atl.).

Var. *densius striata* A. S. (1881). — L. 0,12; B. 0,04 mm. Striæ 11 in 0,01 mm. — Atl. LXX f. 42.

Marine: Jamaica (Atl.).

Var. *laxepunctata* Cl. — L. 0,18; B. 0,05 mm. Striæ 11 in 0,01 mm.; puncta close towards the margin, inwards more distant, forming undulate longitudinal rows, 8 to 9 in 0,01 mm.

Marine: Kobi, Japan (Temp., Perag. Types N:o 188).

43. **N. granulata** Bail. (1854). — V. elliptic-lanceolate. L. 0,045 to 0,07; B. 0,022 to 0,032 mm. Axial area linear, narrowed towards the central nodule and the ends. Central area orbicular. Striæ 10 in 0,01 mm. slightly radiate throughout. Puncta closer near the margins, about 13 in 0,01 mm., more scattered on the depressed parts on both sides of the median line, where they form distant, undulating, longitudinal rows. — Smiths Contr. VII f. 16. *N. polysticta* Grev. Ed. N. Ph. J. X p. 28 Pl. IV f. 12 (1859). *N. Baileyana* A. S. N. S. D. Pl. I f. 31 (1874). Atl. VI f. 26, 27.

Marine: North Sea! Mediterranean Sea (Perag.), Bab el Mandeb! Ceylon! Japan! Sydney! Calif. guano (Grev.).

44. **N. transfuga** Grun. (1883). — V. elliptic-lanceolate with rostrate or subrostrate ends, depressed on both sides of the median line. Depressions large, lunate. L. 0,07 to 0,11; B. 0,045 to 0,06 mm. Axial area indistinct; central area large, dilated outwards, and rounded or not sharply defined. Striæ 9 in 0,01 mm., slightly radiate throughout. Puncta closer near the margins (11 to 12 in 0,01 mm.) than on the depressed areas (about 6 in 0,01 mm.), where they form undulating longitudinal rows. — Cl. Vega p. 511 Pl. XXXV f. 15.

Marine: Bab el Mandeb! Seychelles! China (Weissflog Coll.)! Japan (Brun Coll.)!

Var. *Neupaueri* PANT. (1886). — V. elliptical, with obtuse, not rostrate, ends. Striæ 11 or 12 (middle) to 12 or 13 (ends). — *N. Neupaueri* PANT. I p. 27 Pl. XIV f. 123.

Marine: Hungary, fossil! Japan, fossil (Tempère). Madagascar! China (Grove Coll.).

Var. *plagiostoma* GRUN. (1879). — V. with parallel margins and rostrate ends. L. 0,015 to 0,075; B. 0,022 to 0,032 mm. Axial area narrow. Central area large, more dilated on one half of the valve than on the other. Striæ 10 in 0,01 mm. slightly radiate, parallel at the ends. Puncta about 12 in 0,01 mm. — *Nav. plagiost.* GRUN. in Cl. M. D. N:o 257.

Marine: Virgin Islands! Pensacola! North Carolina!

Forma fossilis PANT. (1889). — L. 0,051; B. 0,024 mm. Striæ 12,5 in 0,01 mm. *N. irrorata v. fossilis* PANT. II p. 49 Pl. VIII f. 147.

Marine: Hungary, fossil (Pant.).

It seems, to judge from the figure, questionable whether the var. fossilis is not an Anomoeoneis.

45. **N. Epsilon** CL. (1893). — V. lanceolate, with rostrate ends. L. 0,08 to 0,1; B. 0,04 mm. Median line with bifid median pores, and terminal fissures turned in opposite directions. Axial area narrow, slightly dilated around the central nodule. Striæ 10 in 0,01 mm., radiate throughout. Puncta near the margins 10 in 0,01 mm., on the depression about 6 in 0,01 mm. disposed in undulating, longitudinal rows. — Diatomiste II p. 12 Pl. I f. 3.

Marine: China (Thum!) Japan (Brun Coll.)!

46. **N. margaritifera** TRUAN a. WITT (1888). — V. elliptical, with acute ends. L. 0,1; B. 0,05 mm. Median line with the ends at some distance from the margin of the valve. Structure: large puncta (about 5 in 0,01 mm.) irregularly scattered over the whole valve. — Jeremie D. p. 17 Pl. IV f. 10.

Marine: Hayti, fossil (Truan and Witt).

This form is very dissimilar to all of this section and its systematic position uncertain. *N. Reusii* PANT. III Pl. XXXIII f. 478 (1893) has also scattered puncta, but with a rim of fine striæ. It may be an allied species, if not *N. glacialis var. septentrionalis.*

47. **N. arabica** GRUN. (1875). — V. with parallel margins and rostrate ends. L. 0,12; B. 0,04 mm. Terminal fissures large, hookshaped. Central area transversely dilated. Striæ 8 in 0,01 mm., slightly radiate throughout. Puncta 7 in 0,01 mm. disposed in undulating, longitudinal rows. — A. S. Atl. VI f. 14.

Marine: Zanzibar (Atl.).

The above description is from the fig. in Atl., which shews terminal fissures of a shape, very dissimilar to those of all other species of this section. Specimens by Grunow determined as *N. arabica*, are identical with *N. brasiliensis var. bicuneata.*

48. **N. oscitans** A. S. (1875). V. elliptical. L. 0,055 to 0,09; B. 0,03 to 0,05 mm. Axial area indistinct; central area irregular, frequently a transverse linear space narrowed outwards. Striæ 9 to 10 in 0,01 mm., radiate throughout, punctate; puncta about 8 in 0,01 mm., closer towards the margin than on the depressed parts on both sides of the median line. — Atl. VI f. 41.

Marine: Balearic Islands! Macassar Straits! Japan, fossil (Brun Coll.)! S:ta Monica, Calif. fossil! Monterey (Atl.).

The fig. 40 Pl. VI in A. S. Atl. from Davis strait belongs probably to *N. oscitans.* I have seen similar forms from S:ta Monica (Deby Coll.) and Redondo (Grove), which I cannot separate from *N. oscitans.*

Var. *subundulata* CL. and GROVE (1891). — V. elliptical, with rounded ends. L. 0,092; B. 0,06 mm. Axial area indistinct, central irregular. Surface of the valve with a slight depression on both sides of the median line. Striæ 7 in 0,01 mm., slightly radiate, composed of puncta, more distant on the depressions (8 in 0,01 mm.) than towards the margin and the median line (18 in 0,01 mm.). Diatomiste I p. 67 Pl. X f. 10.

Marine: Macassar Straits!

This form is perhaps to be considered as a distinct species.

49. **N. impressa** GRUN. (1875). — V. elliptic-lanceolate. L. 0,06 to 0,075; B. 0,034 to 0,045 mm. Axial area indistinct, central area small. Striæ 7 to 9 in 0,01 mm. parallel in the middle, slightly radiate at the ends. Puncta coarse, 7 to 11 in 0,01 mm. On both sides of the median line are large lunate depressions. — A. S. Atl. VI f. 17, 18.

Marine: Campeachy Bay! Sumbava (Kinker Coll.)!

50. **N. sparsipunctata** GROVE and STURT (1886). — V. broadly elliptical, with rounded ends. L. 0,05 to 0,055; B. 0,03 to 0,04 mm. Central nodule very small. Terminal fissures indistinct. Axial area narrow, linear, unilateral. Central area indistinct. Striæ 10 in 0,01 mm. parallel in the middle, radiate at the ends. Puncta coarse, inequidistant, about 6 in 0,01 mm. At some distance from the margin is a narrow, not punctate, space. — Quek. M. Cl. II (2) p. 323 Pl. XVIII f. 1.

Marine: Oamaru, New Zealand, fossil!

This is a very remarkable form, not closely akin to any known species. The median line and the central nodule are especially peculiar.

51. **N. interlineata** GROVE and STURT (1886). V. elliptic-lanceolate. L. 0,1; B. 0,05 mm. Axial area narrow, very slightly dilated around the central nodule. Terminal fissures indistinct. Striæ 8 in 0,01 mm., radiate throughout. Puncta 8 in 0,01 mm. forming irregularly undulating rows. On both sides of the median line is a narrow, arcuate, lateral area, inside which the puncta form more regular longitudinal rows. — J. Quek. M. Cl. II (2) p. 323 Pl. XVIII f. 2.

Marine: Oamaru, New Zealand, fossil!

A very remarkable species, which shews some resemblance to *Diploneis nitida*.

52. **N. fraudulenta** A. S. (1881). V. elliptical with rounded ends. L. 0,03 to 0,045; B. 0,019 to 0,023 mm. Axial area indistinct. Central area small, not sharply defined. Striæ 14 (middle) to 18 (ends) in 0,01 mm. slightly radiate at the ends, composed of puncta, about 13 in 0,01 mm., disposed towards the median line in straight, somewhat distant, longitudinal rows. — N. S. D. III p. 18 (without name). *N. fraudulenta* A. S. Atl. LXX f. 60. *N. restituta* A. S. accord. to Grun. in Cl. M. D. No 102 (1878).

Marine: North Sea! Sebastopol!

A small, very distinct species, not to be mistaken for any other.

53. **N. Novæ Guineænsis** TEMP. (1891). V. broad, biconstricted apiculate. L. 0,04 to 0,05; B. 0,027 mm. Central nodule transversely dilated. Axial area narrow, linear. Central area transversely dilated. Striæ 11 in 0,01 mm., strongly radiate at the ends, composed of coarse puncta, about 7 in 0,01 mm. forming undulating longitudinal rows. — Diatomiste I p. 71, Pl. XI f. 1.

Brackish water: Yule Island (New Guinea)!

This is a very interesting form, not closely connected with any other. The median line has somewhat arcuate components, which suggests that the valve is slightly geniflexed as in Achnanthes. The coarse structure resembles that of *Nav. Tuscula*, but the direction of the terminal rows of puncta is different and there is no appearance of a lineation across the puncta. The dilated central nodule, as well as the strongly inclined striæ, remind one of the lower valve of *Achnanthes danica* and its allies, but the structure is much coarser and the valve strongly silicious.

54. **N. Pi** CL. (1893) — V. rhombic-lanceolate, with obtuse ends. L. 0,08; B. 0,022 mm. Axial area indistinct; central area small. Terminal fissures in the same direction. Striæ 11 (middle) to

12 (ends) in 0,01 mm. almost parallel. Puncta about 12 in 0,01 mm. forming slightly undulating longitudinal rows. Diatomiste II p. 15 Pl. I f. 13.

Marine: China (Van Heurck Coll.)!

55. **N. doljensis** PANT. (1886). — V. lanceolate, with subacute ends. L. 0,112; B. 0,033 mm. Median line with approximate central pores, slightly undulating. Axial area indistinct, central very small, orbicular. Striæ 9 in 0,01 mm., transverse throughout, coarsely punctate, puncta about 9 in 0,01 mm. — PANT. I p. 24 Pl. XXIV f. 219.

Marine: Hungary, fossil (Pant.).

56. **N. Brunii** PANT. (1886). — V. lanceolate, with subobtuse ends. L. 0,084; B. 0,02; mm. Median line straight, with approximate central pores. Axial area indistinct, central a short and narrow transverse fascia. Striæ 9 in 0,01 mm. slightly radiate in the middle, slightly convergent at the ends, coarsely punctate. — PANT. I p. 23 Pl. XXIV f. 217.

Marine: Hungary, fossil (Pant.).

57. **N. Lunula** CL. — V. moderately asymmetrical, with convex dorsal and ventral margins and subacute ends. L. 0,062; B. 0,016 mm. Median line straight. Axial area narrow, not dilated around the central nodule. Striæ 13 in 0,01 mm., slightly radiate, coarsely punctate; puncta 13 in 0,01 mm. Median ventral striæ not ending in isolated puncta. — Part I Pl. V f. 5.

Marine: Java!

Of this form I have seen one specimen only, in a gathering of shell-sand found at Java by Dr. AURIVILLIUS. There were no freshwater forms in the material, so I have no doubt about the marine habitat of this form, which could be placed in *Cymbella*, were not the puncta so distant and the habitat marine.

58. **N. Grundleri** CL. a. GRUN. (1878). — V. broad with almost parallel or very slightly concave sides and broad rounded ends. L. 0,075 to 0,098; B. 0,028 mm. Median line excentric, with large hook-shaped terminal fissures turned in the same directions. Axial area indistinct; central area small and orbicular. Striæ 10 to 12 in 0,01 mm., slightly radiate in the middle and convergent at the ends, coarsely punctate; puncta 9 to 12 arranged in undulating longitudinal rows. — *Alloioneis Gründleri* CL. West Ind. D. p. 7 Pl. II f. 10.

Marine: West Indies! Campeachy Bay! Colon! Fossil: Oamaru, New Zeeland!

Var. *symmetrica* CL. — L. 0,07; B. 0,03 mm. Median line almost central, its terminal fissures small. Striæ 15, puncta 14 in 0,01 mm.

Marine: Oamaru, New Zealand, fossil!

This is a very remarkable species, not nearly akin to any other. The var. *symmetrica*, although in some characteristics differing from the type, can however in my opinion not be separated from *N. Grundleri*, especially as the asymmetrical type occurs also at Oamaru. *N. Grundleri* is a form intermediate to the *Amphoræ* of the section *Psammamphora* or *Amblyamphora*, and has as these, the striæ in the middle between the central and terminal nodules divergent from the median line.

Additional.

N. arverna HÉRIB. a. PERAG. (1893). — V. broadly elliptical, with apiculate ends. L. 0,05; B. 0,013 mm. Axial area narrow. Central area star-like. Striæ 5 in 0,01 mm. radiate in the middle and alternately longer and shorter, transverse at the ends, coarsely punctate. — D. d'Auvergne p. 105 Pl. IV f. 19.

Fresh water? Auvergne, fossil.

Naviculæ Lyratæ Cl.

Valve usually elliptical to lanceolate, rarely constricted in the middle. Median line with curved terminal fissures, rarely in contrary direction, or bayonet-shaped. Axial area indistinct. Central area small, united to two, more or less broad, lateral areas. Structure of the valve: usually distinct puncta, disposed in transverse rows, radiate at the ends of the valve, and in undulating longitudinal rows. Zone not complex.

I have examined some living specimens of *N. Lyra*, *N. spectabilis* and *N. Hennedyii*. All have two chromatophore-plates along the valves. The margins of the plates are strongly indented. From the apices a narrow and deep sinus proceeds towards the central nodule and has at its end an elæoplast. As the plates in some cases were deeply constricted in the middle it seems probable that they divide by a fissure at right angle to the median line.

Nav. Hennedyi with cell-contents, 600 times magnified

Nav. Lyra var. with cell-contents, 600 times magnified

The most important characteristic of this group consists in the lateral areas, which are to be regarded as lateral expansions of the central nodule. They are more silicious than other parts of the valve, and coherent with the mass of the usually small central nodule.

This group, corresponding to the *Hennedyées* and *Lyrées* in Van Heurck's Synopsis, comprises an enormous mass of forms, in which are more transitions than in any other group of naviculoid diatoms. All the characteristics are subject to so much variation, that I am unable to distinguish more than a very few, well defined species, although besides the numerous published figures I have examined at least 300 sketches of forms from all parts of the world.

I have tried to obtain characteristics from the relative number of the striæ and their puncta, but the variation, even in the same species, is too great. The outline of the valve offers no trustworthy characteristics, the same species occurring with rounded, obtuse and rostrate ends. The breadth and form of the lateral areas are also subject to great variations, so that all possible transitions can be traced from the large lunate areas of *N. Hennedyi* to the narrow and linear areas of *N. Lyra*. The presence or absence of markings in the areas offer no characteristics for specific distinction. Inspection of a large number of specimens has induced me to unite in one species a considerable number of forms, hitherto admitted as distinct species. The forms belonging to *N. approximata*, *N. Hennedyi*, *N. spectabilis*, *N. clavata* and *N. Lyra* are numerous, and the simplest and most effective course would perhaps have been to unite these five species, and possibly others; as they all pass by numerous intermediate forms into each other.

The group most nearly connected with the *Nav. Lyratæ* is the *Nav. punctatæ*, both being united by numerous transitional forms. In some cases it is difficult to decide whether a form belongs to the Nav. punctatæ or the Nav. lyratæ. Such forms are for instance *N. transfuga* and *N. carinifera* among the Punctatæ and *N. Schaarschmidtii* among the Lyratæ.

On the other hand the Nav. lyratæ offer some resemblance to the genus *Diploneis*, especially in *D. hyalina*, *D. Hudsonis* and some other forms. The prolongations of the central nodule in Diploneis correspond evidently to the lateral expansions of the central nodule in the Lyratæ, but there are no longitudinal lines in Lyratæ as in Diploneis, and in Diploneis there is no punctate space between the median line and the prolongations of the central nodule.

All the forms of this Section live in salt water, a few only (*N. pygmæa* and some varieties of *N. forcipata*) living in brackish water; so that the forms of this section of Navicula are very characteristic of purely marine deposits. In the older deposits only few occur. From the Barbados deposit I have seen only one specimen, of a species akin to *N. Barbitos*. In the Oamaru deposit there are a few peculiar forms, one of which has the terminal fissures in contrary directions, and another has almost straight terminal fissures. In the deposits of the miocene or oligocene age forms of Lyratæ begin to become numerous, one of the most frequent being *N. prætexta*. In the present age, forms of this Section are very frequent, and the same species have a very wide range of distribution.

Most species of this section being transitional and their characteristics subject to great variation, it is extremely difficult to construct a satisfactory artificial key. Still I believe the following will be of use.

Artificial key.

1.	Lateral areas uniting with the central area	2.
	— — not — — — —	*N. conciliana* Cl.
2.	Puncta forming straight longitudinal rows	*N. Durandi* Kitton.
	— — undulating — —	3.
3.	Lateral areas linear	4.
	— — broader in the middle	20.
4.	Spaces between the areas and the median line striate	5.
	— — — — — not —	*N. Reichardtii* Grun.
5.	Central pores incrassate	6.
	— — not —	7.
6.	Striæ about 13 in 0,01 mm.	*N. forcipata* Grun.
	— 15 to 22 — —	*N. forcipata* var.
	— about 26 — —	*N. pygmæa* Kütz.
7.	Lateral areas short, not reaching to the margin	8.
	— — — reaching — —	11.
8.	Striæ ending at the margin in double rows of small puncta	*N. rudis* Cl.
	— not — — — — — — — —	9.
9.	Axial area narrowed at the ends and in the middle	*N. abrupta* Greg.
	— — indistinct	10.
10.	Valve almost orbicular	*N. H. album* Cl.
	— elliptical	*N. connectens* Grun.
	(*N. australica* A. S., *N. Lyra var. atlantica*, *N. spectabilis, var.*, *Rattrayi var. abbreviata*).	
11.	Valve indented in the middle	*N. distenta* A. S.
	· not — —	12.
12.	Valve narrow, linear with rounded ends	*N. Samoensis* Grun.
	— broad, elliptical or elliptic-lanceolate	13.
13.	Puncta of the median striæ confluent towards the central nodule	*N. genifera* A. S.
	— — — — not	14.
14.	Axial part of the valve elevated towards the ends	*N. Barbitos* A. S. (*N. Lyra v. subcarinata*).
	— — — not	15.
15.	Lateral areas very distant from the median line	*N. diffluens* A. S.
	— — not — — —	16.

16.	Areas well defined	17.
	— not —	19.
17.	Ends of the areas convergent or parallel	*N. irrorata* GRUN.
	— — — divergent	18.
18.	Areas contracted in the middle	*N. inhalata* A. S.
	— not — — —	*N. fluitans* BRUN.
19.	Ends of the areas parallel or divergent	*N. Lyra* EHR.
	— — — convergent	*N. approximata* GREV. (*N. spectabilis var.*).
20.	Lateral areas with a band of short striæ	21.
	— — punctate or dotted	24.
	— smooth	33.
21.	Terminal fissures in contrary directions	*N. variolata* CL.
	— the same —	22.
22.	Puncta twice as close as the striæ	*N. illustra* PANT.
	— and striæ equidistant	23.
23.	Striæ about 9 in 0,01 mm.	*N. copiosa* A. S.
	— 14 —	*N. Sandriana* GRUN.
24.	Axial part of the valve elevated at the ends	25.
	— — not — —	26.
25.	Areas with puncta in short undulating rows	*N. venustissima* KITT.
	— — irregular puncta	*N. venusta* JAN.
26.	Areas narrow	*N. inhalata var. biharensis.*
	— broad	27.
27.	Areas indentate in the middle	*N. spectabilis var. hungarica* and *var. excavata.*
	— not — — —	28.
28.	Areas semiorbicular	*N. oamaruensis* GRUN.
	— semielliptical	29.
29.	Median portion of the areas smooth	*N. Stercus muscarum* CL.
	— — — — punctate	30.
30.	Ends rostrate	*N. clavata var. indica.*
	— non —	31.
31.	Areas with large dots	*N. perfecta* PANT. (*N. Hennedyi var. caliginosa* and *var. Neapolitana*).
	— short, undulating rows of puncta	*N. reticulo-radiata* BR. a. TEMP.
	— irregular puncta	32.
32.	Axial striæ of 2 to 4 puncta	*N. prætexta* EHR. (*N. Hennedyi var. circumsecta*).
	— — — 4 to 8 —	*N. Schaarschmidtii* PANT.
33.	Valve constricted in the middle	*N. clavata var. exul* (*N. Hennedyi var. constricta*).
	— not — — —	34.
34.	Valve rostrate	*N. clavata* GREG.
	— non —	35.
35.	Areas contracted in the middle	*N. spectabilis* GREG.
	— not — — —	36.
36.	Areas broad	*N. Hennedyi* W. SM.
	— narrow	37.
37.	L. 0,047 mm.	*N. turgidula* PANT.
	L. 0,08 to 0,17 mm.	*N. irrorata* GREV.

1. **N. concilians** CL. N. Sp. V. lanceolate, with subrostrate ends. L. 0,045; B. 0,023 mm. Lateral areas not uniting with the central area, linear or narrow lunate, not sharply defined. Marginal striæ 13 to 14 in 0,01 mm. Puncta about 18 in 0,01 mm., becoming more distant towards the areas. — Pl. I f. 25.

Marine: Honolulu!

In this form the lateral areas are separated by a row of puncta from the small central nodule. It is therefore to be considered as a transitional form from the Punctatæ to the Lyratæ. Similar forms are known from Samoa (lanceolate. L. 0,066; B. 0,05 mm. Striæ 12 in 0,01 mm.) and from Madagascar.

2. **N. connectens** GRUN. (1886). — V. elliptical or lanceolate, with rounded or cuneate ends. L. 0.072 to 0.13; B. 0.035 to 0.038 mm. Lateral areas linear, ending at a considerable distance from the ends of the valve. Striæ 8 to 9, puncta 10 in 0.01 mm. — *N. Lyra var. connectens* GRUN. in PANT. I Pl. XXIV f. 221.

Marine: Atlantic City, N. Jersey, fossil (Deby Coll.)! Hungary, fossil (Pant.).

3. **N. H album** CL. N. Sp. V. broadly elliptical, or almost orbicular. L. 0.076; B. 0.052 mm. Terminal fissures at a right angle to the median line. Lateral areas almost parallel, abbreviate, somewhat distant, producing in the middle of the valve a figure resembling the letter H. Marginal striæ 14, axial striæ 18 and puncta 16 in 0.01 mm. — Part I Pl. IV f. 8, 9.

Marine: China (Van Heurck and Deby Coll.)!

4. **N. Schaarschmidtii** PANT. (1886). — V. elliptical. L. 0.075 to 0.13; B. 0.04 to 0.065 mm. Lateral areas not sharply defined, with scattered puncta, and sometimes larger dots. Marginal striæ 9 to 15 in 0.01 mm. Puncta 10 to 14 in 0.01 mm. Axial striæ of 4 to 8 puncta. PANT. I p. 28 Pl. XIV f. 121.

Marine: Hungary, fossil! Japan, fossil (Brun Coll.)! Maryland, fossil (Deby Coll.)!

This species is nearly akin to *N. transfuga* in the group Punctatæ.

5. **N. reticulo-radiata** TEMP. a. BRUN (1889). — V. elliptical. L. 0,1; B. 0.067 mm. Lateral areas large, not sharply defined, with short undulating longitudinal rows of puncta. Marginal striæ 10 in 0.01 mm. Puncta about 8 in 0.01 mm. Axial striæ of single puncta. D. fossiles de Japon p. 44 Pl. V f. 4.

Marine: Japan, fossil! China (Deby Coll.)!

6. **N. Stercus muscarum** CL. N. Sp. — V. elliptical. L. 0.072; B. 0,042 mm. Areas large, lunate, not sharply defined, smooth in the middle and with scattered, larger puncta on their sides. Marginal striæ 10 in 0.01 mm., short, finely punctate. Axial striæ 13 to 14 in 0,01 mm. very short. — Pl. I f. 27.

Marine: China (Van Heurck Coll.)!

7. **N. prætexta** EHR. (1840). — V. elliptical. L. 0.045 to 0,19; B. 0,03 to 0.11 mm. Lateral areas large, semielliptical, not sharply defined, with scattered puncta. Striæ marginal, 6 to 8 in 0,01 mm. Puncta 9 to 10 in 0.01 mm. Axial striæ of 3 to 4 puncta. *Pinn. præt.* EHR. Ber. 1840 M. G. XIX f. 28. *Nav. præt.* GREG. D. of Clyde p. 481 Pl. IX f. 11. DONK. B. D. p. 10 Pl. II f. 1. A. S. Atl. III f. 31—34; CXXIX f. 7. V. H. Syn. p. 92 Pl. IX f. 13. WITT Archangelsk D. Pl. IX f. 4. JAN. Gaz. Exp. XV f. 21.

Marine: North Sea! Mediterranean Sea! Red Sea! Ceylon! Australia! Japan! Kerguelens Land! Cape Horn (Petit)! Macassar Straits! West Indies! North Carolina! Fossil: Archangelsk! Moravian Tegel! Upper tertiary deposits of Hungary! Moron! Japan! Hayti (Truan and Witt), Oamaru, N. Zealand! California!

Var. *abundans* A. S. (1888). — V. rhombic-elliptical. L. 0.1; B. 0.07 mm. Areas not defined, covered with puncta (4 to 5 in 0.01 mm.) in connection with the puncta of the marginal striæ. Marginal striæ 6 in 0.01 mm., their puncta 6 in 0,01 mm. — Atl. CXXIX f. 8.

Marine: Monterey and S:ta Monica, Cal. fossil!

Var. *abnormis* CL. — L. 0,14; B. 0.075. Striæ 11, puncta 14 in 0.01 mm. Marginal striæ in the middle of the valve close, 14 in 0.1 mm.

Marine: Soundings. Lat. 12°24 N., Long. 122°15 Gr. (Rae Coll.)!

Var. *Haytiana* TRUAN and WITT (1888). L. 0,16; B. 0,12 mm. Marginal striæ 8 in 0.01 mm. No axial striæ. — *N. Haytiana* TRUAN a. WITT Jeremie D. p. 17 Pl. IV f. 9.

Marine: Hayti, fossil (Truan a. Witt).

Var *Lanyaczki* Pant. (1886). — L. 0,11; B. 0,05 mm. Striæ 10 in 0,01 mm. interrupted in the middle of the valve. — *N. Lanyae*. Pant. I p. 26 Pl. XIV f. 122. *N. prætexta* Truan a. Witt Jerem. D. p. 17 Pl. IV f. 8.

Marine: Hungary, fossil (Pant.). Hayti (Truan a. Witt.).

N. prætexta is a most variable species, passing into *N. Hennedyi var. circumsecta*.

8. **N. irrorata** Grev. (1859). — V. with parallel margins and cuneate ends, or lanceolate. L. 0,09 to 0,17; B. 0,045 to 0,06 mm. Lateral areas not sharply defined, linear, with straight exterior margins, smooth. Marginal striæ 7 to 10, puncta 6 to 9 in 0,01 mm. Axial striæ of 2 to 5 puncta. — Edinb. N. Ph. J. X p. 27 Pl. IV f. 1. A. S. Atl. II f. 22, 23.

Marine: Adriatic! Sydney! Calif. guano (Grev.). West Indies! Mexico! Campeachy Bay! Florida!

Var. *mexicana* Cl. — Lanceolate. L 0,12; B 0,053. Striæ 7, puncta about 5 in 0,01 mm. — *N. irrorata* A. S. Atl. II f. 19.

Marine: Gulf of Mexico (Atl.).

Var. *substauroneiformis* Grun. (1874). - L. 0,08; 0,04 mm. Striæ 7, puncta 9 in 0,01 mm. Central nodule incrassate and transversely dilated. — *N. approxim. v. substauroneif.* A. S. Atl. II f. 20.

Marine: Campeachy Bay!

Var. *ceylanica* Cl. — Elliptical. L. 0,095; B. 0,05 mm. Marginal striæ 14, their puncta about 21 in 0,01 mm. Axial striæ 17, their puncta 16 in 0,01 mm.

Columbo, Ceylon (Letourneur Coll.)!

Var. *elliptica* Cl. — Elliptical to elliptic-lanceolate. L. 0,075 to 0,13; B. 0,03 to 0,055 mm. Areas with convex exterior margins, convergent. Striæ 9 to 10 in 0,01 mm. Puncta about 9 to 10 inequidistant. — Icon. n. Part I Pl. IV f. 13.

Marine: Colon (Deby Coll.)! Gulf of Mexico! West Indies! China! Manila (Deby Coll.)! Fossil: Hungary, Kekkö (Deby Coll.)!

9. **N. perfecta** Pant. (1886). — V. elliptical. L. 0,116 to 0,14; B. 0,068 to 0,07 mm. Areas not sharply defined, semilanceolate, with large crowded dots. Striæ 9 (10 to 11 accord. to Pant.), puncta about 10 in 0,01 mm. The puncta become less crowded towards the area and are there arranged in almost regular, longitudinal rows. Pant. I p. 28 Pl. XXIII f. 207.

Marine: Hungary, fossil!

Var. *Letourneurii* Pant. (1889). V. slightly constricted in the middle. L. 0,08; B. 0,032 mm. Striæ 12,5, puncta 15 in 0,01 mm. — *N. Letour.* Pant. II p. 49 Pl. XXIV f. 358.

Marine: Hungary, fossil (Pant.).

10. **N. venusta** Jan. Ms. — V. rhombic-lanceolate. L. 0,07 to 0,11; B. 0,05 to 0,04 mm. Axial part elevated. Lateral areas not sharply defined, semilanceolate with scattered puncta. Striæ 13 in 0,01 mm. closely punctate near the margin. - Gazelle Exp. XV f. 17.

Marine: Galapagos Islands!

Var. *intermedia* Cl. — V. elliptical. L. 0,097; B. 0,052 mm. Lateral areas large, semilanceolate, dotted on the part near the axial striæ, punctate on the part near the marginal striæ, puncta distant, gradually passing over to the marginal striæ. Marginal striæ 13, their puncta 18 in 0,01 mm. Axial part less distinctly elevated.

Marine: Mediterranean Sea (Tempère).

This variety seems to connect *N. venusta* with *N. perfecta*.

11. **N. Barbitos** A. S. (1888). — V. strongly silicious, rhombic-lanceolate, with the axial part elevated towards the ends. L. 0,18 to 0,22; B. 0,055 to 0,013 mm. Lateral areas linear, not sharply defined, almost parallel, approximate to the median line. Striæ 12 in 0,01 mm. punctate; puncta closer (about 14 in 0,01 mm.) near the margins than near the lateral area (about 9 in 0,01 mm.), where they form undulating and obscurely decussating longitudinal rows. — Atl. CXXIX f. 5.

Marine: Singapore! Cebu! Sumatra! Sumbava!

12. **N. venustissima** KITTON (1892). V. lanceolate, with elevated axial part. L. 0,13 to 0,2; B. 0,055 mm. Lateral areas not sharply defined, large, semilanceolate, covered with undulating longitudinal rows of puncta. Marginal striæ 10 and their puncta 11 in 0,01 mm. — LEUD. FORTM. D. de la Malaisie p. 17 Pl. II f. 3. Icon. n. Part. I Pl. IV f. 12.

Marine: Penang Harbour! Hongkong (Deby and Rae Coll.)! Samarang (Grove Coll.)!

13. **N. inhalata** A. S. (1874). — V. elliptical. L. 0,07 to 0,08; B. 0,035 to 0,045 mm. Areas not sharply defined, broadly linear, constricted in the middle and convergent at the ends. Striæ 13 to 14, puncta 12 to 14 in 0,01 mm. — Atl. II f. 30.

Marine: Madagascar! Philippines! Samoa (Atl.). Fossil: Moravian Tegel! Hungary (Pant.). S:ta Monica Calif.!

Var. *lanceolata* CL. — V. with rostrate ends. L. 0,065; B. 0,035 mm. Striæ and puncta 12 in 0,01 mm.

Marine: Manilla (Deby Coll.)!

Var.? *biharensis* PANT. (1889). — L. 0,052; B. 0,0265 mm. Areas with scattered puncta. Striæ 12,5 to 13 in 0,01 mm. finely punctate. PANT. II p. 48 Pl. VIII f. 139.

Marine: Hungary, fossil (Pant.).

The var. *biharensis* seems to be more akin to *N. spectabilis*.

14. **N. rudis** CL. (1881). — V. elliptical. L. 0,052 to 0,1; B. 0,032 to 0,08 mm. Areas not sharply defined, linear, abbreviate. Striæ 6 in 0,01 mm. Puncta 6 to 7 in 0,01 mm. closer and in double rows near the margin. — N. R. D. p. 8 Pl. II f. 17. *N. Truani* PANT. I p. 29 Pl. II f. 19 (1886).

Marine: Balearic Islands! Moron, Spain, fossil!

15. **N. fluitans** BRUN (1891). — V. elliptical. L. 0,14 to 0,16; B. 0,05 to 0,06 mm. Areas not sharply defined, linear, extending to the ends. Striæ 9 in 0,01 mm., puncta about 11 in 0,01 mm. — D. Esp. n. p. 34 Pl. XV f. 13.

Marine: Mauritius (Brun). Cabenda, Western Africa (Brun).

16. **N. variolata** CL. (1892). — V. orbicular. L. 0,1 to 0,15; B. 0,096 to 0,12 mm. Median line with terminal fissures in contrary directions. Lateral areas large, semicircular with numerous dots and in the middle a linear band of short, punctate striæ. Marginal striæ 17 to 18, puncta about 22 in 0,01 mm. Axial striæ of 5 to 6 puncta. — Diatomiste I p. 76 Pl. XII f. 7. A. S. Atl. CLXXIV f. 26.

Marine: Oamaru, New Zealand, fossil!

This species, resembling *N. rimosa* and *N. Oamaruensis*, is well distinguished by its terminal fissures.

17. **N. oamaruensis** GRUN. (1888). — V. nearly orbicular. L. 0,06 to 0,11; B. 0,053 to 0,10 mm. Lateral areas semicircular, large with scattered large puncta and dots. Median line with bayonet-shaped terminal fissures. Marginal striæ 10 to 11, puncta 14 in 0,01 mm. Axial striæ of one or two puncta. — A. S. Atl. CXXIX f. 9.

Marine: Oamaru, fossil!

18. **N. Hennedyi** W. SM. (1856). — V. elliptical. L. 0,045 to 0,12; B. 0,03 to 0,053 mm. Lateral areas broad, semilanceolate, with parallel interior margins, smooth. Marginal striæ 9 to 11, puncta 14 to 20 in 0,01 mm. — B. D. II p. 93. GREG. T. M. S. IV Pl. V f. 3 (1856). GRUN. Verh. 1860 III f. 21. DONK. B. D. II f. 3. A. S. N. S. D. I f. 41. Atl. III f. 18. V. H. Syn. p. 93 Pl. IX f. 14.

Marine: Greenland! Finmark! Spitsbergen! Sea of Kara! North Sea! Mediterranean Sea! Red Sea! Madagascar! Cape of Good Hope! Ceylon! Philippines! China! Japan! California! Galapagos Islands! Cape Horn! West Indies! Fossil. Hungary!

Var. *maxima* Cl. — L. 0,21; B. 0,114 mm. Striæ and puncta 9 in 0,01 mm.

Marine: Sendaï, Japan, fossil (Brun Coll.)!

Var. *tenuistriata.* — L. 0,18; B. 0,09 mm. Striæ and puncta 16 in 0,01 mm.

Marine: Mexillones Guano (Deby Coll.)!

Var. *undulata* Cl. (1881). L. 0,07; B. 0,035 mm. Margins triundulate. Striæ 14, puncta 18 in 0,01 mm. N. R. D. p. 7 Pl. II f. 19.

Marine: Galapagos Island!

Var. *Centraster* Cl. — L. 0,125; B. 0,007 mm. Areas broad with a group of 5 to 9 large granules on both sides of the central nodule. Striæ 13, puncta 20 in 0,01 mm. — Part. I Pl. IV f. 14.

Marine: Mexillones Guano (Deby Coll.)!

Var. *Schleinitzii* Jan. (1881). — V. elliptic-lanceolate. L. 0,12; B. 0,075 mm. Lateral areas broad in the middle, narrower towards the ends. Striæ 8 to 9 in 0,01 mm. — *N. Schlein.* A. S. Atl. LXX f. 43. Jan. Gaz. XV f. 1.

Marine: Leton Bank (Atl.), Cape Horn (Petit).

Var. *finitima* Jan. — V. lanceolate, often with slightly triundulate margins. L. 0,11 to 0,14; B. 0,06 mm. Areas broad in the middle, suddenly narrowed towards the ends. Interior margins of the areas convergent. Striæ 9 to 13, puncta 14 to 17 in 0,01 mm. - Gazelle Exp. XV f. 2 to 4, 18.

Marine: Falkland Islands (Deby Coll.)! Morocco! Madagascar! Columbo, Ceylon (Letourneur Coll.)!

Var. *manca* A. S. (1874). — V. elliptical. L. 0,15; B. 0,069 mm. Areas broad with convergent interior margins. Striæ 9, puncta about 12 in 0,01 mm. — Atl. III f. 17.

Marine: Campeachy Bay (Atl.).

Var. *californica* Grev. (1859). — V. elliptical. L. 0,07 to 0,11; B. 0,04 to 0,053 mm. Lateral areas very large, semielliptical, smooth. Striæ 10, puncta 13 in 0,01 mm. — *N. californica* Grev. Edinb. N. Ph. J. X p. 29 Pl. IV f. 5. *N. calif. var. campechiana* Grun. in A. S. Atl. III f. 19.

Marine: California (Grev.), West Indies! Colon (Deby Coll.)! Campeachy Bay!

Var. *circumsecta* Grun. (1874). — V. elliptical. L. 0,06 to 0,19; B. 0,03 to 0,08 mm. Areas large, semilanceolate, with numerous dots and sometimes, large puncta. Striæ 9 to 15; puncta 10 to 18 in 0,01 mm. — *N. polysticta var. circumsecta* Grun. in A. S. N. D. p. 89 Pl. I f. 36, 42. Atl. III f. 27, 28. *N. polysticta* A. S. Atl. III f. 26. *N. californica* A. S. Atl. III f. 6. *N. Henned. var. granulata* Grun. in A. S. Atl. III f. 3. Jan. Gazelle Exp. XV f. 14.

Marine: Finmark! North Sea! Mediterranean Sea! Red Sea! Ceylon! Madagascar! Maryland (Deby Coll.)! Florida! Cape Horn! Galapagos Islands! Mexillones Guano (Deby Coll.)! Hungary, fossil (Deby Coll.)!

Var. *neapolitana* Cl. — V. elliptical with subcuneate ends. L. 0,15; B. 0,078 mm. Areas narrow, about 1/8 of the breadth of the valve, with large, scattered dots. Striæ 7,5, puncta 10 in 0,01 mm.

Marine: Gulf of Naples!

Var. *nebulosa* Greg. (1857). V. elliptical. L. 0,055 to 0,085; B. 0,025 to 0,042 mm. Areas very large, suddenly narrowed at the ends, smooth. Striæ 14 to 16, puncta 16 to 20 in 0,01 mm. — *N. nebulosa* Greg. D. of Clyde p. 480 Pl. IX f. 8. Donk. B. D. p. 11 Pl. II f. 2. A. S. Atl. III f. 14; LXX f. 44. *Nav. Hennedyi* Witt Archangelsk D. IX f. 5.

Marine: North Sea! Morocco! Mediterranean Sea! Madagascar! Ceylon! Galapagos Islands! Florida! Fossil: Archangelsk (Witt).

The *N. Hennedyi var. fossilis* Pant. (II p. 47 Pl. XII f. 207) has a narrower area, and belongs probably to the var. nebulosa, to judge from the fine striation.

Forma bacillifera Pant. (1889). — L. 0,112 to 0,125; B. 0,048 to 0,062 mm. Striæ 16 to 18 in 0,01 mm. Areas with irregular linear markings. — *N. bacillifera* Pant. II p 42 Pl. V f. 80. *N. Hennedyi var. abnorm.* A. S. Atl. CXXIX f. 14.

Marine: Galapagos Islands! Hungary, fossil (Pant.).

The linear markings on the area are of no specific value, as they occur also in other varieties of *N. Hennedyi*. Such a form with 11 striæ and puncta in 0,01 mm. I have found in the Bory deposit (Hungary), this and another form with 12 striæ and 14 puncta in 0,01 mm. from Nossi Bé (Brun Coll.) may be associeted with *N. rugosa* JAN. Gaz. Exp. Pl. XV f. 11 and belong to the *Nar. Hennedyi*-type.

Var.? *difficilis* PANT. (1893). — L. 0,0467; B. 0,03 mm. Striæ 16 in 0,01 mm. (punctation not figured). — *N. difficilis* PANT. III Pl. XLI f. 560.

Marine: fossil Nyermegy (Pant.).

Var. *caliginosa* CL. a. GROVE (1891). — L. 0,08; B. 0,05 mm. Marginal striæ and their puncta 18 in 0,01 mm. Axial striæ 21 in 0,01 mm. Areas large, covered with irregularly scattered dots and with a large punctum on one side of the central nodule. — Diatomiste I p. 67 Pl. X f. 9.

Marine: Macassar Straits (Grove Coll.)!

Var. *constricta* PETIT (1877). — V. slightly constricted in the middle. PETIT Campbell I. D. p. 24 Pl. IV f. 13.

Marine: Campbells Island.

Var. *cuneata* GRUN. (1874). V. with cuneate ends. L. 0,083; B. 0,045 mm. Striæ 9 in 0,01 mm. — A. S. Atl. III f. 4.

Marine: Campeachy Bay (Atl.).

Var. *minuta* CL. (1881). L. 0,027 to 0,05; B. 0,016 to 0,027 mm. Striæ 8 or 10 (marginal) to 9 or 14 (axial) in 0,01 mm. Puncta 13 to 17 in 0,01 mm. Areas narrow. — N. R. D. p. 7 Pl. I f. 15.

Marine: Galapagos Islands! Tahiti!

Var. *tahitensis* CL. (1881). — L. 0,04 to 0,045; B. 0,017 to 0,023 mm. Striæ 13 or 14 (marginal) to 15 or 17 (axial) in 0,01 mm. not distinctly punctate. Areas narrow. — N. R. D. p. 8 Pl. I f. 14.

Marine: Adriatic! Tahiti! Sandwich Islands!

19. **N. coplosa** A. S. (1888). — V. elliptical. L. 0,1 to 0,17; B. 0,048 to 0,09 mm. Lateral areas lunate, with convergent interior margins and with an elongated spot of short striæ in the middle. Marginal striæ and their puncta 7 to 10 in 0,01 mm. Axial striæ of 6 to 7 puncta. — Atl. CXXIX f. 6.

Marine: Mexillones Guano!

This form might be regarded as a variety of *N. Hennedyi* (nearest to the *var. manca*).

20. **N. illustra** PANT. (1892). — V. elliptical. L. 0,13; B. 0,055 mm. Lateral areas broad, lunate, smooth, but with a longitudinal band of coarsely punctate striæ in the middle. Marginal striæ 14, their puncta 27 to 28 in 0,01 mm. Axial band of striæ moderately broad. — PANT. III Pl. II f. 17. *N. Ypsilon* CL. Part I Pl. IV f. 10.

Marine: Bory, Hungary!

This is a very distinct form, remarkable not only for the band of striæ in the middle of the area, but by its extremely finely punctate striæ.

21. **N. Sandriana** GRUN. (1863). — V. elliptical. L. 0,1 to 0,12; B. 0,06 to 0,07 mm. Areas large, semielliptical, with dots, disposed in irregularly curved rows, and in the middle a longitudinal band of punctate striæ. Marginal striæ 14 to 16 and their puncta 15 to 17 in 0,01 mm. Axial striæ of 3 to 8 puncta. — Verh. 1863 p. 153 Pl. IV f. 5. *N. rimosa* GREV. T. M. S. XIV p. 129 Pl. XII f. 25 (1866).

Marine: Adriatic (Grun.). Red Sea (Deby Coll.)!

Var. *lævis* Cl. L. 0,07 to 0,11; B. 0,05 to 0,06 mm. Areas smooth. Marginal striæ 10 to 13 and their puncta 11 to 16 in 0,01 mm. Axial striæ of 3 to 5 puncta. — *N. Sandriana* A. S. Atl. III f. 10; LXX f. 45. Pant. I p. 28 Pl. IX f. 82.

Marine: North Sea (Bohuslän! Sölswig. Atl.). S:t Brieuc (Atl.). Morocco! Balearic Islands! Cannes! Red Sea (Deby Coll.)! Madagascar (Kinker Coll.)! Fossil, Hungary!

22. N. spectabilis Greg. (1857) V. elliptical. L. 0,07 to 0,12; B. 0,03 to 0,06 mm. Lateral areas broad, convergent, narrowed in the middle. Striæ 6 to 14, puncta 10 to 23 in 0,01 mm. D. of Clyde p. 481 Pl. IX f. 10. A. S. Atl. III f. 20-21. Donk. B. D. p. 12 Pl. II f. 5. *N. Hennedii* Janisch Guano p. 28 Pl. II f. 13. *N. mikado* Pant. III Pl. XXIII f. 334 (1893)?

Marine: Greenland! North Sea! Morocco! Mediterranean Sea! Adriatic! Red Sea! Bab el Mandeb! Ceylon! Java! Philippines! Japan! Cape Horn (Petit). Colon (Deby Coll.)! Fossil: Augamos Guano (Jan.), Hungary (Pant.). S:ta Monica. Calif.!

N. spectabilis is extremely variable and comprises forms connecting *N. Hennedyi* and *N. Lyra*, no absolute limit existing between these three species.

Var. *maxima* Cl. V. elliptical. L. 0,18; B. 0,08 mm. Areas linear. Striæ 5 in 0,01 mm. Puncta 7 in 0,01 mm. disposed in longitudinal rows.

Marine: Macassar Straits (Grove Coll.)!

Var. *bullata* Cl. — L. 0,11; B. 0,05 mm. Lateral areas with a row of large puncta. Striæ 10, puncta 17 in 0,01 mm. — *N. bullata var. obtusa* Castr. Voy. Challenger p. 29 Pl. XXVIII f. 10.

Marine: Singapore!

Forma *Mölleriana* Jan. (1881). V. subhexagonal to elliptic-lanceolate. Lateral areas narrow, scarcely narrowed in the middle. L. 0,1 to 0,13; B. 0,05 to 0,053 mm. Striæ 7, puncta 10 in 0,01 mm. — *N. bullata var. Mölleriana* A. S. Atl. LXX f. 51, 52.

Marine: Australia (Atl.).

Var. *madagascarensis* Cl. V. with subcuneate ends. L. 0,125 to 0,155; B. 0,062 to 0,068 mm. Striæ and puncta 13 in 0,01 mm.; the latter forming almost straight longitudinal rows.

Marine: Madagascar (Van Heurck Coll.)! Nossi-Bé (Tempère)!

Var. *controversa* A. S. (1874). L. 0,09; B. 0,035 mm. Lateral areas in the middle linear, dilated and then narrowed towards the margins. Striæ 10, puncta 13 in 0,01 mm. - *N. Hennedyi var. controversa* A. S. Atl. III f. 5.

Marine: Campeachy Bay (Atl.).

Var. *abbreviata* Cl. — V. with slightly constricted middle and broad, cuneate ends. L. 0,083; B. 0,03 mm. Areas short not reaching to the ends of the valve. Striæ 12 (axial and terminal 15), puncta 15 in 0,01 mm.

Marine: Madagascar!

Var. *Rattrayi* Pant. (1889). V. elliptic-lanceolate. L. 0,0775; B. 0,032 mm. Areas as in var. abbreviata. Marginal striæ 10, terminal 15 in 0,01 mm. finely punctate. *N. Rattrayi* Pant. II p. 52 Pl. XXX f. 427.

Marine: Hungary, fossil (Pant.).

Var. *emarginata* Cl. — V. elliptical. L. 0,07 to 0,11; B. 0,03 to 0,042 mm. Areas broad, notched in the middle. Striæ 12, puncta 18 in 0,01 mm. Central nodule sometimes transversely dilated. — *N. excavata* A. S. Atl. III f. 22-25. Janisch Gazelle Exp. XV f. 22.

Marine: Sierra Leone (Deby Coll.)! Japan (Atl.). Campeachy Bay (Atl.). Nottingham. Maryl. fossil (Rae Coll.)!

Var. *Anglorum* Cl. (1881). — V. elliptical. L. 0,085 to 0,2; B. 0,047 to 0,09 mm. Areas broad sinuate in the middle, attenuate towards the ends, smooth. Striæ 7 to 15, puncta 14 to 16 in 0,01 mm. Central nodule sometimes transversely dilated. *N. excavata var. Anglorum* Cl. N. R. D. p. 8 Pl. II f. 20. *N. Oswaldi* Janisch, *N. excavata var. mesoleia* Grun. in A. S. Atl. LXX f. 46 (1881).

Marine: California, fossil (Monterey, S:ta Monica, S:ta Maria, S:n Redondo)! Bolivia Guano! Intermediate forms to typical *Var. excavata* occur in the California earth.

Var. *hungarica* PANT. (1889). — L. 0,114; B. 0,06 mm. Striæ 22, puncta 20 in 0,01 mm. Area with a few scattered dots. *N. Oswaldi* PANT. II p. 52 Pl. XXV f. 370.

Marine: Hungary, fossil (Pant.).

Var. *excavata* GREV. (1866). — L. 0,076 to 0,14; B. 0,065 to 0,07 mm. Areas as in var. *Angelorum*, but with numerous, scattered dots. Striæ 14 to 16; puncta 12 to 14 in 0,01 mm. — *N. excavata* GREV. T. M. S. XIV p. 130 Pl. XII f. 15. *Nav. Oswaldi* JANISCH Gaz. Exp. XV f. 12.

Marine: Red Sea (Grev.), Madagascar! S:ta Monica, Calif., fossil! Hungary, fossil!

23. **N. australica** A. S. (1874). — V. elliptical. L. 0,015; B. 0,022 mm. Lateral areas linear, with slightly concave exterior margins, tapering towards the ends, abbreviate. Striæ 11 in 0,01 mm. Puncta? — Atl. II f. 37. f. 12?

Marine: S:t Vincent (Austr.).

This species, unknown to the author, appears to be a small variety of *N. spectabilis* or a form of *N. Lyra var. atlantica*.

24. **N. genifera** A. S. (1874). — V. lanceolate. L. 0,13 to 0,16; B. 0,05 to 0,06 mm. Lateral areas narrow, constricted in the middle, slightly convergent. Marginal striæ 9 and their puncta 9 in 0,01 mm., the latter forming longitudinal rows. Axial striæ 9 in 0,01 mm. composed of about 3 puncta. Puncta of the striæ are confluent close to the sinuses of the areas. Atl. II f. 6.

Marine: Colon (Deby Coll.)! Puerto Caballo (Atl.).

25. **N. abrupta** GREG. (1857). — V. elliptical. L. 0,055 to 0,085; B. 0,022 to 0,034 mm. Axial areas distinct, narrowed towards the central nodule and the ends. Lateral areas narrow, short, constricted in the middle and with convergent interior margins. Striæ 10 in 0,01 mm., finely punctate; puncta about 23 in 0,01 mm. or indistinct. — *N. Lyra var. abrupta* GREG. D. of Clyde p. 486 Pl. IX f. 14, 14 *b*. *N. abrupta* DONK. B. D. p. 13 Pl. II f. 6. A. S. N. S. D. I f. 37. Atl. III f. 1. 2. V. H. Syn. p. 94 Pl. X f. 4.

Marine: Spitsbergen! Finmark! North Sea! Mediterranean Sea! Adriatic! Black Sea! Red Sea! Labuan! China! Fossil: Hungary (Pant.).

N. abrupta seems to be a distinct species, not closely connected with the others, distinguished by its axial area and the fine punctation of the striæ.

26. **N. clavata** GREG. (1858). — V. elliptical, with rostrate ends. L. 0,04 to 0,09; B. 0,022 to 0,055 mm. Lateral areas usually broad and semilanceolate with divergent ends. Marginal striæ 10 to 14, axial striæ 14 to 16, puncta 16 to 20 in 0,01 mm. — T. M. S. IV p. 46 Pl. V f. 17. DONK. B. D. p. 15 Pl. II f. 8. A. S. N. S. D. I f. 33. Atl. LXX f. 50. *N. Wrighti* O'MEARA M. J. VII p. 116 Pl. V f. 1 (1867). *N. Hennedyi var. clavata* V. H. Syn. p. 93. *N. Lyra var.* A. S. Atl. LXX f. 47.

Marine: North Sea! Mediterranean Sea! Red Sea! Seychelles! Madagascar! Ceylon! Sumatra! Singapore! China! Japan! Samoa! Galapagos Islands! West Indies! Florida! Delaware! Connecticut!

Var. *caribæa* A. S. (1874). — Lateral areas contracted in the middle. L. 0,11; B. 0,044 mm. Striæ 11, puncta 13 in 0,01 mm. — *N. caribæa* A. S. N. S. D. I f. 40. Atl. II f. 17; LXX f. 48.

Marine: North Sea (A. S.), Jamaica (Atl.). Mediterranean Sea (Peragallo).

Forma minor CL. L. 0,065; B. 0,028 mm. Striæ 13 in 0,01 mm. Puncta indistinct.

Marine: Colon (Deby Coll.).

These varieties connect *N. clavata* with *N. spectabilis*.

Var. *excsul* A. S. (1874). — V. constricted in the middle. L. 0,044 to 0,068; B. 0,021 to 0,038 mm. Lateral areas broad, sometimes dotted. Marginal striæ 11 to 14, puncta 17 to 20 in 0,01 mm. Axial striæ 12 to 18 in 0,01 mm. — *N. excsul* A. S. Atl. II f. 13.

Marine: Balearic Islands! Seychelles (Van Heurck Coll.)! Labuan! Galapagos Islands! Florida! Campeachy Bank (Atl.).

Var. *rhombica* Cl. — V. rhomboid or broadly lanceolate. L. 0,105 to 0,125; B. 0,056 to 0,075 mm. Lateral areas broad, tapering from the middle to the ends, where they reach the margin. Striæ 12 to 13, puncta 15 in 0,01 mm. — Part I Pl. IV f. 11.

Marine: Morocco! Galapagos Islands.

Forma minuta. — L. 0,055; B. 0,035 mm. Striæ 19, puncta 22 in 0,01 mm., the latter disposed in longitudinal rows.

Marine: Sumbava (Kinker Coll.)! Seychelles (Van Heurck Coll.)!

Var. *proxima* Jan. — V. broadly lanceolate. L. 0,105 to 0,15; B. 0,056 to 0,07 mm. Lateral areas narrow, subparallel, gradually tapering towards the ends, where they reach the margin. Striæ 9 to 10 in 0,01 mm. — *N. proxima* A. S. Atl. LXX f. 49. Jan. Gazelle Exp. XV f. 5 to 7.

Marine.

This variety is nearly akin to var. *rhombica*, but has narrow lateral areas and connects *N. clavata* with certain forms of *N. Lyra*.

Var. *elongata* Perag. (1888). — V. with rounded not rostrate ends. L. 0,11; B. 0,043 mm. Striæ 14 in 0,01 mm. - Villefr. D. p. 48 Pl. V f. 37.

Marine: Mediterranean Sea (Perag.).

This variety connects *N. clavata* with *N. Hennedyi*.

Var. *indica* Grev. (1862). — V. elliptical, rostrate. L. 0,1 to 0,16; B. 0,056 to 0,068 mm. Lateral areas broad, semilanceolate, with scattered dots. Striæ 12, puncta 16 to 17 in 0,01 mm. *N. indica* Grev. T. M. S. 1862 p. 95 Pl. IX f. 13. Janisch Gazelle Exp. XV f. 15, 19, 20. *N. hibernica* O'Meara M. J. VII p. 115 Pl. V f. 1 (1867). *N. Hennedyi var. granulata* Leud. Fortm. D. de Ceylon IX f. 88.

Marine: Honduras (Grun.). Ceylon! Sumbava (Kinker Coll.)! Macassar Straits! Manilla! Cebu (Rae Coll.)!

27. **N. diffluens** A. S. (1874). — V. elliptical with broad rostrate and truncate ends. L. 0,045; B. 0,023 mm. Lateral areas linear, slightly convergent. Striæ 10 in 0,01 mm., distinctly punctate. The axial striæ form a band, broader than that of the marginal striæ. Central area dilated towards the lateral areas. — Atl. II f. 15.

Marine: Campeachy Bank (Atl.).

28. **N. samoensis** Grun. (1881). — V. linear with rounded ends. L. 0,068; B. 0,012 mm. Lateral areas narrow, more approximate to the margin than to the median line, convergent at the ends. Striæ 10 in 0,01 mm. — A. S. Atl. LXX f. 41.

Marine: Samoa (Atl.).

29. **N. distenta** A. S. (1874). - V. elliptical, rostrate, with slightly convex margins, constricted in the middle. L. 0,06; B. 0,027 mm. Lateral areas narrow, constricted in the middle. Striæ 10 in 0,01 mm. not distinctly punctate. — Atl. II f. 14.

Marine: Campeachy Bank (Atl.).

Seems to be a variety of some of the forms intermediate between *N. clavata* and *N. Lyra.*

30. **N. approximata** Grev. (1859). — V. lanceolate, frequently with cuneate or subrostrate ends, and with parallel margins. L. 0,075 to 0,15; B. 0,04 to 0,08 mm. Lateral areas narrow, convergent at the ends. Striæ 7,5 to 10; puncta 10 to 15 in 0,01 mm.

Forma typica. Broadly linear with cuneate ends. L. 0,11; B. 0,046 mm. Striæ 8, puncta 11 in 0,01 mm. — *N. approximata* Grev. Edinb. N. Ph. J. X p. 28 Pl. IV f. 4. Cl. West. Ind. D. p. 4 Pl. I f. 1. *N. Hennedyi var. nicæensis* Perag. Villefr. D. p. 47 Pl. V f. 39 (1888).

Marine: California guano (Grev.), Florida! West Indies! Connecticut! Ceylon! Madagascar! Tahiti!

Var. *Couperi* Bail. (1850). — V. slightly constricted in the middle. — *Pinnul. Couperi* Bail. Smiths Contr. II p. 39 Pl. II f. 33.

Marine: Florida (Bail.).

Var. *Kittoniana* A. S. (1874). — V. broadly lanceolate. L. 0,075 to 0,15; B. 0,04 to 0,08 mm. Striæ 7,5 to 10, puncta 10 to 15 in 0,01 mm. — *N. Kittoniana* A. S. Atl. II f. 10.

Marine: Brazil (Deby Coll.)! Porto Seguro (Deby Coll.)! Colon (Deby Coll.)! Pensacola! Campeachy Bay! Sierra Leone (Deby Coll.)! Red Sea! Ceylon (Lend. Fortm.). Seychelles (Van Heurck Coll.)! Mauritius (Deby Coll.)!

31. **N. turgidula** Pant. (1893). — V. broadly elliptical with rounded ends. L. 0,047; B. 0,033 mm. Lateral areas narrow, broader in the middle and convergent at the ends. Striæ 13 in 0,01 mm. coarsely punctate. — Pant. III Pl. XXXII f. 462.

Marine: Hungary, fossil (Pant.).

32. **N. Lyra** Ehb. (1843). — V. elliptical with rounded or rostrate ends. L. 0,05 to 0,18; B. 0,026 to 0,06 mm. Lateral areas narrow, linear, constricted in the middle, or not, divergent at the ends or not. Striæ 6 to 14; puncta 7 to 18 in 0,01 mm.

Var. *elliptica* A. S. (1874). — V. elliptical, with rounded to subrostrate ends, or subhexagonal. L. 0,12 to 0,18; B. 0,04 to 0,06 mm. Lateral areas linear, convergent towards the ends. Striæ 6 to 7, puncta 7 to 11 in 0,01 mm. — N. S. D. Pl. I f. 39. Atl. II f. 29. V. H. Syn. X f. 2. Janisch Gazelle Exp. XV f. 23.

Marine: North Sea! Mediterranean Sea! Red Sea! Ceylon! Madagascar! Seychelles (Van Heurck Coll.)! Sumatra (Deby Coll.)! Philippines! Singapore! Fossil: Moravian Tegel!

Forma bullata Norm. (1861). — L. 0,13 to 0,16; B. 0,06 to 0,07 mm. Areas with a row of large puncta. Striæ 6, puncta 11 in 0,01 mm. — *N. bullata* Norm. T. M. S. 1861 p. 8 Pl. II f. 7. A. S. Atl. III f. 8—9.

Marine: Ceylon (Letourneur Coll.)! Macassar Straits (Grove Coll.)! Japan (Atl.), Australia (Norm.). Samoa (Atl.).

Var. *Ehrenbergii* Cl. — V. elliptical, with rostrate ends. L. 0,05 to 0,165; B. 0,026 to 0,054 mm. Lateral areas constricted in the middle, with divergent ends. Striæ 9 to 12, puncta 16 to 21 in 0,01 mm. — *N. Lyra* Ehb. Am. I: I f. 9 *a*. Greg. D. of Clyde Pl. IX f. 13 *b*. Jan. Rabh. Honduras D. III f. 7. Janisch Guano Pl. I A f. 26. Donk. B. D. p. 14 Pl. II f. 7. A. S. Atl. II f. 11, 16, 25. V. H. Syn. p. 93 Pl. X f. 1. Janisch Gazelle Exp. XV f. 13. *N. Gregoryana* Grev. M. J. V. p. 10 Pl. III f. 7 (1857).

Marine: North Sea! Mediterranean Sea! Red Sea! Madagascar! China! Japan! Sumatra! Australia! Samoa! Galapagos Islands! Honduras (Jan. Rabh.). Brazil! Florida! New York! Fossil: Baltchik!

Var. *dilatata* A. S. (1874). — V. elliptical, rostrate. L. 0,08; B. 0,044. Lateral areas slightly convergent. Striæ 11, puncta about 14 in 0,01 mm. — Atl. II f. 26.

Marine: Gulf of Mexico (Atl.).

Var. *denudata* Grun. Ms. — V. elliptic-lanceolate. L. 0,1; B. 0,045 to 0,05 mm. Lateral areas as in the var. *Ehrenbergii*, but dilated as they reach the margins of the valve. Striæ 10, puncta 17 in 0,01 mm.

Marine: S:ta Monica, Calif. fossil!

Var. *atlantica* A. S. (1874). — V. elliptical, with parallel margins and cuneate ends. L. 0,06 to 0,1; B. 0,026 to 0,032 mm. Lateral areas not reaching to the margins of the valve. Striæ 9 to 11 in 0,01 mm. Puncta very close. — N. S. D. I f. 34. Atl. II f. 33? *N. Couperi* Atl. II f. 12? *N. Lyra dilatata perpusilla* Pant. I p. 27 Pl. XVII f. 150. *N. Lyra var. elliptica* A. S. N. S. D. Pl. I f. 35, 38.

Marine: North Sea! Hungary, fossil (Pant.).

This var. graduates into *N. connectens* Grun.

Var. *subelliptica* Cl. — V. elongated, elliptical, non rostrate. L. 0,065 to 0,13; B. 0,035 to 0,048 mm. Lateral areas as in var. *Ehrenbergii*. Striæ 9 to 11, puncta 17 to 22 in 0,01 mm.

Marine: Spitsbergen! Finmark! North Sea! Japan! Philippines! Fossil at Bory Hungary! Monterey and S:ta Monica, Calif.! Mexillones guano (Deby Coll.)!

This variety is nothing but a non-rostrate form of the var. *Ehrenbergii* and graduates into *N. spectabilis*. Such transitional forms are the fig. 9 Pl. XV in Janisch Gazelle Exp. D. *N. Lyra var. producta* Pant. III Pl. XXXIII f. 466 and var. *acuta* f. 468, var. *hungarica* Pant. Pl. XXXIV f. 479. A specimen in Deby's Coll. from Bory in Hungary approaches very near to *N. Hennedyi var. fossilis* Pant. II Pl. XII f. 207.

Var. *insignis* A. S. (1874). — V. elliptical. L. 0,05 to 0,068; B. 0,027 to 0,032 mm. Lateral areas distant, abbreviate. Striæ strongly radiate, 10 (middle) to 13 (ends), puncta 18 in 0,01 mm. — Atl. II f. 27.

Marine: Japan (Atl.). Madagascar!

Var.? *seductilis* A. S. (1874). — V. elliptical with rounded ends. L. 0,05; B. 0,015 mm. Areas slightly convergent. Striæ 14 in 0,01 mm. — *N. sed.* A. S. Atl. II f. 35, f. 36?

Marine: Ceylon (Atl.).

Var. *acuta* Pant. (1889). — V. broadly elliptical, with acute ends. L. 0,09 to 0,040 mm. Striæ 12 in 0,01 mm. — Pant. II p. 50.

Marine: Hungary, fossil (Pant.).

Var. *producta* Pant. (1889). — V. elongate-elliptical. L. 0,145; B. 0,057 mm. Striæ 12 in 0,01 mm., slightly radiate. — Pant. II p. 50.

Marine: Hungary, fossil.

Var. *recta* Grev. (1859). — V. elongated, lanceolate, frequently with slightly rostrate ends. L. 0,135 to 0,21; B. 0,047 to 0,073 mm. Axial part not distinctly elevated towards the ends. Lateral areas linear, parallel, approximate to the median line. Striæ 7 to 12; puncta 10 to 12 in 0,01 mm., forming longitudinal, undulating rows. — Edinb. N. Ph. J. X p. 28 Pl. IV f. 3 (1859). A. S. Atl. II f. 18. Peragallo Villefr. D. p. 49 Pl. IV f. 36. Janisch Gaz. Exp. XV f. 8.

Marine: Mediterranean Sea (Perag.). S:t Peter Hungary, fossil! Rio Janeiro (Deby Coll.)! Gulf of Mexico (Atl.). California guano (Grev.). Seychelles and Samoa (Van Heurck Coll.)!

Forma fornicata A. S. (1874). — Lanceolate. L. 0,15; B. 0,057 mm. Striæ 8, puncta 9 in 0,01 mm., crossed by an arcuate, blank line. — Atl. II f. 9.

Marine.

Forma abnormis A. S. (1874). — Lanceolate. L. 0,165; B. 0,06 mm. Lateral areas moderately broad. Striæ 8, puncta about 10 in 0,01 mm. Median striæ much closer and more finely punctate. — Atl. II f. 8.

Marine: Zanzibar (Atl.).

Var. *subcarinata* Grun. (1874). — As var. *recta*, but with the axial part of the valve elevated. Striæ 11 to 16, puncta 12 to 14 in 0,01 mm. — A. S. Atl. II f. 5.

Marine: Ceylon! Seychelles! Java (Kinker Coll.)! Singapore! Philippines! Samoa! Tahiti!

Var. *signata* A. S. (1874). — As var. *recta*, but with an orbicular spot on both sides of the central nodule, crossed in the middle by a longitudinal, fissure-like marking. L. 0,09 to 0,16; B. 0,035 to 0,07 mm. Striæ and puncta 10 in 0,01 mm. — Atl. II f. 4. *N. Zanzibarica var.* A. S. Atl. CXXIX f. 4. *N. Zanzib. var. zebuana* Castr. Voy. Challenger p. 31 Pl. XXVIII f. 8.

Marine: Gulf of Mexico (Atl.). Elephanta Island (Atl.). Hongkong (Rae Coll.)! Cebu!

Var. *zanzibarica* Grev. (1866). — As. var. *recta*, but with an orbicular spot on both sides of the central nodule, inside which the puncta form a star of radiate lines. L. 0,2 to 0,24; B. 0,06 to 0,07 mm. Striæ and puncta 8 to 9 in 0,01 mm. — *N. zanz.* Grev. T. M. S. 1866 p. 129 Pl. XII f. 24. A. S. Atl. II f. 3.

Marine: Zanzibar! Seychelles! Madagascar! Sumatra!

Var. *Robertsoniana* GREV. (1863). — V. lanceolate. Margins usually with three to four slight undulations. L. 0,1 to 0,15; B. 0,058 to 0,065 mm. Lateral areas linear, parallel, approximate. Striæ 7 to 8, puncta 7 to 9 in 0,01 mm. *N. Rob.* GREV. T. Bot. Soc. Edinb. Vol. VIII p. 235 Pl. III f. 9. A. S. Atl. II f. 7.

Marine: Ceylon! Singapore! Manilla! New Caledonia! Samoa!

Forma bullata CL. — L. 0,165; B. 0,07 mm. Striæ 6, puncta 6 to 7 in 0,01 mm. Lateral areas with a row of large puncta.

Marine: Hongkong (Deby Coll.)!

33. **N. Durandii Kitton** (1888). — V. lanceolate with elevated axial part. L. 0,32; B. 0,1 mm. Lateral areas approximate, parallel, narrow. Striæ 10 in 0,01 mm., very slightly radiate, composed of elongated puncta, forming longitudinal straight rows, 4 in 0,01 mm. Axial striæ 10 in 0,01 mm., composed of 2 to 3 puncta. — A. S. Atl. CXXIX f. 1.

Marine: Singapore! Java (Deby Coll.)!

Var. *intermedia* A. S. (1888). — V. elliptical-lanceolate. L. 0,16; B. 0,063 mm. Lateral areas with a row of large puncta. — Atl. CXXIX f. 3.

Marine: Singapore.

Var. *rhomboides* CASTRAC. (1886). — V. with triundulate margins. L. 0,19 to 0,23; B. 0,06 to 0,076 mm. Lateral areas with a row of large puncta. Striæ 8 in 0,01 mm. — *N. bullata var. rhomb.* CASTRAC. Voyage Challenger p. 30 Pl. XXX f. 17. *N. Durandii var. rhomb.* A. S. Atl. CXXIX f. 2.

Marine: Hongkong! Cebu (Rae Coll.)! Singapore (Atl.).

34. **N. Reichardtii** GRUN. (1879). — V. elliptical. L. 0,022 to 0,029; B. 0,0115 to 0,02 mm. Lateral areas linear, convergent towards the ends, in the middle united by the stauroid transversely dilated central nodule. Striæ 13 to 17 in 0,01 mm., very finely or indistinctly punctate. On the part enclosed by the lateral areas are no, or indistinct, striæ. CL. M. D. 208 to 210. A. S. Atl. LXX f. 23 to 29. V. H. Syn. Pl. X f. 9.

Marine: Norway, Grip! Adriatic!

Var. *Tschutchschorum* CL. (1883). — L. 0,1; B. 0,0065 mm. Striæ 13 in 0,01 mm. — *N. Tsch.* Vega p. 472 Pl. XXXVII f. 18.

Marine: Cape Deschneff!

35. **N. pygmaea** KÜTZ. (1849). — V. hyaline elliptical. L. 0,028 to 0,045; B. 0,016 to 0,024 mm. Lateral areas convergent and constricted in the middle. Striæ fine, about 26 in 0,01 mm. — Sp. Alg. p. 77. W. SM. B. D. II p. 91. DONK. B. D. p. 10 Pl. I f. 10. A. S. N. S. D. I f. 43. Atl. LXX f. 7. V. H. Syn. p. 94 Pl. X f. 7. *N. minutula* W. SM. B. D. I p. 48 XXXI f. 274 (1853).

Brackish water: Spitsbergen! Finmark! Sea of Kara! North Siberian Sea! Baltic! North Sea! Magdeburg (Atl.). Argentina! Galapagos Islands!

36. **N. forcipata** GREV. (1859). — V. elliptical with rounded ends. L. 0,04 to 0,08; B. 0,02 to 0,026 mm. Median line with incrassate median pores. Lateral areas narrow, constricted in the middle, with convergent ends. Striæ 13 in 0,01 mm., finely punctate. — M. J. VII p. 83 Pl. VI f. 10, 11. DONK. B. D. p. 12. Pl. II f. 4. A. S. N. S. D. I f. 45, II f. 16, 18. Atl. LXX f. 17. V. H. Syn. p. 94 Pl. X f. 3.

Marine: Greenland! North Sea! Mediterranean Sea! Black Sea! Red Sea! Cape of Good Hope! Nicobar Islands! Philippines! California! Galapagos Islands! Florida! Fossil, Hungary (Pant.).

Var. *punctata* CL. — L. 0,06; B. 0,025 to 0,03 mm. Striæ 10 in 0,01 mm. punctate, puncta 10 to 16 in 0,01 mm.

Marine: Morocco! Seychelles (Van Heurck Coll.)! Manilla (Deby Coll.)!

Var. *versicolor* Grun. (1874). Lateral areas broader, not constricted in the middle. Striæ 10 in 0,01 mm. punctate, puncta 17 to 20 in 0,01 mm. — *N. versicolor* Grun. A. S. N. S. D. II f. 17. Atl. LXX f. 18 to 22. V. H. Syn. Pl. X f. 6. *N. variguensis* Grun. in Cl. M. D. N:o 209 (1879). *N. seductilis var.* Perag. Villefr. D. p. 49 Pl. II f. 20.

Marine: North Sea! Mediterranean Sea! Adriatic! Sumatra!

Var. *nummularia* Grev. (1859). V. nearly orbicular. L. 0,023 to 0,045; B. 0,017 to 0,038 mm. Striæ 10 in 0,01 mm. finely punctate, puncta about 18 in 0,01 mm. *N. numm.* Grev. Edinb. N. Ph. J. X p. 29 Pl. IV f. 6. *N. forcip. var. nummularoides* Grun. A. S. Atl. LXX f. 30, 31, 39, 40 (1881).

Marine: Adriatic (Atl.), Bab el Mandeb! Madagascar! Cape of Good Hope (Atl.), Java! California guano (Grev.), Florida!

Var. *suborbicularis* Grun. (1880). As var. nummularia, but with closer striæ, 13 to 14 in 0,01 mm. L. 0,018 to 0,036; B. 0,012 to 0,024 mm. V. H. Syn. Pl. X f. 5.

Marine: Spitsbergen! North Sea! Balearic Islands! Seychelles! Zulu Sea (Deby Coll.)! Galapagos Islands!

Var. *densestriata* A. S. (1881). — Eliptical. L. 0,03 to 0,06; B. 0,012 to 0,018 mm. Striæ 15 to 22 in 0,01 mm. – Atl. LXX f. 12 to 16. *N. forc. var. minor* A. S. Atl. LXX f. 32. A. S. N. S. D. I f. 44.

Marine: North Sea! Corsica! Cape of Good Hope! Java! Japan! Campeachy Bank (Atl.).

This variety connects *N. forcipata* and *N. pygmaea*, so that the latter might be regarded as a variety of *N. forcipata*.

Var. *balnearis* Grun. (1880). — V. linear-elliptical. L. 0,037; B. 0,01 mm. Lateral areas not constricted in the middle, and forming by their junction a broad stauros. Striæ 18 in 0,01 mm. *N. pygm. var. balnearis* Grun. in V. H. Syn. X f. 8.

Slightly brackish water: Sweden, Ronneby, fossil!

Additional.

N. seriosa Pant. (III Pl. XXXII f. 464). — Elliptical, rostrate-acuminate. L. 0,047; B. 0,033 mm. Lateral areas moderately broad, with scattered linear markings, very slightly constricted in the middle and convergent at the ends. Striæ 12 in 0,01 mm distinctly punctate.

Marine: Hungary, fossil (Pant.).

Naviculæ Lævistriatæ Cl.

Valve in outline more or less lanceolate. Axial area linear, abruptly dilated around the central nodule to an orbicular space, or transverse fascia, or uniting with the central area in a more or less broad, lanceolate space. Striæ usually coarse, radiate, not distinctly punctate or lineate, not crossed by longitudinal lines or furrows. Terminal fissures of the median line usually small and indistinct. Connecting zone not complex.

This section is remarkable for its apparently smooth striæ, and might on that account have been placed in the genus *Pinnularia*. But most of the species bear a closer relationship to the true Naviculæ than to the Pinnulariæ, and, besides, it is possible that the striæ may be only apparently smooth. *Nav. palpebralis*, which I place in the section, is usually described and figured as having distinctly punctate striæ, but I have never been able to detect any punctate character in its striæ. It does however contain several forms (as for instance *Nav. bituminosa*) which are closely related to species of Pinnularia, belonging to the section *divergentes* of that genus. On the other hand several species shew a close affinity to those of the section *Entoleiæ* of Navicula.

Thus, it appears that the forms of the lævistriatæ are intermediate between the Pinnulariæ and the true Naviculæ.

The species of this group are usually inhabitants of brackish water and æstuaries, but there are also purely marine forms among them.

Artificial key.

1.	Valve sigmoid	*N. Racana* Castr.
	— straight	2.
2.	Axial area abruptly dilated into an orbicular central area or transverse fascia	3.
	Axial and central area uniting into a lanceolate or linear space	7.
3.	Median striæ of equal length	4.
	— — alternately longer and shorter	*N. lauta* Grun.
4.	Central area orbicular	5.
	— — a transverse fascia	6.
5.	Valve acute or rostrate	*N. elegans* W. Sm.
	— obtuse	*N. Chyzeri* Pant., *N. discernenda* Pant., *N. grata* Pant.
6.	Valve large. L. about 0,06 mm	*N. bituminosa* Pant.
	— small. L. about 0,02 mm.	*N. megastauros* Cl.
7.	Valve triundulate	*N. Areschougiana* Grun. (*N. palpebralis v. Bolleriana* Grun.)
	— not —	8.
8.	Striæ radiate throughout	9.
	Terminal striæ convergent or parallel	12.
9.	Median striæ of equal length	10.
	— — alternately longer and shorter	11.
10.	Area very broad	*N. marginulata* Cl.
	— medium sized	*N. palpebralis* Bréb.
11.	Area narrow	*N. Vahliana* Grun.
	— rhombic-lanceolate	*N. solida* Cl.
12.	Valve elliptical	*N. Kochii* Pant.
	— lanceolate	13.
13.	Striæ coarse, distant, 7 to 8 in 0,01 mm.	*N. yarrensis* Grun.
	— closer, 8 to 9 in 0,01 mm.	*N. halionata* Pant.

1. **N. bituminosa** Pant. (1889). — V. linear-lanceolate, with subacuminate ends. L. 0,065; B. 0,0145 mm. Central pores of the median line somewhat approximate. Axial area narrow, linear. Central area a broad suborbicular fascia, almost reaching the margin. Striæ 10 in 0,01 mm., divergent in the middle, convergent at the ends. — Pant. II p. 42 Pl. VII f. 137.

Brackish water: Hungary fossil!

Var. *latecapitata* Pant. (1889). — V. linear, with broad, rostrate ends. L. 0,064; B. 0,0135 mm. Striæ 8,5 to 9 in 0,01 mm. — Pant. II l. c. f. 133.

Brackish water: Gyöngyös Pata. Hungary fossil (Pant.).

Var. *robusta* Pant. (1889). — V. with capitate-rostrate ends. L. 0,085; B. 0,018 mm. Central area lanceolate. Striæ 10 to 11 in 0,01 mm. — Pant. II Pl. XI f. 202.

Brackish water: Erdöbenye, Hungary, fossil (Pant.).

Var. *signata* Pant. (1889). — V. linear-lanceolate, with obtuse ends. L. 0,068; B. 0,018 mm. Central area a transverse fascia reaching nearly to the margin. Striæ 11 to 12,5 in 0,01 mm. Pant. II p. 43. *N. bit. v. valida* Pl. V f. 89.

Brackish water: Gyöngyös Pata, Hungary, fossil (Pant.).

Var. *staurophora* Pant. (1889) — V. lanceolate. L. 0,054 to 0,075; B. 0,013 to 0,015 mm. Central area a broad fascia, reaching to the margin. Striæ 10 to 11 in 0,01 mm. — Pant. II Pl. V f. 87, 88.

Brackish water: Hungary fossil (Pant.).

Var.? *cincta* Pant. (1889). — V. lanceolate, with obtuse ends. L. 0,075; B. 0,016 mm. Area lanceolate, very wide. Striæ 12,5 in 0,01 mm. — *Nav. cincta* Pant. II p. 44 Pl. XI f. 196.

Brackish water: Hungary, fossil (Pant.).

Nav. bituminosa is a variable species, which is closely akin to *Pinnularia*, section *divergentes*. On the other hand some of its varieties seem to be akin to varieties of *Nav. Yarrensis*. The areas are subject to great variation, and there are gradual passages from forms with a perfect transverse fascia, to forms with the central and axial areas uniting in a lanceolate space. As the most extreme form of this kind I regard *Nav. cincta* PANT., which I know only by the figure in PANTOCSEK's work. PANTOCSEK considers it as a distinct species, and if so another name is necessary, as the name *cincta* has been used for another, well known species.

2. **N. Chyzereii** PANT. (1889). — V. elliptic-lanceolate, with obtuse extremities. L. 0,066; B. 0,019 mm. Axial area distinct, linear, abruptly dilated to an orbicular central area. Striæ 8 to 10 in 0,01 mm. divergent in the middle, convergent at the ends. — PANT. II p. 43 Pl. V f. 96.
Brackish water: Hungary, fossil!

3. **N. discernenda** PANT. (1889). — V. linear-elliptical, with subcuneate ends. L. 0,037 to 0,05; B. 0,012 to 0,013 mm. Axial area very narrow; central area large, orbicular. Striæ 12 to 14 in 0,01 mm. divergent in the middle, convergent at the ends. — PANT. II p. 45 Pl. XXII f. 335.
Brackish water: Hungary, fossil!
N. discernenda is closely akin to *N. Chyzerii* and scarcely more than a small variety with somewhat closer striæ.

4. **N. grata** PANT. (1889). — V. narrow, elliptic-lanceolate. L. 0,084; B. 0,015 mm. Median pores distant. Axial area narrow linear, strongly dilated in the middle. Striæ 11 in 0,01 mm., divergent in the middle, convergent at the ends, their terminations angularly bent. — PANT. II p. 46 Pl. II f. 21
Brackish water: Hungary, fossil (Pant.).

5. **N. elegans** W. SM. (1853). — V. lanceolate, with acute ends. L. 0,1; B. 0,027 mm. Median line with distant central pores and semicircular terminal fissures. Axial area very narrow; central area large, orbicular. Striæ 9 in 0,01 mm., strongly divergent in the middle, convergent at the ends. — Br. D. I p. 49 Pl. XVI f. 137. DONK. Br. D. p. 23 Pl. IV f. 4.
Marine to brackish: England! Bohuslän!
Var. *cuspidata* CL. — V. rostrate. L. 0,08; B. 0,02 mm. Striæ closer, about 12 in 0,01 mm.
Brackish water: Atlantic coast of North America!

6. **N. lauta** GRUN. (1888). — V. linear-elliptical, with subcuneate ends. L. 0,095; B. 0,028 mm. Axial area lanceolate, dilated in the middle. Median line with the terminal fissures in contrary directions (Grun.). Striæ 13 (9 to 10 Grun.) in 0,01 mm. divergent in the middle, convergent at the ends, in the middle alternately longer and shorter. — V. H. Types 542 Bot. Centralbl. XXIII p. 324. Icon. n. Part. I Pl. I f. 30.
Brackish water: South Yarra, Australia!

7. **N. megastauros** CL. (1883). — V. elliptic-lanceolate, with subacute ends. L. 0,02; B. 0,008 mm. Axial area indistinct; central large, transverse, dilated to a stauros, reaching nearly to the margin. Striæ 16 in 0,01 mm., strongly divergent in the middle, transverse at the ends. — Vega p. 464 Pl. XXXV f. 19.
Marine: Cape Deschneff!
Stauroneis delicatula LEUD. FORTM. (Ceyl. p. 36 Pl. III f. 34, 1879) is twice as large as *N. megastauros* and seems to be akin to it. I have not seen this species.

8. **N. halionata** PANT. (1886). — V. lanceolate, gradually tapering from the middle to the obtuse ends. L. 0,12 to 0,22; B. 0,03 to 0,048 mm. Area broad, lanceolate. Striæ 8 to 9 in 0,01

mm. divergent in the middle, convergent at the ends; a few shorter striæ are occasionally intercalated among the median. — PANT. I p. 25 Pl. XI f. 94. II Pl. I f. 12.

Marine, brackish: Hungary fossil! Atlantic City, N. Jers. U. S. Amer. foss. (Deby Coll.)!

Var. *robusta* PANT. (1889). — L. 0,117; B. 0,036 mm. Striæ 10 to 12,5 in 0,01 mm. *Nav. robusta* PANT. II p. 53 Pl. IX f. 159.

Brackish water: Hungary, foss. (Pant.).

Var. *directa* PANT. (1889). — V. linear, with cuneate ends. L. 0,11; B. 0,024 mm. Striæ 10 in 0,01 mm. — PANT. II p. 46 Pl. XII f. 211.

Brackish water: Hungary, fossil (Pant.).

Var. *minor* PANT. (1889). — V. elliptic-lanceolate. L. 0,09; B. 0,025 mm. Striæ 10 in 0,01 mm. — PANT. II p. 46 Pl. XXVI f. 381.

Marine: Hungary, fossil (Pant.).

Nav. halionata is a beautiful species, akin to *N. Yarrensis* and *N. palpebralis*, but much larger. Between *N. halionata* and *N. robusta* I am unable to find any difference of importance.

9. **N. Racana** CASTR. (1886). V. lanceolate sigmoid, twisted. L. 0,09 to 0,15; B. 0,035 to 0,04 mm. Area narrow, somewhat dilated in the middle. Striæ smooth, 1,5 to 5 in 0,01 mm. *Pinn. Racana* CASTR. D. Challenger p. 25 Pl. XV f. 3. *Nav. contorta* KITTON Ms.

Brackish water: Ceylon! Singapore! Java! Sumatra! Labuan! Hongkong!

This remarkable form is nearly akin to *N. Yarrensis*, of which it is perhaps a contorted variety.

10. **N. Yarrensis** GRUN. (1876). V. lanceolate, to narrow elliptical, with obtuse ends. L. 0,06 to 0,20; B. 0,02 to 0,038 mm. Median line with small terminal fissures. Area linear to lanceolate, more or less broad. Striæ 4 to 1,5 in 0,01 mm., divergent in the middle slightly convergent towards the ends, where they are a little closer. — A. S. Atl. XLVI f. 1 to 6. PANT. I Pl. II f. 20; II Pl. X f. 178, XII f. 219, XVI f. 274.

Brackish water: Kiel (Atl.), Hungary, fossil! S. Africa! Madagascar! Singapore! Ceylon! Java! Japan! Australia! Florida! Atlantic City N. Jers. U. S. Amer. fossil (L. 0,16; B. 0,03. Striæ 6 in 0,01 mm.). Cameroon!

Var. *americana* CL. — L. 0,09; B. 0,018. Striæ 7 to 8 in 0,01 mm. Area narrow.

Brackish water: Atlantic coast of U. S. Quincy Mass.! Cape May! Connecticut!

Var. *bituminosa* PANT. (1889). — V. elliptic-lanceolate. L. 0,056 to 0,075; B. 0,016 to 0,0185 mm. Area lanceolate, wide. Striæ 5 to 8 in 0,01 mm. — PANT. II p. 55 Pl. IV f. 71.

Brackish water: Gyöngyös Pata etc., Hungary (Pant.).

Var. *gracilior* PANT. (1889). — V. lanceolate. L. 0,062; B. 0,016 mm. Area wide. Striæ 6 in 0,01 mm. — PANT. II p. 55 Pl. XXI f. 323.

Marine: Bory Dept. Hungary (Pant.).

Var. *valida* PANT. (1889). — V. broad, lanceolate. L. 0,057; B. 0,02 mm. Area wide, lanceolate. Striæ 7 to 8,5 in 0,01 mm. — PANT. II p. 55 Pl. XII f. 212.

Brackish water: Szurdok-Püspöki Dept. Hungary (Pant.).

Var. *De Wittiana* KAIN & SCHULTZ. — V. broadly linear with protracted ends. L. 0,11; B. 0,03 mm. Area narrow, lanceolate. Striæ 5 in 0,01 mm. *Nav. De Wittiana* KAIN & SCHULTZ Tor. Bot. Club Aug. 1889 Vol. XVI N:o 8 p. 209 Pl. XCIII f. 5.

Marine: Atlantic City, N. Jers. foss. (Deby Coll.)!

Var.? *aradina* PANT. (1893). — V. lanceolate. L. 0,06; B. 0,02 mm. Area broad, lanceolate. Striæ 5 to 6 in 0,01 mm. — *Nav. aradina* PANT. III Pl. XXX f. 434.

Marine?: Kavna-Bremia, Hungary, fossil (Pant.).

Var.? *Phalangium* PANT. (1893). Linear, with cuneate ends. L. 0,06; B. 0,017 mm. Area narrow-lanceolate. Striæ 6 in 0,01 mm. — *Nav. phalangium* PANT. III Pl. XXX f. 432.

Marine?: Kavna-Bremia, Hungary, fossil (Pant.).

Var. *Simbirskiana* PANT. (1889). V. lanceolate with protracted ends. L. 0,048; B. 0,015 mm. Area lanceolate. Striæ 8 in 0,01 mm. *Nav. Simbirskiana* PANT. II p. 53 Pl. XII f. 216.

Marine: Russia, Ananino, foss. (Pant.).

Var. *heresensis* PANT. (1889). — V. slightly constricted in the middle, with subcuneate ends. L. 0,072; B. 0,015 mm. Area wide, linear. Striæ 6,5 in 0,01 mm. — *Nav. heresensis* PANT. II p. 47 Pl. IV f. 67.

Brackish water: Hungary, foss. (Pant.).

11. **N. Kochii** PANT. (1889). — V. elliptical, with broad, rounded ends. L. 0,017 to 0,014 mm. Median line with approximate central pores, and small curved terminal fissures. Area narrow, linear-lanceolate, widened in the middle. Striæ slightly radiate in the middle, 8 (8 to 12 Pant.) in 0,01 mm., convergent at the ends. PANT. II p. 49 Pl. IV f. 72.

Brackish water: Hungary, foss. (Pant.).

12. **N. Areschougiana** GRUN. (1860). V. narrow, linear, triundulate, with subrostrate, obtuse ends. L. 0,1; B. 0,008 mm. Area linear. Striæ 10 in 0,01 mm. GRUN. Verh. 1860 p. 521 Pl. III f. 23.

Marine: Sweden, Bohuslän (Grun.).

This species is entirely unknown to me, having never seen in the numerous gatherings from west-coast of Sweden, which I have examined, anything similar to the fig. of GRUNOW. I have provisionally placed this form near to *Nav. palpebralis*, among the varieties of which is a triundulate form, viz. *var. Bottериana*.

13. **N. Vahliana** GRUN. (1874). — V. lanceolate, with subrostrate, obtuse ends. L. 0,04; B. 0,011 mm. Area narrow lanceolate. Striæ 13 in 0,01 mm., divergent and alternately longer and shorter in the middle, transverse at the ends. — A. S. N. S. D. Pl. II f. 21.

Marine: North Sea (A. S.).

This speciee is unknown to me, perhaps a variety of *N. palpebralis*.

14. **N. palpebralis** BRÉB. (1853). — V. elliptic-lanceolate, with acute ends. L. 0,038 to 0,08; B. 0,013 to 0,016 mm. Area broad, lanceolate. Striæ 10 in 0,01 mm., radiate throughout, not distinctly punctate. BRÉB. in W. SM. B. D. I p. 50 Pl. XXXI f. 273. GRUN. Verh. 1860 p. 536 Pl. III f. 27. DONK. B. D. p. 25 Pl. IV f. 3. V. H. Syn. p. 96 Pl. XI f. 9.

Marine, usually litoral: Davis Strait! North Sea (coast of England, Norway and Belgium)! Atlantic (Morocco)! Mediterranean (Balearic Islands! Adriatic Grun.), Galapagos Islands! Connecticut!

Var. *Barclayana* GREG. (1857). — V. broad, linear with acuminate-apiculate ends. L. 0,041 to 0,043 (0,1 to 0,11 according to Greg.); B. 0,02 (0,026 to 0,03 according to Greg.) mm. Striæ 11 to 12 in 0,01 mm. *Nav. Barcl.* GREG. D. of Cl. p. 480 Pl. IX f. 9. *Nav. palp. var. Barkl.* V. H. Syn. p. 97 Pl. XI f. 12.

Marine: North Sea (Scotland, Greg., Belgium, V. H.). Mediterr. (Balearic Islands, Adriatic)!

Var. *angulosa* GREG. (1856). V. as the type. L. 0,06 to 0,11; B. 0,014 to 0,021 mm. Area lanceolate, angular in the middle. — *Nav. angulosa* GREG. T. M. S. IV p. 42 Pl. V f. 8. DONK. B. D. p. 26 Pl. IV f. 4. A. S. N. S. D. II f. 19. *Nav. palp. var. angulosa* V. H. Syn. Pl. XI f. 10.

Marine: North Sea (Sweden! Belgium V. H.). Mediterranean (Naples)!

Var. *semiplena* GREG. (1859). — V. narrow, elliptic-lanceolate, with subacute ends. L. 0,06 to 0,075; B. 0,013 to 0,015 mm. Area narrow, lanceolate. — *Pinn. semipl.* GREG. M. J. VII p. 84 Pl. VI f. 12. *Nav. angulosa var. β* GREG. T. M. S. IV p. 42 Pl. V f. 8*. *Nav. semipl.* DONK. B. D. p. 26 Pl. IV f. 5. *Nav. præsecta* A. S. N. S. D. p. 90 Pl. II f. 20?

Marine: Spitsbergen! Finmark! Scotland (Grev.), Morocco! Fossil, Baldjik!

Var. *obtusa* V. H. (1885). — V. lanceolate, with subrostrate, obtuse ends. L. 0,05; B. 0,017 mm. Area lanceolate. — Syn. p. 97 Pl. XI f. 8.

Marine: Belgium (V. H.).

Var. *minor* Grun. (1880). — V. elliptic-lanceolate, with acute ends. L. 0,035 to 0,013; B. 0,011 to 0,012 mm. Area lanceolate. Striæ 10 to 11 in 0,01 mm. — A. D. p. 30 Pl. I f. 23. V. H. S. p. 97 Pl. XI f. 11. *Nav. minor* Greg. D. of Cl. p. 477 Pl. IX f. 1 (1857)?

Marine: Finmark! Belgium (V. H.).

Var. *Botteriana* Grun. (1860). — V. broad, lanceolate, with slightly triundulate margin. L. 0,07 to 0,08; B. 0,02 to 0,023 mm. Area large, lanceolate. Striæ 8 in 0,01 mm. (finely punctate, Grun.). — *Nav. Bott.* Grun. Verh. 1860 p. 535 Pl. III f. 20. *Nav. Esoculus* Schum. P. D. p. 189 Pl. IX f. 53?

Marine: Adriatic (Grun.).

Forma minor Grun. — V. with rostrate ends and triundulate margins. L. 0,04; B. 0,0136 mm. Striæ 12 in 0,01 mm. — l. c. f. 10.

Marine: Adriatic (Grun.).

15. **N. solida** Cl. (1880). — V. elliptic-lanceolate, with subacute ends. L. 0,058; B. 0,024 mm. Area rhombic-lanceolate. Striæ 10 in 0,01 mm., the median alternately longer and shorter. — A. D. p. 13 Pl. I f. 24.

Marine: Finmark!

16. **N. marginulata** Cl. (1881). — V. rhomboid. L. 0,042; B. 0,012 mm. Area very large. Striæ 17 in 0,01 mm. — N. R. D. p. 11 Pl. III f. 29.

Marine: Pensacola, Florida!

Pinnularia Ehb. (1843).

Valve more or less elongated, usually linear, with rounded, obtuse, sometimes capitate, ends. Median line straight or flexuose. Terminal fissures generally large and distinct. Structure: apparently more or less smooth, transverse striæ, usually radiate or divergent in the middle, convergent at the ends. Connecting zone not complex. — The chromatophores form two plates, closely following the interior surface of the connecting zone. At the division of the cell they migrate from the zone to the interior surface of the valves, and are then split up along the longitudinal axis of the valve by fissures, simultaneously in the middle and at the ends (Pfitzer, Bau und Entw. p. 51). — On conjugating, two parallel cells form two small egg-shaped auxospores, one above the other. The auxospores are later on developed into cylindrical transversely annulated bodies, bearing at their ends hemispherical caps (Pfitzer, Bau und Entw. p. 67).

The following description of the structure of the valve is principally an abridged account of the researches of Pfitzer (Bau und Entw. p. 30), Flögel (J. R. M. S. ser. 2 IV p. 505) and especially Otto Müller (Ber. d. D. Bot. Ges. VII p. 169, 1889).

The valve forms a more or less convex shell, and its median part a more or less narrow, structureless area (the *axial area*) usually dilated in the middle to an irregularly rounded space, or to a transverse fascia (the *central area*) and at the ends to a smaller space (the *terminal area* or *nodule*). The axial area is bordered by *striæ*, in most cases radiate in the middle and convergent at the ends. In the middle of the central area is the *central nodule*, and, connecting the central and terminal nodules, the *median line*.

The striæ are thinner parts of the valve and according to Pfitzer furrows on the outside, according to Flögel and Müller channels on the inside, of the valve, closed, except in the middle, where is a large foramen. The foramina form in the large species, a more or less distinct or broad *longitudinal band* across the striæ.

The central nodule consists of a conical silicious mass, projecting in the inside of the cell, usually excentric, so that one margin of its base (the *median margin*) coincides with the axis of the valve. Between the nodules of both valves, in the interior of the cell, is the *median plasma-mass*, containing in its middle the *nucleus*. According to OTTO MÜLLER the central nodule has, on the top of the cone or its median side, an open shallow furrow, in both ends of which is a pore, by which the plasma communicates with a system of closed channels in the central nodule and, by means of similar channels in the median line, with open fissures in the parts of the median line which are between the centre and the ends. From these pores pass vertically, through the solid mass of the nodule, two channels (the *channels of the central nodule*) which terminate on the exterior of the valve as two bulb-shaped pores (the *median pores*). The channels of the central nodule each give rise to two parallel, closed, channels, one above the other (the *exterior* and *interior channels*).

Two similar channels also open into the terminal nodules. The exterior of these channels is at its end bent towards that side of the valve, on which the central nodule is situated, and terminates in an oblique, sometimes spirally twisted, fissure (the *terminal fissure*), which bends round the terminal nodule. The terminal fissures are in most cases turned to the same side, but in some few cases in contrary directions. Their shape is somewhat different in different groups, sometimes curved and comma-like, sometimes straight, giving to the ends of the median line a bayonet-like shape.

On the lower side of the curved end, or opening of the exterior channel, opposite to the terminal fissure, is a triangular fissure (the *funnel*) which passes obliquely through the terminal nodule, and opens with its pore-like apex into the plasma-mass at the ends of the cell. The median part of the funnel communicates with the interior channel of the terminal nodule.

The exterior and interior channels from the central to the terminal nodules are connected by a fissure of more or less complicated structure. In many cases this fissure forms a *filiform* line and seems then to be simply a vertical fissure. In other cases it is broad, and lies in an oblique position. In some of the larger species the fissure is of a more *complex* nature, being formed by the junction of short knife-like laminæ projecting from both halves of the valve. From the half of the valve, on which the central nodule is situated project three, in some cases two, such laminæ, alternating with two (or one) laminæ from the other half of the valve. In some of the larger species the anterior laminæ on the half of the valve which contains the central nodule cover the laminæ on the other half of the valve on two portions of the median line, thus giving rise to a biundulated median line.

The genus Pinnularia comprises a great number of forms, both marine and fresh-water, the latter being very predominant, forming an important and very characteristic part of the fresh-water diatomaceous flora, both recent and fossil. The marine forms are not all closely connected. One group among them is characterized by the peculiar form of the large terminal fissures, projecting from the ends of the median line at an angle of about 90°. To this group belong *P. Trevelyana*, *P. rectangulata*, *P. groenlandica*, and in a less degree *P. cruciformis*. The latter seems to be connected with *P. quadratarea*, having indistinct terminal fissures. Smaller marine forms bear a great resemblance to the smallest fresh-water Pinnulariæ of the group *Parallelistriatæ*. Among the marine forms are a few more or less panduriform, which appear in several respects to be akin to panduriform species of the genus *Caloneis*.

The fresh-water forms pass into one another to a great extent, so that the definition of good or distinct species or groups is a matter of the greatest difficulty or almost impossible. Still, I think some groups of forms may be distinguished, although closely connected with each other. Such groups are the following:

I. *Parallelistriatæ*, which comprises forms generally small, often with capitate or rostrate ends, and with close, parallel or slightly radiate striæ. The axial area is indistinct or very narrow.

Several of these forms resemble small fresh-water species of Caloneis, and it may be in some cases questionable whether they should be classed with Pinnularia, or with the forms of the Caloneis Silicula-type. The only distinction is the absence of the longitudinal line which crosses the striæ of the Caloneis-forms, and which is indeed often seen in these only with great difficulty.

II. *Capitatæ*. Small forms, with capitate or rostrate ends, radiate striæ, and narrow or indistinct axial area.

III. *Divergentes*. Smaller or larger, linear, sublanceolate, or subelliptical forms, with rounded ends and strongly radiate striæ. The axial area, in some species narrow, is in others moderately broad. From the smallest species of this group, *P. Brébissonii*, to the large *P. episcopalis* is a continual series of forms, while on the other side *P. Brébissonii* is closely connected with *P. microstauron* of the Capitatæ. Small forms of *P. Brébissonii* seem also to graduate into the group of

IV. *Distantes*, comprising lanceolate to elliptical, or elliptic-linear forms, remarkable for their distant striæ.

V. *Tabellariceæ*, comprising forms generally linear, narrow, often gibbous in the middle and at the ends. The striæ are usually strongly radiate in the middle, and convergent at the ends. The terminal fissures are more or less bayonet-shaped. The area is distinct but moderately narrow. This group is closely connected with the divergentes, *P. Legumen* being an intermediate form. On the other hand it is also closely allied with the next.

VI. *Brevistriatæ*, comprising linear forms, with very broad axial area and parallel striæ. In *P. hemiptera* this group touches the following.

VII. *Majores*, usually large, linear, and slender forms with parallel or radiate striæ, narrow area, oblique median line and comma-like, terminal fissures.

VIII. *Complexæ*, linear, usually large forms, remarkable for their complex median line.

Several forms belonging to Pinnularia have some apparent resemblance to those belonging to Caloneis, but it is questionable whether they are really connected. The longitudinal structureless depression of *P. Trevelyana* and *P. groenlandica* seem to point to an affinity with some species of Caloneis, which also have smooth striæ, but the terminal fissures of the above named species of Pinnularia are too peculiar to allow of their union.

Among the Naviculæ are some forms, which, on account of their smooth striæ might be placed in Pinnularia, especially *Navicula Yarrensis*, typical specimens of which have some likeness to *P. alpina*; but there is, I believe, no true relation between these forms, the terminal fissures of P. alpina being spirally twisted and large, those of *Nav. Yarrensis* being indistinct.

Among the many fossil forms, recently discovered in Hungary and described by Dr. Pantocsek, are several closely connected with *N. Yarrensis* and with *N. elegans*. These forms are also allied to the group of *Nav. palpebralis*. All these seem to be related to the group of *Nav. lineolatæ*, for which reason I consider it more natural to class *Nav. Yarrensis* and its allied forms in Navicula than in Pinnularia. The small species *Nav. hungarica* and *Nav. costulata* with coarse, apparently smooth, striæ seem naturally to belong to the same group as *Nav. Yarrensis*, although it may not be denied that they are also akin to some forms of the *Lineolatæ*, for instance *Nav. cincta*.

I. Gracillimæ.

Artificial key.

1.	Ends rounded	2.
	— capitate or rostrate	4.
2.	Striæ not interrupted	*P. sublinearis* GRUN.
	— interrupted	3.
3.	Striæ almost parallel	*P. leptosoma* GRUN.[1]
	— in the middle slightly radiate	*P. molaris* GRUN.
4.	Ends capitate	*P. undulata* GREG.
	— rostrate	*P. gracillima* GREG.

1. **P. gracillima** GREG. (1856). — V. linear, triundulate, with rostrate to subcapitate ends. L. 0,026 to 0,03; B. 0,005 mm. Areas indistinct. Striæ, 18 to 22 in 0,01 mm. almost parallel. — M. J. IV Pl. I f. 31. *Nav. gr.* V. H. S. Pl. VI f. 24. *N. mesolyla* SCHUM. Tatra D. Pl. IV f. 51?

Fresh water: Scotland (Greg.), Greenland!

2. **P. undulata** GREG. (1854). — V. linear, with more or less distinctly triundulate margins and broad, capitate ends. L. 0,03 to 0,035; B. 0,006 mm. Axial area indistinct; central area orbicular or a transverse fascia. Striæ 22 in 0,01 mm., almost parallel, convergent at the ends. — M. J. II, Pl. IV f. 10. — CL. D. of Finland p. 30 Pl. II f. 8.

Fresh water: Sweden (Pauträsk in Stensele Lappmark)! Finland, Savitaipale Dept! Scotland (Greg.).

Var. *subundulata* GRUN. — V. with less distinctly undulated margins. Striæ 18 to 21 in 0,01 mm., not interrupted. — V. H. Types N:o 140.

Fresh water: Scotland (V. H. T.).

As far one may judge from the figures *Nav. mesolyla* SCHUM. and *P. gracillima* are the same species, and the only difference between them and *P. undulata* consists in the broad, capitate ends of the latter.

3. **P. sublinearis** GRUN. (1880). — V. narrow, linear, slightly gibbous in the middle, with rounded ends. L. 0,02 to 0,03; B. 0,004 mm. Areas indistinct. Striæ 21 to 24 in 0,01 mm. slightly radiate in the middle, convergent at the ends. — *Nav. subl.* GRUN. V. H. Syn. p. 76 Pl. VI f. 25, 26. *P. tenuis* GREG. M. J. 1854 p. 97 Pl. IV f. 9?

Fresh water: Greenland!

4. **P. leptosoma** GRUN. (1880). — V. narrow, linear, with rounded ends. L. 0,035 to 0,04; B. 0,005 mm. Median line with approximate central pores. Axial area very narrow; central area a broad, transverse fascia. Striæ 14 or 17 (middle) to 16 or 20 in 0,01 mm. (at the ends) almost parallel. *Nav. leptos.* GRUN. in V. H. Syn. XII f. 29.

Fresh water: Sweden (Rimforsa in Westergötland)! Finland!

5. **P. molaris** GRUN. (1863). — V. linear, slender, with rounded or subcuneate ends. L. 0,033 to 0,05; B. 0,005 to 0,008 mm. Axial areal narrow or indistinct; central area a broad, transverse fascia, reaching to the margin. Striæ 15 to 17 in 0,01 mm., slightly radiate in the middle, convergent at the ends. — *Nav. molaris* GRUN. Verh. 1863 p. 149 Pl. IV f. 26. V. H. Syn. Pl. VI f. 19. *Nav. macra* A. S. Atl. XLIV f. 54. *Nav. mesoleia* CL. N. R. D. p. 10 Pl. II f. 26.

Fresh water: Norway (Dovre)! Scotland! Sweden! Denmark (Ringköbing Atl.), Finland! Germany (Grun.), Brazil! Demerara River! Cape Horn! Bengal!

P. molaris is nearly akin to *P. leptosoma*, which differs by nothing except the less radiate median and the closer terminal striæ.

[1] Conf. *P. isostauron* GRUN.

II. Capitatæ.

Artificial key.

1.	Valve rostrate	*P. microstauron* Ehr.
	— capitate	2.
2.	Valve with undulated margins	*P. mesolepta* Ehr.
	— not undulated	3.
3.	Valve linear	*P. interrupta* W. Sm.
	— lanceolate	4.
4.	Capitate ends broad and large	*P. globiceps* Greg.
	— ends small	5.
5.	Valve lanceolate	*P. Braunii* Grun.
	— almost linear	6.
6.	Striæ 16 to 18 in 0,01 mm	*P. appendiculata* Ag.
	— 12 to 13 in 0,01 mm.	*P. subcapitata* Greg.

6. **P. appendiculata** Ag. (1828). — V. linear, gently tapering from the middle to the slightly rostrate-capitate ends. L. 0,018 to 0,036; B. 0,004 to 0,005 mm. Area very narrow, dilated in the middle to a transverse fascia. Striæ 16 to 18 in 0,01 mm., slightly radiate in the middle, convergent at the ends. — *Frustulia app.* Ag. Icon. Alg. Eur. Pl. I (according to Kütz). *Nav. app.* Kütz Bac. p. 93 Pl. III f. 28. V. H. Syn. p. 79 Pl. VI f. 18, 20. *N. app. c. irrorata* Grun. V. H. Syn. Pl. VI f. 30, 31. *Nav. Naveana* Grun. Verh. 1863 p. 149 Pl. IV f. 24. V. H. Syn. Pl. VI f. 29.

Fresh water (moist rocks, mosses etc.): Iceland! Scotland! Sweden (Gothland)! Belgium (V. H.), Brünn (Grun.), Bengal! Australia (Blue Mountains)! Greenland! New Jersey (Hoboken)! Ecuador!

Var. *budensis* Grun. (1880). — V. gibbous in the middle, with distinctly capitate ends. Striæ 20 to 23 in 0,01 mm. — V. H. Syn. Pl. VI f. 27, 28.

Hot springs: Buda-Pesth (Grun.). New Zealand!

P. appendiculata is closely connected with *P. subcapitata* and *P. molaris* and the other hand through the var. *budensis* with *P. Braunii.*

7. **P. Braunii** Grun. (1876). — V. lanceolate, with capitate or subcapitate ends. L. 0,035 to 0,05; B. 0,009 to 0,008 mm. Axial area narrow, gradually increasing in breadth towards the middle of the valve, where it expands to a large and broad, transverse fascia. Striæ 11 to 12 in 0,01 mm. divergent in the middle, convergent at the ends. — *Nav. Brauniana* Grun. in A. S. Atl. XLV f. 77, 78. *Nav. Braunii* Grun. in V. H. Syn. p. 79 Pl. VI f. 21.

Fresh water: Iceland! Sweden (Rosslängen in Kalmar län! Loka. Atl.), Finland! Belgium (V. H.), Bengal! Australia (Blue Mountains)! Argentina! Brazil!

8. **P. subcapitata** Greg. (1856). — V. linear, with subcapitate to capitate ends. L. 0,03 to 0,05; B. 0,005 to 0,006 mm. Axial area narrow or indistinct. Central area a transverse fascia. Striæ 12 to 13, slightly divergent in the middle, convergent at the ends. — M. J. IV p. 9 Pl. I f. 30. *Pin. Hilseana* Janisch in Rabh. Alg. Sachs. N:o 953 (1860). *Nav. Hilseana* A. S. Atl. XLV f. 65. V. H. Syn. p. 77 Suppl. A. f. 11. *Nav. subcapitata* A. S. Atl. XLIV f. 53, 55. V. H. Syn. p. 78 Pl. VI f. 22. A. S. Atl. XLV f. 59, 60.

Fresh water: Spitsbergen! Sweden (Helsingland, Upsala, Marstrand, Gothland)! Finland! Scotland! England! Kiel! Belgium (V. H.). Bengal! Amsterdam Island! Australia (Blue Mountains)! Argentina! Ecuador! Greenland!

Var. *paucistriata* Grun. — Striæ short, gradually shortened towards the middle, where is a very broad transverse fascia. — V. H. Syn. p. 79 Pl. VI f. 23.

Pinn. subcapitata of GREGORY has uninterrupted striæ, but forms with a transverse fascia are much more frequent. This species seems to graduate into *Pinn. interrupta*, from which it differs principally by its smaller size and less distinctly capitate ends.

9. **P. interrupta** W. SM. (1853). — V. linear, with parallel or slightly concave margins and capitate ends. L. 0,05 to 0,076; B. 0,013 mm. Axial area narrow, dilated in the middle to a rhomboid space or transverse fascia. Striæ 10 to 15 in 0,01 mm., strongly radiate in the middle, convergent at the ends.

Forma biceps: central area rhomboid. — *P. biceps* GREG. M. J. IV p. 8 Pl. 1 f. 28 (1856). *P. interrupta* β W. SM. B. D. II p. 96. *Nav. mesolepta* β *producta* GRUN. Verh. 1860 p. 520 Pl. IV f. 22 *a*. *Nav. bicapitata* LAGST. Spitsb. D. p. 23 Pl. 1 f. 5. V. H. Syn. p. 78 Pl. VI f. 14. *Nav. biceps* A. S. Atl. XLV f. 69, 70. *Nav. Termes* A. S. Atl. XLV f. 67. *Nav. mesolepta var. borgana* PANT. III Pl. XXI f. 312.

Fresh water: Spitsbergen! Norway! Sweden! Finland! Scotland (Greg.). Siberia! Japan! Australia, Blue Mountains! Brazil!

Forma stauroneiformis: central area a transverse fascia. *Pinn. interrupta* W. SM. B. D. XIX f. 181. *Nav. int.* A. S. Atl. XLV f. 72, 75, 76. *Nav. Termes var. stauroneif.* V. H. Syn. Pl. VI f. 12, 13. A. S. Atl. XLV f. 71.

Fresh water: Greenland! Norway (Romsdalen)! Sweden! Finland! England (W. Sm.). Germany (Atl.). Bengal! Sandwich Islands! Surinam! Brazil!

Var. *crassior* GRUN. (1880). — V. gibbous in the middle and with broad, capitate ends L. 0,035 to 0,042; B. 0,008 to 0,012 mm. Striæ 13 to 14 in 0,01 mm. *Nav. globiceps var. crassior* GRUN. A. D. p. 27 Pl. 1 f. 13. A. S. Atl. XLV f. 79 (without name).

Brackish water: Jamal (Kara Sea)! Aland (Baltic)!

Pinnul. biceps is closely connected with *P. mesolepta*, which differs only in the triundulate margins. There is the same connection between them as between *P. divergens* and *P. Legumen*.

10. **P. mesolepta** EHR. (1843). — V. triundulated, with capitate ends. L. 0.03 to 0.06; B. 0,011 mm. Axial area narrow, dilated in the middle. Striæ 10 to 14 in 0,01 mm. strongly divergent in the middle and convergent at the ends. — *Nav. mesolepta* EHR. Am. IV: 2 f. 4. KÜTZ Bac. p. 101 Pl. XXVIII f. 73, XXX f. 31. V. H. Syn. p. 79 Pl. VI f. 10–11. *Pinn. mesolepta* W. SM. B. D. XIX f. 182. *Nav. mes. var. α. genuina* GRUN. Verh. 1860 p. 520.

Fresh water: England! Scotland! Greenland! New Zealand!

Var. *stauroneiformis* GRUN. (1860). — Central area a transverse fascia, widened towards the margins. GRUN. Verh. 1860 p. 520 Pl. IV f. 22 *b*. A. S. Atl. XLV f. 52, 53.

Fresh water: Sweden (Rossläugen, Upsala)! Finland! Greenland! Canada! Bridgewater, Maine!

Var. *angusta* CL. — V. narrow linear, triundulate. L. 0,065 to 0.08; B. 0,009 to 0,01 mm. Axial area wider. Striæ 10 to 13 in 0,01 mm. — *Nav. gracillima* A. S. Atl. XLV f. 62. CL. M. D. N:o 103.

Fresh water: Upsala, Sweden! Ringkiöbing, Denmark (Atl.). Harz (Atl.). Maine, Bridgetown! Demerara River! Rio Purus, Brazil!

Var. *polyonca* BRÉB. (1849). — V. triundulate; the median inflation being larger than the others. L. 0.06 to 0,08; B. 0,012 mm. Area narrow, gradually expanded towards the middle to a stauros. Striæ 11 to 12 in 0.01 mm., divergent in the middle, convergent at the ends. — *Nav. polyonca* BRÉB. in Kütz Sp. Alg. p. 85. V. H. Syn. p. 80 Suppl. A. f. 14. *Nav. mesotyla* A. S. Atl. XLV f. 54, 55.

Fresh water: Sweden (Loka, Atl., Upsala!) Belgium (V. H.).

P. mesolepta is nearly connected with *P. interrupta* and analogous to *P. nodosa*, from which latter it differs by its narrower area. The var. *polyonca* is in all respects to *P. mesolepta* what the var. *Formica* is to *P. nodosa*.

11. **P. globiceps** Greg. (1856). — V. strongly gibbous in the middle and with capitate ends. L. 0,03 to 0,04; B. 0,01 mm. Axial area indistinct; central area a broad, transverse fascia, narrowed towards the margin. Striæ 16 to 18 in 0,01 mm., divergent in the middle, convergent at the ends. — M. J. IV Pl. 1 f. 34. *Nav. glob.* V. H. S. Syn. Suppl. A. f. 13.

Brackish water: Scotland (Greg.), Anvers (V. H.). Strehlen (Grun.). Dörrenberg in Saxony! Bengal!

Var. *Krookii* Grun. (1882). — L. 0,015 to 0,028; B. 0,005 to 0,007 mm. Central area a wide lanceolate space. Striæ 15 to 17 in 0,01 mm. in the middle, 19 to 20 near the ends. — *Nav. Krockii* Grun. Foss. D. Österr. Ung. p. 155 Pl. XXX f. 40.

Brackish water: Hungary, (Soos Dept. Grun.), Gulf of Bothnia (Salmis to Tornea)!

12. **P. microstauron** Ehr. (1843). — V. linear, with parallel margins and rostrate, broad ends. L. 0,025 to 0,08; B. 0,007 to 0,009 mm. Axial area very narrow, frequently dilated in the middle to a transverse fascia. Striæ 12 in 0,01 mm., strongly divergent in the middle and convergent at the ends. *Stauroptera microstauron* Ehr. Am. I: 4 f. 1; IV: 2 f. 2, Microg. XVI: 2 f. 4. *Stauroneis micr.* Kütz. Bac. p. 106 Pl. XXIX f. 13. A. S. Atl. XLIV f. 16. *Nav. divergens f. minor* A. S. Atl. XLIV f. 14, 34, 35, XLV f. 31 to 34. *Nav. Brébissonii v. subproducta* V. H. Syn. p. 77 Pl. V f. 9. *Pinn. interrupta* Pedicino Ischia II f. 14. *Nav. bicapitata var. hybrida* V. H. Syn. Pl. VI f. 9. *Nav. Brébissonii* Lagst. Spitsb. D. I f. 2 a. *Pinn. Rabenhorstiana* Hilse Rab. A. Sachs. N:o 812 (1859). *Nav. divergens var. prolongata* Br. a. Héribaud D. d'Auvergne p. 89 Pl. IV f. 1.

Fresh water: Spitsbergen! Finmark! Sweden (Lappland, Areskutan, Skane)! Finland (Lappland to Åbo)! England! Germany! Kamtschatka! Australia (Blue Mountains)! Greenland! North America (Canada, Maine, White Mountains, Sierra Nevada)!

P. microstauron is closely connected with *P. Brébissonii* and *P. interrupta var. stauroneiformis*, which graduates into *P. mesolepta*.

III. Divergentes.

Artificial key.

1.	Terminal fissures in contrary direction	*P. platycephala* Ehr.
	— — in the same direction	2.
2.	Valve with undulated margins	*P. Legumen* Ehr.
	— not undulated	3.
3.	Central area rounded	*P. karelica* Cl.
	— — a transverse fascia	4.
4.	Small forms 0,04 to 0,06 mm.	5.
	Larger forms 0,07 to 0,36 mm.	6.
5.	Striæ very strongly divergent	*P. divergentissima* Grun.
	— somewhat divergent	*P. Brébissonii* Kütz.
6.	Striæ 8 to 9 in 0,01 mm.	7.
	— 11 to 12 in 0,01 mm.	*P. divergens* W. Sm.
7.	Valve linear with parallel margins	8.
	— — gibbous in the middle and at the ends	*P. Hartleyana* Greg.
8.	Striæ strongly radiate	*P. episcopalis* Cl.
	— slightly radiate	*P. Cardinaliculus* Cl.

13. **P. divergentissima** Grun. (1880). — V. lanceolate with obtuse ends. L. 0,03 to 0,035; B. 0,007 mm. Axial area indistinct. Central area a broad fascia. Striæ 13 in 0,01 mm. strongly divergent in the middle and convergent at the ends. – *Nav. nodulosa forma* Lagst. Spitsb. D. p. 22 Pl. II f. 2. *Nav. divergentissima* Grun. in V. H. Syn. Pl. VI f. 32.

Fresh water: Spitsbergen (Ldt), North Iceland! Norway (Dovre)! Finland (Russian Lapland, Åbo)! Greenland! Canada! New Zealand!

This little species is very characteristic and seems to belong to arctic and alpine regions.

14. **P. Brébissonii** Kütz (1844). — V. linear-elliptical, with rounded ends. L. 0,04 to 0,06; B. 0,011 to 0,01 mm. Area narrow, gradually widened in the middle to a transverse fascia, broader towards the central nodule. Striæ 10 to 13 in 0,01 mm., divergent in the middle and convergent towards the ends. *Nav. Brébissonii* Kütz Bac. p. 93 Pl. III f. 49. A. S. Atl. XLIV f. 17, 18. V. H. Syn. p. 77 Pl. V f. 7. Ldt Spitsb. D. Pl. I f. 2 *a'*. Wolle D. of Am. X f. 26? *Pinn. stauroneiformis* W. Sm. Br. D. I p. 57 Pl. XIX f. 178 *a'* (1853). Pedicino, Ischia Pl. II f. 21. *Nav. Mormonorum* Grun. in A. S. Atl. XLIV f. 24 to 26. *Nav. Brébissonii var. fossilis* Pant. III Pl. XIX f. 279 (1893).

Fresh water. (earth and mosses): Beeren Eiland (Ldt). Spitsbergen! Iceland! Norway (Dovre)! Sweden! Scotland! England (W. Sm.), Finland! Belgium (V. H.), Germany (Harz, Atl.), Switzerland! Italy! Greenland! Utah!

Var. *diminuta* V. H. (1880). — Smaller, with gradually narrowed ends. — Syn. p. 77 Pl. V f. 8.

Fresh water: Finland! Scotland! Belgium (V. H.).

Var. *notata* Hérib. a. Perag. (1893). — V. more narrow, slender. L. 0,05 to 0,055; B. 0,008 to 0,009 mm. Striæ 10 to 15 in 0,01 mm. strongly radiate. — *Nav. notata* Hérib. D. d'Auvergne p. 87 Pl. IV f. 11. *P. stauroneif.* Sm. B. D. XIX f. 178 *β*. A. S. Atl. XLIV f. 19.

Fresh water: Iceland! Norway (Romsdalen)! Finland! Germany (Franzenbad, Atl.), Puy de Dôme (foss. Hérib.). Santa Rosa, Cal.!

P. Brébissonii is a very variable species, closely connected with smaller forms of *P. divergens* and with *P. microstauron*. Nearly allied also is *P. appendiculata*.

15. **P. karelica** Cl. (1891). — V. linear, gibbous in the middle, with broad, truncate ends. L. 0,045 to 0,05; B. 0,011 to 0,012 mm. Median line straight, with moderately approximate median pores and hook-shaped terminal fissures, turned in the same direction. Axial area indistinct; central area large, orbicular. Striæ divergent in the middle, convergent at the ends 15 to 16 in 0,01 mm. — Diat. of Finl. p. 28 Pl. I f. 6.

Fresh or slightly brackish water: Norway (Mouth of Tana-elf)! Sweden (Lule Lappmark, Wenern, Rosslängen in Småland, Umea, fossil)! Finl., Karelen!

16. **P. Legumen** Ehr. (1843). — V. linear-lanceolate, with triundulate margins and subrostrate, broad ends. L. 0,07 to 0,011; B. 0,015 to 0,018 mm. Median line filiform, with comma-like terminal fissures. Axial area broad, nearly $^1/_3$ of the breadth of the valve, dilated in the middle. Striæ 10 to 12 in 0,01 mm., strongly divergent in the middle, convergent at the ends. Am. I. I. f. 7? *Nav. Leg.* Ehr. M. G. II: 2 f. 12. A. S. Atl. XLIV f. 44 to 47. V. H. Syn. p. 80 Pl. VI f. 16. *Nav. undulata* Schum. P. D. p. 188 f. 37.

Fresh water: Sweden! Norway (Stavanger, foss.)! Scotland! Belgium (V. H.), France! Italy (S:ta Fiora, foss.)! Bengal! New Zealand! Australia (Murray River, Australian Alps)! Japan! Congo (V. H. Coll.)! North America (Port Hope, Crane Pond, French Pond, Waltham Mass., Illinois)!

Var. *florentina* Grun. (1877). — L. 0,1 to 0,13; B. 0,018 mm. Central area dilated to a transverse fascia. Striæ 8 in 0,01 mm. — *Nav.* (*Esox var.?*) *florent.* Grun. in Cl. M. D. N:o 14. A. S. Atl. XLIV f. 8. *Nav. divergens var. undulata* Hérib. a. Perag. D. d'Auvergne p. 89 Pl. IV f. 2 (1893).

Fresh water: Livorno (Atl.), S:ta Fiora!

Var. *ornata* Cl. — L. 0,07; B. 0,012 mm. Central area a transverse fascia with a row of puncta on each side of the central nodule. Striæ 11 in 0,01 mm.

Fresh water: Bengal!

Pinn. or *Nav. Legumen* Ehr. seems to comprise several different species with triundulate margins, so that it is impossible to say what species may be the true *P. Legumen*. I have adopted the opinion expressed in Van Heurcks synopsis. *P. Legumen* is most variable, the undulations of the margin being often very slight, in which case it is impossible to distinguish it from certain forms of *P. divergens* and *P. stauroptera*.

17. **P. platycephala** Ehr. (1854). — V. linear, 5 to 6 times longer than broad, with broad, subcapitate ends and slightly undulate margins. L. 0,083 to 0,105; B. 0,017 to 0,018 mm. Median line filiform with terminal fissures in contrary directions. Axial area distinct, about 1/3 of the breadth of the valve. Central area a more or less perfect fascia. Striæ divergent in the middle, convergent at the ends, 12 in 0,01 mm. — *Stauroptera platycephala* Ehr. M. G. XVII: II f. 9. *Pinnul. platyc.* Cl. Diat. of Finl. p. 20 Pl. II f. 1.

Fresh water: Sweden: Rosslängen (Calmar län)! Pjesörn Dept. (Skellefteå)! Öjasjö Dept. (Blekinge)! Finl. Suomenniemi Dept. (Viborgs län)! Unrais socken (Vasa)! Pudasjärvi Dept. (Österbotten)! Scotland (Grove), France: Lac Gerardmer (Vosges)!

P. platycephala is an isolated species, which shews no close relation to any known form. It seems to come nearer to *P. divergens* and *P. legumen* than to any other.

18. **P. divergens** W. Sm. (1853). — V. lanceolate, gradually attenuated to the obtuse or slightly capitate ends. L. 0,07 to 0,14; B. 0,015 to 0,02 mm. Median line filiform, with curved terminal fissures. Axial area narrow, distinct, widened in the middle to a transverse fascia. Striæ 11 to 12 in 0,01 mm., strongly divergent in the middle, convergent at the ends. — Br. D. p. 57 Pl. XVIII f. 177. *Nav. div.* A. S. Atl. XLIV f. 9. Wolle D. of N. A. XIX f. 21.

Fresh water: Sweden (Lappland to Blekinge)! Norway (Stavanger)! Scotland (Premney Peat, W. Sm., Dolgelly earth W. Sm., Loch Kinnord!) Finland! Bengal! New Zealand! Sandwich Islands! N. America (Waterford, Maine)! S. America (Demerara River, Santos)!

Var. *cuneata* Grun. (1876). — V. with cuneate, subacute ends. L. 0,075 to 0,1; B. 0,014 to 0,02 mm. Central area a narrow fascia. Striæ 11 in 0,01 mm. — A. S. Atl. XLIV f. 10, 11.

Fresh water: Demerara River!

Var. *sublinearis* Cl. — V. elleptic-linear, gradually tapering from the middle to the obtuse ends. L. 0,08 to 0,10; B. 0,014 to 0,013 mm. Striæ 12 in 0,01 mm. — A. S. Atl. XLIV f. 20, 23. *Nav. procera* Pant. II p. 52 Pl. I f. 8 (1889)?

Fresh water: New Zealand! America (Bemis Lake, White Mountains, Waterford, Maine; Rio Purus, Brazil)!

Var. *elliptica* Grun. (1884). — V. broad, linear to elliptical, with rounded ends. L. 0,075 to 0,15; B. 0,015 to 0,027 mm. Striæ 8 to 11 in 0,01 mm. — *Nav. dir. var. ellipt.* Grun. Fr. Jos. Land D. p. 98 Pl. I f. 19. *Nav. dir.* A. S. Atl. XLIV f. 6—7. *Nav. cardinalis var. africana* Brun D. espèces nov. p. 33 Pl. XVI f. 9. *Nav. viridis var. staurophora* Pant. III Pl. VI f. 96 (1893)?

Fresh water: Franz Jos. Land (Grun.), Norway (Tana Elf, Stavanger)! Sweden (Rosslängen in Kalmar län, Öjasjö in Blekinge)! Finland! Scotland (Island of Lewis)! Australia (Blue Mountains)! Greenland! Monmouth (Atl.), Demerara River! S. W. Africa, Ombika (Brun Coll.)!

Forma ornata Grun. — Central area with a semicircular row of dots on both sides of the central nodule. L. 0,12; B. 0,017 mm. Striæ 10 in 0,01 mm. — Bengal!

Var. *Schweinfurtii* A. S. (1876). — L. 0,11 to 0,12; B. 0,02 mm. Axial area more narrow. Median line oblique. Striæ 11 in 0,01 mm. — *Nav. Schweinfurtii* A. S. Atl. XLIV f. 4, 5.

Fresh water: Scriba Gattas (Atl.).

19. **P. Cardinaliculus** Cl. N. Sp. — V. linear, with parallel margins and rounded ends. L. 0,08 to 0,1; B. 0,015 to 0,018 mm. Median line filiform, with approximate central pores and short, bayonet-shaped terminal fissures. Axial area less than 1/3 as broad as the breadth of the valve in the middle widened to a transverse fascia. Striæ 9 in 0,01 mm., almost parallel or slightly divergent in the middle and convergent at the ends. — Pl. I f. 12.

Fresh water: Scotland (Grove Coll.)! America (Canada, Crane Pond, French Pond, Houghton Mich., Mexico)!

20. **P. Hartleyana** Grev. (1865). — V. linear, gibbous in the middle and at the ends. L. 0,2 to 0,23; B. 0,033 to 0,045 mm. Median line straight, filiform. Axial area linear, less than $^1/_3$ as broad as the valve, in the middle transversely dilated, frequently to a fascia. Striæ 8 in 0,01 mm. divergent in the middle, convergent at the ends. — T. M. S. vol. XIII Pl. VI f. 30.

Fresh water: Liberia (Grev.), Demerara River!

21. **P. episcopalis** Cl. (1891). — V. linear, with parallel margins and broad rounded ends. L. 0,23 to 0,36; B. 0,035 to 0,04 mm. Median line filiform with comma-like terminal fissures. Axial area broad, about $^1/_3$ of the breadth of the valve, in the middle widened to a transverse fascia. Striæ 8 in 0,01 mm., strongly divergent in the middle and convergent at the ends. — *P. cardinalis* Ehr. M. G. XVIII: 1 f. 4. *P. episcopalis* Cl. D. of Finl. p. 27 Pl. I f. 4.

Fresh water: Sweden (Lake Wenern, Lake Rosslängen in Kalmar län, Öjasjö Dept. in Blekinge, interglacial mud from Hernösand)! Finland! Lac Gerardmer, Vosges! Cherryfield, America!

Var. *brevis* Cl. L. 0,18; B. 0,038 mm. Striæ 6 in 0,01 mm. less radiate.

Fresh water: New Zealand (Auckland, Witt Coll.)!

Var. *africana* Cl. — V. smaller. L. 0,115; B. 0,018 mm. Axial area less than a third of the breadth of the valve. Striæ 8 in 0,01 mm.

Fresh water, mouth of rivers: Cameroon, Africa!

P. episcopalis is a very large and beautiful diatom, nearly akin to *P. divergens* and to *P. Hartleyana*.

IV. Distantes.

Artificial key.

1.	Valve lanceolate	*P. alpina* W. Sm.
	— more or less narrow, elliptical	. . . . 2.
2.	Very small forms. L. about 0,01 mm	*P. Balfouriana* Grun.
	Length 0,02 to 0,1 mm. and more	. . . . . 3.
3.	L. 0,1 mm. and more	*P. lata* Bréb.
	L. less than 0,1 mm	. . . . . 4.
4.	Striæ 5 to 6 in 0,01 mm.	. . *P. borealis* Ehr.
	— 8 in 0,01 mm.	*P. intermedia* Lagst.

22. **P. intermedia** Lagst. (1873). — V. linear-elliptical, with rounded ends. L. 0,018 to 0,042; B. 0,06 to 0,08 mm. Axial area narrow; central a transverse fascia. Striæ radiate at the ends, 8 in 0,01 mm. — *Nav. int.* Lagst. Spetsb. D. 23 Pl. I f. 3.

Fresh water: Spitsbergen (Lagst.), Beeren Eiland (Lagst.), Australia (Blue Mountains)!

This form seems, according to Lagerstedt, to graduate into *P. borealis* and *P. Brébissonii*.

23. **P. Balfouriana** Grun. Ms. — V. elliptical. L. 0,008 to 0,01; B. 0,004 mm. Area wide. Striæ distant, 10 in 0,01 mm. — Pl. I f. 18.

Fresh water: Scotland (Grun.), North Iceland!

24. **P. borealis** Ehr. (1843). — V. linear-elliptical, with rounded or subtruncate ends. L. 0,03 to 0,06; B. 0,007 to 0,008 mm. Median line with approximate central pores and hook-shaped terminal fissures. Area narrow. Striæ parallel, 5 to 6 in 0,01 mm. — Am. Pl. I: 2 f. 6. *Nav. borealis* Kütz B. p. 96. Grun. Verh. 1860 p. 518. Lagst. Sp. D. Pl. I f. 4. A. S. Atl. Pl. XLV f. 15—21. V. H. Syn. p. 76 Pl. VI f. 3, 4. Wolle Pl. IX f. 23. *Pinnul. hebridensis* Greg. M. J. 1854 p. 28 Pl. IV f. 13. *Pinn. chilensis* Rabh. Alg. Sachs. 885 (1859).

On mosses, moist earth, in fresh water: Spitsbergen! Beeren Eiland (Lagst.), Greenland! Iceland! Sweden! Finland! Germany! England! Belgium (V. H.), Switzerland! Japan! S:t Pauls Island (Grun.), Sandwich Islands! Australia (Blue Mountains)! New Zealand! South Africa! Argentina! Ecuador! W. Ind. S:t Vincent!

Var. *scalaris* Ehb. (1843). — Narrow, linear. Central area a broad transverse fascia. — *Stauroptera scalaris* Ehb. Am. IV: 2 f. 3. *Nav. borealis var. scalaris* Grun. Verh. 1860 p. 518 Pl. IV f. 15.

Labrador (Ehb.).

Pinn. borealis graduates by intermediate forms into *P. lata*.

25. **P. lata** Bréb. (1838). — V. linear-elliptical, with broad, rounded ends. L. 0,1 to 0,13; B. 0,03 to 0,04 mm. Median line oblique; central pores approximate, terminal fissures hook-shaped. Area large, slightly widened in the middle. Striæ slightly radiate in the middle, 3 in 0,01 mm., transverse at the ends. — *Frustulia lata* Bréb. Cons. p. 18. *P. lata* W. Sm. B. D. I pl. XVIII f. 167. *Nav. lata* Kütz Bac. p. 92. Grun. Franz Jos. Land D. p. 98 Pl. I f. 14. *Nav. lata var. minor* Hérib. a. Perag. D. d'Auvergne p. 86 Pl. IV f. 5. *P. megaloptera* Ehb. M. G. III: 1 f. 4; IV: 2 f. 5 (1854). Abh. 1870 Pl. III f. 16. *Nav. meg.* Hérib. D. d'Auvergne p. 88 Pl. IV f. 6. *P. pachyptera* Ehb. Am. p. 133 Pl. IV: 2 f. 9 (1843). *Nav. pach.* A. S. Atl. XLV f. 5, 8. Pant. III Pl. XX f. 302. *Nav. costata* Hérib. D. d'Auvergne p. 87 Pl. IV f. 7 (1893).

Fresh water: Franz Josefs Land (Grun.), England! Scotland! Ireland! France (Normandy)! Switzerland! Australia (Murray River)! New Zealand! Hungary fossil.

Var. *Rabenhorstii* Grun. (1860). — V. slightly constricted in the middle, with cuneate, truncate ends. L. 0,06; B. 0,015 mm. Striæ parallel, 4 in 0,01 mm. — *Nav. Thuringiaca* Rabh. Fl. E. A. p. 205. *Nav. Rabenhorstii* Grun. Verh. 1860 p. 515, Pl. IV f. 13. *Nav. borealis var. fossilis* Pant. III Pl. V f. 73 (1893).

Fresh water: Thüringen (Rabh.).

Var. *latestriata* Greg. (1854). V. narrow-linear, with subcuneate extremities. L. 0,04 to 0,06; B. 0,012 mm. Striæ 4 in 0,01 mm. — *Pinn. latestr.* Greg. M. J. II p. 98 Pl. IV f. 12. *Nav. borealis var.? producta* Grun. Verh. 1860 p. 518 Pl. IV f. 14.

Fresh water: Mull Dept.

Var. *minor* Grun. (1878). — L. 0,045; B. 0,013 mm. Area narrow. Striæ 4—5 in 0,01 mm. — Grun. Cap. S. Alg. Pl. IV f. 22. Fr. Jos. L. D. p. 98 Pl. I f. 16, 17. *Nav. lata* V. H. S. p. 76 Pl. VI f. 1—2.

Fresh water: Spitsbergen! Franz Jos. Land (Grun.), Casp. Sea (Grun.).

Var. *curta* Grun. (1884). — V. elliptical. Grun. Fr. Jos. L. D. f. 15.

Fresh water: Franz Jos. Land (Grun.).

26. **P. alpina** W. Sm. (1853). — V. elliptic-lanceolate, with rounded, obtuse ends. L. 0,1 to 0,18; B. 0,038 to 0,05 mm. Median line oblique; central nodule large; terminal fissures spirally twisted. Axial area wide (less than 1/3 of the breadth of the valve) lanceolate. Striæ radiate, 3,5 in 0,01 mm., transverse at the ends. B. D. I p. 55 XVIII f. 168. *Nav. alpina* Donk. B. D. p. 27 IV f. 6. A. S. Atl. XLV f. 1 to 4.

Fresh water (subalpine regions): Scotland! Ireland! Erzgebirge! Switzerland!

V. Tabellarieæ.

Artificial key.

1. { Central area with a linear mark on each side of the central nodule . . . . 2.
   { — — without — — — — — — . . . . 3.
2. { Valve not undulate . . . . *P. stomatophora* Grun.
   { — slightly triundulate . . . . *P. Brandelii* Cl.
3. { Valve lanceolate, broad . . . . 4.
   { — linear, narrow . . . . 6.
4. { Large. L. 0,14 to 0,15 mm. . . . . *P. Sillimanorum* Ehb.
   { Small. L. 0,04 to 0,075 mm. 5.

5.	Striæ 6 in 0,01 mm.	*P. Thorax* Brun.
	— 13 — —	*P. lignitica* Cl.
6.	Valve narrow lanceolate	*P. subsolaris* Grun.
	— linear	7.
7.	Ends subcapitate	8.
	— rounded	12.
8.	Central area broad	*P. stauroptera* Grun.
	— — narrow	9.
9.	Valve large. L. 0,1 to 0,2 mm.	10.
	— smaller. L. 0,05 to 0,08 mm.	11.
10.	Axial area very narrow	*P. luculenta* A. S.
	— — 1/3 as broad as the valve	*P. Tabellaria* Ehb.
11.	Central area small	*P. gibba* Ehb.
	— — large	*P. mesogongyla* Ehb.
12.	Striæ parallel	*P. spitsbergensis* Cl.
	— radiate	13.
13.	Striæ 8 to 10 in 0,01 mm.	*P. rangoonensis* Grun.
	— 12 in —	*P. bogotensis* Grun.

27. **P. spitsbergensis** Cl. N. Sp. — V. linear, with parallel margins and rounded ends. L. 0,058 to 0,067; B. 0,007 to 0,008 mm. Median line filiform with somewhat distant, bayonet-shaped, terminal fissures. Axial area distinct, less than 1/3 of the breadth of the valve, linear, slightly widened around the central nodule, or transversely dilated to a fascia. Striæ 16 to 17 in 0,01 mm., almost parallel. Pl. I f. 13.

Fresh water: Spitsbergen (Cl. M. D. N:o 159). Jenissey!

Var. *stomatophora* Cl. — Central area with a linear marking on each side of the central nodule. — Fresh water: Spitsbergen.

28. **P. luculenta** A. S. (1876). — V. linear, slightly gibbous in the middle and at the ends. L. 0,1; B. 0,014 mm. Median line filiform, with approximate central pores, and bayonet-shaped terminal fissures. Axial area very narrow; central area small, orbicular. Striæ 13 in 0,01 mm. strongly divergent in the middle and convergent at the ends. — *Nav. luculenta* A. S. Atl. XLIII f. 12.

Fresh water: Bengal (Kyan-Zoo, Atl.).

29. **P. gibba** (Ehb.?) W. Sm. (1853). — V. linear, gradually tapering from the middle to the subcapitate ends. L. 0,05 to 0,08; B. 0,007 to 0,008 mm. Median line filiform, with approximate median pores and slightly curved terminal fissures. Axial area narrow, linear, slightly dilated in the middle. Striæ 10 to 11 in 0,01 mm. slightly divergent in the middle and convergent at the ends, frequently interrupted in the middle. — *Stauroptera gibba* Ehb. Am. I: 2 f. 3 (1843)? *P. gibba* W. Sm. B. D. I Pl. XIX f. 180. *Nav. Proserpinæ* Pant. III Pl. XVIII f. 260 (1893). *Nav. appendiculata* Pant. III Pl. III f. 46 (1893)?

Fresh water: England (Cornwall)! Scotland (W. Sm.), Ireland (Mourne Mountains)! Australia (Blue Mountains)! N. America (Waterford, Maine)! Brazil (Caldas)!

30. **P. stauroptera** Grun. (1860). — V. slender, gradually tapering from the middle to the subcapitate ends. L. 0,09 to 0,12; B. 0,012 to 0,013 mm. Median line filiform, with approximate median pores and slightly curved terminal fissures. Area wide, about a third of the breadth of the valve. Striæ 9,5 to 10 in 0,01 mm. strongly divergent in the middle and convergent at the ends. — *Nav. stauroptera* Grun. Verh. 1860 p. 516. *Nav. gibba* Donk. B. D. p. 70 Pl. XII f. 3. A. S. Atl. XLV f. 48 to 50. *Nav. gibba var. hyalina* Hérib. a. Perag. D. d'Auvergne p. 92 Pl. IV f. 14.

Fresh water: Iceland! Sweden! Norway (Stavanger, foss.)! Finland! Holstein! Australia (Murray River, Blue Mountains)! N. America (Canada, Massachusetts, New Hampshire, Sierra Nevada)! Brazil!

Var. *semicruciata* CL. — Striæ in the middle unilaterally interrupted. *Nav. gibba β Peckii* GRUN. Verh. 1860 p. 517 Pl. IV f. 17.

Fresh water: Sweden (Öjasjö. Blekinge)! Norway (Stavanger Dept.)! America (Canada West., Waltham Mass., Caldas Brazil)!

Var. *interrupta* CL. — Striæ interrupted on both sides of the central nodule. *Nav. Stauroptera* GRUN. Verh. 1860 p. 516 Pl. IV f. 18 (f. gracilis) f. 19 (f. parva) Fr. Jos. Land D. Pl. 1 f. 18. A. S. Atl. XLIV f. 41. V. H. Syn. p. 77 Pl. VI f. 7, f. 6 (f. parva). *Nav. Tabellaria* V. H. Syn. f. 8. *Nav. abaujensis* PANT. II p. 41 Pl. III f. 51 (1889).

Fresh water: Franz Josef's Land (Grun.). Sweden! Finland! Norway! Scotland! France (Lac Gerardmer Vosges)! New Zealand! Hawaii! Demerara! Surinam! North America (Waltham Mass., Troy, New Hampshire)! Ecuador!

Var. *sancta* GRUN. Ms. — V. strongly gibbous in the middle. L. 0,11; B. 0,015 mm. Area very wide. Striæ 10 to 11 in 0,01 mm.

Fresh water: Santos, Brazil! Bengal!

31. **P. rangoonensis** GRUN. Ms. — V. linear. with broad, rounded ends. L. 0,07 to 0,10; B. 0,012 to 0,014 mm. Median line filiform, with approximate central pores and comma-like, terminal fissures. Axial area distinct, but narrow, in the middle dilated to an elliptical space, or on one or both sides, to a transverse fascia. Striæ 8 to 10 in 0,01 mm. divergent in the middle, convergent at the ends. — *Stauroptera semicruciata* EHB. M. G. XXXIII: 2 f. 7*?

Fresh water: Rangoon!

This form is scarcely specifically distinct from *P. stauroptera*. The same is also the case with *Nav. Troyana* GRUN. (in Cl. and Möller Diat. N:o 275) and *Nav. Förarmensis* GRUN. (Cl. and Möller Diat. N:o 140), which I am unable to distinguish from *P. rangoonensis*. The only differences between these forms and *P. stauroptera* consist in the shape of the valve and in the terminal fissures, which are more curved in *P. rangoonensis*. I hav efound such forms from the following localities: Greenland, Sweden (Förarm. Småland), Troy (New Hampshire), Demerara River, New Zealand, Blue Mountains (Australia).

32. **P. Brandelii** CL. (1891). — V. linear gibbous in the middle and at the ends, often with tri-undulate margins. Ends broadly rounded, frequently subclavate. L. 0,07 to 0,08; B. 0,007 to 0,009 mm. Median line filiform, with semicircular terminal fissures. Area distinct, narrow, linear, in the middle widened to a broad transverse fascia, having a linear marking on each side of the central nodule. Striæ 14 in 0,01 mm., divergent in the middle, convergent at the ends. — D. of Finl. p. 26 Pl. 1 f. 8, 9.

Fresh water: Sweden (Ålmten in Kalmar län)! Finland! France (Lac Gerardmer, Vosges)!

33. **P. stomatophora** GRUN. (1876). — V. linear-lanceolate, gradually tapering from the middle to the rounded ends. L. 0,07 to 0,11; B. 0,09 to 0,011 mm. Median line with bayonet-shaped terminal fissures. Axial area narrow, linear, widened in the middle to a narrow transverse fascia, where is on each side of the central nodule a linear marking. Striæ 12 to 13 in 0,01 mm., strongly divergent in the middle and convergent at the ends. — *Nav. stomatophora* GRUN. in A. S. Atl. XLIV f. 27 to 29.

Fresh water: Iceland, Scotland (Island of Lewis)! Norway (Dovre, Atl.)! Sweden (Rosslängen in Kalmar län)! Finland! Germany (Harz. Atl.). New Zealand! America (Canada, Crane Pond, French Pond)!

Var. *continua* CL. — L. 0,07 to 0,12; B. 0,009 to 0,014 mm. Striæ 13 in 0,01 mm., not interrupted.

Fresh water: Loch Kinnord, Scotland! Sweden (Lake Rosslängen in Kalmar län)!

34. **P. bogotensis** GRUN. (1876). — V. linear, with rounded ends. L. 0,1 to 0,11; B. 0,013 mm. Median line with approximate central pores and bayonet-shaped terminal fissures. Axial

area narrow, widened in the middle to a broad, transverse fascia. Striæ 12 in 0,01 mm. strongly divergent in the middle and convergent at the ends. — *Nav. bogotensis* A. S. Atl. XLIV f. 30 to 32.

Fresh water: New Grenada (Atl.), French Pond, Maine (Atl.).

35. **P. subsolaris** Grun. (1882). V. linear-lanceolate, with obtuse ends. L. 0,065 to 0,07; B. 0,01 to 0,011 mm. Median line with bayonet-shaped terminal fissures. Axial area narrow, widened in the middle to a large suborbicular space. Striæ 10 to 11 in 0,01 mm. strongly divergent in the middle and convergent at the ends. — *Nav. decurrens?* A. S. Atl. XLV f. 29, 30. *Nav. Legumen var. undulata* V. H. Syn. Pl. VI f. 17. *Nav. (decurrens* Ehb. *var.?) subsolaris* Grun Foss. D. Öster. Ung. p. 143. *Nav. scythica* Pant. III Pl. XXIII f. 335 (1893).

Fresh water: Norway (Stavanger, foss.)! Scotland! Hungary (Dubravica Dept. Grun.), New Zealand! Canada! Dana's Pond (Grun.). Demerara River!

Var. *brevistriata* Grun. (1882). Area broader. Striæ less radiate. — *Nav subs. var. br.* Foss. D. Österr. Ung. p. 143 Pl. XXX f. 38.

Fresh water: Hungary (Dubravica Dept. Grun.).

Var. *australiensis* Cl. — L. 0,096; B. 0,012 mm. Striæ 14 in 0,01 mm.

Fresh water: Rieva Lagoons. Australian Alps!

Var. *linearis* Cl. — V. linear, with parallel margins and broad, subtruncate ends. L. 0,12; B. 0,017 mm. Striæ 10 in 0,01 mm.

Fresh water: Finland (Lojo)! Rangoon! New Zealand!

36. **P. Tabellaria** Ehb. (1843). - V. slender, gibbous in the middle and at the ends. L. 0,1 to 0,2; B. 0,015 to 0,02 mm. Median line filiform, slightly oblique, with approximate central pores and bayonet-shaped terminal fissures. Axial area linear, less than $^1/_3$ as broad as the valve, widened in the middle to an elliptical space. Striæ 11 to 14 in 0,01 mm. strongly divergent in the middle, convergent at the ends. Am. p. 131 Pl. II: 5 f. 26. M. G. II: 3 f. 6. *Nav Tab.* A. S. Atl. XLIII f. 4.

Fresh water: N. America (Cherryfield, Waltham Mass., Bemis Lake, White Mountains, Crane Pond) S. America, Brazil, Caldas! South Africa, Ombika (Brun Coll.)!

37. **P. mesogongyla** Ehb. (1870). — V. linear, gibbous in the middle and gradually tapering to the subcapitate, broad ends. L. 0,08 to 0,08; B. 0,013 mm. Median line filiform, with somewhat approximate central pores and slightly curved terminal fissures. Area narrow, widened in the middle to an orbicular space. Striæ 11 in 0,01 mm. strongly divergent in the middle and convergent at the ends. Ber. 1870 II f. 16. Cl. D. of Finland p. 25 Pl. I f. 11. *Nav.* (without name) A. S. Atl. XLV f. 45. *Nav. decurrens* Cl. Vega XXXVI f. 20. *Nav. gibba* V. H. Syn. Suppl. A f. 12.

Fresh water: Iceland! Scotland, Lock Cannor (Atl.). Finmark! Norway, Dovre! East Cape! Utah (Ehb.).

Var. *interrupta* Cl. (1891). L. 0,06; B. 0,01 mm. Striæ 12 in 0,01 mm. interrupted by a broad, transverse fascia. Cl. D. of Finland p. 26 Pl. I f. 10.

Fresh water: Finland!

P. mesogongyla of Ehrenberg comprises several different species, among which are *P. nobilis* and *P. major*. As the forms figured in Ber. 1870 seems to be the same as ours, I have adopted Ehrenberg's name. Grunow believes this form to be *P. decurrens* of Ehrenberg, but the latter is too insufficiently figured to admit of identification. *P. decurrens* seems to be a form of *P. stauroptera*.

38. **P. Sillimanorum** Ehb. (1843). V. lanceolate, with large, capitate ends. L. 0,14 to 0,15; B. 0,034 to 0,035 mm. Median line filiform with distant median pores and bayonet shaped terminal fissures. Axial area large, dilated around the central nodule, on both sides of which are some rugosities. Striæ 10 in 0,01 mm., strongly divergent in the middle, and there alternately

longer and shorter, very convergent at the ends. — Am. p. 133. M. G II: 2 f. 13. *Nav. Sill.* LEWIS Proceed. Acad. Nat. Scienc. Philad. Pl. II f. 8. WALKER a. CHASE N. a. R. D. Pl. II p. 6 Pl. II f. 2.

Fresh water: North America, Crane Pond! New Hampshire (Ehb.), Wolfboro (Lewis).

39. **P. lignitica** CL. N. Sp. - V. lanceolate, with protracted, broad and rounded ends. L. 0,075; B. 0,019 mm. Terminal nodules hook-shaped. Axial area uniting with the central area in a lanceolate space. Striæ 13 in 0,01 mm., slightly radiate, at the ends convergent. Pl. I f. 15.

Fresh water: Japan, lignite (Brun Coll.)!

Nav. transylvanica PANT. (III Pl. I f. 7) and its var. *producta* (l. c. Pl. XXIII f. 345) may be akin to this species, if they do not represent a Caloneis allied to *C. formosa*, which I am unable to decide from the figures.

40. **P. Thorax** BRUN (1891). -- V. lanceolate, with more or less protracted, obtuse ends. L. 0,04 to 0,0065; B. 0,017 to 0,02 mm. Terminal fissures small and indistinct. Axial and central areas uniting in a lanceolate space. Striæ 6 in 0,01 mm., slightly radiate, convergent, and closer near the ends. -- *Nav. Thorax* BRUN D. espèces n. p. 41 Pl. XVI f. 6.

Fresh water: Japan, lignite (Brun Coll.)!

VI. Brevistriatæ.

Artificial key.

1. { Margins of the valve undulate . . . . . . *N. nodosa* EHB.
   { — — — not — . . . . . . 2.
2. { Area punctate . . . . . . *N. acrosphæria* BRÉB.
   { — not — . . . . . . 3.
3. { Ends cuneate . . . . . . 4.
   { — not — . . . . . . 5.
4. { Median line straight . . . . . . *P. singularis* A. S.
   { — — flexuose . . . . . . *P. integra* GRUN.
5. { Linear lanceolate, tapering from the middle . . . . . . 6.
   { -- narrowed towards the ends . . . . . . 7.
6. { Striæ 10 to 11 in 0,01 mm. . . . . . . *P. parva* EHB.
   { -- 21 to 22 - -- . . . . . . *P. modesta* GRUN.
7. { Striæ 8 to 10 in 0,01 mm. . . . . . . 8.
   { — 14 to 15 — — . . . . . . *P. pauleusis* GRUN.
8. { L. 0,1 to 0,12 mm. . . . . . . *P. brevicostata* CL.
   { L. 0,05 to 0,08 mm. . . . . . . *P. hemiptera* KÜTZ.

41. **P. hemiptera** KÜTZ (1844). -- V. elliptic-linear to linear, narrowed towards the often subcuneate ends. L. 0,05 to 0,08; B. 0,012 to 0,013 mm. Axial area generally wide, more or less lanceolate. Terminal fissures semicircular. Striæ 8 to 10 in 0,01 mm. slightly radiate or almost parallel. — *Nav. hem.* KÜTZ Bac. p. 97 Pl. XXX f. 11. A. S. Atl. XLIII f. 28, XLV f. 9. *P. acuminata* W. SM. B. D. XVIII f. 164. *Nav. instabilis* A. S. Atl. XLIII f. 35 to 40. *Nav. debilis* PANT. II p. 44 Pl. XII f. 214 (1889). *Nav. hybrida* HÉRIB. a. PERAG. D. d'Auvergne p. 85 Pl. IV f. 9 (1893). *Nav. hybrida var. Bielawskii* HÉRIB. a. PERAG. l. c. p. 85 Pl. IV f. 10.

Fresh water: Sweden (Lapland to Skane)! Finland (Russian Lapland to Åbo)! Norway! Iceland! Great Britain (Premnay Peat, Loch Kinnord)! Italy (S:ta Fiora Dept.)! Hongkong (Atl.), New Zealand! Australia (Blue Mountains)! America (Waltham Mass., Crane Pond, Demerara River, Brazil, Trinidad)!

Var. *interrupta* CL. — Striæ uni- or bilaterally interrupted in the middle by a transverse fascia.

Fresh water: Japan, lignite (Brun Coll.)!

This species is of very frequent occurence and very variable, especially as to the breadth of the axial area, which sometimes becomes very broad as in the form named by A. S. *Nav. instabilis.*

42. **P. paulensis** GRUN. Ms. — V. linear, slightly narrowed to the obtuse, rounded ends. L. 0,065 to 0,14; B. 0,011 to 0,014 mm. Median line filiform, with approximate central pores and slightly curved, elongate, terminal fissures. Axial area wide, about a third of the breadth of the valve, linear. Striæ 14 to 15 in 0,01 mm., almost transverse to the ends. — A. S. Atl. XLIII f. 7, 8, 9 (without name). Icon. n. Pl. I f. 20.

Fresh water: America (Greenland, White Mountains, Cherryfield, Monmouth, Ducks Pond, Maine, Sierra Nevada, Demerara River, Brazil, Caldas, San Paolo)!

43. **P. brevicostata** CL. (1891). V. linear, with parallel margins and broad, rounded ends. L. 0,1 to 0,12; B. 0,016 mm. Median line almost filiform. Terminal fissures comma-like. Area very broad, irregularly lanceolate. Striæ 8 to 9 in 0,01 mm. parallel throughout. *Nav. hemiptera* A. S. Atl. XLIII f. 26, 27. *Pinn. brevicostata* CL. D. of Finl. p. 25 Pl. I f. 5.

Fresh water: Sweden (Rosslängen in Kalmar län)! Finland! Bengal!

Var. *leptostauron* CL. (1891). — L. 0,075 to 0,01; B. 0,013 mm. Striæ 10 in 0,01 mm., interrupted in the middle. A. S. Atl. XLIII f. 25 (without name). D. of Finl. p. 25.

Fresh water: Sweden (Stensele Lappmark, Rosslängen in Kalmar län, Öjasjö in Blekinge)! Finland (Tavastland)! Scotland (Ordie Dept.)! Germany (Laacher See, Atl.), France (Lac de Gerardmer, Vosges)!

Var. *Demeraræ* CL. V. linear, attenuated towards the subcuneate ends. L. 0,07; B. 0,01 mm. Area about a third as broad as the valve. Central area a transverse fascia. Striæ 10 in 0,01 mm.

Fresh water: Demerara River!

44. **P. acrosphæria** BRÉB. (1838). — V. linear, more or less gibbous in the middle and at the ends. L. 0,032 to 0,18; B. 0,008 to 0,02 mm. Median line filiform, its central pores approximate and its terminal fissures semicircular. Axial area about a third as broad as the valve, finely punctate. Striæ 9 to 14 in 0,01 mm. parallel, or slightly radiate at the ends.

Forma maxima. — L. 0,15 to 0,18; B. 0,02 mm. Striæ 9 in 0,01 mm. — *Nav. acrosph. var. sandvicensis* A. S. Atl. XLIII f. 14, 15.

Fresh water: Java (eatable earth)! New Zealand! Sandwich Islands (Atl.).

Forma genuina — L. 0,1; B. 0,012 mm. Striæ 10 to 12 in 0,01 mm. *Frustulia acrosphæria* BRÉB. Considér. p. 19. *Nav. acrosph.* KÜTZ Bac. p. 97 Pl. V f. 2. DONK. Br. D. p. 72 Pl. XII f. 2. W. SM. B. D. XIX f. 183. A. S. Atl. XLIII f. 16 (22?).

Fresh water: Sweden (Rosslängen in Kalmar län)! Finland (Savolaks)! Scotland (Atl.), Bengal! Illinois! Brazil (Caldas)! Ecuador!

Forma minor. — L. 0,035 to 0,07; B. 0,008 to 0,01 mm. Striæ 13 to 14 in 0,01 mm. — A. S. Atl. XLIII f. 23.

Fresh water: Bengal! Australia (Blue Mountains)! Pensacola (Atl.), California!

Var. *turgidula* GRUN. Ms. V. strongly gibbous in the middle. L. 0,048 to 0,07; B. 0,012 mm. Striæ 12 in 0,01 mm.

Fresh water: Waltham Mass.!

Var. *undulata* CL. — V. with three slight inflations. L. 0,11; B. 0,012 mm. Striæ 12 in 0,01 mm.

Fresh water: Sweden (Lake Rosslängen in Kalmar län)!

Var. *lævis* CL. L. 0,083; B. 0,017 mm. Area smooth. Striæ 8 to 12 in 0,01 mm. — A. S. Atl. XLIII f. 18.

Fresh water: New Zealand! Australia (Blue Mountains)!

45. **P. singularis** A. S. (1876). — V. gibbous in the middle, with cuneate and capitate ends. L. 0,106; B. 0,019 mm. Median line straight, with approximate central pores and comma-

like terminal fissures. Area very broad, linear, slightly widened in the middle. Striæ 8 in 0,01 mm. — A. S. Atl. XLIII f. 20.

Fresh water: Celebes (Atl.).

46. **P. integra** Grun. Ms. — V. linear, with parallel margins, or slightly gibbous in the middle. Ends cuneate, often subcapitate. L. 0,11 to 0,12; B. 0,016 to 0,017 mm. Median line flexuose, with approximate central pores and small, semicircular, terminal fissures. Area broad, linear, gently dilated in the middle. Striæ 7 in 0,01 mm., almost parallel, not interrupted. — A. S. Atl. XLIII f. 19.

Fresh water: America (Crane Pond, Waltham Mass.)! French Pond (Atl.).

The median line is bordered on each side by a silicious rib.

47. **P. nodosa** Ehr. (1838). — V. more or less distinctly triundulate, with capitate to rostrate ends. L. 0,055 to 0,075; B. 0,009 to 0,012 mm. Median line filiform, with approximate median pores and semicircular terminal fissures. Axial area wider than a third of the breadth of the valve. Striæ 8 to 10 in 0,01 mm. parallel, more or less convergent at the ends, interrupted or not.

Forma genuina. — Ends rostrate. Striæ 8 to 9 in 0,01 mm. parallel throughout, uni- or bilaterally interrupted. — *Nav. nodosa* Ehr. Inf. p. 179 Pl. XIII f. 9? M. G. XVII: 2 f. 12, 13. Grun. Verh. 1860 p. 521, Pl. IV f. 21. *N. (Pinn.) nodosa* Greg. M. J. 1856 Pl. I f. 5. A. S. Atl. XLV f. 56 to 58.

Fresh water: Scotland (Greg.)! France (Lac Gerardmer, Vosges)! America (Canada, French Pond, Albany)!

Forma capitata. — Ends capitate. Area often punctate. Striæ 10 to 11 in 0,01 mm., convergent at the ends. — *Pinnularia isocephala* Ehr. M. G. V: 3 f. 21? *P. monile* Ehr. M. G. XVII: 1 f. 12?

Fresh water: Sweden (Lake Rosslängen in Kalmar län)! America (Houghton, Michigan)!

Var. *Formica* Ehr. (1843). — V. triundulate, with strongly inflated middle and capitate ends. L. 0,08 to 0,09; B. 0,014 mm. Striæ 9 in 0,01 mm., interrupted in the middle, convergent at the ends. — *Nav. Formica* Ehr. Am. p. 130. M. G. IV: 3 f. 8. *Pinnul. polyonca* Lewis Proc. Ac. N. Sc. Philad. 1861 p. 67 Pl. II f. 7. *Nav. peripunctata* Brun. D. Esp. n. p. 37 Pl. XVI f. 11, 1891.

Fresh water: N. America (Waltham, Mass.! N. Jersey to Savannah, Lewis).

48. **P. parva** (Ehr. 1843?) Greg. (1854). — V. linear, gradually tapering from the middle to the obtuse or capitate ends. L. 0,04 to 0,07; B. 0,007 to 0,013 mm. Median line filiform with approximate central pores and semicircular terminal fissures. Axial area broad, lanceolate. Striæ 9 to 10 in 0,01 mm., almost parallel, convergent at the ends, frequently uni- or bilaterally interrupted. — *Stauroptera parva* Ehr. Am III: 1. f. 19? *P. parva* Greg. M. J. II Pl. IV f. 11. *Nav. parvula* Ralfs Pritch. Inf. p. 908 (1861). Grun. Foss. D. Öst. Ung. p. 143 Pl. XXX f. 37. *Nav. gibba var. brevistriata* V. H. Syn. p. 78 Pl. VI f. 5. A. S. Atl. XLIII f. 21. *Nav. gibba forma. curta* Bleisch Rabh. Alg. Sachsens N:o 951 (1860). *Nav. biglobosa* Schum. P. D. II Nacht. f. 48? *Nav. curtestriata* Pant. III Pl. XII f. 188 (1893). *Nav. (peregrina var.?) curtestr.* Pant. II p. 44 Pl. II f. 19 (1889).

Fresh water: Sweden! Finland! Scotland (Greg.). Holstein! Dresden! Hungary, foss. Grun., Java! Australian Alps! New Zealand! North America (Crane Pond, Illinois)! Argentina!

Var. *Lagerstedtii* Cl. — L. 0,025 to 0,033; B. 0,005 to 0,008 mm. Striæ 8,5 to 10 in 0,01 mm. — *Nav. parvula* Lagst. Spitsb. D. p. 26 Pl. II f. 4 1873.

Fresh water: Beeren Eiland, Spitsbergen (Lagst.).

Var. *Novæ Zealandiæ* Cl. — L 0,032; B. 0,008 mm. Striæ 12 in 0,01 mm. interrupted on both sides of the central nodule.

Fresh water: New Zealand (Rotomahana)!

49. **P. modesta** Grun. (1882). — V. linear-lanceolate with obtuse ends. L. 0,035; B. 0,007 mm. Median line with approximate central pores. Area broad, lanceolate. Striæ 21 to 22 in

0,01 mm. parallel, convergent at the ends. -- *Nav. modesta* GRUN. Foss. D. Öster. Ung. p. 143 Pl. XXX f. 39.

Fresh water: Hungary, foss. Grun., Ecuador (Riobamba)!

VII. Majores.

Artificial key.

1.	Terminal fissures in contrary directions	2.
	— — — the same	3
2.	Ends broad, rounded	*P. Flamma* A. S.
	-- subcapitate	*P. Flammula* A. S.
3.	Striæ parallel or slightly radiate	4.
	-- radiate	5.
4.	Area broad	*P. macilenta* EHB.
	narrow	*P. secernenda* A. S.
5.	Band across the striæ broad	6.
	-- — -- narrow or indistinct	7.
6.	Elliptic-lanceolate	*P. Dactylus* EHB.
	Linear with broad, rounded ends	*P. lateritata* CL.
7.	Area very narrow	8.
	- moderately broad	9.
8.	Striæ slightly radiate	*P. conspicua* A. S.
	strongly —	*P. oregonica* CL.
9.	Valve with undulate margins	*P. Esox* EHB.
	Margins not undulate	10.
10.	Ends triangular	*P. trigonocephala* CL.
	— rounded or subcuneate	*P. major* KÜTZ.

50. **P. macilenta** (EHB. 1843) CL. --- V. linear, with broadly obtuse ends. L. 0,11 to 0,15; B. 0,017 to 0,02 mm. Median line broad, oblique, not complex; its central pores approximate and the terminal fissures comma-like. Axial area wide, less than a third of the breadth of the valve, linear, scarcely widened in the middle. Striæ parallel, 8 to 9 in 0,01 mm. crossed by a narrow band. - EHB. Am. 21 f. 23? M. G. I f. 7; I: 3 f. 13. CL. Diat. of Finland p. 24 Pl I f. 27.

Fresh water: Sweden (Lake Wenern, Lake Rosslängen in Kalmar län)! Finland (Nyland, Pudasjärvi)! Hungary (Bory, fossil)! America (Pine spring, Hermico Co. Va, Deby Coll.)!

51. **P. secernenda** A. S. (1876). — V. linear, with broadly rounded subcapitate ends and slightly gibbous middle. L. 0,17; B. 0,021 mm. Median line oblique with approximate central pores. Axial area narrow, not dilated around the central nodule. Striæ 7 to 8 in 0,01 mm. almost parallel. — *Nav. sec.* A. S. Atl. XLIII f. 13.

Fresh water: Laconia U. S. A. (Atl.).

52. **P. trigonocephala** CL. N. Sp. -- V. linear, gibbous in the middle and at the broadly cuneate, subcapitate ends. L. 0,17 to 0,2; B. 0,026 mm. Median line narrow, its central pores approximate. Terminal fissures comma-shaped. Axial area narrow, linear, slightly dilated in the middle. Striæ 7 in 0,01 mm. slightly divergent in the middle and convergent at the ends. Bands not visible. -- Pl. I f. 21.

Fresh water: America (Waltham Mass., Hudson River, Deby Coll., Big Lake S. Calif. Deby Coll.)!

53. **P. conspicua** A. S. (1876). V. linear, gibbous in the middle and at the ends. L. 0,11 to 0,13; B. 0,018 to 0,019 mm. Median line filiform, with approximate central pores and semi-circular terminal fissures. Area very narrow, slightly dilated around the central nodule. Striæ 11 in 0,01 mm. slightly divergent in the middle, elsewhere almost parallel. - *Nav conspicua* A. S. Atl. XLIII f. 10, 11.

Fresh water: Demerara River!

54. **P. Flamma** A. S. (1876). — V. linear, with broadly rounded ends. L. 0,14 to 0,15; B. 0,025 to 0,02 mm. Axial area very narrow, central orbicular. Striæ subparallel, flexuose, in the middle radiate, 7 to 9 in 0,01 mm., crossed by a broad band. — *Nav. Flamma* A. S. Atl. XLII f. 27, 28.

Fresh water: Demerara River!

55. **P. Flammula** A. S. (1876). — V. linear, with somewhat dilated and capitate ends. L. 0,1; B. 0,015 mm. Axial area narrow, central orbicular. Striæ radiate, 9 in 0,01 mm. *Nav. Flammula* A. S. Atl. XLII f. 26.

Fresh water: Demerara River!

Seems to be only a smaller form of the preceding.

56. **P. oregonica** Cl. N. Sp. — V. linear, slightly triundulate, with cuneate, subacute ends. L. 0,113; B. 0,015 mm. Median line filiform with approximate median pores, and semicircular terminal fissures. Axial area very narrow, widened in the middle to a rhomboid-lanceolate central area. Striæ 11 in 0,01 mm. divergent in the middle, convergent at the ends. — A. S. Atl. XLIII f. 31.

Fresh water: Oregon, fossil!

57. **P. major** Kütz (1833). — V. slender, linear, gibbous in the middle, and at the rounded ends. L. 0,2 to 0,3; B. 0,03 mm. Median line not complex, oblique; terminal fissures commashaped. Area linear somewhat less than a third of the breadth of the valve, scarcely widened in the middle, convergent at the ends, crossed by a narrow band. *Frustulia major* Kütz Syn. p. 19 f. 25? *Nav. maj.* Kütz Bac. p. 97 Pl. IV f. 19, 21. Donk. B. D. p. 69 Pl. XI f. 2. V. H. Syn. p. 73 Pl. V f. 3, 4. A. S. Atl. XLII f. 8.

Fresh water (usually larger lakes): Sweden (Lapland to Skane)! Finland (Russian Lapland to Nyland)! Novaja Zemla! France! Switzerland (Lac Leman)! Japan! New Zealand! America (Canada, Albany, Michigan, Washington Territory)!

Var. *linearis* Cl. — V. linear, not gibbous in the middle, or ends. Area narrower. Striæ 7 in 0,01 mm. — *Pinn. maj.* W. Sm. B. D. XVIII f. 162. *Nav. maj. var. andesitica* Pant. III Pl. VII f. 113 (1893).

Fresh water: Sweden (Lake Rosslängen)! Norway (Stavanger, foss.)! England Sm. Finland (Pudasjärvi, foss.)! Holstein! Germany! Africa (Congo, V. H. Coll.)! America (Monticello New York, Waltham Mass., Demerara)!

Var. *heroina* A. S. (1876). — V. gibbous in the middle and at the subcuneate ends. L. 0,26; B. 0,035 mm. Median line broad, oblique. Area narrow. Striæ 8 in 0,01 mm. slightly divergent in the middle, and convergent at the ends. Bands indistinct. — *Nav. heroina* Atl. XLIII f. 2.

Fresh water: Demerara River!

Var. *asymmetrica* Cl. — V. linear, with broad, obtuse ends. L. 0,14 to 0,26; B. 0,02 to 0,03 mm. Median line asymmetrical, the two halves of it meeting each other in an obtuse angle. — Pl. I f. 22.

Fresh water: America (Eralton Lake Canada, Waltham Mass., Crane Pond, Montgomery Alabama)!

Var. *subacuta* Ehr. (1854). — V. linear, with parallel margins and cuneate ends. Area narrow. Striæ 7 to 7,5 in 0,01 mm. *Pinnul. subacuta* Ehr. M. G. XXXV A 6 f. 12. — A. S. Atl. XLIII f. 30 to 32.

Fresh water: Demerara River! Caldas, Brazil!

Var. *turgidula* Cl. — V. strongly gibbous in the middle and at the ends. L. 0,17 to 0,28; B. 0,034 to 0,04 mm. Striæ 7 to 8 in 0,01 mm.

Fresh water: America (Monticello, Troy, Sierra Nevada)!

This form is very similar to *P. latevittata var. Domingensis*, from which it differs only by a narrower band across the striæ.

Var. *transversa* A. S. (1876). — V. very slender. L. 0,17 to 0,22; B. 0.02 mm. Median line very broad and oblique. Striæ 9 in 0,01 mm. *Nav. transversa* A. S. Atl. XLIII f. 5 to 6.

Fresh water: Finland (Sodankylä)! America (Monticello)! Australia (South Yarra)!

58. **P. Esox** Ehb. (1843). — V. triundulate, with obtuse ends. L. 0,08 to 0,145; B. 0,012 to 0,022 mm. Median line not complex, narrow. Terminal fissures comma-like. Area linear, narrow, less than $^1/_3$ of the breadth of the valve. Striæ 8 to 10 in 0.01 mm., divergent in the middle, convergent at the ends, crossed by a narrow band. — Am. I: 2 f. 4? Schum. Pr. D. I Pl. IX f. 36? Cl. Diat. of Finl. p. 24 Pl. I f. 3. Hérib. D. d'Auvergne p. 82 Pl. IV f. 4.

Fresh water: Sweden (Älmten in Kalmar län)! Finland (Sodankylä)! Greenland! Puy de Dôme, fossil (Hérib.), America (Maine, Brun Coll.)!

59. **P. latevittata** Cl. N. Sp. — V. linear, with broad, rounded ends. L. 0,18; B. 0,033 mm. Median line not complex, oblique; terminal fissures comma-shaped. Axial area broad, less than $^1/_3$ of the breadth of the valve, widened in the middle. Striæ 6 in 0.01 mm., divergent in the middle, convergent at the ends, crossed by a very broad band. - A. S. Atl. XLII f. 5.

Fresh water: Puerto Monte, Chile, foss.! Ecuador!

Var. *Domingensis* Cl. V. slender, gibbous in the middle and at the ends. L. 0.15 to 0,36; B. 0,022 to 0,04 mm. Striæ 6 to 8 in 0,01 mm. — A. S. Atl. XLIII f. 3. Cl. Diatomiste II Pl. VII f. 3.

Fresh water: North America (Cherryfield, Atl.), West Indies, Jamaica and St. Vincent (Grove Coll.)! San Domingo (Witt Coll.)! Ecuador!

60. **P. Dactylus** Ehb. (1843). V. subelliptic-linear, with rounded, obtuse ends. L. 0,17 to 0,32; B. 0,03 to 0,05 mm. Median line gently undulate, not complex. Central nodule large, excentric; terminal fissures comma-shaped. Axial area moderately wide, about $^1/_3$ as broad as the valve, irregularly linear-lanceolate. Striæ 4,5 to 5 in 0,01 mm., crossed by a broad band. — Am. p. 132 Pl. IV: 1 f. 3. *P. Gigas* Ehb. Am. p. 133, II: 3 f. 1. *Navicula Dactylus* A. S. Atl. XLII f. 3, 4, 6. *Nav. Dac. forma maxima* V. H. Syn. Pl. V f. 1. *Nav. Gigas* A. S. Atl. XLII f. 1.

Fresh water: Sweden (Lapland to Halland)! Norway! Finland! Scotland (Premnay Peat)! France (Lac Gerardmer Vosges)! America (common: most diatomaceous earths)!

Var. *horrida* Hérib. a. Perag. (1893). — L. 0,16; B. 0,025 mm. Area with irregularly scattered spines. Striæ 7 in 0,01 mm. *Nav. maj. var. horr.* Hérib. a. Perag. D. d'Auvergne p. 83 Pl. IV f. 3.

Fresh water: Puy de Dôme (fossil).

Var. *Demeraræ* Cl. Linear, with subcuneate ends. L. 0,14; B. 0,034 mm. Striæ 5,5 in 0,01 mm. — A. S. Atl. XLIII f. 29.

Fresh water: South America (Demerara River)!

Var. *Dariana* A. S. (1876). — V. lanceolate, with obtuse ends. L. 0,18 to 0,21; B. 0,044 0,045 mm. Median line oblique, not complex, with comma-shaped terminal fissures. Axial area broad, less than $^1/_3$ of the breadth of the valve, widened in the middle. Striæ 7 to 8 in 0,02 mm., divergent in the middle, convergent at the ends, crossed by a broad band. *Nav. Dariana* A. S. Atl. XLII f. 24, 25.

Fresh water: America, Crane Pond! Sebasta Co. Calif.! Neuse River (Atl.), Darien (Atl.).

VIII. Complexæ.

Artificial key.

1.	Central area a transverse fascia.	2.
	— — not — —	4.

2. { Valve large. L. 0,15 to 0,2 mm. . . . . *P. cardinalis* Ehb.
   { — small L. 0,08 to 0,12 mm. . . . . 3.

3. { Striæ 7 to 7,5 in 0,01 mm. . . . . *P. æstuarii* Cl.
   { 9 to 12 — — . . . . *P. isostauron* Grun.

4. { Valve gibbous in the middle and at the ends . . . . 5.
   { — not — — — — — . . . . 6.

5. { Striæ 4,5 to 5 in 0,01 mm. . . . . *P. nobilis* Ehb.
   { — 7 in 0,01 mm. . . . . *P. gentilis* Donk.

6. { Striæ parallel or slightly radiate . . . . 7.
   { — strongly radiate . . . . *P. distinguenda* Cl.

7. { Valve with parallel margins . . . . *P. streptoraphe* Cl.
   { — — convex — . . . . 8.

8. { Striæ 4,5 to 5 in 0,01 mm. . . . . *P. flexuosa* Cl.
   { — 6,5 (to 15) in 0,01 mm. *P. viridis* Nitzsch.

61. **P. viridis** Nitzsch (1817). — V. elliptic-linear, with parallel margins, attenuated towards the rounded ends. L. 0,14 to 0,17; B. 0,02 to 0,024 mm. Median line complex; terminal fissures comma-shaped. Axial area linear, narrow, about 1/5 of the breadth of the valve, slightly widened around the central nodule. Striæ 6,5 to 7,5 in 0,01 mm. slightly divergent in the middle and convergent at the ends, else almost parallel, crossed by a distinct band, about 1/3 of the length of the striæ. — *Bacillaria viridis* Nitzsch Pl. IV f. 1 to 3. *Pinnul. viridis* Ehb. Inf. p. 182. *Nav. viridis* Kütz Bac. p. 97 Pl. XXX f. 12. A. S. Atl. XLII f. 11 to 14, 19, 21, 22, 23. V. H. Syn. p. 73 Pl. V f. 5. *Pinnul. medioconstricta* Rabh. A. Sachsens N:o 952 (1860). *Nav. Gutwinskii* Pant. III Pl. XIV f. 217 (1893)?

Fresh water: Sweden (Lapland to Skane)! Norway! Finland (Russian Lapland to Ladoga)! Belgium (V. H.), Germany (Franzenbad Dept.)! Hungary (Dubravica Dept. Grun.). Italy (Livorno, Atl.), Australia (Talbot River, Victoria)! New Zealand! America (Illinois, California, Ecuador, Brazil)!

Var. *intermedia* Cl. (1891). — V. linear. L. 0,075 to 0,11; B. 0,014 to 0,015 mm. Area about 1/4 of the breadth of the valve. Striæ 8 to 9 in 0,01 mm. divergent in the middle, convergent at the ends, crossed by a narrow band. *Nav. major* A. S. A. Atl. XLII f. 9, 10. *Pinn. virid. var. int.* Cl. D. of Finl. p. 22. *Nav. viridis* Pant. III Pl. VII f. 119 (1893)?

Fresh water: Sweden (Lapland, Småland)! Finland! Scotland (Atl.), Congo (V. H. Coll.)! Java! Australia (Blue Mountains)!

Var. *commutata* Grun. (1876). — V. linear. L. 0,05 to 0,09; B. 0,01 mm. Area narrow, widened in the middle. Striæ 10 to 12 in 0,01 mm. divergent in the middle, convergent at the ends. Bands indistinct. — *Pinnul. viridis* W. Sm. XVIII f. 163 *a'*. *Nav. commutata* Grun. A. S. Atl. XLV f. 35 to 37. *Pinn. Heufleri* Pedicino Ischia Pl. II f. 17 (1867). *Pinn. sudetica* Hilse Rab. A. Eur. N:o 1023 (1861). *Nav. decumana* Pant. III Pl. XXXV f. 499 (1893)?

Fresh water: Sweden (Upsala, Rosslängen in Smaland)! Finland (Russian Lapland to Ladoga)! England Sm., Scotland (Lock Canmor Atl.), Germany (Harz, Atl.), France (Lac Gerardmer, Vosges)! Tasmania! America (Canada, Waltham Mass., S:ta Rosa Calif., Sierra Nevada, Rio Purus Brazil)!

Similar to *Pinn. vir. var. commutata* is *Pinn. oblongo-linearis* Kostowsky (Materialy 1888 p. 23 Pl. XVII f. 5) but this form has wider striæ, about 6 in 0,01 mm.

Var. *leptogongyla* (Ehb.?) Grun. (1876). — V. linear with parallel margins, or slightly gibbous in the middle. Ends rounded. L. 0,08; B. 0,01 mm. Area narrow, strongly dilated in the middle to a rhomboid-orbicular space. Median line filiform. Terminal fissures semicircular. Striæ 10 in 0,01 mm., divergent in the middle, convergent at the ends. — *Nav. leptogongyla* Grun. in A. S. Atl. XLV f. 26 to 28. *Nav. Tabellaria* Donk. B. D. p. 70 Pl. XII f. 4?

Slightly brackish water: Eger, Franzenbad foss.!

Var. *fallax* Cl. — L. 0,045 to 0,095; B. 0,009 to 0,016 mm. Area very narrow. Striæ 10 to 12 in 0,01 mm., almost parallel, frequently uni- or bilaterally interrupted. — *Pinnul. viridis* β W. Sm.

Br. D. XVIII f. 163 *β*. *Nav. semicruciata* A. S. Atl. XLIV f. 43? XLIII f. 24. *Nav. viridis var. commutata* V. H. S. p. 73 Pl. V f. 6. A. S. Atl. XLV f. 10, 11.

Fresh water: Sweden (Lapland to Småland)! Belgium (V. H.), Germany (Harz Atl., Eisleben Atl.). Australia (Waltham Mass., Monticello, Sierra Famatina Argent., Rio Purus Brazil)!

According to VAN HEURCK's Syn. the valves of the same frustule are dissimilar, the striæ being in one uninterrupted and in the other unilaterally interrupted. This variety, confounded with the preceding, is distinguished by its almost parallel striæ.

Var. *semicruciata* GRUN. (1882). — V. large. Striæ unilaterally interrupted. — *Nav. viridis var. semicruciata* GRUN. Foss. D. Öster. Ung. p. 143.

Fresh water: Hungary, foss. (Grun.).

Var. *rupestris* HANTZSCH (1861). — L. 0,04 to 0,065; B. 0,007 to 0,012 mm. Area very narrow. Striæ 13 to 15 in 0,01 mm. divergent in the middle, convergent at the ends. — *Pinnul. rup.* HANTZSCH Rab. Alg. E. N:o 1203. *Nav. rup.* A. S. Atl. XLV f. 38 to 44.

Fresh water: Sweden (Top of the mountain Åreskutan! Vernamo, foss., Atl.), Norway! Finland! Denmark (Ringkiöbing, Atl.). Holstein! Iceland! Scotland (Braemar, Edinburgh, Loch Canmor, Atl.). Saxony! America (Cherryfield)! Martinique!

Var. *dispar* SCHUM. (1862). — Area unilateral. L. 0,05 to 0,06 mm. Striæ 7 in 0,01 mm. — *Nav. dis.* SCHUM. P. D. I Nachtr. p. 189 f. 50.

Fresh water: Königsberg, foss. (Schum.).

62. **P. distinguenda** CL. (1891). — V. linear to elliptic-linear, with rounded ends. L. 0,10 to 0,18; B. 0,02 to 0,026 mm. Median line distinctly complex; central nodule large, excentric; terminal fissures comma-like. Axial area broad, about $^1/_3$ of the breadth of the valve, irregularly linear-lanceolate, unilaterally widened in the middle. Striæ 7 in 0,01 mm., strongly divergent in the middle and convergent at the ends, crossed by indistinct bands. — *Nav. viridis* KÜTZ. Bac. IV f. 18. *Pinnul. viridis* W. SM. f. 163 *a*. *Pinnul. viridis var. distinguenda* CL. D. of Finl. p. 22 Pl. I f. 1. *Nav. Hyrtlii* PANT. III Pl. XVII f. 257 (1893)? *Nav. viridis var. fossilis* PANT. III Pl. XII f. 193 (1893). *Nav. paripinnata* PANT. III Pl. XVIII f. 263 (1893)?

Brackish or fresh water: Sweden (Carlshamn and Södertelge Depts.)! Finland! Hungary (Bory Dept.)! Kamtschatka! Africa (Congo V. H. Coll.)! Australia (South Yarra, Tasmania)! New Zealand! America (Houghton foss., Michigan Shasta Co and S:ta Rosa Cal., Washington Territory, Sierra Famatina, Argent.)!

63. **P. gentilis** DONK. (1873). — V. linear, with parallel margins and broadly rounded ends. L. 0,14 to 0,25; B. 0,022 to 0,036 mm. Median line slightly complex, with somewhat approximate central pores and comma-shaped terminal fissures. Axial area narrow, less than $^1/_3$ of the breadth of the valve. Striæ 7 in 0,01 mm., divergent in the middle, convergent at the ends, crossed by a moderately broad, not very distinct, band. — *Nav. gentilis* DONK. Br. D. p. 69 Pl. XII f. 1. A. S. Atl. XLII f. 2.

Fresh water: Sweden (Lapland to Upland)! Finland! England (Donk., Atl.), Schlesien (Gronowitz foss.)! United States (Salem Mass., Waltham Mass.)!

64. **P. nobilis** EHR (1840). — V. linear, slightly gibbous in the middle and at the broadly rounded ends. L. 0,25 to 0,35; B. 0,034 to 0,05 mm. Median line complex, with somewhat approximate central pores and comma-shaped terminal fissures. Axial area linear, less than $^1/_3$ of the breadth of the valve, slightly widened around the central nodule. Striæ 4,5 to 5 in 0,01 mm. divergent in the middle, convergent at the ends, crossed by a distinct band, $^1/_3$ as broad as the length of the striæ. — Ber. 1840 p. 214. W. SM. Br. D. XVIII f. 161. *P. mesogongyla* EHR. p. p. M. G. VI: I f. 5. *Nav. nobilis* KÜTZ Bac. p. 98 Pl. IV f. 24. DONK. Br. D. p. 68 Pl. XI f. 1. V. H. Syn. p. 73 Pl. V f. 2. A. S. Atl. XLIII f. 1.

Fresh water: Sweden (Lapland to Småland)! Norway (Stavanger Dept.)! Finland! England! Scotland! Ireland! France! Switzerland (Br.), Italy (Livorno, foss.)! America (Salem and Boxford Mass., Big Lake Cal. Montgommery Ala., Washington Terr. all foss.)!

Var. *neogena* GRUN. (1882). L. 0,215; B. 0,032 to 0,036 mm. Area broader. Striæ 5 in 0,01 mm. — *Nav. nob. var. neog.* GRUN. Foss. Diat. Öster. Ung. p. 143 Pl. XXX f. 41. PANT. III Pl. IX f. 159.

Fresh water: Dubravica, Hungary, foss. (Grun.).

Var. *fossilis* PANT. (1889). — L. 0,12 to 0,21; B. 0,018 to 0,033 mm. Striæ 6,5 to 8 in 0,01 mm. — PANT. II p. 51.

Fresh water?: Bory Hungary (Pant.).

65. **P. flexuosa** CL. N. Sp. — V. linear to elliptic-linear, with rounded ends. L. 0,22 to 0,27; B. 0,04 to 0,048 mm. Median line complex. Central nodule large, excentric; terminal fissures comma-shaped. Axial area broad, somewhat less than 1/3 of the breadth of the valve, not, or very slightly, widened in the middle. Striæ 4,5 to 5 in 0,01 mm., slightly divergent in the middle and convergent at the ends, crossed by broad, distinct bands. — Pl. I f. 23.

Fresh water: Canada (Eralton Lake)! United State (Cherryfield, Crane Pond)!

This form is nearly akin to *P. nobilis*, but closely resembles *P. Dactylus*, from which species it differs principally by its complex median line.

66. **P. streptoraphe** CL. (1891). — V. linear with parallel margins and broad, rounded extremities. L. 0,18 to 0,26; B. 0,03 mm. Median line strongly complex; terminal fissures comma-shaped. Axial area moderately narrow, less than 1/3 of the valve, not widened in the middle. Striæ almost parallel, 5 in 0,01 mm., crossed by a broad and distinct band. — *Nav. sp.* A. S. Atl. XLII f. 7. *Nav. viridis var. sublinearis* GRUN. Franz Jos. L. D. p. 98 Pl. I f. 22. *Pin. streptoraphe* CL. Diat. of Finl. p. 23.

Fresh water: Franz Jos. Land (Grun.), Sweden (common in most diatomaceous earths from Lapland to Småland)! Finland! England (Premnay Peat, Loch Leven)! France (Lac de Grandlieu Loire infér.)! N. America (common in most diatomaceous earths, for inst. Nova Scotia, New York, Massachusetts, California)!

Var. *styliformis* GRUN. (1884). L. 0,116; B. 0,0125 mm. Striæ 7 in 0,01 mm. Area narrow. — EHB. M. G. XXXVIII: 17 f. 6? *Nav. viridis var. stylif.* GRUN. Franz Jos. L. D. p. 98 Pl. I f. 21.

Fresh water: Franz Josefs Land (Grun.).

Var. *minor* CL. (1891). — L. 0,055 to 0,1; B. 0,015 to 0,016 mm. Area distinct. Striæ slightly radiate, 6,5 in 0,01 mm., interrupted on one or both sides of the central nodule. *Nav. viridis* A. S. Atl. XLII f. 20. *Pinnul. viridis var. minor* CL. Diat. of Finl. p. 22 Pl. I f. 2.

Fresh water: Sweden (Rosslängen Smål., Ebbetorp Dept. Smål.)! Finland!

67. **P. isostauron** (EHB. 1843?) GRUN. (1880). — V. linear, with parallel margins and rounded ends. L. 0,03 to 0,07; B. 0,008. Median line flexuose, axial area narrow, widened around the central nodule to a transverse fascia. Striæ parallel 9 to 12 in 0,01 mm. — *Stauroptera isostauron* EHB. Am. p. 135 f. 1. M. G. XVI: 1 f. 7? *Nav. viridis var. icostauron* GRUN. A. D. p. 27 Pl. I f. 14. *Nav. icostauron var. conifera* BRUN a. HÉRIB. D. d'Auvergne p. 91 Pl. II f. 2.

Fresh water: Greenland! Iceland! Kara Sea (Grun.), Sweden (Förarm in Asnen, Upsala)! Finland! Puy du Dôme (fossil). Colorado (Brun Coll.)!

Stauroptera isostauron of EHRENBERG is very doubtful and may perhaps denote some forms of *Pinn. divergens*, scarcely the species of GRUNOW, which is closely related to *P. Aestuarii* CL. *P. isostauron* may perhaps more properly be placed in the group *Gracillimæ*.

68. **P. Aestuarii** CL. N. Sp. — V. linear, with parallel margins and rounded ends. L. 0,10 to 0,12; B. 0,016 mm. Median line flexuose; terminal fissures semicircular. Axial area moderately

broad, linear. Central area a transverse fascia, reaching to the margin. Striæ parallel, 7 to 7,5 0,01 mm. — Pl. 1 f. 16.

Slightly brackish water: Sweden (postglacial deposit of Ebbetorp in Kalmar Län)! Mouth in of Delaware! Connecticut!

69. **P. cardinalis** Ehr. (1840). — V. linear, with broad, rounded ends. L. 0,15 to 0,2; B. 0,03 to 0,035 mm. Median line distinctly complex, central pores approximate, terminal fissures comma-shaped, small. Axial area wide; central area a broad transverse fascia, reaching to the margin. Striæ 5 in 0,01 mm., slightly divergent in the middle and convergent at the ends, crossed by a broad band. — *Stauroptera cardinalis* Ehr. Berl. Abh. 1840 p. 213 (accord. to Chase). *Pinnul. cardinalis* W. Sm. Br. D. I Pl. XIX f. 166. *Nav. cardinalis* A. S. Atl. XLIV f. 1, 2. V. H. Syn. p. 74 Suppl. Pl. A f. 5.

Fresh water: Sweden (Lapland to Småland foss.)! Finland! Ireland, Scotland (Loch Leven, Ordie Deposit), Belgium (V. H.), Italy (Livorno, Atl.), Switzerland (Brun).

IX. Marinæ.

Artificial key.

1.	Asymmetrical	2.
	Symmetrical	3
2.	Striæ strongly radiate	*P. Stauntonii* Grun.
	— slightly —	*P. ambigua var. Digitus* A. S.
3.	Axial area broad	4.
	— narrow or indistinct	5.
4.	Valve narrow	*P. ambigua* Cl.
	— broad	*P. Temperei* Brun.
5.	Central nodule stauroid	*P. bistriata* Leud. Fortm.
	— not —	6.
6.	Central area large, orbicular	7.
	— — a transverse fascia	10.
7.	Striæ crossed by a blank band	8.
	— not — — —	9.
8.	Valve linear	*P. Trevelyana* Donk.
	— lanceolate	*P. Grœnlandica* Cl.
9.	Striæ 3 to 4 in 0,01 mm.	*P. excellens* Cl.
	— 8 to 10 — —	*P. rectangulata* Greg.
10	Valve biconstricted	*P. Claviculus* Greg.
	— constricted in the middle	11.
	— not or slightly constricted in the middle	12.
11.	L. 0,1 mm.	*P. lobata* Grove a. Sturt.
	L. about 0,035 mm.	*P. constricta* Cl.
12.	Axial area indistinct	13.
	— — narrow	14.
13.	Striæ parallel	*P. quadratarea* A. S.
	— radiate in the middle, convergent at the ends	*P. cruciformis* Donk.
14.	Striæ 12 in 0,01 mm.	*P. cruciata* Cl.
	— 15 to 20 —	*P. floridana* Cl.

70. **P. ambigua** Cl. N. Sp. V. linear, with rounded ends. L. 0,033 to 0,078; B. 0,007 to 0,008 mm. Central nodule small, terminal nodules small, approximate to the margin. Area broad, linear, not widened in the middle. Striæ short, parallel, 8 to 9 in 0,01 mm., with capitate terminations. — *Nav. retusa* Grun. A. D. p. 38 (1880). Cl. Vega p. 470 Pl. XXXVI f. 35.

Marine: Lysekil (Bohuslän, Sweden, Grun.), Oldenburg (Grun.), Cape Wankarema!

The frustule is according to Grunow, in the zone-view more or less constricted in the middle and more or less broad. The connecting zone has numerous punctate longitudinal divisions

Nav. retusa Brén. seems to be a form, akin to *Nav. cancellata*, and therefore entirely different from this species, which I have, with much hesitation, placed in Pinnularia.

Var. (*Amphora*) *Digitus* A. S. (1875). — V. asymmetrical. L. 0,05 to 0,1; B. 0,007 to 0,012 mm. Axial area asymmetrical, a little broader on the dorsal side. Striæ 8 in 0,01 mm., not distinctly punctate. Frustule rectangular. Connecting zone with several faint longitudinal divisions, which are finely transversely lineate; lineolæ 24 in 0,01 mm. *Amphora Digitus* A. S. Atl. XXVI f. 30. Cl. and Grove Diatomiste I p. 67 Pl. X f. 11 to 13.

Marine: North Sea! Guernsey (Grove Coll.)! Balearic Islands! Macassar Straits! China!

71. **P. bistriata** Leud. Fortm. (1879). — V. linear, with rounded ends. L. 0,055 to 0,065; B. 0,009 mm. Central nodule transversely dilated. Axial area narrow; central area a broad, transverse fascia. Striæ 10 in 0,01 mm. radiate in the middle, transverse or convergent at the ends. — *Stauroneis bistriata* Leud. Fortm. D. Ceylon Pl. IX f. 89.

Marine: Mediterranean Sea (Barcelona)! Ceylon (Leud. Fortm.). Labuan!

I have seen only two valves of this characteristic form and I have placed it in Pinnularia with great hesitation.

72. **P. quadratarea** A. S. (1874). — V. narrow, linear, with parallel margins and broad rounded extremities. L. 0,04 to 0,09; B. 0,011 mm. Median line with small terminal fissures. Axial area indistinct or very narrow; central area a broad fascia. Striæ parallel, 8 to 10 in 0,01 mm. — *Nav. Pinnularia* Cl. (1868) Sv. N. D. p. 224 Pl. IV f. 1, 2. *Nav. quadrat.* A. S. N. S. D. p. 90 Pl. II f. 26.

Marine: Arctic Seas (Arctic America, Spitsbergen, Finmark, Novaja Zembla, Cape Wankarema)! North Sea (Bohuslän, Sweden)! Mediterr. (Balearic Islands)! Australia Sydney!

This species was first described by me as *Nav. Pinnularia*, and later by A. Schmidt as *Nav. quadratarea*, but as my specific name would be inadmissible I have given preference to the name of A. Schmidt. It is a very variable species, of which a great number of forms has been described as distinct species, but as they are closely connected I have united them. The chief distinction consists in the outline and the number of striæ. Closely connected with some of the varieties (Var. *fluminensis* etc.) are *P. floridana* Cl. and *P. cruciata*. On the other hand the var. *Théelii* approaches to *P. cruciformis* Donk. The varieties may be arranged in the following series.

A. *Forms with linear, not constricted valves.*

Var. *baltica* Grun. (1880). — B. 0,008. Striæ 9 in 0,01 mm. — *Nav. Pinn. var. balt.* Grun. A. D. p. 27.

Brackish water: Baltic (Grun.).

Var. *Seychellensis* Grun. (1880). — V. short, linear, with rounded ends. B. 0,011 mm. Striæ 12 in 0,01 mm. — *Nav. Pinn. var. Seych.* Grun. A. D. p. 28.

Marine: Seychelles (Grun.).

Var. *Söderlundii* Cl. (1880). — V. linear, with rounded ends. L. 0,036 to 0,045; B. 0,006 to 0,007 mm. Striæ 13 to 16 in 0,01 mm. — *Nav. Pinn. var. Söderl.* Cl. A. D. p. 28.

Marine: Davis Strait! Balearic Islands! Tahiti!

Var. *Tahitensis* Grun. (1880). — V. linear, with subcuneate ends. B. 0,009 mm. Striæ 13 in 0,01 mm. — *Nav. Pinn. var. Tah.* Grun. A. D. p. 28.

Marine: Tahiti (Grun.).

Var. *interrupta* Cl. (1883). — V. linear, with subcuneate ends. L. 0,08; B. 0,02 mm. Striæ 9 in 0,01 mm., crossed by irregular, longitudinal, blank bands. — *Nav. Pinn. var. interr.* Cl. Vega p. 463 Pl. XXXVI f. 21.

Marine: Cape Wankarema!

Var. *asymmetrica* CL. (1883). — V. linear, with subcuneate ends. L. 0,08; B. 0,018 mm. Axial area narrow, unilateral. Striæ 8 in 0,01 mm. — *Nav. Pinn. var. asym.* CL. Vega p. 463.

Marine: Cape Wankarema!

Var. *subproducta* GRUN. (1880). — V. linear, with somewhat rostrate ends. B. 0,01 mm. Striæ 12 in 0,01 mm. — *Nav. Pinn. var. subp.* GRUN. A. D. p. 28.

Brackish water: Baltic (Grun.).

Var. *amphiglottis* GRUN. (1884). — V. linear, with protracted ends. L. 0,115 mm. — *Nav. Stuxbergii var. amphigl.* GRUN. Franz Josefs Land D. p. 104.

Brackish water: North Siberia (Grun.).

B. *Forms with subelliptical to sublanceolate valves.*

Var. *Stuxbergii* CL. (1880). — V. lanceolate, with broad, rounded or subcuneate ends. L. 0,059 to 0,1; B. 0,016 to 0,017 mm. Striæ 10 to 12 in 0,01 mm. (finely punctate according to Grunow). — *Nav. Stuxbergii* CL. A. D. p. 13 Pl. I f. 15.

Marine: Sea of Kara! Cape Wankarema!

Var. *leptostauron* GRUN. (1884). — V. elliptic-linear. L. 0,04 to 0,057; B. 0,012 to 0,013 mm. Central fascia with three indistinct striæ. Striæ 11 in 0,01 mm. — *Nav. Stuxbergii var. leptost.* GRUN. F. Jos. Land D. p. 103 Pl. I f. 32.

Marine: Franz Josefs Land (Grun.).

Var. *subcontinua* GRUN. (1884). — V. elliptic. L. 0,04; B. 0,014 mm. Central fascia with one or two indistinct striæ. — *Nav. Stuxbergii var. subc.* GRUN. Fr. Jos. Land D. p. 103 Pl. I f. 33.

Marine: Franz Josefs Land (Grun.).

Var. *Theelii* CL. (1880). — V. lanceolate, with rostrate, obtuse ends. L. 0,055; B. 0,017 mm. Striæ slightly radiate, 10 to 12 in 0,01 mm. — *Nav. Theelii* CL. A. D. p. 13 Pl. I f. 22.

Marine: Kara! Cape Deschneff.

C. *Forms constricted in the middle.*

Var. *fluminensis* GRUN. (1860). — V. linear, slightly constricted in the middle, with broad, rounded extremities. L. 0,047; B. 0,008 mm. Striæ 11 in 0,01 mm. — *Nav. fluminensis* GRUN. Verh. 1860 p. 520 Pl. III f. 7. A. D. p. 28.

Marine: Kara! Adria (Grun.), Ceylon! Seychelles!

Var. *kerguelensis* GRUN. (1880). — V. linear, constricted in the middle. L. 0,057; B. 0,009 (middle) to 0,012 (end) mm. Striæ 8,5 to 10 in 0,01 mm. — *Nav. fluminensis var. kerg.* GRUN. A. D. p. 28.

Marine: Kerguelens Land!

Var. *minor* GRUN. (1880). — L. 0,032; B. 0,005 (middle) to 0,006 (end) mm. Striæ 15 in 0,01 mm. — *Nav. flumin. var. minor* GRUN. A. D. p. 28 Pl. I f. 12.

Marine: Finmark!

Var. *Lóczyi* PANT. (1889). — V. linear, slightly constricted in the middle, with cuneate ends. L. 0,081; B. 0,007 (middle) to 0,0145 (ends) mm. Striæ 17,5 in 0,01 mm. — *Nav. Lóczyi* PANT. II p. 50 Pl. VI f. 114.

Marine: Bremia Dept. Hungary (Pantoczek).

I have not seen original specimens and am therefore uncertain whether this form really belongs to *P. quadratarea* or whether it is a *Caloneis*.

73. **P. Claviculus** GREG. (1857). — V. linear, with two constrictions, dividing the valve into three segments, of which the median one is the smallest. L. 0,038 to 0,048; B. in the middle 0,006, at the ends 0,007 mm. Median line with approximate central pores and distant terminal pores. Axial area indistinct; central area a broad, transverse fascia. Striæ parallel, 12 to 13 in

0,01 mm., radiate at the ends. *Nav. Clavic.* GREG. D. of Clyde p. 478 Pl. IX f. 5. A. S. N. S. D. Pl. II f. 28. PANT. II Pl. VI f. 110.

Marine: North Sea (Coasts of Scotland Greg.) Sweden! Balearic Islands! Bremia, foss. Hungary (Pant.).

Var. *javanica* CL. — L. 0,04; B. 0,009 mm. Striæ 18 in 0,01 mm. parallel. — Pl. I f. 24.

Marine: Java!

74. **P. cruciformis** DONK. (1861). V. linear, often slightly inflated in the middle, with broad, rounded ends. L. 0,03 to 0,12; B. 0,01 to 0,014 mm. Median line with rather approximate central pores, and hook-shaped, large terminal fissures. Axial area indistinct, central area a broad fascia, dilated outwards and reaching to the margin. Striæ 10—12 in 0,01 mm. radiate in the middle, convergent at the ends, crossed by a faint longitudinal depression. — *Nav. cruc.* DONK. M. J. (N. S.) I p. 10 Pl. I f. 7. B. D. p. 65 Pl. X f. 4. A. S. N. S. D. Pl. II f. 25. V. H. Syn. p. 74 Suppl. A f. 8.

Marine: Finmark! North Sea (coasts of Sweden, England and Belgium)! Baltic (Travemünde Dannf.). West Indies! Cape Horn! Seychelles!

Var. *brevior* CL. (1883). — L. 0,035; B. 0,009 mm. Striæ 14 in 0,01 mm. — CL. Vega p. 464 Pl. XXXV f. 18.

Marine: Cape Deschneff!

Var. *upolensis* GRUN. (1880). — L. 0,058; B. 0,01 mm. Striæ 14 in 0,01 mm., slightly radiate. — GRUN. A. D. p. 28.

Var. *Seychellensis* GRUN. (GRUN. 1880). — V. lanceolate, with broad, rounded ends. L. 0,043; B. 0,01 mm. Striæ 10 to 12 in 0,01 mm., strongly radiate. — *l. c.*

Nav. elata LEUD. FORTM. (D. de Ceylon p. 27 Pl. III f. 28, 1879) seems to belong either to *P. cruciformis* or to *Achnanthes inflata* GRUN.

75. **P. cruciata** CL. (1881). — V. linear, slightly constricted in the middle. L. 0,087; B. 0,017 (in the middle 0,014) mm. Median line with small terminal fissures, and approximate central pores. Axial area narrow; central a broad fascia, narrowed outwards. Striæ 12 in 0,01 mm. parallel. — *Nav. cruc.* CL. N. R. D. p. 6 Pl. I f. 11.

Marine: Greenland(?)

76. **P. floridana** CL. (1881). — V. slightly constricted in the middle. L. 0,045 to 0,075; B. 0,01 to 0,012 (ends), 0,008 to 0,009 (middle) mm. Axial area narrow, distinct; central area a broad, transverse fascia. Striæ almost parallel, 15 (middle) to 20 (ends) in 0,01 mm. *Nav. fluminensis var. floridana* CL. N. R. D. p. 6 Pl. I f. 10.

Marine: Pensacola (Florida)!

77. **P. excellens** CL. (1890). V. linear, slender, slightly constricted in the middle, with cuneate ends. L. 0,3; B. 0,03 (middle) to 0,043 (ends). Median line with approximate central pores and small, curved terminal fissures. Axial area narrow, linear, slightly widened in the middle, where on each side of the central nodule is a linear marking. Striæ almost parallel, 3 in 0,01 mm., slightly radiate at the ends. — CL. Diatomiste I p. 31 Pl. V f. 6.

Marine: Oamaru Dept., New Zealand (Tempère).

Var. *interrupta* CL. (1890). — L. 0,21; B. 0,022 to 0,029 mm. Striæ 4 in 0,01 mm. Central area a broad, transverse fascia, reaching to the margin. — CL. l. c. p. 31.

Marine: Oamaru Dept., New Zealand (Deby Coll.)!

78. **P. lobata** GROVE a. STURT (1887). — V. panduriform, with subelliptical segments. L. 0,09 to 0,12; B. 0,025 to 0,03; at the constr. 0,015 mm. Median line with approximate central pores and small terminal fissures. Axial area narrow, linear; central area a broad fascia reaching to the

margin and with a linear marking on each side of the central nodule. Striæ 4 in 0,01 mm., slightly divergent in the middle and at the ends. — *Nav. lobata* GROVE a. STURT J. Q. M. Cl. (2) III p. 133 Pl. X f. 12. *Nav. spathifera* GROVE a. STURT A. S. Atl. CLXXIV f. 23.

Marine: Oamaru Dept., New Zealand! San Pedro Dept. (Kinker Coll.)!

79. **P. constricta** CL. N. Sp. — V. small, constricted in the middle, with apiculate ends. L. 0,035; B. 0,01 mm. (at the constr. 0,005 mm.). Terminal fissures small. Axial area narrow; central a transverse, broad fascia. Striæ 8 to 9 in 0,01 mm., parallel. — Pl. I f. 14.

Marine: Galapagos Islands!

80. **P. Temperei** BRUN (1889). — V. broad, with parallel or slightly concave margins, and cuneate, obtuse ends. L. 0,14 to 0,15; B. 0,045 to 0,055 mm. Median line with distant central pores and small, hook-shaped, terminal fissures, bordered on each side by lines, divergent towards the middle of the valve. Area wide, lanceolate, dilated around the central nodule. Striæ 7 to 8 in 0,01 mm. in the middle radiate, and sometimes alternately longer and shorter, parallel at the ends. *Nav. Temperei* BRUN Diat. du Japon p. 45 Pl. V f. 1. A. S. Atl. CLXXIV f. 24.

Marine: Sendaï Dept. Japan!

81. **P. Trevelyana** DONK. (1861). — V. linear, slightly gibbous in the middle and at the broad, rounded ends. L. 0,1 to 0,15; B. 0,02 to 0,025 mm. Median line excentric towards the ends and somewhat flexuose, bordered on each side by a longitudinal line. Terminal fissures large, hook-shaped. Axial area narrow, linear. Central area large, orbicular. Striæ strongly radiate in the middle and convergent at the ends, 10 in 0,01 mm., crossed by a narrow depression. — *Nav. Trev.* DONK. M. J. I (N. S.) p. 8 Pl. I f. 2. Br. D. p. 66 Pl. X f. 6. V. H. Syn. p. 74 Suppl. A f. 5, 6. *Pinn. T.* Rabh. E. A. p. 210.

Marine: North Sea (Coasts of Sweden, England, Scotland, Belgium)! Florida (Pensacola)! Japan!

Var. *angusta* CL. — V. linear. L. 0,1 to 0,16; B. 0,01 to 0,015 mm. Striæ 9 to 10 in 0,01 mm. *Nav. Trev. var. hungarica* PANT. III Pl. XLII f. 575 (1893)?

Marine: Gulf of Naples! Sumatra (Deby Coll.)! Galapagos Islands! Bermudas (Rae Coll.)!

Stauroneis Brébissonii CASTR. (Chall. Voy. p. 24 Pl. XV f. 4) appears to be akin to *P. Trevelyana.*

82. **P. groenlandica** CL. (1881). — V. lanceolate, with rounded ends. L. 0,117; B. 0,023 mm. Median line central, angularly bent towards the central nodule. Terminal fissures hook-shaped. Axial area narrow, linear; central area large, orbicular. Striæ strongly radiate in the middle, convergent towards the ends, 6 to 7,5 in 0,01 mm., crossed by a narrow lateral area. *Nav. groenl.* CL. N. R. D. p. 7 Pl. I f. 13.

Marine: Davis Strait!

83. **P. rectangulata** GREG. (1857). — V. linear, frequently slightly gibbous in the middle and at the ends. L. 0,065 to 0,1; B. 0,015 to 0,02 mm. Median line central, with strong, hook-shaped terminal fissures. Axial area indistinct; central area large, rounded-quadrate. Striæ strongly radiate in the middle, convergent at the ends, 8 to 10 in 0,01 mm. — *Nav. rect.* GREG. D. of Clyde p. 479 Pl. IX f. 7. DONK. B. D. p. 66 Pl. X f. 5. V. H. Syn. p. 74 Suppl. A f. 7. *Nav. Regula* GRUN. in Cl. D. West Ind. p. 5 Pl. I f. 3. *Nav. lumen* PERAG. Villefr. p. 45 Pl. II f. 19. *Pinnul. rect.* RABH. E. A. p. 215.

Marine: North Sea (Coasts of Sweden, Scotland, England, Belgium)! Mediterranean (Perag.). Labuan! West Indies! Campeachy Bay (Grun.).

Forma *subundulata* GRUN. (1882). V. with slightly undulate margins. — CL. M. D. No 301.

Marine: Firth of Tay!

84. **P. Stauntonii** GRUN. (1882). V. asymmetrical, linear, convex, slightly gibbous in the middle, with broad, rounded ends. L. 0,053; B. 0,01 mm. Median line excentric, with hook-shaped

terminal fissures. Axial area indistinct; central area a broad fascia, widened towards the margins. Striæ strongly radiate in the middle, convergent at the ends, 9 to 10 in 0.01 mm. Zonal view of the frustule rectangular with strongly divergent striæ. — *Alloioneis Stauntonii* GRUN. Cl. M. D. 304. Foss. D. Öst. Ung. p. 142 Pl. XXX f. 36. *Amphora naviculacea* DONK. M. J. 1861 p. 11 Pl. 1 f. 12?

Marine, æstuaries: Scotland!

Amphora EHR. (1840).

The first known species of Amphora is *A. ovalis*, described as *Navicula Amphora* by EHRENBERG 1831. The genus *Amphora* was established by the same author 1840 (Ber. p. 11). In the »Bacillarien» KÜTZING 1844 described 18 species only, but this number was greatly increased by GREGORY (Diat. of Clyde 1857), who named 32 new species and first made the distinction between forms with complex and not complex connecting zone. Several other authors have since added new species and in the year 1873 Professor H. L. SMITH published (Lens p. 65) a synopsis of all the known forms. By the issue of the plates XXV to XXVIII (1875) and XXXIX, XL (1876) of A. SCHMIDT'S Atlas the number of species was greatly increased. Since then new species have been added, and in the Sylloge of DE TONI (1891) the number amounts to 221.

An inspection of these species shews that it is impossible to give any diagnosis of the genus Amphora, which is sufficient to distinguish it from Cymbella. The following seems to be the only possible diagnosis of Cymbella and Amphora together:

Naviculoid diatoms, with both valves similar and asymmetrical along the longitudinal axis.

The distinction between *Amphora* and *Cymbella* is, so far I can see, no other than the degree of asymmetry; the ventral and dorsal side of Cymbella being in the same plane, but in Amphora in planes crossing each other in an angle, which is variable.

Amphora and Cymbella are only asymmetrical forms of Naviculæ, belonging to different types. There are in the same species gradual passages from perfectly symmetrical to asymmetrical amphora-like forms (as in *Trachyneis aspera*). In several groups of Navicula more or less asymmetrical forms occur (for instance *Pinnularia Stauntonii* and others, formerly named *Alloioneis*) so closely connected with the symmetrical that it would be unnatural to separate them. The asymmetrical form is not a sufficient characteristic for a natural family, but is merely a facies, which may occur in groups of very different types and seem to depend on the method of growth, Amphoræ occuring attached to algæ and other objects. This genus is in short to be considered, as well as *Achnanthes* and *Cocconeis*, as degenerated forms. To trace the origin of these forms is in most cases difficult, as the intermediate passages are lost or unknown, but we may get some approximate knowledge of the original types by the study of the structure of the valve and by comparing it with that of different types of Navicula.

The Cymbellæ appear, to a great extent, to be asymmetrical forms of the section *Naviculæ lineolatæ*, and the same may be the case with the still imperfectly known *Amphora labuensis*.

Amphora Clevei is no doubt nearly akin to the genus *Trachyneis*.

Amphora elegans PERAG. is with great probability allied to the section *Naviculæ orthostichæ*.

As to the other large number of Amphoræ, they may be classed in forms with and without longitudinal lines. Those with lines are probably asymmetrical forms of *Diploneis* or allied genera. There are in some species of this section forms with a structure so closely resembling that of Diploneis that the idea of their connection presents itself at once to the mind, notwithstanding the different shape of the valves. In the large *Amphora nodosa* we have a form with coarse, transverse costæ, alternating with rows of ocelli, as in *Diploneis Beyrichiana*, *D. lesi-*

nensis and *D. prisca*. In others, as in *Amphora egregia*, we meet with transverse costæ, alternating with double rows of puncta or alveoli, exactly as in *Diploneis gemmata*, and many others. The space between the longitudinal and median lines correspond to the furrows of Diploneis. The ventral side of the valve, which has been more modified than the dorsal side, retains still in many cases a longitudinal crest, although all other structure has disappeared. In some forms the longitudinal line of the dorsal side fades away, and there is left of it only a blank space, as in forms of *Amphora ovalis:* in others no trace of it is perceptible, although other characteristics remain marking the affinity with forms which possess distinct longitudinal lines. The forms with longitudinal lines on the dorsal side may be classed in two groups, viz. with complex, and not complex, connecting zone. I propose for the former the name *Diplamphora*, founded on their supposed relation to Diploneis, and for the latter I reserve the name *Amphora*, sensu strictiori.

There is another group of forms, which have a longitudinal crest not on the dorsal, but on the ventral side. These forms, which I include in the group *Calamphora*, are of doubful relationship.

Akin to Calamphora is a group of forms with a row of costæ on the ventral side but without the longitudinal crest. All of these, known at present, are fossil, and I propose for them the name *Archiamphora*.

A large group of Amphora is of the type of *A. coffæiformis* or *A. salina*. They are without longitudinal lines, but have a complex zone, protracted, and frequently, capitate ends. Their striæ are more or less distinctly punctate. I include these forms in the group *Halamphora*, but am unable to trace their connection with any of the divisions of Navicula.

Another group of *Amphora*, characterized by a complex zone, absence of longitudinal lines, and distinctly punctate striæ, constitutes the the group *Oxyamphora*. There can scarcely be any doubt that this group of forms, many of which have a stauros, is akin to the *Microstigmaticæ* among the Naviculæ, particularly the subdivision *Stauroneis*.

The same may be the case with the two groups *Amblyamphora* and *Psammamphora*, both characterized by the direction of the median line, absence of longitudinal lines, by their finely punctate striæ, but differing in the simple or complex nature of the zone.

As *Cymbamphora* I regard forms, which have great resemblance to *Cymbellæ*, but not distinctly punctate striæ. The zone is simple, not complex. I am unable to trace their connection with other groups of naviculoid diatoms.

There remain some forms, which I cannot comprise under groups above named, and which I treat of in an appendix.

If the above named large groups of Amphoræ were admitted as distinct genera, which I believe they ought to be, the synonymy would be still more intricate than it is at present. I propose for this reason, that the species of the different groups should retain their generic name Amphora, which in all cases signifies that they are asymmetrical Naviculæ. This will also afford an opportunity of testing my views, which are entirely new, before admitting the proposed new genera.

In many Amphoræ, belonging to different groups, a peculiar, structureless, very hyaline limbus occurs, which seems to be a flat plate projecting from the dorsal side of the valve. I am in doubt how to regard this peculiar organ, which perhaps may correspond to the wing in the genus *Tropidoneis*. As specimens of the same species are found with and without this limbus, it seems not to be of great importance for the distinction of species.

Subgenus **Amphora** Cl.

Frustules in outline usually elliptical, with truncate ends. Connecting zone broader on the dorsal than on the ventral part, without longitudinal divisions and not transversely striate or costate. Valve asymmetrical, more or less lunate. Median line biarcuate. Dorsal part of the valve in some species with a keel at a longer or shorter distance from the median line, in some with a more or less distinct, blank, narrow band across the striæ, in some without any keel or longitudinal band. Structure: usually rows of coarse puncta or strong, transverse costæ crossed by longitudinal costæ, producing a network of more or less regular quadrate alveoli. Ventral part of the valve without a keel, but in some cases with a narrow blank band across the striæ, rarely without striæ, frequently with short, radiate striæ.

A. Proteus with cell-contents (ventral and dorsal side) 600 times magnified.

The living cell is known in few forms only. *A. ovalis*, contains a single chromatophore-plate along the ventral side of the zone and the inside of the valves. At the end of the ventral side it has a broad and deep sinus. It has also a narrow and deep sinus from the margin towards the central nodule. Central plasma-mass and nucleus distinct (PFITZER Bau and Entw. p. 82 Pl. IV f. 8, 9). *A. Proteus* has also a single chromatophore-plate along the ventral side of the zone and extending along the valves towards the dorsal side. — On conjugating, two frustules form two auxospores, the longitudinal axis of which crosses the longitudinal axis of the mothercells (CARTER, Ann. a. Mag. Nat. Hist. 2 ser. XVII 1856 p. 2 Pl. I f. 13 to 20. BORSCOW Süssw. Bac. p. 111 Pl. 13 f. 2 *a* to *g* 1873).

Artificial key.

1. { Very small forms. L. 0,006 to 0,01 mm . . . . *A. perpusilla* GRUN.
Length 0,02 to 0,04 mm. . . . . 2.
— more than 0,04 mm. . . . . 4.

2. { Ventral side not striate . . . . *A. behringensis* CL.
— — striate . . . . 3.

3. { Central area distinct . . . . *A. ovalis var. Pediculus.*
— — indistinct . . . . *A. Pusio* CL.

4. { Frustule rather rectangular . . . . 5.
— — elliptical . . . . 7.

5. { Ventral side striate in its whole length . . . . 6.
— — — at the ends only . . . . *A. Weinckii* JAN.

6. { Longitudinal line distinct . . . . *A. javanica* A. S.
— — indistinct . . . . *A. arenicola* GRUN.

7. { Dorsal side longitudinally angularly bent . . . . *A. dubia* A. S.
— — not — — — . . . . 8.

8. { Median line on an elevated keel . . . . *A. Schmidtii* GRUN.
— — not very elevated . . . . 9.

9. { Longitudinal line on the dorsal side distinct . . . . 10.
— — — — — not — . . . . 13.

10. { Striæ (or costæ) 4 in 0,01 mm. . . . . *A. nodosa* BR.
— — 6 to 7 — — . . . . 11.

11. { Central area large . . . . *A. Oculus* A. S.
— — indistinct . . . . 12.

12. { Ventral side throughout striate . . . . *A. mexicana* A. S.
— — striate along the median line and at the ends . . . . *A. gigantea* GRUN.

13. { Striæ 6 to 7 in 0,01 mm. . . . . 14.
— 10 to 14 — — . . . . 15.

14. { Ventral side striate . . . . *A. robusta* GREG.
— — not — . . . . *A. valida* PER.

15. { Ventral side striate . . . . 16.
— — not — . . . . *A. Ovum* CL.

16. { Marine species . . . . 17.
Fresh water — . . . . *A. ovalis* KÜTZ.

17. { Striæ on the ventral side crossed by a blank line . . . . *A. Proteus* GREG.
— — — — not — — — — *A. marina* V. H. (*A. Proteus v. contigua*).

1. **A. behringensis** CL. N. Sp. Frustule elliptical, with truncate ends. L. 0,028; B. 0,014 mm. V. lunate, acute. L. 0,028; B. 0,006 mm. Median line nearly straight. Axial area of the dorsal side broad. Ventral side not striate, very narrow. Dorsal striæ 15 to 16 in 0,01 mm. not crossed by a longitudinal line. — Pl. III f. 34, 35.

Marine: Behring Island!

This small species seems to connect this group with the Cymbamphora.

2. **A. Ovum** CL. N. Sp. — Frustule broadly elliptical, very convex. L. 0,04; B. 0,025 mm. Median line nearly straight, approximate to the ventral margin. Axial area on the dorsal side not distinct. Striæ on the dorsal side 10 to 11 in 0,01 mm. composed of obscure granules and not crossed by a longitudinal line. Ventral side narrow, structureless. — A. S. Atl. XXVI f. 40 (without name). Icon. n. Pl. IV f. 12.

Marine: Balearic Islands! Java (Atl.).

3. **A. dubia** (GREG. 1857?) A. S. (1875). Frustule in outline elliptical. L. 0,04 to 0,08; B. 0,016 to 0,02 mm. Zone very narrow. V. angularly bent along a line combining the ends, so that it, if seen from the end, appears composed of two laminæ in an angle of about 60°. Outline of the valve lunate, with arcuate exterior, straight interior margins and acute ends. Median line straight, approximate to the ventral margin. Axial area moderately broad on the dorsal side of the median line. Ventral part of the valve linear, narrow, without striæ and longitudinal line. Dorsal side strongly transversely striate, especially on the exterior part. Striæ 10 in 0,01 mm. coarsely punctate; puncta 12 in 0,01 mm. — D. of Clyde p. 514 Pl. XIII f. 76? A. S. Atl. XXVII f. 20 to 26. Icon. n. Pl. IV f. 5, 6.

Marine: Coasts of Norway! Balearic Islands! Barcelona! Adriatic! Campeachy Bay (Atl.), Singapore (Atl.), Java!

A. dubia of GREGORY seems to be some species of Amphora in the state of division, scarcely the very characteric and isolated species, figured in Atlas. The form of the valve is generally difficult to make out, but I succeded with the aid of slides, mounted, by Mr THUM in which the valves were placed on their extremities. They presented themselves like segments of an orange. There is no species akin to *A. dubia*.

4. **A. valida** PERAG. (1888). — Frustule broadly elliptical, with rounded ends. L. 0,07 to 0,08 mm. Valve broadly lunate. Median line approximate to the ventral margin. Axial area on the dorsal side indistinct. Ventral side not striate. Dorsal side with 5 to 6 coarsely punctate striæ in 0,01 mm. — D. Villef. p. 40 Pl. III f. 25.

Marine: Villefranche, Medit. (Perag.).

This species, unknown to me, has the form of *A. Ovum* but is much larger.

5. **A. Weisckii** JAN. (1876). — Frustule rectangular, with parallel margins. L. 0,06; B. 0,013 mm. Valve linear, with gibbous ends. Median line straight. Axial area narrow, on the dorsal side moderately broad, with some few oblique striæ at the ends. Dorsal part with about 14 striæ in 0,01 mm. — A. S. Atl. XXXIX f. 20.

Marine?

This species, which I know only from the A. S. Atl., seems to be very characteristic and requires a more complete examination.

6. **A. Pusio** CL. — Frustule in outline broadly elliptical, with truncate ends. L. 0,025 to 0,027; B. 0,017 mm. Median line strongly biarcuate. Central nodule large. Axial and central areas not distinct. Dorsal and ventral side with strong striæ, about 14 in 0,01 mm., not interrupted and not distinctly punctate. — Pl. III f. 40.

Brackish water, marine: Coast of Sweden (Cl. M. D. N:o 157); Balearic Islands! Hilo, Sandwich Islands (in almost fresh water).

This little form scarcely belongs to *A. ovalis* and is remarkable for the strongly striate dorsal and ventral sides, as well as for the absence of central area. Perhaps a small form of the following. *A. Proteus var. parvula* FLÖGEL Pommerania Exp. p. 89 f. 10 may represent this form.

7. **A. marina** (W. SM. 1857?) V. H. (1880). — Frustule in outline elliptical or orbicular, with truncate ends. L. 0,04; B. 0,025 mm. V. lunate, with subacute ends and slightly concave ventral margin. L. 0,04 to 0,06; B. 0,01 to 0,013 mm. Median line slightly biarcuate. Axial and central areas not distinct on the dorsal side. Striæ 15 in 0,01 mm. coarsely punctate, not interrupted or crossed by a longitudinal line. Ventral side narrow, striate as the dorsal side. A. N. H. 1857 p. 7 Pl. I f. 2? V. H. Syn. p. 58 Pl. I f. 16. A. S. Atl. XXVII f. 14, 17, 18. *A. pellucida* GREG. D. of Clyde p. 513 Pl. XII f. 73? *A. nana* FLÖGEL Pommerania Exp. p. 90 f. 12?

Marine: North Sea! Balearic Islands! Seychelles! China! Porto Seguro (Deby Coll.)!

A. marina of W. SM. is too badly figured for identification. According to ARNOTT (M. J. VI p. 206) *A. marina* is identical with *A. Proteus* of GREG., but if so the striæ are incorrectly stated as 40 in 0,001". *A. pellucida* GREG. is too imperfectly described and figured for admitting of identification, but it seems to be the same as *A. marina*. *A. marina* is doubtful as a species, probably a form of A. Proteus.

8. **A. Proteus** GREG. (1857). Frustule elliptical with truncate ends, about twice as long as broad. Valve lunate, obtuse. L. 0,04 to 0,065; B. 0,005 to 0,016 mm. Median line biarcuate. Axial area indistinct on the dorsal side. No central area. Striæ on the dorsal side 9 to 13 in 0,01 mm. not interrupted and coarsely punctate. Ventral side striate, especially towards the ends. Striæ radiate, approximate to the median line and crossed by a narrow, blank band. — D. of Clyde p. 518 Pl. XIII f. 81. A. S. Atl. XXVII f. 3. *A. Prot. var. Kariana* GRUN. A. D. p. 21 Pl. I f. 7 (1880). *A. hexagonalis* O. WITT Mus. Godeffroi I p. 66 Pl. VIII f. 12? *A. speciosa* CASTR. Voyage Challenger p. 17 Pl. XXVII f. 1?

Marine: Greenland! Spitsbergen! Finmark! Sea of Kara! Cape Deschneff! North Sea! S:t Helena! Campeachy Bay! Mediterranean Sea! Black Sea! Seychelles! China! Galapagos Islands!

Var. *contigua* CL. — Striæ on the ventral side not crossed by a blank, narrow band. — A. S. Atl. XXVII f. 7 to 9. Probably also XXVIII f. 4.

Marine: North Sea! Adriatic! Labuan! New Caledonia!

Var. *alata* CL. — V. L. 0,13; B. 0,032 mm. Dorsal side with a projecting hyaline limbus in the middle. Striæ 12 in 0,01 mm.

Marine: Baltjic Dept. (Van Heurck Coll.)!

9. **A. robusta** GREG. (1857). — Frustule in outline broadly elliptical, with truncate ends. L. 0,065 to 0,17; B. 0,038 to 0,12 mm. Valve lunate with arcuate dorsal margin and straight ventral margin. Median line strongly biarcuate. Axial and central area indistinct on the dorsal side. Dorsal side with strong striæ, 6 to 7 in 0,01 mm., not crossed by a longitudinal line, coarsely punctate; puncta about 8 in 0,01 mm. Ventral side broad, with a more or less broad band of coarse radiate striæ along the median line. — D. of Clyde p. 516 Pl. XIII f. 79.

Marine: Spitsbergen (striæ 10 in 0,01 mm.)! North Sea! Mediterranean Sea! Adriatic! Macassar Straits! Japan (fossil)! Samoa!

Var. *fusca* CL. — Connecting zone with a number of small, irregular puncta, giving it a brownish colour. L. 0,12; B. 0,075 mm. Striæ 6 in 0,01 mm.

Marine: China (Deby Coll.)!

Var. *subplicata* CL. — Connecting zone with traces of longitudinal divisions and longitudinal rows of puncta. L. 0,115; B. 0,045 mm. Striæ 8 in 0,01 mm.

Marine: S:ta Monica, Cal. fossil (Deby Coll.)!

A. robusta is nearly related to *A. Proteus* and differs principally by the coarse striæ and larger size. *A. oblonga* GREG. (D. of Clyde p. 515 Pl. XIII f. 78) seems to be a form of *A. robusta*, but I have never met with any perfectly similar form.

10. **A. javanica** A. S. (1875). — Frustule rectangular, about three times longer than broad. L. 0,045 to 0,06; B. 0,017 to 0,02 mm. Zone not complex. Axial area narrow, dilated on the dorsal side around the central nodule. Keel or longitudinal line on the dorsal side very distinct. Striæ 12 in 0,01 mm. composed of elongated distant puncta. Ventral side striate, except in the middle. Striæ 12 in 0,01 mm. curved, composed of some few elongated, large puncta or crossed by an undulating narrow line. — Atl. XXVII f. 27, 30 to 33.

Marine: Java!

This form is very nearly akin to *A. arenicola*, of which it may be a variety.

11. **A. arenicola** GRUN. (1882). — Frustule nearly rectangular, three times longer than broad. L. 0,038 to 0,07; B. 0,017 to 0,021 mm. Valve in breadth 0,01 mm., linear, with broad, unilaterally rounded ends. Median line slightly biarcuate, distant from the ventral margin. Axial area indistinct on the dorsal side. Central area none or orbicular. Dorsal side with 10 to 14 coarsely punctate, not interrupted, striæ in 0,01 mm. Longitudinal line indistinct. Ventral side broad, with radiate, coarsely punctate striæ, sometimes crossed by a narrow, blank band. — *A. marina var. arenicola* GRUN. in Cl. M. D. N:o 310. *A. marina* Pritch Inf. Pl. V f. 59? *A. arenic.* Icon. n. Pl. IV f. 19, 20.

Marine: Coasts of England and Belgium! China (Deby Coll.)!

Var. *major* CL. — V. in L. 0,1; in B. 0,026 mm. Striæ 8 to 9 in 0,01 mm. composed of large, distant puncta. — *A. robusta* A. S. Atl. XXVII f. 39 to 41. *A. Lima* PANT. III Pl. XXIII f. 347 (1893).

Brackish water: Baltic!

Var. *oculata* CL. — Frustule in L. 0,07; in B. 0,036 mm. Central area on the dorsal side large, rounded. Striæ 11 in 0,01 mm. composed of large, distant puncta. — Pl. IV f. 21.

Marine: Sebastopol!

Var. *subæqualis* CL. — Frustule linear elliptical. L. 0,075; B. 0,032 mm. Median line biarcuate, very distant from the ventral margin, so that the ventral side is almost as broad as the dorsal. Dorsal side with 10 striæ in 0,01 mm., composed of large puncta, 10 in 0,01 mm. Ventral side entirely covered with coarsely punctate striæ. — Pl. IV f. 22.

Marine: China (Deby Coll.)!

12. **A. ovalis** KÜTZ (1833). — Frustule broadly elliptical, with truncate ends. L. 0,01 to 0,06; B. 0,0045 to 0,033 mm. Valve lunate with subacute ends. Median line slightly biarcuate. Axial and central areas on the dorsal side indistinct or distinct. Dorsal side twice as broad as the ventral. Ventral side with a row of short striæ. Dorsal part with 10 to 16 striæ in 0,01 mm. Striæ punctate, not interrupted, or crossed by a somewhat irregular blank band.

Forma typica. Frustule in L. 0,045 to 0,06; B. 0,024 to 0,033 mm. No axial and central area, no longitudinal band on the dorsal side. Striæ 10 to 11 in 0,01 mm. composed of distinct puncta (about 9 in 0,01 mm.). — *A. ovalis* KÜTZ Syn. f. 5, 6. Bac. p. 107. V. H. Syn. p. 59 Pl. I f. 1. H. L. Sm. Types N:o 40.

Fresh water: Sweden! England! France! Germany! Switzerland (Brun), Baltic (Gulf of Bothnia!) Australia, Lake Muir!

Var. *gracilis* EHB. (1843). — As the type, but smaller. L. 0,027; B. 0,01 mm. Striæ about 12 in 0,01 mm. — *A. gracilis* EHB. Am. p. 122 Pl. III: 1 f. 43. *A. ovalis var. gr.* V. H. Syn. p. 59 Pl. I f. 3. A. S. Atl. XXVI f. 101.

Fresh water: Belgium (V. H.), Harz (Atl.).

Var. *libyca* EHB. (1840). — V. lunate. L. 0,055 to 0,08; B. 0,011 to 0,017 mm. Median line slightly biarcuate. Central area distinct on the dorsal side, frequently uniting with an irregular, blank band across the striæ. Striæ on the dorsal side 10 to 11 in 0,01 mm. coarsely punctate; puncta about 8 in 0,01 mm., often uniting near the central nodule. *A. libyca* EHB. Ber. 1840 p. 11 (fide Kütz). KÜTZ Bac. p. 107. *A. affinis* KÜTZ Bac. p. 107. *A. ovalis var. affinis* V. H. Syn. p. 59 Pl. I f. 2. *A. ovalis* A. S. Atl. XXVI f. 102 to 111; Pl. XXVII f. 4, 5? *A. abbreviata* BLEISCH RABH. A. E. 1489 (1863). *A. Szontaghii* PANT. II p. 39 Pl. VII f. 138? *A. Proteus var.* A. S. Atl. XXVIII f. 1? *A. Staubii* PANT. III Pl. X f. 171 (1893)? *A. verrucosa* PANT. III Pl. X f. 166 (1893)? *A. scaris* PANT. III Pl. XXVIII f. 416 (1893)?

Fresh or brackish water: Spitsbergen (Atl.), Greenland! East Cape! Sweden! England! France! Belgium (V. H.), Germany (Saline Dürrenberg! Königsberg, foss.!) Hungary foss. (Pant.)?

Var. *Pediculus* KÜTZ (1844). — Frustule in outline broadly elliptical. Valve lunate. L. 0,02 to 0,04; B. 0,006 to 0,008 mm. Median line slightly biarcuate. Central area distinct and central nodule strong. Striæ 14 to 16 in 0,01 mm. coarsely punctate. Ventral side striate. — *Cymbella? Pediculus* KÜTZ Bac. p. 80 Pl. V f. 8. *A. ovalis δ Pediculus* V. H. Syn. p. 59 Pl. I f. 6. *A. ovalis γ affinis f. minor* (*A. Pediculus major* GRUN.) V. H. Syn. p. 59 Pl. I f. 4, 5. *A. minutissima* W. SM. B. D. p. 20 Pl. II f. 30 (1853). *A. borealis* SCHUM. P. D. I Nachr. p. 23 f. 31 (1863). *A. globosa* SCHUM. P. D. II Nachr. p. 55 Pl. I f. 24 (1867). *A. sp. n.?* A. S. Atl. XXVI f. 102. *A. libyca var. interrupta* PANT. II p. 37 Pl. II f. 28.

Fresh or slightly brackish water, usually attached to larger diatoms, as Nitzschia sigmoidea, or on algæ: Sweden! Finland! England! Belgium! Germany! India (Atl.), New Zealand! Tasmania! Hungary, fossil (Pant.).

Although these varieties are at first sight very dissimilar to each others, they are so intimately connected by intermediate forms that I am entirely of the opinion of GRUNOW and VAN HEURCK that they should be united.

13. **A. perpusilla** GRUN. (1880). Frustule in outline nearly orbicular. L. 0,006 to 0,01; B. 0,004 to 0,005 mm. Valve lunate, with arcuate dorsal, and straight ventral, margin. Central nodule strong. Dorsal striæ 16 to 20 in 0,01 mm. almost transverse. Central area usually not distinct. Ventral side without striæ. — *A. (globulosa var.) perpusilla* GRUN. V. H. Syn. Pl. I f. 11. *A. perp.* V. H. Types N:o 4. *A. ovalis var. δ Pediculus forma minor and exilis* V. H. Syn. p. 59 Pl. I f. 8, 9, 10. *A. Pediculus* A. S. Atl. XXVI f. 99. CL. M. D. 126, 137. *A. globulosa* SCHUM. Preuss. D. II Nachr. p. 55 Pl. I f. 25. A. S. Atl. XXVI f. 100.

Fresh water, moist earth etc.: Sweden (Upsala, Dalsland!) Prussia (Schum.), Belgium (V. H.), England, Swansea! France, Meudon! Hungary, Plattensee (Atl.).

14. **A. mexicana** A. S. (1875). — V. lunate with arcuate dorsal and straight ventral margin. L. 0,15 to 0,20; B. 0,035 mm. Median line more or less biarcuate. Axial area not distinct; central area small and rounded on the dorsal side. Dorsal side with a longitudinal line more or less approximate to the median line. Striæ 6 to 8 in 0,01 mm. coarsely punctate; puncta 6 to 7 in 0,01 mm. Ventral side entirely covered with somewhat radiate striæ. — A. S. Atl. XXVII f. 47 to 48. Icon. n. Pl. IV f. 15. *A. boryana* PANT. III Pl. XXXVIII f. 531 (1893).

Marine: Morocco! Gulf of Naples! Sumatra (Deby Coll.!), China! Galapagos Islands! Gulf of Mexico (Atl.).

Var. *fusca* CL. — Zone with small irregular puncta giving it a brownish colour. L. 0,14; B. 0,075 mm. Striæ 8 in 0,01 mm.

Marine: Macassar Straits!

I am not quite sure about the identification, as the fig. in Atl. shews a more distant longitudinal line than in my specimens. *A. lima* A. S. Atl. Probetaf. f. 14. which is unknown to me, seems to be allied to *A. mexicana*.

15. **A. gigantea** GRUN. (1875). Frustule broadly elliptical with truncate ends. V. lunate, with straight ventral margin. L. 0,09 to 0,17; B. 0,025 to 0,035. Median line strongly biarcuate.

No axial nor central area on the dorsal side. Longitudinal line closely approximate to the median line. Dorsal striæ 6 to 7 in 0,01 mm. coarsely punctate; puncta 7 in 0,01 mm. Ventral side with a row of short striæ along the median line and towards the ends of the valve. Ventral striæ frequently crossed by a longitudinal line. — A. S. Atl. XXVII f. 46. *A. gigantea var. andesitica* PANT. II p. 36; III Pl. XVII f. 243.

Marine: Gulf of Naples! Java! Japan! San Pedro Calif., fossil (Kinker), Campeachy Bay! Pensacola! Colon (Deby Coll.)! Hungary, Bory fossil (Pant.)?

Var. *obscura* CL. V. in L. 0,10 to 0,20, in B. 0,015 to 0,04 mm. Striæ on the dorsal side 6 to 7 in 0,01 mm.; puncta coarse, about 5 in 0,01 mm. forming longitudinal undulating lines. Ventral side with a row of short, radiate striæ along the whole median line. A. S. Atl. Pl. XXVIII f. 20 (without name). Icon. n. Pl. IV f. 28, 29.

Marine: Balearic Islands! Gulf of Naples (Deby Coll.)! Sambava (Kinker Coll.)! Sumatra (Deby Coll.)! Macassar Straits! Campeachy Bay (Atl.).

Forma *minor*. Striæ 8 in 0,01 mm. L. 0,11 mm. — A. S. Atl. XL f. 28, 29.

Marine: S:t Peter, Hungary (fossil)! Leton Bank (Atl.).

Var. *fusca* A. S. (1875). V. in L. 0,07 to 0,12 mm. Dorsal striæ 10 in 0,01 mm. coarsely punctate; puncta 8 in 0,01 mm. Longitudinal line somewhat obscure. Ventral part broad, structureless, except at the ends, where are short sets of oblique, granulate striæ. Zone with irregular small puncta, giving it a brownish colour. *A. fusca* A. S. Atl. XXVII f. 68.

Marine: Gulf of Naples! Red Sea (Van Heurck Coll.)! Java! Labuan! Macassar Straits! Gulf of Mexico (Atl.). Bahia! Galapagos Islands!

16. **A. nodosa** BRUN. (1891). — V. with strongly arcuate dorsal margin, straight ventral margin and broad, rounded ends. L. 0,12 to 0,15; B. 0,042 mm. Median line slightly biarcuate. Dorsal side without axial and central areas, divided into two parts by a longitudinal line (or crest), of which the interior bears short rows of large puncta, and the exterior strong costæ (4 in 0,01 mm.) alternating with rows of large ocelli (4 to 5 in 0,01 mm.), which form longitudinal, slightly undulating lines. Ventral side of the valve narrow, with short and strong costæ. — D. espèces nouv. p. 9 Pl. XII f. 2.

Marine: Nossibé (Brun Coll.)! Japan (Brun). Samoa! Macassar Straits!

One of the largest and stoutest forms of Amphora. The strong central nodule, the crest enclosing, on the dorsal side of the valve, a furrow, recal Diploneis, as does also the structure of transverse costæ, alternating with ocelli.

17. **A. Oculus** A. S. (1875). — V. lunate, with obtuse ends. L. 0,07 to 0,15; 0,02 to 0,04 mm. Median line approximate to the ventral margin, straight or slightly biarcuate. Axial area indistinct; central area large, rounded. Longitudinal line at a considerable distance from the median line. Striæ on the dorsal side 7 to 10 in 0,01 mm., coarsely punctate; puncta about 8 in 0,01 mm. Ventral side narrow, with coarse striæ in its whole length. — Atl. XXVII f. 52. *A. Oc. var. fossilis* PANT. I p. 22 Pl. XIV f. 127. *A. Wachenhusenii* JANISCH A. S. Atl. XL f. 38 (1876).

Marine: Gulf of Naples (Deby, Brun Coll.)! Seychelles (Van Heurck Coll.)! Sumbava (Kinker Coll.)! China (Deby Coll.)! Japan (Atl.), Campeachy Bay (Atl.).

Var. *Farcimen* A. S. (1875). — L. 0,06 to 0,07; B. 0,019 mm. Central area less distinct. Striæ 11 in 0,01 mm.; puncta 10 in 0,01 mm. — *A. Farc.* A. S. Atl. XXVII f. 56, 57.

Marine: Seychelles (Van Heurck Coll.)! Samoa (Atl.). Galapagos Islands! Campeachy Bay (Atl.).

18. **A. Schmidtii** GRUN. (1875). — Frustule in outline elliptical with truncate ends. L. 0,09; B. 0,04 mm. Median line elevated to a biarcuate keel. Dorsal side with coarsely punctate striæ, 9 in 0,01 mm. reaching to the median line. Ventral side also with coarsely punctate striæ. Zone with two or more longitudinal rows of large puncta. — A. S. Atl. XXVIII f. 2.

Marine: China! Samoa (Atl.). Bahia, Rio Janeiro, Porto Seguro (Deby Coll.)!

Forma *major*. — Frustule in L. 0,133; B. 0,06 mm. Striæ 7 in 0,01 mm. — *A. Schm.* A. S. Atl. XXVIII f. 3.

Marine: Campeachy Bay (Atl.).

Forma *minor*. — Frustule in L. 0,07; B. 0,025 mm. Striæ 12 in 0,01 mm.

Marine: Pensacola! Labuan!

Var. *alata* Cl. — As the type, but with a hyaline limbus projecting from the dorsal side L. 0,055; B. 0,035 to 0,045 mm. Striæ 10 in 0,01 mm.

Marine: China! Japan (Brun Coll.)! Barbados! Florida!

Var. *Schleinitzii* Jan. (1876). — Frustule in L. 0,12 to 0,15, in B. 0,066 mm. Zone without puncta. Dorsal side with a hyaline limbus. The striæ 8 in 0,01 mm. coarsely punctate; puncta 7 in 0,01 mm. — *A. Schleinitzii* A. S. Atl. XXXIX f. 9, 10.

Marine: Gulf of Naples (Deby Coll.)! Samoa (Atl.).

I am unable to find any specific difference between *A. Schmidtii* and *A. Schleinitzii*. The structure of the connecting zone is variable. In some specimens I have seen, besides the longitudinal rows of large pearls, very fine scattered puncta, giving it a brownish colour. The absence or presence of a limbus seems also not be of any specific value.

A. Schmidtii is a form of a peculiar type, remarkable for the elevation of the valve to a keel bearing on its summit the median line as in *Auricula*.

Subgenus **Diplamphora** Cl.

Frustule in outline usually elliptical, or rectangular, with rounded, truncate, or rostrate ends, sometimes indented in the middle. Zone with more or less numerous longitudinal divisions, more or less coarsely, transversely, costate or striate. Valve linear to semilanceolate, with obtuse or protracted ends; its dorsal side with one (or two) longitudinal lines. Structure: transverse costæ or rows of puncta. Ventral side structureless, punctate, or costate, with or without longitudinal line.

This group comprises a number of species, very different in appearance, but agreeing in the complex connecting zone and the longitudinal line on the dorsal side. They are nearest akin to Amphora, sensu stricto, but differ in the complex zone. Whether this characteristic be of such importance that the two groups are to be regarded as distinct genera, I cannot at present state with certainty. There are among the Amphoræ some forms with tendency to a complex zone, for instance *A. robusta var. subplicata* and *A. Schmidtii*. In all cases *Amphora* and *Diplamphora* are to be considered as allied groups, having in common a more or less distinct longitudinal line or keel on the dorsal, and frequently also on the ventral, side of the valve. This characteristic as well as the structure of the valve point to a relation to the genus *Diploneis*, although no intermediate forms have hitherto been discovered.

The species of this subgenus are very variable in size and form, and the valves in many cases present very different appearances according to the position, in which they lie. These circumstances make the distinction of species and the construction of an artificial key extremely difficult. All forms of this group are marine and occur in all seas, but in the greatest variety in the tropical. Many of them are found in a fossil state in Hungary, Japan and New-Zealand.

Artificial key.

1.	Frustle indented in the middle	2.
	— not —	9.
2.	Central nodule stauroid	3.
	— — not —	7.
3.	Axial area broad	*A. exsecta* Grun.
	— — narrow or indistinct	4.

4.	Ends of the valve broad and incurved .	. . *A. vetusta* Cl.
	— — not — — . . .	. . . . 5.
5.	Zone dissimilar on the dorsal and ventral side	*A. cuneata* Cl.
	— not — — — — —	. . . . 6.
6.	L. 0,01 to 0,017 mm. . . .	. *A granulifera* Cl.
	L. 0,1 to 0,113 mm. . . .	. *A. Weissflogii* A. S.
7.	Ends of the valve reflexed	. . . *A. Janischii* A. S.
	— — — not	. . . . 8.
8.	Striæ crossed by broad lateral areas .	*A. margaritifera* Cl.
	— not — .	. . *A. alata* Per.
9.	Ends of the valve broad, obtuse, or incurved	10.
	— . not — — .	. . . 20.
10	Structure: quadrate alveoli in longitudinal and transverse rows	*A. tesselata* Grove a. Sturt.
	transverse costæ or rows of puncta	11.
11.	Ventral side of the valve without puncta or costæ .	12.
	— — — with	. . . 13.
12	Costæ 2,3 to 3 in 0,01 mm.	. . *A. Pecten* Brun.
	10 in 0,01 mm.	*A inornata* Cl. (*A. crassa var.*, *A. egregia var.*)
13	Ventral side with two longitudinal rows of puncta	14.
	with punctate or costate striæ . . .	. . . 15.
14.	Dorsal side with one longitudinal line	*A. Gründleri* Grun.
	— — several — lines	. *A. prismatica* Cl.
15.	Ventral side punctate	16.
	— — costate	18.
16.	Rows of puncta on the ventral side crossed by a blank band	. . . 17.
	— — not	*A. crassa* Greg.
17.	Dorsal striæ of large, distant puncta	*A. comorensis* Cl.
	apparently smooth .	*A ornata* Leud. Fortm.
18.	Costæ 4 to 7 in 0,01 mm.	. . . . . . 19.
	12 in — —	. *A. decipiens* Cl.
19	Costæ alternating with double rows of puncta .	. . . . . . *A. egregia* Ehb.
	— not — — — . .	*A. inelegans* Cl. a. Grove.
20.	Dorsal side with two longitudinal lines	21.
	— — — one line	. . . . 22.
21.	Axial area indistinct . .	. . . . *A. areolata* Grun.
	— — distinct	. *A. Lendugeriana* Per.
22.	Longitudinal line approximate to the median line	*A. diaphana* Cl.
	— distant from — — .	23.
23.	Space between the median and longitudinal lines suddenly dilated in the middle	24.
	— — — not — — . . .	26.
24.	Central area structureless .	. . . . 25.
	with scattered puncta	*A. subpunctata* Grove a. Sturt
	— faint striæ .	. . . *A. bioculata* Cl.
25.	Dorsal margin arcuate	*A. gemmifera* Petit.
	— sinuose .	*A. Sturtii* Grun.
26.	Central nodule dilated to a stauros .	*A. capensis* A. S.
	— not stauroid .	. . 27.
27.	Ends of the valve protracted .	28.
	— not	. . . . 29.
28.	Striæ reaching to the longitudinal line	. . *A. proboscidea* Cl.
	across	*A. Grevilleana* Greg.
29.	Striæ 19 to 20 in 0,01 mm	*A. truncata* Cl.
	— 11 to 14 —	. . . . 30.
30.	L. 0,05 to 0,06 mm. . .	. . *A. sulcata* Cl.
	L. 0,1 to 0,13 mm.	. *A Graeffii* Cl.

1. **A. decipiens** Cl. N. Sp. Frustule nearly rectangular, about 3 times as long as broad. L. 0,055; B. 0,02 mm. Zone with distant rows (6 in 0,01 mm.) of puncta (about 11 in 0,01 mm.). V. gibbous in the middle of the ventral margin. L. 0,035 to 0,06; B. 0,02 mm. Ends obtuse. Axial area distinct on the dorsal and ventral side, somewhat dilated in the middle. Crest or

longitudinal line distinct on the dorsal side, at some distance from the median line. Ventral side **striate.** Striæ 12 in 0,01 mm. not distinctly punctate. Striæ crossed by an obsolate longitudinal **band.** — Pl. IV f. 16, 17, 18.

Marine: Labuan!

This species resembles *A. javanica*, from which it differs by the scarcely punctate striæ and the complex zone.

2. **A. crassa** GREG. (1857). Frustule linear-elliptical, with rounded ends. L. 0,05 to 0,1; B. 0,02 to 0,03 mm. Zone with about 3 divisions in 0,01 mm transversely costate; costæ 5 in 0,01 mm. V. linear with obliquely rounded, or subcapitate and incurved, ends. L. 0,015 to 0,09; B. 0,008 to 0,02 mm. Median line biarcuate. Axial and central areas indistinct on the dorsal side. Striæ 5 to 8 in 0,01 mm. punctate, crossed on the dorsal side by a longitudinal line. Ventral side with somewhat radiate rows of puncta. T. M. S. V. p. 72 Pl. I f. 35. D. of Clyde p. 524 Pl. XIV f. 91. FLÖGEL Pommerania Exp. p. 90 f. 11. *A. crassa var.* A. S. Atl. XXXIX f. 30. *A. crassa var. punctata* A. S. Atl. XXVIII f. 30 to 33. PANT I p. 21 Pl. VI f. 46. *A. biseriata* GREG. T. M. S. V p. 71 Pl. I f. 32 (1857)? *A. sulcata* ROPER M. J. VI p. 24 Pl. III f. 7 (1858). *A. thaitiana* CASTR. Voyage Challenger D p. 19 Pl. XXVII f. 15 (1886)?

Marine: Greenland! Spitsbergen! North Sea! Mediterranean! Adriatic! Sumatra! China! Hungary, fossil (Pant.).

Var. *elongata* CL. — V. in L. 0,15 to 0,19; B. 0,02 to 0,022 mm. Rows of puncta 4 to 5 in 0,01 mm.; puncta about 8 in 0,01 mm.

Marine: Gulf of Naples (Deby Coll.)! Macassar Straits!

Var. *campechiana* GRUN. (1875). V. in L. 0,1 to 0,15; B. 0,02 mm. Dorsal striæ 7 to 11 in 0,01 mm. punctate. Longitudinal line distinct. Ventral side with rows of puncta, more distant than on the dorsal striæ. A. S. Atl. XXVIII f. 16.

Marine: Macassar Straits! Campeachy Bay (Atl.). Pensacola!

Var. *interlineata* GROVE and STURT (1887). V. in L. 0,09 to 0,17; B. 0,015 to 0,017 mm. Dorsal striæ 9 in 0,01 mm. punctate; puncta about 20 in 0,01 mm. Longitudinal line distinct. Ventral side with a row of marginal short striæ or puncta. Zone with about 5 divisions in 0,01 mm. transversely striate; striæ 10 in 0,01 mm. *A. interlineata* GROVE and STURT Quek. M. C. J. (2) III p. 131 Pl. X f. 2.

Marine: Oamaru, New Zealand, fossil!

Var. *sölswigiensis* PETIT (1888) p. p. V. in L. 0,13; B. 0,019 mm. Striæ 6 in 0,01 mm. coarsely punctate. Ventral side with a marginal row of small puncta. A. S. Atl. XXVIII f. 17. PETIT D. de Cap Horn p. 120 Pl. X f. 15.

Marine: North Sea (Atl.).

This form is nearly akin to the var. *interlineata*. PETIT quotes as *A. solswigiensis* the fig. 17 and 18 in Atl. Pl. XXVIII, which represent distinct forms, if not species. PETITS own figure (D. de Cap Horn Pl. X f. 15) is too indistinct for deciding what form the author denotes.

Var. *modesta* CL. V. in L. 0,065; B. 0,02 mm. Dorsal side with 6 rows of coarse puncta in 0,01 mm. Longitudinal line distinct. Ventral side with a row of marginal striæ. — A. S. Atl. XXVIII f. 23?

Marine: Tamatave (Kinker Coll.)!

Var. *euprepes* PANT. (1886). V. in L. 0,08 to 0,1; B. 0,018 mm. Dorsal side with 5 to 8 rows of distant puncta reaching to the median line, where the puncta become strong. Longitudinal line indistinct. Ventral side striate at the ends. PANT. I p. 21 Pl. XIV f. 128.

Marine: Morocco (striæ 8 in 0,01 mm.); Hungary, fossil (striæ 5 in 0,01 mm. Pant.).

Var. *degenerata* CL. — L. 0,05 to 0,07; B. 0,009 mm. Dorsal striæ coarse, punctate, 7 to 8 in 0,01 mm. Longitudinal line distinct. Ventral side smooth.

Marine: China! Galapagos Islands!

Var. *seychellensis* Cl. — V. in L. 0,036; B. 0,01 mm. with capitate, incurved ends. Dorsal side with 15 punctate striæ in 0,01 mm. Longitudinal line distinct, approximate to the median line. Ventral side smooth.

Marine: Seychelles (Van Heurck Coll.)!

Var. *minor* Pant. (1889). L. of V. 0,051; B. 0,009 mm. Striæ 15 in 0,01 mm. Ventral side with rows of distant puncta. — Pant. II p. 36 Pl. III f. 51.

Marine: Fossil, Hungary (Pant.).

Var. *spuria* Cl. — V. in L. 0,065 to 0,1 mm.; B. 0,013 to 0,017 mm. Striæ 6 to 7 in 0,01 mm. not distinctly punctate outside the longitudinal line, coarsely punctate inside the longitudinal line. Ventral side with longer or shorter striæ. A. S. Atl. XXVIII f. 21?

Marine: Sumatra (Deby Coll.)! Macassar Straits! Samoa! Magellan's Strait! Colon (Deby Coll.)!

3. **A. Pecten** Brun (1891). Frustule rectangular, twice as long as broad, with somewhat convex margins and truncate ends. Connecting zone with numerous divisions, 2 in 0,01 mm., crossed by smooth, transverse costæ, about 2,5 in 0,01 mm. V. linear with inflated and incurved, acuminate ends. L. 0,16 to 0,22; B. 0,03 mm. Dorsal side with strong, transverse costæ, 2,5 to 3 in 0,01 mm. Spaces between the costæ smooth. Median line biarcuate. Longitudinal line approximate to the median line. Furrow between both lines with a row of large ocelli. Ventral side broad, smooth and with a strong longitudinal line. — D. espèces nouvelles p. 9 Pl. XII f. 4. Cl. a. Grove Diatomiste I p. 157 Pl. XXII f. 5 to 7. *A. prævalida* Janisch Gazelle Exp. Pl. XX f. 21. *A. alveolata* Leud. Fortm. D. de Ceylon p. 19 Pl. I f. 8? *A. scalaris* Castr. Voyage Challenger D. p. 18 Pl. XXVII f. 19?

Marine: Colombo, Ceylon (Le Tourneur Coll.)! Madagascar (Kinker and Van Heurck Coll.)! Nossi Bé (Brun Coll.)! Macassar Straits (Grove Coll.)! Fossil: Oamaru, N. Zeal. (Grove Coll.)! Sn Pedro Calif. (Kinker Coll.)!

Var. *Argus* Cl. — L. of the V. 0,13 to 0,17; B. 0,02 to 0,025 mm. Costæ of the dorsal side 4 in 0,01 mm. alternating with a few ocelli, arranged in longitudinal rows. Ventral side with a strong keel.

Marine: Madagascar (Van Heurck, Brun, Kinker Coll.)! Colon (Deby Coll.)!

4. **A. inornata** Cl. N. Sp. Frustule elliptical. L. 0,056; B. 0,023 mm. Divisions of the zone broad, 5 to 6 in 0,01 mm. Striæ 18 in 0,01 mm. Valve linear, with obtuse ends curved inwards L. 0,065 to 0,166; B. 0,01 to 0,02 mm. Median line almost straight. Longitudinal line rather near the median line. No areas on the dorsal side. Dorsal striæ 10 to 15 in 0,01 mm. smooth. Ventral side structureless. — Pl. IV f. 35, 36, 37, 38.

Marine: Java! Macassar Straits (Grove Coll.)!

5. **A. egregia** (Ehr. 1861?) A. S. (1875). Frustule rectangular with rounded ends, about 2 or 3 times longer than broad. Zone with 2 to 4 divisions in 0,01 mm.; its transverse costæ 5 to 6 in 0,01 mm. V. linear with broad, obtuse ends curved inwards. L. 0,06 to 0,17; B. 0,014 to 0,03 mm. Dorsal side without axial area. Costæ 4 to 6 in 0,01 mm. alternating with double rows of small puncta, about 18 in 0,01 mm., and crossed by a distinct longitudinal line. Ventral side usually with a row of strong, costate striæ, on larger specimens frequently also with a number of minute, irregular puncta. No longitudinal line on the ventral side. Ber. 1861 p. 294 fide Chase? A. S. Atl. XXVIII f. 13, 14. *A. sp.* Atl. XXVIII f. 12, 18. *A. crassa var.* Atl. XXXIX f. 31. *A. sp.* Atl. XXXIX f. 27. *A. exornata* Jan. A. S. Atl. XXXIX f. 26. *A. bistriata* Leud. Fortm. D. de Ceylon p. 20 Pl. I f. 12 (1879). *A. egregia var. neogradensis* Pant. II p. 38 Pl. IV f. 61 (1889). *A. zebrata* Temp. and Brun D. f. du Japon p. 16 Pl. VII f. 14 (1889).

Marine: Morocco! Mediterranean Sea! Ceylon! Seychelles! Nossibé! Singapore! Java! Sumbava! Macassar Straits! China! Samoa (Atl.), Galapagos Islands! Campeachy Bay! West Indies! Fossil: Hungary (Pant.), Oamaru, New Zealand!

This species is very variable and comprises a number of forms, which however are so closely connected, that I am unable, after comparison of a large number of sketches, to group them in separate species or varieties. Besides, the form, and appearance of the valve, especially of the ends, changes much according to its position. The ventral side, which in larger specimens has a row of short costate striæ, has in some forms a few striæ at the ends only and in others none at all. The double rows of puncta alternating with the costæ are in some specimens not distinct. Smaller forms are closely connected with *A. crassa var. spuria*.

6. **A. tesselata** Grove and Sturt (1887). — V. linear, with inwards curved, obtuse ends. L. 0,10; B. 0,015 mm. Median line biarcuate. Dorsal side with strong, smooth transverse costæ, 5,5 in 0,01 mm. crossed by longitudinal costæ, about 7 in 0,01 mm. Ventral side with coarse, costate striæ. — Q. M. Cl. III (2) p. 131 Pl. X f. 1.

Marine: Oamaru, N. Zealand, fossil!

This peculiar form seems to me certainly to belong to the group of *A. crassa*, but differs from all other forms by its peculiar structure. The dorsal side of the valve seems to be covered with quadrate alveoli, disposed in transverse and longitudinal rows. The specimens I have seen were mounted in a position, not favourable for examination of the ventral side. Still I succeeded by means of very oblique light in seeing on the ventral side, a row of strong, costate striæ and on the dorsal side not far from the median line a longitudinal line, the space between the lines being crossed by transverse costate striæ.

7. **A. inelegans** Cl. and Grove (1891). – V. sublunate, with incurved, obtuse ends. L. 0,09; B. 0,03 mm. Median line biarcuate. Axial and central areas indistinct on the dorsal and ventral side. Dorsal side with 7 costate striæ in 0,01 mm. crossed by a narrow, blank longitudinal line. Ventral side without central area and with strong, costate striæ, divergent, between the central nodule and the ends, towards the median line. Diatomiste I p. 68 Pl. X f. 15.

Marine: Macassar Straits!

Var.? *polita* Cl. V. stout, elongated, with broad, obtuse and incurved ends. L. 0,06; B. 0,015 mm. Median line biarcuate. Dorsal side with strong, smooth, costate striæ, 6 in 0,01 mm., reaching to the median line and crossed by a narrow, blank line. Ventral side with rounded central area and strong, costate striæ, crossed by a narrow, blank line. Pl. IV f. 40.

Marine: Java!

This form is very dissimilar to the type, but it is difficult to find any specifically distinct characteristic.

8. **A. ornata** Leud. Fortm. (1879). – V. linear, with incurved, obtuse ends. L. 0,1; B. 0,02 mm. Dorsal side with 8 costate striæ in 0,01 mm. crossed by a linear furrow and reaching to the median line. Ventral side with inclined rows (7 in 0,01 mm.) of puncta, crossed by a longitudinal, narrow area. — D. de Ceylon p. 20 Pl. I f. 9.

Marine: Ceylon (Le Tourneur Coll.)!

I have seen a single valve only, the opaque structure of which did not admit of a close examination of the dorsal side. Still there can be no doubt that this form is a distinct species, belonging to the group of *A. crassa*.

9. **A. comorensis** Cl. N. sp. — V. broadly linear, with obliquely rounded and slightly incurved ends. L. 0,14 to 0,19; B. 0,025 mm. Median line strongly biarcuate and elevated. Dorsal side with transverse rows (7 in 0,01 mm.) of large puncta (10 in 0,01 mm.) not reaching to the median line. Ventral side with curved rows of large and distant puncta, crossed by a narrow blank area.

Marine: Nossibé (Brun Coll.)! Tamatave (Kinker Coll.)!

This is a large and distinct form, akin to *A. ornata*. The opaque structure and the elevation to a keel of the median line made the examination of the dorsal side difficult. Still I believe that the dorsal rows of puncta are crossed by a keel or longitudinal line.

10. **A. Gründleri** GRUN. (1875). Frustule rectangular, with broad, truncate ends. L. 0,065 to 0,136; B. 0,03 to 0,05 mm. Zone with several longitudinal divisions, about 3 in 0,01 mm., transversely striate; striæ 9 to 10 in 0,01 mm. Median line strongly arcuate. V. linear with prominent, subcapitate and incurved ends. Dorsal side with 9 to 10 indistinctly punctate striæ in 0,01 mm., not reaching to the median line and crossed by a narrow longitudinal band. Ventral side with two rows of puncta, one along the median line and one near the ventral margin. — A. S. Atl. XXVIII f. 24 to 27; XXXIX f. 25.

Marine: Gulf of Naples! Madagascar! Colombo, Ceylon (Le Tourneur Coll.), Manilla (Deby Coll.)! Galapagos Islands! Campeachy Bay! Gulf of Mexico! Fossil: Hungary (Pant.).

Var. *trachytica* PANT. (1889). V. in L. 0,09 to 0,1; B. 0,015 mm. Striæ on the dorsal side reduced to two rows of puncta. — PANT. II p. 37 Pl. VII f. 132.

Marine: Hungary, fossil (Pant.).

Var. *approximata* CL. — V. in L. 0,13; B. 0,017 mm. Dorsal striæ 12 in 0,01 mm. Ventral rows of puncta approximate to the median line.

Marine: Island of Rhea, near Singapore (Van Heurck Coll.)!

Var. *robusta* CL. — V. in L. 0,1 to 0,17; B. 0,02 to 0,03 mm. Striæ 6 to 7 in 0,01 mm.

Marine: Nossibé (Brun Coll.)! Macassar Straits (Grove Coll.)! Fossil: Oamaru, N. Zealand (Grove Coll.)!

11. **A. prismatica** CL. N. sp. — V. elongated, with prominent, rounded and incurved ends. L. 0,12 to 0,17; B. 0,018 to 0,027 mm. Dorsal side with distinct axial area and several longitudinal blank bands. Striæ not distinctly punctate, 10 to 12 in 0,01 mm. Ventral side with two longitudinal rows of short striæ. — Pl. IV f. 26.

Marine: Gulf of Naples (Deby Coll.)! Oamaru, N. Zealand, fossil (Grove Coll.)!

12. **A. diaphana** CL. N. Sp. Frustule elliptical, with truncate ends. L. 0,048; B. 0,027 mm. Zone complex, its divisions about 7 in 0,01 mm., striate. Striæ 14 in 0,01 mm. V. with strongly arcuate dorsal and straight ventral margin; ends not protracted. L. 0,048 to 0,065; B. 0,01 to 0,017 mm. Median line strongly biarcuate. No axial area on the dorsal side, where there is close to the median line a strong longitudinal line. Striæ 15 in 0,01 mm. finely punctate. Ventral side structureless, broad, with a longitudinal line. Pl. IV f. 27.

Marine: Java! Colon (Deby Coll.)!

13. **A. truncata** GREG. (1857?) CL. — Frustule elliptical with truncate ends. L. 0,05 to 0,055; B. 0,025 to 0,028 mm. Zone with about 4 divisions in 0,01 mm., transversely striate; striæ 22 in 0,01 mm. V. with arcuate dorsal margin and straight ventral margin. Ends not protracted. Axial area moderately broad on the dorsal side. Striæ 19 to 20 in 0,01 mm. Ventral side structureless, or with faint traces of striation. D. of Clyde p. 515 Pl. XIII f. 77? Icon. n. Pl. III f. 17, 18.

Marine: Finmark! Sebastopol!

What *A. truncata* GREG. may exactly denote is not possible to make out without original specimens, but it is certainly a form nearly akin to *A. Grevilleana*. The same may be the case with *A. quadrata* GREG. (D. of Clyde p. 521 Pl. XIII f. 85) and also with *A. sulcata* BRÉB. (1854).

14. **A. sulcata** (BRÉB. 1854)? CL. — Frustule elliptic-rectangular, with truncate ends. L. 0,053 to 0,06; B. 0,026 mm. Zone with about 3 divisions in 0,01 mm., striate; striæ 15 to 16 in 0,01 mm. V. with arcuate dorsal and straight ventral margin. Axial area distinct on the dorsal side of the median line. Striæ 11 to 12 in 0,01 mm. Longitudinal line indistinct. Ventral side structureless. Longitudinal line not distinct. BRÉB. Notes sur quelques D. de Cherb. f. 8 (1854)?

Marine: Balearic Islands!

As above stated it is impossible to make out what form *Brébisson* denotes by the name *A. sulcata*, for which reason I have adopted this name for a form, which in all points is nearly akin to it. *A. elongata* GREG. (D. of Clyde p. 521 Pl. XIII f. 84) seems to be an elongated variety of this species, which is nearly related to the following.

15. **A. Græffii** (GRUN. 1875) CL. — Frustule elliptical to rectangular, with broad, truncate ends. L. 0,1; B. 0,05 mm. Zone with about 2 divisions in 0,01 mm. striate; striæ 17 in 0,01 mm. V. lunate, with almost straight ventral margin and not protracted ends. L. 0,1 to 0,13; B. 0,013 to 0,025 mm. Median line biarcuate. Axial area more or less broad on the dorsal side. Striæ 11 to 14 in 0,01 mm., not distinctly punctate, and crossed by a conspicuous, narrow blank line. Ventral side structureless or with a row of faint and short striæ. No distinct longitudinal line. *A. Græffii var.* A. S. Atl. XXV f. 40. *A. truncata?* Atl. XXVIII f. 5? *A. Debyi* LEUD. FORTM. D. de la Malaisie p. 10 Pl. I f. 4 (1892)?

Marine: Gulf of Naples (Brun Coll.)! Zanzibar (Atl.), Sumatra (Deby Coll.)! China! Galapagos Islands!

A. Græffii GRUN. in A. S. Atl. is to judge from the figures the same species as *A. Grevilleana*. At least I am not able to discover any distinctive characteristics. I understand *A. Græffii* to represent a form, nearly akin to *A. Grevilleana* but with closer, not distinctly punctate striæ, and not protracted ends. The zones appear to differ in the divisions, which in *A. Græffii* are contiguous, but in *A. Grevilleana* are separated by an intermediate, blank, longitudinal band. This requires further investigation.

Var. *staurophora* CL. — Central nodule transversely dilated to a short stauros.

Marine: Gulf of Naples (Brun Coll.)!

16. **A. Grevilleana** GREG. (1857). — Frustule more or less rectangular, with truncate ends. L. 0,1 to 0,16; B. 0,035 to 0,1 mm. Zone with about 3 divisions in 0,01 mm. transversely striate; striæ 6 to 17 in 0,01 mm. V. with arcuate dorsal margin and more or less produced ends. L. 0,10 to 0,22; B. 0,02 to 0,03 mm. Median line biarcuate. Axial area more or less broad on the dorsal side. Dorsal side with 6 to 10 striæ in 0,01 mm. Striæ coarsely punctate, crossed by a distinct longitudinal line or keel. Ventral side structureless, with a strong longitudinal line. T. M. S. V. p. 73 Pl. I f. 36. D. of Clyde p. 522 Pl. XIII f. 89. A. S. Atl. XXV f. 41. *A. sulcata* GREG. D. of Clyde Pl. XIII f. 92? *A. complexa* GREG. l. c. f. 90. *A. fasciata* GREG. l. c. f. 91. *A. Græffii* GRUN. A. S. Atl. XXV f. 42 (1875). *A. Grev. var. prominens* GRUN. A. S. Atl. XXV f. 43, 44. *Var. campechiana* GRUN. l. c. f. 45. *A. (Grevill. var.?) sepulta* PANT. I p. 22 Pl. XXIV f. 223 (1886). *A. sumatrensis* LEUD. FORTM. D. de la Malaisie p. 10 Pl. I f. 5 (1892)?

Marine: Spitsbergen (small form L. 0,1 mm. Striæ 12 on the valve, 17 on the zone in 0,01 mm.)! North Sea! Guernsey! Morocco! Gulf of Naples! China! Magellans Strait! S:ta Monica Calif., foss. (Deby Coll.)! Galapagos Islands! Campeachy Bay (Atl.).

A. Grevilleana is a somewhat variable species, closely connected with *A. Græffii*, from which it is distinguished by larger size, more prominent ends and the coarsely punctate striæ. On larger specimens the latter seem under high power to be costate and alternate with double rows of puncta (about 9 in 0,01 mm.).

Var. *contracta* CL. — V. with straight ventral, and in the middle deeply sinuose dorsal margin. Ends rostrate-capitate. L. 0,085 to 0,125; B. 0,02 to 0,028 mm. Median line almost straight. Axial area moderately wide on the dorsal side. Striæ 8 in 0,01 mm., costate and alternating with double rows of puncta, 13 in 0,01 mm. Keel across the striæ strong. Ventral side narrow. — A. S. Atl. Pl. XL f. 33.

Marine: Barcelona! Grip, Norway (Atl.).

17. **A. proboscidea** (GREG. 1857?) CL. — Frustule elliptical, with truncate ends. L. 0,065 to 0,07; B. 0,034 mm. Zone with 3 sharply defined divisions in 0,01 mm., transversely striate; striæ about 10 in 0,01 mm. V. with rostrate and incurved ends. Median line biarcuate. Axial

area large on the dorsal side. Striæ 9 in 0,01 mm., ending at the longitudinal line. — D. of Clyde p. 526 Pl. XIV f. 98? Icon. n. Pl. III f. 19, 20, 21.

Marine: Porto Seguro, Bahia (Deby Coll.)! Java!

This form, which of all Amphoræ observed by me has the greatest resemblance to *A. proboscidea* of Gregory, is nearly akin to *A. Græffii*.

18. **A. bioculata** Cl. Frustule elliptical with truncate ends. L. 0,07; B. 0,04 mm. Zone with broad divisions (1,5 in 0,01 mm.) transversely striate; striæ 17 in 0,01 mm. finely punctate. V. lunate with broad, obtuse and incurved ends. Median line biarcuate. Axial area narrow. Longitudinal line strong, bent from the central nodule. Striæ 14 in 0,01 mm., costate, and alternating with rows of puncta (15 in 0,01 mm.) faint on the space between the longitudinal and median line. Ventral side structureless, broad. Pl. III f. 36, 37, 38.

Marine: Balearic Islands! Sumatra (Deby Coll.)!

19. **A. gemmifera** Petit (1888). — V. with arcuate dorsal and straight ventral margin. Ends rostrate. L. 0,06 to 0,072; B. 0,008 to 0,012 mm. Axial area on the dorsal side narrow; central triangular, striæ 7 in 0,01 mm. crossed by a longitudinal line, bent around the central nodule. — D. de Cape Horn p. 120 Pl. X f. 12.

Marine: Cape Horn (Petit).

This species is unknown to the author, possibly a var. of *A. Grevilleana* or perhaps a var. of the following species.

20. **A. Sturtii** Grun. (1888). V. with straight ventral margin, gibbous in the middle, sinuose dorsal margin and capitate ends. L. 0,14; B. 0,025 mm. Axial area narrow, central triangular. Striæ 7 in 0,01 mm. not distinctly punctate (on corroded specimens), crossed by a strong longitudinal line bent around the central nodule. — Bot. Centralbl. Bd. 34 p. 36. *A. contracta?* Grove a. Sturt J. Quek. M. C. Vol. III Ser. II p. 131 (1887) Pl. X f. 4.

Marine: Oamaru, New Zealand foss. (Grove Coll.)!

21. **A. subpunctata** Grove and Sturt (1887). — V. with arcuate dorsal and straight ventral margins, obtuse and incurved ends. L. 0,19; B. 0,028 mm. Axial and central areas uniting on the dorsal side in a broad semilanceolate space, covered with large and scattered dots. Longitudinal line strong, bent from the central nodule. Striæ 6 to 7 in 0,01 mm. coarsely punctate. J. Quek. M. C. Vol. III Ser. II p. 131 Pl. X f. 3.

Marine: Oamaru, New Zealand, fossil (Grove Coll.)!

22. **A. Lendugeriana** Petit (1888). — V. narrow, with arcuate dorsal and straight ventral margins. Ends rostrate-capitate, incurved. L. 0,08 to 0,11; B. 0,014 to 0,016 mm. Median line straight, approximate to the ventral margin. Axial area linear, rather broad. Longitudinal lines two. Striæ 7 to 8 in 0,01 mm. not distinctly punctate. Ventral side not striate. — D. de Cape Horn p. 119 Pl. X f. 13.

Marine: Cape Horn (Petit) Magellans Strait!

This form is nearly connected with small forms of *A. arcolata*, from which it differs by the broader axial area.

23. **A. arcolata** Grun. (1876). — Frustule rectangular, with slightly convex sides and truncate ends. L. 0,09 to 0,16; B. 0,02 to 0,035 mm. Connecting zone with 2,5 to 3 divisions in 0,01 mm., crossed by strong, transverse costæ, a little closer than the costæ of the valve. V. with arcuate dorsal, and straight central, margins. Ends protracted, rostrate or subcapitate, according to the position of the valve. Median line straight or slightly biarcuate, approximate to the ventral margin. Axial area indistinct. Longitudinal lines two, strong, not bent around the central nodule. Striæ costate, 3,5 to 6,5 in 0,01 mm. Intermediate spaces smooth or with a double row of obsolete puncta. Ventral part not striate, but with a strong longitudinal line.

Var. *maxima* Cl. a. Grove (1892). — L. of V. 0,13 to 0,16; B. 0,02 to 0,03 mm. Striæ 3,5 to 4,5 in 0,01 mm. — Diatomiste I p. 156 Pl. XXII f. 1 to 4.

Marine: Tamatave (Kinker Coll.)! Sumbava (Kinker Coll.)! Macassar Straits (Grove Coll.)!

Var. *curta* Cl. — L. of V. 0,068 to 0,093; B. 0,017 to 0,024 mm. Striæ 5 in 0,01 mm. — *A. areolata* Grun. A. S. Atl. XXXIX f. 28. *A. megapora* Pant., II p. 38 Pl. XXIX f. 418 (1889).

Marine: Campeachy Bay (Atl.). Hungary, fossil (Pant.).

Var. *minor* Cl. — L. of V. 0,08 to 0,1; B 0,017 mm. Striæ 5 to 6,5 in 0,01 mm.

Marine: Java! Porto Seguro (Deby Coll.)! Colon (Deby Coll.)! Pensacola (Cl. M. D. N:o 320).

24. **A. capensis** A. S. (1875). — Frustule elliptical with broad, rostrate ends. L. 0,06; B. 0,03 mm. Zone with distant longitudinal rows of puncta. V. with arcuate dorsal, and centrally gibbous ventral, margins. Ends rostrate and reflexed. B. 0,07 mm. Median line near the ventral margin. Axial area very narrow. Central nodule incrassate on the dorsal side. Striæ 10 in 0,01 mm. coarsely punctate. — Atl. XXV f. 49, 50.

Marine: Cape of Good Hope (Atl.).

I have not seen this species, and the diagnosis has been constructed from the figures in the Atlas. It seems to be akin to *A. Janischii*.

25. **A. Janischii** A. S. (1875). — Frustule broad, elliptic-linear, with rostrate and broadly truncate ends, indented in the middle. L. 0,08; B. 0,027 mm. Zone with about 3 divisions in 0,01 mm. coarsely striate; striæ about 10 in 0,01 mm. V. with arcuate dorsal, straight or centrally gibbous ventral, margins and rostrate, reflexed ends. Median line near the ventral margin. Central nodule incrassate but not dilated into a stauros. Above the nodule is an oblong depression. Axial area narrow, dilated around the central nodule. Longitudinal line distinct. Striæ 11 in 0,01 mm. of distant but obscure puncta. Ventral side narrow; striæ 12 in 0,01 mm. — Atl. XXV f. 51, 52, 53, 56; XL f. 30, 32. H. L. Sm. T. N:o 32. *A. contracta* Grun. A. S. Atl. XXV f. 54, 55, 57.

Marine: Leton Bank! Seychelles (V. Heurck Coll.)! Campeachy Bay (Atl.), Barbados (Cl. M. D. N:o 118), Yokohama (Atl.), Macassar Straits!

26. **A. alata** Perag. (1881). — Frustule rectangular, indented in the middle. L. 0,06 to 0,07; B. 0,04 mm. Zone with numerous divisions, about 4 in 0,01 mm., transversely striate; striæ 10 to 11 in 0,01 mm. Hyaline limbus distinct in the middle of frustule. Valve narrow, with capitate, inflected ends. Median line close to the ventral margin. Axial area distinct. Central nodule not dilated to a stauros. Longitudinal line distinct. Striæ 9 to 10 in 0,01 mm., finely punctate. Ventral side structureless, with a longitudinal line. — D. de Villefranche p. 41 Pl. II f. 11. A. S. Atl. XXV f. 61?

Marine: Norway Grip (valve not winged)! Morocco! Balearic Islands! Macassar Straits!

Var. *major* Cl. — L. 0,09 mm. Striæ distinctly punctate, 8 in 0,01 mm.

Marine: Galapagos Island!

Var. *aptera* Cl. — L. 0,05 mm. Dorsal side without limbus. Striæ 12 in 0,01 mm.

Marine: Pensacola (Cl. M. D. N:o 320).

27. **A. vetusta** Cl. — Frustule in outline broadly linear elliptical, indented in the middle. L. 0,075; B. 0,03 mm. Zone with 4 longitudinal divisions in 0,01 mm. transversely striate; striæ 10 in 0,01 mm. V. narrow, linear with broad, capitate and incurved ends. L. 0,09 to 0,13; B. 0,014 to 0,02 mm. Central nodule transversely dilated into an obscure stauros. Axial and central areas indistinct. Longitudinal line strong, at some distance from the median line. Striæ 7 to 9 in 0,01 mm., transverse and coarsely, but obscurely punctate. Ventral side with a longitudinal line (specimen from S:ta Monica) or a longitudinal row of short striæ (specimen from Oamaru). Otherwise structureless. — Pl. IV f. 30, 31, 32.

Marine: Oamaru, New Zealand, fossil (Grove Coll.)! S:ta Monica, Calif. (Deby Coll.)!

28. **A. exsecta** Grun. (1875). Frustule in outline more or less rectangular to elliptical, indented in the middle. L. 0,06 to 0,065; B. 0,022 to 0,03 mm. Zone with numerous divisions, about 5 in 0,01 mm., striate: striæ 11 to 12 in 0,01 mm. Dorsal margin without limbus. V. with arcuate dorsal and straight ventral margins, and somewhat rostrate, slightly incurved ends. Median line straight, near the ventral margin. Longitudinal line on the dorsal side distinct. Central nodule transversely dilated to the longitudinal line. Axial area broad. Striæ 10 to 11 in 0,01 mm. composed of coarse puncta, about 11 in 0,01 mm., forming undulating, longitudinal rows. Ventral side structureless. — A. S. Atl. XXVII f. 54, 55. Icon. n. Pl. III f. 26—29. *A. kamorthensis var. minor* A. S. Atl. XXV f. 81?

Marine: Campeachy Bay (Atl.), China (Van Heurck and Deby Coll.)!

A. milesiana Greg. (D. of Clyde p. 521 Pl. XIII f. 83) seems to be a nearly related form, with less distinctly indented centre. I have seen a specimen, somewhat resembling the fig. in Greg. D. of Clyde, from the west-coast of Sweden, but the complex membrane prevented the examination of the valve. The fig. 13 Pl. XXXIX in A. S. Atl. seems to represent this form.

29. **A. Weissflogii** A. S. (1875). — Frustule rectangular, indented in the middle, with conspicuous and broad hyaline limbus. Zone complex, with about 4 divisions in 0,01 mm., coarsely striate; striæ 8 in 0,01 mm. V. with arcuate dorsal and straight ventral margins, and more or less rostrate-capitate ends. L. 0,1 to 0,113; B. 0,014 mm. Median line near the ventral margin. Longitudinal line distant from the median line. Central nodule incrassate and transversely dilated towards the longitudinal line. Axial area narrow; central area triangular. Striæ 8 in 0,01 mm. coarsely punctate outside, with distant puncta inside, the longitudinal line. (Ventral side not observed). — Atl. XXV f. 58.

Marine: Baldjik, foss. (Van Heurck Coll.)!

This species is no doubt nearly akin to *A. exsecta*, and the small form figured in A. S. Atl. f. 59 appears to be more nearly connected with *A. exsecta* than with the type. *A. kamorthensis* Grun. (Nov. p. 99 Pl. I A f. 12; 1867) seems to be an allied species, of which I have not seen specimens.

30. **A. cuneata** Cl. (1876). — Frustule elongated, truncate, constricted or indented in the middle. L. 0,03 to 0,08; B. 0,013 mm. Zone with about 4 divisions in 0,01 mm., transversely striate on the ventral side of the frustule (striæ about 12 in 0,01 mm.) transversely costate on the dorsal side (costæ 5 to 8 in 0,01 mm.). Hyaline limbus small, at the constriction of the valve, frequently indistinct. V. narrow, with sinuose dorsal margin, arcuate in the middle, and subcapitate ends. Central nodule incrassate, dilated to a stauros. Axial and central areas indistinct. Longitudinal line on the back of the dorsal side. Striæ 10 to 11 in 0,01 mm., coarsely punctate. Ventral side narrow, structureless, with a longitudinal line. — A. S. Atl. XXXIX f. 29. Icon. n. Pl. III f. 23—25. *A. lyrata* Greg. D. of Clyde p. 520 Pl. XIII f. 82 (1857)? A. S. Atl. XXVI f. 2 (small form?). *A. decora* Castr. Voyage Challenger D. p. 18 Pl. XXVII f. 14.

Marine: Balearic Islands! Adriatic! Macassar Straits! Pensacola!

This species by its peculiar connecting zone suggests *A. Peragalli*.

31. **A. granulifera** Cl. N. Sp. — Frustule in outline lanceolate, constricted in the middle. Ends rostrate-truncate. L. 0,04 to 0,047; B. 0,015 mm. Zone with about 4 divisions in 0,01 mm., transversely costate, costæ about 7 in 0,01 mm. V. with arcuate dorsal and straight ventral margins. Ends rostrate. L. 0,028 to 0,046; B. 0,007 to 0,01 mm. Median line straight, near the ventral margin. Axial area indistinct; central area a short fascia on the dorsal side of the nodule. Longitudinal line near the dorsal margin. Striæ 10 in 0,01 mm.; inside the longitudinal line resolved into large, distinct puncta. Ventral side narrow, linear, structureless. — Pl. III f. 32, 33.

Marine: Java (Cl. M. D. No 147).

32. **A. margaritifera** Cl. N. Sp. — Frustule indented in the middle, bicuneate, with broad, truncate ends. L. 0,027 to 0,04; B. 0,015 mm. Zone with about 4 divisions in 0,01 mm. coarsely transversely striate. Striæ 8 in 0,01 mm., composed of distinct puncta. V. with arcuate dorsal, slightly convex ventral margin, and rostrate ends. L. 0,035; B. 0,01 mm. Median line straight. Longitudinal line indistinct. Central nodule not stauroid. Axial area indistinct; central small rounded. Dorsal striæ 8 in 0,01 mm., composed of a few large puncta, crossed by a broad, blank area. Ventral side with a row of small puncta along the margin (10 to 11 in 0,01 mm.). — Pl. III f. 30, 31.

Marine: Galapagos Islands!

Subgenus **Halamphora** Cl.

Frustule elongated, sometimes constricted in the middle. Connecting zone complex. Valve boat-shaped, usually with rostrate or capitate ends. Median line close to the ventral margin. Axial area usually indistinct. No longitudinal line on the dorsal or ventral side. Structure: puncta disposed in transverse striæ.

This subgenus, to which belongs *A. salina* of W. Smith, comprises a large number of forms, closely connected in part. They differ from *Cymbamphora* by the zone being complex, by the, usually, capitate ends and the distinctly punctate striæ. The small terrestrial *A. Normani* seems to be related to *A. perpusilla* of the subgenus *Amphora*, so also *A. veneta* and *A. commutata*, otherwise there is no close connection between this and any other group of Amphora.

Artificial key.

1. Striæ crossed by a longitudinal band . . . . . *A. intersecta* A. S.
   — — by several blank lines . . . . . *A. czekehazensis* Pant.
   — not — — . . . . . 2.
2. Striæ with distant puncta . . . . . 3.
   — closely punctate . . . . . 4.
3. Dorsal margin slightly triundulate . . . *A. Grunowii* A. S.
   — — not undulate . . *A. corpulenta* Cl. a. Grove.
4. Valve constricted . . . . . 5.
   — not — . . . . . 11.
5. Valve with one constriction . . . 6.
   — two constrictions . . . . . *A. Jeschkei* Jan.
   — — several — . . . . . 10.
6. Zone on the dorsal side reticulate . . . . . *A. Peragalli* Cl.
   — — — not — . . . . . 7.
7. Constriction with a median gibbosity . . . . . *A. bullata* Cl.
   — without — — 8
8. Divisions of the zone faint . . . . . *A. bigibba* Grun.
   — — distinct . . . . . 9.
9. Dorsal striæ about 13 in 0,01 mm. . . . . . *A. trinodis* Greg.
   — — 9 to 10 — . . . . . *A. angularis* Greg.
10. Undulations equal . . . . . *A. tetragibba* Cl.
    Median undulation larger than the others . . . . . *A. sarniensis* Grev.
11. Striæ 5 in 0,01 mm. . . . . . *A. clara* A. S.
    — 9 to 10 in 0,01 mm. . . . . . 12.
12. Ends of the valve not capitate . . . . . 13.
    — — — capitate, not curved inwards . . . . . 18.
13. Ends not rostrate . . . . . 14.
    — rostrate, curved inwards . . . . . 16.
14. Striæ 20 in 0,01 mm. . . . . . *A. veneta* Kütz.
    — 12 to 14 in 0,01 mm. . . . . . 15.

15.	Median line approximate to the ventral margin	*A. Lagerheimii* Cl.
	— — distant from — —	*A. æstuarii* Cl.
16.	Frustule almost orbicular	*A. Szaboi* Pant.
	— elongate-elliptical	17.
17.	L. 0,02 to 0,035 mm.	*A. Normani* Rabh.
	L. 0,05 to 0,085 mm.	*A. commutata* Grun.
18.	Frustule orbicular . . .	19.
	— elongated	20.
19.	L. 0,03 mm.	*A. turgida* Greg.
	L. 0,045 to 0,08 mm. .	*A. costata* W. Sm.
20.	Striæ 7 to 9 in 0,01 mm.	21.
	9 to 13 — —	22.
	— 13 to 20 —	24.
21.	Striæ indistinctly punctate	*A. Terroris* Ehr.
	— distinctly —	*A. Eunotia* Cl.
22.	Zone with longitudinal rows of coarse puncta	*A. granulata* Greg.
	transversely striate . .	23.
23.	L. 0,025 to 0,04 mm. .	*A. exigua* Greg.
	L. 0,04 to 0,12 mm. .	*A. macilenta* Greg.
24.	Zone with faint divisions . .	*A. Normani* Rabh.
	— distinct —	25.
25.	Zone delicately striate . . .	*A. coffeiformis* Ag.
	distinctly	*A. acutiuscula* Kütz.

1. **A. æstuarii** Cl. (1891). Frustule elliptical, with broad, truncate ends. L. 0,05; B. 0,03 mm. Zone apparently smooth, with 4 to 5 broad divisions. V. lunate, acute, with somewhat gibbous ventral margin. Median line arcuate in the middle of the valve. Axial area broad, on the dorsal side frequently dilated around the central nodule. Dorsal side with 14 not distinctly punctate, striæ in 0,01 mm., not crossed by a longitudinal line. Ventral side broad, with a median row of short striæ, about 17 in 0,01 mm. — Diatomiste II p. 146 Pl. IX f. 10, 11.

Brackish water (mouth of rivers): Africa, Cameroon!

This species which resembles in the outline *A. sulcata* or *A. truncata* is remarkable for its very broad, ventral side, in which characteristic it agrees with *Cymbella*.

2. **A. Lagerheimii** Cl. (1891). Frustule elliptical, with broad, truncate ends. L. 0,05 to 0,07 mm. Zone with about 4 punctate (puncta 16 in 0,01 mm.) lines (divisions) in 0,01 mm. Valve lunate, gradually tapering from the middle to the narrow ends. Dorsal margin arcuate; ventral straight. Median line near the ventral margin. Axial area very large, apparently scabrous. Dorsal side at the margin with a short stauros, reaching to the area, and marginal striæ, 12 in 0,01 mm. Ventral side smooth, except at the margin, where are short striæ, 16 in 0,01 mm. (perhaps belonging to the zone). — Diatomiste II p. 99 Pl. VII f. 2.

Fresh water, moist rocks: Ecuador, Banos!

This is a very curious species, remarkable for the short dorsal stauros. There is no nearly akin form, as far as I know. Perhaps it is most nearly related to *A. veneta*, through different in most respects.

3. **A. veneta** Kütz (1844). — Frustule elliptical with rounded truncate ends. L. 0,02 to 0,06; B. 0,011 to 0,018 mm. Zone with several distinct divisions, about 12 in 0,01 mm., which are more or less distinctly, transversely striate; striæ 26 or more in 0,01 mm. V. with convex dorsal and straight or slightly concave ventral margin. Ends subacute, not protracted or rostrate. Central nodule strong, elongated. Median line straight close to the ventral margin; its central pores distant. Dorsal side striate, ventral not. Dorsal striæ 20 in 0,01 mm., more distant in the middle, punctate. Bac. p. 108 Pl. III f. 25. V. H. Syn. p. 58 Pl. I f. 17. *A. fasciata* Ehr. 1840 (according to H. L. Smith). *A. Hohenackeri* Rabenh. Süss. D. p. 31 Pl. IX f. 11 (1853). *A. quadricostata* Rabh. Süssw. D. Pl. IX f. 5 (1853). A. S. Atl. XXVI f. 74 to 80. *A. tumidula*

GRUN. Rab. A. E. N:o 1,716 (1864). H. L. SM. T. N:o 616. *A. hyalina var. parvula* GRUN. Rab. A. E. N:o 1,722 (1864). *A. coffeiformis* H. L. SM. T. N:o 31. *A. libyca* H. L. SM. T. N:o 34.

Fresh or brackish water: Sweden (Visby, Bohuslän)! England (Kew gardens!) France (Caen!) Germany (Berlin!) Sardinia (Atl.), Nile Delta! Persia! New Zealand! Ecuador! Argentina! N. America (Michigan!)

A. ovalis is well characterized by its elongated central nodule and distant median striæ. The connecting zone is variable in its structure. Frequently the divisions are difficult to see, sometimes they are clear and distinctly transversely striate.

4. **A. Szaboi** PANT. (1889). — Frustule in outline orbicular with slightly rostrate ends. L. 0,035; B. 0,028 mm. Zone with numerous divisions, about 5 in 0,01 mm., transversely striate; striæ 19 in 0,01 mm. V. broad, lunate, with straight or slightly concave ventral margin and subrostrate obtuse ends, curved inwards. L. 0,03 to 0,06; B. 0,013 mm. Median line almost straight, approximate to the ventral margin. Axial area distinct, frequently dilated in the middle on the dorsal side of the central nodule. Striæ on the dorsal side 13 to 17 in 0,01 mm. coarsely punctate. Striæ on the ventral side 17 in 0,01 mm. short, marginal. — PANT. II p. 39 Pl. II f. 20. *A. hercsensis* PANT. II p. 37 Pl. II f. 32, Pl. III f. 46, Pl. IV f. 68. *A. Wiesneri* PANT. II p. 40 Pl. III f. 45. *A. arcuata* PANT. II p. 35 Pl. IV f. 70. *A. minuta* PANT. II p. 38 Pl. I f. 16. *A. coffeiformis var. fossilis* PANT. II Pl. IV f. 69?

Brackish water: Hungary, fossil (Szakdoe!)

I have united all the above named species of PANTOCSEK, being unable to find in the figures or descriptions any difference of importance. They differ only in size and, slightly, in the number of striæ. This species seems to me to be nearest akin to *A. ovalis*, from which it is however quite distinct.

5. **A. Normani** RABH. (1864). — Frustule elliptical, truncate, frequently with somewhat rostrate ends. L. 0,02 to 0,035; B. 0,01 mm. Connecting zone with numerous, frequently indistinct, divisions (about 12 in 0,01 mm.). V. narrow, lunate, with more or less distinctly capitate ends curved inwards. L. 0,22 to 0,03; B. 0,004 to 0,005 mm. Central nodule strong. Median line at some distance from the ventral margin. Striæ on the dorsal side 17 in 0,01 mm. Ventral side structureless. — F. E. Alg. p. 88. V. H. Syn. p. 56. V. H. T. N:o 5. *A. humicola* GRUN. A. S. Atl. XXVI f. 90 to 92 (1875). V. H. Syn. Pl. I f. 12. *A. humic. var. javanica* GRUN. A. S. Atl. XXVI f. 89. *A. humic. var. caldariorum* GRUN. in Cl. M. D. N:o 191.

Moist earth: Sweden, Upsala! Belgium! Harz (Atl.), Java (Atl.).

6. **A. bullata** CL. — Frustule subrectangular, truncate, centrally contracted on the ventral side with a gibbosity in the sinus. L. 0,025 to 0,055; B. 0,01 to 0,012 mm. Zone with about 5 divisions in 0,01 mm. obscurely striate. V. with protracted, subcapitate and somewhat incurved ends. Median line at some distance from the ventral margin. Dorsal side obscurely striate; striæ about 17 in 0,01 mm. Ventral side not striate.

Marine: Macassar Straits!

7. **A. commutata** GRUN. (1880). — Frustule elongated, linear elliptical, with rounded ends. L. 0,05 to 0,085; B. 0,02 to 0,026 mm. Zone with longitudinal rows (5 in 0,01 mm.) of short, fine striæ (29 in 0,01 mm.). V. linear, with rostrate, incurved ends. Median line biarcuate. Axial area moderately large on the dorsal side. Ventral side without striæ or with a row of short, marginal striæ, about 15 in 0,01 mm. Dorsal side with 9 to 10 striæ in 0,01 mm. — V. H. Syn. p. 58 Pl. I f. 14. *A. affinis* W. SM. B. D. I p. 19 Pl. II f. 27. H. L. Sm. Typ. N:o 28. *A. pellucida* A. S. Atl. XXVII f. 11? 36, 37. *A. robusta* A. S. Atl. XXVII f. 38. *A. robusta var. minor* DANNF. D. of Baltic p. 20 Pl. I f. 7.

Brackish water: Baltic! Mansfelder See! England! Belgium! France!

Var. *fossilis* PANT. (1889). — V. L. 0,065 to 0,071; B. 0,008 to 0,0115 mm. Striæ about 16 in 0,01 mm. — *A. fossilis* PANT. II p. 36 Pl. I f. 2. *A. curvata* PANT. II p. 36 Pl. I f. 11.

Brackish water: Hungary, fossil (Pant.).

This species, very frequent in brackish water, is of uncertain position in the system. It differs from other forms of *Halamphora* in its strongly biarcuate median line and broad, ventral side. It has some resemblance to the species of the subgenus *Amphora*, but the zone is complex, although the divisions are seen only with difficulty. The only species, with which it seems to be connected, is *A. Normani.* I am unable to discover any differences between *A. fossilis* and *A. curvata* PANT. and both differ from *A. commutata* in somewhat closer striæ only.

8. **A. bigibba** GRUN. (1875). — Frustule strongly constricted in the middle, truncate. L. 0,02 to 0,046; B. 0,014 to 0,018 mm. Zone with numerous, more or less distinct divisions. V. with straight ventral margin and protracted ends. Median line closely approximate to the ventral margin. Dorsal striæ delicate, 15 in 0,01 mm. — A. S. Atl. XXV f. 66, 67, 69, 70 to 77.

Marine: Balearic Islands! Adriatic! Japan (Atl.). Chile (Atl.), Galapagos Islands! West Indies! Campeachy Bay!

Var. *interrupta* GRUN. (1875). — L. 0,05 mm. Striæ 13 in 0,01 mm. interrupted in the middle of the valve. — A. S. Atl. XXV f. 65.

Marine: Campeachy Bank.

9. **A. sarniensis** GREV. (1862). — Frustule with a strong constriction in the middle and a shallow one between the middle and the ends, which are rostrate-truncate. L. 0,04 to 0,05; B. 0,017 mm. Zone with about 4 divisions in 0,01 mm., transversely striate; striæ 9 to 13 in 0,01 mm. V. with about 10 to 14 striæ in 0,01 mm. — T. M. S. 1862 p. 95 Pl. IX f. 12.

Marine: Guernsey (Grove Coll.)! Macassar Straits (Grove Coll.)!

Var.? *sinuata* GREV. (1863). — L. 0,07 mm. Margin with 7 constrictions. — *A. sinuata* GREV. E. N. Ph. J. XVIII p. 183 f. 5.

Marine: Queensland (Grev.).

Var.? *flexuosa* GREV. (1863). — L. 0,056 mm. Margin with 5 constrictions. — *A. flex.* GREV. E. N. Ph. J. XVIII p. 183 f. 4.

Marine: Queensland (Grev.).

10. **A. tetragibba** CL. N. Sp. — Frustule subrectangular, with four undulations on the margins. L. 0,035; B. 0,019 mm. V. with four equal undulations on the dorsal side. Ends capitate and incurved. Median line close to the ventral margin. Striæ about 10 in 0,01 mm. — *A. sarniensis?* A. S. Atl. XXV f. 80. *A. sinuata* aff. GRUN. A. S. Atl. XXV f. 78, 79.

Marine: Baltjik (Atl.), Japan (Atl.).

11. **A. coffeæformis** AG. (1827). — Frustule lanceolate, 2 to 3 times longer than broad, truncate. L. 0,03 to 0,05 mm. Zone with numerous, close divisions, 10 to 16 in 0,01 mm., very delicately striate; striæ about 21 in 0,01 mm. V. narrow with arcuate dorsal, somewhat concave ventral margin, and protracted, capitate ends. Median line close to the ventral margin. Dorsal striæ about 20 in 0,01 mm. — *Frustulia coffeæformis* AG. in Regensb. Flora 1827 II p. 627 (according to Kütz). KÜTZ Bac. p. 108. A. S. Atl. XXVI f. 56, 58. *A. aponina* KÜTZ Bac. p. 108 (1844). *A. salina* W. SM. B. D. p. 19 Pl. XXX f. 251 (1853). V. H. Syn. p. 57 Pl. I f. 19. *A. lineata* GREG. T. M. S. p. 71 Pl. I f. 33 (1857). *A. Neupaueri* PANT. II p. 38 Pl. I f. 7 (1889)? *A. Taylori* GRUN. V. H. T. No 13.

Hot springs and brackish water: Sea of Kara! Baltic! Salines of Saxony! Iceland! Sandwich Islands! Australia, Fischie River! West Indies!

Var.? *perpusilla* GRUN. (1884). — L. 0,009 to 0,011 mm. Striæ more than 30 in 0,01 mm. — GRUN. Fr. Jos. Land D. p. 102. A. S. Atl. XXVI f. 98.

Marine: Franz Josephs Land (Grun.). Nice (Atl.).

Var. *borealis* KÜTZ (1844). — L. 0,013 to 0,025 mm. Striæ 21 to 24 in 0,01 mm. — *A. borealis* KÜTZ Bac. p. 108 Pl. III f. 18. V. H. Syn. Pl. I f. 20. *A. salina β minor* V. H. Syn. p. 57.

Fresh or brackish water: Helgoland (Kütz). Gulf of Bothnia!

Var. *fossilis* PANT. (1889). — L. 0,032 mm. Striæ 22,5 in 0,01 mm. — *A. salina var. fossilis* PANT. II p. 39 Pl. III f. 47.

Brackish water: Hungary, fossil (Pant.).

Var. *angularis* V. H. (1880). — Frustule in L. 0,025 to 0,043; B. 0,01 to 0,015 mm. slightly constricted in the middle. Striæ 20 to 23 (18 according to Van Heurck) in 0.01 mm. Divisions of the zone about 14 in 0,01 mm., distinctly striate. *A. angularis* V. H. Syn. p. 57 Pl. I f. 21. *A. angulosa var. lyrata* V. H. Syn. f. 22. *A. hybrida* GRUN. V. H. Syn. p. 57 V. H. T. N:o 12. *A. bullosa var. lineolata* H. L. SMITH T. N:o 611.

Marine: England! Belgium!

Var. *hungarica* CL. — V. in length 0,044; B. 0,01. Ventral margin straight. Striæ 20 in 0,01 mm. — *A. acutiuscula var. fossilis* PANT. II p. 35 Pl. II f. 29.

Brackish water: Hungary, fossil (Pant.).

Var. *protracta* PANT. (1889). L. of V. 0,08; B. 0,007 mm. Ventral margin convex. Ends protracted, capitate. Striæ distinctly punctate 17,5 to 19 in 0,01 mm. — *A. protracta* PANT. II p. 39 Pl. I f. 5.

Brackish water: Hungary, fossil (Pant.).

12. **A. acutiuscula** KÜTZ (1844). — Frustule elliptic-lanceolate, with subrostrate and truncate ends. L. 0,035 to 0,07; B. 0,019 mm. Zone with numerous divisions, about 11 in 0,01 mm., transversely striate; striæ 18 to 20 in 0,01 mm. V. narrow, 10 to 12 times as long as broad, with subcapitate ends and straight ventral margin. Median line close to the ventral margin. Striæ 13 to 18 in 0,01 mm. finely, but distinctly punctate. Bac. p. 108 Pl. V f. 32. V. H. Syn. p. 57 Pl. I f. 18. *A. lineata* GREG. Diat. of Clyde p. 512 Pl. XII f. 70 (1857) A. S. Atl. XXVI f. 59. *A. coffeiformis var. Salinarum* GRUN. Foss. D. Österr. Ung. p. 148 (1882). *A. striata* PANT. II p. 39 Pl. II f. 31 (1889)? *A. striolata* PANT. II p. 39 Pl. II f. 25 (1889)? *A. juvenalis* PANT. III Pl. XIII f. 199 (1893).

Brackish and marine: Greenland! Spitsbergen! Finmark! Sea of Kara! Baltic! North Sea! Morocco! Balearic Islands! Caspian Sea (Grun.), Hungary, fossil Czekehaza! Cape May! Samoa!

Var.? *subconstricta* GRUN. (1878). Frustule slightly constricted in the middle. L. 0,035 to 0,045; B. 0,011 to 0,012 mm Striæ 15 to 17 in 0,01 mm., on the zone fine. — Casp. Sea Alg. p. 8 Pl. III f. 5.

Brackish water: Caspian Sea (Grun.), N. Wales.

Var.? *constricta* GRUN. (1878). Larger than the var. *subconstricta*. Striæ 12 to 14 in 0,01 mm. — Casp. Sea Alg. p. 8.

Marine: Tahiti, Tonga Islands, Samoa (Grun.), Seychelles (Van Heurck Coll.!)

A. acutiuscula differs from *A. coffeiformis* in its larger size, coarser striæ, and distinctly striate zone, but all these characteristics are variable, and in fact both species are connected by intermediate forms, as is also the case with *A. macilenta* GREG.

PANTOCSEK has described under the name *A. Loczyi* (II p. 37 Pl. V f. 93) a form that seems to belong to *A. acutiuscula*, but the description does not agree with the figure, as the striæ are according to the description 11 in 0,01 mm. and on the fig. 14 to 15 in 0,01 mm. The variety *subconstricta* may be identical with *A. angularis* and the var. *constricta* with *A. binodis*.

13. **A. macilenta** GREG. (1857). — Frustule in outline lanceolate, with truncate ends. L. 0,037 to 0,12 mm. Zone with numerous divisions, 7 to 8 in 0,01 mm., transversely striate: striæ 11 to 15 in 0,01 mm. V. semilanceolate with rostrate-capitate ends. Median line close to the ventral margin. Striæ 9 to 12 in 0,01 mm., obscurely punctate.

Var. *typica* CL. — Frustule with narrow zone, 3 to 4 times longer than broad. Striæ on the zone 15 to 17 in 0,01 mm. V. in L. 0,087 to 0,13; B. 0,007 to 0,015 mm Striæ 11 to 12 in 0,01 mm. *A. macilenta* GREG. D. of Clyde p. 510 Pl. XII f. 65.

Marine: Coasts of Sweden and Scotland! Baltjik, fossil! Labuan! Seychelles! Behring Island!

Var. *cygadensis* GREG. (1857). — Frustule 3 to 4 times longer than broad, with narrow zone. L. 0,06 to 0,089; B. 0,019 mm. Striæ of the zone 15 in 0,01 mm. V. about 12 times longer than broad; its striæ 9 in 0,01 mm. *A. cygadensis* GREG. D. of Clyde p. 512 Pl. XII f. 71.

Marine: Scotland (Greg.), Balearic Islands! Baltjik foss.! Macassar Straits!

A. macilenta and *A. cygadensis* are badly represented by GREGORY, and their identification from the figures is doubtful. From the description of the number of striæ, it seems possible that GREGORY denotes these forms, which are nearly akin to *A. acutiuscula* and differ from that species in coarser striæ and larger size only.

14. **A. Eunotia** CL. (1873). — Frustule broad, with truncate ends. L. 0,08 to 0,12; B. 0,05 mm. Zone with numerous divisions, about 6 in 0,01 mm. distinctly striate; striæ 11 in 0,01 mm. V. semilanceolate, with slightly rostrate ends, about 6 times longer than broad. Median line close to the ventral margin. Striæ on the dorsal side 7,5 to 8 in 0,01 mm., distinctly punctate; puncta about 10 in 0,01 mm. Ventral side not striate. D. of Arctic Sea p. 21 Pl. III f. 17. Icon. n. Pl. IV f. 2, 3. *A. cymbifera* CL. Vega p. 462. *A. cymb. var.* A. S. Atl. XXV f. 35.

Marine: Greenland! Spitsbergen! Bohuslän! Bab el Mandeb! Labuan!

Var. *gigantea* GRUN. — V. in L. 0,15; B. 0,026 mm. Striæ 7 in 0,01 mm.; puncta 6 in 0,01 mm. Ventral side with marginal puncta, 10 in 0,01 mm. — *A. cymbifera var. gigantea* GRUN. in V. H. T. No 516.

Marine: Baldjik. foss.! Sumbava (Kinker Coll.!).

15. **A. clara** A. S. (1875). V. semilanceolate with straight ventral margin and rostrate ends. L. 0,10 to 0,14; B. 0,023 to 0,028 mm. Median line straight, close to the ventral margin. Striæ 5 in 0,01 mm. composed of large puncta, 5 to 6 in 0,01 mm. Atl. XXV f. 20.

Marine: Japan (Atl.), Macassar Straits (Grove Coll.)!

16. **A. costata** W. SM. (1853). Frustule in outline broadly lanceolate, with rostrate and truncate ends. L. 0,045 to 0,08; B. 0,03 to 0,065 mm. Zone with about 3 divisions in 0,01 mm., coarsely striate, striæ 10 in 0,01 mm. V. lunate with somewhat concave ventral margin and rostrate ends. Median line close to the ventral margin. Striæ on the dorsal side 9 in 0,01 mm. composed of large puncta, 7 in 0,01 mm. Ventral side very narrow, with 10 striæ in 0,01 mm. — B. D. I p. 20 Pl. XXX f. 253. GREG. D. of Clyde p. 527 Pl. XIV f. 99. H. L. SMITH Lens II p. 83. *A. inflata* GRUN. A. S. Atl. XXV f. 29 to 30 (1875).

Marine: North Sea! Mediterranean Sea (Perag.), Adriatic! Sumatra (Deby Coll.)! New Haven (H. L. Smith), Pensacola! Colon! Campeachy Bay! Porto Seguro! Galapagos Islands!

A. monilifera GREG. (D. of Clyde p. 511 Pl. XII f. 69) is probably a frustule of *A. costata* or *Terroris* in the state of division. The same may be the case with *A. monilifera* in A. S. Atl. XXVI f. 32.

17. **A. Terroris** EHR. (1853). — Frustule lanceolate with rostrate-truncate ends. L. 0,045 to 0,07; B. 0,018 to 0,02 mm. Zone with about 5 divisions in 0,01 mm. striate; striæ 11 in 0,01 mm. V. semilanceolate with rostrate-capitate ends. Striæ 8 to 9 in 0,01 mm., not distinctly punctate. — B. Ak. 1853. *A. Erebi* EHR. M. G. Pl. XXXV A 23 f. 2 (1854). CL. Vega p. 462. *A. cymbifera* GREG. D. of Clyde p. 526 Pl. XIV f. 97 (1857). A. S. Atl. XXVI f. 33; XXXIX f. 18; XXV f. 17 to 19, 33, 34, 36. *A. Lightsmithiana* O'MEARA M. J. XIV Pl. VIII f. 8 (1874)?

Marine: Arctic America! Greenland! Spitsbergen! Finmark! Sea of Kara! East Cape! North Sea! Mediterranean Sea! Macassar Straits! Gulf of Mexico!

Var. *limbata* Cl. Frustule in L. 0,05 to 0,08; B. 0,03 to 0,05 mm. Striæ of the zone 10 to 11 in 0,01 mm. V. in L. 0,09; B. 0,015 mm. Striæ 7 in 0,01 mm. Dorsal side with a narrow hyaline limbus.

Marine: Indian Ocean (Deby Coll.)! China (Deby Coll.)!

18. **A. exigua** Greg. (1857). — Frustule linear-lanceolate, with rostrate, truncate ends. L. 0,025 to 0,04; B. 0,011 to 0,012 mm. Zone with about 8 divisions in 0,01 mm. delicately striate; striæ 17 to 20 in 0,01 mm. V. with arcuate dorsal, straight ventral, margins and rostrate, capitate ends. Striæ 12 to 14 in 0,01 mm. not distinctly punctate. Median line close to the ventral margin. — D. of Cl. p. 511 Pl. XII f. 75.

Brackish and marine: Scotland (Greg.), Arctic America! Bessels Bay! Adriatic! Sandwich Islands! Tahiti! West Indies!

A. exigua is figured by Gregory in a manner which admits of no trustworthy identification, but as the striæ are stated to be 11 in 0.01 mm. I believe that Gregory denotes this species, which differs from smaller forms of *A. acutiuscula* in its smaller size, more delicately striate zone, and not distinctly punctate striæ.

19. **A. granulata** Greg. (1857). Frustule linear-lanceolate, with rostrate, truncate ends. L. 0,038 to 0,04 (0,045 to 0,077 Greg.); B. 0,013 to 0,018 (0,02 to 0,033 Greg.) in 0,01 mm. Zone with 7 to 11 divisions in 0,01 mm. and longitudinal rows of large puncta, 10 to 13 in 0,01 mm. V. with straight median line, closely approximate to the ventral margin. Striæ 13 (10 to 14 Greg.) in 0,01 mm. not distinctly punctate. — D. of Clyde p. 525 Pl. XIV f. 96.

Marine: Java! Macassar Straits!

20. **A. Jeschkei** Jan. (1876). — Frustule about 3 times longer than broad, with triundulate margins and broadly truncate ends. L. 0,04; B. 0,0135 mm. Zone with about 4 longitudinal rows of large puncta (about 11 in 0,01 mm.) in 0,01 mm. Valve narrow with protracted and capitate, incurved ends. Striæ 12 in 0,01 mm. — A. S. Atl. XXXIX f. 14.

Marine:?

21. **A. turgida** Greg. (1857). — Frustule in outline almost orbicular, with rostrate ends. L. 0,025 to 0,035; B. 0,015 to 0,02 mm. Zone with longitudinal divisions. V. in L. 0,02 to 0,04; B. 0,0075 to 0,009 mm. with broad, arcuate dorsal margin, straight ventral margin and rostrate ends. Median line close to the ventral margin. Striæ 13 (9 Greg.) in 0,01 mm., not distinctly punctate. D. of Clyde p. 510 Pl. XII f. 63. A. S. Atl. XXV f. 24, 25.

Marine: Scotland (Greg.), Norway! Red Sea! Java! Macassar Straits! Labuan!

A. turgida is nearly akin to *A. exigua*, differing scarcely in anything but its greater breadth. Grunows *A. fluminensis* (Verh. 1863 p. 12 Pl. XIII f. 15) agrees in size and outline with *A. turgida*, but has closer striæ, 21 in 0,01 mm. The latter species is unknown to me.

22. **A. Grunowii** A. S. (1874). — V. broad with straight ventral margin and elevated, slightly triundulate dorsal margin. Ends capitulate. L. 0,054; B. 0,021 mm. Striæ 10 in 0,01 mm. composed of large, distant puncta. Median line closely approximate to the ventral margin. Atl. Probet. f. 15.

Marine: Java (Atl.).

23. **A. corpulenta** Cl. a. Grove (1891). — V. with almost straight ventral margin, very elevated dorsal margin, and acuminate ends. L. 0,096; B. 0,045 mm. Median line close to the ventral margin. Dorsal side with 6 striæ in 0,01 mm. composed of distant puncta (4 to 5 in 0,01 mm.). Ventral side very narrow, with about 8 striæ in 0,01 mm. — Diatomiste I p. 68 Pl. X f. 14.

Marine: Macassar Straits!

24. **A. binodis** Greg. (1857). — Frustule lanceolate, truncate, constricted in the middle. L. 0,044 to 0,05; B. 0,0127 mm. Zone with numerous delicate divisions (10 in 0,01 mm.) finely striate; striæ about 28 in 0,01 mm. V. with straight ventral margin. Median line close to the ventral margin. Dorsal side with 13 not distinctly punctate striæ in 0,01 mm. Ventral side with faint and closer striæ; about 19 in 0,01 mm. D. of Clyde p. 510 Pl. XII f. 67.

Marine: Scotland (Greg.), Balearic Islands!

25. **A. angularis** Greg. (1855). — Frustule constricted in the middle, with broad, rostrate ends. L. 0,04 to 0,06; B. 0,02 to 0,025 mm. Zone with about 9 divisions in 0,01 mm., very finely striate. V. with slightly concave ventral margin, arcuate, and centrally sinuose dorsal margins, and capitate ends. L. 0,042; B. 0,008 mm. Median line close to the ventral margin. Dorsal striæ 9 to 10 in 0,01 mm. not distinctly punctate. — M. J. III p. 39 Pl. IV f. 6? A. S. Atl. XXV f. 83.

Marine: Bohuslän (Atl.), Java! Macassar Straits!

Gregory's figure is scarcely sufficient for identification and Grunow believed it to represent a form of *A. coffæiformis*, but it has much coarser striæ.

26. **A. Peragalli** Cl. N. Sp. Frustule elongated, slightly constricted in the middle, with truncate ends. L. 0,055 to 0,065; B. 0,022 to 0,025 mm. Zone very dissimilar on the dorsal and ventral side; on the dorsal side with about 5 longitudinal costæ in 0,01 mm. connected by transverse costæ, 4 to 5 in 0,01 mm.; on the ventral side with about 12 longitudinal ribs in 0,01 mm. and transversely striate, striæ 24 in 0,01 mm. V. with the median line close to the ventral margin. Its striæ 11 in 0,01 mm. not distinctly punctate. *Amphora sp. n.?* Perag. D. de Villefranche p. 10 Pl. III f. 26 (1888).

Marine: Mediterranean, Balearic Islands! Villefranche (Per.), Adriatic, Rovigno!

The figure given by Peragallo does not exactly correspond with our species, as it has closer (15 in 0,01 mm.), and distinctly punctate, striæ; nevertheless I have no doubt about the identity.

27. **A. czekehazensis** Pant. (1889). V. with arcuate dorsal and straight ventral margin. Ends rostrate. L. 0,06 to 0,0625; B. 0,01 to 0,0105 mm. Median line closely approximate to the ventral margin. Striæ 20 in 0,01 mm. not distinctly punctate, but crossed by numerous, undulating blank bands. — Pant. II p. 36 Pl. I f. 6.

Brackish water: Czekehaza, Hungary, fossil!

28. **A. intersecta** A. S. (1875). Frustule linear, with truncate ends. L. 0,16; B. 0,04 mm. Zone with about 4 to 5 divisions in 0,01 mm., striate; striæ 18 in 0,01 mm. V. about 7 times longer than broad, with slightly arcuate dorsal margin, straight ventral margin, and capitate ends. L. 0,11 to 0,14; B. 0,02 mm. Median line near the ventral margin. Axial area distinct on the dorsal side. Dorsal side with 8 striæ in 0,01 mm. Striæ obscurely punctate and crossed by two or three longitudinal blank bands. Ventral side narrow, with short marginal striæ, about 11 in 0,01 mm. — Atl. XXV f. 37, 38. Pant. III Pl. XII f. 190.

Marine: Baltjik, foss.! Bory, Hungary, fossil!

Var. *sarmatica* Pant. (1886). — Striæ strongly punctate. Pant. I p. 21 Pl. XV f. 135.

Marine: Dolje, Hungary fossil (Pant.).

Var.? *striata* Pant. (1886). L. 0,095; B. 0,015 mm. Striæ 10 in 0,01 mm. composed of 4 distant puncta. — Pant. I p. 22 Pl. XVII f. 156.

Marine: Dolje, Hungary, fossil (Pant.).

Subgenus **Oxyamphora.**

Frustule usually broadly elliptical, with truncate ends and complex connecting zone. Valves lunate, acute. Median line approximate to the ventral margin. Central nodule transversely dilated to a stauros or not. Axial and central areas usually indistinct. No longitudinal lines or keels on the dorsal side of the valve. Structure of the dorsal side: usually fine puncta, arranged in parallel, or slightly radiate, transverse striæ, and in undulating, longitudinal lines. Ventral side with, usually, much closer striæ than the dorsal side.

A. hyalina with cell-contents, frustule in zonal view, in state of division, and in valvular view; 600 times magnified.

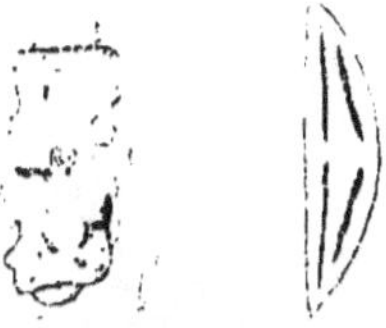

A. ostrearia with cell-contents; 600 times magnified.

Cell-contents. I have examined living specimens of *A. hyalina*, *A. ostrearia* and *A. quadrata*. In *A. hyalina* there is, along the ventral side of the connecting zone, a flat chromatophore-plate, the extremities of which are deeply indented and at the ends of which a single elæoplast constantly occurs. On the dorsal side of the plate and on its centre the nucleus occurs enclosed in a plasma-mass, from which radiate fine threads towards the wall of the frustule. On dividing, the plate and terminal elæoplasts are longitudinally cloven. If the living frustule be stained with methylene-blue, numerous, intensely coloured granules make their appearance in the primordial stratum of the plasma. *A. ostrearia* has two chromatophore-plates, one along the dorsal wall of the connecting zone. Both are deeply constricted in the middle. *A. quadrata* has instead of chromatophore-plates a large number of small, rounded discs, gathered below the central plasma-mass and at the extremities. It is thus, as to its cell-contents, a coccochromatic diatom.

A. quadrata with cell-contents; 600 times magnified.

This subgenus comprises a number of forms with or without stauros, which in other respects are too closely connected to be placed in different sections. From the subgenus *Amblyamphora* they differ by the very narrow ventral side and by the acute, frequently apiculate, ends of the valve. In the genus *Navicula* they correspond to *Stauroneis* and *Libellus*.

Artificial key.

1.	Zone with some few inordinate stigmas	*A. magnifica* GREV.
	— without — — —	2.
2.	Without stauros	3.
	With —	10.
3.	Thin and membranaceous	4.
	Silicious	6.

4.	Frustule globose .	. . . . *A. hyalina* Kütz.
	— rectangular	. . . . 5.
5.	Divisions of the zone close (10 in 0,01 mm.) . . .	. . . *A. lineolata* Ehb.
	— less — (7 in 0,01 mm.) .	*A. bacillaris* Greg.
6.	Striæ on the ventral side as close as on the dorsal side	7.
	— — — closer than — —	. . . 8.
7.	L. 0,05 to 0,08 mm.	. . *A. Arcus* Greg.
	L. 0,13 to 0,26 mm.	. . . *A. rhombica* Kitt.
8.	Striæ of distant puncta (5 to 6 in 0,01 mm.) .	. . . . . *A. mæandrina* Cl.
	— close (10 to 12 in 0,01 mm.) .	. . . . 9.
9.	Rows of puncta reaching to the median line .	*A. grœnlandica* Cl.
	— not	. . . . *A. aspera* Pet.
10.	Striæ oblique . . .	*A. decussata* Grun.
	— transverse	. . . 11.
11.	Median line straight . .	12.
	— — arcuate	15.
12.	Median line close to the margin	13.
	— — distant from —	. 14.
13.	Striæ of very distant puncta (4 to 5 in 0,01 mm.)	*A. micans* A. S.
	— not very distant puncta (10 in 0,01 mm.)	*A. acuta* Greg.
14.	Striæ 14 to 17 in 0,01 mm., of distant puncta . .	*A. Lunula* Cl.
	20 — — finely punctate . .	*A. staurophora* Cl.
15.	Striæ coarsely punctate	. *A. ostrearia* Bréb.
	— finely —	*A. lævis* Greg.

1. **A. lineolata** Ehb. (1838). — Frustule rectangular or elliptical with broad, truncate ends, membranaceous. L. 0,032 to 0,045; B. 0,015 to 0,023 mm. Zone with numerous divisions, 10 in 0,01 mm. Central nodule not dilated into a stauros. Dorsal part of the valve finely striate. Striæ 20 to 23 in 0,01 mm. — Inf. Pl. XIV f. 4 (?) Kütz Bac. p. 107 Pl. V f. 36. V. H. Syn. p. 57 Pl. I f. 13, 23. A. S. Atl. XXVI f. 51. *A. plicata* Greg. T. M. S. V p. 70 Pl. I f. 31 (1857). A. S. Atl. XXVI f. 50. *A. Rabenhorstii* Rabh. Alg. Eur. No 1.931 (1866). *A. hyalina* H. L. Sm. Types No 614. *A. sulcata* Dannf. Baltic D. Pl. I f. 8 (1882). *A. tenuis* Flögel Pomerania Exp. p. 90 f. 13 (1873)?

Brackish water: Sea of Kara! Coasts of Scotland, England and Sweden. Belgium! Baltic! Saxony, Halle! Caspian Sea (Grun.). Adriatic! Java! China! California!

Var. *chinensis* A. S. (1875). Frustule with more convex margins. Central nodule slightly transversely dilated. *A. chinensis* A. S. Atl. XXVI f. 12.

Marine: China.

Var. *undata* H. L. Sm. (1873). Frustule slightly constricted in the middle. L. 0,043; B. 0,019 mm. Striæ 21 in 0,01 mm. — *A. undata* H. L. Sm. Lens II p. 70 Pl. I f. 21.

Brackish water: Baltic at Westervik! New Haven Conn. Sm.

According to H. L. Smith (Lens 1873 p. 74) Ehrenbergs name denotes partly *A. ovalis* and partly another species. *A. lineolata* Kütz seems me to be this species, but *A. lineolata* Donk. is another species, or *Psammamphora arenaria var.* *A. incurva* Greg. (M. J. III p 39 Pl. IV f. 5) may represent detached valves of this or some other species, impossible to decide. *A. tenera* W. Sm. (B. D. I p. 20 Pl. XXX f. 252) may be a small form of *A. lineolata* or *Cymbamphora cymbelloides*, impossible to decide without original specimens. Prof. Hamilton Smith believes it to represent some *Navicula*. It seems questionable whether *A. hyperborea* Grun. (Franz Josefs Land D. p. 55 Pl. I f. 10, 1884) may be a variety of *A. lineolata*, or belong to *Navicula complanata*.

2. **A. magnifica** Grev. (1863). — Frustule quadrate. L. 0,102; B. 0,14 mm. V. very narrow. Median line arcuate. Zone with numerous divisions, about 4 in 0,01 mm. dotted with large scattered puncta. Edin. N. Ph. J. XVIII p. 182 f. 4.

Marine: Queensland (Grev.).

3. **A. hyalina** Kütz (1844). — Frustule membranaceous, more or less orbicular in outline. L. 0,05 to 0,08 mm. Zone with numerous divisions. Valve semicircular with straight ventral margin and somewhat apiculate ends. Median line close to the ventral margin. Striæ about 23 in 0,01 mm. — Bac. p. 108 Pl. XXX f. 18. W. Sm. B. D. I Pl. II f. 28. A. S. Atl. XXVI f. 52 to 55. *A. hemisphaerica* Grun. in Hedwigia VI p. 24 (1867).

Marine: Spitsbergen! North Sea! Mediterranean Sea! Adriatic! Cape May! Barbados! Honduras (Grun.).

4. **A. bacillaris** Greg. (1857). — Frustule almost rectangular. L. 0,05; B. 0,017 to 0,02 mm. Zone with 7 divisions in 0,01 mm. transversely striate; striæ 20 in 0,01 mm. Valve narrow. Central nodule not dilated into a stauros. Striæ radiate, 18 to 19 in 0,01 mm. not crossed by a longitudinal line. — D. of Clyde p. 527 Pl. XIV f. 100. Icon. n. Pl. IV f. 40, 41. *A. bac. var scotica* Cl. M. D. N:o 310.

Marine: Coasts of Scotland!

This form agrees pretty well with Gregory's *A. bacillaris*. As I have seen no detached valves, I have not been able to give a complete description, for which reason this species requires a more accurate examination.

5. **A. arcus** Greg. (1854). — Frustule more or less elliptic-rectangular, with broad, truncate ends. L. 0,05 to 0,08; B. 0,032 to 0,04 mm. Zone with numerous divisions, 5 to 6 in 0,01 mm., which are transversely striate. V. narrow, lunate, acute. Median line biarcuate. Striæ of equal number on the dorsal and ventral side, distinctly punctate.

Forma *typica* Cl. — Striæ of the zone 10, of the valve 9 to 10 in 0,01 mm. composed of moderately coarse puncta. — *A. arcus* Greg. T. M. S. V. p. 75 Pl. I f. 37. D. of Clyde p. 522 Pl. XIII f. 88. Icon. n. Pl. IV f. 4.

Marine: Spitsbergen! Finmark! Scotland! Sumatra (Deby Coll.)! Japan, fossil (Brun).

Var. *sulcata* A. S. (1875). — Striæ of the zone 16 to 20 in 0,01 mm., of the valve 14 to 20 in 0,01 mm. finely punctate; puncta about 25 in 0,01 mm., forming undulate, longitudinal lines. — *A. sulcata* A. S. Atl. XXVI f. 46, 47.

Marine: Rovigno, Adriatic! Rembang Bay (Deby Coll.)! Barbados (Cl. M. D. N:o 149).

The variety *sulcata* is akin to *A. lineolata* but more silicious and connected with the type by intermediate forms. It cannot be *A. sulcata* Greg. D. of Clyde (p. 523 Pl. XIII f. 92 and 92 *b*), which seems to represent some form of *A. Grevilleana* and has much broader divisions.

6. **A. rhombica** Kitton (1876). — V. semi-rhomboidal, apiculate. L. 0,13 to 0,26; B. 0,021 to 0,05 mm. Median line closely approximate to the ventral margin. Striæ on the dorsal side 10 to 12 in 0,01 mm., radiate, frequently alternately longer and shorter near the dorsal margin, composed of elongated puncta, forming undulate, longitudinal lines. Ventral side very narrow, striate; striæ a little closer (11 to 13 in 0,01 mm.) than on the dorsal side. — A. S. Atl. XL f. 39.

Marine: Mediterranean Sea (Perag.). Island of Rhea! Sumbava (Kinker Coll.)! Sumatra (Deby Coll.)! Macassar Straits (Grove Coll.)! China! Colon (Deby Coll.)!

Var. *gracilior* Cl. — V. in L. 0,11 to 0,14; B. 0,024 mm. Dorsal striæ 16 to 17, ventral 18 in 0,01 mm.

Marine: Tahiti! Campeachy Bay (Brun Coll.)!

Var *intermedia* Cl. — L. 0,09 to 0,1; B. 0,017 mm. Dorsal striæ 14 and ventral 16 in 0,01 mm.

Marine: Cette (Temp., Perag. Types N:o 447).

7. **A. mæandrina** Cl. N. Sp. — V. lunate, apiculate. L. 0,18; B. 0,035 mm. Central nodule strong. Median line close to the ventral margin. Dorsal part with about 12 striæ in 0,01 mm. composed of distant, elongated puncta, about 5 to 6 in 0,01 mm., forming undulate, longitudinal rows. Ventral part narrow, with 19 to 20 transverse striæ in 0,01 mm. — Pl. IV f. 14.

Marine: Colon (Deby Coll.)!

8. **A. aspera** PETIT (1877). — V. semilanceolate. L. 0,057 to 0,085; B. 0,013 to 0,018 mm. Ventral margin straight, somewhat gibbous in the middle. Central nodule strong. Dorsal side with 16 striæ in 0,01 mm. composed of distant (about 10 in 0,01 mm.) puncta, forming undulate, longitudinal lines. Ventral side narrow, finely striate. Striæ 22 to 23 in 0,01 mm — D. de l'île Campbell p. 19 Pl. IV f. 9. Icon. n. Pl. III f. 22. *A. undata* LEUD. FORTM. D. de la Malaisie p. 11 Pl. II f. 4 (1892).

Marine: Gulf of Naples (Deby Coll.)! N. Zealand (Petit).

9. **A. groenlandica** CL. N. Sp. — V. narrow, lunate, with subacute ends. L. 0,09; B. 0,016 mm. Ventral margin straight. Median line approximate to the ventral margin. Central nodule not transversely dilated. Striæ of the dorsal side 14 (at the ends 15 to 16) in 0,01 mm. composed of puncta (12 in 0,01 mm.) forming slightly undulating, longitudinal rows. Ventral part with 23 striæ in 0,01 mm. — Pl. IV f. 4.

Marine: Davis Strait!

10. **A. acuta** GREG. (1857). Frustule subquadrate. Divisions of the zone about 4 in 0,01 mm. finely transversely striate; striæ about 21 in 0,01 mm. V. lunate, with arcuate dorsal margin, straight ventral margin and apiculate ends. L. 0,089 to 0,15; B. 0,03 mm. Central nodule transversely dilated into a stauros. Striæ on the dorsal side 12 to 14 in 0,01 mm., composed of puncta, about 10 in 0,01 mm., forming undulating, longitudinal rows. Ventral side very narrow, finely striate; striæ about 26 in 0,01 mm. — D. of Clyde p. 524 Pl. XIV f. 93. A. S. Atl. XXVI f. 19, 20 (21, 22?).

Marine: Greenland! Spitsbergen! Finmark! North Sea! Morocco! Mediterranean Sea! China! Magellan's Strait!

Var. *neogena* PANT. (1889). L. 0,084 to 0,092; B. 0,018 to 0,02 mm. Striæ 17,5 in 0,01 mm. — PANT. II p. 35.

Marine: Hungary, Bory fossil (Pant.).

Var. *arcuata* A. S. (1875). V. with recurved ends. L. 0,06 to 0,15; B. 0,012 to 0,028 mm. Dorsal striæ 9 to 12 in 0,01 mm., composed of distant puncta (about 7 in 0,01 mm.). Ventral striæ very close. — *A. arcuata* Atl. XXVI f. 27 to 29.

Marine: Balearic Islands! Seychelles (Van Heurck Coll.)! Macassar Straits (Grove Coll.)! Samoa (Atl.), Mazatlan (Atl.), Gulf of Mexico (Atl.).

Var. *labyrinthica* GRUN. (1880). — V. in L. 0,1 to 0,13. Dorsal striæ 14 to 17 in 0,01 mm., composed of distinct puncta (10 in 0,01 mm.) forming undulating lines. Ventral striæ 26 in 0,01 mm. — *A. labyr.* GRUN. A. D. p. 25. Icon. n. Pl. IV f. 23.

Marine: Balearic Islands!

In the Diatoms of Clyde GREG. has 1857 figured (p. 521 Pl. XIII f. 87) a form, named *A. nobilis*, which seems to represent an entire frustule of *A. acuta*.

11. **A. micans** A. S. (1875). V. hyaline, with strongly arcuate dorsal margin and straight ventral margin. Ends apiculate. L. 0,12; B. 0,028 mm. Median line approximate to the ventral margin. Central nodule dilated into a stauros. Dorsal striæ 14 in 0,01 mm., distinctly visible near the median line, but on the valve broken up into small, scattered puncta, 4 to 5 in 0,01 mm. Ventral side very narrow; its striæ close, about 26 in 0,01 mm. — Atl. XXVI f. 18. Icon. n. Pl. IV f. 7—9.

Marine: Campeachy Bay (Atl.), Macassar Straits (Grove Coll.)!

12. **A. decussata** GRUN. (1867). Frustule thin, elliptical with truncate ends, about twice as long as broad. Zone with numerous divisions. V. lunate with acute ends. L. 0,05 to 0,17; B. 0,011 to 0,03 mm. Median line close to the ventral margin. Central nodule dilated into a transverse stauros. Dorsal side with very oblique striæ, about 17 in 0,01 mm., turned in opposite directions from the stauros and crossed by undulating, narrow, transverse blank bands. Ventral

side very narrow. Its striæ 15 in 0,01 mm. — Hedwigia VI p. 23. M. J. 1877 p. 178 Pl. CXCV f. 9. A. D. p. 25. Icon. n. Pl. IV f. 10.

Marine: Balearic Islands! Adriatic! China! Honduras (Grun.), Barbados!

Var. *brioeensis* LEUD. FORTM. Ms. — Frustule elliptical, with truncate ends. L. 0,015; B. 0,02 mm. Zone with about 8 divisions in 0,01 mm. transversely striate; striæ 15 in 0,01 mm. Dorsal oblique striæ 21 in 0,01 mm. — Pl. IV f. 11.

Marine: The Eng. Channel (Deby Coll.)!

13. **A. Lunula** CL. N. Sp. — V. lunate, with subacute ends and straight ventral margin. L. 0,13 to 0,15; B. 0,018 to 0,02 mm. Median line straight, not very closely approximate to the ventral margin. Central nodule transversely dilated into a stauros. Striæ on the dorsal side almost parallel, 14 to 17 in 0,01 mm., composed of distinct puncta, about 13 in 0,01 mm. Ventral side striate; striæ 12 to 15 in 0,01 mm. punctate. — Pl. IV f. 13.

Marine: Balearic Islands! Sumatra (Deby Coll.)! Colon (Deby Coll.)!

14. **A. staurophora** (CASTR. 1886?) CL. — Frustule hyaline, in outline quadrate to rectangular. V. slightly indented in the middle of the dorsal margin, narrow, with obtuse ends. L. 0,05 to 0,055; B. 0,01 mm. Median line straight, at some distance from the ventral margin. Central nodule dilated to a transverse stauros. Striæ delicate, punctate, about 20 in 0.01 mm. — *A. sp.* A. S. Atl. XXV f. 85, 86. *A. staurophora* CASTR. Voyage Challenger p. 20 Pl. XXVII f. 6? Icon. n. Pl. IV f. 33. 34.

Marine: Davis Straits (Atl.), North Sea (Atl.), Morocco! Balearic Islands! Pensacola!

This form is only imperfectly known and requires further investigations.

15. **A. ostrearia** BRÉB. (1849). — Frustule silicious, in outline elliptical to quadrate, or rectangular. Zone with numerous divisions, 3 to 9 in 0,01 mm., distinctly striate. V. of various apparent shapes, depending on its positions. L. 0,03 to 0,17; B. 0,005 to 0,02 mm. Median line biarcuate. Central nodule transversely dilated to a stauros. Dorsal and ventral side with about equinumerous, distinctly punctate striæ, 10 to 17 in 0,01 mm.

A. ostrearia is very variable in size and in the number of striæ. The valves have very different shapes in different positions, and for these reasons a large number of forms have been, often in a very incomplete manner, described or figured as distinct species.

Var. *vitrea* CL. (1868). — L. of frustule 0,036 to 0,1; B. 0,068 mm. Zone with 4 to 5 divisions in 0,01 mm. its striæ 10 to 11 in 0.01 mm. Striæ on the dorsal and ventral side 9 to 10 in 0,01 mm. composed of puncta, about 10 in 0.01 mm. — *A. vitrea* CL. Svenska och N. D. p. 237 Pl. IV f. 5. A. S. Atl. XXVI f. 25. *A. Nova Caledonica* GRUN. A. S. Atl. XXVI f. 16 (1875). *A. Porcellus* KITTON A. S. Atl. XXXIX f. 15 to 17. *A. Treubii* LEUD. FORTM. D. de la Malaisie p. 11 Pl. I f. 7 (1892)?

Marine: Spitsbergen! Bohuslän! Mediterranean Sea! Labuan! Japan (Atl.). New Caledonia (Atl.), West Indies!

Var. *typica* CL. — Frustule 0,035 to 0,08 mm. in length and 0,02 to 0,06 mm. in breadth. Zone with 3 to 5 divisions in 0.01 mm. Its striæ about 13 in 0.01 mm. Striæ of the valve 11 to 13 in 0.01 mm.; their puncta about 12 in 0,01 mm. — *A. ostrearia* KÜTZ Sp. Alg. p. 94. GRUN. A. D. p. 25. A. S. Atl. XXVI f. 23. V. H. Syn. p. 55 Pl. I f. 25. *A. membranacea* W. SM. B. D. I p. 20 Pl. II f. 29 1853 (striæ are stated to be 31 in 0.01 mm., but are distinct on the figure at an enlargement of 400 only). *A. quadrata* BRÉB. Kütz Sp. Alg. p. 95 (1849)? *A. elegans* GREG. T. M. S. V p. 70 Pl. I f. 30 (1857)? *A. litoralis* DONK. T. M. S. VI p. 30 Pl. III f. 15 (1858). *A. Petitii* TEMP. and BRUN D. foss. du Japon p. 15 Pl. IX f. 16 (1889). *A. Nova Caledonica* PANT. III Pl. XV f. 227 (1893).

Marine: Finmark! North Sea! Mediterranean Sea! Sumatra! Labuan! China (Deby Coll.)! Japan (Brun. Coll.)!

Var. *lineata* CL. — L. of V. 0,085; B. 0,015 mm. Striæ 12 to 13 in 0,01 mm., composed of puncta (about 9 in 0,01 mm.) forming straight, longitudinal rows. — *A. litoralis* CL. M. D. N:o 255.

Marine: Mouth of Somme!

Var. *minor* GRUN. (1880). — Frustule elliptical, truncate. L. 0,03 to 0,037; B. 0,017 to 0,019 mm. Divisions about 8 in 0,01 mm. Striæ 17 in 0,01 mm. — A. D. p. 25. CL. M. D. N:o 142.

Marine: West coast of Sweden!

Var. *belgica* GRUN. (1880). — Frustule rectangular. L. 0,033 to 0,048; B. 0,021 to 0,022 mm. Divisions of the zone about 9 in 0,01 mm. Striæ on the zone 18 in 0,01 mm. Valve with 16 to 17 finely punctate striæ in 0,01 mm. — V. H. Syn. p. 56 V. H. T. N:o 74.

Marine: Belgium!

16. **A. lævis** GREG. (1857). — Frustule hyaline and membranaceous, rectangular, with more or less truncate ends. L. 0,04 to 0,09; B. 0,02 to 0,04 mm. Zone with numerous divisions, 6 to 9 in 0,01 mm. Striæ fine, about 22 in 0,01 mm. — D. of Clyde p. 514 Pl. XII f. 71 *a, b, c*. A. S. Atl. XXVI f. 10. GRUN. A. D. p. 24 Pl. I f. 8 (var of *A. ostrearia*?). DANNF. D. of the Baltic p. 20 Pl. I f. 5.

Brackish and marine: Finmark! North Sea! Balearic Islands! Java (A. S. Atl.).

A. lævis differs from *A. ostrearia* by being more transparent and thin. The striæ are much more delicate, and scarcely visible on the connecting zone. In some specimens the stauros is only imperfectly developed, in which case *A lævis* offers a remarkable likeness to *A. lineolata*. Akin to *A. lævis* is probably *A. nobilis* FLÖGEL Pommerania Exp. p. 88 f. 9.

Var. *lævissima* GREG. (1857). — F. very thin. L. 0,06 to 0,076; B. 0,023 mm. Divisions of the zone obscure. Striæ 27 to 28 in 0,01 mm. — *A. lævissima* GREG. D. of Clyde p. 513 Pl XII f. 72. A. S. Atl. XXVI f. 3. 13. 14. V. H. T. N:o 8.

Brackish and marine: Sea of Kara! Finmark! Scotland! England!

Var. *minuta* CL. — Frustule in L. about 0,035; B. 0,02 mm. Striæ very delicate. — *A. lævissima* H. L. SM. T. N:o 615.

Marine: Helgoland!

Var. *perminuta* GRUN. — Frustule in L. 0,016 to 0,018; B. 0,0085 mm. Striæ very delicate. — *A. læviss. var. permin.* GRUN. in V. H. T. N:o 9. *A. hians* FLÖGEL? (Grun.).

Marine: Swansea Docks, Schleswig (Grun.).

To *A. lævis* seems to belong *A. excisa* GREG. (D. of Clyde p. 521 Pl. XIII f. 86, 1857) and A. S. Atl. XXXIX f. 3.

17. **A. quadrata** BRÉB. (1889). — Frustule very thin and membranaceous, rectangular, with broad, truncate ends. L. 0,09; B. 0,03 mm. Stauros narrow. Zone with numerous, strongly marked divisions, about 6 in 0,01 mm. Striæ exceedingly fine. — KTZ Sp. Alg. p. 94? V. H. Syn. p. 56 Pl. I f. 24. *A. parallela* FLÖGEL Pommerania Exp. p. 88 f. 8 (1873)? *A. polyzonata* CASTR. D. of Challenger Exp. p. 8 Pl. XXVII f. 18 (1856)?

Marine: Belgium (V. H.). Sweden, Fiskebäckskil!

This species is remarkable for its cell-contents, the chromatophores being numerous rounded discs, as in the coccochromatic diatoms. It differs from *A. ostrearia* in its rectangular outline and exceedingly fine structure, and from *A. lævis* in its strongly marked divisions.

Subgenus **Amblyamphora**.

Frustule more or less rectangular. Connecting zone complex. Valves linear to lunate, with obtuse, usually broad ends. Components of the median line divergent towards the dorsal margin. Axial and central areas indistinct. Structure: fine puncta arranged in transverse striæ, which on the ventral side usually diverge towards the median line. No longitudinal lines.

The forms comprised in this subgenus agree in all respects, except in the complex nature of the zone, with *Psammamphora*, for which reason it is impossible to decide whether detached valves belong to one or other of the subgenera.

Artificial key.

1.	Striæ on the dorsal side furcate . . .	*A. spectabilis* GREG.
	— not —	. . . . . . 2.
2.	Valve reniform	*A. obesa* CL. a. GROVE.
	— linear	. . . . 3.
3.	Valve about 20 times longer than broad	*A. inflexa* BRÉB.
	— 6 to 7 — — — —	*A. obtusa* GREG.

1. **A. inflexa** BRÉB. (1849). Frustule linear, elongated, with truncate ends. Connecting zone with close and fine divisions. V. arcuate, linear, with rounded ends. L. 0,13; B. 0,007 mm. Median line more approximate to the dorsal than to the ventral margin. Central nodule elongated. No areas. Striæ 20 in 0,01 mm. parallel, convergent at the ends, where they are closer, very finely punctate. -- *Amphipleura inflexa* BRÉB., KÜTZ Sp. Alg. p. 88. *Amphora inflexa* H. L. SM. Lens II p. 78 Pl. II f. 16 (1873). *Okedenia inflexa* EULENST. Ms. CL. M. D. N:o 192 (1879). V. H. T. N:o 167.

Marine (pelagic): Firth of Tay! Adriatic!

The fig. in The Lens does not give any idea of the appearance of this isolated and strange form. The complex nature of the zone is very difficult to discover, and I am indebted to Prof. VAN HEURCK for photographs of specimens, mounted in realgar, which shew it pretty well.

2. **A. obtusa** GREG. (1857). -- Frustule in outline elliptic-rectangular, somewhat more than twice as long as broad. V. linear, obliquely rounded. L. 0,065 to 0,26; B. 0,01 to 0,035 mm. Median line not dilated to a stauros. Striæ 11 to 20 in 0,01 mm.

Forma *typica* CL. — L. of valve 0,075 to 0,14; B. 0,035 to 0,05 mm. Dorsal and ventral striæ 18 to 20 in 0,01 mm., composed of puncta, 15 to 24 in 0,01 mm. *A. obtusa* GREG. T. M. S. V p. 72 Pl. I f. 34. A. S. Atl. XL f. 4 to 7, 11 to 13. *Amphiprora maxima* RAB. JAN. Honduras D. p. 3 Pl. II f. 4 (1862). *Toxonidea lævis* WITT J. Mus. Godeff. p. 70 Pl. VIII f. 9 (1873). *Amphora permagna* PANT. II p. 38 Pl. VI f. 113 (1889).

Marine: North Sea! Mediterranean Sea! Adriatic! Black Sea! Red Sea! Seychelles! Madagascar! Labuan! Celebes! China! Cape May! North Carolina! West Indies! Campeachy Bay! Mexico! Porto Seguro! Fossil: Hungary, Czekehaza! Oamaru (Striæ 17 to 18 in 0,01 mm.).

Forma *minuta* CL. -- Frustule 0,063 in length and in breadth 0,03. B. of the valve 0,03 mm. Striæ 25 in 0,01 mm.; puncta about 21 in 0,01 mm.

Marine: Macassar Straits!

Var. *oceanica* CASTR. (1886). — V. in L. 0,13 to 0,26; in B. 0,028 to 0,035 mm. Striæ 15 in 0,01 mm., composed of puncta, about 15 in 0,01 mm., which form undulating, longitudinal rows. — *A. oceanica* CASTR. Challenger Exp. D. p. 20 Pl. XXVII f. 20. *A. fallax* TEMP. et BRUN D. du Japon p. 14 Pl. VII f. 13 (1889). *A. cyclops* LEUD. FORTM. D. de Ceylon Pl. VIII f. 82 (1879)?

Marine: Gulf of Naples (Deby Coll.)! Ceylon (Le Tourneur Coll.)! Sumatra (V. H. Coll.)! China (Deby Coll.)! Sydney (Castr.). Japan, fossil (Temp. a. Brun).

Var. *Lanyaeskii* PANT. (1889). — L. 0,129; B. 0,028 mm. Striæ 9 to 9,5 in 0,01 mm. — *A. Lan.* PANT. II p. 38; III Pl. XXXV f. 498.

Marine: Hungary, fossil (Pant.).

Var. *transfuga* CL. -- V. in L. 0,18 and B. 0,023 mm. Striæ 11 to 12 in 0,01 mm.; puncta 19 in 0,01 mm. — *Amphora obtusa* A. S. Atl. XL f. 16, 17?

Marine: Madagascar! Macassar Straits!

Var. *Radula* Cl. — V. in L. 0,14, in B. 0,021 mm. Striæ 12 in 0,01 mm.; puncta 9 in 0,01 mm.

Marine: Gulf of Naples (Petit and Deby Coll.)!

3. **A. spectabilis** Greg. (1857). — Frustule elliptic-rectangular. L. 0,11; B. 0,05 mm. Zone finely transversely striate; striæ about 12 in 0,01 mm. finely punctate. V. narrow. L. 0,07 to 0,11; B. 0,02 mm. linear, with obliquely rounded ends. Striæ on the dorsal side of the valve 5 to 6 in 0,01 mm., furcate, composed of coarse puncta, about 14 in 0,01 mm. Striæ on the ventral part 8 to 9 in 0,01 mm. D. of Clyde p. 516 Pl. XIII f. 80 *a* and *c*. A. S. Atl. XL f. 18 to 23. *A. furcata* Leud. Fortm. D. de Ceylon p. 20 Pl. I f. 11 (1879).

Marine: North Sea! Mediterranean Sea! Ceylon! Borneo! Seychelles! Madagascar! China! Samoa! West Indies! Davis Straits! Macassar Straits!

The description of this species in D. of Clyde agrees very well with this species, as do also the fig. *a* and *d*, but *b* and *c* belong probably to another species and fig. *c* seems to represent *A. obtusa*.

4. **A. obesa** Cl. and Grove (1892). V. with almost semicircular dorsal, and straight ventral margins, and obtuse, broad ends. L. 0,09 to 0,167; B. 0,03 to 0,07 mm. Components of the median line divergent from the central nodule at an angle of about 140. Striæ 9,5 in 0,01 mm., curved and composed of puncta, about 8 in 0,01 mm. Ventral striæ divergent on the portion between the central and terminal nodules. — Diatomiste I p. 157 Pl. XXII f. 8.

Marine: Macassar Straits!

Of this curious form valves only are known at present, so it cannot be decided whether it belongs to Amblyamphora or Psammamphora, but as the striæ are coarse, I believe it is more nearly related to *A. obtusa* than to *A. arenaria*.

Subgenus **Psammamphora** Cl.

Frustule more or less rectangular. Connecting zone not complex. Median line arcuate. Central nodule frequently transversely dilated to a stauros. No axial or central areas. No longitudinal lines. Structure fine puncta disposed in transverse rows or striæ on the dorsal and ventral side of the valve.

This subgenus, named after one of the typical species, *A. arenaria* Donk., comprises forms with or without stauros, which is no characteristic of generic value. It is well defined, and closely analogous to the subg. *Amblyamphora*, the zone of which is complex.

Among the Naviculas the group *Stauroneis*, and the non-complex *Microstigmaticæ* are probably in near relation to this section.

Artificial key.

1.	Central nodule dilated to a stauros	2.
	— not —	3.
2.	Puncta arranged in decussating striæ	*A. Pleurosigma* Temp. a. Brun.
	— — transverse —	4.
	— indistinct	*A. hians* Flogel.
3.	Marine species	*A. ocellata* Donk.
	Fresh water species	*A. delphinea* A. S.
4.	Marine species	5.
	Fresh water species	*A. Berggrenii* Cl.
5.	Valve not inflated or with a single median inflation	*A. arenaria* Donk.
	— with two median inflations	*A. biggibosa* Cl.

1. **A. biggibosa** CL. N. Sp. V. with two gibbosities on the middle of the dorsal side. L. 0,1; B. 0,016 mm. Central nodule not dilated into a stauros. Striæ 18 in 0,01 mm., punctate; puncta 20 in 0,01 mm. — *A. sp.* A. S. Atl. XL f. 11.

Marine: Gulf of Naples (Brun Coll.)! Gulf of Mexico (A. S. Atl.).

I have not seen entire frustules, so I cannot decide whether this species really belongs to the section *Psammamphora* or *Amblyamphora*. To judge from the fig. in Atl., which represents an entire frustule, the zone is not complex, and in such case this species is akin to *A. arenaria*.

2. **A. arenaria** DONK. (1853). Frustule hyaline, rectangular. L. 0,1 to 0,15; B. 0,01 mm. V. linear, with broad ventral side. Striæ very fine, 24 to 27 in 0,01 mm. parallel.

Forma *typica*. — Frustule with rounded angles and somewhat gibbous middle. L. 0,1 to 0,15; B. 0,04 mm. Striæ 27 in 0,01 mm. — *A. arenaria* DONK. T. M. S. VI p. 31 Pl. III f. 16. A. S. Atl. XL f. 8, 9, 10, 12. V. H. T. N:o 13. H. L. SM. I N:o 30.

Marine (æstuaries): North Sea! Hungary, fossil (Pant.).

Var. *Donkinii* RABH. (1864). — Frustule elliptic-rectangular to rectangular. L. 0,076 to 0,1; B. 0,03 to 0,04 mm. Striæ 24 to 25 in 0,01 mm. — *A. lineolata* DONK. Q. M. J. I. N. S. p. 12 Pl. I f. 13 (1861). *A. Donkinii* RABH. F. E. A. p. 96.

Marine æstuaries: North Sea! Cape May!

Var. *Rattrayi* CL. (1882). Frustule rectangular, with truncate ends. L. 0,035 to 0,04; B. 0,015 to 0,017 mm. Striæ extremely fine. *A. Rattrayi* CL. M. D. N:o 310.

Marine: Æstuaries: Scotland! Belgium!

3. **A. ocellata** DONK. (1861). — Frustule rectangular. L. 0,06 to 0,11; B. 0,028 to 0,035 mm. Valve in breadth 0,05 mm. linear. Central nodule on the dorsal side dilated into a stauros. Terminal fissures small. Striæ 17 to 21 in 0,01 mm. punctate. Ventral side as broad as the dorsal, finely striate. Striæ in the middle between the central nodule and the ends divergent towards the median line.

Var. *typica* CL. — L. 0,06 to 0,09 mm. Striæ 21 in 0,01 mm. composed of puncta, about 24 in 0,01 mm. — *A. ocell.* DONK. Q. M. J. N. S. I p. 11 Pl. I f. 11. V. H. Syn. p. 56 Pl. I f. 26.

Marine: Coasts of Sweden! Belgium! England! Adriatic!

Var. *cingulata* CL. (1878). — L. 0,085 to 0,12; B. 0,015 mm. Striæ 17 in 0,01 mm.; puncta 20 in 0,01 mm. — *A. cingulata* CL. D. W. Ind. Arch. p. 9 Pl. III f. 15. A. S. Atl. XXVI f. 17. Icon. n. Pl. III f. 39.

Marine: Gulf of Mexico! Pensacola! West Indies! N. Carolina!

Var.? *interrupta* PANT. (1886). — V. more lunate. L. 0,079; B. 0,013 mm. Striæ 20 in 0,01 mm. — *A. (ostrearia?) interrupta* PANT. I p. 21 Pl. XV f. 131.

Marine: Hungary, fossil (Pant.).

As entire frustules have not been seen, it is doubtful whether this form really belongs to *A. ocellata*. A very similar valve in VAN HEURCK's Coll. from Sumatra has 17 striæ and 17 puncta in 0,01 mm.

Var.? *oamaruensis* CL. V. in L. 0,18; B. 0,026 mm. Stauros obscure. Transverse striæ 16, puncta 14 in 0,01 mm.

Marine: Oamaru (Grove Coll.)!

As *A. staurophora* DANNFELDT (Baltic D. p. 20 Pl. I f. 9) has described a very small Amphora (only 0,014 mm. in length), which seems to belong to this section, but having had no opportunity of examining it, I am unable to decide about its affinities.

4. **A. Pleurosigma** TEMP. and BRUN (1889). — Frustule thin and flat, rectangular, with rounded angles. L. 0,12 to 0,16; B. 0,042 mm. V. in breadth about 0,02 mm. Ventral side appearently broader than the dorsal. Central nodule dilated to a stauros. Structure, fine puncta disposed in lines crossing each other in the angle of 65°. — D. Foss. du Japon p. 15 Pl. VII f. 8.

Marine: Japan, fossil (Br. et Temp.).

5. **A. delphinea** (BAIL. 1861?) A. S. Atl. (1876). — Frustule silicious, broadly elliptic-rectangular, frequently gibbous in the middle. L. 0,076 to 0,12; B. 0,05 to 0,068 mm. Valve linear to lunate, with obliquely rounded ends. Central nodule dilated to a stauros. Terminal fissures deep. Striæ 27 to 28 in 0,01 mm., on the dorsal side parallel, on the ventral divergent towards the median line. — Bost. Jour. Nat. Hist. VII Pl. I f. 1 (fide H. L. Sm.). A. S. Atl. XL f. 26, 27.

Fresh water: Demerara River!

Var. *minor* CL. — V. in L. 0,06; B. 0,012 mm. Striæ 24 in 0,01 mm. — A. S. Atl. XL f. 25.

Fresh water: North America, Crane Pond! Demerara River!

Var. *jamalinensis* CL. a. GRUN. (1880). — V. more linear, with gibbous middle. L. 0,048 to 0,057; B. 0,01 to 0,011 mm. Striæ very fine. — *A. ocellata var. jamal.* A. D. p. 21 Pl. I f. 6. A. S. Atl. XL f. 24?

Brackish water: Sea of Kara! Pensacola (Atl.)?

It is difficult to find any specific distinction between this species and *A. ocellata*. Yet they cannot be regarded as the same species. *A. ocellata* is thinner, has somewhat coarser striæ, and less deeply impressed terminal fissures. Moreover *A. delphinea* is a freshwater form and *A. ocellata* marine.

6. **A. Berggrenii** CL. (1878). Frustule silicious, subrectangular with rounded ends. L. 0,065; B. 0,025 mm. Median line with distant median pores; its terminal fissures deep and flexuose. Central nodule not dilated into a stauros. Dorsal striæ parallel, 17 in 0,01 mm., ventral striæ divergent towards the median line. CL. a. M. D. N:o 90. CL. N. R. D. p. 4 Pl. I f. 3 (1881). H. L. SM. T. N:o 610.

Fresh water: New Zealand, Arthur's Pass, foss.!

This remarkable species is evidently akin to *A. delphinea*, although its central nodule is not dilated to a stauros.

7. **A. hians** FLÖGEL (1873). Frustule elliptical, in the middle slightly constricted, with truncate ends. L. 0,045; B. 0,015 mm. V. narrow with slightly reflexed ends. Central nodule a transverse stauros. Striæ not seen. — Pommerania Exp. p. 88 f. 7.

Marine: Knarrhöi, Kattegat (Flögel).

Subgenus **Cymbamphora.**

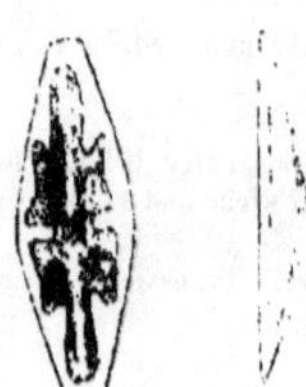

A. angusta var. ventricosa with cell-contents; 600 times magnified.

Valve narrow elongated, semilanceolate, gradually tapering from the middle to the acute or subacute ends. Median line straight, approximate to the ventral margin. Striæ not crossed by longitudinal lines. Connecting zone without divisions. — Living specimens of *A. angusta var. ventricosa* have a chromatophore-plate along the ventral side of the connecting zone. Another plate occurs on the dorsal side. Both are deeply constricted in the middle.

This subgenus, in which the valves have a considerable likeness to some Cymbellæ, comprises marine forms only, so closely connected that many of the reputed species differ in nothing but the number of striæ, size of the valve, and such trifling characteristics.

Artificial key of species

1.	Striæ very fine 20 or more in 0,01 mm.	2.
	— coarser less than 20 in 0,01 mm.	3.
2.	Frustule short, narrow elliptical	*A. cymbelloides* GRUN.
	— very elongated, linear	*A. arcta* A. S.

3. { Striæ distinctly punctate . . . . *A. magellanica* Per.
   { — not distinctly punctate 4
4. { Axial area distinct . . . . *A. angusta* Cl.
   { — — not distinct . . . . 5.
5. { Median line straight . . . . *A. cymbiformis* Cl.
   { — — slightly biarcuate . . . . *A. bituminosa* Pant.

1. **A. angusta** (Greg. 1857) Cl. — V. narrow, semilanceolate, acute or subacute. L. 0,01 to 0,13; B. 0,005 to 0,018 mm. Median line straight, parallel and approximate to the ventral margin. Axial area distinct and frequently moderately broad on the dorsal side, indistinct or small on the ventral side. Striæ 7 to 17 in 0,01 mm., not distinctly punctate. Both the dorsal and the ventral sides of the valve are striate.

This species comprises a number of forms.

Var. *typica* Cl. — B. of the frustule 0,01. L. of the valve 0,05 to 0,055; B. 0,005 to 0,007 mm. Striæ 17 to 18 in 0,01 mm. — *A. angusta* Greg. D. of Clyde p. 510 Pl. XII f. 66. *A. angusta var. gracilenta* Grun. A. S. Atl. XXV f. 15. *A. Eulensteinii var. fossilis* Pant. 1889 II p. 36 Pl. I f. 3. Pl. III f. 49. *Cymbella marina* Castr. Chall. Exp. D. p. 31. Pl. XXVII f. 13?

Marine: Scotland (Greg.), Spitsbergen! Sea of Kara! Quincy, Massachusetts! Czekehaza, Hungary (fossil)! Jamaica (Grove Coll.).

The figure of *A. angusta* in Diat. of the Clyde is not sufficient for identification without original specimens, but as in the description is stated that it has 17 to 18 striæ in 0,01 mm. I think that *A. angusta* Greg. may denote this form. *A. Eulensteinii var. fossilis* is described as having 20 to 22,5 striæ in 0,01 mm. I found 18 only in specimens from Czekehaza. *Cymbella marina* Castr. may be this or another form of *A. angusta*, it is impossible to decide which from the figure and the description.

Var. *oblongella* Grun. (1878). — Frustule in breadth 0,008 to 0,013. V. in L. 0,032 to 0,068; B. 0,006 to 0,01 mm. Striæ 14 to 15 in 0,01 mm. — *A. oblongella* Grun. Casp. Sea D. p. 7 Pl. IV f. 20. *A. exigua* Greg. D. of Clyde p. 514 Pl. IV f. 75? *A. angusta var. arctica* Grun. A. D. p. 24 Pl. I f. 9 (1880). *A. lanceolata var. minor* Cl. Vega p. 462 (1883).

Marine and brackish: Sweden (Bohuslän)! Firth of Tay! East cape! Behrings Island! Balearic Islands! Caspian Sea (Grun.). Campeachy Bay! Pensacola! Honolulu!

A. exigua Greg. may be this form although the striæ are stated to be 11 in 0,01 mm., but it is impossible to decide without original specimens.

Var. *Eulensteinii* Grun. (1875). — L. of the valve 0,08 to 0,121; B. 0,016 to 0,02 mm. Striæ 11 to 12 in 0,01 mm. somewhat closer on the ventral side, or about 14 in 0,01 mm. — *A. Eulensteinii* A. S. Atl. XXV f. 1 to 3; XL f. 35 to 37.

Marine: China! Japan! Govans Bay; Raised March; Leton Bank (Atl.), Cape May!

Var. *diducta* A. S. (1875). — V. gibbous in the middle. L. 0,082; B. 0,015 mm. Dorsal striæ 10 to 11 in 0,01 mm. — *A. did.* A. S. Atl. XXV f. 13. *A. cymbelloides var. latior* Grun. Atl. XXV f. 8.

Marine: Java, Japan (Atl.).

Var. *ventricosa* Greg. (1857). — V. in L. 0,059 to 0,13; B. 0,013 to 0,018 mm. Dorsal striæ 8 to 9 in 0,01 mm., ventral somewhat closer. — *A. ventricosa* Greg. D. of Clyde p. 511 Pl. XII f. 68. *A. lanceolata* Cl. D. from Spitsb. p. 667 Pl. XXIII f. 2 (1864). *Cymbella criophila* Castr. Chall. Exp. D. p. 21 Pl. XXVII f. 5 1886 (striæ distinctly punctate)? *Cymbella marina* Pant. III Pl. XIX f. 274?

Marine: Greenland! Spitsbergen! Sea of Kara! Finmark! Coasts of Scotland, Norway and Bohuslän! Adriatic! Bab el Mandeb! Monterey (Atl. XXV f. 6).

The fig. in Diat. of the Clyde is insufficient for identification, still I have little doubt that Gregory denotes this form. An intermediate form between *Var. ventricosa* et *Var. Eulensteinii* is fig. 5 Pl XXV in A. S Atl.

Var. *incurvata* BRUN (1891). Valve arcuate. L. 0,1 to 0,13; B. 0,011 mm. Striæ 6 in 0,01 mm. — *A. lanceolata var. incr.* BRUN D. espèces n. p. 8 Pl. XII f. 3.

Marine: Japan! Western Africa (Brun).

Var. *zebrina* A. S. (1875). — V. gibbous in the middle. L. 0,075; B. 0,009 mm. Striæ 6 (dorsal) to 7 (ventral) in 0,01 mm. — *A. zebrina* A. S. Atl. XXV f. 11.

Marine: Baltjik Dept. (Atl.).

2. **A. cymbiformis** CL. N. Sp. — V. semilanceolate, acute. L. 0,045 to 0,07; B. 0,007 to 0,013 mm. Axial area indistinct. Striæ 14 to 17 in 0,01 mm. — A. S. Atl. Pl. XXV f. 9.

Marine: Port Jackson! Labuan!

3. **A. cymbelloides** GRUN. (1867). — Hyaline. L. of the frustule 0,038 to 0,084; B. of the frustule 0,011 to 0,013, of the valve 0,008 to 0,011 mm. Striæ very fine, 29 in 0,01 mm. or more. — Hedw. 1867, VI p. 24. *A. angusta var. minuta* GRUN. A. S. Atl. XXVI f. 65, 66. DANNF. Baltic D. Pl. I f. 10? *A. angusta var. glaberrima* GRUN. A. S. Atl. XXVI f. 61, 62.

Marine: Seychelles! Honduras (Grun.), Barbados!

The original *A. cymbelloides* of GRUNOW is a very delicately striate form, of which the author several years ago sent me a sketch, agreeing with *A. angusta var. minuta*, or *var. glaberrima* in A. S. Atl. More coarsely striate forms have since been published as *A. cymbelloides* (Atl. XXV f. 8, 11) which belong to *A. angusta*. The *var. mauritiana* GRUN. (Hedwigia l. c. p. 25) cannot belong to the same species as it has a longitudinal line across the striæ.

4. **A. arcta** A. S. (1875). — Hyaline. Frustule almost linear with truncate ends. L. 0,094; B. 0,012 mm. Striæ delicate. — Atl. XXVI f. 63.

Marine: Australia, Port Lincoln (Atl.).

5. **A. magellanica** PETIT (1888). — V. semilanceolate, acute. L. 0,061 to 0,063; B. 0,01 to 0,011 mm. Median line straight, approximate to the ventral margin. Axial area indistinct; central small, rounded. Striæ 12 in 0,01 mm. finely punctate. — D. de Cape Horn p. 119 Pl. X f. 14. A. S. Atl. XXV f. 4 (no name).

Marine: Magellan's Straits!

6. **A. bituminosa** PANT. (1889). — Frustule elongated, elliptical. L. 0,016 to 0,018; B. 0,012 to 0,014 mm. Median line approximate to the ventral margin, slightly biarcuate. Axial and central areas indistinct. Striæ 14 to 15 in 0,01 mm. not distinctly punctate and not interrupted or crossed by a longitudinal line. Connecting zone not complex. — PANT. II p. 35 Pl. I f. 1. Pl. II f. 23.

Brackish water: Szardoc, Hungary, fossil!

It is doubtful whether this species be correctly placed in this subgenus or in the subgenus Amphora, as the median line is not perfectly straight.

Subgenus **Calamphora** CL.

Frustule rectangular, with more or less rounded ends. Zone complex, with more or less numerous, transversely striate or costate divisions. Valves linear, obtuse, or with obliquely rounded ends. Median line biarcuate, not closely approximate to the ventral margin. Dorsal side with transverse striæ, not crossed by a longitudinal line. Ventral side structureless, but with a longitudinal line.

This subgenus comprises complex forms, the dorsal striæ of which are not crossed by a keel or line. From *Halamphora* and *Oxyamphora* they differ by the broader ventral side, which has a longitudinal line, and by the non-protracted or non-rostrate ends.

Artificial key.

1.	L. 0,03 to 0,05 mm.	*A. pusilla* Cl.
	L. 0,045 to 0,075 mm.	2.
2.	Central nodule stauroid	*A. sendaiana* Brun.
	— — not —	3.
3.	Valve constricted in the middle	5.
	— not — — —	4.
4.	Costæ 8 to 9 in 0,01 mm.	*A. formosa* Cl.
	— 5 to 6 — —	*A. Scala* Cl. a. Grove.
5.	Slightly constricted	6.
	Strongly —	7.
	Triconstricted	*A. dorsalis* Cl. a. Grove.
6.	Valve with a hyaline wing	*A. limbata* Cl. a. Grove.
	— without — —	*A. Grovei* Cl.
7.	Striæ 8 in 0,01 mm.	*A. Camelus* Cl. a. Grove.
	— 10 — —	*A. biconvexa* Jan.

1. **A. pusilla** (Greg. 1857?) Cl. — Frustule linear-elliptical, with rounded ends. L. 0,032 to 0,053; B. 0,01 to 0,02 mm. V. with obtuse and gibbous ends. Median line biarcuate, at some distance from the ventral margin. Dorsal side striate; striæ 12 in 0,01 mm. not distinctly punctate. Ventral side not striate. — D. of Clyde p. 525 Pl. XIV f. 95? Diatomiste I p. 159 Pl. XXIII f. 3, 4.

Marine: Macassar Straits!

It is doubtful what *A. pusilla* Greg. may denote. It is described as having coarser striæ (9 in 0,01 mm.) than *A. bacillaris* Greg., to which it otherwise bears a considerable resemblance. There is some doubt about the exact position of this little form, as the ventral side of the valve has, so far as I have hitherto seen, no distinct longitudinal line.

2. **A. Camelus** Cl. and Grove (1892). — Frustule of rectangular outline. L. 0,073; B. 0,035 mm. Zone with a number of longitudinal divisions (2 in 0,01 mm.) transversely striate; striæ 9 in 0,01 mm. V. with slightly arcuate median line and the dorsal margin sinuose in the middle. Ends capitate. Dorsal side with 8 striæ in 0,01 mm. — Diatomiste I p. 158 Pl. XXII f. 9 to 12.

Marine: Macassar Straits!

3. **A. biconvexa** Jan. 1875. — V. with straight ventral margin. Dorsal margin sinuose in the middle, and with rostrate-truncate or capitate ends. L. 0,1 to 0,14; B. 0,017 to 0,025 mm. Median line straight, approximate to the ventral margin. Dorsal striæ 9 to 11 in 0,01 mm. alternating with single rows of obscure puncta, about 18 in 0,01 mm. Ventral side without striæ. — A. S. Atl. XXV f. 68.

Marine: Macassar Straits (Grove Coll.)! Nossibé (Brun Coll.)! Carpentaria Bay (Atl.).

This form, of which valves only have been observed, is still imperfectly known, and its place in the system is consequently not well established. The median striæ of the dorsal side are often approximate, giving the appearance of a stauros.

4. **A. dorsalis** Cl. and Grove (1892). Frustule rectangular. L. 0,09; B. 0,03 mm. Zone with a number of longitudinal divisions (about 3 in 0,01 mm.) transversely and coarsely striate; V. with capitate ends and quadri-undulated dorsal margin. Striæ 10 in 0,01 mm. Diatomiste I p. 158 Pl. XXII f. 13 to 15.

Marine: Macassar Straits!

This species seems to be akin to *A. undulata* Grev. (Ed. N. Phil. J. XVII p. 182 f. 3 1863) from Queensland. The latter has however much coarser striæ and a not complex zone.

5. **A. limbata** Cl. and Grove (1892). — Frustule in outline rectangular, slightly constricted in the middle. L. 0,045 to 0,075; B. 0,02 to 0,035 mm. Zone with several longitudinal divisions

(5 to 8 in 0,01 mm.), coarsely, transversely striate; striæ 8 to 9 in 0,01 mm. On both sides of the longitudinal margins is a broad hyaline limbus. V. narrow, linear, with broad capitate ends. Median line slightly biarcuate. Dorsal side with 8 striæ in 0,01 mm., coarsely but obscurely punctate. Ventral side without striæ, and with a longitudinal line close to the median line. — Diatomiste I p. 159 Pl. XXIII f. 1, 2.

Marine: Norway, Grip! Morocco! Balearic Islands! Macassar Straits! Galapagos Islands!

The frustule has a considerable resemblance to *A. exsecta* GRUN., but the valves are different. *A. limpida* JAN. (A. S. Atl. XXXIX f. 8) is probably allied with this species, or is perhaps a small variety of it, but the figure it not sufficient for identification.

6. **A. sendaiana** BRUN (1891). — V. linear with obliquely rounded ends. L. 0,19; B. 0,02 mm. Median line biarcuate. Central nodule strong, dilated on the dorsal side to a stauros. Dorsal side with 11, finely punctate striæ in 0,01 mm. Ventral side without striæ, and with a longitudinal line. — D. espèces nov. p. 9 Pl. XII f. 1.

Marine: Japan, fossil!

According to Prof. BRUN there is a line across the striæ, which I have not noted in an original specimen, sent by him. If this line be not the margin of the frustule, and really crosses the striæ, this species may be removed from this group and placed in Diplamphora.

7. **A. Grovei** CL. (1892). — Frustule, of rectangular outline, gibbous on the back. L. 0,105; B. 0,05 mm. Zone with several divisions, transversely striate; striæ 18 in 0,01 mm. V. linear, with gibbous dorsal margin and broad ends. L. 0,10 to 0,12; B. 0,015 mm. Striæ on the dorsal side 10 to 11 in 0,01 mm., finely punctate. Ventral side not striate and with a longitudinal line. — Diatomiste I p. 158 Pl. XXII f. 16, 17.

Marine: Seychelles! Java! Sumbava (Kinker Coll.)! China! Macassar Straits!

8. **A. formosa** CL. (1875). — Frustule rectangular with rounded angles. L. 0,14; B. 0,07 mm. Zone with few, broad divisions, about 12 in 0,01 mm., finely transversely striate; striæ 8 to 9 in 0,01 mm. V. linear with obliquely rounded, spathulate, or clavate ends, according to the position of the valve. L. 0,09 to 0,2; B. 0,025 to 0,035 mm. Median line biarcuate. Dorsal side with 8 to 9 costate striæ in 0,01 mm., alternating with more or less distinct puncta, 15 to 18 in 0,01 mm. Ventral side structureless, with a longitudinal line. — A. S. Atl. XXVIII f. 34, XXXIX f. 2. *A. Studeri* JANISCH A. S. Atl. XXXIX f. 1 (1876).

Marine: Mediterranean Sea (Balearic Islands, Gulf of Naples)! Madagascar (Kinker Coll.)! Ceylon (Colombo, Le Tourneur Coll.)! Sumatra (Deby Coll.)! Singapore! Sumbava (Kinker Coll.)! Macassar Straits! Galapagos Islands! Colon (Deby Coll.)! Fossil: S:ta Monica, Calif.

Var. *minuta* CL. — L. of the frustule 0,085; B. 0,045 mm. Costæ 9 in 0,01 mm.

Marine: Macassar Straits! Bahia (Deby Coll.)!

The valves of this very large and beautiful diatom have a very different shape according to the position. *A. Petiti* LEUD. FORTM. (De de la Malaisie p. 10 Pl. I f. 3) may be a small form of this species, which I am unable to decide without original specimens.

9. **A. Scala** CL. and GROVE (1892). — Frustule of rectangular outline, with slightly concave sides and rounded ends. L. 0,14; B. 0,05 mm. Zone with broad divisions (about 2 in 0,01 mm.) which are transversely costate (costæ about 5,5 in 0,01 mm.). V. in B. 0,015 mm. Dorsal side with smooth, costate striæ, 5 to 6 in 0,01 mm.; intermediate space not distinctly punctate. Ventral side smooth with a strong longitudinal line. — Diatomiste I p. 158 Pl. XXII f. 18, 19.

Marine: Macassar Straits! Porto Seguro (Deby Coll.)!

Var. *alata* CL. — Dorsal side of the valve with a hyaline limbus. L. of the V. 0,24; B. 0,018 mm. Striæ 6 in 0,01 mm.

Marine: Macassar Straits!

Subgenus **Archiamphora.**

Frustule unknown. Valves as in Calamphora, but the ventral side is without longitudinal lines, and has a row of short striæ or puncta, either along the median line or between the median line and the margin.

The species of this subgenus are all found in a fossil state at Oamaru, New Zealand, always as detached valves. Yet they bear a considerable likeness to the forms of *Calamphora*, so that it is possible that the zone may be complex; and, indeed, in specimens of *A. fimbriata* fragments of the zone are found which tend to show that it is similar to those of the subgenus *Calamphora*.

Artificial key.

1.	Costæ 4 to 5 in 0,01 mm.	2.
	— 6 to 7 — —	*A. fimbriata* Cl. a. Grove.
	— 11 — —	*A. antiqua* Cl. a. Grove.
2.	Puncta 9 in 0,01 mm.	*A. rectilineata* Cl. a. Grove.
	— 11 — —	*A. prisca* Cl. a. Grove.

1. **A. antiqua** Cl. a. Grove N. Sp. V. linear, with obliquely rounded ends. L. 0,13; B. 0,013 mm. Dorsal side with parallel costate striæ, 11 in 0,01 mm., alternating with rows of puncta, 24 in 0,01 mm. Ventral side smooth, with a longitudinal median row of short striæ, 11 in 0,01 mm.
Marine: Oamaru, New Zealand, fossil (Grove Coll.)!

2. **A. rectilineata** Cl. a. Grove N. Sp. — V. linear with obliquely rounded ends. L. 0,09; B. 0,015 mm. Dorsal side with parallel costæ, 4 in 0,01 mm., alternating with double rows of puncta, 9 to 10 in 0,01 mm., forming longitudinal rows. Ventral side smooth, with a median band of short, puncta-like striæ, 6 in 0,01 mm. — Pl. IV f. 24, 25.
Marine: Oamaru, New Zealand, fossil (Grove Coll.)!

3. **A. fimbriata** Cl. a. Grove N. Sp. — V. linear with obliqely rounded ends. L. 0,14 to 0,18 mm. Dorsal side with parallel striæ, 6 to 7 in 0,01 mm. Ventral side with a row of short striæ, close to the median line.
Marine: Oamaru, New Zealand, fossil (Grove Coll.)!

4. **A. prisca** Cl. a. Grove N. Sp. — V. linear, with obliquely rounded ends. L. 0,14 to 0,16; B. 0,016 to 0,022 mm. Dorsal side with parallel costate striæ, 4 to 5 in 0,01 mm. Intermediate spaces transversely lineate; lineolæ 11 in 0,01 mm. Ventral side with a row of short radiate striæ along the median line, otherwise structureless.
Marine: Oamaru, New Zealand, fossil (Grove Coll.)!

Additional.

Amphoræ, which cannot for the present be grouped in any of the above subgenera.

1. **Amphora elegans** Perag. (1894). — Frustule elongated, narrow, with slightly convex margins and truncate ends. L. 0,09; B. 0,015 mm. Zone not complex. V. narrow lunate, acute. L. 0,08; B. 0,01 mm. Central nodule dilated into a stauros. No areas and no longitudinal lines. Striæ equidistant on the dorsal and ventral side, 22 in 0,01 mm. distinctly punctate; puncta 25 in 0,01 mm. arranged in straight longitudinal rows. — Temp. a. Perag. Types N:o 414. Diatomiste II p. 56 Pl. III f. 8.
Marine: Cabours.

This remarkable species has the same structure as the Naviculæ of the section *Orthostichæ* and might be considered as an asymmetrical form of this section.

2. **A. gibba** A. S. (1876). V. rectangular, somewhat constricted in the middle. L. 0,03; B. 0,015 mm. Median line close to the ventral margin. No areas and no longitudinal line. Striæ transverse in the middle, radiate at the ends, about 8 in 0,01 mm., composed of distant puncta about 6 in 0,01 mm. — Atl. XXXIX f. 32.

Marine: Galapagos Islands! Campeachy Bay (Atl.).

This is a characteristic and easily recognized form, evidently akin to *A. Reichardtiana*. As entire frustules are unknown, and the ventral side of the valve not has been seen, it is impossible to decide its place in the system. In the striation it resembles of *A. corpulenta*.

3. **A. Reichardtiana** GRUN. (1867). V. linear with broad, rounded ends. L. 0,04 to 0,07; B. 0,01 to 0,02 mm. Median line close to the ventral margin. No areas and no longitudinal line. Striæ slightly radiate, punctate, 10 in 0,01 mm. — Hedwigia VI p. 25. A. S. Atl. XXXIX f. 33, 34.

Marine: Adriatic! Cape of Good Hope! Campeachy Bay! Pensacola!

An easily recognized form, but too imperfectly known to be placed in any of the larger sections of Amphora.

4. **A. scabriuscula** CL. a. GROVE (1893). — V. lunate, obtuse. L. 0,057; B. 0,01 mm. Dorsal side with rather broad axial area, without longitudinal line. Structure coarse and transversely lineate alveoli, arranged in somewhat radiate rows, 10 in 0,01 mm. Ventral side throughout striate. Striæ 10 in 0,01 mm. Diatomiste II p. 56 Pl. III f. 7.

Marine: Macassar Straits!

This species is evidently nearly akin to the genus *Trachyneis*.

5. **A. Clevei** GRUN. (1875). Frustule rectangular. L. 0,10 to 0,16; B. 0,04 mm. Zone not complex. V. linear-lanceolate or (according to the position) semilanceolate and rostrate. Median line very excentric, slightly biarcuate (or according to the position of the valve, straight, and close to the margin). Central nodule on the dorsal side a short stauros, expanding outwards, on the ventral irregularly rounded. Axial area narrow, linear on the dorsal side. Central area of the outline of the central nodule. Alveoli in almost transverse or slightly curved rows (8 to 9 in 0,01 mm.). Spaces between them very narrow, forming longitudinal undulating lines. Longitudinal striæ very fine. A. S. Atl. XXV f. 46 to 48.

Marine: North Carolina! Florida! West Indies!

This peculiar form is an *Amphora* with the characteristics of *Trachyneis*.

6. **A. Wittsteinii** A. S (1876). — Frustule rectangular, with large, hyaline limbus. L. 0,058 to 0,065; B. 0,023 mm. Zone complex, on the ventral side with 6 to 7, on the dorsal with 4, divisions in 0,01 mm. Dorsal divisions punctate; puncta 10 in 0,01 mm. V. narrow, with 7 striæ in 0,01 mm. — Atl. XXXIX f. 6, 7.

Marine: ?

This is a characteristic form, of which no detached valves have been examined. It is therefore impossible to decide as to its place in the system. It may belong to the subgenus *Calamphora*.

7. **A. Mülleri** A. S. (1875). — V. almost linear, subacute. L. 0,075; B. 0,009 mm. Median line almost straight. Dorsal side with a pretty broad axial area. Striæ 8 in 0,01 mm., short, coarsely granulate. Ventral side with a row of puncta along the margin. — Atl. XXVI f. 31.

Marine: North Sea (Atl.).

8. **A. labuensis** CL. (1883). Frustule rectangular, with parallel margins. L. 0,08; B. 0,02 mm. Zone not complex. Components of the median line divergent from the central nodule to the corners of the frustule. V. linear, in B. 0,01 mm. Transverse striæ 6 in 0,01 mm. finely transversely lineate. — Vega p. 493 Pl. XXXV f. 1. *A. lab. var. fusiformis* LEUD. FORTM. D. de la Malaisie p. 11 Pl. I f. 8 (1892)?

Marine: Labuan!

This characteristic form is but imperfectly known, as no valves in a favourable position have been examined. It seems impossible to find a place for this species in any of the above subgenera, the nature of the striation being entirely different, and closely similar to that of the *Lineolatæ* of Navicula, of which section it might be an asymmetrical form.

9. **A. Naumanni** JAN. (1876). — Frustule sublinear, with slightly rostrate ends. L. 0,05; B. 0,012 mm., bordered with a narrow limbus. Zone on the dorsal side with two rows of puncta. V. narrow; its dorsal side with about 10 striæ in 0,01 mm. Ventral side smooth with a longitudinal line. — A. S. Atl. XXXIX f. 19.

Marine:?

It is impossible to decide the position of this form, which I know only from the figs. in Atl. representing entire frustules. It may be akin to *A. pusilla* CL. or to *A. Wittstrinii.*

Amphoræ placed in the other genera.

A. Digitus A. S., *Pinnularia ambigua* CL.

A. naviculacea DONK., *Pinnularia Stauntonii* GRUN.

Doubtful, or imperfectly known, Amphoræ.

A. acuta var. neogena PANT. (III Pl. XII f. 187 1893); belongs to the subgenus *Oxyamphora.*

A. amphioxys BAIL. (Smiths. Contr. 1852 p. 39 Pl. II f. 20 to 22) is according to HAMILTON SMITH *Hantzschia amphioxys*, which appears to be beyond doubt.

A. andesitica PANT. (III Pl. XIII f. 205; 1893).

A. Argus PANT. (III Pl. XXII f. 329; 1893) seems to be akin to *A. ovalis.*

A. Beccarii. DE NOTARIS (Exb. Crit. ital. Ser. II N:o 633) unknown to the author.

A. badayana PANT. (III Pl. XXIII f. 336).

A. bullosa. FIOR. MAZZ. (Atti. Soc. crit. ital. 1879 p. 104. *Colletonema bullosum* Fior. Mazz. Atti. Acad. Pont. N. Lincei 1861 Pl. I fig. 1—5) unknown to the author, not having seen the original paper.

A. cingulata PANT. (II Pl. XXV f. 369; 1889) is an indeterminable fragment of some diatom.

A. coarctata LEUD. FORTM. (D. de Ceylon Pl. II f. 18; 1879) impossible to identify.

A. cristata PETIT (D. de Campbell p. 18 Pl. IV f. 8; 1877) is unknown to me, but seems to be a remarkable species, which however is too imperfectly figured and described to decide as to its place in the system.

A. cunotiæformis GRUN. (A. S. Atl. XXXIX f. 5) seems to be a *Navicula* akin to *Nav. rhombica.*

A. invidenda PANT. (III Pl. XIV f. 210; 1893).

A. Kossuthii PANT. (III Pl. X f. 169; 1893).

A. lutea LEUD. FORTM. (D. de Ceylon Pl. I f. 10; 1879) an indeterminable connecting zone of some diatom.

A. munda A. S. (Atl. XL f. 15; 1876) no *Amphora*, but a frustule of a *Tropidoneis*, akin to *T. Lepidoptera.*

A. naviformis LEUD. FORTM. (D. de Malaisie Pl. I f. 6; 1892) probably *Hantzschia marina.*

A. obtecta BAIL. (H. L. Smith Lens p. 77 Pl. II f. 12) cannot be identified. Possibly a form of *A. Grevilleana.*

A. obtusiuscula GRUN. (A. S. Atl. XXV f. 7; 1875) seems to be a *Navicula* of the section *Fusiformes.*

A. rectangularis GREG. (T. M. S. 1857 p. 70 Pl. I f. 29) represents in HAMILTON SMITHS opinion, in which I agree, some *Stauroneis.*

A. rimosa EHB. (Am. p. 79; 1843; M. G. V: 1 f. 27).

A. Schmidtii PETIT (Campbell D. p. 17 A. S. Atl. XXVII f. 51).

A. sejuncta PANT. (III Pl. XXXV f. 495; 1893) probably the half valve of some *Navicula*, belonging to the section *Punctatae*.

A. staurophora PANT. (III Pl. XV f. 228; 1893).

A. strigata PANT. (III Pl. XI f. 181; 1893).

A. tertiaria PANT. (III Pl. XV f. 225; 1893).

A. transylvanica PANT. (III Pl. I f. 12; 1893) similar to *A. ovalis*, but with a stauroid central nodule.

A. vittata PANT. (III Pl. XXII f. 326; 1893) akin to *A. ovalis*?

Mastogloia THWAITES (1848).

Valve linear, lanceolate or orbicular, frequently with rostrate or capitate ends, symmetrical. Median line usually undulate. Axial area usually indistinct. Central area small. Structure: transverse punctate striæ, usually subparallel, the puncta so disposed as to form obliquely decussating, or straight, or undulating, longitudinal, striæ. Connecting zone not complex. Between the zone and the valve there is a marginal septate plate. In conjugation two mothercells form two auxospores (Lüders Beob. p. 557). — Cell-contents (of *M. Smithii*) have along the valves two chromatophore-plates, extending from the apices towards the central nodule. They have a narrow sinus reaching from the ends half-way to the centre. In F. V. the plates are bent near the extremities. On staining with methylene-green a number of small, intensely coloured plastids make their appearance at the surface-stratum of the plasma. (Conf. A. S. Atl. Pl. CLXXXV f. 32).

Mastogloia Smithii with cell-contents; 500 times magnified.

As early as 1833 one species of Mastogloia was named by AGARDH *Frustulia elliptica*, and in 1844 another (probably *M. lanceolata* THW.) was described by KÜTZING (Bac. Pl. XXX f. 37) as *Navicula meleagris*. In 1848 a third species was described by THWAITES (Ann. 2d Ser. Vol. 1) under the name *Dickieia Dansei*, but on W. SMITH pointing out the great difference between the mamillate mucous cushion constituting the nidus of this form, and the leaf-like fronds of Dickieia, THWAITES created the new Genus *Mastogloia* for its reception and that of two additional species discovered by Smith.

W. SMITH (S. B. D. Vol. II p. 63) was the first to call attention to the most characteristic feature of the new Genus, viz the septate marginal plate attached, according to him, to the connecting zone. This plate can easily be isolated in preparation, and appears to be placed between the zone and the valves. The septa, in SMITH's view, are small cubical chambers or »loculi» opening outwards, which is probable, as in mounting they are frequently filled with air.

In 1860 GRUNOW placed this Genus in the Naviculaceæ, but in 1867 (Nov. Exp p. 16) he removed it to the Cocconeidæ and created the Genus *Orthoneis* for elliptical cocconeiform species of Mastogloia with a band of numerous loculi, and a subgenus *Stictoneis* for similar forms with a few lunate loculi only. In 1880 (Arct. Diat. p. 17) GRUNOW formed a separate family, the *Mastogloiaceæ*, comprising Mastogloia, with the addition of the forms hitherto classed by him in Orthoneis; and Orthoneis, comprising only the forms with a few lunate loculi which he had before placed in Stictoneis.

As however I do not see sufficient generic difference between Mastogloia and Orthoneis either in respect of the elliptical, or lanceolate, outlines, or of the fewer or greater number of the lunate, or rectangular, loculi, I propose here to unite them in one Genus, Mastogloia.

Considerable differences exist in the structure in Mastogloia, some species having decussating lines of puncta, while others have the puncta in transverse and longitudinal rows. Transitions, however, occur between these types, and I see no reason for splitting up the genus on this account. Among other Naviculoids no kindred forms are known, except in the genus Cocconeis of which some species seems to be degenerate forms of Mastogloia.

The species of Mastogloia live in gelatinous mammillate masses, the formation of which seems to have some connection with the loculi. A few only inhabit perfectly fresh water. Some as *M. Smithii, M. elliptica, M. exigua, M. lanceolata* are abundant in brackish water. A. small number of species are found in the Arctic seas, but the majority occur in tropical seas.

I have placed the small *Diadesmis gallica* W. SM. in Mastogloia, on the supposition that the marginal puncta of this species are loculi, which is not easy to decide as the form is so exceedingly small [1]).

Artificial key.

1.	Structure double, of costæ and puncta	2.
	— simple, of puncta only	3.
2	Valve linear with cuneate ends	*M. Grevillei* W. SM.
	— elliptic-lanceolate	*M. Castracanei* PANT.
3.	Puncta arranged in decussating rows	4.
	— not —	22.
4.	Ends subacute, more or less rostrate	5.
	— broad, rounded	13.
5.	Striæ about 22 in 0,01 mm.	6.
	— — 13 — —	8.
6.	Loculi 9 in 0,01 mm.	*M. decussata* GRUN.
	— 6 — —	*M. delicatula* CL.
	— 3 to 4 —	7.
7.	Valve with longitudinal furrows	*M. sulcata* CL.
	— without — —	*M. Kjellmanii* CL.
8.	Ends rostrate	9.
	— subacute,	*M. Grovei* CL. (*M. Bahamensis* CL., *M. Jelineckiana* GRUN.).
9.	Loculi lunate	*M. Rhombus* PET.
	— quadrate or rectangular	10.
10.	Median loculi larger than the others	*M. angulata* LEWIS.
	— not — — —	11.
11.	Terminal loculi larger	*M. rostellata* GRUN.
	— — not —	12.
12	Rim of loculi reaching to the ends	*M. asperula* GRUN.
	— — not — — —	*M. Szontaghii* PANT.
13.	Loculi lunate	14.
	— quadrate	16.
14.	Loculus single unilateral	*M. binotata* GRUN.
	Loculi few	15.
15.	Central area a transverse fascia	*M. Crucicula* GRUN.
	— — not — —	*M. fimbriata* BTW.
16.	Median line between two rows of puncta	17.
	— — not enclosed between rows of puncta	18.
17.	Puncta along the median line rounded	*M. Wrightii* O'M.
	— — — — — elongated	*M. Barbadensis* GREV.
18.	Transverse rows of puncta ending near the margin in double rows of small puncta	19.
	— — — not — — — — — — —	20.
19.	Rows of puncta 5 to 6 in 0,01 mm.	*M. Clevei* GRUN.
	— — — 8 — —	*M. splendida* GREG.

[1]) The following monograph was already completed, when the plates 185 to 188 of A. SCHMIDT's *Atlas* were issued, in which a considerable number of Mastogloiæ are figured. Before printing this monograph I have completed the text with quotations, but I could not change the artificial key, as most of the new species are not represented in sufficient detail for being admitted into the system. The reader will find at the end of this monograph a list of the new species, which I am unable to identify with known forms.

20. Rows of puncta 7 to 10 in 0,1 mm. . . . . *M. cribrosa* Grun.
— — 14 to 15 — . . . . 21.

21. Loculiferous rim broad . . . . *M. cocconeiformis* Grun.
— — narrow . . . . *M. Horvathiana* Grun.

22. Valve elliptical . . . . 23.
— lanceolate . . . . 24.

23. Valve with irregular large puncta . . . . *M. oamaruensis* Cl.
— — close striæ . . . . *M. ovata* Grun.

24. Valve without axial or lateral areas . . . . 25.
— with — — — . . . . 65.

25. Striæ crossed by several longitudinal furrows . . . . 26.
— not — — — — — . . . . 27.

26. Valve elliptic-lanceolate or rhomboid . . . . *M. quinquecostata* Grun.
— lanceolate, acuminate . . . . *M. seriata* Cl.

27. Puncta in straight longitudinal rows, stronger than the transverse . . . . 28.
Transverse rows of puncta stronger than the longitudinal . . . . 31.

28. Transverse striæ 12 in 0,01 mm. . . . . *M. lineata* Cl. a. Grove.
— — 17 to 30 in 0,01 mm. . . . . 29.

29. Loculiferous rim distant from the margin . . . . *M. acuta* Grun.
— — marginal . . . . 30.

30. Central area distinct . . . . *M. ovata* Cl.
— — indistinct . . . . *M. exarata* Cl.

31. Valve with longitudinal lines parallel to the median line . . . . 32.
— without — — — — — — . . . . 38.

32. Longitudinal lines combined with the central area . . . . 33.
— — not — — — . . . . 35.

33. Small. L. 0,025 to 0,028 mm. . . . . *M. pumila* Grun.
Larger. L. 0,04 to 0,095 mm. . . . . 34.

34. Loculi about 8 in 0,01 mm. . . . . *M. Debyi* Cl.
— — 5 — — . . . . *M. Braunii* Grun.

35. Longitudinal lines close to the median line . . . . 36.
— — distant from — — . . . . 37.

36. Valve elliptic-lanceolate . . . . *M. apiculata* W. Sm.
— linear with cuneate ends . . . . *M. labuensis* Cl.
— broad, elliptical, rostrate . . . . *M. Citrus* Cl.
— lanceolate, rostrate . . . . *M. baltica* Grun.

37. Loculi 4 in 0,01 mm. . . . . *M. Pisciculus* Cl.
— 8 — — . . . . *M. Peragalli* Cl.

38. Loculi of equal size . . . . 39.
— — unequal — . . . . 61.

39. Valve very small. L. 0,01 mm. . . . . *M. gallica* W. Sm.
— larger. L. 0,02 mm. and more . . . . 40.

40. Loculi few . . . . 41.
— numerous . . . . 42.

41. Loculi 2 on each side . . . . *M. capitata* Grun.
— 4 — — . . . . *M. exigua* Lewis.

42. Loculiferous rim inside the margin . . . . *M. paradoxa* Grun. (*M. Smithii var.*).
— — marginal . . . . 43.

43. Valve constricted in the middle . . . . *M. constricta* Cl.
— not — — — . . . . 44.

44. Valve rostrate or apiculate . . . . 45.
— not — . . . . 51.

45. Puncta forming almost straight longitudinal rows . . . . 46.
— not — — — — — . . . . 48.

46. Median line strongly undulating . . . . *M. undulata* Grun.
— — slightly — or straight . . . . 47.

47. Ends rostrate-capitate . . . . *M. Goesii* Cl.
— slightly rostrate . . . . *M. fallax* Cl.

48. Median line strongly flexuose . . . . 49.
— — slightly — . . . . 50.

49. Striæ about 18 in 0,01 mm. . . . . . *M. flexuosa* Cl.
— — 25 — — . . . . . . *M. cuspidata* Cl.

50. Valve apiculate . . . . . . *M. minuta* Grun.
— rostrate . . . . . . *M. Smithii* Thwaites

51. Valve rhomboidal . . . . . . 52.
— linear with cuneate ends . . . . . . *M. elliptica v. Dansei*
— elliptical to lanceolate . . . . . . 55.

52. Loculi almost as close as the striæ . . . . . . 53.
less — than — . . . . . . 54.

53. L. about 0,045 mm. . . . . . . *M. bahamensis* Cl.
L. — 0,075 mm. . . . . . . *M. affirmata* Leud. Fortm.

54. Loculi 4, striæ 13 in 0,01 mm. . . . . . . *M. Lancettula* Cl.
— 4, — 21 — — . . . . . . *M. Rhombulus* Cl.
— 6, — 11 — — . . . . . . *M. rhombica* Cl.
8, — 14 — — . . . . . . *M. pulchella* Cl.

55. Loculi less than 7 in 0,01 mm. . . . . . . 56.
— more than 7 — — . . . . . . 58.

56. Striæ coarse, of distant puncta . . . . . . *M. affinis* Cl.
— of close puncta . . . . . . 57.

57. Loculi lunate . . . . . . *M. notata* Pant.
— rectangular . . . . . . *M. laminaris* Ehb.

58. L. 0,09 mm. . . . . . . *M. Portieriana* Grun.
L. 0,05 mm. or less . . . . . . 59.

59. Striæ about 15 in 0,01 mm. . . . . . . *M. elegans* Lewis
— — 20 — — . . . . . . 60.

60. Striæ radiate in the ends . . . . . . *M. elliptica* Ag. (*M. Smithii var.*).
— convergent — — . . . . . . *M. lanceolata* Thwaites.

61. Loculi closer in one end than in the other . . . . . . *M. inæqualis* Cl.
Terminal loculi equal in both ends . . . . . . 62.

62. Loculi between the middle and the ends largest . . . . . . *M. erythræa* Grun.
Median loculi largest . . . . . . 63.

63. Loculi 3 in 0,01 mm. . . . . . . *M. kariana* Grun.
— about 8 in 0,01 mm. . . . . . . 64.

64. Valve linear . . . . . . *M. pusilla* Grun.
— elliptical . . . . . . *M. floridana* Cl.

65. Valve with axial area . . . . . . 66.
— — lateral areas . . . . . . 68.

66. Axial area narrow . . . . . . 67.
— — broad . . . . . . *M. eulotcia* Cl.

67. Loculi marginal . . . . . . *M. japonica* Cl.
— inside the margin . . . . . . *M. antiqua* Cl.

68. Lateral areas structureless . . . . . . 69.
— — punctate or striate . . . . . . 74.

69. Lateral and central areas uniting . . . . . . 70.
— — — — not — . . . . . . 73.

70. Central nodule stauroid . . . . . . 71.
— — not — . . . . . . 72.

71. Striæ 9 in 0,01 mm. . . . . . . *M. cruciata* Leud. Fortm.
— 17 — — . . . . . . *M. cuaina* Cl.
— 22 — — . . . . . . *M. Macdonaldii* Grev.

72. Striæ finely punctate . . . . . . *M. submarginata* Cl. a. Grun.
— coarsely — . . . . . . *M. baldjikiana* Grun.

73. Loculi 5 to 6 in 0,01 mm. . . . . . . *M. bisulcata* Grun.
— 10 — — . . . . . . *M. rimosa* Cl.

74. Areas with faint puncta . . . . . . *M. Jelineckii* Grun.
— — longitudinal rows of elongated puncta . . . . . . 75.

75. Rows of puncta few . . . . . . 76.
— — — numerous . . . . . . 78.

76. { Valve broadly lanceolate, acuminate . . . . *M. obesa* Cl.
{ rhombic-lanceolate to rhomboid 77

77. { Puncta and striæ equidistant . . . . *M. Lemniscata* Leud. Fortm.
{ more distant than the striæ . . . . *M. javanica* Cl.

78. { Valve elliptical to lanceolate . . . . 79.
{ rhombic-lanceolate . . . . 80.

79. { Striæ 10 in 0,01 mm. . . . . *M. Temperei* Cl.
{ 11 to 15 in 0,01 mm. . . . . *M. Kelleri* Pant.

80. { Puncta in the longitudinal rows largest in the middle . . . *M. Craveni* Leud. Fortm.
{ — — — — of equal size . . . . *M. Leudugeri* Cl. a. Grove.

1. **M. Grevillei** W. Sm. (1856). — V. linear, with cuneate, obtuse ends. L. 0,035 to 0,06; B. 0,01 to 0,012 mm. Central area rounded. Axial area narrow, linear. Median line flexuose. Loculi 6 to 7 in 0,01 mm. forming a band ending near the cuneate extremities. Costæ 10 in 0,01 mm., very slightly radiate, alternating with double rows of puncta arranged in oblique lines, about 20 in 0,01 mm. — W. Sm. B. D. II p. 65 Pl. LXII f. 389. V. H. Syn. p. 71 Pl. IV f. 20. A. S. Atl. CLXXXV, 1, 2.

Fresh or slightly brackish water: Pentland Hills (Grove Coll.)! Belgium (V. H.), St Gallen (Atl.).

This species resembles *M. elliptica var. Dansei* but has a different structure of the valve.

2. **M. Castracanei** Pant. (1889). — V. elliptic-lanceolate, with very slightly rostrate ends. L. 0,065; B. 0,021 mm. Axial area very narrow, lanceolate. Loculi(?) along the whole margin, alternately larger and smaller, the former 3 in 0,01 mm. Structure: transverse, slightly radiate costæ, 6 to 7,5 in 0,01 mm., alternating with double rows of small puncta, arranged in decussating lines. Connecting zone with two longitudinal rows of coarse puncta. — *Alloioneis Castr.* Pant. II Pl. XXIII f. 311, III Pl. XXV f. 374. *M. Castr.* A. S. Atl. CLXXXVIII, 30.

Marine: Bory, Karand Hungary, fossil (Pant.).

I have not examined this remarkable species, which I have placed provisionally in *Mastogloia*, as the figure in the zonal view shews something, which appears to be loculi. The structure of the valve resembles that of *M. Grevillei*.

3. **M. delicatula** Cl. (1893). — V. lanceolate, acuminate. L. 0,037; B. 0,014 mm. Median line slightly flexuose. Areas indistinct. Loculi quadrate, 6 in 0,01 mm., equal, forming a marginal band, reaching nearly to the ends. Striæ 21 in 0,01 mm. parallel, formed of puncta arranged in decussating rows. — Cl. Diatomiste Vol. II p. 16 Pl. I f. 20.

Marine: Bahamas (Grove Coll.)!

4. **M. Rhombus** Petit (1867). — V. broadly lanceolate, acuminate. L. 0,046 to 0,058; B. 0,025 to 0,035 mm. Loculi with convex inner margin, 3 to 4 in 0,01 mm., equal, forming a row along the whole margin of the valve. Striæ 13 in 0,01 mm. composed of elongated puncta, forming decussating rows, about 9 in 0,01 mm. — *Nav. Rhombus* Petit D. Campbell p. 23 Pl. IV f. 12. *Mastog. Rh.* Cl. and Grove Diatomiste I p. 58 Pl. IX f. 12. A. S. Atl. CLXXXVII 33 to 35.

Marine: Nossibé (Brun Coll.)! Manilla (Deby Coll.)! Macassar Straits (Grove Coll.)! China (Thum.)! Campeachy Bay!

5. **M. asperula** Grun. (1892). — V. elliptical or lanceolate, with acuminate, rostrate or subcapitate ends. L. 0,03 to 0,05; B. 0,023 to 0,027 mm. Median line straight. No axial area. Central area small, rounded. Loculi equal, quadrate, 4 in 0,01 mm. forming a band reaching to the ends. Striæ 13 in 0,01 mm. parallel, slightly radiate at the ends, of elongated alveoli, arranged in obliquely decussating rows. — Cl. Diatomiste I p. 161 Pl. XXIII f. 12. *M. Phaitiana* (instead of *thaitiana* Castr.) A. S. Atl. CLXXXVII, 46, 47 (variety?).

Marine: Balearic Islands! Seychelles (Van Heurck Coll.)! Java! Cebu (Grove Coll.)!

Var. *Gilberti* A. S. (1893). — V. elliptic-lanceolate, rostrate. L. 0,03; B. 0,012 mm. Median line straight. No axial and central areas. Loculi about 5 in 0,01 mm., forming a band along the whole margin. Striæ 12 in 0,01 mm. very slightly radiate, of some few elongated alveoli. — Atl. CLXXXVII f. 14, 15.

Marine: Kings Mill Island (Atl.), Barcelona!

6. **M. rostellata** Grun. (1877). — V. lanceolate, frequently slightly constricted in the middle, with acuminate, rostrate ends. L. 0,042 to 0,06; B. 0,02 mm. Loculi 3 in 0,01 mm. with somewhat convex interior margin, almost equal (terminal loculi somewhat larger than the others), forming a marginal band reaching nearly to the ends of the valve. Striæ 11 in 0,01 mm. slightly radiate at the ends, composed of elongated alveoli, arranged in somewhat irregular, decussating rows. — Grun. M. J. 1877 p. 174 Pl. CXCV f. 2.

Marine: Honduras (Grun), Campeachy Bay! Florida!

7. **M. angulata** Lewis (1860). — V. elliptical to lanceolate, rostrate. L. 0,04 to 0,08; B. 0,025 to 0,029 mm. Median line straight. No areas. Loculi of unequal size, the median largest, 3 in 0,01 mm. forming a band reaching almost to the ends. Striæ 12 in 0,01 mm.; puncta arranged in decussating rows. — Lewis Proceed Ac. Nat. Sc. Philadelphia 1861 p. 65 Pl. II f. 4. A. S. Atl. CLXXXVII, 4 to 11. *M. thaitiana* Castr. Voyage Challenger p. 22 Pl. XXVI f. 11? *M. apiculata* Grun. Verh. 1860 p. 577 Pl. VII f. 9 (non W. Sm.).

Marine: Atlantic coasts of North America! Honduras (Atl.), Mediterranean, Adriatic, Black and Red Seas! Australia (Atl.).

Var. *pusilla* Grun. (1877). — L. 0,026; B. 0,014 mm. Loculi 4 to 5 in 0,01 mm. oblique striæ 14 to 16 in 0,01 mm. — *M. apicul. var. pus.* Grun. M. J. 1877 p. 175 Pl. CXCV f. 3.

Marine: Honduras (Grun.), Adriatic!

8. **M. Szontághii** Pant. (1890). — V. broadly linear, with cuneate ends. L. 0,083; B. 0,025 mm. Loculi about 2 in 0,01 mm. confined to the middle of the margin, quadrate. Striæ 11,5 in 0,01 mm. composed of coarse puncta, forming oblique rows. — Pant. II p. 41 Pl. XXIX f. 116. A. S. Atl. CLXXXVII, 12.

Marine: Hungary, fossil (Pant.).

9. **M. sulcata** Cl. (1892). — V. lanceolate, acuminate, with slightly triundulate margins. L. 0,08 to 0,085; B. 0,027 to 0,028 mm. Central nodule small, transversely dilated. Loculi, about 3 in 0,01 mm., elongated, forming a narrow band along the whole margin. Striæ 22 in 0,01 mm. parallel, convergent in the ends, finely punctate; puncta forming very fine, decussating striæ. The striæ are crossed, between the middle and the ends of the valve, by a linear furrow, parallel to the median line and halfway between it and the margin. — Cl. Diatomiste I p. 162 Pl. XXIII f. 13, 14. A. S. Atl. CLXXXVII f. 51.

Marine: Philippines (Grove Coll.), Java!

10. **M. decussata** Grun. (1892). — V lanceolate, acute. L. 0,07 to 0,078; B. 0,022 to 0,027 mm. Loculi 9 in 0,01 mm., equal, rectangular, forming a band along the whole margin. Striæ 22 to 25 in 0,01 mm. finely punctate; puncta forming decussating lines. — Cl. Diatomiste I p. 162 Pl. XXIII f. 17. A. S. Atl. CLXXXVI, 40, 41.

Marine: Seychelles (V. H. Coll.)! Sandwich Islands!

11. **M. Kjellmanii** Cl. (1883). — V. linear-lanceolate, rostrate. L. 0,06; B. 0,014 mm. Loculi 4 in 0,01 mm. almost equal, with somewhat convex interior margin, forming a narrow band along the whole margin of the valve. Striæ 22 in 0,01 mm. finely punctate; puncta forming oblique rows. — Vega p. 495 Pl. XXXV f. 6.

Marine: Labuan!

12. **O. (Stictoneis) binotata** Grun. (1863). V. elliptical. L. 0,033; B. 0,022 mm. Loculus single in the middle of one of the margins (entire frustules shew one loculus on each side), large with convex interior margin. Central area transversely dilated to a short pseudostauros. Striæ 13 in 0,01 mm., radiate near the ends, punctate; puncta about 11 in 0,01 mm. forming curved, oblique rows. — *Cocconeis Scutellum γ* Roper M. J. VI p. 24 Pl. III f. 9. *Cocc. binotata* Grun. Verh. 1863 p. 145 Pl. IV f. 13 *a, b*. *Orthon. binot.* Grun. Novara p. 15. V. H. Syn. Pl. XXVIII f. 7.

Marine: England! France! Mediterranean Sea! Adriatic Sea! Red Sea (Grun.), Nicobar Islands (Grun.). Island of Rhea! Australia! Cape Good Hope (Grun.), West Indies!

Var. *atlantica* Grun. — V. elliptical to elliptic-lanceolate. Loculi elongated. Striæ finer. — Novara p. 15 Pl. I f. 11.

Marine: Atlantic. Honduras (Grun.).

On living specimens a long horn of mucoid substance projects from the loculus.

13. **O. (Stictoneis) Crucicula** Grun. (1877). — V. elliptical. L. 0,011 to 0,017; B. 0,008 to 0,01 mm. Loculi along the whole margin, 4 on each side, with invard margins convex. Central nodule transversely dilated into a stauros. Striæ 22 in 0,01 mm., slightly radiate, finely punctate (puncta in decussating lines?) — M. J. 1877 p. 177 Pl. CXCV f. 8.

Marine: Honduras. Adriatic (Grun.).

14. **O. (Stictoneis) fimbriata** Btw. (1859). V. elliptical. L. 0,02 to 0,05; B. 0,017 to 0,033 mm. Loculi large, 3 to 6 on each side, with interior margin convex. Striæ 7 to 8 in 0,01 mm. coarsely punctate; puncta 7 to 8 in 0,01 mm. forming oblique and curved lines. The rows of puncta end near the margin in double rows of small puncta. — *Coccon. fimbr.* M. J. VII p. 179 Pl. IX f. 13. *Mastogloia cribrosa* Grun. Verh. 1860 p. 577 Pl. VII f. 10 *d*.

Marine: Mediterranean and Adriatic Sea! Mauritius! Madagascar! Sumbava! Japan! China! Australia! Oceania! Honduras and Brazil (Grun.).

15. **O. Clevei** Grun. (1880). — V. elliptical. L. 0,046; B. 0,03 mm. Loculi 2,5 in 0,01 mm. narrower outwards. Striæ 8 in 0,01 mm. of large puncta, about 8 in 0,01 mm. forming oblique rows. The striæ end at the margin in double rows of small puncta. — V. H. Syn. Pl. XXVIII f. 4.

Marine: Mauritius! Seychelles! Java! Barbados (Grun.).

Resembles *O. fimbriata*, but has shorter, more numerous loculi, which become narrow outward.

16. **O. splendida** Greg. (1857). — V. elliptical. L. 0,07 to 0,17; B. 0,052 to 0,13 mm. Loculi 2 to 3 in 0,01 mm., narrowed outwards. Their inner margin straight. The ends of the median line curved in the same direction. Striæ 5 to 6 in 0,01 mm. slightly radiate, composed of large puncta, forming elegantly curved and decussating rows, 4 to 5 in 0,01 mm., ending near the margin in double rows of small puncta. — *Cocc. splendida* Greg. D. of Clyde p. 193 Pl. IX f. 29. *Cocc. punctatissima* Grev. M. J. V p. 8 Pl. III f. 4 (1857). *M. cribrosa* Grun. Verh. 1860 p. 577 Pl. VII f. 10 *a*. *Orthon. splend.* Grun. Novara p. 15 (1867). V. H. Syn. Pl. XXVIII f. 1, 2. Truan a. Witt D. of Jeremie Pl. IV f. 13. Pant. II Pl. XXIV f. 352.

Marine: Scotland (Greg.). Bohuslän! Mediterranean Sea! Adriatic! Red Sea! Seychelles! Madagascar! Sumatra! China! Japan! Oceania! Galapagos Islands! Honduras (Rabh.), Colon! West Indies! Fossil: Hungary! Moravia! Nankoori! California! Jeremie (Truan a. Witt), Oamaru!

Widely distributed and easily recognized species. Fossil specimens from Moravia and Hungary attain a gigantic size.

17. **O. Wrightii** O'Meara (1867). — V. broadly elliptical. L. 0,027 to 0,034; B. 0,018 to 0,025 mm. Median line straight, not reaching to the margin and enclosed between two rows of puncta, 12 to 13 in 0,01 mm. Loculi 8 in 0,01 mm. equal, quadrate, forming a marginal rim. Puncta of

the valve forming transverse and decussating rows. Transverse rows 9, oblique rows 8 in 0,01 mm. Marginal puncta frequently double. — *Cocc. Wr.* O'M. M. J. N. S. VII Pl. VII f. 6? PETIT D. Campbell p. 12. Pl. IV f. 3? *O. barbadensis var. nankoorensis* GRUN. Novara p. 98 Pl. I *A* f. 10 (1867)?

Marine: Cape Horn (Petit Coll.)!

None of the figures corresponds exactly with this species, so that the identification is doubtful. As *Orthoneis Pethöi* PANTOCSEK has figured (III Pl. IX f. 148) a similar, but acuminate form.

18. **O. barbadensis** GREV. (1864). — V. elliptical to orbicular. L. 0,05 to 0,08; B. 0,03 to 0,05 mm. Loculi? Median line slightly undulate. Puncta more crowded near the margin, where they form short striæ, about 8 in 0,01 mm., transversely elongated at the median line (9 in 0,01 mm.), where they form a longitudinal band on both sides of the line. The puncta of the valve are larger towards the median line than towards the margin and form elegantly curved decussating rows. — *Cocc. barbadensis* GREV. T. M. S. XII p. 14 Pl. II f. 10. *Cocc. naviculoides* GREV. T. M. S. XIII p. 34 Pl. IV f. 24 (1865).

Marine: Barbados, foss.! Oamaru. New Zealand, fossil!

Var.(?) *tenuipunctata* BRUN (1893). — L. 0,12 to 0,15 mm. Striæ 10 to 12 in 0,01 mm. Diatomiste I p. 176 Pl. XXIV f. 8.

Marine: Oamaru, fossil.

19. **O. Grovei** CL. (1892). — V. elliptic-lanceolate, subacute. L. 0,1 to 0,11; B. 0,04 to 0,045 mm. Central area small, subquadrate. Median line undulating. Loculi subequal, quadrate, about 3 in 0,01 mm., forming a band along the margin. Transverse rows of puncta 9 in 0,01 mm.; oblique rows 10 in 0,01 mm. Transverse rows not ending with double rows. Puncta along the median line not elongated. — *M. Grovei* CL. Diatomiste I p. 161 Pl. XXIII f. 10.

Marine: Barbados, foss.!

Var. *rhombica* CL. — V. rhombic-lanceolate. L. 0,1; B. 0,025 mm. Central area small, with some isolated puncta. Striæ as in the type, but near the margin crossed by a narrow blank line. — Pl. II f. 14.

Marine: Barbados, fossil (Deby Coll.)!

20. **O. cribrosa** GRUN. (1860). — Elliptical. L. 0,034 to 0,05; B. 0,027 to 0,03 mm. Loculi quadrate, 2 to 4 in 0,01 mm. forming a band along the margin. Median line straight. Central area indistinct. Transverse rows of puncta 7 to 10 in 0,01 mm. not ending with double rows of small puncta. Oblique rows of puncta gently curved. — *Mastogl. cribrosa* GRUN. Verh. 1860 p. 577 Pl. VII f. 10 c. *Orthon. cribr.* GRUN. Novara p. 16 (1867). V. H. Syn. Pl. XXVIII f. 6.

Marine: Adriatic! Nicobar Islands (Grun.), Port Jackson! Japan! Samoa! Tahiti!

O. cribrosa greatly resembles *O. fimbriata*, but the loculi are entirely different, and there are no double rows of small puncta at the end of the transverse rows.

21. **O. Horvathiana** GRUN. (1860). — Elliptical. L. 0,035; B. 0,024 mm. Loculi 5 to 8 in 0,01 mm., rectangular, forming a broad band along the margin. Transverse rows of puncta 15 in 0,01 mm. Oblique rows gently curved. — *Mast. Horvath.* GRUN. Verh. 1860 p. 578 Pl. VII f. 13. A. S. Atl. CLXXXVIII f. 41.

Marine: Red Sea (Grun.), Samoa! Tahiti (Grun.), Honduras (Grun.), Java (Atl.).

Nearly akin to *O. cribrosa* and differing in its closer loculi and finer striations. This may probably be regarded as *O. cribrosa var.*

22. **O. cocconeiformis** GRUN. (1860). — Orbicular. L. 0,036; B. 0,028 to 0,03 mm. Loculi 8 in 0,01 mm., rectangular, forming a broad band along the margin. Puncta forming radiate

rows, 14 to 15 in 0,01 mm., curved oblique rows and, near the slightly undulating median line, almost longitudinal rows. — *Mastogl. coccon.* GRUN. Verh. 1860 p. 578 Pl. VII f. 14. A. S. Atl. CLXXXVIII f. 43. Icon. n. Pl. II f. 20.

Marine: Red Sea! Madagascar! Bahamas (Grove Coll.)!

23. **O. oamaruensis** CL. N. Sp. — V. elliptical. L. 0,05; B. 0,03 mm. Loculi? Median line undulating. V. with very distant large puncta, along the median line 5 in 0,01 mm. Margin with double-rows (4 in 0,01 mm.) of small puncta. — Pl. II f. 19.

Marine: Colombo, Ceylon (Le Tourneur Coll.)! Oamaru, New Zealand, fossil!

Coccon. armata GREV. (T. M. S. XIV p. 126 Pl. XI f. 13, 1866) is, to judge from the figure, nearly akin to *O. oamaruensis* and to *O. barbadensis*. The marginal tubercles of this form, mentioned by GREVILLE are beyond doubt loculi. All these forms are only insufficiently described and figured. In this species the puncta are not arranged in decussating rows, so that it strictly does not belong to this division, but in other respects is nearly akin to the latest described species.

24. **M.? (Diadesmis) gallica** W. SM. (1857). — V. linear elliptical, with rounded ends. L. 0,09 to 0,015; B. 0,003 to 0,004 mm. Loculi small, about 12 in 0,01 mm. forming a band of puncta along the margin. Striæ about 28 in 0,01 mm. — *Diad. gallica* W. SM. Ann. Mag. N. Hist. XIX p. 11 Pl. II f. 16. V. H. Syn. Pl. XIV f. 39. *Navicula parvula* H. L. SMITH Am. Q. J. M. 1878 p. 14 Pl. III f. 4.

Fresh water, moist earth etc.: Spetsbergen (Lagst.), Upsala! Brussells (V. H.), Havre (W. Sm.), America (H. L. Sm.).

One of the smallest diatoms, characterized by the marginal granulation, which I believe to be loculi. The frustules occur in long bands.

25. **M. marginulata** GRUN. (1867). — V. narrow lanceolate or linear, obtuse. L. 0,025 to to 0,08; B. 0,0057 to 0,011 mm. Loculi 12 to 14 in 0,01 mm. Striæ 22 in 0,01 mm. transverse. — Novara p. 16 Pl. I f. 12. M. J. 1877 p. 175. A. S. Atl. CLXXXVI, 30.

Marine: Adriatic, Australia, Samoa, Tahiti, New Zealand, Chile, Honduras (Grun.).

I have not seen this small form, which seems to be widely distributed. It may perhaps be the same as *M. inæqualis* CL.

26. **M. inæqualis** CL. — V. narrow lanceolate, obtuse. L. 0,05; B. 0,01 mm. Loculi in one half (valve imagined cut along the transverse axis) of the valve quadrate, 10 in 0,01 mm., in the other more narrow (15 in 0,01 mm.) forming a band along the whole margin. Striæ parallel about 30 in 0,01 mm. Pl. II f. 15.

Marine: Australia (Möller), Java! Rodriguez!

I have seen many specimens all agreeing, so that the different size of the loculi seems to be a characteristic feature.

27. **M. Rhombulus** CL. N. Sp. — V. rhomboid acute. L. 0,03; B. 0,008 mm. Loculi 4 in 0,01 mm. with straight interior margin, forming a narrow marginal band. Median line slightly undulating. Striæ 21 in 0,01 mm. not distinctly punctate.

Marine Pensacola (Grove Coll.)!

28. **M. Lancettula** CL. (1892). — V. rhomboid, subacute. L. 0,03 to 0,045; B. 0,008 to 0,01 mm. Central area small, rounded. Median line undulating. Loculi 4 in 0,01 mm., narrow, with somewhat convex interior margins, in a band along the whole margin. Striæ 13 in 0,01 mm. composed of distinct puncta forming longitudinal rows, 13 to 20 in 0,01 mm. — Diatomiste I p. 163 Pl. XXIII f. 18. A. S. Atl. CLXXXVIII f. 24.

Marine: Cebu, Philippines! Java!

29. **M. affinis** Cl. N. Sp. — V. narrow lanceolate. L. 0,035; B. 0,01 mm. Loculi 4 in 0,01 mm., almost equal, with inner margin convex, forming a band reaching to the ends. Striæ 12 in 0,01 mm. composed of 4 to 5 elongated puncta. — Diatomiste I p. 163 Pl. XXIII f. 19.

Marine: Galapagos Islands!

This small species is nearly akin to *M. kariana*, but has closer loculi and more coarsely punctate striæ. In the shellsand from Norway (Cl. M. D. 311) a similar form occurs frequently without loculi, which may possibly have been destroyed in the cleaning processes.

30. **M. kariana** Grun. (1880). — V. lanceolate. L. 0,05; B. 0,011 mm. Central area small, orbicular. Loculi 3 in 0,01 mm. larger in the middle, with convex interior margin. Striæ 11,5 in 0,1 mm. parallel, finely punctate. — A. D. p. 17 Pl. I f. 3.

Marine: Sea of Kara (Grun.).

31. **O. notata** Pant. (1889). — V. elliptical. L. 0,035; B. 0,0205 mm. Loculi 6 on each side, with convex interior margin. Striæ 15 in 0,01 mm., subradiate, punctate. — Pant. II p. 57 Pl. XXVII f. 392.

Marine: Bory, Hungary, foss. (Pant.).

Species entirely unknown to me. As the punctation is not described, it is impossible to say what are its affinities.

32. **M. floridana** Cl. (1894). — V. elliptical, rostrate. L. 0,043; B. 0,015 mm. Median line straight. Axial area indistinct. Central area small, orbicular. Loculi unequal, the two to four median much larger than the others (8 to 9 in 0,01 mm.), which form a narrow marginal band, reaching nearly to the ends. Striæ 14 to 16 in 0,01 mm., very slightly radiate, distinctly punctate; puncta, about 11 in 0,01 mm., forming longitudinal rows. — *M. florida* (name altered by the editor) Diatomiste II p. 55 Pl. III f. 1.

Marine: Pensacola (Grove Coll.)!

33. **M. pusilla** Grun. (1878). — V. narrow, linear-elliptical to lanceolate, rostrate. L. 0,02 to 0,035; B. 0,006 mm. Loculi about 7 in 0,01 mm., 7 to 16 in each row, the median ones larger. Striæ 14 to 17 in 0,01 mm. slightly radiate, finely punctate. — *M. Smithii var.? pusilla* Grun. Casp. Sea Alg. p. 14 Pl. III f. 10. Cl. M. D. N:o 206. A. S. Atl. CLXXXV, 34. Icon. n. Pl. II f. 8.

Brackish and marine: Caspian Sea (Grun.), Adriatic!

34. **M. minuta** Grev. (1857). — V. elliptical, apiculate. L. 0,02 to 0,035; B. 0,01 to 0,013 mm. Loculi 6 to 9 in 0,01 mm. of equal size, quadrate to rectangular, forming a band reaching nearly to the ends. Striæ 15 to 16 in 0,01 mm. parallel, not interrupted, distinctly punctate. — M. J. V. p. 12 Pl. III f. 10. A. S. Atl. CLXXXVII, 22. Icon. n. Pl. II f. 7.

Marine! Seychelles! Java! Samoa! Sandwich Islands (Grun.), Honduras! Trinidad (Grun.)! Bahamas (Grove Coll.)! Valparaiso (Atl.).

35. **M. (Stigmaphora) capitata** Br. (1891). — V. narrow, lanceolate, capitate-rostrate. L. 0,03 to 0,035; B. 0,01 mm. Loculi two on each side, in the middle of the margin, rounded. Striæ? — D. espèces nouv. p. 45 Pl. XI f. 13.

Marine: Java, parasitical on Rhizosolenia (Brun).

36. **M. exigua** Lewis (1861). — V. fusiform to lanceolate. L. 0,025 to 0,04; B. 0,011 mm. Loculi few, 2 to 6 in the middle of each margin, 4 in 0,01 mm., with somewhat rounded interior edges. Striæ 20 to 24 in 0,01 mm. slightly radiate. — Proc. Acad. Nat. Sc. Philad. 1861 p. 65 Pl. II f. 5. V. H. Syn. p. 70 Pl. IV f. 25, 26. A. S. Atl. CLXXXV f. 33. *M. amygdala* Leud. Fortm. D. Malaise p. 19 Pl. II f. 7 (1892).

Brackish and marine: Baltic (Gothland)! Belgium (V. H.), Atlantic coast of America! Behring Island!

37. **M. Smithii** THWAITES (1848 fide W. SM.). — V. lanceolate, more or less rostrate, or rostrate-capitate. L. 0,027 to 0,053; B. 0,01 to 0,016 mm. Loculi 6 to 8 in 0,01 mm. of equal size, quadrate, forming a band ending at some distance from the ends of the valve. Striæ 18 to 19 in 0,01 mm., almost parallel, or radiate at the ends, punctate; puncta about 24 in 0,01 mm. forming longitudinal rows. Central area small, rounded. — W. SM. B. D. II p. 65 Pl. LIV f. 341. V. H. Syn p. 70 Pl. IV f. 13. *M. lanceolata var.* GRUN. Verh. 1860 p. 576 Pl. VII f. 6. *M. lanceolata var. hungarica* PANT. II p. 41 Pl. VII f. 136 (1889).

Brackish water: Baltic (from Tornea to Rügen)! Saxony! Caspian Sea (Grun.). England! Australia! Tasmania! Fossil: Hungary (Czekehaza! etc.).

Var. *lacustris* GRUN. (1878). — Central area transverse, moderately large. Striæ 15 to 16 in 0,01 mm., slightly radiate. — Caspian Sea Alg. p. 14. V. H. Syn. Pl. IV f. 14. *M. antiqua* SCHUM. Preuss. D. p. 190 Pl. IX f. 58 *c*, *e* (1862).

Fresh water: Spitsbergen! Gulf of Bothnia! Iceland! England! Belgium (V. H.).

Var. *lanceolata* GRUN. (1878). — V. linear lanceolate, slightly rostrate. L. 0,045 to 0,05; B. 0,008 mm. Loculi 6 in 0,01 mm. Striæ 18 to 19 in 0,01 mm. radiate. — CL. M. D. N:o 161. *M. Smithii* PANT. III Pl. XXXVII f. 520.

Brackish water: Gothland!

Var. *amphicephala* GRUN. (1878). — V. with capitate ends. — *M. Smithii β W. Sm.* *M. Sm. var. amphic.* GRUN. in Cl. M. D. N:o 161. V. H. Syn. Pl. IV f. 27. A. S. Atl. CLXXXV, 13, 14. *M. capitata* GREV. M. J. N. S. II p. 235 Pl. X f. 11, 12?

Brackish: Baltic! England, Scotland Sm., Morocco (Atl.).

Var. *intermedia* GRUN. (1878). — V. lanceolate, slightly rostrate. L. 0,032 to 0,037; B. 0,0125 mm. Central area very small. Loculi 8 in 0,01 mm. Striæ 18 to 19 in 0,01 mm., somewhat radiate. — Caspian Sea Alg. p. 13.

Brackish: Caspian Sea (Grun.). South Africa (Cl. M. D. N:o 197). Karand, Hungary, fossil!

Var. *abnormis* GRUN. (1878). — V. lanceolate, rostrate. L. 0,065; B. 0,02 mm. Loculi 6 in 0,01 mm. in a band at some distance from the margin. Central nodule slightly transversely dilated. Striæ 17 in 0,01 mm. coarsely punctate; puncta 17 in 0,01 mm. — Casp. Sea Alg. p. 14. Icon. n. Pl. II f. 17.

Brackish: Caspian Sea (Grun.). Marine: Hungary, Karand, fossil (Deby Coll.).

Description from a specimen from Karand.

Var. *doljensis* PANT. (1886). — V. elliptic-lanceolate. L. 0,03 to 0,04; B. 0,001 mm. Central nodule transversely dilated into a stauros. Loculi 6 to 8 in 0,01 mm. Striæ 27,5 in 0,01 mm. parallel (radiate on the figure given by Pant.). — PANT. I p. 22 Pl. X f. 88.

Brackish: Dolje, Hungary, fossil (Pant.).

38. **M. elliptica** AG. (1833). — V. elliptical. L. 0,022 to 0,045; B. 0,01 to 0,018 mm. Central area orbicular, small, but distinct. Loculi 7 to 8 in 0,01 mm. of equal size, forming a band, which ends at some distance from the ends. Striæ 20 in 0,01 mm. radiate throughout, in the middle alternately longer and shorter, finely punctate. — *Frustulia elliptica* AG. in KÜTZ. Syn. p. 10. *M. Dansei var. elliptica* V. H. Syn. Pl. IV f. 19. DANNF. Baltic D. Pl. IV f. 19. *M. obtusa* PANT. II p. 41 Pl. VII f. 134 (1889).

Brackish water: Sweden (Baltic, extremely abundant)! Saxony! England! Belgium! Ecuador (Baños, Tesalia)!

Var. *australis* CL. — L. 0,032 to 0,036; B. 0,01 to 0,013 mm. Loculi 9 in 0,01 mm. Striæ 14 to 15 in 0,01 mm. coarsely punctate; puncta about 16 in 0,01 mm.

Slightly brackish water; Mitchell River, Australia! Rioja, rep. Argentina!

Var. *Dansei* THW. (1856). — V. narrow, linear with cuneate ends. L. 0,035 to 0,04; B. 0,01 to 0,012 mm. Striæ 18 in 0,01 mm., finely punctate. — *M. Dansei* THW SM. B. D. II p. 64

Pl. LXII f. 388. V. H. Syn. p. 70 Pl. IV f. 18. A. S. Atl. CLXXXV, 5 to 8. *M. antiqua* SCHUM. Preuss. D. Pl. IX f. 58 *a* (1862).

Brackish, or almost fresh water: Sweden (Gothland)! England! Belgium (V. H.), Saxony! Tasmania! Australia (Atl.).

Var. *punctata* CL. — Linear, with cuneate ends. L. 0,04 to 0,065; B. 0,01 to 0,012 mm. Striæ 15 in 0,01 mm.; puncta 16 in 0,01 mm.

Almost fresh water: Australia (Mitchell River)! Gothland!

39. **M. lanceolata** THWAITES (1848 fide W. SM.). - V. lanceolate, frequently acuminate. L. 0,04 to 0,05; B. 0,017 to 0,019 mm. Central area not distinct. Median line slightly undulating. Loculi 9 to 10 in 0,01 mm. rectangular, of equal size, forming bands ending near the extremities. Striæ about 19 in 0,01 mm. parallel, convergent at the ends, punctate; puncta 25 in 0,01 mm. forming longitudinal rows. — W. SM. B. D. II p. 64 Pl. LIV f. 340. GRUN. Casp. Sea Alg. p. 14 Pl. III f. 11. V. H. Syn. p. 70 Pl. IV f. 15 to 17. A. S. Atl. CLXXXVI, 21, 22.

Brackish and marine: Baltic (Rügen)! Caspian Sea (Grun.). England! Adriatic Sea! Labuan! Port Jackson! Pensacola!

40. **M. fallax** CL. N. Sp. — V. lanceolate, slightly rostrate. L. 0,045 to 0,047; B. 0,018 mm. Median line slightly undulating. Axial area indistinct. Central area small. Loculi 10 in 0,01 mm. forming a marginal band ending near the extremities. Striæ 16 in 0,01 mm., radiate throughout, the median shorter, composed of elongated puncta forming longitudinal rows, closer at the margins. — Pl. II f. 16.

Marine: Seychelles (V. H. Coll.)! Java!

This species resembles *M. lanceolata*, but its striæ are radiate throughout and have a different punctation. In outline it resembles GRUNOW'S *Rhaphoneis dubia* (Novara p. 99 Pl. 1 A f. 6) which seems to be a *Mastogloia*, but has coarser striæ than *M. fallax*.

41. **M. laminaris** EHB. (1843). - V. lanceolate, frequently slightly acuminate. L. 0,03 to 0,05; B. 0,01 to 0,015 mm. Median line very slightly undulating or straight. Central area not distinct. Loculi 4 to 5 in 0,01 mm. of equal size, forming bands ending near the extremities. Striæ about 21 in 0,01 mm., almost parallel, very finely punctate. — *Ceratoneis lamin.* EHB. Am. Pl. III: 7 f. 24 (fide Grun.). CL. Vega p. 494. CL. M. D. N:o 153.

Marine: Adriatic! Corsica! Labuan! Java! Pensacola (Grove Coll.)!

Var. *intermedia* CL. — L. 0,035; B. 0,015 mm. Loculi 8 in 0,01 mm. Striæ 21 in 0,01 mm. — Pl. II f. 10.

Marine: Japan!

M. laminaris resembles *M. lanceolata*, but has larger loculi and finer striæ. The var. *intermedia* takes an intermediate position.

42. **M. Portierana** GRUN. (1863). — V. lanceolate, slightly rostrate. L. 0,095; B. 0,027 mm. Loculi 7 in 0,01 mm. equal, forming a band reaching to the apices. Striæ fine, more than 22 in 0,01 mm. finely punctate. — Verh. 1863 p. 157 Pl. IV f. 3.

Marine: Red Sea (Grun.).

Unknown to me, seems to be allied to *M. lanceolata* or *laminaris*.

43. **M. pulchella** CL. N. Sp. — V. rhomboid, acute. L. 0,1; B. 0,028 mm. Median line undulating. Axial area indistinct; central area small, irregular. Loculi quadrate, 8 in 0,01 mm. forming a marginal band reaching to the ends. Striæ 14 in 0.01 mm. finely punctate, crossed by several faint longitudinal lines. — Pl. II f. 27, 28, 29.

Marine: Java.

44. **M. elegans** Lewis (1865). — V. lanceolate, subacute or subrostrate. L. 0,066; B. 0,026 mm. Loculi 3 to 7 in 0,01 mm., delicate, frequently rudimentary, forming a band along the whole margin. Median line almost straight, or very slightly undulating. Central area very small, or indistinct. Striæ about 15 in 0,01 mm. almost parallel throughout, punctate; puncta about 15 in 0,01 mm. forming longitudinal rows. — Proced. Acad. Nat. Sc. Philadelphia 1865 p. 13 Pl. I f. 9. — Grun. Foss. D. Öst. Ungarns p. 150 Pl. XXIX f. 20. A. S. Atl. CLXXXVI f. 19, 20.

Marine: Atlantic coast of U. St.! Java! Pensacola! Foss. Bory, Hungary!

45. **M. paradoxa** Grun. (1878). — V. linear-lanceolate, rostrate. L. 0,055; B. 0,014 mm. Loculi 4 in 0,01 mm. equal, forming a band at some distance from the margin, and ending at a considerable distance from the extremities. Striæ 26 to 29 in 0,01 mm. — Cl. M. D. N:o 153. *M. Seychellensis* Grun. Casp. Sea Alg. p. 14.

Marine: Corsica (Grun.). Seychelles (Grun.).

This species is unknown to me, having failed in finding it in Cl. M. D. N:o 153. The above description is from a sketch sent by Grunow, who does not indicate whether the striæ are longitudinal, straight, or oblique, for which reason its place in the system is uncertain.

46. **M. erythræa** Grun. (1860). — V. lanceolate with acuminate or apiculate ends. L. 0,04; B. 0,01 to 0,013 mm. Loculi about 12 in 0,01 mm., forming a band interrupted in one or two places by one, to three, larger loculi. Median line undulating. Areas indistinct. Striæ 21 in 0,01 mm. almost parallel, punctate; puncta forming undulating longitudinal rows, about 14 in 0,01 mm. — Verh. 1860 p. 577 Pl. VII f. 4. M. J. 1877 p. 174 Pl. CXCIV f. 12 to 14. A. S. Atl. CLXXXVI f. 25, 26. *M. bullata* A. S. Atl. CLXXXVI f. 36 (1893).

Marine: Mediterranean, Adriatic and Black Seas! Red Sea (Grun.). Honduras (Grun.). Bahamas (Grove Coll.)!

Var. *biocellata* Grun. (1877). — The larger loculi in the middle of the band. Striæ 24 in 0,01 mm. — M. J. 1877 l. c. f. 15.

Marine: Honduras (Grun.).

Var.? *interrupta* Hantzch (1862). — Larger loculi 4 to 6. — *M. inter.* Hantzsch Ost Ind. Arch. D. p. 20 Pl. VI f. 5. A. S. Atl. CLXXXVI f. 37.

Marine: East Indies (Hantzsch), Nicobar Islands (Grun.).

47. **M. constricta** Cl. (1892). — V. elongated, with cuneate ends, constricted in the middle. L. 0,06; B. 0,011 at the constriction 0,0065 mm. Loculi 6 in 0,01 mm. of equal size and with straight interior margins. Median line undulating. Central area very small. Striæ 21 in 0,01 mm. transverse, punctate; puncta about 20 in 0,01 mm. forming undulating longitudinal rows. — Diatomiste I p. 159 Pl. XXIII f. 5.

Marine: Java!

48. **M. flexuosa** Cl. N. Sp. — V. linear to elliptical with rostrate to acuminate ends. L. 0,03 to 0,045; B. 0,011 to 0,01 mm. Median line strongly sinuose. Loculi 7 to 8 in 0,01 mm. of equal size, quadrate, forming a band ending near the apices. Central area very small, orbicular. Striæ 16 to 20 in 0,01 mm. parallel, of coarse elongated puncta, not forming straight lines. — Pl. II f. 12.

Marine: Pithyusian Islands! Mediterranean!

This small species is remarkable for the strong flexure of its median line, near the central nodule.

49. **M. cuspidata** Cl. (1893). — V. elliptical, apiculate. L. 0,026; B. 0,01 mm. Median line strongly flexuose. Axial and central areas indistinct. Loculi 6 in 0,01 mm. equal, quadrate, forming a marginal band, ending below the extremities of the valve. Striæ 25 in 0,01 mm., parallel, not distinctly punctate. — Diatomiste II p. 16 Pl. I f. 18.

Marine: Bahamas (Grove Coll.)!

50. **M. bisulcata** GRUN. (1877). — V. elliptic-lanceolate, rostrate. L. 0,017 to 0,03; B. 0,09 to 0,011 mm. Loculi 5 to 6 in 0,01 mm., of equal size, quadrate, forming bands not reaching to the extremities. Median line undulating. Striæ 10,5 in 0,01 mm. slightly radiate, finely punctate, crossed on both sides of the median line by a narrow, arcuate furrow. M. J. 1877 p. 176 Pl. CXCV f. 6.

Marine: Honduras (Grun.).

Var. *corsicana* GRUN. (1878). — V. elliptic-lanceolate, apiculate. L. 0,025 to 0,032; B. 0,008 to 0,011 mm. Loculi 5 in 0,01 mm. Median line slightly undulating. Striæ 11 to 15 in 0,01 mm. crossed by one or two, narrow, longitudinal furrows. — *M. corsic.* GRUN. Cl. M. D. N:o 153. *M. bisulc. var. cors.* GRUN. V. H. Syn. Pl. IV f. 28.

Marine: Mediterranean!

51. **M. rimosa** CL. (1893). — V. rhombic-lanceolate, with apiculate ends. L. 0,037; B. 0,013 mm. Median line flexuose. Axial area narrow, distinct. Loculi rectangular, about 10 in 0,01 mm., forming a broad band, reaching to the apiculi. Striæ 11 in 0,01 mm. slightly radiate, convergent at the ends and crossed by a longitudinal furrow, not distinctly punctate. — Diatomiste vol. II p. 15 Pl. I f. 15. A. S. Atl. CLXXXVIII f. 25.

Marine: Bahamas (Grove Coll.)!

52. **M. Goësii** CL. (1878). — V. elliptical with rostrate to capitate ends. L. 0,036 to 0,06; B 0,013 to 0,02 mm. Loculi 8 in 0,01 mm., forming a narrow marginal band reaching to the apices. Median line straight. Areas not distinct. Striæ 16 to 18 in 0,01 mm. of elongated puncta forming parallel, longitudinal rows, about 12 in 0,01 mm. *Nav. Goësii* CL. West Ind. D. p. 6 Pl. I f. 7. *Mastogl. Goësii* CL. Diatomiste I p. 160 Pl. XXIII f. 6. A. S. Atl. CLXXXVIII f. 23?

Marine: Seychelles (Van Heurck Coll.)! Cebu, Philippines! West Indies!

53. **M. undulata** GRUN. (1860). — V. broadly lanceolate, rostrate. L. 0,03 to 0,045; B. 0,012 to 0,018 mm. Loculi 9 to 12 in 0,01 mm. equal, forming bands, reaching to the apices. Median line strongly undulating. No distinct areas. Striæ 17 to 18 in 0,01 mm., almost parallel, of elongated puncta, forming longitudinal rows, about 9 in 0,01 mm. — Verh. 1860 p. 576 Pl. VII f. 5. M. J. 1877 p. 176 Pl. CXCV f. 5. PERAG. D. Villfranche p. 44 Pl. III f. 24.

Marine: Mediterranean Sea! Adriatic! Seychelles (Grun.), Australia and Oceania (Grun.), Honduras (Grun.).

54. **M. rhombica** CL. (1883). — V. rhomboid, with a shallow longitudinal depression on each side of the median line. L. 0,048; B. 0,02 mm. Loculi 6 in 0,01 mm. equal, quadrate, forming bands reaching to the ends. Median line undulating. Striæ 11 in 0,01 mm. coarsely punctate; puncta 17 in 0,01 mm. forming undulating longitudinal rows. — Vega p. 494 Pl. XXXV f. 9.

Marine: Labuan!

55. **M. affirmata** LEUD. FORTM. (1879). — V. rhomboid to lanceolate. L. 0,07 to 0,085; B. 0,035 to 0,04 mm. Median line undulating, unilaterally dilated at the central nodule. Loculi 9 to 11 in 0,01 mm., equal, forming broad bands, reaching to the ends. Striæ 10 in 0,01 mm., parallel or slighly radiate at the ends, crossed by parallel longitudinal striæ, 8 to 9 in 0,01 mm. — *Navic. affirm.* LEUD. FORTM. D. de Ceylan p. 24 Pl. II f. 22. *M. affirm.* CL. Diatomiste I p. 162 Pl. XXIII f. 15. *M. squamosa* BR. A. S. Atl. CLXXXVIII f. 19, 31 (1893).

Marine: Ceylon, Colombo (Le Tourneur Coll.)! Philippines! Rodriguez (Atl.).

56. **M. bahamensis** CL. (1893). — V. rhombic-lanceolate. L. 0,045; B. 0,022 mm. Median line dilated near the central nodule. Loculi 12 in 0,01 mm., equal, rectangular, forming a band, which reaches the ends of the valve. Striæ 13 in 0,01 mm., composed of coarse, elongated puncta, forming longitudinal, or irregularly decussating, rows, about 8 in 0,01 mm. — Diatomiste II p. 16 Pl. I f. 17. A. S. Atl. CLXXXVIII f. 20, 21.

Marine: Bahamas (Grove Coll.)!

Closely akin to *M. affirmata* in all characteristics, but much smaller. Perhaps a forma minuta of this species.

57. **O. ovata** Grun. (1860). V. elliptical. L. 0,035 to 0,036; B. 0,018 to 0,02 mm. Loculi 4 to 5 in 0,01 mm, equal, quadrate, forming a rim along the margin. No areas. Striæ 17 in 0,01 mm, transverse or slightly radiate at the ends, composed of elongated puncta, forming longitudinal rows, about 11 in 0,01 mm. — *Mast. ovata* Grun. Verh. 1860 p. 578 Pl. VII f. 12. A. D. p. 17 Pl. I f. 2. *Orthon. ov.* Grun. Novara p. 98.

Marine: Sea of Kara (Grun.). Mediterranean, Adriatic and Black seas! Madagascar! Java! Samoa! Honduras (Grun.).

Allied to *O. ovata* is probably *M. ovalis* A. S. (Atl. CLXXXV f. 30) from Japan. L. 0,03; B. 0,018 mm. Striæ 12 and loculi 4 in 0,01 mm. It is distinguished from *O. ovata* principally by the short bands of 7 loculi, which end at a considerable distance from the extremities of the valve.

58. **M. lineata** Cl. a. Grove (1891). V. lanceolate, acute or apiculate. L. 0,093; B. 0,034 mm. Loculi 2,5 in 0,01 mm. equal, delicate, with convex interior edges, along the whole margin of the valve. Median line slightly undulate. Central area very small, rounded. Striæ 12 in 0,01 mm. parallel, composed of elongated puncta, forming straight, parallel, longitudinal rows, 7 in 0,01 mm. — Diatomiste I p. 59 Pl. IX f. 11.

Marine: Macassar Straits (Grove Coll.)! Manilla (Deby Coll.)! Cebu!

59. **M. exarata** Cl. N. Sp. — V. lanceolate, apiculate. L. 0,065 to 0,08; B. 0,027 to 0,028 mm. Loculi 5 in 0,01 mm. delicate, with straight interior edges forming a narrow band along the margin. No areas. Median line straight. Striæ 21 in 0,01 mm. parallel, of elongated puncta forming longitudinal, parallel, straight rows, 11 to 12 in 0,01 mm. — Pl. II f. 35. A. S. Atl. CLXXXVII f. 38.

Marine: China (Van Heurck Coll.)! Japan (Brun Coll.)!

Similar to *M. lineata*, but differs by its closer loculi and finer striæ.

60. **M. arata** Cl. N. Sp. — V. rhomboid. L. 0,09 to 0,11; B. 0,035 mm. Loculi 3,5 in 0,01 mm. delicate, equal, with straight interior edges, forming a band along the whole margin. Central area moderately large, rounded. Median line undulating. Striæ 17 in 0,01 mm. transverse, composed of elongated puncta, forming straight, parallel longitudinal rows, 11 in 0,01 mm. — Pl. II f. 9.

Marine: Island of Rhea, near Singapore!

61. **M. acuta** Grun. (1883). — V. lanceolate to rhomboid. L. 0,04; B. 0,015 mm. Loculi of unequal size, larger in the middle, forming a band at some distance from the margin and ending at a distance from the apices. No areas. Striæ about 30 in 0,01 mm., crossed by more distant longitudinal furrows, about 17 in 0,01 mm. — Vega p. 494 Pl. XXXV f. 8. Icon. n. Pl. II f. 13.

Marine: Seychelles (Grun.), Labuan!

M. lineolata A. S. (Atl. CLXXXVI f. 33) from Malabar resembles somewhat *M. acuta*, but the figure is too little detailed for identification.

62. **M. baltica** Grun. (1880). — V. lanceolate, with broad, rostrate ends. L. 0,03 to 0,04; B. 0,013 to 0,016 mm. Loculi 6 in 0,01 mm. equal, quadrate, forming a band, ending at some distance from the extremities. Median line straight enclosed between two approximate longitudinal ribs. No areas. Striæ 20 to 21 in 0,01 mm. finely punctate; puncta forming longitudinal rows. — V. H. Syn. Pl. IV f. 24. *M. lanceolata var. elliptica* and *var. amphicephala* Danne. Baltic D. p. 16 Pl. I f. 2?

Brackish water: Baltic (Gothland, Rügen)! South Africa!

This species has a close resemblance to ***M. Smithii***, from which it is however distinguished by the longitudinal lines close to the median line. The following three species are nearly akin to *M. baltica* and all may perhaps more properly be considered as varieties of *M. apiculata*.

63. **M. Citrus** Cl. (1883). — V. broadly elliptical, apiculate. L. 0,03 to 0,04; B. 0,016 to 0,024 mm. Loculi about 9 in 0,01 mm., of equal size, quadrate, forming a band reaching to the apiculi. Striæ 18 or 19 (middle) to 23 (ends) in 0,01 mm. slightly radiate. *M. baltica var.? Citrus* Cl. Vega p. 495 Pl. XXXV f. 7. *M. suborbicularis* Leud. Fortm. D. de Malaisie p. 19 Pl. II f. 6 (1892)? *M. Citrus* A. S. Atl. CLXXXVII f. 16 to 19. Icon. n. Pl. II f. 6.
Marine: Adriatic! Labuan! Sandwich Islands! Vera Cruz (Atl.), Jamaica (Grove Coll.)!

64. **M apiculata** W. Sm. (1856). — V. elliptic-lanceolate, frequently rostrate. L. 0,05 to 0,09; B. 0,023 mm. Loculi 7 to 8 in 0,01 mm. equal, quadrate, forming a band, ending near the extremities. Median line straight, enclosed between two approximate longitudinal ribs. No areas. Striæ 15 to 19 in 0,01 mm., almost parallel, finely punctate; puncta 19 to 23 in 0,01 mm., forming fine, longitudinal rows. — B. D. II p. 65 Pl. LXII f. 387. A. S. Atl. CLXXXV f. 13, CLXXXVI f. 23. Icon. n. Pl. II f. 24, 25. *M. acutiuscula* Grun. in Cl. Vega p. 495. *M. angulata* Perag. D. de Villefr. Pl. III f. 22 (1888). *M. balkanica* Br A. S. Atl. CLXXXVII f. 40 (1893)?
Marine: North Sea (England, Sweden)! Cherbourg (Grun.), Mediterranean Sea! Sebastopol! China!

65. **M. labuensis** Cl. (1883). — V. linear, with cuneate ends. L. 0,064 to 0,075; B. 0,015 to 0,016 mm. Median line straight, enclosed between two approximate longitudinal ribs. No areas. Loculi 7 to 8 in 0,01 mm. equal, quadrate, forming bands reaching nearly to the extremities. Striæ 15 to 17 in 0,01 mm. parallel, or slightly radiate towards the extremities, coarsely punctate, puncta 17 in 0,01 mm., forming straight, longitudinal rows. — *M. acutiusc. var. lab.* Cl. Vega p. 495 Pl. XXXV f. 5. *M. lab.* A. S. Atl. CLXXXV f. 4? CLXXXVII f. 2. Icon. n. Pl. II f. 5.
Marine: Labuan! Philippines!

66. **M. Peragalli** Cl. (1892). — V. elliptic-lanceolate, rostrate. L. 0,052 to 0,058; B. 0,0025 to 0,0027 mm. Median line undulating, enclosed between two, not very approximate longitudinal ribs. No axial area. Central area small. Loculi 8 in 0,01 mm., almost equal, rectangular, forming bands, reaching to the apices and with slightly undulating interior edges. Striæ 18 in 0,01 mm. parallel, or slightly radiate towards the ends, punctate; puncta about 20 in 0,01 mm., forming straight, parallel, longitudinal rows. — *M. sp.?* Perag. D. Villefranche p. 44 Pl. III f. 23. *M. Perag.* Cl. Diatomiste I p. 160 Pl. XXIII f. 7.
Marine: Mediterranean Sea (Perag.), Sumatra (Deby Coll.)! Japan!

67. **M. Pisciculus** Cl. (1894). V. lanceolate, subacuminate. L. 0,035; B. 0,015 mm. Median line sinuose. Axial area indistinct. Central area orbicular, small. Loculi 4 in 0,01 mm., quadrate, equal, forming a marginal band, ending below the extremities of the valve. Striæ 21 in 0,01 mm. almost parallel, radiate at the ends, finely punctate, puncta forming longitudinal rows. The striæ are crossed by a longitudinal line at some distance from the median line. The striæ inside the longitudinal lines faint. — Diatomiste II p. 55 Pl. III f. 2.
Marine: Pensacola (Grove Coll.)!

68. **M. pumila** Grun. (1880). — V. elliptic-lanceolate. L. 0,025 to 0,028; B. 0,01 mm. Central nodule large, quadrate, prolonged into narrow horns, parallel to the margin. Loculi 6 to 8 on each side, of unequal size, the median being largest. Striæ 23 in 0,01 mm. parallel. — *M. Braunii var. pumila* Grun. V. H. Syn. p. 71 Pl. IV f. 23. A. S. Atl. CLXXXV f. 36, 37.
Slightly brackish water: Baltic (Dannf.), Hawaii!

69. **M. Braunii** Grun. (1863). V. elliptic-lanceolate. L. 0,04 to 0,035; B. 0,014 to 0,027 mm. Central nodule large, quadrate, prolonged into narrow horns, as to form a lyriform figure. Loculi 4,5 to 6 in 0,01 mm. quadrate, equal, or the median larger, forming a band ending near the extremities. Striæ 18 to 22 in 0,01 mm. parallel, radiate towards the ends, finely punctate; puncta about 25 in 0,01 mm. — Verh. 1863 p. 156 Pl. IV f. 2. Dannf. Balt. D. Pl. I f. 4. V. H. Syn. p. 71 Pl. IV f. 21, 22. A. S. Atl. CLXXXV f. 39, 40, 45; CLXXXVIII f. 4 to 12. *M. Kinsmannii* Lewis Proced. Ac. Nat. Hist. Philad. p. 13 Pl. II f. 15 (1865).

Brackish water: Spitsbergen! Baltic! Caspian Sea! Saxony! North Sea! Mediterranean, Adriatic and Black Seas! Red Sea (Grun.). Japan! Pensacola! Cape May (Lewis).

70. **M. Debyi** Cl. (1892). — V. narrow, rhombic-lanceolate. L. 0,055; B. 0,014 mm. Median line strongly flexuose. Central area quadrate, expanded into narrow, linear lateral areas, parallel to the median line. Loculi 8 in 0,01 mm. quadrate, forming a narrow band reaching to the ends. Striæ 15 in 0,01 mm. slightly radiate, finely punctate. — Diatomiste I p. 161 Pl. XXIII f. 11. *Nav. perducta* Pant. III Pl. XVIII f. 262 (1893). *M. rhomboidalis* Pant. III Pl. XLI f. 563 (1893)?

Marine: Karand, Hungary, fossil (Deby Coll.)!

71. **M. baltjikiana** Grun. (188 ?). — V. elliptical to elliptic-lanceolate, subacute. L. 0,042; B. 0,02 mm. Median line undulating. Central area broad, transverse, merging into two narrow, lunate lateral areas. Loculi 6 to 8 in 0,01 mm., equal, rectangular, forming bands, ending at some distance from the apices. Striæ 16 to 17 in 0,01 mm., slightly radiate, coarsely punctate; puncta about 16 in 0,01 mm. *M. Braunii var. baltjikiana* Grun. in V. H. Types №o 545. *M. baltj.* A. S. Atl. CLXXXVIII f. 2. Icon. n. Pl. II f. 11. *M. Pethöi* Pant. III Pl. XXXVII f. 519 (1893). *M. neogena* Pant. III Pl. XLI f. 559 (1893). *M. Kinkerii* Pant. III Pl. XLI f. 562 (1893). *Navicula Orphei* Pant. III Pl. XLII f. 580 (1893).

Marine: Baltjik, foss.!

Var. *ballata* Cl. — Areas with some few scattered, large puncta. L. 0,09; B. 0,024 mm. Striæ 17 in 0,01 mm. Puncta 16 in 0,01 mm.

Marine: Russia, fossil (Deby Coll.)!

72. **M. Macdonaldii** Grev. (1865). V. lanceolate to rhomboid, subacute. L. 0,035 to 0,045; B. 0,013 to 0,017 mm. Median line slightly undulating. Central nodule transversely dilated into a broad stauros. Loculi 3 in 0,01 mm., decreasing in size towards the extremities and with slightly rounded interior edges. Striæ 22 in 0,01 mm. slightly radiate throughout, crossed by large, semi-lanceolate areas, punctate; puncta about 22 in 0,01 mm. forming somewhat undulating longitudinal rows. — T. Bot. Soc. Edinb. Vol. VIII p. 237 Pl. III f. 15. A. S. Atl. CLXXXVII f. 42, 43. Icon. n. Pl. II f. 21.

Marine: Corsica! Adriatic! Philippines! Australia (Grev.).

73. **M. euxina** Cl. (1892). — V. lanceolate. L. 0,07; B. 0,026 mm. Median line undulating. Axial area narrow. Central nodule transversely dilated into a short stauros. Axial area narrow; central area prolonged into the narrow, lunate lateral areas. Loculi 5 in 0,01 mm. equal, quadrate, forming a band reaching nearly to the ends. Striæ 17 in 0,01 mm. coarsely punctate; puncta about 18 in 0,01 mm. forming undulating longitudinal rows. Axial striæ short. — Diatomiste I p. 160 Pl. XXIII f. 9.

Marine: Baltjik, fossil!

74. **M. entoleia** Cl. (1892). V. lanceolate. L. 0,07; B. 0,025 mm. Loculi 4 in 0,01 mm. of equal size, rectangular, forming bands ending at some distance from the extremities. Median line undulating. Axial area lanceolate, moderately broad. Striæ 17 in 0,01 mm. punctate; puncta, about 14 in 0,01 mm., forming longitudinal undulating rows. Diatomiste I p. 160 Pl. XXIII f. 8. A. S. Atl. CLXXXVIII f. 15 to 17.

Marine: Baltjik, foss.!

A similar, not described, and insufficiently figured, form seems to be *M. obtusa var. fluviatilis* Brun in A. S. Atl. CLXXXVIII f. 18.

75. **M. antiqua** Cl. (1893). — V. rhomboid. L. 0,08; B. 0,03 mm. Median line slightly undulating. Axial area a narrow, lanceolate space. Loculi 6 in 0,01 mm., equal, quadrate, forming a band inside the margin and ending at some distance from the extremities. Striæ 18 in 0,01 mm. parallel, very slightly radiate at the ends, punctate; puncta 18 in 0,01 mm., forming undulating longitudinal rows. Diatomiste II p. 16 Pl. I f. 19.

Marine: Karand, Hungary, fossil (Deby Coll.)!

76. **M. cruciata** Leud. Fortm. (1879). — V. rhomboid. L. 0,085 to 0,122; B. 0,053 to 0,057 mm. Central nodule transversely dilated into a stauros, not reaching to the margins. Median line slightly undulating. Loculi? Lateral areas large, semilanceolate, crossed by faint striæ. Striæ marginal and axial. Marginal striæ 8 to 9 in 0,01 mm. punctate; puncta 12 in 0,01 mm. Axial striæ short. — *Nav. cruc.* Leud. Fortm. D. Ceylan p. 25 Pl. II f. 19. *Mast. cruc.* Cl. Diatomiste I p. 65 Pl. X f. 4 (1891). A. S. Atl. CLXXXVII f. 50.

Marine: Ceylon (Le Tourneur Coll.)! Manilla (Deby Coll.)! Philippines!

77. **M. Craveni** Leud. Fortm. (1879). — V. rhombic-lanceolate. L. 0,111; B. 0,056 to 0,06 mm. Median line almost straight. Central area irregularly rounded, moderately large. Loculi? Lateral areas large, with numerous and irregular longitudinal rows (about 7 in 0,01 mm.) of elongated puncta. Striæ marginal and axial. Marginal striæ 12 in 0,01 mm. punctate; puncta about 14 in 0,01 mm. — *Navicula Crav.* Leud. Fortm. D. Ceylan p. 25 Pl. II f. 20. *Mastogl. Crav.* Cl. Diatomiste I p. 66 Pl. X f. 5.

Marine: Colombo, Ceylon (Le Tourneur Coll.)!

78. **M. Leudugeri** Cl. a. Grove (1891). V. rhombic-lanceolate. L. 0,12; B. 0,06 mm. Median line undulating. Central area small, subquadrate. Axial area very narrow. Loculi 3 in 0,01 mm., quadrate, equal, forming a band, reaching to the extremities. Lateral areas broad, semilanceolate, with numerous longitudinal rows (about 7 in 0,01 mm.) of short striæ. Striæ marginal and axial, 14 in 0,01 mm. punctate; puncta 15 in 0.01 mm. forming undulating, longitudinal rows. — Diatomiste I p. 65 Pl. X f. 3. A. S. Atl. CLXXXVI f. 13.

Marine: Macassar Straits! Singapore! Java!

79. **M. lemniscata** Leud. Fortm. (1879). — V. rhombic-lanceolate. L. 0,05 to 0,088; B. 0,025 to 0,043 mm. Median line slightly undulating. Loculi 5 to 6 in 0,01 mm. quadrate, forming a band reaching to the ends. Central area small, quadrate. Lateral areas large, semilanceolate, with a few (3 to 4) longitudinal rows of short striæ. Striæ 15 to 16 in 0,01 mm. punctate; puncta 15 to 20 in 0,01 mm. — D. de Ceylon p. 35 Pl. III f. 29. A. S. Atl. CLXXXVI f. 14. Icon. n. Pl. II f. 26. *M. decora* Leud. Fortm. l. c. f. 32.

Marine: Madagascar (Van Heurck and Kinker Coll.)! Ceylon! Sumbava (Kinker Coll.)! Manilla (Deby Coll.)! Macassar Straits (Grove Coll.)! Carpentaria Bay! Japan! Colon (Deby Coll.)!

80. **M. javanica** Cl. (1893). — V. rhomboid-lanceolate. L. 0,11; B. 0,032 mm. Median line slightly undulating. No axial or central areas. Loculi 3 in 0,01 mm. equal, rectangular, forming a narrow band, reaching to the ends. Striæ 16 in 0,01 mm. parallel, slightly radiate at the ends, composed of elongated puncta, forming longitudinal, parallel, straight rows, 12 in 0,01 mm. Surface of the valve with a shallow, narrow, longitudinal depression, close to the median line. The longitudinal rows of puncta are more distant on the depression. — A. S. Atl. CLXXXVIII f. 38. Icon. n. Pl. II f. 22, 23.

Marine: Java! Sumatra (Grove Coll.)!

81. **M. obesa** CL. (1893). — V. broadly lanceolate, acuminate. L. 0,04; B. 0,024 mm. Median line slightly undulate. Axial area very narrow. Central area quadrate, extending into narrow, lunate lateral areas. Loculi 6 in 0,01 mm. equal, quadrate forming a band, ending near the extremities. Striæ 12 in 0,01 mm. composed of coarse and distant puncta. Between the striæ and the lateral areas are a few rows of elongated puncta. — Diatomiste II p. 15 Pl. I f. 16.

Marine: Java!

82. **M. Temperei** CL. (1890). — V. elliptic-lanceolate. L. 0,11; B. 0,04 mm. Median line undulate. Axial and central areas indistinct. Loculi? Lateral areas lunate with about 5 undulating longitudinal rows of elongated puncta. Striæ 10 in 0,01 mm. punctate; puncta 10 in 0,01 mm. forming undulate longitudinal rows. — Diatomiste I p. 23 Pl. III f. 3.

Marine: Japan, fossil!

Nearly akin to *M. Jelineckii*, probably a variety of it.

83. **M. Jelineckii** GRUN. (1863). — V. rhombical. L. 0,06 to 0,11; B. 0,025 to 0,045 mm. Median line almost straight. Axial area small, transverse. Loculi 3 to 4 in 0,01 mm. delicate, with rounded interior edges, forming a narrow band, reaching to the apices. Lateral areas large, with faint prolongations of the striæ. Striæ 13 to 14 in 0,01 mm punctate; puncta 10 to 18 in 0,01 mm. forming irregular, oblique rows. — *Navic. Jel.* GRUN. Verh. 1863 p. 151 Pl. V f. 12. *Mastogl. Jel.* GRUN. Novara p. 99 Pl. I f. 11. T. M. Soc. 1877 p. 174 Pl. CXCV f. 1. A. S. Atl. CLXXXVII f. 49. *Nav. quarnerensis var. dilatata* PETIT D. Campbell p. 21 Pl. V f. 24? *Nav. subrhomboidea* CASTR. Voyage challenger D. p. 30 Pl. XX f. 4? *Mastogl. Jel. var. italica* B. A. S. Atl. CLXXXVII f. 48.

Marine: Mediterranean Sea! Seychelles (Van Heurck Coll.)! Madagascar (Van Heurck Coll.)! Java! Sumbava (Kinker Coll.)! Manilla (Deby Coll.)! China! West Indies! Brazil!

Var. *fossilis* CL. — L. 0,07; B. 0,03 mm. Striæ 12 in 0,01 mm. the median alternately longer and shorter. Puncta 14 in 0,01 mm.

Marine: Russia, fossil (Deby Coll.)!

Var. *marina* (JAN. a. RABH.?) CL. — V. rhomboid. L. 0,04 to 0,07; B. 0,017 to 0,025 mm. Loculi 4 to 5 in 0,01 mm. Lateral areas narrow, frequently with a row of short striæ at their exterior edges. Striæ 17 to 18 in 0,01 mm. finely punctate; puncta 25 in 0,01 mm. *Nav. mar.* JAN. RABH. D. Honduras p. 10 Pl. II f. 16? Icon. n. Pl. II f. 18.

Marine: Honduras (Jan. Rabh.). Manilla (Deby Coll.)! Java! Philippines (Grove Coll.):

84. **M. submarginata** CL. and GRUN. (1881). — V. lanceolate subacute. L. 0,04 to 0,055; B. 0,017 to 0,018 mm. Median line straight. Central area quadrate, merging into the lunate, structureless, or faintly striate, large lateral areas. Loculi rudimentary 5 to 8 in 0,01 mm. Striæ 19 in 0,01 mm. punctate; puncta 23 in 0,01 mm. — N. R. D. p. 4 Pl. I f. 2.

Marine: Galapagos Islands! Campeachy Bay (Grun.).

85. **M. Kellerii** PANT. (1889). — V. elliptic-lanceolate. L. 0,09 to 0,12; B. 0,033 to 0,036 mm. Median line undulate. Central and axial areas small or indistinct. Loculi 4 in 0,01 mm., equal, quadrate, forming a band extending along the whole margin. Depressed lateral areas lunate with crowded longitudinal rows (6 in 0.01 mm.) of short striæ. Striæ 14 to 15 in 0,01 mm. punctate; puncta about 10 in 0,01 mm. — *Navicula Kellerii* PANT. II p. 49 Pl. XXIII f. 351.

Marine: Hungary, fossil, Bory!

86. **M. japonica** CL. (1892). — V. elliptic-lanceolate. L. 0,045 to 0,065; B. 0,02 to 0,027 mm. Median line strongly undulate. Axial area narrow, distinct. Loculi 6 in 0,01 mm. equal, quadrate, forming a band, ending in the apices. Striæ 16 in 0,01 mm., of elongated puncta, forming longitudinal parallel rows, 12 in 0,01 mm.; the two rows next to the median line more distant. — Diatomiste I p. 162 Pl. XXIII f. 16.

Marine: Japan (Tempère)!

87. **M. seriata** Cl. a. Grove (1891). — V. broadly lanceolate, acuminate. L. 0,06; B. 0,036 mm. Median line undulate. Central area small, rounded. Loculi 4 in 0,01 mm. equal, quadrate, forming a band reaching to the ends. Surface of the valve with 5 to 6 shallow, longitudinal furrows on each side of the median line. Striæ 16 in 0,01 mm., radiate throughout, in the middle alternately longer and shorter, finely punctate. — Diatomiste I p. 68 Pl. X f. 6.

Marine: Macassar Straits (Grove Coll.)!

All these species from *M. Lendugeri* are intimately connected. *M. seriata* combines them with *M. quinquecostata var. rhombica*

88. **M. quinquecostata** Grun. (1860). — V. elliptical to subrhomboid. L. 0,057 to 0,104; B. 0,022 to 0,05 mm. Median line more or less undulate. Central area small. Loculi 4 to 5 in 0,01 mm. almost equal, forming a band reaching nearly to the ends. Striæ 16 in 0,01 mm., slightly radiate, finely punctate; puncta forming close, undulate, longitudinal rows. Striæ crossed on each side of the median line by 2 or 3 longitudinal, narrow depressions. — Verh. 1860 p. 578 Pl. VII f. 8. Hantzsch D. Ostind. Arch. p. 20 f. 6. Perag. D. Villefranche Pl. III f. 21. *Navic. olivacea* Leud. Fortm. D. Ceylan p. 32 Pl. II f. 23 (1879). *Mast. obscura* Leud. Fortm. l. c. p. 36 Pl. III f. 33 (1879). *Navic. Egeria* Pant. III Pl. XLII f. 578 (1893)? *Mast. Grunowii* A. S. Atl. CLXXXVI f. 1 to 7.

Marine: Mediterranean and Adriatic Seas! Cape of Good Hope! Kerguelen's Land (Castr.), Sumbava! Java! Samoa!

Var. *kerguelensis* Castr. (1886). — Elliptical. L. 0,03 to 0,045; B. 0,018 mm. Loculi 5 in 0,01 mm. Striæ 27 in 0,01 mm. *M. kerg.* Castr. Voyage Challenger D. p. 22 Pl. XV f. 11.

Marine: Labuan! Upolu (Grun.), Kerguelen's Land (Castr.).

Var. *concinna* A. S. (1893). — V. almost rhomboid. L. 0,05; B. 0,022 mm. Loculi somewhat unequal, forming an undulate band along the margin. Striæ 22 to 23 in 0,01 mm. — *M. conc.* A. S. Atl. CLXXXVI f. 9.

Marine: Corsica! Pithyusian Islands! Samoa!

Var. *elongata* Leud. Fortm. (1879). — V. narrow, rhombic-lanceolate. L. 0,105 to 0,111; B. 0,03 mm. Striæ 15 in 0,01 mm. Puncta about 19 in 0,01 mm. forming longitudinal rows. — *M. elong.* Leud. Fortm. D. Ceylan p. 35 Pl. III f. 31. A. S. Atl. CLXXXVI f. 12.

Marine: Madagascar (Van Heurck Coll.)! Ceylon (Leud. Fortm.).

Var. *rhombica* Cl. — V. rhomboid. L. 0,072; B. 0,036 mm. Median line slightly undulate. Central nodule very small. Loculi 3,5 to 4 in 0,01 mm. Striæ 15 in 0,01 mm., slightly radiate, stronger at the margin, fainter inwards, crossed by about 4 longitudinal shallow depressions, punctate; puncta about 20 in 0.01 mm.

Marine: Ceylon! Madagascar!

M. *quinquecostata* is a very variable species, closely connected with all the above forms from *M. cruciata*. More or less connected with *M. quinquecostata* are *M. quinquecostata var. neapolitana* Brun (A. S. Atl. CLXXXVI f. 10), *M. sinuata* A. S. (l. c. f. 11), *M. mauritiana* Brun (A. S. Atl. l. c. f. 28), *M. sansibarica* A. S. (l. c. CLXXXVII f. 44), all forms, of which I have had no opportunity of examining original specimens.

Additional.

M. Brunii A. S. (1893) — appears to be allied with *M. fallax* — Atl. CLXXXVIII f. 27.

M. chersonensis A. S. (1893) — seems to be related to *M. elegans*, but the figure is insufficient for identification. — Atl. CLXXXVI f. 31. 32.

M. divergens A. S. (1893) — a characteristic form, which however I cannot class in the system as the figure is not sufficient. — Atl. CLXXXVII f. 52.

M.? dubia CL. N. Sp. — V. broadly lanceolate, with cuneate ends. B. 0,07; B. 0,03 mm. Median line straight. No axial area. Central area small, orbicular. Along the median line is a row of elongated puncta. Striæ 16 in 0,01 mm. composed of distant, elongated puncta, forming undulating, longitudinal rows, about 12 in 0,01 mm. Loculi not seen. — Pl. II f. 38.

Marine: Barbados, foss.!

This form, of which I have found one specimen only, is perhaps a Navicula, but if so I know of no allied form, nor am I acquainted with any kindred species of Mastogloia.

M. egregia A. S. (1893) — a form of the group of *M. lemniscata*. — Atl. CLXXXVI f. 16.

M. electa A. S. (1893). — V. lanceolate, subapiculate. L. 0,056; B. 0,022 mm. Axial area narrow, but distinct. Transverse striæ 12 in 0,01 mm., slightly radiate throughout, composed of puncta, arranged in obliquely decussating rows. Loculi 3 in 0,01 mm. of equal size, quadrate, forming a band extending to the extremities. Atl. CLXXXVII f. 3. Seems to be akin to *M. rostellata* and *M. asperula*.

Marine: Sandwich Islands (Atl.).

M. Foliolum BRUN (1893). — The figure is insufficient for description. — A. S. Atl. CLXXXVII f. 45.

M. funafutensis A. S. (1893). — V. lanceolate, apiculate. L. 0,046; B. 0,018 mm. Median line straight. No areas and no furrows. Striæ 9 in 0,01 mm. almost parallel, of coarse equidistant puncta, 9 in 0,01 mm. Loculi 7 in 0,01 mm. rectangular, forming a marginal band, extending to the extremities. — Atl. CLXXXVII f. 13. Characteristic species.

Marine: Funafuti (Atl.).

M. Gründleri A. S. (1893). V. rhomboid-lanceolate. L. 0,045; B. 0,018 mm. Central nodule unusually elongated. No areas. Striæ 13 in 0,01 mm. transverse, composed of distinct puncta. Loculi 5 in 0,01 mm., quadrate, in a marginal row reaching to the ends of the valve. — Atl. CLXXXVIII f. 26. Seems to be akin to *M. affinis*.

Marine: Campeachy Bay!

M. intersecta A. S. (1893) resembles *M. erythræa*, but the fig. which shews longitudinal lines, is too little detailed for description and identification. — Atl. CLXXXVI f. 38.

M. (Orthoneis) latericia A. S. (1893). — V. broadly elliptical, with subrostrate ends. L. 0,07; B. 0,04 mm. Median line straight. No areas. Transverse rows of alveoli 7 in 0,01 mm. slightly radiate. Alveoli rectangular, arranged in obliquely decussating, curved rows. Loculi 4 in 0,01 mm. rounded quadrate, of equal size, forming a marginal band, extending to the extremities. — Atl. CLXXXVIII f. 40. A remarkable species, in some respects allied with *M. asperula*.

Marine: Kings Mill Island (Atl.).

M. peracuta JANISCH (1893). An apiculate form, apparently akin to *M. Rhombus*, but the figure is too little detailed for identification — Atl. CLXXXVII f. 37.

M. radians A. S. (1893). — Probably no Mastogloia, but a small form of Diploneis nitescens, at any rate too insufficiently figured to be admitted in to the system. — Atl. CLXXXVIII f. 28.

M. remota A. S. (1893). — The figure is not sufficient for description. — Atl. CLXXXVIII f. 29.

M. tumescens A. S. (1893). — This form is too imperfectly figured to be admitted into the system. — Atl. CLXXXVII f. 20.

Stigmaphora WALLICH (1860). This genus, of which I have not seen any species, was founded by WALLICH (T. M. S. VIII p. 43). It seems to be akin to Mastogloia and comprises two pelagic species:

1. *S. rostrata* WALLICH (1860). — V. lanceolate, slightly gibbous in the middle, abruptly constricted between the middle and the ends. L. 0,09 to 0,095; B. 0,014 to 0,015 mm. Along the median line is a row of equidistant puncta. Loculi 2 on each side, small, cuneate. — T. M. S. VIII p. 43 Pl. II f. 5, 6. — Pelagic: Indian Ocean (W.), Honduras (Grun.).

2. *S. lanceolata* WALLICH (1860). — V. lanceolate, acute. Median line without puncta, otherwise as *S. rostrata*. — L. c. f. 7, 8. - Pelagic: Indian Ocean.

Achnantheæ.

Frustule with dissimilar valves, the upper without, the lower with, central nodule and median line, usually bent along the longitudinal (*Cocconeis*) or along the transverse axis (*Achnanthes*).

As early as 1783 O. F. MÜLLER observed an Achnanthes, named by him *Conferva armillaris* (= *A. longipes*). Another species was in 1819 named by LYNGBYE *Echinella stipitata* (*A. brevipes*). The generic name *Achnanthes* was given in 1822 by BORY ST. VINCENT. In his Conspectus criticus diat. 1832, J. AGARDH defined the genus as »frustilla (l. articuli) convexa, pauca, in frondem vexilliformem (vexillum) stipitatum coadunata» (coordinata?) KÜTZING, who correctly observed that the lower valves only of *Achnanthes* and *Cocconeis* have a central nodule, formed in 1844 a section »*Monostomaticeæ*» (Bac. p. 70) comprising the *Cocconeideæ*, with the genera *Cocconeis* and *Doryphora*, and the *Achnantheæ*, including the genera *Achnanthes*, *Achnanthidium* and *Cymbosira*, distinguished by the genuflexed frustules, *Achnanthes* comprising stipitate, *Achnanthidium* free living forms, and *Cymbosira* those, in which the frustules are connected as in *Diatoma*. HEIBERG (Consp. Crit. Diat. 1863) rejected these distinctions, as founded exclusively on the manner in which the frustules occur in the living state, but retained the names *Achnanthes* and *Achnanthidium*, the former for those forms which have a double structure, of costæ, alternating with double rows of puncta; the latter for those which have no costæ. This view has not been adopted. GRUNOW (Verh. 1860 p. 511) included in the family *Achnantheæ*, besides *Achnanthes* and *Achnanthidium*, both in the sense of KÜTZING, also *Cocconeis*, and *Rhoicosphenia*, a genus formed for receiving *Gomphonema curvatum* of older authors; but in the year 1862 (Verh. p. 116) he separated as a distinct family *Cocconeideæ*, comprising *Cocconeis*, *Campyloneis* and *Rhaphoneis*. He published in 1880 (Arct. Diat. p. 17) a very valuable synopsis of *Achnanthes*, retained *A. longipes* in the same genus as *A. subsessilis*, but reserved the name *Achnanthidium* for *A. flexellum*, or *Cocconeis Thwaitesii* W. SM.

The genus *Cocconeis* was formed in 1838 by EHRENBERG. The species of this genus usually have a broad, elliptical outline, and live attached to algæ by their lower valves, which is probably the cause that the frustules are genuflexed along the longitudinal axis, thus differing from *Achnanthes*, in which genus the frustules are genuflexed along the transverse axis. In course of time a number of diatoms with elliptical outline were described by authors as Cocconeis, although their valves were similar, and in 1867, GRUNOW (Novara p. 8) tried to bring order into this chaos. He there defined the family Cocconeideæ as follows:

»Naviculoid diatoms, attached by their flatter side to algæ, with or without gelatinous envelopes; with dissimilar and bent, or similar and straight valves. Interior costate stratum of the lower or of both valves absent, present in a rudimentary state, or strongly developed by the vertical elevation of the ribs into marginal loculi».

He included in this family *Campyloneis*, *Cocconeis*, *Orthoneis* and *Mastogloia*. In the genus *Anorthoneis*, formed for receiving *Cocconeis excentrica*, he sees a connecting link between *Cocconeideæ* and *Cymbelleæ*. In the year 1880 (Arct. Diat. p. 16) he separated *Mastogloia* and *Orthoneis*, including them in a new family, *Mastogloieæ*.

The true Cocconeideæ and Achnantheæ resemble each other in the dissimilarity of their valves, the lower being naviculoid, the upper without central nodule and median line, but with an axial pseudo-raphe or area. The only respect in which they differ is in the manner in which the frustules are genuflexed, but the latter characteristic is not of generic importance. One may easily feel inclined to unite in one group or family all diatoms with dissimilar valves, and form new genera of species which are related. Although this course appears to me to be the only one, by which one may hope to bring order into the chaos of forms. I consider that such a family would be far from a natural one, and would comprise widely different types. The dissimilarity of the valves appears to me, just as the asymmetry, rather as a facies common to different types, than a characteristic of allied forms. There are among the true naviculoid diatoms several more or less arcuate forms with slightly or strongly dissimilar valves, although both have a central nodule and a median line. For such forms, belonging to the sections Lineolatæ and Microstigmaticæ of Navicula GRUNOW formed the genus *Rhoiconeis*, and PERAGALLO has recently proved that the valves of *Gyrosigma compactum* are very dissimilar. In *Rhoicosphenia*, which belongs to the true Achnantheæ, we meet with a form, which in many characteristics, especially of the cell-contents, appears to be nearly akin to *Gomphonema*. Many of the species of *Cocconeis* have a loculiferous rim and are so nearly akin to the elliptical forms of *Mastogloiæ*, that it seems justifiable to believe them to be *Mastogloiæ*, degenerated by their parasitical habits. It thus appears that the flexure of the frustule is connected with a dissimilar development of the valves, and the differences become more striking, when the frustules are stipitate or attached to algæ or other objects. The lower valve maintains its naviculoid characteristics, but the upper undergoes more or less complete changes. From this it seems probable that the forms of *Cocconeis* and *Achnanthes* are *Naviculæ* degenerated by their manner of living. The original Naviculæ probably belonged to very different types and have undergone analogous changes. I think it evident that *Cocconeis* and *Achnanthes* comprise forms which frequently have very little real affinity. The classification offers many difficulties, but I believe that to this end the structure of the lower valve is of more importance than that of the upper valve. A characteristic, which appears to me to be also of importance, is the presence or absence of a marginal rim, which occurs in *C. Placentula*, *C. Scutellum* and others, and is probably of the same nature as the loculiferous plates in *Mastogloia*. Some forms are probably akin to the section *Mesoleiæ* of Navicula, as *C. minor* to *Navicula Rotaeana*. Others, such as *C. reticulata* seem to be connected with the section *Punctatæ*. The curious *A. danica* is remarkable for the highly inclined striæ of the lower valve and resembles in this respect the section *Heterostichæ* of Navicula. If we consider also that *Rhoicosphenia* is a *Gomphonema*-like *Achnanthes*, we feel that the family Achnantheæ represents rather a facies belonging to widely different types than a family of allied species. The interior of the cells and the formation of the auxospores point to the same conclusion. There is a great resemblance in this respect between *Cocconeis Pediculus* and *Achnanthes lanceolata*, both having a single chromatophore-plate along the upper valve, but in *Achnanthes brevipes* the chromatophore-plates are two, placed along the walls of the connecting zone, as in *Navicula*.

It is possible that by a long continued degeneration, the lower valve of the frustule may also lose its central nodule and median line, in which case the form would become a *Rhaphoneis*. Some points of resemblance between *Achnanthes* and *Rhabdonema* (and its allied genera) seem to exist. In *Gephyria* we meet with the arcuate and stipitate frustule of *Achnanthes*. The structure of the upper valve of *A. groenlandica* and *A. longipes* is the same as in *Rhabdonema*. The zone of both forms is striate, and rudiments of septa exist in *A. groenlandica* and *A. baccata*, also in *Rhoicosphenia curvata*. There is certainly a great difference between *Rhabdonema* (and allied genera) and *Achnanthes* in the cell-contents, but it may be observed that the chromatophore-plate of *Cocconeis* by its marginal incisions seems to have a tendency to become split up in several patches.

In a truly natural system the genera, belonging to the Achnantheæ, would be distributed in widely distant places, but I think it advisable, to avoid a too intricate synonymy, to keep them provisionally together in a family, and to retain for the forms the old generic names of Cocconeis and Achnanthes, under which they are usually known. For the new subgenera, which I propose, I give the following key:

1.	Valves asymmetrical	2.
	— symmetrical	3.
2.	Asymmetrical to the longitudinal axis	*Anorthoneis* GRUN.
	— transverse	*Rhoicosphenia* GRUN.

3.	Frustules with an interior skeleton	*Campyloneis* GRUN
	— — a marginal rim	4
	— without skeleton or rim	5.
4.	Upper valve costate, costæ alternating with double rows of puncta	. . . *Pleuroneis* CL.
	— — punctate-striate	. . *Cocconeis* CL.
5.	Lower valve with costæ alternating with double rows of puncta	. . *Achnanthes* BORY
	— ecostate	. . . . . 6.
6.	Upper valve costate	7.
	— — not costate	. . . . 8.
7.	Axial area of the upper valve broad or lanceolate .	*Heteroneis* CL.
	— — — — — narrow or a rib .	. . . . 10.
8.	Valve broadly elliptical	*Eucocconeis* CL.
	— narrow, linear or lanceolate	. . . 9.
9.	Structure: finely punctate striæ	*Microneis* CL.
	- coarsely punctate striæ	*Achnanthidium* CL.
10.	Valve elliptical	. . . *Disconeis* CL.
	— lanceolate or rhomboid	. *Actinoneis* CL.

Rhoicosphenia GRUN. (1860).

Valves dissimilar, strongly asymmetrical to the transverse axis, clavate. Upper valve without central nodule and median line, but with an axial area. Lower valve with central nodule and longitudinal line. Structure of both valves: transverse, finely punctate striæ. Frustule usually stipitate, cuneate, with short diaphragms at the ends. Connecting zone not complex.

Cell-contents a single chromatophore-plate along one of the interior walls of the zone and both valves, with the opening along the other wall of the zone, with slight sinuses at the base and the ends, and also towards the ventral nodule; but there is no deep fissure below the median line. Division of the plate as in Gomphonema (PFITZER, Bau u. Entw. p. 91). In conjugating the cells behave as Gomphonema, but when the auxospores attain to the length of the mother-cells they become enclosed in a silicious, transversely costate, membrane, inside which the primordial cells originate (Thwaites).

The species which for long was the only one in this genus was in 1833 named by KÜTZING *Gomphonema minutissimum*, or *G. curvatum*, and was first (1860) by GRUNOW removed as *Rhoicosphenia curvatum* to the family Achnantheæ. Notwithstanding the dissimilarity of the valves *Rhoicosphenia* bears a close resemblance to *Gomphonema* both in exterior and interior respects. There is also some affinity to the *Tabellariea*, especially in the diaphragms at the ends of the frustule.

1. **R. curvata** KÜTZ (1833). — V. clavate, with rounded, obtuse upper end, and more narrow, attenuated, obtuse base. L. 0,015 to 0,025; B. 0,003 to 0,045 mm. Upper V. with narrow, centrally placed axial area, and parallel striæ, about 16 in 0,01 mm. Lower V. with narrow or indistinct axial, and small elongated, central area. Median line with somewhat distant central pores, and about 15 striæ in 0,01 mm., radiate throughout and stronger in the middle. — *Gomphonema minutissimum* KÜTZ. Dec. N:o 76 (1833) according to Lagst. *G. curvatum* KÜTZ. Linnæa X p. 567 Pl. XVI f. 51 (1833), according to Lagst. W. SM. B. D. p. 81 Pl. XXIX f. 245, 246. *Rhoicosphenia curvata* V. H. Syn p. 127 Pl. XXVI f. 1 to 3. *Gomph. marinum* W. SM. B. D. I p. 81 Pl. XXIX f. 246.

Fresh and brackish water: Arctic America! Greenland! Spitsbergen! Finmark! Cape Deschneff! Behring Island! Europe generally, Baltic and Caspian seas! Atlantic coasts of Europe and America! Cape Good Hope (Grun.). New Zealand (Grun.). S:t Pauls Island! Honduras (Jan. Rabh.).

Var. *major* CL. — L. 0,07; B. 0,008 mm. Striæ 9 in 0,01 mm.

Fresh water: Pitt River, Oregon!

Var. *fracta* SCHUM. (1862). V. almost symmetrical, gibbous in the middle, from which it tapers to the ends. L. 0,034 to 0,047; B. 0,005 to 0,007 mm. Striæ 9 in 0,01 mm. — *Gomph. fractum* SCHUM. P. D. p. 187 f. 32.

Fresh and brackish water: Königsberg, Baltic (Schum.), Caspian Sea (Grun.).

2. **R. Van Heurckii** GRUN. (1881). — V. slightly clavate or broadly lanceolate, obtuse. L. 0,007 to 0,009; B. 0,003 to 0,005 mm. Upper V. with broad, lanceolate area, and radiate marginal striæ, 14 to 15 in 0,01 mm. Lower V. without distinct area, and radiate striæ, 18 in 0,01 mm. V. H. Syn. p. 127 Pl. XXVI f. 5 to 9.

Fresh water: Belgium (V. H.).

Anorthoneis GRUN. (1867).

Valves dissimilar, orbicular. Upper valve without central nodule and median line, but with an excentric axial area. Lower valve with excentric median line and central nodule. Structure of both valves similar: puncta arranged in radiate striæ.

This genus was proposed by GRUNOW (Nov. p. 9) for *Cocconeis excentrica* DONK., the closer affinities of which species are obscure, although there is some resemblance in the structure to *Mastogloia cribrosa*.

1. **A. excentrica** DONK. (1858). V. orbicular, 0,025 to 0,045 mm. in diameter. Upper valve with a narrow axial area not reaching to the margin and dilated in the middle to a small, rounded central area. Striæ 10 in 0,01 mm. radiate throughout, in the middle alternately longer and shorter, distinctly punctate; puncta 10 in 0,01 mm. forming longitudinal or irregularly oblique rows. Striæ and puncta closer towards the margin, about 13 in 0,01 mm., which gives the valve the appearance of being bordered with a rim. Lower V. thinner, with distinct median line, the ends of which do not reach the margin. Central pores approximate. Axial and central area indistinct. Striation as in the upper valve. *Coccon. excentr.* DONK. T. M. S. VI p. 25 Pl. III f. 11. A. S. Atl. CXCIII, 57.

Marine, æstuaries: Firth of Tay! English Channel! Mount Desert Island, Maine!

This species lives free among the sands of the beach, not attached to algæ.

2. **A. eurystoma** CL. N. Sp. — Upper V. almost orbicular, about 0,04 mm. in diameter. Axial area large, lanceolate. Striæ throughout radiate and alternately longer and shorter, 14 (at the margin) or 10 (at the area) in 0,01 mm., composed of puncta, larger towards the area (about 10 in 0,01 mm.) than at the margin (about 12 in 0,01 mm.) and forming undulating longitudinal rows. — Pl. III f. 12.

Marine: Pensacola!

Of this species I have seen some few upper valves only, but GRUNOW sent me, many years ago, a sketch of a similar valve with central nodule and median line under the ms. name of *Alloioneis cocconeiformis* N. Sp. It seems to be nearly allied to the symmetrical *Cocconeis Kinkeri* A. S. Atl. CXCI, 37.

Campyloneis GRUN. (1862).

Valves dissimilar, in outline elliptical or orbicular. Upper valve without central nodule and median line, with radiate rows of coarse puncta or alveoli. Lower valve with central nodule and median line, with radiate, finely punctate striæ. Between both valves, and connected to the lower valve by some vertical processes, is an interior silicious skeleton of more or less complicated structure.

C. Grevillei was described 1853 by W. SMITH as *Cocconeis*, but in 1862 (Verh. p. 115) GRUNOW placed it in *Campyloneis*, a new genus which he formed for the reception of an allied form, *C. Argus*, now considered as a variety of *C. Grevillei*. The most striking feature in *Campyloneis* is the interior silicious skeleton, which is frequently found isolated from the valves. This skeleton, which varies greatly in its form, is in the entire frustule attached by some vertical processes to the lower valve. It is evidently analogous to the annulus of several *Cocconeis*-forms and to the loculiferous plate of *Mastogloia*.

Campyloneis lives attached to marine algæ and occurs in temperate and tropical seas, where it is plentiful, and occurs in a great variety of forms, which are all closely connected, however different they may appear.

1. **C. Grevillei** W. SM. (1853). — V. broadly elliptical, with rounded ends. L. 0,02 to 0,01; B. 0,017 to 0,09 mm. Upper V. with or without a depressed axial part, with transverse rows of puncta or alveoli. Lower valve with straight median line, not reaching to the margin; its central pores approximate. Striation much finer than on the upper valve.

This most variable species comprises a number of forms, which may be distributed in the following varieties:

Var. *Argus* GRUN. (1862). — L. 0,03 to 0,05; B. 0,025 to 0,05 mm. Upper valve with a more or less distinct, narrow axial area. Transverse rows of puncta about 6 in 0,01 mm. Longitudinal rows 5 to 6 in 0,01 mm. Lower V. with 14 striæ and 18 puncta in 0,01 mm. Interior skeleton of distinct transverse ribs, united to an axial rib. — *Campyl. Argus* GRUN. Verh. 1862 p. 429 Pl. VII f. 9, 10. Novara p. 10. V. H. Syn. Pl. XXVIII f. 16. *Rhaphoneis suborbicularis* O'MEARA M. J. (n. s.) VII Pl. VII?

Marine: English Channel! Galway (Grove Coll.)! Iceland (Grun.)! Island of Rhea (Singapore)!

Var. *typica* CL. — L. 0,03 to 0,06; B. 0,025 to 0,04 mm. Upper V. with a depressed, lanceolate area. Striæ 6 in 0.01 mm., outside of the area composed of distinct puncta, inside of short ribs, formed of fused puncta. Lower V. as in *Var. Argus*. Striæ about 18 in 0,01 mm. Skeleton of transverse ribs connected by an axial and, usually, by several lateral ribs. — *Coccon. Grev.* W. SM. B. D. I p. 22 Pl. III f. 35. *Campyl. Grev.* GRUN. Novara p. 11 1867. PETIT D. de Campbell Pl. IV f. 5. V. H. Syn. Pl. XXVIII f. 10, 11. *Camp. Grev. var. obliqua* GRUN. Nov. p. 11 Pl. I f. 5 (small form). *Coccon. villosa* PERAG. D. de Villefranche Pl. IV f. 35 (lower valve)?

Marine: S:t Pauls Island (Grun.), New Zealand! Sandwich Islands! Japan! Ceylon! Galapagos Islands! Monterey! West Indies! Eng. Channel (W. Sm.).

Var. *microsticta* GRUN. (1881). — L. 0,04 to 0,05; B. 0,032 to 0,035 mm. Upper valve as in *Var. Argus*, skeleton as in *Var. typica*. Striæ 7 in 0,01 mm. — V. H. Syn. Pl. XXVIII f. 8, 9.

Marine: King Georges Sound!

Var. *regalis* GREV. (1859). Almost orbicular. L. 0,07 to 0,1; B. 0,05 to 0,09 mm. Upper valve with depressed lanceolate area, the interior part of which forms a structureless, more or less narrow space. Alveoli rectangular, inside finely punctate, forming radiate rows, about 4 in 0,01 mm., on the depressed area, at least at its marginal part, prolonged. Lower V. as in the other varieties, but more coarsely striate, striæ 8 in 0,01 mm. Puncta of the striæ 8 in 0,01 mm. Interior skeleton very complicated, having at the margin radiate costæ 1½ to 2 in 0,01 mm., which send off numerous short lateral branches. — *Cocconeis regalis* GREV. M. J. VII p. 156 Pl. VII f. 1. V. H. Syn. XXVIII f. 13, 14 (small form).

Marine: Japan! Californian guano (Grev.), S:ta Monica, fossil!

The varieties of *Camp. Grevillei* are exceedingly variable. The interior skeleton especially is subject to great variations. *Cocconeis radiata* GREG. (T. M. S. V p. 68 Pl. IV f. 26; 1857) is probably the interior skeleton of *C. Grevillei*. In the deposit of Oamaru occur very complicated skeletons of a form akin to the *var. regalis*. A similar skeleton is named by BRUN *Cocconeis*

Tolarae Diatomiste II Pl. VI f. 5. As *Campyoneis notabilis* BRUN has described a form from Rodriguez, which, to judge from the figure seems not to differ essentially from *C. Grevillei*.

Cocconeis (EHB.) CL.

Valve in outline broadly elliptical. Upper valve ecostate, with a more or less narrow longitudinal axial area. Structure: puncta or alveoli arranged in transverse and, frequently, longitudinal rows. Lower valve usually with a marginal line or marginal area. Between the valves is a more or less rudimentary, loculiferous annulus. Frustules usually bent along the longitudinal axis. Cell-contents (of *C. Pediculus*) a single chromatophore-plate, along the inside of the upper valve, lacerate at the margin and with a deep sinus from the margin to the centre, where the nucleus is embedded in the central plasma-mass (PFITZER, Bau u. Entw. p. 87). In conjugation two cells split at the lower valve and secrete a voluminous gelatinous mass, inside which is formed a large globular auxospore, the exosporium of which is hyaline and without ribs. The interior of the auxospores contains a lacerate endochrome-plate (BORSCOW: Süssw. Bac. p. 97).

This genus comprises the most common species of the old genus Cocconeis. The obsoletely loculiferous rim indicates that these species are akin to *Mastogloia*, probably degenerated forms of that genus. In several forms of *C. Scutellum* the rows of puncta end near the margin in short double rows of smaller puncta, as is also the case with *Mastogloia* (*Orthoneis*) *splendida*.

All these forms, *C. gibbocalyx* perhaps excepted, live attached to algæ and other objects in the water by the lower valve. *C. Placentula*, *C. Pediculus* and *C. Disculus* live in fresh, but also, especially *C. Pedic.*, in brackish water. The other species are marine, but *C. Scutellum* also occurs in brackish water.

Artificial key.

1. { Median line sigmoid . . . . *C. australis* PET.
   — straight . . . . 2.
2. { Axial area of the upper valve lanceolate . . . . 3.
   — — — — linear . . . . 4.
3. { Area very broad. Marine . . . . *C. grata* A. S.
   — moderately broad. Freshwater habitat . . . . . . *C. Disculus* SCHUM.
4. { Upper valve finely striate . . . . 5.
   — — with coarse puncta or alveoli . . . . . . 6.
5. { Upper valve with a marginal line . . . . *C. Placentula* EHB.
   — — without . . . . *C. Pediculus* EHB.
6. { Upper valve coarsely reticulate . . . . *C. Van Heurckii* CL.
   — — — punctate . . . . 7.
7. { Margin of the upper valve finely striate . . . . 8.
   — — — not — . . . . 9.
8. { Rows of puncta in the upper valve 4 to 5 in 0,01 mm. . . *C. granulifera* GREV.
   — — — — 8 to 9 — — . . *C. cruciata* PANT.
9. { Valve lanceolate . . . . *C. gibbocalyx* BRUN.
   — elliptical . . . . 10.
10. { Puncta of the upper valve forming equidistant transverse and (usually) straight longitudinal rows *C. Scutellum* EHB.
   — — — not — — — — . . . . . . *C. distans* GREG.

1. *C.* **granulifera** GREV. (1861). Outline elliptical, with broad, rounded ends. L. 0,028 to 0,057; B. 0,018 to 0,038 mm. Upper V. with finely striate margin (striæ 17 in 0,01 mm.), narrow axial area and radiate rows (4 to 5 in 0.01 mm.) of large puncta (about 5 in each row). Lower V. with finely striate margin (striæ 20 in 0,01 mm.). Axial area indistinct; central area small rounded. Median line straight, reaching to the margin. Striæ about 13 in 0,01 mm. strongly

radiate and distinctly punctate. Marginal area narrow. — T. M. S. IX p. 73 Pl. VIII f. 19. A. S. Atl. CXCIII. 34. Icon. n. Pl. II f. 36. 37. *C. distans* GREG. D. of Clyde p. 490 Pl. IX f. 23 (1857). Pritch. Inf. Pl. VII f. 38. *C. regalis* PER. D. de Villefranche p. 37 Pl. II f. 12?

Marine: Coasts of Scotland (Greg. Grev.) and Norway! Balearic Islands! Galapagos Islands!

2. **C. Pediculus** EHR. (1838). — Outline broadly elliptical, frequently subrhomboidal or malformate. L. 0,015 to 0,03; B. 0,01 to 0,02 mm. Upper V. with a linear, axial area somewhat constricted in the middle. Striæ 17 to 18 in 0,01 mm. finely punctate; puncta forming undulate, longitudinal rows. Lower V. frequently with traces of a loculiferous rim. Axial area indistinct. Central area small, suborbicular. Striæ 16 to 17 in 0,01 mm. finely punctate, radiate, not reaching to the margin, where is a hyaline, narrow rim. Annulus with rudimentary loculi. — Inf. p. 194. Pl. XXI f. 11. W. SM. B. D. I Pl. III f. 31. V. H. Syn. p. 133 Pl. XXX f. 28 to 30. A. S. Atl. CXCII. 56, 58 to 63. *Cocc. sigmoidea* SCHUM. P. D. II Nachtr. Pl. I f. 14? *C. tenera* SCHUM. II Nachtr. p. 54 f. 15? *C. Placentula var. baltica* DANNF. p. 14 Pl. I f. 1 (1882)? *C. excentrica* GUTW. Mater. p. 27 f. 22?

Fresh or brackish water: throughout Europe! Baltic! Caspian Sea (Grun.)! Michigan! Ecuador!

Var. *Salinarum* PANT. (1889). — L. 0,021; B. 0,012 mm. Striæ of the lower valve 25 in 0,01 mm. — PANT. II p. 58 Pl. XXVII f. 393.

Brackish water: Hungary, fossil (Pant.).

3. **C. Placentula** EHR. (1838). — Outline elliptical. L. 0,0125 to 0,035; B. 0,008 to 0,02 mm. Upper V. with narrow, linear, not constricted, axial area. Striæ 25 in 0,01 mm. finely punctate; puncta forming undulate, close longitudinal rows. Lower V. with distinct marginal line, frequently also a loculiferous rim (loculi 15 in 0,01 mm.). Median line straight, not reaching to the ends. Striæ 23 in 0,01 mm. — Inf. p. 194. W. SM. B. D. I Pl. III f. 32. V. H. Syn. p. 133 Pl. XXX f. 26. 27. A. S. Atl. CXCII. 38 to 51. *C. punctata* SCHUM. Tatra D. p. 60 Pl. II f. 20. *C. producta* A. S. Atl. CXCI, 2.

Fresh or brackish water: throughout Europe! Baltic! Caspian Sea (Grun.), Tasmania! New Zealand! Illinois! California! Mexico! Ecuador!

Var. *intermedia* HÉRIB. a. PERAG. (1893). — L. 0,05 to 0,07 mm. Upper V. with coarser rows of puncta, 12 (margin) to 15 (axial part) in 0,01 mm. — *C. intermedia* HÉRIB. a. PERAG. D. d'Auvergne p. 44 Pl. III f. 1, 2.

Fresh water: Puy de Dôme, fossil.

Forma minor HÉRIB. a. PERAG. l. c. L. 0,02 to 0,03 mm.

Fresh water: Puy de Dôme, fossil.

Var *Rouxii* BRUN a. HÉRIB. (1893). — L. 0,04 to 0,09; B. 0,025 to 0,055 mm. Upper V. with coarse striæ, about 11 in 0,01 mm. crossed on each side of the axial area by 5 to 6 blank undulating bands. Lower V. with about 14 striæ in 0,01 mm. Their puncta about 16 in 0,01 mm. — *C. Rouxii* BR. a. HÉRIB. D. d'Auvergne p. 45 Pl. I f. 3.

Fresh water: Auvergne, Puy de Dôme fossil and living.

Var. *trilineata* HÉRIB. a. PERAG. (1883). — L. 0,02 to 0,025; B. 0,01 to 0,013 mm. Upper V. with about 16 striæ in 0,01 mm. crossed by 3 broad longitudinal, blank bands. Lower V. with 15 to 17 striæ in 0,01 mm. — *C. trilineatus* HÉRIB. a. PERAG. D. d'Auvergne p. 47 Pl. III f. 4. 5.

Fresh water: Puy de Dôme fossil.

Var. *lineata* EHR. (1843). — L. 0,04 to 0,07; B. 0,03 to 0,04 mm. Striæ of the upper valve punctate, puncta forming 4 to 6 longitudinal, undulating rows. Striæ of the lower valve 17 in 0,01 mm. — *C. lineata* EHR. Am. p. 81. V. H. Syn. p. 133 Pl. XXX f. 31, 32. *C. lin. var. minor* PANT. III Pl. XXI f. 311 (1893). *C. lin. var. pygmea* PANT. l. c. Pl. VIII f. 140.

Fresh water: Belgium (V. H.), Mexico, Oregon, Guatemala, foss.!

Var. *caelypta* EHR. (1854). — L. 0,026; B. 0,017 mm. Striæ of the upper valve crossed by 4 to 5 longitudinal, blank bands. Striæ of the lower valve 19 in 0,01 mm. — *C. cael.* EHR. M. G. XXXIV A. f. 2. V. H. Syn. XXX f. 33, 34. GRUN. Franz Josefs Land Diat. Pl. I f. 3.

Fresh water: Franz Josefs Land (Grun.). Belgium (V. H.). Mexico! Tasmania! Australia (Daintree River)!

4. C. **Scutellum** EHR. (1838). — Outline broadly elliptical. Upper V. with coarse puncta arranged in transverse rows, usually ending at the margin in an elongated or triangular, finely punctate space, and in longitudinal, usually straight and equidistant, rows. Lower V. delicate with a marginal, frequently loculiferous, rim or line. Median line straight. Central nodule rounded or stauroid. Striæ radiate, becoming obsolete towards the median line, finely punctate.

Var. *genuina* CL. — L. 0,045 to 0,06; B. 0,03 to 0,04 mm. Upper V with narrow, linear axial area. Puncta 7 to 8 in 0,01 mm. forming, slightly radiate, transverse and almost equidistant, straight longitudinal rows. Transverse striæ ending at the margin with larger, finely punctate alveoli. Lower V. with a rim of obsolete loculi. Central area rounded, small. Striæ 8 to 9 in 0,01 mm. radiate, finely punctate. — *C. Scutellum* EHR. Inf. 194 Pl. XIV f. 8. W. SM. B. D. I p. 22 Pl. III f. 34. V. H. Syn. p. 132 Pl. XXIX f. 1 to 3. A. S. Atl. CXC, 17 to 20. *C. Scut. var. gemmata* A. S. Atl. CXC, 23, 24; *var. dilatata* A. S. l. c. 25, 26.

Marine: Arctic America! Spitsbergen! Finmark! Sea of Kara! East Cape; Behrings Island! Baltic! Caspian Sea (Grun.), North Sea! Mediterranean! Adriatic! Black Sea! Japan! South Australia! Magellans Straits! California!

Var. *minutissima* GRUN. (1881). — L. 0,008; B. 0,006 mm. Rows of puncta about 17 in 0,01 mm. Marginal alveoli not larger than the puncta. Axial area narrow. — V. H. Syn. Pl. XXIX f. 12. GRUN. Franz Josefs Land D. p. 55 Pl. I f. 1.

Marine: Franz Josefs Land (Grun.).

Var. *parva* GRUN. (1881). — L. 0,018 to 0,02; B. 0,01 to 0,017 mm. Upper V. with 11 rows of puncta in 0,01 mm. Marginal puncta elongated. Axial area narrow. — V. H. Syn. Pl. XXIX f. 8, 9. *C. consociata* and *C. aggregata* KÜTZ. according to Grun. *C. transversalis* GREG. M. J. III p. 39 Pl. IV f. 7; 1854? *C. Scut. var. minor* A. S. Atl. CXC. 22.

Marine: Baltic! East Cape! Adriatic (Atl.).

Var. *stauroneiformis* W. SM. (1853). — L. 0,022; B. 0,013 to 0,018 mm. Upper valve with narrow axial area. Marginal puncta not larger than the others. Transverse and straight longitudinal rows of puncta 10 in 0,01 mm. Lower V. central area dilated into a transverse fascia. — B. D. I Pl. XXX f. 24 β. V. H. Syn. Pl. XXIX f. 10, 11. *C. paniformis* A. S. Atl. CLXXXIX 16. 21 (1894).

Marine: Arctic America! Spitsbergen! Finmark! East Cape! North Sea! Mediterranean Sea (Peragallo). New Zealand (Grun.). England (W. Sm.).

Var. *ampliata* GRUN. (1881). — L. 0,05; B. 0,04 mm. Upper V. with somewhat broad axial area. large marginal alveoli and 5 to 6 puncta in 0,01 mm, arranged in equidistant transverse and longitudinal rows. Lower V. with distinct marginal area. Striæ 6,5 in 0,01 mm., becoming fainter towards the axial area, strongly radiate. — V. H. Syn. XXIX f. 4. *C. adjuncta* A. S. Atl. CXC, 15, 16?

Marine: Kerguelens Land!

Var. *ornata* GRUN. (1867). — L. 0,037 to 0,047; B. 0,026 to 0,033 mm. Upper V. with narrow axial area. Puncta 5 to 6 in 0,01 mm., arranged in radiate transverse, and curved longitudinal, rows. The transverse striæ end at the margin in double rows of small puncta. Lower V. with a loculiferous rim. Striæ slightly radiate and finely punctate, 10 in 0,01 mm. — Novara p. 12. V. H. Syn. Pl. XXIX f. 6, 7. *Rhaphoneis marginata* GRUN. Verh. 1862 p. 383 Pl. IV f. 13.

Marine: Kamtschatka and North Pacific Ocean (Grun.).

Var. *baldjikiana* Grun. (1888). — L. 0,055; B. 0,04 mm. Upper V. with narrow axial area. Puncta (about 6 in 0,01 mm.) arranged in slightly radiate striæ and curved longitudinal rows. The striæ end at the margin in triangular, finely punctate spaces. Lower V. with 7 finely punctate striæ in 0,01 mm., becoming fainter towards the median line. — Bot. Centrb. 1888 p. 324. V. H. T. N:o 546 *C. Morrisii* W. Sm. Q. J. M. S. V p. 8 (1857)? *C. Haradae* Pant. III Pl. XXIV f. 368 (1893)? *C. Pethői* Pant. III Pl. XXXVI f. 504 (1893). *C. baldjikiana* A. S. Atl. CXC f. 7 to 10.

Marine: Baltjik, foss.!

Var. *Rařana* Pant. (1889). — L. 0,048; B. 0,036. Upper V. with somewhat broader axial area and larger marginal alveoli than in Var. *baldjikiana*, otherwise similar. *C. Rařana* Pant. II p. 59 Pl. XXIV f. 354.

Marine: Hungary, fossil!

Var.? *dubia* Grun. (1884). — L. 0,018 to 0,03; B. 0,012 to 0,023 mm. Striæ 8 to 11 in 0,01 mm. Puncta in the lower V. 14, in the upper 10 in 0,01 mm. Lower V. without marginal rim. — Franz Josefs Land D. p. 55.

Marine: Tafel Suimpe (Grun.).

Var. *californica* Grun. (1878). L. 0,02 to 0,027; B. 0,015 to 0,016 mm. Upper V. with narrow axial area. Puncta 13 in 0,01 mm., arranged in equidistant longitudinal and transverse rows, the latter interrupted by a broad, marginal area. Lower V. with distinct marginal line. Striæ 11 in 0,01 mm. finely punctate, radiate. — *C. ambigua var. calif.* Grun. in Cl. M. D. N:o 70. V. H. Syn. Pl. XXX f. 8, 9. A. S. Atl. CXCI. 40 to 43.

Marine: California!

Var. *doljensis* Pant. (1886). — L. 0,04 to 0,08; B. 0,04 to 0,059 mm. Upper V. with narrow axial area. Puncta arranged in somewhat undulating longitudinal rows and transverse striæ, 7 (at the margin) or 12 (at the area) in 0,01 mm., ending in elongated triangular, finely punctate alveoli. — Pant. I p. 32 Pl. XVIII f. 161.

Marine: Hungary, fossil (Pant.).

Var. *maxima* Grun. (1863). — L. 0,04 to 0,09; B. 0,033 to 0,055 mm. Upper V. with more or less broad, linear axial area. Puncta coarse, arranged in more or less undulating longitudinal and transverse rows, the latter about 6 in 0,01 mm., composed of 3 to 5 puncta and ending in punctate alveoli, which form a broad marginal band, frequently separated by a furrow from the striæ. Lower V. thin, with a loculiferous rim (loculi 3 in 0,01 mm.). Striæ about 11 in 0,01 mm. finely punctate. — *Mastogloia maxima* Grun. Verh. 1863 Pl. IV f. 1 (lower valve). *C. Scut. var. fossilis* Pant. II p. 59 Pl. XXIV f. 353; 1890 (upper valve). *C. Lorenziana* A. S. Atl. CXCI f. 28 to 34.

Marine: Black Sea! Adriatic! Galapagos Islands! Hungary, fossil (Pant.).

Cocconeis Scutellum is extremely variable and comprises a number of very different forms, which I, however, am not inclined to separate as distinct species. Many insufficiently described or figured species of *Cocconeis* and *Rhaphoneis* are probably mere varieties of *C. Scutellum*, as *C. Portii* O'Meara (T. M. J. VII Pl. VII f. 7; 1867). *C. Grantiana* Grev. (T. M. S. N. S. IX p. 72 Pl. VIII f. 18). *C. ornata* Greg. (D. of Clyde p. 491 Pl. IX f. 24). *C. Grunowii* Pant. (II p. 58 Pl. XXV f. 364; 1889). *Rhaphoneis Jonesii* O'Meara (M. J. N. S. Vol. VII Pl. VII f. 10), *Rhaphoneis Moorii* O'Meara (M. J. N. S. Vol. VII f. 11). *Navicula Allmaniana* Greg. (D. of Clyde p. 488 Pl. IX f. 21) and *C. crebrestriata* (Grev. M. J. V. p. 9 Pl. III f. 2; 1857) (both perhaps *Orthoneis fimbriata*), *C. boryana* Pant. III Pl. II f. 33 (1893) and *C. californica var. hungarica* Pant. III Pl. X f. 164 (1893). *Cocconeis (ambigua var.?) californica* Grun. appears certainly to be a form of *C. Scutellum*, but *C. californica var. meliniticu* Pant. (II p. 58 Pl. IV f. 71 Pl. VII f. 123) represents upper valves, which are much too finely punctate for that species. *C. ambigua* Grun. (Novara p. 14 Pl. I f. 9, 22) is doubtful. The fig. 22 appears to represent the upper valve of *C. pellucida*.

5. **C. cruciata** PANT. (1886). Outline elliptical. L. 0,03 to 0,046; B. 0,02 to 0,027 mm. Upper V. with finely striate margin (15 striæ in 0,01 mm.). Axial area lanceolate, in the middle dilated to a fascia. Striæ 8 to 9 in 0,01 mm. composed of large, distant puncta, arranged in longitudinal, undulating rows. — PANT. I p. 31 Pl. XVI f. 148.

Marine: Ceylon (Le Tourneur Coll.)! Hungary, fossil (Pant.).

6. **C. gibbocalyx** BRUN. (1891). — Outline broadly elliptic-lanceolate. Ends subcuneate. L. 0,032 to 0,045; B. 0,024 to 0,032 mm. Upper V. with narrow, linear-lanceolate axial area. Striæ 7 in 0,01 mm., composed of few, large puncta, and ending at the margin in large costæ forming a rim. Lower V. with straight median line, ending in the conical and elevated extremities. Central pores distant. Axial area narrow. Central area rounded, large. Striæ about 9 in 0,01 mm., radiate throughout, composed of distinct puncta, 8 to 12 in 0,01 mm., becoming smaller towards the median line and arranged in longitudinal rows, more or less parallel with the margin. Margin of the valve finely striate (striæ 16 to 22 in 0,01 mm.). — D. espèces nouv. p. 17 Pl. XVIII f. 1 A. S. Atl. CXC f. 35? CXCIII f. 54 to 55.

Marine: Zanzibar (Brun). Manilla (Deby Coll.)! Mauritius (Brun Coll.)! Galapagos Islands! West Indies, Tortola!

This is a very remarkable and isolated species. Both valves have not been seen in contact, so that it is somewhat doubtful whether the upper valve, which has some resemblance to *Cocc. Scutellum*, really corresponds to the valve here described as the lower.

7. **C. grata** A. S. (1894). — Outline elliptic-lanceolate. L. 0,01 to 0,06; B. 0,03 to 0,044 mm. Upper V. with a broad, lanceolate axial area. Striæ 10 to 11 in 0,01 mm. composed of distinct puncta, about 16 in 0,01 mm. Lower V. with an annulus of rudimentary loculi, about 5 in 0,01 mm. Median line straight, reaching to the margin. Striæ 15 in 0,01 mm. radiate, finely punctate, becoming fainter towards the median line. — Pl. II f. 30, 31. A. S. Atl. CXC f. 36. CXCII f. 65.

Marine: Campeachy Bay! Mediterranean Sea! Grip in Norway!

C. andesitica PANT. (III Pl. X f. 170; 1893) appears to be akin to this species or to *C. dirupta*.

8. **C. distans** (GREG. 1857?) A. S. 1874. — Outline elliptical to elliptic-lanceolate. L. 0,05 to 0,07; B. 0,03 to 0,04 mm. Upper V. with narrow, lanceolate axial area. Puncta elongated, forming slightly radiate transverse (about 7 in 0,01 mm.) and undulating longitudinal rows (about 4 in 0,01 mm.). Lower V. unknown. — N. S. D. Pl. III f. 22, 23 (1871). Atl. CXCIII f. 29, 36, 40. *C. dist. forma minima* PERAG. D. de Villefranche p. 37 Pl. II f. 13.

Marine: Arctic America! Sea of Kara! North Sea! Mediterranean Sea! Madagascar! Java! Florida! Campeachy Bay!

C. distans GREG. (M. J. III p. 39 Pl. IV f. 9; 1855) is a mere variety of *C. Scutellum*. *C. distans* GREG. (T. M. J. 1857 Vol. V Pl. I f. 25 and D. of Clyde p. 190 Pl. IX f. 23) seems not to differ from *C. granulata* GREG. The species I consider as *C. distans* has been figured by A. SCHMIDT, but is a small variety, named by PERAGALLO var. *minima*. SCHMIDT figures one specimen with median line and central nodule, but this fig. certainly represents an entire frustule. I have seen in a gathering from Java an entire frustule, but the coarse structure of the upper valve prevented me from examining the lower one, which seems to be very delicate. *C. lamprosticta* GREG. (T. M. S. V. p. 69 Pl. I f. 28, 1857) represents either this species or a form of *Cocc. Scutellum*.

9. **C. Disculus** SCHUM. (1864). — Upper V. broadly elliptical. L. 0,02; B. 0,015 mm. Axial area lanceolate. Striæ 8 in 0,01 mm. composed of two to four large elongated puncta. Lower V. unknown. — *Navicula Disculus* SCHUM. Preuss. D. 1 Nachtr. p. 21 f. 23.

Fresh or slightly brackish water: Domblitten and Spirding, Prussia, fossil! Sweden, (baltic deposits from the Ancylus-epoch)!

This small and characteristic form is figured by SCHUMANN with median line and central nodule, of which I have never seen a trace.

10. **C. australis** PETIT (1877). Outline elliptical. L. 0,0264; B. 0,0242 mm. Upper V. unknown. Lower V. with sigmoid median line and the terminal nodules in contrary directions, at some distance from the margin. Margin with rudimentary loculi. Striae fine. — D. de Campbell p. 11 Pl. IV f. 2.

Marine: New Zealand (Petit).

This species has the appearance of being very distinct, but it is, unfortunately, incompletely described and figured.

11. **C. Van Heurckii** CL. N. Sp. Elliptical. L. 0,035 to 0,04; B. 0,015 to 0,024 mm. Upper V. with a straight axial silicious rib, sending off on both sides strong costae, 4 to 5 in 0,01 mm., connected by longitudinal silicious ribs, 2 to 4 on each side, thus forming a reticulum of large, quadrate alveoli. Lower V. with straight median line, not reaching to the margin, and a narrow, but distinct marginal area. Axial area indistinct. Central area small, rounded. Striae 18 in 0,01 mm. slightly radiate, punctate. — Pl. II f. 32, 33, 34.

Marine: Madagascar!

The very peculiar upper valve of this species makes it doubtful whether it really belongs to this group, but on the other hand the lower valve resembles that of *C. Scutellum*. This species may be the same as *Cocc. surirelloides* GRUN. (Novara p. 98 Pl. I A f. 27, 28; 1867) but the descriptions and figure are insufficient for identification.

Eucocconeis CL. N. G.

Valves elliptical, rarely rostrate, without a marginal rim, ecostate, usually not very dissimilar. Striation of both valves unusually delicate. Upper valve with a narrow axial area. Lower valve with straight or sigmoid median line.

This group comprises most species of the old genus Cocconeis. Its affinities are difficult to decide. In outline of the valves it resembles *Cocconeis* CL., from which it is distinguished by the absence of the loculiferous rim[1]). In the usually fine striation of both, not very dissimilar, valves, it approaches *Microneis*. *C. flexella* and *C. minuta* are isolated forms recalling *Navicula depressa* and *N. Rotaeana*.

Artificial key.

1.	Upper valve with lateral areas or furrows	9.
	— without	2.
2.	Upper valve with an unilateral horseshoe-shaped marking	3.
	— — without	4.
3.	Striation fine, median line straight	*C. Calcar* CL.
	— coarse, — sigmoid	*C. notata* PET.
4.	Median line straight	5.
	— sigmoid	7.
5.	Median line reaching to the margin	6.
	— — not	*C. molesta* KÜTZ.
6.	Striae of the upper valve fine (20 in 0,01 mm.)	*C. finmarchica* GRUN.
	— — — coarse (8 —)	*C. septentrionalis* GRUN.
7.	Marine habitat	*C. dirupta* GREG.
	Fresh water habitat	8.
8.	Axial area dilated in the middle	*C. minuta* CL.
	— — not — —	*C. flexella* BRÉB.

[1]) In the collection of E. GROVE I have seen some specimens of *C. dirupta* from Australia which had rudimentary loculi.

9.	Median line sigmoid	10.
	— straight	13.
10.	Valve with an annulus at the side of the centre	*C. cyclophora* Grun.
	without	11.
11.	Striæ of the upper valve coarse (9 to 11 in 0,01 mm.)	12.
	— — — — fine 25 — — —)	*C. heteroidea* Hantsch.
12.	Central nodule transversely dilated	*C. arctica* Cl.
	— — not — —	*C. soluta* Br.
13.	Lateral areas connected to a broad marginal annulus	14.
	— not — — — —	15.
14.	Striæ of the upper valve composed of coarse puncta	*C. antiqua* Br.
	— — — costate with a median punctum	*C. interrupta* Grun.
15.	Upper valve with longitudinal furrows or depressions	16.
	— — without	18.
16.	With several, strong furrows	*C. pellucida* Hantsch.
	— — a lunate depression	17.
17.	Striæ fine (16 to 21 in 0,01 mm.) punctate	*C. pseudomarginata* Greg.
	— coarse (10 in 0,01 mm.) costate, with a median punctum	*C. citrea* Brun.
18.	Lateral areas crossed by two oblique rows of puncta	*C. praecellens* Past.
	— not — — — —	*C. Letourneuri* Cl.

1. **C. molesta** (Kütz. 1844) Grun. (1881). — Outline elliptical, with broad, rounded ends. L. 0,017 to 0,019; B. 0,007 to 0,008 mm. Upper V. with narrow axial area. Striæ more than 30 in 0,01 mm. finely punctate, puncta forming zig-zag-lines. Lower V. with straight median line, not reaching to the ends. Central area very small. Striæ more than 30 in 0,01 mm. punctate, puncta forming fine, longitudinal striæ. — Bac. p. 71 Pl. V f. 7, 11, 12. V. H. Syn. Pl. XXX f. 18, 19. A. S. N. S. D. Pl. III f. 20?

Marine: Venice (Kütz.).

Var. *crucifera* Grun. (1881). — L. 0,015 to 0,025; B. 0,008 to 0,016 mm. Central area of the lower valve dilated to a transverse fascia. — V. H. Syn. Pl. XXX f. 20, 23. *C. diaphana* W. Sm. B. D. p. 22 Pl. XXX f. 254 (partim) 1853. A. S. Atl. CXCIII, 48 to 51.

Marine: England! Coasts of France!

Var. *amygdalina* (Bréb.) Grun. (1881). — L. 0,035 to 0,045; B. 0,018 to 0,02 mm. Upper V. with about 20 striæ in 0,01 mm. Lower V. with slightly dilated central area and about 27 striæ in 0,01 mm. — *C. diaphana* W. Sm. B. D. I p. 22 Pl. XXX f. 254 (partim). *C. amygdalina* Grun. in V. H. Syn. XXX f. 5, 35.

Marine: French coast of the English Channel!

2. **C. finmarchica** Grun. (1880). — Elliptical. L. 0,012 to 0,015; B. 0,0055 to 0,007 mm. Upper V. with linear axial area. Striæ 20 in 0,01 mm. slightly radiate. Lower V. with straight median line, ending near the margin. Central area a fascia, not reaching to the margin. Striæ 24 in 0,01 mm. slightly radiate. — A. D. p. 16 Pl. I f. 1.

Marine: Arctic America! Finmark!

3. **C. septentrionalis** Grun. (1884). — Elliptical. L. 0,022 to 0,036; B. 0,012 to 0,023 mm. Upper V. with narrow axial area. Striæ 8 in 0,01 mm. almost parallel, punctate; puncta 11 in 0,01 mm., larger at the margin, not arranged in longitudinal rows. Lower V. with straight median line. Central area a narrow, transverse fascia. Striæ radiate, 9 in 0,01 mm. punctate; puncta 16 in 0,01 mm. — Franz Josefs Land D. p. 55 Pl. I f. 2.

Marine: Assistance Bay (Grun.).

4. **A. Calcar** Cl. (1891). — Broadly elliptical. L. 0,012; B. 0,009 mm. Upper V. with straight, narrow axial area. Central area on one side of the nodule dilated into a spurlike projection, on the other bifid, forming an horseshoe-like marking. Lower V.(?) with straight median

line, reaching to the margin, no areas and fine striæ, radiate throughout, about 25 in 0,01 mm. Diat. of Finland p. 51 Pl. III f. 8 (9?)

Fresh water: Sweden (Ryssby in Calmar Län, baltic freshwater deposit from the Ancylus-epoch), Åbo, Finland!

5. **C. dirupta** Greg. (1857). — Broadly elliptical to almost orbicular. Upper V. with linear, usually sigmoid, axial area. Lower V. with more or less distinctly sigmoid median line and the terminal fissures in contrary directions. Central nodule transversely dilated to an outwardly narrowing fascia.

Var. *typica* Cl. — L. 0,026 to 0,061; B. 0,018 to 0,05 mm. Upper V. with linear not sigmoid axial area. Striæ about 17 in 0,01 mm. punctate; puncta forming undulate longitudinal rows. Lower V. with very slightly sigmoid median line. Central area transversely dilated to a fascia not reaching to the margin. Striæ 20 in 0,01 mm. *C. dirupta* Greg. D. of Clyde p. 491 Pl. IX f. 25. A. S. N. S. D. Pl. III f. 21. V. H. Syn. p. 133 Pl. XXIX f. 13 to 15. *C. diaphana* W. Sm. B. D. p. 22 Pl. XXX f. 251 partim (1853)? *C. delicata* A. S. Atl. CXCVI, 24? Probably also *C. oceanica*, *C. limbata* and *C. fasciata* Ehr.

Marine: Greenland! North Sea! Mediterranean Sea! China! Behring's Island! Tahiti (Grun.). Cape of Good Hope (Grun.), California! Galapagos Islands! Colon!

Var. *dubia* Grun. (1867). — Smaller. Striæ 22 0,01 mm. Central nodule rarely, terminal nodules never, transversely dilated. — Novara p. 14.

Marine: S:t Paul (Grun.).

Var.? *Beltmeyeri* Jan. (1894). -- L. 0,04; B. 0,027 mm. Upper V. with lanceolate, not sigmoid area. Striæ 12 in 0,01 mm. crossed by 4 to 8 blank bands. — A. S. Atl. CXCVI, 22, 23.

Marine: Leton Bank (Atl.), Pensacola (Atl.)?

Var. *flexella* Jan. Rab. (1862). — L. 0,02 to 0,03; B. 0,02 to 0,03 mm. Upper V. with narrow, lanceolate axial area. Striæ 20 in 0,01 mm. crossed on each side of the area by about 4 linear, curved blank bands. Lower V. with sigmoid median line, reaching to the ends, and transverse central area. Striæ about 19 in 0,01 mm. - *C. flexella* Jan. Rab. D. Honduras p. 7 Pl. I f. 11. *C. dir. var. flex.* V. H. Syn. Pl. XXIX f. 16, 17.

Marine: Mediterranean Sea! Adriatic! Honduras (Jan. Rab.).

Var. *antarctica* Grun. (1881). — L. 0,042; B. 0,035 mm. Upper V. with narrow, linear axial area. Striæ about 15 in 0,01 mm., punctate; puncta forming longitudinal rows, about 13 in 0,01 mm. Lower V. with nearly straight median line, ending at some distance from the margin in transverse terminal areas, turned in contrary directions. Striæ 11 in 0,01 mm. distinctly punctate; puncta forming irregularly undulating longitudinal rows, about 11 in 0,01 mm. - V. H. Syn. Pl. XXIX f. 18, 19. *C. dir. var. major* Grun. Novara p. 14?

Marine: New Zealand (Grun.). China!

Var. *californica* Cl. — L. 0,045 to 0,07; B. 0,03 to 0,06 mm. Upper V. with slightly sigmoid, lanceolate axial area not dilated in the middle. Striæ 11 to 16 in 0,01 mm. of large, distant puncta, forming undulating, longitudinal rows, about 9 in 0,01 mm. — A. S. Atl. CXCVI, 17, 18(?)

Marine: California fossil at S:ta Martha and S:ta Monica (Deby Coll.)! Moron, Spain, fossil (Grove Coll.)!

Var. *decipiens* Cl. (1873). L. 0,025 to 0,06; B. 0,034 to 0,04 mm. Upper valve with sigmoid axial area in the middle dilated to an orbicular space. Striæ 16 to 20 in 0,01 mm. punctate; puncta (10 in 0,01 mm.) forming irregularly decussating rows (14 in 0,01 mm.). Lower V. with sigmoid median line reaching nearly to the ends. Striæ 11 to 12 in 0,01 mm. punctate: puncta, about 14 in 0,01 mm., becoming larger outwards. — *C. decip.* Cl. D. Arct. Sea p. 14 Pl. I f. 6 (Lower V.). *C. arcticum* Cl. l. c. Pl. II f. 11 *a* (Upper V.).

Marine: Arctic America! Greenland! Finmark! Behring's Island!

Var. *Fulgur* BRUN (1891). — Almost orbicular. L. 0,03 to 0,04; B. 0,027 to 0,036 mm. Upper V. with narrow axial area, and large irregular central area. Striæ 12 in 0,01 mm. radiate, punctate; puncta 11 in 0,01 mm. Lower V. with sigmoid median line and transverse, outwardly dilated, central area. Striæ 14 in 0,01 mm., radiate, coarsely punctate; puncta 13 in 0,01 mm. becoming larger towards the margin. — *C. Fulgur* BRUN D. espèces nov. p. 17 Pl. XVIII f. 3.

Marine: Mogador. Cabenda (Western Africa), Magellan's Straits (Brun).

Var. *Sigma* PANT. (1886). — Almost orbicular. L. 0,04 to 0,065; B. 0,03 to 0,05 mm. Upper V. with sigmoid axial area, in the middle dilated to a rhomboidal, or irregularly orbicular, central area. Striæ radiate 12 to 13 in 0,01 mm. coarsely punctate; puncta about 9 in 0,01 mm. forming irregular zig-zag-lines. Lower V. with sigmoid median line and transversely dilated central area. Striæ 12 to 14 in 0,01 mm. radiate. *C. Sigma* PANT. I p. 32 Pl. VIII f. 68. *C. Oculus Catis* BRUN Diat. esp. nouv. p. 18 Pl. XVIII f. 5 (1891). *C. sigmo-radians* TEMP. BRUN D. foss. du Japon p. 33 Pl. VIII f. 4 (1889). A. S. Atl. CXCVI, 11.

Marine: Ceylon (Le Tourneur Coll.)! Fossil: Japan (Brun Coll.)! S:ta Monica, Calif. (Brun), Atlantic City (Brun).

Var. *sparsipunctata* BRUN (1891). — Broadly elliptical. L. 0,05 to 0,09; B. 0,04 to 0,07 mm. Upper V. with not well defined lanceolate area, large and distant puncta, forming 3 to 4 irregular, undulating longitudinal rows. Margin with a row of close puncta (10 in 0,01 mm.). Lower V. with sigmoid median line and narrow, transverse, central area. Axial area indistinct. Striæ 11 in 0,01 mm. punctate; puncta 14 in 0,01 mm. equidistant. — *C. spars.* BRUN D. espèces nouv. p. 18 Pl. XVIII f. 8. A. S. Atl. CXCVI, 13 to 15.

Marine: Japan, fossil (Brun Coll.)!

6. **C. notata** PETIT (1877). — Upper V. elliptical. L. 0,02 to 0,026; B. 0,01 to 0,013 mm. with sigmoid axial area, in the middle dilated into a fascia, on one side branched near the margin as to form a horseshoe-like marking. Striæ about 17 in 0,01 mm. coarsely punctate; puncta forming about 5 longitudinal rows on each side of the area. D. de Campbell p. 10 Pl. IV f. 4.

Marine: New Zealand (Petit). China!

7. **C. Letourneuri** CL. N. Sp. — Outline elliptical. L. 0,04 to 0,05; B. 0,03 to 0,033 mm. Upper V. with straight, linear axial area, separated by two rows of puncta from the narrow, lunate lateral areas. Striæ marginal, 9 in 0,01 mm., of coarse puncta, 7 to 8 in 0,01 mm. Lower Valve with straight median line, ending at some distance from the ends. Axial and central areas indistinct. Striæ 10, radiate at the ends, punctate; puncta about 16 in 0,01 mm. — Pl. III f. 10, 11.

Marine: Colombo, Ceylon (Le Tourneur Coll.)!

8. **C. arctica** CL. (1873). — Elliptical. L. 0,03 to 0,04; B. 0,02 mm. Upper V. with slightly sigmoid axial area. Striæ 11 in 0,01 mm., coarsely punctate, crossed on each side of the area by large, lunate depressions, across which the striæ continue faintly. Lower V. with sigmoid median line, and transversely dilated central area. Striæ 12 in 0,01 mm. radiate, coarsely punctate; puncta becoming larger towards the margin. — D. of arctic sea p. 11 Pl. II f. 11 *b* (Upper V.). Vega p. 460 Pl. XXXV f. 4. *C. inflexa* A. S. Atl. CXCVI, 10?

Marine: Arctic America! Greenland! Finmark!

9. **C. præcellens** PANT. (1886). — Broadly elliptical. L. 0,0299 to 0,045; B. 0,0187 to 0,034 mm. Upper V. with broad axial area and large lateral areas separated by three longitudinal rows of large puncta. Striæ 16 in 0,01 marginal, composed of about three puncta. Lower V. with straight median line, reaching to the margin, otherwise similar to the upper valve, except that there are two rows of small puncta divergent from the central nodule across the lateral areas. — PANT. I p. 31 Pl. VIII f. 69.

Marine: Hungary, fossil (Pant.).

10. **C. antiqua** Temp. and Brun (1889). — Elliptical. L. 0,06 to 0,08; B. 0,04 to 0,06 mm. Upper V. with straight lanceolate axial area connected with the lateral areas, which form an annular space at some distance from the margin. Striæ 9 in 0,01 mm., coarsely punctate (puncta 6 in 0,01 mm.) crossed by the lateral areas. Lower V. with straight median line ending at some distance from the margin in small lunate terminal areas. Central area transverse. Striæ 10 to 11 in 0,01 mm. distinctly punctate; puncta 15 in 0,01 mm. D. foss. du Japon p. 32 Pl. VIII f. 5. — A. S. Atl. CXCI, 49, 52.

Marine: Japan, fossil (Brun Coll.)!

Var. *fossilis* Cl. — L. 0,05 to 0,085; B. 0,035 to 0,058 mm. Upper V. with linear axial area. Striæ 10 and puncta 7 to 9 in 0,01 mm. — A. S. Atl. CXCI, 44 to 46.

Marine: S:ta Monica Cal. and Oamaru, New Zealand, fossil!

Nearly akin, if not identical, *Cocc. Jimboi* Pant. (III Pl. II f. 24; 1893) appears to be. The figure represents the lower valve. *C. japonica* Pant. (III Pl. XLII f. 582; 1893) seems to be the upper valve.

11. **C. voluta** Br. (1894). — Orbicular. Diam. 0,08. Upper V. with lanceolate axial area not reaching to the margin and with one or two lateral areas on each side of the axial area. Striæ 10 to 11 in 0,01 mm. punctate; puncta 9 to 10 in 0,01 mm. Lower V. with slightly sigmoid median line, small rounded terminal areas at some distance from the margin. Striæ 12 in 0,01 mm., radiate throughout, punctate; puncta 11 to 12 in 0,01 mm. — A. S. Atl. CXCVI f. 25, 26 (left figure *Cocc. probata* A. S.).

Marine: California, S:ta Monica, fossil (Deby Coll.)!

12. **C. interrupta** Grun. (1863). — Elliptical. L. 0,032 to 0,062; B. 0,024 to 0,04 mm. Upper V. with short, narrow, axial area slightly widened in the middle, connected with the very broad lateral areas. Striæ 9 to 10 in 0,01 mm. at the margin and at the axial area, costate with a median punctum. Lower V. with straight median line, ending at some distance from the margin in small lunate terminal areas. Axial area indistinct. Central area transverse (and frequently unilateral). Striæ 9 in 0,01 mm. radiate and curved towards the ends, distinctly punctate. Verh. 1863 p. 141 Pl. IV f. 14. V. H. Syn. Pl. XXX f. 3, 4. A. S. Atl. CXCIV f. 17. *C. Crux.* Pet. D. de Campbell Pl. IV f. 4?

Marine: Kamtschatka!

13. **C. vitrea** Brun (1891). — Elliptical. L. 0,06 to 0,07; B. 0,04 to 0,05 mm. Upper V. with narrow lanceolate axial area, and narrow lunate lateral areas. Striæ between the areas 10 in 0,01 mm., having a large median punctum. Marginal striæ also with a median punctum. Lower V. with straight median line, ending at some distance from the margin. Axial and terminal areas indistinct. Central area irregularly rounded. Striæ 18 in 0,01 mm. radiate, punctate; puncta about 17 in 0,01 mm. — D. esp. nouv. p. 19 Pl. XVIII f. 2. A. S. Atl. CXCIV f. 10, 11. *C. De Toniana* Pant. III Pl. XXXIV f. 482 (1893). *C. pseudomarginata* A. S. Atl. CXCIV f. 8.

Marine: Japan and Hungary, fossil (Brun).

Var.? *verrucosa* Brun (1891). — L. 0,05 to 0,06; B. 0,035 to 0,05 mm. Upper V. with lanceolate axial area, and broad lunate lateral areas, marked with some large scattered dots. Striæ 15 in 0,01 mm. with a median punctum. Marginal striæ short. Lower V. with straight median line, ending at some distance from the ends in pyriform terminal areas. Axial and central areas indistinct. Striæ 18 in 0,01 mm. radiate and curved at the ends, punctate; puncta 17 in 0,01 mm. — *C. sp.* Brun Temp. D. du Japon Pl. VIII f. 9. *C. verruc.* Brun D. espèces nouv. p. 18 Pl. XVIII f. 7. A. S. Atl. CXCIV f. 14.

Marine: Japan, fossil (Brun Coll.)! Indian Ocean (Brun).

A somewhat similar, but much smaller, valve is *C. Kinkeri* PANT. (III Pl. II f. 30; 1893) too imperfectly known to be placed in the system.

14. **C. pellucida** HANTZSCH (1862). Broadly elliptical. L. 0,03 to 0,1; B. 0,02 to 0,07 mm. Upper V. with rather broad linear, and straight axial area, on both sides of which are about 5 longitudinal parallel rows of short striæ, 30 in 0.01 mm. Lower V. with a marginal line and straight median line, ending at a distance from the margin in lunate terminal areas. Terminal fissures in contrary directions. Striæ 21 in 0.01 mm., slightly radiate, finely punctate. — Ostind. Archip. D. p. 21 f. 11. GRUN. Novara p. 12. WITT a. TRUAN Jeremie D. p. 15 Pl. IV f. 11 (f. 12, 20, 21 varieties with less numerous furrows) A. S. Atl. CXCIV f. 2; CXCV f. 1 to 6. *C. oceanica* EHR. Pritch. Inf. Pl. XII f. 42? *C. notabilis* PANT. III Pl. XXXV f. 492 (1893). *C. circumcincta* A. S. Atl. CXCV f. 7 to 9 (1894).

Marine: Nicobar Islands (Grun.), Java! Sumatra! Singapore! Sandwich Islands! Behrings Island! Madagascar! New Zealand (Grun.). Fossil: Nankoori (Grun.), Hungary (Pant.), Hayti (Witt).

Var. *minor* GRUN. (1867). L. 0,019 to 0,04; B. 0,013 to 0,03 mm. Upper V. with about 4 strong furrows on each side of the axial area. Lower V. with straight, or slightly sigmoid median line, reaching almost to the margin. Striæ 20 in 0.01 mm. Novara p. 13 Pl. I f. 7. *C. lineata* EHR. M. G. VI. 1, 10.

Marine: Red Sea! S:t Pauls Island (Grun.), Cape Good Hope (Grun.), Nicobar Islands (Grun.), New Zealand (Grun.), Trinidad!

Var. *nankoorensis* GRUN. (1867). L. 0,055 to 0,12; B. 0,045 to 0,09 mm. Upper V. with about four furrows on each side of the area. Striæ 11 to 14 in 0.01 mm. — Novara p. 98. A. S. Atl. CXCIV f. 15. *C. pell. var. fossilis* PANT. III Pl. XXXII f. 465 (1893). *C. Lungacsekii* PANT. III Pl. XLI f. 564 (1893).

15. **C. pseudomarginata** GREG. (1857). — Elliptical. L. 0,038 to 0,084; B. 0,026 to 0,076 mm. Upper V. with narrow, lanceolate axial area and on each side of it lunate depressions. Striæ 16 to 21 in 0.01 mm., punctate. Lower V. with straight median line, ending at some distance from the margin in small, lunate terminal areas. Axial area narrow, central small orbicular. Striæ 20 to 24 in 0.01 mm. radiate, punctate. — D. of Clyde p. 492 Pl. IX f. 27 (entire frustule) Pritch. Inf. Pl. VII f. 39. V. H. Syn. XXIX f. 20, 21. A. S. Atl. CXCIV, 5 to 7. *C. major* GREG. D. of Clyde Pl. IX f. 28 (lower V.). *C. pellucida* GRUN. Verh. 1863 p. 145 Pl. IV f. 6. *C. Kirchenpaueriana* JAN. and RABH. D. of Honduras p. 7 Pl. I f. 9? *C. Henrioti* PER. D. de Cape Horn p. 117 Pl. X f. 7 (1888)?

Marine: Greenland! Spitsbergen! Sea of Kara! North Sea! Mediterranean! Red Sea! Seychelles! Madagascar! China! Galapagos Islands! Sandwich Islands! Honduras (Rabh.). Hungary, fossil (Pant.).

Var. *intermedia* GRUN. (1867). L. 0,05 to 0,06; B. 0,04 to 0.045 mm. Lower V. with slightly sigmoid median line. Striæ 20 in 0.01 mm. — Novara p. 13 Pl. I f. 6. *C. duplex* A. S. Atl. CXCIV, 4.

Marine: Corsica! Cape Good Hope (Grun.). Nicobar Islands (Grun.), Philippines (Grun.). Sandwich Islands! Tahiti (Grun.), Japan!

16. **C. heteroidea** HANTZSCH (1862). Broadly elliptical to almost orbicular. L. 0,035 to 0,07; B. 0,025 to 0,065 mm. Upper V. with broadly linear, more or less distinctly sigmoid, or oblique axial area, on both sides of which are 3 to 5 arcuate furrows. Striæ 25 in 0.01 mm. Lower V. with sigmoid median line, not reaching to the margin. Axial area narrow, central area small, frequently transversely dilated into a narrow fascia. Striæ 18 to 22 in 0,01 mm. radiate. Terminal areas lunate, frequently prolonged into a line parallel to the margin of the valve. Ostind. Arch. D. p. 21 f. 10. GRUN. Novara p. 12. A. S. Atl. CXCVI f. 2, 33 to 37, 40, 41. *C. lunata* LEUD. FORTM. D. de Ceylon Pl. I f. 3. *C. recurva* A. S. Atl. CXCVI 31, 32 (1894). *C. tenella* A. S. l. c. f. 38. *C. transversa* A. S. l. c. f. 39.

Marine: Seychelles! Madagascar! Mauritius! Nicobar Islands (Grun.). Singapore! Japan! China! Sandwich Islands! Samoa! West Indies! Colon!

Var. *curvirotunda* TEMP. and BRUN (1889). — L. 0,1 to 0,12; B. 0,09 to 0,105 mm. Lower V. with fine, slightly sigmoid median line, ending at some distance from the margin in lunate, small areas. Central area small and orbicular. Striæ 13 in 0,01 mm. — *C. (pell. var.?) curvirotunda* BR. and TEMP. D. foss. du Japon p. 32 Pl. VIII f. 6. A. S. Atl. CXCV f. 10 to 17? *C. composita* A. S. Atl. CXCVI f. 4, 5?

Marine: Japan, fossil (Brun).

Var. *sigmoidea* GRUN. (1867). — L. 0,025; B. 0,02 mm. Median line sigmoid; central area transversely dilated. — *C. pelluc. var. sigmoidea* GRUN. Novara p. 13 Pl. I f. 8. *C. parthenopaea* PEDIC. Rab. Alg. Eur. N:o 2223 (1870).

Marine: Naples! Red Sea! Tahiti (Grun.).

Var. *conspicua* A. S. (1894). — Lower V. with a row of large puncta between the median line and the margin. — *C. consp.* Atl. CXCVI, 27, 28.

Marine: Kings Mill Island, Singapore, Samoa (Atl.).

17. **C. cyclophora** GRUN. (1879). Broadly elliptical. L. 0,017 to 0,028; B. 0,01 to 0,018 mm. Upper V. with sigmoid lanceolate axial area, lunate lateral areas, and on one side of the centre a large circular annulus. Striæ 16 in 0,01 mm. of decussating puncta. Lower V. with sigmoid median line and narrow axial area, not dilated in the middle. Striæ 28 in 0,01 mm. of small puncta, forming decussating lines. Close to the central nodule is a large, circular annulus. — CL. M. D. N:o 254. GRUN. A. D. p. 16. V. H. Syn. XXX f. 24, 25.

Marine: South Australia!

Var. *Challengeri* CL. — L. 0,055 to 0,07; B. 0,01 to 0,06 mm. Upper V. with scarcely sigmoid, in the middle transversely dilated, axial area, on both sides of it a lunate lateral area, and on one side of the middle a circular annulus. Striæ 17 in 0,01 mm. coarsely punctate; puncta 13 in 0,01 mm. Lower V. with slightly sigmoid median line, and narrow axial area not dilated in the centre. Striæ 24 in 0,01 mm. punctate; puncta 16 in 0,01 mm. On one side of the central nodule a circular annulus.

Marine: Off Marion Island Challenger St. 145 (Comber Coll.)!

18. **C. flexella** KÜTZ (1844). — Rhomboid-elliptical, with obtuse broad ends. L. 0,04 to 0,05; B. 0,02 mm. Upper V. with narrow sigmoid linear axial area not centrally dilated. Striæ radiate throughout 16 in 0,01 mm. Lower V. with sigmoid median line, narrow axial area, small and elongated central area. Striæ 17 in 0,01 mm. radiate throughout, punctate, in the middle alternately longer and shorter. — *Cymbella flexella* KÜTZ. Bac. p. 80 Pl. IV f. 11. *Cocconeis Thwaitesii* W. SM. B. D. I p. 21 Pl. III f. 33 (1853). *Achnanthidium flexellum* BRÉB. in Kütz. Sp. Alg. p. 54. GRUN. A. D. p. 17. V. H. Syn. p. 128 Pl. XXVI f. 29 to 31. *Navicula Semen* EHB. partim. *Navicula Macula* GREG. T. M. S. IV p. 43 Pl. V f. 9? *Achnanthidium naviculoides* REINSCH (accord. to Grun.).

Fresh water: Spitsbergen (Lagst.). Beeren Eiland (Lagst.), Arctic America! Sweden! Finland! England! Belgium! Switzerland (Brun.).

19. **C. minuta** CL. (1891). — Elliptical with broad, rounded ends. L. 0,021 to 0,029; B. 0,01 to 0,012 mm. Upper V. with narrow linear axial area, dilated in the middle to a large, orbicular central area. Striæ 20 in 0,01 mm., almost parallel. Lower V. without axial area. Central area large, rounded. Striæ radiate, 20 (middle) to 25 (ends) in 0,01 mm. — *Cocconeis Thwaitesii var. β arctica* LAGST. Spitsb. D. p. 41 Pl. II f. 16 (1873). *Achnanthidium minutum* CL. D. of Finl. p. 53 Pl. III f. 6, 7 (1891). *N. dissimilis* W. SM. Ann. Mag. Nat. XIX p. 8 Pl. II f. 6; 1857?

Fresh water: Spitsbergen (Lagst.). Finland (Åbo)! Sweden (Wenern)!

This form resembles greatly *Nav. Rotaeana var. oblongella.*

Var. *alpestris* Br. (1880). — L. 0,027 to 0,033; B. 0,012 to 0,015 mm. V. truncate, with strongly sigmoid axial area, dilated in the middle to a large subquadrate central area. Striæ about 23 in 0,01 mm. Lower V. with small central area, striæ about 25 in 0,01 mm. — *Ach. flex.* B. D. des Alpes Pl. III f. 26. Diatomiste II p. 72 Pl. V f. 15.

Alpine regions: Switzerland! Norway (Br.), Auvergne (Br.).

Disconeis Cl. N. G.

Valves in outline elliptical, without marginal rim, very dissimilar. Upper valve coarsely costate, with narrow axial area. Lower valve without axial area, and with punctate radiate striæ.

The forms placed in this genus are not closely connected. As to their affinities it may be noted that the lower valve of *C. Lyra* perfectly resembles a small form of *Navicula Hennedyi*, and that of *C. reticulata* a small form of the section *Punctatæ* of Navicula. The lower valve of *C. pinnata* has a great resemblance to *C. Pediculus* or *C. pseudomarginata*, and *C. formosa* in its lower valve recalls *C. costata*.

Artificial key.

1. { Costæ of the upper valve anastomosing into a reticulum . . . . 2.
   { — not — — — — . . . . 3.
2. { Axial area narrow, lanceolate . . . . *C. formosa* Brun.
   { — — a silicious rib . . . . *C. reticulata* Cl.
3. { Axial area of the upper valve very narrow . . . . 4.
   { — — — — — lanceolate . . . . 5.
4. { Costæ alternating with double rows of coarse puncta . . . . *C. Lyra* A. S.
   { crossed by fine oblique striæ . . . . *C. hexagona* Br. Cl.
5. { Costæ alternating with rows of short lines . . . . *C. versicolor* Br.
   { — — — double rows of fine puncta . . . . *C. pinnata* Greg.

1. **A. hexagona** Br. a. Cl. (1891). — Outline broadly linear, with cuneate ends. L. 0,042; B. 0,02 mm. Upper V. with very narrow axial area. Striæ 11 in 0,01 mm., parallel in the middle, radiate at the ends, crossed by a set of close oblique striæ, about 25 in 0,01 mm. Lower V. with very narrow axial area. Median line straight; central nodule transversely dilated to a stauros not reaching the margin. Striæ 13 in 0,01 mm., transversely lineate, strongest near the margin, faint on other parts of the valve. — D. espèces nouv. p. 5 Pl. XIX f. 3 *a*, *b*.

Marine: Western Africa and Nossibé (Brun.), Yokohama (Brun Coll.)!

The lower valve has some resemblance to *C. costata*, but the upper differs in its structure, and especially in the absence of the marginal ring.

2. **C. Lyra** A. S. (1871). — Outline elliptical. L. 0,023 to 0,06; B. 0,014 to 0,033 mm. Upper V. without area, but with an axial rib sending off on both sides parallel (at the ends radiate) costæ (about 7 in 0,01 mm.) alternating with double rows of puncta, about 15 in 0,01 mm., forming longitudinal rows. Lower V. with straight median line, and transverse central area, united on both sides to a broad linear area, so as to form a lyre-shaped figure. Striæ 15 in 0,01 mm. not distinctly punctate. — N. S. D. p. 93 Pl. III f. 19 (right figure, lower valve). *C.?* l. c. f. 18 (upper figure, upper valve). *C. norvegica* Grun. Cl. M. D. N:o 102 (1878) upper valve.

Marine: Grip and Bergen, Norway!

This curious and isolated form has exceedingly different valves, which I have found together in the same frustule. The lower valve resembles a small form of *Navicula Hennedyi*.

3. **C. reticulata** Cl. N. Sp. — Outline elliptical. L. 0,03 to 0,035; B. 0,017 to 0,02 mm. Upper valve with an axial rib sending off, laterally, transverse costæ (about 6 in 0,01 mm.) ana-

stomosing with longitudinal costæ, thus forming a net-work of quadrate alveoli. Lower V. with indistinct axial area, small orbicular central area and 9 striæ in 0,01 mm., composed of distinct puncta, about 9 in 0,01 mm. -- Pl. III f. 6, 7.

Marine: Galapagos Islands!

4. **C. formosa** Brun (1891). — L. 0,075 to 0,1; B. 0,05 to 0,07 mm. Upper V. with narrow, lanceolate axial area, and slightly radiate costæ, 5 in 0,01 mm., anastomosing into a net-work of rectangular alveoli, 4 in 0,01 mm. Lower V. with straight median line, and indistinct axial area. Central area transverse, narrow lanceolate. Terminal areas small and near the margin. Striæ 6,5 in 0,01 mm. slightly radiate, coarsely punctate (puncta 8 to 9 in 0,01 mm.) and ending with double rows of puncta. — D. espèces nouv. p. 16 Pl. XVIII f. 6. Pant. III Pl. XXXII f. 457. A. S. Atl. CXCIII, 42 to 47.

Marine: Japan, fossil (Brun Coll.)! Indian Ocean (Brun), Wemlats (Pant.).

A peculiar form, the lower valve of which resembles *C. costata*, from which it differs by the absence of a marginal annulus. There is also some resemblance to *C. versicolor*, but the upper valves are entirely dissimilar.

5. **C. versicolor** Brun (1891). — Elliptical. L. 0,05 to 0,065; B. 0,035 to 0,04 mm. Upper V. with narrow, lanceolate axial area, and strongly radiate costæ, 5,5 in 0,01 mm. Intercostal spaces transversely lineate, lineolæ 13 in 0,01 mm. Lower V. with straight median line reaching to the margin. Axial area indistinct; central area narrow, transverse. Striæ 7 in 0,01 mm. slightly radiate, punctate; puncta 14 in 0,01 mm. Median striæ shorter than the others. -- D. espèces nouv. p. 19 Pl. XVIII f. 1. A. S. Atl. CXC f. 12 to 14.

Marine: Japan, fossil (Brun Coll.)! Mogador (Brun).

6. **C. pinnata** Greg. (1859). — Elliptical. L. 0,024 to 0,04; B. 0,019 to 0,03 mm. Upper V. with broad, axial area and strong, slightly radiate costæ, 4 to 5 in 0,01 mm. Intercostal spaces with double rows of puncta, arranged in oblique lines. Lower V. as in Cocc. pseudo-marginata, but smaller and with closer striation (according to Grunow). *C. pinnata* Greg. M. J. VII p. 79 Pl. VI f. 1. V. H. Syn. Pl. XXX f. 6, 7. A. S. Atl. CLXXXIX f. 1 to 5. *C. Lorenziana* Perag. D. de Villefranche Pl. V f. 38? *C. denticulata* Leud. Fortm. D. de Ceylon Pl. I f. 2? *Rhaphoneis Archeri* O'Meara Quek. M. J. Vol. VII ser. 2 Pl. VII f. 12?

Marine: Spitsbergen! Finmark! North Sea! Mediterranean Sea! Adriatic! Seychelles! Island of Rhea near Singapore!

Pleuroneis Cl. N. G.

Frustules with a marginal rim. Valves broadly elliptical to orbicular. Upper valve with more or less narrow axial area and radiate costæ, alternating with double rows of puncta, forming oblique, decussating lines. Lower valves with radiate rows of finer puncta.

1. **C. britannica** Nægeli (1849). Broadly elliptical. L. 0,025 to 0,05; B. 0,022 to 0,037 mm. Upper V. with very narrow axial area. Costæ 6 to 10 in 0,01 mm., alternating with double rows of small puncta (about 18 in 0,01 mm.) forming oblique lines. Lower V. with distinct median line, not reaching to the margin. Axial area indistinct. Central area very small and orbicular. Striæ about 10 in 0,01 mm. Rim with about 5 costæ in 0,01 mm. — *C. brit.* Ktz. Sp. Alg. p. 890. V. H. Syn. Pl. XXX f. 1, 2. *C. coronata* Btw. M. J. VII p. 179 Pl. IX f. 2? *C. pseudo-marginata* Jan. Rab. Honduras D. Pl. I f. 16? *C. scutelliformis* Grun. in Cl. M. D. 148, 151, 208 -210. *C. costata* var. A. S. Atl. CLXXXIX f. 8? *C. eximia* A. S. Atl. CXCII f. 31?

Marine: Mediterranean Sea! Adriatic (Grun.)! Barbados!

This species resembles, under a low power, *C. Scutellum*, from which it is however widely different. *C. Singaporensis* Petit (Mém. Soc. Cherbourg XXIII p. 207 Pl. I a. 1881) perhaps represents *C. britannica* (the upper valve seems to be some Coscinodiscus). Also *C. fraterna* A. S. (Atl. CLXXXIX f. 27) seems to be a form of *C. britannica*.

2. **C. costata** GREG. (1855). More or less elliptical to orbicular. Upper V. with narrow axial area and strong, transverse costæ, alternating with double rows of obliquely arranged puncta. Lower V. with the median line reaching nearly to the margin. Axial area narrow. Central area transversely dilated to a fascia narrowed outwardly. Striæ radiate, distinctly punctate.

Var. *typica* CL. — L. 0.015 to 0.038; B. 0.009 to 0.018 mm. Upper V. with linear axial area connected with the margin by strong costæ, 5 to 6 in 0.01 mm., alternating with double rows of puncta, forming oblique lines, about 17 in 0.01 mm. Lower V. with indistinct axial area and transversely dilated central area. Striæ 15 in 0.01 mm. slightly radiate and distinctly punctate; puncta about 16 in 0.01 mm. — *C. costata* GREG. T. M. S. III p. 39 Pl. IV f. 10. Vol. V p. 68 Pl. I f. 27. A. S. Atl. CLXXXIX f. 6, 7. V. H. Syn. Pl. XXX f. 11, 12. *Surirella quarnerensis* GRUN. Verh. 1862 p. 456 Pl. IX f. 10 (1862). *Rhaphoneis scutelloides* GRUN. Verh. 1862 p. 383 Pl. IV f. 34.

Marine: Arctic America! Greenland! Davis Straits! Canada! Spitsbergen! Finmark! Behring Island! North Sea! Mediterranean Sea! Adriatic! Auckland (Grun.).

Var. *hexagona* GRUN. (1881). — V. broad, linear, with cuneate ends. L. 0.015 to 0,02; B. 0.009 mm. Costæ of the upper valve 8 in 0,01 mm. — *C. costata var. hex.* GRUN. V. H. Syn. Pl. XXX f. 15 to 17.

Marine?

Var. *pacifica* GRUN. (1867). Elliptical. L. 0.027 to 0.05; B. 0.015 to 0.035 mm. Upper V. with linear axial area and strong costæ, 5 to 6 in 0.01 mm., radiate at the ends, crossed on both sides of the area by a longitudinal line and alternating with double rows of puncta, 12 to 16 in 0.01 mm. Lower V. with transversely dilated central area connected with a marginal blank band, crossing the faint and finely punctate striæ, about 8 in 0.01 mm. — *C. pacif.* GRUN. Novara p. 11 Pl. I f. 10. V. H. Syn. Pl. XXX f. 13, 14. *C. Imperatrix* A. S. Atl. CLXXXIX f. 11 to 15 (1894). *C. Janischii* A. S. Atl. l. c. f. 33? *C. excoptata* A. S. Atl. CXC f. 31? *C. præstans* A. S. Atl. CXC f. 32?

Marine: Ceylon! Magellans Straits! Chile (Grun.). Oamaru, fossil!

Var. *kerguelensis* PET. (1888). Elliptical to orbicular. L. 0.055 to 0.1; B. 0,05 to 0.085 mm. Upper V. with narrow, linear axial area. Costæ 4 to 6 in 0,01 mm. alternating with double rows of puncta, about 10 in 0,01 mm., forming oblique lines. Lower V. with the median line ending near the margin. Axial area very narrow. Central area a transverse, outwardly narrowed fascia. Striæ 4 in 0.01 mm. composed of double rows of puncta, 10 to 12 in 0,01 mm. and crossed near the margin by a narrow blank band. — *C. kerguelensis* PET. D. de Cape Horn p. 116 Pl. X f. 5. A. S. Atl. CLXXXIX f. 9. *C. Reginæ* JOHNS. M. J. VIII p. 13 Pl. I f. 12? *C. extravagans* JAN. A. S. Atl. CLXXXIX f. 28 to 32.

Marine: Kerguelens Land! Magellans Straits!

The var. *kerguelensis* cannot in my opinion be separated as a distinct species from *C. costata*, however different it may look at the first glance. The important characteristics are the same for both, and the differences consist only in size, number of costæ and striæ. The difference in size is enormous, *C. kerguelensis* being gigantic compared to *C. costata*.

Heteroneis CL. N. G.

Frustule without rim. Valves very dissimilar, in outline elliptical or elliptic-lanceolate. Upper valve striate or costate, with a large area. Lower valve either without, with uniting axial and central or without axial and with quadrate central, area.

This subgenus comprises forms, which appear not to be very closely connected. *A. hyperborea* seems to be akin to the linear forms of *Microneis*. *A. gibberula* and *A. Holstii* are probably allied to the section *Mesoleiæ* of *Navicula* and ought perhaps to be placed by the side of *C. minuta*. To *C. quarnerensis* and the others I am unable to find any allied forms among the *Naviculæ*.

Artificial key.

1. { Valve linear . . . . *A. hyperborea* GRUN.
    — lanceolate or rhomboidal . . . . 2.
    — elliptical . . . . 5.

2. { Area of the upper valve granulate . . . . *A. Lilljebergii* GRUN.
    — — — not . . . . 3.

3. { Upper valve with an horseshoe-like mark . . . . *A. Vaszaryi* PANT.
    — — without — . . . . 4.

4. { Striæ of the upper valve 22 in 0,01 mm . . . . *A. gibberula* GRUN.
    — — — — 14 — — . . . . *A. Holstii* CL.

5. { L. about 0,01 mm. . . . . 6.
    L. 0,02 mm. or more . . . . 7.

6. { Striæ of the upper valve unilaterally interrupted . . . . *A. americana* CL.
    — — — — not — — . . . . *C. pygmæa* SCHUM.

7. { Upper valve with an horseshoe-like mark . . . . *A. Lagerheimii* CL.
    — — without — — — . . . . 8.

8. { Striæ of the upper valve 9 in 0,01 mm. . . . . *C. quarnerensis* GRUN.
    — — — — 11 to 12 in 0,01 mm. . . . . 9.

9. { Area of the upper valve dilated in the middle . . . . *C. biharensis* PANT.
    — — — not — — — . . . . *C. Pelta* A. S.

1. **A. Vaszaryi** PANT. (1893). — Outline rhomboid, subacute. L. 0,06; B. 0,03 mm. Upper V. unknown. Lower V. with narrow axial area and transverse, outwardly fimbriate central area. Median striæ transverse and of unequal length, 13 in 0,01 mm. Other striæ strongly radiate throughout, about 20 in 0,01 mm., punctate. *Nav. Vaszaryi* PANT. III Pl. XVI f. 239.

Habitat? Nyermegy (Pant.).

Var. *oregonica* CL. (1893). — Outline lanceolate with subrostrate, obtuse ends. L. 0,03; B. 0,013 mm. Upper V. with lanceolate axial area, a third as broad as the valve, and with a unilateral horseshoe-shaped marking. Costæ slightly radiate, about 16 in 0,01 mm. alternating with fine obliquely arranged puncta, about 30 in 0,01 mm. Lower valve without axial area and with a large central area, fimbriate outwards. Median striæ of unequal length and transverse, about 18 in 0,01 mm. Striæ of the other portions of the valve very radiate, becoming closer towards the ends, about 26 in 0,01 mm. — Diatomiste II p. 57 Pl. III f. 15, 16.

Fresh water: Oregon, fossil!

This is a very interesting species, the lower valve of which perfectly resembles that of Actinoneis. It appears to be akin to *A. heteromorpha* of the subgenus *Actinoneis*. There can be no doubt that *Nav. Vaszaryi* PANT., which represents the lower valve, is very nearly related to the form from Oregon, of which I have examined an entire frustule. The differences are slight, as to the size, the outline, and the coarseness of the striation, for which reason I am not inclined to consider them as distinct species.

2. **A. hyperborea** GRUN. (1882). — Outline linear, with broad, sometimes cuneate, ends, slightly constricted in the middle. L. 0,026 to 0,028; B. 0,0065 to 0,008 mm. slightly arcuate. Upper V. with obsolete median line and broad, linear area. Striæ 27 in 0,01 mm., radiate at the ends. Lower V. without areas. Median striæ 24, terminal 30 in 0,01 mm. — CL. M. D. N:o 314. Franz Josefs Land D. p. 102 Pl. I f. 4, 5.

Marine: Franz Josefs Land (Grun.).

3. **A. gibberula** Grun. (1880). — Lanceolate, with obtuse ends. L. 0,018 to 0,02; B. 0,0045 to 0,005 mm. Upper V. with wide, lanceolate area. Striæ 22 in 0,01 mm. Lower V. with narrow, lanceolate axial area, centrally not transversely dilated. Striæ about 22 in 0,01 mm. radiate, more distant in the middle than towards the ends. In the zonal view the upper margin of the lower valve is gibbous in the middle. — A. D. p. 22. V. H. Syn. Pl. XXVII f. 47 to 49.

Hot springs: East Indies (Grun.).

Var. *angustior* Grun. — Valves narrower. V. H. T. N:o 139.

Fresh water: Stuttgart.

4. **A. Holstii** Cl. (1881). Lanceolate, with obtuse, subrostrate ends. L. 0,028; B. 0,009 mm. Upper V. with broad and lanceolate axial area. Striæ 14 in 0,01 mm. subradiate in the middle, parallel at the ends. Lower V. with very narrow axial area, dilated in the middle to a central area not reaching to the margin. Striæ 13 (middle) to 14 or 15 (ends) in 0,01 mm., radiate. D. from Greenl. and Arg. p. 13 Pl. XVI f. 6, 7.

Fresh water: Greenland, Kornak!

5. **A. marginulata** Grun. (1880). — Elliptical. L. 0,011 to 0,022; B. 0,005 to 0,008 mm. Upper V. with broad, lanceolate area. Striæ 24 in 0,01 mm. marginal. Lower V. with very narrow or indistinct axial area. Central area large, quadrate. Striæ 23 to 27 in 0,01 mm. — A. D. p. 21. V. H. Syn. Pl. XXVII f. 45, 46. *Achnanthidium delicatulum* Schum. Tatra p. 61 Pl. II f. 22?

Fresh water, alpine regions: Arctic America! Greenland! Norway (Dovre)! Russian Lapland (Fiskarehalfön).

6. **A. americana** Cl. (1893). Broadly elliptical with obtuse or subtruncate ends. L. 0,013; B. 0,006 mm. Upper V. with broad, lanceolate area and about 16 striæ in 0,01 mm., unilaterally interrupted. Lower V. with lanceolate area. Striæ about 17 in 0,01 mm., radiate and shortened in the middle of the valve. Diatomiste II Pl. III f. 17, 18.

Fresh water: Crane Pond, North America!

7. **C. biharensis** Pant. (1889). Elliptical. L. 0,023 to 0,026; B. 0,013 to 0,016 mm. Upper V. with lanceolate area, transversely dilated in the middle, and distinct median line. Striæ 11 to 12,5 in 0,01 mm. radiate. Lower V. with marginal, costate and radiate striæ, 8 to 12,5 in 0,01 mm. and with a row of parallel striæ (12,5 in 0,01 mm.) along the median line, separated from the marginal striæ by narrow lateral areas. — Pant. II p. 57 Pl. V f. 90, 94.

Marine: Bory, Hungary (Pant.).

Var. *minor* Pant. (1889). — L. 0,016; B. 0,08 mm. Upper V. with a row of short striæ, 11 in 0,01 mm., at some distance from the margin, and enclosing a broad, lanceolate area without median line. Lower V. with 11 striæ in 0,01 mm., reaching to the median line. Pant. II Pl. IV f. 75, 76.

Marine: Hungary, fossil (Pant.).

8. **C. pygmaea** Schum. (1864). — Broadly elliptical, with rounded ends. L. 0,007 to 0,011 mm. Striæ 15 in 0,01 mm. Upper V. with broad, lanceolate area. Lower V. with narrow area. - Preuss. D. I Nachtr. p. 19 Pl. II f. 11.

Brackish water: Baltic (Schum.).

9. **C. Pelta** A. S. (1874). — Broadly elliptical. L. 0,02; B. 0,015 mm. Upper V. with broad, lanceolate area. Striæ 12 in 0,01 mm. marginal. Lower V. with straight median line. — N. S. D. p. 93 Pl. III f. 17. Atl. CXCI, 6 to 9.

Marine: North Sea (A. S.).

10. **C. quarnerensis** Grun. (1862). Elliptical. L. 0,022 to 0,035; B. 0,012 to 0,016 mm. Upper V. with very large, usually irregularly punctate area. Striæ 9 in 0,01 mm., marginal, not

punctate. Lower V. with straight median line, ending near the margin. Its central pores somewhat distant. Axial area narrow; central large, orbicular. Striæ 8 to 9 in 0,01 mm. slightly radiate, not distinctly punctate. — *Rhaphoneis quarn.* GRUN. Verh. 1862 p. 381 Pl. IV f. 24. *C. quarn.* A. S. N. S. D. p. 93 Pl. III f. 15 to 16. Atl. CXCII. p. 20 to 24. *Navicula Orulum* A. S. N. S. D. Pl. II f. 12. *C. clavigera* O'MEARA M. J. (n. s.) VII Pl. VII f. 5?

Marine: Greenland! Spitsbergen! Finmark! North Sea! Mediterranean Sea! Adriatic! Fossil: Karand, Hungary (a small form L. 0,015 mm.)!

11. **A. Lilljeborgii** GRUN. (1881). — Lanceolate, obtuse. L. 0,017 to 0,046; B. 0,008 to 0,01 mm. Upper V. strongly silicious, with lanceolate axial area, one third of the breadth of the valve, with coarse scattered granules. Costæ 8 to 9 in 0,01 mm., slightly radiate, not punctate. Lower valve thin, with lanceolate narrow axial area. Striæ 12 in 0,01 mm., radiate in the middle, where some are of unequal length, parallel at the ends, finely punctate. — Bot. Centralbl. 1881 p. 68. CL. a. M. D. N:o 102. 311. Diatomiste II Pl. III f. 19, 20.

Marine: Grip and Bergen, Norway! Ile de Bréhat, the Channel (Grunow).

12. **C. Lagerheimii** CL. (1893). — Outline elliptical. L. 0,02 to 0,028; B. 0,01 to 0,015 mm. Upper V. with lanceolate axial area, having in its middle two longitudinal rows of coarse puncta. Striæ costate, 8 in 0,01 mm., the two median unilaterally united into a horseshoe-like marking. Lower V. delicate with straight median line. Central area uniting with very large lunate lateral areas. Striæ fine, 25 in 0,01 mm. — Diatomiste II Pl. III f. 21, 22. A. S. Atl. CXC, 46?

Fresh water: Ecuador, Sn. Nicolas, reg. trop.!

Actinoneis CL. N. G.

Outline rhomboid to lanceolate. Valves very dissimilar. Upper valve with strong costæ and narrow axial area. Lower valve delicate, with finely punctate and strongly radiate striæ. No marginal rim.

This group comprises a number of peculiar diatoms, the upper and lower valves being exceedingly dissimilar. The lower valves are finely punctate-striate and the striæ are usually alternately longer and shorter in the middle, and strongly radiate throughout. Valves of such a character are met with only in the group of *Naviculæ microstigmaticæ* and *heterostichæ*, and in a less degree in the *Naviculæ lineolatæ* (*Nar. Gastrum* for instance).

Artificial key.

1. { Upper valve with an unilateral horseshoe-shaped marking . . . . 2.
   { — — without — — — — . . . . 3.
2. { Lower valve with lateral areas . . . . *A. inopinata* CL.
   { — without — . . . . *A. heteromorpha* GRUN.
3. { Axial area of the upper valve lanceolate . . . . *A. Lorenziana* GRUN.
   { — — — — — narrow linear 4
4. { Valve apiculate or rostrate . . . . 5.
   { — not — — . . . . 6.
5. { Costæ 6 in 0,01 mm. . . . . *A. mammalis* CASTR.
   { — 10 — — . . . . *A. dispar* CL.
6. { Valve short, rhomboid . . . . *A. baldjikii* BRW.
   { — elongated — or lanceolate . . . . 7.
7. { Axial and central area of the lower valve indistinct . . . . *A. Clevei* GRUN.
   { — — — — — — — distinct . . . . 8.
8. { Axial area suddenly dilated to a fimbriate central area . . . . *A. danica* FLÖGEL.
   { — — lanceolate . . . . *A. bottnica* CL.

1. **A. Clevei** Grun. (1860). — Lanceolate, obtuse. L. 0,013 to 0,024; B. 0,006 to 0,009 mm. Upper V. with linear, narrow axial area (sometimes with rudimentary central nodule, Grun.). Costæ 9 to 11 in 0,01 mm., radiate; intermediate spaces distinctly punctate. Lower V. with very narrow axial area and very small or indistinct central area. Striæ 18 to 24 in 0,01 mm. strongly radiate, punctate. Median striæ more distant than the others. — A. D. p. 21. V. H. Syn. Pl. XXVII f. 5, 7.

Fresh water: Billingen (Westergötland, Sweden)! Gulf of Bothnia at Torneå!

2. **A. bottnica** Cl. (1891). — Lanceolate, subacute. L. 0,017 to 0,032; B. 0,005 to 0,01 mm. Upper V. with narrow, linear axial area, and parallel transverse costæ, 11 to 12 in 0,01 mm.; intermediate spaces coarsely punctate (puncta 18 in 0,01 mm.). Lower V. with lanceolate axial area. Striæ 17 (middle) to 25 in 0,01 mm., radiate throughout. Among the median striæ some shorter ones are frequently intercalated. — *A. Clevei var. bottn.* — Cl. D. of Finl. p. 52 Pl. III f. 4, 5.

Slightly brackish water: Gulf of Bothnia, at Torneå!

3. **A. dispar** Cl. (1891). — Elliptical or lanceolate, with rostrate ends. L. 0,023; B. 0,009 mm. Upper V. with linear, narrow axial area. Costæ parallel, 19 in 0,01 mm., not distinctly punctate. Median costæ abbreviate. Lower V. with indistinct axial area and orbicular central area. Striæ about 19 in 0,01 mm. strongly radiate throughout, and in the middle alternately longer and shorter. — D. of Finl. p. 52 Pl. III f. 2, 3.

Brackish water: Gulf of Bothnia, at Torneå!

4. **A. inopinata** Cl. (1893). — Rhomboid, acute. L. 0,027; B. 0,009 mm. Upper V. with narrow axial area and, unilaterally, a horseshoe-shaped marking in the middle. Costæ 12 in 0,01 mm. almost parallel, not punctate. Lower V. with narrow axial area and quadrate central area, uniting with lunate lateral areas. Striæ 14 in 0,01 mm., radiate, not distinctly punctate. — Diatomiste II p. 57 Pl. III f. 13, 14.

Marine: Baldjik (near Varna) fossil!

5. **A. heteromorpha** Grun. (1880). — Rhomboid to lanceolate. L. 0,046 to 0,08; B. 0,02 to 0,025 mm. Upper V. with narrow axial area and a horseshoe-shaped, unilateral marking in the middle. Costæ 8 to 10 in 0,01 mm., slightly radiate, indistinctly (finely Grun.) punctate. Lower V. with broad lanceolate central area. Striæ 7 (middle) to 9 (ends) in 0,01 mm. strongly radiate throughout. — A. D. p. 23. Cl. Diatomiste II Pl. III, 11, 12.

Fresh water: Demerara River!

6. **A. danica** Flögel (1873). — Rhomboid, acute. L. 0,036 to 0,05; B. 0,011 to 0,015 mm. Upper V. with narrow axial area. Costæ 8 to 13 in 0,01 mm. slightly radiate or almost parallel, alternating with fine lineolæ, twice as close as the costæ. Lower V. with narrow axial area and transverse central area, fimbriate at the ends. Striæ about 26 in 0,01 mm. strongly radiate throughout, in the middle alternately longer and shorter. — *C. danica* Flögel Pommerania D. p. 91 f. 14. *Ach. danica* Grun. A. D. p. 21 (1880). *A. heteropsis* Grun. Cl. M. D. N:o 154 (1878). *Stauroneis cornuta* Leud. Fortm. D. de Ceylon p. 37 Pl. III f. 36 (1879). *Schizostauron fimbriatum* Grun. Hedwigia 1867 p. 28.

Marine: North Sea (Grip in Norway)! Mediterranean Sea! Adriatic (Grun.), Florida!

Var. *major* Cl. L. 0,07 to 0,08; B. 0,03 to 0,035 mm. Upper V. with 9 subradiate and anastomosing costæ in 0,01 mm. Lower V. with 16 distinctly punctate striæ in 0,01 mm. — Pl. III f. 8, 9.

Marine: Baldjik, fossil!

7. **A. Lorenziana** Grun. (1862). — Lanceolate, subacute. L. 0,04 to 0,05; B. 0,022 mm. Upper V. with narrow lanceolate axial area, and strong, very slightly radiate costæ, 7 in 0,01

mm. Intercostal spaces finely punctate (puncta about 23 in 0,01 mm.), frequently apparently smooth. Lower V. with straight median line, very narrow axial area. Central area transversely dilated. Striæ in the middle 18, at the ends much closer, about 27 in 0,01 mm. — *Rhaphoneis Lorenziana* GRUN. Verh. p. 381. *Rhaph. fluminensis* GRUN. l. c. Pl. IV f. 5. V. H. Syn. Pl. XXXVI f. 31. *C. robusta* LEUD. FORTM. D. de Ceylon I f. 1? *Achn. danica* PANT. II Pl. IV f. 66? *Rhaphoneis Scutellum* PETIT D. de Ningpo Pl. III f. 6?

Marine: Barcelona. Balearic Islands! Adriatic (Grun.). Bab el Mandeb! Macassar Straits (Grove Coll.)!

This species is in the index to the plates in GRUNOW's monograph erroneously named *R. fluminensis*. I have seen an entire frustule in GROVE's collection, but the coarse structure of the upper valve made the examination of the lower very difficult. It is doubtless no *Rhaphoneis*, but a species nearly akin to *A. danica*.

8. **A. mammalis** CASTR. (1886). — Elliptical, apiculate. L. 0,045 to 0,053; B. 0,02 to 0,038 mm. Upper V. with narrow, linear axial area and slightly radiate costæ (6 in 0,01 mm.) alternating with double rows of small puncta, 11 to 14 in 0,01 mm. Lower V. with very narrow axial area. Central area transverse, widening outward, and laciniate. Striæ 21 (middle) to 25 (ends) in 0,01 mm. in the middle alternately longer and shorter, finely punctate. *Rhaphoneis mammalis* CASTR. D. Voy. Chall. p. 48 Pl. XXVI f. 3 (upper valve). *Stauroneis tahitiana* CASTR. l. c. Pl. XX f. 16 (lower valve)? *Stauroneis apiculata* GREG. Ed. N. Phil. J. X (n. s.) 1859 p. 30 Pl. IV f. 8 (lower valve)? *Stauroneis? obesa* GREV. T. Bot. Soc. V. VIII p. 237 Pl. III f. 12 (lower valve)? *A. mammalis* Icon. n. Pl. III f. 13, 14, 15.

Marine: Galapagos Islands! Macassar Straits (Grove Coll.)!

Var. *reticulata* CL. — Upper V. without rows of puncta between the costæ, but connected by longitudinal costæ, forming an irregular reticulum. — Pl. III f. 16.

Marine: Macassar Straits (Grove Coll.)! Galapagos Islands!

Of the var. *reticulata* I have seen, besides upper valves, an entire frustule, with distinct median line and transverse central area, but the coarse structure of the upper valve prevented the exact examination of the lower valve, which however seems to have the same structure as the type, although that of the upper valves is so different. The outline of both forms is exactly the same.

9. **A. baldjikii** BRW. (1859). — Rhomboid. L. 0,045; B. 0,03 mm. Upper V. with linear axial area and strong radiate costæ (7 in 0,01 mm.) without intercostal puncta, and in the middle alternately longer and shorter. Lower V. without axial area, central area small rounded. Striæ 10 to 11 in 0,01 mm., strongly radiate throughout, punctate, in the middle alternately longer and shorter. — *Odontidium Bald.* BRW. M. J. VII p. 180 Pl. IX f. 10. *Rhaphoneis Bald.* GRUN. Verh. 1862 p. 379. *Achn. bald.* GRUN. A. D. p. 21. PANT. III Pl. XIII f. 204. Icon. n. Pl. III f. 4, 5. *A. bald. var. subquadrata* PANT. III Pl. XIII f. 202. *Dimeregramma baldj.* WALKER and CHASE N. R. D. Pl. I f. 3; 1886.

Marine: Baldjik near Varna, fossil!

Microneis CL. N. G.

Valves small, linear to lanceolate, not very dissimilar. Upper valve with fine, parallel striæ and central, straight, narrow axial area. Lower valve with fine, almost parallel striæ. No marginal rim. Frustule genuflexed.

This group comprises a number of usually very small diatoms, partly stipitate, partly free and frequently genuflexed. Most of them inhabit fresh water, hot springs and brackish water. As to their affinities, they seem to be most nearly akin to the *Naviculæ minusculæ* and *Naviculæ mesolciæ*.

Artificial key.

1.	Valve biconstricted	*A. trinodis* Arn.
	— not constricted	2.
2.	Lower valve with a transverse fascia	3.
	— — without	4.
3.	Valve narrow, linear-lanceolate	*A. affinis* Grun.
	— narrow, elliptical	*A. hungarica* Grun.
	elliptical, rostrate	*A. exigua* Grun.
4.	Valve broad and short	5.
	— narrow and elongated	7.
5.	Striæ fine (25 in 0,01 mm.)	*A. Biasolettiana* Kütz.
	coarse (10 to 14 in 0,01 mm.)	6.
6.	Valve broadly lanceolate	*A. delicatula* Kütz.
	— elliptical	*A. Hauckiana* Grun.
7.	Striæ 12 to 16 in 0,01 mm.	8.
	— 21 or more	9.
8.	Valve lanceolate	*A. Hudsonis* Grun.
	— linear	*A. glabrata* Grun.
9.	Striæ 21 in 0,01 mm.	*A. exilis* Kütz.
	— 21 or more in 0,01 mm	10.
10.	Valve with parallel margins	11.
	— — slightly convex	12.
11.	Fresh water habitat	*A. linearis* W. Sm.
	Marine	*A. tæniata* Grun.
12.	Ends subcapitate	*A. microcephala* Kütz.
	— obtuse	*A. minutissima* Kütz.

1. **A. minutissima** Kütz. (1833). — Linear with somewhat attenuate and obtuse ends. L. 0,015 to 0,02; B. 0,003 to 0,004 mm. Upper V. with narrow, linear axial area. Striæ about 26 in 0,01 mm. parallel. Lower V. without axial area and with small, transverse central area. Striæ about 25 in 0,01 mm., stronger in the middle, slightly radiate. — Dec. N:o 75 (1833) according to Lagst. Grun. A. D. p. 23. V. H. Syn. p. 131 Pl. XXVII f. 35 to 38. *A. exilis* W. Sm. B. D. II Pl. XXXVII f. 303.

Fresh water: Sweden! Germany! England! Belgium (V. H.). probably common everywhere.

Var. *cryptocephala* Grun. — Smaller, with slightly capitate ends. L. 0,012 to 0,018; B. 0,002 to 0,003 mm. Striæ about 30 in 0,01 mm. — V. H. Syn. Pl. XXVII f. 41 to 44.

Fresh water: Finland!

2. **A. microcephala** Kütz. (1844). — Linear lanceolate, with subcapitate ends. L. 0,009 to 0,026; B. 0,003 mm. Upper valve with linear axial area and parallel striæ, 30—36 in 0,01 mm., the median striæ abbreviated. Lower V. without axial area and with small transverse central area. Striæ about 32 in 0,01 mm. slightly radiate. — *A. microcephalum* Kütz. Bac. 75 Pl. III f. 13, 19 (1844). Grun. A. D. p. 22. V. H. Syn. p. 131 Pl. XXVII f. 20 to 23. *Navicula pachycephala* Schum. Preuss. D. 2:te N. II f. 44?

Fresh water: Sweden (Helsingland)! Belgium (V. H.).

Achnanthidium microcephalum W. Sm. B. D. is probably *Anomœoneis exilis* Grun.

3. **A. linearis** W. Sm. (1855). — Linear with rounded ends. L. 0,01 to 0,02; B. 0,003 to 0,004 mm. Upper V. with narrow, linear axial area and parallel striæ, 24 to 27 in 0,01 mm. Lower V. without axial area and with small and transverse central area. Striæ 22 to 28 in 0,01 mm. — *Achnanthidium lin.* W. Sm. Ann. and Mag. Nat. Hist. 1855 p. 8 Pl. I f. 9. B. D. II p. 31 Pl. LXI f. 381. *Achnanthes lin.* Grun. A. D. p. 23. V. H. Syn. p. 131 Pl. XXVII f. 31, 32.

Fresh water: Norway (Dovre)! England! Belgium (V. H.).

Var. *pusilla* GRUN. (1880). — L. 0,013 to 0,017; B. 0,003 to 0,004 mm. Striæ 18 to 23 in 0,01 mm. — A. D. p. 23. V. H. Syn. Pl. XXVII f. 33, 34.

Fresh water: Greenland! Norway (Dovre)!

Var. *Jackii* RABH. (1861). - Broader. L. 0,015; B. 0,0045 mm. Striæ about 25 to 26 in 0,01 mm. — *Achnanthidium Jackii* RABH. Alg. E. N:o 1063. V. H. Syn. Pl. XXVII f. 24.

Fresh water: Baden (Rabh.)!

4. **A. exilis** KÜTZ. (1833). — Linear-lanceolate, with rounded ends. L. 0,015 to 0,03; B. 0,008 to 0,009 mm. Upper V. with narrow, axial area slightly dilated at the middle. Striæ parallel, about 21 in 0,01 mm. Lower V. without axial area and with small and rounded central area. Striæ slightly radiate throughout, in the middle 20, at the ends 27 in 0,01 mm. — Dec. N:o 12 (according to Lagst.). GRUN. A. D. p. 22. V. H. Syn. Pl. XXVII f. 16 to 19. *A. subhungaricum* GUTW. Materialy p. 29 Pl. I f. 26?

Fresh water: Belgium (V. H.), Germany!

5. **A. glabrata** GRUN. (1863). — Linear, with rounded ends. L. 0,012 to 0,046; B. 0,0068 to 0,013 mm. Upper V. with 12 to 13 striæ in 0,01 mm. Lower V. with 13 to 15 striæ in 0,01 mm, coarser in the middle than elsewhere. Frustule with broad connecting zone, and rudimentary diaphragms at the ends. — Verh. 1863 p. 146 Pl. IV f. 17. A. D. p. 22.

Marine: California (Cl. M. D. N:o 120). Pacific Ocean, New Zealand, North and South America (Grun.).

Var. *auklandica* GRUN. (1880). — L. 0,035 to 0,04 mm. Striæ 22 to 24 in 0,01 mm. Median striæ more distant, 10 to 11 in 0,01 mm. — A. D. p. 22.

Marine: Auckland (Grun.).

Akin to this species is probably the incompletely described and figured *Cymbosira minutula* GRUN. (Verh. 1863 p. 146 Pl. IV f. 27).

6. **A. Biasolettiana** KÜTZ. (1844). - Broadly lanceolate, with obtuse, rounded-truncate ends, somewhat gibbous in the middle. L. 0,055 to 0,031; B. 0,0065 to 0,007 mm. Upper V. with narrow linear axial area. Striæ parallel, about 25 in 0,01 mm. Lower V. without axial area; central area small, rounded. Striæ 25 in 0,01 mm. slightly radiate in the middle. — *Synedra Bias.* KÜTZ. Bac. p. 63 Pl. III f. 22. *Achn. Bias.* GRUN. A. D. p. 22. V. H. Syn. p. 130 Pl. XXVII f. 27, 28.

Fresh water: Hungary (Grun.). Belgium (V. H.).

Forma *minuta* GRUN. (1880). L. 0,012 to 0,013; B. 0,0045. Striæ 24 in 0,01 mm. — A. D. p. 22.

Fresh water: Triest (Grun.).

Var. *sublinearis* GRUN. — Linear, narrowed at the ends. L. 0,014; B. 0,004 mm. Striæ 17 to 22 in 0,01 mm. — V. H. T. N:o 11.

Brackish water: Belgium (V. H. T.).

7. **A. tæniata** GRUN. (1880). — Frustule scarcely arcuate. V. linear, with rounded ends. L. 0,02 to 0,03; B. 0,005 mm. Lower V. without areas. Striæ about 24 in 0,01 mm. more distant in the middle and closer towards the ends. -- A. D. p. 22 Pl. I f. 5.

Marine: Sea of Kara (Grun.).

8. **A. Hudsonis** GRUN. (1881). — Linear-lanceolate or subelliptical, with broad and obtuse, frequently subrostrate, ends. L. 0,015 to 0,035; B. 0,005 to 0,008 mm. Upper V. with narrow, linear axial area and parallel striæ, 15 to 16 in 0,01 mm. Lower V. with narrow axial area; small and orbicular or subrhomboidal central area. On each side of the central nodule is a lunate marking. Striæ 14 in 0,01 mm., slightly radiate. V. H. Syn. XXVII f. 25, 26.

Brackish water: Hudson River!

9. **A. trinodis** ARNOTT (1861). — Linear, gibbous in the middle and at the broad ends. L. 0,015 to 0,02; B. 0,005 mm. Upper V. with narrow axial area dilated in the middle to an almost orbicular, small central area. Striæ about 30 in 0,01 mm. parallel. Lower V. without distinct axial area and with small central area. Striæ about 30 in 0,01 mm. parallel. — *Achnanthidium trinode* PRITCH. Inf. p. 872 Pl. VIII f. 9. *Nav. trinodis* GRUN. Verh. 1860 p. 551 Pl. IV f. 8. *Rhoicosneis trin.* GRUN. Verh. 1863 p. 147. *Achn. trin.* V. H. Syn. Pl. XXVII f. 50 to 52.

Fresh water: England. Tyrol (Grun.).

10. **A. delicatula** KÜTZ. (1844). — Elliptic-lanceolate, frequently with subrostrate ends. L. 0,01 to 0,02; B. 0,005 to 0,011 mm. Upper V. with narrow, linear axial area. Striæ 14 to 15 in 0,01 mm. almost parallel. Lower V. with indistinct axial area and very small, orbicular central area. Striæ 17 to 19 in 0,01 mm. the median shorter. — *Achnanthidium delicatulum* KÜTZ. Bac. p. 75 Pl. III f. 21. *Achnanthes delic.* GRUN. A. D. p. 22, 1880. V. H. Syn. p. 130 Pl. XXVII f. 3, 4.

Brackish water: Greenland! Arctic America! North Sea! English Channel! Balearic Islands! San Francisco!

11. **A. Hauckiana** GRUN. (1880). — Elliptical to elliptic-lanceolate. L. 0,012 to 0,031; B. 0,006 to 0,008 mm. Upper V. with linear, narrow axial area. Striæ 10 to 12 in 0,01 mm., parallel. lower V. without axial area and with small central area. Striæ 10 to 13 in 0,01 mm. radiate. A. D. p. 21. *Achn. Hauckii* GRUN. V. H. Syn. Pl. XXVII f. 14, 15.

Hot springs and brackish water: Triest (Grun.), Canada! New Zealand! Tasmania! Cape Horn!

12. **A. affinis** GRUN. (1880). — Linear-lanceolate, obtuse. L. 0,015 to 0,023; B. 0,003 to 0,0035 mm. Upper V. with narrow, linear axial area. Striæ parallel 27 to 30 in 0,01 mm. Lower V. with narrow axial area. Central area a transverse fascia, reaching to the margin. Striæ about 30 in 0,01 mm. radiate throughout. — A. D. p. 20. V. H. Syn. p. 130 Pl. XXVII f. 39, 40.

Fresh water: Belgium (V. H.). Tasmania! North America, White Mountains!

Var. *jamalinensis* GRUN. (1880). — L. 0,037; B. 0,005 mm. Striæ of the lower V. 16 in 0,01 mm. — *A. hungarica var.? jamal.* GRUN. A. D. p. 20.

Marine(?): Sea of Kara (Grun.).

13. **A. exigua** GRUN. (1880). — Broadly elliptic-lanceolate, with rostrate, obtuse ends. L. 0,013 to 0,017; B. 0,005 to 0,006 mm. Upper V. with narrow, linear axial area. Striæ about 22 in 0,01 mm. parallel. Lower V. with very narrow axial area. Central area a transverse fascia, reaching to the margin. Striæ about 25 in 0,01 mm. slightly radiate throughout. — *Stauroneis exilis* KÜTZ. Bac. p. 105 Pl. XXX f. 21. SCHUM. Preuss. D. II Nachtr. Pl. II f. 59. *Ach. exigua* GRUN. A. D. p. 21. V. H. Syn. Pl. XXVII f. 29, 30.

Fresh water, hot springs: Sweden (Hernösand, interglacial deposit)! Germany (Berlin)! Brazil! Ecuador! Surinam! Java! New Zealand! Hawaii!

14. **A. hungarica** GRUN. (1863). — Narrow elliptical or linear-lanceolate with subcuneate ends. L. 0,02 to 0,03; B. 0,006 to 0,007 mm. Upper V. with narrow axial area, in the middle dilated to a narrow, short, transverse central area. Striæ about 21 in 0,01 mm., parallel. Lower V. with narrow axial area. Central area a broad fascia. Striæ about 21 in 0,01 mm., slightly radiate. — *Achnanthidium hungaricum* GRUN. Verh. 1863 p. 146 Pl. IV f. 8. *Achnanthes hung.* A. D. p. 20. V. H. Syn. p. 130 Pl. XXVII f. 1, 2. *Achnanthidium neglectum* SCHUM. Preuss. D. II Nachtr. p. 54 Pl. I f. 17?

Fresh water: Sweden (Grun.), Belgium (V. H.). Hungary (Grun.). Illinois! Brazil! Ecuador! Australian Alps (Rieva Lagoon)!

To this group may belong *Achnanthes Gregoryana* GREV. (M. J. VII p. 84 Pl. VI f. 13, 14) if this form, of which the zonal view is figured, be really an *Achnanthes*, but it appears more probable that it may represent an arcuate *Gyrosigma* perhaps *G. arcticum*.

Achnanthidium (Kütz. 1844) Heib. 1863.

Outline more or less linear, rarely elliptical. Valves dissimilar. Upper valve without central nodule and median line, but with narrow, frequently asymmetrical axial area, not costate (except A. groenlandica). Structure transverse rows of puncta (except A. groenlandica). Lower valve with straight, central median line. Central nodule usually stauroid. Central area a transverse fascia. Structure: transverse rows of puncta. Frustule genuflexed, without rim. Connecting zone usually with longitudinal rows of short striæ.

Cell-contents (of *A. lanceolata*) a single chromatophore-plate along the inside of the upper valve or (as in *A. brevipes*) two plates, deeply sinuose in the middle along the inside of the connecting zone. In conjugation one cell (*A. brevipes*) gives origin according to Lüders to one auxospore (Pfitz. Bau und Entw. p. 85).

This group comprises most of the stipitate species of *Achnanthes* of authors. They agree in outline with the true Achnanthes, which have an entirely different structure. Whether the genus formed by me is natural is somewhat doubtful, the cell-contents of *A. lanceolata* being very similar to those of *Cocconeis*, and those of *A. brevipes* agreeing with those of *Navicula*. On the other hand *A. groenlandica* differs in the costate upper valve and is remarkable for the rudimentary diaphragms at the ends of the frustule, which point to some affinity with the Tabellariæ (*Entopyla*). The exact position of this group in a natural system is impossible to define at present.

Artificial key [1]).

1.	Margin of the upper valve with a horseshoe-shaped mark	*A. lanceolata* Bréb. (*A. Peragalli* Bréb. a. Hérib.).
	— — — — without — — —	2.
2.	Margin crenulated	*A. crenulata* Grun. (*A. brevipes var. subcrenulata*).
	— not —	3.
3.	Upper valve with transverse costæ	*A. groenlandica* Cl.
	— — — — rows of puncta	4.
4.	Axial area of the upper valve central	5.
	— — — — excentric	6.
5.	Valve linear	*A. mesogongyla* Grun.
	— lanceolate	*A. margaritarum* Cl.
6.	Valve centrally gibbous	*A. inflata* Grun.
	— — not —	7.
7.	Valve small and constricted	*A. coarctata* Bréb.
	— — — elliptical or large, and constricted, or not	*A. brevipes* Ag.

1. **A. margaritarum** Cl. (1893). — V. not arcuate, lanceolate, with slightly protracted ends. L. 0,05 to 0,06; B. 0,02 mm. Upper V. with central, narrow axial area. Striæ 10 (middle) to 13 (ends) in 0,01 mm. very slightly radiate, composed of distinct puncta, arranged in straight, longitudinal rows, 15 in 0,01 mm. Lower V. with straight median line, indistinct, axial and small, orbicular central area. Striæ 10 (middle) to 15 (ends) in 0,01 mm. composed of puncta, arranged in straight longitudinal rows, 13 in 0,01 mm. — Diatomiste II p. 57 Pl. III f. 9, 10.

Marine: Pearl Islands (near Java?)!

This remarkable species is not akin to any other. The upper valve has some resemblance of *Rhaphoneis amphiceros*.

2. **A. lanceolata** Bréb. (1849). — Narrow, elliptic-lanceolate to broadly elliptical, with rounded, obtuse, rarely rostrate, ends. L. 0,017 to 0,035; B. 0,005 to 0,008 mm. Upper V. with

[1]) The incompletely known *Ach. hercata* Leud. Fortm., *A. agglutinata* Grun. and *Cocconeis perpusilla* Pant. not included.

linear, central axial area, on one side of which, in the middle of the valve, there is a horseshoe-shaped area. Striæ 13 in 0,01 mm. almost parallel, coarsely punctate. Lower V. with narrow axial area and broad, quadrate or rectangular central area. Striæ 14 in 0,01 mm., slightly radiate, coarsely punctate. — *Achnanthidium lanceolatum* KÜTZ. Sp. Alg. p. 54. W. SM. B. D. II Pl. XXXVII f. 301. *Achnanthes lanc.* GRUN. A. D. p. 23. V. H. Syn. p. 13) Pl. XXVII f. 8 to 11. *Stauroneis truncata* SCHUM. Preuss. D. I Nachtr. p. 22 f. 28.

Fresh water: Throughout Europe! Amsterdam Island! Tasmania! New Zealand! Australia (North Australia, Daintree River, Australian Alps)! Illinois! Ecuador!

Var. *dubia* GRUN. (1880). Broadly lanceolate. L. 0,015 to 0,017; B. 0,007 to 0,0072 mm. Striæ 13 to 14 in 0,01 mm. A. D. p. 23. V. H. Syn. p. 132 Pl. XXVII f. 12, 13.

Fresh water: Belgium (V. H.), Austria (Grun.)!

Var. *elliptica* CL. (1891). — Elliptical. L. 0,012 to 0,016; B. 0,007 to 0,009 mm. Upper V. with 16 striæ in 0,01 mm. — D. of Finland p. 51 Pl. III f. 10, 11.

Fresh water: Abo in Finland!

Var. *Haynaldii* SAABSCH. (1881). — Inflated in the middle, with rostrate-capitate ends. L. 0,025 to 0,027; B. 0,007 mm. Striæ 16 in 0,01 mm., indistinctly punctate. — *Achn. Haynaldii* SAABSCH. Spec. Phyc. Aequat. p. 8 (according to De Toni Syll. p. 478). CL. Diatomiste II Pl. VII f. 14.

Fresch water: Ecuador, Antisana!

3. **A. Peragalli** BRUN. a. HÉRIB. (1893). — Broadly elliptical, inflated, with protracted apiculate or subcapitate ends. L. 0,012 to 0,016; B. 0,006 to 0,008 mm. Upper V. with narrow, linear and central axial area, on one side of which in the middle of the valve there is a horseshoe-shaped area. Striæ 17 in 0,01 mm. slightly radiate. Lower V. with large, outward dilated central area. Striæ very fine and oblique. — D. d'Auvergne p. 50 Pl. I f. 4.

Fresh water: Puy de Dôme, living (Brun. Coll.)!

A very small, but distinct species, resembling *A. lanc. var. Haynaldii.*

4. **A. mesogongyla** GRUN. (1879). — Narrow, elongated, inflated in the middle, with rounded ends. L. 0,08 to 0,09; B. 0,013 to 0,014 mm. Upper V. with central, narrow axial area and transverse, coarsely punctate striæ, 10 in 0,01 mm. (puncta 18 in 0,01 mm.). Lower V. with broad central fascia. Striæ 11 in 0,01 mm. punctate; puncta 18 in 0,01 mm. — CL. M. D. N:o 193. A. D. p. 19. Icon. nost. Pl. III f. 2.

Fresh water: Brazil!

5. **A. coarctata** BRÉB. (1855). — Linear, slightly constricted in the middle, with broad, truncate ends. L. 0,04; B. 0,008 mm. Upper V. with very excentric, narrow, frequently inframarginal, axial area. Striæ 11 to 14 in 0,01 mm. punctate. Lower V. with broad central fascia. Striæ 12 to 15 in 0,01 mm. slightly radiate, punctate. — *Achnanthidium coarct.* Ann. Mag. Nat. Hist. [2] Vol. XV p. 8 f. 10. W. SM. B. D. Pl. LXI f. 379. *Achnanthes coarct* GRUN. A. D. p. 20. V. H. Syn. p. 130 Pl. XXVI f. 17 to 20. *Achnanthidium coarct. var. elineata* LAGST. Spitsb. D. p. 49 Pl. I f. 16. *Achn. binodis* EHR. M. G. Pl. XXXIV, 5, B, 12.

Fresh water, moist earth, on mosses: Spitsbergen! Beeren Eiland (Lagst.). Arctic America! Sweden (Upsala)! England! France! Belgium (V. H.).

6. **A. inflata** KÜTZ. (1844). — Elongated, gibbous in the middle, with rounded capitate ends. L. 0,045 to 0,065; B. 0,015 to 0,018 mm. Upper V. with very excentric axial area. Striæ 9 to 10 in 0,01 mm. parallel, composed of coarse puncta, about 9 in 0,01 mm. Lower V. with broad fascia. Striæ about 10 in 0,01 mm. slightly radiate; puncta about 10 in 0,01 mm. — *Stauroneis inflata* KÜTZ. Bac. 105 Pl. XXX f. 22. *Achnanthes ventricosa* EHR. M. Geol. p. 226. *Monogramma ventr.* EHR. M. Geol. Pl. I. II. f. 9, Pl. III f. 18, 19, *b, c.* GREV. T. Bot. Soc. Edinb. Vol. VIII

p. 439 Pl. VI f. 6, 7. *Achnanthes inflata* GRUN. A. D. p. 19. *Navicula elata* LEUD. FORTM. D. de Ceylon Pl. III f. 28. *Achn. brevipes var. tumidula* GRUN. A. D. p. 19.

Fresh water, in tropical and subtropical regions: South Tyrol (Grun.). Pompeii (Grun.), Java! Australia! Tasmania! New Zealand! Tahiti! Brazil! Ecuador! Cuba (Grun.). Bourbon and Mauritius (Ehb.).

Var. *Smithiana* GREV. (1866). — Ends cuneate. Striæ coarser. — *Monogramma Smithiana* GREV. T. Bot. Soc. Edinb. Vol. VIII Pl. VI f. 3 to 5.

Fresh water: Mauritius and New Hebrides (Grun.). Cameroon, Africa!

7. **A. brevipes** AG. (1824). — Linear-lanceolate, frequently slightly constricted in the middle, with cuneate ends. Upper V. with somewhat excentric axial area and transverse rows of coarse puncta forming irregular longitudinal rows. Lower V. with indistinct axial area. Central nodule transversely dilated into a stauros, reaching to the margin. Striæ slightly radiate. Frustule genuflexed, stipitate. Connecting zone finely and transversely striate.

Var. *parvula* KÜTZ. (1844). — Elliptical. L. 0,01 to 0,02; B. 0,005 to 0,007 mm. Upper V. with 12 to 18 striæ in 0,01 mm. Lower V. with about 15 striæ in 0,01 mm. — *A. parvula* KÜTZ. Bac. p. 76 Pl. XXI f. 5. GRUN. A. D. p. 19. V. H. Syn. p. 129 Pl. XXVI f. 25 to 28. *A. pachypus* MONT. Ann. Sc. nat. (2) T. VIII p. 348 (accord. to Kütz.). KÜTZ. Bac. p. 76 Pl. XXI f. 2.

Brackish water: Trondhjem! England! Ostend (V. H.), Calvados! Galapagos Islands!

Var. *Leudugeri* TEMP. a. BRUN (1889). Broadly lanceolate with obtuse ends. L. 0,075 to 0,095; B. 0,03 to 0,037 mm. Striæ of the lower V. 6 in 0,01 mm. — *Achn. Leud.* D. foss. du Japon p. 9 Pl. IX f. 11.

Marine: Japan, fossil (Temp. Br.).

Var. *typica* CL. — Linear with cuneate ends, frequently constricted in the middle. L. 0,07 to 0,1; B. 0,02 mm. Upper V. with slightly excentric axial area. Striæ 7 to 8 in 0,01 mm. coarsely punctate; puncta 7 to 8 in 0,01 mm. forming undulating longitudinal rows. Lower V. with indistinct axial area. Central area a narrow fascia, reaching to the margin. Striæ 7 to 9 in 0,01 mm. slightly radiate and coarsely punctate. — *A. brevipes* AG. Syst. Alg. p. 1. KÜTZ. Dec. N:o 77, 78 (according to Lagst.) 1833. W. SM. B. D. II Pl. XXXVII f. 301. V. H. Syn. p. 129 Pl. XXVI f. 10 to 12. *A. salina* KÜTZ. Linnaea 1838 p. 72.

Brackish water: Arctic America! Greenland! Spitsbergen! Finmark! North Sea! Baltic! Caspian Sea (Grun.), Japan, fossil! Monterey and Mauritius (Grun. forma contracta A. D. p. 19).

Var. *marginata* CL. — Rhomboid-lanceolate, subacute. L. 0,12; B. 0,05 mm. Upper V. with excentric, linear axial area and transverse striæ, 7 in 0,01 mm., composed of large quadrate alveoli. Parallel to the margin and close to it, is an elevated line or keel. Connecting zone with longitudinal rows of coarse puncta, 6 to 7 in 0,01 mm.

Marine: Madagascar!

Var. *capensis* CL. — Narrow, linear lanceolate, tapering from the middle. L. 0,05; B. 0,01 mm. Upper V. with very excentric axial area and 9 granulate striæ in 0,01 mm. Lower V. with 11 almost parallel striæ in 0,01 mm. composed of about 13 puncta in 0,01 mm.

Marine: Cape of Good Hope!

Var. *subcrenulata* CL. (1891). — Narrow elliptic-linear, obtuse, with crenulated margin. L. 0,047; B. 0,012 mm. Upper V. with very excentric axial area and parallel striæ, 8 in 0,01 mm., composed of large puncta (7 to 8 in 0,01 mm.). Lower V. with 11 striæ in 0,01 mm. Puncta 11 to 12 in 0,01 mm. — Diatomiste I p. 50 Pl. IX f. 5, 6.

Brackish water: New Guinea!

Var. *intermedia* KÜTZ. (1833). — Linear-elliptical, with rounded ends. L. 0,03 to 0,05; B. 0,01 to 0,011 mm. Striæ about 10 in 0,01 mm. — *Achn. int.* KÜTZ. Dec. N:o 21 (according to Lagst.). LAGST. Öfvers. K. Sv. Vet.-Akad. Förh. X f. 2 *a*. *A. subsessilis* KÜTZ. Dec. N:o 42 (1833) according to Lagst. W. Sm. B. D. II Pl. XXXVII f. 302. V. H. Syn. p. 129 Pl. XXVI f. 21 to 24. *A. multiarticulata* Ag. Consp. p. 59 (1832). *A. capensis* Kütz. Bac. p. 76 Pl. XXI f. 1 (1844). *Achnanthidium arcticum* Cl. D. Arctic Sea p. 25 Pl. IV f. 22 (1873). *Achn. Lóczyi* Pant. II p. 57 Pl. XII f. 217 (1889).

Brackish and marine: Finmark! Coasts of Britain (Sm.). North Sea! Baltic! Caspian Sea (Grun.). Mediterranean Sea! Amsterdam Island (Grun.).

Var. *seriata* Ag. (1827). — Frustules concatenated into Diatoma-like series. Valves elongated, narrow, frequently broader at one end than at the other. — *A. seriata* Ag. Bot. Zeitung 1827. Consp. p. 60. *Cymbosira Agardhii* Kütz. Bac. p. 77 Pl. XX f. 3 (1844). *A. ser. var.? cuneata* Grun. A. D. p. 19. *A. subsessilis var. cuerris* Petit Mém. de la Soc. de Cherb. p. 207 Pl. XXIII Pl. III f. 2?

Marine: Adriatic (Kütz), Java! Labuan! Pacific Ocean (Grun.).

Var. *angustata* Grev. (1859). Elongated, narrow. L. 0,07 to 0,15; B. 0,005 to 0,01 mm. Striæ 10 to 15 in 0,01 mm. *A. angustata* Grev. M. J. VII p. 163 Pl. VIII f. 9. *A. pennata* Cl. Vega p. 504 Pl. XXXV f. 2.

Marine: Californian guano (Grev.). Ceylon!

Greville figures two coherent frustules in the zonal view, for which reason the identificatation with *A. pennata* Cl., the figure of which represents a lower valve, is somewhat doubtful.

Var.? *pennæformis* Grev. (1865). — Frustule biarcuate, long and narrow. Lower valve linear obtuse. L. 0,15; B. 0,01 mm. Striæ parallel, 12 in 0,01 mm. punctate, puncta 13 in 0,01 mm. *Achnanthes pennæf.* Grev. T. Bot. Soc. Edinb. Vol. VIII p. 438 Pl. VI f. 11 to 13.

Marine: Sandwich Islands!

Var. *indica* Brun (1893). — Centrally constricted, with cuneate ends. L. 0,06 to 0,075; B. 0,02 mm. Striæ and puncta 8 to 9 in 0,01 mm. — *Achnanthes indica* Brun Diatomiste I p. 173 Pl. XXIV f. 14.

Marine: Rodriguez (Brun).

A. brevipes is an exceedingly variable species, on the varieties of which a great number of new species, usually imperfectly described and figured, has been founded. The characteristics, by which these reputed species differ, are such trifling ones as the shape of the valve, the size of the stipes, the excentricity of the axial area of the upper valve, etc. But as all these characteristics are very variable, I am unable to separate as species the above named varieties. *A. inflata*, *A. crenulata* and *A. coarctata*, are so nearly allied to *A. brevipes* that it is difficult to state any stable characteristics for their distinction. *Achn. parallela* Castr. (Voy. Challenger p. 41 Pl. XIX f. 11) and *A. kerguelensis* Castr. (l. c. Pl. XX f. 41) would seem to belong to the varieties of *A. brevipes*, were not the area of the upper valves represented as central, and the striæ of the latter so fine.

8. **C. perpusilla** Pant. (1889). V. broadly lanceolate. L. 0,015; B. 0,008 mm. Lower V. with narrow axial area. Central area a narrow transverse fascia, reaching to the margin. Median line straight. Striæ 17,5 in 0,01 mm. punctate, slightly radiate throughout. Upper V.? Pant. II p. 58 Pl. IV f. 73.

Marine: Hungary, fossil (Pant.).

A small form, unknown to me, resembling a small variety of *Achnanthes subsessilis*.

9. **A. agglutinata** Grun. (1880). — V. narrow, lanceolate. L. 0,022 to 0,028; B. 0,004 to 0,005 mm. Upper V. with 13 punctate striæ in 0,01 mm. Lower V. with 15 punctate striæ in 0,01 mm. — A. D. p. 19.

Marine: Triest.

This, to me unknown form, resembles according to Grunow *A. subsessilis*, but occurs attached by the lower valve to seaweeds, not on gelatinous stalks as *A. subsessilis*.

10. **A. baccata** Leud. Fortm. (1879). — Linear, with broad, rounded ends. L. 0,1; B. 0,025 mm. Lower V. with wide and irregular axial area. Central area large and irregularly transverse. Striæ 7 in 0,01 mm. formed of large puncta, arranged in undulating, longitudinal rows. — *Stauroneis baccata* Leud. D. de Ceylan p. 37 Pl. III f. 35. *Achnanthes curvata* Leud. l. c. Pl. I f. 5? *A. bacc.* Icon. n. Pl. III f. 3.

Marine: Colombo, Ceylon (Le Tourneur Coll.)!

11. **A. groenlandica** Cl. (1873). — Linear with rounded ends. L. 0,04 to 0,06; B. 0,005 to 0,007 mm. Upper V. with narrow axial area and strong costate striæ, 1,5 to 6 in 0,01 mm. crossed by a longitudinal line. Lower V. with indistinct axial area. Central area a broad transverse fascia. Central pores of the median line somewhat distant. Striæ 5 to 6 in 0,01 mm. slightly radiate, formed by 3 to 4 large, distant puncta. Frustule genuflexed. Connecting zone with a row of puncta, 6 to 7 in 0,01 mm. Lower valve with rudimentary diaphragms. — *Achnanthidium groenlandicum* Cl. A. D. p. 25 Pl. IV f. 23. *Achnanthes gr.* Grun. A. D. p. 20. Cl. Vega p. 460 Pl. XXXV f. 3.

Marine: Arctic America! Greenland! Spitsbergen! Finmark! Behrings Island!

12. **A. crenulata** Grun. (1880). — Elliptical to elliptic-linear, obtuse, with crenulated margin (2,5 to 3 undulations in 0,01 mm.). L. 0,034 to 0,076; B. 0,015 to 0,02 mm. Upper V. with very excentric and narrow axial area. Striæ parallel, 6 to 6,5 in 0,01 mm. coarsely punctate; puncta 6 to 7 in 0,01 mm. Lower V. with narrow but distinct axial area. Central area a transverse fascia. Striæ 6 to 7 in 0,01 mm. slightly radiate throughout, punctate; puncta 6 to 7 in 0,01 mm. — A. D. p. 20. Cl. Diatomiste I p. 50 Pl. IX f. 3, 4.

Fresh or brackish water: New Guinea! Samoa! Australia (Daintree River)!

Achnanthes Bory S:t Vincent (1822).

Outline linear to elliptical or lanceolate. Upper valve with central and narrow axial area, without central nodule and median line. Lower valve with median line and stauroid central nodule. Axial area narrow. Structure similar in both valves: transverse costæ, alternating with double rows of small puncta, arranged in decussating rows. Frustule genuflexed, stipitate. No annulus. Connecting zone transversely striate. The cell-contents of *A. longipes* have a number of scattered, rounded or elongated chromatophore-granules.

Achnanthes longipes with cell-contents. 500 times magnified.

Achnanthes, limited as above, has a great resemblance to *Achnanthidium*, as regards the manner of living and the form of the frustule and the valves, but the structure is different. Of the affinities of *Achnanthes* little can be stated. The structure of *A. javanica* and of *A. bengalensis*, which, according to Grunow, have longitudinal lines, has some resemblance to that of *Scoliotropis* and *Gomphoneis*. *Mastogloia Grevillei* has a similar structure, but differs greatly in other respects. There is also some resemblance to *Mastoneis*, the central nodule of which also forms a stauros, although short.

1. **A. longipes** C. Ag. (1832). — Linear-elliptical, with broad, rounded and frequently cuneate ends, usually slightly constricted in the middle. L. 0,005 to 0,18; B. 0,012 to 0,027 mm. Upper V. convex. Axial area a central, linear silicious rib. Costæ 7 to 8 in 0,01 mm. parallel.

alternating with double rows of puncta, 9 in 0,01 mm. Lower V. with almost indistinct axial area. Central nodule a narrow stauros, not bifid at the margin. Costæ 6,5 in 0,01 mm. puncta 10 in 0,01 mm. Connecting zone finely striate. — Consp. cr. p. 58. KÜTZ. Bac. p. 77 Pl. XX f. 1. PRITCH Inf. Pl. VII f. 42. W. SM. B. D. II p. 26 Pl. XXXV f. 300; Pl. XXXVI f. 300. V. H. Syn. p. 129 Pl. XXVI f. 13 to 16. *A. Carmichaeli* GREV. according to Kütz.

Brackish water and marine: Coasts of Britain (Sm.). Baltic! Mansfelder Seen in Saxony! North Sea! Adriatic! Mediterranean Sea! Belgium (V. H.). S:t Pauls Island (Grun.).

2. **A. javanica** GRUN. (1878). — Broadly elliptical to lanceolate, gradually tapering to the obtuse or subacute ends. L. 0,03 to 0,08; B. 0,013 to 0,025 mm. Upper V. with narrow axial area. Costæ 5 to 6 in 0,01 mm., puncta 11 to 12 in 0,01 mm. Near the margin are two obsolete longitudinal lines (according to Grunow). Lower V. with very narrow axial area. Central nodule transversely dilated into a stauros, bifid near the margin. Costæ 6 to 7 in 0,01 mm. radiate in the middle and transverse at the ends, alternating with double rows of puncta, 13 in 0,01 mm. CL. M. D. N:o 147. A. D. p. 18.

Marine: Java! China!

Var. *rhombica* GRUN. — Rhomboid-lanceolate. L. 0,088; B. 0,035 mm. Costæ of the lower V. 4,5 to 5 in 0,01 mm. — A. D. p. 18.

Marine: Java!

3. **A. bengalensis** GRUN. (1880). Linear with rounded ends. L. 0,028 to 0,05; B. 0,008 to 0,009 mm. Upper V. with narrow axial area and 5 to 6 costæ in 0,01 mm., crossed between the area and the margin by a longitudinal line. Puncta about 13 in 0,01 mm. At each end of the valve is a small blank spot on both sides of the area. Lower V. with narrow axial area and narrow stauros. Costæ 8 in 0,01 mm., alternating with double rows of puncta, about 20 in 0,01 mm. — A. D. p. 18.

Brackish water: Bengal (Grun.).

Achn. costata GREV. (T. Bot. Soc. Edinb. Vol. VIII p. 438 Pl. VI f. 8 to 10: 1866) figured as having a single row of puncta between the costæ, is probably an allied form.

Imperfectly known species, which cannot, for the present, be admitted in the above monograph.[1])

Cocconeis æmula A. S. Atl. CXCIV f. 18.

C. arcta A. S. l. c. CXCI f. 1 seems to be a new species belonging to Microneis (nearest to *A. Hudsonis*), but the figure does not shew the finer structure.

C. biflexa A. S. Atl. CXCIII f. 25.

C. biradiata BR. A. S. Atl. CXC f. 1 an indeterminable, probably corroded, upper valve.

C. blandicula A. S. Atl. CXCII f. 17.

C. campechiana GRUN. A. S. Atl. CXCII f. 1.

C. cincta A. S. Atl. CXC f. 38 (Campylodiscus sp.?).

C. coarctata A. S. Atl. CXC f. 37.

C. comis A. S. Atl. CXCII f. 2.

C. conterminа A. S. Atl. CXCVI f. 21.

C. discrepans A. S. Atl. CXCIII f. 26 to 28.

C. dispar A. S. Atl. CXCIII f. 41.

C. egena A. S. Atl. CXCIII f. 24.

C. Febigeri BR. A. S. Atl. CXCIII f. 58 (*Diploneis microtatos* PANT.).

[1]) No reference has been taken to the plates CXCVII—VIII of A. S. Atl

C. glacialis A. S. Atl. CLXXXIX f. 22. Seems to be a Mastogloia, indeterminable for the want of structure.

C. Grovei A. S. Atl. CXCIV f. 3.

C. Granovii A. S. l. c. f. 20.

C. illustris A. S. Atl. CXCII f. 32. resembles *Mastogloia Horvathiana*, but has no central nodule.

C. insueta A. S. Atl. l. c. f. 3.

C. japonica A. S. Atl. CXC f. 30 appears to be a var. of *C. Scutellum*.

C. moronensis A. S. Atl. CXCIV f. 9.

C. notabilis A. S. Atl. l. c. f. 13 allied with *C. pellucida var. mankoorensis*.

C. nutans A. S. Atl. CXCVI f. 9.

C. Pensacolæ A. S. Atl. CXCII f. 4.

C. præcellens A. S. Atl. CXCVI f. 1. Doubtful whether the same as Pantocsek's species.

C. Reichelttii A. S. Atl. CXCII f. 37 probably *C. Placentula*.

C. rivalis A. S. Atl. CXCIV f. 4.

C. Schleinitzii Jan. A. S. Atl. CXC f. 5, 6.

C. semipolita A. S. Atl. CXCII f. 18.

C. vetusta A. S. Atl. CXCVI f. 8.

Index.

PLATE I.

Fig. 1. Amphipleura pellucida var. Truani V. H. — Spain, $^{500}/_{1}$
2. Pleurosigma præ-longum CL. — Greenland, $^{225}/_{1}$
3, 4. Gyrosigma arcticum CL. var. — Kerguelens Land, $^{500}/_{1}$
5. G. sciotense Sull. — Hudson River, $^{500}/_{1}$
6. G. diaphanum CL. — Ile de Bréhat, $^{500}/_{1}$
7. Caloneis Beccariana GRUN. — Bengal, $^{1000}/_{1}$
8. C. Anderssonii CL. — Galapagos Islands, $^{500}/_{1}$
9. C. Musca var. eurynota CL. — Rio Janeiro, $^{500}/_{1}$
10. C. Hardmaniana CL. — Campeachy Bay, $^{500}/_{1}$
11. N. Omicron CL. — Galapagos Islands, $^{500}/_{1}$
12. Pinnularia cardinaliculus CL. — Waltham, Mass.
13. P. spitsbergensis CL. Spitsbergen, $^{1000}/_{1}$
14. P. constricta CL. — Galapagos Islands, $^{500}/_{1}$
15. P. lignitica CL. — Japan, $^{1000}/_{1}$
16. P. Aestuarii CL. Connecticut, $^{500}/_{1}$
17. Navicula My CL. — China, $^{1000}/_{1}$
18. Pinnularia Balfouriana GRUN. — Aberdeen [1]), $^{750}/_{1}$
19. Navicula brasiliensis GRUN. var. bicuneata CL. — Pensacola, $^{500}/_{1}$
20. Pinnularia paulensis GRUN. — Demerara River, $^{1000}/_{1}$
21. P. trigonocephala CL. Big Lake, Cal., $^{500}/_{1}$
22. P. major var. asymmetrica CL. — Waltham Mass., $^{500}/_{1}$
23. P. flexuosa CL. — Crane Pond, $^{500}/_{1}$
24. P. Claviculus var. javanica CL. — Java, $^{1000}/_{1}$
25. Navicula concilians CL. — Honolulu, $^{500}/_{1}$
26. N. Schulzii Kain var. californica CL. — San Pedro, Cal., $^{500}/_{1}$
27. N. Stercus muscarum CL. — China, $^{500}/_{1}$
28. N. glacialis CL. — Matotchin Scharr, $^{1000}/_{1}$
29. N. Chi CL. — Balearic Islands, $^{1000}/_{1}$
30. N. Rhaphoneis GRUN. Samoa, $^{1000}/_{1}$
31. N. Amicorum GRUN. — Samoa, $^{1000}/_{1}$
32. N. subalata GRUN. — Seychelles, $^{500}/_{1}$
33. N. Formenteræ CL. — Balearic Islands, $^{1000}/_{1}$
34. N. Phi CL. — Seychelles, $^{1000}/_{1}$
35. N. centroster CL. — Madagascar, $^{1000}/_{1}$
36. N. pennata A. S. var. maxima CL. — Naples, $^{500}/_{1}$
37. N. leptostigma EHB. — Oregon, $^{1000}/_{1}$
38. N. annulata GRUN. — Demerara River, $^{500}/_{1}$

[1]) From a sketch sent by GRUNOW.

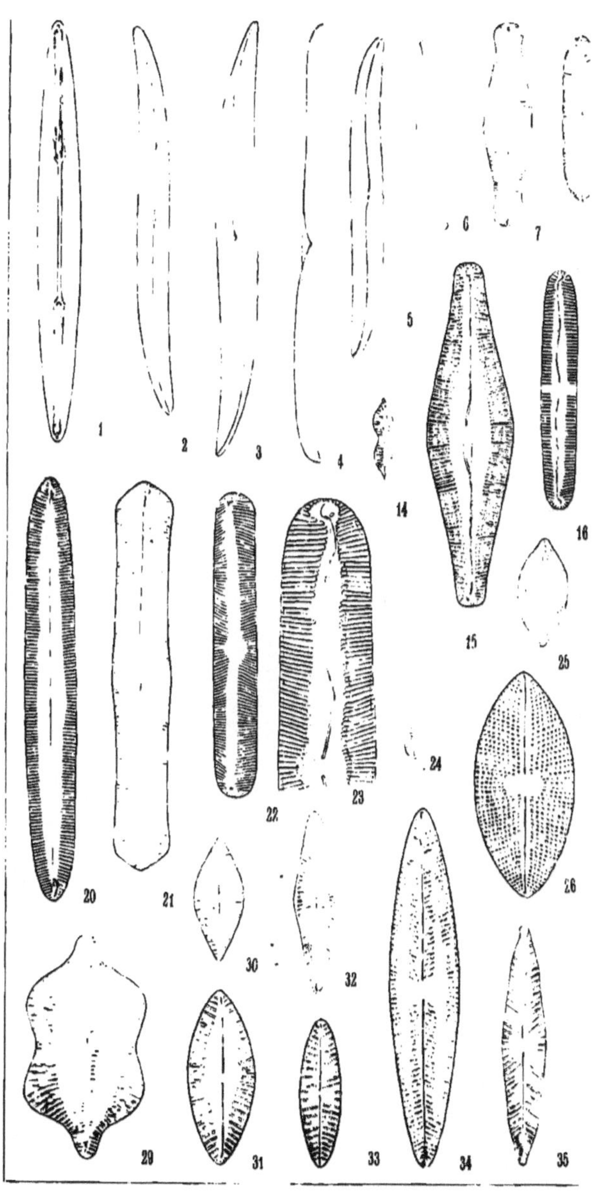
1
2
3
4
5
6
7
14
15
16
20
21
22
23
24
25
26
29
30
31
32
33
34
35

Plate II.

PLATE II.

Fig.		Page.
Fig. 1.	Navicula surinamensis CL. — Surinam, $^{1000}/_{1}$	9.
2.	N. peregrina var. calcuttensis GRUN. — Calcutta, $^{500}/_{1}$	18.
3.	N. Pusio CL. — New Zealand, $^{1000}/_{1}$	9.
4.	N. oviformis CL. — Madagascar, $^{1000}/_{1}$	24.
5.	Mastogloia labuensis CL. — Cebu, $^{1000}/_{1}$	157.
6.	M. Citrus CL. — Adriatic, $^{1000}/_{1}$	157.
7.	M. minuta GREV. — Java, $^{1000}/_{1}$	151.
8.	M. pusilla GRUN. — Pensacola, $^{1000}/_{1}$	»
9.	M. arata CL. — Island of Rhea, $^{500}/_{1}$	156.
10.	M. laminaris EHB. var. intermedia CL. — Japan, $^{1000}/_{1}$	153.
11.	M. baldjikiana GRUN. — Baldjik, $^{1000}/_{1}$	158.
12.	M. flexuosa CL. — Adriatic, $^{1000}/_{1}$	154.
13.	M. acuta GRUN. — Labuan, $^{1000}/_{1}$	156.
14.	M. Grovei CL. var. rhombica CL. — Barbados, $^{500}/_{1}$	149.
15.	M. inæqualis CL. — Australia, $^{1000}/_{1}$	150.
16.	M. fallax CL. — Java, $^{1000}/_{1}$	153.
17.	M. Smithii THW. var. abnormis GRUN. — Karand, $^{1000}/_{1}$	152.
18.	M. Jelineckii var. marina RABH. — Cebu, $^{1000}/_{1}$	160.
19.	M. (Orthoneis) oamaruensis CL. — Oamaru, $^{500}/_{1}$	150.
20.	M. (Orthoneis) cocconeiformis GRUN. — Red Sea, $^{1000}/_{1}$	149.
21.	M. Mac Donaldii GREV. — Cebu, $^{1000}/_{1}$	158.
22.	M. javanica CL. — Java, $^{500}/_{1}$	159.
23.	» $^{1000}/_{1}$	
24.	M. apiculata W. SM. — Cumbræ, $^{1000}/_{1}$	157.
25.	» » » var. — Balearic Islands, $^{1000}/_{1}$	»
26.	M. lemniscata LEUD. FORTM. — Cebu, $^{1000}/_{1}$	159.
27.	M. pulchella CL. — Java, $^{500}/_{1}$	153.
28, 29	» » » $^{1000}/_{1}$	
30, 31	Cocconeis grata A. S. — Campeachy Bay, $^{1000}/_{1}$	172.
32, 33, 34	C. Van Heurckii CL. — Madagascar, $^{1000}/_{1}$	173.
35.	Mastogloia exarata CL. — China, $^{1000}/_{1}$	156.
36, 37.	Cocconeis granulifera GREV. — Galapagos Islands, $^{1000}/_{1}$	168.
38.	Mastogloia(?) dubia CL. — Barbados, $^{1000}/_{1}$	162.

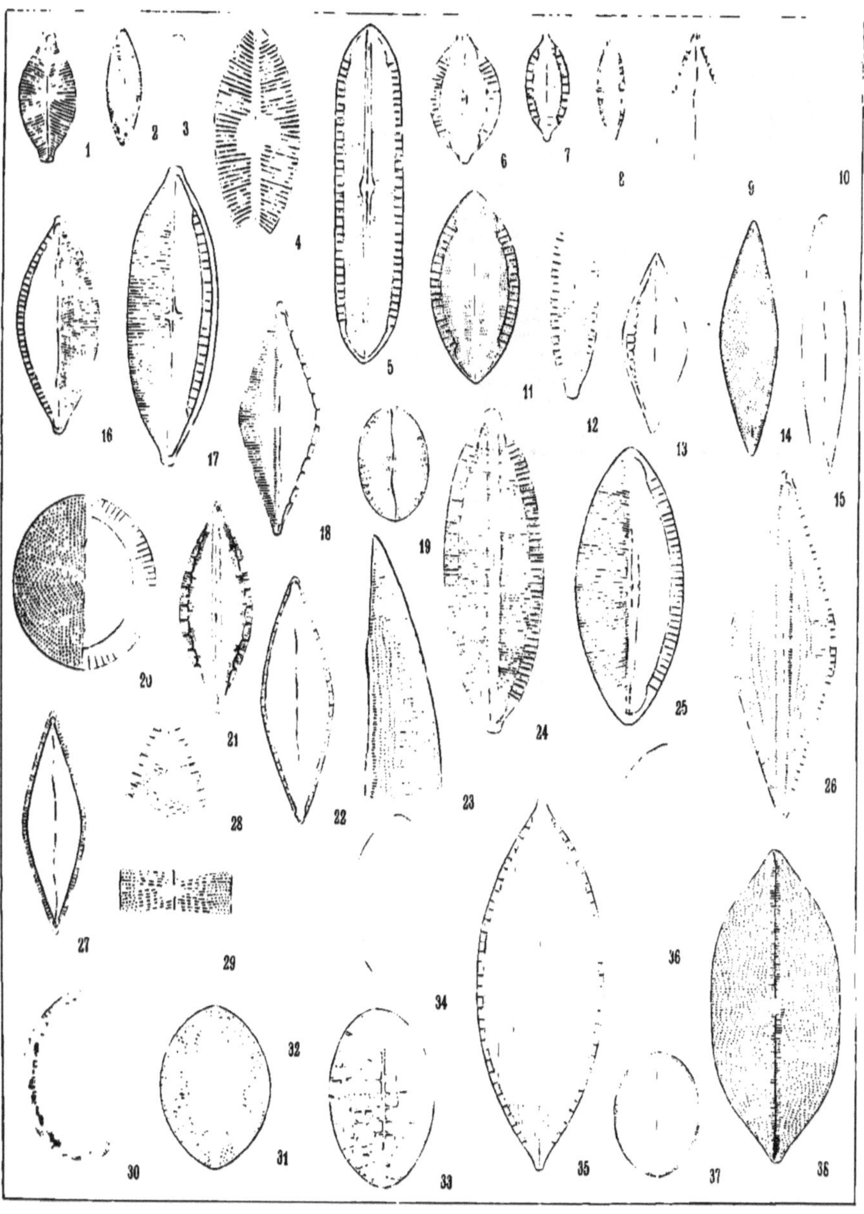

PLATE III.

		Page.
Fig. 1, 2.	Achnanthes mesogongyla GRUN. — Brazil, $\frac{1000}{1}$	192.
3.	A. baccata LEUD. FORTM. Ceylon, $\frac{500}{1}$	195.
» 4, 5.	A. (Actinoneis) baldjikii BTW. — Baldjik, $\frac{1000}{1}$	187.
6, 7.	Cocconeis (Disconeis) reticulata CL. — Galapagos Islands, $\frac{1000}{1}$	180.
8, 9.	Achnanthes (Actinoneis) danica FLÖGEL var. major CL. — Baldjik, $\frac{1000}{1}$	186.
» 10, 11.	Cocconeis (Eucocconeis) Letourneurii CL. — Ceylon, $\frac{1000}{1}$	176.
» 12.	Anorthoneis eurystoma CL. — Pensacola, $\frac{1000}{1}$	166.
13, 14.	Achnanthes (Actinoneis) mammalis CASTR. — Macassar Straits, $\frac{500}{1}$	187.
15.	» portion of the valve, $\frac{1000}{1}$	»
» 16.	A. (Actinoneis) mammalis CASTR. var. reticulata CL. — Macassar Straits. Entire frustule, $\frac{500}{1}$	»
17, 18.	Amphora (Diplamphora) truncata (GREG.?) CL. — Sebastopol, $\frac{1000}{1}$	112.
19.	A. (Dipl.) proboscidea (GREG.?) CL. — Java, $\frac{500}{1}$	113.
20, 21	» » » Bahia, $\frac{500}{1}$	»
22.	A. (Oxyamphora) aspera PETIT. — Naples, $\frac{1000}{1}$	128.
» 23.	A. (Dipl.) cuneata CL. — Java, $\frac{500}{1}$	116.
24, 25.	» » Macassar Straits, $\frac{500}{1}$	»
26, 27, 28, 29.	A. (Dipl.) exsecta GRUN. — China, $\frac{500}{1}$	116.
30, 31.	A. (Dipl.) margaritifera CL. — Galapagos Islands, $\frac{1000}{1}$	117.
» 32, 33.	A. (Dipl.) granulifera CL. — Java, $\frac{1000}{1}$	116.
» 34, 35.	A. behringensis CL. — Behrings Straits, $\frac{1000}{1}$	102.
» 36.	A. (Diplamphora) bioculata CL. — Balearic Islands, $\frac{1000}{1}$	114.
37, 38.	» » » » $\frac{500}{1}$	115.
39.	A. (Psammamphora) ocellata DONK. var. cingulata CL. — Pensacola, $\frac{500}{1}$	133.
40.	A. Pusio CL. — Sandwich Islands, $\frac{1000}{1}$	102.

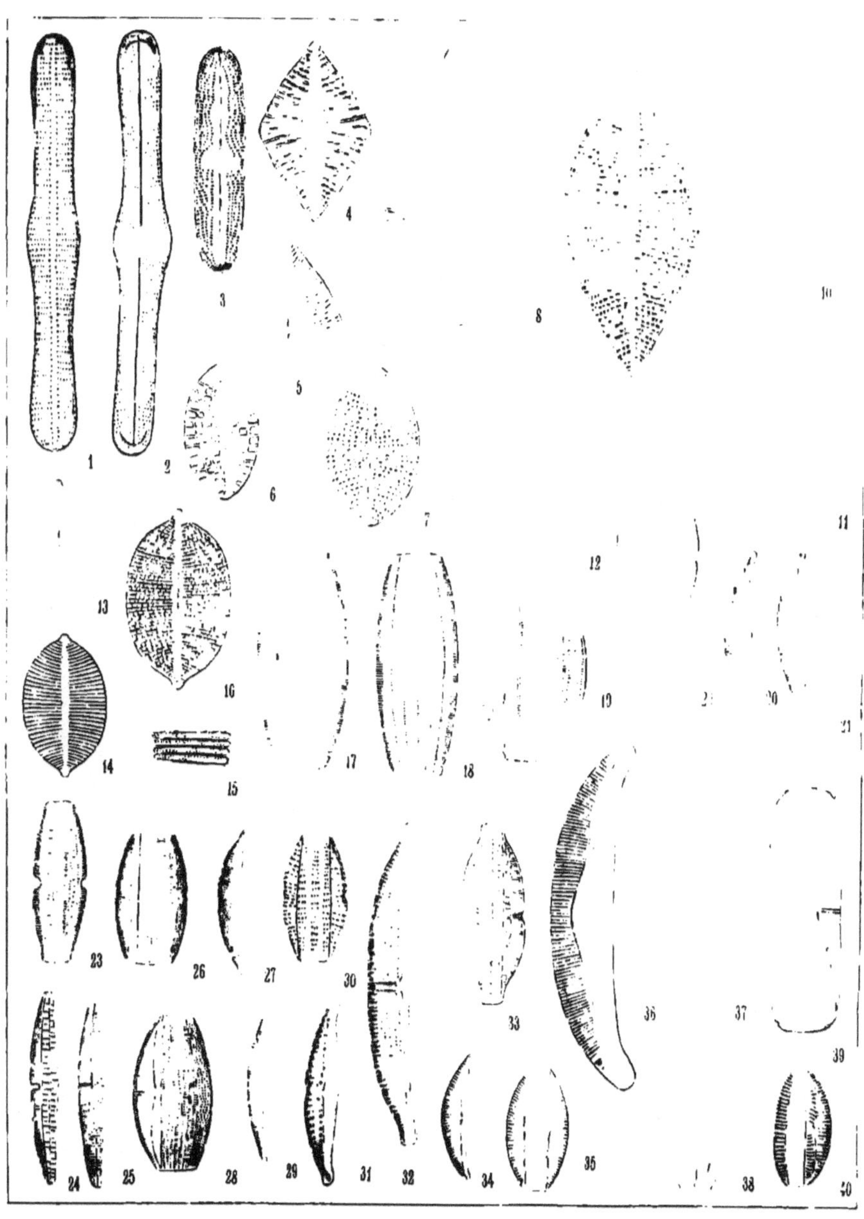

PLATE IV.

Fig.		Page.
1.	Amphora (Oxyamphora) groenlandica CL. Davis Straits, $^{1000}/_{1}$	128.
2, 3.	A. (Halamphora) Eunotia CL. — Spitsbergen, $^{500}/_{1}$	122.
4.	A. (Oxyamphora) Arcus GREG. — Sumatra, $^{500}/_{1}$	127.
5, 6.	A. dubia A. S. — Barcelona, $^{500}/_{1}$	102.
7.	A. (Oxyamphora) micans A. S. — Macassar Straits. $^{500}/_{1}$	128.
8, 9.	(portion of the margin and end) $^{1000}/_{1}$	»
10.	A. (Oxyamphora) decussata GRUN. — Adriatic, $^{500}/_{1}$	128.
11.	» » var. briocensis LEUD. FORTM. — The English channel, $^{1000}/_{1}$	129.
12.	A. Ovum CL. — Balearic Islands, $^{1000}/_{1}$	102.
13.	A. (Oxyamphora) Lunula CL. — Sumatra, $^{1000}/_{1}$	129.
14.	A. (Oxyamphora) Maeandrina CL. — Colon, $^{500}/_{1}$	127.
15.	A. mexicana A. S. — Naples, $^{500}/_{1}$	105.
16, 17, 18.	A. (Diplamphora) decipiens CL. — Labuan, $^{1000}/_{1}$	108.
19, 20.	Arenicola GRUN. — South Pembroke, $^{500}/_{1}$	104.
21.	» » » var. oculata CL. — Sebastopol, $^{800}/_{1}$	»
22.	» » var. subæqualis CL. — China, $^{500}/_{1}$	»
23.	A. (Oxyamphora) acuta var. labyrinthica GRUN. — Balearic Islands, $^{1000}/_{1}$	128.
24, 25.	A. (Archiamphora) rectilineata CL. a. GROVE — Oamaru, $^{500}/_{1}$	»
26.	A. (Diplamphora) prismatica CL. — Naples, $^{500}/_{1}$	112.
27.	A. (Diplamphora) diaphana CL. — Colon, $^{500}/_{1}$	»
28, 29.	A. gigantea var. obscura CL. — Naples, $^{500}/_{1}$	106.
30, 31, 32.	A. (Diplamphora) vetusta CL. a. GROVE, — Oamaru $^{500}/_{1}$	115.
33.	A. (Oxyamphora) staurophora CASTR. — Morocco, $^{500}/_{1}$	129.
34.	» » » Pensacola, $^{500}/_{1}$	»
35.	A. (Diplamphora) inornata CL. — Macassar Straits, $^{500}/_{1}$	110.
36, 37, 38.	» » Java, $^{500}/_{1}$	»
39.	A. (Diplamphora) inelegans var.? polita CL. — Java, $^{1000}/_{1}$	111.
40.	A. (Oxyamphora) bacillaris (GREG.?) CL. — Firth of Tay, $^{500}/_{1}$	127.
41.	» » (portion of the dorsal side of the connecting zone) $^{1000}/_{1}$	»

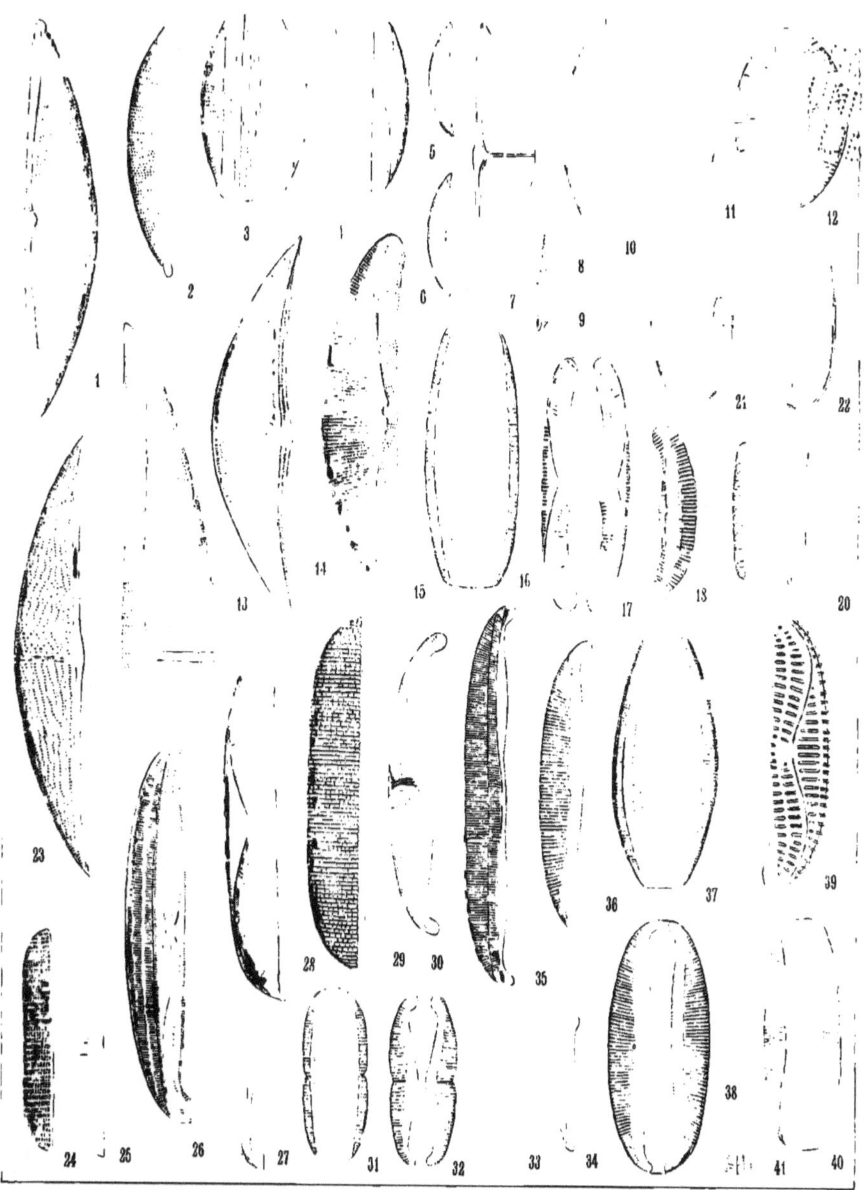

www.ingramcontent.com/pod-product-compliance
Lightning Source LLC
Chambersburg PA
CBHW022144300426
44115CB00006B/342

9783337724160